Teacher's Edition

Español
Santillana

fans del Español

SANTILLANA USA

Español Santillana is a collaborative effort by two teams specializing in the design of Spanish-language educational materials. One team is located in the United States and the other in Spain.

Editorial Staff in the United States

Anne Silva
Ana Isabel Antón

Editorial Staff in Spain

Susana Gómez
Belén Saiz
Clara Alarcón

Mercedes Fontecha
M.ª Antonia Oliva

Published in the United States of America.

Español Santillana
Teacher's Edition Level 4
ISBN-13: 978-1-62263-245-9
ISBN-10: 1-62263-245-1

Illustrator: **Bartolomé Seguí**
Picture Coordinator: **Carlos Aguilera**

Cartographers: **José Luis Gil, Tania López**
Cartographic Coordinator: **Ana Isabel Calvo**

Production Manager: **Ángel García Encinar**

Production Coordinator: **Julio Hernández**

Design and Layout: **Jorge Borrego, Pedro Valencia, Raquel Sánchez, Eva Hernández**

Proofreaders: **Nuria del Peso, Elizabeth A. Pease, Marta López**

Photo Researchers: **Mercedes Barcenilla, Amparo Rodríguez**

Santillana USA Publishing Company, Inc.
2023 NW 84th Avenue, Doral, FL 33122

Printed by Worzalla, Wisconsin

1 2 3 4 5 6 7 8 9 10   19 18 17 16 15 14

Linguistic and Cultural Advisers in Latin America and in the United States

Antonio Moreno
Content Director, Santillana México

Mayra Méndez
Content Director, Santillana Puerto Rico

Claudia Noriega
Content Director, Santillana Guatemala

Cecilia Mejía
Content Director, Santillana Perú

Graciela Pérez de Lois
Content Director, Santillana Argentina

Rodolfo Hidalgo
Content Director, Santillana Chile

Mario Núñez
Director of Professional Development, Santillana USA

Reviewers

Gabriel Alfaro
Houston, TX

Luis Altamirano
San Diego, CA

Esteban Longoria
Houston, TX

John W. McNulty
Chicago, IL

Maria L. Rodriguez-Burns
Bernalillo, NM

Tina Thymai Dong
Austin, TX

Writers (Teacher's Edition)

Paloma Lapuerta
New Britain, CT

María Lourdes Casas
New Haven, CT

Elizabeth Millán
Highland Park, IL

María Á. Pérez
Tenerife, Spain

Lisa Berliner
Farmington, CT

Jan Ferrier Sands
North Granby, CT

Writers (Student Book)

Paloma Lapuerta
teaches Spanish Language, Literature and Culture at Central Connecticut State University. She graduated from the University of Salamanca, Spain, and received her PhD from the University of Geneva, Switzerland. She has taught in different countries and is co-author of several Spanish textbooks.

María Lourdes Casas
received her Masters of Arts and PhD in Spanish at the University of Wisconsin-Madison. Dr. Casas has taught Spanish Language and Literature at the University of Wisconsin-Madison, Connecticut College, and Southern Connecticut State University. Currently she is an Assistant Professor at Central Connecticut State University.

Lisa Berliner
received her MA in Educational Leadership from Central Connecticut State University. She is currently pursuing a Masters degree in Spanish. She teaches Spanish at the secondary level in Avon, CT.

Jan Ferrier Sands
received her BS in Spanish and MS in Curriculum and Supervision from Central Connecticut State University. She is a career teacher of Spanish at Simsbury High School, Simsbury, CT. From 2005 to 2008, she served as the World Languages Teacher-in-Residence at the Connecticut State Department of Education.

María Á. Pérez
received her MA in Spanish from Portland State University. She was the assistant director for the Spanish Basic Language Program at the University of Illinois in Chicago. She has taught college-level Spanish at several institutions, and has worked as an editor and writer for various publishers.

Contributing Writers

Ana Isabel Antón
Miami, FL

Susana Gómez
Madrid, Spain

M.ª Antonia Oliva
Madrid, Spain

Anne Silva
Miami, FL

Clara Alarcón
Madrid, Spain

Mercedes Fontecha
Madrid, Spain

Belén Saiz
Madrid, Spain

Contributors

Janet L. Glass
Dwight-Englewood School
Englewood, NJ

Jan Kucerik
Pinellas County Schools
Largo, FL

Carol McKenna Semonsky
Georgia State University
Atlanta, GA

Anne Nerenz
Eastern Michigan University
Ypsilanti, MI

Gerardo Piña-Rosales
North American Academy of the Spanish Language
The City University of New York, New York, NY

Paul Sandrock
ACTFL
Madison, WI

Emily Spinelli
AATSP
University of Michigan-Dearborn, Dearborn, MI

Brandon Zaslow
Occidental College
Los Angeles, CA

Advisers

Paula Hirsch
Windward School, Los Angeles, CA

María Orta
Kennedy High School, Chicago, IL

Developmental Editor
María Á. Pérez and Belén Saiz

Editorial Coordinator
Anne Silva

Editorial Director
Enrique Ferro

Índice

Español Santillana. Presentation

Scope and Sequence

Key Ideas for Today's Language Classroom

Diego Rivera. *Sueño de una tarde dominical en la Alameda Central* (1947).

1. A motivating story

1. *Español Santillana* tells a story of travels and challenges.

Four pairs of enthusiasts of the Spanish language and Hispanic culture want to explore the Spanish-speaking world: its people, its cities, its regions, and its cultures. Because of this, they have decided to create the *Fans del español* website and to travel to different countries in order to discover and show unique aspects of each place. In each country, the four teams compete, taking on different *desafíos*, or challenges, that they must complete.

The community of *Fans* has grown, and in Levels 3 and 4, new fans will take on all-new challenges with the same objective: to get to know the places, the cultures, and the lifestyles of Spanish-speaking countries.

2. The challenges present exceptionally motivating situations and fascinating places.

Each unit presents several challenges (four in Levels 1 and 2; three in Levels 3 and 4) related to the people, the regions, or the cultures of a country or geographic area. For example, the teams participate in the ritual of the *voladores de Papantla* in Mexico (Level 1), act in a *telenovela* in Buenos Aires (Level 2), prepare a typical dish of *ropa vieja* with a recipe from the Canary Islands (Level 3), and participate in the ritual of preparing and drinking *mate* (Level 4).

3. The students decide which team wins the challenge in each unit.

In Levels 1 and 2, students discuss the challenges at the beginning of each unit, and make predictions about which pair will win. At the end of the unit, students take a vote to decide the winners of the challenge according to a previously established criterion: the most original, the most fun, the most relevant, and so on.

In Levels 3 and 4, students get to choose one of the pairs' challenges in order to perform a task related to it.

Active participation in the storyline promotes student involvement and motivation.

⚑→ TU DESAFÍO

The *Tu desafío* section that appears on certain pages of Levels 1 and 2 is intended to motivate students and promote independent work. Upon accessing the *Fans del español* website to do the proposed activity, students earn points, which they can accumulate throughout the year.

In Levels 3 and 4, the students' challenges are linked to the challenges that the three pairs take on in each unit.

¿Quién ganará?

4 **Los desafíos**

▶ **Habla.** What will be the challenge for each pair? Think about this question and discuss it with your classmates.

DESAFÍO ①
La máscara de jade

Diana y Rita

DESAFÍO ②
Vamos de compras

Patricia y Tess

DESAFÍO ③
Tres trajes típicos

Mack y Tim

DESAFÍO ④
Un mercado especial

Janet y Andy

5 **Las votaciones**

▶ **Decide.** You decide. You will vote to choose the most interesting challenge. Who do you think will win?

Interesante

Tu desafío

88 **Los desafíos**

¿Recuerdas los desafíos que Andy y Tess les plantearon a los personajes? ¿Cuál te gusta más? Elige una de estas opciones y resuelve tu desafío.

DESAFÍO Ⓐ
Escribe y dibuja una historieta gráfica. Incluye adjetivos de descripción física o de personalidad. Si quieres, puedes hacerla sobre uno de estos personajes de autores hispanos.

Mot (Nacho y Azpiri)
Este simpático monstruo, capaz de viajar a otras dimensiones, apareció en 1988 en un suplemento para niños del diario español El País. Sus historietas se adaptaron después a la televisión y a los videojuegos.

Máximo Chambónez (Themo Lobos)
Según el diccionario, Chambón significa «persona de poca habilidad en el juego». Esta definición retrata bien a este personaje inocente y de buenas intenciones, al que nada le sale bien.

DESAFÍO Ⓑ
Elige uno de estos dos cuadros, busca información en Internet y elabora una audioguía. Debes describir el cuadro e incluir algo de información sobre el pintor.

Pablo Picasso (España). La familia de saltimbanquis.

Diego Rivera (México). Baile en Tehuantepec.

DESAFÍO Ⓒ
Inventa y escribe una leyenda utilizando los tiempos de pasado. Debes incluir alguno de estos elementos:

- Personajes: una princesa, un rey, un monstruo, un mago.
- Acontecimientos: una boda, una muerte, un viaje, una mentira.
- Lugares: un bosque, una selva, un desierto, un país muy lejano.

2. The integration of culture into the units

1. Culture is the framework for learning Spanish.

Culture is present throughout the unit: in the challenges, in the boxes that feature the five Cs of language learning, in the section titled *Mapa cultural*, in the readings, and in the final project.

Culture is also present in the practice activities: students analyze the cultural perspectives, practices, and products of a country or cultural area, compare it with their own country, and transfer what they have learned to their own reality.

Find a jade mask in Antigua.

2. Culture is presented in an original way.

Each challenge features a **cultural element** related to the theme of the unit. For example, *Desafío 1* in Guatemala (Level 1) showcases an element of traditional Guatemalan culture: jade masks.

Elements of the culture related to the theme of the unit are also presented in an organized way in the *Mapa cultural* section.

3. Culture is recognized in all its richness.

Culture is explored as a perspective, a practice, and a product. For example, students reflect about the festivals, customs, traditions, family dynamics, table manners, courtesy expressions, dances, foods, etc.

Culture is exhibited from a variety of angles:

▶ Major cities such as Mexico City, San Juan in Puerto Rico, Antigua in Guatemala, Santo Domingo, Cartagena de Indias, Buenos Aires, Seville, etc.

▶ Archeology, architecture, and the fine arts: Teotihuacan, Tikal, Machu Picchu, the Zócalo in Mexico City, the El Morro fortress in San Juan, the Alhambra, Frida Kahlo, Diego Rivera, Pablo Picasso, Fernando Botero, etc.

▶ Customs such as festivals, traditional clothing, foods, and sports.

▶ Youth culture, such as music and fashion.

▶ Social relationships and societal organization.

An example of the integration of culture

Level: 1   **Country:** Guatemala   **Theme:** Shopping and clothing

DESAFÍO ②

Vamos de compras

Patricia y Tess

Buy articles of clothing in a mall in Guatemala.

DESAFÍO ③

Tres trajes típicos

Mack y Tim

Acquire three traditional garments in Tikal.

DESAFÍO ④

Un mercado especial

Janet y Andy

Locate a bag of worry dolls in the Chichicastenango market.

3. An organization based on motivation and learning

1. The units are organized around *Desafíos*.

The units are organized by sections called *Desafíos*. Each *Desafío* presents a challenge that a pair of characters must resolve. In this way, the *Desafíos* contextualize learning in a motivating, meaningful storyline.

The *Desafío* is the cultural and communicative context in which language learning happens.

▶ Each *Desafío* revolves around a **cultural topic** that is related to the theme of the unit: living spaces, clothing, food, health, work, free time, nature, history, politics, society, etc. Culture is the core of each *Desafío*.

▶ Each *Desafío* is focused on a certain **communicative function**: identifying oneself, describing people, describing places, expressing states and feelings, expressing obligation, giving orders or advice, etc.

2. Vocabulary and grammar are presented in context within the framework of each *Desafío*.

Vocabulary and grammar are presented in short, well-defined sections within each *Desafío*. This system facilitates focus on the topic being studied.

Communicative function

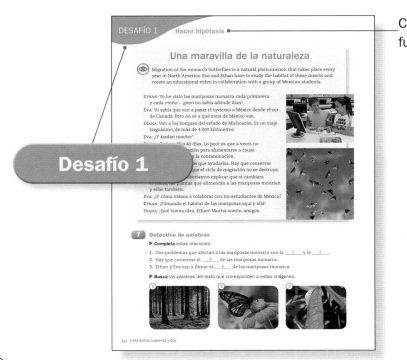

Desafío 1

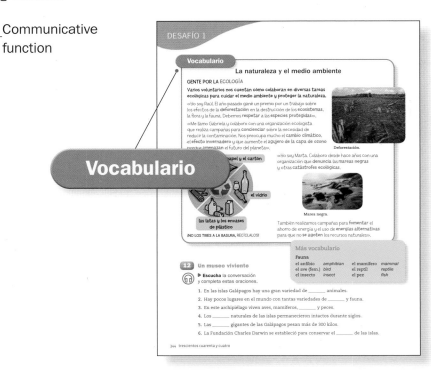

Vocabulario

Some of the characters' challenges

Level 1

- Dress like Frida Kahlo (Mexico).
- Perform as a Papantla Flyer (Mexico).
- Find the most colorful house in Old San Juan (Puerto Rico).
- Find an ancient Mayan jade mask (Guatemala).
- Buy worry dolls in a market in Guatemala.
- Prepare Peruvian *ceviche*.
- Get the autograph of the leader in the Tour of Spain bicycle race.
- Play a game of dominoes on Calle 8 in Miami.
- Spend the night in the Hispanic Society of America Museum in New York.
- Take a trip on the Train to the Clouds in Salta, Argentina.
- Find the fake *moai* on Easter Island (Chile).
- Participate in the Stairs Marathon in Valparaiso, Chile.

Level 2

- Find the tallest woman in León, Nicaragua.
- Find Sir Francis Drake's scale in Santo Domingo, Dominican Republic.
- Participate in a serenade in Ponce, Puerto Rico.
- Participate in the Oruro Carnival (Bolivia).
- Prepare Day of the Dead bread (Mexico).
- Participate in a chili contest in San Antonio, Texas.
- Find a *margarita cubista* in the Picasso Museum in Barcelona, Spain.
- Find *El Dorado* in Colombia.
- Drive a bus through the streets of Caracas, Venezuela.
- Act in a *telenovela* (Argentina).
- Cross the Panama Canal in a kayak.
- Help baby sea turtles in Tortuguero National Park (Costa Rica).

The tasks

In Levels 3 and 4, the *Desafíos* propose tasks that the characters and students have to complete: create a comic strip, write a legend, make an audio guide about a painting, compose an invitation, write an e-mail, design a flag, describe an Andalusian patio, present a typical dish, design a webpage, prepare an interview, present a character, respond to an ad, write a report, make a poster, write an essay, create a brochure, etc.

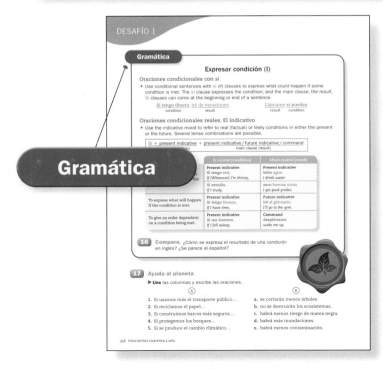

Gramática

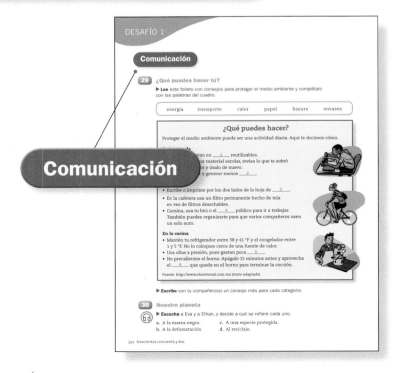

Comunicación

The Unit: Levels 1 and 2

Outline of the unit (Levels 1 and 2)

The units are organized in three major blocks.

1. The linguistic nucleus. This is the fundamental and most extensive part of the unit. It is centered around the vocabulary, the grammar, and the practice of communication in the context of the travels and the challenges. It contains these sections:

▶ *La llegada.* The characters arrive at the destination, which serves as the geographic framework of the unit. This section presents the unit's target vocabulary and grammar in context, as well as some *expresiones útiles* (useful expressions).

▶ *Los Desafíos.* Each pair of characters receives a challenge. In this section, the vocabulary and grammar are presented in detail. Following the *Desafíos* is a section called *Todo junto*, with culminating communicative activities.

▶ *El encuentro.* The pairs are reunited to discuss the tasks they have completed, and students choose the winning team.

2. An in-depth look into culture. This has as its core the *Mapa cultural*. This section presents some of the characteristic cultural aspects of a country (Level 1) or a region (Level 2).

The *Mapa cultural* is complemented by a *Lectura* section, in which students learn about a cultural aspect while practicing reading comprehension skills and strategies.

3. Putting knowledge into action: the *Repaso* pages and the *Proyecto.* Students review the vocabulary and grammar of the unit, then do a project in which they integrate the unit's key linguistic and cultural concepts in a communicative way.

Each unit takes place in a country or region and discusses a particular theme.

La llegada

Los desafíos

Todo junto

El mapa

Los repasos

In Levels 1 and 2, there are four *desafíos* per unit.

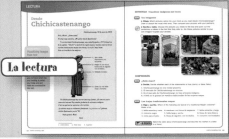

El encuentro

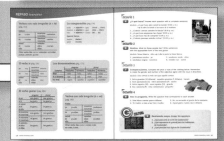

La lectura

El proyecto

The Unit: Levels 3 and 4

The units maintain the organization in three major blocks.

1. **The linguistic nucleus.** It is centered around the vocabulary, the grammar, and the practice of communication in the context of the *Desafíos*. It contains these sections:

   - **Las tareas.** The characters receive the tasks they will complete throughout the unit. This section presents the unit's target vocabulary and grammar in context, introduces some *expresiones útiles* (useful expressions), and reviews previously learned vocabulary related to the theme.

   - **Los Desafíos.** In addition to the Vocabulary and Grammar, this part includes a **Lectura** section that systematically alternates between a dialogue, an informative text, or a literary text.

   - **Para terminar.** Includes **Todo junto** and **Tu desafío**. In this last part, the students must complete one of the challenges presented to the characters.

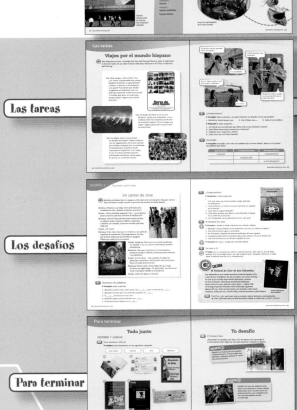

2. **An in-depth look into culture.** The **Mapa cultural** presents different practices, products, and perspectives of the Spanish-speaking world, related to the theme of the unit.

   The *Mapa cultural* is complemented by an **Escritura** section. In this section, students practice and extend their writing skills, and apply the vocabulary and grammar they have learned in the unit.

3. **Putting knowledge into action:** the **Repaso** pages and the **Proyecto.** Students review the vocabulary and grammar of the unit, then do a project in which they integrate the unit's key linguistic and cultural concepts in a communicative way.

The unit closes with preparation for the AP* Spanish Language and Culture Exam.

In Level 4, each unit focuses on one specific portion of the AP* Exam.

In Levels 3 and 4, there are three *desafíos* per unit.

La escritura

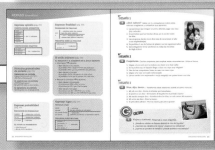

El proyecto

*AP is a registered trademark of the College Board, which was not involved in the production of, and does not endorse, this product.

Each *Desafío* consists of culture, vocabulary, and grammar.

The *Desafío* is the story of each team's challenge, and is therefore the basis of the storyline. It also develops key vocabulary and grammar around a communicative function in a cutural setting.

1. *El desafío* (presentation)

The **Desafío** begins with a text in which the characters talk about their challenge using the target vocabulary and grammar in a context. The context allows the students to become familiar with the new words and structures, and to make hypotheses about their meaning and their usage.

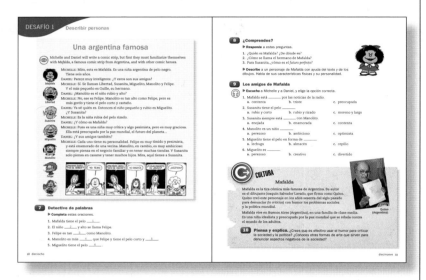

2. *El vocabulario*

On the **vocabulary** pages, the new words and phrases are presented with the support of images and language context. Students use the vocabulary in follow-up activities.

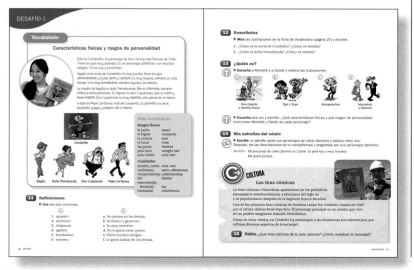

3. *La gramática*

On the **grammar** pages, students are given explanations of key structures, which are practiced along with the key vocabulary.

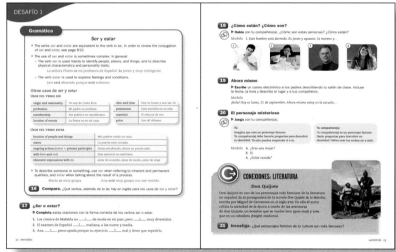

4. *La lectura*

In Levels 3 and 4, **reading** is practiced in each *Desafío* via a written dialogue, an informative text, or a literary text.

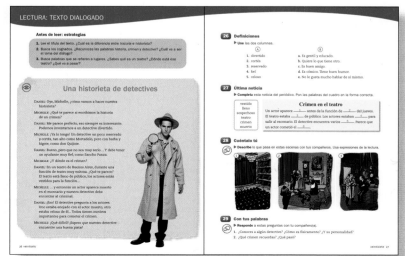

5. *La comunicación*

On the **communication** pages, there are progressively more open-ended activities that allow students to apply the key vocabulary and grammar in communicative situations.

6. *Final del desafío*

The *Desafío* ends with a *fotonovela*, which is a continuation of, and a conclusion to, the initial text.

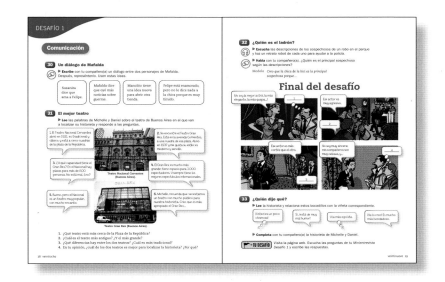

The "C-Boxes"

The linguistic material presented in each *Desafío* is complemented with boxes in which four of the five C's from the standards are developed: **Culture**, **Comparisons**, **Communities**, and **Connections**.

Communication is developed throughout the book in the vocabulary and grammar activities. A section at the end of each *Desafío* is also dedicated to Communication.

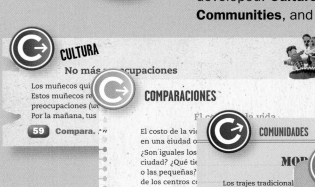

Alfredo Gálvez. *Tejedoras de Atitlán.*

The Vocabulary

A careful selection.

Key vocabulary has been selected, considering the specifications of organizations dedicated to the instruction and evaluation of Spanish, including the *Instituto Cervantes* and the American Association of Teachers of Spanish and Portuguese (AATSP).

In general, the most commonly used and standard Spanish terms have been chosen, rather than regional variants. Whenever possible, words close to their English counterparts (cognates) have been included.

The basic criteria for the selection of vocabulary were frequency of use and relevance to students' everyday life, interests, and needs.

Organization by topic or situations.

The vocabulary is organized by topic or by situations related to the theme of the unit. For example, a unit dedicated to the theme of food includes words relating to foods and beverages, meals, and food stores.

Level 2, Unit 4. Theme: Food

Desafío 1	**Foods**: los pescados, los mariscos, el salmón, los camarones, el atún, los cereales, el pan, la pasta, el arroz, la carne, los frijoles, las lentejas, los guisantes, los lácteos, el queso, la leche, el yogur, la mantequilla, las frutas, las fresas, las uvas, la sandía, el melón, la piña, la pera, las verduras, las hortalizas…
Desafío 2	**Food containers**: un bote, una lata, una caja, una bolsa, una botella, un paquete. **Actions, measures, and other words related to buying food**: comprar, hacer la compra, vender, costar, pedir, pensar, hacer cola / fila; un kilo, un litro; la lista de la compra, el precio.
Desafío 3	**Condiments**: el aceite, el vinagre, la sal, la pimienta, el azúcar, la salsa de tomate, la mayonesa, la mostaza. **Actions in the kitchen**: pelar, cortar, echar, mezclar, batir, cocer, hervir, freír, asar.
Desafío 4	**In the restaurant**: el menú del día, de primero, de segundo. **At the table**: el mantel, la servilleta, el cuchillo, el tenedor, el vaso, la cuchara. **Describing foods and beverages**: agrio(a), dulce, picante, salado(a), soso(a), amargo(a), bueno(a), malo(a), delicioso(a), caliente, frío(a), fresco(a). **Preparing food**: frito(a), asado(a), a la plancha, cocido(a), hervido(a), empanado(a).

The instructional focus: work on many levels.

1. *Fotonovelas* and *Desafío* presentation texts

These include new vocabulary words and expressions that students can understand through their visual or verbal context. The activities help students focus on the lexical items and formulate hypotheses about their meaning.

2. *Vocabulario*

The new words and expressions are presented on the vocabulary pages in each *Desafío* with the support of images and / or language contexts.

Students practice the vocabulary first in closed-ended activities (less difficult) and then in open-ended activities (more difficult), where they can apply the vocabulary in real-life situations.

3. *Gramática*, *Comunicación*, and *Todo junto*

Key vocabulary is reinforced and used in different contexts, along with recycled vocabulary from previous units.

4. *Repaso*

At the end of the unit, vocabulary is reviewed and pre-assessment activities are included.

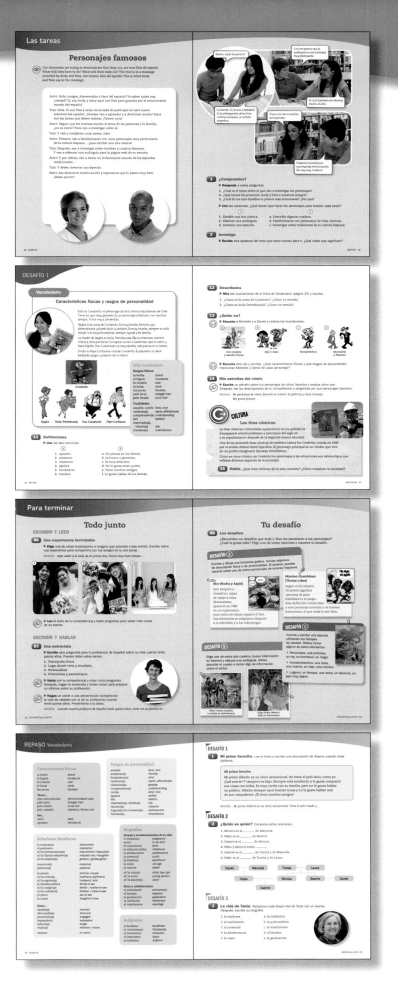

The Grammar

A decision guided by experience.

The selection and sequence of the grammatical elements was determined keeping three fundamental criteria in mind: the use of the structures, their productivity in communicative contexts, and their difficulty.

For example, the verbs *ser*, *estar*, and *tener* are presented before the verb *gustar* because they are more frequently used, they are more productive, and they present fewer difficulties for English speakers than the verb *gustar*.

Organization: grammar linked to communicative functions.

In general, the presentation of grammar is linked to a communicative function. For example, in Level 2, Unit 1, dedicated to the theme of personal life, the following functions and structures are learned:

Gramática

Verbos con raíz irregular (e > ie)

Verbos irregulares

- Irregular verbs do not follow typical conjugation patterns. Ser and tener, for example, are irregular verbs.

  ser → yo soy, tú eres...

  tener → yo tengo, tú tienes...

- Irregular verbs may change the stem or the endings. Remember: To identify the stem of a verb, delete the -ar, -er, -ir endings from the infinitive form.

  lav -a̶r̶   prend -e̶r̶   abr -i̶r̶

Verbos con raíz irregular (e > ie)

- Some verbs, like cerrar (to close), require a stem change from e to ie.

VERBO CERRAR (TO CLOSE). PRESENTE

Singular		Plural	
yo	**cierro**	nosotros nosotras	**cerramos**
tú	**cierras**	vosotros vosotras	**cerráis**
usted él ella	**cierra**	ustedes ellos ellas	**cierran**

Note: The e > ie stem change affects all the present tense forms except nosotros, nosotras and vosotros, vosotras. This is why these verbs are called "boot or shoe verbs."

- Other verbs like cerrar are:

  empezar (to begin) → yo empiezo
  entender (to understand) → yo entiendo
  pensar (to think) → yo pienso

  preferir (to prefer) → yo prefiero
  querer (to want) → yo quiero

15 **Comparación.** What irregular English verbs do you know? Give three examples and explain why they are irregular.

Level 2, Unit 1. Theme: Personal Life

Desafío 1 Identifying yourself and others	Possessive adjectives and pronouns
Desafío 2 Describing people	Adjectives and nouns
Desafío 3 Expressing states and feelings	Comparison and superlatives
Desafío 4 Asking questions	Interrogatives

Didactic focus: the use of concise and organized information.

1. *Fotonovelas* and *Desafío* presentation texts

The beginning texts of each *Desafío* include new structures that students can comprehend by their visual or linguistic context. The activities help students to focus on these structures and to formulate hypotheses about their meaning and usage.

2. *Gramática*

The grammar boxes contain explicit information about the structures presented in the initial text. They present the information supported by concise, visually organized graphics, tables, and diagrams. Each grammar box concludes with a comparison between Spanish and English.

The grammar activities are sequenced according to difficulty, from closed-ended activities to open-ended and personalized activities.

3. *Comunicación* and *Todo junto*

Key grammatical structures are reinforced by their application in open-ended, communicative activities.

4. *Repaso*

Key grammar is reviewed at the end of the unit by means of pre-assessment activities.

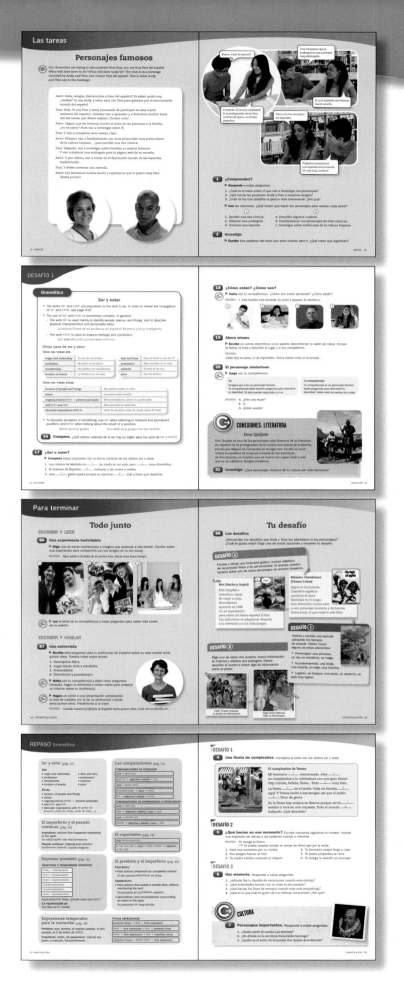

The *Mapas Culturales*

The *Mapas culturales* propose a systematic study.

The *Mapa cultural* is the section in which students study Hispanic cultures in an organized and systematic way.

In Levels 1 and 2, the *Mapa cultural* is based on the study of a country (Mexico, Puerto Rico, Spain, etc.) or a geographical region with cultural similarities (Central America, the Antilles, the Río de la Plata region, etc).

The first page contains **general information** about the country or cultural area which is being studied: its location, size, the countries in this region, main cities, etc.

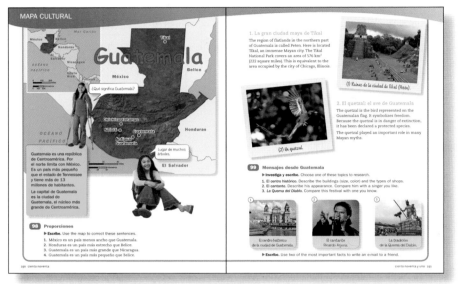

The *Mapa cultural* offers a selection of representative cultural aspects: places, people, traditions, customs, and folklore.

In Levels 3 and 4, the *Mapa cultural* compares a cultural practice or product in different Spanish-speaking countries: the festivals (the *Desfile de Llamadas* in Uruguay, the *Grito de Dolores* in Mexico, the *castells* in Spain), the traditional sports (*tejo* in Colombia, the *charreada* in Mexico, *pato* in Argentina, stone lifting in Spain), urbanism in colonial cities, the universities, etc. The integrated thematic structure allows students to make comparisons and to appreciate the richness and diversity of the Spanish-speaking world.

Level 1

México	La antigua Tenochtitlán El sur: la población indígena
Puerto Rico	El Viejo San Juan La salsa, la esencia de Puerto Rico
Guatemala	La gran ciudad maya de Tikal El quetzal: el ave de Guatemala
Perú	Los incas, reyes de las montañas Las líneas de Nazca
España	Madrid: paraíso de pintores El sur: la herencia árabe
Estados Unidos	Huellas hispanas en los Estados Unidos Estados con historia hispana Concentración hispana en las ciudades
Argentina	El tango Buenos Aires
Chile	La Isla de Pascua Pablo Neruda Los chinchineros

Level 2

Centroamérica	Mestizaje y cultura Riqueza natural
Las Antillas	Barrios coloniales Música caribeña
Andes centrales	Quechuas y aymaras Los equecos Las islas Galápagos
Norteamérica	El Camino Real de Tierra Adentro Los chicanos
España	Paisaje mediterráneo La Noche de San Juan Las lenguas romances
Caribe continental	Símbolos nacionales El mestizaje y los bailes Cocina del Caribe: color y sabor
Río de la Plata	Influencia italiana Cultura rioplatense El chipá
La Panamericana	Variedad geográfica El mundo hispano

Level 3

La población latinoamericana	Indígenas, europeos, africanos El mestizaje
La fiesta: expresión comunitaria	El Desfile de Llamadas (Uruguay) El Grito de Dolores (México) Los castells (España)
La ciudad colonial	El modelo urbanístico de las ciudades coloniales
Alimentos básicos en el mundo hispano	El maíz (México y Centroamérica), el trigo (España), la papa (Perú), la yuca (Paraguay)
Universidades hispanas	Universidad de Chile Universidad de Alcalá (España) Universidad Autónoma de México
Deportes con tradición	El tejo (Colombia), la charreada (México), el pato (Argentina), el levantamiento de piedras (España)
Espacios naturales singulares	Cabo de Hornos (Chile) Lanzarote (España) Las Yungas (Argentina) Arrecife Alacranes (México)
Una ciudad con historia: Barcelona	La antigua Barcino La Barcelona medieval La Barcelona moderna La Barcelona actual

Level 4

Unidad y variedad del español	Variaciones léxicas Variaciones gramaticales
Sistemas de salud en el mundo hispano	Cobertura sanitaria en México Turismo sanitario en Costa Rica El sistema de salud en España
La economía de Latinoamérica	Los países de clima tropical Los países de clima templado Los países extractores
El turismo en Latinoamérica	Riviera Maya Bariloche y la Patagonia argentina Santo Domingo
La inmigración hispana en los Estados Unidos	Los mexicanos Los cubanos Los dominicanos
El «boom» de la novela latinoamericana	Gabriel García Márquez Mario Vargas Llosa Carlos Fuentes

Reading

Reading materials, linked to a comprehension strategy, build competency for reading in Spanish.

The reading materials present an opportunity to practice the given vocabulary and grammatical structures, while improving students' ability to interpret new vocabulary and grammatical structures in context. The use of numerous cognates makes the context more understandable and helps students to increase their vocabulary.

In Levels 1 and 2, each unit focuses on a specific reading strategy to understand Spanish texts: identifying cognates, identifying key concepts, making inferences, and so on.

Level 1

Theme	Type of Text
• Teotihuacán	An informative text.
• El Morro	A travel blog.
• Desde Chichicastenango	A letter.
• Festividad inca del Inti Raymi	A travel brochure.
• El *Guernica*, de Pablo Picasso	An art catalog.
• Celebramos la Herencia Hispana	An invitation.
• *La vuelta al mundo de Cinthia Scoch*	A short story.
• *Oda a la manzana,* de Pablo Neruda	A poem.

Level 2

Theme	Type of Text
• El blog de Ichxel	A personal blog.
• Estilo de vida caribeño	A travel magazine.
• Textiles andinos bolivianos	A museum brochure.
• La receta del guacamole	An instructional text.
• *Figura en una ventana,* de Salvador Dalí	A descriptive text.
• El Dorado, ecos de una leyenda	An informative text.
• Un cuento de Benedetti	A narrative text.
• El Tapón de Darién	An argumentative text.

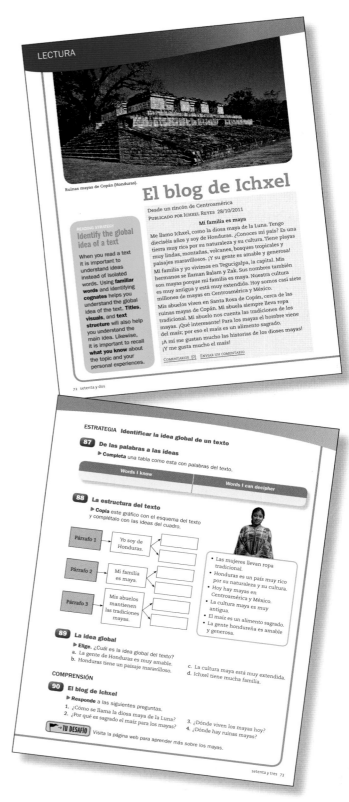

The readings work with different types of texts.

In Levels 1 and 2, the readings are linked to the culture of a country or cultural area, or with the theme of the unit, and represent different writing genres: narrative, descriptive, instructional, literary texts, etc.

In Levels 3 and 4, reading is practiced systematically in each unit with three types of texts: a written dialogue, an informative text, and a literary text.

Level 3

Textos informativos	Textos literarios
• Una breve biografía de Frida Kahlo	• *Los hermanos Ayar* (leyenda inca)
• Juegos precolombinos	• *El mensaje*
• Guía de viajeros: un hotel inolvidable	• *La casa de muñecas*
• El blog personal de Sara	• *La leyenda del maíz* (leyenda azteca)
• Manuel Jalón, un inventor humanista (reportaje)	• *Música*, de Ana María Matute
• Historia de los Juegos Panamericanos	• *Galletitas*, de Jorge Bucay
• Las tradiciones del Sol	• *El eclipse*, de Augusto Monterroso
• Entrevista a Debra McKeon	• *La muralla*, de Nicolás Guillén

Level 4

Textos informativos	Textos literarios
• *El oficio más romántico: escribir cartas de amor por encargo*	• *El diario a diario*, de Julio Cortázar
• *El cáncer y su prevención*	• *La piedra mágica* (cuento popular)
• *La globalización económica* (artículo de economía)	• *El constructor de ecuaciones*, de Juan Bonilla
• *Como la vida misma*, de Rosa Montero	• *Vivir para contarla*, de Gabriel García Márquez
• *María Eva Duarte de Perón* (biografía)	• *El exiliado*, de Cristina Peri Rossi
• *Rafael Moneo* (entrevista)	• *El sur*, de Jorge Luis Borges

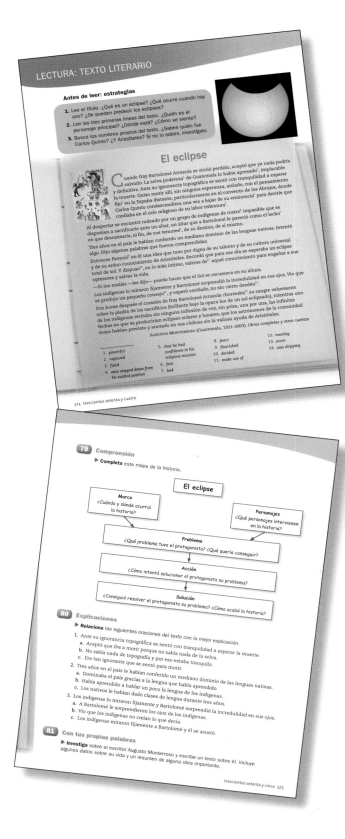

Writing

Writing moves toward the production of more complex texts.

In Levels 1 and 2, writing is practiced at several points throughout the unit:

▶ In the *Comunicación* and *Todo junto* pages within the framework of the *Desafíos*.

▶ In the project.

Students are faced with increasingly more complex texts, which range from writing simple lists (such as a shopping list), to more elaborate texts, such as a diary entry, a script, or a travelogue.

In Levels 3 and 4, there is an additional composition included and the students are required to create somewhat more complex compositions: a character sketch, an essay, a short story, a report, an opinion article, etc.

Through these activities, students have the opportunity to express their ideas and become accustomed to formal and creative writing in Spanish.

Writing Tasks. Examples

Level 1

- Describe people or places.
- Write an Instant Messenger conversation with a classmate.
- Write a post to introduce oneself.
- Make lists with different items.
- Write a postcard to a friend.
- Write informal and formal e-mails.
- Write a radio ad.
- Write a review of a restaurant.
- Write a note.
- Write a blog entry.
- Narrate actions or events.
- Write a plan for a vacation.
- Write a summary of a story.
- Write a travelogue.

Level 2

- Write a menu.
- Write dialogues.
- Write a summary of events.
- Write a poem.
- Write a short story.
- Write a newspaper ad.
- Write a shopping list.
- Write a diary entry.
- Write a chat conversation.
- Write slogans.
- Write a recipe.
- Write a news article.
- Write a script.
- Write a post in a travel blog.
- Write an e-mail or a letter.
- Write a weather report.

Compositions are developed within the framework of the writing process.

In Levels 3 and 4, writing is developed in a four-step process:

1 *Piensa* **2** *Escribe* **3** *Revisa* **4** *Comparte*

In this process, students frequently exchange their writing with their peers in the tasks of planning and revision, thus taking full advantage of collaborative work.

Writing Program

Level 3

- Un personaje interesante (bosquejo biográfico)
- ¿Un poema o un dibujo? ¡Un caligrama!
- Un ensayo de moda
- Una receta típica
- Una carta formal
- Un cuento
- Un reportaje medioambiental
- Y tú, ¿qué opinas? (un texto de opinión)

Level 4

- Un correo de presentación
- Recomendaciones de viajes
- Un currículum vítae
- Un blog de viajes
- Un ensayo
- Una reseña

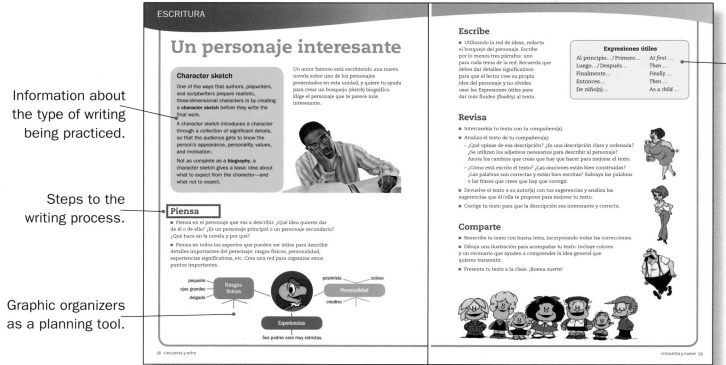

Information about the type of writing being practiced.

Steps to the writing process.

Graphic organizers as a planning tool.

Useful vocabulary.

The Project

The project provides an opportunity for integrating and applying knowledge.

Each unit closes with a project that encourages students' creativity and communicative capacity, while activating vocabulary and grammatical structures that students have learned. Each project develops a communicative activity that integrates cultural and linguistic information.

The activities are separated into steps.

Each project develops from a set of activities presented sequentially in separate steps. Each step is clearly defined and includes guidelines to help students complete the activities.

Una exposición de muñecos quitapenas

PASO 1	**Crea tus muñecos quitapenas**
PASO 2	**Prepara una exposición de muñecos**
PASO 3	**Dramatiza la compra y venta de muñecos**

Project Tasks
Level 1

México	Una presentación sobre Diego Rivera
Puerto Rico	Una visita guiada por la Casa Blanca
Guatemala	Una exposición de muñecos quitapenas
Perú	Nuestros restaurantes
España	Un póster sobre hábitos de higiene
Estados Unidos	Un cartel sobre un hispano famoso
Argentina	Crónica de un viaje
Chile	Un póster sobre animales en peligro

Project: *Una exposición de muñecos quitapenas*

Vocabulary	• Clothing. Characteristics, materials, and colors of clothing • Shopping
Grammar	• The verb *gustar* • Demonstrative adjectives • Comparisons • Present tense of irregular verbs
Culture	• Indigenous traditions • Traditional handicrafts from Guatemala

Level 2

Centroamérica	Una historia sobre personajes de Guatemala
Las Antillas	Un juego en las calles de Santo Domingo
Andes centrales	Una revista sobre moda andina
Norteamérica	Un menú con ingredientes americanos
España	Una presentación sobre hábitos de alimentación
Caribe continental	Un folleto sobre la laguna de Guatavita
Río de la Plata	Un guión para una telenovela
La Panamericana	Un boletín sobre la predicción meteorológica

Level 3

Las personas y la familia	Un álbum de fotos de tu vida
Vida social	Un plan de actividades con tus amigos
La ropa y la vivienda	Una feria sobre ciudades coloniales hispanas
La alimentación y la salud	Una guía para una vida saludable
El trabajo y las profesiones	Un proyecto de una organización solidaria
El tiempo libre y los viajes	Un plan para un viaje de estudios
La naturaleza y el medio ambiente	Una campaña publicitaria en favor del medio ambiente
Historia, política y sociedad	Una presentación sobre un país de Latinoamérica

Level 4

Relaciones sociales y comunicación	Una página web de nuestra clase de Español
Los alimentos y la salud	Un cómic sobre la salud
Los estudios y el trabajo	Un premio a la empresa hispana del año
El ocio y los viajes	Un anuncio para promocionar un país
Historia y sociedad	Un manifiesto para solucionar un problema de tu comunidad
Arte y literatura	Una exposición de las obras de arte favoritas

The unit closes with a self-evaluation.

At the end of each unit is a self-evaluation section with questions that correspond to the unit objectives, so that students can reflect upon their progress.

Presentation of the task.

Steps.

Project instructions.

Self-evaluation.

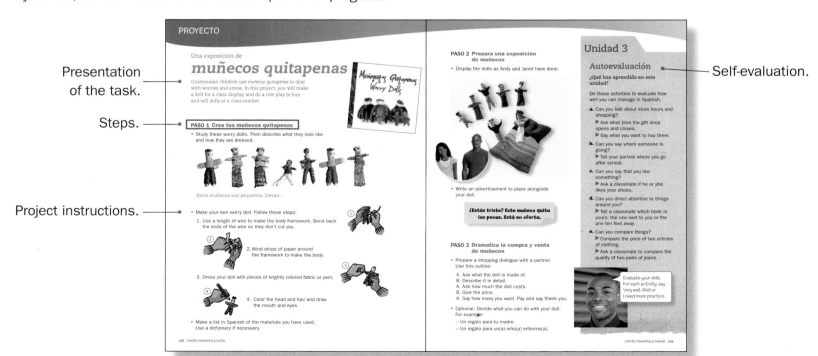

T29

Instruction is centered around the development of communicative skills.

Español Santillana places heavy emphasis on communicative aspects of language. Beginning in the first unit of Level 1, students undertake activities that strengthen the development of speaking, listening, reading, writing, and interacting skills. These activities are the springboard by which students can reach the level of excellence in Spanish required by the AP* Exam.

The Level 4 Student Book offers preparation specifically geared toward the AP* Exam.

Each unit in Level 4 ends with a section called *Hacia el AP* Exam*, which is designed specifically to prepare students for the test. In this section, students learn about the structure of the test and the characteristics of each activity type, as well as strategies for performing well in each section. It also contains a sample exercise so that students can practice taking each type of activity on the exam.

Hacia el AP* Exam

Interpretive Communication: Print Texts

Presentación

En el examen AP* vas a realizar una prueba de comprensión de lectura. Consta de varios textos seguidos de preguntas de opción múltiple.

Los textos proceden de fuentes auténticas: periódicos, revistas, páginas web u otras publicaciones del mundo hispano. Pueden estar acompañados por tablas u otros gráficos.

En las preguntas que siguen a cada texto, hay que escoger la opción que mejor contesta cada pregunta. Estas preguntas están basadas en los objetivos de aprendizaje establecidos por los organizadores del examen. Es importante leer cada opción cuidadosamente, porque a veces se parecen mucho.

> **Estrategias**
>
> **Prelectura**
> - Realiza una lectura rápida del texto para tener una idea general de cuál es el tema.
> - Lee las preguntas y las opciones de respuesta.
>
> **Lectura**
> - Lee el texto cuidadosamente, intentando captar tanto los datos más importantes como el mensaje y el propósito básico del texto.
> - Vuelve a leer el texto y localiza la información o palabras clave.
> - Si hay alguna palabra que no entiendas, intenta concentrarte en la idea general de la oración, no en la palabra específica.
>
> **Preguntas**
> - Para responder las preguntas de opción múltiple, guíate por las palabras clave que señalaste en el texto.

Instrucciones para el examen

Directions: You will read a print text. The passage is followed by a number of comprehension questions. For each question, select the answer that is best according to the reading passage.

Instrucciones: Vas a leer un texto. El texto va seguido de varias preguntas de comprensión. Para cada pregunta, elige la mejor respuesta de acuerdo con el texto.

Introducción

Este texto fue publicado originalmente en http://www.informativoweb.com y se refiere a la presentación del primer diccionario de abreviaturas utilizadas en los SMS.

*AP is a registered trademark of the College Board, which was not involved in the production of, and does not endorse, this product.

Nace 'exo x ti y xa ti', el primer diccionario de abreviaturas SMS

El proyecto diccionarioSMS.com, presentado como una iniciativa de la Asociación de Usuarios de Internet (AUI) con motivo del próximo Día de Internet, pretende recoger los términos y las abreviaturas que emplean los jóvenes cuando escriben mensajes en sus teléfonos móviles o a través de la Red (messenger, correo electrónico, chat, etc.), en lo que se ha configurado como «una especie de dialecto propio, práctico, instantáneo y trasgresor», según Miguel Pérez Subías, presidente de esta asociación. «Queremos ayudar a los padres, profesores y lingüistas a no ignorar, sino conocer mejor esta realidad».

Ns vms n la fsta sta trd. qdms a ls 8. bss

diccionarioSMS.com permitirá consultar y traducir términos SMS en castellano, catalán, euskera y gallego, así como conocer qué términos son los más utilizados, además de incorporar comentarios colaborativos, al estilo de Wikipedia. Puede consultarse tanto por Internet en diccionarioSMS.com como por teléfono móvil enviando un mensaje corto al 5857 seguido de la palabra clave ddi y del término SMS que se quiere consultar.

Paralelamente, los organizadores han anunciado las bases del concurso diario entre todos los usuarios que registren los términos y abreviaturas. El lote de premios diarios consiste en 21 teléfonos móviles de última generación, 10.000 horas de descarga de música, 10 juegos para la plataforma xBox, una consola xBox, y bonos para enviar hasta 9.000 SMS desde el PC al móvil.

José de la Peña, director de Acción Institucional de Telefónica Móviles España, ha destacado «las posibilidades del móvil como una herramienta de comunicación inmediata, rápida y muy personal, que ha facilitado que los usuarios, principalmente los jóvenes, hayan creado un lenguaje específico. diccionarioSMS.com contribuirá a ordenar, entender y clarificar este nuevo lenguaje, de uso cada vez más frecuente».

«Las comunicaciones online y sms se están introduciendo en los hábitos de los jóvenes, a las que dedican cada vez más tiempo. Con este diccionarioSMS.com nos acercamos a esta realidad con un completo manual que nos ayudará a entender mejor este nuevo «lenguaje», declara Víctor Castro, Country Manager de MSN España. Por su parte, Sisco Sapena, director ejecutivo de Lleida.net, ha subrayado que «los jóvenes adaptan constantemente las nuevas tecnologías a sus formas de comunicación y a sus relaciones interpersonales. El proceso de elaboración de este primer diccionario SMS, de elaboración popular, será una muestra palpable de este fenómeno social.»

«Esta iniciativa es una demostración de que el uso de los teléfonos móviles forma parte del modo de comunicarse de los jóvenes actuales, como lo demuestra el uso masivo que hacen del servicio de mensajes cortos», ha asegurado Joaquín Mollinedo, Director Corporativo de Relaciones Institucionales y Regulación de Grupo Auna.»

«Cada 90 segundos se envía un millón de SMS en todo el mundo, con un lenguaje universal,» ha explicado Miguel Udaondo, director de Relaciones Corporativas de Vodafone España. «Los usuarios nos hemos adaptado al terminal para ser entendidos, suprimiendo en el mensaje todo aquello que no es necesario.»

Nuevos usos que interesan y mucho en los colegios. «Me preocupa el uso que se hace de nuestro idioma por el alejamiento que supone de la uniformidad del idioma creando un código que dificulte la comunicación», explica Concha Badía, profesora de Lengua del Colegio Ramón y Cajal, «pero por otra parte, considero que la lengua está viva y es, sobre todo, de los hablantes y por tanto suya y, como tal, pueden transformarla. Quiero con esto decir que hay que escuchar y plantearse si hay una parte valiosa en su forma de comunicación. Un rechazo frontal no creo que nos condujera a nada.»

Fuente: http://www.informativoweb.com

A targeted workbook.

The series is complemented with an *AP* Preparation Workbook,* which systematically practices each one of the skills measured by the AP* Exam:

Interpretive Communication	Print Texts.
Interpretive Communication	Print and Audio Texts (combined).
Interpretive Communication	Audio Texts.
Interpersonal Writing	E-mail Reply.
Presentational Writing	Persuasive Essay.
Interpersonal Speaking	Conversation.
Presentational Speaking	Cultural Comparison.

The workbook provides strategies for taking each portion of the test, sample answers, and practice activities.

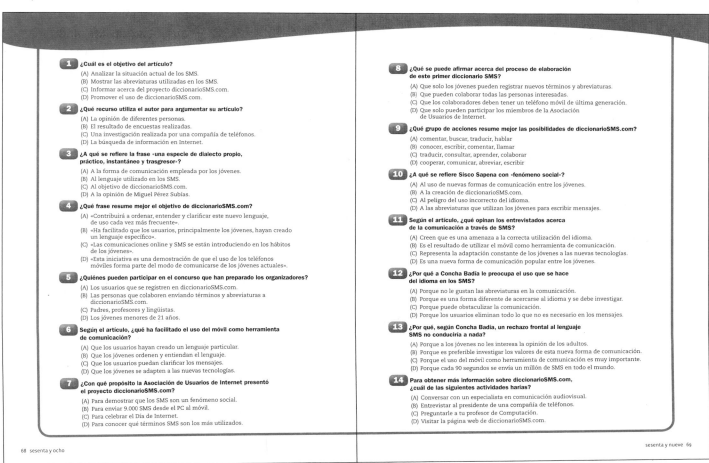

1 ¿Cuál es el objetivo del artículo?

(A) Analizar la situación actual de los SMS.
(B) Mostrar las abreviaturas utilizadas en los SMS.
(C) Informar acerca del proyecto diccionarioSMS.com.
(D) Promover el uso de diccionarioSMS.com.

2 ¿Qué recurso utiliza el autor para argumentar su artículo?

(A) La opinión de diferentes personas.
(B) El resultado de encuestas realizadas.
(C) Una investigación realizada por una compañía de teléfonos.
(D) La búsqueda de información en Internet.

3 ¿A qué se refiere la frase «una especie de dialecto propio, práctico, instantáneo y trasgresor»?

(A) A la forma de comunicación empleada por los jóvenes.
(B) Al lenguaje utilizado en los SMS.
(C) Al objetivo de diccionarioSMS.com.
(D) A la opinión de Miguel Pérez Subías.

4 ¿Qué frase resume mejor el objetivo de diccionarioSMS.com?

(A) «Contribuirá a ordenar, entender y clarificar este nuevo lenguaje, de uso cada vez más frecuente».
(B) «Ha facilitado que los usuarios, principalmente los jóvenes, hayan creado un lenguaje específico».
(C) «Las comunicaciones online y SMS se están introduciendo en los hábitos de los jóvenes».
(D) «Esta iniciativa es una demostración de que el uso de los teléfonos móviles forma parte del modo de comunicarse de los jóvenes actuales».

5 ¿Quiénes pueden participar en el concurso que han preparado los organizadores?

(A) Los usuarios que se registren en diccionarioSMS.com.
(B) Las personas que colaboren enviando términos y abreviaturas a diccionarioSMS.com.
(C) Padres, profesores y lingüistas.
(D) Los jóvenes menores de 21 años.

6 Según el artículo, ¿qué ha facilitado el uso del móvil como herramienta de comunicación?

(A) Que los usuarios hayan creado un lenguaje particular.
(B) Que los jóvenes ordenen y entiendan el lenguaje.
(C) Que los usuarios puedan clarificar los mensajes.
(D) Que los jóvenes se adapten a las nuevas tecnologías.

7 ¿Con qué propósito la Asociación de Usuarios de Internet presentó el proyecto diccionarioSMS.com?

(A) Para demostrar que los SMS son un fenómeno social.
(B) Para enviar 9.000 SMS desde el PC al móvil.
(C) Para celebrar el Día de Internet.
(D) Para conocer qué términos SMS son los más utilizados.

8 ¿Qué se puede afirmar acerca del proceso de elaboración de este primer diccionario SMS?

(A) Que solo los jóvenes pueden registrar nuevos términos y abreviaturas.
(B) Que pueden colaborar todas las personas interesadas.
(C) Que los colaboradores deben tener un teléfono móvil de última generación.
(D) Que solo pueden participar los miembros de la Asociación de Usuarios de Internet.

9 ¿Qué grupo de acciones resume mejor las posibilidades de diccionarioSMS.com?

(A) comentar, buscar, traducir, hablar
(B) conocer, escribir, comentar, llamar
(C) traducir, consultar, aprender, colaborar
(D) cooperar, comunicar, abreviar, escribir

10 ¿A qué se refiere Sisco Sapena con «fenómeno social»?

(A) Al uso de nuevas formas de comunicación entre los jóvenes.
(B) A la creación de diccionarioSMS.com.
(C) Al peligro del uso incorrecto del idioma.
(D) A las abreviaturas que utilizan los jóvenes para escribir mensajes.

11 Según el artículo, ¿qué opinan los entrevistados acerca de la comunicación a través de SMS?

(A) Creen que es una amenaza a la correcta utilización del idioma.
(B) Es el resultado de utilizar el móvil como herramienta de comunicación.
(C) Representa la adaptación constante de los jóvenes a las nuevas tecnologías.
(D) Es una nueva forma de comunicación popular entre los jóvenes.

12 ¿Por qué a Concha Badía le preocupa el uso que se hace del idioma en los SMS?

(A) Porque no le gustan las abreviaturas en la comunicación.
(B) Porque es una forma diferente de acercarse al idioma y se debe investigar.
(C) Porque puede obstaculizar la comunicación.
(D) Porque los usuarios eliminan todo lo que no es necesario en los mensajes.

13 ¿Por qué, según Concha Badía, un rechazo frontal al lenguaje SMS no conduciría a nada?

(A) Porque a los jóvenes no les interesa la opinión de los adultos.
(B) Porque es preferible investigar los valores de esta nueva forma de comunicación.
(C) Porque el uso del móvil como herramienta de comunicación es muy importante.
(D) Porque cada 90 segundos se envía un millón de SMS en todo el mundo.

14 Para obtener más información sobre diccionarioSMS.com, ¿cuál de las siguientes actividades harías?

(A) Conversar con un especialista en comunicación audiovisual.
(B) Entrevistar al presidente de una compañía de teléfonos.
(C) Preguntarle a tu profesor de Computación.
(D) Visitar la página web de diccionarioSMS.com.

The *Teacher's Edition*

Keys for teaching and learning.

The pages at the beginning of each unit offer a broad overview as well as tools for the organization and planning of school activities.

Objectives, contents, and evaluation criteria.

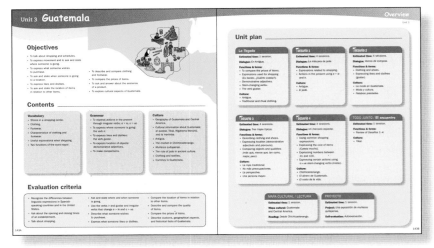

Outline of the unit and estimated time for completing each section.

Detailed description of the standards for learning Spanish in the unit.

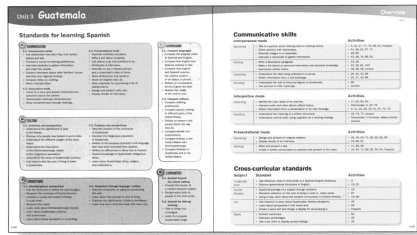

Communicative abilities practiced in the unit classified by skill (speaking, writing, listening, and reading) and by use (interpersonal, interpretative, and presentational).

Standards for other areas also discussed.

Detailed lesson plans for 50- and 90-minute classes.

Audio scripts.

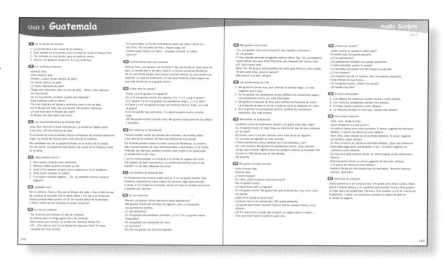

The instructional guides offer numerous resources for making the teacher's job easier.

General overview of the section.

Explanation of key educational and methodological solutions for interpreting the material.

Additional information about the cultural topics discussed.

Methodological proposals and suggestions: how to present the material, what to do with the class, how to prevent common errors, etc.

Differentiated instruction: developing learners, expanding learners, heritage language learners, special-needs learners, cooperative learning, multiple intelligences, critical thinking, etc.

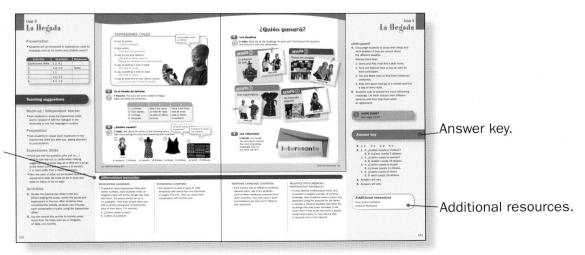

Answer key.

Additional resources.

Technology

A wide variety of technological resources.

Español Santillana relies on broad technological support, including digital versions of print materials (books, workbooks, and teacher's guides), plus an extensive offering of specific resources: visual presentations, videos, audio materials, a webpage, and more.

Visual presentations in the *fotonovelas* and the challenges.

The *fotonovelas* that present the characters' arrival in the country and their challenges are supported by visual presentations that replicate the dialogues and the story. The visual presentations offer an excellent method for improving students' listening comprehension ability.

Videos for enjoying the Spanish-speaking world's cultures.

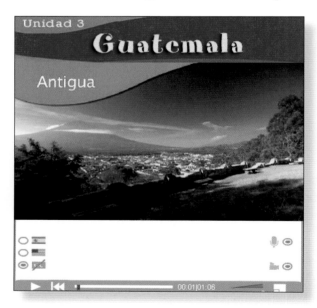

The unit begins with a video that gives students an overview of the country or cultural area and the challenges that the characters will undertake. Each *Mapa cultural* is also accompanied by a video that offers a detailed view of the country or cultural area, its landscapes, and its most outstanding characteristics. In addition, each unit includes two other videos on significant cultural topics: the house of Frida Kahlo (Mexico), Old San Juan (Puerto Rico), the market of Chichicastenango (Guatemala), and so on. The videos are highly evocative, serving to motivate students and reinforce their listening skills while promoting learning.

The audios, an invaluable tool.

The books are accompanied by Audio CDs containing recordings of all the listening activities. The *Speaking and Listening Workbook* (see page T37) is also accompanied by Audio CDs.

The webpages are a fundamental element of *Español Santillana.*

The webpage **Fans del español** (www.fansdelespañol.com) features the basic plot of the story. The characters decide to create the website *Fans del español* in order to share what they know about the Spanish-speaking world. Characters post information about themselves and about challenges that students can access on this webpage. In this manner, fiction becomes reality.

Additionally, the **Español Santillana** series is supported by the **eLearning Center**, which offers countless activities, photogalleries, games, and other resources for the student, as well as an extensive bank of assessment activities for the teacher to use (Online Assessments).

The digital versions provide a complete multimedia experience.

Both the Student Book and Teacher's Edition are available in an interactive digital format:

▶ The **Interactive Student Book** contains numerous multimedia resources that enhance and complement learning Spanish: videos, visual presentations, audios, photogalleries, flashcards, etc. Students can listen to the pronunciation of the dialogues and vocabulary words, and can also use interactive tools such as highlighters and sticky notes.

▶ The **All-in-One Digital Teacher's Edition** brings together all of the elements that the teacher needs to plan and teach a class:

- The *Interactive Student Book* and its multimedia resources. This version of the *Student Book* is designed so that the teacher can project the pages onto a screen and can also activate the videos, the visual presentations, the audios, and other features.
- The *Teacher's Edition* pages.
- The *Teacher's Annotated Edition* of the *Practice Workbook* and the *Speaking and Listening Workbook*, with its corresponding audio tracks.
- The Assessment Program, with answer keys for the teacher.
- An editable version of the Lesson Plans, so that the teacher can personalize the lesson plans to his or her needs.

The workbooks are also available in digital format.

The Workbooks

Three workbooks to practice with.

Español Santillana features three student workbooks for each level: the *Practice Workbook*, the *Speaking and Listening Workbook*, and the workbook for heritage Spanish speakers (the *Cuaderno para hispanohablantes*). Additionally, High School Level 4 is complemented by the *AP* Preparation Workbook* (see page T31).

The *Practice Workbook* deepens the study of the language independently.

This is the perfect complement to the Student Book. Here students will find many opportunities to work with the linguistic and cultural contents of the series. It contains all the information (word glossaries and grammar summaries) that students need, and the activities have been designed so that students can work them out without having to consult other sources.

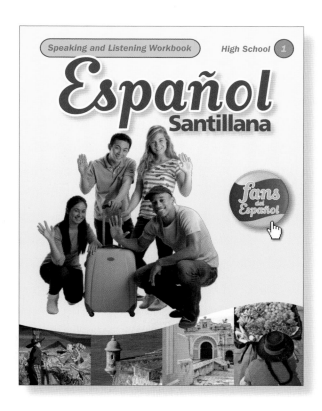

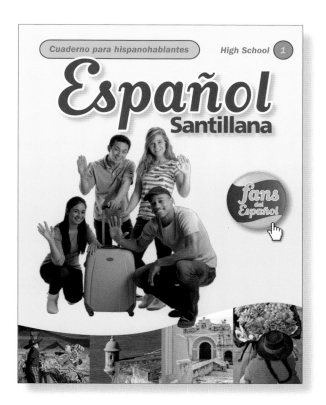

The *Speaking and Listening Workbook* consolidates two fundamental skills.

This workbook deals specifically with comprehension and verbal expression.

The listening activities can be used in the classroom or at home. The Audio CD that accompanies the workbook allows the students to work independently. In contrast, the speaking activities are designed to be used in the classroom.

The speaking and listening activities allow students to practice the key vocabulary and grammatical structures presented in the books.

The workbook for heritage Spanish speakers improves their reading comprehension and writing ability.

This workbook complements the *Español Santillana* textbook and is for heritage Spanish speakers capable of completing an activity in Spanish by themselves. The workbook maintains the themes and structures of the Student Book, allowing heritage Spanish speakers to work with the textbook in class while completing tasks appropriate to their language level in the workbook.

The objectives of the workbook are the following:

- To develop reading comprehension (Reading).
- To expand students' vocabulary (Vocabulary).
- To improve students' handling of written expression for various purposes (Spelling, Writing).
- To encourage understanding of and appreciation for differences in cultural origins (Connections, Communities).

Scope and Sequence High School 1

Contents

Unidad	Vocabulario
Unit 1 **México** 30–85	• People • Physical characteristics • Personality traits • Family • States and conditions
Unit 2 **Puerto Rico** 86–143	• The house • Furniture and objects in a house • Household chores • Leisure activities
Unit 3 **Guatemala** 144–199	• The shopping center • Clothing and footwear • Describing clothing and footwear • Shopping
Unit 4 **Perú** 200–255	• Foods and beverages • Food stores • At the table • Describing food
Unit 5 **España** 256–309	• Parts of the body • Personal hygiene • Symptoms and illnesses • Basic remedies • Healthy habits
Unit 6 **Estados Unidos** 310–363	• The world of work • Hobbies • Free time • Sports
Unit 7 **Argentina** 364–417	• Transportation • Travel • Destinations and lodging • The city. Location and directions
Unit 8 **Chile** 418–471	• The universe • Geography • Political divisions • Numbers from 101 to 1,000 • Nature and the environment

Gramática		Cultura	

• Subject pronouns
• The verb *ser*
• Adjectives
• The verb *tener*
	• Expressing possession:
	  – Possessive adjectives
	  – The preposition *de*
	• The verb *estar*
		• *Mapa cultural:* Mexico
		  • Mexico City: Tenochtitlan
		  • The south: the indigenous population
			• *Lectura: Teotihuacán, ciudad de los dioses*

• Nouns
• Articles. Agreement with nouns
• Expressing existence. The verb *haber*
• Expressing location
• Regular *-ar* verbs, present tense
	• Regular *-er* and *-ir* verbs, present tense
	• Expressing obligation:
	  – *Tener que* + infinitive
	  – *Hay que* + infinitive
	• Adverbs of frequency
		• *Mapa cultural:* Puerto Rico
		  • Old San Juan
		  • Salsa, the essence of Puerto Rico
			• *Lectura: El Morro: Blog de viajes*

• Stem-changing verbs (*e > ie*)
• The verb *ir*
• The verb *gustar*
• Demonstratives
	• Comparison. Comparative adjectives
	• Stem-changing verbs (*o > ue*)
		• *Mapa cultural:* Guatemala
		  • The great Mayan city of Tikal
		  • The quetzal, national bird of Guatemala
			• *Lectura: Desde Chichicastenango*

• Adverbs of quantity
• Expressing want, preference, and rejection. The verbs *querer* and *preferir*
	• Irregular verbs in the *yo* form
	• Direct object pronouns
	• Indirect object pronouns
	• Stem-changing verbs (*e > i*)
		• *Mapa cultural:* Peru
		  • The Incas, kings of the mountains
		  • The Nazca lines
			• *Lectura: Festividad inca del Inti Raymi*

• The verbs *ver, oír, oler,* and *decir*
• Reflexive verbs
• The verb *doler*
	• The verb *sentirse*
	• Affirmative *tú* commands. Regular verbs
		• *Mapa cultural:* Spain
		  • Madrid: a painter's paradise
		  • The south: an Arabic heritage
			• *Lectura: El Guernica, de Pablo Picasso*

• Affirmative commands. Irregular verbs
• *Ir a* + infinitive. Time markers in the future
• The present progressive
	• The present participle
	• Stem-changing verbs (*u > ue*)
		• *Mapa cultural:* United States
		  • Hispanic influence in the United States
		  • States with Hispanic history
			• Concentration of Hispanic people in cities
			• *Lectura: Celebramos la Herencia Hispana*

• The preterite tense of regular *-ar* verbs
• The preterite tense of regular *-er* and *-ir* verbs
	• Time markers in the past
	• The preterite tense of the verbs *ser* and *ir*
	• Negative commands
		• *Mapa cultural:* Argentina
		  • The tango
		  • Buenos Aires
			• *Lectura: La vuelta al mundo de Cinthia Scoch*

• Expressing cause: *porque* and *por*
• Expressing quantity. Indefinites
• Irregular verbs in the preterite. *Decir* and *hacer*
	• Irregular verbs in the preterite. *Estar* and *tener*
	• Expressing permission and prohibition
		• *Mapa cultural:* Chile
		  • Easter Island
		  • Pablo Neruda
		  • The chinchineros
			• *Lectura: Oda a la manzana*

Scope and Sequence High School 2

Contents

Unidad	Vocabulario
Unit 1 **Centroamérica** 28–79	• Personal and family relationships • Physical characteristics and personality traits • Emotional states and feelings • Personal information
Unit 2 **Las Antillas** 80–131	• The house. Household chores • Furniture and objects in a house • Electrical appliances • The neighborhood. Places and services
Unit 3 **Andes centrales** 132–183	• Clothing and accessories • Describing clothes • Stores and establishments • Shopping
Unit 4 **Norteamérica** 184–235	• Foods • Buying food • In the kitchen • In the restaurant
Unit 5 **España** 236–287	• Parts of the body • Personal hygiene • Health: symptoms and illnesses • Healthy habits
Unit 6 **Caribe continental** 288–339	• Trips and excursions • On the train and on the plane • The car • The hotel. The bank
Unit 7 **Río de la Plata** 340–391	• The school • Professions • Hobbies, free time activities, and entertainment • Sports
Unit 8 **La Panamericana** 392–443	• Geography • Countries • The weather • Nature and environment

Gramática		Cultura	

• Possessives
• Adjectives and nouns
	• Comparisons and superlatives
	• Interrogatives
		• *Mapa cultural:* Centroamérica
		  • Mestizaje y cultura
		  • Riqueza natural
			• *Lectura: El blog de Ichxel*

• The present progressive
• Direct object pronouns
	• Indirect object pronouns
	• Demonstratives
		• *Mapa cultural:* Las Antillas
		  • Barrios coloniales
		  • Música caribeña
			• *Lectura: Estilo de vida caribeño*

• The preterite tense of regular
  -ar verbs
• The preterite tense of regular
  -er and *-ir* verbs
	• The preterite tense of the verbs *ser, ir,*
	  decir, tener, estar, and *hacer.*
	• The preterite tense of
	  stem-changing *-ir* verbs
		• *Mapa cultural:* Andes centrales
		  • Quechuas y aymaras
		  • Los equecos
		  • Las islas Galápagos
			• *Lectura: Textiles andinos bolivianos*

• Expressing amount. Indefinites
• Singular affirmative commands
	• Plural affirmative commands
	• Negative commands
		• *Mapa cultural:* Norteamérica
		  • El Camino Real de Tierra Adentro
		  • Los chicanos
			• *Lectura: La receta
			  del guacamole*

• The past participle
• Adverbs ending in *-mente*
	• *Por* and *para*
	• Making recommendations
		• *Mapa cultural:* España
		  y el Mediterráneo
		  • Paisaje mediterráneo
		  • La Noche de San Juan
		  • Las lenguas romances
			• *Lectura:* Figura en una ventana,
			  de Salvador Dalí

• The imperfect tense
• The preterite tense of the verbs
  dar, poder, poner, querer, saber,
  and *venir*
	• Talking about past actions. The preterite
	  and imperfect tenses
	• Talking about past actions and describing
	  in the past. The preterite and imperfect
	  tenses
		• *Mapa cultural:* Caribe continental
		  • Símbolos nacionales
		  • El mestizaje y los bailes
		  • Cocina del Caribe: color
		  y sabor
			• *Lectura: El Dorado, ecos
			  de una leyenda*

• Expressing existence. Indefinites
• The present subjunctive
  of regular verbs
	• The present subjunctive of
	  stem-changing verbs
	• The present subjunctive of
	  irregular verbs
		• *Mapa cultural:* El río de la Plata
		  • Influencia italiana
		  • Cultura rioplatense
		  • El chipá
			• *Lectura: Un cuento de Benedetti*

• The relative superlative
• Expressing plans
  and intentions
	• The future tense
	• Hiding the agent. The pronoun *se*
		• *Mapa cultural:* La ruta Panamericana
		  • Variedad geográfica
		  • El mundo hispano: unidad
		  y diversidad
			• *Lectura: El Tapón de Darién:
			  un corte en la ruta Panamericana*

Scope and Sequence High School 3

Contents

Unidad	Vocabulario
Unit 1 **¿Cómo eres?** 12–65	• Physical characteristics and personality traits • Family relationships • Biographies
Unit 2 **Entre amigos** 66–119	• Personal relationships • Introductions. Expressions to invite, accept, and reject an invitation • Phone calls
Unit 3 **Tus cosas** 120–173	• Clothing • Describing objects • Household chores and professions
Unit 4 **Vida sana** 174–227	• Foods • Healthy habits • The doctor's office. The human body
Unit 5 **¿Trabajas?** 228–281	• Jobs and professions • Work and technology • Volunteering and community service
Unit 6 **Tus aficiones** 282–335	• Free time and events • Sports • Travel and lodging
Unit 7 **Nuestro planeta** 336–389	• Nature and the environment • The weather. The universe • Natural disasters. Natural resources
Unit 8 **En sociedad** 390–443	• Historical figures, events, civilizations • Politics and government • Society

Gramática		Cultura		Escritura
• *Ser* and *estar* • Comparatives and superlatives • The imperfect and the past progressive	• Expressing possession • The preterite and the imperfect tenses • Time expressions for narration	• Lectura informativa: *Una breve biografía* • Lectura literaria: *Los hermanos Ayar* (leyenda inca)	• Mapa cultural: La población latinoamericana	Un bosquejo biográfico
• Direct object and indirect object pronouns • Reflexive and reciprocal verbs • Expressing wishes, likes, and preferences	• Non-reflexive verbs used with pronouns • Expressing need and obligation • Speaking about the future	• Lectura informativa: *Juegos precolombinos* • Lectura literaria: *El mensaje*	• Mapa cultural: La fiesta: expresión comunitaria	Un caligrama
• The past participle • Talking about recent actions. The present perfect tense • Indefinites	• Impersonal constructions. The pronoun *se* • The past perfect tense • Demonstratives	• Lectura informativa: *Guía de viajeros: un hotel inolvidable* • Lectura literaria: *La casa de muñecas*	• Mapa cultural: La ciudad colonial	Un ensayo
• Commands • Verbs that express change • *Para* and *por*	• Making value statements • The conditional tense • Giving advice and recommendations	• Lectura informativa: *El blog personal de Sara* • Lectura literaria: *La leyenda del maíz* (leyenda azteca)	• Mapa cultural: Alimentos básicos en el mundo hispano	Una receta
• Expressing certainty and doubt • The imperfect subjunctive • Giving details. The relative pronoun *que*	• The gender of nouns • Expressing feelings • Expressing difficulty	• Lectura informativa: *Manuel Jalón, un inventor humanista* • Lectura literaria: *Música* (Ana María Matute)	• Mapa cultural: Universidades hispanas	Una carta formal
• Expressing opinion • Grammatical forms of courtesy • Expressing probability	• Expressing purpose • Indirect speech • Expressing place	• Lectura informativa: *Historia de los Juegos Panamericanos* • Lectura literaria: *Galletitas* (Jorge Bucay)	• Mapa cultural: Deportes con tradición	Un cuento
• Expressing condition (I) • Expressing condition (II) • Expressing time	• The present perfect subjunctive • Expressing cause and consequence • The personal *a*	• Lectura informativa: *Las tradiciones del Sol* • Lectura literaria: *El eclipse* (Augusto Monterroso)	• Mapa cultural: Espacios naturales singulares	Un reportaje
• The passive voice • The past tenses (review) • Referring to the stages of an action	• Uses of the indicative (review) • Articles • Uses of the subjunctive (review)	• Lectura informativa: *Entrevista a Debra McKeon* • Lectura literaria: *La muralla* (Nicolás Guillén)	• Mapa cultural: Una ciudad con historia: Barcelona	Un texto de opinión

Scope and Sequence High School 4

Contenidos

Unidad	Vocabulario
Unidad 1 **Nos relacionamos** 12–69	• Características físicas y rasgos de personalidad • La oficina de correos • Los medios de comunicación
Unidad 2 **Nos cuidamos** 70–127	• En el restaurante • La sala de urgencias • Estados físicos y anímicos
Unidad 3 **Trabajamos** 128–183	• La escuela • La economía • Trabajo y profesiones
Unidad 4 **Nos divertimos** 184–239	• Ocio y espectáculos. Deportes y tiempo libre • Los viajes • El alojamiento. El tiempo meteorológico
Unidad 5 **Participamos** 240–297	• Historia • Política y gobierno • Problemas sociales y medioambientales
Unidad 6 **Creamos** 298–353	• Arte y pintura • Arquitectura y escultura • Literatura

Gramática		Cultura		Escritura	Hacia el AP* Exam
• Expresar gustos, intereses, sentimientos y emociones • Los adjetivos • Los verbos pronominales	• Los verbos reflexivos y recíprocos • Hablar de acciones en curso • Expresar cantidad	• Lectura informativa: *El oficio más romántico: escribir cartas de amor por encargo* (reportaje) • Lectura literaria: *El diario a diario* (Julio Cortázar)	• Mapa cultural: Unidad y variedad del español	Un correo de presentación	Interpretación de textos escritos
• Las construcciones impersonales. El pronombre *se* • Los pronombres de OD y OI • Los verbos con preposición	• Los artículos • La voz pasiva • *Ser y estar*	• Lectura informativa: *El cáncer y su prevención* (artículo científico) • Lectura literaria: *La piedra mágica* (cuento popular)	• Mapa cultural: Sistemas de salud en el mundo hispano	Recomendaciones de viajes	Interpretación de textos orales
• El participio pasado • El presente perfecto y el pluscuamperfecto • Los pronombres relativos	• El futuro perfecto • Expresar deseos • Expresar condición	• Lectura informativa: *La globalización económica* (artículo de economía) • Lectura literaria: *Un constructor de ecuaciones* (Juan Bonilla)	• Mapa cultural: La economía de Latinoamérica	Tu currículum ideal	Interacción escrita
• Expresar frecuencia • Expresar probabilidad (I) • Expresar probabilidad (II)	• El presente perfecto de subjuntivo • Expresar causa • Expresar consecuencia	• Lectura informativa: *Como la vida misma* (Rosa Montero; columna periodística) • Lectura literaria: *Vivir para contarla* (Gabriel García Márquez)	• Mapa cultural: El turismo en Latinoamérica	Un blog de viajes	Interacción oral
• Los numerales ordinales • Expresar certeza y duda • Expresar finalidad	• Expresar dificultad • Expresar condición. El pluscuamperfecto de subjuntivo • Expresar tiempo	• Lectura informativa: *María Eva Duarte de Perón* (biografía) • Lectura literaria: *El exiliado* (Cristina Peri Rossi)	• Mapa cultural: La inmigración hispana en los Estados Unidos	Un ensayo	Presentación escrita
• Las comparaciones • El artículo neutro *lo* • Expresar opinión	• Hacer valoraciones • Los diminutivos • Dar consejos y hacer recomendaciones	• Lectura informativa: *Rafael Moneo* (entrevista) • Lectura literaria: *El Sur* (Jorge Luis Borges)	• Mapa cultural: El «boom» de la literatura latinoamericana	Una reseña	Presentación oral

The Spanish Language of the United States

Gerardo Piña-Rosales The North American Academy of the Spanish Language

First of all, dear reader, let us focus on the title of this essay: "The Spanish Language *of* the United States" instead of "The Spanish Language *in* the United States." The difference between these two prepositions is an essential one: it implies that we have begun to speak of a United States Spanish with its own characteristics, as one more of the multiple variants of the Spanish language spoken around the world.

Spanish Speakers in the United States

It is estimated that there are some 45 million Spanish-speaking people in the United States, which translates into 15 percent of the nation's population, and it is expected that this figure will rise to more than 150 million Spanish speakers by 2050. In other words, it is highly probable that the United States will become the country with the largest number of Spanish-speaking inhabitants on our planet. More than half of the 45 million Spanish speakers were born in this country, and they make up a younger-than-average portion of the overall population: 48 percent of Hispanics are younger than 25 years of age. Whether or not a minority language replaces the language spoken by the majority depends, above all, on the new generations; thus, the relative youth of the Hispanic population will undoubtedly influence the future of the Spanish language in the United States.

Spanish Variants

When we speak of the Spanish language of the United States, it is important to point out that we are not referring to a monolithic, uniform language, but to one that encompasses a number of variants. In this regard, we can divide the country into several linguistic areas, each with its own distinct characteristics. In the West and Southwest, where 60 percent of Hispanics reside, a *chicano* variant of Spanish is spoken; in Florida, and especially in Miami, a Cuban variant of Spanish is heard. In the Northeast, including New York, New Jersey, and Connecticut, a Caribbean form of Spanish is spoken. Furthermore, one can hear *isleño* Spanish in Louisiana and a distinctive form of Spanish spoken in the region of the Sabine River (Louisiana and Texas).

English Influences

The massive influence of English has imparted a unique imprint on the Spanish language of the United States, which contrasts with that of other Spanish-speaking countries. This particular influence is manifested in new vocabulary, much of it based on "borrowed" words, which have contributed to the incorporation of *anglicisms* into the Spanish spoken in those countries.

English Influence at Work

Hispanic immigrants try to learn and speak English at their workplace and in their associations with Americans. This effort to communicate tends to facilitate the use of *Spanglish*. In time, if they have a certain level of education, they learn both languages well and become bilingual. There is a desire to acquire a better knowledge not only of English but also of the Spanish of their heritage.

Spanglish

A distinctive characteristic of the Spanish language of the United States is the so-called "code-switching," which consists of a speaker's use of both languages during a conversation. Since this means of communication has not been methodically studied until recently, a certain notion exists—both among the general public and among certain educators—that it is a random mixture of languages, i.e., *Spanglish*. In fact it is a process with its own structural conventions, one that also plays a unique role among bilingual Spanish speakers, precisely as an alternative to communicating in a single language. The economic importance of the Spanish language of the United States is greater than that of any other Spanish-speaking country. The Spanish language would survive if only for the United States.

Bibliography

Amastae, Jon and Lucía Elías-Olivares. *Spanish in the United States: Sociolinguistic Aspects.* Cambridge: Cambridge University Press, 1982.

Elías-Olivares, Lucía, ed. *Spanish in the U.S. Setting: Beyond the Southwest.* Rosslyn, VA: National Clearinghouse for Bilingual Education, 1983.

Lipski, John M. *Varieties of Spanish in the United States.* Washington DC: Georgetown University Press, 2008.

López-Morales, Humberto, ed. *Enciclopedia del español en los Estados Unidos.* Madrid: Instituto Cervantes/Santillana, 2008.

Teaching and Learning: Language and Culture

Janet Glass Dwight Englewood School, Englewood, New Jersey, Rutgers University

Alfred Nobel's Peace Prize wished to reward "the person who shall have done the most or the best work for fraternity between nations." What could be more critical today? As teachers of world languages, our medium is language, but our message is one of cultural ambassador. Besides, what is more intriguing to a student than to learn how to make a new friend from another culture, to enter another world? This motivation is what stimulates our students' curiosity and helps them master the language. But once hooked, how can we make the most of their interest?

Five-Senses Culture

We can start by integrating culture into the whole language instruction process, making sure that culture underscores every language activity and is at the core of the unit. We can go beyond cultural "awareness" and try to experience the target culture in the classroom with smells, touches, simulations, tastes, rhythms, and video clips. Learning is enhanced when exchanges with people from the target culture happen early and often. As Byram et al. say in "Developing Intercultural Competence in Practice," "the task is rather to facilitate learners' interactions with some small part of another society and its cultures … and encouraging them to investigate for themselves the otherness around them." Let's lift it off the page!

Measuring Culture

When it comes to culture, students are always asking, "Does it *count*?" Although we have currently come a long way in measuring the language proficiency of our students, we are challenged to do as well with testing cultural appropriateness. Culture has to be taught systematically and then, assessed. How powerful it is to show students evidence of their own cultural competence, yet more exploration of how to best assess cultural competence is needed.

Seeing Our Own Culture with New Eyes

As language teachers, we also make the most of students' interest when we show how language shapes our thoughts, and leads to how we behave. Most of us don't become aware of our own cultural assumptions until confronted by another world view. When I was in Japan, for example, people frequently apologized as part of their daily conversation. They said, "Sorry I disturbed you" when calling someone on the phone. How does this habit of polite language reflect its culture? Accepting responsibility is a very high priority in Japan. As a result, we find it is a culture that discourages blame and is relatively free of lawsuits. Cultural instincts become internal, hidden, and subconscious. Through the target language, we strive to have our students uncover these influences, empathize with the people, and be able to interact in culturally appropriate ways.

Research Says

Meanwhile, research has confirmed what we have sensed. In a survey of young students studying language and culture, their responses to "People from other countries are scary" and "Hearing a language that's not English makes me nervous" was a resounding "No!" Students not in the program answered "Maybe" and "Yes."

So, as we make the foreign become familiar, the familiar will become a bit more foreign. By bringing cultural experiences into the classroom, measuring the outcomes, aiming for deep understanding and exchanges, we put linguistic and cultural abilities together and at the forefront of our shrinking world. *¡Sí, se puede!*

Bibliography

Byram, Michael, A. Nichols, and D. Stevens. "Developing Intercultural Competence in Practice." *Multilingual Matters Ltd*. 3 (2001).

Kennedy, Teresa, et al. "The FLES Attitudinal Inventory." *Foreign Language Annals*, ACTFL 33(3), May/June 2000: 278–289.

Wright, David A. "Culture as Information and Culture as Affective Process: A Comparative Study." *Foreign Language Annals*, ACTFL 33(3), May/June 2000: 330–341.

The Integration of Language, Culture, and Content in the Three Modes of Communication

Brandon Zaslow Site Director, California Foreign Language Project, Department of Education, Occidental College, Los Angeles, California

Work with teachers who are implementing a standards-based instructional approach shows that the integration of language, culture, and content is the area of greatest challenge and the aspect of standards-based practice that has the most transformative effect on student learning.

Preparing students to use language for real-world purposes in culturally appropriate ways requires that teachers specify the tasks students will need to carry out in order to function in target-language communities. The most efficient way to gain access to language, culture, and content is through the use of authentic materials, those that are designed for individuals who speak the language and share the culture and its perspectives on content. Semi-authentic video, audio, or print media are often used to ensure that all of the language, culture, and content necessary for successful real-world language use are available for learning.

Interpretive Mode

Teachers use a variety of strategies for making language, culture, and content comprehensible. They prepare students for interpretation by interesting them in the theme of the lesson, building on previous knowledge, and previewing key language, culture, and content. They ask students to make predictions, provide non-linguistic supports to meaning, and work with texts multiple times using different interpretive tasks that focus student attention on language, culture, or content. Often teachers break up texts into smaller segments in order to help students skim for main ideas and then scan for supporting details. Texts with storylines or content that can be divided into logical parts are easier to understand and recall.

Interpersonal Mode

When learners understand the materials used during interpretive communication, they need a great deal of practice to use the language, content, and cultural knowledge and skills to participate in real-world tasks. In order to gain proficiency in interpersonal communication, learners need to practice carrying out real-world tasks in multiple settings combining various elements of language, culture, and content. Recycling communicative elements that will occur in culminating tasks ensures that students will be successful in spontaneous, unrehearsed interpersonal communication. As students gain proficiency using their language in a variety of culturally-authentic settings, teachers integrate language, culture, and content in more demanding simulations or real-world interpersonal tasks.

Presentational Mode

When students have had an opportunity to practice with others and carry out a number of interpersonal tasks using language, culture, and content, they will have developed the skills necessary to carry out real-world presentational tasks with sufficient clarity and accuracy to be successfully understood by a target-culture audience. Presentational tasks can be oral or written or combine both speech and writing. It is important when constructing presentational tasks to focus learner attention on culturally appropriate behavior and target-culture audiences. In written presentational tasks, rubrics are useful to guide the many drafts that may be necessary to produce a clear and accurate text that communicates effectively with the target audience.

Conclusion

Although challenging, the integration of language, culture, and content in interpretive, interpersonal, and presentational communication will transform world language classrooms and prepare students to function effectively in target-language communities.

Bibliography

National Standards in Foreign Language Education Project. *Standards for Foreign Language Learning in the 21st Century*. Lawrence, KS: Allen Press, Inc., 1999.

Anderson, Nancy, ed. *Spanish for Native Speakers*. AATSP, 2000.

Ballman, Terry L., Judith E. Liskin Gasparro, and Paul B. Mandell, eds. *The Communicative Classroom*. AATSP, 2001.

Birckbichler, Diane W. and Robert M. Terry, eds. *Reflecting on the Past to Shape the Future*. ACTFL, 2000.

Galloway, Vicky, ed. *Teaching Cultures of the Hispanic World: Products and Practices in Perspective*. AATSP, 2001.

Gunterman, Gail, ed. *Teaching Spanish with the Five C's: A Blueprint for Success*. ACTFL, 2000.

Heining-Boynton, Audrey L., ed. *2005-2015: Realizing Our Vision of Languages for All*. ACTFL, 2006.

Lafayette, Robert C., ed. *National Standards: A Catalyst for Reform*. ACTFL, 1996.

Omaggio-Hadley, Alice. *Teaching Language in Context*, 3rd ed. Boston: Heinle and Heinle, 2001.

Shrum, Judith L. and Eileen W. Glisan, *Teacher's Handbook: Contextualized Language Instruction*, 4th ed. Boston: Heinle and Heinle, 2010.

Teaching Vocabulary and Grammar Using Authentic Literary Texts and Other Reading Selections

Emily Spinelli Executive Director, American Association of Teachers of Spanish and Portuguese. Professor Emerita of Spanish, University of Michigan-Dearborn

For many years the foreign language profession viewed the teaching of language and the teaching of literature as two very separate and distinct activities. At all educational levels the reading of literary texts was often seen as a task that only very advanced students could undertake. As a result, the early years of instruction were generally devoted to learning the language so that students could study literature in upper-level courses.

Authentic Texts Defined

In the 1970s this separation of language and literature teaching was challenged as researchers in language acquisition advocated for the use of authentic texts and materials in the language classroom. Widdowson pointed out that the language presented to students does not need to be simplified for easy access. He further stated that, "Nowadays there are recommendations that the language presented should be authentic." Wallace later defined authentic language as that found in "…real-life texts, not written for pedagogic purposes." Soon thereafter, authentic materials gradually made their way into textbooks in the form of advertisements, brochures, menus, schedules, and other items utilized in daily life. However, literature was still not viewed as suitable material for language learning.

Contemporary View of Literary Texts

Recently, a report from the Modern Language Association called for an end to the separation of language courses and literature courses and recommended a curriculum "in which language, culture, and literature are taught as a continuous whole." This contemporary view of the role of literature reinforces the notion that literary texts can be used to teach language beginning at the earliest levels. In addition to providing language models for students, literary selections also provide authentic cultural information, help critical thinking skills, and emphasize historical and literary traditions.

Reading Strategies and Activities to Promote Comprehension

It is now generally accepted that literary and other authentic texts should not be simplified or modified in order to help students comprehend them. Rather, students should be provided with reading strategies and activities prior to reading the selection. In turn, these strategies and activities will help students comprehend the authentic material.

Pre-reading, During-reading, and Post-reading Activities

Generally the strategies, explanations, and activities related to a reading selection fall into three categories called pre-reading, during-reading, and post-reading activities, depending on when they are used in relation to reading the selection. Pre-reading strategies provide students with reading techniques such as reading for gist, understanding the genre of the text, or forming hypotheses about the theme or topic of the text. Pre-reading activities can involve a presentation or review of vocabulary or grammar structures used within the literary selection. Vocabulary activities typically focus on cognate recognition, word families, prefixes and suffixes and other information designed to assist students with comprehending individual words. Grammar activities generally focus on recognition of parts of speech, verb forms and tenses, and word order. Other pre-reading activities focus on cultural information that have students compare or contrast cultural products, practices or perspectives found in the text with those found in their own cultures. During-reading activities generally help students focus on the pre-reading strategies and other information taught or reviewed in the pre-reading phase. Finally, the post-reading activities focus on comprehension and ask students to demonstrate what they learned while reading.

By helping students comprehend authentic texts through the use of pre-reading strategies and activities, we expand their language capabilities while strengthening their cross-cultural and literacy skills.

Bibliography

Bernardo, Sacha Anthony. "The Use of Authentic Materials in the Teaching of Reading." *The Reading Matrix* 6 (2006): 60–69.

Foreign Languages and Higher Education: New Structures for a Changed World. New York: Modern Language Association, 2006.

Wallace, Catherine. *Reading.* Oxford: Oxford University Press, 1992.

Widdowson, Henry G. *Aspects of Language Teaching.* Oxford: Oxford University Press, 1990.

Motivation

Jan Kucerik Pinellas County Public Schools, Pinellas County, Florida

A seventh grade student known to his Spanish teacher as "Juanito" ambles reluctantly into his beginning Spanish classroom. He greets the teacher, not with an enthusiastic "Buenos días, señora," but instead with the question on the mind of many of his classmates, "What are we doing in here today?" Although we would like to believe that the question has been posed out of genuine interest in the classroom activities, we realize that Juanito's question is motivated by self-preservation. He worries that he might be unprepared for, or embarrassed by, the activities Señora has planned for the day.

What Motivates Our Students

Motivation is crucial to teaching and learning. Whenever we feel a desire or need for something, we are in a state of motivation. Juanito is motivated to survive the class period, and his teacher wants him to thrive and share her passion for the Spanish language and Hispanic culture. He has a need to feel safe, yet his teacher understands that he must take risks in order to acquire language. He wants to avoid struggle, and she knows that great effort is involved in negotiating meaning and learning from mistakes. Although human beings are motivated to learn from birth, students are often not motivated to learn what we want them to learn in the way that we want them to learn it. They do, however, select information and learning experiences that are important to them every day. Teachers continue to work tirelessly to motivate their students, but most focus on extrinsic motivators, which may not be enough to truly engage students in the long term. How do we make students feel connected to learning? How do we make them feel as if the learning could not happen without them? How do we create excitement for learning, resulting in students eagerly entering our classrooms each day?

Relationships Are Key

We rely on the standards and performance guidelines to articulate authentic tasks and clear goals. We persevere in our commitment to adjust the learning environment and the content to attract students. Most importantly, we recognize that our relationships with our students and their relationship with the learning process are crucial. Students must believe that they can be successful and experience incremental growth through learning experiences carefully designed around small chunks of meaningful language, leading to purposeful communication. Learning must be fun. Students are more likely to retain the language they acquire in a learning context that they enjoy.

They must feel that they are part of the learning environment, that they belong to the target culture, while they are acquiring their new language. They must understand the purpose of the lesson and have the freedom to select language that is important to them along the way.

Motivation and Learning

Students are motivated to take part in Spanish class when the context through which the language is presented and practiced is meaningful, serves a purpose, and relies on the students to bring it to life. Effective teachers understand the link between motivation and learning, and select language and cultural contexts that rely on the students to tell the story. "What are we doing in here today, Señora?" "We need you, Juanito, to help guide us on our learning journey."

Bibliography

Blaz, Deborah. *Foreign Language Teacher's Guide to Active Learning.* Larchmont, NY: Eye on Education, Inc., 1999.

———. *Bringing the Standards for Foreign Language Learning to Life.* NY: Eye on Education, Inc., 2002.

Curtain, Helena, and Carol A. Dahlberg. *Languages and Children—Making the Match.* Boston: Allyn and Bacon, 2004.

High, Julie. *Second Language Learning through Cooperative Learning.* San Clemente, CA: Kagan Publishing, 1993.

Marzano, Robert J., Debra J. Pickering, and Jane E. Pollock. *Classroom Instruction that Works.* Baltimore: ASCD, 2001.

Omaggio, Alice H. *Teaching Language in Context.* Florence, KY: Cengage and Heinle, 2000.

Patrick, Paula. *The Keys to the Classroom.* Alexandria, VA: The American Council on the Teaching of Foreign Languages, 2007.

Rogers, Spence. *21 Building Blocks Critical to Leaving No Child Left Behind.* Evergreen, CO: PEAK Learning Systems, Inc., 2003.

Rogers, Spence, Jim Ludington, and Becky Graf. *Teaching and Training Techniques: Lighting the Way to Performance Excellence.* Evergreen, CO: PEAK Learning Systems, Inc., 2003.

Rogers, Spence, Jim Ludington, and Shari Graham. *Motivation and Learning: A Teacher's Guide to Building Excitement for Learning and Igniting the Drive for Quality.* Evergreen, CO: PEAK Learning Systems, Inc., 1999.

Shrum, Judith L., and Eileen W. Glisan. *Teacher's Handbook: Contextualized Language Instruction.* Florence, KY: Cengage and Heinle, 2005.

Features of Backwards Design Found in *Español Santillana*

Carol McKenna Semonsky Associate Professor Emerita, Georgia State University

Principles of Backwards Design

Backwards Design, developed by Grant Wiggins and Jay McTighe, is an approach to unit development that puts the emphasis on big ideas and enduring understandings rather than on discrete skills and coverage. It has three main steps: 1) identify desired results; 2) determine acceptable evidence; and 3) plan learning experiences and instruction. Assessments are performance-based, reflect the big ideas, and are designed before the instructional activities.

Step One: Identify Desired Results

In step one, teachers define the unit's goals, its essential questions and enduring understandings, as well as the key language skills students will acquire as a result of the unit. Enduring understandings are those that have value in real life beyond the classroom, that have a potential for engaging students, and that include core tasks that are essential and integral to the subject matter. For world language teachers, national, state, and local standards as well as thematic planning provide essential guidelines and contexts when defining desired results.

Español Santillana's overall format, that of thematic units centered around young people traveling in various Spanish-speaking countries, addresses enduring understandings, such as, "Who are the Spanish-speaking peoples of the world and how do they live?" and "How are our lives similar and different?" The themes are broad and reflect cultural perspectives. For instance, in Level 1, *Unidad 3*, the stated theme is "shopping in the context of Mayan cultures and Guatemala's historic cities."

Step Two: Determine Acceptable Evidence

In step two, teachers decide which evidence will show that students have a grasp of the big ideas and enduring understandings. Wiggins and McTighe suggest that performance tasks provide the best evidence. For world language teachers, performance-based assessments, focused on student use of extended, communicative language in authentic situations, are recommended. However, the use of extended language requires initial skill building where core vocabulary and structures are mastered first.

Español Santillana offers a wide selection of contextualized formative assessments centered on these core skills as well as summative assessments that prompt extended and authentic language. Students are given an opportunity to reflect on their accomplishment of the goals by using the *Autoevaluación* at the end of each unit.

Step Three: Plan Learning Experiences and Instructions

It is in step three, in the planning for learning experiences, where *Español Santillana* excels. Both the textbook and ancillaries offer plentiful and contextualized practice of essential skills that form the building blocks necessary for meaningful communication. Practice exercises represent real-life situations. Daily plans found in the Teacher's Edition facilitate planning for both regular and block scheduling. The Teacher's Edition directly links unit content to standards and offers many ideas to address individual differences, including suggestions for reaching all learners via multiple intelligences and differentiated instruction. *Español Santillana* has a selection of ancillary materials, including websites, DVDs, and other multimedia from which teachers may choose in order to design the most effective instruction, matching both their initial desired results and their students' individual needs.

Bibliography

Center for Advanced Research on Language Acquisition. *Creating an Assessment Unit Process: Backwards Design.* University of Minnesota. July, 2010. <http://www.carla.umn.edu/assessment/vac/CreateUnit/p_1.html>.

National Standards in Foreign Language Education Project. *Standards for Foreign Language Learning in the 21st Century.* Lawrence, KS: Allen Press, Inc., 1999.

Wiggins, Grant and Jay McTighe. *Understanding by Design.* Power Point presentation. Winter 2004. <http://www.grantwiggins.org/documents/mtuniontalk.pdf>.

———. *Understanding by Design, Expanded 2nd Edition.* Alexandria, VA: Association for Supervision and Curriculum Development, 2005.

Contextualization in the Language Classroom

Anne Nerenz, Eastern Michigan University

American educator John Dewey wrote: "We only think when we are confronted with a problem." In some subject areas, students have difficulty connecting what they are learning with real-life situations in which the knowledge and skills are needed. When taught as a collection of isolated bits and pieces, vocabulary and grammar rules are meaningless abstractions to be "covered" in class but never used. In contrast, contextualized learning sets each new word or grammatical structure in an age-appropriate, relevant situation and highlights its usefulness. Knowing what to say, when, and to whom can only be acquired through practice in carrying out increasingly complex real-world tasks. Research shows that by contextualizing learning, students can more easily acquire knowledge and skills and transfer their knowledge and skills to new and different situations.

Making Learning Meaningful

There are several ways to contextualize learning. First, we can make learning meaningful simply by stating at the beginning of each lesson why and for what purpose the vocabulary and grammar will be needed. Instead of saying: "Today, we'll be learning about adjective agreement," we make learning relevant by saying: "By the end of class today, you'll be able to describe someone's appearance." Contextualized learning focuses students' attention on the tasks they will be able to complete.

Emphasizing the Cultural Context

In addition to stating our lesson objective as a communication task, we can also make learning meaningful by emphasizing cultural situations in which vocabulary and grammar would be needed. Rather than teaching vocabulary for fruits, vegetables, meat or desserts in an alphabetical list, in one lesson we could teach only the items that would typically be sold in a single store. For example, the communication task might be "asking for and stating a price;" the cultural context might be "at the bakery." In addition to learning about culturally specific products that are sold in a bakery and the expressions and cultural practices used to purchase something in a bakery, students can compare this daily life situation with the way in which they complete a similar task in their own communities (Standards 2.1, 2.2, and 4.2).

Making Connections to Other Disciplines

One final way to contextualize what students learn is to incorporate content from other academic disciplines. Using art as an example, when learning articles of clothing and colors, students might focus on the tasks "asking for a description" and "identifying and describing clothing" by analyzing clothing items and painting styles from the target culture. In addition to learning to accomplish meaningful language tasks and learning about important cultural products, students also make connections to art as they observe artists' use of color, light, background, and detail (Standards 3.1 and 3.2).

Teaching in Context

By focusing instruction on meaningful language tasks, situating lessons in engaging cultural contexts, and making connections to other disciplines, we capture students' attention and make learning relevant for them. Teaching in context helps all students to move seamlessly from *acquiring* skills to *applying* those skills as they work their way more and more smoothly through the business of life in the target culture.

Bibliography

American Council on the Teaching of Foreign Languages (ACTFL). *Standards for Language Learning.* Yonkers, NY: Author, 1999.

Bransford, John D., Ann L. Brown, and Rodney R. Cocking, eds. *How People Learn: Brain, Mind, Experience, and School*. Washington, DC: National Academy Press, 1999.

Glaser, Robert. "Expert Knowledge and Processes of Thinking." *Enhancing Thinking Skills in the Sciences and Mathematics*. Ed. Diane F. Halpern. Hillsdale, NJ: Erlbaum, 1992. 63–75.

Greeno, James G., Lauren Resnick, and Allan Collins. "Cognition and Learning." *Handbook of Educational Psychology*. Eds. David Berliner and Robert Calfee. New York: Simon & Schuster Macmillan, 1997. 15–46.

Hartman, Hope J., ed. *Metacognition in Learning and Instruction: Theory, Research and Practice*. Norwell, MA: Kluwer Academic Publishers, 2001.

Merrifield, Juliet. *Equipped for the Future Research Report: Building the Framework*, 1993–1997. Washington, DC: National Institute for Literacy, 2000.

Pressley, Michael, and Vera Woloshyn. *Cognitive Strategy Instruction That Really Improves Children's Academic Performance*. Cambridge, MA: Brookline Books, 1995.

Wenger, Etienne. *Communities of Practice: Learning, Meaning, and Identity*. New York: Cambridge University Press, 1998.

Learning Languages: Pathway to Common Core Literacy

Paul Sandrock Director of Education. American Council on the Teaching of Foreign Languages

The *Common Core State Standards for English Language Arts and Literacy* describe a pathway to develop college- and career-ready high school graduates. The building blocks of that pathway are the four strands of reading, writing, speaking and listening, and language.

Common Core and World Languages

Language educators also have a set of national standards that form a core common across most states' standards: the five C goal areas of Communication, Cultures, Connections, Comparisons, and Communities. The standards that describe Communication match the strands of the Common Core State Standards, not just superficially, but at a deeper conceptual level and with many commonalities for implementation:

- Reading corresponds to the Interpretive Mode
- Writing corresponds to the Presentational Mode
- Speaking and Listening correspond to the Interpersonal Mode, and also to the Presentational (speaking) and Interpretive (listening) modes

By emphasizing the purpose behind the communication, the language learning standards move away from isolated skill building and situate the development of language usage in that purpose. When these standards guide curriculum, assessment, and instruction, learners are on a pathway to literacy.

The fourth strand of the Common Core—Language—corresponds to the overarching description of how proficiency develops. How learners improve their language performance (increasing their vocabulary, awareness of language conventions, and control of language functions) is captured in the ACTFL Proficiency Levels: Novice, Intermediate, Advanced, Superior, and Distinguished. Making this conceptual link of language standards with Common Core is easy. To actually put this into practice implies important changes in our assessment and instruction. The Common Core State Standards, just like the national language standards, do not describe content to teach but rather outline the competencies that need to be developed in a standards-based program.

National Standards and the AP* Program

The National Standards for Learning Languages are now the framework for the Advanced Placement* language and culture courses and exams. With this common emphasis on the three communication modes (interpersonal, interpretive, and presentational) and an engaging context through the other four Cs, the AP* language and culture course connects to the vertical development of the same language performance across every grade level and learning experience.

The Common Core Standards and *Español Santillana*

The Santillana materials supporting language learning and Advanced Placement* follow this approach to developing literacy:

- **Interpersonal mode.** Language learners develop Common Core literacy in listening and speaking when they practice strategies to initiate and maintain a conversation, negotiate meaning, ask follow-up questions, ask for clarification, and come to agreement. This requires creating a need to engage in conversation, find out information, exchange ideas, and come to consensus.
- **Interpretive mode.** Language learners develop Common Core literacy in listening and reading when they practice strategies to figure out what the writer, speaker, or producer wants them to understand. Learners need to acquire a variety of strategies to access meaning, including skimming and scanning for key words and phrases, predicting what might be in the "text," looking for clues from the context, verifying if potentially true statements are logical, and hypothesizing about the meaning and then verifying as more evidence emerges.
- **Presentational mode.** Language learners develop Common Core literacy in speaking and writing when they practice strategies to plan and organize their content, self-correct and peer-edit, research and present findings, and develop and carefully construct an argument.

Conclusion

Using the Standards for Learning Languages as a guide, language educators are poised to support the development of learners' literacy as described in the Common Core State Standards, simultaneously helping students acquire and practice the strategies that will improve their use of both native and target languages.

Bibliography

Aligning the National Standards for Learning Languages with the Common Core State Standards. 2012. <http://cort.as/6WMd>.

American Council on the Teaching of Foreign Languages. *ACTFL Proficiency Guidelines.* 2012. <http://actflproficiencyguidelines2012.org/>.

Common Core State Standards for English Language Arts & Literacy in History/Social Studies, Science, and Technical Subjects. 2010. <http://www.corestandards.org/ELA-Literacy>.

National Standards in Foreign Language Education Project. *Standards for Foreign Language Learning in the 21st Century.* Lawrence, KS: Allen Press, Inc., 2006.

Santillana USA. *The Common Core State Standards & World Languages.* 2013. <http://cort.as/6WMv>.

Español
Santillana

fans del Español

SANTILLANA USA

Español Santillana is a collaborative effort by two teams specializing in the design of Spanish-language educational materials. One team is located in the United States and the other in Spain.

Published in the United States of America.

Español Santillana
Student Book Level 4
ISBN-13: 978-1-62263-242-8
ISBN-10: 1-62263-242-7

Illustrator: **Bartolomé Seguí**
Picture Coordinator: **Carlos Aguilera**

Cartographer: **José Luis Gil, Tania López**
Cartographic Coordinator: **Ana Isabel Calvo**

Production Manager: **Ángel García Encinar**

Production Coordinator: **Julio Hernández**

Design and Layout: **Victoria Lucas, Raquel Sánchez, Eva Hernández**

Proofreaders: **Elizabeth A. Pease, Marta López**

Photo Researchers: **Mercedes Barcenilla, Amparo Rodríguez**

Santillana USA Publishing Company, Inc.
2023 NW 84th Avenue, Doral, FL 33122

1 2 3 4 5 6 7 8 9 10   19 18 17 16 15 14

Editorial Staff in the United States
Anne Silva
Ana Isabel Antón

Editorial Staff in Spain
Susana Gómez
Clara Alarcón
Belén Saiz
Mercedes Fontecha
M.ª Antonia Oliva

Linguistic and Cultural Advisers in Latin America and in the United States

Antonio Moreno
Content Director, Santillana México

Mayra Méndez
Content Director, Santillana Puerto Rico

Claudia Noriega
Content Director, Santillana Guatemala

Cecilia Mejía
Content Director, Santillana Perú

Graciela Pérez de Lois
Content Director, Santillana Argentina

Rodolfo Hidalgo
Content Director, Santillana Chile

Mario Núñez
Director of Professional Development, Santillana USA

Reviewers

Gabriel Alfaro
Houston, TX

Luis Altamirano
San Diego, CA

Esteban Longoria
Houston, TX

John W. McNulty
Chicago, IL

Maria L. Rodriguez-Burns
Bernalillo, NM

Tina Thymai Dong
Austin, TX

Writers

Paloma Lapuerta
teaches Spanish Language, Literature and Culture at Central Connecticut State University. She graduated from the University of Salamanca, Spain, and received her PhD from the University of Geneva, Switzerland. She has taught in different countries and is co-author of several Spanish textbooks.

María Lourdes Casas
received her Masters of Arts and PhD in Spanish at the University of Wisconsin-Madison. Dr. Casas has taught Spanish Language and Literature at the University of Wisconsin-Madison, Connecticut College, and Southern Connecticut State University. Currently she is an Associate Professor at Central Connecticut State University.

Lisa Berliner
received her MA in Educational Leadership from Central Connecticut State University. She is currently pursuing a Masters degree in Spanish. She teaches Spanish at the secondary level in Avon, CT.

Jan Ferrier Sands
received her BS in Spanish and MS in Curriculum and Supervision from Central Connecticut State University. She is a career teacher of Spanish at Simsbury High School, Simsbury, CT. From 2005 to 2008, she served as the World Languages Teacher-in-Residence at the Connecticut State Department of Education.

María Á. Pérez
received her MA in Spanish from Portland State University. She was the assistant director for the Spanish Basic Language Program at the University of Illinois in Chicago. She has taught college-level Spanish at several institutions, and has worked as an editor and writer for various publishers.

Contributing Writers

Ana Isabel Antón
Miami, FL

Clara Alarcón
Madrid, Spain

Susana Gómez
Madrid, Spain

Mercedes Fontecha
Madrid, Spain

M.ª Antonia Oliva
Madrid, Spain

Belén Saiz
Madrid, Spain

Anne Silva
Miami, FL

Contributors

Janet L. Glass
Dwight-Englewood School
Englewood, NJ

Jan Kucerik
Pinellas County Schools
Largo, FL

Carol McKenna Semonsky
Georgia State University
Atlanta, GA

Anne Nerenz
Eastern Michigan University
Ypsilanti, MI

Gerardo Piña-Rosales
North American Academy of the Spanish Language
The City University of New York, New York, NY

Paul Sandrock
ACTFL
Madison, WI

Emily Spinelli
AATSP
University of Michigan-Dearborn, Dearborn, MI

Brandon Zaslow
Occidental College
Los Angeles, CA

Advisers

Paula Hirsch
Windward School, Los Angeles, CA

María Orta
Kennedy High School, Chicago, IL

Developmental Editor
Susana Gómez

Editorial Coordinator
Anne Silva

Editorial Director
Enrique Ferro

Bienvenidos a

Las parejas

Eva Bishop y Ethan Thomas

Nosotros somos fans del español por el arte y la música. Nos encantan.

Daniel García y Michelle Liu

A nosotros nos interesan las costumbres y las tradiciones del mundo hispano.

Español Santillana

Quiénes somos

Somos una comunidad de fans del español y de la cultura hispana. Nuestro objetivo es dar a conocer el mundo que habla español: sus gentes, sus ciudades, sus fiestas y tradiciones, sus alimentos... Y para eso hemos creado la página web Fans del Español (www.fansdelespañol.com).

Nuestra historia

Nuestra página web nació hace unos años con los primeros fans del español: Andy y su hermana Janet; Tess y su madre Patricia; Diana y su tía Rita; y Tim y su abuelo Mack. Las cuatro parejas decidieron viajar por los países hispanohablantes para resolver unos desafíos: encontrar los lugares más sorprendentes, los vestidos más exóticos, las costumbres y tradiciones más divertidas...

Los desafíos continúan

Hoy formamos una gran comunidad con muchas personas que quieren participar y saber más sobre Latinoamérica y sobre España.

Este año nuestros protagonistas son tres parejas: Eva y Ethan; Daniel y Michelle; y Asha y Lucas. Los seis están estudiando High School y son grandes fans del español. Por eso están dispuestos a enfrentarse a nuevos desafíos. Su objetivo: mejorar su español y conocer mejor la cultura y las formas de vida de los países hispanos.

¿Quieres pertenecer a nuestra comunidad? Puedes seguir nuestras aventuras a través de este libro y de nuestra página web. Tú también tienes Tu Desafío.

Asha Patel y Lucas Cardoso

Los veteranos

Andy, Tess, Diana y Tim

Queremos viajar por el mundo hispano. Hay lugares increíbles.

¡Adelante!

(1) Cataratas del Iguazú (Argentina)

(2) Carnavalito (Perú)

(3) El caballito (México D. F.)

Los temas de los desafíos

Las tres parejas y los veteranos han hecho un listado de temas de su interés. Seguro que tú ya sabes algo sobre esos temas.

Comunicación y relaciones sociales

¿Qué celebraciones típicas del mundo hispano conoces? ¿En cuáles te gustaría participar? ¿Por qué?

Los alimentos y la salud

¿Qué alimentos del mundo hispano te gustan más? ¿Qué sabes de su origen?

Los estudios y el trabajo

¿Qué profesionales hispanos destacados conoces? ¿Por qué son conocidos? ¿Qué estudios realizaron?

El ocio y los viajes

¿Qué géneros musicales hispanos conoces? ¿Qué sabes de su historia? ¿Quiénes son los intérpretes más destacados?

Historia y sociedad

¿Qué sabes de la época precolombina y del período colonial en las Américas? ¿Y qué sabes de la independencia de Hispanoamérica?

Arte y literatura

¿Qué artistas y escritores hispanos conoces? ¿Cuáles son tus obras favoritas? ¿Por qué?

Los escenarios de los desafíos

Usa tus conocimientos de la geografía de Hispanoamérica y de España para responder a estas preguntas:

1. ¿Qué tres países de habla hispana forman parte de la región del Río de la Plata?

2. Menciona cuatro países de Centroamérica y tres de las Antillas donde se hable español.

3. ¿Qué país de Suramérica tiene mayor extensión de costa?

4. ¿Qué océanos y mares rodean España?

Tu desafío

Tú también tienes unos desafíos que resolver. En cada unidad vas a elegir un desafío de una pareja para hacer una tarea relacionada con él. Ese será TU DESAFÍO.

Hacia el AP* Exam

Preparación para el AP* Spanish Language and Culture Exam

¿Vas a prepararte para tomar el *AP* Spanish Language and Culture Exam*? Español Santillana te va a ayudar de distintas maneras.

1. En las unidades encontrarás muchas actividades marcadas con estos íconos:

Estas actividades te ayudarán a desarrollar y practicar las destrezas comunicativas necesarias para tener éxito en las distintas pruebas del *AP* Exam*.

2. Al final de cada unidad encontrarás una sección específica titulada "Hacia el *AP* Exam*" que se dirige específicamente a la preparación de la prueba. En ella encontrarás información sobre la estructura del examen y las características de cada ejercicio, y algunas estrategias para resolverlo con éxito. Y encontrarás también unos ejercicios modelo que te ayudarán a familiarizarte con las distintas pruebas del examen.

- Actividades de interpretación de textos escritos reales (*Interpretive Communication: Print Texts*).

- Actividades de interpretación de textos orales reales (*Interpretive Communication: Audio Texts*).

- Actividades de interacción escrita (*Interpersonal Writing: E-mail Reply*).

- Actividades de presentación escrita (*Presentational Writing: Persuasive Essay*).

- Actividades de interacción oral (*Interpersonal Speaking: Conversation*).

- Actividades de presentación oral (*Presentational Speaking: Cultural Comparison*).

Además, la serie cuenta con un *"AP* Preparation Workbook"* con el que podrás preparar a fondo el examen. En el cuaderno encontrarás instrucciones para resolver las pruebas, modelos de examen resueltos y diferentes pruebas para practicar.

Contenidos

Gramática	Cultura		Escritura	Hacia el AP* Exam
• Expresar gustos, intereses, sentimientos y emociones • Los adjetivos • Los verbos pronominales • Los verbos reflexivos y recíprocos • Hablar de acciones en curso • Expresar cantidad	• Lectura informativa: *El oficio más romántico: escribir cartas de amor por encargo* (reportaje) • Lectura literaria: *El diario a diario* (Julio Cortázar)	• Mapa cultural: Unidad y variedad del español	Un correo de presentación	Interpretación de textos escritos
• Las construcciones impersonales. El pronombre *se* • Los pronombres de OD y OI • Los verbos con preposición • Los artículos • La voz pasiva • *Ser* y *estar*	• Lectura informativa: *El cáncer y su prevención* (artículo científico) • Lectura literaria: *La piedra mágica* (cuento popular)	• Mapa cultural: Sistemas de salud en el mundo hispano	Recomendaciones de viajes	Interpretación de textos orales
• El participio pasado • El presente perfecto y el pluscuamperfecto • Los pronombres relativos • El futuro perfecto • Expresar deseos • Expresar condición	• Lectura informativa: *La globalización económica* (artículo de economía) • Lectura literaria: *Un constructor de ecuaciones* (Juan Bonilla)	• Mapa cultural: La economía de Latinoamérica	Tu currículum ideal	Interacción escrita
• Expresar frecuencia • Expresar probabilidad (I) • Expresar probabilidad (II) • El presente perfecto de subjuntivo • Expresar causa • Expresar consecuencia	• Lectura informativa: *Como la vida misma* (Rosa Montero; columna periodística) • Lectura literaria: *Vivir para contarla* (Gabriel García Márquez)	• Mapa cultural: El turismo en Latinoamérica	Un blog de viajes	Interacción oral
• Los numerales ordinales • Expresar certeza y duda • Expresar finalidad • Expresar dificultad • Expresar condición. El pluscuamperfecto de subjuntivo • Expresar tiempo	• Lectura informativa: *María Eva Duarte de Perón* (biografía) • Lectura literaria: *El exiliado* (Cristina Peri Rossi)	• Mapa cultural: La inmigración hispana en los Estados Unidos	Un ensayo	Presentación escrita
• Las comparaciones • El artículo neutro *lo* • Expresar opinión • Hacer valoraciones • Los diminutivos • Dar consejos y hacer recomendaciones	• Lectura informativa: *Rafael Moneo* (entrevista) • Lectura literaria: *El Sur* (Jorge Luis Borges)	• Mapa cultural: El «boom» de la literatura latinoamericana	Una reseña	Presentación oral

Nos relacionamos

Comunicación y relaciones sociales

www.fansdelespañol.com

Nos cuidamos

Los alimentos y la salud

www.fansdelespañol.com

UNIDAD 3

Trabajamos

Los estudios y el trabajo

www.fansdelespañol.com

UNIDAD 4

Nos divertimos

El ocio y los viajes

www.fansdelespañol.com

fans del Español

Participamos

Historia y sociedad

www.fansdelespañol.com

Creamos

Arte y literatura

www.fansdelespañol.com

Objectives

- To talk about current actions and situations.
- To describe routines.
- To narrate past actions.
- To use regular and irregular verbs properly.
- To compare and contrast information.
- To initiate and engage in meaningful conversations.
- To talk about personal experiences in the past.
- To talk about the future.
- To give orders and instructions.
- To give advice or make recommendations.

Contents

Vocabulary
- Daily routines.
- Free-time activities.
- Archeology and civilizations.
- Travel vocabulary.
- Professions and work.
- Natural resources and the environment.
- Healthy habits.

Grammar
- The present tense.
- The preterite tense.
- The imperfect tense.
- The future tense.
- Informal and formal affirmative commands.

Evaluation Criteria

- Recognize and use verbs in the present tense.
- Answer questions appropriately.
- Recognize and use regular and irregular verbs in the preterite tense.
- Recognize and use regular and irregular verbs in the imperfect tense.
- Understand informative texts such as news and blog entries.

- Write a text based on an image.
- Form sentences using appropriate verb tenses.
- Talk about personal experiences in the past.
- Engage in conversations to elicit or provide information.
- Write a short text about personal experiences.

- Describe past vacations or travel experiences.
- Recognize and use regular and irregular verbs in the future tense.
- Compare information orally.
- Talk about predictions and plans about the future.
- Tell someone to do something.
- Give advice or make recommendations.

Unit Plan

Presentación del nivel/ Páginas preliminares

Estimated time: 1 session.

Level 4 presentation: Pages IV–VII.

Unit presentation: Unit opener.

1. CONTAR HECHOS ACTUALES

Estimated time: 1 session.

Functions & forms:
- To talk about current actions.
- The present tense.

2. CONTAR HECHOS PASADOS

Estimated time: 1 session.

Functions & forms:
- To talk about actions completed in the past.
- The preterite tense.

3. DESCRIBIR EN EL PASADO

Estimated time: 1 session.

Functions & forms:
- To describe actions in the past.
- The imperfect tense.

4. HABLAR DEL FUTURO

Estimated time: 1 session.

Functions & forms:
- To talk about future actions.
- The future tense.

5. DAR ÓRDENES E INSTRUCCIONES / EVALUACIÓN

Estimated time: 1 session.

Functions & forms:
- To give orders and instructions.
- Informal and formal affirmative commands.

Assessment: Test.

Standards for Learning Spanish

COMMUNICATION

1.1. Interpersonal mode

- Discuss what students learned in the previous course and what they will learn in this course.
- Engage in oral conversations using personal knowledge and experience.
- Compare and contrast information with a partner.
- Exchange personal opinions and experiences.
- Talk about future plans with a partner.

1.2. Interpretive mode

- Demonstrate understanding of oral and written expressions.
- Understand written exchanges.
- Understand and obtain information from audio recordings.
- Demonstrate understanding and extract information from informative texts.
- Obtain information from charts or images.

1.3. Presentational mode

- Write sentences or paragraphs about personal experiences.
- Complete sentences or texts with correct verb tenses.
- Write answers to given questions.
- Write predictions about the future.
- Write sentences giving orders or advice.
- Write sentences or a paragraph summarizing information.
- Organize and present a plan for a celebration in the school.

CULTURE

2.1. Practices and perspectives

- Learn about activities young people do in their leisure time.

2.2. Products and perspectives

- Learn about the ancient history of Peru.

CONNECTIONS

3.1. Interdisciplinary connections

- Understand the similarities and differences between some aspects of grammar in English and in Spanish.
- Reinforce grammatical concepts.
- Conjugate verbs in different verb tenses.

- Read about food and health.
- Use reading strategies and previous knowledge to help comprehend texts.

3.2. Viewpoints through language / culture

- Learn about the use of language in social networks.

COMPARISONS

4.1. Compare languages

- Compare the formation and use of various verb tenses in English and in Spanish.

4.2. Compare cultures

- Compare leisure activities in Hispanic cultures and in the United States.

COMMUNITIES

5.1. Spanish within and beyond the school setting

- Imagine situations in which Spanish could be used.
- Discuss leisure activities done in one's community.
- Discuss past actions experienced outside the classroom.

5.2. Spanish for lifelong learners

- Reflect on how Spanish can be used in future life experiences.
- Discuss future professions and actions.

Communicative Skills

Interpersonal Mode

		Activities
Speaking	• Engage in conversation with a classmate. • Compare and contrast information with a classmate. • Exchange personal opinions and experiences.	• 2, 7, 10, 13, 14, 18 • 13 • 7, 13
Writing	• Write a text summarizing information from a conversation.	• 18
Listening	• Understand and obtain information from oral exchanges.	• 2, 6, 7, 10, 13, 14, 18
Reading	• Understand an informative text and use it to talk with a classmate.	• 10, 13

Interpretive Mode

		Activities
Listening	• Obtain information from conversations. • Understand informative audios. • Understand narrative or descriptive sentences.	• 1, 15 • 4 • 9
Reading	• Understand informative sentences or texts. • Demonstrate comprehension of written exchanges.	• 5, 10, 12 • 16
Viewing	• Obtain information from a chart. • Write a text based on an image. • Connect information to images.	• 3 • 6, 12 • 12

Presentational Mode

		Activities
Speaking	• Present information to the class.	• 18
Writing	• Write an informative text. • Write predictions about the future. • Write sentences giving orders or advice.	• 6, 10 • 12, 13 • 15, 17

Cross-Curricular Standards

Subject	Standard	Activities
Language Arts	• Write a text summarizing information.	• 18
Social Studies	• Learn about the ancient history of Peru.	• 4

Lesson Plans (50-Minute Classes)

Day	Objectives	Sessions	Activities	Time	Standards	Resources / Homework
1	To introduce Level 4 and the *Unidad preliminar*	**Introduction** • *Bienvenidos a Español Santillana Level 4* (IV-VII) • Unit presentation: Unit opener (1)		30 m. 20 m.	1.2	
2	To talk about current actions and situations	**1. Contar hechos actuales** (2–3) • Warm-Up: Independent Starter • *Gramática: El presente de indicativo*	1–3	5 m. 45 m.	1.1, 1.2, 1.3, 2.1, 3.1, 3.2, 5.1	Audio Practice Workbook
3	To talk about actions completed in the past	**2. Contar hechos pasados** (4–5) • Warm-Up: Independent Starter • *Gramática: El pretérito*	4–7	5 m. 45 m.	1.1, 1.2, 1.3, 2.1, 2.2, 3.1, 3.2, 5.1	Audio Practice Workbook
4	To describe actions in the past	**3. Describir en el pasado** (6–7) • Warm-Up: Independent Starter • *Gramática: El imperfecto*	8–10	5 m. 45 m.	1.1, 1.2, 1.3, 2.2, 3.1	Audio Practice Workbook
5	To talk about future actions	**4. Hablar del futuro** (8–9) • Warm-Up: Independent Starter • *Gramática: El futuro*	11–14	5 m. 45 m.	1.1, 1.2, 1.3, 3.1, 5.1, 5.2	Audio Practice Workbook
6	To give orders and instructions	**5. Dar órdenes e instrucciones / Assessment** (10–11) • Warm-Up: Independent Starter • *Gramática: El imperativo afirmativo* • Test	15–18	5 m. 35 m. 10 m.	1.1, 1.2, 1.3, 3.1, 5.2	Audio Practice Workbook

Lesson Plans (90-Minute Classes)

Day	Objectives	Sessions	Activities	Time	Standards	Resources / Homework
1	To introduce Level 4 and the *Unidad preliminar*, and to talk about current actions and situations	**Introduction / 1. Contar hechos actuales** (1–3) • *Bienvenidos a Español Santillana Level 4* (IV-VII) • Unit presentation: Unit opener (1) • *Gramática: El presente de indicativo*	1–3	25 m. 20 m. 45 m.	1.1, 1.2, 1.3, 2.1, 3.1, 3.2, 5.1	Audio Practice Workbook
2	To talk about actions completed in the past and to describe actions in the past	**2. Contar hechos pasados / 3. Describir en el pasado** (4–7) • Warm-Up: Independent Starter • *Gramática: El pretérito* • *Gramática: El imperfecto*	4–7 8–10	5 m. 40 m. 45 m.	1.1, 1.2, 1.3, 2.1, 2.2, 3.1, 3.2, 5.1	Audio Practice Workbook
3	To talk about future actions and to give orders and instructions	**4. Hablar del futuro / 5. Dar órdenes e instrucciones** (8–11) • Warm-Up: Independent Starter • *Gramática: El futuro* • *Gramática: El imperativo afirmativo*	11–14 15–18	5 m. 45 m. 40 m.	1.1, 1.2, 1.3, 3.1, 5.1, 5.2	Audio Practice Workbook
4	To assess student proficiency	**Review / Assessment** • Oral presentation • Test		60 m. 30 m.	1.1, 1.2, 1.3, 2.1, 2.2, 5.1, 5.2	

Audio Scripts

Icons

The (🎧) symbol is used to refer to audio activities. The audio scripts for these activities are found in each unit at the end of the Overview section.

The (💬) symbol is used to refer to speaking activities. These activities require spoken expression by the student and do not follow any particular script.

1 ¡Vaya día!

Hola, Eva. ¿Qué te pasa? Te veo un poco estresada.

–Sí, estoy algo estresada.

–¿Por qué?

–Pues porque tengo un día de mucho trabajo.

–¿Qué haces hoy?

–Hoy tengo siete clases.

–Y este año, además de Español, tomas Francés, ¿no?

–Sí. Y también estoy en el club de Ciencias, y después de clase participo en actividades de voluntariado en la comunidad.

–¿No te parece que es demasiado?

–Quizás... Pero si veo que no puedo con todo, puedo dejar algunas actividades. ¿Y tú, cómo tienes hoy el día?

–Pues bastante ocupado. También tengo siete clases.

–Tienes guitarra por la mañana, ¿no?

–Sí, pero no hoy. Solo son dos días a la semana.

–Nos vemos luego, Ethan, que llego tarde a clase.

–Hasta luego, Eva. Suerte.

4 Descubrimiento arqueológico en Perú

Un grupo de arqueólogos peruanos descubrió un conjunto de tumbas de la cultura wari en el sur de Perú. El descubrimiento se realizó en una zona de la selva del Amazonas en la que hasta ese momento solo se habían descubierto ruinas incas.

La civilización wari fue anterior al imperio inca. Se cree que varios aspectos de la organización social y política de los waris sirvieron de modelo para los incas.

En las tumbas se encontraron valiosos objetos de oro y plata, numerosas piezas de cerámica, armas y una máscara. Una de las tumbas pertenecía a un gobernante wari. Por los análisis de sus dientes se supo que tenía entre 25 y 35 años de edad cuando murió. La prensa y el público le dieron el nombre de «Señor de Wari».

9 Vacaciones en la playa

1. Llovía a cántaros.
2. Y hacía viento.
3. Al principio no me gustó el lugar.
4. Pero el hotel estaba bien.
5. Y la gente era muy amable.
6. Al día siguiente, por fin salió el sol.
7. Y pudimos ir a la playa.
8. Sí. Fueron unas vacaciones estupendas.

12 Eventos futuros

1. En dos años mi esposo y yo nos jubilaremos. Por fin podremos viajar.
2. En seis años tendré una profesión. Trabajaré en algo relacionado con las Ciencias.
3. Mi esposa está embarazada. Tendremos nuestro primer hijo en seis meses.
4. Cumplo años en un mes. Lo celebraré con una fiesta a la que vendrán todos mis amigos.
5. La semana que viene será mi aniversario de bodas. Mi esposo y yo lo celebraremos con una cena romántica.
6. Este fin de semana saldré con mis nietos al parque.

15 Una fiesta sorpresa

–Planifiquemos la fiesta sorpresa de Carlos. Ya no tenemos mucho tiempo.

–Es verdad. Falta muy poco para su cumpleaños. Elige tú la música.

–¡Música para bailar, por supuesto! ¿Te parece bien poner ritmos latinos? Salsa, merengue, cumbia...

–Sí, perfecto. Oye, hay que pensar en la comida y la bebida. Decide qué vamos a comprar.

–Yo no sé nada de comida. Mejor encárgate tú de eso.

–De acuerdo. Entonces pide tú el dinero a los invitados para comprar el regalo.

–Mejor pidámoslo los dos, así nos hacen más caso.

–Sí, buena idea. Oye, ¿y la lista de invitados?

–Todavía no la tenemos. Hagámosla también entre los dos.

–Bien, pero entonces envía tú las invitaciones.

–Vale, no hay problema. Haré una invitación electrónica.

–Yo creo que eso es todo, ¿no?

–No sé..., déjame pensar.

Preliminary Unit
Llegamos a la meta

The Unit

- This unit is a review of the main objectives of Spanish Levels 2 and 3. Students will review the following topics:
  - The present tense to talk about current actions, describe routines, and talk about free-time activities.
  - The regular and irregular preterite tense conjugations to talk about actions completed in the past.
  - The imperfect tense to describe past events and set the scene.
  - The future tense to talk about future plans.
  - The regular and irregular affirmative command forms to tell someone to do something.

Activities	Standards	Resources
Llegamos a la meta	1.2	

Teaching Suggestions

Preparation

- Invite students to introduce themselves to the class. Then direct their attention to the pictures on these pages. Do they remember the participants' names? And the veterans' names? You may want to give students a few moments to look at the information on pages IV and V so that they can acquaint or reacquaint themselves with the three pairs and with the veterans of *Fans del español*. Consider providing students with some information about the participants' ages, hometowns, interests, etc.

- Direct students to page VI and introduce them to the topics or themes of Spanish Level 4. Explain that they will learn new and exciting information about each of these topics, but that there are also many things they already know about the Spanish-speaking world and these topics. Divide the class into six groups, assign each group one of the topics, and have them answer the questions posed for their topic. Encourage students to go beyond the questions and brainstorm more information about their assigned topic, since they will surely know more.

UNIDAD

preliminar

Llegamos a la meta

¡¡Hola, fan del español!! ¡¡Y felicidades: ya estás en 4º!! Eso quiere decir que has hecho un buen trabajo.

Hemos recorrido juntos un largo camino en el que has aprendido a hablar, a leer, a escribir, a comunicarte en español. Y has conocido muchos aspectos de los países hispanos: su geografía, sus lugares, sus costumbres, su cultura.

Este año vamos a profundizar en lo que ya sabes. Nuestro objetivo es que puedas expresarte en español de una manera precisa y efectiva, que puedas participar en conversaciones, intercambiar opiniones y argumentar tus puntos de vista con mayor fluidez, con mayor naturalidad y con mayor corrección. Y que sigas profundizando también en el conocimiento de la cultura hispana.

¡Acompáñanos en nuestra aventura!

The Veterans

ANDY DOUGLAS

Andy used to travel with his sister, Janet. He is from Atlanta, GA.

DIANA ROBLES

Diana used to travel with her aunt, Rita. She is from Lawrenceville, NJ.

TESS WILLIAMS

Tess used to travel with her mother, Patricia. She is from San Antonio, TX.

TIM TAYLOR

Tim used to travel with his grandfather, Mack. He is from San Francisco, CA.

The Participants

EVA BISHOP

Age: 18 years old

Hometown: Chula Vista, CA

Interests: science and technology

Spanish-language experience: Started studying Spanish in middle school.

ETHAN THOMAS

Age: 19 years old

Hometown: Chula Vista, CA

Interests: writing and playing guitar

Spanish-language experience: Started studying Spanish in 10th grade.

Preliminary Unit
Llegamos a la meta

Este año te esperan muchas sorpresas de la mano de Eva, Ethan, Daniel, Michelle, Lucas y Asha, nuestros fans del español. Ellos te guiarán por los nuevos desafíos y te ayudarán a descubrir nuevos lugares y nuevas costumbres del mundo hispano. Y te acercarán a la actualidad de Latinoamérica y de España, a su economía, a su literatura, a su historia, a sus problemas sociales.

¿Estás preparado(a)? Pues adelante. Pero antes de empezar, vamos a recordar algunas de las cosas que ya sabes.

¡Adelante!

1. Contar hechos actuales
El presente de indicativo

2. Contar hechos pasados
El pretérito

3. Describir en el pasado
El imperfecto

4. Hablar del futuro
El futuro

5. Dar órdenes e instrucciones
El imperativo afirmativo

uno 1

MICHELLE LIU
Age: 18 years old
Hometown: Tallahassee, FL
Interests: traveling and art
Spanish-language experience: Started studying Spanish in 9th grade.

DANIEL GARCÍA
Age: 18 years old
Hometown: Tallahassee, FL
Interests: cooking and art
Spanish-language experience: Started studying Spanish two years ago, but his family speaks Spanish at home.

ASHA PATEL
Age: 17 years old
Hometown: New York, NY
Interests: music and soccer
Spanish-language experience: Started studying Spanish in kindergarten.

LUCAS CARDOSO
Age: 18 years old
Hometown: New York, NY
Interests: nature and basketball
Spanish-language experience: Started studying Spanish in 8th grade, but he already knew some Spanish.

- After students have answered the questions in their groups and recorded any additional information, call on each group to share their information with the class. If some students in the class have personal knowledge of any of the topics, invite them to share their experiences with the class.
- Ask students to read silently the objectives for this unit listed on page 1. Then, in order to assess your students' proficiencies, give them this performance pretest. If students are not able to perform certain tasks, this will be a good indication that you might need to spend some extra class time reviewing the corresponding structures.

1. Contar hechos actuales
- Have students
  - Describe their daily school routines and schedules this semester.
  - Describe what they do in their leisure time (e.g., on the weekend, during their summer vacation).

2. Contar hechos pasados
- Have students
  - Retell a news story, specifying the sequence of events that took place.
  - Talk about the last time they did something and tell what happened.

3. Describir en el pasado
- Have students
  - Talk about their last outing with friends or family, describing the weather, the people who accompanied them, their feelings before and after the outing, etc.

4. Hablar del futuro
- Have students
  - Talk about what they think their lives will be like in ten years.

5. Dar órdenes e instrucciones
- Have students
  - Tell a classmate what to do to foster the learning of Spanish.
  - Offer their advice for healthy living to their Spanish teacher.

Objectives

- In this unit, students will
  - Express actions and routines in the present tense.
  - Talk about actions completed in the past.
  - Describe past events.
  - Talk about future plans.
  - Give recommendations and advice.

1

Preliminary Unit

1. CONTAR HECHOS ACTUALES

Gramática – El presente de indicativo

Presentation

- In this section, students will review the present tense to talk about current actions, describe routines, and talk about the future when referring to timetables, pre-arranged events, and when presenting the information as a fact.

Activities	Standards	Resources
Gramática	1.2, 3.1	
1.	1.2, 1.3	Audio
2.	1.1, 1.2, 1.3, 5.1	
3.	1.2, 1.3, 2.1, 3.2	

Teaching Suggestions

Warm-Up / Independent Starter

- Have students think about a typical week and ask them to list eight different activities they do during the week. To get them started, you may want to give them some verbs, such as *estudiar, trabajar, leer, ver la tele, hacer deporte, salir, ir al cine...*

Preparation

- Divide the class into small groups and have them exchange their lists from the Independent Starter. Ask students to work on a group list in which they include the activities that all of them do, as well as the activities that only one or two of them do. Invite groups to report their findings to the class. For example: *En nuestro grupo, todos estudiamos y salimos con nuestros amigos los fines de semana, pero solo Andy trabaja los sábados.* If you feel it is appropriate, discuss your weekly routine and have students compare it with theirs.

- Write a few of the students' sentences on the board and review some of the present tense conjugations with them. Remind students that in Spanish we use the present tense in some cases where the present progressive is used in English. For example: *¿Qué estudias?* (What are you studying?) *Este sábado voy de compras.* (This Saturday, I'm going shopping.) In Spanish, the present progressive indicates an action in progress at the moment of speaking.

2

Gramática

El presente de indicativo

- Usamos verbos en presente en estos casos:
  - Para hablar de acciones y situaciones que ocurren cuando se habla.
    Ahora **voy** a ver a mi hermana.
  - Para describir rutinas o acciones que se repiten.
    Los domingos **duermo** hasta las 10:00 a. m.
  - Para describir situaciones estables o hacer afirmaciones de valor universal.
    Madrid **es** la capital de España.
    Dos y dos **son** cuatro.
  - Para presentar como actuales hechos pasados.
    Colón **llega** a América el 12 de octubre de 1492.
  - Para hablar de horarios y de eventos futuros previstos o planificados.
    Este verano **vamos** a México.

- Algunos verbos irregulares tienen cambios vocálicos en el presente:
  - e > ie: querer → quiero   – o > ue: contar → cuento
  - i > ie: adquirir → adquiero   – u > ue: jugar → juego
  - e > i: pedir → pido

- Otros tienen irregular la forma yo:
  hacer → hago   poner → pongo   salir → salgo   traer → traigo
  conocer → conozco   ver → veo   saber → sé

Repasa la conjugación del presente en las páginas R12 (verbos regulares) y R13 (verbos irregulares).

TERMINACIONES DEL PRESENTE

Verbos regulares en -*ar*:

-o	-amos
-as	-áis
-a	-an

Verbos regulares en -*er*:

-o	-emos
-es	-éis
-e	-en

Verbos regulares en -*ir*:

-o	-imos
-es	-ís
-e	-en

1 ¡Vaya día!

 ▶ **Escucha** la conversación entre Ethan y Eva, y decide si estas oraciones son ciertas o falsas. Después, corrige las oraciones falsas.

1. Eva está estresada porque tiene un examen de Ciencias.
2. Ethan tiene siete clases y Eva tiene seis.
3. Eva estudia dos idiomas este año.
4. Ethan piensa que Eva está demasiado ocupada.
5. Eva planea dejar alguna de sus actividades si ve que no puede con todo.
6. Ethan tiene clase de guitarra por la tarde.

Differentiated Instruction

DEVELOPING LEARNERS

- For additional practice with verbs in the present tense to describe routines, provide students with the following sentence starters: *Los sábados..., Los domingos..., Entre semana...* Have students complete the sentences, describing what they do on those days.
- Then ask students to get together with a partner and compare their statements. Finally, ask students to write a one-paragraph summary of this comparison. Invite volunteers to share their paragraphs with the class.

EXPANDING LEARNERS

- Have students create a survey to find out the class's favorite summer vacation activities. Suggest that they prepare a chart with the activities that they think are most common among students their age. They should also leave space in their charts so that they can take note of other activities their classmates may do. Then, have students interview their classmates and note the answers in their charts. Allow students time to analyze the results of their survey and to write a summary. Finally, ask students to present their results to the class.

2 **Un sábado típico en la familia de Eva**

▶ **Escribe.** ¿Qué hacen Eva y su familia un sábado típico?

Modelo   1. *Eva y su familia desayunan juntos.*

desayunar juntos   hacer la compra   poner la lavadora

lavar los platos   leer   ir al cine

 ▶ **Habla** con tu compañero(a). ¿Cómo es un sábado típico en tu casa?

3 **Cosas de jóvenes**

 ▶ **Lee** los resultados de una encuesta realizada a jóvenes mexicanos y responde a las preguntas.

Encuesta Nacional de Juventud (2010)

Jóvenes entre 12 y 29 años según la principal actividad que realizan en su tiempo libre para divertirse.

Actividad	Porcentaje
Reunirse con amigos	22,2%
Ver la tele	12,9%
Salir con su pareja	12,4%
Hacer deporte	11,4%
Escuchar música	8,9%
Ir a bailar	4,4%
Jugar a los videojuegos	3,7%

Fuente: Instituto Mexicano de la Juventud

1. ¿Cuál es la actividad preferida por los jóvenes mexicanos?
2. ¿Qué actividades realizan en grupo? ¿E individualmente?
3. ¿Qué haces tú en tu tiempo libre?
4. ¿Qué actividades de tiempo libre son más populares entre los jóvenes de tu país?

tres **3**

HERITAGE LANGUAGE LEARNERS

• Have students work with a partner to compile a list of stem-changing verbs in the present tense. Encourage them to include high-frequency verbs that their classmates may not know. Suggest that they first concentrate on listing as many stem-changing verbs as they can remember, and then choose ten verbs for each stem change pattern based on their usefulness (e.g., *atravesar, descender, extender, sugerir, aprobar, morder, devolver*). Ask students to share their list with the class. You may want to post the list in the classroom and add verbs to it as the semester progresses.

MULTIPLE INTELLIGENCES:
Verbal-Linguistic Intelligence

• Have students hypothesize about the present tense conjugations of the following verbs: *consentir* (to consent), *encerrar* (to enclose), *envolver* (to wrap up), *recostarse* (to lie back), *descontar* (to discount), *despedir* (to fire). Ask students to think of reasons for the conjugation patterns they noticed for these verbs. Are they able to extrapolate a rule from these patterns? Students should associate these verbs with the core verb (e.g., *consentir → sentir*).

Gramática – El presente de indicativo

Activities

1. Have students read the six statements before playing the audio. Then play the audio twice. Tell students to simply listen to the audio the first time and complete the activity the second time.

3. You may wish to organize a class survey to find out the class's top five leisure activities. Then, have students compare and contrast their findings with those of the survey on page 3. Encourage students to come up with theories for any similarities as well as differences between themselves and young adults in Mexico.

AUDIO SCRIPT
See page XXIF.

Answer Key

1. 1. F. Eva está estresada porque tiene un día de mucho trabajo.
2. F. Los dos tienen siete clases.
3. C.
4. C.
5. C.
6. F. Tiene clase de guitarra por la mañana dos días a la semana.

2. 2. Eva y su padre hacen la compra.
3. Su padre pone la lavadora.
4. Su hermana lava los platos.
5. Sus padres leen.
6. Eva y sus amigos van al cine.
▶ Answers will vary.

3. 1. Reunirse con sus amigos.
2. En grupo: reunirse con sus amigos, salir con su pareja, hacer deporte, ir a bailar. Individualmente: ver la tele, escuchar música, jugar a los videojuegos.
3. Answers will vary.
4. Answers will vary.

Additional Resources

Fans Online activities
Practice Workbook

2. CONTAR HECHOS PASADOS

Gramática – El pretérito

Presentation

- In this section, students will review the preterite tense to talk about past actions or events that are presented as completed.

Activities	Standards	Resources
Gramática	1.2, 3.1	
4.	1.2, 2.2, 3.2	Audio
5.	1.2, 3.1, 3.2	
6.	1.1, 1.3, 2.1	
7.	1.1, 5.1	

Teaching Suggestions

Warm-Up / Independent Starter

- Give students exactly two minutes to list in sequence everything they did yesterday. Tell them to list the actions using verbs conjugated in the *yo* form of the preterite (e.g., *me levanté, desayuné, salí, llegué, saludé, leí*). Students should not use their textbooks. Call time at two minutes and have students stop writing.

Preparation

- Ask students to exchange their lists from the Independent Starter with a partner and correct each other's verbs. They can now use their textbooks as reference. Then, have students count the number of correct verbs. Who was the class champion? Call on volunteers to share their lists with the class. You may want to write on the board some of the irregular verbs students mention (e.g., *fui, tuve, hice, estuve*). If needed, allow students time to review the irregular preterite conjugations.

- Discuss with the class what all of the actions they listed have in common (i.e., they refer to past events that are presented as completed). Go over the grammar presentation and discuss with students the reason for the use of the preterite in the dialogue between Michelle and Daniel. Then remind students of some of the time expressions that are generally paired with verbs in the preterite tense: *ayer, anoche, anteayer, la semana pasada, el mes/año pasado, el 15 de septiembre de 2010...*

Gramática

El pretérito

- Usamos verbos en pretérito para hablar sobre acciones o eventos pasados que se presentan como completos:

   Ayer **discutí** con mi novio porque me **mintió**.

- Los verbos que terminan en -car, -gar y -zar requieren un cambio ortográfico en la forma yo del pretérito:

   bus**car** → bus**qué**   lle**gar** → lle**gué**   empe**zar** → empe**cé**

- Algunos verbos muy comunes son irregulares en el pretérito:

pedir → pidió pidieron	estar → estuve	dar → di	
dormir → durmió durmieron	saber → supe	ir → fui	
	poder → pude	ser → fui	
	tener → tuve		
decir → dije	poner → puse		
querer → quise	traer → traje		
hacer → hice			
venir → vine			

TERMINACIONES DEL PRETÉRITO

Verbos regulares en -ar:

-é	-amos
-aste	-asteis
-ó	-aron

Verbos regulares en -er, -ir:

-í	-imos
-iste	-isteis
-ió	-ieron

Repasa la conjugación del pretérito en las páginas R16 y R17 (verbos regulares y verbos irregulares).

 ¿Qué **pasó** ayer en la telenovela? **Estuve** muy ocupada y no **pude** verla.

 ¡**Pasaron** muchísimas cosas! Arturo **tuvo** un accidente de tráfico. Carmen no **fue** a la entrevista de trabajo. Silvia **rompió** con su novio...

---

4 **Descubrimiento arqueológico en Perú**

 ▶ **Escucha** una noticia sobre un descubrimiento arqueológico en Perú y une las dos columnas.

Ⓐ
1. Los arqueólogos...
2. La civilización wari...
3. Los incas...
4. En las tumbas waris...
5. El «Señor de Wari»...
6. La prensa y el público...

Ⓑ
a. siguieron algunas prácticas de los waris.
b. fue un gobernante wari.
c. se encontraron objetos de oro y plata.
d. fue anterior al imperio inca.
e. eligieron el nombre del «Señor de Wari».
f. descubrieron varias tumbas waris en la selva de Perú.

Differentiated Instruction

DEVELOPING LEARNERS

- Give students a few moments to think of a scene from a TV program, movie, or book that comes to mind. Next, ask them to list the sequence of events that took place in the scene. Then have students work their sentences into a narrative by adding connectors such as *primero, poco después, luego, por último*. You may wish to ask those students who are artistically inclined to illustrate their narratives to create a comic strip. Invite volunteer students to share their work with the class. Can the class identify the source of the scene?

EXPANDING LEARNERS

- Have pairs select a historical event that they feel was important for their country or the world (e.g., the Declaration of Independence, the first man on the Moon, the invention of the personal computer). Ask students to go on the Internet and research some facts. Next, have them write a two-paragraph summary of the event. For example: *El 4 de julio de 1776, el Congreso firmó la Declaración de Independencia. Esa misma tarde...* Ask volunteer pairs to share their narratives with the class. Hold a class vote to choose the three most important events.

5 Una buena noticia

▶ **Completa** esta noticia. Usa la forma correcta del pretérito de estos verbos.

> informar   colocar   perder   durar   participar   lograr

El Universal, 8 de junio de 2012

Un éxito, el primer trasplante de brazos

Gabriel Granados, de 52 años, ____1____ los brazos a causa de una descarga eléctrica ocurrida en enero de 2011. Sin embargo, una nueva cirugía de trasplante de extremidades superiores realizada por un grupo de especialistas del Instituto Nacional de Ciencias Médicas y Nutrición «Salvador Zubirán» ____2____ que Gabriel volviera a tener brazos y manos. Este novedoso trasplante ____3____ a México como el primer país en América Latina en aplicar esta técnica.

Martín Iglesias Morales, jefe del Servicio de Cirugía Plástica del Instituto, ____4____ que la operación ____5____ 17 horas y que en ella ____6____ al menos 19 especialistas.

Fuente: http://www.eluniversal.com.mx (selección)

---

6 ¿Qué pasó?

▶ **Elige** una de estas fotografías y escribe una noticia explicando qué pasó.

Modelo   *Ayer a las seis de la tarde tuvo lugar el desfile de…*

7 Una anécdota

▶ **Habla** con tu compañero(a) sobre algo que te sucedió. Puedes usar las ideas del cuadro.

> tu primer día de clase
> un pequeño accidente
> un viaje de vacaciones
> una entrevista de trabajo
> una celebración o un evento

> Este verano hice camping con mi familia y me pasó algo gracioso.

> ¿Un oso les robó la comida?

Gramática – El pretérito

Activities

4. Ask further questions regarding this archaeological discovery. Had students heard of the ancient Wari civilization of the south-central Andes? Encourage them to research this culture and share what they have learned with the class.

6. Ask students to share their news with a classmate. Then, have partners help each other to rewrite the news for a "broadcast." Give students time to practice reading the news aloud, imitating the intonation and mannerisms of a TV news anchor. Assist them with pronunciation and fluency issues. Then ask students to deliver their news in front of the class. You may want to set up an area in the classroom for the "broadcasts."

7. Invite volunteer pairs to act out some of their dialogues for the class. After each presentation, ask the class comprehension questions, such as *¿Adónde fueron de vacaciones? ¿Por qué se asustó Jane?* If time allows, hold a class vote to choose the funniest story, the scariest, the happiest, etc.

> **AUDIO SCRIPT**
> See page XXIF.

Answer Key

4. 1. f   3. a   5. b
     2. d   4. c   6. e

5. 1. perdió   4. informó
     2. logró   5. duró
     3. colocó   6. participaron

6. Answers will vary.

7. Answers will vary.

Additional Resources

Fans Online activities
Practice Workbook

HERITAGE LANGUAGE LEARNERS

- Have students think of an important historical figure from their heritage country (e.g., Simón Bolívar, Benito Juárez, Gabriela Mistral). Ask them to go on the Internet and research some facts about their chosen person. Then, have students use the information they have gathered and what they know about the person to write a four-paragraph biography. You may wish to collate students' work to make a booklet of influential Hispanics that can be shared with the class. Or, you may choose to publish the biographies on the class website.

TOTAL PHYSICAL RESPONSE (TPR)

- Tell students that they will play a game to practice the preterite. Ask them to stand and, going by rows, ask the first student to say a verb in the preterite. The next student must say a meaningful sentence with that verb. For example: *llegó → Alicia llegó tarde.* If the sentence is incorrect, the student must sit down and the following student gets a turn. Upon a correct response, that student says another verb in the preterite and the next student uses it in a sentence. The winners are those students who are standing when you call time.

3. DESCRIBIR EN EL PASADO

Gramática – El imperfecto

Presentation

- In this section, students will review the imperfect tense to talk about habitual and repeated actions in the past and to describe and explain the circumstances surrounding a past event.

Activities	Standards	Resources
Gramática	1.2, 3.1	
8.	1.2, 1.3	
9.	1.2, 3.1	Audio
10.	1.1, 1.2, 1.3, 2.2	

Teaching Suggestions

Warm-Up / Independent Starter

- Have students think about an important event in their lives. Next, ask them to think of the background and the circumstances surrounding the event (e.g., What was the weather like that day? Who was there?) Have students jot down the information, but tell them not to conjugate the verbs or write in complete sentences.

Preparation

- Go over the grammar presentation with the class. If students have difficulties understanding some of the examples, you may want to contrast the sentences with a similar sentence that requires the use of the preterite. For example: *Vivimos en Texas de 2009 a 2013.* vs. *Antes vivíamos en Texas.*

- Focus students' attention on the photo of Ethan and explain that he is writing a short story for a school assignment. Call on a student to read the text in the speech bubble aloud. Then, as a class, analyze the use of the imperfect tense in the text. Elicit that the text is describing the character and explaining the circumstances surrounding an event.

- Ask students to take out their notes from the Independent Starter and use them to write a paragraph describing the setting, characters, and circumstances surrounding an important event in their lives. Invite students to share their narratives with the class.

6

---

3. DESCRIBIR EN EL PASADO

Gramática

El imperfecto

- Usamos el imperfecto en estos casos:
  - Para hablar de acciones pasadas que son habituales o que ocurren repetidamente.

    Cuando era niño, **jugaba** al fútbol todos los sábados.
  - Para hablar de acciones pasadas como acciones que duran un tiempo indeterminado, sin mencionar su final.

    Antes **vivíamos** en Texas.
  - En las narraciones, para describir personajes y lugares y para explicar las circunstancias que rodean a un evento.

    Ernesto **salía** muy poco, pero ese día decidió dar un paseo a pesar de que **llovía** y no **había** nadie en la calle.

- Solo hay tres verbos irregulares en el imperfecto:
  - ir → iba, ibas, iba, íbamos, ibais, iban.
  - ser → era, eras, era, éramos, erais, eran.
  - ver → veía, veías, veía, veíamos, veíais, veían.

Repasa la conjugación del imperfecto en la página R17.

TERMINACIONES DEL IMPERFECTO

Verbos regulares en -ar:

-aba	-ábamos
-abas	-abais
-aba	-aban

Verbos regulares en -er, -ir:

-ía	-íamos
-ías	-íais
-ía	-ían

Elena **llegaba** siempre tarde al trabajo. **Sabía** que **podían** despedirla, pero no **era** capaz de levantarse cuando **sonaba** el despertador. Una mañana...

8 Mi niñez

▶ **Completa** estas oraciones con la forma correcta del imperfecto.

Cuando era niña...

1. ... __1__ de vacaciones a Florida, donde __2__ mis abuelos.
   (1: ir) (2: estar)

2. ... __3__ todos los fines de semana con mi amiga Alicia.
   (3: jugar)

3. ... __4__ clases de *ballet* porque mis padres __5__ , pero a mí no me __6__
   (4: tomar) (5: querer) (6: gustar)

4. ... mi familia y yo __7__ en una casa que __8__ de dos plantas.
   (7: vivir) (8: ser)

6 seis

Differentiated Instruction

DEVELOPING LEARNERS

- Ask students to think about a childhood friend or a pet they used to have, and ask them to write a short description of this person or pet. If necessary, break the task down into steps: 1. Students make a list of physical characteristics and personality traits. 2. Students then write sentences out. 3. Students use their sentences to compose one or two paragraphs. You may wish to give them an example: *Toby era un gato muy tranquilo. Estaba un poco gordo porque se pasaba casi todo el día tumbado en el sofá...*

EXPANDING LEARNERS

- Have students look at online newspapers in Spanish and select a piece of news that catches their attention. Give them time to skim through the article and note the main event. Then ask students to make up the background information and circumstances surrounding the event, and write an introduction to the news. Encourage them to be creative. For instance, if the news is about a traffic accident, students may focus on one of the people involved. For example: *Sarah tenía 30 años y detestaba el tráfico. Siempre evitaba esa autopista, pero hoy...*

3. DESCRIBIR EN EL PASADO

Gramática – El imperfecto

9. Vacaciones en la playa

 ▶ **Escucha** y clasifica los verbos de las oraciones en una tabla como esta.

	Pretérito	Imperfecto
1		llovía
2		
3		
4		
5		
6		
7		
8		

10. Tu opinión cuenta

▶ **Lee** las entradas de este blog de viajes y responde a las preguntas.

Hacienda Orquídea: Opiniones de los huéspedes

Viajera 25

Estupenda, pero muy aislada ★★★★ 6/08/13
Buscaba un hotel exclusivo en la zona cafetera de Colombia. Esta hacienda parecía cumplir con esos requisitos, y así fue. Sin embargo, estaba más lejos de los centros urbanos de lo que pensaba.

Viajero 13

La hacienda bien, la comida regular ★★★ 25/07/13
La comida era un poco repetitiva. El menú diario variaba muy poco. Por lo demás, la habitación era amplia y cómoda, y el baño estaba bien equipado. La decoración colonial le daba un aire muy elegante a la hacienda.

Viajero 32

Ideal para desconectar ★★★★ 15/07/13
Se respiraba mucha paz. Los jardines estaban muy bien cuidados y había también senderos para caminar en plena naturaleza. Mi única queja es que no había cobertura wifi en la habitación. Tenía que ir a a la recepción cuando necesitaba acceso a Internet, y la conexión era lenta.

1. ¿Cómo eran las habitaciones y los baños de este hotel?
2. ¿Qué tipo de hotel era? ¿Cómo era la decoración?
3. ¿Cómo eran las zonas verdes? ¿Qué actividades podían realizarse allí?
4. ¿Qué aspectos positivos mencionan los viajeros? ¿Y negativos?
5. ¿Para qué tipo de viajeros crees que es recomendable este hotel? ¿Por qué?

▶ **Escribe** una entrada de blog similar sobre un hotel donde te hayas alojado.

Activities

9. To extend this activity, play the recording again and ask students to write one more descriptive sentence after #5 and one more action after #7. Have volunteers share their sentences.

10. Have students use a star system (from 0 to 5) to categorize the hotel they stayed in. Then collect students' entries and arrange them from best to worst hotel based on the stars awarded to each hotel. Invite the class to look at the reviews and choose one hotel they would like to stay in and one they would never stay in.

 AUDIO SCRIPT
See page XXIF.

Answer Key

8.

1. iba	4. tomaba	7. vivíamos
2. estaban	5. querían	8. era
3. jugaba	6. gustaba	

9. Pretérito: 3. gustó; 6. salió; 7. pudimos; 8. fueron.
Imperfecto: 1. llovía; 2. hacía; 4. estaba; 5. era.

10. Answers will vary. Sample answers:
1. Las habitaciones eran amplias y cómodas. Los baños estaban bien equipados.
2. Era una hacienda exclusiva. La decoración era colonial y muy elegante.
3. Había jardines bien cuidados y senderos para caminar.
4. Positivos: hotel exclusivo, buenas habitaciones y baños, decoración colonial, mucha paz, zonas verdes bien cuidadas, senderos. Negativos: lejos de centros urbanos, comida repetitiva, no wifi en las habitaciones, conexión a Internet lenta.
5. Answers will vary.
▶ Answers will vary.

Additional Resources

Fans Online activities
Practice Workbook

HERITAGE LANGUAGE LEARNERS

• Ask students to interview a family member about his or her life growing up in their country of origin. Encourage students to get a detailed description of their relative's hometown, the school this person attended, daily life, the celebrations they used to have, etc. Then, ask students to organize the information in an appealing way to present it to the class. They may, for instance, bring in pictures or they may video record their interviews and show excerpts to the class.

MULTIPLE INTELLIGENCES:
Visual-Spatial Intelligence

• Show students an image of an event that took place some time ago in your community or state. Explain briefly what happened and give students a few moments to think of the background and circumstances surrounding the event. Encourage students to be creative. Then, have them draw the background (e.g., the setting, weather, passers-by). Finally, invite students to show their art to the class and encourage the class to describe the scene. For example: *Hacía frío, por eso todos llevaban abrigo...*

4. HABLAR DEL FUTURO

Gramática – El futuro

Presentation

- In this section, students will review the future tense to refer to future events and to talk about things that will happen at some point in the future.

Activities	Standards	Resources
Gramática	1.2, 3.1	
11.	1.3	
12.	1.2, 1.3	Audio
13.	1.1, 1.3, 5.1	
14.	1.1, 5.2	

Teaching Suggestions

Warm-Up / Independent Starter

- Provide students with the following list of objects and ask them to write down what they think those objects will be like in ten years. For example: *las impresoras 3D → todos tendremos una*; *la aspiradora → desaparecerá.*
  - *– el teléfono fijo*
  - *– la tableta*
  - *– el teléfono celular*
  - *– el coche*
  - *– el libro en papel*
  - *– el televisor*

Preparation

- Ask students to get together with a partner and compare their Independent Starters. Did they make similar predictions? Then discuss the students' predictions as a class. Encourage students to justify their conclusions. For example: *El teléfono fijo desaparecerá porque ya no será necesario. Usaremos solo celulares.*

- Have students read the grammar explanation silently, and then ask a volunteer to read it aloud. Next, ask for two volunteers to role-play the conversation between Asha and Lucas. Point out the use of these time expressions in the dialogue: *en diez años, para entonces.* Then remind students of some of the time expressions that are generally paired with verbs in the future tense: *esta tarde/noche, mañana, pasado mañana, la próxima semana, el mes/año que viene, dentro de cinco/diez años...* For further practice, ask students to use their predictions from the Independent Starter to create two more sentences to continue Asha and Lucas's dialogue.

Gramática

El futuro

- Usamos el futuro para hablar de eventos que ocurrirán en el futuro:

  Mañana **hará** mucho calor.
  Este fin de semana no **saldré** porque tengo que estudiar.

- Algunos futuros tienen la raíz irregular:

caber → cabr-	haber → habr-	saber → sabr-
poder → podr-	poner → pondr-	tener → tendr-
salir → saldr-	valer → valdr-	venir → vendr-
decir → dir-	hacer → har-	querer → querr-

  Repasa la conjugación del futuro en la página R18.

TERMINACIONES DEL FUTURO

Verbos regulares en *-ar, -er, -ir*:

-é	-emos
-ás	-éis
-á	-án

- Para hablar de eventos futuros, usamos también la estructura: *ir a + infinitivo* conjugando el verbo *ir* en presente.

  El año que viene mis padres **van a vender** la casa.

En diez años, este teléfono que ahora es tan moderno no **valdrá** nada y nadie lo **querrá**.

¡Claro! Para entonces los teléfonos **tendrán** pantalla flexible y **serán** tan finos como una hoja de papel.

11 ¿Qué pasará?

▶ **Escribe** oraciones para contar hechos futuros. Utiliza las tres columnas.

Modelo   *El próximo verano mi profesora irá de viaje a otro país.*

(A)	(B)	(C)
el próximo verano	los médicos	tener una casa
el mes que viene	yo	ir de viaje a otro país
en cincuenta años	mi mejor amigo(a)	salir a cenar
este fin de semana	mis padres y yo	hacer un examen
en cinco años	mis compañeros(as)	poder hablar español perfectamente
dentro de diez años	mi profesor(a)	curar todos los tipos de cáncer

---

Differentiated Instruction

DEVELOPING LEARNERS

- For additional practice with irregular verbs, ask students to complete the following sentences with the correct future tense form of the verbs in parentheses:
  1. *En cien años, no (haber) petróleo en la Tierra. (habrá)*
  2. *Pasado mañana mis amigos y yo (salir) a cenar. (saldremos)*
  3. *En cinco años, la gasolina (valer) más de $6.00 el galón. (valdrá)*
  4. *Cuando el niño tenga tres años, no (caber) en la cuna. (cabrá)*
  5. *Dentro de diez años, yo (tener) 27 años. (tendré)*

EXPANDING LEARNERS

- Ask students to use the future tense to write two paragraphs describing a popular future technology that is still in its infancy or that has not been invented yet. Students should include supporting details that justify why they think that this technology will be successful. They will also need to describe the objects that will use this technology. Encourage creativity and the use of humor in their compositions. Students may include a drawing or diagram depicting the technology or explaining how it is used.

12 Eventos futuros

 ▶ **Escucha** y relaciona cada oración con la fotografía correspondiente.

 A

 B

 C

 D

 E

 F

▶ **Elige** dos de las fotografías y escribe más predicciones sobre esas personas.

Modelo   *El niño será arquitecto. Sus padres tendrán dos hijos más y...*

13 ¿Te atreves a predecir el futuro?

▶ **Completa** una tabla como esta con tus predicciones para el futuro.

	En 10 años	En 100 años
1. El clima de mi región.		
2. El medio ambiente de mi región.		
3. Los recursos naturales de mi estado.		
4. Las actividades económicas de mi país.		
5. El nivel de vida de mi país.		

 ▶ **Intercambia** tu tabla con tu compañero(a) y comenten sus predicciones. ¿Quién tiene una visión más optimista del futuro? ¿Y más pesimista? ¿Por qué?

14 Tus planes

 ▶ **Habla** con dos compañeros(as) sobre sus planes y objetivos futuros en estas áreas.

Educación   Trabajo

Familia   Vivienda

¿Ya sabes qué estudiarás o qué profesión tendrás?

Estoy segura de que estudiaré algo relacionado con el medio ambiente.

HERITAGE LANGUAGE LEARNERS

• Have students imagine that they have been commissioned by a Hollywood studio to write the script for a science fiction movie set in their community in the year 2200. Ask students to write an outline describing the setting (i.e., their community in the year 2200), the people, the businesses and jobs people will have, leisure-time activities they will enjoy, etc. Then have students exchange their outline with a partner who will look at it from the point of view of a Hollywood producer and give feedback to the "writer."

MULTIPLE INTELLIGENCES:
Intrapersonal Intelligence

• Ask students to write a journal entry that focuses on their future and how they hope to reach their personal and professional goals. They may start with their goals regarding education, work, living arrangements, and family. For example: *Estudiaré Derecho Corporativo. Trabajaré en un prestigioso bufete de abogados...* Then, students should specify how they are planning to reach those goals. For example: *Asistiré a la Facultad de Derecho de la Universidad de Michigan. Me graduaré con matrícula de honor...*

---

4. HABLAR DEL FUTURO

Gramática – El futuro

Activities

11. To extend this activity, ask students to add three statements to each column. Then have them exchange their activities with a partner and complete each other's statements.

12. Before playing the audio, ask students to look at the pictures and write down one possible sentence using a verb in the future tense for each picture. Then play the audio and have students complete the activity.

14. Ask students to exchange the results of their interviews in small groups. Then have groups compile the results and share them with the class. In a class discussion, analyze the results. What professions do the majority of students plan to have? Where are most of them planning to live? Encourage students to think of reasons for these trends.

 AUDIO SCRIPT
See page XXIF.

Answer Key

11. Answers will vary. Sample answers:
  - El mes que viene mi mejor amiga hará un examen.
  - En cincuenta años los médicos curarán todos los tipos de cáncer.
  - Este fin de semana mis padres y yo saldremos a cenar.
  - En cinco años mis compañeros podrán hablar español perfectamente.
  - Dentro de diez años yo tendré una casa.

12. 1. E   3. A   5. F
     2. C   4. D   6. B
  ▶ Answers will vary.

13. Answers will vary.
  ▶ Answers will vary.

14. Answers will vary.

Additional Resources

Fans Online activities
Practice Workbook

5. DAR ÓRDENES E INSTRUCCIONES

Gramática – El imperativo afirmativo

Presentation

- In this section, students will review both the informal and formal affirmative command forms.

Activities	Standards	Resources
Gramática	1.2, 3.1	
15.	1.2, 1.3	Audio
16.	1.2, 1.3	
17.	1.3, 5.2	
18.	1.1, 3.1, 5.2	

Teaching Suggestions

Warm-Up / Independent Starter

- Have students think of five golden rules for learning Spanish (e.g., *Ten amigos hispanos. Lee en español*).

Preparation

- Go over the grammar presentation as a class. Then give students a few moments to revise their sentences from the Independent Starter. Call on volunteers to read their sentences aloud, and decide on the top seven rules as class.

Activities

16. As a class, discuss the effectiveness of the advice Julia Mari is receiving from her fellow forum participants. Encourage students to think of other recommendations they could make. Alternatively, have students write three more recommendations for Julia Mari.

17. To expand this activity, have students choose one of the cases and elaborate on their recommendations. Encourage them to begin with a brief introduction explaining the importance of following their advice. Invite students to share their work with the class.

AUDIO SCRIPT
See page XXIF.

10

Gramática

El imperativo afirmativo

- Usamos las formas del imperativo afirmativo *(informal or formal affirmative commands)* para dar órdenes o pedir a una persona que haga algo.

  Ten paciencia.   **Lleguen** a tiempo.
  Coma frutas y verduras.   **Practiquen** algún deporte.

- Usamos la forma nosotros(as) del imperativo para expresar lo que tenemos que hacer o para sugerir algo.

  Vayamos al gimnasio esta tarde.

- Algunos verbos muy comunes son irregulares en el imperativo:

  decir → di, diga, digan   dar → da, dé, den
  poner → pon, ponga, pongan   ser → sé, sea, sean
  tener → ten, tenga, tengan   ir → ve, vaya, vayamos,
  hacer → haz, haga, hagan   vayan
  salir → sal, salga, salgan
  venir → ven, venga, vengan

  Repasa la conjugación del imperativo afirmativo en las páginas R22 (verbos regulares) y R23 (verbos irregulares).

TERMINACIONES DEL IMPERATIVO AFIRMATIVO

Verbos regulares en -ar:

-a	tú
-e	usted
-emos	nosotros(as)
-ad	vosotros(as)
-en	ustedes

Verbos regulares en -er:

-e	tú
-a	usted
-amos	nosotros(as)
-ed	vosotros(as)
-an	ustedes

Verbos regulares en -ir:

-e	tú
-a	usted
-amos	nosotros(as)
-id	vosotros(as)
-an	ustedes

Yo voy a diseñar las invitaciones. Y tú, **pide** presupuesto para alquilar el salón y **piensa** en la decoración.

Pero primero, ¡**hagamos** la lista de invitados!

15 **Una fiesta sorpresa**

▶ **Escucha** a Eva y a Ethan, y decide quién va a realizar estas tareas. Después, escribe dos órdenes más para ellos.

	Eva	Ethan	Los dos
Planificar la fiesta sorpresa.			✔
Elegir la música.			
Comprar la comida y la bebida.			
Pedir el dinero para el regalo.			
Hacer la lista de invitados.			
Enviar las invitaciones.			

10 diez

Differentiated Instruction

DEVELOPING LEARNERS

- Ask students to write six affirmative informal commands telling someone what to do to lead a healthful lifestyle. However, tell students to give bad advice. Then have them exchange papers with a partner who has to correct the advice. To get students started, offer these examples:

1. *Come alimentos ricos en grasas saturadas.* → *Reduce el consumo de alimentos ricos en grasas saturadas.*

2. *Ten siempre varias botellas de refresco en el refrigerador.* → *Elimina los refrescos de tu dieta.*

EXPANDING LEARNERS

- Tell students to imagine that they have been asked to write a short inspirational piece for their school newspaper to promote good eating habits and to offer tips for healthful living among their classmates. Students should use their own knowledge and common sense when making suggestions for exercise, reducing stress, getting proper rest, and avoiding a sedentary lifestyle. The suggestions should make use of affirmative informal commands. Students may look for images on the Internet to illustrate their articles, or create their own art. When they finish, display their work in the classroom.

16 **¿Qué me recomiendan?**

▶ **Lee** este foro y complétalo con las formas correctas del imperativo de estos verbos.

| hacer | preparar | trabajar | dar | sembrar | decir | aumentar | disminuir |

Autor	Mensaje
JuliaMari 🗎 Publicado: 10/09/2013 7:00 p. m.	Hola a todos. Acabo de descubrir que tengo un nivel alto de colesterol y debo cambiar mis hábitos alimenticios. ¿Qué me recomiendan? ____1____ me ideas, por favor.
Lola15 🗎 Publicado: 10/09/2013 7:15 p. m.	Hola, JuliaMari. Te felicito por tu decisión de cambiar. Antes que nada, ____2____ las grasas saturadas de tu dieta y ____3____ el consumo de frutas y verduras. Y ____4____ ejercicio al menos tres veces por semana.
JuliaMari 🗎 Publicado: 10/09/2013 7:25 p. m.	Gracias, Lola15. Tengo un pequeño jardín detrás de la casa y he pensado en sembrar algunas verduras. A lo mejor así animo también a mi hijo de 8 años y a mi esposo a comer más hortalizas.
PedroDíaz 🗎 Publicado: 10/09/2013 8:00 p. m.	Hola, JuliaMari. ¡Excelente idea! ____5____ juntos en el pequeño jardín familiar. Estoy seguro de que eso los animará a comer de forma más saludable. ¡Y es un buen ejercicio!
Lola15 🗎 Publicado: 10/09/2013 8:05 p. m.	Yo también siembro verduras, pero en macetas porque no tengo jardín. ____6____ distintas verduras y así tendrán variedad. ____7____ le a tu hijo qué minerales y vitaminas tiene cada verdura y ____8____ platos juntos.

17 **Consejos para todos**

▶ **Escribe** tres recomendaciones para cada caso.

Modelo   1. *Haga ejercicio tres o cuatro veces a la semana. Reduzca...*

1. Tu profesor(a) quiere ponerse en forma y bajar de peso.

2. Tu mejor amigo(a) quiere aprender bailes latinos.

3. Tus compañeros(as) y tú quieren sacar mejores notas.

18 **Una semana dedicada a la salud**

▶ **Habla** con tu compañero(a). Planeen una «Semana de la Salud» en la escuela.

Diseña una página web para el evento. Eres tan buena con las computadoras...

Sí, pero ayúdame con el contenido. Y decidamos juntos qué actividades incluir.

▶ **Escriban** el plan y después preséntenlo a la clase.

HERITAGE LANGUAGE LEARNERS

• Ask students to research a typical dish from their country of origin, including any anecdotal information about its origin. Then have students write a description of the dish and the recipe. They should include step-by-step instructions on how to prepare the dish. For example: *Primero mezcla la masa de maíz con agua y déjala reposar media hora. Después, fríe...* Ask the class to take notes and encourage them to prepare this dish at home and share their experiences with their classmates.

COOPERATIVE LEARNING

• Have students work in small groups to come up with a list of seven recommendations for fostering a well-balanced life (i.e., having a good work-life balance). They should first write the rules using informal command forms *(tú)* and then rewrite them using formal commands *(ustedes)*. Have groups read their recommendations to the class and afterward engage them in a discussion about the effectiveness and practicality of each rule. Finally, hold a class vote to select the seven most effective rules.

---

5. DAR ÓRDENES E INSTRUCCIONES

Gramática – El imperativo afirmativo

Answer Key

15. Eva: elegir música, enviar las invitaciones.
Ethan: comprar la comida y la bebida.
Los dos: pedir el dinero para el regalo, hacer la lista de invitados.

16.
1. Den
2. disminuye
3. aumenta
4. haz
5. Trabajen
6. Siembra/Siembren
7. Di
8. preparen

17. Answers will vary.

18. Answers will vary.
▶ Answers will vary.

Assessment (Lesson Plans for 90-Minute Classes)

■ In addition to the unit test, you may want to ask students to do an oral presentation in order to evaluate their oral proficiency. Explain that they will choose a topic related to one of the themes presented in this unit and speak for three minutes in front of the class. Provide students with this list of topics: 1. talk about their daily routines; 2. describe leisure activities of students their age; 3. tell an anecdote; 4. deliver important news; 5. describe their last vacation; 6. describe a scene from their favorite movie; 7. give their predictions for the next decade; 8. talk about their future plans; 9. offer their advice for applying to college; 10. tell what to do to stay healthy.

■ Allow students time to prepare their speeches. They may prepare a basic outline, but should avoid reading as they deliver their speeches. Assess students on organization, content, correct use of target vocabulary and grammar structures, and pronunciation and fluency.

Additional Resources

Fans Online activities
Practice Workbook

Unit 1 Nos relacionamos

Objectives

- To describe people's physical characteristics and personality traits.
- To express likes, interests, feelings, and emotions.
- To use descriptive adjectives correctly.
- To express habitual actions.
- To talk about the postal service.
- To learn pronominal verbs.

- To learn reflexive and reciprocal verbs.
- To talk about actions in progress.
- To talk about different means of communication.
- To express quantity.
- To identify main ideas and significant details in a variety of texts.

- To write a wide variety of texts, including a personal letter or e-mail.
- To know and apply the different stages of the writing process: planning, writing, revising, and sharing.
- To explore variations of the Spanish language.

Contents

Vocabulary

- Useful expressions used to greet people, to say goodbye, and to express good wishes when ending a conversation.
- Review: Words for physical characteristics, personality traits, and personal relationships.
- Physical characteristics and personality traits.
- Post office and mail.
- Means of communication.

Grammar

- To express likes, interests, feelings, and emotions using several verbs like *gustar*.
- Descriptive adjectives: position and meaning.
- Pronominal verbs.
- Reflexive and reciprocal verbs.
- To describe actions in progress in the past, present, or future.
- To express quantity using indefinite adjectives or pronouns, adverbs of quantity, and other expressions.

Culture

- The Mexican tradition of *piñatas*.
- Emotive language in Hispanic countries.
- Mariachi music.
- *Las mañanitas*.
- The Peruvian *chasquis*.
- Juan Rulfo.
- *La carta a los Reyes Magos*.
- The Gomeran whistle.
- *¿Prensa digital o prensa en papel?*
- Social networks in Spanish.
- Julio Cortázar.

Evaluation Criteria

- Describe people's physical characteristics and personality traits.
- Express likes, interests, feelings, and emotions using verbs similar to *gustar*.
- Recognize and use descriptive adjectives that change meaning before and after nouns.
- Describe postal products and services.
- Recognize the meaning of verbs depending on their use with pronouns.

- Recognize and use reflexive and reciprocal verbs.
- Identify technology and practices related to different means of communication.
- Use progressive tenses to talk about actions in progress in the past, present, and future.
- Use indefinite adjectives and pronouns, adverbs of quantity, and other expressions to express quantity.

- Express understanding of Spanish language variations.
- Write a personal e-mail to introduce yourself to a host family.
- Read different types of texts and identify main ideas and significant details in them.
- Write guided texts giving information, describing, or narrating events.

Unit Plan

Las tareas/Antes de empezar

Estimated time: 2 sessions.

Text: *Ritos y celebraciones.*

Functions & forms:
- Useful expressions to greet people, to say goodbye, and to express good wishes when ending a conversation.
- Review of known vocabulary for physical characteristics, personality traits, and personal relationships.

DESAFÍO 1

Estimated time: 6 sessions.

Text: *Un cumpleaños importante.*

Functions & forms:
- To describe people.
- Physical characteristics and personality traits.
- To express likes, interests, feelings, and emotions.
- Descriptive adjectives: Position and meaning.

Culture:
- *Las piñatas.*
- *Los diminutivos.*
- *El mariachi (México).*

Reading: *Las mañanitas.*

DESAFÍO 2

Estimated time: 6 sessions.

Text: *Los nuevos chasquis.*

Functions & forms:
- To express habitual actions.
- Post office and mail.
- Pronominal verbs.
- Reflexive and reciprocal verbs.

Culture:
- *Los chasquis (Perú).*
- *Juan Rulfo.*
- *La carta a los Reyes Magos.*

Reading: *El oficio más romántico: escribir cartas de amor por encargo.*

DESAFÍO 3

Estimated time: 6 sessions.

Text: *Un extraño lenguaje.*

Functions & forms:
- To talk about actions in progress.
- Means of communication.
- To describe actions in progress.
- To express quantity.

Culture:
- *El silbo gomero.*
- *¿Prensa digital o prensa en papel?*
- *Redes sociales en español.*

Reading: *El diario a diario.*

Para terminar

Estimated time: 2 sessions.

Todo junto:
- Review of *Desafíos* 1–3.

Tu desafío:
- *Desafío A:* Write an e-mail to a best friend asking for his or her help in planning a traditional Mexican birthday party.
- *Desafío B*: Create a poster to promote the postal service in your city.
- *Desafío C*: Research the Gomeran whistle.

MAPA CULTURAL

Estimated time: 1 session.

Mapa cultural: *Unidad y variedad del español.*

ESCRITURA

Estimated time: 1 session.

Writing: *Un correo de presentación.*

PROYECTO / EVALUACIÓN

Estimated time: 2 sessions.

Project: *Una página web de nuestra clase de Español.*

Self-evaluation: *Autoevaluación.*

HACIA EL *AP* EXAM*

Estimated time: 2 sessions.

Test: Interpretive Communication: Print Texts.

Standards for Learning Spanish

COMMUNICATION

1.1 Interpersonal mode
- Exchange personal opinions and experiences.
- Engage in oral conversations using personal knowledge and experience.
- Talk about habitual actions.
- Compare information with a partner.
- Ask and answer questions on different topics orally.
- Prepare and conduct an interview.
- Ask a partner questions, take notes, and present a summary to the class.
- Invent a story with a classmate.
- Write an e-mail to a friend.

1.2. Interpretive mode
- Demonstrate understanding of oral and written idiomatic expressions.
- Demonstrate understanding of questions relating to familiar and less familiar topics.
- Understand and obtain information from audio or video recordings.
- Understand written exchanges.
- Extract information from a journalistic report.
- Identify main ideas and significant details from a literary story.
- Draw conclusions and make judgments from oral and written texts.
- Interpret texts on other cultures and relate them to personal knowledge and experience.
- Write sentences to explain images.

1.3. Presentational mode
- Produce and present an original creation orally.
- Write an explanatory text about own experiences or as result of a research activity.
- Use a chart to present information.
- Design and present a webpage.
- Create a literary story or a beginning and an end for a literary story.
- Write slogans or brief promotional texts.
- Write verses for a song.
- Write a formal e-mail to introduce oneself.
- Dramatize a dialogue.

CULTURE

2.1. Practices and perspectives
- Read about cultural celebrations related to birthdays and saint's days in Hispanic countries.
- Learn about historical communication practices of the Incas.
- Learn about the Hispanic tradition of the Three Kings Day.
- Learn how people use traditional and new media to stay informed or to communicate in Spanish.

2.2. Products and perspectives
- Learn about mariachi music.
- Learn about important Hispanic writers.
- Read about traditional Hispanic legends and understand their cultural significance.
- Read about and research relevant Hispanic writers.
- Learn about the whistled language of La Gomera in the Canary Islands, Spain.

CONNECTIONS

3.1. Interdisciplinary connections
- Understand the similarities and differences between some aspects of grammar in English and in Spanish.
- Learn about relevant Hispanic writers.
- Learn about traditional Mexican music.
- Use the writing process to produce a written work.
- Learn about mass media used in Hispanic communities.
- Create a webpage.

3.2. Viewpoints through language / culture
- Read dialogues, informative texts, and literary texts in Spanish that provide insight into Hispanic cultures.
- Learn about how geography influences language and communication.

COMPARISONS

4.1. Compare languages
- Compare the uses of diminutives in English and in Spanish.
- Compare how to express likes and feelings in English and in Spanish.
- Compare the meaning of certain adjectives according to their position.
- Compare pronominal and non-pronominal verb forms in English and in Spanish.
- Compare progressive tenses in English and in Spanish.
- Compare the use of quantity expressions in English and in Spanish.

4.2. Compare cultures
- Compare birthday and saint's day celebrations in Hispanic countries and in the United States.

COMMUNITIES

5.1. Spanish within and beyond the school setting
- Use language to express feelings and emotions.
- Conduct research on the Internet or in a library.
- Write a formal letter or an e-mail in Spanish.

5.2. Spanish for lifelong learners
- Encourage the knowledge of Hispanic history and cultural traditions.
- Promote interest in Hispanic means of communication.
- Learn the writing process.
- Use technology to learn.

Communicative Skills

Interpersonal Mode

		Activities
Speaking	• Exchange opinions or experiences with a classmate. • Compare and contrast information or your own texts with a classmate. • Ask and answer questions with a partner. • Invent a story with a classmate or discuss a topic with the class.	• 9, 27, 29, 48, 52, 72, 73, 76 • 6, 9, 18, 25, 26, 27, 51, 52, 75 • 35, 41, 59, 74 • 23, 73
Writing	• Write questions for an interview. • Take notes from an interview or write a summarizing text of an interview. • Write an e-mail to a friend.	• 41, 78 • 59, 78 • 79
Listening	• Understand and obtain information from oral exchanges.	• 9, 27, 29, 35, 41, 48, 52, 59, 72, 73, 74, 76, *Escritura*
Reading	• Understand personal information in an e-mail.	• *Escritura*

Interpretive Mode

		Activities
Listening	• Obtain information from a conversation. • Understand oral informative audios.	• 3, 9, 13, 17, 28, 39, 64, 68 • 58, 73
Reading	• Demonstrate comprehension of written exchanges or longer written dialogues. • Infer meanings based on a text. • Reflect on cultural topics in relation to personal knowledge and experience. • Understand a descriptive text. • Obtain information and draw conclusions from an informative text. • Research using outside sources. • Understand a literary story or a stanza of a song.	• 1, 8, 12, 24, 29, 31, 52, 54, 76 • 2, 7, 11, 47, 57, 71 • 10, 19, 36, 45, 56, 60, 65 • 5, R1 • 27, 32, 44, 46, 55, 64, 77, *Hacia el* AP* Exam • 26, 33, 73, 79 • 50, 69, 70
Viewing	• Connect information or descriptions to images. • Write sentences to describe images.	• 4, 6, 30, 34, 39 • 23, 40, 49

Presentational Mode

		Activities
Speaking	• Act out a dialogue. • Present information or an original creation to the class.	• 80 • 78, 79, *Proyecto*
Writing	• Write a descriptive or an explanatory text. • Write a literary story or a beginning and an end for a literary story. • Write promotional slogans or a brief promotional text for a poster. • Write an introduction e-mail or an informative text for a webpage.	• 9, 26 • 50, 72 • 52, 79 • *Escritura, Proyecto*
Visually Representing	• Create a poster or a webpage.	• 79, *Proyecto*

Cross-Curricular Standards

Subject	Standard	Activities
Language Arts	• Compare elements of Spanish grammar with English equivalents. • Use the writing process to write a formal introduction e-mail. • Learn about variations of the Spanish language.	• 14, 15, 20, 25, 37, 42, 61, 66 • *Escritura* • *Mapa cultural*
Literature	• Read about and research relevant Hispanic writers.	• 36, *Lectura D3*
Social Studies	• Learn about the history and culture of the Incan civilization.	• *Lectura D2*, 32, 33

Lesson Plans (50-Minute Classes)

Day	Objectives	Sessions	Activities	Time	Standards	Resources / Homework
1	To introduce social relationships and the characters' challenges	**Nos relacionamos / Las tareas** (12–15) • Warm-Up: Topic orientation • Presentation: *Ritos y celebraciones*	1–2	15 m. 35 m.	1.1, 1.2, 1.3, 2.1, 2.2, 4.1	Video Practice Workbook
2	To learn useful expressions related to the unit topic and to review learned vocabulary	**Antes de empezar** (16–17) • Warm-Up: Independent Starter • *Expresiones útiles* • *Recuerda*	3–4 5–6	10 m. 15 m. 25 m.	1.1, 1.2, 1.3, 2.1	Audio Practice Workbook
3	To describe people	**Desafío 1 – Un cumpleaños importante** (18–19) • Warm-Up: Independent Starter • *Texto: Un cumpleaños importante* • *Cultura: Las piñatas*	7–9 10	5 m. 35 m. 10 m.	1.1, 1.2, 2.1, 2.2, 3.2, 4.2, 5.2	Audio
4	To talk about physical characteristics and personality traits	**Desafío 1 – Vocabulario** (20–21) • Warm-Up: Independent Starter • *Vocabulario: Características físicas y rasgos de personalidad* • *Conexiones: Los diminutivos*	11–13 14	5 m. 35 m. 10 m.	1.1, 1.2, 1.3, 2.1, 3.1, 4.1, 5.1	Audio Practice Workbook
5	To learn several verbs to express likes, interests, feelings, and emotions	**Desafío 1 – Gramática** (22–23) • Warm-Up: Independent Starter • *Gramática: Expresar gustos, intereses, sentimientos y emociones* • *Cultura: El mariachi (México)*	15–18 19	5 m. 35 m. 10 m.	1.1, 1.2, 1.3, 2.1, 2.2, 3.1, 3.2, 4.1, 5.1	Audio Practice Workbook
6	To learn descriptive adjectives that change meaning before and after nouns	**Desafío 1 – Gramática** (24–25) • Warm-Up: Independent Starter • *Gramática: Los adjetivos. Posición y significado*	20–23	5 m. 45 m.	1.1, 1.2, 1.3, 3.1, 4.1	Practice Workbook
7	To understand a written dialogue	**Desafío 1 – Lectura** (26–27) • Warm-Up: Independent Starter • *Lectura: Las mañanitas*	24–26	5 m. 45 m.	1.1, 1.2, 1.3, 2.1, 2.2, 3.2, 4.1, 5.1, 5.2	Audio
8	To integrate vocabulary and grammar and to assess student proficiency	**Desafío 1 – Comunicación / Evaluación** (28–29) • Warm-Up: Independent Starter • *Comunicación*: Review • *Final del desafío* • Quiz on *Desafío 1*	27–28 29	5 m. 25 m. 10 m. 10 m.	1.1, 1.2, 1.3, 2.1, 2.2, 3.2, 4.2, 5.1	Audio Practice Workbook

Day	Objectives	Sessions	Activities	Time	Standards	Resources / Homework
9	To talk about habitual actions	**Desafío 2 – Los nuevos chasquis** (30–31) • Warm-Up: Independent Starter • *Texto: Los nuevos chasquis* • *Cultura: Los chasquis (Perú)*	30–32 33	5 m. 35 m. 10 m.	1.1, 1.2, 2.1, 2.2, 3.1, 3.2	Audio
10	To describe postal products and services	**Desafío 2 – Vocabulario** (32–33) • Warm-Up: Independent Starter • *Vocabulario: La oficina de correos* • *Conexiones: Juan Rulfo*	34–35 36	5 m. 35 m. 10 m.	1.1, 1.2, 1.3, 2.2, 3.1, 3.2, 5.1, 5.2	Practice Workbook
11	To learn pronominal verbs	**Desafío 2 – Gramática** (34–35) • Warm-Up: Independent Starter • *Gramática: Los verbos pronominales*	37–41	5 m. 45 m.	1.1, 1.2, 1.3, 3.1, 4.1	Audio Practice Workbook
12	To learn reflexive and reciprocal verbs	**Desafío 2 – Gramática** (36-37) • Warm-Up: Independent Starter • *Gramática: Los verbos reflexivos y recíprocos* • *Cultura: La carta a los Reyes Magos*	42–44 45	5 m. 35 m. 10 m.	1.1, 1.2, 1.3, 2.1, 3.1, 4.1, 4.2, 5.1	Practice Workbook
13	To understand information in a journalistic report	**Desafío 2 – Lectura** (38–39) • Warm-Up: Independent Starter • *Lectura: El oficio más romántico: escribir cartas de amor por encargo*	46–48	5 m. 45 m.	1.1, 1.2, 1.3, 2.1, 3.2, 5.1	
14	To integrate vocabulary and grammar and to assess student proficiency	**Desafío 2 – Comunicación / Evaluación** (40–41) • Warm-Up: Independent Starter • *Comunicación*: Review • *Final del desafío* • Quiz on *Desafío 2*	49–51 52	5 m. 25 m 10 m. 10 m.	1.1, 1.2, 1.3, 2.1, 2.2, 3.2, 5.1	Audio Practice Workbook
15	To talk about actions in progress	**Desafío 3 – Un extraño lenguaje** (42—43) • Warm-Up: Independent Starter • *Texto: Un extraño lenguaje* • *Cultura: El silbo gomero*	53–55 56	5 m. 35 m. 10 m.	1.1, 1.2, 1.3, 2.1, 2.2, 3.2	
16	To talk about different means of communication	**Desafío 3 – Vocabulario** (44–45) • Warm-Up: Independent Starter • *Vocabulario: Los medios de comunicación* • *Conexiones: ¿Prensa digital o prensa en papel?*	57–59 60	5 m. 35 m. 10 m.	1.1, 1.2, 1.3, 3.1, 5.1	Audio Practice Workbook
17	To learn and use progressive tenses	**Desafío 3 – Gramática** (46–47) • Warm-Up: Independent Starter • *Gramática: Hablar de acciones en curso* • *Comunidades: Redes sociales en español*	61–64 65	5 m. 35 m. 10 m.	1.1, 1.2, 1.3, 2.1, 2.2, 3.1, 3.2, 4.1, 4.2, 5.1, 5.2	Audio Practice Workbook

Unit 1 Nos relacionamos

Day	Objectives	Sessions	Activities	Time	Standards	Resources / Homework
18	To learn indefinite adjectives and pronouns, and other quantity expressions	**Desafío 3 – Gramática** (48–49) • Warm-Up: Independent Starter • *Gramática: Expresar cantidad*	66–69	5 m. 45 m.	1.1, 1.2, 1.3, 2.2, 3.1, 3.2, 4.1, 5.2	Audio Practice Workbook
19	To understand a literary story	**Desafío 3 – Lectura** (50–51) • Warm-Up: Independent Starter • *Lectura: El diario a diario*	70–72	5 m. 45 m.	1.1, 1.2, 1.3, 2.2, 3.1, 3.2	
20	To integrate vocabulary and grammar and to assess student proficiency	**Desafío 3 – Comunicación / Evaluación** (52–53) • Warm-Up: Independent Starter • *Comunicación:* Review • *Final del desafío* • Quiz on *Desafío 3*	73–75 76	5 m. 25 m. 10 m. 10 m.	1.1, 1.2, 1.3, 2.1, 2.2, 3.1, 3.2, 4.2, 5.1, 5.2	Audio Practice Workbook
21	To integrate language in context	**Para terminar** (54–55) • Warm-Up: Independent Starter • *Todo junto* • *Tu desafío*	77–78 79	5 m. 25 m. 20 m.	1.1, 1.2, 1.3, 2.1, 2.2, 3.1, 3.2, 4.2, 5.1, 5.2	Practice Workbook *Tu desafío* work
22	To integrate language in context and to assess student proficiency	**Tu desafío / Evaluación** (55) • Warm-Up: Prepare *Tu desafío* • *Tu desafío* presentations • Quiz on *Desafíos 1–3*		5 m. 25 m. 20 m.	1.2, 1.3, 2.1, 2.2, 3.2, 5.1, 5.2	
23	To learn about variants of the Spanish language	**Mapa cultural** (56–57) • Warm-Up: Independent Starter • *Mapa cultural: Unidad y variedad del español*	80	5 m. 45 m.	1.1, 1.2, 1.3, 2.1, 2.2, 3.2	Practice Workbook
24	To write an introduction e-mail	**Escritura** (58–59) • Warm-Up: Independent Starter • *Escritura: Un correo de presentación*		5 m. 45 m.	1.1, 1.2, 1.3, 2.1, 5.1, 5.2	Project work
25	To create a webpage for the Spanish class	**Proyecto** (64–65) • Warm-Up: Prepare project presentations • Project presentations		10 m. 40 m.	1.1, 1.2, 1.3, 2.1, 2.2, 3.1, 5.1, 5.2	**Repaso–Vocabulario** (60–61) **Repaso–Gramática** (62–63)
26	To assess student proficiency	**Assessment** • *Autoevaluación* (65) • Test		10 m. 40 m.	1.1, 1.2, 1.3, 2.1, 2.2, 5.1, 5.2	
27	To prepare for the AP* Exam	**Hacia el AP* Exam** (66–69) • Warm-Up: Test introduction • Test: Interpretive Communication: Print Texts		10 m. 40 m.	1.2, 2.1, 2.2, 3.1, 3.2, 5.1, 5.2	
28	To prepare for the AP* Exam	**Hacia el AP* Exam** (66–69) • Warm-Up: About the test • Review and correction of the test		10 m. 40 m.	1.2, 2.1, 2.2, 3.1, 3.2, 5.1, 5.2	

Lesson Plans (90-Minute Classes)

Day	Objectives	Sessions	Activities	Time	Standards	Resources/ Homework
1	To introduce social relationships and the characters' challenges, to learn useful expressions, and to review learned vocabulary	***Nos relacionamos/Las tareas/ Antes de empezar*** (12–17) • Warm-Up: Topic orientation • Presentation: *Ritos y celebraciones* • *Expresiones útiles* • *Recuerda*	 1–2 3–4 5–6	 15 m. 35 m. 15 m. 25 m.	1.1, 1.2, 1.3, 2.1, 2.2, 4.1	Audio Practice Workbook
2	To describe people and to talk about physical characteristics and personality traits	***Desafío 1 – Un cumpleaños importante/ Vocabulario*** (18–21) • Warm-Up: Independent Starter • *Texto: Un cumpleaños importante* • *Cultura: Las piñatas* • *Vocabulario: Características físicas y rasgos de personalidad* • *Conexiones: Los diminutivos*	 7–9 10 11–13 14	 5 m. 30 m. 10 m. 35 m. 10 m.	1.1, 1.2, 1.3, 2.1, 2.2, 3.1, 3.2, 4.1, 4.2, 5.1, 5.2	Audio Practice Workbook
3	To learn several verbs to express likes, interests, feelings, and emotions, and to learn descriptive adjectives that change meaning before and after nouns	***Desafío 1 – Gramática*** (22–25) • Warm-Up: Independent Starter • *Gramática: Expresar gustos, intereses, sentimientos y emociones* • *Cultura: El mariachi (México)* • *Gramática: Los adjetivos. Posición y significado*	 15–18 19 20–23	 5 m. 35 m. 10 m. 40 m.	1.1, 1.2, 1.3, 2.1, 2.2, 3.1, 3.2, 4.1, 5.1	Audio Practice Workbook
4	To understand a dialogue, to integrate vocabulary and grammar, and to assess student proficiency	***Desafío 1 – Lectura/Comunicación/ Evaluación*** (26–29) • Warm-Up: Independent Starter • *Lectura: Las mañanitas* • *Comunicación: Review* • *Final del desafío* • Quiz on *Desafío 1*	 24–26 27–28 29	 5 m. 40 m. 25 m. 10 m. 10 m.	1.1, 1.2, 1.3, 2.1, 2.2, 3.2, 4.1, 4.2, 5.1, 5.2	Audio Practice Workbook
5	To talk about habitual actions and to describe postal products and services	***Desafío 2 – Los nuevos chasquis/ Vocabulario*** (30–33) • Warm-Up: Independent Starter • *Texto: Los nuevos chasquis* • *Cultura: Los chasquis (Perú)* • *Vocabulario: La oficina de correos* • *Conexiones: Juan Rulfo*	 30–32 33 34–35 36	 5 m. 30 m. 10 m. 35 m. 10 m.	1.1, 1.2, 1.3, 2.1, 2.2, 3.1, 3.2, 5.1, 5.2	Audio Practice Workbook

Unit 1 Nos relacionamos

Day	Objectives	Sessions	Activities	Time	Standards	Resources / Homework
6	To learn pronominal, reflexive, and reciprocal verbs	**Desafío 2 – Gramática** (34–37) • Warm-Up: Independent Starter • *Gramática: Los verbos pronominales* • *Gramática: Los verbos reflexivos y recíprocos* • *Cultura: La carta a los Reyes Magos*	37–41 42–44 45	5 m. 35 m. 40 m. 10 m.	1.1, 1.2, 1.3, 2.1, 3.1, 4.1, 4.2, 5.1	Audio Practice Workbook
7	To understand information in a journalistic report, to integrate vocabulary and grammar, and to assess student proficiency	**Desafío 2 – Lectura/Comunicación/ Evaluación** (38–41) • Warm-Up: Independent Starter • *Lectura: El oficio más romántico: escribir cartas de amor por encargo* • *Comunicación:* Review • *Final del desafío* • Quiz on *Desafío 2*	46–48 49–51 52	5 m. 40 m. 25 m. 10 m. 10 m.	1.1, 1.2, 1.3, 2.1, 2.2, 3.2, 5.1	Audio Practice Workbook
8	To talk about actions in progress and to talk about different means of communication	**Desafío 3 – Un extraño lenguaje/ Vocabulario** (42–45) • Warm-Up: Independent Starter • *Texto: Un extraño lenguaje* • *Cultura: El silbo gomero* • *Vocabulario: Los medios de comunicación* • *Conexiones: ¿Prensa digital o prensa en papel?*	53–55 56 57–59 60	5 m. 30 m. 10 m. 35 m. 10 m.	1.1, 1.2, 1.3, 2.1, 2.2, 3.1, 3.2, 5.1	Audio Practice Workbook
9	To learn and use progressive tenses and to learn indefinite adjectives and pronouns and other quantity expressions	**Desafío 3 – Gramática** (46–49) • Warm-Up: Independent Starter • *Gramática: Hablar de acciones en curso* • *Comunidades: Redes sociales en español* • *Gramática: Expresar cantidad*	61–64 65 66–69	5 m. 40 m. 10 m. 35 m.	1.1, 1.2, 1.3, 2.1, 2.2, 3.1, 3.2, 4.1, 4.2, 5.1, 5.2	Audio Practice Workbook
10	To understand a literary story and to integrate vocabulary and grammar	**Desafío 3 – Lectura/Comunicación/ Evaluación** (50–53) • Warm-Up: Independent Starter • *Lectura: El diario a diario* • *Comunicación:* Review • *Final del desafío* • Quiz on *Desafío 3*	70–72 73–75 76	5 m. 40 m. 25 m. 10 m. 10 m.	1.1, 1.2, 1.3, 2.1, 2.2, 3.1, 3.2, 4.2, 5.1, 5.2	Audio Practice Workbook **Para terminar – Tu desafío** (55)

Day	Objectives	Sessions	Activities	Time	Standards	Resources/ Homework
11	To integrate language in context and to assess student proficiency	**Para terminar/Evaluación** (54–55) • Warm-Up: Independent Starter • *Todo junto* • *Tu desafío*: work and presentations • Quiz on *Desafíos 1–3*	77–78 79	5 m. 25 m. 40 m. 20 m.	1.1, 1.2, 1.3, 2.1, 2.2, 3.1, 3.2, 4.2, 5.1, 5.2	Practice Workbook
12	To learn about variants of the Spanish language and to write an introduction e-mail	**Mapa cultural / Escritura** (56–59) • Warm-Up: Independent Starter • Mapa cultural: *Unidad y variedad del español* • Escritura: *Un correo de presentación*	80	5 m. 40 m. 45 m.	1.1, 1.2, 1.3, 2.1, 2.2, 3.2, 5.1, 5.2	Practice Workbook **Repaso–Vocabulario** (60–61) **Repaso–Gramática** (62–63) Project work
13	To create a webpage for the Spanish class and to assess student proficiency	**Proyecto/Assessment** (64–65) • Warm-Up: Prepare project presentations • Project presentations • *Autoevaluación* • Test		10 m. 45 m. 10 m. 25 m.	1.1, 1.2, 1.3, 2.1, 2.2, 3.1, 5.1, 5.2	
14	To prepare for the AP* Exam	**Hacia el AP* Exam** (66–69) • Warm-Up: Test Introduction • Test: Interpretive Communication: Print Texts • Review and correction of the test		10 m. 40 m. 40 m.	1.2, 2.1, 2.2, 3.1, 3.2, 5.1, 5.2	

Unit 1 Nos relacionamos

3 ¡Cuánto tiempo sin verte!

1. –Hola, Sandra.
   –Hola, Jaime. ¿Cómo estás?
2. –¡Hola, Javier! ¡Qué sorpresa verte aquí!
   –¡Cuánto tiempo, Andrea!
3. –¿Quieres que vayamos a visitar a Carla esta tarde? Está enferma.
   –Sí, buena idea. ¿Nos vemos esta tarde al salir de la escuela?
   –De acuerdo. Oye, me voy a clase.
4. –Buenos días, profesor Sánchez.
   –Buenos días, chicos.
5. –Señora Núñez, tómese estas píldoras, se sentirá mucho mejor. Y vuelva a verme la próxima semana.
   –De acuerdo, doctora.
6. –¿Te vas a Perú, Rafael?
   –Sí, me voy mañana. Me quedaré en casa de mi familia un mes.
   –Escríbenos para saber cómo te va, ¿eh?
   –Sí, claro.

9 Organizando la fiesta

–Lucas, ¿qué tal los preparativos para la fiesta de Margarita?
–Bien. Averigüé algunas cosas más sobre las piñatas. ¿Sabes que las piñatas tradicionales tienen forma de estrella de siete puntas?
–No, no lo sabía. ¿Y de dónde viene esta tradición?
–He leído que la costumbre de romper la piñata llegó a América con los conquistadores europeos y que era un juego lleno de simbolismo y significado religioso.
–¿Y has visto cómo son esas piñatas? ¡Tenemos que hacer una para Margarita!
–Sí, he encontrado muchas fotos; puedo mostrártelas. Son muy vistosas y muy bonitas. Y he visto en Internet que en Navidad colocan una piñata tradicional en la plaza del Zócalo de la Ciudad de México. Es una piñata enorme y por la noche está iluminada. ¡Me encanta, pero no será fácil hacer una piñata así!
–Tal vez tengamos que pedir ayuda…
–¿Y tú qué tal vas con la canción?
–Bueno, regular. Solo sé que es una canción muy popular en México y que también se canta en las fiestas de cumpleaños en otros países de Latinoamérica. Pero aún no me la he aprendido.

13 Entre amigos

1. –Alejandro, ¿estás enojado con Martín?
   –Bueno, el fin de semana pasado discutimos. Habíamos quedado para ir al cine y llegué tarde, así que nos perdimos la película. Le pedí disculpas e intenté explicarle que había tenido un problema con el autobús, pero no quería escucharme. Y, de repente, se fue y me dejó allí hablando solo. Es tan impulsivo… Pero hoy me llamó y me pidió disculpas, así que está todo arreglado.

2. –Andrea, ¿cómo conociste a Rafa?
   –Lo conocí en la universidad. Al principio no me cayó muy bien. Me parecía que siempre quería ser el centro de atención. Claro, ¡como yo soy tan tímida! Él es muy seguro y tiene mucha personalidad. Pero me ayudó mucho y ahora es mi mejor amigo.

3. –Jimena, ¿qué te pasó con Marta?
   –Ya no somos amigas.
   –¡¿Qué?! ¡Pero si ustedes estaban siempre juntas…! Vestían igual, pensaban igual… Como dos hermanas gemelas. ¡Parecían dos gotas de agua!
   –Sí, pero Marta es tan terca… No puedes hablar con ella: ¡siempre tiene que tener razón!
   –Bueno, Jimena, tú también tienes mucho carácter.
   –Sí, tienes razón, y soy muy apasionada defendiendo mis ideas. ¡Pero ella no me deja ni hablar!

17 Cine y teatro

–Sara, me apetece ir al teatro este fin de semana. ¿Vamos juntas?
–Es que prefiero ir al cine, Paula. Me interesa mucho el cine argentino y esta semana hay un ciclo de cine rioplatense en la universidad. El sábado y el domingo proyectan algunas películas muy buenas y me da pena perdérmelas.
–La última película argentina que vi me encantó. Me emocionó la actuación de Ricardo Darín. Pero lo que realmente me fascina es el teatro.
–¿Y no vas con tu novio?
–No, a Gabriel le encanta ir a conciertos o a la ópera, pero le aburre el teatro y no me divierte nada ir con él. Además, me enfada que hable durante la representación. ¡Parece un niño pequeño!
–En el cine mucha gente come y habla… ¡y hasta suenan los celulares! Me molesta muchísimo oír ruidos durante la proyección de la película. Oye, Paula, ¿qué te parece si vamos al teatro el sábado y al cine el domingo?
–¡Sí, qué buena idea! Me alegra mucho que hagamos cosas juntas.
–¡A mí también! Lo vamos a pasar muy bien.

25 Tu versión

Estas son las mañanitas
que cantaba el rey David,
hoy por ser día de tu santo,
te las cantamos a ti.

Despierta mi bien, despierta,
mira que ya amaneció.
Ya los pajarillos cantan,
la luna ya se metió.

28 Titulares de prensa

–¿Qué haces, Fernando?

–Estoy hojeando el periódico. ¡Hay unas noticias curiosísimas!

–¿Sí?

–Verás… Detenido un hombre invisible al intentar robar un banco. Parece que utilizó jugo de limón para hacerse invisible.

–¿De verdad? ¿Y qué pasó?

–Pues que la policía lo vio y lo detuvo. ¡Estaba muy sorprendido porque él pensaba que era invisible!

–¡Increíble!

–Escucha. Esta es muy interesante. En distintos lugares públicos de México y en algunas ciudades de otros países van a poner esculturas que fusionan la tradición maya con las visiones más contemporáneas del país. La intención es ofrecer una nueva imagen de México a través del arte.

–¡Ojalá traigan una escultura a nuestra ciudad! Me interesa mucho el arte.

–Y mira esta otra noticia. Encontraron en Utah el esqueleto de un dinosaurio gigante con cuernos.

–¿Con cuernos? ¿Cómo un toro?

–Sí, pero con quince cuernos. ¡Quince!

–¡Qué miedo!

–Ahora estaba leyendo las páginas de deportes. ¿Conoces a Lionel Messi?

–¿El jugador de fútbol argentino?

–Sí, es argentino y juega en un equipo español, el Fútbol Club Barcelona. Ayer fue la gran figura en un partido contra Uruguay. Marcó tres goles.

–A mí no me divierte mucho el fútbol, pero la verdad es que Messi juega muy bien.

–¡Pues a mí el fútbol me fascina!

31 Un sistema muy bien organizado

–Si nuestro desafío es hacer un cartel de una carrera de chasquis, ¿no te parece que todavía tiene que haber chasquis?

–No lo sé, Eva… El imperio inca tuvo su esplendor en el siglo XV y llegó a su fin en 1532. ¡Hace casi quinientos años!

–¡Pero cuánto sabes del imperio inca!

–Bueno, es que este asunto de los chasquis me parece muy misterioso… Tampoco entiendo muy bien cómo funciona ese quipu que aparece en la estampilla de tu carta… ¿Una cuerda con nudos que sirve para transmitir mensajes?

–He leído que el quipu era un conjunto de cuerdas de varios colores y nudos de distintos tipos que tenían diferentes significados.

–Ah, entonces las cuerdas y los nudos eran como símbolos.

–Eso es. Los incas utilizaban el quipu para recordar y contar, y, según algunos estudiosos, el quipu era también un sistema de escritura. Es increíble la cantidad de información que podía contener. ¡Como un libro!

–Parece muy complejo. No había sobres ni estampillas. ¡Ni aviones, ni barcos…! ¿Los chasquis iban a caballo?

–No, iban a pie. Los aztecas tenían un sistema de comunicación similar. Bueno, y los griegos, y los romanos…

–Es verdad.

–Los chasquis se preparaban para este trabajo desde niños. Dicen que eran capaces de recorrer dos mil kilómetros en cinco días.

–Pero Eva, ¡una persona no puede recorrer dos mil kilómetros a pie en cinco días sin descansar!

–Una sola persona no, claro. Por eso había un sistema de «tambos» muy bien organizado.

–¿Tambos?

–Sí, eran lugares en los que los chasquis descansaban y había nuevos mensajeros para llevar el mensaje a su destino.

–Ah, como una carrera de relevos.

–Eso es.

–¡Qué eficientes! Mira, Eva, he encontrado una noticia sobre una carrera de chasquis que se celebró el año pasado.

39 ¿Qué hacen?

1. –Raquel, tengo una fiesta esta noche. ¿Me puedes ayudar a decidir el vestido?

   –¿Qué tal este azul, Sofía?

   –¿No es muy corto?

   –No, te queda muy bien.

   –De acuerdo, el azul entonces.

   –¿Volverás tarde?

   –No. No me quedaré hasta muy tarde porque mañana tengo que levantarme temprano.

2. –Rosa, ¿a qué hora es la reunión de vecinos?

   –Acordamos reunirnos a las ocho.

   –¿A las ocho? ¡Qué tarde!

   –Sí, preguntaron quién quería reunirse a las seis, pero nadie levantó la mano.

   –La última vez pasó igual y acabamos muy tarde.

3. –César, la sopa está sosa. ¿Dónde está la sal?

   –Lo siento, Luisa, se acabó ayer y se me olvidó comprarla. Si quieres voy al supermercado mientras tú pones la mesa. No tardaré mucho.

   –De acuerdo.

Unit 1 Nos relacionamos

49 Servicios postales

1. –Buenos días. Quería mandar este paquete a Lima.
   –¿Por correo aéreo?
   –Sí. ¿Cuánto tarda aproximadamente?
   –Una semana o semana y media.
   –¿Y si lo mando urgente?
   –Unos cinco días.
   –Entonces prefiero enviarlo urgente. ¿Puede decirme cuánto es el franqueo?
   –Vamos a ver cuánto pesa. Señora, ha olvidado escribir el remitente...
   –¡Uy, es verdad!

2. –Jesús, ¿escribiste las tarjetas de Navidad?
   –Sí, Alicia, estoy escribiendo la última. Pero no tengo estampillas para todas.
   –Bueno, ahora las compramos en la oficina de correos.
   –¿Tienes la dirección y el código postal de los primos de Canarias? Es que no la encuentro.
   –Sí, espera... Aquí la tienes.

3. –Papá, el buzón está lleno de correspondencia. Mira, los sobres se salen del buzón.
   –Sí, Carlos, siempre ocurre lo mismo al volver de vacaciones. Vamos a recogerlos.
   –A ver si ha llegado una tarjeta postal de mi amigo Pedro...

58 El noticiero

1. El presidente del gobierno ha anunciado que la semana próxima viajará a Canadá para reunirse con el primer ministro en un viaje oficial que durará cuatro días.
2. La Organización Mundial de la Salud ha publicado un estudio que revela que el uso excesivo de los celulares puede estar relacionado con el riesgo de sufrir tumores cerebrales.
3. El jugador Pau Gasol, que ha estado casi un mes alejado de las canchas a causa de una lesión, volverá a jugar este fin de semana. Gasol ha declarado que está muy contento de poder volver a competir con sus compañeros.
4. La Agencia Internacional de la Energía anunció el pasado martes que en 2017 el carbón podrá superar al petróleo como principal fuente de energía en todo el mundo.

64 Informe policial

–Por favor, señora Rodríguez, cuénteme con detalle cómo sucedieron los hechos, qué vio y qué oyó cuando estaba preparando la cena en su casa.

–Recuerdo que eran las ocho cuando llegué a casa. Nada más entrar me quité el abrigo y los zapatos, y estaba subiendo las escaleras para ir a mi habitación cuando sonó el teléfono. No llegué a tiempo, así que saltó el contestador automático. Era mi marido; en el mensaje decía que estaba saliendo del trabajo y que venía hacia casa. Me cambié de ropa y bajé a la cocina para hacer la cena. Mientras preparaba la carne y las verduras, estuve escuchando el noticiero en la radio y se me pasó el tiempo muy rápido. Miré varias veces por la ventana para ver si llegaba mi marido. Vi a dos personas un poco extrañas, pero no me pareció importante. Luego, cuando estaba sacando la cena del horno, oí un ruido inusual. Entonces apagué la radio y me quedé quieta unos segundos, intentando entender lo que decían.

–¿Y pudo usted oír algo?

–Estuve escuchando atentamente un buen rato y me pareció oír la voz de dos hombres que estaban discutiendo. Luego, uno dijo algo así como: «Quédate quieto, no grites y no te pasará nada». A continuación, oí cómo se cerraban con fuerza las puertas de un auto y a otro hombre que gritaba: «¡Socorro, socorro, que alguien me ayude!». Inmediatamente corrí a la ventana de la cocina y vi un auto saliendo a gran velocidad del garaje de mis vecinos. Después los llamé a ustedes por teléfono.

–¿Y su marido, señora Rodríguez?

–No lo sé. Cuando estaba saliendo del trabajo me llamó desde su celular, y de esto hace más de dos horas. Estuve esperando hasta que llegaron ustedes, pero él no llegó. ¿Piensan que le ha podido pasar algo? ¿Creen que lo estaban esperando en la puerta de casa y lo han secuestrado? Por favor, ayúdenme, estoy muy preocupada.

68 El doble y la mitad

1. –¿Qué tal el fin de semana?
   –Muy bien. El sábado estuve en un concierto muy divertido en la escuela. Algunos estudiantes del último curso han formado un grupo musical. Tiene muchos componentes; la mitad de ellos son chicas y la otra mitad, chicos.
   –¿Qué instrumentos tocan?
   –Hay una batería, dos guitarras eléctricas y un piano. Y cantan en inglés y en español.
   –¿Y qué cantan?
   –La mayoría de las canciones son temas de otros cantantes de música pop, como Rihanna, Michael Jackson, Juanes o Shakira. Lo pasamos muy bien. Todos cantamos con ellos.
   –¿Y duró mucho?
   –Uy, sí, el concierto duró el doble del tiempo previsto: ¡casi tres horas!

2. –¿Qué tal el partido de baloncesto de ayer?
   –¡Fue muy emocionante. Nuestro equipo jugó muy bien.
   –¿Pero ganó?
   –¿Que si ganó? ¡Arrasó! Consiguió el triple de puntos que el equipo visitante.

–¿Y había muchos aficionados?

–Sí, había cuatro veces más de público que en el último partido. Solo un tercio de los aficionados eran del equipo visitante.

69 **¿Todo o nada?**

1. Fuente: Mai Meneses. «Con lo poco que quedaba»

Con lo poco que quedaba
de lo mucho que empezó
se terminó nuestro amor.
Yo lo mío, tú lo tuyo.
Algo tuyo, algo mío
hemos perdido los dos.
Tanta emoción racionalizada
que acabé sin sentir nada.

2. Fuente: Leiva. «Matar al cartero»

Nada es suficiente y no sé por qué
me falta algo y no sé qué.
Tengo de todo, dentro de un orden,
pero, en el fondo, nada que importe.

73 **Medios de comunicación hispanos**

La población hispana es la de mayor crecimiento en los Estados Unidos y supera ya los cincuenta millones de personas. Y mientras la población hispana sigue creciendo, se lanzan nuevos medios de comunicación en español. En los últimos años los medios de comunicación hispanos han conseguido mantenerse e, incluso, crecer.

En general, la prensa diaria hispana vio aumentar su difusión mientras los diarios en inglés registraban pérdidas. Las ciudades con mayor población hispana tienen hoy diarios consolidados e importantes; es el caso de *El Nuevo Herald* en Miami, *El Diario La Prensa* en Nueva York o *La Opinión* en Los Ángeles.

El número de emisoras de radio también aumentó, hasta tal punto que prácticamente toda la población hispana de los Estados Unidos puede sintonizar al menos una emisora de radio con programación en español.

Las cadenas con más oyentes son Univisión Radio, Hispanic Radio Network y Entravisión Radio.

En el ámbito de la televisión, las versiones en español de canales en inglés, como la CNN o la MTV, compiten con cadenas de habla hispana muy potentes, como Univisión, Telemundo o la mexicana Galavisión. Una cuarta parte de los hispanos que hablan inglés en sus hogares y casi la mitad de los que hablan principalmente español en casa ven la televisión en español entre una y tres horas por día. Telenovelas, noticieros, deportes, programas de variedades, películas y *reality shows* son parte sustancial de la programación de estas cadenas, que registraron importantes avances. Univisión y Telemundo, dos de las cadenas con mayor audiencia, alcanzaron importantes beneficios económicos en concepto de publicidad.

A todo ello hay que añadir los sitios web de medios hispanos: QuePasa.com, Univision.com y Terra.com son algunos de los más visitados. Hay que tener en cuenta que la mayoría de los medios impresos hispanos cuelgan casi todos sus artículos en páginas web.

Los medios de comunicación en español muestran la importancia que está adquiriendo el español en contextos más formales de la vida norteamericana y son importantes para una población hispana que está cambiando y que es cada vez más numerosa y está más preparada.

Unit 1
Nos relacionamos

The Unit

- The themes for Unit 1 are social relationships and communication. The participants will describe people and learn to express likes, interests, feelings, and emotions. They will also learn about different modes of communication, talk about actions in progress, and express quantity.
- Tim, a veteran of *Fans del español*, will give the participants their tasks.
  - *Desafío 1.* Asha and Lucas have to plan a traditional Mexican birthday party for a classmate.
  - *Desafío 2.* Eva and Ethan have to design a poster and come up with a slogan for a *chasqui* race that takes place in Huancayo, Peru.
  - *Desafío 3.* Michelle and Daniel have to learn a phrase in a mysterious language from the Canary Islands, Spain.

Activities	Standards	Resources
Nos relacionamos	1.2, 2.1, 2.2	

Teaching Suggestions

Warm-Up / Independent Starter

- Ask students to look at the photos and come up with a short description for one of the images.

Preparation

- Call on volunteers to read their descriptions from the Independent Starter, and ask the class to try to guess the picture that is being described. Then have students read the captions and predict what the topic for each challenge might be. For instance, they may answer that the first image shows several piñatas, so the topic might be birthday celebrations; the topic for the second challenge might be indigenous cultures, etc.
- Have students read each *Desafío's* objective, as well as the vocabulary and grammar goals, then discuss how each image might relate to these objectives and goals.

12

Nos relacionamos
Comunicación y relaciones sociales

DESAFÍO 1

Grabado con un chasqui indígena (Perú).

CORE ON·MAJOR·IMENOR
HATVNCHASQVICHVRV
~ MVLLO·CHAS QVI·CVRACA ~

▶ **Describir personas**

Vocabulario
Características físicas y rasgos de personalidad

Gramática
Expresar gustos, intereses, sentimientos y emociones

Los adjetivos. Posición y significado

DESAFÍO 2

▶ **Expresar acciones habituales**

Vocabulario
La oficina de correos

Gramática
Los verbos pronominales

Los verbos reflexivos y recíprocos

Grupo de piñatas (México).

12 doce

The Challenge

DESAFÍO 1

Grupo de piñatas

Piñatas seem to have originated in China, where they were used to celebrate the New Year. Marco Polo may have taken them to Italy in the 14th century and, from there, the tradition spread to Spain and then to Mexico. The first documented use of piñatas in Mexico places them in the town of Acolman, in the late 16th century. Catholic priests in Acolman were looking for ways to Christianize the indigenous population, and began to include piñatas in their Christmas celebrations. Today, piñatas are especially popular in Mexico during Christmas and at birthday parties.

DESAFÍO 2

Grabado con un chasqui indígena

Persia, China, and Rome were some of the ancient powers that used a network of postal relay stations for sending and delivering mail. In the Americas, the Incas had created a similar system to carry messages—using specialized runners, called *chasquis*, and a vast network of roads that linked all parts of the empire. In some places, this system operated at altitudes of over 12,000 ft. above sea level. Working at these altitudes represents a great physical challenge. For this reason, only the fittest and strongest males were chosen to be *chasquis*, and their training began in boyhood.

DESAFÍO
3

▶ **Hablar de acciones en curso**

Vocabulario
Los medios de comunicación

Gramática
Hablar de acciones en curso

Expresar cantidad

Escolares de la isla de
La Gomera practicando
el silbo (España).

DESAFÍO 3

**Escolares de la isla de La Gomera
practicando el silbo**

In response to a harsh terrain, the inhabitants
of the Canary island of La Gomera came up with
a whistled language to communicate across
deep valleys. The sounds produced by whistling
travel farther than the human voice, making it
a good means for delivering short messages
across the mountains. In the Gomeran whistle,
several vowels and consonants from Spanish are
replaced by tones, which are then whistled
at different frequencies. Most whistled languages
have been lost, but Gomerans still use and
teach theirs.

Nos relacionamos

Picture Discussion

- Have students look at the images again and review their predictions about each topic. Then ask them to share their predictions and any information they may have on these topics in a class discussion.

Grupo de piñatas (México)

- Ask students to identify the objects pictured. (piñatas) Then have them describe the piñatas in terms of color, shape, animal, or object each piñata represents. Call on different volunteers to explain how and when piñatas are used. If there are students in your class who have celebrated their birthdays with a piñata, invite them to share their experiences with the class.

Grabado con un chasqui indígena (Perú)

- Focus students' attention on the image and have them describe it. What is the man wearing? What is he carrying? What is he blowing? Explain that this is a 16th-century engraving. Then focus students' attention on the first line of text in the engraving. Explain that it is written in Old Castilian, but they might be able to decipher it by reading it aloud. (*correo mayor y menor*) Does this phrase help students determine the profession of the man pictured?

Escolares de la isla de La Gomera practicando el silbo (España)

- Have students focus on the people in the image and ask them what they think these people are doing. (whistling) If students cannot tell, ask them to focus on the sculpture. What does it represent? Why might these people be whistling? Encourage students to come up with different explanations and share them with the class.

Objectives

- By the end of Unit 1, students will be able to
  - Describe people and talk about personal and social relationships.
  - Express likes, interests, feelings, and emotions.
  - Talk about the postal service.
  - Talk about customary actions and routines.
  - Talk about modes of communication.
  - Talk about ongoing actions.
  - Express quantity.
  - Talk about birthday traditions, music, writers, and historical and modern methods of communication of the Spanish-speaking world.

Las tareas

Presentation

- In this section, the three pairs read a message sent by Tim, a former participant, who describes the challenges that lie ahead. Students will preview useful expressions for greeting someone, responding to greetings, saying goodbye, and expressing good wishes.

Activities	Standards	Resources
Texto	1.2, 2.1, 2.2	
1.	1.1, 1.2, 1.3, 2.1, 2.2	
2.	1.2, 4.1	

Teaching Suggestions

Warm-Up / Independent Starter

- Have students scan the text and the dialogue on these pages, and list any phrases that express likes, interests, feelings, or emotions (e.g., *estoy encantado, les van a encantar*).

Preparation

- Acquaint or reacquaint students with Tim. Explain that he is from San Francisco, CA, and that he used to travel with his grandfather, Mack.

- Invite volunteers to share their Independent Starters. Discuss the differences between *estoy encantado* and *les van a encantar*, and between *será fascinante* and *me fascinan*. Elicit that *encantado* and *fascinante* are adjectives; and *encantar* and *fascinan* are verbs, which are conjugated in the same way as the verb *gustar*.

- You may want to review some of the following idiomatic expressions: *echar de menos* (to miss someone or something), *apetecer* (to feel like), *¿Qué les parece?* (What do you think?), *¿Qué será(n)...?* (I wonder...).

Texto: Ritos y celebraciones

- Read the introduction to the text aloud. Then prepare a three-column chart on the board with the following headings: *Tarea 1, Tarea 2, Tarea 3*. Ask students to scan the text on page 14 and point out the tasks that the three pairs have been assigned.

Ritos y celebraciones

Los personajes quieren seguir aprendiendo más cosas sobre el mundo y la cultura hispana. Esta vez han decidido investigar sobre antiguos ritos y costumbres que aún se conservan. Lee el mensaje de Tim y averigua qué desafíos les propone.

Hola, amigos. ¿Cómo les va? Estoy encantado de que quieran seguir aprendiendo con nosotros. El tema de la comunicación y las relaciones sociales es apasionante, así que les van a encantar los desafíos que les he preparado. ¿Están listos?

Asha y Lucas me contaron que tienen una nueva compañera de clase que es mexicana y que pronto va a ser su cumpleaños. Seguramente ella echa de menos su país de origen, así que van a prepararle una fiesta típica mexicana para celebrar su cumpleaños. Deberán hacer una piñata y aprender una canción tradicional de México para felicitarla.

Ethan y Eva van a hacer un cartel y un eslogan para promocionar una carrera de chasquis que se celebrará en unos días en Huancayo (Perú). Seguramente se están preguntando qué es un chasqui, ¿verdad? Pues no se lo voy a decir, eso sería demasiado fácil. Tendrán que descubrirlo ustedes. Les aseguro que será fascinante.

Para terminar, Michelle y Daniel van a aprender a decir una frase en un misterioso lenguaje de las islas Canarias (España). La frase es: «¡Somos los mejores fans del español!» ¿Qué les parece?

Ya saben que estaré aquí para ayudarlos. Mucha suerte y, sobre todo... ¡que se diviertan!

Differentiated Instruction

DEVELOPING LEARNERS

- Read or write the following false statements and ask students to correct them:
  1. *Asha y Lucas van a preparar una fiesta de despedida.* (una fiesta de cumpleaños)
  2. *Asha y Lucas van a aprender a tocar la guitarra.* (una canción tradicional de México)
  3. *Ethan no tiene interés en hacer un cartel.* (tiene mucho interés / le apetece mucho)
  4. *Eva piensa que quizá los chasquis sean músicos.* (autos o algún animal)
  5. *Daniel y Michelle van a promocionar el turismo en Canarias.* (aprender a decir una frase en un lenguaje misterioso de Canarias)

EXPANDING LEARNERS

- Help students expand their vocabulary by listing as many synonyms as they can for the following verbs that appear in the text. Encourage students to write or say a sentence with some of the synonyms.
  1. *seguir* (continuar, proseguir)
  2. *contar* (decir, relatar, narrar)
  3. *echar de menos* (extrañar)
  4. *celebrar* (festejar)
  5. *promocionar* (promover, fomentar, darle publicidad)
  6. *asegurar* (garantizar)
  7. *terminar* (acabar, finalizar, concluir)

> Este es un buen desafío, ¿no?

> Sí. A Margarita le encantará que le preparemos una fiesta mexicana.

> Me apetece mucho hacer un cartel y un eslogan, pero... ¿qué serán los chasquis?

> No tengo ni idea, la verdad. Quizá sean autos o algún animal...

> ¿Habías oído hablar alguna vez de un lenguaje misterioso de las islas Canarias?

> No, ¡pero me fascinan los enigmas!

1 ¿Comprendes?

▶ **Escribe.** ¿Qué tiene que hacer cada pareja?

1. Lucas y Asha...   2. Ethan y Eva...   3. Michelle y Daniel...

▶ **Responde** a estas preguntas.

1. ¿Qué le parece el desafío a Asha?
2. ¿Sabes qué es una piñata?
3. ¿Qué saben Ethan y Eva sobre los chasquis?
4. ¿Qué le fascina a Daniel?

▶ **Explica.** ¿Qué desafío te parece más interesante? ¿Por qué?

2 Investiga

▶ **Escribe** tres palabras del texto que sean nuevas para ti. ¿Qué crees que significan?

quince **15**

Las tareas

■ After reading the text and the dialogues, have students add details to the columns on the board. For example: 1. *Deben hacer una piñata y aprenderse una canción.* 2. *La carrera de chasquis se celebrará en Huancayo, Perú.* 3. *La frase que deben aprenderse es: ¡Somos los mejores Fans del español!* Then discuss with students the participants' reactions to the challenges.

Activities

1. Have students use the chart they prepared for the *Texto* section to answer the first part of this activity. Then ask students to share their opinions about the tasks. Which pair of participants seems most self-assured about their assigned task? What do students think about the level of difficulty of each task?

Answer Key

1. 1. Deberán hacer una piñata y aprender una canción tradicional de México para celebrar el cumpleaños de una compañera mexicana.
   2. Van a hacer un cartel y un eslogan para promocionar una carrera de chasquis que se celebrará en Huancayo, Perú.
   3. Van a aprender a decir una frase en un misterioso lenguaje de las islas Canarias, España.

   ▶ Answers will vary. Sample answers:
   1. Le parece que es un buen desafío.
   2. Es un recipiente lleno de dulces, típico de las fiestas de cumpleaños. Los asistentes a la fiesta, con los ojos vendados, le pegan con un palo hasta romperla y recogen los dulces que caen.
   3. No saben nada.
   4. Le fascinan los enigmas.

   ▶ Answers will vary.

2. Answers will vary.

Additional Resources

Fans Online activities
Practice Workbook

HERITAGE LANGUAGE LEARNERS

• Ask students to think about their favorite family celebration; it could be a birthday, an important holiday, or any other special event. Have them describe to the rest of the class how their families observe this day. If possible, ask students to bring in photos or videos from one of these past celebrations and explain the significance of what is happening. After students make their presentations, ask them to compare and contrast how they celebrate this and other family events in this country and in their family's country of origin.

CRITICAL THINKING

• Ask students to think about the different ways people have communicated with one another in the past and how they communicate today. How do they think certain kinds of news were transmitted before formal mail service and the telephone? Have students brainstorm some logical ways and discuss their efficacy. Then, based on the photos from the unit opener and what students already know about ancient Peruvian cultures and the traditional customs among some residents of the Canary Islands, have them project how the two related challenges are linked to communication.

Antes de empezar

Presentation

- In this section, students will learn a variety of useful expressions to greet someone, say goodbye, and express good wishes.
- Students will also review vocabulary for physical characteristics and personality traits, as well as vocabulary to talk about personal relationships.

Activities	Standards	Resources
Expresiones útiles	1.2, 2.1	
3.	1.2	Audio
4.	1.1	
Recuerda	1.2	
5.	1.2, 1.3	
6.	1.1, 1.3	

Teaching Suggestions

Warm-Up / Independent Starter

- Have students write two phrases they use to greet people and two they use to say goodbye. To get them started you may want to suggest the following examples: *¡Hola! ¿Qué tal estás?* / *Adiós. Nos vemos luego.*

Preparation

- Call on volunteers to read their Independent Starters. You may want to start two lists on the board: *Saludos* and *Despedidas*. Then have students write their phrases under the corresponding heading. How many different phrases do they know? Encourage students to use some of the phrases on the board to compose several short conversations. Then, as a class, go over the *expresiones útiles*. Model pronunciation and clarify any questions students may have.
- Give students a few moments to read the *Recuerda* box silently. Then have them work in small groups to create a word web to classify the words. Suggest that they add more categories to the web. For example: *Características físicas → Hombres → bigote, barba, apuesto...; Mujeres → pelo largo, bonita...; Ambos → pecas, lunar...* For the personality traits, students may want to categorize the traits into positive, negative, and neutral.

EXPRESIONES ÚTILES

Para saludar y responder al saludo:

—¿Cómo te va?
—Muy bien, gracias. ¿Y tú, qué tal?

—¡Cuánto tiempo! Me alegro de verte. ¿Cómo estás?
—Bien, como siempre. ¿Y tú?

Para despedirse:

Hasta luego.
Hasta el lunes./Hasta la semana que viene.
Hasta pronto./Hasta la vista.

Para expresar buenos deseos al despedirse:

Que tengas un buen día.
Que te vaya bien.
Que descanses.
Que se diviertan.

Que pasen un buen fin de semana.
Que tengas buen viaje.
Que te mejores. [cuando alguien está enfermo]

3 **¡Cuánto tiempo sin verte!**

▶ **Escucha** y decide. ¿Cómo continúa cada diálogo?

a. ¿Cómo están?
b. Hasta luego, Marta.
c. Hasta la semana que viene.
d. Hasta pronto, amigos.
e. Muy bien, gracias. ¿Y tú?
f. Me alegro de verte.

4 **Buenos deseos**

▶ **Escribe** buenos deseos para las personas de las fotografías.

Differentiated Instruction

DEVELOPING LEARNERS

- Ask students to work with a partner and create other scenarios for some of the expressions listed on page 16. The first student will describe the scene; for example, *Llevo tres días enferma con la gripe*. The partner will offer a logical response; for example, *Que te mejores pronto*. Allow students five minutes to create as many dialogues as they can and have them present some of these mini-conversations to the class.

EXPANDING LEARNERS

- Explain to students that they are going to play a game to guess a celebrity's identity. Divide students into teams. Each student will have secretly selected a celebrity who might be someone from the past, present, or even from fiction. Select one team member to go first while teammates take turns asking questions about the celebrity. Encourage students to add to the adjectives listed on the page that describe physical characteristics and personality traits, and the verbs that deal with personal relations. Set the number of questions or limit the questions to two minutes before calling time.

RECUERDA

Características físicas

la barba	pelo lacio/rizado/castaño
el bigote	calvo(a)
la cicatriz	apuesto
el lunar	
las pecas	

Rasgos de personalidad

amable	impaciente
amistoso(a)	perezoso(a)
cariñoso(a)	reservado(a), tímido(a)
comprensivo(a)	sincero(a)
egoísta	trabajador(a)
fiel	seguro(a) de sí mismo(a)
generoso(a)	travieso(a)

Relaciones personales

la amistad	el abrazo
el amor	el beso
la confianza	
la fidelidad	
apoyar	llevarse bien/mal
apreciar	mentir
discutir	pedir perdón
echar la culpa	querer
enamorarse	reconciliarse
equivocarse	respetar
estar celoso(a)	romper
estar enamorado(a)	tener razón

5 Así son mis hermanos

▶ **Completa** el texto.

Cuatro hermanos

Mi hermano mayor se llama Felipe. Es serio y no le gusta mucho hablar de sí mismo; es muy ___1___. Entre Felipe y yo está Juana. Ella tiene muchos amigos y siempre piensa en los demás. Es muy ___2___. Siempre está hablando por teléfono con Jonás, su novio; creo que los dos están muy ___3___. Nuestra hermana pequeña se llama Luisa. Es muy divertida, pero no está quieta ni un minuto; es bastante ___4___. Los cuatro somos muy diferentes, pero nos ___5___ bien y nos queremos mucho.

6 ¿Cuánto sabes?

▶ **Fíjate** en el cuadro Recuerda y escribe tres palabras para cada fotografía. Después, compara tu lista con la de tu compañero(a) y añade más palabras.

① ② ③

Antes de empezar

■ Next, ask students to think of other words they already know to talk about physical characteristics, personality traits, and personal relationships and add those words to their webs. Once students have finished, have groups come together and share their word webs as a class. Then, have the class create a master web that displays all of their words.

Activities

3. To expand this activity, have students work with a partner to create short dialogues similar to those in the recording. Remind students to add a polite phrase at the end. Then invite volunteer pairs to role-play their dialogues for the class.

6. You may want to convert this activity into a competition. Have partners list as many words as they can think of to describe each picture. They can be creative, and they can also use other vocabulary they know, but the words must make sense for the photo. For instance, *el abrazo, apoyar, apreciar,* and *reconciliarse* are all possible choices for picture #2, but *pelearse* and *enojarse* would not be acceptable word choices for this picture.

 AUDIO SCRIPT
See page 11K.

Answer Key

3. 1. e   2. f   3. b   4. a   5. c   6. d

4. Answers will vary.

5. Answers will vary. Sample answers:
1. reservado   4. traviesa
2. generosa   5. llevamos
3. enamorados

6. Answers will vary. Sample answers:
1. barba; bigote; pelo lacio
2. amistad; cariñosas; se abrazan
3. discuten; se llevan mal; piden perdón

Additional Resources

Fans Online activities
Practice Workbook

HERITAGE LANGUAGE LEARNERS

• Ask students to write a letter to an advice columnist, asking for help in a troubled relationship with a friend or family member. The writer should describe the personality traits as well as some physical characteristics of the other person in this relationship, and use as a starting point some of the verbs that are listed on page 17. Then ask students to exchange their letters with a partner, who will respond with good or humorous advice. Allow student pairs to read their letters and replies aloud.

TOTAL PHYSICAL RESPONSE (TPR)

• Have students play "Charades" with the words listed in the *Recuerda* feature on page 17, plus any others that are appropriate. Divide the class into even-numbered teams who will play against each other. Write the words on slips of paper and place them in a bag or box. Then ask each member of the teams to select one. Establish a time limit for guessing the word and have the winning teams play against each other to see who is class champion.

DESAFÍO 1

Describir personas

Presentation

- In *Desafío 1*, Asha and Lucas will plan a traditional Mexican birthday party for a classmate. Students will preview language used for descriptions.

Activities	Standards	Resources
Texto	1.2, 2.1, 2.2	
7.	1.2, 2.1, 2.2	
8.	1.1, 1.2, 2.1, 2.2	
9.	1.2, 2.1, 2.2	Audio
10. Cultura	1.1, 1.2, 2.1, 2.2, 3.2, 4.2, 5.2	

Teaching Suggestions

Warm-Up / Independent Starter

- Ask students to jot down some of the things they did to celebrate their last birthday. Have them save these notes for later use.

Preparation

- Read the title aloud and ask students for ideas on how to celebrate an "important birthday." Encourage students from different cultural backgrounds to contribute their ideas. Are there some common elements, such as music and food, in the celebrations students propose? Why might this be?

Texto: Un cumpleaños importante

- Have students look at the pictures of Asha and Lucas and mention two personality traits for each one. Then call on a student to read the introduction. Invite students to share with the class what they know about piñatas and *Las mañanitas*. Then, have two volunteers read the dialogue. What other personality traits can be gleaned from the dialogue? As a class, discuss Asha and Lucas's plans for the party.

Activities

7. In addition to the meaning, ask students to compare the position and spelling of *grande* in both sentences. Then, provide these examples: 1. *Tengo un coche grande.* 2. *Tengo un gran coche.* Can students see a pattern? Encourage them to extrapolate a rule.

Un cumpleaños importante

Asha y Lucas tienen que preparar una fiesta de cumpleaños para Margarita, una nueva compañera de clase que es mexicana. Además de encargarse de los preparativos para la fiesta, tendrán que hacer una piñata tradicional y aprenderse la canción *Las mañanitas* para felicitar a su compañera.

LUCAS: Hola, Asha. ¿Ya has enviado las invitaciones? Margarita me dijo que una vieja amiga suya viene de visita ese fin de semana y le gustaría que la invitáramos.

ASHA: Sí, ya las mandé. Pero no te preocupes, invitaré también a su amiga. Oye, he visto unas piñatas grandes con forma de muñecos en el supermercado. ¿Compro una?

LUCAS: ¿Con forma de muñecos? ¡No! Hay que hacer una piñata tradicional, una piñata de barro.

ASHA: Ah, no sabía que las piñatas fueran de barro.

LUCAS: Es que las piñatas son una tradición muy antigua. Unos dicen que proceden de los pueblos originarios de México. Otros creen que proceden de China y que fue Marco Polo quien las llevó a Europa, desde donde pasaron a México. Tendré que investigar un poco.

ASHA: Si te parece, tú puedes encargarte de averiguar más cosas sobre las piñatas y yo me ocupo de aprenderme la canción *Las mañanitas*. Se me da muy bien cantar.

LUCAS: Es una gran idea, pero... ¿tenemos que cantar los dos? Es que lo hago tan mal...

7 **Detective de palabras**

▶ **Completa** estas oraciones.

1. Asha vio en el supermercado unas piñatas _____ con forma de muñecos.

2. A Lucas le parece una _____ idea que Asha se ocupe de aprenderse *Las mañanitas*.

▶ **Explica.** ¿Qué significa la palabra que has escrito en cada oración?

Differentiated Instruction

DEVELOPING LEARNERS

- Ask students the following questions:

1. *¿Quién mandó las invitaciones? (Asha.)*

2. *¿Por qué quiere invitar Lucas a la vieja amiga de Margarita? (Se lo pidió Margarita.)*

3. *¿Dónde pensaba Asha comprar una piñata? (En el supermercado.)*

4. *¿Quién sabe más de piñatas, Asha o Lucas? ¿Por qué lo sabes? (Lucas, porque sabe de qué están hechas y algo sobre su historia.)*

5. *¿Qué piensa investigar Lucas? (El origen de las piñatas.)*

6. *¿Por qué no quiere cantar* Las mañanitas *Lucas? (Porque canta mal.)*

EXPANDING LEARNERS

- Ask students to rewrite the dialogue between Lucas and Asha as a third-person narrative. Remind students that they should use a variety of connecting words to link the statements as well as make use of synonyms for *decir* (e.g., *comentar, añadir, explicar*). Explain to students that they may set the narrative in the present or past tense. Call on volunteers to read their compositions to the rest of the class.

- Discuss which format, dialogue or narrative, is more effective and why.

¿Comprendes?

▶ **Responde** a estas preguntas.

1. ¿A quién quiere invitar Lucas a la fiesta de cumpleaños de Margarita?
2. ¿Cómo eran las piñatas que vio Asha en el supermercado?
3. ¿De qué están hechas las piñatas tradicionales?
4. ¿De dónde proceden las piñatas?
5. ¿Qué idea le propone Asha a Lucas?
6. ¿Qué tal canta Lucas?

9 Organizando la fiesta

▶ **Escucha** la conversación entre Asha y Lucas, y elige la opción correcta.

1. Las piñatas tradicionales tienen forma de _____.
   a. muñeco   b. estrella   c. animales
2. La costumbre tradicional consiste en _____ la piñata.
   a. romper   b. quemar   c. esconder
3. Según Lucas, las piñatas tradicionales son bonitas y _____.
   a. luminosas   b. enormes   c. vistosas
4. La canción *Las mañanitas* se canta en las fiestas de _____.
   a. Navidad   b. graduación   c. cumpleaños

▶ **Escribe** un párrafo describiendo cómo sueles celebrar tu fiesta de cumpleaños.

▶ **Habla** con tu compañero(a). ¿Cómo celebra él / ella su cumpleaños? ¿Cuáles son las semejanzas y las diferencias entre su celebración y la tuya?

CULTURA

Las piñatas

Las piñatas son muy populares en México, en América Central y en el sur de los Estados Unidos. Su origen es incierto, pero muchos dicen que proceden de China y que fueron llevadas a las Américas por los conquistadores europeos.

Las piñatas mexicanas son ollas de barro o cajas de cartón que contienen dulces, frutas y pequeños regalos. La piñata se adorna con papeles de colores y se cuelga o se coloca en un lugar alto, para que una persona con los ojos vendados *(blindfolded)* la rompa con un palo *(stick)* y haga caer su contenido. El momento de romper la piñata es el punto central en los cumpleaños y en las fiestas infantiles.

10 Explica. ¿Conoces alguna tradición similar a la costumbre de romper la piñata? ¿Has participado alguna vez en una fiesta con piñata? ¿Te parece divertido?

diecinueve 19

HERITAGE LANGUAGE LEARNERS

- Ask students to share other traditional songs or customs for birthdays or other family celebrations in their family's country of origin. Students may bring in recordings of these songs or sing them to the rest of the class. Encourage all students to learn the lyrics to their favorite songs and sing them on classmates' birthdays.

COOPERATIVE LEARNING

- Have students work in small groups and come up with a new and original tradition for a birthday celebration. All students will contribute their ideas to the group, discuss them, and select one. Different tasks may be assigned according to students' comfort level and expertise in composing a description, using graphics, making a video, etc. All group members will participate in a presentation of their new "tradition" to the class. You may want to honor some of these traditions on the upcoming birthdays of students.

Describir personas

9. For the speaking part, have students take out their notes from the Independent Starter. Compile a class list of the most original birthday celebrations.

 AUDIO SCRIPT
See page 11K.

 CULTURA

Las piñatas

In Mexico, most birthday celebrations include a piñata. Participants are encouraged to break open the piñata while the rest of the group sings, *Dale, dale, dale. No pierdas el tino, porque si lo pierdes, pierdes el camino.* Piñatas are also important cultural symbols. The town of Acolman, in the state of Mexico, hosts an annual National Piñata Fair. More than 200 artisans take pride in continuing a tradition that, according to some accounts, began in this town more than 400 years ago.

Answer Key

7. 1. grandes   2. gran
   ▶ En el primer caso se refiere al tamaño. En el segundo, indica que es una buena idea.

8. 1. A una vieja amiga de Margarita.
   2. Eran grandes, con forma de muñecos.
   3. De barro.
   4. Unos dicen que son originarias de México y otros creen que son de China.
   5. Le propone que se encargue de averiguar más cosas sobre las piñatas.
   6. Lo hace muy mal.

9. 1. b   2. a   3. c   4. c
   ▶ Answers will vary.
   ▶ Answers will vary.

10. Answers will vary.

Additional Resources

Fans Online activities

Unit 1

DESAFÍO 1

Vocabulario – Características físicas y rasgos de personalidad

Presentation

- In this section, students will learn words that describe physical characteristics and personality traits.

Activities	Standards	Resources
Vocabulario	1.2	
11.	1.2	
12.	1.1, 1.2	
13.	1.1, 1.2, 1.3, 5.1	Audio
14. Conexiones	1.1, 1.2, 2.1, 3.1, 4.1	

Teaching Suggestions

Warm-Up / Independent Starter

- Have students look at the pictures on this page and describe each person with four adjectives.

Preparation

- Read the words in the *Más vocabulario* box aloud and have students repeat them after you. Then do the same with the highlighted words and phrases. Point out that many of these new words are defined in the reading (e.g., *pelo ondulado = casi rizado*). For those words that are not defined, use body language to help students comprehend their meanings.
- Have students read Asha's e-mail silently. On the board, draw a cluster diagram for each character mentioned in the e-mail. As a class, discuss Juan Pablo's physical characteristics and personality traits and list them in the corresponding ovals of one of the diagrams. Then do the same for Mr. Rodríguez. Clarify any vocabulary questions students may have.

Activities

11. To expand this activity, have students list a synonym for each word (e.g., *humilde = modesto*). If there are words for which students don't know a synonym, allow them to provide a short definition.

13. For the second part of this activity, ask each pair to share with the class the two traits they like best in a friend and the two they find least attractive.

Vocabulario

Características físicas y rasgos de personalidad

De: Asha
Para: Emi

¡Hola, Emi!

¿Cómo te va? ¿Estás contenta en tu nueva escuela? Yo estoy muy emocionada; hoy comenzaron las clases y tengo muchas cosas que contarte.

Este año hay un chico nuevo en la clase. Se llama Juan Pablo. Es moreno y tiene el pelo ondulado, casi rizado. ¡Y se parece a Orlando Bloom! Bueno, a mí me parece que son idénticos, ¡como dos gotas de agua! Siempre está haciendo cosas sin pensar demasiado: es muy impulsivo. A Elena le cae mal porque dice que siempre está haciendo bromitas y tomándole el pelo. Pero a mí me parece que tiene mucho sentido del humor porque me hace reír. Es apasionado y tiene personalidad. Me cae bien.

Nuestro profesor de Español es el señor Rodríguez. ¿Te acuerdas de él? Es mayor. No tiene el pelo blanco, pero tiene muchas canas y algunas arrugas en la cara. Es muy seguro. Algunos chicos dicen que es un poco vanidoso y parece muy estricto, pero es sensible y bondadoso. ¡Me gustan sus clases!

Escríbeme y cuéntame qué tal en tu nueva escuela.

Hasta pronto. Besos.

Asha

Más vocabulario

Características físicas

ciego(a)	blind
mudo(a)	mute
sordo(a)	deaf
diestro(a)	right-handed
zurdo(a)	left-handed

Rasgos de personalidad

astuto(a)	shrewd
cobarde	cowardly
envidioso(a)	envious
humilde	modest, humble
indeciso(a)	indecisive
maleducado(a)	bad-mannered
terco(a)	stubborn
valiente	brave

¡Atención!

sensato(a)	sensible
sensible	sensitive

11 Palabras relacionadas

▶ **Une** las palabras con sus opuestos.

(A)	(B)
1. valiente	a. vanidoso
2. humilde	b. seguro
3. terco	c. razonable
4. indeciso	d. cobarde
5. estricto	e. flexible

20 veinte

Differentiated Instruction

DEVELOPING LEARNERS

- Help students reinforce their comprehension of the vocabulary in the e-mail and the *Más vocabulario* feature by having them match each word in the first column with its antonym in the second.

1. *ondulado* (d)	a. *soso*
2. *idéntico* (g)	b. *zurdo*
3. *impulsivo* (f)	c. *correcto*
4. *astuto* (e)	d. *lacio*
5. *estricto* (h)	e. *ingenuo*
6. *apasionado* (a)	f. *tranquilo*
7. *diestro* (b)	g. *contrario*
8. *maleducado* (c)	h. *flexible*

EXPANDING LEARNERS

- Ask students to think of at least five people from real life or fictional characters from literature, movies, or radio/television. Then have students write a few sentences describing these people, without revealing who they are, by using some of the physical characteristics or personality traits mentioned on page 20. Encourage students to include other descriptive adjectives. Ask students to read their sentences aloud and have their classmates try to guess each person's or character's identity.

12 **¿Comprendes?**

▶ **Lee** de nuevo el mensaje de Asha y responde a estas preguntas.

1. ¿Cómo tiene el pelo Juan Pablo?
2. ¿Cómo es la personalidad de Juan Pablo?
3. ¿Qué tal se llevan Asha y Juan Pablo? ¿Y Elena y Juan Pablo?
4. ¿Cómo es físicamente el señor Rodríguez?
5. ¿Qué piensa Asha del señor Rodríguez?

13 **Entre amigos**

 ▶ **Escucha** y completa las oraciones con la forma correcta de estos adjetivos.

tímido(a)	terco(a)	impulsivo(a)	apasionado(a)	seguro(a)

1. Martín es...
2. Rafa es...
3. Andrea es...
4. Marta es...
5. Jimena es...

 ▶ **Habla** con tu compañero(a). ¿Cómo es tu mejor amigo(a)? ¿Qué es lo que más te gusta de él/ella? ¿Y qué es lo que menos te gusta?

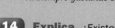

CONEXIONES: LENGUA

Los diminutivos

En español, muchas palabras admiten el sufijo diminutivo *-ito(a)* para expresar que algo es de tamaño pequeño. Pero el diminutivo puede añadir otros matices *(nuances)*, como expresar afecto, restar importancia o, incluso, mostrar desprecio. Según las zonas, se emplean también otros sufijos diminutivos como *-illo(a)*, *-ico(a)* o *-ín(a)*.

Me he comprado un bolsito precioso para ir a tu fiesta.
Esta tarde vamos a visitar a mi abuelita.
Papá, tengo que contarte una cosita.
Tú siempre gastando bromitas...

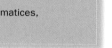

14 **Explica.** ¿Existen diminutivos en inglés? ¿Pueden expresar distintos matices, como en español?

veintiuno **21**

HERITAGE LANGUAGE LEARNERS

• Explain that the diminutive suffix *-illo* may also be used to give words a special meaning. For example: *ventana* (window) and *ventanilla* (ticket window). Have students explain the meaning of the following words. Then ask them to add the suffix *-illo(a)* and explain how this changes each word's meaning.

1. *la bomba (la bombilla)* (bomb/pump; light bulb)
2. *la caja (la cajetilla)* (box/cash register; pack)
3. *la cama (la camilla)* (bed; stretcher)
4. *la manzana (la manzanilla)* (apple; chamomile)
5. *el palo (el palillo)* (stick; toothpick)

SPECIAL-NEEDS LEARNERS

• Distribute large index cards to students who are having difficulty with their vision and ask them to write the highlighted words, along with those in the *Más vocabulario* feature, on one side. You might also have them include vocabulary from page 17. Then ask them to work with a heritage language learner and write the English-language equivalent on the other side. Ask students to read the words in both languages. Then ask them to work with a partner and test each other on this vocabulary.

Vocabulario – Características físicas y rasgos de personalidad

 AUDIO SCRIPT
See page 11K.

CONEXIONES: LENGUA

Los diminutivos

Diminutives in Spanish are used to talk to young children, indicate something is small, express affection, and give a friendly tone to an utterance. Diminutives are also used to provide a nuance of meaning that is difficult to translate into English. For instance, diminutives can be used to express politeness (e.g., *Ahorita lo atiendo*), diminish a pejorative (e.g., *Está gordito*), and as intensifiers (e.g., *Es igualito a su padre*). Diminutives can also convey irony (e.g., *¡Vaya cochecito!*) and even contempt (e.g., *Se compró un cochecillo*).

Answer Key

11. 1. d 2. a 3. c 4. b 5. e

12. 1. Lo tiene ondulado.
  2. Es impulsivo.
  3. Asha y Juan Pablo se llevan bien. A Elena le cae mal Juan Pablo.
  4. Tiene canas y algunas arrugas.
  5. Que es muy seguro, sensible y bondadoso.

13. 1. impulsivo   4. terca
  2. seguro   5. apasionada
  3. tímida
  ▶ Answers will vary.

14. Answers will vary. Sample answer:
  En inglés se usa el adjetivo *little* para formar el diminutivo. Muchos nombres tienen también diminutivos (e.g., Jimmy, *doggie*), pero los diminutivos no son tan comunes como en español.

Additional Resources

Fans Online activities
Practice Workbook

DESAFÍO 1

Gramática – Expresar gustos, intereses, sentimientos y emociones

Presentation

■ In this section, students will review verbs used to express likes, interests, feelings, and emotions.

Activities	Standards	Resources
Gramática	1.2, 3.1	
15.	1.2, 3.1, 4.1	
16.	1.2	
17.	1.2, 1.3	Audio
18.	1.1, 1.3, 5.1	
19. Cultura	1.1, 1.2, 2.1, 2.2, 3.1, 3.2	

Teaching Suggestions

Warm-Up / Independent Starter

■ Ask students to write their reactions to these things. For example: *la ópera → Me aburre.*
  – *las películas de terror* – *leer*
  – *los vanidosos* – *el chocolate*

Preparation

■ Have students read the grammar presentation silently. Then ask them to revise their Independent Starters, making sure that the verb agrees with the subject. Call on several students to share their answers with the class. For further practice with verbs like *gustar*, write the following pairs of sentences on the board and have students determine the subject for each sentence and contrast the meaning:

1. *Me fascinas.* 2. *Nos caemos bien.*
   ¿Te fascino? *Me caen bien.*

Activities

17. Before playing the audio, have students draw a three-column chart with these headings: Sara, Paula, Gabriel. Then, ask them to list these characters' likes and dislikes in the appropriate column as they listen to the audio.

18. Hold a whole-class discussion session to comment on students' interests. Then share with them some of your generation's interests when you were your students' age. Invite the class to compare and contrast the interests.

Gramática

Expresar gustos, intereses, sentimientos y emociones

Los verbos como *gustar* (*a mí me...*)

■ Muchos verbos que expresan gustos, intereses, sentimientos y emociones siguen el modelo del verbo gustar: se conjugan generalmente en tercera persona (singular o plural) y llevan un pronombre de objeto indirecto: me, te, le, nos, os, les.

VERBOS COMO GUSTAR

aburrir	encantar
alegrar	enfadar
apetecer	enojar
asustar	extrañar
caer bien/mal	fascinar
dar miedo	importar
dar pena	interesar
deprimir	molestar
divertir	parecer
doler	preocupar
emocionar	sorprender

PRONOMBRE	VERBO EN 3.ª PERSONA	ALGO O ALGUIEN (SUJETO)
Me	gustan	los helados.
Nos	encanta	ser tus amigos.
Les	preocupa	que no estudie.

Observa que el sujeto va generalmente detrás del verbo.

■ La mayoría de estos verbos se pueden conjugar también en primera y en segunda persona.

Tú **me gustas** mucho.   Yo **te sorprendo** cada día.

■ Los verbos como gustar se pueden conjugar en diferentes tiempos (*tenses*), igual que cualquier otro verbo.

PRESENTE	A mi amiga Carla **le encantan** las películas románticas.
PRETÉRITO	**Nos molestó** la actitud agresiva del vendedor.
IMPERFECTO	Cuando era niño, **me asustaban** las tormentas.
FUTURO	Creo que a ustedes **les aburrirá** esa película.

15 **Piensa.** ¿Cómo traduces las siguientes oraciones al inglés?
  a. Me interesan las matemáticas.   **b.** Nos sorprendió el final de la película.

16 **Gustos y emociones**

▶ **Completa** las oraciones con estos verbos. Usa el presente y los pronombres adecuados.

encantar	deprimir
dar miedo	molestar
apetecer	preocupar

1. A mis padres _____ mucho los ruidos.
2. La crisis económica _____ a todo el mundo.
3. A Elsa y a mí _____ las películas de terror; no nos gustan nada.
4. A mí _____ hacer deporte al aire libre.
5. Eva, ¿_____ ir conmigo al cine esta tarde?
6. A Juan _____ los días lluviosos, se pone muy triste.

Differentiated Instruction

DEVELOPING LEARNERS

• Ask students to work with a partner. Each one will describe a classmate by using some of the verbs listed on the page, as well as any others that express this person's likes, interests, feelings, and emotions. Students should not reveal the classmate's identity to one another. Give students time to guess the classmates' identities and, based on this description, have each partner write a short descriptive paragraph about the "mystery" student.

EXPANDING LEARNERS

• Direct students' attention to *Los verbos como gustar* feature and ask them to select a minimum of ten verbs and write a sentence for each one that reflects their own likes, interests, feelings, or emotions. Then have them exchange these brief descriptions with a partner who will use the same verbs to write what is true about him or herself. Have partners discuss their similarities and differences. For example:

A. *Esa película que ponen en el cine Central me aburrió muchísimo.*

B. *¡No me digas! Me pareció buenísima y me fascinó.*

17 Cine y teatro

 ► **Escucha** la conversación y decide si estas afirmaciones son ciertas o falsas. Después, corrige las falsas.

1. A Sara le fascina el cine argentino.
2. A Sara le aburre el teatro.
3. A Gabriel le encanta la ópera.
4. A Paula le gusta mucho ir al teatro con Gabriel.
5. A Sara le molesta que la gente haga ruido en el cine.
6. A Paula le alegra ir al cine con Sara.

 ► **Escucha** de nuevo y escribe oraciones que expresen los gustos, intereses y emociones de Sara, Paula y Gabriel.

Modelo   *A Paula le apetece ir al teatro.*

a. Ir al teatro.
b. El cine argentino.
c. La última película argentina que vio.
d. Ir con Gabriel al teatro.
e. Oír ruidos durante la proyección.
f. Hacer cosas juntas.

18 ¿Qué te gusta a ti?

► **Escribe** un párrafo sobre tus gustos e intereses. Piensa también en algunas experiencias que hayas tenido y escribe qué sentiste.

 ► **Habla** con tu compañero(a) sobre lo que han escrito. Comparen sus gustos y emociones.

Modelo   A. *A mí me emociona ver jugar a mi equipo de fútbol.*
         B. *¡A mí también! Y me divertí mucho viendo la última final con mis amigos.*

CULTURA
El mariachi (México)

Las fiestas populares y las celebraciones familiares en México suelen ir acompañadas de música de mariachi. Este género musical forma parte de la identidad nacional y es una de las expresiones culturales del país más reconocidas en el mundo.

El mariachi procede de la región occidental de México, en el actual estado de Jalisco. Originariamente se tocaba con instrumentos de cuerda, pero después se incorporaron instrumentos de viento, como la característica trompeta. Algunas de las canciones más conocidas interpretadas por mariachis son *Cielito lindo*, *El rey* y *Las mañanitas*.

19 **Explica.** Escucha alguna canción mariachi. ¿Qué instrumentos reconoces? ¿Qué temas y sentimientos tratan las canciones?

veintitrés 23

Gramática – Expresar gustos, intereses, sentimientos y emociones

AUDIO SCRIPT
See page 11K.

CULTURA
El mariachi (México)

The sounds of mariachi music originated in Mexico's colonial times, but mariachi as we know it today is a 20th century phenomenon. Mariachi ensembles generally include trumpets, violins, vihuelas (a five-string guitar), and a guitarrón (a large bass guitar). Most mariachi bands are all male, but co-ed and even all-female bands are becoming more common. Mariachi songs talk about love, betrayal, death, revolutionary heroes, and country life.

Answer Key

15. a. *I'm interested in mathematics.*
     b. *The movie's ending surprised us.*
16. 1. les molestan   4. me encanta
     2. le preocupa   5. te apetece
     3. nos dan miedo   6. le deprimen
17. 1. F. A Sara le interesa el cine argentino.
     2. F. A Gabriel le aburre el teatro.
     3. C.
     4. F. A Paula no le divierte nada ir con él.
     5. C.
     6. C.
     ► Answers will vary.
18. Answers will vary.
     ► Answers will vary.
19. Answers will vary.

Additional Resources

Fans Online activities
Practice Workbook

HERITAGE LANGUAGE LEARNERS

• Ask students to think about a traditional or contemporary Spanish-language song that best expresses their likes, interests, feelings, or emotions. Have students bring this song to class and share it with the rest of the students. Ask the heritage language learners to explain the lyrics and describe the instruments used in the music to the other students and offer them some anecdotal information about the composer/lyricist or singer. Then have students write at least one paragraph describing how this song relates to them.

MULTIPLE INTELLIGENCES:
Intrapersonal Intelligence

• Have students keep a diary in which they will record their feelings, both positive and negative, during the week. Ask them to write a few lines every day describing their emotions and what triggers them. Encourage students to use the verbs listed on the page as well as any others that reflect how they feel or what interests them. Suggest that students come up with a solution for any negative feelings they may have. For example: *Me deprime ver a tantos niños hambrientos en el mundo.* (*Me encantaría participar en una campaña contra la hambruna.*)

DESAFÍO 1

Gramática – Los adjetivos. Posición y significado

Presentation

- In this section, students will learn about adjective placement in Spanish and the differences in meaning associated with adjective placement.

Activities	Standards	Resources
Gramática	1.2, 3.1	
20.	1.2, 3.1, 4.1	
21.	1.2	
22.	1.2	
23.	1.1, 1.3	

Teaching Suggestions

Warm-Up / Independent Starter

- Have students read the grammar presentation silently. Encourage them to take notes on any material they have trouble understanding.

Preparation

- Go over the grammar presentation as a class. Adjective placement is a complex grammar topic, so you may want to offer additional explanations. As a general rule, a descriptive adjective following a noun distinguishes that object or person from others. For instance, *Vivo en la casa roja* implies that I live in a house that is painted red rather than any other color. Placing a descriptive adjective before a noun implies that the quality is naturally associated with the noun. For instance, *Vimos la roja sangre de la víctima*, confirms what we know about blood (i.e., it is red). For further practice, have students give a reason for each adjective placement in these sentences:
  1. a. *Ella vive en una casa <u>blanca</u>.*
     b. *La <u>blanca</u> nieve cubre las calles.*
  2. a. *Tuve un sueño <u>horrible</u>.*
     b. *El <u>horrible</u> monstruo destruyó el pueblo.*
- Although changes in meaning due to adjective placement are rare in English, they do exist. You may want to give students these examples to help them understand the concept: a. They want to hire a <u>responsible person</u>. b. The <u>person responsible</u> for the accident should pay. Then analyze the different examples provided in the presentation.

Gramática

Los adjetivos. Posición y significado

Posición de los adjetivos calificativos

- En español, los adjetivos que expresan clases (día festivo) y cualidades o propiedades propias de uno o varios individuos (persona sensible) van detrás del nombre.

  Cartagena de Indias es una ciudad **turística**.   Tengo una amiga **argentina**.

  En cambio, los adjetivos que expresan una cualidad típica del nombre van delante.

  A lo lejos se veían las **altas montañas**.

- Muchos adjetivos se pueden poner delante o detrás del nombre por razones estilísticas, pero algunos tienen significados distintos según su posición.

ADJETIVOS CON CAMBIO DE SIGNIFICADO

Adjetivo	Antes del nombre	Después del nombre
antiguo(a)	*former, ex-* un antiguo compañero	*ancient, antique* un mueble antiguo
viejo(a)	*long-standing* una vieja canción	*old, elderly* una casa vieja
nuevo(a)	*different, other* una nueva computadora	*brand new* una computadora nueva
gran/grande	*great, famous* un gran amigo	*big, large* un edificio grande
pobre	*unfortunate* un pobre hombre	*penniless* un hombre pobre
único(a)	*only* un único libro	*unique* un libro único

Los adjetivos apocopados

- Los adjetivos bueno, malo y grande tienen formas cortas: buen, mal y gran. Las formas cortas se usan delante de los nombres en estos casos:

bueno → buen malo → mal	+ nombre masculino singular	Jaime es un **buen** compañero.
grande → gran	+ nombre singular	Meryl Streep es una **gran** actriz.

20 **Compara.** ¿Hay adjetivos en inglés que cambien de significado según su posición?

21 **Antes o después**

▶ **Explica** el significado de los adjetivos destacados en estas oraciones.
1. Admiro mucho a tu padre. Es un **viejo** amigo y una **gran** persona.
2. Espero tener una **nueva** oportunidad de viajar a Perú el año próximo.
3. Este viaje es una ocasión **única**, no te lo puedes perder.

Differentiated Instruction

DEVELOPING LEARNERS

- Have students complete the following sentences with the correct form and placement of the adjective shown:
  1. *Solo tengo un libro. (único) Es mi … libro… (único libro)*
  2. *Ana es mi amiga desde hace 25 años. (vieja) Es una … amiga… (vieja amiga)*
  3. *(grande) Cervantes fue un … escritor… (gran escritor)*
  4. *(antiguo) El Sr. López es un … profesor … de este colegio. (antiguo profesor)*
  5. *(nuevo) ¿Has leído la … novela … de J.K. Rowling? (nueva novela)*

EXPANDING LEARNERS

- Review with students some other adjectives that change meaning according to their placement, and have them write two sentences with each adjective.

	After Noun	Before Noun
medio	average	half
mismo	himself	same
puro	pure, clean	sheer
simple	simple-minded	simple, mere
triste	sad	miserable
valiente	brave	great (ironically)
varios	various, assorted	several

22 Parejas

▶ **Completa** las oraciones con una palabra de cada cuadro en la forma y el orden correctos.

Adjetivos	
nuevo	bueno
único	grande
antiguo	viejo

Nombres	
libro	auto
compañero	amigo
casa	actor

1. Mis padres ya no viven allí. Su _____ es ahora una tienda de ropa.
2. Robert de Niro es un _____. Me encantan todas sus películas.
3. Antonio tiene un _____. Se ha comprado el último modelo, qué suerte.
4. David es un _____. Siempre está ahí cuando lo necesito.
5. *El Quijote* de mi amigo Francisco es un _____ en el mundo. No hay otro igual.
6. Elisa y yo somos _____. Las dos íbamos a la misma escuela.

23 Una historia en imágenes

▶ **Escribe** oraciones para describir estas imágenes. Cada oración debe incluir al menos un adjetivo delante o detrás del nombre.

①

②

③

④

⑤

⑥

▶ **Escribe** una historia breve usando las oraciones que has creado en el apartado anterior.

 ▶ **Habla** con tu compañero(a). Comparte con él/ella tu historia. Después, inventen una nueva historia usando sus relatos y cuéntensela a la clase.

veinticinco 25

Activities

21. To extend this activity, have students write six pairs of sentences using the six adjectives listed under *Adjetivos con cambio de significado*. Then have students exchange their sentences with a partner and explain the meaning of each one.

22. Once students have finished this activity, ask them to rewrite the sentences reversing the adjective order. Explain that they may need to change both sentences so that they make sense. For example: 1. *Mis padres acaban de comprar una <u>casa antigua</u>.* 2. *Marlon Brando era un <u>actor grande</u>. Llegó a pesar más de 300 libras.* Call on students to share their new sentences with the class.

23. For further practice with adjectives, ask students to rewrite their stories, changing the adjectives to the opposite. For instance, if their original story began with a sentence such as, *La astuta anciana...*, students should change it to *La ingenua joven...* Invite students to share these new stories with the class. Then hold a vote to choose the funniest story.

Answer Key

20. Hay muy pocos casos. Por ejemplo: *She is <u>late</u>. I loved my <u>late</u> grandfather.*

21. 1. *long-standing; great*
  2. *another*
  3. *unique*

22. 1. antigua casa 4. buen amigo
  2. gran actor 5. libro único
  3. auto nuevo 6. viejas compañeras

23. Answers will vary.
  ▶ Answers will vary.
  ▶ Answers will vary.

Additional Resources

Fans Online activities
Practice Workbook

HERITAGE LANGUAGE LEARNERS

• Remind students that certain adjectives are always placed in front of a noun, and review with them these common examples: *ambos, mucho, otro, poco, tanto*. Then introduce some less frequently used adjectives: *llamado, mero, pleno, presunto, pretendido, sendos*, and give an example with each (*los llamados conservadores, la mera idea, en pleno desarrollo, la presunta asesina, los pretendidos ganadores, traen sendos libros*). Next, ask students to write their own sentences using adjectives that should only be placed before the noun. Have a partner check their work.

COOPERATIVE LEARNING

• Sponsor a sentence-writing competition in the classroom. Divide the class into teams of four or five and include students of different learning abilities in each one. Explain that they are going to write original sentences illustrating the correct placement of adjectives that change meaning according to their position with the noun. Establish a time period in which students must complete as many sentences as they can. Then have groups read their sentences aloud and have classmates correct them if necessary. The winning team is the one that wrote the most sentences correctly.

LECTURA: TEXTO DIALOGADO

Presentation

- In this section, students will read a dialogue, translate the song *Las mañanitas* into English, and research a Hispanic tradition, as well as answer comprehension questions based on the reading.

Activities	Standards	Resources
Lectura: texto dialogado	1.1, 1.2, 2.1, 2.2, 3.2	
24.	1.1, 1.2, 2.1, 2.2	
25.	1.2, 4.1, 5.1, 5.2	Audio
26.	1.1, 1.3, 2.1, 5.1	

Teaching Suggestions

Warm-Up / Independent Starter

- Have students read the *Antes de leer* strategies silently. Then ask them to think about possible answers to the questions.

Preparation

- Call on a volunteer to answer the first question in the *Antes de leer* section. Sample response: Las mañanitas *es una canción que se canta en los cumpleaños en México.* Ask students to think of a reason for the use of the diminutive in *mañanitas*. Elicit that in this case, the diminutive is used as an intensifier to indicate that it is very early in the morning.

- Once students have located the song excerpt in the dialogue, discuss with them the use of the diminutive in this case: *Ya los pajarillos cantan.* What would be an equivalent in English? (birdies, little birds)

- If students have difficulties coming up with an explanation for the song's title, focus their attention on this phrase: *Despierta mi bien, despierta, mira que ya amaneció.* What time in the morning do they think it is? Would they like to be awakened to an early morning serenade on their birthday?

- Read the dialogue aloud, modeling correct pronunciation and intonation. Then call on several pairs to alternate reading the dialogue aloud. Offer suggestions to improve their oral reading.

LECTURA: TEXTO DIALOGADO

Antes de leer: estrategias

1. Lee el título y recuerda. ¿Qué son *Las mañanitas*?
2. Mira el texto y localiza un fragmento de *Las mañanitas*.
3. Comenta con tus compañeros(as). ¿Por qué creen que esta canción tiene ese título?

Las mañanitas

LUCAS: ¿Ya te aprendiste la canción *Las mañanitas*?

ASHA: ¡Sí! La escuché en Internet y tomé nota de la letra. Hay varias versiones, pero creo que esta es la más popular. Te la voy a cantar:

Estas son las mañanitas
que cantaba el rey David,
hoy por ser día de tu santo,
te las cantamos a ti.

Despierta mi bien, despierta,
mira que ya amaneció.
Ya los pajarillos cantan,
la luna ya se metió.

LUCAS: ¡Qué bonita! ¿Y sabes algo de su origen?

ASHA: Es una canción tradicional mexicana que se canta desde antes de la Revolución. Pero no averigüé nada de su autor.

LUCAS: ¿Y por qué dice «Hoy por ser día de tu santo…»?

ASHA: Pues creo que porque antes a los niños les solían poner el nombre del santo de ese día, así que el santo solía coincidir con el cumpleaños.

LUCAS: ¿El santo?

ASHA: Sí, he leído que en los países de tradición católica cada día del año está asociado a los nombres de algunos santos y santas. Las personas que se llaman como ellos celebran el santo ese día.

LUCAS: ¡Qué curioso!

ASHA: Por ejemplo, el santo de Lucía se celebra el 13 de diciembre, el de Juan el 24 de junio, y el tuyo…

LUCAS: ¿El mío?

ASHA: Sí, lo he buscado y el tuyo se celebra el 18 de octubre.

LUCAS: ¡Ah, qué bien! ¿Y sabes por qué la canción se titula *Las mañanitas*?

ASHA: Porque antes se cantaba para despertar al cumpleañero.

LUCAS: ¡Qué divertido! ¡Podemos despertar así a Margarita el día de su cumpleaños!

26 veintiséis

Differentiated Instruction

DEVELOPING LEARNERS

- Have students work in small groups and take turns reading the dialogue aloud. After they read a few lines, ask them to explain in their own words what Lucas and Asha are saying. For example, the first line could be: *Lucas le pregunta a Asha si ella ya se ha aprendido la canción.* Verify students' accuracy of what is being said in the dialogue as well as their correct use of verb tenses.

EXPANDING LEARNERS

- Asha and Lucas are both looking forward to Margarita's birthday celebration. Ask students to write an e-mail to a *fan del español* from either Asha's or Lucas's point of view. Students should explain how they are going to celebrate their friend's birthday. They should also describe Margarita: her physical characteristics, her personality traits, her likes and dislikes, as well as how the writer feels about preparing this event.

24 ¿Comprendes?

▶ **Responde** a estas preguntas.

1. ¿Existe una sola versión de la canción *Las mañanitas*?
2. ¿Se sabe quién es el autor de la canción y cuándo se escribió?
3. ¿Por qué dice «Hoy por ser día de tu santo...» si es una canción de cumpleaños?
4. ¿Por qué se titula *Las mañanitas*?

25 Tu versión

 ▶ **Escucha** la canción *Las mañanitas* y traduce la letra al inglés. Ten en cuenta que debe encajar en la melodía.

Las mañanitas

Estas son las mañanitas
que cantaba el rey David,
hoy por ser día de tu santo,
te las cantamos a ti.

Despierta mi bien, despierta,
mira que ya amaneció.
Ya los pajarillos cantan,
la luna ya se metió.

 ▶ **Canta** tu versión de *Las mañanitas* a tus compañeros(as). ¿Cuál les gusta más?

26 Con tus propias palabras

▶ **Investiga** sobre la celebración del santo en los países hispanos y escribe un texto breve explicándolo. Además, si el nombre de tus amigos y familiares se corresponde con el de algún santo, anota quién era y cuándo se celebra.

▶ **Comenta** con tus compañeros(as) lo que has averiguado.

Activities

24. There are a couple of historical references in the dialogue. If time allows, you may want to discuss them. Asha says that the song has been around since before the Mexican Revolution. Ask students to research the Mexican Revolution and get some general information (e.g., years, reasons for the fight, revolutionary heroes). Have them share what they found out with the class. There is also a historical reference in the song itself: *Estas son las mañanitas que cantaba el rey David*. Do students know who King David was? Elicit that King David is a Biblical figure. It is believed that he ruled over the Kingdom of Israel around the year 1000 BCE.

26. Some students may want to know who their patron saint is. You will find a list of saints for each day of the year by doing an Internet search for *santoral católico*. Is there any student in your class whose name is the same as his or her patron saint? What other traditions regarding names do students know?

AUDIO SCRIPT
See page 11K.

Answer Key

24. 1. No. Hay varias versiones.
2. No se sabe ni quién es su autor ni cuándo se escribió. Es una canción tradicional mexicana, que se canta desde antes de la Revolución.
3. Porque antes a los niños al nacer les ponían el nombre del santo de ese día.
4. Porque antes se cantaba para despertar al cumpleañero.

25. Answers will vary.
▶ Answers will vary.

26. Answers will vary.
▶ Answers will vary.

Additional Resources

Fans Online activities

HERITAGE LANGUAGE LEARNERS

• Ask students to expand their initial research on the Mexican Revolution by focusing on some of the key players in this ten-year struggle, such as Pancho Villa, Emiliano Zapata, Porfirio Díaz, and Francisco Madero. Students might work in pairs or small groups and compile both biographical information on their historical figure and an explanation of his role in the Revolution. Students should be prepared to make a brief oral presentation to the rest of the class.

MULTIPLE INTELLIGENCES:
Musical-Rhythmic Intelligence

• After students listen to the song *Las mañanitas*, ask them to work in small groups and come up with a new melody and lyrics for a song that celebrates a birthday or other special occasion for friends or family. If any students play a musical instrument, encourage them to accompany one of the groups. After allowing time for students to rehearse, ask them to make their musical debut in front of the class.

DESAFÍO 1

Comunicación

Presentation

- In this section, students will integrate the vocabulary and grammar skills from *Desafío 1* in order to describe personality traits and express likes, interests, feelings, and emotions.

Activities	Standards	Resources
27.	1.1, 1.2, 1.3, 2.1, 2.2, 3.2, 4.2, 5.1	
28.	1.2, 1.3	Audio
29. Final del desafío	1.1, 1.2, 2.1, 2.2, 3.2	

Teaching Suggestions

Warm-Up / Independent Starter

- Have students answer these questions:
  1. *¿Cómo te apetece celebrar tu próximo cumpleaños?*
  2. *¿Te gustaría invitar a algún antiguo compañero?*
  3. *¿Qué te apetece: una fiesta con muchos invitados o una reunión íntima entre amigos? ¿Por qué?*

Preparation

- Go over the vocabulary and grammar topics from this *Desafío*. Clarify any questions students may have. Then, as you go over their answers to the questions in the Independent Starter, you may extend this activity by adding more questions. For example: *¿Hay algo que te moleste de las fiestas de cumpleaños? ¿Tienes alguna tradición que sigas siempre? ¿Qué nuevas actividades te gustaría incorporar a tu próxima fiesta?* Monitor students' answers and review any vocabulary or grammar structures that are causing them difficulties.

Activities

27. To help students answer question #2, have them create a two-column chart with these headings: *Celebración mexicana* and *Mi celebración*. As they read Julieta's e-mail, ask them to complete the column corresponding to the Mexican celebrations. Then, have students complete the second column and answer the question. For question #3, students add additional columns for each country.

28

Comunicación

27 **Un cumpleaños mexicano**

▶ **Lee** el texto y escribe seis oraciones sobre los sentimientos que expresa Julieta. Usa estos verbos.

alegrar · divertir · dar pena · apetecer · encantar · emocionar

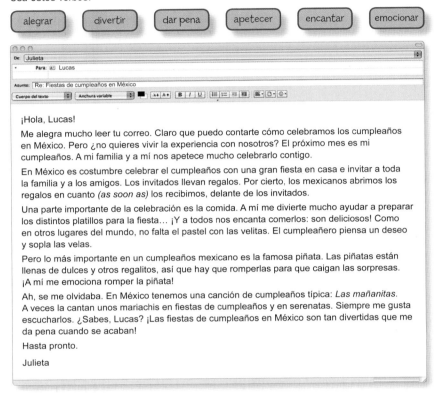

De: Julieta
Para: Lucas
Asunto: Re: Fiestas de cumpleaños en México

¡Hola, Lucas!

Me alegra mucho leer tu correo. Claro que puedo contarte cómo celebramos los cumpleaños en México. Pero ¿no quieres vivir la experiencia con nosotros? El próximo mes es mi cumpleaños. A mi familia y a mí nos apetece mucho celebrarlo contigo.

En México es costumbre celebrar el cumpleaños con una gran fiesta en casa e invitar a toda la familia y a los amigos. Los invitados llevan regalos. Por cierto, los mexicanos abrimos los regalos en cuanto *(as soon as)* los recibimos, delante de los invitados.

Una parte importante de la celebración es la comida. A mí me divierte mucho ayudar a preparar los distintos platillos para la fiesta… ¡Y a todos nos encanta comerlos: son deliciosos! Como en otros lugares del mundo, no falta el pastel con las velitas. El cumpleañero piensa un deseo y sopla las velas.

Pero lo más importante en un cumpleaños mexicano es la famosa piñata. Las piñatas están llenas de dulces y otros regalitos, así que hay que romperlas para que caigan las sorpresas. ¡A mí me emociona romper la piñata!

Ah, se me olvidaba. En México tenemos una canción de cumpleaños típica: *Las mañanitas*. A veces la cantan unos mariachis en fiestas de cumpleaños y en serenatas. Siempre me gusta escucharlos. ¿Sabes, Lucas? ¡Las fiestas de cumpleaños en México son tan divertidas que me da pena cuando se acaban!

Hasta pronto.

Julieta

▶ **Habla** con tu compañero(a). Utilicen estas preguntas como guía.

1. ¿Cómo celebras tu cumpleaños?
2. ¿Qué semejanzas y qué diferencias hay entre la celebración típica de México y la tuya?
3. ¿Conoces costumbres de cumpleaños propias de otros países?

▶ **Compartan** sus comentarios con la clase. Hagan entre todos una tabla comparando las costumbres para celebrar el cumpleaños en los distintos países.

28 veintiocho

Differentiated Instruction

DEVELOPING LEARNERS

- Ask students to imagine they have a close friend who is the exact opposite of them in personality traits, physical characteristics, and even in interests, likes, and dislikes. First, have students write a description of themselves, including their physical and emotional characteristics, traits, likes, and dislikes. Then, have them write a profile of this "opposite" friend. Encourage students to be creative; they do not need to portray themselves accurately but they do need to reflect their friend's opposite characteristics in their descriptions.

- Call on some volunteers to read their descriptions aloud.

EXPANDING LEARNERS

- After students read Julieta's e-mail, ask them to write a response either accepting or declining her kind invitation. If students are declining, they should include the reason, but they also need to extend their good wishes to Julieta and ask her some relevant questions about the celebration. If they are accepting, they need to pose some questions as to the logistics of Julieta's party: the date, time, place, and where they can stay for a few days.

- Call on volunteers to read their e-mails to the rest of the class.

28 **Titulares de prensa**

▶ **Escucha** y completa estos titulares con un nombre y un adjetivo.

> Detenido un « __1__ » al intentar robar un banco

> __2__ de México a través del arte

> Descubren en los Estados Unidos un __3__ con quince cuernos

> El jugador del F. C. Barcelona fue la __4__ contra Uruguay

▶ **Escribe** cuatro sentimientos que te provoquen estas noticias.

Final del desafío

Lucas: Asha, encontré mucha información y algunos videos para hacer una piñata. Además, le pregunté a mi amiga mexicana. Ella es muy __1__ y me regaló esta vasija de barro.

Asha: Yo traje lo que me pediste: papel de periódico, papel de colores y pegamento.

Lucas: Estupendo... Yo compré un montón de dulces y regalitos para poner dentro de la piñata. No creas que soy nada __2__.

Asha: ¡Noooo, cómo voy a pensar eso...! Si tú eres siempre el primero en comprar y en invitar...

Lucas: ¡No me tomes el pelo!

Asha: ¿Y qué tal *Las mañanitas*? ¿Ensayamos la canción? Que no te dé vergüenza, Lucas. ¡Tienes que ser menos __3__ y más __4__!

Lucas: Gracias, Asha, pero es que... ¡canto tan mal!

Asha: No seas __5__, Lucas, no insistas más.

29 **Desafíos muy artísticos**

▶ **Completa** el texto del final del desafío. Usa estos adjetivos.

> terco   valiente   generosa   indeciso   egoísta

▶ **Habla** con tu compañero. ¿Crees que Asha y Lucas lograron su desafío? ¿Por qué?

---

28. Invite students to share their reactions to the headlines with the class. Encourage them to elaborate on their answers. For example: *El «hombre invisible» me da mucha risa. Me asombra que alguien sea tan tonto.*

29. Call on volunteers to role-play Asha and Lucas's dialogue in front of the class. Then, as a conclusion to the dialogue, ask the class to join in singing *Las mañanitas*. You may wish to play the music for the song (you'll find it online) to help students stay on key and sound their best.

 AUDIO SCRIPT
See page 11L.

Answer Key

27. Answers will vary. Sample answers:
1. Le alegra mucho leer el correo de Lucas.
2. Le divierte preparar los platillos de la fiesta.
3. Le da pena cuando se acaban las fiestas.
4. A Julieta y a su familia les apetece celebrar el cumpleaños con Lucas.
5. A todos les encanta comer los platillos.
6. Le emociona romper la piñata.
▶ Answers will vary.
▶ Answers will vary.

28. 1. hombre invisible
2. Nueva imagen
3. dinosaurio gigante
4. gran figura
▶ Answers will vary.

29. 1. generosa
2. egoísta
3. indeciso
4. valiente
5. terco
▶ Answers will vary.

Additional Resources

Fans Online activities
Practice Workbook

HERITAGE LANGUAGE LEARNERS

- Ask students to search the Internet for a newspaper from a Spanish-speaking country, or find a local Spanish-language paper and look for colorful headlines that make good use of the placement of adjectives. Have students choose two of these headlines, read them to the class, and give an oral or written synopsis of the accompanying news story. Students should also be prepared to explain the placement of the adjectives.

SPECIAL-NEEDS LEARNERS

- Give a copy of the audio script for activity 28 to students with auditory impairments, and do this for all other activities of this type. Have students listen to the audio as many times as needed, while following along on the printed page. Make sure that these students are seated in a quiet area of the classroom, away from distractors such as windows or doors.

Unit 1

DESAFÍO 2

Expresar acciones habituales

Presentation

- In *Desafío 2*, Ethan and Eva have to create a poster and a slogan to promote a *chasqui* race. Students will preview vocabulary about the postal service.

Activities	Standards	Resources
Texto	1.2, 2.1, 2.2	
30.	1.2	
31.	1.2, 2.1, 2.2	Audio
32.	1.1, 1.2, 2.1, 3.2	
33. Cultura	1.1, 1.2, 2.1, 2.2, 3.1	

Teaching Suggestions

Warm-Up / Independent Starter

- Ask students to list three examples of postal service use. Then have them answer this question in writing: *¿Por qué se sigue usando el correo postal?*

Preparation

- Invite students to share their Independent Starters. What do they think about the future of the postal service? As a class, discuss other forms of communication. Which ones do students use the most? Why? Encourage students to think of ways in which modes of communication have changed with the passing of time.

Texto: Los nuevos chasquis

- Read the title and the introduction to the dialogue. Then ask students to speculate on what or who the *chasquis* might be.
- Have students read the dialogue silently. Then discuss the passages that shed light on the identity of the *chasquis*. What do students think about the possible existence of *chasquis* in Peru today?

Activities

31. Before playing the recording, have students read the statements and, based on their previous knowledge and the dialogue on page 30, note the ones they think are false.

32. Ask additional questions: *¿Qué hacían los chasquis del imperio inca? ¿Qué es un tambo? ¿A qué velocidad por hora iban los corredores?* Then have students revisit their opinions about the existence of *chasquis*. Were they correct?

30

Los nuevos chasquis

Ethan y Eva tienen que preparar un cartel y un eslogan para promocionar una carrera de chasquis. Pero antes deben averiguar qué es un chasqui...

CARTERO: Buenas tardes. Traigo una carta certificada para Eva Bishop. ¿Es usted?

EVA: Sí, soy yo. Muchas gracias. Mira, Ethan. El cartero me trajo una carta, pero no está escrito el nombre del remitente. Solo sé que viene de Lima. ¿Tú conoces a alguien allí?

ETHAN: No, qué va.

EVA: Fíjate, la estampilla es muy rara. Tiene una especie de cuerda con nudos.

ETHAN: A lo mejor es una pista para el desafío. Venga, abre el sobre, a ver qué dice la carta.

EVA: Tenías razón. Aquí dice que la estampilla muestra un quipu, que es un objeto que usaban los incas para contar y también como forma de escritura. Pero no sé qué tiene que ver eso con nuestro desafío. Por cierto, ¿averiguaste lo que son los chasquis?

ETHAN: Sí. Eran los mensajeros del imperio inca. Transmitían noticias y mensajes de un lugar a otro.

EVA: O sea, que eran como los carteros de hoy en día.

ETHAN: Sí. Tal vez los chasquis llevaban quipus para contar las historias.

EVA: Tiene sentido. Pero todo esto es muy raro. Tenemos que hacer el cartel de una carrera de chasquis. ¿Tú crees que todavía existen?

ETHAN: No creo...

30 Detective de palabras

▶ **Busca** en el diálogo las palabras que corresponden a estas imágenes.

30 treinta

Differentiated Instruction

DEVELOPING LEARNERS

- To reinforce students' comprehension of the dialogue, have them work with a partner and practice reading it aloud (the student playing Ethan may also read the line for *el cartero*). Monitor their pronunciation and intonation as they read. Encourage students to add a few additional lines of dialogue to the original; for example, students might elaborate their ideas on the current role of *los chasquis*. Allow students time to rehearse and then have them present the dialogue to the rest of the class.

EXPANDING LEARNERS

- Ask students to research the Pony Express, one of the early cross-country mail services in the United States. Have them prepare a written report including information about the routes, riders, horses, perils, distances covered, and time taken, as well as the purpose of the messages. Then, ask students to compare this system with that of the *chasquis*. After students complete their research, you might ask them to calculate the time it would take a Pony Express rider to cover the same 25 kilometers covered in the *chasqui* race in Huancayo, Peru.

31 Un sistema muy bien organizado

 ▶ **Escucha** a Eva y a Ethan, y decide si estas afirmaciones son ciertas o falsas. Después, corrige las afirmaciones falsas.

1. Eva piensa que los chasquis existen todavía.
2. El quipu era un libro donde los chasquis anotaban sus mensajes.
3. Los colores y los nudos del quipu tenían diferentes significados.
4. Los incas fueron la única civilización antigua que utilizaba mensajeros.
5. Los tambos eran lugares para el relevo (*changing*) de los chasquis.

32 Los chasquis hoy

 ▶ **Lee** la noticia y escribe la respuesta a estas preguntas.

Sábado, 23 de junio de 2012

En Huancayo reviven carrera de ancestrales chasquis

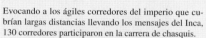

Evocando a los ágiles corredores del imperio que cubrían largas distancias llevando los mensajes del Inca, 130 corredores participaron en la carrera de chasquis.

La competencia comenzó en el puente centenario que une los distritos de Huancayo y El Tambo, donde históricamente existía un lugar de aprovisionamiento y descanso para los corredores.

Los competidores cubrieron una distancia de 25 kilómetros entre avenidas y caminos rurales en 1 h 15 min, con relevos cada 2 kilómetros aproximadamente. El ganador fue el equipo de chasquis «Los amigos de Huancayo».

Fuente: http://www.rpp.com.pe (texto adaptado)

1. ¿De qué competencia habla la noticia? ¿Dónde se celebró y cuántos participantes hubo?
2. ¿Cuántos kilómetros recorrieron los participantes? ¿Cuánto tiempo tardaron?
3. ¿Existen chasquis hoy en día?

 **CULTURA**

Los chasquis (Perú)

Los chasquis eran mensajeros al servicio del soberano del imperio inca. Su misión era llevar los mensajes reales desde rincones distantes del imperio hasta su capital, Cuzco, recorriendo grandes distancias en un breve período de tiempo.

Los chasquis registraban la información en un *quipu*, formado por una serie de cuerdas de distintos colores y con nudos que indicaban cantidades. También llevaban un *pututu*, que era una trompeta hecha con una caracola (*conch*), y un textil o *qëpi* a la espalda.

33 Investiga. ¿Para qué necesitaban los chasquis el *pututu* y el *qëpi*?

HERITAGE LANGUAGE LEARNERS

• Explain that it was a great honor to be chosen as a *chasqui*, and boys were selected for their athletic physique, healthy lungs, and the ability to run fast. Training started from childhood and was very demanding: running up and down hills to help build stamina, increase speed, and gain strength. Ask students to imagine that they are living in the Inca empire and dream of being chosen to be a *chasqui*. Ask them to write a few entries in their journals that reflect their desire to be chosen, their ambition to complete their training, and their thoughts on the actual job.

CRITICAL THINKING

• Have students think about a current news event and how its developments are being made known to the public. Then have students discuss how a similar event would have been made known to the public in the past. Do students think the delivery of news via *chasquis* was the most effective way to communicate hundreds of years ago? Why? Have them think of other methods that would have been equally or more effective. What do students think of our 24/7 news coverage today? Do they think that society has become a bit obsessed with such constant coverage?

Expresar acciones habituales

 AUDIO SCRIPT
See page 11L.

 CULTURA

Los chasquis (Perú)

The Incas established posts at even intervals along a complex road system. A *chasqui*, or running courier, would run the distance separating each post station at full speed, and then pass the message onto another runner. This rapid relay system allowed for a message to be taken as far as 250 miles in a single day. *Chasquis* were chosen based on their physique and running abilities, and they were trained from boyhood.

Answer Key

30. 1. sobre   3. remitente
2. estampilla   4. cartero

31. 1. C.
2. F. Era un conjunto de cuerdas de varios colores con nudos que servía para transmitir mensajes.
3. C.
4. F. Los aztecas, los griegos y los romanos también utilizaban mensajeros.
5. C.

32. 1. De una carrera de chasquis. Se celebró en Huancayo y hubo 130 corredores.
2. Recorrieron 25 km en 1h 15 min.
3. No.

33. Answers will vary. Sample answer:
El *pututu* era para anunciar su llegada y el *qëpi* era una especie de mochila para llevar paquetes.

Additional Resources

Fans Online activities

DESAFÍO 2

Vocabulario – La oficina de correos

Presentation

- In this section, students will learn vocabulary related to the postal service.

Activities	Standards	Resources
Vocabulario	1.2	
34.	1.3	
35.	1.1, 1.2, 5.1	
36. Conexiones	1.1, 1.2, 2.2, 3.1, 3.2, 5,2	

Teaching Suggestions

Warm-Up / Independent Starter

- Have students specify how they send each of these items: *un paquete, una carta, una invitación, una tarjeta* (e.g., *un paquete → por correo*).

Preparation

- Have students share their Independent Starters in small groups. Do they have similar responses? Then ask students to read the words in the *Más vocabulario* feature and the highlighted words in the dialogue silently. Have students point out the cognates, as well as any false cognates (e.g., *carta* = letter; *tarjeta* = card) they find.
- Call on two students to read Eva and Ethan's dialogue. Ask questions to verify comprehension: *¿Por qué está Ethan en la oficina de correos? ¿Cómo va a enviar el paquete? ¿Es caro el envío?* Then ask students to guess the cost of sending Ethan's package from their location to Buenos Aires, Argentina, assuming the package weighs two pounds. Then have students look up this information on the U.S. Postal Service website (www.usps.com). Did anyone guess correctly? Is it expensive?

Activities

35. Ask students to think of different reasons to send someone a card. Then list these card classifications: *amor y amistad, buenos deseos, días festivos, felicitación, gracias, invitación, perdón, saludos.* Ask students to think of one or two examples for each type of card (e.g., *En los cumpleaños enviamos tarjetas de felicitación*).

Vocabulario

La oficina de correos

EVA: ¿A quién vas a enviar ese paquete, Ethan?
ETHAN: A un amigo que vive en Argentina. Este jueves es su cumpleaños y le voy a mandar un regalo. Me gustaría que el cartero se lo entregara el mismo día de su cumpleaños.
EVA: Seguro que se alegrará mucho. A mí me emociona recibir cartas y paquetes. ¿Se lo vas a mandar por correo aéreo?
ETHAN: Sí, por correo aéreo certificado y urgente, para asegurarme de que llega a tiempo.
EVA: Pero el envío será muy caro, ¿no?
ETHAN: No creo, el paquete no es muy pesado ni frágil.
EVA: Claro, tienes razón. ¿Y sabes cuánto tiempo tardará en llegar?
ETHAN: Se lo preguntaré al empleado de correos.

La carta

la estampilla
el destinatario
el remitente
la dirección
el sobre
el código postal

Más vocabulario

El correo

la balanza	scale
el buzón	mailbox
la correspondencia	mail
la tarjeta postal	postcard
la tarjeta de felicitación	greeting card
la tarjeta navideña	Christmas card
el franqueo	postage

¡Atención!

la firma	signature
firmar	to sign

34 **Servicio postal**

▶ **Escribe** los verbos correspondientes a estas acciones. Después, escribe un pie de foto para cada fotografía.

Differentiated Instruction

DEVELOPING LEARNERS

- Ask students to work with a partner and prepare a short dialogue or story to accompany one of the photographs on the page. As a starting point, students may use some of the words highlighted in the dialogue as well as those listed in the *Más vocabulario* feature and the photograph, but should include other vocabulary related to the topic. Encourage creativity and, if there is time, ask student pairs to present their work to the class.

EXPANDING LEARNERS

- Explain that today many people choose to send greeting cards and invitations by e-mail rather than through the regular mail service. Tell students that some of them will participate in a group debate to defend one of these delivery systems. Assign to each student the delivery system they must defend. Give each one in the group two minutes to present his or her arguments, then allow the opposing side the same time. Allow one minute for rebuttal. Those students who are not participating in the debate will vote on the most effective presentation.

35 Mi relación con el correo postal

▶ **Completa** los bocadillos con las palabras del cuadro.

buzones	cartas personales	cartero	correspondencia	envíos
franqueo	tarjeta de felicitación	paquetes	tarjetas navideñas	correo

Me llamo Mario Hernández y soy ___1___. Mi profesión ha cambiado mucho en los últimos años, ya que el número de ___2___ postales ha descendido notablemente. Cada día reparto la ___3___, pero los ___4___ no se llenan nunca, ni siquiera (*even*) en diciembre con las ___5___.

Me llamo Lucía y me encanta el correo postal. Aunque utilizo mucho el ___6___ electrónico, no he dejado de escribir ___7___ a mis amigos y siempre les mando una ___8___ por su cumpleaños. También envío ___9___ a mi familia de Argentina. A veces son muy pesados y el ___10___ es alto, ¡pero la alegría es mayor!

▶ **Habla** con tu compañero(a). Por turnos, hagan preguntas y respondan sobre el uso que hacen ustedes y sus familias del correo postal.

CONEXIONES: LITERATURA

Juan Rulfo

El escritor mexicano Juan Rulfo (1917-1986) está considerado uno de los autores más influyentes del siglo XX por su novela *Pedro Páramo*. Poco después de su muerte, su esposa, Clara Aparicio, decidió publicar las cartas que él le escribió los primeros años de su noviazgo. Son poemas y cartas de amor en las que él le describía su vida, su trabajo y su pasión por la fotografía, y que nos permiten conocer más aspectos de la vida de este gran autor.

*D*esde que te conozco, hay un eco en cada rama que repite tu nombre; en las ramas altas, lejanas; en las ramas que están junto a nosotros, se oye. Se oye como si despertáramos de un sueño en el alba. Se respira en las hojas, se mueve como se mueven las gotas del agua. Clara: corazón, rosa, amor...

Juan Rulfo. *Cartas a Clara.*
Editorial RM.

36 Explica.
Lee este fragmento de una de las cartas de Juan Rulfo a Clara Aparicio. ¿Qué te parece? ¿Alguna vez has escrito una carta de amor? ¿Crees que las cartas de amor van a desaparecer?

---

36. Have students share their answers to the last question (*¿Crees que las cartas de amor van a desaparecer?*) with the class. Ask them to write their names on sticky notes. Then create a bar graph on the board using the students' sticky notes. Which opinion is more prevalent among students? Invite students from each side of the argument to justify their opinions.

CONEXIONES: LITERATURA

Juan Rulfo

Juan Rulfo's literary production consists of two slim books, *El llano en llamas* (1953) and *Pedro Páramo* (1955). However, their impact on Latin American fiction has been enormous. The "magic realism" of Gabriel García Márquez and Carlos Fuentes, among others, owes much to Rulfo's work. His stories depict the harsh realities of life in rural Mexico; his language is sparse and his characters show little emotion. At the same time, there are usually surrealist elements in Rulfo's narrative.

Answer Key

34. 1. pesar
2. enviar / mandar
3. entregar

35.
1. cartero	6. correo
2. envíos	7. cartas personales
3. correspondencia	8. tarjeta de felicitación
4. buzones	9. paquetes
5. tarjetas navideñas	10. franqueo

▶ Answers will vary.

36. Answers will vary.

Additional Resources

Fans Online activities
Practice Workbook

HERITAGE LANGUAGE LEARNERS

- Ask students to work with a partner and write a love letter and a suitable response to it. Both students will select two fictional characters from literature, movies, TV, or comics. One student will write the love letter from one of these characters to the other. The contents may be serious or humorous, but should be an attempt at romanticism. The other student (i.e., the recipient) will write a suitable response, either accepting or rejecting the would-be suitor. Ask students to read their letters aloud.

MULTIPLE INTELLIGENCES:
Visual-Spatial Intelligence

- Have students work in small groups and design and write the message for a greeting card. They may select from a variety of topics: birthday, congratulations, Valentine's Day and other holidays, thank you, get well, missing you, or cards that express friendship. Allow them to draw their designs or use a suitable computer graphics program. The message may be sentimental or humorous, but should be appropriate to the occasion. Display students' cards in the classroom.

DESAFÍO 2

Gramática – Los verbos pronominales

Presentation

- In this section, students will review verbs that can be used pronominally or not pronominally. They will also learn some verbs that are always pronominal.

Activities	Standards	Resources
Gramática	1.2, 3.1	
37.	1.2, 3.1, 4.1	
38.	1.2	
39.	1.2, 1.3	Audio
40.	1.3	
41.	1.1, 1.3	

Teaching Suggestions

Warm-Up / Independent Starter

- Ask students to determine the meaning of each underlined verb.
  1. a. *Anoche dormí bien.*
     b. *Anoche me dormí tarde.*
  2. a. *Aprendí a leer a los seis años.*
     b. *Nunca me aprendí la tabla periódica.*

Preparation

- Have students read the grammar presentation silently, take notes on any material they do not understand, and review the conjugation of pronominal verbs. For the verbs that are always pronominal in Spanish, clarify that their usage is idiomatic. These verbs should not be confused with reflexive verbs.

- Ask students to share their Independent Starters with a partner. As a class, discuss the meaning differences between the verbs. If students are having difficulties, ask them to contrast these sentences: I saw Peter yesterday. I saw myself as a famous actor. Students should note that the use of the reflexive pronoun changes the meaning of the verb slightly in the second example.

Activities

38. Once students have finished, ask them to write a sentence for each verb that they didn't use (i.e., *quedarse, parecer, dormir*). Then, call on three students to share their sentences.

34

Gramática

Los verbos pronominales

Los verbos pronominales (yo me...)

- Los verbos que se conjugan con un **pronombre reflexivo** (me, te, se, nos, os, se) que se refiere al sujeto se llaman verbos pronominales. Estos verbos tienen la forma yo me..., tú te..., él se...

  Me despierto a las 7:00 a. m.　　　Los amigos **se saludaron** con un beso.

- Los verbos pronominales tienen el pronombre se en el infinitivo (despertarse, saludarse) y se pueden conjugar en cualquier tiempo verbal.

PRESENTE	Siempre **me levanto** de buen humor.
PRETÉRITO	Mi amigo Carlos y yo **nos conocimos** en la escuela.
IMPERFECTO	De pequeña **me llevaba** muy mal con mi hermana mayor.
FUTURO	Tú y yo no **nos pelearemos** nunca.

Verbos con cambio de significado

- Algunos verbos se conjugan siempre con un pronombre reflexivo.

  ¿**Te atreves** a viajar a países lejanos?

- Otros verbos se pueden conjugar con pronombres reflexivos o sin ellos, pero el significado cambia.

VERBOS CON PRONOMBRE REFLEXIVO

arrepentirse	to regret
atreverse	to dare
enterarse	to find out
esforzarse	to make an effort
fugarse	to run away
quejarse	to complain

VERBOS CON CAMBIO DE SIGNIFICADO

acabar	to finish	acabarse	to end, to run out	parecer	to seem	parecerse	to look like
acordar	to agree	acordarse	to remember	poner	to put	ponerse	to put on
aprender	to learn	aprenderse	to memorize	quedar	to arrange to meet	quedarse	to stay
dormir	to sleep	dormirse	to fall asleep	romper	to break something	romperse	to get broken
estudiar	to study	estudiarse	to learn	salir	to leave, to go out	salirse	to go beyond the limits
ir	to go	irse	to leave, to go away				
levantar	to lift	levantarse	to get up	volver	to come back	volverse	to turn

37 **Piensa.** ¿Existe en inglés una forma de expresar la diferencia entre Luis **rompió** un vaso y Luis **se rompió** un dedo?

38 **Con pronombre**

▶ **Completa** las oraciones con el verbo correcto en la forma adecuada.

1. ¿Vamos de compras esta tarde? Si quieren, _____ a las cinco.
   quedar/quedarse

2. Sandra _____ mucho a su hermana mayor.
   parecer/parecerse

3. No vi toda la película; estaba tan cansada que _____ en el cine.
   dormir/dormirse

Differentiated Instruction

DEVELOPING LEARNERS

- To give students more practice, have them translate the following sentences:
  1. Juan looks a lot like his grandfather. (*Juan se parece mucho a su abuelo.*)
  2. Isabel fell asleep watching TV. (*Isabel se durmió viendo la tele.*)
  3. When did you find out? (*¿Cuándo te enteraste?*)
  4. Where did they put the keys? (*¿Dónde pusieron las llaves?*)
  5. I ran out of milk. (*Se me acabó la leche.*)
  6. I get along with all my neighbors. (*Me llevo bien con todos mis vecinos.*)

EXPANDING LEARNERS

- Explain that se can add a shade of meaning to certain verbs. Have students explain the differences between the following pairs of verbs and to write a sentence with each one.

  aguantar / aguantarse (to tolerate / to put up with something)

  creer / creerse (to believe / to have an unfounded belief)

  imaginar / imaginarse (to conceive of / to suppose, guess)

  pasar / pasarse (to pass by / to overdo it)

  probar / probarse (to try / to try on [clothes])

  saltar / saltarse (to jump / to skip, bypass)

DESAFÍO 2

Gramática – Los verbos pronominales

---

 39 **¿Qué hacen?**

 ▶ **Escucha** los diálogos y une las tres columnas. Después, escribe oraciones completas.

(A)	(B)	(C)
1. Raquel va a...	acabar	ayer.
2. Raquel no...	acabarse	de comprar sal.
3. Raquel tiene que...	acordar	de que está sosa.
4. Los vecinos...	acordarse	en la fiesta hasta muy tarde.
5. Nadie...	levantar	la mano para reunirse a las seis.
6. La última reunión de vecinos...	levantarse	muy tarde.
7. Luisa prueba la sopa y...	ponerse	reunirse a las ocho.
8. La sal...	quedarse	temprano al día siguiente.
9. César no...	quejarse	un vestido azul para la fiesta.

40 **¡Vaya día!**

▶ **Escribe** una oración para explicar cada imagen. ¿Qué le pasó a Silvia ayer?

41 **Para conocernos mejor**

▶ **Escribe** diez preguntas para saber más cosas sobre tu compañero(a). Usa verbos de la ficha de Gramática.

Modelo   *¿Te acuerdas del cumpleaños de todos tus amigos?*

▶ **Habla** con tu compañero(a). Túrnense para hacerse las preguntas y responder.

---

39. Before playing the recording, have students look at the verbs in column B. Then ask them to read the statements in columns A and C. Explain that reading the questions helps them predict the answers and tells them what information to focus on when listening.

40. To expand this activity, have students use their six sentences, plus two of their own creation, to compose a narrative about Silvia's eventful day. Remind students to use transition words (e.g., *para empezar, luego, después, por último*). Then have students share their stories with the class.

AUDIO SCRIPT
See page 11L.

Answer Key

37. En inglés se usa el mismo verbo en ambos casos: *Luis broke a glass. Luis broke a finger*. Pero se puede usar un posesivo en el segundo caso para aclarar el significado: *Luis broke <u>his</u> finger*.

38. 1. quedamos   3. me dormí
2. se parece

39. 1. Raquel va a ponerse un vestido azul.
2. Raquel no se quedará en la fiesta hasta muy tarde.
3. Raquel tiene que levantarse temprano.
4. Los vecinos acordaron reunirse a las ocho.
5. Nadie levantó la mano.
6. La última reunión de vecinos acabó tarde.
7. Luisa prueba la sopa y se queja de que está sosa.
8. La sal se acabó ayer.
9. César no se acordó de comprar sal.

40. Answers will vary.

41. Answers will vary.
▶ Answers will vary.

Additional Resources

Fans Online activities
Practice Workbook

HERITAGE LANGUAGE LEARNERS

• Ask students to work with a partner and, based on their collective knowledge plus researching grammar texts and dictionaries, have them compose a master list of verbs that can be used with both pronominal and non-pronominal forms. Students should include the shades of meaning expressed by the two forms of all the verbs listed and write a sample sentence for each one. Display their work in the classroom and encourage other students to study the verbs listed.

MULTIPLE INTELLIGENCES:
Verbal-Linguistic Intelligence

• Divide the class into teams and have them play against each other. Write a pronominal verb on each of several index cards and place them face down in a pile. Team members will take turns picking up a card and using the verb in a sentence. If the sentence is correct, students keep the card; if not, they must return it to the bottom of the pile. The winning team is the one with the most cards after you call time.

DESAFÍO 2

Gramática – Los verbos reflexivos y recíprocos

Presentation

- In this section, students will review and practice reflexive and reciprocal verbs.

Activities	Standards	Resources
Gramática	1.2, 3.1	
42.	1.3, 3.1, 4.1	
43.	1.3	
44.	1.2, 1.3, 2.1, 5.1	
45. Cultura	1.1, 1.2, 2.1, 4.2	

Teaching Suggestions

Warm-Up / Independent Starter

- Ask students to complete these sentences with the correct form of the verb in parentheses:

  1. *Ana nunca (maquillarse). (se maquilla)*
  2. *Los amigos (saludarse) con un beso. (se saludan)*
  3. *Ella (ducharse) antes de acostarse. (se ducha)*
  4. *Mis amigos y yo (ayudarse). (nos ayudamos)*

Preparation

- Call on volunteers to read aloud one bulleted item each in the *Gramática* feature. Clarify that when the subject is plural and the part of the body is singular, we use a singular noun (e.g., *Nosotros nos lavamos la cara*). However, if the part of the body is plural, a plural noun is used (e.g., *Nosotros nos lavamos las manos*).

- Have students share their Independent Starters. Ask them to circle the reflexive verbs and underline the reciprocal ones. How do they know which is which?

Activities

43. Have students think of reciprocal uses for the reflexive verbs. For instance, *Los bebés se despiertan* could be both reflexive and reciprocal. For a reciprocal meaning, we would add a clarification: *Los bebés se despiertan el uno al otro*.

44. Have students exchange their letters with a classmate. Then have partners write a reply as if they were one of the Wise Men. Students should make up all sorts of excuses for not granting the wishes.

Gramática

Los verbos reflexivos y recíprocos

Los verbos reflexivos

- Los verbos reflexivos son verbos pronominales que expresan una acción que se refleja en el sujeto.

  ¿A qué hora **te despertaste?**   **Vístete**, por favor.

- Muchos verbos reflexivos se refieren a hábitos y a la higiene personal.

  Me lavo el pelo dos veces por semana.

- El nombre que funciona como objeto directo de un verbo reflexivo puede ir en singular (uno) o en plural (varios). Y, a diferencia del inglés, cuando se refiere a partes del cuerpo o al vestido lleva delante un artículo, no un adjetivo posesivo.

  Me lavaré **el pelo** con champú.   Ella se puso **la camisa** al revés.
  Ellos se lavaron **la cara.**   Él se puso **los zapatos** nuevos.

VERBOS REFLEXIVOS
acostarse
bañarse
ducharse
lavarse
levantarse
maquillarse
vestirse

Los verbos recíprocos

- Los verbos recíprocos son verbos pronominales que expresan acciones recíprocas *(each other, one another).*

  Ana y Luis **se quieren** (uno al otro).

- Los verbos recíprocos se conjugan como los verbos reflexivos, pero siempre en plural (nosotros(as) nos…, vosotros(as) os…, ustedes se…, ellos(as) se…).

  Ellos **se conocieron** en una fiesta el año pasado.
  Antes mi novio y yo **nos llamábamos** todos los días.
  ¡Abrácense y perdónense!

VERBOS RECÍPROCOS	
abrazarse	hablarse
apoyarse	llamarse
ayudarse	mirarse
besarse	odiarse
conocerse	pelearse
contarse	perdonarse
despedirse	quererse
entenderse	saludarse
escribirse	verse

42 **Piensa.** Traduce al español estas oraciones.

a. *They always get up late.*

b. *My grandparents used to write each other letters.*

43 **¿Reflexivos o recíprocos?**

▶ **Decide** si estos verbos son reflexivos o recíprocos, y escribe una oración con cada uno.

1. ayudarse
2. despertarse
3. hablarse
4. saludarse
5. levantarse
6. escribirse
7. maquillarse
8. vestirse

Differentiated Instruction

DEVELOPING LEARNERS

- Ask students to imagine that they have a little brother who is always saying or doing the opposite of everyone else. Have students rewrite these sentences from the little brother's point of view.

  1. *Mis amigos y yo nos saludamos. (Mis amigos y yo nos despedimos.)*
  2. *Siempre nos peleamos. (Siempre nos perdonamos.)*
  3. *Nos entendemos. (No nos comprendemos.)*
  4. *Nos queremos. (Nos odiamos.)*
  5. *Me pongo los zapatos. (Me quito los zapatos.)*

EXPANDING LEARNERS

- Write or say the following verbs and ask students to explain the difference in their meanings. Then have students select five of these pairs and write a sentence with each one. Call on volunteers to read one of their sentence pairs aloud.

acostar / acostarse	negar / negarse
aburrir / aburrirse	perder / perderse
preocupar / preocuparse	cansar / cansarse
despedir / despedirse	sentir / sentirse
enamorar / enamorarse	tirar / tirarse
involucrar / involucrarse	

44 **Una carta muy particular**

▶ **Lee** la carta de Paula y complétala con los verbos del cuadro en presente.

ayudarse	levantarse	llevarse	hablarse
peinarse	pelearse	perdonarse	quererse

Queridos Reyes Magos de Oriente:

Este año me estoy portando muy bien. Todos los días ___1___ temprano para llegar a tiempo a la escuela. Mis hermanos y yo ___2___ bien y ___3___ mucho con las tareas. Aunque algunas veces ___4___... Ahora mi hermano Javi y mi hermano Leo están enfadados y no ___5___ porque Javi se puso un suéter de Leo sin pedirle permiso. ¡Siempre están igual! Pero seguro que pronto ___6___. Si pueden traerles algo de ropa, seguro que les gustará mucho y así no discutirán.

Mis padres ___7___ mucho, ¡y yo los quiero mucho también! Me gustaría que les trajeran un auto nuevo. Y para mí... Bueno, me gusta mucho un chico de otra clase, que ___8___ como Justin Bieber y es guapísimo. Me gustaría conocerlo. ¿Pueden ayudarme?

Muchas gracias y ¡hasta el año que viene!

Paula

▶ **Lee** de nuevo la carta y completa estas oraciones.

1. Todos los días Paula...
2. Paula y sus hermanos...
3. Javi y Leo...
4. Los padres de Paula...

▶ **Escribe** tu carta a los Reyes Magos. Usa verbos reflexivos y recíprocos.

CULTURA

La carta a los Reyes Magos

En España y en muchos países hispanos es tradición que los niños reciban regalos de los Reyes Magos la noche del 5 al 6 de enero. Para ello deben escribir una carta pidiéndoles lo que desean. La condición para recibirlos es haberse portado bien; si se portaron mal, solo recibirán carbón dulce.

Los niños pueden entregar sus cartas directamente a los Reyes Magos o echarlas a uno de los buzones especiales que se instalan en las oficinas de correos y en los centros comerciales. Desde hace unos años también es posible escribirles una carta virtual a través de Internet o de las redes sociales.

45 **Explica.** ¿Conoces tradiciones similares a las de los Reyes Magos? ¿Quién trae los regalos navideños en tu país?

DESAFÍO 2

Gramática – Los verbos reflexivos y recíprocos

CULTURA

La carta a los Reyes Magos

According to Christian tradition, Melchior (representing Europe), Caspar (representing Asia), and Balthazar (representing Africa), traveled to Bethlehem by horse, camel, and elephant to present baby Jesus with gifts. This gift-giving tradition continues in many Spanish-speaking countries on Three Kings Day. In Mexico City, families go to an area close to Alameda Park before January 6th. There, balloons are sold so children can attach their letters to them and have them fly up to the sky, carrying their petitions to *los Reyes Magos*.

Answer Key

42. a. Ellos(as) siempre se levantan tarde.
b. Mis abuelos se escribían cartas.

43.
1. recíproco	5. reflexivo
2. reflexivo	6. recíproco
3. recíproco	7. reflexivo
4. recíproco	8. reflexivo

44.
1. me levanto	5. se hablan
2. nos llevamos	6. se perdonan
3. nos ayudamos	7. se quieren
4. nos peleamos	8. se peina

▶ 1. ... se levanta temprano.
2. ... se llevan bien.
3. ... se pelean.
4. ... se quieren mucho.

▶ Answers will vary.

45. Answers will vary.

Additional Resources

Fans Online activities
Practice Workbook

HERITAGE LANGUAGE LEARNERS

• Have students work with a partner or in small groups and collectively write a story. After the first student writes the opening line, others will contribute in turn. Students have the freedom to choose the topic, plot, and verb tenses, but they must include pronominal verbs that are used reflexively or reciprocally. Set a time limit for students to complete this writing task and have them read the fruit of their creative efforts to the class.

CRITICAL THINKING

• Ask students to think about gift-giving during certain holidays or on other special occasions. Even though people enjoy receiving and giving gifts, do students think that our culture has become too focused on material gift-giving and has lost sight of what these holidays and special occasions mean? Do they think a gift of sharing time with a loved one is more valuable than a gift certificate? Lead a classroom discussion on this topic and encourage all students to contribute their thoughts.

LECTURA: TEXTO INFORMATIVO

Presentation

- In this section, students will read an article about a woman who writes love letters for a living. Students will also answer comprehension questions based on the reading as well as learn several idiomatic expressions.

Activities	Standards	Resources
Lectura: texto informativo	1.2, 1.3, 2.1, 3.2	
46.	1.1, 1.2, 2.1	
47.	1.1	
48.	1.1, 2.1, 5.1	

Teaching Suggestions

Warm-Up / Independent Starter

- Have students read the *Antes de leer* strategies silently and jot down the answers to the first two questions.

Preparation

- Call on volunteers to share their Independent Starters. Then have them get together with a classmate to work on the third question. Ask them to write the phrases in bold on a piece of paper and then read them aloud. Based on the information provided by these phrases, what is the reading about? Invite pairs to share their answers with the class.

- Ask students to read the first sentence in the third paragraph. Then have them look at the phrase *se decidió a entrar*. Explain that *decidió entrar* is also possible, but the meaning is slightly different. Have students analyze the use of the pronominal form (*decidirse*) and compare it with the non-pronominal form (*decidir*). (*decidirse* = to make up one's mind; *decidir* = to decide)

- Then have students read the text individually. Encourage them to use context clues to determine the meaning of unknown words. Then, to further expand the comprehension of the text, have students work in groups to summarize each of the paragraphs with their own words. Be sure groups are heterogeneous, containing both males and females and students of different ability levels.

Antes de leer: estrategias

1. Lee el titular *(headline)* del reportaje. ¿Qué otros oficios y profesiones te parecen románticos?
2. Lee la entradilla *(lead)*. ¿Qué detalles te gustaría conocer de esta historia?
3. Lee las partes del texto destacadas en negrita *(bold)*. Resume con tus palabras la información que has obtenido.

El oficio más romántico: escribir cartas de amor por encargo

Una mujer cubana lleva 15 años escribiendo cartas románticas a clientes de 20 países distintos

A mano, con sentimiento y buena letra, como en los mejores romances clásicos, **una periodista cubana** escribe cartas de enamorados. Lleva 15 años haciéndolo, y es que posee uno de los trabajos más románticos que se pueden tener: **redacta cartas de amor por encargo**, convencida de que en la era informática «la gente aún no ha perdido la fe» en ellas, según cuenta a la prensa de su país.

Se llama **Liudmila Quincose**, tiene 34 años y es poetisa. Le encanta escribir y utiliza su talento para ayudar a los demás. «**Una carta de amor es una necesidad para cualquier persona. Cuando las escribo, siempre pienso en quien la va a recibir, en la emoción o el alivio**[1] **que va a sentir**», asegura. Defensora del amor, un día de junio de 1994 decidió colgar un singular cartel a las puertas de su casa, en Sancti Spíritus (Cuba): «Escribanía[2] Dollz. Se escriben cartas de amor a cualquier hora. Cartas de negocios y cartas de suicidas de 8:30 a. m.

a 3:00 p. m.» Un primer cartel un tanto serio, pero que le ha valido el reconocimiento y la fama de ser **la mejor «Cupido» del país**.

Aquella vez tuvo que esperar un mes hasta que alguien se decidió a entrar en la escribanía. Su primer cliente fue un hombre, bastante desesperado, que creía perder a su esposa. «Eran cerca de las 10 de la noche; entró, se acomodó en un sillón y me contó casi toda su vida. Aquello me sorprendió. **Él esperaba que yo hiciera un milagro**». Afortunadamente, la carta hizo su mágico efecto, todo salió bien, consiguió reconciliarse con su mujer y recuperó la tranquilidad.

Una idea que en un principio le pareció graciosa, pero que pronto se convirtió en un negocio y, lo más importante, en una vía[3] para dar rienda suelta[4] a la «**mucha necesidad de comunicación**» que Liudmila encuentra en la sociedad. Desde aquella primera historia, cientos de personas han pasado ya a visitar

Una mujer cubana posee uno de los trabajos más románticos: escribe cartas de amor por encargo.

a Liudmila. Tiene **fama en toda Cuba** porque sus cartas siempre resultan eficaces. Su secreto está en su gran sensibilidad[5], en poner todas sus energías en cada una de las historias de amor y, por supuesto, en su gran dominio de la escritura.

Las cartas «más fáciles son las que se regalan para decirle a otra persona cuánto se le quiere», y

Differentiated Instruction

DEVELOPING LEARNERS

- To strengthen students' working vocabulary, ask them to complete this chart with words related to those found in the article.

Verbo	Nombre
redactar	(la redacción)
(encargar)	el encargo
(aliviar)	el alivio
(reconocer)	el reconocimiento
reconciliarse	(la reconciliación)
(tranquilizar)	la tranquilidad
(dominar)	el dominio
evolucionar	(la evolución)

EXPANDING LEARNERS

- Ask students to work with a partner and, using the information from the text as well as other data researched on Internet, have them prepare an interview with Liudmila Quincose. One student will be the interviewer, and the other the letter writer. Although the facts presented in the interview must be accurate, students are free to contribute their own opinions and anecdotal stories of Liudmila's clients. Give students some time to rehearse their interviews and have them present these in front of the class.

«las más difíciles son cuando las parejas están peleadas», explica Liudmila, que perdió la cuenta de «cuántas» ha redactado en estos 15 años y no asume el raro oficio como «un medio[6] de vida», asegura.

«Cada vez que una persona viene, yo siento una felicidad muy grande. No es un medio de vida porque de esto yo no vivo; si tienen cinco pesos, me los pagan, pero por ejemplo, las que yo respondo, que son más que las que vendo, son totalmente gratis», explica la mujer, cuya escribanía atiende pedidos de unos 20 países.

Preguntada por el éxito de sus amorosas cartas, Liudmila es humilde: **«El amor todo lo perdona, lo salva, no pone peros[7].»**

¿Podríamos decir que es una escribana[8] en pleno siglo XXI? «De los viejos escribanos envidio el trazo[9] de sus letras, los dibujos de sus firmas. Sus cartas eran bellas, yo solo escribo en un papel especial», cuenta.

Eso sí, Liudmila agradece que el hecho de hacer cartas de amor por encargo le ha aguzado[10] los sentidos. Se ha ido adentrando[11] en un mundo creativo cada vez más rico, que le

permite evolucionar como escritora y también ayudar a sus clientes. Liudmila necesita inspiración, pero, como ha contado a la prensa cubana, le gusta ver las caras a las personas. **Tal y como ellos hablan, ella escribe**. «No puedes hacer una carta muy elevada[12] para alguien medio. Hay gente muy práctica y no debes redactarle un mensaje muy poético, porque se da cuenta el que la recibe.» Una mujer convertida en mensajera del amor, probablemente el oficio más dulce del mundo.

Fuente: http://www.hola.com
(selección)

---

1. consuelo
2. *writing desk*
3. manera, modo
4. *to give free rein*
5. delicadeza
6. manera, modo
7. *find fault*
8. *scribe*
9. dibujo
10. *sharpened*
11. metiendo
12. formal, erudita

---

46 ¿Comprendes?

▶ **Responde** a estas preguntas.

1. ¿Cuál es la profesión de Liudmila? ¿De qué vive realmente?
2. ¿Por qué escribe cartas de amor?
3. ¿Sus cartas suelen causar el efecto deseado? Pon un ejemplo.
4. ¿Qué tipo de cartas le cuesta más escribir a Liudmila?
5. ¿Qué estilo emplea Liudmila al escribir las cartas?

47 Palabras y expresiones

▶ **Busca** en el texto las palabras destacadas en estas oraciones y responde a las preguntas.

1. ¿Qué otras cosas se suelen hacer **a mano**?
2. ¿Qué se puede comprar **por encargo**?
3. Cuando lloramos, ¿a qué sentimientos **damos rienda suelta**?
4. ¿Qué otros **medios de vida** inusuales conoces?

48 Con tus propias palabras

▶ **Habla** con tus compañeros(as). ¿Le encargarías una carta de amor a Liudmila? ¿En qué situación? ¿Crees que el oficio de Liudmila tiene futuro? Justifica tus respuestas.

treinta y nueve 39

Activities

46. To expand this activity, ask further comprehension and discussion questions.

1. *¿Cómo se anunció Liudmila? ¿Qué te llamó más la atención de su anuncio?*
2. *¿Cuál es el secreto del éxito de Liudmila?*
3. *¿Qué admira Liudmila de los antiguos escribanos?*
4. *¿Qué efecto ha tenido su trabajo en ella?*

48. Hold a class discussion on the usefulness of Liudmila's job. This can also be done in the form of a debate, with some students for and others against Liudmila's profession. Give each group a few minutes to prepare their arguments and then begin with the pro side.

Answer Key

46. Answers will vary. Sample answers:

1. Es periodista y poetisa, y escribe cartas de amor por encargo.
2. Porque cree que las cartas de amor son una necesidad del ser humano.
3. Sí. Su primer cliente fue un hombre que pensaba que iba a perder a su esposa. La carta que escribió Liudmila logró la reconciliación.
4. Las cartas de las parejas que están peleadas.
5. Trata de emplear un estilo que se adapte a la persona que hace el encargo.

47. Answers will vary. Sample answers:

1. Los arreglos florales, una vasija de cerámica, una pintura.
2. Un traje de novia, un mueble, un pastel.
3. Damos rienda suelta al dolor, a la tristeza y a la frustración.
4. Hay personas que trabajan como adivinos (*psychics*). También hay personas que son asesores de *feng shui*.

48. Answers will vary.

Additional Resources

Fans Online activities

HERITAGE LANGUAGE LEARNERS

• Ask students to think about a letter they or a family member wrote or responded to. The letter might have been upbeat or melancholic, and was a response to situations that range from congratulatory to disappointing, or difficult or challenging. Topics might be the announcement of a wedding or acceptance into college, the illness or death of a loved one, a romantic breakup, or the academic or professional success of a family member. Have students describe this letter and its effect on themselves or a member of their family.

SPECIAL-NEEDS LEARNERS

• Help students who have difficulty staying focused when they are reading long passages by having them work with a partner with advanced language skills. Partners will monitor students as they read aloud, and ask them to paraphrase what they have read.

DESAFÍO 2

Comunicación

Presentation

- In this section, students will integrate the vocabulary and grammar skills from *Desafío 2* in order to read a letter, propose a commemorative stamp, and write a slogan to advertise a *chasqui* race.

Activities	Standards	Resources
49.	1.2, 1.3	Audio
50.	1.1, 1.2, 1.3, 2.2, 3.2	
51.	1.1, 1.3, 5.1	
52. Final del desafío	1.1, 1.2, 1.3, 2.1, 2.2	

Teaching Suggestions

Warm-Up / Independent Starter

- Have students answer these questions:
  1. *¿Cuándo fue la última vez que te quejaste? ¿De qué te quejaste?*
  2. *¿Te arrepientes de algo? ¿De qué?*
  3. *¿Te pareces a alguien de tu familia o a algún famoso?*

Preparation

- Spend some time reviewing the grammar topics of this *Desafío* and answer any questions students may have. Then call on volunteers to share their Independent Starters. As you go over students' answers, you may expand this activity by adding more questions. For example: *¿Te quejas a menudo? ¿Qué haces cuando te arrepientes de algo? ¿A qué persona famosa te gustaría parecerte?*

- Have students write a two-paragraph narrative of an experience at the post office. They may make it up. Ask them to use pronominal, non-pronominal, and reflexive verbs, as appropriate. For example: *El martes pasado fui a la oficina de correos a enviarle un paquete a un amigo. Hice fila sin quejarme. Mientras esperaba me aprendí todos los carteles que había en las paredes...*

- Call on volunteers to read their narratives aloud. As students read, you may want to write on the board some of the vocabulary and grammar structures from this *Desafío* that they used.

Comunicación

49 **Servicios postales**

▶ **Escucha** los diálogos y relaciona las personas con las imágenes correspondientes.

1. la señora
2. Jesús y Alicia
3. Carlos y su padre

(A)

(B)

(C)

(D)

(E)

(F)

▶ **Escribe** una oración explicando cada imagen y su relación con cada persona.

Modelo   *La señora quiere enviar un paquete a Lima.*

50 **¿A quién le escribo?**

▶ **Lee** este fragmento de un cuento y responde a las preguntas.

Una carta a Dios

Lencho era un hombre rudo y trabajaba como una bestia en los campos, pero sin embargo sabía escribir. El domingo, con la luz del día, empezó a escribir una carta que él mismo llevaría al pueblo para echarla al correo.

«Dios —escribió— si no me ayudas, pasaré hambre con toda mi familia durante este año. Necesito cien pesos para volver a sembrar y vivir mientras viene la nueva cosecha, porque el granizo...». Escribió «A Dios» en el sobre, metió la carta y, todavía preocupado, fue al pueblo. En la oficina de correos, le puso una estampilla a la carta y echó esta en el buzón. Un empleado, que era cartero y también ayudaba en la oficina de correos, llegó riéndose mucho ante su jefe, y le mostró la carta dirigida a Dios. El jefe de la oficina —gordo y amable— también empezó a reír, pero muy pronto se puso serio.

GREGORIO LÓPEZ Y FUENTES. *Cuentos campesinos de México.* (http://fhuhs.org) (texto adaptado)

1. ¿Cómo es Lencho? ¿Cuál es su profesión?
2. ¿Qué problema tiene? ¿Qué hace para solucionarlo?
3. ¿Cómo reaccionan los empleados de la oficina de correos? ¿Por qué?

▶ **Escribe** un principio y un final para la historia de Lencho.

Differentiated Instruction

DEVELOPING LEARNERS

- Ask the following questions:
  1. *¿Dónde trabaja Lencho? (En el campo.)*
  2. *¿Quién llevó la carta de Lencho a la oficina de correos? (Él mismo.)*
  3. *¿Qué necesita Lencho? (Cien pesos.)*
  4. *¿Qué hizo Lencho en la oficina de correos? (Le puso una estampilla a la carta y la echó.)*
  5. *¿Es Lencho pesimista u optimista? ¿Por qué? (Las respuestas variarán.)*
  6. *¿Hizo bien el empleado al abrir la carta que escribió Lencho? ¿Por qué? (Las respuestas variarán.)*

EXPANDING LEARNERS

- Ask students to think about to whom they might write a letter but will never receive a response; for example, fictional characters (Harry Potter, Don Quijote) or those who are no longer living (Abraham Lincoln, Cristóbal Colón). Have students choose a character from fiction or a historical figure and write a letter to him or her. Then have students exchange letters with a partner, who will write a response. Call on pairs to read their letters aloud.

51 Estampillas conmemorativas

▶ **Haz** una lista de personajes famosos de la actualidad que te gustaría que aparecieran en una estampilla de correos y piensa por qué.

▶ **Habla** con tu compañero(a). Elijan el personaje que más les gusta de sus listas y hagan su propuesta a la clase justificando su elección.

Final del desafío

EVA: Estoy escribiendo eslóganes para nuestro cartel.

ETHAN: Estupendo, Eva. Yo estaba buscando información y algunas imágenes. En realidad, las carreras de chasquis se organizan para celebrar diversos eventos: el Día del Cartero, el Día del Indígena…

EVA: Yo creo que suelen ser una celebración de la herencia cultural indígena.

ETHAN: Sí, y a veces también son un homenaje a la tierra, ¿no? ¿Tú ___1___ de que en Perú celebran el Día del Campesino con carreras de chasquis?

EVA: Sí, es un evento tradicional. Y normalmente los corredores ___2___ como los antiguos chasquis.

ETHAN: Deberíamos dibujar un chasqui en nuestro cartel.

EVA: Mejor que lo hagas tú, Ethan; yo no ___3___ a dibujar, se me da muy mal.

ETHAN: De acuerdo, voy a ___4___ para hacer un buen dibujo. Pero si no me sale bien, luego no puedes ___5___, ¿eh?

EVA: No, hombre. Te voy a leer mis eslóganes, a ver qué te parecen. Mira, este es el primero: *Tu pasado es tu futuro.* Otro es: *Todos somos chasquis.* Y el último, jugando con las palabras: *Tan rápidos como un CHASQUIdo (snap).*

ETHAN: ¡El último, sin duda!

52 Preparando el cartel

▶ **Completa** el diálogo poniendo estos verbos en la forma correcta.

acordarse	atreverse	esforzarse	quejarse	vestirse

▶ **Habla** con tu compañero(a). ¿Cuál de los eslóganes de Eva les gusta más? ¿Por qué?

▶ **Escribe** tres eslóganes más con tu compañero(a) para ayudar a Ethan y a Eva. Después, compártanlos con el resto de la clase y voten para elegir el mejor.

HERITAGE LANGUAGE LEARNERS

• Ask students to bring in some stamps from their family's country of origin and to be prepared to describe what or who is depicted on them. Have students share this information with the rest of the class and also explain the importance of each event, person, place, or thing that is depicted. Students should also be able to describe the currency shown and convert this amount to the currency used in this country. Finally, have students compare and contrast the stamps shown with those used in this country.

MULTIPLE INTELLIGENCES:
Visual-Spatial Intelligence

• Explain to students that they are going to design a postage stamp that will commemorate an event, person, place, animal, plant, or something else of significance in their community. Have students work with a partner or in small groups and first discuss the possibilities. After they draw the image, ask them to prepare a concise paragraph that gives some background information about what is depicted, and why it was selected. Display students' stamps in the classroom.

Activities

50. Have student pairs work on the second part of this activity. Encourage partners to exchange ideas, be creative, and try out different beginnings and endings before they settle on one. Then ask them to share their stories with the class. Hold a class vote to choose the best beginning and the best ending.

52. In addition to coming up with the slogans, have students design a logo for their campaign. Ask them to use what they know about the *chasquis* and the Inca empire for inspiration.

> **AUDIO SCRIPT**
> See page 11M.

Answer Key

49. 1. La señora: C, F.

2. Jesús y Alicia: A, E.

3. Carlos y su padre: B, D.

▶ Answers will vary.

50. Answers will vary. Sample answers:

1. Es un hombre rudo, pero sabe escribir. Es agricultor.

2. El granizo dañó su cosecha y necesita cien pesos para volver a sembrar y vivir mientras nace la nueva cosecha. Le escribe a Dios pidiéndole ayuda.

3. Se ríen porque les hace gracias ver la carta dirigida a Dios.

▶ Answers will vary.

51. Answers will vary.

▶ Answers will vary.

52. 1. te acordabas   4. esforzarme

2. se visten   5. quejarte

3. me atrevo

▶ Answers will vary.

▶ Answers will vary.

Additional Resources

Fans Online activities
Practice Workbook

41

Unit 1
DESAFÍO 3
Hablar de acciones en curso

Presentation

- In *Desafío 3*, Michelle and Daniel have to learn a phrase in a whistled language from the Canary Islands, Spain. Students will preview vocabulary related to the media.

Activities	Standards	Resources
Texto	1.2, 2.1, 2.2	
53.	1.2, 2.1, 2.2	
54.	1.1, 1.2, 2.2	
55.	1.2, 1.3, 2.2, 3.2	
56. Cultura	1.1, 1.2, 2.1, 2.2, 3.2	

Teaching Suggestions

Warm-Up / Independent Starter

- Ask students to list the languages, in addition to Spanish, that are spoken in Latin America and Spain.

Preparation

- Have students share their Independent Starters with the class. Remind them that there are several countries where Spanish coexists with indigenous languages. Then, display a map of Europe and Africa, and guide students to locate the Canary Islands. Call on volunteers to share what they know about this Spanish archipelago.

Texto: Un extraño lenguaje

- Read the introduction to the dialogue aloud. Invite students to speculate on what this mysterious language might be. Then have them get together with a partner and read the dialogue.
- Ask students to compare the information they learned in the dialogue with their guesses. Invite them to comment on advantages and disadvantages of such a language.

Activities

54. Remind students that in Spain, Catalan, Euskera, and Galician have co-official status in the regions where they are spoken. Then, discuss with students how easy or difficult they think this *Desafío* will be.

42

Un extraño lenguaje

Michelle y Daniel tienen que aprender a decir una frase en un extraño lenguaje de las islas Canarias (España). Daniel está ansioso por aprender más sobre ese lenguaje misterioso, pero Michelle tiene otra preocupación…

MICHELLE: Daniel, en las islas Canarias se habla español. ¿No será que tenemos que aprender algo en español?

DANIEL: Ya hablamos español. No creo que nos hayan dado un desafío tan fácil.

MICHELLE: En España hay otras lenguas, además del español. Quizá el desafío se refiere a una de ellas.

DANIEL: No creo, porque en Canarias solo se habla español.

MICHELLE: Tengo un mensaje de voz de Tim. Voy a poner el altavoz para que puedas escucharlo.

DANIEL: Y sube el volumen para oírlo bien. ¡Uy! Qué raro. En esta grabación no se oyen palabras, solo silbidos (whistles).

MICHELLE: ¡Ya sé lo que es! La profesora de Español nos contó que en La Gomera, una de las islas Canarias, se creó hace siglos un sistema de comunicación basado en silbidos.

DANIEL: ¿Por qué?

MICHELLE: Porque los habitantes de la isla necesitaban comunicarse entre ellos salvando (overcoming) los precipicios que los separaban. Piensa que entonces no había teléfonos ni computadoras.

DANIEL: ¿Entonces tenemos que aprender a silbar como ellos? ¡Qué divertido!

MICHELLE: Sí, pero es un desafío bastante difícil. ¡Sobre todo si uno no sabe silbar!

---

53 **Detective de palabras**

▶ **Completa** estas oraciones.

1. Michelle puso el ___1___ para que Daniel pudiera escuchar el ___2___ de Tim.
2. Daniel le pidió a Michelle que subiera el ___3___ para oír bien el mensaje.
3. En la ___4___ de Tim solo se oían silbidos.
4. En una isla canaria se creó hace siglos un ___5___ basado en silbidos.
5. Los silbidos servían para comunicarse a distancia cuando no había ___6___ ni computadoras.

Differentiated Instruction

DEVELOPING LEARNERS

- Ask students to match the words from the dialogue and readings in the first column with a synonym in the second. Then ask students to write or say a sentence with each of these words.

1. *crear* (d)	a. *nombrar*
2. *comunicarse* (e)	b. *difundir*
3. *declarar* (a)	c. *resaltar*
4. *sustentar* (f)	d. *inventar*
5. *destacar* (c)	e. *hablar*
6. *transmitir* (b)	f. *apoyar*

EXPANDING LEARNERS

- Explain to students that they are going to participate in a debate on language. The topic is whether to recognize only one official language in a nation, or recognize several. Divide the class into four teams and assign one side of this issue to team members. Allow some students to serve as judges in order to evaluate the debate. Assign a time slot for opening arguments, follow-up, and rebuttal. Then have the judges evaluate each team's performance and name a winner.

Maqueta de La Gomera.

54 **¿Comprendes?**

▶ **Responde** a estas preguntas.

1. ¿En qué cree Michelle que consiste el desafío?
2. ¿Qué se oye en el mensaje de voz de Tim?
3. ¿Para qué usaban los silbidos en la isla de La Gomera?
4. ¿En qué consiste el desafío de Michelle y Daniel?

55 **Un lenguaje de silbidos**

▶ **Lee** este artículo y escribe. ¿Por qué el silbo de La Gomera es un legado cultural tan valioso? Explícalo usando tus propias palabras.

CULTURA

El silbo gomero, declarado por la UNESCO Patrimonio de la Humanidad

El silbo gomero ha sido declarado Patrimonio Cultural Inmaterial de la Humanidad en una reunión celebrada por la UNESCO en Abu Dhabi (Emiratos Árabes). El Gobierno de Canarias explica que la candidatura se sustentó en que el silbo gomero tiene un valor excepcional como muestra del genio creador humano, presenta una gran complejidad técnica y estética, y es expresión de la cultura po-

pular de un territorio. Además destacó su valor como producto cultural y por su capacidad para ser transmitido de unas generaciones a otras. El Gobierno también resalta que el silbo gomero es una parte viva dentro de la actividad social de la comunidad gomera y su origen está en las tradiciones y necesidades de un pueblo.

Fuente: http://www.laopinion.es (selección)

 **CULTURA**

El silbo gomero

El silbo gomero es el lenguaje silbado (*whistled*) de la isla canaria de La Gomera. Es el único lenguaje silbado del mundo completamente desarrollado y practicado en una comunidad numerosa.

El silbo gomero reproduce la lengua de los habitantes de La Gomera, es decir, el español, y se creó para transmitir noticias, convocar a fiestas y funerales, etc. Ha sido transmitido de unas generaciones a otras durante siglos y hoy se enseña en las escuelas. En 2009 fue declarado Patrimonio Inmaterial de la Humanidad por la UNESCO.

56 **Piensa y explica.** ¿Por qué es útil un lenguaje de silbidos en La Gomera? ¿Crees que se conservará en el futuro?

cuarenta y tres **43**

Unit 1

DESAFÍO 3

Hablar de acciones en curso

55. You may want to have a class discussion on different forms of ancient, long-distance communication (e.g., smoke signals, fire messages, Inca quipus, homing pigeons, heliographs). If time allows, divide the class into small groups and have each group research a form of communication and report their findings back to the class.

 CULTURA

El silbo gomero

The Gomeran whistled language consists of combinations of whistled vowels and consonants. Rising and falling tones and broken and continuous pitches help to convey meaning. The sounds can travel up to two miles, which makes it possible to send messages across canyons and deep valleys quickly. It was widely used as a means of communication on the island up until the 1950s. Today, people in La Gomera do not need to whistle to communicate, but they have chosen to preserve this whistled language as part of their distinctive cultural heritage.

Answer Key

53. 1. altavoz
2. mensaje de voz
3. volumen
4. grabación
5. sistema de comunicación
6. teléfonos

54. 1. En aprender algo en español.
2. Se oyen silbidos.
3. Para comunicarse a distancia.
4. En aprender una frase en silbo gomero.

55. Answers will vary. Sample answer: El silbo gomero es un ejemplo de la creatividad humana para superar los obstáculos. Se transmite de una generación a otra y es parte de la cultura gomera.

56. Answers will vary.

Additional Resources

Fans Online activities

43

DESAFÍO 3

Vocabulario – Los medios de comunicación

Presentation

- In this section, students will learn and use target vocabulary to talk about the media and communications technology.

Activities	Standards	Resources
Vocabulario	1.2	
57.	1.3	
58.	1.2, 1.3	Audio
59.	1.1, 1.3, 5.1	
60. Conexiones	1.1, 1.2, 3.1, 5.1	

Teaching Suggestions

Warm-Up / Independent Starter

- Ask students to list the different communication devices they use and how frequently they use each one.

Preparation

- Read the words in the *Más vocabulario* feature aloud to model correct pronunciation and have students repeat. Ask them which ones are easily decodable. Then do the same with the highlighted words in the texts. Next, ask three volunteers to play the roles of the people in the vocabulary presentation and read their parts aloud.

- Have students share their Independent Starters. Then, based on their use of technology, ask them to choose the person they most resemble from the vocabulary presentation.

Activities

57. Have students share their definitions with the class. Then ask them to group the vocabulary into new categories of their own choosing.

58. Play the recording again and have students write one more headline for each piece of news (e.g., 1. *El viaje durará 4 días*). Invite students to share their new headlines with the class.

59. Ask the class to take notes on their classmates' presentations. Then, have students use their notes to determine: top Spanish-language movie the class has seen, most popular movie channel, and most popular TV series.

Vocabulario

Los medios de comunicación

«Mi pasión son las nuevas tecnologías.»
Andrea, 35 años

Yo soy una apasionada de las nuevas tecnologías. Soy periodista y trabajo en prensa digital. Escribo **artículos** para la **sección internacional** y colaboro en la **sección de finanzas** porque me interesa mucho la economía. En el futuro me encantaría escribir **editoriales** para la **sección de opinión**.

«Estoy loco por el cine.»
David, 27 años

Me encanta ir al cine. Veo muchas películas extranjeras en **versión original** con **subtítulos**. En casa también veo **canales** de cine y sigo algunas **series** y **programas** en distintas **cadenas** de televisión. También suelo ver los **noticieros** para estar bien informado, pero la **programación** me parece bastante mala, en general.

«Vivo pegado al teléfono.»
Ricardo, 40 años

En mi trabajo utilizo mucho el teléfono porque hablo con muchos clientes. Y en el auto activo el **altavoz** de mi celular para seguir hablando. Siempre tengo mensajes en mi **buzón de voz** y en casa voy con el **teléfono inalámbrico** de un lado a otro. Tengo que admitir que vivo pegado al teléfono.

Más vocabulario

La televisión

el concurso	game show
el documental	documentary
el botón	button
el control remoto	remote control
el sonido	sound
el volumen	volume

La prensa

la noticia	news
el titular	headline
la primera plana	front page

¡Atención!

comentar	to discuss
discutir	to argue, to discuss

57 **Definiciones**

▶ **Escribe** definiciones que ayuden a comprender el significado de estas palabras.

Modelo *El teléfono inalámbrico sirve para hablar por teléfono desde cualquier lugar de casa porque puedes llevarlo de un sitio a otro.*

1. el teléfono inalámbrico
2. el altavoz
3. el noticiero
4. la serie de televisión
5. el titular
6. el editorial

44 cuarenta y cuatro

Differentiated Instruction

DEVELOPING LEARNERS

- Have students complete these sentences:
  1. *En la sección ... del periódico podemos leer noticias de todo el mundo. (internacional)*
  2. *Los periodistas escriben ... para opinar. (editoriales)*
  3. *Si no entiendes el idioma de la película, puedes leer... (los subtítulos)*
  4. *Las noticias más importantes del periódico están en... (la primera plana)*
  5. *Me encantan ... que tratan hechos históricos. (los documentales)*
  6. *Siempre veo las películas hispanas en versión... (original)*

EXPANDING LEARNERS

- Ask students to imagine what a day would be like without their electronic devices. Ask them to describe how this would affect their studies, social life, and connection with what is happening in the world. How would they communicate with their friends? Would they write a letter, or wait for the day to end and call them first thing in the morning? Would they forgo the news, or buy a paper? If they had to do research for a school project, would they go to their local library? Have students write at least two paragraphs describing their reactions and what they would do.

58 **El noticiero**

 ▶ **Escucha** las noticias y completa estos titulares.

> **El presidente viaja a Canadá para reunirse con el primer** ___1___

> **La OMS alerta sobre el uso excesivo de los** ___2___

> **Gasol vuelve a las** ___3___

> **El carbón superará al** ___4___ **como primera fuente de energía en 2017**

▶ **Clasifica.** ¿A qué sección del periódico corresponde cada titular?

> FINANZAS   SALUD   POLÍTICA   DEPORTES

59 **Una entrevista**

 ▶ **Entrevista** a tu compañero(a) usando estas preguntas y toma nota de sus respuestas.

1. ¿Sueles ir al cine? ¿Qué películas has visto en español?
2. ¿Ves canales de cine en la televisión? ¿Cuáles?
3. ¿Sigues alguna serie de televisión? ¿En qué cadena?
4. ¿Utilizas mucho el teléfono? ¿A quién sueles llamar?

▶ **Escribe** un resumen de la entrevista. Después, preséntalo a la clase.

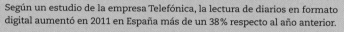

CONEXIONES: TECNOLOGÍA

¿Prensa digital o prensa en papel?

Según un estudio de la empresa Telefónica, la lectura de diarios en formato digital aumentó en 2011 en España más de un 38% respecto al año anterior.

Muchos usuarios prefieren los periódicos en papel a las versiones digitales porque les resultan más fiables, más completos o porque los pueden leer en cualquier sitio y disfrutar más de la lectura. En cambio, los lectores de diarios en la red los prefieren por el precio, porque pueden acceder a noticias muy recientes o de hace tiempo, y porque Internet les permite personalizar sus preferencias de lectura.

60 **Explica.** ¿Cómo prefieres leer las noticias: en periódicos impresos o digitales? ¿Crees que el futuro de los periódicos en papel está en peligro? ¿Por qué?

HERITAGE LANGUAGE LEARNERS

• Ask students to go online and find a newspaper from their family's heritage country and then find a local paper. Have students compare and contrast the two. They should point out the similar sections as well as any distinguishing ones. Ask them to review an article that deals with the same topic in both papers and then make a comparison between them. How do the papers deal with images and advertising? Is there more focus on local or international news? Students may write a report or make an oral presentation in front of the class.

CRITICAL THINKING

• Explain to students that they are going to discuss cell phones. First, ask students to define proper cell phone etiquette and, based on their contributions, have them establish some cell phone rules that they promise to observe. Then, encourage a discussion on the phenomenon of some people's need to be constantly connected and communicating with someone. Do students think that the cell phone and other devices have weakened face-to-face conversations? Encourage all students to share their opinions.

Vocabulario – Los medios de comunicación

 AUDIO SCRIPT
See page 11M.

CONEXIONES: TECNOLOGÍA

¿Prensa digital o prensa en papel?

Some analysts think that newspapers—both printed and digital—will slowly fade into oblivion. There are, however, some who think newspapers have the edge in local and community news. In fact, in most cities, there is only one newspaper, which is a big competitive advantage. Large and well-established newspapers also have brand name recognition and a loyal readership. But, most strikingly, newspapers have existed for over 400 years, long before the advent of radio, television, and the Internet.

Answer Key

57. Answers will vary. Sample answers:
  2. El altavoz sirve para amplificar el sonido.
  3. En el noticiero transmiten las noticias más importantes del momento.
  4. Las series son obras creadas para la televisión que se transmiten en capítulos.
  5. El titular es el título de una noticia.
  6. El editorial es un artículo que expresa la opinión de la dirección de un periódico.

58. 1. ministro   3. canchas
      2. celulares   4. petróleo
  ▶ 1. Política   3. Deportes
      2. Salud   4. Finanzas

59. Answers will vary.
  ▶ Answers will vary.

60. Answers will vary.

Additional Resources

Fans Online activities
Practice Workbook

45

DESAFÍO 3

Gramática – Hablar de acciones en curso

Presentation

- In this section, students will use the present, past, and future progressive tenses in order to talk about ongoing actions.

Activities	Standards	Resources
Gramática	1.2, 3.1	
61.	1.2, 3.1, 4.1	
62.	1.3, 3.1	
63.	1.2, 1.3	
64.	1.2, 1.3	Audio
65. Comunidades	1.1, 1.2, 2.1, 2.2, 3.1, 3.2, 4.2, 5.1, 5.2	

Teaching Suggestions

Warm-Up / Independent Starter

- Ask students to write a sentence about something that was happening to them yesterday when something else took place, and a sentence about what they are doing at this very moment.

Preparation

- Have students share their Independent Starters. Write some of their examples on the board, and circle the present and imperfect progressive forms. Review the uses of each tense. Then have students read the grammar presentation silently.

- Remind students that in Spanish, progressive tenses denote "I am / I was / I will be <u>in the process of</u>…" Explain that the imperfect progressive tense is often interchangeable with the simple imperfect.

Activities

63. To expand this activity, have students rewrite the sentences using a different progressive tense. Call on students to share their sentences with the class. Review any problematic areas.

64. Before playing the recording, allow students a couple of minutes to read the report and list the progressive actions. Check the list with the class and have students identify the tense for each progressive form.

Gramática

Hablar de acciones en curso

La conjugación progresiva

- La conjugación progresiva se utiliza para hablar de acciones pasadas, presentes o futuras que están en desarrollo.

  Ahora María **está leyendo** y antes **estaba haciendo** la comida.

- Los tiempos progresivos *(progressive tenses)* se forman con el verbo estar y el gerundio *(present participle)* de un verbo. Repasa la formación del gerundio en la página R11.

PRESENTE PROGRESIVO

> estar (en presente) + gerundio

Ahora Bill **está escuchando** música.

PRETÉRITO PROGRESIVO

> estar (en pretérito) + gerundio

Ayer **estuve leyendo** hasta las 9:00 p. m.

IMPERFECTO PROGRESIVO

> estar (en imperfecto) + gerundio

Estaba **comiendo** cuando me llamaste.

FUTURO PROGRESIVO

> estar (en futuro) + gerundio

Mañana a esta hora **estaré trabajando**.

Uso de la conjugación progresiva

- En español, la conjugación progresiva es frecuente con actividades dinámicas que duran cierto tiempo (hablar, leer, escribir, mirar, pensar, trabajar, llover…) o que admiten progreso (crecer, acercarse, enfadarse…). En cambio, no se suele usar con los verbos ir, venir, conocer, saber o creer.

  Vengo de mi casa y ahora voy a la escuela.

- Para expresar planes futuros, usamos el futuro o la expresión voy a…, no el futuro progresivo. En cambio, utilizamos el futuro progresivo para expresar probabilidad.

  Mañana **voy a ir** a una fiesta. A estas horas **estaré bailando**.

61 **Compara.** ¿Cómo se forman los tiempos progresivos en inglés? ¿Tienen los mismos usos que en español?

62 **Todos estudiamos**

▶ **Une** las columnas y escribe oraciones completas.

Ⓐ

1. No puedo ir porque estoy estudiando…
2. Javier estuvo estudiando…
3. Isabel y yo estábamos estudiando…
4. Ana y Jimena estarán estudiando…

Ⓑ

a. cuando Natalia vuelva a casa.
b. cuando llamó Luis.
c. en la biblioteca ayer.
d. para el examen de mañana.

▶ **Escribe** cuatro oraciones usando los cuatro tiempos de la ficha de Gramática.

Differentiated Instruction

DEVELOPING LEARNERS

- Ask students to write five or six questions using the progressive tenses in the present, imperfect, preterite, and future. The questions should be aimed at a partner. Then have them get together with the partner, exchange sentences, and answer each other's questions in writing. Be sure students use the correct tense of the progressive.

EXPANDING LEARNERS

- Have students work with a partner and create a short dialogue. Explain to students that in order to practice all the progressive tenses in the indicative, the conversation should focus on what the speakers are doing at this moment, were doing at some point in the past, and will be doing by some point in the future. Give students time to write and practice their lines. Then, have them present their mini-conversation in front of the class.

63 **¿Estamos o estaremos?**

▶ **Completa** las oraciones poniendo los verbos del cuadro en presente o en futuro progresivo.

organizar	proyectar	trabajar	ver	vivir	volar

1. Mis profesores _____ un ciclo de cine hispanoamericano para el próximo otoño.
2. Cuando empieces tus estudios en la universidad, yo ya _____ como abogada.
3. Hoy _____ una película mexicana en versión original en el taller de cine de la escuela.
4. El domingo a esta hora Antonio y Cecilia _____ a su país.
5. Mi hermano siempre quiere cambiar de canal cuando yo _____ la televisión.
6. El año que viene nosotros _____ en Sydney.

64 **Informe policial**

 ▶ **Escucha** la declaración de la señora Rodríguez y localiza los errores en este informe que hizo un policía. Después, escríbelo de nuevo.

INFORME

La señora Rodríguez llegó a su casa a las ocho de la tarde. Cuando estaba abriendo la puerta, sonó el teléfono. Era su marido. Estuvo hablando con él algunos minutos; él le dijo que estaba saliendo del trabajo y que se dirigía a casa. Mientras preparaba la cena, la señora Rodríguez estuvo viendo el noticiero. Después estuvo mirando por la ventana para ver si llegaba su marido. Entonces, vio a dos personas extrañas, pero no le pareció importante. Estaba viendo la televisión cuando oyó un ruido inusual. Estuvo escuchando atentamente un buen rato y le pareció oír a dos hombres que estaban riéndose. Luego oyó que un hombre decía: «Quédate quieto, no grites y no te pasará nada», y a otro hombre que gritaba pidiendo ayuda. Inmediatamente, miró por la ventana y vio un auto deportivo que estaba entrando en el garaje de sus vecinos. A continuación, llamó a la policía. Estuvo esperando a su marido, pero él no llegó.

 **COMUNIDADES** f Sonico

REDES SOCIALES EN ESPAÑOL

Las redes sociales suponen (signify) una verdadera revolución en el mundo de la comunicación y son una herramienta (tool) indispensable en el mundo laboral, los negocios, la publicidad y los medios de comunicación.
Facebook y Twitter, las redes sociales con más millones de seguidores, están disponibles en español. Pero además, varios países hispanos han creado sus propias redes sociales, algunas de ellas muy populares, como la argentina Sonico o la española Tuenti.

65 **Explica.** ¿Utilizas las redes sociales habitualmente? ¿Para qué las usas? ¿Qué redes sociales hispanas conoces? ¿Participas en alguna de ellas?

HERITAGE LANGUAGE LEARNERS

• Have students describe some social networks they are familiar with from their family's heritage country and compare them to, for example, Twitter or Facebook. If students are not familiar with any such social networks, encourage them to research some or ask family members for descriptions. Have students explain how they and their family members stay in touch with relatives who live abroad.

MULTIPLE INTELLIGENCES:
Verbal-Linguistic Intelligence

• Ask students to reread the *Informe* with the corrections in place. Then, have them think about who the two men were and what they were doing, and what might have happened to *señora* Rodríguez's husband. Next, have them write their own conclusion to the story, using the progressive tenses where applicable. Finally, call on volunteers to read their endings aloud.

DESAFÍO 3

Gramática – Hablar de acciones en curso

 AUDIO SCRIPT
See page 11M.

 COMUNIDADES

Redes sociales en español

Hispanics are avid social media users. In fact, Spanish is the second most widely used language on Twitter, and Facebook has over 80 million Spanish-speaking users. However, there is still ample room for growth, since Internet penetration in Latin America is below 50%. In the United States, Hispanics are already the most active users on social networks. As a result, marketers and multinational corporations are increasing their social media presence in Spanish.

Answer Key

61. Se forman con el auxiliar *to be* y el verbo principal terminado en *-ing*. Cuando se usan para hablar de acciones en desarrollo, tienen los mismos usos que en español.

62. 1. d   2. c   3. b   4. a
  ▶ Answers will vary.

63. 1. están organizando   4. estarán volando
  2. estaré trabajando   5. estoy viendo
  3. están proyectando   6. estaremos viviendo

64. – Cuando estaba subiendo las escaleras…
  – No estuvo hablando con su marido.
  – Mientras preparaba la cena estuvo escuchando el noticiero.
  – Estaba sacando la cena del horno cuando oyó un ruido inusual.
  – Le pareció oír la voz de dos hombres que estaban discutiendo.
  – Vio un auto que estaba saliendo del garaje.

65. Answers will vary.

Additional Resources

Fans Online activities
Practice Workbook

DESAFÍO 3

Gramática – Expresar cantidad

Presentation

- In this section, students will review and practice the use of numbers and indefinites to express quantity.

Activities	Standards	Resources
Gramática	1.2, 3.1	
66.	1.2, 3.1, 4.1	
67.	1.2	
68.	1.2, 1.3	Audio
69.	1.1, 1.2, 2.2, 3.1, 3.2, 5.2	Audio

Teaching Suggestions

Warm-Up / Independent Starter

- Have students answer these questions in writing:
  1. *¿Cuántos televisores hay en tu casa?*
  2. *¿Ves alguna serie?*
  3. *¿Te interesan mucho o poco los noticieros?*

Preparation

- Ask students to share their Independent Starters. On the board, write some of their sentences and underline the words that express quantity (e.g., *Hay tres televisores; No veo ninguna serie*). Then have students get together with a partner to read the grammar presentation. Encourage them to use the sentences on the board and their own sentences as examples of ways to express quantity. Clarify any explanations students did not understand.

- Explain that in most sentences with this structure, "singular quantifier + *de* + plural noun," the verb can be either singular or plural (e.g., *La mayor parte de mis amigos usa/usan las redes sociales*). In these cases, the verb tends to be plural when the component members of the plural noun are considered separately; and singular, when the group is handled as a unit.

Activities

68. Have student pairs choose one of the two events described in the conversations. Then ask them to use the sentences they wrote about the event, plus three more of their own creation, to compose a short, original narrative.

48

Gramática

Expresar cantidad

Los cuantificadores numerales

- Para expresar cantidad de una manera precisa, usamos los numerales *(numbers)*: uno, cien, mil, un millón…

- Algunos numerales expresan una parte:

| medio
la mitad (de) | un tercio (de)
la tercera parte (de) | un cuarto (de)
la cuarta parte (de) | un quinto (de)
la quinta parte (de) |

- Otros numerales sirven para multiplicar:

$\times 2$ el doble / dos veces más $\times 3$ el triple / tres veces más $\times 4$ el cuádruple / cuatro veces más

Los cuantificadores indefinidos

- Para expresar cantidad de una manera imprecisa, usamos los adjetivos y los pronombres indefinidos, y los adverbios de cantidad.

  – Los **adjetivos** y los **pronombres indefinidos** (algún, poco, mucho, todo…) se refieren a un nombre y concuerdan *(agree)* con él en género y en número.

  Este verano he visto **bastantes películas** en español.

  Repasa los adjetivos y pronombres indefinidos más comunes en la página R4.

  – Los **adverbios de cantidad** (poco, mucho, demasiado…) se refieren a un verbo o a un adjetivo. Los adverbios no tienen variación de género ni de número.

  Estas revistas son **bastante buenas**.

  Repasa los adverbios de cantidad más comunes en la página R7.

- Las expresiones la mayoría o la mayor parte también se refieren a una cantidad imprecisa.

  La mayor parte de mis amigos **tiene/tienen** celular.

66 **Piensa.** ¿Cómo dices en inglés La mayoría de los estudiantes lee/leen en español?

67 **Cantidades**

▶ **Completa** estas oraciones.

1. No estoy cansado porque he dormido _____ horas.
2. Vino mucha gente a la fiesta, pero no vi a _____ amigo tuyo.
3. No me encuentro bien porque he comido _____ pollo.
4. Pregunté tres veces por Cristina, pero no respondió _____.

bastantes
demasiado
nadie
ningún

Differentiated Instruction

DEVELOPING LEARNERS

- Ask partners to translate the following:
  1. a lot of rain *(mucha lluvia)*
  2. too many rules *(demasiadas reglas)*
  3. she worries too much *(se preocupa demasiado)*
  4. the second half of the first book *(la segunda mitad del primer libro)*
  5. They don't eat too much, but they eat too much pizza. *(No comen demasiado, pero comen demasiada pizza.)*
  6. The majority of my neighbors have a dog. *(La mayoría de mis vecinos tiene/tienen perro.)*

EXPANDING LEARNERS

- Ask students to translate these phrases. They may need to look up certain terms in the dictionary.
  1. the first three sentences *(las tres primeras oraciones)*
  2. there are too many people *(hay demasiadas personas/hay demasiada gente)*
  3. a hundredth of a second more *(una centésima de segundo más)*
  4. it's 150 square feet *(mide ciento cincuenta pies cuadrados)*
  5. that wall is too red *(esa pared es demasiado roja)*

68 El doble y la mitad

▶ **Escucha** los diálogos y une las columnas.

Ⓐ   Ⓑ

1. la mitad   a. de las canciones del grupo
2. la mayoría   b. de los aficionados
3. el doble   c. de los componentes del grupo musical
4. el triple   d. del tiempo previsto
5. cuatro veces más   e. de público
6. un tercio   f. de puntos

▶ **Escucha** de nuevo y escribe oraciones con los elementos que has unido.

69 ¿Todo o nada?

▶ **Lee** estas estrofas de dos canciones de grupos musicales españoles y complétalas con los indefinidos de los cuadros.

> Con lo __1__ que quedaba
> de lo __2__ que empezó
> se terminó nuestro amor.
> Yo lo mío, tú lo tuyo.

> __3__ tuyo, __4__ mío
> hemos perdido los dos.
> Tanta emoción racionalizada
> que acabé sin sentir __5__.
>
> Nena Daconte

algo
algo
mucho
nada
poco

> Nada es __6__ y no sé por qué
> me falta __7__ y no sé qué.
> Tengo de __8__, dentro de un orden *(within limits)*,
> pero, en el fondo *(deep inside)*, __9__ que importe.
>
> Pereza

algo
nada
suficiente
todo

▶ **Escucha** y comprueba tus respuestas.

▶ **Habla** con tu compañero(a). Respondan a estas preguntas.

1. ¿De qué sentimiento habla la primera canción? ¿Qué experiencia vivieron sus protagonistas?
2. ¿Qué le pasa al protagonista de la segunda canción? ¿Qué sentimiento expresa?

▶ **Escribe** una estrofa similar expresando el sentimiento que tú quieras: amor, desamor, amistad, desengaño, etc. Usa indefinidos.

cuarenta y nueve 49

HERITAGE LANGUAGE LEARNERS

• Ask students to work with a partner and write a dialogue on any topic that makes good use of expressing quantity by using numbers, indefinite pronouns, and adjectives, as well as adverbs of quantity. Students might make comparisons between what they have, where they live, and what they do in their free time.

A. *Aunque tenemos varias computadoras en casa, ninguna funciona.*

B. *Lo siento. Solo tenemos una, pero funciona bastante bien.*

• Call on pairs to present their dialogues in front of the class.

MULTIPLE INTELLIGENCES:

Verbal-Linguistic Intelligence

• Turn students' attention to some of the words that appear in either song: *algo*, *nada*, *todo*, *mucho*, and *poco*. Explain that these words are often found in love songs or poems, either praising *el ser querido* or lamenting a lost love. Ask students to write a poem lamenting a "lost love," but explain that the "love" does not have to be a person; it could be a pet, a sports team, or any suitable article (e.g., an old pair of jeans, a book). Encourage creativity, but tell students to include as many indefinites and adverbs of quantity as they can.

Unit 1

DESAFÍO 3

Gramática – Expresar cantidad

69. For further practice with quantifiers, ask students to change as many of the quantifiers as they can in the two songs. They may need to change the sentences a bit. For example: *Con la tercera parte que quedaba de la mitad que empezó...* Invite volunteers to share their new versions of the songs with the class.

AUDIO SCRIPT
See page 11M.

Answer Key

66. Se dice: *The majority of students read Spanish.*

67. 1. bastantes   3. demasiado
     2. ningún   4. nadie

68. 1. c   2. a   3. d   4. f   5. e   6. b

▶ Answers will vary. Sample answers:
1. La mitad de los componentes del grupo musical son chicas.
2. La mayoría de las canciones del grupo son temas de otros cantantes.
3. El concierto duró el doble del tiempo previsto.
4. Su equipo consiguió el triple de puntos que el equipo visitante.
5. Había cuatro veces más de público que en el último partido.
6. Un tercio de los aficionados eran del equipo visitante.

69. 1. poco   6. suficiente
     2. mucho   7. algo
     3. Algo   8. todo
     4. algo   9. nada
     5. nada

▶ Answers will vary.
▶ Answers will vary.

Additional Resources

Fans Online activities
Practice Workbook

49

Unit 1

LECTURA: TEXTO LITERARIO

Presentation

- In this section, students will read a short story by Argentinean author Julio Cortázar. They will also write their own short story about an everyday object.

Activities	Standards	Resources
Lectura: texto literario	1.2, 1.3, 2.2, 3.1, 3.2	
70.	1.2, 1.3	
71.	1.3	
72.	1.1, 1.3	

Teaching Suggestions

Warm-Up / Independent Starter

- Ask students to read the *Antes de leer* strategies silently and answer the first question.

Preparation

- Call on a volunteer to share his or her Independent Starter. Do students understand the play on words in the title of this short story? Ask them if they know of another object called *diario*. (a diary or journal) Then have students think of expressions with the word *diario*, such as *de diario* (everyday), *el consumo diario* (daily consumption), *la vida diaria* (daily life).

- Have students work on the second question of the *Antes de leer* individually. If they are not familiar with the word *tranvía*, clarify that it refers to a streetcar or trolley. Then discuss their answers as a class. Encourage students to think of an alternative beginning, using what is common in their community. For example: *Un señor toma el auto y sale de su casa. Pasa por un...*

- Read the story aloud to model pronunciation and have students follow along in their books. Then call on individual students to each read a paragraph aloud. Offer assistance with pronunciation as needed. Then give students a couple of minutes to read the biographical reference about Julio Cortázar. As a class, discuss some of the elements that characterize Cortázar's short stories, especially those elements present in the short story students have just read.

50

Antes de leer: estrategias

1. Lee el título y observa la fotografía. ¿Qué significa *diario*? ¿Y la expresión *a diario*?
2. Lee el primer párrafo del cuento. ¿Describe una imagen frecuente en la actualidad? Justifica tu respuesta.

El diario a diario

Un señor toma el tranvía después de comprar el diario y ponérselo bajo el brazo. Media hora más tarde desciende con el mismo diario bajo el mismo brazo.

Pero ya no es el mismo diario, ahora es un montón de hojas impresas que el señor abandona en un banco de la plaza.

Apenas queda solo en el banco, el montón de hojas impresas se convierte otra vez en un diario, hasta que un muchacho lo ve, lo lee y lo deja convertido en un montón de hojas impresas.

Apenas queda solo en el banco, el montón de hojas impresas se convierte otra vez en un diario, hasta que una anciana lo encuentra, lo lee y lo deja convertido en un montón de hojas impresas. Luego se lo lleva a su casa y en el camino lo usa para empaquetar medio kilo de acelgas[1], que es para lo que sirven los diarios después de estas excitantes metamorfosis.

JULIO CORTÁZAR. *Historias de cronopios y de famas*

---
1. *Swiss chard*

Julio Cortázar (Bruselas, 1914-París, 1984)

El escritor argentino, nacionalizado francés, Julio Cortázar destaca sobre todo como autor de libros de relatos breves, caracterizados por la fantasía, el humor, la paradoja y el juego con los conceptos del tiempo y el espacio. Entre ellos sobresalen *Bestiario* (1951), *Final del juego* (1956) e *Historias de cronopios y de famas* (1962).
Cortázar escribió también algunas novelas, entre ellas *Rayuela* (1963), que es una referencia fundamental de la literatura hispanoamericana. Esta obra se puede leer siguiendo el orden normal de los capítulos o siguiendo el orden que da el autor; según el orden elegido, la obra tiene distintas interpretaciones.

Differentiated instruction

DEVELOPING LEARNERS

- Have students answer these questions:

1. *La historia se cuenta desde el punto de vista...* (b)
   a. *del señor*   b. *del narrador*

2. *¿Qué hace el muchacho con el periódico?* (a)
   a. *Lo lee.*   b. *Lo devuelve.*

3. *¿Qué hace la señora con el periódico?* (b)
   a. *Lo lee y lo deja.*   b. *Lo lee, lo deja y lo vuelve a usar.*

4. *¿A qué se refieren «estas excitantes metamorfosis»?* (b)
   a. *A los diarios.*   b. *A los cambios del diario.*

EXPANDING LEARNERS

- Ask students to rewrite this short story, but this time from the point of view of *el diario*. Students should keep in mind the feelings that the paper may have, how it deals with its metamorphoses, possibly its attitude toward those who have used it and then abandoned it, and what it was doing when it was picked up by others, as well as what it might be doing in the future after it is definitively abandoned. Call on volunteers to read their stories aloud.

50

70 ¿Comprendes?

▶ **Decide** en cada caso. ¿Qué es el periódico según el relato: un diario o un montón de hojas impresas?

1. Una persona compra un _____ para leerlo.
2. Un señor va con un _____ que aún no ha leído.
3. Una persona está leyendo un _____.
4. Alguien deja en un banco un _____ porque ya lo ha leído.
5. Hay un _____ abandonado en un banco que alguien puede encontrar y leer.
6. Cuando se utiliza para envolver cosas, es un _____.

▶ **Explica** con tus palabras. ¿Qué convierte un montón de hojas impresas en un diario según el relato?

71 Palabras y expresiones

▶ **Reescribe** estas oraciones sustituyendo las palabras destacadas por otras equivalentes.

1. Media hora más tarde **desciende** con el mismo diario bajo el mismo brazo.
2. Ahora es un montón de hojas impresas que el señor **abandona** en un banco.
3. Apenas queda solo en el banco, el montón de hojas impresas **se convierte** otra vez en un diario.
4. Hasta que un muchacho lo ve, lo lee, y lo **deja** convertido en un montón de hojas impresas.
5. En el camino lo usa para **empaquetar** medio kilo de acelgas.

72 Con tus propias palabras

▶ **Habla** con tus compañeros(as). ¿Qué otros objetos cotidianos sufren a diario una transformación similar?

▶ **Escribe** un relato similar a *El diario a diario* que tenga como protagonista alguno de los objetos de los que han hablado. Completa cuatro párrafos que empiecen así:

> Un señor...
>
> Pero ya...
>
> Apenas...
>
> Luego...

HERITAGE LANGUAGE LEARNERS

• Ask students to share information they may have about the life of Julio Cortázar and his literary works. If they are not familiar with this author, assign one or more of his short stories for them to read, as well as some biographical information. Explain that they should be prepared to make a summary of the author's life and these literary pieces, and to share their impressions of this work with the rest of the class. If time permits, have students read one of the short stories aloud.

COOPERATIVE LEARNING

• Students will work in small groups and come up with a plan for an author reading and signing. The author will be Cortázar, who is publicizing his "new" collection of short stories in which *El diario a diario* appears. Each member of the group will have a task; some will prepare advertising flyers, others will make a poster to welcome the public. Students will also prepare a short biographical introduction to the author and one will do an expert reading of the short story. Afterward, have students welcome questions or comments from the audience.

LECTURA: TEXTO LITERARIO

Activities

70. To help students with this activity, suggest that they create a two-column chart with the following headings: *Diario, Montón de hojas*. Then, have them reread the story and classify the actions related to the newspaper in the appropriate column of their charts. For example: *Diario → señor lo compra; muchacho lo ve; anciana lo encuentra. Montón de hojas → señor lo abandona; muchacho lo deja; anciana lo usa para empaquetar acelgas.*

72. Ask students to exchange their stories with a partner and proofread each other's work. Then invite volunteers to read their stories aloud. You may wish to collect the stories and compile a short story anthology for the class.

Answer Key

70.
1. diario
2. diario
3. diario
4. montón de hojas
5. diario
6. montón de hojas

▶ Answers will vary. Sample answer: Es un diario cuando aún no se ha leído. Al leerse se convierte en un montón de hojas.

71. Answers will vary. Sample answers:
1. Media hora más tarde baja con el mismo diario bajo el mismo brazo.
2. Ahora es un montón de hojas impresas que el señor deja en un banco.
3. Apenas queda solo en el banco, el montón de hojas impresas se transforma otra vez en diario.
4. Hasta que un muchacho lo ve, lo lee y lo abandona convertido en un montón de hojas impresas.
5. En el camino lo usa para envolver medio kilo de acelgas.

72. Answers will vary.
▶ Answers will vary.

Additional Resources

Fans Online activities

Unit 1
DESAFÍO 3
Comunicación

Presentation

- In this section, students will integrate the vocabulary and grammar skills from *Desafío 3* in order to understand a radio broadcast about Spanish-language media in the United States, express quantity, and describe what they will be doing at different points in the future.

Activities	Standards	Resources
73.	1.1, 1.2, 2.1, 2.2, 3.1, 3.2, 4.2, 5.1, 5.2	Audio
74.	1.1, 1.3, 5.1	
75.	1.1, 1.3, 5.1	
76. Final del desafío	1.1, 1.2, 1.3, 2.1, 2.2, 5.1	

Teaching Suggestions

Warm-Up / Independent Starter

- Ask students to complete the following sentences:
  1. *Solo leo los ... del periódico. (titulares)*
  2. *No me gusta activar el ... del celular. (altavoz)*
  3. *Me aburren las ... de televisión. (series)*
  4. *No veo películas con... (subtítulos)*

Preparation

- Call on different volunteers to share a sentence from the Independent Starter. Then give students a few moments to review the vocabulary on page 44. Even though most words are cognates, the stress may be placed on a different syllable (e.g., orig*in*al, *bo*tón, documen*tal*). Make students aware of any word they are not pronouncing correctly.

- Go over the grammar topics from this *Desafío*. Clarify any questions students may have. Then, for additional practice with quantifiers, ask students to complete these sentences. Explain that several answers are possible for each sentence and remind them to use the preposition *de* if needed.
  1. *Un ... de los estudiantes no tiene celular.*
  2. *Asistió ... más público del esperado.*
  3. *Veo ... películas extranjeras.*
  4. *... de los jóvenes usa las redes sociales.*

DESAFÍO 3

Comunicación

73 Medios de comunicación hispanos

 ▶ **Escucha** un reportaje sobre los medios de comunicación hispanos en los Estados Unidos y decide si estas afirmaciones son ciertas o falsas.

1. El crecimiento de la población hispana ha significado un crecimiento de los medios de comunicación en español.
2. La mayoría de los medios de comunicación hispanos no han podido crecer en los últimos años.
3. Univisión y Telemundo son dos de las cadenas hispanas con mayor audiencia.
4. La publicidad proporcionó importantes beneficios a las cadenas de televisión.
5. La prensa diaria en español registró pérdidas en las principales ciudades estadounidenses con población hispana y por eso cuelga sus artículos en Internet.
6. Los medios de comunicación son un reflejo de los cambios que se están produciendo en la población hispana de los Estados Unidos.

 ▶ **Investiga y habla** con tus compañeros(as). ¿Qué medios de comunicación hispanos conocen? ¿Siguen espacios de noticias o de entretenimiento a través de algunos de estos medios? ¿Qué les interesa de ellos?

 ▶ **Debate** con tus compañeros(as). ¿Qué medio te parece mejor? ¿Por qué?

 la prensa escrita vs. la radio   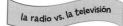 la radio vs. la televisión    la televisión vs. Internet

74 Tus cantidades

▶ **Completa** estas oraciones. Después, escribe cinco oraciones más sobre ti con expresiones de cantidad.

1. La mayoría de los jóvenes...
2. Un cuarto de la población de los Estados Unidos...
3. Un tercio de los estudiantes de mi clase...
4. La mitad de mi familia...
5. Me gusta diez veces más...
6. Tardo el doble de tiempo en...

 ▶ **Comparte** con tu compañero(a) lo que has escrito y hazle preguntas para saber más sobre él/ella.

Differentiated Instruction

DEVELOPING LEARNERS

- Ask students to complete the following sentences with the correct progressive tense of the verb in parentheses:
  1. *Yo (leer) un libro cuando me llamaron por teléfono. (estaba leyendo)*
  2. *Mañana a esta hora nosotros (aterrizar) en Madrid. (estaremos aterrizando)*
  3. *¿En qué (pensar) cuando dijiste eso? (estabas pensando)*
  4. *Ana (estudiar) hasta las tres ayer. (estuvo estudiando)*
  5. *Ahora no quiero salir porque (ver) un documental interesantísimo. (estoy viendo)*

EXPANDING LEARNERS

- Expand the Independent Starter activity by asking students the following questions:
  1. *¿Por qué solo lees los titulares del periódico? ¿Por qué no te interesa enterarte bien de lo que ocurre?*
  2. *¿Por qué no te gusta activar el altavoz del celular? ¿Te molesta si otras personas activan el altavoz de su teléfono, o te agrada?*
  3. *¿Por qué te aburren esos programas? ¿Cuáles prefieres ver? ¿Por qué?*
  4. *¿Por qué no ves películas con subtítulos? ¿Prefieres las películas dobladas? ¿Por qué? ¿Te molesta leer los subtítulos? ¿Por qué?*

75 **¿Cómo te imaginas el futuro?**

 ▶ **Escribe** seis oraciones siguiendo el modelo. Utiliza el futuro progresivo. Después, compara tu futuro con el de tu compañero(a). ¿Qué coincidencias tienen?

Modelo 1. *Mañana a esta hora estaré haciendo las tareas de la clase de Español.*

1. mañana a esta hora
2. el próximo domingo por la tarde
3. el 4 de julio del próximo año
4. el día de tu 25 cumpleaños
5. el 31 de diciembre de 2030
6. el día de las próximas elecciones presidenciales

Final del desafío

MICHELLE: Yo creo que en La Gomera hay ___1___ personas con celular. Con el silbo, no necesitan teléfono para comunicarse... ¡Y no tienen ___2___ problema con la cobertura (range) o la batería del celular!

DANIEL: Desde luego, este sistema de comunicación me parece fantástico. ¿Y sabes que con el silbo podemos decir también palabras en ___3___ lenguas? ¡Podemos comunicarnos con el silbo en inglés!

MICHELLE: ¡Pero yo no sé silbar, Daniel! ¡Y no sabemos qué dice el mensaje de la grabación! ¡Me parece un desafío ___4___ difícil!

DANIEL: Bueno, Michelle, no te desanimes. ___5___ los niños de La Gomera aprenden a silbar en la escuela, así que nosotros también aprenderemos. Vamos a escuchar de nuevo la grabación.

MICHELLE: ___6___ sonidos son graves y ___7___ agudos... A veces los sonidos se unen y a veces se cortan...

DANIEL: Tenemos que encontrar a ___8___ que nos enseñe.

76 **Otra forma de comunicarse**

▶ **Completa** el diálogo con las palabras del cuadro.

| alguien | algunos | demasiado | ningún | otros | otras | pocas | todos |

 ▶ **Habla** con tu compañero(a).

1. ¿Qué les parece el desafío de Michelle y Daniel? ¿Creen que lo conseguirán?
2. ¿Les gustaría a ustedes aprender el silbo gomero? ¿Por qué?

HERITAGE LANGUAGE LEARNERS

• Explain to students that they are going to design their own newspaper. They will have to come up with a name for their publication, decide on the focus (news, sports, entertainment, etc.), and the targeted age group. Students will also need to determine if it will be print or digital. Ask students to write the headlines and lead articles for the first page, and to include other pertinent information on it (publisher, city, weather, index, price, etc.). Display students' first pages throughout the classroom.

MULTIPLE INTELLIGENCES:
Interpersonal Intelligence

• Explain to students that they will not be able to communicate with one another verbally or by writing for a period of time you will specify. However, they must devise an original way to communicate, either by gestures, whistles, or any other means. Have students work in small groups and devise a communication plan. Allow them to communicate this way with one another for a few minutes. Then call time and have each group explain and demonstrate their new method.

Activities

73. Ask students to take notes as they listen to help them complete the activity. Then, play the audio a second time and have students check their answers. For the second part of this activity, you may want to show students some websites of well-known Spanish-language media outlets (e.g., eldiariony.com, univision.com, latino.msn.com, telemundo.com, yosoyraza.com). What do students know about these media? Then, for the third part of this activity, divide the class into six groups to debate the pros and cons of each medium.

75. To expand this activity, have students write new sentences for the following situations: 1. *ayer a esta hora*; 2. *el 4 de julio del año pasado*; 3. *el día de mi último cumpleaños*. Check students' sentences, paying special attention to the use of the imperfect progressive or the preterite progressive. Both options may be possible, depending on what students want to express. For example: *Ayer a esta hora estuve leyendo un rato. / Ayer a esta hora estaba leyendo cuando me llamó mi novia.*

AUDIO SCRIPT
See page 11N.

Answer Key

Additional Resources

Fans Online activities
Practice Workbook

53

Para terminar

Presentation

- In this section, students will review the unit objectives and put them into practice. They will read a newspaper article and conduct an interview. Students will also select one of the following *desafíos* to develop: plan a traditional Mexican birthday party, design a poster to promote the postal service, or research the whistled language of La Gomera and do a class presentation.

Activities	Standards	Resources
77.	1.1, 1.2, 1.3, 2.1, 2.2, 3.1, 3.2, 4.2	
78.	1.1, 1.3, 5.1	
79. Tu desafío	1.2, 1.3, 2.1, 2.2, 3.2, 5.1, 5.2	

Teaching Suggestions

Warm-Up / Independent Starter

- Have students go back and review the vocabulary and grammar sections in this unit. Then ask them to write a paragraph describing various modes of communication available today.

Preparation

- Call on volunteers to share their paragraphs from the Independent Starter. Then hold a brief class discussion to talk about the pros and cons of the modes of communication they mentioned. Based on this discussion, have the class vote on the most effective method of communication.

- Have students close their textbooks. Then write the following list of tasks on the board and have students complete them in their notebooks:

  1. *Describe a tu mejor amigo(a) y comenta qué gustos comparten y en qué son distintos ustedes dos.*
  2. *Describe tu rutina diaria en un día escolar y en el fin de semana.*
  3. *Describe tu medio de comunicación favorito y explica por qué te gusta tanto.*

  Ask students to share their answers in small groups and check their work together. They may open their textbooks now and review any topic that they have not yet mastered.

Para terminar

Todo junto

LEER

77 Cumpleaños en México

 ▶ **Lee** esta noticia y escribe las respuestas a las preguntas.

Miércoles, 7 de marzo de 2012

Gabo: 85 cumpleaños en México rodeado de los suyos

El premio nobel de literatura colombiano Gabriel García Márquez celebró ayer su 85 aniversario en su residencia de la capital mexicana. *Gabo*, vestido con traje de cuadros, camisa negra y corbata gris, recibió a sus familiares y amigos en la casa del sur de Ciudad de México, donde entre 1965 y 1966 escribió su obra cumbre, *Cien años de soledad*.

Según fotografías publicadas por el diario mexicano *La Jornada*, el escritor colombiano festejó el domingo por anticipado (*in advance*) sus 85 años con un pastel adornado con mariposas amarillas que podrían haber sali-do de una de las páginas de *Cien años de soledad*. *Gabo* sopló las velitas rodeado de sus amigos y la cantante peruana Tania Libertad entonó *Las mañanitas*. En el pastel se colocaron seis velitas entre las mariposas y *Gabo* levantó una copa mirando hacia la cámara en el brindis (*toast*).

Fuente: http://www.elmundo.es (texto adaptado)

1. ¿Quién es *Gabo*? ¿Cómo es? Describe su aspecto físico en esta fotografía e imagina algunos rasgos de su personalidad.
2. ¿Dónde celebró *Gabo* su 85 cumpleaños? ¿Cómo y con quién lo celebró? Imagina tres cosas que le gustan a *Gabo*.
3. ¿Qué elementos de esta celebración son comunes a las fiestas de cumpleaños de tu país?

ESCRIBIR Y HABLAR

78 Con permiso...

▶ **Escribe** doce preguntas para tu compañero(a) sobre su vida y sus relaciones personales. Usa estos verbos.

1. arrepentirse
2. levantarse
3. parecerse
4. quejarse
5. despedirse
6. escribirse
7. atreverse
8. ayudarse
9. ponerse
10. acordarse
11. pelearse
12. contarse

 ▶ **Haz** las preguntas a tu compañero(a) y toma nota de sus respuestas. Después, presenta un resumen a la clase.

Differentiated Instruction

DEVELOPING LEARNERS

- Have students complete these sentences:

  1. *Esa fiesta se parece / parece divertida.* (parece)
  2. *Marcos durmió / se durmió en seguida.* (se durmió)
  3. *¿A qué hora quedaste / te quedaste con tus amigos?* (quedaste)
  4. *Isabel y Hugo conocieron / se conocieron el año pasado.* (se conocieron)
  5. *El jefe se acordó / acordó subirles el sueldo a todos.* (acordó)
  6. *Margarita puso / se puso la mesa.* (puso)
  7. *El vaso rompió / se rompió.* (se rompió)

EXPANDING LEARNERS

- Ask students to think about the special abilities or characteristics participants should have in order to complete the *desafíos* successfully. Then, have students write a brief profile of the ideal participant. Students should include the person's special abilities as well as personality traits and physical characteristics. For example: *Para investigar sobre los chasquis, la persona debe ser paciente porque la investigación toma su tiempo. Para cantar* Las mañanitas, *es importante que tenga buena voz y que no sea tímida. Para reproducir el silbo gomero, debe aprenderse ciertos sonidos.*

Tu desafío

79 **Los desafíos**

¿Recuerdas los desafíos que Tim les planteó a los personajes? ¿Cuál te gusta más? Elige una de estas opciones y resuelve tu desafío.

DESAFÍO Ⓐ

Vas a organizar en tu casa una fiesta de cumpleaños al estilo mexicano. Escribe un correo electrónico a tu mejor amigo(a) para que te ayude a organizarla. Explica:

- A quién te apetece invitar y por qué. Ten en cuenta que los invitados deben llevarse bien.
- Qué elementos típicos de México debe haber en la fiesta.
- Qué vas a preparar tú y en qué te puede ayudar él/ella.

DESAFÍO Ⓑ

Diseña un cartel para promocionar el servicio de correo postal de tu ciudad. Incluye un dibujo o una fotografía y un eslogan convincente. Escribe también un breve texto o una lista con los beneficios que aporta este servicio.

DESAFÍO Ⓒ

Investiga sobre el silbo gomero y toma notas. Si puedes, mira algún video en Internet para ver cómo suena y cómo lo practican los habitantes de La Gomera.

Haz una presentación en clase explicando qué es y qué representa este lenguaje silbado.

Una tradición de antes para el mañana
El Silbo Gomero
Patrimonio Cultural Inmaterial de la Humanidad

cincuenta y cinco **55**

Activities

77. To elicit a more complete description for question #1, you may want to show students several pictures of García Márquez (you will find them online). Then, to help them with the description of Márquez's personality, read the following excerpt from an interview he gave to Rita Guibert: *El recuerdo más antiguo que tengo es que dibujaba cómics y ahora me doy cuenta que posiblemente lo hacía porque todavía no sabía escribir. Siempre he buscado medios para contar y me he quedado con la literatura, que es el más accesible. Pero pienso que mi vocación no es la de escritor sino la de contador de cuentos.*

79. For those students who choose the third *desafío*, suggest that they watch this video: http://cort.as/6KY5. Display students' work in the classroom and have the class vote on the best entry in each category.

Answer Key

77. Answers will vary. Sample answers:
1. Es el Nobel de Literatura colombiano Gabriel García Márquez. Tiene bigote y el pelo blanco y ondulado. Tienes algunas arrugas. Parece que tiene mucho sentido del humor y mucha personalidad.
2. Lo celebró en su casa de Ciudad de México, donde escribió *Cien años de soledad*, con un pastel con mariposas amarillas y rodeado de sus amigos y familiares. Creo que le interesa mucho la literatura. También me parece que le gustan las celebraciones en familia y, como vive en México, seguramente le gusta celebrar el cumpleaños con *Las mañanitas*.
3. Los pasteles con velitas son típicos en las fiestas de cumpleaños de mi país.

78. Answers will vary.
▶ Answers will vary.

79. Answers will vary.

HERITAGE LANGUAGE LEARNERS

- Have students discuss the following quote from García Márquez and explain to them that it appears in his memoirs: *La vida no es la que uno vivió, sino la que uno recuerda y cómo la recuerda para contarla*. Do students think that this implies that one might not be entirely truthful in writing one's autobiography? Or does it imply that one's memories are more accurate than the life one seemingly lived? Encourage students to share their opinions.

CRITICAL THINKING

- Ask students to think about the three *desafíos* presented in this unit. Ask them which one they think is the most culturally significant. Then, ask them to explain its cultural impact and why they believe it is more significant than the other two challenges. Students need to write at least two paragraphs and present their reasons convincingly. Invite volunteers to read their work aloud.

Additional Resources

Fans Online activities
Practice Workbook

MAPA CULTURAL

Unidad y variedad del español

Presentation

- This section presents information about dialectal varieties of the Spanish language. The images serve as a reference point for additional cultural readings and activities that expand on the skills students learned in this unit.

Activities	Standards	Resources
Mapa cultural	1.2, 2.1, 2.2, 3.2	
80.	1.1, 1.2, 1.3, 2.1	

Cultural Topics

- **Variaciones léxicas entre el español de España y de Hispanoamérica.** There are a few words that are common to all Spanish speakers in the Americas, but are different from the terms used in Spain. For example (the Latin American term appears first): cellular phone – *celular*, *móvil*; computer – *computadora* or *computador*, *ordenador*; juice – *jugo*, *zumo*; plumber – *plomero*, *fontanero*; potato – *papa*, *patata*. In some cases, there are differences in stress. For instance, in Spain, the words *chófer* and *pudin* are stressed on the second-to-last syllable; whereas in the Americas, these words are stressed on the last syllable (i.e., *chofer*, *pudín*).

- **Spanglish.** In areas of the United States where Spanish and English speakers have been in contact for many years, these two languages have combined in a particular way. In most cases, English words are adapted to Spanish pronunciation. For example: *lonche – almuerzo*; *parquear – estacionar*; *rufo – techo, tejado*; *troca – camioneta*; *wachimán – vigilante*. There are also cases of a literal translation into Spanish of English phrases, such as *esto no trabaja* (this does not work) for *esto no funciona* and *te llamo para atrás* (I'll call you back) for *te devuelvo la llamada*.

Teaching Suggestions

Warm-Up / Independent Starter

- Write these two sets of words on the board and have students guess the two things they name: 1. *anteojos, espejuelos, gafas, lentes*; 2. *bizcocho, pastel, queque, tarta, torta*. (eyeglasses, cake)

Unidad y variedad del español

El español es la lengua materna de unos 450 millones de personas en más de 20 países. Esta amplia distribución geográfica produce variaciones en el vocabulario, en la gramática y en la pronunciación.

Variaciones léxicas

Más del 80 por ciento del vocabulario es común a todos los hispanohablantes, pero hay diferencias que pueden dar lugar a malentendidos. A veces, una misma palabra tiene distintos significados según las regiones. Y, a veces, en distintos lugares se emplean palabras diferentes para expresar un mismo concepto.

¿Qué significa?

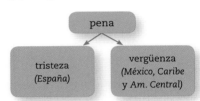

pena

tristeza (España)

vergüenza (México, Caribe y Am. Central)

¿Cómo se dice?

bañador (España) malla (Argentina, Chile) traje de baño (México) trusa (Cuba)	alberca (México) pileta (Argentina) piscina (España)
camiseta (España) franela (Venezuela) playera (México, Nicaragua) polera (Chile, Bolivia) remera (Argentina, Chile)	autobús (España) bus (Chile, Colombia) camión (México) colectivo (Argentina) guagua (Cuba, islas Canarias, Rep. Dom.)
amigo (España) compadre (Chile) cuate (México, Guatemala) llave (Colombia) mano (varios países)	caucho (Venezuela) goma (varios países) llanta (México) neumático (España)

Differentiated Instruction

DEVELOPING LEARNERS

- In pairs, have students review the highlighted words on page 56. Explain to them that they will choose a country or a geographical area mentioned on the page and create a short dialogue using some of these words. Encourage them to use their dictionaries to find more regional variants; for example, "errands" is *recados* in Spain, *mandados* throughout most of Latin America, and *diligencias* in parts of South America. Invite students to present their dialogues to the rest of the class.

EXPANDING LEARNERS

- Give students practice with *el voseo*. Write some on these forms on the board: *decís, podés, hacés, callás, comés, querés, vivís*, and ask students to identify the pattern. The irregular forms *vas* and *sos* correspond to *ir* and *ser*. Then, ask students to work with a partner and create a short dialogue that takes place in *el Cono Sur*. Invite pairs to present their conversations to the rest of the class.

Variaciones gramaticales

Las variaciones gramaticales no son tan numerosas como las variaciones léxicas, y no suelen impedir la comprensión entre los hablantes. Afectan sobre todo a los pronombres.

> **El voseo**
>
> En Argentina, Uruguay y Paraguay se usa *vos* en lugar de *tú*. Este fenómeno se llama voseo y provoca también un cambio en la forma verbal: *vos cantás* (en lugar de *tú cantas*); *vos sos* (en lugar de *tú eres*).

> **El uso de *vosotros* y de *ustedes***
>
> En el centro y el norte de España se distingue entre *vosotros* (tratamiento de confianza) y *ustedes* (tratamiento de respeto).
>
> En el sur de España y en las Américas se usa solo *ustedes* como forma de confianza y de respeto.

80 **Una lengua muy diversa**

▶ **Investiga.** Con tu compañero(a), busca palabras que se usan para hablar de la ropa y el calzado, la alimentación, las profesiones… en estas ciudades.

- Ciudad de México
- Buenos Aires
- Caracas
- Madrid

▶ **Escribe** un breve diálogo con tu compañero(a) usando las palabras que encontraste. Después, represéntenlo.

HERITAGE LANGUAGE LEARNERS

- Native speakers often confuse the following letters when spelling: *b/v, c/s/z, g/j, y/ll*, and omit or add *h* or written accents incorrectly. Explain to students that you are going to give them a spelling test (you might also make this a spelling bee). Say the following words:

1. *uvas*	6. *prohíbe*	11. *la enzima*
2. *garaje*	7. *jirafa*	12. *atropello*
3. *cazador*	8. *cebra*	13. *encima de*
4. *crujir*	9. *hacha*	14. *jeringa*
5. *una vez*	10. *realicé*	15. *imagen*

MULTIPLE INTELLIGENCES:
Visual-Spatial Intelligence

- Students will draw their own cartoon or cartoon strip. Have them work with a partner and create a character similar to Mafalda, and who is equally concerned with world issues, or one who is diametrically opposed to such concerns. Students are free to choose the topic, but must use the *voseo* form in their dialogues. Students may draw their cartoons by hand or use computer graphics. As always, encourage creativity and display students' work in the classroom.

Preparation

■ Invite students to share their Independent Starters. Did most guess correctly? Explain that, in some cases, lexical differences are due to loan words from indigenous languages. For instance, *ananás* (from Guarani *naná*) is the word for *piña* (pineapple) in most of South America. Other examples of the influence of indigenous languages include: 1. *calabaza* (pumpkin) → *auyama* (from Carib *auyamá*) in parts of the Caribbean basin, *ayote* (from Nahuatl *ayotli*) in parts of Central America, *zapallo* (from Quechua *sapallu*) in parts of South America; 2. *pimiento* (pepper) → *ají* (from Taino *haxi*) in the Antilles and most of South America, *chile* (from Nahuatl *chilli*) in Mexico and parts of Central America.

■ If there are heritage language learners in your class, invite them to share with the class other examples of lexical variations from their heritage country. Students might mention some localisms (i.e., words peculiar to a particular locality). In some cases, localisms are used to name things not found anywhere else (e.g., *pupusa, arepa, chipá, hallaca, tamal, mate, huipil, nopal*).

Activities

80. To get students started, provide these examples: *alubia* (Spain), *caraota* (Venezuela), *frijol* (Mexico, Central America), *habichuela* (Antilles), *poroto* (parts of South America). To expedite students' online search, suggest that they look for *Diccionario del español de* [name of country]. You may want to supervise students while they search online, since there are many sites that specialize in slang and swear words.

Answer Key

80. Answers will vary.
▶ Answers will vary.

Additional Resources

Fans Online activities
Practice Workbook

Unit 1
ESCRITURA
Un correo de presentación

Presentation

- In this section, students will practice and extend their writing skills. They will apply the vocabulary and grammar they have learned in this unit in order to write an e-mail introducing themselves.

Activities	Standards	Resources
Escritura	1.1, 1.2, 1.3, 2.1, 5.1, 5.2	

Teaching Suggestions

Warm-Up / Independent Starter

- Ask students to think of different reasons for sending someone an e-mail (e.g., to request information, to send a job application).

Preparation

- Invite students to share their Independent Starters. Then ask them to read the title of this page and the introduction silently. Had students thought of this kind of e-mail? Give students a few moments to imagine the situation (i.e., they are spending a month as exchange students in Mexico). As a class, discuss students' apprehensions about being in a foreign country, in the home of a family they do not know. Then ask students to look at the situation from the host family's point of view. How might the family feel about hosting a foreign student? Encourage students to think about these issues as they write their messages.

- Ask for a volunteer to read *La correspondencia personal* box aloud. As a class, discuss the language and style that is expected in this kind of correspondence. Clarify that personal correspondence is not synonymous with careless writing. Students should strive to write a thoughtfully crafted message.

Step-by-Step Instructions

Piensa

- If access to the Internet is available, encourage students to look for samples of introduction e-mails online. Then have them use the class discussion from the Preparation section to help them select the information they will include in their messages.

Un correo de presentación

La correspondencia personal

La correspondencia personal está formada por las cartas, mensajes y correos electrónicos que utilizamos en nuestra vida cotidiana para hacer una invitación, felicitar, agradecer, presentarnos, etc.

Al escribir una carta o un mensaje personal hay que tener muy en cuenta a quién nos dirigimos y con qué propósito, con el fin de elegir el tratamiento, el tono y el registro adecuados.

Imagina que vas a pasar un mes con una familia mexicana como estudiante de español. Vas a escribir un correo electrónico para presentarte.

La presentación y la corrección ortográfica dicen mucho de tu forma de ser, así que debes cuidarlas especialmente. Además, es importante que seas educado(a) y expreses tu agradecimiento por poder vivir con ellos durante tu estancia en el extranjero.

Piensa

- ¿Qué aspectos de ti mismo, de tu familia y de tu vida crees que debe conocer la familia de acogida? Selecciona los que te parezcan más adecuados y añade los que creas necesario.

Presentación
– Nombre, edad, lugar de residencia…
– Rasgos de personalidad.
– Estudios.
– Aficiones.
– Razones por las que estudias español.
– Razones por las que quieres ir a su país.

Descripción de tu familia
– Sus miembros (nombre, edad, profesión, etc.).
– Tu relación con ellos.
– Qué cosas hacéis juntos.

Otra información de interés
– Horarios.
– Alergias.

- ¿Qué te gustaría a ti saber de ellos? ¿Qué dudas te surgen? Haz una lista.

Modelo

Sobre la familia: ¿Cuántos miembros la componen? ¿Hay alguien de mi edad?
Sobre la casa: ¿La casa está cerca de la escuela a la que iré? ¿Tendré una habitación individual?
Sobre el barrio: ¿Hay algún centro deportivo? ¿Hay alguna biblioteca cerca?

Rubric for Evaluation

	Content	Organization	Conventions
1 point	Main purpose of the message is not clear. It has missing information. Word choice and tone are inappropriate.	Does not follow suggested format. No apparent organization, hard to follow. Very few or no transitions used.	Many errors in spelling, punctuation, grammar, and usage. Errors obscure meaning.
3 points	Main purpose of the message is clear. It is mostly complete. Word choice and tone are mostly appropriate for audience.	Format is close to the suggested model. Organization is clear, but some ideas may not be in the right sequence. Some transitions used.	Some errors in spelling, punctuation, grammar, and usage. Errors don't interfere with meaning.

Escribe

- Utiliza las ideas que anotaste en el paso anterior y escribe la primera versión de tu mensaje.

- Recuerda utilizar la forma *usted*, ya que no conoces a la familia a la que va dirigido el mensaje.

- No olvides agradecer a la familia su acogimiento.

Expresiones útiles

Saludo:

Querido(a)... / Estimado(a)...   *Dear ...*

Cuerpo:

Me dirijo a usted(es)...   *I am addressing you ...*
Me pongo en contacto   *I have contacted you ...*
  con usted(es) ...

Despedida y firma:

Un saludo.   *Regards ...*
Reciba(n) un cordial saludo.   *Please accept my*
        cordial greetings.
A la espera de sus noticias,   *I look forward to*
  le(s) saluda...   *hearing from you ...*

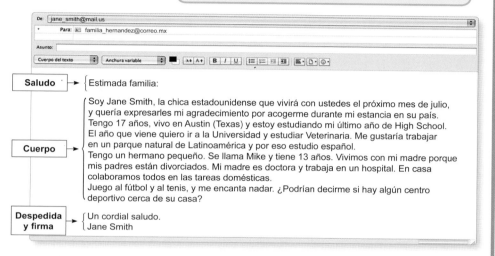

De: jane_smith@mail.us
Para: familia_hernandez@correo.mx
Asunto:

Saludo → Estimada familia:

Cuerpo →
Soy Jane Smith, la chica estadounidense que vivirá con ustedes el próximo mes de julio, y quería expresarles mi agradecimiento por acogerme durante mi estancia en su país. Tengo 17 años, vivo en Austin (Texas) y estoy estudiando mi último año de High School. El año que viene quiero ir a la Universidad y estudiar Veterinaria. Me gustaría trabajar en un parque natural de Latinoamérica y por eso estudio español.
Tengo un hermano pequeño. Se llama Mike y tiene 13 años. Vivimos con mi madre porque mis padres están divorciados. Mi madre es doctora y trabaja en un hospital. En casa colaboramos todos en las tareas domésticas.
Juego al fútbol y al tenis, y me encanta nadar. ¿Podrían decirme si hay algún centro deportivo cerca de su casa?

Despedida y firma →
Un cordial saludo.
Jane Smith

Revisa

- Intercambia tu mensaje con tu compañero(a) y revisa su correo.
  - ¿El texto cumple el objetivo? ¿La información está bien organizada?
  - ¿Ha empleado un vocabulario y unas construcciones gramaticales correctas?
  Devuelve el mensaje a su autor(a) con tus sugerencias.

- Revisa tu trabajo e incorpora los cambios que sean necesarios para escribir la versión definitiva.

Comparte

- Lee tu mensaje a la clase. ¿Qué opinan tus compañeros(as)? ¿Creen que tu mensaje refleja bien cómo eres? ¿Ofrece una buena imagen de ti mismo(a)?

cincuenta y nueve 59

	Content	Organization	Conventions
5 points	Main purpose of the message stands out. It is complete, clear, and concise. Word choice and tone are appropriate for audience.	Follows the suggested model. Organization is clear. Ideas are well sequenced. Uses transitions smoothly.	Few, if any, errors in spelling, punctuation, grammar, and usage. Excellent command of the Spanish language.

ESCRITURA

Un correo de presentación

- Encourage students to address both their own and the family's concerns in their message. However, their tone should not be apprehensive. Remind students that this is the first time they are communicating with this family and they should aim to make a positive impression.

Escribe

- Tell students that tone is very important in this kind of message. Have them analyze the *expresiones útiles* and determine the slight differences in tone between the different expressions. For instance, the word *estimado(a)* is slightly more formal and emotionally detached than *querido(a)*.

- As students compose their messages, remind them that the text should flow. They should strive to develop a picture of who they are, rather than simply listing their likes and interests.

Revisa

- Before students exchange their messages with a classmate, have them look at the format to make sure that they have included all the sections and information needed. Then ask them to read the first paragraph to themselves. Is the purpose of the message clearly stated in this first paragraph? Then have students exchange their texts and evaluate each other's message.

- Have students read their partner's text through before they mark anything. Then ask them to read the text again, looking at the content and organization. After this first evaluation, have students read the text one more time, looking for spelling, punctuation, grammar, vocabulary, and usage errors.

Comparte

- Emphasize the importance of selecting the right tone. Encourage students to transmit their message's tone when they read it aloud to their classmates. Ask students to pay attention to their body language and use it to help them convey their message.

Evaluation

- Distribute copies of the rubric to students and discuss the evaluation criteria. Ask students to refer to the rubric as they prepare their writing and as they evaluate their classmates' messages.

Unit 1

REPASO

Vocabulario

Presentation

■ In this section, students will review all key vocabulary from the unit, organized by themes, to prepare for an assessment. Students will complete practice activities for each of the three *Desafíos*.

Activities	Standards	Resources
1.	1.2, 1.3	
2.	1.2	
3.	1.1, 1.2	

Teaching Suggestions

Warm-Up / Independent Starter

■ Ask students to write a short description on a piece of paper of a historical figure or well-known personality. They should include both a physical description and a list of personality traits. Tell students not to name the person.

Preparation

■ Go over the *Repaso* presentation with the class. Then give students a couple of minutes to make a list of vocabulary words that come from other words they know. Next, have students write a short definition using both words. For example: *ondulado: de la palabra* onda, *que tiene ondas*; *apasionado: de la palabra* pasión, *que siente mucha pasión*; *titular: de título, el título de un artículo de prensa*. Invite volunteers to share some of their definitions with the class.

■ Collect students' papers from the Independent Starter and redistribute them to different students. Give the class a few moments to read their papers silently and think of an answer. Then call on individual students to read their papers aloud and make a guess. Ask them to justify their answers. If there are students in the class who do not agree, invite them to explain why and give their opinions. For example: *No creo que sea Abraham Lincoln porque Lincoln no era impulsivo. Creo que la persona es...* If all students agree on the identity of the person, have them come up with additional descriptive words that apply to the person. Encourage students to think of synonyms for words already mentioned.

60

REPASO Vocabulario

Características físicas y rasgos de personalidad

Características físicas

Ser...

ciego(a)	blind
mudo(a)	mute
sordo(a)	deaf
diestro(a)	right-handed
zurdo(a)	left-handed
como dos gotas de agua	identical

Tener...

arrugas	wrinkles
canas	grey hairs
el pelo	
ondulado	wavy hair

Rasgos de personalidad

Ser...

apasionado(a)	passionate
astuto(a)	shrewd
cobarde	cowardly
envidioso(a)	envious
estricto(a)	strict
humilde	modest, humble
impulsivo(a)	impulsive
indeciso(a)	indecisive
maleducado(a)	bad-mannered
terco(a)	stubborn
valiente	brave
vanidoso(a)	vain

¡Atención!

sensato(a)	sensible
sensible	sensitive

caer bien/mal	to like/dislike
tener personalidad	to have personality
tener sentido del humor	to have a sense of humor
tomarle el pelo a alguien	to trick, to tease someone

La oficina de correos

El correo

la balanza	scale
el buzón	mailbox
el/la cartero(a)	mail carrier
el correo aéreo	air mail
la correspondencia	mail
el envío	shipment
el franqueo	postage
el paquete	package
la tarjeta de felicitación	greeting card
la tarjeta navideña	Christmas card
la tarjeta postal	postcard
frágil	fragile
pesado(a)	heavy
certificado(a)	certified
urgente	urgent

La carta

el código postal	ZIP code
el/la destinatario(a)	addressee
la dirección	address
la estampilla	stamp
el/la remitente	sender
el sobre	envelope

Acciones

entregar	to deliver	recibir	to receive
enviar,		tardar	to delay
mandar	to send		

¡Atención!

la firma	signature	firmar	to sign

Los medios de comunicación

La prensa

el artículo	article
el editorial	editorial
la noticia	news
la primera plana	front page
la sección...	
de opinión	opinion section
de finanzas	finance section
internacional	international news
el titular	headline

La televisión

la cadena	network
el canal	channel
el concurso	game show
el documental	documentary
el noticiero	news
el programa	program
la programación	programming
la serie	series
el botón	button
el control remoto	remote
el sonido	sound
el volumen	volume

El cine

con subtítulos	with subtitles
en versión original	in the original version

El teléfono

el altavoz	loudspeaker
el teléfono inalámbrico	wireless telephone

¡Atención!

comentar	to discuss
discutir	to argue, to discuss

60 sesenta

Differentiated Instruction

DEVELOPING LEARNERS

• Ask students to write a description of someone and read it to a partner, who will draw a portrait of that person based on the description given, including personality traits. Then, a third student will write a description of the person based on the illustration. Next, have the three students compare the second written description with the original. Do they match? Are there major differences? If so, what are they? Is the inaccuracy in the drawing or in a student's misinterpretation of it? Have students discuss this among themselves.

EXPANDING LEARNERS

• Ask students to expand activity 2 by creating more clues for post office vocabulary, and by including words to describe *características físicas, rasgos de personalidad,* and *medios de comunicación*. You may want to have students work in teams and play against each other. For example: *Si tienen que devolverte una carta que mandaste, hay que incluir esto. (el remitente) Lo veo en la tele si quiero saber lo que está pasando en el mundo. (el noticiero) Es una persona que nunca cambia de opinión. (Es terca.) Las suelo mandar cuando estoy de vacaciones. (las tarjetas postales)*

DESAFÍO 1

1 **¡Qué diferentes!** Describe a cada persona usando otros adjetivos que expresen las mismas ideas.

Modelo *Raúl tiene el pelo ondulado y, aunque es joven...*

Raúl tiene el pelo casi rizado y, aunque es joven todavía, tiene algunas canas. Él cree que es muy atractivo y muy inteligente; no es nada humilde. Raúl pone mucha pasión en las cosas que hace y sabe bien lo que quiere.

A Marisa le encanta salir con sus amigos. Siempre piensa en cómo se sienten los demás y qué necesitan. Nunca tiene miedo. A veces hace las cosas sin pensar demasiado, pero siempre está haciendo bromas y es muy divertida.

DESAFÍO 2

2 **Adivínalo.** Escribe. ¿A qué palabras se refieren estas oraciones?

1. Las necesito para franquear una carta. Representan símbolos o emblemas de un país: escudos o banderas, flores, animales, personajes públicos, etc.
2. Cuando viajo, siempre compro algunas como recuerdo. Me gustan las que representan monumentos o paisajes típicos de un lugar. Y suelo escribirles una a mis familiares.
3. ¡Si no lo escribo en el sobre, la carta no llega! ¿Cómo van a saber en la oficina de correos a quién enviársela?
4. El empleado de correos la utiliza para pesar las cartas y los paquetes.
5. Va de casa en casa entregando las cartas y los paquetes postales.

DESAFÍO 3

3 **Ocio y comunicación.** Completa los bocadillos con las palabras del cuadro.

artículos	series	editoriales	noticieros	versión original	prensa

Yo practico el español siempre que puedo. Me gusta ver las películas en ___1___ y sigo varias ___2___ de televisión en español.

Yo veo los ___3___ en la televisión y leo la ___4___ todos los días. Me interesan los ___5___ de la sección internacional y los ___6___ .

HERITAGE LANGUAGE LEARNERS

- Ask students to imagine that a crime has been committed in the post office and they are journalists or TV reporters sent to cover the story. Encourage them to use as many terms from the vocabulary categories as they can to describe the crime, the setting, the presumed culprit and others who were there, and what they were doing. You might ask students to either write a news story complete with a headline, or make an on-the-scene report for TV.

MULTIPLE INTELLIGENCES:
Verbal-Linguistic Intelligence

- Have students play "Jeopardy." Display the following categories: *la oficina de correos, rasgos de personalidad, características físicas, medios de comunicación,* and assign a value to them based on difficulty. Prepare questions and answers for each of these categories, or ask students to prepare them for other contestants. Four to five students will play against each other, or have teams of several players play. Example statements/questions include: *Te ayudan a entender una película extranjera. / ¿Qué son subtítulos?; Sirve para pesar las cartas. / ¿Qué es una balanza?*

Unit 1
REPASO
Vocabulario

- Organize a game to practice words related to the postal service. Divide the class into small groups. Write words on small index cards, put them in a bag, and have one student from each group pick a card. The student will then write the word vertically on the board, and within a given time limit, write words using each letter of the original word as the initial letter for a word. For example: sobre → **s**ensible; **o**rgulloso; **b**onita; **r**ecibir; **e**stricto.

Activities

1. To expand this activity, have students add a paragraph to each description. In their paragraphs, ask students to elaborate on the original description by adding physical characteristics and personality traits. Tell students to justify some of their choices. For example: *Raúl seguramente es impulsivo porque la gente apasionada suele ser también impulsiva*. Invite students to share their paragraphs with the class.

2. Ask students to work with a partner to complete this activity. Then have pairs interview each other regarding their use of communication devices and the media.

Answer Key

1. Answers will vary. Sample answers:
   1. Tiene el pelo ondulado. Cree que es muy guapo y muy astuto; es vanidoso. Es apasionado y seguro de sí mismo.
   2. Marisa es amistosa. Es sensible y valiente. Es un poco impulsiva, pero tiene sentido del humor.

2.
   1. las estampillas
   2. las tarjetas postales
   3. el destinatario
   4. la balanza
   5. el cartero

3.
   1. versión original
   2. series
   3. noticieros
   4. prensa
   5. artículos
   6. editoriales

Additional Resources

Fans Online activities
Practice Workbook

REPASO

Gramática

Presentation

- Students will review grammatical structures presented in the unit. Each grammar point is cross-referenced to the corresponding page on which it was introduced. The activities here provide systematic practice by *Desafío*.

Activities	Standards	Resources
4.	1.1, 1.2	
5.	1.2	
6.	1.3	
7. Cultura	1.1, 1.2, 2.1, 2.2	

Teaching Suggestions

Warm-Up / Independent Starter

- Give students a couple of minutes to review the grammar topics on this page silently.

Preparation

- Ask students to get together with a classmate. Then have them close their textbooks and answer the following questions in writing:

  1. Tell your partner your likes and interests regarding media communication, including social media. Then compare each other's interests.

  2. Translate these sentences into Spanish:
     a. They have a grand house. *(Tienen una gran casa.)* b. They have a big house. *(Tienen una casa grande.)*

  3. Translate these sentences into Spanish:
     a. He regrets some of the things he did in his youth. *(Se arrepiente de algunas cosas que hizo en su juventud.)* b. Two criminals ran away from prison. *(Dos criminales se fugaron de la prisión.)*

  4. Compare your daily routine with your partner's.

  5. Tell your partner one thing you will be doing this coming Saturday at this time.

  6. Talk to your partner about some statistics (e.g., number of attendees, scores, percentage of men and women) from the last sports or musical event you attended or watched.

  Ask students to open their textbooks and check their answers. Are most of their answers correct? Provide additional practice as necessary.

REPASO Gramática

Expresar gustos, intereses, sentimientos y emociones (pág. 22)

me te le nos os les	gustar encantar + preocupar molestar sorprender	+ infinitivo + que + subjuntivo

Verbos pronominales (pág. 34)

VERBOS CON CAMBIO DE SIGNIFICADO

acabar/acabarse
acordar/acordarse
aprender/aprenderse
dormir/dormirse
estudiar/estudiarse
ir/irse
levantar/levantarse

parecer/parecerse
poner/ponerse
quedar/quedarse
romper/romperse
salir/salirse
volver/volverse

Verbos reflexivos y recíprocos (pág. 36)

VERBOS REFLEXIVOS

acostarse   lavarse   vestirse
bañarse   levantarse
ducharse   maquillarse

VERBOS RECÍPROCOS

abrazarse   despedirse   odiarse
apoyarse   entenderse   pelearse
ayudarse   escribirse   perdonarse
besarse   hablarse   quererse
conocerse   llamarse   saludarse
contarse   mirarse   verse

Expresar cantidad (pág. 48)

LOS CUANTIFICADORES NUMERALES

medio / la mitad (de)
un tercio, un cuarto, un quinto
la tercera parte, la cuarta parte, la quinta parte
el doble, el triple, el cuádruple
dos / tres / ... veces más

Los adjetivos. Posición y significado (pág. 24)

POSICIÓN DE LOS ADJETIVOS CALIFICATIVOS

- Detrás del nombre, los adjetivos que expresan clases y cualidades.
  Cartagena de Indias es una ciudad turística.

- Delante del nombre, los adjetivos que expresan una cualidad típica.
  A lo lejos se veían las altas montañas.

ADJETIVOS CON CAMBIO DE SIGNIFICADO

Adjetivo	Antes del nombre	Después del nombre
antiguo(a)	former, ex-	ancient, antique
viejo(a)	long-standing	old, elderly
nuevo(a)	different, other	brand new
gran / grande	great, famous	big, large
pobre	unfortunate	penniless
único(a)	only	unique

Hablar de acciones en curso (pág. 46)

PRESENTE PROGRESIVO

estar (en presente) + gerundio

PASADO PROGRESIVO

estar (en imperfecto) + gerundio

estar (en pretérito) + gerundio

FUTURO PROGRESIVO

estar (en futuro) + gerundio

LOS CUANTIFICADORES INDEFINIDOS

algún, alguno(a)(os)(as)   bastante(s)   alguien
ningún, ninguno(a)   suficiente(s)   nadie
poco(a)(os)(as)   todo(a)(os)(as)   algo
mucho(a)(os)(as)   varios(as)   nada
demasiado(a)(os)(as)   otro(a)(os)(as)
                             cualquier(a)

Differentiated Instruction

DEVELOPING LEARNERS

- Ask students which word does not belong.

  1. enfadarse   divertirse   enojarse *(divertirse)*
  2. abrazarse   pelearse   besarse *(pelearse)*
  3. gustar   encantar   doler *(doler)*
  4. volverse   irse   fugarse *(volverse)*
  5. alegrar   dar pena   deprimir *(alegrar)*
  6. acabar   terminar   quedar *(quedar)*
  7. molestar   caer bien   gustar *(molestar)*
  8. asustar   caer mal   dar miedo *(caer mal)*
  9. interesar   fascinar   preocupar *(preocupar)*
  10. enterarse apoyarse   darse cuenta *(apoyarse)*

EXPANDING LEARNERS

- Ask students to explain the difference between the following pairs of sentences:

  1. *El jefe despidió a Juan. / Juan y yo nos despedimos.*
  2. *El ruido me despertó. / Ayer me desperté a las 5:00 a. m.*
  3. *Acosté al niño después de cenar. / Me acosté temprano.*
  4. *Ana maquilla a las modelos. / Esta joven se maquilla muy mal.*
  5. *Los políticos acordaron reunirse. / ¿Se acuerdan de su serie favorita?*
  6. *¿Por qué se fueron tan deprisa? / ¿Fueron al museo ya?*

DESAFÍO 1

4 **Gustos y emociones.** Completa estas oraciones.

1. A mi hermana _____ mi maleta roja.
   encantar
2. A sus amigos _____ el cine español.
   interesar
3. Ayer vi a Rosa en el teatro y _____ que no me saludara.
   extrañar
4. A Sara y a Jaime _____ nuestros antiguos compañeros de la escuela.
   caer bien
5. Vengan conmigo a la montaña el próximo sábado, _____ sus paisajes únicos.
   fascinar

DESAFÍO 2

5 **¿Con o sin pronombre?** Elige la opción correcta.

1. Este paquete es muy pesado, casi no puedo _____.
   a. levantarse   b. lo levanto   c. levantarlo
2. La profesora _____ el nombre de todos los alumnos el primer día de clase.
   a. aprendió   b. aprende   c. se aprendió
3. Ayer no _____ muy tarde de la fiesta porque estaba muy cansado.
   a. me fui   b. fue   c. fui
4. Este objeto es frágil; si no lo llevas con cuidado, puede _____.
   a. romperlo   b. romper   c. romperse
5. No _____ leche en el refrigerador.
   a. le quedan   b. queda   c. se queda

DESAFÍO 3

6 **Acciones en curso.** Completa usando el presente, el pasado o el futuro progresivo.

1. Ayer, mientras esperaba a Javier…
2. Ahora mismo yo…
3. Cuando Luisa salga del trabajo, tú y yo…
4. Cuando tú fuiste de vacaciones a Costa Rica, yo…
5. El día que tú tomes el avión a Nueva York, mi familia y yo…

CULTURA

7 **Tradiciones.** Responde a estas preguntas.

1. ¿De qué están hechas las piñatas tradicionales? ¿Qué contienen?
2. ¿Cómo se llamaban los mensajeros del imperio inca?
3. ¿Qué lengua reproduce el silbo gomero? ¿Para qué se creó este lenguaje silbado?

HERITAGE LANGUAGE LEARNERS

• Ask students to imagine that they have been given the opportunity to complete one of the *desafíos* in this unit. Then, ask them to write an e-mail to a friend explaining why they have chosen this challenge and how they plan to go about completing it. Next, ask students to imagine that they have completed the *desafío* and have them write another e-mail to their friend describing their experience, including how they resolved the challenge, and whether they completed it successfully.

CRITICAL THINKING

• Facilitate a classroom discussion on the role that traditions, such as birthday celebrations, preserving the language of one's ancestors, and observing ancient customs have had and continue to have on cultures. You might ask students these or similar questions: *¿Qué significa para ustedes la celebración del cumpleaños? ¿Por qué creen que la gente disfruta de estas celebraciones? ¿Es importante conservar vivo un idioma único como el silbo gomero? ¿Por qué? ¿Qué aprendemos al observar costumbres antiguas como las carreras de los chasquis?*

REPASO

Gramática

■ Go over the *Repaso* presentation with the class. Then invite volunteer pairs to share some of their answers to the Preparation activity with the class and identify the different grammar structures being reviewed in this *Repaso*.

Activities

5. To expand this activity, have students come up with a sentence for each option they did not use. For example: 1. *Carlos no quiere <u>levantarse</u> temprano. / Si algo es liviano, <u>lo levanto</u> fácilmente.* Invite students to share their sentences with the class.

6. Once students have completed this activity, ask them to create a questionnaire to interview a classmate. For example: 1. *¿Qué estabas haciendo ayer mientras almorzabas?* 2. *¿Qué estás haciendo ahora mismo?* 3. *¿Qué estarás haciendo mañana a esta hora?* Then have them pair up with another student and interview each other. After the interview, students will write a paragraph summarizing their partner's responses.

Answer Key

4. 1. le encanta   4. les caen bien
   2. les interesa   5. les fascinarán
   3. me extrañó

5. 1. c   2. c   3. a   4. c   5. b

6. Answers will vary. Sample answers:
   1. … estuve leyendo.
   2. … estoy escribiendo.
   3. … estaremos viendo una película en el cine.
   4. … estaba trabajando en el banco.
   5. … estaremos volando a Londres.

7. Answers will vary. Sample answers:
   1. Son de barro y contienen dulces.
   2. Se llamaban chasquis.
   3. Reproduce el español. Se creó para poder comunicarse de un pueblo a otro, ya que la isla es muy montañosa.

Additional Resources

Fans Online activities
Practice Workbook

Unit 1

PROYECTO

Nuestra clase de Español

Presentation

- In this section, students will apply the vocabulary, grammar, and cultural information they have learned in this unit to design a webpage for their Spanish class.

Activities	Standards	Resources
Paso 1	1.1, 1.3, 5.1, 5.2	
Paso 2	1.1, 1.3, 2.1, 5.1, 5.2	
Paso 3	1.1, 3.1, 5.1, 5.2	
Paso 4	1.1, 1.3, 2.1, 5.1, 5.2	
Paso 5	1.1, 1.3, 2.1, 3.1, 5.1, 5.2	

Teaching Suggestions

Warm-Up / Independent Starter

- Ask students to read the introduction to the project silently. Then have them think about webpages they visit often and the features they like best about those pages.

Preparation

- Invite students to share their thoughts from the Independent Starter. You may wish to record on the board any commonalities in students' answers (e.g., design, ease of use, relevance of content, opportunities to interact with other users). Then give students a few moments to list some of the things they do in their Spanish class. Next, ask them to think about the users of the site (i.e., their classmates) and list what they think would be of interest to their classmates about the study of Spanish and their Spanish class. Call on students to share their lists with the class. Then divide the class into groups of three or four to work on the project.

Step-by-Step Instructions

Paso 1

- During this step, students should think through the whole webpage and make a list of all that needs to be included in it. They may find it useful to first determine the page's purpose as well as its intended audience. Encourage students to think of ways in which their page can promote interaction between the users.

64

PROYECTO

Una página web de

nuestra clase de Español

En este proyecto vas a diseñar una página web para tu clase de Español. En ella deberás recoger información útil e interesante para ustedes.

PASO 1 Elige las secciones

- Reúnete con tres o cuatro compañeros(as) y decidan qué secciones les gustaría que tuviera su página web. Aquí tienen algunas sugerencias:

> información sobre la escuela y la clase de Español

> información sobre los desafíos

> lo que más les gusta del español

> lo que más les gusta de la cultura hispana

> consejos para aprender mejor

> trabajos y proyectos realizados en clase

> fotos o videos de momentos importantes del curso

> enlaces a páginas web interesantes

- Decidan si quieren incluir un foro en su página web donde sus compañeros(as) puedan hacer comentarios y escribir sus opiniones.

PASO 2 Prepara la información de las secciones

- Escriban una primera versión de los textos para cada una de las secciones elegidas.
- Busquen fotos e imágenes para ilustrar cada sección.

Nuestra clase de EspaÑol

| Conócenos | Los desafíos | Galería de fotos | Tu opinión |

Conócenos

En esta página web encontrarás información útil sobre la clase de Español. También podrás participar y expresar tus opiniones.

Rubric for Evaluation

	Content	Organization	Presentation
1 point	Information is incomplete or not focused. Little consideration was put into image choices and design.	Inefficient use of time. Site is disorganized, unclear, and difficult to navigate.	Unclear communication, not fluent. Many errors in vocabulary and grammar.
3 points	Relevant and focused information, but some of it lacks significance. Some consideration was put into image choices and design.	Time is used well. Site is mostly organized but it lacks some clarity. Relatively easy to navigate.	Clear communication, mostly fluent. Mostly correct vocabulary and grammar.

PASO 3 Decide el diseño

- Definan el diseño de su página web. Piensen en los colores, en el tipo de letra…
- Diseñen los iconos que van a aparecer en la página.

PASO 4 Desarrolla las secciones

- Revisen los textos que prepararon en el Paso 2 y escriban la versión final. Después, seleccionen las imágenes definitivas para cada sección.

Conócenos

En esta página web encontrarás toda la información de la clase de Español: horarios, libros de texto, actividades, excursiones…

Además, tú podrás participar en este espacio aportando tus opiniones, comentarios, experiencias y mucho más.

¡Seguro que este curso lo disfrutaremos todos!

PASO 5 Presenta tu página web

- Presenten su página web a la clase y contesten las preguntas y dudas de sus compañeros(as). Pueden hacer un póster, una presentación de Power Point…
- Entre todos(as), elijan la página web que más les guste. Deben explicar las razones de su elección.
- ¿Cuál ha sido la página favorita? ¿Por qué no la hacen entre todos(as)? Así podrán utilizarla durante el curso.

Unidad 1

Autoevaluación

¿Qué has aprendido en esta unidad?

Haz estas actividades para comprobar tu progreso.

Evalúa tus habilidades. Para cada punto, di Muy bien, Bien o Necesito practicar más.

a. ¿Puedes describir personas?

▶ Describe las características físicas y los rasgos de personalidad de tu personaje favorito de ficción.

▶ Compara este personaje con tu primer(a) amigo(a). ¿Qué cosas te sorprenden de esta comparación?

b. ¿Puedes expresar acciones habituales?

▶ Explica qué hace una persona en la oficina de correos.

▶ Describe una relación por correspondencia real o imaginaria con un(a) amigo(a); cómo se comunican ustedes, qué se dicen en sus cartas, etc.

c. ¿Puedes hablar de acciones en curso?

▶ ¿Qué estás haciendo en este curso? Escribe un párrafo explicando con detalle lo que estás haciendo.

Nuestra clase de Español

Paso 2

- To make more efficient use of time, suggest to students that they assign a different section to each group member, who must then develop its content and look for images. Once they have finished, students discuss their texts and art choices as a group.

Paso 3

- Remind students that colors, font choices, and size help organize the information and allow for easy reading. The page should be visually appealing and have visual coherence.

Paso 4

- Emphasize the importance of correct punctuation, spelling, and grammar. Errors distract from the content. As students decide on the images, remind them that their visuals should enhance the content of their page and create interest.

Paso 5

- Ask students to try to anticipate the kind of questions that their classmates might ask and prepare themselves by taking notes that will help them answer these questions. Rehearsals should enable students to present confidently and fluently. If a real webpage cannot be developed, students can create a mock-up webpage on a poster.

Evaluation

- Distribute copies of the rubric to students. Discuss the evaluation criteria and explain how this project will be graded. Encourage students to refer to the rubric as they prepare their projects.

Content

- Explain that the page's content should reflect its purpose. Students should select information that is relevant, interesting, and current. The page should also be easy to read and understand.

Organization

- Users should be able to find topics easily. Encourage students to include an outline of topics covered. Navigation should be clear and logical.

Presentation

- Remind students to speak clearly and to pause often to give their audience time to process the information. Once they have finished, ask students to thank their audience and invite questions.

	Content	Organization	Presentation
5 points	Relevant, focused, and interesting information. Images and design are interesting and creative.	Time is used wisely. Site is well organized, clear, and very easy to navigate.	Clear communication. Fluent delivery. Correct and complete vocabulary and grammar.

HACIA EL AP* EXAM

Interpretive Communication: Print Texts

Presentation

- These pages present students with a sample activity from the "Interpretive Communication: Print Texts" portion of the AP* Spanish Language and Culture Exam. Students will read an authentic text from the Spanish-speaking world and answer several multiple-choice questions based on the reading.

Activities	Standards	Resources
Interpretive Communication: Print Texts	1.2, 2.1, 2.2, 3.1, 3.2, 5.1, 5.2	

Preparing for the Exam

The Exam

- The AP* Spanish Language and Culture Exam tests students' ability to communicate in the three modes of communication: Interpretive, Interpersonal, and Presentational. Students are asked to read, listen, write, and speak in Spanish on a variety of topics. The exam has six sections and lasts for a total of approximately three hours. For more information, you may wish to visit apcentral.collegeboard.com.

About This Section

- The "Interpretive Communication: Print Texts" section of the AP* Exam requires students to read authentic journalistic or literary text sources and answer multiple-choice questions based on their comprehension. This section of the exam lasts approximately 40 minutes, and contains a total of 30 questions distributed among several reading selections. In this section of the Student Book, however, students will only be asked to answer questions for one reading selection. You may wish to prepare additional activities in order to simulate the Print Texts section of the AP* Exam.

- In the multiple-choice questions of this section of the exam, students will be asked to identify the text's main ideas and significant details, as well as make inferences and predictions. Reading critically is especially important.

Hacia el AP* Exam

Interpretive Communication: Print Texts

Presentación

La primera prueba del examen AP* es una prueba de comprensión de lectura. Consta de varios textos seguidos de preguntas de opción múltiple.

Los textos proceden de fuentes auténticas: periódicos, revistas, páginas web u otras publicaciones del mundo hispano. Pueden estar acompañados por tablas u otros gráficos.

En las preguntas que siguen a cada texto, hay que escoger la opción que mejor contesta cada pregunta. Estas preguntas están basadas en los objetivos de aprendizaje establecidos por los organizadores del examen. Es importante leer cada opción cuidadosamente, porque a veces se parecen mucho.

Estrategias

Prelectura

- Realiza una lectura rápida del texto para tener una idea general de cuál es el tema.
- Lee las preguntas y las opciones de respuesta.

Lectura

- Lee el texto cuidadosamente, intentando captar tanto los datos más importantes como el mensaje y el propósito básico del texto.
- Vuelve a leer el texto y localiza la información o palabras clave.
- Si hay alguna palabra que no entiendas, intenta concentrarte en la idea general de la oración, no en la palabra específica.

Preguntas

- Para responder las preguntas de opción múltiple, guíate por las palabras clave que señalaste en el texto.

Instrucciones para el examen

Directions: You will read a print text. The passage is followed by a number of comprehension questions. For each question, select the answer that is best according to the reading passage.

Instrucciones: Vas a leer un texto. El texto va seguido de varias preguntas de comprensión. Para cada pregunta, elige la mejor respuesta de acuerdo con el texto.

Introducción

Este texto fue publicado originalmente en http://www.informativoweb.com y se refiere a la presentación del primer diccionario de abreviaturas utilizadas en los SMS.

---

*AP is a registered trademark of the College Board, which was not involved in the production of, and does not endorse, this product.

Language Expansion

VOCABULARY

- Students may have difficulty with these words and phrases from the reading:

SMS	→	mensaje de texto
trasgresor	→	que viola las leyes
castellano	→	español
euskera	→	lengua del País Vasco
lote	→	partes de una lotería
subrayado	→	enfatizado
palpable	→	evidente
suprimiendo	→	eliminando
alejamiento	→	distanciamiento
plantearse	→	considerar
valiosa	→	de mucho valor
rechazo	→	no aceptación

GRAMMAR STRUCTURES:
Subjects and Verbs within Sentences

- In Spanish, the subject of a sentence may be found relatively far from the verb, and this may make understanding the text more difficult. Ask students to identify the subject of each sentence in the article and note the verb that accompanies it. Have students rephrase certain sentences, placing the subject directly before the verb: *El proyecto diccionarioSMS.com, presentado como una iniciativa de la Asociación de Usuarios de Internet (AUI) con motivo del próximo Día de Internet, pretende recoger...* → *El proyecto diccionarioSMS.com pretende recoger...*

Nace 'exo x ti y xa ti', el primer diccionario de abreviaturas SMS

El proyecto diccionarioSMS.com, presentado como una iniciativa de la Asociación de Usuarios de Internet (AUI) con motivo del próximo Día de Internet, pretende recoger los términos y las abreviaturas que emplean los jóvenes cuando escriben mensajes en sus teléfonos móviles o a través de la Red (messenger, correo electrónico, chat, etc.), en lo que se ha configurado como «una especie de dialecto propio, práctico, instantáneo y trasgresor», según Miguel Pérez Subías, presidente de esta asociación. «Queremos ayudar a los padres, profesores y lingüistas a no ignorar, sino conocer mejor esta realidad».

diccionarioSMS.com permitirá consultar y traducir términos SMS en castellano, catalán, euskera y gallego, así como conocer qué términos son los más utilizados, además de incorporar comentarios colaborativos, al estilo de Wikipedia. Puede consultarse tanto por Internet en diccionarioSMS.com como por teléfono móvil enviando un mensaje corto al 5857 seguido de la palabra clave ddi y del término SMS que se quiere consultar.

Paralelamente, los organizadores han anunciado las bases del concurso diario entre todos los usuarios que registren los términos y abreviaturas. El lote de premios diarios consiste en 21 teléfonos móviles de última generación, 10.000 horas de descarga de música, 10 juegos para la plataforma xBox, una consola xBox, y bonos para enviar hasta 9.000 SMS desde el PC al móvil.

José de la Peña, director de Acción Institucional de Telefónica Móviles España, ha destacado «las posibilidades del móvil como una herramienta de comunicación inmediata, rápida y muy personal, que ha facilitado que los usuarios, principalmente los jóvenes, hayan creado un lenguaje específico. diccionarioSMS.com contribuirá a ordenar, entender y clarificar este nuevo lenguaje, de uso cada vez más frecuente».

Ns vms n la fsta sta trd. qdms a ls 8. bss

«Las comunicaciones online y sms se están introduciendo en los hábitos de los jóvenes, a las que dedican cada vez más tiempo. Con este diccionarioSMS.com nos acercamos a esta realidad con un completo manual que nos ayudará a entender mejor este nuevo «lenguaje», declara Víctor Castro, Country Manager de MSN España. Por su parte, Sisco Sapena, director ejecutivo de Lleida.net, ha subrayado que «los jóvenes adaptan constantemente las nuevas tecnologías a sus formas de comunicación y a sus relaciones interpersonales. El proceso de elaboración de este primer diccionario SMS, de elaboración popular, será una muestra palpable de este fenómeno social.»

«Esta iniciativa es una demostración de que el uso de los teléfonos móviles forma parte del modo de comunicarse de los jóvenes actuales, como lo demuestra el uso masivo que hacen del servicio de mensajes cortos», ha asegurado Joaquín Mollinedo, Director Corporativo de Relaciones Institucionales y Regulación de Grupo Auna.»

«Cada 90 segundos se envía un millón de SMS en todo el mundo, con un lenguaje universal,» ha explicado Miguel Udaondo, director de Relaciones Corporativas de Vodafone España. «Los usuarios nos hemos adaptado al terminal para ser entendidos, suprimiendo en el mensaje todo aquello que no es necesario.»

Nuevos usos que interesan y mucho en los colegios. «Me preocupa el uso que se hace de nuestro idioma por el alejamiento que supone de la uniformidad del idioma creando un código que dificulte la comunicación», explica Concha Badía, profesora de Lengua del Colegio Ramón y Cajal, «pero por otra parte, considero que la lengua está viva y es, sobre todo, de los hablantes y por tanto suya y, como tal, pueden transformarla. Quiero con esto decir que hay que escuchar y plantearse si hay una parte valiosa en su forma de comunicación. Un rechazo frontal no creo que nos condujera a nada.»

Fuente: http://www.informativoweb.com

More Practice

FINDING ADDITIONAL SOURCES

- You can find additional print texts online in order to give students further practice at reading authentic texts. Look for a wide variety of text genres, such as informative articles, short works of fiction, poems, graphs and tables, and publicity (posters, announcements, etc.). Most texts will be around one page long.

ADDITIONAL SOURCES

- You may find interesting print texts at the following news websites:
  El País (Spain): elpais.com
  BBC Mundo: www.bbc.co.uk/mundo
  El Nuevo Herald (Miami): www.elnuevoherald.com
  El Diario (New York): www.eldiariony.com
  El Tiempo (Colombia): www.eltiempo.com
- Be sure to review the texts to make sure the topic, length, and reading level are appropriate for your students.

HACIA EL AP* EXAM

Interpretive Communication: Print Texts

Strategies: Reading

- Have students read the *Presentación* section silently. Ask them to brainstorm ways that authentic text sources might be different from translations or texts written specifically for second-language learners.

- Ask students to read the *Estrategias* box with a partner, then discuss which strategies they think will be the most useful. Do they know of any other useful reading strategies? Have the pairs share their ideas and compile a class list.

- Have students read the instructions to this activity carefully. What aspect do they feel the most anxious about: the text difficulty, the time limit, or something else? Reading with a strict time limit gives many students difficulty, regardless of their language proficiency. In order to prepare students for a reduced time limit, begin giving them time expectations for their classwork and homework. Help them learn to use skimming and scanning techniques to orient themselves when reading.

Extension Activities

- After having students complete the reading comprehension activity, you may wish to use the reading passage in a variety of other ways in order to give students practice for the exam.

  - Have students create two more multiple-choice questions about the reading, then exchange them with a classmate. Identifying the questions that may be asked on an exam is a good way to be sure students have understood the most critical points of the text.

  - Ask students to send an e-mail reaction to this reading to a classmate. In their e-mail, they should briefly summarize the article, then react to what they read.

  - Allow student pairs to have a two-minute conversation about the article in which they each explain what they understood, aspects that surprised or confused them, and further questions they have about the topic.

Additional Resources

Español Santillana AP* Preparation Workbook

HACIA EL AP* EXAM

Interpretive Communication: Print Texts

Presentation

- The fourteen multiple-choice questions on these pages comprise the reading comprehension activity that accompanies the text selection on the previous page. Students have the opportunity to read the selection and answer the comprehension questions based on the reading.

Activities	Standards	Resources
Interpretive Communication: Print Texts	1.2, 2.1, 2.2, 3.1, 3.2, 5.1, 5.2	

Preparing for the Exam

Critical Reading

- The AP* Spanish Language and Culture Exam requires students to not only understand the authentic text selections presented, but also read the texts critically, employing literacy skills as well as language skills. While some of the questions will naturally be particular to the specific text presented, there are some types of questions and tasks that may be commonly asked. By identifying these topics and presenting them to students frequently during regular classwork and homework, students may be more readily able to answer them during a testing scenario as well. These include:
  - Who is the intended audience for this text?
  - What is the tone of the article?
  - What is the article's objective?
  - What literary device does the author use?
  - How does the author achieve his or her objective?
  - What does (a particular word or phrase) mean in this context?
  - What does (a particular word or phrase) refer to in this article?
  - How could you best summarize the article?
- Additionally, encourage students to use context clues and word and sentence structure. This will help them to decipher unknown vocabulary and will enhance their comprehension of the content.

1 **¿Cuál es el objetivo del artículo?**
- (A) Analizar la situación actual de los SMS.
- (B) Mostrar las abreviaturas utilizadas en los SMS.
- (C) Informar acerca del proyecto diccionarioSMS.com.
- (D) Promover el uso de diccionarioSMS.com.

2 **¿Qué recurso utiliza el autor para argumentar su artículo?**
- (A) La opinión de diferentes personas.
- (B) El resultado de encuestas realizadas.
- (C) Una investigación realizada por una compañía de teléfonos.
- (D) La búsqueda de información en Internet.

3 **¿A qué se refiere la frase «una especie de dialecto propio, práctico, instantáneo y trasgresor»?**
- (A) A la forma de comunicación empleada por los jóvenes.
- (B) Al lenguaje utilizado en los SMS.
- (C) Al objetivo de diccionarioSMS.com.
- (D) A la opinión de Miguel Pérez Subías.

4 **¿Qué frase resume mejor el objetivo de diccionarioSMS.com?**
- (A) «Contribuirá a ordenar, entender y clarificar este nuevo lenguaje, de uso cada vez más frecuente».
- (B) «Ha facilitado que los usuarios, principalmente los jóvenes, hayan creado un lenguaje específico».
- (C) «Las comunicaciones online y SMS se están introduciendo en los hábitos de los jóvenes».
- (D) «Esta iniciativa es una demostración de que el uso de los teléfonos móviles forma parte del modo de comunicarse de los jóvenes actuales».

5 **¿Quiénes pueden participar en el concurso que han preparado los organizadores?**
- (A) Los usuarios que se registren en diccionarioSMS.com.
- (B) Las personas que colaboren enviando términos y abreviaturas a diccionarioSMS.com.
- (C) Padres, profesores y lingüistas.
- (D) Los jóvenes menores de 21 años.

6 **Según el artículo, ¿qué ha facilitado el uso del móvil como herramienta de comunicación?**
- (A) Que los usuarios hayan creado un lenguaje particular.
- (B) Que los jóvenes ordenen y entiendan el lenguaje.
- (C) Que los usuarios puedan clarificar los mensajes.
- (D) Que los jóvenes se adapten a las nuevas tecnologías.

7 **¿Con qué propósito la Asociación de Usuarios de Internet presentó el proyecto diccionarioSMS.com?**
- (A) Para demostrar que los SMS son un fenómeno social.
- (B) Para enviar 9.000 SMS desde el PC al móvil.
- (C) Para celebrar el Día de Internet.
- (D) Para conocer qué términos SMS son los más utilizados.

More Information

ABOUT SMS

- While the concept of SMS (short message service), or text messages, was developed in 1984, the first text message was not sent until 1992, when Neil Papworth—a software engineer at Sema Group—sent Richard Jarvis, the then director of Vodafone, two words typed from his PC: "Merry Christmas." In 1995, Americans sent an average of only 0.4 text messages per month. By 2013, that number had risen to around 570.
- The abbreviation SMS will appear in the 23rd edition of the *Diccionario de la lengua española* published by the *Real Academia Española*.

COMMON SMS ABBREVIATIONS IN SPANISH

a2	→ adiós	k qrs?	→ ¿qué quieres?
aki	→ aquí	k tl?	→ ¿qué tal?
b	→ bien	mxo	→ mucho
bss	→ besos	nl	→ en el / en la
d	→ de	pq	→ por qué, porque
dnd	→ dónde	q	→ que
ers 2	→ ¿eres tú?	tas ok?	→ ¿estás bien?
exo	→ hecho	tb	→ también
find	→ fin de semana	tq	→ te quiero
hl	→ hasta luego	xfa	→ por favor
hla	→ hola	+	→ más
kls	→ clase	−	→ menos

8 **¿Qué se puede afirmar acerca del proceso de elaboración de este primer diccionario SMS?**

(A) Que solo los jóvenes pueden registrar nuevos términos y abreviaturas.
(B) Que pueden colaborar todas las personas interesadas.
(C) Que los colaboradores deben tener un teléfono móvil de última generación.
(D) Que solo pueden participar los miembros de la Asociación de Usuarios de Internet.

9 **¿Qué grupo de acciones resume mejor las posibilidades de diccionarioSMS.com?**

(A) comentar, buscar, traducir, hablar
(B) conocer, escribir, comentar, llamar
(C) traducir, consultar, aprender, colaborar
(D) cooperar, comunicar, abreviar, escribir

10 **¿A qué se refiere Sisco Sapena con «fenómeno social»?**

(A) Al uso de nuevas formas de comunicación entre los jóvenes.
(B) A la creación de diccionarioSMS.com.
(C) Al peligro del uso incorrecto del idioma.
(D) A las abreviaturas que utilizan los jóvenes para escribir mensajes.

11 **Según el artículo, ¿qué opinan los entrevistados acerca de la comunicación a través de SMS?**

(A) Creen que es una amenaza a la correcta utilización del idioma.
(B) Es el resultado de utilizar el móvil como herramienta de comunicación.
(C) Representa la adaptación constante de los jóvenes a las nuevas tecnologías.
(D) Es una forma de comunicación que debemos rechazar.

12 **¿Por qué a Concha Badía le preocupa el uso que se hace del idioma en los SMS?**

(A) Porque no le gustan las abreviaturas en la comunicación.
(B) Porque es una forma diferente de acercarse al idioma y se debe investigar.
(C) Porque puede obstaculizar la comunicación.
(D) Porque los usuarios eliminan todo lo que no es necesario en los mensajes.

13 **¿Por qué cree Concha Badía que un rechazo frontal al lenguaje SMS no conduciría a nada?**

(A) Porque a los jóvenes no les interesa la opinión de los adultos.
(B) Porque es preferible investigar los valores de esta nueva forma de comunicación.
(C) Porque el uso del móvil como herramienta de comunicación es muy importante.
(D) Porque cada 90 segundos se envía un millón de SMS en todo el mundo.

14 **Para obtener más información sobre diccionarioSMS.com, ¿cuál de las siguientes actividades harías?**

(A) Conversar con un especialista en comunicación audiovisual.
(B) Entrevistar al presidente de una compañía de teléfonos.
(C) Preguntarle a tu profesor de Computación.
(D) Visitar la página web de diccionarioSMS.com.

Interpretive Communication: Print Texts

Strategies: Answering Comprehension Questions

- Have students refer back to the *Estrategias* box on page 66, specifically to the strategy related to *Preguntas*. Have they used this strategy before? What are some strategies they use in their other classes while answering multiple-choice questions? Have them brainstorm a list and see which strategies are applicable in Spanish class as well.

- One of the most useful strategies for answering multiple-choice questions, especially given the time constraints of the AP* Exam, is to immediately narrow down the choices to two viable options. In general, the students should be able to do that before referring back to the reading. Then, they can look back to the applicable part of the text in order to decide between the two remaining options. Have them practice this strategy aloud with a partner while answering two or three questions. Can they use this strategy in other contexts as well?

Answer Key

1. C	**8.** B
2. A	**9.** C
3. B	**10.** A
4. A	**11.** C
5. B	**12.** C
6. A	**13.** B
7. C	**14.** D

Additional Resources

Español Santillana AP* Preparation Workbook

Differentiated Instruction

DEVELOPING LEARNERS

- While reading both the text and the questions, students may have difficulty deciphering key vocabulary words, which can impede understanding. As students read, ask them to note any of these difficult vocabulary words (e.g., *alejamiento*). After completing the activity, have them see if they can infer the meaning of the words. Ask them to brainstorm synonyms (e.g., *distanciamiento*) as well as related words (e.g., *lejos, lejano*), and keep a list of these words in their notebooks for future review.

EXPANDING/HERITAGE LANGUAGE LEARNERS

- Expanding and heritage language learners can take advantage of authentic text sources to expand both their vocabulary and their use of sophisticated language structures. While completing the reading comprehension activity, have students make a list of the words and phrases that catch their attention. Afterward, have them define these expressions in Spanish and use them in writing a summary of what they have read. They should try to use these words and phrases in future classwork and homework.

Unit 2 Nos cuidamos

Objectives

- To talk about foods.
- To communicate in a restaurant setting.
- To use the impersonal pronoun *se*.
- To use pronouns for direct and indirect objects.
- To talk about health.
- To talk about illnesses, medical conditions, and practices in the emergency room.
- To learn verbs with prepositions.

- To use definite or indefinite articles or to use no article.
- To talk about changes and states.
- To express physical conditions and moods.
- To form and use sentences in the passive voice.
- To identify main ideas and significant details in a variety of texts.

- To write a wide variety of texts, including a travel guide.
- To know and apply the different stages of the writing process: planning, writing, revising, and sharing.
- To explore health-care systems in Hispanic countries.

Contents

Vocabulary

- Useful expressions used to say that a meal is delicious, that you do not want to eat more, and that someone eats a lot.
- Review: Words for food, health, moods, illnesses and symptoms, the doctor's office, and medical specialists.
- In the restaurant.
- Emergency room. Illnesses and symptoms, and medical specialists.
- Physical conditions and moods. The life cycle.

Grammar

- Impersonal constructions. The pronoun *se*.
- Direct object and indirect object pronouns.
- Verbs with prepositions.
- Articles.
- The passive voice.
- The verbs *ser* and *estar*.

Culture

- The ritual of preparing and drinking *mate*.
- *Las tapas españolas.*
- *Inca Kola.*
- The Colombian scientist, Manuel Patarroyo.
- Drugstore hours in Hispanic countries.
- Journalistic language in Hispanic newspapers.
- Traditional wedding celebrations in Mexico.
- The Inca rite of passage ceremony.
- Latin American family structure.
- Health-care systems in Hispanic countries.

Evaluation Criteria

- Talk about foods and meals.
- Communicate in a restaurant setting.
- Express an action using the impersonal pronoun *se*.
- Use object pronouns to replace the direct object and the indirect object.
- Talk about health, illnesses, and health care.

- Talk about medical conditions and practices in the emergency room.
- Recognize and use verbs followed by a preposition.
- Use definite or indefinite articles or no article.
- Talk about physical conditions and moods, and express changes in state.

- Use and differentiate the verbs *ser* and *estar* correctly.
- Express understanding of health-care systems in different Hispanic countries.
- Write a travel guide.
- Read different types of texts and identify main ideas and significant details in them.
- Write guided texts giving information, describing, or narrating events.

Unit Plan

Las tareas/Antes de empezar

Estimated time: 2 sessions.

Text: *Desafíos para todos los gustos.*

Functions & forms:
- Useful expressions used to say that a meal is delicious, that you do not want to eat more, and that someone eats a lot.
- Review of known vocabulary about food, health, moods, illnesses and symptoms, the doctor's office, and medical specialists.

DESAFÍO 1

Estimated time: 6 sessions.

Text: *Se vende mate.*

Functions & forms:
- To talk about food.
- In the restaurant.
- The impersonal pronoun *se*.
- Direct and indirect object pronouns.

Culture:
- *El mate.*
- *Las tapas españolas.*
- *Inca Kola.*

Reading: *El ritual del mate.*

DESAFÍO 2

Estimated time: 6 sessions.

Text: *Un científico con corazón.*

Functions & forms:
- To talk about health.
- Emergency room. Illnesses and symptoms and medical specialists.
- Verbs with prepositions.
- Articles.

Culture:
- *Manuel Patarroyo.*
- *Los horarios de las farmacias.*
- *El lenguaje periodístico.*

Reading: *El cáncer y su prevención.*

DESAFÍO 3

Estimated time: 6 sessions.

Text: *Una boda impresionante.*

Functions & forms:
- To refer to changes and states.
- Physical conditions, moods, and life stages.
- The passive voice.
- The verbs *ser* and *estar*

Culture:
- *Las bodas en México.*
- *La celebración de la madurez.*
- *Estructura familiar en Latinoamérica.*

Reading: *La piedra mágica.*

Para terminar

Estimated time: 2 sessions.

Todo junto: Review of *Desafíos 1–3.*

Tu desafío:
- *Desafío A:* Prepare a poster or a brochure to present a Hispanic dish in a culinary competition.
- *Desafío B:* Research and prepare a presentation about an important Hispanic scientist.
- *Desafío C:* Create a presentation with photographs or drawings about a traditional celebration in a Hispanic country.

MAPA CULTURAL

Estimated time: 1 session.

Mapa cultural: *Sistemas de salud en el mundo hispano.*

ESCRITURA

Estimated time: 1 session.

Writing: *Recomendaciones de viajes.*

PROYECTO/EVALUACIÓN

Estimated time: 2 sessions.

Project: *Un cómic sobre la salud.*

Self-evaluation: *Autoevaluación.*

HACIA EL *AP* EXAM*

Estimated time: 2 sessions.

Test: Interpretive Communication: Audio Texts.

Unit 2 Nos cuidamos

Standards for Learning Spanish

 COMMUNICATION

1.1. Interpersonal mode
- Exchange personal opinions and experiences.
- Engage in oral conversations using personal knowledge and experience.
- Talk about food and meals, and plan a menu.
- Compare information with a partner.
- Ask and answer questions on different topics.
- Ask a partner questions, take notes, and present a summary to the class.
- Write a story with a classmate.
- Write a dialogue with a partner.
- Write the script for a comic.

1.2. Interpretive mode
- Demonstrate understanding of oral and written idiomatic expressions.
- Demonstrate understanding of questions relating to familiar and less familiar topics.
- Understand and obtain information from audio or video recordings.
- Understand written exchanges.
- Identify main ideas and significant details in a variety of texts.
- Draw conclusions and make judgments from oral and written texts.
- Interpret texts about other cultures and relate them to personal knowledge and experience.
- Use words or expressions, or write sentences to explain images.

1.3. Presentational mode
- Produce and present an original creation orally.
- Dramatize a dialogue.
- Tell a story to classmates.
- Write an explanatory text about own experiences or as result of a research activity.
- Write a story.
- Write a formal invitation e-mail.
- Write a travel guide.
- Create a poster or a brochure.
- Design and present a comic.

 CULTURE

2.1. Practices and perspectives
- Learn about preparing and drinking *mate*.
- Learn about Hispanic cultural traditions related to food and meals.
- Learn about traditional Mexican weddings.
- Read about the Inca rite of passage ceremony.
- Learn about health-care systems in Hispanic countries.
- Read about the composition of the family in Latin American society.

2.2. Products and perspectives
- Learn about *yerba mate*.
- Read about the Peruvian soft drink Inca Kola.
- Learn about important Hispanic scientists and their research.

CONNECTIONS

3.1. Interdisciplinary connections
- Understand the similarities and differences between some aspects of grammar in English and in Spanish.
- Use the writing process to produce a written work.
- Read about cultural traditions related to food.
- Learn about some traditional celebrations in the Spanish-speaking world.
- Read about and research relevant Hispanic scientists.
- Learn about illnesses and prevention.
- Create a comic.

3.2. Viewpoints through language / culture
- Read dialogues, informative texts, and literary texts in Spanish that provide insight into Hispanic cultures.
- Learn about cultural roots in present-day celebrations.
- Learn about the importance of health care in Hispanic societies.
- Learn about healthy habits and prevention of illnesses.

 COMPARISONS

4.1. Compare languages
- Compare how to express an accidental or involuntary action in English and in Spanish.
- Compare the use of object pronouns in English and in Spanish.
- Compare the use of passive voice in English and in Spanish.
- Compare the uses of the Spanish verbs *ser* and *estar* with the English verb *to be*.

4.2. Compare cultures
- Compare food and drink traditions in Hispanic countries and in the United States.
- Compare drugstores in the United States and in Hispanic countries.
- Compare traditions for weddings in the United States and in Hispanic countries.

 COMMUNITIES

5.1. Spanish within and beyond the school setting
- Communicate in a restaurant.
- Promote a positive attitude toward other cultures.
- Learn about emotional changes in adolescence.
- Research and obtain information on the Internet.

5.2. Spanish for lifelong learning
- Encourage the knowledge of the cultural traditions in Hispanic countries.
- Learn about healthy habits and illness prevention.
- Learn the writing process.
- Use technology to learn.

Communicative Skills

Interpersonal Mode

		Activities
Speaking	• Exchange ideas, opinions, or experiences with classmates.	• 2, 12, 13, 18, 22, 25, 27, 30, 37, 44, 49, 51, 55, 72, 73, 75, 76, 79
	• Compare and contrast descriptions or information with a classmate.	• 55, 69, 74
	• Plan a menu or talk about food and meals with a classmate.	• 12, 13
	• Interview a classmate.	• 59
Writing	• Write a dialogue, a story, or the end of a story with a classmate.	• 6, 18, 26, 69, *Proyecto*
	• Write a summarizing text or write an ad.	• 37, 51
	• Write questions for an interview or take notes from an interview.	• 52, 59
Listening	• Understand and obtain information from oral exchanges.	• 2, 12, 13, 18, 22, 25, 27, 30, 37, 44, 49, 51, 55, 59, 69, 72, 73, 74, 75, 76, 77, 79, *Proyecto*

Interpretive Mode

		Activities
Listening	• Obtain information from conversations or take notes from audio recordings.	• 5, 20, 26, 33, 36, 44, 55
	• Understand descriptive or informative audios.	• 57, 63, 68, 76
Reading	• Demonstrate comprehension of written exchanges or longer written dialogues.	• 1, 3, 8, 23, 29, 32, 52, 54, 75
	• Infer meanings based on a text.	• 2, 24, 48, 71
	• Reflect on cultural topics in relation to personal knowledge and experience.	• 10, 14, 22, 25, 38, 56, 59, 65
	• Understand the information in an e-mail, a diary, or in a blog entry.	• 21, 27, 40
	• Research using outside sources.	• 25, 34, 49, 56, 79
	• Obtain information and draw conclusions from an informative text.	• 47, 50, 73
	• Understand a descriptive text, a story, or a passage from a diary.	• 67, 70, 72, 77, R2, R3, R5
Viewing	• Write sentences to describe images or obtain information from an image.	• 4, 9, 18, 41, 58, 69, 74, 77

Presentational Mode

		Activities
Speaking	• Act out a dialogue or tell a story to the class.	• 6, 72
	• Present information or an original creation to the class.	• 25, 28, 59, *Escritura, Proyecto*
Writing	• Write a descriptive or an explanatory text.	• 28, 55, 64
	• Create a list of rules or write promotional slogans.	• 17, 22
	• Summarize a narrative or an informative text.	• 44, 73
	• Write a formal invitation e-mail, a story, or a travel guide.	• 45, 77, *Escritura*
Visually Representing	• Create a poster or a brochure.	• 78
	• Create a comic.	• *Proyecto*

Cross-Curricular Standards

Subject	Standard	Activities
Language Arts	• Compare elements of Spanish grammar with English equivalents.	• 15, 19, 61, 66
	• Use the writing process to write a travel guide.	• *Escritura*
Art	• Design a comic.	• *Proyecto*
Social Studies	• Learn about Hispanic cultural traditions related to food and meals.	• 7, 8, 9, 10, 14, 22, *Lectura D1*
	• Read about and research traditional celebrations in the Spanish-speaking world.	• 53, 54, 55, 56, 60, 78
	• Learn about health-care systems in Hispanic countries.	• *Mapa cultural*
Science	• Read about Hispanic scientists and learn about illnesses and prevention.	• 31, 32, 33, 34, 47, 48, 49, 50, 78

Lesson Plans (50-Minute Classes)

Day	Objectives	Sessions	Activities	Time	Standards	Resources / Homework
1	To introduce food and healthy living and the characters' challenges	**Nos cuidamos / Las tareas** (70–73) • Warm-Up: Topic orientation • Presentation: *Desafíos para todos los gustos*	1–2	15 m. 35 m.	1.1, 1.2, 1.3, 2.1, 2.2	Practice Workbook
2	To learn useful expressions related to the unit topic, and to review learned vocabulary	**Antes de empezar** (74–75) • Warm-Up: Independent Starter • *Expresiones útiles* • *Recuerda*	3–4 5–6	10 m. 15 m. 25 m.	1.1, 1.2, 1.3, 2.1	Audio Practice Workbook
3	To talk about food	**Desafío 1 – Se vende mate** (76–77) • Warm-Up: Independent Starter • *Texto: Se vende mate* • *Cultura: El mate*	7–9 10	5 m. 35 m. 10 m.	1.1, 1.2, 1.3, 2.1, 2.2, 3.1, 3.2, 4.2	Audio
4	To communicate in a restaurant setting	**Desafío 1 – Vocabulario** (78–79) • Warm-Up: Independent Starter • *Vocabulario: En el restaurante* • *Cultura: Las tapas españolas*	11–13 14	5 m. 35 m. 10 m.	1.1, 1.2, 1.3, 2.1, 2.2, 3.2, 4.2	Practice Workbook
5	To learn the impersonal construction with the pronoun se	**Desafío 1 – Gramática** (80–81) • Warm-Up: Independent Starter • *Gramática: Las construcciones impersonales. El pronombre 'se'*	15–18	5 m. 45 m.	1.1, 1.2, 1.3, 3.1, 4.1, 5.1	Practice Workbook
6	To learn direct and indirect object pronouns	**Desafío 1 – Gramática** (82–83) • Warm-Up: Independent Starter • *Gramática: Los pronombres de objeto directo e indirecto* • *Cultura: Inca Kola*	19–21 22	5 m. 35 m. 10 m	1.1, 1.2, 1.3, 2.1, 2.2, 3.1, 3.2, 4.1, 4.2, 5.2	Audio Practice Workbook
7	To understand a written dialogue	**Desafío 1 – Lectura** (84–85) • Warm-Up: Independent Starter • *Lectura: El ritual del mate*	23–25	5 m. 45 m.	1.1, 1.2, 1.3, 2.1, 2.2, 4.2	
8	To integrate vocabulary and grammar, and to assess student proficiency	**Desafío 1 – Comunicación / Evaluación** (86–87) • Warm-Up: Independent Starter • *Comunicación*: Review • *Final del desafío* • Quiz on *Desafío 1*	26–28 29–30	5 m. 25 m. 10 m. 10 m.	1.1, 1.2, 1.3, 2.1, 2.2, 5.2	Audio Practice Workbook
9	To talk about health	**Desafío 2 – Un científico con corazón** (88–89) • Warm-Up: Independent Starter • *Texto: Un científico con corazón* • *Conexiones: Manuel Patarroyo*	31–33 34	5 m. 35 m. 10 m.	1.1, 1.2, 1.3, 2.2, 3.1, 3.2	Audio

Day	Objectives	Sessions	Activities	Time	Standards	Resources / Homework
10	To talk about illnesses, medical conditions, and practices in the emergency room	**Desafío 2 – Vocabulario** (90–91) • Warm-Up: Independent Starter • *Vocabulario: La sala de urgencias* • *Comparaciones: Los horarios de las farmacias*	35–37 38	5 m. 35 m. 10 m.	1.1, 1.2, 1.3, 2.1, 2.2, 3.1, 4.2, 5.1, 5.2	Audio Practice Workbook
11	To learn verbs with prepositions	**Desafío 2 – Gramática** (92–93) • Warm-Up: Independent Starter • *Gramática: Los verbos con preposición*	39–41	5 m. 45 m.	1.2, 1.3, 3.1	Practice Workbook
12	To refer to known or unknown objects or persons	**Desafío 2 – Gramática** (94–95) • Warm-Up: Independent Starter • *Gramática: Los artículos* • *Conexiones: El lenguaje periodístico*	42–45 46	5 m. 35 m. 10 m.	1.1, 1.2, 1.3, 2.1, 2.2, 3.1	Audio Practice Workbook
13	To understand information about illnesses and prevention	**Desafío 2 – Lectura** (96–97) • Warm-Up: Independent Starter • *Lectura: El cáncer y su prevención*	47–49	5 m. 45 m.	1.1, 1.2, 1.3, 3.1, 3.2, 5.1, 5.2	
14	To integrate vocabulary and grammar, and to assess student proficiency	**Desafío 2 – Comunicación / Evaluación** (98–99) • Warm-Up: Independent Starter • *Comunicación: Review* • *Final del desafío* • Quiz on *Desafío 2*	50–51 52	5 m. 25 m. 10 m. 10 m.	1.1, 1.2, 1.3, 2.2, 3.1, 3.2, 5.1, 5.2	Practice Workbook
15	To talk about changes and states	**Desafío 3 – Una boda impresionante** (100–101) • Warm-Up: Independent Starter • *Texto: Una boda impresionante* • *Cultura: Las bodas en México*	53–55 56	5 m. 35 m. 10 m.	1.1, 1.2, 1.3, 2.1, 2.2, 4.2, 5.1	Audio
16	To talk about physical conditions and moods	**Desafío 3 – Vocabulario** (102–103) • Warm-Up: Independent Starter • *Vocabulario: Estados físicos y anímicos* • *Cultura: La celebración de la madurez*	57–59 60	5 m. 35 m. 10 m.	1.1, 1.2, 1.3, 2.1, 2.2, 3.2, 4.2	Audio Practice Workbook
17	To form and use sentences in the passive voice	**Desafío 3 – Gramática** (104–105) • Warm-Up: Independent Starter • *Gramática: La voz pasiva* • *Comunidades: Estructura familiar en Latinoamérica*	61–64 65	5 m. 35 m. 10 m.	1.2, 1.3, 2.1, 2.2, 3.1, 3.2, 4.1, 4.2	Audio Practice Workbook
18	To learn the uses of the verbs *ser* and *estar*	**Desafío 3 – Gramática** (106–107) • Warm-Up: Independent Starter • *Gramática: 'Ser' y 'estar'*	66–69	5 m. 45 m.	1.1, 1.2, 1.3, 3.1, 4.1	Audio Practice Workbook
19	To understand a literary story	**Desafío 3 – Lectura** (108–109) • Warm-Up: Independent Starter • *Lectura: La piedra mágica*	70–72	5 m. 45 m.	1.1, 1.2, 1.3, 3.2, 4.2, 5.2	

Day	Objectives	Sessions	Activities	Time	Standards	Resources / Homework
20	To integrate vocabulary and grammar, and to assess student proficiency	**Desafío 3 – Comunicación / Evaluación** (110–111) • Warm-Up: Independent Starter • *Comunicación:* Review • *Final del desafío* • Quiz on *Desafío 3*	73–74 75	5 m. 25 m. 10 m. 10 m.	1.1, 1.2, 1.3, 2.1, 2.2, 3.1, 5.1, 5.2	Practice Workbook
21	To integrate language in context	**Para terminar** (112–113) • Warm-Up: Independent Starter • *Todo junto* • *Tu desafío*	76–77 78	5 m. 25 m. 20 m.	1.1, 1.2, 1.3, 2.1, 2.2, 3.1, 3.2, 4.2, 5.1, 5.2	Audio Practice Workbook *Tu desafío* work
22	To integrate language in context, and to assess student proficiency	**Tu desafío / Evaluación** (113) • Warm-Up: Prepare *Tu desafío* presentations • *Tu desafío* presentations • Quiz on *Desafíos 1–3*		5 m. 25 m. 20 m.	1.2, 1.3, 2.1, 2.2, 3.1, 3.2, 5.1, 5.2	
23	To learn about health-care systems in Hispanic countries	**Mapa cultural** (114–115) • Warm-Up: Independent Starter • *Mapa cultural: Sistemas de salud en el mundo hispano*	79	5 m. 45 m.	1.1, 1.2, 2.1, 2.2, 3.1, 3.2, 4.2, 5.1, 5.2	Practice Workbook
24	To write a travel guide	**Escritura** (116–117) • Warm-Up: Independent Starter • *Escritura: Recomendaciones de viajes*		5 m. 45 m.	1.1, 1.2, 1.3, 2.1, 2.2, 3.1, 3.2, 5.1, 5.2	Project work
25	To create a comic to inform about health topics	**Proyecto** (122–123) • Warm-Up: Prepare project presentations • Project presentations		10 m. 40 m.	1.1, 1.2, 1.3, 2.1, 2.2, 3.1, 5.2	**Repaso – Vocabulario** (118–119) **Repaso – Gramática** (120–121)
26	To assess student proficiency	**Assessment** • *Autoevaluación* (123) • Test		10 m. 40 m.	1.1, 1.2, 1.3, 2.1, 2.2, 5.1, 5.2	
27	To prepare for the AP* Exam	**Hacia el AP* Exam** (124–127) • Warm-Up: Test introduction • Test: Interpretive Communication: Audio Tests		5 m. 45 m.	1.1, 1.2, 2.1, 2.2, 3.1, 3.2, 5.1, 5.2	Audio
28	To prepare for the AP* Exam	**Hacia el AP* Exam** (124–127) • Warm-Up: About the test • Review and correction of the test		5 m. 45 m.	1.1, 1.2, 2.1, 2.2, 3.1, 3.2, 5.1, 5.2	Audio

Lesson Plans (90-Minute Classes)

Day	Objectives	Sessions	Activities	Time	Standards	Resources / Homework
1	To introduce food and healthy living and the characters' challenges, to learn useful expressions related to the unit topic, and to review learned vocabulary	***Nos cuidamos / Las tareas / Antes de empezar*** (70–75) • Warm-Up: Topic orientation • Presentation: *Desafíos para todos los gustos* • *Expresiones útiles* • *Recuerda*	 1–2 3–4 5–6	 15 m. 35 m. 15 m. 25 m.	1.1, 1.2, 1.3, 2.1, 2.2	Audio Practice Workbook
2	To talk about food and to communicate in a restaurant setting	***Desafío 1 – Se vende mate / Vocabulario*** (76–79) • Warm-Up: Independent Starter • *Texto: Se vende mate* • *Cultura: El mate* • *Vocabulario: En el restaurante* • *Cultura: Las tapas españolas*	 7–9 10 11–13 14	 5 m. 30 m. 10 m. 35 m. 10 m.	1.1, 1.2, 1.3, 2.1, 2.2, 3.1, 3.2, 4.2	Audio Practice Workbook
3	To learn the impersonal construction with the pronoun se and to learn direct and indirect object pronouns	***Desafío 1 – Gramática*** (80–83) • Warm-Up: Independent Starter • *Gramática: Las construcciones impersonales. El pronombre 'se'* • *Gramática: Los pronombres de objeto directo e indirecto* • *Cultura: Inca Kola*	 15–18 19–21 22	 5 m. 35 m. 40 m. 10 m.	1.1, 1.2, 1.3, 2.1, 2.2, 3.1, 3.2, 4.1, 4.2, 5.1, 5.2	Audio Practice Workbook
4	To understand a written dialogue, to integrate vocabulary and grammar, and to assess student proficiency	***Desafío 1 – Lectura / Comunicación / Evaluación*** (84–87) • Warm-Up: Independent Starter • *Lectura: El ritual del mate* • *Comunicación: Review* • *Final del desafío* • Quiz on *Desafío 1*	 23–25 26–28 29–30	 5 m. 40 m. 25 m. 10 m. 10 m.	1.1, 1.2, 1.3, 2.1, 2.2, 4.2, 5.2	Audio Practice Workbook
5	To talk about health and to talk about illnesses, medical conditions, and practices in the emergency room	***Desafío 2 – Un científico con corazón / Vocabulario*** (88–91) • Warm-Up: Independent Starter • *Texto: Un científico con corazón* • *Conexiones: Manuel Patarroyo* • *Vocabulario: La sala de urgencias* • *Comparaciones: Los horarios de las farmacias*	 31–33 34 35–37 38	 5 m. 30 m. 10 m. 35 m. 10 m.	1.1, 1.2, 1.3, 2.1, 2.2, 3.1, 3.2, 4.2, 5.1, 5.2	Audio Practice Workbook
6	To learn verbs with prepositions and to refer to known or unkown objects or persons	***Desafío 2 – Gramática*** (92–95) • Warm-Up: Independent Starter • *Gramática: Los verbos con preposición* • *Gramática: Los artículos* • *Conexiones: El lenguaje periodístico*	 39–41 42–45 46	 5 m. 35 m. 40 m. 10 m.	1.1, 1.2, 1.3, 2.1, 2.2, 3.1	Audio Practice Workbook

Unit 2 Nos cuidamos

Day	Objectives	Sessions	Activities	Time	Standards	Resources / Homework
7	To understand information about illnesses and prevention, to integrate vocabulary and grammar, and to assess student proficiency	**Desafío 2 – Lectura / Comunicación / Evaluación** (96–99) • Warm-Up: Independent Starter • *Lectura: El cáncer y su prevención* • *Comunicación:* Review • *Final del desafío* • Quiz on *Desafío 2*	47–49 50–51 52	5 m. 40 m. 25 m. 10 m. 10 m.	1.1, 1.2, 1.3, 2.2, 3.1, 3.2, 5.1, 5.2	Practice Workbook
8	To talk about changes and states and to talk about physical conditions and moods	**Desafío 3 – Una boda impresionante / Vocabulario** (100–103) • Warm-Up: Independent Starter • *Texto: Una boda impresionante* • *Cultura: Las bodas en México* • *Vocabulario: Estados físicos y anímicos* • *Cultura: La celebración de la madurez*	53–55 56 57–59 60	5 m. 30 m. 10 m. 35 m. 10 m.	1.1, 1.2, 1.3, 2.1, 2.2, 3.2, 4.2, 5.1	Audio Practice Workbook
9	To form and use sentences in the passive voice and to learn the uses of the verbs *ser* and *estar*	**Desafío 3 – Gramática** (104–107) • Warm-Up: Independent Starter • *Gramática: La voz pasiva* • *Comunidades: Estructura familiar en Latinoamérica* • *Gramática: 'Ser' y 'estar'*	61–64 65 66–69	5 m. 40 m. 10 m. 35 m.	1.1, 1.2, 1.3, 2.1, 2.2, 3.1, 3.2, 4.1, 4.2	Audio Practice Workbook
10	To understand a literary story and to integrate vocabulary and grammar	**Desafío 3 – Lectura / Comunicación / Evaluación** (108–111) • Warm-Up: Independent Starter • *Lectura: La piedra mágica* • *Comunicación:* Review • *Final del desafío* • Quiz on *Desafío 3*	70–72 73–74 75	5 m. 40 m. 25 m. 10 m. 10 m.	1.1, 1.2, 1.3, 2.1, 2.2, 3.1, 3.2, 4.2, 5.1, 5.2	Practice Workbook ***Para terminar – Tu desafío*** (113)
11	To integrate language in context and to assess student proficiency	**Para terminar / Evaluación** (112–113) • Warm-Up: Independent Starter • *Todo junto* • *Tu desafío:* work and presentations • Quiz on *Desafíos 1–3*	76–77 78	5 m. 25 m. 40 m. 20 m.	1.1, 1.2, 1.3, 2.1, 2.2, 3.1, 3.2, 4.2, 5.1, 5.2	Audio Practice Workbook
12	To learn about health-care systems in Hispanic countries and to write a travel guide	**Mapa cultural / Escritura** (114–117) • Warm-Up: Independent Starter • *Mapa cultural: Sistemas de salud en el mundo hispano* • *Escritura: Recomendaciones de viajes*	79	5 m. 40 m. 45 m.	1.1, 1.2, 1.3, 2.1, 2.2, 3.1, 3.2, 4.2, 5.1, 5.2	Practice Workbook ***Repaso –Vocabulario*** (118–119) ***Repaso – Gramática*** (120–121) Project work

Day	Objectives	Sessions	Activities	Time	Standards	Resources / Homework
13	To create a comic to inform about health topics and to assess student proficiency	**Proyecto / Assessment** (122–123) • Warm-Up: Prepare project presentations • Project presentations • *Autoevaluación* • Test		10 m. 45 m. 10 m. 25 m.	1.1, 1.2, 1.3, 2.1, 2.2, 3.1, 5.1, 5.2	
14	To prepare for the AP* Exam	**Hacia el AP* Exam** (124–127) • Warm-Up: Test Introduction • Test: Interpretive Communication: Audio Tests • Review and correction of the test		10 m. 55 m. 25 m.	1.1, 1.2, 2.1, 2.2, 3.1, 3.2, 5.1, 5.2	Audio
15	To practice oral skills in social interactions	**Final Activity** • Warm-Up: Presentation of the activity • Role-play activity		15 m. 75 m.	1.1, 1.2, 1.3, 2.1, 2.2, 4.2, 5.1, 5.2	

Final Activity (Day 15)

Presentation

▪ Explain to students that they will be participating in a role-play situation related to one of the topics covered in this unit. Suggested situations include:

1. being the dinner guests of a Hispanic friend whose family has prepared a menu consisting of foods the guests do not know;
2. resolving a misunderstanding regarding delivery of the wrong order to a table at a restaurant in a Spanish-speaking country;
3. having a minor accident while traveling in a Spanish-speaking country that requires a visit to the emergency room;
4. volunteering as doctors and nurses for Doctors Without Borders in a rural area in a Spanish-speaking country;
5. making a faux pas at the wedding of a Mexican couple;
6. being in charge of the food and music of the *quinceañera* party for a friend.

Preparation

▪ Divide the class into small groups and assign a situation to each group. Ask students to brainstorm the details of their assigned situation and the different characters that will take part in it. Then allow students time to write the script cooperatively. They should plan for a role-play of about five to six minutes.

Revision and Rehearsal

▪ Ask students to revise their scripts, paying attention to accurate use of vocabulary and grammar structures. At this point, students may also correct any inconsistencies in the storyline, add a punch line, or make other minor changes they deem appropriate. Then allow for rehearsal time. Explain to students that they will be able to improvise, or ad-lib. However, rehearsing their lines a few times will give them confidence and improve their fluency.

Dramatization and Evaluation

▪ Call on each group to role-play their assigned situation. Assess students on fluency, pronunciation, content, organization, and correct use of target vocabulary and grammar. You may want to prepare a short evaluation questionnaire that the class fills in at the end of each role-play. If time permits, discuss as a class the real-life situations upon which the role-plays were based.

6 Síntomas

–A ver, dígame lo que siente.

–Pues, me siento mal desde hace unos días. Me duele el estómago y estoy mareado.

–¿Ha comprobado si tiene fiebre? ¿Siente escalofríos?

–No, no tengo fiebre, pero estoy muy cansado y no tengo hambre.

–¿Y no le duele la cabeza?

–Pues ahora que lo dice…, sí, de vez en cuando.

–Es posible que tenga un virus. Le aconsejo que descanse, que beba mucha agua y que coma comidas ligeras. Por ejemplo, un poco de pescado hervido y un yogur. Pero, sobre todo, tiene que rehidratarse, así que no se olvide de tomar mucha agua, té o incluso un refresco, si le apetece.

9 ¡Cuántas variedades de mate!

–La primera variedad de mate que podemos hacer es el mate endulzado con azúcar. Algunos piensan que el mate amargo es más auténtico, pero en varias zonas de Argentina y Chile se toma dulce.

–Pues primero haremos una variedad con azúcar y otra sin azúcar.

–He leído que también hay un mate de leche, que se hace sustituyendo el agua por leche. También en este caso se añade azúcar, claro.

–A mí me encanta el té con leche, así que creo que esta variedad me gustará mucho… Yo tengo un amigo argentino que me habló de dos variedades muy interesantes. Una se prepara añadiendo rodajas o corteza de limón o de naranja.

–¡Mate de limón y mate de naranja, qué refrescantes! Tengo ganas de probarlos. ¿Y la otra variedad?

–Pues parece ser que el mate también se toma frío. Se llama tereré.

–No tenía ni idea. ¿Y cómo se prepara?

–Se añade al agua jugo de limón o de toronja y azúcar. ¡Y hielo, claro! Es ideal para combatir el calor.

–Bueno, pues ya tenemos bastantes variedades para nuestra cata, ¿no te parece?

20 Soluciones para todo

1. –¿Por fin te has cambiado de casa?
   –Sí, ya estoy instalada en mi nuevo apartamento.
   –¡Qué bien! ¿Y qué hiciste con el sofá que no te cabía?

2. –Antonio, ¿no tienes diccionario de español?
   –No, no lo he comprado todavía.
   –¿Y qué haces si lo necesitas en la clase?

3. –Susana, ¿has comprado el regalo para Patricia?
   –No, lo siento. No he tenido tiempo.
   –Yo voy esta tarde al centro comercial. ¿Quieres que se lo compre yo?

4. –Michelle y Daniel quieren aprender a preparar mate.
   –¿Ah, sí? ¿Y tienen yerba mate?

–Sí, pero no saben cómo se prepara.

–Bueno, yo puedo ayudarlos. Bebo mate todos los días.

5. –Mamá, ¿has visto mis guantes?
   –¿Unos de color verde?
   –Sí. Los dejé encima de la mesa del salón, pero ya no están allí.

6. –¿Dónde están las guías de viaje de Argentina? No las veo.
   –En la estantería del comedor, ¿no?
   –No, aquí no están.

26 En el restaurante

–Buenas noches. ¿Tienen ustedes reserva?

–¡Ay, no! Se me olvidó reservar mesa. ¿Tiene alguna disponible?

–¿Cuántas personas son?

–Somos dos…

–Sí, hay una mesa estupenda en el rincón. Acompáñenme. ¿Qué les parece?

–Perfecta, gracias.

–Yo prefería sentarme junto a la ventana…

–Sofía, por favor, no seas tan exigente; quedémonos aquí… Es la única mesa libre.

–Está bien.

–¿Qué te apetece comer?

–No sé qué pedir.

–¿Por qué no pedimos el menú del día?… Solo cuesta 30 pesos y está todo incluido: el primer plato, el segundo, el postre, el pan, una bebida y el café.

–Me parece una buena idea. ¿Qué me recomiendas?

–¿De primer plato? Las berenjenas. Aquí las hacen riquísimas.

–¿Cómo se preparan?

–Están rellenas de carne molida y hongos.

–Es que yo no como carne, soy vegetariana. ¿No te acuerdas?

–Uy, no me acordaba. Pues mira, los huevos revueltos con espárragos son exquisitos aquí; es la especialidad de la casa.

–Seguro que están buenísimos, pero yo nunca los como por la noche. Solo los como para desayunar.

–¡Pruébalos! Te van a encantar.

–No sé…

–¿Y si pides un plato combinado? Mira, este no lleva carne.

–Ya, pero es que no me gustan los pimientos.

–Ay, Sofía, qué difícil me lo pones…

33 El trabajo de Patarroyo

–Buenos días, profesor Ramírez.

–Buenos días, Ethan. ¿Qué tal?

–Bien, pero estoy un poco preocupado por lo del ciclo de charlas. Eva y yo todavía no hemos invitado a nadie.

–Pues no tienen mucho tiempo, así que deben tomar una decisión. ¿Tienen alguna idea?

–Sí, hemos pensado invitar a Manuel Patarroyo porque descubrimos que desarrolló la vacuna contra la malaria.

–Me parece estupendo. Sería maravilloso si Patarroyo participara en el ciclo de charlas.

–¿Usted cree?

–¡Claro! Su desarrollo de la vacuna es histórico. Lo que diferencia a este científico es que se ha dedicado a la investigación de vacunas contra enfermedades que afectan a países con menos recursos. Muchos científicos se concentran en los países más desarrollados, donde hay más dinero para financiar la investigación y se puede lograr un importante beneficio económico al vender las vacunas. En cambio, él dedicó más de treinta años de trabajo a investigar sobre la malaria y, en lugar de vender la patente de la vacuna, la donó a la Organización Mundial de la Salud.

–Eva y yo conocemos la historia, pero también hemos leído que la vacuna y su uso son controversiales porque muchos dicen que no es efectiva en el cien por cien de los casos.

–Es cierto, pero la malaria afecta a unos doscientos millones de personas al año y causa unas seiscientas mil muertes, así que aunque la vacuna no logre curar todos los casos, su uso es fundamental. Además, Manuel Patarroyo sigue trabajando para mejorarla. Creo que sería una suerte tenerlo en el ciclo de charlas.

–Gracias por su ayuda, profesor. Vamos a ponernos en contacto con él para invitarlo.

–No hay de qué. Estas charlas van a ser muy interesantes.

36 En la consulta

–Buenas tardes, señor Vargas.

–Buenas tardes, doctor.

–Por favor, explíqueme sus síntomas.

–Me siento muy mal. Tengo náuseas y he vomitado. Y llevo todo el día muy mareado.

–¿Ha perdido el conocimiento en algún momento?

–No.

–¿Tiene fiebre?

–Sí. Empezó anoche.

–Le voy a tomar el pulso y la presión arterial.

–Muy bien.

–A ver… El pulso es regular y la presión arterial no está alta.

–¿Tengo algo grave, doctor?

–No, no se preocupe. Lo que tiene es gripe, así que tendrá que guardar cama unos días.

–¿Nada más?

–Nada más. Procure descansar y beba mucho líquido. En tres o cuatro días se sentirá mejor. Lo que sí le aconsejo es que se ponga la vacuna contra la gripe cada otoño.

–Gracias, doctor. Lo tendré en cuenta.

44 Eva está enferma

–Hola, Ethan.

–¿Qué tal, Eva? No viniste a la escuela hoy. ¿Estás bien?

–Pues no, la verdad. Cuando me levanté esta mañana no me sentía bien. Me dolía la cabeza y el estómago, y también tenía náuseas. Me tomé una pastilla para calmar el dolor, pero no me ayudó.

–¿Y qué hiciste?

–Pues llamé a mi madre, que se había ido a trabajar. Ella regresó a casa y me llevó al hospital porque me había subido bastante la fiebre. Fuimos a urgencias.

–¿Qué te dijeron?

–La médica me tomó la temperatura y la presión arterial. Y me hizo muchas preguntas sobre los síntomas que tenía.

–¿Y qué tienes?

–Parece que solo es un virus del estómago. Quizás comí algo en mal estado. Me han recetado unas pastillas.

–¿Entonces no vas a asistir a clase mañana?

–No estoy segura.

–Tranquila, yo te prestaré mis apuntes.

–Gracias, Ethan, pero estoy preocupada por el desafío. Todavía no hemos invitado al señor Patarroyo. ¿Te imaginas que no pueda venir?

–Bueno, tú descansa, que yo me ocupo de todo. Mañana te llamo y te cuento.

–Vale, gracias. ¡Hasta mañana!

55 ¡Cuántos preparativos!

–Necesito comer algo ya. Estoy mareado.

–¡Lucas, por favor! ¡No seas tan impaciente! Disfruta de la boda. Todo está perfecto. Los novios y sus familias trabajaron meses en los preparativos.

–Ya, pero tengo hambre. Asha, dime que van a servir la comida ya.

–Sí, la ceremonia está a punto de terminar y enseguida vas a probar el plato tradicional típico: el mole.

–El mole… ahora recuerdo, me parece que el chile es uno de los ingredientes básicos, ¿verdad? ¡Qué hambre!

–Sí. Mira, ahí llegan los mariachis. ¡Ojalá canten una ranchera!

–Ah, ¿también hay música?

–Pues claro, Lucas. En una boda típica mexicana no puede faltar el show de mariachis. Pero recuerda, según la tradición los invitados no podemos empezar a bailar antes que los novios.

57 ¿Cómo se sienten?

1. Hace un calor horrible. Hace más de tres horas que no bebo nada y no veo ningún lugar abierto para comprar agua o un refresco.

2. Estoy muy enojada con mi amiga Gabriela. Siempre le presto mis cosas y nunca me las devuelve. Anteayer le dejé mi vestido favorito, ¡y ahora ella lo ha perdido! Ya no vuelvo a prestarle nada más.

3. Hoy estuve todo el día estudiando en la biblioteca porque esta semana tengo tres exámenes. Pero no sé si lograré aprobarlos todos. Las asignaturas son difíciles, tengo poco tiempo... No sé...

4. Estoy en casa descansando en el sofá, tomando un chocolate caliente y leyendo un buen libro. ¿Qué más puedo pedir?

5. Hoy todo me sale mal. Me olvidé de poner el despertador, me dormí y llegué tarde a la escuela. Y mañana tengo que entregar un informe para la clase de Ciencias y acabo de darme cuenta de que dejé mis notas en la clase. ¡Vaya día!

6. ¡Qué cansancio! Creo que por hoy ya he estudiado suficiente. Me voy a dormir.

63 **Quinceañera**

–Rocío, ¿dónde celebraste tu quinceañera? ¿Fue aquí, en los Estados Unidos?

–Lo pensé, pero al final la celebramos en México, en el pueblo donde nació mi mamá, en el estado de Morelos. Es un pueblo precioso. Recuerdo con mucho cariño mi fiesta. Mi familia más cercana y mis mejores amigos estuvieron allí. Fue un día muy especial y todo salió a la perfección.

–Cuéntame qué hicieron.

–La ceremonia fue oficiada por mi tío Pedro, que es sacerdote. Después de la misa fuimos a una hacienda preciosa que estaba decorada con un montón de flores.

–Qué lindo.

–Sí. No faltó ningún detalle. Todas mis canciones favoritas fueron interpretadas por unos mariachis y bailamos todos sin parar. Tocaron rancheras, corridos...

–¿Y no bailaste el vals?

–Sí, claro. Todavía me emociono cuando pienso en el momento en el que mi papá me puso los zapatos de tacón y salimos a bailar. ¿Sabes que los zapatos fueron hechos a mano?

–¿En serio? Uff, me imagino que todo eso sería carísimo...

–Supongo que sí. Lo pagaron todo mis padrinos, José y Manuela. Mira, aquí tengo unas fotos.

–A ver, a ver...

68 **Descripciones**

1. ¡Qué duro está este tomate! Todavía no se puede comer.
2. Los padrinos pagaron todos los gastos de la boda y les regalaron a los novios un viaje de tres semanas por Europa.
3. Lucas no necesita estudiar tantas horas como otros chicos. Él lee una vez los temas y es capaz de recordar toda la información importante.
4. A la mejor amiga de Asha no le gusta hablar de sí misma y tampoco le gusta ir a fiestas en las que hay mucha gente.
5. Michelle no puede asistir al concierto porque tiene fiebre y le duele mucho la garganta.

6. El bibliotecario de la escuela siempre saluda a todo el mundo, te ayuda a encontrar los libros que buscas y se preocupa por el buen funcionamiento de la biblioteca.

76 **Un programa gastronómico**

Fuente: Radio Caracol, Colombia

Pues es que les quiero contar que acaba de salir una publicación que se llama *Cocina colombiana para Navidad y otras recetas internacionales*. Hemos invitado a su autora, doña Clara Inés de Arango. Es experta en la preparación de alimentos para fotografía.

–Este libro... Bueno, lo consiguen en cualquier parte, en cualquier librería.

–Sí, en cualquier librería.

–Bueno, para armar... Díganos un menú, que a usted le gustaría preparar.

–Uno sencillo, que cualquier ama de casa en estos momentos pueda sentarse rápidamente y decir: esto voy a hacer de Navidad.

–Pues en el libro hay unas, hay unas...

–¿Propuestas?

–... propuestas. En la parte de atrás hay unas propuestas. Pero, por ejemplo, a mí realmente el lomo de cerdo me parece delicioso. Para que no sea simplemente el pernil, que todo el mundo lo puede tener en cuenta. El lomo de cerdo con salsa de moras es muy, muy rico. Además, la combinación de una salsa dulce con cerdo es maravillosa. Le pueden hacer el arroz con almendras, que ahí está...

–Ah, sí.

–O unas papas que hay con puerro. También son deliciosas. Es un pastel de papa. También le podríamos...

–Un postrecito.

–Ah, no, ya. Sí, los postres, cualquiera, porque tenemos tortas. Tenemos la torta navideña, que es una delicia. Como una torta negra, ¿sí? Con frutas, es muy rica. La consabida natilla, que no nos falte.

–Bueno, y todos los postres, todas las comidas, siempre van acompañadas de buenas bebidas, ¿no? ¿Hay algo de eso en el libro, con qué se debe acompañar?

–Sí, también están las bebidas. Mire, de los postres me gustaría rescatar uno que es maravilloso, que es el brazo de reina o el pionono, como le dicen en mi tierra, que es el rollo, el brazo de reina.

–Con cremita.

–Con cremita o relleno de arequipe, también puede ser.

–Bueno, pues muchas recetas, unas fotos espectaculares, pasos muy fáciles...

–Y todas se pueden comer. Todas se pudieron comer en el momento de las fotografías.

–Lo importante es tener buen apetito.

–Bueno, muy bien. Pues, doña Clara Inés de Arango, muchas gracias por su atención. No olviden el libro *Cocina colombiana para Navidad y otras recetas internacionales*.

Hacia el *AP* Exam*

Fuente: Cadena SER, España

—Seguro que si os ponéis a pensarlo os surgen un montón de ejemplos, muchas situaciones en las que la comida acaba en un vertedero. No hace falta irse muy lejos para encontrar esos ejemplos. Simplemente basta con pensar, por ejemplo, en el *buffet* del hotel que esté cerca de vuestra casa, el *catering* que degustan los invitados de una de las muchas convenciones que se organizan en la semana en toda España... En fin, toneladas de comida reconvertida en basura como ocurre, por ejemplo también, con la comida que dan en los aviones. Se preparan muchos platos, muchas bandejas, pero no todos los pasajeros quieren pagar por comer mientras van volando y por eso, después de cada vuelo, esa comida acaba en la basura. En este contexto y con este escenario de fondo, nuestra primera conexión de esta noche es con Agustín Alberti. Es miembro de la Federación Española del Banco de Alimentos. Agustín, ¿qué tal? Buenas noches.

—¿Qué tal? Buenas noches.

—Bueno, en primer lugar, no sé si nos podríais decir si se tira o no mucha comida al cabo de un día aquí en España.

—Ya. Eso es muy difícil de saber. Pero, indudablemente, se puede afirmar que son muchos. Entre otras cosas porque, por ejemplo, por ley no se pueden entregar, pues los restos de los restaurantes o de los *caterings*... Porque, claro, nadie garantiza que eso esté luego bien conservado y todo esto. Luego, hay muchos supermercados, por ejemplo, pues que por la noche sacan los productos a la basura, los productos perecederos que no han podido entregar ese día. Sobre todo los supermercados pequeños. Al lado de mi casa, por ejemplo, pues por la noche se puede ver más de una o dos personas escarbando en los restos de un supermercado.

—Comentabas que aquí, en España, no está permitido, al menos por ley, poder reutilizar, llamémoslo así, esa comida que sobra de algunos restaurantes o de algún *catering*. Pero, si no me equivoco, creo que algún otro país sí que lo permite.

—Bueno, es raro pero, por ejemplo, en Italia se hizo una campaña precisamente por la Fundación Bancos de Alimentos (Banca Alimentaria de Italia) que consiguió que el Parlamento italiano votara una ley que permitiera, en determinadas condiciones y con las garantías suficientes, pues poder acceder a ese tipo de alimentos para las personas necesitadas. Pero las condiciones tienen que ser muy estrictas porque, claro, son alimentos que están ya, como si dijéramos, en circulación, ya condimentados y tal, y que es necesario que se consuman rápidamente.

—Agustín, sí me gustaría también que nos cuentes un poco por qué unas empresas sí que optan por esta vía y otras no. Ya sé que no te pedimos que te pongas en el papel de todas las empresas, pero sí al menos conocer por qué unas sí y otras no.

—Sí, hay razones muy equivalentes. Por ejemplo, hay empresas, primero, que tienen una conciencia social, de responsabilidad social corporativa, muy acusada. No quiero decirte empresas concretas porque si me dejo algunas luego me vendrían a mí con el... Pero, vamos, hay algunas empresas, de grandes superficies sobre todo, que tienen una responsabilidad social muy acusada. Luego hay otro mecanismo... Claro, es que en muchas ocasiones sale más caro realmente el eliminar, porque por ley tienen que eliminarlos de determinados procedimientos, no pueden dejar ahí tirados un montón de alimentos en cualquier lado, ¿no?, sino que hay que reciclarlos. Y eso sale más caro que cedérnoslos a nosotros, que tenemos unos mecanismos ya muy bien establecidos para repartirlos rápidamente.

—Y, Agustín, te quiero pedir ahora que nos entiendas y te voy a poner en un pequeño aprieto. Igual que nos has mencionado algún ejemplo de las empresas que de alguna forma sí que tienen algún tipo de conciencia solidaria, también te quería preguntar si, por la otra parte, te surge el nombre de alguna empresa que echáis en falta y que os gustaría que también se sumase a este tipo de proyectos solidarios donando alimentos o productos alimenticios para la gente que lo necesita.

—Pues mira, realmente sería injusto si te dijera nombres concretos porque eso responde mucho a la política de cada empresa. Hay empresas comerciales que devuelven a las empresas productoras..., le devuelven los productos que no han vendido. Y, claro, pues ahí nosotros no tenemos nada que rascar, como quien dice, ¿no?, nada que obtener. Pero muchas veces yo creo que es por desconocimiento de los mecanismos de los bancos de alimentos. Para eso, fíjate, se está creando en la facultad, en la Escuela Superior de Ingenieros Agrónomos, no me acuerdo ahora del nombre de la catedrática, pero se está haciendo un programa muy interesante, una especie de red social especializada en todo el tema agrícola, y eso puede ser un instrumento muy bueno para... Una especie de red social, que es lo que está de moda, y además que funciona muy bien y es muy eficaz, pues ponernos en contacto con empresas que a lo mejor para nosotros serían desconocidas y nosotros seríamos desconocidos para ellas.

—Pues veremos a ver, Agustín, dónde llega esa red social como decías tan de moda ahora mismo para, de alguna forma, poneros en contacto. Me parece un sistema por lo menos interesante para ver si se amplía esta red del banco de alimentos a todas las empresas.

—Sí, es un instrumente eficaz, ¿eh?

—Pues Agustín Alberti, miembro de la Federación Española de Bancos de Alimentos, gracias por acompañarnos esta noche en este repaso a la comida que desafortunadamente se tira pero también a la comida que se reutiliza y se aprovecha bien. Gracias.

—Muchísimas gracias a vosotros.

Unit 2
Nos cuidamos

The Unit

- The themes for Unit 2 are food and health. The participants will learn about traditions associated with food, drink, and weddings. They will also learn to express themselves in a medical situation and to describe both physical and emotional states.

- Tess, a veteran of *Fans del español*, will give the participants their tasks.

  – *Desafío 1.* Michelle and Daniel have to participate in an international food fair. They have to compete with a food or drink from the Spanish-speaking world.

  – *Desafío 2.* Eva and Ethan have to help organize a conference at their school. They have to invite an important Hispanic scientist to give a talk at the conference.

  – *Desafío 3.* Asha and Lucas have to attend a Mexican wedding and make a photographic report of the ceremony and reception.

Activities	Standards	Resources
Nos cuidamos	1.2, 2.1, 2.2	

Teaching Suggestions

Warm-Up / Independent Starter

- Have students look at the photos and come up with a one-paragraph description for one of the images. This will reactivate the vocabulary they have previously learned about food, health, and the life cycle.

Preparation

- Ask students to read the captions and predict what the topic for each challenge might be. For example, they may answer that the first image is about healthy eating; the second is about science or medicine; and the last image is about traditional ceremonies or rituals related to the life cycle.

- Have students read each *Desafío's* objective, as well as the vocabulary and grammar goals, then discuss how each picture might relate to these objectives and goals.

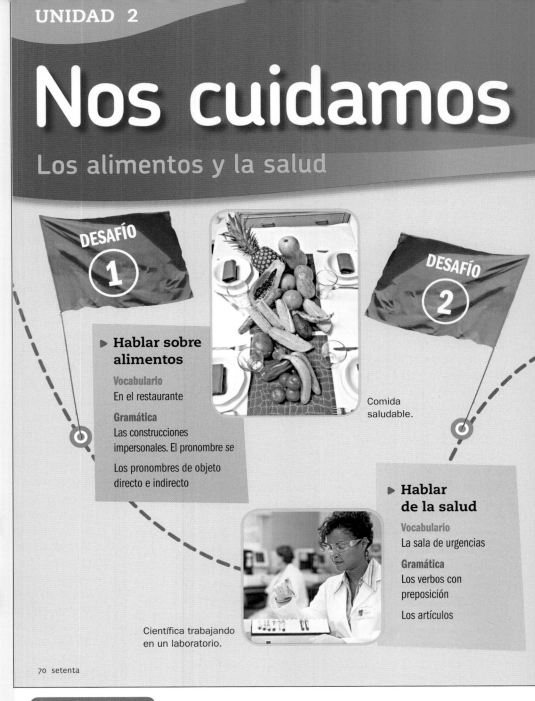

UNIDAD 2
Nos cuidamos
Los alimentos y la salud

DESAFÍO 1

▶ **Hablar sobre alimentos**

Vocabulario
En el restaurante

Gramática
Las construcciones impersonales. El pronombre *se*

Los pronombres de objeto directo e indirecto

DESAFÍO 2

Comida saludable.

▶ **Hablar de la salud**

Vocabulario
La sala de urgencias

Gramática
Los verbos con preposición

Los artículos

Científica trabajando en un laboratorio.

The Challenge

DESAFÍO 1

Comida saludable

Research has shown that the traditional Mediterranean diet—consisting of fruits, vegetables, whole grains, legumes, nuts, fish, and olive oil—reduces the risk of heart disease. Additionally, several fruits and vegetables native to the Americas are among some of the healthiest foods we can eat. For instance, avocados are rich in vitamin E and omega-3 fatty acids, tomatoes are rich in antioxidants, papayas contain a digestive enzyme, pumpkins and sweet potatoes are rich in vitamin A, and potatoes are rich in vitamin C and vitamin B6.

DESAFÍO 2

Científica trabajando en un laboratorio

There has been a growing effort in the Spanish-speaking world to improve the quality and quantity of its scientific pool. This is being attained in several ways: funding doctoral fellowships to train and educate scientists, supporting international exchanges of qualified scientists and technologies, setting aside a higher percentage of the national budget for research and development, and promoting international investments in scientific projects. There is still much to be done, but these efforts are beginning to bear fruit in the growth in scholarly output for the region.

Nos cuidamos

DESAFÍO 3

▶ Referirse a cambios y estados

Vocabulario
Estados físicos y anímicos

Gramática
La voz pasiva

Ser y estar

Boda tradicional
de Yucatán (México).

setenta y uno 71

Picture Discussion

- Have students look at the images again and review their predictions about each topic. Then ask them to read their descriptions from the Independent Starter and share their predictions and any information they may have on these topics in a class discussion.

Comida saludable

- Have students identify the different foods pictured. Some students might need help identifying the root vegetable (*yuca*) as well as some of the tropical fruits (*mamey, papaya, mango*). Then invite different students to describe the taste, texture, and appearance of the fruits and vegetables that they are familiar with from this picture. You may need to prompt students with questions such as, *¿Es dulce o ácida? ¿Es dura o blanda? ¿Tiene mucha fibra? ¿Tiene muchas calorías? ¿Cambia de color cuando madura?*

Científica trabajando en un laboratorio

- Brainstorm with students a list of specializations in science (e.g., *biología, química, bioquímica, genética, microbiología*). Write down some responses and call students' attention to the fact that most of these words are cognates. Then ask students to speculate on a possible specialization for the scientist pictured. Ask students to justify their choices.

Boda tradicional de Yucatán (México)

- Have students identify the elements in this picture that are usually associated with weddings (e.g., *color blanco, flores, velo*). Then ask them to focus on what is different or unusual (e.g., *la ropa del novio, el tipo de vestido de la novia*). Do students know the name of the shirt the groom is wearing? (*guayabera*) Discuss with students the mix of cultures in Yucatán (i.e., Spanish and Maya) and how this mix is reflected in this image.

Objectives

- By the end of Unit 2, students will be able to
  - Talk about food dishes and restaurant menus.
  - Express involuntary or accidental actions.
  - Talk about health, medicine, and medical specialists.
  - Express physical and emotional states.
  - Describe a ceremony or ritual in detail.
  - Talk about some foods, drinks, scientists, and ceremonies of the Spanish-speaking world.

DESAFÍO 3

Boda tradicional de Yucatán

The state of Yucatán, located in southern Mexico, is famous for its mix of Maya and Spanish cultures. A traditional Yucatán wedding, or *boda mestiza*, is a good example of this mix. The bride wears a white *terno*—a variation of the traditional formal attire of indigenous Maya women. Her dress is complemented with some items of European origin, such as a veil and the bridal bouquet. The groom wears a white *guayabera* and white cotton pants. A large red scarf, called *paliacate*, hangs from one of his pants pockets.

Las tareas

Presentation

- In this section, the three pairs chat with Tess, a former participant, who describes the challenges that lie ahead. Students will preview ways to express that a dish or food is very tasty, that they have had enough to eat, and that someone has eaten too much.

Activities	Standards	Resources
Texto	1.2, 2.1, 2.2	
1.	1.1, 1.2, 1.3, 2.2	
2.	1.1, 1.2, 1.3	

Teaching Suggestions

Warm-Up / Independent Starter

- To activate students' previous knowledge about the themes of this unit, have them list, in a three-column chart, the following items from the Spanish-speaking world: food dishes, scientists, and rituals or celebrations that mark the different stages of life. You may want to get them started with the following examples:

Comidas	Científicos	Celebraciones
ropa vieja	Ellen Ochoa	quinceañera

Preparation

- Acquaint or reacquaint students with Tess. Explain that she is from San Antonio, TX, and that she used to travel with her mother, Patricia.
- Invite volunteers to share their Independent Starters. Congratulate them on their knowledge of the foods, peoples, and traditions of the Spanish-speaking world, and discuss some of the dishes, scientists, and celebrations they mentioned.

Texto: Desafíos para todos los gustos

- Read the title aloud and ask students to explain what they think the phrase *para todos los gustos* means. You may want to share with students these related proverbs: *Para gustos hay colores. Sobre gustos no hay nada escrito.* Discuss the meaning with the class. (It's a question of taste. There is no accounting for taste.) Do they agree with these proverbs?

Las tareas

Desafíos para todos los gustos

Los personajes quieren aprender más sobre costumbres hispanas relacionadas con los alimentos y la salud. Lee el chat para saber qué desafíos les propone Tess.

Mostrar mensajes de: Hoy | Esta semana | Últimos 30 días | Todos

Tess dice: 9:45
Hola, chicos. En nuestros viajes por el mundo hispano tuvimos la oportunidad de probar comidas y bebidas buenísimas típicas de varios países. Mmmm, se me hace la boca agua solo de pensarlo.

Ethan dice: 9:47
No me extraña. A mí también me encanta probar comidas nuevas. Hace poco estuve en un restaurante peruano y pedí ceviche. ¡Estaba delicioso!

Michelle dice: 9:48
¿Quieren dejar de hablar de comida, por favor? ¡Acabo de cenar y no puedo pensar en comer más! Estoy llena.

Tess dice: 9:50
¡Ja, ja! De acuerdo, hablemos de sus desafíos. No van a viajar como nosotros, pero van a vivir experiencias similares en sus propias ciudades. Tú y Daniel van a participar en una feria de gastronomía internacional. Hay un premio para el mejor puesto. ¡Espero que lo consigan!

Daniel dice: 9:51
¿Gastronomía internacional? ¡Qué divertido!

Tess dice: 9:52
Ethan y Eva van a ayudar a organizar una serie de charlas con hispanos relevantes en su escuela. Tienen que encontrar un científico hispano e invitarlo a participar.

Ethan dice: 9:55
¿Invitar a un científico famoso? ¡Qué interesante!

Tess dice: 9:56
Asha, Lucas, ¿a ustedes también les gusta la buena comida? Espero que sí, porque van a darse una comilona... ¡en una boda mexicana! Pero no van a asistir a la boda solo para eso. Tienen que hacer un reportaje fotográfico que muestre las costumbres de las bodas mexicanas. ¡Buena suerte!

▼ Conectado

Differentiated Instruction

DEVELOPING LEARNERS

- Ask students to correct the following false statements:
  1. *Ethan no tiene interés en probar comidas nuevas. (Le encanta.)*
  2. *Michelle tiene mucha hambre. (Está llena.)*
  3. *Ethan y Eva van a organizar una serie de charlas con gastrónomos. (con científicos hispanos)*
  4. *Asha y Lucas van a hacer invitaciones para una boda. (Van a hacer un reportaje fotográfico de una boda.)*
  5. *Michelle es una buena cocinera. (No se le da bien cocinar.)*

EXPANDING LEARNERS

- Review the false cognates on page 72 (i.e., *probar, varios, asistir*) and ask students what they mean (to try, several, to attend) and what words they are often confused with (to probe, various, to assist). Have students write the English-language equivalent of each of the following words, along with the false cognate and its Spanish translation:
  1. *actual* (present, current; actual: *real*)
  2. *balón* (ball; balloon: *globo*)
  3. *disgusto* (unpleasantness; disgust: *asco*)
  4. *éxito* (success; exit: *salida*)
  5. *pretender* (to expect; pretend: *fingir*)
  6. *sensible* (sensitive; sensible: *sensato*)

> Michelle, tenemos que pensar en algo que le guste a todo el mundo.

> Ya, pero a mí no se me da bien cocinar.

> La boda será este sábado. ¿Alguna vez has asistido a una boda mexicana?

> Sí, mi prima se casó con un mexicano. ¡El evento fue tan lindo...!

> Me encanta nuestro desafío, Ethan.

> A mí también. ¡Pero no se me ocurre ningún científico hispano al que podamos invitar!

1 ¿Comprendes?

▶ **Responde** a estas preguntas.

1. ¿En qué tipo de restaurante estuvo Ethan hace poco? ¿Qué comió?
2. ¿Por qué Michelle no quiere oír hablar de comida?
3. ¿Qué tienen que hacer Michelle y Daniel?
4. ¿En qué consiste el desafío de Ethan y Eva?
5. ¿Para qué tienen que ir Asha y Lucas a una boda mexicana?

▶ **Escribe.** ¿Cuál de los tres desafíos te parece más interesante? ¿Por qué?

2 Investiga

 ▶ **Busca** en el texto estas expresiones relacionadas con la comida. ¿Qué crees que significan? Coméntalo con tu compañero(a) y escribe una oración con cada expresión.

> hacérsele (a alguien) la boca agua

> estar lleno(a)

> darse una comilona

HERITAGE LANGUAGE LEARNERS

- Ask students to imagine that they are among the pairs who are completing one of the *desafíos*. Have them work with a partner and create a dialogue in which they will describe and discuss their doubts about completing the challenge successfully. Students may voice concerns about their inability to cook; or their dislike of going to gatherings where they will be with strangers; or their concern that they will not be able to identify any Hispanic scientists. Call on pairs to present their dialogues to the class.

MULTIPLE INTELLIGENCES:
Intrapersonal Intelligence

- Ask students to imagine that they are Michelle, who is going to take part in an international food festival but does not know how to cook. Have students write journal entries that reflect Michelle's concern about her non-existent skills in the kitchen and her worry that she might fail her partner. Students may write entries over a period of several days. Invite students to read their journals aloud.

- Read the introduction to the text aloud, and then ask for five volunteers to read the chat aloud. Write down the following words on the board and ask students to associate a participant pair with each of these words according to their tasks: *feria, charla, boda.* (Michelle and Daniel, Eva and Ethan, Asha and Lucas)

Activities

1. Encourage students to express themselves by asking related questions. For example: *A Ethan le encantó el ceviche peruano. ¿Qué platos de la cocina hispana les gustan a ustedes? ¿Han asistido a alguna feria o evento de comida? ¿Qué comidas había? ¿A qué científico hispano les gustaría conocer? ¿Han asistido a alguna boda? ¿Cómo fue la ceremonia? ¿Hubo fiesta después?*

2. To expand this activity, have students use their sentences to write a short dialogue where they use these expressions. Invite volunteer pairs to role-play their dialogues for the class.

Answer Key

1. 1. En un restaurante peruano. Comió ceviche.
   2. Porque acaba de cenar y está llena.
   3. Tienen que participar en una feria de gastronomía internacional.
   4. Van a ayudar a organizar una serie de charlas en su escuela. Tienen que encontrar un científico hispano e invitarlo a participar.
   5. Para hacer un reportaje fotográfico de las bodas mexicanas.
   ▶ Answers will vary.

2. Answers will vary. Sample answers: Hacérsele la boca agua: desear comer cuando se piensa en ello. Darse una comilona: comer mucho y bien. Estar lleno(a): haber comido tanto que ya no puedes comer más.

Additional Resources

Fans Online activities
Practice Workbook

Unit 2

Antes de empezar

Presentation

- In this section, students will learn a variety of useful expressions to indicate that a dish or food is very tasty, that they have had enough to eat, and that someone has eaten too much.

- Students will also review vocabulary for talking about food, health and medicine, and emotional states.

Activities	Standards	Resources
Expresiones útiles	1.2, 2.1	
3.	1.2, 2.1	
4.	1.3, 2.1	
Recuerda	1.2	
5.	1.3	
6.	1.1, 1.2, 1.3	Audio

Teaching Suggestions

Warm-Up / Independent Starter

- Have students write six sentences expressing their opinions about different foods they like (e.g., *El postre es lo más rico de una comida*).

Preparation

- Go over the *expresiones útiles* with the class. Explain that most of these expressions are metaphors or similes. For instance, *se me hace la boca agua*, describes what happens in our mouths when we think about food we love (the mouth waters). If students have difficulties with the expression *ponerse las botas*, suggest that they think about this phrase, which is used in some English-speaking countries: "Fill your boots." In the context of a meal, it is an invitation to eat as much as the person wishes, which is similar to the meaning of *ponerse las botas*.

- Ask students to use their Independent Starters and the *expresiones útiles* they have just learned to create new sentences. For example: *Cuando pienso en el postre, ¡se me hace la boca agua!*

- For the *Recuerda* vocabulary, divide the class into five groups and assign each group one of the vocabulary categories, except for *Salud*, which all the groups can use. Have students add other words they know to their assigned vocabulary list.

74

EXPRESIONES ÚTILES

Para decir que una comida está muy rica:
> Se me hace la boca agua.
> Este plato está **para chuparse los dedos**.

Para decir que ya no quieres comer más:
> Estoy lleno(a).

Para decir que alguien come mucho:
> Tess **come como una fiera / como una lima**.
> **Nos pusimos las botas** en aquel restaurante tan bueno.
> El día de Acción de Gracias **nos dimos una comilona / un atracón**.

3 Cosas de la comida

▶ **Completa** los diálogos poniendo estas expresiones en la forma correcta.

   a. hacérsele (a alguien) la boca agua   c. darse un atracón
   b. estar lleno(a)   d. comer como una lima

1. —Diego, ¿quieres un trozo de pastel?
   —No, gracias, Lucía. He comido muchísimo arroz ¡y dos platos de pollo! _____.

2. —Pablo ha crecido mucho, ¿verdad?
   —Sí. Es un chico muy atlético. Hace mucho deporte y además _____.

3. —¿Tienes hambre, Sara? Estoy preparando una comida muy rica.
   —¡Qué bien huele, David! _____.

4. —Pedro, ¿dónde está tu hermano?
   —Está enfermo. Ayer _____ y hoy no se encuentra bien.

4 Diálogos

▶ **Escribe** un diálogo para estas fotografías usando las expresiones útiles.

74 setenta y cuatro

Differentiated Instruction

DEVELOPING LEARNERS

- Explain to students that they are going to take a class survey to see who among them has ever pigged out (*darse un atracón*) on certain foods or drinks such as *helado, refrescos, chocolate,* or *pizza* as well as some of those listed in the *Recuerda* feature. Ask them to work with a partner or in small groups to question their classmates (*¿Con cuál de estas comidas te has dado un atracón?*) and to include their own favorite pig-out foods. Have them present the results to the class.

EXPANDING LEARNERS

- Give student pairs more practice with the phrases in the *Expresiones útiles* section by having them develop a dialogue focusing on food and eating habits. Encourage students to review or find other expressions that describe overeating. You might introduce some of these expressions: *ponerse morado / ciego de algo* (to pig out); *la gula, la glotonería* (gluttony); *glotón, tragón* (glutton); *tener un hambre voraz / insaciable* (to have an insatiable appetite); *comer con avidez / ávidamente* (to eat eagerly). Invite pairs to present their dialogues to the class.

RECUERDA

Alimentación

el aceite	el melón
el arroz	el pollo
el atún	el queso
la carne de cerdo	el salmón
la carne de res	la sandía
las fresas	las uvas
los frutos secos	el vinagre
los guisantes	la zanahoria

Salud

aumentar de peso	entrenar
bajar de peso	hacer ejercicio
cuidarse	relajarse
descansar	respirar

Estados de ánimo

aburrido(a)	nervioso(a)
contento(a)	relajado(a)
enojado(a)	tranquilo(a)
estresado(a)	triste

Enfermedades y síntomas

la alergia	la fiebre
el catarro	la gripe
doler	estornudar
estar hinchado(a)	picar
estar mareado(a)	tener escalofríos
estar roto(a)	toser

La consulta médica

el análisis de sangre	las píldoras
el antibiótico	la radiografía
el diagnóstico	la receta
el examen físico	la revisión médica

Especialistas médicos

el/la dentista
el/la oculista
el/la pediatra
el/la psicólogo(a)

---

 5 **¿Cuánto sabes?**

▶ **Fíjate** en el cuadro Recuerda. ¿Conoces más vocabulario sobre esos temas? Escríbelo.

Modelo *Alimentación: lechuga, espinacas, frijoles...*

 6 **Síntomas**

 ▶ **Escucha** el diálogo, e indica qué síntomas tiene el paciente.

1. Le duele la cabeza.
2. Tiene escalofríos.
3. Tiene fiebre.
4. Se siente mal.
5. Está mareado.
6. Tiene alergia.

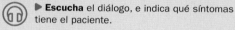 ▶ **Escucha** el diálogo de nuevo y escribe tres recomendaciones que le da la médica al paciente.

▶ **Escribe** con tu compañero(a) un diálogo similar y represéntenlo ante la clase.

setenta y cinco 75

Antes de empezar

■ Then have groups create a word web on poster board to classify their list of words. For example: *Especialistas médicos → dentista; Especialidad → dientes, muelas...; Síntomas que trata → dolor de dientes/muelas...; Tratamiento → tomar analgésicos, cepillarse los dientes tres veces al día...* Invite groups to present their word webs.

Activities

3. To extend this activity, have student pairs choose one of the dialogues and add a few more lines to create a brief conversation in which they use other *expresiones útiles.* For instance, dialogue #2 might continue as follows:

—*Sí, en la barbacoa del Día de la Independencia se dio un atracón de hamburguesas.*

—*Es cierto. Cuando ve una hamburguesa, ¡se le hace la boca agua!*

6. For the third part of this activity, encourage students to use available props to make their role-plays as realistic as possible.

 AUDIO SCRIPT
See page 69K.

Answer Key

3. 1. Estoy lleno.
   2. come como una lima
   3. Se me hace la boca agua.
   4. se dio un atracón

4. Answers will vary.

5. Answers will vary.

6. Le duele la cabeza.
   Se siente mal.
   Está mareado.
   ▶ Answers will vary. Sample answer:
   Le aconseja que descanse, que coma comidas ligeras y que beba mucha agua.
   ▶ Answers will vary.

Additional Resources

Fans Online activities
Practice Workbook

75

DESAFÍO 1

Hablar sobre alimentos

Presentation

- In *Desafío 1*, Michelle and Daniel learn about *mate,* a South American drink. Students will preview language used to talk about food and drink preparation.

Activities	Standards	Resources
Texto	1.2, 2.1, 2.2	
7.	1.2, 1.3, 3.1	
8.	1.1, 1.2, 2.1, 2.2	
9.	1.2, 2.1	Audio
10. Cultura	1.1, 1.2, 2.1, 2.2, 3.2, 4.2	

Teaching Suggestions

Warm-Up / Independent Starter

- Have students brainstorm and list dishes from the Spanish-speaking world that they have heard of or have tried before.

Preparation

- Ask students to share their Independent Starters in small groups. Then groups will write five or six sentences describing how to prepare one of the dishes. As students discuss the recipes, take the opportunity to review some food vocabulary.

Texto: Se vende mate

- Read the introduction, and then ask students to think of a possible dish or drink that Michelle and Daniel could take to the fair. Emphasize that it has to be something that is not too common.
- Call on several pairs of volunteers to alternate reading the dialogue. Then ask students to explain, in their own words, what *mate* is and how it is prepared.

Activities

8. Have students answer these questions: *¿Qué ingredientes y utensilios se usan en la preparación del mate? ¿De qué otros alimentos o bebidas se pueden hacer catas? ¿Creen que Michelle y Daniel tendrán éxito en la feria con la «cata de mate»?* Hold a whole-class discussion to answer this last question.

Se vende mate

Daniel y Michelle van a participar en una feria de gastronomía internacional. Tienen que presentar una comida o una bebida de algún país hispano, pero los concursantes ya eligieron las más conocidas. ¿Qué llevarán ellos?

MICHELLE: Daniel, no sé qué podemos llevar a la feria.

DANIEL: ¿Has probado el mate?

MICHELLE: No, ¿qué es?

DANIEL: Es como un té, pero con un sabor un poco amargo. Se toma mucho en Argentina, en Uruguay y en Paraguay.

MICHELLE: ¿Y cómo se prepara? Espero que no sea muy difícil.

DANIEL: Creo que es muy sencillo, aunque me parece que hay distintas formas de prepararlo.

MICHELLE: ¿Qué tal si hacemos una cata *(tasting)* para que todos puedan probar varios tipos de mate y elijan el que más les guste?

DANIEL: ¡Qué creativa, Michelle! ¡Seguro que ganamos! Pero primero tenemos que aprender a prepararlo. Aquí dice que el mate es una infusión de yerba mate. Se prepara en un recipiente que también se llama mate, que tradicionalmente se fabricaba con calabazas.

MICHELLE: ¿Con calabazas? ¡Qué curioso! ¿Y cómo se prepara?

DANIEL: Se ponen dentro las hojas de yerba mate y se echa agua caliente. Y para beberlo se coloca la bombilla, que es una especie de pajita *(straw)* metálica.

MICHELLE: ¿Y no se pone nada más? Pues no parece muy difícil.

7   Detective de palabras

▶ **Completa** estas oraciones.

1. El mate ____1____ en Argentina, en Uruguay y en Paraguay.
2. El mate ____2____ en un recipiente que también ____3____ mate.
3. Para prepararlo, ____4____ las hojas de yerba mate en el recipiente, ____5____ agua caliente y ____6____ la bombilla.

▶ **Escribe.** ¿Qué tienen en común las seis formas verbales del apartado anterior? ¿Sabes por qué se usa esa estructura verbal?

Differentiated Instruction

DEVELOPING LEARNERS

- Ask students to say whether the following statements are true *(cierto)* or false *(falso).* Have them correct the false ones.
  1. *Michelle no sabe qué es el mate.* (C)
  2. *Según Daniel, el mate es más dulce que el té.* (F; es más amargo)
  3. *Solo hay una forma de prepararlo.* (F; hay distintas formas)
  4. *Piensan hacer una cata para que todos prueben varios tipos de mate.* (C)
  5. *Se coloca una calabaza en el mate para beberlo.* (F; se coloca una bombilla)

EXPANDING LEARNERS

- Review some irregular and stem-changing verbs with students. Point out the verb *elegir* and the forms that are used in the dialogue: *eligieron, elijan.* Ask students to write the following verbs in the third-person plural of the preterite: *sentir (sintieron), morir (murieron), referir (refirieron), producir (produjeron).* Then ask them to write these verbs in the first person of the present subjunctive: *caber (quepa), cocer (cueza), oler (huela), proteger (proteja).* After you check their spelling, have students write six sentences using these verbs. Call on volunteers to read their sentences aloud.

8 ¿Comprendes?

▶ **Responde** a estas preguntas.

1. ¿En qué países es costumbre tomar mate?
2. ¿Cómo se prepara el mate?
3. ¿Qué se necesita para tomarlo?
4. ¿Qué crees que se le puede añadir al mate para preparar algunas variantes?

9 ¡Cuántas variedades de mate!

▶ **Escucha** y anota cuáles de estos ingredientes necesitan Michelle y Daniel para preparar las distintas variedades de mate.

① leche ② dulce de leche ③ rodajas de limón ④ azúcar

⑤ corteza de naranja ⑥ canela ⑦ moras ⑧ jugo de toronja ⑨ miel

CULTURA

El mate

El término *mate* tiene su origen en la palabra quechua *mati*, que significa *calabacita*. El mate es la infusión de la yerba mate, que se elabora con una planta originaria de la cuenca del Río de la Plata. Era consumido ya en la época precolombina por los indígenas guaraníes y forma parte del patrimonio cultural de Argentina, Paraguay y Uruguay. En el español de esta zona, se llama *matear* a tomar el mate, prepararlo es *cebarlo* y la persona que lo prepara es el *cebador*. El mate representa un auténtico ritual familiar y social.

10 **Investiga.** ¿Qué comida o bebida representa un ritual social en tu cultura?

setenta y siete 77

HERITAGE LANGUAGE LEARNERS

• Ask students to research some other foods or beverages that originated in the Americas (e.g., *el tomate, el aguacate, la papa, el chile o ají, el chocolate, el maíz, la piña*), but have made their way into international cuisine. Have students describe the food, its place of origin, how it traveled from country to country, the dishes made with it, and any other historical, gastronomical, or anecdotal information. Encourage students to present their findings with visuals and, if possible, bring some samples of the food or beverage to class.

SPECIAL-NEEDS LEARNERS

• Allow students with slight or moderate hearing loss to read the audio script before they listen to the recording, and to follow along with the script as they listen. You may also wish to read the script to them aloud as they read along silently. You may consider doing this for all of the activities that have an audio portion. Ask students to look at the illustrations as you play the recording.

Hablar sobre alimentos

9. Once students have completed the activity, take a vote to see which version of *mate* most of the class would like to try. Can students think of other possible versions? Encourage creativity (e.g., *mate con crema y vainilla, mate frío con menta*).

AUDIO SCRIPT
See page 69K.

CULTURA

El mate

The *mate* plant is a tree, which is pruned to a shrub-like shape. The leaves and twigs are harvested, dried—usually over a fire—and then finely chopped for consumption. *Yerba mate* has a bitter, woody flavor and a strong aftertaste, which prompts most first-time users to add sugar or honey, but the traditional *mate* is consumed without sugar. *Mate* is a beverage for sharing, and the practice of a group using the same gourd and straw reinforces its communal aspect.

Answer Key

7. 1. se toma 4. se ponen
2. se prepara 5. se echa
3. se llama 6. se coloca
▶ Answers will vary. Sample answer: Usan el pronombre *se*. Son construcciones impersonales.

8. 1. En Argentina, Uruguay y Paraguay.
2. Se ponen las hojas de yerba mate en un recipiente y se echa agua caliente.
3. Un mate y una bombilla.
4. Answers will vary.

9. 1, 3, 4, 5, 8

10. Answers will vary.

Additional Resources

Fans Online activities

DESAFÍO 1

Vocabulario – En el restaurante

Presentation

- In this section, students will learn vocabulary to talk about food, dishes, and restaurant menus.

Activities	Standards	Resources
Vocabulario	1.2	
11.	1.2	
12.	1.1, 1.3	
13.	1.1, 1.3	
14. Cultura	1.1, 1.2, 2.1, 2.2, 3.2, 4.2	

Teaching Suggestions

Warm-Up / Independent Starter

- Ask students to create a three-column chart and label the columns with these headings: *Primeros platos, Segundos platos, Postres*. Then have them list dishes they associate with each category.

Preparation

- Go over the vocabulary presentation with students. Then, see if students can come up with a list of ingredients for some of the dishes. If necessary, review some of the vocabulary for condiments (e.g., *sal, pimienta, salsa de tomate, aceite, ajo, cebolla*). Next, ask students to choose one dish from the menu, based on what they like. Then have them think about the preparation of the dish, and ask them to jot down four or five steps. Call on individual students to share their recipes with the class. Does the rest of the class agree? Encourage students to give their opinion (e.g., *Yo creo que el jamón se fríe antes de añadir los huevos*).

- Ask students to share their Independent Starters in small groups. Then have groups agree on three *primeros platos*, three *segundos platos*, and three *postres* to create a menu similar to the one from the vocabulary presentation.

Activities

11. To expand this activity, have students make other associations (e.g., color, degree of spiciness, flavor, price of the item) for the food in the vocabulary presentation and other foods they know.

Vocabulario

En el restaurante

Restaurante El mate

Primeros platos	Segundos platos	Postres

Ensalada de lentejas con pepino y aguacate

Chuletas de cordero con papas y pimientos

Helado de mora y de frambuesa

Huevos revueltos con calabacita y jamón

Pechuga de pavo asada con ciruelas

Durazno al horno con canela

Berenjenas rellenas de carne molida y hongos

Filete de bacalao con langostinos

Nueces con miel

Más vocabulario

Carne

las alitas de pollo	*chicken wings*
el filete de pavo	*turkey fillet*
el lomo de ternera	*veal loin*

Pescado y marisco

el cangrejo	*crab*
la langosta	*lobster*
el pez espada	*swordfish*

Fruta

las cerezas	*cherries*
las pasas	*raisins*
la toronja	*grapefruit*

11 **Asociaciones**

▶ **Busca** el intruso en cada grupo. Justifica tu respuesta.

1. frambuesas cerezas pepino durazno

2. lentejas berenjenas pimientos hongos

3. cordero bacalao jamón ternera

78 setenta y ocho

Differentiated Instruction

DEVELOPING LEARNERS

- Ask students to find the word that does not belong. Have them justify their answers.

   1. *pimientos* *toronjas* *pepinos (toronjas)*
   2. *cordero* *ternera* *bacalao (bacalao)*
   3. *cerezas* *durazno* *canela (canela)*
   4. *lentejas* *ciruelas* *moras (lentejas)*
   5. *langosta* *cangrejo* *hongos (hongos)*
   6. *chuletas* *nueces* *filetes (nueces)*
   7. *pechuga* *helado* *lomo (helado)*
   8. *calabacita* *jamón* *carne (calabacita)*

EXPANDING LEARNERS

- Students are going to play a word game. Divide the class into teams and have them play against each other. Assign each team one of the *primeros platos* or *segundos platos* described on the page. Then, have them write as many words as they can that are spelled by using the letters in the meal. For example, the following are some of the words found in *nueces con miel*: *mes, cuece, cueces, cuecen, leo, lees, lee, leemos, leen, mil, come, comen, seco, mi, es, son, uso, use, usen*. The game continues until you call time.

12 **Ricos platos**

▶ **Fíjate** en todos los ingredientes de la ficha de Vocabulario y haz una lista de otros platos que se pueden preparar con ellos. Puedes añadir otros ingredientes.

 ▶ **Habla** con tu compañero(a) y, con sus listas, elaboren estos tipos de menús completos (primer plato, segundo plato y postre).

Modelo *Para el menú vegetariano te sugiero una ensalada de aguacate, lechuga y piña.*

	Primer plato	Segundo plato	Postre
Menú vegetariano	Ensalada de aguacate, lechuga y piña.		
Menú económico			
Menú navideño			
Menú infantil			

13 **Decisiones**

▶ **Habla** con tu compañero(a). Van a visitar el restaurante El mate y tienen que decidir qué van a pedir. Utilicen el menú de la página 78 para conversar sobre los platos.

▶ **Escribe** un párrafo contando tu experiencia en El mate: ¿Con quién fuiste? ¿Qué comieron? ¿Quién pagó? ¿Dejaron propina?

 **CULTURA**

Las tapas españolas

Las tapas son parte fundamental de la cultura gastronómica de España. Una tapa es una pequeña porción de comida que se sirve para acompañar la bebida y se toma como aperitivo. Desde las sencillas aceitunas o las tradicionales croquetas hasta recetas más modernas y sofisticadas, la cantidad y variedad de tapas es casi infinita.

El origen de las tapas se sitúa en la Edad Media. El rey Alfonso X ordenó que en los mesones se sirviera algo de comida con el vino. Entonces se empezó a poner una loncha de jamón o de queso tapando la jarra de vino. De ahí el nombre de *tapa*.

14 **Investiga.** ¿De dónde viene el nombre de una comida típica de tu cultura?

Vocabulario – En el restaurante

12. Encourage students to be creative and think of unusual combinations. They may also wish to consider a dish's visual appeal. A salad that combines green leafy vegetables, red fruits, and bright yellow corn could be an attractive choice for a *primer plato*. Ask students to share their menus with the class, and hold a vote to choose the best menu for each category.

13. You may want to ask students to role-play a scene at this restaurant. Divide the class into small groups and have them come up with a short script for their scene. Then, have groups act out their scenes for the class.

 CULTURA

Las tapas españolas

Tapas can be practically any type of dish, served in small portions. The *tapeo* tradition—strolling with a group of friends from *tapas* bar to *tapas* bar, tasting a large variety of *tapas*—is as important as the food. Conversation is an integral part of this ritual, and is common that both friends and strangers engage in lively discussions. In most *tapas* bars, guests eat standing up, crowded around the counter where the *tapas* are on display.

Answer Key

11. 1. pepino: no es fruta, sino verdura
2. lentejas: no es verdura, sino legumbre
3. bacalao: no es carne, sino pescado

12. Answers will vary.
▶ Answers will vary.

13. Answers will vary.
▶ Answers will vary.

14. Answers will vary.

Additional Resources

Fans Online activities
Practice Workbook

HERITAGE LANGUAGE LEARNERS

• Ask students to select a *primer plato, segundo plato,* and *postre* from the foods listed on the vocabulary presentation; this will be their dinner. Then, have them refer to the MyPlate food guidelines and describe what foods they should have at breakfast and lunch in order to comply with the recommendations for healthful eating. You might also ask students to design a weekly meal plan, again making sure they follow MyPlate's recommendations. Discuss their choices and make suggestions as needed.

MULTIPLE INTELLIGENCES:
Visual-Spatial Intelligence

• Have students imagine that they are the public relations team for *El mate* Restaurant. They will work in small groups and make an ad for the opening of their restaurant. Students will need to describe some dishes that are not mentioned on the page, address prices and practical information of location, phone, e-mail, and hours. They will need to include background information on the chef and owner as well as a description of the restaurant's decor and what distinguishes it from other dining establishments.

DESAFÍO 1

Gramática – Las construcciones impersonales. El pronombre *se*

Presentation

- In this section, students will review and practice how to use the pronoun *se* in impersonal and passive voice constructions, and with certain verbs to express accidental or involuntary actions.

Activities	Standards	Resources
Gramática	1.2, 3.1	
15.	1.2, 3.1, 4.1	
16.	1.2	
17.	1.3	
18.	1.1, 1.3, 5.1	

Teaching Suggestions

Warm-Up / Independent Starter

- On the board, draw a two-column chart and add these headings: *Se puede... No se puede...* Have students write a list of things they can and cannot do in a vegetarian restaurant.

Preparation

- Have two volunteers read aloud the first two sections of the grammar presentation. Then review with students the examples they produced for their Independent Starters. Next, have students rewrite some of their examples using *se* and a verb in the third person. Encourage them to adapt the sentences so that they can use different verb tenses. For example: *En ese restaurante antes se podía comer carne, pero ahora es vegetariano y no se sirven platos con carne.* Be sure that students make proper use of the third person singular and plural.

- Have students read the third section of the grammar presentation silently. Write the following pairs of sentences on the board and have students tell the difference in meaning:
  1. a. *Rompimos la computadora.*
     b. *Se nos rompió la computadora.*
  2. a. *Me olvidé de llamarte.*
     b. *Se me olvidó llamarte.*

  In the second example, both sentences would be translated into English as "I forgot to call you." But, in example b, the person is not taking responsibility for the act of forgetting.

Gramática

Las construcciones impersonales. El pronombre *se*

El pronombre *se* impersonal

- En inglés, cuando hablamos de una acción sin decir exactamente quién la hace, usamos la voz pasiva o un sujeto como *you, it, one, they* o *people*: *Spanish is spoken; it said that...* En español, esa misma idea se expresa con la construcción *se + verbo en 3.ª persona.*

se + verbo en 3.ª persona

Se habla español en más de 20 países.
Se dice que habrá una exposición en la escuela.

Uso de *se* + verbo en tercera persona

- En las construcciones con *se + verbo en 3.ª persona* el verbo puede ir en singular o en plural:
  - Delante de un infinitivo o de una cláusula que comienza por *que*, el verbo va en singular:

    Se prohíbe comer en clase.

    Se sabe que las verduras son saludables.

  - Cuando el verbo se refiere a un nombre, concuerda con él en número (singular o plural):

    Se vende casa de campo.

    Se necesitan cocineros con experiencia.

- La construcción *se + verbo en 3.ª persona* se puede conjugar en cualquier tiempo verbal.

PRESENTE	Se dice que el pescado azul es beneficioso.
PRETÉRITO	Se exportaron dos millones de toneladas de trigo.
IMPERFECTO	Antes se comía bien en ese restaurante.
FUTURO	En el futuro se venderán más alimentos por Internet.

El pronombre *se* de involuntariedad

- Con verbos como *caer, olvidar, perder, romper...* usamos el pronombre *se* para presentar la acción como un accidente o como algo involuntario. En estos casos, *se* va seguido de un pronombre de objeto: *me, te, le, nos, os, les.* Ese pronombre representa a quien experimenta la acción y concuerda en número con el nombre al que se refiere.

VERBOS DE INVOLUNTARIEDAD

acabarse	*to run out of*
caerse	*to drop*
olvidarse	*to forget*
perderse	*to lose*
romperse	*to break*

se + pronombre de objeto indirecto + verbo en 3.ª persona

Mi padre perdió las llaves. → A mi padre **se le perdieron** las llaves.

15 **Compara.** ¿Cómo expresas en inglés que una acción fue involuntaria o accidental?

Differentiated Instruction

DEVELOPING LEARNERS

- Ask students to match the sentences in the first column with those in the second.

  1. *Olvidé las entradas.* (d)   a. *Se me acabó.*
  2. *Perdí el dinero.* (e)   b. *Se te olvidó.*
  3. *No tengo arroz.* (a)   c. *Se me cayeron.*
  4. *Olvidaste la llave.* (b)   d. *Se me olvidaron.*
  5. *Dejé caer los vasos.* (c)   e. *Se me perdió.*

EXPANDING LEARNERS

- Have students list ten annoying issues with their least favorite restaurant. They should use the pronoun *se* to describe the restaurant's policies and the behavior of the wait staff. Ask them to offer suggestions to remedy the situation. For example: *Se recogen los platos antes de que hayas terminado de comer.* → *Se debe esperar a que el cliente termine de comer. A los meseros se les olvida lo que habías pedido.* → *Los meseros deben escribir los pedidos. No se sirven verduras frescas.* → *Se debe comprar verduras frescas todos los días.*

16 ¿Singular o plural?

▶ **Completa** estas oraciones.

1. En muchas guías se _____ que el restaurante Casa Botín de Madrid es el restaurante más antiguo del mundo.
   <small>decir</small>

2. En casa siempre se _____ las carnes y los pescados al horno.
   <small>preparar</small>

3. En Argentina se _____ mucho mate.
   <small>beber</small>

4. Cuando era pequeño, no se _____ llevar comida de casa a la escuela.
   <small>poder</small>

17 El restaurante ideal

▶ **Escribe** una lista con diez reglas para el restaurante ideal. Usa el pronombre *se*.

Modelo

> **Las diez reglas del restaurante ideal**
>
> 1. Solo se contrata a cocineros profesionales.
> 2. Se compran ingredientes de primera calidad.
> 3. Cada día se sirven...

18 ¡Qué mala suerte!

▶ **Escribe** una oración para cada ilustración explicando qué le pasó a Mike. Usa estos verbos.

| caerse | olvidarse | perderse | acabarse |

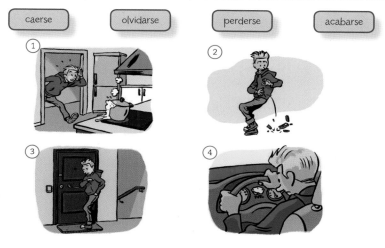

▶ **Escribe** con tu compañero(a) la historia completa de Mike.

 ▶ **Habla** con tu compañero(a). ¿Alguna vez te ha pasado algo similar? Cuéntaselo y hazle preguntas para conocer más detalles de su anécdota.

Gramática – Las construcciones impersonales. El pronombre *se*

Activities

16. To extend this activity, have students rewrite the sentences specifying a subject. For example:
1. *Las guías dicen que...*
2. *Nosotros siempre preparamos...*

17. Once students have finished, have them get together in small groups of three or four and share their lists of rules. Then, ask groups to decide on a group list to present to the class. Hold a class vote to choose the most attractive restaurant.

18. For the third part of this activity, ask students to take notes on their partner's anecdote. Then give students a few moments to organize their notes in the order in which the events took place. Finally, ask students to report their partner's anecdote to the class.

Answer Key

15. Normalmente, en inglés no se especifica. Pero se puede añadir una aclaración para indicar que algo fue accidental o involuntario. Por ejemplo: Se me cayó el lápiz. → *I accidentally dropped my pencil.*

16. 1. dice 3. bebe
2. preparan 4. podía

17. Answers will vary.

18. Answers will vary. Sample answers:
1. A Mike se le olvidó apagar la cocina.
2. A Mike se le cayó el celular.
3. A Mike se le perdieron las llaves.
4. A Mike se le acabó la gasolina.
▶ Answers will vary.
▶ Answers will vary.

Additional Resources

Fans Online activities
Practice Workbook

HERITAGE LANGUAGE LEARNERS

• Ask students to list at least ten suggestions to correct *las costumbres de un(a) compañero(a) de mesa insoportable*. Explain that students must use the pronoun *se*. Some of these suggestions may include: *Se prohíbe hablar por el celular; se prohíbe tocarse la nariz; no se debe comer con los dedos; se prohíbe sorber la sopa; no se le debe caer la comida de la boca; se debe usar la servilleta para limpiarse la boca; se debe masticar con la boca cerrada.*

COOPERATIVE LEARNING

• Have students imagine that they are the owners of a new restaurant and will need to hire a full staff, from busboys and valet attendants to general managers. Ask students to work in small groups and create some want ads for their business. Students should use the pronoun *se*; for example: *Se busca gerente con mínimo de 5 años de experiencia. Se necesitan dos pasteleros.* Students should elaborate on the experience required and benefits offered. They should also include a brief description of their restaurant.

81

DESAFÍO 1

Gramática – Los pronombres de objeto directo e indirecto

Presentation

- In this section, students will review the direct and indirect object pronouns and their placement in a sentence.

Activities	Standards	Resources
Gramática	1.2, 3.1	
19.	1.2, 3.1, 4.1	
20.	1.2, 1.3	Audio
21.	1.2, 2.1, 2.2, 3.1	
22. Cultura	1.1, 1.2, 2.2, 3.2, 4.2, 5.2	

Teaching Suggestions

Warm-Up / Independent Starter

- Ask students to rewrite these sentences using both direct and indirect object pronouns:
  1. *Le pedí el postre al mesero. (Se lo pedí.)*
  2. *Tráiganos la bebida, por favor. (Tráiganosla.)*
  3. *No le pongas azúcar al mate. (No se lo pongas.)*
  4. *Estamos bebiendo café. (Estamos bebiéndolo.)*

Preparation

- Call on volunteers to share their Independent Starters. Remind students that they can find the direct object of the verb by asking *¿qué?* or *¿quién?* For example: *¿Qué le pediste al mesero? (el postre)* They can find the indirect object by asking *¿a quién/qué?* or *¿para quién?* For example: *¿A quién le pediste el postre? (al mesero)*

- Provide these sentences to students: a. *El mesero le dio a él la cuenta.* b. *El mesero le dio la cuenta.* Explain that both sentences are possible, but *El mesero dio a él la cuenta* would be incorrect in Spanish. In this case, both the indirect object pronoun and the indirect object must be stated.

Activities

20. Before playing the audio, ask students to read the statements and come up with the indirect object pronouns (*le, le, le, les, le*). Then, suggest that they focus on the direct object as they listen.

Gramática

Los pronombres de objeto directo e indirecto

Los pronombres de objeto

- Con frecuencia, los nombres de objeto directo y objeto indirecto se sustituyen por un pronombre para evitar repeticiones.

  —¿Compraste la fruta? —¿Le traigo el postre al niño?
  —Sí, la compré. —Sí, tráigaselo.

- El pronombre de objeto es obligatorio con los verbos pronominales y también en estos casos:
  - Cuando el objeto indirecto es a + *pronombre* (a mí, a ti, a usted...) o a + *nombre*: Le envié un mensaje a Pedro.
  - Cuando el nombre objeto va delante del verbo:

    Estas fresas las compré ayer.

PRONOMBRES DE OBJETO DIRECTO	
me	nos
te	os
lo, la	los, las

PRONOMBRES DE OBJETO INDIRECTO	
me	nos
te	os
le	les

Posición de los pronombres de objeto

- Los pronombres de objeto se colocan así:
  - Delante del verbo conjugado, excepto en las formas del imperativo *(affirmative commands)*:

    No le compres nada. Ella se los da. Los vimos ayer.

  - Detrás de un imperativo, un infinitivo o un gerundio, unidos a la forma verbal:

    Dímelo. Comprársela fue un acierto. Pensándolo bien, tienes razón.

- En las construcciones de *verbo + infinitivo* o *verbo + gerundio*, los pronombres pueden ir delante del verbo conjugado o detrás del infinitivo o del gerundio.

  Ella se los va a dar./Ella va a dárselos. Ella se los está dando./Ella está dándoselos.

- Si un mismo verbo lleva dos pronombres de objeto, el de objeto indirecto va delante:

  Le pido la cuenta al mesero. → Se la pido.

  Observa en el ejemplo que cuando hay dos pronombres de objeto, le (y también les) se convierte en se.

19 **Compara.** Traduce estas oraciones al inglés. ¿Los pronombres funcionan igual que en español?

  a. La llamo por teléfono todos los días. b. Le añadí sal a la sopa.

20 **Soluciones para todo**

 ▶ **Escucha** los diálogos. ¿Cómo continúan? Escribe oraciones completas siguiendo el modelo.

Modelo 1. *Se lo regalé a mi amiga Berta.*

1. regalar (a mi amiga Berta)
2. pedir (a mi compañero)
3. comprar (para Patricia)
4. explicar (a Michelle y a Daniel)
5. dar (a tu hermana)
6. prestar (a mi primo)

Differentiated Instruction

DEVELOPING LEARNERS

- Have students answer the following questions in the affirmative:
  1. *¿Encontraste las llaves del coche? (Sí, las encontré.)*
  2. *¿Sabes preparar esos platos? (Sí, sé prepararlos / los sé preparar.)*
  3. *¿Debo leer la lista de ingredientes? (Sí, debes leerla / la debes leer.)*
  4. *¿Explicamos el problema bien? (Sí, lo explicaron bien.)*
  5. *¿Piensas pedir las chuletas? (Sí, pienso pedirlas / las pienso pedir.)*

EXPANDING LEARNERS

- Have students reword the following sentences as quickly as possible, using both the direct and indirect object pronouns:
  1. *¿Te sirvo la langosta? (¿Te la sirvo?)*
  2. *Le dijeron la verdad. (Se la dijeron.)*
  3. *Te di buenos consejos. (Te los di.)*
  4. *Juan me dio el libro. (Me lo dio.)*
  5. *¿Te pongo canela? (¿Te la pongo?)*
  6. *¿Le escribió la carta? (¿Se la escribió?)*

21 El arte de matear

▶ **Lee** el mensaje de Michelle y complétalo con los pronombres de objeto directo e indirecto correctos.

De: Michelle
Para: ✉ Tess
Asunto: ¡Necesitamos ayuda!

Cuerpo del texto ▾ | Anchura variable ▾ | ■ A+ A+ | B I U | ☰ ☱ ☲ | 🔳 🔲 ◉

¡Hola, Tess!

¿Cómo estás? ___1___ escribo para ver si puedes _ayudar_ _2___ a Daniel y a mí. Hemos elegido el mate para la feria de gastronomía. Como queremos tener mucho éxito, no queremos _preparar_ _3___ de la forma tradicional y hemos decidido hacer algunas variedades de mate para organizar una cata. ¿Qué te parece?

Tenemos muchas ideas: podemos _servir_ _4___ solo con las hojas de yerba mate. Pero a la infusión también ___5___ podemos añadir azúcar, corteza de naranja, jugo de limón (esta es una variedad fría; hay que _poner_ _6___ hielo), un poco de leche y azúcar... Ahora solo nos falta practicar. Hemos conseguido la yerba mate, pero no pudimos encontrar suficientes mates para la cata. Daniel dice que podemos preparar las variedades en otro recipiente y _servir_ _7___ en vasos para la cata, pero yo creo que no saldrá igual.

La feria es dentro de poco y no sabemos de dónde sacar tantos mates. Estuvimos en varias tiendas de la ciudad, pero no ___8___ encontramos. Y si ___9___ pedimos a través de Internet, me temo que no llegarán a tiempo. ¿Se ___10___ ocurre algo? Si tienes alguna idea, _cuéntanos_ _11___, por favor. Nos encanta el desafío, pero no sé si ___12___ podremos lograr.

Un beso.

Michelle

 CULTURA

Inca Kola

Inca Kola es el nombre de un refresco muy popular en Perú. Se hace con hierba luisa *(lemon verbena)* y tiene un sabor muy dulce. Este refresco se ha convertido en la bebida de Perú, tal como muestran algunos de sus eslóganes:

– *Inca Kola, solo hay una y no se parece a ninguna.*
– *Hay una sola y el Perú sabe por qué.*
– *Destapa el sabor del Perú.*

Es tan popular que en los años noventa venció a los gigantes del sector (Coca-Cola y Pepsi) y Coca-Cola tuvo que comprar parte de la compañía para poder competir en Perú.

22 Explica.
¿Hay alguna bebida o plato típico en la región donde vives? Prepara un eslogan para popularizarlo y comparte tus ideas con la clase.

ochenta y tres 83

HERITAGE LANGUAGE LEARNERS

• Have students write a reply to Michelle's e-mail to Tess. The message should be upbeat and encouraging. "Tess" should first congratulate both Michelle and Daniel on their choice of beverage for the *feria*, and then offer some suggestions for finding more *mates* in order to complete their *desafío*. Her suggestions should be concrete; she should mention the name of the store or person who might have some, where it is, and how to initiate contact. Call on students to read their e-mails aloud.

CRITICAL THINKING

• Initiate a classroom discussion on what many believe is the unhealthful habit of consuming large quantities of sugary drinks. What other foods are often consumed in abusive amounts and pose a danger to one's health? After your discussion, have students work with a partner and come up with a poster and slogan to make the public aware of these dangers to their health. Take a class vote to select the most effective message and exhibit all students' work in the classroom.

Gramática – Los pronombres de objeto directo e indirecto

21. Before beginning this activity, have students scan the e-mail and point out clues that will help them to determine the correct object pronoun. For example: 1. *escribo (a ti)* → *te*; 2. *a Daniel y a mí* → *nos*. Then have students work with a partner to answer Michelle's e-mail.

 AUDIO SCRIPT
See page 69K.

 CULTURA

Inca Kola

Inca Kola was first marketed in 1935, and by the 1940s it was already a market leader in Peru. Other popular soft drinks in Latin America include the Mexican brand Jarritos— first marketed in 1950 and one of Mexico's largest soft drink companies. Jarritos is the best-selling Latin American soft drink in the United States. The island of Puerto Rico also boasts a homegrown soft drink, Coco Rico, made with coconut concentrate.

Answer Key

19. a. *I call her every day.*
b. *I added salt to the soup.*
En el primer caso, el pronombre funciona igual que en español. En el segundo caso no se usa el pronombre en inglés.

20. 2. Se lo pido a mi compañero.
3. Sí, cómpraselo.
4. Sí explícaselo.
5. Se los di a tu hermana.
6. Se las presté a mi primo.

21.
1. Te	4. lo	7. las	10. te
2. nos	5. le	8. los	11. la
3. lo	6. le	9. los	12. lo

22. Answers will vary.

Additional Resources

Fans Online activities
Practice Workbook

LECTURA: TEXTO DIALOGADO

Presentation

- In this section, students will read a dialogue, learn about the tradition of drinking *mate*, and research and discuss other traditions related to foods or drinks of the Spanish-speaking world or their own cultures. Students will also answer comprehension questions based on the reading.

Activities	Standards	Resources
Lectura: texto dialogado	1.1, 2.1, 2.2	
23.	1.1, 1.2, 2.1, 2.2	
24.	1.2, 2.1, 2.2	
25.	1.1, 1.2, 1.3, 2.1, 2.2, 4.2	

Teaching Suggestions

Warm-Up / Independent Starter

- Have students list three things they have learned so far about the tradition of drinking *mate*.

Preparation

- Call on students to share their Independent Starters. You may want to start a list on the board with their answers. Then focus students' attention on the second question of the *Antes de leer* section and have them use their Independent Starters and the list on the board to come up with words they already know related to the tradition of drinking *mate*. As a class, discuss the first and third questions of *Antes de leer*.

- Remind students that using context clues is one way to identify the correct meaning of unknown words in a text. Have students scan the text and list words or phrases they don't know. Next, have them use context clues to determine the meaning of each unknown word or phrase they listed. Call on volunteers to share their lists with the class and explain how they used context clues to determine the meaning. For example: *de buena educación* – the sentence says, *que la bombilla esté orientada hacia él.* The person who is preparing *mate* is doing something nice for the person drinking it, so it seems that *de buena educación* means "good manners."

Antes de leer: estrategias

1. Lee el título del texto. ¿Qué es un ritual?
2. Anota todas las palabras que ya conoces relacionadas con el mate.
3. Fíjate en la fotografía. ¿Qué muestra sobre el ritual del mate?

El ritual del mate

Grupo de amigos tomando mate.

DANIEL: Ahora que ya tenemos pensado los tipos de mate que vamos a preparar, tenemos que averiguar cómo se toma.

MICHELLE: Creo que es muy común que el mate se tome en grupo. Fabio, mi amigo argentino, dice que es una muestra de amistad y de bienvenida para las visitas.

DANIEL: ¿Y cómo se toma entonces? ¿Se le da un recipiente a cada uno?

MICHELLE: A veces sí, pero también se puede hacer una rueda de mate entre un grupo de gente que se reúne para charlar.

DANIEL: ¿Y todos beben del mismo mate?

MICHELLE: Sí. El cebador, que es la persona que lo prepara, se lo pasa a la persona que va a tomarlo. Creo que es de buena educación que la bombilla, que es la caña que se utiliza para sorber (*sip*) el mate, esté orientada hacia él.

DANIEL: ¿Y qué debe hacer después de beber?

MICHELLE: Pues debe devolvérselo al cebador para que vuelva a llenar el recipiente, o cebarlo, como ellos dicen, y se lo entregue al siguiente. Esto es una ronda de materos. ¡Ah! Y creo que está mal visto limpiar la bombilla cada vez que alguien toma.

DANIEL: Es todo un arte esto de matear.

MICHELLE: Ya lo creo. Y un detalle importante: no se le agradece al cebador cada mate. Cuando una persona dice «gracias» en el momento de devolver el mate, quiere decir que ya no quiere seguir tomando.

Differentiated Instruction

DEVELOPING LEARNERS

- To confirm students' comprehension of the dialogue, ask them to read several exchanges aloud and then restate the information in their own words. For example, the first two exchanges might be summarized as follows: *Daniel y Michelle ya saben qué tipos de mate van a preparar, pero deben averiguar cómo se toma el mate. Un amigo argentino de Michelle le explicó que tomar el mate es una muestra de amistad y de bienvenida.*

- You may want to pair these students with heritage speakers, who will verify their work.

EXPANDING LEARNERS

- Initiate a classroom discussion on students' interpretation of these sayings:
  - *Que la comida sea tu alimento y el alimento tu medicina (Hipócrates).*
  - *La perfecta hora de comer es, para el rico, cuando tiene ganas; y para el pobre, cuando tiene que comer (Luis Vélez de Guevara).*
  - *El rico come, el pobre se alimenta (Francisco de Quevedo).*
  - *Nunca es lo mismo una comida recalentada ni una amistad reconciliada (Anónimo).*

- Then, encourage students to write their own sayings.

LECTURA: TEXTO DIALOGADO

23 ¿Comprendes?

▶ **Responde** a estas preguntas.

1. ¿Con qué tipo de gente se suele compartir el mate?
2. ¿Hay un recipiente para cada persona?
3. ¿Cómo se debe colocar la bombilla al entregar el mate?
4. ¿Qué se hace después de haberlo tomado?
5. ¿Qué se debe decir cuando ya no quieres tomar más?

▶ **Resume** el ritual que se sigue para tomar mate.

Persona cebando el mate.

24 Palabras y expresiones

▶ **Busca** en el texto las palabras que se corresponden con estas definiciones.

1. Tomar el mate.
2. Añadir agua caliente al mate para prepararlo.
3. Persona que prepara el mate.
4. Utensilio que se utiliza para sorber el mate.
5. Recipiente en el que se prepara el mate.
6. Persona aficionada a tomar mate.

25 Con tus propias palabras

▶ **Habla** con tus compañeros(as). ¿Qué piensas que significa esta afirmación de Laura Esquivel, autora de la novela *Como agua para chocolate*? ¿Te parece que podría aplicarse al ritual del mate? ¿Por qué?

> «Uno es lo que come, con quien lo come y como lo come.»

▶ **Investiga** sobre otro ritual relacionado con comidas o bebidas de tu cultura o del mundo hispano. Haz una presentación para tus compañeros(as) explicándolo y comparándolo con el ritual del mate. Ten en cuenta estos aspectos:

– Qué comida o bebida se sirve.
– Cuándo se toma.
– Qué se necesita para prepararla.
– Quién la prepara.
– Quién la sirve.
– A quién se le prepara.
– Qué se considera de mala o de buena educación durante la ceremonia.

Familia comiendo el Roscón de Reyes (España).

ochenta y cinco 85

HERITAGE LANGUAGE LEARNERS

• Have students imagine that they and a good friend have been invited by some friends from Argentina to *una rueda de mate*. The problem is that their friend is a germaphobe and is not aware that the same *bombilla* will be shared by all. Ask students to work with a partner and come up with some creative, but polite, excuses for not drinking *mate* with the group. Then, have pairs present their excuses in a dialogue and ask the class to vote on the most original.

SPECIAL-NEEDS LEARNERS

• For students with difficulties staying focused while reading longer passages, copy the dialogue and cut it into shorter exchanges between the speakers. Then, have students work with a partner and read each exchange in order. Next, have students mix up the exchanges and put them back together in the correct sequence (they may tape them onto a sheet of paper). Finally, assign each student a role to interpret in the dialogue.

■ Read the dialogue aloud to students, modeling correct pronunciation and intonation. Then call on several pairs of students to alternate reading the dialogue aloud. Offer suggestions to improve their oral reading.

Activities

24. Once students have finished, ask them to use their answers and the pictures on these pages to explain the *mate*-drinking ritual. For example: *Primero, el cebador ceba el mate. Es decir, pone agua caliente…* Invite volunteer students to share their descriptions with the class.

25. Divide the class into small groups to work on this activity. Try to make the groups as heterogeneous as possible. You may want to make sure that each group is working on a different tradition or ritual so that the information is not duplicated. Encourage students to look for images and to organize their information and pictures in a visually appealing way to do a class presentation.

Answer Key

23. 1. Con amigos y visitas, ya que es una muestra de amistad y de bienvenida.
2. A veces sí, pero también pueden beber del mismo recipiente.
3. La bombilla debe estar orientada hacia la persona que va a tomar el mate.
4. Se devuelve al cebador para que lo vuelva a llenar y se lo entregue a la siguiente persona.
5. Se debe decir «gracias» en el momento de devolver el mate.
▶ Answers will vary.

24. 1. Sorber el mate. 4. La bombilla.
2. Cebar el mate. 5. Calabaza o mate.
3. El cebador. 6. Matero.

25. Answers will vary.
▶ Answers will vary.

Additional Resources

Fans Online activities

85

DESAFÍO 1

Comunicación

Presentation

- In this section, students will integrate the vocabulary and grammar skills from *Desafío 1* in order to talk about food and eating habits.

Activities	Standards	Resources
26.	1.2, 1.3	Audio
27.	1.1, 1.2, 1.3, 5.2	
28.	1.3	
29. Final del desafío	1.1, 1.2, 2.1, 2.2	
30.	1.1, 1.2, 2.1, 2.2	

Teaching Suggestions

Warm-Up / Independent Starter

- Write the following proverbs on the board:
  1. *Más vale ir bien comido que bien vestido.*
  2. *Desayunar como un rey, comer como un príncipe y cenar como un mendigo.*

  Ask students to use the vocabulary and grammar structures they learned in this *Desafío* to write a brief explanation for each of the two proverbs.

Preparation

- As a class, discuss students' answers to the Independent Starter. What do they think *bien comido* implies? Encourage students to think not only in terms of quantity of food, but of quality. Could eating one's fill of French fries be considered *bien comido*? For the second proverb, have students design a breakfast menu for a king, lunch for a prince, and dinner for a beggar. What health benefits might eating in this way provide?

Activities

26. Since students need to make up the mother's lines, encourage them to use some of those lines to describe Sofía. For instance, the mother might say, *Me parece que Sofía es muy egoísta y un poco maleducada.* In this way, students will recycle vocabulary from Unit 1. Then invite volunteer pairs to role-play their dialogues for the class.

Comunicación

26 **En el restaurante**

▶ **Escucha** una conversación en un restaurante y toma notas sobre lo que pasa.

▶ **Imagina** qué le contó Ana a su madre al día siguiente sobre la cena con Sofía y escribe el diálogo con tu compañero(a).

Modelo —*Mamá, se me olvidó reservar una mesa anoche.*
—*¿Y había mesas libres?*
—*Sí. Nos sentaron en una mesa perfecta, pero a Sofía no le gustó.*

27 **El ritual de la comida**

▶ **Lee** esta entrada de blog y decide si las oraciones que siguen son ciertas o falsas. Después, corrige las falsas.

> **Recupera tu comida y transforma tu día**
>
> Me ha llamado la atención una iniciativa que acaba de poner en marcha una organización norteamericana llamada *The Energy Project*. Se llama *Recupera tu comida y transforma tu día*. Según datos de esta organización, el 60 % de los 1.200 profesionales encuestados respondieron que comen en menos de 20 minutos, y un 20 % en menos de 10. Una cuarta parte reconoció que no abandona su mesa de trabajo durante el almuerzo y que come frente al ordenador.
>
>
>
> Este grupo acaba de lanzar una iniciativa que consiste en organizar cada miércoles una comida colectiva nacional en parques de todo el país. Esto nos puede parecer algo ridículo, pero somos cada vez más los que comemos delante del ordenador. A veces estamos tan obsesionados con el trabajo que ponemos en riesgo nuestra salud física y mental. Tal vez no sea mala idea prestar más atención al ritual de la comida.
>
> Fuente: http://www.vidasencilla.es (texto adaptado)

1. Según la encuesta, la mayoría de los profesionales comen en menos de diez minutos.
2. Se dice que el 25 % de los profesionales siguen trabajando mientras comen.
3. La organización ha propuesto hacer una reunión semanal para restablecer el ritual de la comida.

▶ **Habla** con tus compañeros(as) sobre el problema presentado en el blog y propongan soluciones.

Differentiated Instruction

DEVELOPING LEARNERS

- Tell students that recognizing cognates makes it easier to comprehend new words and strengthens the student's vocabulary in his or her native language. Ask students to look for cognates in the blog and list them. Next to each one, have them write the English-language equivalent. See how many they can find. You might start students off with the following: *recupera* (recuperate); *transforma* (transform); *atención* (attention); *iniciativa* (initiative). Encourage students to write these words and other cognates they find in the articles in their notebooks.

EXPANDING LEARNERS

- According to The Energy Project, having lunch in front of the computer poses a certain risk to one's health. Ask students to think of other bad habits people often have about eating and ask them to write a list of *consejos para no poner en riesgo la salud a la hora de comer*. Ask them to use the pronoun *se* when describing these bad habits (e.g., *No se debe comer y manejar al mismo tiempo*). Call on students to read their lists aloud.

28 Una receta especial

▶ **Escribe** las características de tu plato preferido. Explica cómo se prepara, qué ingredientes y utensilios se necesitan para prepararlo, cuándo se come, etc.

▶ **Presenta** tu receta a tus compañeros(as). Después, decide los tres platos que más te gustaría probar y explica por qué.

Final del desafío

FABIO: Ya veo que consiguieron las calabazas secas y limpias, chicos. Excelente.

MICHELLE: ¿Ya podemos preparar el mate? Tenemos todos los ingredientes: el azúcar, los limones y las naranjas, la leche, el hielo...

FABIO: No seas impaciente, Michelle. Como las calabazas son nuevas, tenemos que curarlas.

MICHELLE: ¿Curarlas? No sabía que esto fuera tan complicado. ¿Cómo se hace?

FABIO: Es muy fácil. Se llenan los recipientes con yerba mate, se echa agua caliente y se deja reposar. Al día siguiente se tira la yerba y el agua, se limpian bien los mates para quitar los restos y se repite el mismo proceso.

DANIEL: ¿Nos dará tiempo? Recuerda que la feria es dentro de unos días.

FABIO: Claro, yo los ayudaré. Vamos a empezar.

29 Una solución muy creativa

▶ **Responde** a estas preguntas.

1. ¿Qué problema tenían Daniel y Michelle al principio del desafío? ¿Qué idea tuvieron para resolver el problema?

2. ¿A qué los va a ayudar Fabio?

30 Expertos materos

▶ **Habla** con tu compañero(a). Escriban los ingredientes que Daniel y Michelle van a añadir al mate para preparar distintas variedades. ¿Cuál les gustaría probar?

▶ **Habla** con tus compañeros(as). ¿Qué creen que significa la expresión argentina «Con bombilla hacia atrás, para que no volvás»?

ochenta y siete 87

Comunicación (Teacher notes)

27. Before reading the blog, ask students to read the title of the selection and the first two statements of the comprehension activity. Have a brief discussion with students about these two statements. If some students think the statements are false, have them make a guess. Then, once students have read the passage and answered the questions, revisit their predictions. Did they guess correctly?

28. For the second part of this activity, have students work in small groups and select one dish for the group. Then have each group present their chosen dish to the class. Hold a class vote to select three dishes students would like to try. Encourage students to prepare these dishes at home.

 AUDIO SCRIPT
See page 69K.

Answer Key

26. Answers will vary.

27. 1. F. El 20% come en menos de diez minutos.
2. C.
3. F. Ha propuesto organizar cada miércoles una comida colectiva en parques de todo el país.
▶ Answers will vary.

28. Answers will vary.
▶ Answers will vary.

29. 1. No encontraban mates (recipientes) para la cata en las tiendas a las que fueron. Consiguieron unas calabazas secas y limpias.
2. Los va a ayudar a curar las calabazas.

30. Answers will vary.
▶ Answers will vary.

Additional Resources

Fans Online activities
Practice Workbook

HERITAGE LANGUAGE LEARNERS

• Ask students to take a survey among their friends or family to explore their lunchtime habits. Have them ask the following questions: *¿Dónde sueles comer? (Sentado/a a la mesa; Delante del televisor; En un restaurante; En el auto; Delante de la computadora; Otro; No almuerzo) ¿Con quién sueles comer? (Solo/a; En familia; Con amigos/as) ¿Cuánto tiempo tardas en comer? (Una hora o más; Entre 30 y 59 minutos; Menos de 30 minutos; Menos de 20 minutos)* Ask students to share their findings with the class.

TOTAL PHYSICAL RESPONSE (TPR)

• Write a direct object pronoun on each of several index cards and do the same for the indirect object pronouns. Distribute the cards to students and explain that they are going to play a game of *Pronombres*. Have other students prepare sentences such as *Le doy el libro a Luis,* read them aloud, and explain that the players must reword the sentences using both the direct and indirect object pronouns they may be holding. For this particular example, students who have the cards with *se* and *lo* will stand and read the correct answer: *Se lo doy.*

Unit 2
DESAFÍO 2

Hablar de la salud

Presentation

- In *Desafío 2*, Eva and Ethan have to invite a well-known Hispanic scientist to give a talk at their school. Students will preview vocabulary to talk about health and medicine.

Activities	Standards	Resources
Texto	1.2, 2.2	
31.	1.2, 1.3	
32.	1.1, 1.2, 2.2	
33.	1.2, 1.3, 2.2	Audio
34. Conexiones	1.1, 1.2, 2.2, 3.1, 3.2	

Teaching Suggestions

Warm-Up / Independent Starter

- Ask students to think of three important scientists and their research or discoveries.

Preparation

- Call on students to talk about one of the scientists from their Independent Starters. Discuss, as a class, the importance of these scientists' contributions. Then have students read the title and ask them why having a good heart might be an important trait for a scientist.

Texto: Un científico con corazón

- Read the introduction aloud. Then, in a class discussion, decide on the criteria for selecting a scientist to give a talk at their school (e.g., *su descubrimiento tiene que haber contribuido a salvar vidas, debe servir de ejemplo a los jóvenes*).
- Call on different volunteers to read the dialogue aloud. What criteria did Eva and Ethan use for selecting Manuel Patarroyo for their school talk?

Activities

31. To extend this activity, ask students to come up with a definition for each word. Then, invite volunteers to share their definitions.

33. Have students write a brief paragraph describing Dr. Patarroyo's work. Then have them add a statement indicating the importance of this scientist's work.

88

Un científico con corazón

La escuela de Ethan y Eva está organizando un ciclo de charlas con personajes hispanos relevantes. Ellos tienen que invitar a un científico hispano, pero ¿a quién elegirán?

EVA: ¿Por dónde empezamos a buscar un científico hispano? Yo no conozco a ninguno.

ETHAN: Mi dermatóloga es de Nicaragua... Podemos invitarla a ella.

EVA: Tu dermatóloga no es famosa, Ethan. Tenemos que encontrar a alguien que haya hecho descubrimientos importantes. Por ejemplo, una persona que haya investigado sobre una enfermedad grave, como el cáncer.

ETHAN: O alguien que haya desarrollado una vacuna. Mira, aquí dice que la primera vacuna contra la malaria la desarrolló un investigador colombiano.

EVA: Ah, pues ese es un gran descubrimiento. La malaria es una enfermedad muy grave. Hay millones de enfermos cada año. ¿Y quién es ese investigador?

ETHAN: Manuel Patarroyo. Es de un pequeño pueblo de Colombia, pero estudió Medicina aquí, en los Estados Unidos. Y mira qué interesante: decidió donar la patente de la vacuna a la Organización Mundial de la Salud en lugar de vendérsela a una compañía farmacéutica.

EVA: Vaya, eso sí es un científico con corazón... Bueno, pues invitemos a Manuel Patarroyo a dar una charla. ¿Crees que aceptará?

Manuel Elkin Patarroyo.

31 **Detective de palabras**

▶ **Completa** estas oraciones.

1. Ethan y Eva tienen que invitar a un _____ hispano.
2. La _____ de Ethan es de Nicaragua.
3. Eva propone buscar a alguien que haya investigado sobre una enfermedad como el _____.
4. Ethan sugiere que inviten a un científico que haya desarrollado una _____.
5. Un _____ colombiano desarrolló la vacuna contra la malaria.
6. La malaria es una enfermedad muy _____.

88 ochenta y ocho

Differentiated Instruction

DEVELOPING LEARNERS

- Ask students to correct the following false statements:
  1. *Eva conoce a muchos científicos. (No conoce a ninguno.)*
  2. *El dermatólogo de Ethan es de Nicaragua. (la dermatóloga)*
  3. *Un oncólogo desarrolló la primera vacuna contra la malaria. (un investigador)*
  4. *Hay pocos enfermos de malaria hoy en día. (Hay millones de enfermos.)*
  5. *Patarroyo donó la patente de la vacuna a la Universidad de Yale. (a la Organización Mundial de la Salud)*

EXPANDING LEARNERS

- Allow students to read the dialogue a second time, and then ask them to write a summary of it as a third-person narrative. Remind students to include a description of the setting and a brief introduction as to why Eva and Ethan are having this conversation about Hispanic scientists. Allow students to decide if they want to place the action in the present or past tense. Call on volunteers to read their summaries aloud.

32 **¿Comprendes?**

▶ **Responde** a estas preguntas.

1. ¿Qué actividad organiza la escuela de Ethan y Eva?
2. ¿Por qué no quiere Eva invitar a la dermatóloga de Ethan?
3. ¿Qué sugiere Ethan?
4. ¿Qué desarrolló Manuel Patarroyo?
5. ¿Qué enfermedades se mencionan en el diálogo?
6. ¿Por qué dice Eva que Patarroyo es «un científico con corazón»?

33 **El trabajo de Patarroyo**

▶ **Escucha** la conversación entre Ethan y su profesor, y decide si estas oraciones son ciertas o falsas. Después, corrige las oraciones falsas.

1. El profesor piensa que invitar a Manuel Patarroyo es una buena idea.
2. Patarroyo ha investigado sobre las enfermedades que afectan a los países más industrializados.
3. El equipo de Patarroyo dedicó unos 10 años a desarrollar la vacuna de la malaria.
4. La vacuna de la malaria es controversial porque no es efectiva en todos los casos.
5. La malaria es una enfermedad que afecta a pocas personas.
6. El profesor va a invitar personalmente a Manuel Patarroyo al ciclo de charlas.

 CONEXIONES: CIENCIAS

Manuel Patarroyo

Manuel Elkin Patarroyo nació en 1946 en un pequeño pueblo de Colombia. Estudió en Bogotá y en la Universidad de Yale (Estados Unidos). Su interés por la investigación biomédica lo llevó a crear un laboratorio que después se convirtió en la Fundación Instituto de Inmunología de Colombia, que dirige actualmente. Él y su equipo han centrado su trabajo en las vacunas contra enfermedades como la malaria, pero investigan también en otras áreas, como el diagnóstico del cáncer de útero.
Patarroyo es Doctor Honoris Causa por varias universidades y ha recibido numerosos premios y reconocimientos en todo el mundo.

34 **Investiga.** Visita la página web de la Fundación Instituto de Inmunología de Colombia (www.fidic.org) y busca más información sobre sus actividades.

HERITAGE LANGUAGE LEARNERS

• Ask students to work with a partner and research diseases transmitted by insects, including information on the vector (carrier), causative organism, host, symptoms, regions affected, treatment, and prevention. Suggest that students make a chart. An example follows for malaria: *Enfermedad: malaria (paludismo); Vector/Portador: mosquito; Organismo causativo: parásitos del género* Plasmodium; *Huésped: ser humano; Zonas: (sub)trópico; Síntomas: dolor de cabeza, fiebre; Tratamiento: prevención y medicamentos contra la malaria; Prevención: evitar picaduras de mosquitos.*

COOPERATIVE LEARNING

• Have students work in small groups and research the impact that malaria and yellow fever had on the workers who were building the Panama Canal. Ask them to document the number of workers affected, the early treatments of these diseases and their side effects (e.g., quinine was usually given to those affected, but large doses resulted in deafness). Ask students to include early preventive measures and the pioneers who tried to eradicate these diseases. Have students make a presentation to the class and encourage them to accompany their reports with visuals.

DESAFÍO 2

Hablar de la salud

 AUDIO SCRIPT
See page 69K.

 CONEXIONES: CIENCIAS

Manuel Patarroyo

When Manuel Patarroyo was nine years old, his parents gave him a book entitled *Luis Pasteur: descubridor de vacunas, benefactor de la humanidad*. This book inspired the young Patarroyo to work on the development of vaccines. Dr. Patarroyo's malaria vaccine has an overall effectiveness rate in South America of about 30%. He is currently working on a new formulation that is scheduled to go on trial in 2014.

Answer Key

31. 1. científico   4. vacuna
2. dermatóloga   5. investigador
3. cáncer   6. grave

32. 1. Un ciclo de charlas con hispanos relevantes.
2. Porque no es famosa.
3. Sugiere invitar a alguien que haya desarrollado una vacuna.
4. La primera vacuna contra la malaria.
5. El cáncer y la malaria.
6. Porque donó la patente de la vacuna a la OMS.

33. 1. C.
2. F. Que afectan a los países con menos recursos.
3. F. Dedicó más de 30 años.
4. C.
5. F. Afecta a unos 200 millones.
6. F. Eva y Ethan van a invitarlo.

34. Answers will vary.

Additional Resources

Fans Online activities

Unit 2

DESAFÍO 2

Vocabulario – La sala de urgencias

Presentation

- In this section, students will learn vocabulary related to health and medicine.

Activities	Standards	Resources
Vocabulario	1.2	
35.	1.2, 3.1	
36.	1.2, 1.3	Audio
37.	1.1, 1.3, 5.1, 5.2	
38. Comparaciones	1.1, 1.2, 2.1, 2.2, 4.2	

Teaching Suggestions

Warm-Up / Independent Starter

- Provide students with the following list of symptoms and have them come up with a medical diagnoses:
  - tos y escalofríos
  - brazo hinchado
  - dolor de garganta
  - dolor de estómago

Preparation

- Call on several volunteers to share their Independent Starters. Does the rest of the class agree with their diagnoses? Encourage students to come up with other symptoms associated with each of the illnesses mentioned. For example: gripe → tos y escalofríos, fiebre, estornudar.

- Call on five students to read aloud the speech bubbles for the three situations presented on page 90. Then, discuss with students the symptoms and possible health problems of the people featured in the vocabulary presentation. Invite students to speculate on the severity of each case and the treatment the doctor might prescribe.

- Have students work with a partner to classify the vocabulary, including Más vocabulario, as follows:

Verbo	Nombre	Adjetivo
tomar	infarto	grave

Then ask partners to come up with sentences using the vocabulary they have just classified. Invite students to share their sentences with the class.

90

Vocabulario

La sala de urgencias

Creo que mi esposa está sufriendo un infarto. Siente molestias en el pecho y en el brazo.

Le voy a tomar la presión arterial mientras viene la cardióloga.

Mi hija se cortó con un cuchillo. El corte sangraba mucho y, al verlo, me mareé y perdí el conocimiento. Creo que me hice un esguince en el tobillo.

¿Es grave, doctora? ¿Me van a ingresar en el hospital?

No, tranquilo, pero es una enfermedad contagiosa. ¿Sabe si sus familiares se pusieron la vacuna de pequeños?

Más vocabulario

Enfermedades y síntomas

el asma	asthma
las náuseas	nausea
la quemadura	burn
tener el colesterol alto	to have high cholesterol
vomitar	to throw up

Especialistas

el/la dermatólogo(a)	dermatologist
el/la oncólogo(a)	oncologist

¡Atención!

asistir (a)	to attend (to)
ayudar	to assist

35 ¿Qué es?

▶ Une las dos columnas.

Ⓐ
1. Desarrollo anormal e incontrolado de ciertas células.
2. Concentración excesiva de azúcar en la sangre.
3. Excesiva acumulación de grasa en el sistema circulatorio.
4. Obstrucción de las arterias.
5. Dificultad al respirar y tos.

Ⓑ
a. diabetes
b. colesterol alto
c. cáncer
d. asma
e. infarto

90 noventa

Differentiated Instruction

DEVELOPING LEARNERS

- Ask students to match the words.

  1. cardiólogo (e)   a. ataque al corazón
  2. dermatólogo (c)   b. herida producida por el fuego
  3. náuseas (d)   c. especialista de la piel
  4. oncólogo (f)   d. asco
  5. quemadura (b)   e. especialista del corazón
  6. infarto (a)   f. especialista en cáncer

EXPANDING LEARNERS

- Ask students to work with a partner and prepare two or three short dialogues that could take place en la sala de urgencias. Ask pairs to incorporate as many of the new words as they can, but also encourage them to use known vocabulary from previous units and levels and to look up some other conditions or situations they might find in an emergency room. Give pairs time to practice and then ask them to present their new dialogues to the class.

36 En la consulta

▶ **Escucha** la conversación y completa estas oraciones.

1. El paciente tiene _____ y está muy mareado.
2. El paciente no ha perdido el _____.
3. El doctor le toma el pulso y la _____ arterial.
4. El paciente pregunta si tiene alguna enfermedad _____.
5. El doctor le dice que tiene _____.
6. El doctor le aconseja que se ponga la _____ contra la gripe cada año.

37 Mi experiencia personal

▶ **Habla** con tu compañero(a) sobre alguna experiencia personal relacionada con una de las dolencias del cuadro. Incluye esta información:

un corte
un esguince
una quemadura

1. ¿Cómo ocurrió?
2. ¿Cómo te sentías?
3. ¿Cómo reaccionaron tus padres o tus amigos?
4. ¿Fuiste al médico o al hospital? ¿Por qué?
5. ¿Qué hiciste para curarte?
6. ¿Cuánto tiempo tardaste en recuperarte?

▶ **Escribe** un párrafo contando la historia de tu compañero(a). Al final, incluye algunas recomendaciones para evitar ese tipo de dolencia en el futuro.

COMPARACIONES

Los horarios de las farmacias

Como sucede en otros establecimientos comerciales, los horarios de las farmacias en los países hispanos son cada vez más amplios y no es raro encontrar algunas que abren las 24 horas del día. No obstante, desde hace tiempo es obligatorio que las farmacias se turnen para ofrecer un servicio de urgencias durante las noches y los días feriados. Es lo que se conoce como *farmacias de guardia* o *farmacias de turno*.

Aparte de medicamentos, en la mayoría de las farmacias se venden otros productos relacionados con la salud y la cosmética, como cremas, colonias, pañales (*diapers*) o curitas (*adhesive bandages*), que suelen estar al alcance del público.

38 **Compara.** ¿Qué diferencias y semejanzas encuentras entre las farmacias en los Estados Unidos y en el mundo hispano?

HERITAGE LANGUAGE LEARNERS

• Encourage heritage speakers to describe a typical *farmacia* in their family's country of origin. Ask them to share photos of the pharmacy or its website. Students should be prepared to discuss the hours, kinds of products sold (in addition to medicine), and the special role the pharmacists play in dispensing medicine and advice on health. Should students have a family member who has worked in a pharmacy in the heritage country, invite that person to talk about the schedules and products of *la farmacia*, as well as the pharmacist's role.

MULTIPLE INTELLIGENCES:
Visual-Spatial Intelligence

• Ask students to imagine that they are the owners of a pharmacy in a Spanish-speaking country. In addition to the standard medicine and products that all pharmacies sell, their *farmacia* will offer customers some items that promise miraculous results. Ask students to create a webpage, print ad, or flyer for their pharmacy. Encourage students' creativity in describing the cures or promised results these products offer and suggest that they do some research to see what natural products are often offered in the country selected.

Activities

35. To extend this activity, ask students to provide a short definition for the following words: *náusea, quemadura, presión arterial, esguince, corte, vacuna.*

37. Have student pairs work together on a script to role-play their anecdotes. Allow for rehearsal time, and then invite volunteer pairs to act out their dialogues.

AUDIO SCRIPT
See page 69L.

COMPARACIONES

Los horarios de las farmacias

In Spain, pharmacies are owed and managed by independent pharmacists. However, in most of Latin America, chain stores are now common. These pharmacies follow the American business format; that is, they offer a wide range of products and many are open 24 hours a day. FASA—with more than 1,200 stores in Chile, Mexico, and Peru—operates the largest chain of pharmacies in Latin America. It was founded in Chile in 1968, but in 2010 was bought by a Mexican corporation for U.S. $637 million.

Answer Key

35. 1. c   2. a   3. b   4. e   5. d
36. 1. náuseas   3. presión   5. gripe
       2. conocimiento   4. grave   6. vacuna
37. Answers will vary.
   ▶ Answers will vary.
38. Answers will vary.

Additional Resources

Fans Online activities
Practice Workbook

DESAFÍO 2

Gramática – Los verbos con preposición

Presentation

- In this section, students will learn and practice verbs that require the use of a preposition as well as verbs that do not take a preposition.

Activities	Standards	Resources
Gramática	1.2, 3.1	
39.	1.2, 3.1	
40.	1.2, 1.3, 3.1	
41.	1.3, 3.1	

Teaching Suggestions

Warm-Up / Independent Starter

- Have students complete the following sentences with the appropriate preposition:
  1. *La enfermera va … tomarle la presión. (a)*
  2. *El virus se convirtió … una epidemia. (en)*
  3. *No estamos de acuerdo … ustedes. (con)*
  4. *Ya terminé … hacer la tarea. (de)*

Preparation

- Ask students to share their Independent Starters with the class. Then have them explain how they knew which preposition was required in each case. Elicit that these verb-preposition combinations have to be memorized.

- Have students read the grammar presentation silently. Reassure them that mastering prepositional verbs (i.e., verbs that require the use of a preposition) takes time. Explain that this grammar presentation focuses on cases where there is a mismatch between English and Spanish.

Activities

39. To extend this activity, ask students to write sentences showing how the use of different prepositions indicates the direction of the movement. For example: *Vamos de aquí para allá. Voy a la tienda.* You may want to provide additional verbs, such as *salir, entrar, subir, bajar,* and *venir.* Then, discuss some of the students' examples and compare the verb-preposition combinations for these verbs in Spanish and in English.

Gramática

Los verbos con preposición

- Muchos verbos necesitan un complemento que va introducido por una preposición. A veces, esta preposición es la misma en español y en inglés, pero a veces es diferente.

Me **niego a** irme.	Ella se **quejó del** hospital.
I **refuse to** leave.	She **complained about** the hospital.

- Estos son algunos verbos que llevan una preposición específica:

VERBOS CON LA PREPOSICIÓN A

acostumbrarse a (to get used to)	No me **acostumbro a** levantarme temprano.
asistir a (to attend)	Los empleados **asistieron a** la reunión.
atreverse a (to dare)	Lola se **atrevió a** probar la salsa picante.
ayudar a (to help)	Este jarabe **ayuda a** calmar la tos.
renunciar a (to give up)	**Renunciaré a** los dulces para adelgazar.

VERBOS CON LA PREPOSICIÓN CON

amenazar con (to threaten to)	La actriz **amenaza con** dejar la serie.
casarse con (to marry)	María se **casó con** su novio de toda la vida.
contar con (to count on)	Puedes **contar con** mi ayuda.
enojarse con (to get mad at)	Javier se **enojó con** su mejor amigo.
soñar con (to dream of)	Raúl **sueña con** ser un psiquiatra famoso.

VERBOS CON LA PREPOSICIÓN DE

acordarse de (to remember)	No me **acordé de** la cita médica.
alegrarse de (to be pleased to)	Me **alegro de** conocerte.
darse cuenta de (to realize)	Elsa se **dio cuenta de** su error.
depender de (to depend on)	El precio **depende de** la calidad.
despedirse de (to say good-bye to)	Se **despidió de** su familia y se fue.

VERBOS CON LA PREPOSICIÓN EN

confiar en (to trust)	**Confiamos en** nuestros amigos y familiares.
consistir en (to consist of)	Tu tarea **consiste en** ordenar tu cuarto.
fijarse en (to notice)	Siento llegar tarde; no me **fijé en** la hora.
insistir en (to insist on)	Kim **insiste en** comprar un auto deportivo.
pensar en (to think about)	Roberto se pasa el día **pensando en** su novia.

- Algunos verbos se construyen sin preposición cuando llevan complemento de cosa:

CONSTRUCCIONES SIN PREPOSICIÓN

agradecer (to be grateful for)	**Agradezco** la atención médica que recibí.	esperar (to wait for)	Los viajeros **esperan** el tren, pero no llega.
buscar (to look for)	Estoy **buscando** las llaves.	mirar (to look at)	Los niños **miran** las ilustraciones del libro.
escuchar (to listen to)	Siempre **escuchas** la misma música.	pedir (to ask for)	Después de comer, **pedimos** la cuenta.

39 **Piensa.** ¿Qué preposiciones se pueden emplear con el verbo *ir*? ¿Y con el verbo *to go*? ¿Qué indican esas preposiciones?

Differentiated Instruction

DEVELOPING LEARNERS

- Ask students to supply the preposition where needed.
  1. *Todo depende … ti. (de)*
  2. *Ayer no asistimos … clase. (a)*
  3. *Se alegró … verte. (de)*
  4. *¿Pediste … la cuenta ya? (X)*
  5. *Contamos … tu ayuda. (con)*
  6. *¿Te atreves … pedírselo? (a)*
  7. *Sueño … estudiar en Madrid. (con)*
  8. *¿… qué consiste la tarea? (En)*
  9. *Confío … ti completamente. (en)*

EXPANDING LEARNERS

- Ask students to translate the following sentences:
  1. She realized her error. *(Se dio cuenta de su error.)*
  2. Don't get angry at Juan. *(No te enojes con Juan.)*
  3. I'm grateful for your help. *(Agradezco tu ayuda.)*
  4. What does the price depend on? *(¿De qué depende el precio?)*
  5. I never got used to living there. *(Nunca me acostumbré a vivir allí.)*
  6. Did you notice her? *(¿Te fijaste en ella?)*

40 **La boda de mi primo**

▶ **Completa** el blog de Martín. Pon los verbos en la forma correcta del pasado o del presente, y añade la preposición cuando sea necesario.

atreverse	asistir	darse cuenta	casarse
pensar	depender	soñar	pedir

¡La boda del año!

PUBLICADO POR MARTÍN, 17 DE NOVIEMBRE

El sábado pasado, mi familia y yo ___1___ la boda de mi primo Diego. A las doce de la mañana él ___2___ su novia Teresa. Fue una boda espectacular. Diego y Teresa se conocieron cuando él tenía solo 18 años. Al principio, él no ___3___ hablar con ella, pero por fin se decidió y le ___4___ una cita. Diego dice que enseguida ___5___ que ella era la chica perfecta, así que se casaron solo dos años después.

Yo todavía no ___6___ el matrimonio, soy demasiado joven. ___7___ graduarme de la universidad a los 23 años y conseguir un buen trabajo antes de casarme. Aunque a lo mejor eso ___8___ mi futura novia, ja, ja.

COMENTARIOS (0)   ENVIAR UN COMENTARIO

▶ **Lee** de nuevo el blog y responde a las preguntas.

1. ¿A qué evento asistió Martín el sábado?

2. ¿Por qué se casaron tan jóvenes Diego y Teresa?

3. ¿Por qué Martín no piensa aún en el matrimonio?

4. ¿Con qué sueña Martín?

41 **¿Qué ocurre?**

▶ **Escribe** oraciones para explicar cada imagen. Utiliza los verbos de la ficha de Gramática.

noventa y tres 93

41. To expand this activity, have students work with a partner to choose one of the images and come up with a story. Encourage them to use as many of the verbs from page 92 as possible. Tell students not to write an ending for their stories. For example: *La madre amenazó a su hija con no dejarla ir a la fiesta. Estaba muy enojada con ella porque se había dado cuenta de que…* Have pairs exchange their stories with another pair, who will come up with an ending for the story.

Answer Key

39. Algunas preposiciones que se pueden usar con el verbo *ir* son: a, de, desde, hacia, para. En el caso del verbo *to go*, se podría usar *to, toward, from*. Estas preposiciones indican la dirección del movimiento.

40. 1. asistimos a   5. se dio cuenta de
2. se casó con   6. he pensado / pienso en
3. se atrevía a   7. Sueño con
4. pidió   8. dependerá de

▶ 1. Asistió a la boda de su primo Diego.
2. Porque Diego se dio cuenta de que ella era la chica perfecta.
3. Porque es demasiado joven.
4. Sueña con graduarse de la universidad a los 23 años y conseguir un buen trabajo.

41. Answers will vary. Sample answers:
1. Ellos se alegran de la victoria de su equipo.
2. Ellos esperan el autobús.
3. Se despide de su madre.
4. La madre amenaza a su hija con no dejarla ir a la fiesta.
5. Busca algo.
6. Ayuda a una anciana.

Additional Resources

Fans Online activities
Practice Workbook

HERITAGE LANGUAGE LEARNERS

• To expand their vocabulary, ask students to explain the difference between the following pairs of verbs: *casar / casarse con; contar / contar con; deber / deber de; despedir / despedirse de; entrar / entrar a (en); pensar en / pensar de; salir con / salir de.* Then have students write a sentence for each pair to confirm their understanding of both verbs. Invite students to read some of their sentences aloud.

TOTAL PHYSICAL RESPONSE (TPR)

• Divide the class into teams named for the prepositions *a, con, de,* and *en.* Also designate one team to be *sin preposición.* Explain to students that you are going to read a series of sentences leaving out the prepositions that follow some of the verbs (you might assign this task to several students who will not be playing). On hearing the sentence, students will stand if the missing preposition, or no preposition, corresponds to their team. Award one point for each correct answer.

93

DESAFÍO 2

Gramática – Los artículos

Presentation

- In this section, students will review and expand their knowledge of the usage of articles in Spanish.

Activities	Standards	Resources
Gramática	1.2, 3.1	
42.	1.2, 3.1	
43.	1.2, 3.1	
44.	1.1, 1.2, 1.3, 3.1	Audio
45.	1.3, 2.2	
46. Conexiones	1.1, 1.2, 2.1, 3.1	

Teaching Suggestions

Warm-Up / Independent Starter

- Have students write a sentence for each of the following phrases:
  - *el coche azul / un coche azul*
  - *la cardióloga / cardióloga / una cardióloga*

Preparation

- Ask students to read the grammar presentation silently. Then give them a few moments to review their sentences from the Independent Starter. Ask for volunteers to write their sentences on the board. Use the sentences to provide a battery of examples. For further practice, have students write sentences with these phrases: 1. *dolor de cabeza / un dolor de cabeza*; 2. *el pan / pan / un pan*. Possible answers: 1. *Tengo dolor de cabeza. Tengo un dolor de cabeza muy fuerte.* 2. *Me gusta el pan. No tengo pan en casa. Compré un pan para hacerme un bocadillo.*

Activities

44. To expand this activity, have students analyze the use of each article in their summaries. For example: *le dolía el estómago y la cabeza → partes del cuerpo; se tomó una pastilla → objeto que no había sido nombrado antes.*

45. Once students have finished, ask them to exchange letters with a partner and then compose a letter using the best parts of each one of their letters. Ask pairs to share their letters with the class and hold a class vote to select the most convincing letter—one that Dr. Patarroyo can't say no to.

Gramática

Los artículos

- Los **artículos indefinidos** (un, una, unos, unas) se usan delante de seres, objetos o entidades que no son conocidos, no están determinados o no han sido nombrados antes: un niño, una ciudad… En cambio, los **artículos definidos** (el, la, los, las) se usan delante de seres, objetos o entidades que son únicos (el sol, la luna), que están determinados (la ciudad de San Diego), que son conocidos o que han sido nombrados antes. Por tanto, el artículo indefinido sirve para presentar el nombre; una vez presentado, se utiliza el artículo definido.

  Ayer fui a comprar una falda. Las faldas que me probé me quedaban muy bien.

- A diferencia del inglés, en español se usa artículo en estos casos:

USO DEL ARTÍCULO EN ESPAÑOL

INGLÉS (SIN ARTÍCULO)	ESPAÑOL (CON ARTÍCULO)
Con los nombres abstractos y los nombres usados en un sentido general.	• El amor es el sentimiento más fuerte. • Me gusta el queso, pero no los huevos.
Con las partes del cuerpo y las prendas de vestir.	• Lleva un suéter en la mano.
Con los títulos, salvo don y doña.	• El doctor García es un médico muy conocido.
Con los días, las horas y las fechas.	• Los viernes salgo del trabajo a las 4:00 p. m. Pero Hoy es lunes, 12 de octubre.
Con los nombres de las calles, los parques, etc.	• Vivo en la calle Mayor, frente al parque Sol.
Con los porcentajes y los números.	• El 80 por ciento aprobó el examen. • Abre la página 80 del libro, en el capítulo 2.

Ausencia del artículo

- En español es frecuente utilizar el nombre sin artículo para referirnos a seres o a objetos no específicos y el nombre con artículo para referirnos a seres o a objetos específicos:

  Compra helado (helado en general, sin especificar tipo o cantidad).
  Compra un helado (un helado cualquiera).
  Compra el helado (un helado concreto y conocido).

- El uso sin artículo es frecuente con verbos como comprar, necesitar, querer, dar, traer, hacer, etc., para hablar de nombres no contables en singular (quiero sopa) o de nombres contables en plural (necesito camisas).

- Tampoco se utiliza el artículo en estos casos:
  - Con el verbo ser, para hablar de oficios, cargos y ocupaciones: es médico; es directora. Pero si el nombre lleva un adjetivo calificativo o un complemento, usamos el artículo: es un médico famoso; es la directora de la escuela.
  - Con verbos como tener, llevar o ponerse, para referirnos al atuendo (lleva falda) o a propiedades típicas de un objeto (esa casa tiene ascensor).

 42 **Piensa.** Explica por qué se usa o no artículo en Carla es profesora, Carla es una profesora excelente y Carla es la profesora de mi hermano.

Differentiated Instruction

DEVELOPING LEARNERS

- Ask students to complete the following sentences with the correct article, if needed:
  1. *Hoy llevo … corbata. (X)*
  2. *Voy a comprar … verduras para hacer … sopa. (X; una/la)*
  3. *Jorge se hizo … esguince en … muñeca. (un; la)*
  4. *… diabetes no es … enfermedad contagiosa. (La; una)*
  5. *Ana es … profesora de francés; también es … buena traductora. (X; una)*
  6. *Vivimos en … tercer piso, al lado de … Gómez. (el; los)*

EXPANDING LEARNERS

- Ask students to imagine that they are Dr. Manuel Patarroyo. Have them work with a partner and exchange the e-mails they composed for activity 45. Then, ask them to write a response, accepting Ethan's invitation and asking for more details as to the character and scope of the conference. If time permits, you may wish to have partners answer Dr. Patarroyo's queries.

43 Recomendaciones del médico

▶ **Completa** cada oración con el artículo apropiado cuando sea necesario.

1. Si usted tiene diabetes, es necesario seguir ___1___ dieta con poco azúcar.
2. Cuando ___2___ niños no se sienten bien, no deben comer ___3___ dulces.
3. ___4___ señora García es ___5___ enfermera. Ella va a examinarle ___6___ garganta.

44 Eva está enferma

▶ **Escucha** la conversación entre Ethan y Eva, y toma notas. Después, escribe un resumen. Usa los artículos definidos e indefinidos necesarios.

Modelo *Ethan llamó a Eva porque ella no había ido a la escuela. Eva le contó que le dolía el estómago y...*

▶ **Habla** con tu compañero(a). ¿Has tenido una experiencia como la de Eva? Describe los síntomas que experimentaste.

45 La invitación

▶ **Escribe.** Ethan prepara el borrador de un correo electrónico para invitar a Manuel Patarroyo al ciclo de charlas de su escuela. Lee el principio y termínalo.

> *Estimado señor Patarroyo:*
>
> *Mi nombre es Ethan Thomas y soy estudiante de High School. Le escribo porque la escuela a la que asisto organiza un ciclo de conferencias y...*

CONEXIONES: LENGUA

El lenguaje periodístico

En los periódicos, especialmente en Latinoamérica, es frecuente encontrar titulares donde se omite el artículo en casos donde en el lenguaje habitual habría que utilizarlo. Este uso se explica por la necesidad de condensar la información en un espacio muy limitado.

> **Presidente se reúne con trabajadores**

46 Investiga.
Busca en Internet páginas de periódicos latinoamericanos y escribe ejemplos de titulares donde se omite el artículo.

 AUDIO SCRIPT
See page 69L.

 CONEXIONES: LENGUA

El lenguaje periodístico

Journalistic style is characterized by its conciseness, clarity, and accuracy. In order to unify standards and keep consistency, most large newspapers have a *Manual de estilo* (Style Guide). One difference in style between Spanish-language and American newspapers is capitalization rules for headlines. In Spanish, only the first word and any proper noun should be capitalized.

Answer Key

42. El primer ejemplo se refiere solo a la profesión (*es profesora*). En el segundo ejemplo, un adjetivo calificativo (*excelente*) modifica el nombre. En el tercer ejemplo el nombre lleva un complemento (*de mi hermano*).

43.
1. una	3. X	5. X
2. los	4. La	6. la

44. Answers will vary. Sample answer:
… la cabeza, y también tenía náuseas. Eva se tomó una pastilla, pero como no se mejoraba, fue al hospital. La médica le tomó la temperatura y la presión, y luego le recetó unas pastillas. Eva tenía un virus de estómago.

▶ Answers will vary.

45. Answers will vary.

46. Answers will vary.

Additional Resources

Fans Online activities
Practice Workbook

HERITAGE LANGUAGE LEARNERS

- Ask students to review the e-mails generated from activity 45. Then, based on the information contained, ask them to write an article for the local Spanish-language newspaper, along with a headline, announcing the conference and the participation of Dr. Manuel Patarroyo. Ask students to include details that answer the questions *¿qué?, ¿cuándo?, ¿dónde?,* and *¿quién?* Encourage them to offer more details that will entice the public to attend.

CRITICAL THINKING

- Explain to students that conferences and symposiums offer a means to exchange information, ideas, and opinions on topics of shared interest. They also offer the public an opportunity to become informed on these matters. Have students brainstorm topics for a symposium they would like to organize for the Spanish classroom. After they agree on a topic, have them consider which outstanding leaders from the community and beyond would make ideal participants and describe what contributions these individuals would make.

LECTURA: TEXTO INFORMATIVO

Presentation

- In this section, students will read an article about cancer and some of its causes as well as preventive measures. They will learn vocabulary related to the topic, answer comprehension questions based on the reading, and research one of several types of cancers that affect young adults.

Activities	Standards	Resources
Lectura: texto informativo	1.2, 3.1	
47.	1.2, 1.3, 3.1	
48.	1.2, 1.3	
49.	1.1, 1.2, 3.1, 3.2, 5.1, 5.2	

Teaching Suggestions

Warm-Up / Independent Starter

- Have students read the *Antes de leer* strategies silently. Then ask them to think of an answer for question #1, and to complete question #2.

Preparation

- Ask students to share their answers for question #1 with the class. You may wish to list some of their ideas about cancer prevention on the board, and then revisit these ideas once students have read the article. Next, focus students' attention on the graphic. Many medical terms have Greek or Latin origin and share similar spelling and meaning in English and Spanish. However, students may not be familiar with some of these terms in English, so allow them to share with the class their lists of words and definitions from question #2 of the *Antes de leer* section. Familiarizing themselves with this vocabulary will enhance their comprehension of the reading and expand their vocabulary in English.

- Read the text aloud to model pronunciation, intonation, and stress. Then ask for seven volunteers to each read a paragraph. You may want to ask students to pause after each paragraph, and call on a different volunteer to paraphrase the content.

LECTURA: TEXTO INFORMATIVO

Antes de leer: estrategias

1. Lee el título del texto. ¿De qué manera crees que se puede prevenir el cáncer?
2. Observa el gráfico. Busca las palabras que no conozcas en el diccionario.

El cáncer y su prevención

El cáncer es una enfermedad causada por la proliferación de células[1] anormales que invaden y destruyen algunos tejidos[2].

Hablamos de tumor cuando se forma una masa[3] de células indiferenciadas (cancerosas) en alguna parte del organismo. Este tumor es benigno si está localizado, es de crecimiento lento y no invade otros tejidos; y maligno o canceroso si invade otros tejidos y puede provocar en ellos crecimientos secundarios, denominados metástasis.

Existen varias causas de cáncer: predisposición genética, los virus, las radiaciones, algunas sustancias químicas, etc.

Las investigaciones recientes parecen mostrar que el cáncer tiene un cierto componente hereditario. Al parecer, lo que se hereda no es la enfermedad, sino la propensión a padecerla.

En muchos casos, el cáncer se desencadena[4] por determinados agentes que se llaman cancerígenos; el tabaco, por ejemplo, es uno de los agentes cancerígenos más peligrosos. En otros casos puede aparecer como consecuencia de una lesión o de forma espontánea, sin una causa clara.

Todos los médicos están de acuerdo en que la principal arma de la lucha contra el cáncer es la prevención y la detección precoz[5]. Algunos hábitos saludables, como evitar la vida sedentaria y el consumo de alcohol y tabaco, protegerse adecuadamente de los rayos solares o incluir frutas y verduras en la dieta, pueden ayudar a prevenir el cáncer.

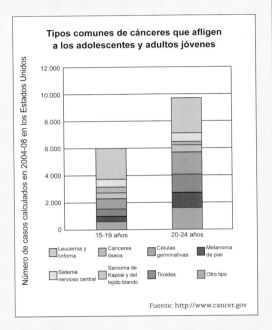

Tipos comunes de cánceres que afligen a los adolescentes y adultos jóvenes

Número de casos calculados en 2004-08 en los Estados Unidos

15-19 años · 20-24 años

Leucemia y linfoma · Cánceres óseos · Células germinativas · Melanoma de piel · Sistema nervioso central · Sarcoma de Kaposi y del tejido blando · Tiroides · Otro tipo

Fuente: http://www.cancer.gov

Differentiated Instruction

DEVELOPING LEARNERS

- Pair students with heritage speakers or with classmates who have superior language skills and ask them to read the article together. Then, ask the developing learner to identify to his or her partner the topic as well as the main idea of each paragraph, plus the supporting details. Explain that using this reading strategy will help them better comprehend the material.

EXPANDING LEARNERS

- Ask students to answer the following questions:
  1. ¿Qué es una enfermedad congénita? ¿Crónica? ¿Contagiosa? Da ejemplos.
  2. ¿Cuál es la diferencia entre una infección bacterial y una viral?
  3. ¿Para qué sirven los antibióticos?
  4. ¿Qué indica la presión arterial?
  5. ¿Qué problemas de salud podría tener una persona con la presión arterial alta?
  6. ¿Es importante controlar el nivel de colesterol? ¿Por qué?

Si un cáncer es diagnosticado a tiempo, puede ser eliminado por diversos medios (normalmente mediante una intervención quirúrgica[6]). A continuación, los médicos prescriben un tratamiento con unos fármacos especiales que impiden la actividad de las células cancerosas y frenan[7] su dispersión. Este tratamiento se denomina quimioterapia y tiene el inconveniente de que es muy agresivo con el organismo. En algunos casos se realiza un tratamiento con rayos (radioterapia) como complemento del anterior.

Fuente: *La enciclopedia del estudiante. Ciencias de la vida.* Santillana

1. *cells*
2. *tissues*
3. *mass*
4. *se produce*
5. temprana
6. operación
7. *slow*

47 ¿Comprendes?

▶ **Explica.** ¿De qué habla el texto? ¿Qué información da?

▶ **Responde** a estas preguntas. Justifica tus respuestas.

1. ¿Qué es el cáncer?
2. ¿Qué dos tipos de tumores hay?
3. ¿Qué es la metástasis?
4. ¿Se pueden prevenir todos los tipos de cáncer?
5. ¿Cuáles pueden ser las causas del cáncer?
6. ¿Qué medidas podemos adoptar para prevenirlo?

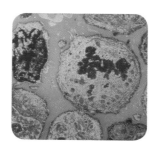

Células cancerígenas.

48 Palabras y expresiones

▶ **Explica** con tus palabras estos términos y expresiones que aparecen en el texto.

1. proliferación
2. causas genéticas
3. propensión
4. agentes cancerígenos
5. detección precoz
6. vida sedentaria

49 Con tus propias palabras

▶ **Elige** uno de los tipos de cáncer del gráfico de la página 96. Busca información sobre él y haz una breve presentación explicando en qué consiste la enfermedad y su tratamiento.

▶ **Busca** testimonios de adolescentes o jóvenes que hayan superado un cáncer. Comenta con tus compañeros(as) su historia y lo que has aprendido de ella.

HERITAGE LANGUAGE LEARNERS

• Have students find information on the most recent research for a cure for cancer, as well as some alternative treatments that may be controversial and even prove to be dangerous. Ask students to prepare a brief oral summary of the data found and present this information to the rest of the class. Afterward, enable a classroom discussion on the research and these so-called miracle treatments.

COOPERATIVE LEARNING

• Have students work in small groups and explain that they are in charge of a nonprofit organization that deals with health-care issues. First, they need to discuss the services their organization offers and give it a name. Then, they will prepare an ad that generates both interest and participation in their organization. Finally, students need to discuss what kind of fundraiser they will organize in order to finance some of their projects or research. Students will self-assign themselves a role to complete this project and then make a joint presentation to the class.

LECTURA: TEXTO INFORMATIVO

Activities

47. You may want to divide the class into small groups and have each group come up with three additional comprehension questions. Collect the questions and redistribute them to different groups. Ask each group to answer all nine questions. Then invite groups to share their answers with the class.

48. Have students write a two-paragraph summary of the article and use the six terms listed in this activity in their summaries.

49. Divide the class into seven groups and assign a different type of cancer to each group. Encourage groups to include graphics, statistics, and prognosis information in their presentations.

Answer Key

47. Answers will vary.
▶ Answers will vary. Sample answers:
1. Es una enfermedad causada por la proliferación de células anormales.
2. Hay tumores benignos y malignos.
3. Es cuando el cáncer invade otros tejidos y provoca crecimientos secundarios.
4. No. Hay cánceres que tienen un componente hereditario; otros pueden aparecer de forma espontánea.
5. Los virus, las radiaciones, sustancias químicas y la propensión genética.
6. Podemos evitar la vida sedentaria, y el consumo de alcohol y tabaco. También es bueno protegerse de los rayos solares y consumir frutas y verduras.

48. Answers will vary. Sample answers:
1. Reproducción, expansión de algo.
2. Causas hereditarias.
3. Tener tendencia a algo.
4. Cosas que pueden provocar cáncer.
5. Descubrir a tiempo algo.
6. Hacer muy poco ejercicio.

49. Answers will vary.
▶ Answers will vary.

Additional Resources

Fans Online activities

DESAFÍO 2

Comunicación

Presentation

- In this section, students will integrate the vocabulary and grammar from *Desafío 2* in order to read an article about the use of a smartphone application in medicine, talk about illness prevention, and come up with questions for Dr. Patarroyo.

Activities	Standards	Resources
50.	1.1, 1.3, 3.1, 3.2	
51.	1.1, 1.3, 3.1, 5.1 5.2	
52. Final del desafío	1.1, 1.2, 1.3, 2.2, 3.1	

Teaching Suggestions

Warm-Up / Independent Starter

- Have students write a description of one of the following medical episodes. Students should include the symptoms, specialist or health-care provider consulted, treatment prescribed, and results of that treatment. For example: *La paciente sentía dolor en el pecho y molestias en el brazo izquierdo. Fue al hospital, donde la atendió un cardiólogo…*
  - *un infarto*
  - *un ataque de asma*
  - *quemaduras por insolación*

Preparation

- Go over the vocabulary and grammar topics from this *Desafío*. Clarify any questions students may have regarding verb-preposition combinations and the use or omission of articles in Spanish. Alternatively, have students work in small groups to discuss the grammar topics and help answer each other's questions.

- Call on volunteers to share their Independent Starters. Try to get a description for each of the three medical episodes. Then have students analyze their paragraphs for uses of vocabulary related to health, verbs with prepositions, and articles. You may want to write some of students' sentences on the board to illustrate some of the topics from this *Desafío*.

Comunicación

50 **Un avance tecnológico**

▶ **Lee** esta noticia y complétala con los artículos definidos e indefinidos necesarios.

TECNOLOGÍA   Lunes, 9 de enero de 2012

Diagnosticar la malaria con el móvil

Evaluar una prueba de imagen, controlar los niveles de glucosa, detectar ___1___ enfermedad en la piel... Todas estas «tareas» médicas ya pueden realizarse de una forma ágil y sencilla con la simple ayuda de ___2___ teléfono móvil.

Las aplicaciones sanitarias cada vez ganan más terreno en el creciente mundo de ___3___ *smartphones* y algunas de estas nuevas propuestas tienen el potencial de mejorar las técnicas de diagnóstico e incluso el acceso a ___4___ atención en muchas zonas del mundo. Es el caso de un reciente desarrollo realizado desde EEUU que permite diagnosticar ___5___ malaria solo con la ayuda de un móvil.

Según sus creadores, investigadores de *Lifelens Project*, su tecnología detecta ___6___ enfermedad de forma rápida y con ___7___ precisión mayor que la que proporcionan los test de diagnóstico rápido.

___8___ aplicación funciona colocando una gota de sangre del paciente en una tira que contiene un marcador reactivo al parásito de la malaria. Después, se toma una imagen de esa tira con un teléfono inteligente equipado con ___9___ pequeñas lentes que permiten ampliar la fotografía hasta 350 veces.

Un *software* especial permite identificar ___10___ células sanguíneas en esa imagen y comprobar si el paciente está afectado por la enfermedad. Además, la aplicación también hace posible subir esos datos a Internet, lo que, según sus creadores, puede ayudar a realizar un seguimiento del trastorno y conocer qué zonas están más afectadas.

Fuente: http://www.elmundo.es
(selección)

▶ **Lee** la noticia de nuevo y responde a las preguntas.

1. ¿Qué dos ventajas ofrecen las aplicaciones sanitarias de los *smartphones*, según el texto?
2. ¿Para qué sirve la aplicación creada por *Lifelens Project*?
3. ¿Por qué se puede decir que esta aplicación es mejor que una prueba de sangre tradicional?
4. ¿Qué se necesita para realizar la prueba?
5. ¿Qué beneficios tiene subir los datos de la prueba a Internet?

▶ **Resume** el procedimiento que se sigue para diagnosticar la malaria con el móvil.

Differentiated Instruction

DEVELOPING LEARNERS

- Ask students whether the following statements are true (*cierto*) or false (*falso*). Have them correct the false ones.
  1. *La tecnología de* Lifelens Project *detecta la malaria lentamente. (F; rápido)*
  2. *Se detecta la malaria colocando una muestra de la piel en una tira. (F; una gota de sangre)*
  3. *La tira contiene un marcador reactivo al virus de la malaria. (F; al parásito de la malaria)*
  4. *Las lentes amplían las fotos 350 veces. (C)*
  5. *La tecnología descrita permite realizar un seguimiento de la enfermedad. (C)*

EXPANDING LEARNERS

- After students complete activity 52, have them work in groups of three and answer the questions Ethan and Eva have asked Dr. Patarroyo. Allow students some time to organize their responses and rehearse their lines. Ask them to imagine that Dr. Patarroyo is being interviewed on television. Then, call on some groups to conduct their interviews in front of the class.

La prevención es
la mejor medida

Gripe A

 51 Una campaña de prevención

 ▶ **Habla** con tu compañero(a). Hagan una lista de consejos para prevenir enfermedades.

Modelo   *Para prevenir las enfermedades más graves lo mejor es vacunarse.*

▶ **Escribe** con tu compañero(a) un anuncio sobre la prevención de una enfermedad. Incluyan un eslogan y presenten el anuncio a la clase.

Final del desafío

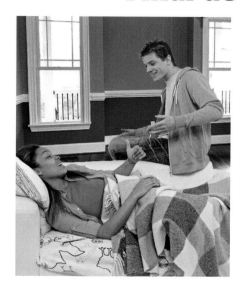

ETHAN: Ayer escribí a Manuel Patarroyo para invitarlo al ciclo de charlas de la escuela.

EVA: ¡Qué bien, Ethan! ¿Y ya te contestó?

ETHAN: ¡Pues claro! Dice que podemos contar con él y que quiere asistir a todas las charlas.

EVA: ¡Fabuloso!

ETHAN: Me alegro de que podamos contribuir a este evento tan importante de la escuela.

EVA: Yo también. Y te agradezco el trabajo que hiciste redactando tú solo el mensaje.

ETHAN: No ha sido nada. Siempre soñé con conocer a un científico muy famoso.

EVA: Tenemos que preparar las preguntas que le vamos a hacer. Yo me ocupo.

ETHAN: ¡Pero tú estás enferma, tienes que descansar!

EVA: No, no. Insisto en ayudarte.

ETHAN: De acuerdo. ¡Pues a trabajar!

52 Respondió que sí

▶ **Lee** el diálogo y responde a estas preguntas.

1. ¿Quién invitó a Manuel Patarroyo al ciclo de charlas?

2. ¿Aceptó la invitación? ¿Qué palabras del diálogo justifican tu respuesta?

 ▶ **Escribe** con tu compañero(a) tres preguntas que Ethan y Eva pueden hacerle a Manuel Patarroyo. Después, preséntenlas a la clase.

Modelo   *¿Ha habido más investigaciones para mejorar la vacuna de la malaria?*

noventa y nueve 99

Unit 2
DESAFÍO 2
Comunicación

Activities

51. Have students work in small groups. To make their presentations more relevant, encourage groups to choose an illness or a medical issue of importance to young adults. Remind students to consider the lifestyle of students their age and tailor their campaign accordingly. Suggest that groups create a catchy tune for their campaign slogan. After the presentations, hold a class vote to select the best campaign.

52. You may want to keep a record on the board of the questions students have for Dr. Patarroyo. Then, as a class, select five questions that students find particularly interesting. Next, divide the class into five groups and assign a question to each group to research. Finally, have groups report their findings back to the class.

Answer Key

50.
1. una	4. la	7. una	10. las
2. un	5. la	8. La	
3. los	6. la	9. unas	

▶ 1. Mejoran las técnicas de diagnóstico y el acceso a la atención en muchas zonas del mundo.
  2. Sirve para diagnosticar la malaria.
  3. Porque detecta la malaria de forma rápida y con mayor precisión.
  4. Se necesita un teléfono inteligente equipado con unas pequeñas lentes.
  5. Ayuda a realizar un seguimiento de la enfermedad y conocer qué zonas están más afectadas.

▶ Answers will vary.

51. Answers will vary.
▶ Answers will vary.

52. 1. Ethan.
  2. Sí. Pueden «contar con él».
▶ Answers will vary.

Additional Resources

Fans Online activities
Practice Workbook

HERITAGE LANGUAGE LEARNERS

• Have students think about a famous, living person from a Spanish-speaking country they would like to interview without revealing that person's identity. Then, have students write a series of questions they would ask and have them read their questions aloud. Next, see if other students can guess the interviewee's identity by the questions alone, or by asking the interviewer no more than three new questions.

CRITICAL THINKING

• Ask students to research and then discuss the impact malaria has had and continues to have on world health. For example, malaria infects between 300 and 500 million people a year, and is the leading cause of death in children under the age of five. Ask students to find organizations, such as the Bill and Melissa Gates Foundation, that are helping to eradicate this disease. After students do their research, ask them to work in small groups and discuss the history and magnitude of malaria, as well as the effectiveness of measures to eradicate it.

DESAFÍO 3

Referirse a cambios y estados

Presentation

■ In *Desafío 3*, Asha and Lucas have to make a photographic report of a Mexican wedding. Students will preview language used to describe people's feelings and human body positions.

Activities	Standards	Resources
Texto	1.2, 2.1	
53.	1.2, 2.1	
54.	1.2, 1.3, 2.1	
55.	1.1, 1.2, 1.3, 2.1, 2.2, 4.2, 5.1	Audio
56. Cultura	1.1, 1.2, 2.1, 2.2, 4.2	

Teaching Suggestions

Warm-Up / Independent Starter

■ Ask students to list the main characteristics of the weddings they are familiar with.

Preparation

■ Have students share their Independent Starters. Are there any common elements (e.g., music, food, dance, dress) in students' descriptions?

Texto: Una boda impresionante

■ Read the introduction to the dialogue. Ask students to pay attention to Asha's description of the wedding. Have students read the dialogue silently. Then, as a class, discuss the main elements of the wedding Asha and Lucas are attending. How is this wedding different from the weddings students have attended?

Activities

54. After students finish, have pairs come up with a list of important moments that they think Asha and Lucas should photograph.

55. Before students listen to the audio, have them read the questions and, using the dialogue on page 100 and what they know about Mexican celebrations, speculate on possible answers. Also, if there are students who are familiar with Mexican weddings, invite them to share their knowledge with the class.

Una boda impresionante

Asha y Lucas tienen que asistir a la boda de una vecina mexicana y hacer un reportaje fotográfico del evento que muestre las costumbres típicas.

ASHA: ¡Qué elegantes están todos! Y la iglesia se ve hermosa, ¿no crees?

LUCAS: Sí, yo nunca había estado en una boda católica. Mira, ahí está el novio.

ASHA: Ese no es el novio, Lucas, es el padrino. Los padrinos son las personas que acompañan y ayudan a los novios durante la ceremonia. La madrina es esa mujer que está de pie hablando con el novio. Anda, sácales una foto.

LUCAS: Ya está. También hay padrinos en los bautizos, ¿no?

ASHA: Sí. Mira, ya viene la novia. Lleva un vestido blanco precioso. ¡Y qué ramo de flores tan lindo! Date prisa, hazle una foto.

LUCAS: Oye, Asha, esta boda es muy larga... Y estoy muerto de hambre.

ASHA: Shhh... ¡Calla, Lucas, me estás avergonzando!

LUCAS: Es que me quiero enterar. ¿Qué hacen ahora? ¿Qué le está dando el novio a la novia?

ASHA: Le está presentando las arras, que son trece monedas simbólicas. Su madre me contó que esas arras son muy antiguas y que las han utilizado en todas las bodas de su familia desde hace muchísimos años.

LUCAS: ¡Y yo me siento como si lleváramos años aquí sentados! Oye, parece que los padrinos están atando a los novios con una cuerda. No sabía que era tan literal el compromiso...

ASHA: Ay, Lucas, eso es el lazo. También es un símbolo. No seas bobo...

53 ### Detective de palabras

▶ **Completa** estas oraciones.

1. Todos ___1___ elegantes en la boda.
2. La madrina ___2___ una mujer que ___3___ de pie.
3. Asha opina que el ramo de flores de la novia ___4___ muy lindo.
4. La boda ___5___ larga y Lucas ___6___ muerto de hambre.
5. El novio ___7___ presentando las arras a la novia.
6. Asha le explica a Lucas que el lazo que ponen a los novios ___8___ un símbolo.

Differentiated Instruction

DEVELOPING LEARNERS

• To reinforce students' comprehension of the dialogue, ask whether the following statements are true (*cierto*) or false (*falso*). Have them correct the false ones.
1. *Lucas confunde al padrino con el novio. (C)*
2. *Los padrinos son los padres de la pareja. (F; son amigos o familiares de la pareja)*
3. *Lucas dice que está muerto de sueño. (F; muerto de hambre)*
4. *Asha avergüenza a Lucas. (F; Lucas la avergüenza)*
5. *Entregan 14 arras. (F; 13)*
6. *Atan a los novios con una cuerda. (F; con un lazo)*

EXPANDING LEARNERS

• After students complete activity 55, ask them to write at least two paragraphs describing an ideal wedding. This celebration could be their future wedding, or one they would organize as wedding planners. Encourage them to accompany their writing with photos taken from magazines, the Internet, or their own drawings. Call on volunteers to share their paragraphs and visuals with the class, and take a class vote to see which wedding is the most creative, the most romantic, or the one more students would like to attend.

54 **¿Comprendes?**

▶ **Responde** a estas preguntas.

1. ¿A qué ceremonia asisten Asha y Lucas?
2. ¿Dónde se celebra esa ceremonia?
3. ¿Quiénes son los padrinos?
4. ¿Qué lleva la novia en la mano?
5. ¿Qué son las arras?
6. ¿De qué otro símbolo hablan Asha y Lucas?

55 **¡Cuántos preparativos!**

▶ **Escucha** la conversación entre Asha y Lucas, y responde a las preguntas.

1. ¿Cómo se encuentra Lucas?
2. ¿Cuánto tiempo tardaron los novios en organizar la boda?
3. ¿Cuál va a ser el plato principal en la comida?
4. ¿Cuál es uno de los ingredientes básicos del plato principal?
5. ¿Qué tipo de música van a tocar?
6. ¿Por qué no pueden empezar a bailar Asha y Lucas?

▶ **Escribe** un párrafo describiendo la última boda a la que asististe. Incluye explicaciones y detalles sobre los ritos y costumbres que viste.

▶ **Habla** con tu compañero(a). ¿Qué diferencias y semejanzas hay entre las bodas que han descrito?

CULTURA

Las bodas en México

México es un país de gran diversidad y esto se ve reflejado en sus celebraciones. En las bodas de la región de Guadalajara, por ejemplo, es frecuente que el novio se vista de charro y llegue a la iglesia a caballo. Otros ritos propios de las bodas están más extendidos por todo el país, como la costumbre de que la novia tenga dos ramos de flores: uno para llevarlo como adorno en la ceremonia religiosa y otro para ofrecérselo a la Virgen de Guadalupe. También es frecuente que actúen unos mariachis durante la ceremonia o en la celebración posterior.

56 **Investiga.** ¿Conoces alguna tradición (de boda o de otra ceremonia) propia de alguna región de tu país? ¿Sabes cómo comenzó? Busca información y prepara una presentación sobre ella.

ciento uno **101**

Referirse a cambios y estados

AUDIO SCRIPT
See page 69L.

CULTURA

Las bodas en México

The *arras* the groom puts into the bride's cupped hands **represent his ability to support her**. The *lazo*, which is usually a white rope or a rosary, is a symbol of the couple's commitment to always be together. At some wedding receptions, guests "pay" to dance with the newlyweds. As they dance, the guests pin money on the bride's or groom's clothes. The money collected is generally used for the honeymoon or setting up the new home.

Answer Key

53.
1. están   4. es   7. está
2. es   5. es   8. es
3. está   6. está

54.
1. A la boda de una vecina mexicana.
2. En una iglesia católica.
3. Las personas que acompañan a los novios en la ceremonia.
4. Lleva un ramo de flores.
5. Son trece monedas simbólicas.
6. De un lazo.

55. Answers will vary. Sample answers:
1. Está mareado.
2. Tardaron meses.
3. El mole.
4. El chile.
5. Música de mariachi.
6. Porque aún no han empezado a bailar los novios.
▶ Answers will vary.
▶ Answers will vary.

56. Answers will vary.

Additional Resources

Fans Online activities

HERITAGE LANGUAGE LEARNERS

- Ask students to share courtship, engagement, and wedding customs from their family's country of origin. Encourage students to compare and contrast their grandparents' or great-grandparents' traditions with those that are observed today, and with customs in this country. Suggest that students bring in photos and other memorabilia that highlight these events. If possible, they may invite a family member who has taken part in these traditions and is willing to share experiences with the students.

CRITICAL THINKING

- Ask students to write an essay to answer the following question: *¿Qué importancia tiene mantener las costumbres y tradiciones de tu familia y pasárselas a las próximas generaciones?* Students should write an introductory paragraph that answers this question. Then, they will offer several arguments to justify their answer in the following paragraphs. Students will end with a conclusion that summarizes their arguments. Call on volunteers to read their essays aloud.

DESAFÍO 3

Vocabulario – Estados físicos y anímicos

Presentation

- In this section, students will learn key vocabulary to describe human body positions and emotional and physical states.

Activities	Standards	Resources
Vocabulario	1.2	
57.	1.2, 1.3	Audio
58.	1.3	
59.	1.1, 1.3	
60. Cultura	1.1, 1.2, 2.1, 2.2, 3.2, 4.2	

Teaching Suggestions

Warm-Up / Independent Starter

- Ask students to create a list of words that express emotional states.

Preparation

- Read aloud the first paragraph from the vocabulary presentation. Then ask for different volunteers to represent the highlighted words by adopting the corresponding position. Call on students to guess which position each student is representing. Next, call on three volunteers to read aloud the chat entries. Then read aloud the words in the *Más vocabulario* feature and have students repeat them after you.

- Have students use a two-column chart to classify the words from the vocabulary presentation that describe an emotional state. Suggest that they label the columns *Emociones positivas* and *Emociones negativas*. Ask students to add their list of words from the Independent Starter to their charts. Then invite volunteers to share their charts with the class. Did they list more positive or negative emotions?

Activities

58. Ask students to use their sentences to write a short narrative about three of the pictures. Then have them find a classmate who has at least one picture in common with them. Ask partners to combine their narratives for the picture into a short story.

Vocabulario

Estados físicos y anímicos

Amigos   Ver todos

Marta García

Pongan la televisión en el canal 1 y vean el documental que están emitiendo. Me ha puesto furiosa ver cómo estamos destruyendo el planeta. Por favor, ¡RECICLEN!

Me gusta · Comentar

  Ismael Arribas ▶ Marta García

Sí, yo también lo estoy viendo y me avergüenza lo que estamos haciendo. Estoy muy desanimado y un poco harto de nuestro comportamiento.

Me gusta · Comentar

  Ana Alcaraz ▶ Marta García

Pues yo estoy esperanzada porque los niños de ahora están muy concienciados. Estamos mejorando y creo que hay que alegrarse por ello.

Estos son mis compañeros de clase. La chica que está de pie es mi mejor amiga, María, y el chico que está a su lado de perfil es su novio, Sergio. Los que están agachados son Julio y Nuria. La chica que está de rodillas es Belén, mi otra mejor amiga. Y el chico que está acostado es Javi. Ah, yo soy la que está sentada a su derecha.

Publicar

Más vocabulario

Estados físicos y anímicos

(in)cómodo(a)	(un)comfortable
(des)contento(a)	(un)happy
de buen/mal humor	in a good/bad mood
estar muerto(a) de hambre/sed	very hungry/thirsty
estar muerto(a) de sueño	very sleepy

Ciclo de la vida

crecer	to grow
envejecer	to get old
morir	to die

¡Atención!

avergonzado(a)	embarrassed
embarazada	pregnant

57 **¿Cómo se sienten?**

 ▶ **Escucha** a los personajes y completa las oraciones con las palabras y expresiones del cuadro.

1. Lucas…
2. Eva…
3. Asha…
4. Ethan…
5. Daniel…
6. Michelle…

está cómodo(a)
está de mal humor
está desanimado(a)
está harto(a)
está muerto(a) de sed
está muerto(a) de sueño

Differentiated Instruction

DEVELOPING LEARNERS

- Ask students to match the antonyms.
  1. alegrarse (g)   a. derecho
  2. feliz (f)   b. muerto
  3. acostado (e)   c. de frente
  4. avergonzado (h)   d. sentado
  5. vivo (b)   e. levantado
  6. de pie (d)   f. descontento
  7. de perfil (c)   g. entristecerse
  8. agachado (a)   h. orgulloso

EXPANDING LEARNERS

- Have students complete the following sentences with what is true for them:
  1. Me pongo furioso(a) cuando…
  2. A menudo me avergüenzo de…
  3. A veces estoy desanimado(a) porque…
  4. Estoy esperanzado(a) cuando…
  5. Me alegro de…
  6. Me gusta estar sentado(a) en…
  7. … me pone de mal humor.
  8. … me pone de buen humor.
  9. Me siento incómodo(a) cuando…

58 Posturas

▶ **Escribe** oraciones para describir a estas personas. Incluye detalles sobre su aspecto físico, su postura, dónde están y qué están haciendo.

59 Tu perfil

▶ **Entrevista** a tu compañero(a). Hazle las siguientes preguntas y toma nota de sus respuestas. Luego, comenta a la clase lo que más te haya llamado la atención.

1. ¿Cuándo y dónde naciste? ¿Dónde creciste?
2. ¿En qué lugar del mundo te gustaría envejecer?
3. ¿Cómo te sientes en este momento?
4. ¿Hay algo que te avergüence fácilmente?
5. ¿De qué puedes decir que estás harto(a)?
6. ¿Qué te pone de buen humor? ¿Y de mal humor?

CULTURA

La celebración de la madurez

En muchas civilizaciones y culturas del mundo hay ritos y ceremonias para celebrar la llegada de una persona a la vida adulta. Los antiguos incas realizaban el Warachikuy para celebrar el paso de la adolescencia a la madurez. Este rito consistía en superar una serie de duras pruebas físicas en las que los jóvenes demostraban sus capacidades como futuros guerreros. En la actualidad, el Warachikuy se representa en el parque arqueológico de Sacsayhuamán (Perú) y en él participan unos 1.500 jóvenes que se preparan con meses de antelación.

60 Explica. ¿Conoces alguna celebración antigua o actual que marque el paso a otra etapa de la vida? ¿Dónde se celebra? ¿En qué consiste?

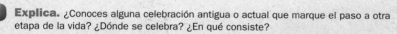

ciento tres 103

Vocabulario – Estados físicos y anímicos

59. You may wish to choose two or three questions and have students report their partner's answers for those questions. Then have students use the answers to describe the class's "personality."

AUDIO SCRIPT
See page 69L.

CULTURA

La celebración de la madurez

When Aztec children reached the age of 15, they were required to attend one of several schools: a *cuicacalli*, where boys and girls were taught to sing and dance; a *calmecac*, where boys and girls from the noble classes were trained in religion, science, administration, and government; or a *telpochcalli*, where boys from the lower classes trained for warfare. Upon completion of their schooling, young adults were considered ready to marry.

Answer Key

57. 1. … está muerto de sed.
2. … está harta.
3. … está desanimada.
4. … está cómodo.
5. … está de mal humor.
6. … está muerta de sueño.

58. Answers will vary.

59. Answers will vary.

60. Answers will vary.

Additional Resources

Fans Online activities
Practice Workbook

HERITAGE LANGUAGE LEARNERS

- Ask students to research other ceremonies throughout the Spanish-speaking world that celebrate a rite of passage. Have them find information on the history of the ceremony or ritual, where it was or still is practiced, who the participants are, and what cultural importance did, or does, this ceremony have. Ask students to make a presentation of their findings to the class and accompany their presentation with visuals.

TOTAL PHYSICAL RESPONSE (TPR)

- Divide the class into two or more teams to play "Charades." Write the new vocabulary on slips of paper and distribute them to students. Have players take turns pantomiming the word or words for their teammates. Set a time limit and award one point for each correct answer. Establish a gesture that students may use to indicate an antonym for their selected word; for example, they might show their full face to their team to indicate the antonym for *de perfil*.

DESAFÍO 3

Gramática – La voz pasiva

Presentation

- In this section, students will review how to use the passive voice.

Activities	Standards	Resources
Gramática	1.2, 3.1	
61.	1.2, 3.1, 4.1	
62.	1.2	
63.	1.2, 1.3, 2.1, 2.2	Audio
64.	1.3, 2.1, 4.2	
65. Comunidades	1.2, 2.1, 3.2, 4.2	

Teaching Suggestions

Warm-Up / Independent Starter

- Ask students to read the following pairs of sentences and compare the use of the active voice and the passive voice:
  1. a. *Cervantes escribió* El Quijote.
     b. *El Quijote fue escrito por Cervantes.*
  2. a. *Un chef famoso hizo el pastel.*
     b. *El pastel fue hecho por un chef famoso.*

Preparation

- Review the Independent Starter. First, have students identify which sentences are written in the active voice and which are written in the passive voice. Then, as a class, discuss how the sentences are different.
- Divide the class into small groups and ask them to read through the grammar presentation aloud. They should then go back over each point, restating it in their own words.

Activities

63. To extend this activity, have students imagine that they are writing a news report for the school newspaper. Ask them to write a summary of Rocío's *quinceañera* party. For example: *Rocío celebró su quinceañera en el pueblo de su mamá, en México. La ceremonia fue oficiada por...*

64. Try to pair up students from different cultural backgrounds so that they can share different experiences. Then invite students to report their partner's experiences back to the class.

Gramática

La voz pasiva

- La voz pasiva es una construcción que presenta al sujeto como receptor de la acción, no como agente. La cláusula pasiva suele constar de tres elementos:
  – Un sujeto que recibe la acción (**sujeto paciente**).
  – Un **verbo en voz pasiva**.
  – Un complemento con la preposición por que nombra a quien realiza la acción (**complemento agente**).

El ratón	fue atacado	por el gato.
sujeto paciente	verbo en voz pasiva	complemento agente

- La voz pasiva de los verbos se forma en español de la misma manera que en inglés: con el verbo ser + *participio*. El participio concuerda con el sujeto en género y número.

Voz pasiva verbo ayudar. Presente de indicativo

yo	soy **ayud**ado(a)	nosotros(as)	somos **ayud**ados(as)
tú	eres **ayud**ado(a)	vosotros(as)	sois **ayud**ados(as)
usted, él, ella	es **ayud**ado(a)	ustedes, ellos(as)	son **ayud**ados(as)

- La voz pasiva se puede conjugar en cualquier tiempo verbal.

Presente	La boda **es oficiada** por el alcalde.
Pretérito	La boda **fue oficiada** por el alcalde.
Imperfecto	Todas las bodas **eran oficiadas** por el alcalde.
Futuro	La boda **será oficiada** por el alcalde.

Uso de la voz pasiva

- En español, la pasiva con ser es menos común que en inglés; se usa poco en estos casos:
  – Con un objeto indirecto: Los clientes le dejaron propina **al mesero**.
  – Con los tiempos progresivos: El chef **está preparando** la comida.
  – Con verbos de percepción (ver, oír, sentir...) o emoción (querer, odiar...): Ayer **vi** una película interesante.
- Tampoco se usa en instrucciones. En este caso se prefiere la construcción se + *verbo en 3.ª persona*: **Se ruega** silencio.

61 **Compara.** ¿Cuándo se usa la voz pasiva en inglés?

62 **¿Voz activa o voz pasiva?**

▶ **Traduce** estas oraciones al español.

1. The cake is being baked by my grandmother.
2. She was given a present by her friends.

Differentiated Instruction

DEVELOPING LEARNERS

- Ask students to change the following sentences to the passive voice:
  1. *El comité presenta los premios. (Los premios son presentados por el comité.)*
  2. *Ana pintó la casa. (La casa fue pintada por Ana.)*
  3. *Hice el postre. (El postre fue hecho por mí.)*
  4. *El pueblo celebra la boda. (La boda es celebrada por el pueblo.)*
  5. *Ayudarás al vecino. (El vecino será ayudado por ti.)*

EXPANDING LEARNERS

- Ask students to think of a family celebration such as a wedding, anniversary, birthday, or holiday and the steps involved in planning it. Ask them to list these steps and then, beside each one, explain if the task still needs to be done or has been completed, and by whom. Ask students to use the passive voice. For example: *Enviar las invitaciones.* → *Las invitaciones fueron enviadas por mi hermana.* Then, have students reword these statements using the active voice and/or se plus a verb in the third person.

63 Quinceañera

 ▶ **Escucha** la conversación y elige la opción correcta.

1. La quinceañera de Rocío se celebró…
   a. en el pueblo de su papá.
   b. en un pueblo del estado de Morelos.
   c. en los Estados Unidos.

2. La celebración comenzó con…
   a. música de mariachi.
   b. una comida en una hacienda.
   c. una ceremonia religiosa.

3. El sacerdote de la ceremonia religiosa era…
   a. el padrino de Rocío.
   b. el tío de Rocío.
   c. el sacerdote del pueblo.

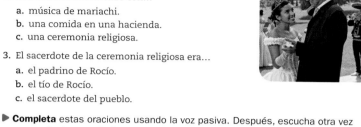

 ▶ **Completa** estas oraciones usando la voz pasiva. Después, escucha otra vez y comprueba los resultados.

1. La ceremonia _____ por mi tío Pedro.
   oficiar

2. Todas mis canciones favoritas _____ por unos mariachis.
   interpretar

3. Los zapatos _____ a mano.
   hacer

64 Presentación en sociedad

▶ **Escribe.** ¿Has ido alguna vez a una fiesta de quinceañera o a una celebración similar? Cuenta tu experiencia. Usa la voz pasiva cuando sea posible.

 **COMUNIDADES**

ESTRUCTURA FAMILIAR EN LATINOAMÉRICA

En las sociedades latinoamericanas es muy habitual que los abuelos convivan con sus hijos y sus nietos en la misma casa. También es común que los parientes más próximos vivan cerca, lo que favorece que distintas unidades familiares conformen una gran familia.
A diferencia de los Estados Unidos, en los países hispanos muchos jóvenes no se independizan hasta que se casan.

65 Explica. ¿Qué ventajas y desventajas encuentras en este tipo de estructura familiar?

Gramática – La voz pasiva

 AUDIO SCRIPT
See page 69M.

 COMUNIDADES

Estructura familiar en Latinoamérica
Family structure is rapidly changing in Latin America, especially in urban areas. The fertility rate has plummeted across the region, from an average of 6 children per family in 1960 to 2.3 children in 2010. Also, the age at which women have their first child has increased in the last decades. There has also been an increase in the number of single-parent households headed by women, and the absolute number of one-person households has doubled. However, nuclear families are still predominant, with a 61.9% share of the total.

Answer Key

61. Answers may vary. Sample answer:
Al igual que en español, se usa para enfatizar el objeto de una acción o cuando no se sabe quién la realizó. Pero, en inglés sí se usa con objetos indirectos, verbos de percepción y tiempos progresivos.

62. 1. Mi abuela está haciendo/horneando un pastel. (tiempo progresivo)
2. Sus amigos le dieron un regalo. (objeto indirecto)

63. 1. b   2. c   3. b
   ▶ 1. fue oficiada
      2. fueron interpretadas
      3. fueron hechos

64. Answers will vary.

65. Answers will vary.

Additional Resources

Fans Online activities
Practice Workbook

HERITAGE LANGUAGE LEARNERS

• Enable a discussion on the changing dynamics of the extended family structure when families move from their country of origin and settle elsewhere. What impact might this have on family members who either no longer share the same house or live in close proximity to one another? How do these families maintain their strong family ties? Does this weaken or perhaps strengthen inter-generational bonds? Encourage students to share their personal experiences. Engage non-heritage speakers in the discussion.

CRITICAL THINKING

• Ask students to write a letter to an advice columnist describing a family member's inability to adapt to his or her new country. Writers should ask for suggestions to help the relative cope with the new environment and what other family members can do to help. Have students exchange letters with a partner and ask the partner to respond with some sensible advice. Call on pairs to read their letters aloud.

DESAFÍO 3

Gramática – *Ser y estar*

Presentation

- In this section, students will review the uses of the verbs *ser* and *estar*. They will also learn how certain adjectives change meaning when used with either *ser* or *estar*.

Activities	Standards	Resources
Gramática	1.2, 3.1	
66.	1.2, 3.1, 4.1	
67.	1.2, 3.1	
68.	1.2, 1.3	Audio
69.	1.1, 1.3	

Teaching Suggestions

Warm-Up / Independent Starter

- Ask students to read these pairs of sentences and use context clues to try to determine the meaning of each underlined adjective:
  1. a. *Ya nos vamos. ¿Estás lista?*
     b. *Es muy lista, por eso saca tan buenas notas.*
  2. a. *Es orgulloso y muy antipático.*
     b. *Él está orgulloso de su familia.*

Preparation

- Review students' Independent Starters and then call on volunteers to explain the meaning of each adjective, the context clues that helped them determine the meaning, and the verb used with each adjective. Students should note that the use of either *ser* or *estar* changes the meaning of these adjectives. Finally, have students translate the sentences into English. Does English use different adjectives in each case?

- Have students read the grammar presentation silently. Encourage them to take notes on any material they have trouble understanding. Then have students get together with a partner and help answer each other's questions. Monitor their discussions. Next, to help students practice the material, ask them to complete the following sentences:
  1. *La boda … este sábado. (es)*
  2. *Todo … listo para la celebración. (está)*
  3. *La novia … mexicana. (es)*
  4. *… muy emocionada. (Está)*
  5. *El novio … muy simpático. (es)*

DESAFÍO 3

Gramática

Ser y estar

- El verbo ser se usa principalmente para hablar de los **rasgos** o las **cualidades** propios de las personas (origen, nacionalidad, religión, profesión, parentesco, afiliación, apariencia, personalidad…), los animales, las ideas y las cosas.

  > Santiago **es** abogado y **es** de Panamá. **Es** apuesto y muy cariñoso.
  > El cristal **es** frágil.

- En contraste, el verbo estar se usa:
  - Para expresar el **lugar** donde están las personas o las cosas: Mis padres **están** en casa.
  - Para expresar **sentimientos y estados**: **Estoy** muy contento.
  - Para hablar del **resultado de un proceso**: La casa ya **está** ordenada.

- Además, el verbo ser y el verbo estar tienen otros usos en español:

EL VERBO SER

Para decir la fecha y la hora.	Hoy **es** martes y **son** las tres de la tarde.
Para expresar posesión.	Ese auto azul **es** de mi hermano.
Para localizar eventos.	La fiesta **es** en el club náutico.
Para expresar precio o material.	**Son** quince dólares con cincuenta centavos. El vestido de la novia **es** de seda.
En igualdades matemáticas.	Dos más dos **son** cuatro.
Con propósito o función (con para)	El sillón **es** para sentarse.

EL VERBO ESTAR

Para expresar estado.	Sue **está** delgada porque se puso a dieta.
Con bien y mal.	¿**Estás** bien?
En los tiempos progresivos.	Lucas **está** cocinando.
En expresiones idiomáticas con de.	estar muerto(a) de hambre, estar de buen / mal humor…

Adjetivos que cambian de significado con *ser* o *estar*

- Muchos adjetivos cambian de significado cuando se usan con ser o con estar.

  > El kiwi **es verde** (*green*) por dentro y, cuando **está verde** (*unripe*), es muy ácido.

66 **Piensa.** ¿Cuál es la diferencia entre *Andrés es feliz* y *Andrés está feliz*? ¿Cómo se expresa esta diferencia en inglés?

ADJETIVOS QUE CAMBIAN DE SIGNIFICADO

	SER	ESTAR
atento(a)	*courteous*	*alert*
callado(a)	*reserved*	*quiet*
listo(a)	*smart*	*ready*
malo(a)	*bad*	*sick, ill*
orgulloso(a)	*arrogant*	*proud*
rico(a)	*rich*	*delicious*
seguro(a)	*safe*	*sure, certain*
verde	*green*	*unripe*
vivo(a)	*bright, sharp*	*alive*

Differentiated Instruction

DEVELOPING LEARNERS

- Ask students to complete the following sentences with the present tense of *ser* or *estar*:
  1. *Estos niños … atentos y corteses. (son)*
  2. *Ese chico … listo porque lee mucho. (es)*
  3. *Mi vecino nunca … de buen humor. (está)*
  4. *… una niña alegre, pero hoy … muy triste. (Es; está)*
  5. *Yo … segura de que este vecindario … seguro. (estoy; es)*
  6. *Una persona arrogante … orgullosa. (es)*
  7. *¡Ay! Son las nueve y ustedes no … listos. (están)*

EXPANDING LEARNERS

- Ask students to complete the following sentences with the correct form of *ser* or *estar*:
  1. *Ana … muy guapa esta noche. (está)*
  2. *Espero que los recién casados … muy felices. (sean)*
  3. *¿Pero qué dices? ¿… de broma? (Estás)*
  4. *La reunión … en el auditorio y … a punto de empezar. (es; está)*
  5. *Presta atención. Hay que … atento en esta clase. (estar)*
  6. *¿… callado porque eres tímido o porque no tienes nada que decir? (Estás)*

67 **Mi mejor amiga**

▶ **Completa** este texto con las formas apropiadas de los verbos *ser* o *estar*.

Laura ___1___ mi mejor amiga. Tiene 16 años y ___2___ de Ecuador, pero ahora ___3___ en los Estados Unidos porque su familia se mudó aquí. ___4___ muy linda y tiene unos ojos preciosos; ___5___ verdes y muy grandes. Laura ___6___ muy lista y siempre ___7___ atenta en las clases. Y me gusta porque no ___8___ orgullosa.

68 **Descripciones**

 ▶ **Escucha** las descripciones y elige la opción correcta. Después, escribe ejemplos con las respuestas que no seleccionaste.

1. **a.** Es verde.
   b. Está verde.

2. **a.** Son ricos.
   b. Están ricos.

3. **a.** Es listo.
   b. Está listo.

4. **a.** Es callada.
   b. Está callada.

5. **a.** Es mala.
   b. Está mala.

6. **a.** Es atento.
   b. Está atento.

69 **¡Qué mala pata!**

▶ **Escribe** oraciones para describir cada dibujo. Describe a los personajes y di qué están haciendo y cómo están.

▶ **Habla** con tu compañero(a) y comparen sus descripciones.

▶ **Escribe** con tu compañero(a) un final para esta historia describiendo la escena y a los personajes detalladamente.

ciento siete 107

Activities

67. After students have completed the activity, ask them to cite the rule for using each of these verbs. For example: *es mi mejor amiga* – to identify people (relationship); *es de Ecuador* – to identify people (origin); *está en los Estados Unidos* – to express location of people.

69. Encourage students to be creative and think of a surprising or unusual ending. Then have students share their stories with the class. Alternatively, ask students to role-play their stories for the class. Then hold a class vote to choose the favorite story.

 AUDIO SCRIPT
See page 69M.

Answer Key

66. Andrés es feliz. → *Andrés is a happy person.*
Andrés está feliz. → *Andrés is feeling happy.*

67.
1. es	4. Es	7. está
2. es	5. son	8. es
3. está	6. es	

68. 1. b   2. a   3. a   4. a   5. b   6. a
Answers will vary. Sample answers:
1. La hierba es verde.
2. Probé los postres, y están ricos.
3. Carlos ya tiene la tarjeta de embarque; está listo para tomar el avión.
4. La niña estuvo llorando, pero ahora está callada.
5. La programación de la televisión es mala.
6. El niño está atento en clase.

69. Answers will vary.
▶ Answers will vary.
▶ Answers will vary.

Additional Resources

Fans Online activities
Practice Workbook

Unit 2

LECTURA: TEXTO LITERARIO

Presentation

- In this section, students will read a folktale. As they read, they will review vocabulary related to food and cooking.

Activities	Standards	Resources
Lectura: texto literario	1.2, 1.3, 3.2	
70.	1.1, 1.3	
71.	1.2, 1.3	
72	1.1, 1.2, 1.3, 4.2, 5.2	

Teaching Suggestions

Warm-Up / Independent Starter

- Ask students to read the title and jot down their ideas regarding the type of story they think this is as well as its theme.

Preparation

- Call on individual students to share their Independent Starters. Have them explain their reasoning for their particular predictions. Then discuss with students some of the main characteristics of folktales, such as magical elements, simple plots, repetitive patterns, themes that teach a lesson. Encourage students to look for some of these elements as they read.

- Have students work with a partner to answer the *Antes de leer* questions. Ask students to create a two-column chart and list in the left column the ingredients they mentioned for question #2. Tell students to keep this chart for activity 70.

- Call students' attention to the following verbs from the reading, and have them identify the verb form: *tenéis, tomad, llenadla, ponedla*. Elicit that these verbs are conjugated in the *vosotros* form, which is used in most of Spain to refer to "you all" in informal situations.

- Call on individual students to each read a section of the story aloud. Alternatively, assign the different roles (*narrador, granjeros, guerrero, granjera, hija mayor*) to different students and have them do a cold reading (i.e., a reading aloud from the script without any rehearsal).

108

Antes de leer: estrategias

1. Observa la fotografía. ¿Qué crees que es? ¿Para qué se utiliza?
2. ¿Qué ingredientes suele tener una sopa? Haz una lista.

La piedra mágica

Un guerrero que regresaba de la guerra llegó a un pueblo. Como tenía mucha hambre, se paró delante de la primera granja que encontró y pidió que le dieran algo de comer. Los granjeros le dijeron:

—No podemos darte nada. No tenemos ni siquiera[1] para nosotros.

Pero el guerrero no estaba dispuesto a[2] quedarse sin comer.

—Pero sí tendréis al menos una marmita[3] —dijo.

—Eso sí —le respondieron.

—¿Y tenéis agua para echar en la marmita?

—Claro —respondió la granjera.

—Entonces, todo arreglado[4] —dijo el guerrero—. Tomad la olla, llenadla de agua y ponedla al fuego. Yo traigo una piedra que hace sopa.

Muerto de curiosidad, el padre tomó rápidamente la marmita, la llenó de agua y la puso encima del fuego. Entonces el guerrero metió la mano en uno de sus bolsillos, sacó una piedra y la echó en la marmita.

—Ya está —dijo el guerrero—. Ahora solo hay que esperar a que hierva el agua.

Toda la familia se sentó, asombrada[5], alrededor del fuego.

Después de un rato, el guerrero preguntó:

—¿No tendríais un poquito de sal para la sopa?

—Sí, claro —dijo la granjera—. Y le dio un tarro de sal.

El guerrero tomó un buen puñado[6] y lo echó en la marmita.

Poco después, el guerrero comentó:

—Algunas zanahorias darían mejor gusto a la sopa.

El granjero se levantó y trajo un hermoso manojo[7] de zanahorias. Mientras las zanahorias se cocían, el guerrero comenzó a contar aventuras.

Tras unos minutos dijo:

—¿No pensáis que algunas patatas[8] espesarían[9] la sopa?

—Nos quedan algunas patatas —dijo la hija mayor—. Voy a buscarlas.

Las patatas entraron en la marmita y de nuevo se esperó a que la sopa hirviera.

108 ciento ocho

Differentiated Instruction

DEVELOPING LEARNERS

- Ask students to imagine that they are one of the *granjeros* in the story. Then, ask them to rewrite the story from the *granjero's* or *granjera's* point of view. Encourage students to add additional details, or even ingredients, to *la sopa de piedra*. Suggest that students may change the time, place, or setting of the tale. Call on volunteers to read their stories aloud.

EXPANDING LEARNERS

- Engage students in a discussion of *moralejas* and *máximas*. Remind them that *moralejas* are often part of fables and children's literature. The lessons they teach may be explicit, as in the fable of the hare and the tortoise, whose maxim is "slow and steady wins the race," or implicit, as in *La piedra mágica*. Discuss the moral of the story they have just read, as well as any others they may know. Then, invite students to write a short story or fable that has a *moraleja*. Ask students to read their stories aloud.

En ese momento llegó el hijo mayor; volvía de cazar con dos hermosas liebres[10].

—He aquí lo que nos falta para enriquecer la cena —dijo el guerrero.

Y en un instante las liebres fueron despiezadas[11] y metidas en la marmita.

Al fin, la sopa estuvo preparada; era, en efecto, excelente y había suficiente para satisfacer el hambre de todos, incluso la de los vecinos. Los granjeros estaban asombrados.

—Es una piedra maravillosa —decía el granjero.

—Es una piedra milagrosa —decía su mujer.

—Sí, es verdad —afirmó el guerrero—. Y hace siempre sopa si se sigue la fórmula que ya sabéis.

Cuando llegó la hora del adiós, el guerrero dio la piedra a la mujer para agradecer sus atenciones. Ella no quería aceptarla, pero el guerrero insistía:

—Es poca cosa, mujer. Tomadla, os lo ruego[12].

Ante tales palabras, la mujer aceptó quedársela. El guerrero continuó entonces su camino sin la milagrosa piedra, pero totalmente feliz y seguro de que encontraría otra antes de llegar al siguiente pueblo.

Basado en F. PINTO y A. JIMÉNEZ. *Bajo la Jaima. Cuentos populares del Sáhara*. 1996

1. *not even*
2. no quería
3. olla, cazuela
4. preparado
5. sorprendida
6. *handful*
7. *bunch*
8. papas (en España)
9. harían más densa
10. *hares*
11. cortadas en trozos
12. *I beg*

---

70 ¿Comprendes?

▶ **Escribe** la receta de la sopa del cuento. Incluye la lista de los ingredientes y los pasos para realizarla.

71 Palabras y expresiones

▶ **Busca** en el texto las palabras y expresiones destacadas, y responde a las preguntas.

1. ¿Qué otros platos se pueden preparar en una **olla** o **marmita**?
2. ¿En qué otros platos hay que **hervir agua** para prepararlos?
3. ¿Qué otras cosas se guardan en **tarros**?
4. ¿De qué otras cosas puedes tomar un **puñado**?
5. ¿Qué otras cosas se compran en **manojos**?
6. ¿Qué otros ingredientes hay que **despiezar** para cocinarlos?

72 Con tus propias palabras

▶ **Explica** con tus palabras la enseñanza que se desprende del cuento y coméntala con tus compañeros(as).

▶ **Habla** con tus compañeros(as). ¿Conoces otros cuentos populares con moraleja *(moral)*? Elige uno y cuéntalo.

ciento nueve **109**

Activities

70. Have students take out their charts from the Preparation activity and ask them to list the ingredients for the soup described in the story in the right column. Then have them compare and contrast the lists. Are there any ingredients common to both soups?

72. For the second part of this activity, you may want to organize a storytelling session. Have the class sit in a circle and invite different students to share a folktale, fable, fairy tale, legend, or myth with the class.

Answer Key

70. Answers will vary. Sample answer:
Ingredientes: agua, piedra que hace sopa, un puñado de sal, un manojo de zanahorias, patatas, dos liebres.
Pasos: 1. Se llena de agua una olla y se pone al fuego. Luego se le pone una piedra de hacer sopa. 2. Cuando hierva el agua se añade la sal. 3. Luego se le añaden las zanahorias, y poco después las patatas. 4. Por último, se limpian y despiezan dos liebres y se le añaden a la sopa. 5. Cuando esté, se retira del fuego y se sirve.

71. Answers will vary. Sample answers:
1. Un estofado de carne, una sopa de pollo con fideos, unas lentejas.
2. Para hacer pasta (espaguetis, tallarines) hay que hervir primero el agua.
3. La salsa de tomate, la mayonesa.
4. De azúcar, de harina, de arroz.
5. El perejil, el cilantro, los espárragos.
6. El pollo, la carne.

72. Answers will vary.
▶ Answers will vary.

Additional Resources

Fans Online activities

HERITAGE LANGUAGE LEARNERS

- The words *tarros, puñados,* and *manojos* are used to describe how certain foods are measured or how they are sold or presented. Ask students to share some other examples, including nonfoods. Suggest these examples: a wad of bills – *un fajo de billetes*; a pinch of salt – *una pizca de sal*; a loaf of bread – *una barra de pan*; a clove of garlic – *un diente de ajo*; a bunch of grapes – *un racimo de uvas*; a sprig of parsley – *una ramita de perejil*. Ask all students to write these words in their notebooks.

CRITICAL THINKING

- Read the following anonymous quote to students and have them relate it to the story they have just read: *Quien comparte su comida, no pasa solo la vida.* Then, engage students in a discussion on sharing, from meals and their time to material possessions and ideas, and how this can strengthen one's friendships and family ties. Encourage all students to participate.

109

DESAFÍO 3

Comunicación

Presentation

- In this section, students will integrate the vocabulary and grammar skills from *Desafío 3* in order to talk about adolescence, as well as to describe a photo in detail, and to discuss Lucas and Asha's photographic report.

Activities	Standards	Resources
73.	1.1, 1.2, 1.3, 3.1, 5.1, 5.2	
74.	1.1, 5.1	
75. Final del desafío	1.1, 1.2, 2.1, 2.2	

Teaching Suggestions

Warm-Up / Independent Starter

- Ask students to imagine that they have to report on their school's graduation ceremony. Have them jot down five or six things they think should be included in their news piece.

Preparation

- Have pairs share their notes from the Independent Starter, and then use them to come up with a three-paragraph description of the graduation ceremony. Encourage students to include the most important moments of the ceremony, give a snapshot of the participants—including some of their emotional reactions during the ceremony—and include details about the time and location. Have pairs read their paragraphs aloud.

- Before starting with the activities, give students a few minutes to review the vocabulary and grammar structures covered in this *Desafío*. Clarify any questions students may have and provide additional examples as needed.

Activities

73. Suggest that students put the article aside when writing the summary. This will force them to use their own words and not follow the article too closely. The first sentence of the summary should state the main idea of the article. Then they should include important details and finish with a thesis statement that restates the main idea of the article.

Comunicación

73 **Cambios de humor**

▶ **Lee** el artículo y complétalo con estas palabras. Ten en cuenta que no todas son válidas.

adolescencia	cambios	incómodos	enojas	confusión	alegría
preocupación	adolescente	divertido	humor	cómodos	solo

¿Por qué estoy de tan mal humor?

¿Te ocurre alguna vez que te ___1___ con facilidad sin tener ninguna razón? ¿O que cambias de ___2___ y te sientes triste sin saber por qué? Cambiar de la tristeza al enfado y de vuelta a la ___3___ en cuestión de minutos puede hacer que los adolescentes se sientan como si estuvieran perdiendo el control. ¿Por qué estos cambios tan bruscos de sentimientos son tan comunes entre los adolescentes?

Tener que hacer frente a ___4___ y presiones constantes es parte de la respuesta. Quizás has comenzado a asistir a una nueva escuela y no has podido ver a tus antiguos amigos tanto como quisieras. Obtener buenas notas o querer mejorar en los deportes u otras actividades puede ser una ___5___ para muchos. Es posible que se sientan como si no tuvieran tiempo suficiente para hacer todo.

Ser adolescente significa luchar con la identidad y la imagen de uno mismo. Ser aceptado por los amigos es percibido como algo sumamente importante. Quizás quieras tomar tus propias decisiones, pero al mismo tiempo puede ser abrumador y hacer que te sientas ___6___ de vez en cuando. Así como este período de tu vida puede ser ___7___ y excitante, también es una temporada de ___8___ y conflicto. Puede tomar algún tiempo para que los adolescentes y sus familiares se sientan ___9___ ante la transición entre la niñez y la edad adulta.

Entender que casi todas las personas atraviesan cambios en su estado de ánimo durante la ___10___ puede que haga que estos momentos sean más fáciles de manejar.

Fuente: © The Nemours Foundation/Kidshealth (texto adaptado)

 ▶ **Piensa.** ¿Cuál es la idea fundamental del texto? Escribe un resumen.

 ▶ **Habla** con tus compañeros(as). ¿Te identificas con lo que dice el texto? ¿Crees que se da una imagen real de los adolescentes y sus problemas? Justifica tu opinión.

Differentiated Instruction

DEVELOPING LEARNERS

- Ask students to match the following words from the article with the appropriate meaning:

1. *constante* (g)	a. *súbito*
2. *de vuelta a* (d)	b. *comprender*
3. *abrumador* (j)	c. *pasar*
4. *percibir* (b)	d. *otra vez*
5. *temporada* (f)	e. *afrontar*
6. *transición* (i)	f. *tiempo*
7. *brusco* (a)	g. *persistente*
8. *atravesar* (c)	h. *emocionante*
9. *hacerle frente* (e)	i. *cambio*
10. *excitante* (h)	j. *agobiante*

EXPANDING LEARNERS

- Explain to students that they will write an article similar to *¿Por qué estoy de tan mal humor?* but from different points of view. Students may elect to write about someone from their grandparents' generation who is facing or experiencing retirement and possibly some health issues. Or, students may prefer to change the title to *¿Por qué estoy de tan buen humor?* and write from the optimistic perspective of someone getting older or someone who is going through adolescence, but justifying why they feel good about it.

74 Un día importante

▶ **Busca** una foto de tu familia y tráela a la clase. Piensa en los detalles del día en el que se sacó: lugar, personas, actividades, sentimientos, etc.

 ▶ **Habla** con tu compañero(a) y cuéntale todos los detalles de la fotografía. ¿Qué tienen en común sus familias?

Final del desafío

LUCAS: Ven, Asha. Acabo de descargar las fotos de la boda en mi computadora. Ahora tenemos que seleccionarlas. ¿Me ayudas?

ASHA: Claro. A ver... Esta foto ___1___ muy bien. Se ve a los novios y a los padrinos. Y todos ___2___ muy alegres.

LUCAS: También se ve a los invitados que ___3___ sentados en la iglesia. ¡Había mucha gente!

ASHA: Esta puede ser la primera foto del reportaje.

LUCAS: ¿___4___ segura? ¿No prefieres esta otra de los novios?

ASHA: No. Recuerda que el reportaje ___5___ para mostrar las tradiciones y ahí no se ve nada especial. ¿Recuerdas lo que ocurrió cuando los novios ___6___ saliendo de la iglesia?

LUCAS: Ah, sí. ¡Pobres novios! Los invitados comenzaron a tirarles un montón de arroz. Aquí está.

ASHA: La foto ___7___ muy buena. Parece que está nevando sobre los novios. El arroz ___8___ un símbolo de prosperidad y de buena suerte.

LUCAS: Entonces, seleccionada también.

ASHA: Sigamos...

75 El reportaje

▶ **Completa** el diálogo usando la forma correcta de los verbos *ser* o *estar*.

▶ **Habla** con tu compañero(a). ¿Crees que Asha y Lucas están haciendo una buena selección de fotos? ¿Qué incluirías tú para que el reportaje fuera lo más completo posible?

ciento once **111**

---

74. Tell students in advance that they should bring a photo to class to complete this activity. Then, before students begin, give them a few moments to observe the photo and reminisce silently. Encourage them to jot down their memories and feelings as they look at the picture. They can then use their notes as they describe the picture to their partners. For students who feel uncomfortable talking about their own families, suggest that they look for pictures of families in magazines or on the Internet and make up the details about these families.

75. For the second part of this activity, have students work in small groups. Ask them to search on the Internet for photographic reports of weddings to get ideas. Then have groups decide on the photos they would include in their reports. Encourage them to justify their choices. Call on groups to share their decisions with the class. Is there a consensus among students regarding the photos they would include in the report?

Answer Key

73.
1. enojas	6. solo
2. humor	7. divertido
3. alegría	8. confusión
4. cambios	9. cómodos
5. preocupación	10. adolescencia

▶ Answers will vary.

▶ Answers will vary.

74. Answers will vary.

▶ Answers will vary.

75.
1. está	5. es
2. están	6. estaban
3. están	7. es
4. Estás	8. es

▶ Answers will vary.

Additional Resources

Fans Online activities
Practice Workbook

HERITAGE LANGUAGE LEARNERS

• Ask students to compare and contrast the trials and tribulations that adolescents go through with those of their elders—perhaps their grandparents—who are entering old age (*la tercera edad*). Who do they think have more of a struggle? Which age group has a better support system to deal with emotional and physical changes? Who has a better coping mechanism? Encourage students to talk to their older family members and discuss this with them. Then, have students share this information with their classmates.

MULTIPLE INTELLIGENCES:
Interpersonal Intelligence

• Ask students to conduct a survey among classmates and friends or relatives who are teenagers. They will ask them: *¿Cuál es tu mayor preocupación? ¿Qué es lo que más te abruma en tu vida escolar? ¿Y en tu vida familiar? ¿Y con tus amistades? ¿Qué es lo que más te divierte? ¿Qué es lo que más temes?* After students conduct the survey, have them get together in small groups, and compile their results in a chart or graph. Invite groups to present their findings to the rest of the class and discuss.

111

Unit 2
Para terminar

Presentation

- In this section, students will review the unit objectives and put them into practice. They will learn about traditional Christmas dishes from Colombia and talk about food dishes for special occasions. They will also select one of the following *desafíos* to develop: choose a favorite dish from a Hispanic country and create a poster or brochure about the dish to enter a food competition, research an important scientist of the Spanish-speaking world and prepare a class presentation, or prepare a visual presentation of a typical celebration of the Hispanic world and present it to the class.

Activities	Standards	Resources
76.	1.1, 1.2, 2.1, 2.2, 3.2, 4.2	Audio
77.	1.1, 1.2, 1.3	
78. Tu desafío	1.2, 1.3, 2.1, 2.2, 3.1, 3.2, 5.1, 5.2	

Teaching Suggestions

Warm-Up / Independent Starter

- Have students review the vocabulary and grammar sections in this unit. Then ask them to think of a famous Hispanic they would like to interview. Have students write six or more questions, incorporating some of the verbs listed on page 92. Encourage students to include questions about the person's life, his or her most important experiences, and the things this person is most passionate about.

Preparation

- Have students read their questions from the Independent Starter aloud to a partner. Then ask the partner to answer the questions as if he or she were the famous Hispanic person. Call on volunteer pairs to present their interviews. Can the class tell the identity of the person being interviewed?

- You may want to use some of the students' questions and answers from the previous activity to assess their command of the vocabulary and grammar structures presented in this unit. Provide additional examples and explanations for those areas that need reinforcement.

112

Todo junto

ESCUCHAR Y HABLAR

76 **Un programa gastronómico**

▶ **Escucha** este fragmento de un programa de radio y elige la opción correcta.

1. En el programa hablan sobre...
   - a. cocina internacional.
   - b. una cocinera colombiana.
   - c. un libro de cocina.

2. La receta del lomo de cerdo lleva una salsa de...
   - a. peras.
   - b. moras.
   - c. almendras.

3. A la invitada le gusta la receta del lomo de cerdo porque...
   - a. mezcla sabores distintos.
   - b. es muy exitosa.
   - c. es fácil de hacer.

4. La torta navideña se hace con...
   - a. frutas.
   - b. natilla.
   - c. crema.

5. El brazo de reina también se llama...
   - a. rollo.
   - b. cremita.
   - c. pionono.

▶ **Habla** con tu compañero(a) de los platos que asocias a alguna celebración o ritual. Explica qué ingredientes llevan y en qué ocasiones especiales se comen.

ESCRIBIR Y LEER

77 **Una boda accidentada**

▶ **Mira** esta ilustración. ¿Qué crees que ha pasado? Escríbelo.

▶ **Escribe** la historia completa incluyendo detalles sobre lo que ocurrió y cómo se sentían los personajes.

▶ **Lee** la historia de tu compañero(a) y ponle un título.

112 ciento doce

Differentiated Instruction

DEVELOPING LEARNERS

- Ask students which word does not belong.

  1. *esperanzado* *desanimado* *harto* (esperanzado)
  2. *agachado* *de rodillas* *de pie* (de pie)
  3. *esguince* *infarto* *nuez (nuez)*
  4. *molestias* *náuseas* *vacunas* (vacunas)
  5. *quemadura* *corte* *asma* (asma)
  6. *moras* *toronjas* *lentejas* (lentejas)
  7. *meteorólogo* *cardiólogo* *oncólogo* (meteorólogo)

EXPANDING LEARNERS

- Ask students to consider the *desafíos* in this unit. What characteristics and special abilities would someone ideally need to have in order to carry them out successfully? Did any of the challenges deal with something that they have always wanted to do, or that has always interested them? Ask them to explain why. Also ask students to name and describe a family member or friend with whom they would have liked to participate, and why this person would make a good partner.

Tu desafío

78 Los alimentos y la salud

¿Recuerdas los desafíos de los personajes? ¿Cuál te gusta más? Elige una de estas opciones y resuelve tu desafío.

DESAFÍO Ⓐ

Elige un plato de un país hispano que te guste mucho y prepara un cartel o un folleto para presentarlo a un concurso gastronómico. Incluye estos datos:

- El nombre del plato y una breve historia sobre su origen, cuándo se come, etc.
- Los utensilios que se necesitan para prepararlo.
- Los ingredientes que lleva.
- La forma de prepararlo.

Tacos de pollo.

DESAFÍO Ⓑ

Investiga sobre un(a) científico(a) importante del mundo hispano (por ejemplo, Mariano Barbacid) y prepara una presentación para la clase. Debes explicar:

- ¿Quién es? ¿De dónde es? ¿A qué se dedica?
- ¿Por qué es una figura relevante? ¿Ha inventado o descubierto algo importante?

Conferencia de Mariano Barbacid.

DESAFÍO Ⓒ

Haz una presentación sobre una celebración típica de un país hispano con fotografías y dibujos. Explica:

- Cuándo y dónde se celebra.
- Quiénes participan.
- En qué consiste.
- Cómo deben ir vestidos los participantes. Si hay platos o bebidas típicas...

Día de los difuntos (México).

ciento trece **113**

Para terminar

Activities

76. As students listen to the audio, have them take notes on the dishes mentioned—the name of each dish and ingredients. Before students answer the questions, have them get together with a partner and compare and contrast their notes. Then ask them to answer the questions individually. For the second part of this activity, you may want to have students work in small groups to agree on a celebration and design a menu that incorporates some of the dishes traditionally associated with the celebration. Then have groups present their menus to the class. Tell students to be prepared for questions from their classmates about the celebration, participants, traditions associated with it, etc.

77. To expand this activity, have students rewrite their partner's story offering a different version of the incident. They may, for instance, make the incident sound more dramatic or choose a more lighthearted tone. Invite volunteer students to share with the class both the first and second versions of their stories. Have the class vote on their favorite version.

78. Display students' work in the classroom and have the class vote on the best entry in each category.

🎧 **AUDIO SCRIPT**
See page 69M.

Answer Key

76. 1. c   2. b   3. a   4. a   5. c
▶ Answers will vary.
77. Answers will vary.
▶ Answers will vary.
▶ Answers will vary.
78. Answers will vary.

Additional Resources

Fans Online activities
Practice Workbook

HERITAGE LANGUAGE LEARNERS

- Ask students to describe another *desafío* that is related to the themes of this unit and one which the characters could have faced. To do this, students might research some other Hispanic food or beverage, scientific contributions made by Spanish speakers, or how people celebrate family events in the Americas or Spain. Students will make their suggestions to the class, which will vote on the best one. Then students will work in small groups or with a partner to compile more information and develop the *desafío*.

COOPERATIVE LEARNING

- Ask students to work in small groups and write ten questions related to Hispanic customs that have to do with food, health, or celebrations. Students will use these questions to survey their classmates. The questions may touch on healthful diets, medical symptoms, treatments, medical innovations, or celebrations, and may be taken from the activities, articles, and cultural features. Then assign groups to survey two other groups and note their opinions. Finally, have students tabulate all the responses. This could serve as a review of the unit topics.

MAPA CULTURAL

Sistemas de salud en el mundo hispano

Presentation

- This section presents information about different health-care systems from the Spanish-speaking world.

Activities	Standards	Resources
Mapa cultural	1.2, 2.1, 2.2, 3.1, 3.2, 5.1	
79.	1.1, 1.2, 2.1, 2.2, 3.1, 3.2, 4.2, 5.1, 5.2	

Cultural Topics

- **Científicos destacados.** Numerous Hispanic scientists have made important contributions to the field of medicine. Bernardo Houssay (Argentina) won the Nobel Prize in 1947 for his research on the role of pituitary hormones. Severo Ochoa (Spain) was awarded the Nobel Prize in 1959 for his research on the synthesis of RNA. María del Socorro Flores (Mexico) won the MEXWII 2006 award for her work on the diagnosis of amebiasis, a parasitic disease. In 2012, Susana López (Mexico) received the L'Oréal-UNESCO Award for her research on rotavirus disease, the second-leading cause of death among children.

- **Centros médicos destacados.** An increasing number of clinics and hospitals in Latin America are being recognized internationally. Clínica Alemana, in Santiago, Chile, is one of the best hospitals in the region. Fundación Santa Fe, a university hospital in Bogotá, is where Colombia's first liver and heart transplants were performed. Hospital Clínica Bíblica, located in San José, Costa Rica, was the second hospital in Latin America to receive accreditation by the Joint Commission International. ABC Medical Center, in Mexico City, has notable cardiovascular and neurological services.

Teaching Suggestions

Warm-Up / Independent Starter

- Ask students to jot down what they know about health care in their country (e.g., health-care system, insurance coverage, hospital networks).

Sistemas de salud en el mundo hispano

La salud es fundamental para el bienestar. Un sistema sanitario avanzado es una muestra del desarrollo económico y social de los pueblos. Durante los últimos años, los países hispanos han hecho progresos hacia la universalización de los sistemas de salud.

Hospital en Guadalajara (México).

El sistema mexicano: cobertura sanitaria universal

En México hasta 2004 la atención médica solo estaba disponible para los ciudadanos que pudieran pagar sus cuotas de la seguridad social a través de su empleo, o para quienes disponían de un seguro privado. En 2012, se logró la cobertura universal a través del Sistema de Protección Social en Salud (SPSS). Desde entonces, cada mexicano tiene acceso a una protección sanitaria en los centros de salud y hospitales de los Servicios Estatales de Salud.

Premio Príncipe de Asturias de Investigación Científica y Técnica

El doctor Arturo Álvarez-Buylla, licenciado en Investigación Biomédica por la Universidad Nacional Autónoma de México, recibió el Premio Príncipe de Asturias en 2011. Su principal campo de trabajo es el cerebro humano.

Turismo sanitario en Costa Rica

La diferencia entre los distintos sistemas sanitarios es la causa del llamado turismo sanitario: algunos pacientes aprovechan sus vacaciones para someterse a algún tratamiento médico en otro país en el que pueden encontrar servicios médicos de calidad a un precio más barato.

En América, uno de los destinos preferidos por los ciudadanos norteamericanos es Costa Rica, que ofrece un sistema sanitario de prestigio con precios y tiempo de espera mucho menores que en otros países. Los servicios más demandados son los tratamientos cosméticos y dentales, y otros tratamientos médicos y quirúrgicos más avanzados.

Hospital en San José (Costa Rica).

Differentiated Instruction

DEVELOPING LEARNERS

- Ask students to create a four-column chart to organize the information in the *Mapa cultural*. Each column will represent one of the paragraphs and the life expectancy chart. Students should copy the text titles and summarize the information contained therein. The main idea, plus the supporting details of each paragraph, will contribute to the summary. Review students' work for accuracy and then ask them to restate the information in their own words.

EXPANDING LEARNERS

- Have students do some more research on one or more of the scientists cited (Arturo Álvarez, Severo Ochoa, Bernardo Houssay, María del Socorro Flores, Susana López). You might also suggest the following Nobel Prize winners: Santiago Ramón y Cajal (Spain, 1906) and Mario Molina (Mexico, 1995). In addition to some biographical data, students should include a summary of the scientists' research and highlight their most important contributions to their respective fields. Encourage students to include some interesting anecdotal information on these scientists' lives or their work.

El Sistema Nacional de Salud de España

En España la atención sanitaria es pública, gratuita y universal, es decir, para todos los ciudadanos.

El Sistema Nacional de Salud se organiza en dos niveles asistenciales: la atención primaria, a través de los Centros de Salud, y la atención especializada, que se presta en Centros de especialidades y en hospitales.

La Organización Nacional de Trasplantes

España es líder mundial en la realización de trasplantes de órganos. La Organización Nacional de Trasplantes (ONT), creada en 1980, coordina la donación y el trasplante de órganos, tejidos y células en el conjunto del Sistema Sanitario Español.

Desde la creación de la ONT, el número de donantes en España se ha incrementado en un 280%. Los trasplantes que más se realizan son los de riñón, hígado, corazón y pulmón.

¿Sabías que...?

La esperanza de vida es el promedio de años que se calcula que puede llegar a vivir un recién nacido. Es un buen indicador del nivel de vida de una población.

ESPERANZA DE VIDA EN EL MUNDO HISPANO

	Hombres	Mujeres		Hombres	Mujeres
España	78	85	Argentina	72	79
Costa Rica	77	81	Uruguay	72	79
Chile	76	82	Paraguay	72	77
Estados Unidos	76	81	Venezuela	71	78
Cuba	76	80	Nicaragua	71	77
Panamá	74	79	República Dominicana	71	72
Perú	74	77	El Salvador	68	76
Colombia	73	80	Honduras	67	73
Ecuador	73	78	Guatemala	66	73
México	73	78	Bolivia	66	70

Datos de 2009. Fuente: Organización Mundial de la Salud (OMS). http://www.who.int/es/

79 **Sistemas sanitarios**

▶ **Investiga** y compara el sistema sanitario de tu país con el de otro país hispano. Después, comenta tus conclusiones con tus compañeros(as).

– Tipo de sistema de asistencia sanitaria (público o privado; universal o no; gratuito o no).
– Organización (atención primaria, atención especializada, etc.).
– Prestación farmacéutica (gratuidad de los medicamentos).
– Datos relevantes sobre la salud de la población (esperanza de vida, principales enfermedades, factores de riesgo, etc.).

HERITAGE LANGUAGE LEARNERS

• Assign some pairs of students a report on the rotavirus disease, and others one on amebiasis. Their reports should include the cause(s) of the disease and how it is spread, the symptoms, the primary victims, what tests and treatments are available, how prevention can be effected, complications, and what parts of the world are usually affected. Select two pairs to make a brief presentation in front of the class.

CRITICAL THINKING

• Ask students to study the life expectancy chart on the page. What factors do they think contribute to the longevity in some of these nations, and a shorter life span in others? Do they think good genes play a role? Or do a healthful diet and lifestyle have more impact? Does a lack of adequate health care influence longevity? Engage students in a whole-class discussion on this topic.

MAPA CULTURAL

Sistemas de salud en el mundo hispano

Preparation

■ Invite students to share their Independent Starters. On the board, list some of the things students mention regarding the health-care system, insurance coverage, hospitals, etc. Then, as a class, go over the two (from Mexico and from Spain) health-care systems mentioned in the *Mapa cultural*, and compare those systems to the system in this country. Although the two systems presented in the *Mapa cultural* are public, there are other countries in Latin America that offer universal health care through dual (public and private) systems. You may want to mention the Chilean health system, where about 68% of the population is covered by the public system and the remaining 32% is covered by private insurance plans or not-for-profit agencies.

■ Focus students' attention on the *Esperanza de vida* chart on page 115 and give them a few moments to read it. Explain that advances in medicine and health care have dramatically increased life expectancy in Latin America. According to a report published by the Pan American Health Organization, the average life expectancy in the region has risen 45 years—from 29 years in 1900 to 74 years in 2010.

Activities

79. You may want to divide the class into small groups and assign each group a different Spanish-speaking country to research. Then, groups come together in a whole-class session and report their findings. The comparison between the different health-care systems can be done as a class. To conclude the discussion, you may wish to have the class select the best three systems. Have them justify their choices.

Answer Key

79. Answers will vary.

Additional Resources

Fans Online activities
Practice Workbook

115

ESCRITURA

Recomendaciones de viajes

Presentation

- In this section, students will practice and extend their writing skills. They will apply the vocabulary and grammar they have learned in this unit to create the health section of a travel guide.

Activities	Standards	Resources
Escritura	1.1, 1.2, 1.3, 2.1, 2.2, 3.1, 3.2, 5.1, 5.2	

Teaching Suggestions

Warm-Up / Independent Starter

- Ask students to think about the last trip they took—it may be an international, domestic, or local trip. Have them list the things they did to prepare for the trip as well as the things they wished they had done to prepare themselves better.

Preparation

- Have students share their Independent Starters with the class. Did any of the students look for information about health-related issues before their trip? Most students do not think about these issues when traveling. Therefore, to get them thinking about this topic, you may want to discuss some of these questions with the class: *¿Qué tipo de emergencias médicas podrían surgir en un viaje? ¿Qué se debe saber antes de viajar sobre la asistencia sanitaria en el país de destino? ¿Qué problemas pueden surgir en algunos países al beber agua del grifo o consumir ciertos alimentos? ¿Cómo podemos prepararnos si hay enfermedades endémicas (e.g., dengue, malaria, rabia) en nuestro destino?* Then, discuss with students good sources of information where they would find the answers to these or similar questions.

- Ask for a volunteer to read the *Textos prescriptivos* box aloud. Explain that process texts are expository. The purpose of these texts is to explain, define, instruct, or share information with readers. The writing style is formal, but the language is simple and easy to understand. In a process text, sentences are generally short and direct, and explanations are clear and succinct.

Recomendaciones de viajes

Textos prescriptivos

Los textos prescriptivos tienen como objetivo explicar al lector cómo hacer algo. Este tipo de textos están muy presentes en la vida cotidiana: recetas de cocina, instrucciones para usar un aparato, normas de comportamiento, leyes, reglamentos, etc.

La información de los textos prescriptivos debe formularse de forma sencilla, clara, precisa y fácil de seguir, evitando ambigüedades e interpretaciones erróneas.

En estos textos se utilizan con frecuencia los verbos en imperativo o en infinitivo, y las construcciones con *hay que* o con *se*.

En las guías de viajes se da todo tipo de información de interés para el viajero sobre el país o la ciudad: museos y monumentos, mapas y transporte, hoteles, restaurantes, tiendas, etc. Y también suelen ofrecer datos de utilidad y recomendaciones relativas a horarios, cambio de moneda, clima, costumbres, salud o seguridad.

En esta unidad vas a escribir la sección de salud para una guía de viajes de algún país hispanohablante.

Piensa

- Elige un país hispanohablante que te gustaría visitar. ¿Qué necesitarías saber sobre cuestiones relacionadas con la salud si viajaras a ese país? Escribe al menos seis preguntas sobre estos temas u otros que se te ocurran:

  - Posibles enfermedades.
  - Vacunación.
  - Botiquín de primeros auxilios.
  - Sistema de asistencia sanitaria.
  - Emergencias, hospitales y farmacias.
  - Consumo seguro de alimentos.

  Modelo
  ¿Debo contratar un seguro médico para viajar a Perú?

- Busca en Internet las respuestas a las preguntas que escribiste. Consulta fuentes fiables, como portales oficiales de turismo o de salud, guías de viajes, etc.

- Selecciona algunas imágenes que podrían ilustrar tu guía para hacerla más didáctica y atractiva.

116 ciento dieciséis

Rubric for Evaluation

	Content	Organization	Conventions
1 point	Irrelevant or inaccurate information. Inappropriate images. Limited or inaccurate word choices.	Confusing organization. Information is not easy to locate. Random formatting. Transitions are not present.	Many errors in spelling, punctuation, grammar, and usage. Errors obscure meaning.
3 points	Mostly relevant information. Some images lack significance. Some inaccurate word choices.	Organization is clear, but some information may not be easy to locate. Appropriate formatting. Some transitions are present.	Some errors in spelling, punctuation, grammar, and usage. Errors don't interfere with meaning.

Escribe

■ Redacta el borrador de tu texto respondiendo a las preguntas que escribiste en el paso anterior.

Utiliza construcciones impersonales con *se* y las expresiones del cuadro.

■ Pon un título atractivo al texto y cita al final las fuentes que utilizaste.

Expresiones útiles

Se recomienda…	*It's recommended …*
Es aconsejable…	*It's advisable …*
Se debe…	*You/One should …*
Es necesario…	*It's necessary …*

Si viajo a Perú…

¿Debo contratar un seguro médico?

Casi todos los hospitales peruanos exigen el pago al contado de los tratamientos, y la estancia en una clínica privada puede resultar muy cara, así que se recomienda contratar un seguro de viaje con antelación.

¿Cómo puedo evitar el mal de altura?

Para evitar el mal de altura o soroche, se recomienda ascender gradualmente para la debida aclimatación, descansar el día de llegada, consumir comidas ligeras, beber abundante líquido y tener a mano caramelos de limón o chicles. Si sufre del corazón, consulte con su médico antes de viajar.

Fuentes: *Perú. Guías visuales.* El País Aguilar (2012) y http://www.peru.travel/es

Revisa

■ Cuando termines de escribir tu texto, revísalo.

– ¿La información es clara y comprensible? ¿Está bien organizada?
– ¿Empleaste un vocabulario y unas construcciones gramaticales correctas?

■ Intercambia tu texto con tu compañero(a). Lee el suyo y completa una tabla como esta con valores del 1 al 5 (5 es la mejor puntuación).

Criterio	Guía de preguntas	Puntuación
Información	¿Es completa? ¿Echas de menos alguna información relevante?	
Redacción	¿El texto está redactado de manera clara y comprensible? ¿Hay alguna parte que no entiendas? ¿Se repiten mucho algunas palabras?	
Gramática y ortografía	¿Está bien escrito el texto? ¿Tiene algún error gramatical u ortográfico? ¿Se usan bien los signos de puntuación?	
Presentación	¿La guía resulta atractiva? ¿Son relevantes las imágenes seleccionadas?	

■ Devuelve el texto a su autor(a). Revisa el tuyo y pásalo a limpio.

Comparte

■ Presenta tu trabajo a la clase. Entre todos(as), elijan las secciones de salud más completas y visualmente más atractivas.

ciento diecisiete **117**

	Content	Organization	Conventions
5 points	Relevant and complete information. Images complement the text effectively. Precise and clear word choices.	Well-organized information, easy to locate. Excellent formatting. Uses appropriate transitions when needed.	Few, if any, errors in spelling, punctuation, grammar, and usage. Excellent command of the Spanish language.

Step-by-Step Instructions

Piensa

■ As students research their topics, remind them that they should name their sources. A good source of information for American citizens traveling abroad is the U.S. Department of State website (travel.state.gov). Tell students to go to the International Travel link, and then select a country.

■ Encourage students to think of a caption for each photo they decide to include in their guides. Images are often the first element a reader notices, and the captions that accompany those images should provide the reader with some context for the information he or she is about to read.

Escribe

■ Remind students to spend some time developing a good introduction. They should catch the reader's attention, give some background information about their topic, and explain the importance of the information they are about to share with the reader.

■ Ask students to consider adding graphic aids to help the reader find information. A logical order and strong organization will also contribute to clear and easy-to-locate information. Remind students to include contact information for the traveler.

Revisa

■ In addition to the peer-editing chart provided in this section, have students answer these questions as they review their classmates' guides: Is the guide well put together? Are the images placed appropriately? Do graphics, fonts, color, and headings lead to a better understanding of the information?

Comparte

■ Ask students to be prepared for questions from the class. They may write some additional information on index cards to help them answer questions they might get from classmates. Allow for rehearsal time and stress the importance of using time wisely.

Evaluation

■ Distribute copies of the rubric to students and discuss the evaluation criteria. Ask students to refer to the rubric as they prepare their writing and as they evaluate their classmates' guides.

117

REPASO

Vocabulario

Presentation

- In this section, students will review all key vocabulary from the unit, organized by themes, to prepare for an assessment. Students will complete practice activities for each *Desafío*.

Activities	Standards	Resources
1.	1.2	
2.	1.2, 3.1	
3.	1.2	

Teaching Suggestions

Warm-Up / Independent Starter

- Have students express their reactions, in writing, to the following situations: *sacar malas notas, no comer en todo el día, ganar un premio, los amigos que mienten.*

Preparation

- Ask students to share their answers from the Independent Starter in small groups, and then have one student from each group report to the class. You may want to keep track of students' answers on the board. Have groups come up with other situations that would prompt other reactions that have not been mentioned. Students may also use body positions in their examples (e.g., *estar agachado un largo rato*). Then have groups share their situations with the class and have the class react with expressions from the vocabulary list.

- Have students choose six words from *En el restaurante* to describe their last experience at a restaurant. Ask for volunteers to share their six words, then have the rest of the class try to reconstruct the experience.

Activities

1. To extend this activity, have student pairs create a menu with the foods mentioned in the activity. They can add two or three drinks and a few dessert choices, but the first and main courses should be variations of the foods from this activity (e.g., *pechuga de pavo rellena de puré de berenjena, lomo de ternera con huevos revueltos*). Have students share their menus with the class. Then, hold a class vote to select the most creative menu.

REPASO Vocabulario

En el restaurante

Carne

las alitas de pollo	*chicken wings*
la carne molida	*ground beef*
las chuletas de cordero	*lamb chops*
el filete de pavo	*turkey fillet*
el jamón	*ham*
el lomo de ternera	*veal loin*
la pechuga de pavo	*turkey breast*

Pescado y marisco

el bacalao	*cod*
el cangrejo	*crab*
la langosta	*lobster*
los langostinos	*prawns*
el pez espada	*swordfish*

Verduras y hortalizas

el aguacate	*avocado*	el pepino	*cucumber*
la berenjena	*eggplant*	el pimiento	*pepper*
la calabacita	*squash*		

Fruta

la cereza	*cherry*	la mora	*blackberry*
la ciruela	*plum*	la pasa	*raisin*
el durazno	*peach*	la toronja	*grapefruit*
la frambuesa	*raspberry*		

Otros alimentos

la canela	*cinnamon*	las lentejas	*lentils*
los hongos	*mushrooms*	la miel	*honey*
los huevos revueltos	*scrambled eggs*	la nuez	*nut*

Preparación de los alimentos

al horno	*baked*	relleno(a)	*filled*

La sala de urgencias

Enfermedades y síntomas

el asma	*asthma*
el corte	*cut*
el esguince	*sprain*
el infarto	*heart attack*
las molestias	*ache*
las náuseas	*nausea*
la quemadura	*burn*
marearse	*to get dizzy*
perder el conocimiento	*to lose consciousness*
sangrar	*to bleed*
tener el colesterol alto	*to have high cholesterol*
vomitar	*to throw up*
contagioso(a)	*contagious*
grave	*serious*

Especialistas

el/la cardiólogo(a)	*cardiologist*
el/la dermatólogo(a)	*dermatologist*
el/la oncólogo(a)	*oncologist*

Diagnóstico y tratamiento

ingresar	*to hospitalize*
tomar la presión arterial	*to take one's blood pressure*
la vacuna	*vaccine*

¡Atención!

asistir (a)	*to attend (to)*
ayudar	*to assist*

Estados físicos y anímicos

(in)cómodo(a)	*(un)comfortable*
(des)contento(a)	*(un)happy*
de buen/mal humor	*in a good/bad mood*
desanimado(a)	*depressed*
esperanzado(a)	*hopeful*
harto(a) (de)	*fed up (with)*
muerto(a) de hambre	*very hungry*
muerto(a) de sed	*very thirsty*
muerto(a) de sueño	*very sleepy*
alegrarse	*to be happy*
avergonzar	*to embarrass*
ponerse furioso(a)	*to become furious*

Ciclo de la vida

crecer	*to grow*
envejecer	*to get old*
morir	*to die*

Posturas

acostado(a)	*lying down*
agachado(a)	*crouching*
de perfil	*in profile*
de pie	*standing*
de rodillas	*kneeling*
sentado(a)	*seated*

¡Atención!

avergonzado(a)	*embarrased*
embarazada	*pregnant*

Differentiated Instruction

DEVELOPING LEARNERS

- Explain to students that many verbs and nouns have mutually related terms. For example: *gritar → el grito*. Ask students to review the nouns and verbs in the vocabulary list and prepare a word family chart like the one below.

Verbo	Nombre
cortar	el corte
sangrar	la sangre
avergonzarse	la vergüenza

- Then have students write sentences with five of these word pairs.

EXPANDING LEARNERS

- Divide the class into two teams to play a word game. One player from each team chooses a word from the new vocabulary (e.g., *desanimado*) and writes it on the board for his or her team only. By turns, teammates will say a word that starts with each letter in *desanimado* (e.g., *divertido, esperanzada, sentado, acuerdo, niño, incómodo, morir, antipático, día, otro*). For every correct word, the team scores one point; two points if it is listed on the *Repaso* page. If a player fails to name a word, his or her team loses one point.

DESAFÍO 1

1 **¡A comer!** Une las palabras de las dos columnas.

(A)	(B)
1. lomo	a. revueltos
2. berenjenas	b. de ternera
3. alitas	c. de cordero
4. chuletas	d. de pollo
5. pechuga	e. rellenas
6. huevos	f. de pavo

DESAFÍO 2

2 **¿Qué le pasa?** Adivina qué enfermedad tienen o qué les pasó a estas personas.

1. Tengo que comer alimentos sin grasa, comer más fruta y verdura, y hacer ejercicio.

2. Me mareé y me caí... Y cuando abrí los ojos, no recordaba qué había pasado. Me sorprendió verme en el suelo.

3. Tengo ataques de tos y dificultad para respirar.

4. Esta mañana estaba corriendo y me hice mucho daño en el pie. Lo tengo muy hinchado.

5. Estaba cortando la verdura y, de pronto, sentí un gran dolor y empecé a sangrar.

6. Me dolía el brazo y tenía molestias en el pecho.

DESAFÍO 3

3 **Mi diario.** Completa este fragmento del diario de Sonia.

de buen humor	de pie	desanimada
sentada	muerta de sueño	furiosa

Lunes, 28 de octubre

Ayer estaba triste y ___1___, pero hoy me siento bien y estoy ___2___. Esta mañana, estaba ___3___ en un banco a la puerta de la escuela cuando vi a Jeff. Yo estaba ___4___, como todos los lunes, pero al verlo, me desperté de golpe *(suddenly)*. Y vi que venía hacia mí, ¡qué nervios! Entonces Amanda, que estaba ___5___ junto a la puerta, me miró con una cara horrible. Y cuando vio que Jeff hablaba conmigo, se puso ___6___ y se marchó. Creo que a Amanda le gusta Jeff... Pero es que yo estoy enamorada de él. ¡Y creo que le gusto! ☺

ciento diecinueve 119

---

2. Have students work with a partner to come up with a script for one of the situations described in this activity. In the dialogue, the patient explains his or her symptoms and the incident that gave rise to these symptoms. The health professional asks relevant questions, gives a diagnosis, and prescribes a treatment. The patient should ask the health professional for clarification of some aspects of the diagnosis or treatment. Invite volunteer pairs to role-play their dialogues for the class.

3. Have students write an ending for this story. Will Sonia and Jeff end up together or will Amanda come between them? Or, perhaps Jeff has other plans. Call on individual students to share their endings with the class.

Answer Key

1. 1. b 2. e 3. d 4. c 5. f 6. a

2. Answers will vary. Sample answers:
   1. Parece que tiene el nivel de colesterol alto.
   2. Perdió el conocimiento.
   3. Probablemente tenga asma y quizás tuvo un ataque de asma.
   4. Es posible que tenga un esguince en el tobillo.
   5. Se cortó con el cuchillo y tiene un corte en el dedo.
   6. Quizás tenga principios de infarto.

3. 1. desanimada 4. muerta de sueño
     2. de buen humor 5. de pie
     3. sentada 6. furiosa

Additional Resources

Fans Online activities
Practice Workbook

HERITAGE LANGUAGE LEARNERS

• Direct students to the vocabulary on page 118 and ask them to come up with other words or expressions that are similar. Encourage them to ask family members for suggestions, or to use their dictionaries for examples. These examples might include: *de buen humor: contento; de pie: parado; desanimado: deprimido, abatido, sin ganas; muerto de sueño: agotado, exhausto, no poder más; furioso: de muy mal genio, violento.* Have students share these words with their classmates, who should write them in their notebooks.

TOTAL PHYSICAL RESPONSE (TPR)

• In small groups, students will play a version of "Jeopardy." You will give them answers and they will supply the corresponding questions by standing up and being the first to ask them. You may use the vocabulary, grammar topics, and cultural information discussed while working on this unit. For example:
   1. *Duraznos, toronjas y ciruelas. (¿Qué son frutas?)*
   2. *Desarrolló una vacuna contra la malaria. (¿Quién es Manuel Patarroyo?)*
   3. *Se bebe con una bombilla. (¿Qué es el mate?)*

119

Unit 2
REPASO
Gramática

Presentation

- Students will review grammatical structures presented in the unit. Each grammar point is cross-referenced to the corresponding page on which it was introduced. The activities here provide systematic practice by *Desafío*.

Activities	Standards	Resources
4.	1.2, 3.1	
5.	1.2, 3.1	
6.	1.2	
7. Cultura	1.2, 1.3, 2.1, 2.2, 3.1	

Teaching Suggestions

Warm-Up / Independent Starter

- Ask students to analyze the following sentences and jot down what they think each one expresses. Explain that context clues are not provided so that they focus on the use and meaning of *ser* and *estar* in each case.
  1. *Jessica es alegre, pero está triste.*
  2. *Soy buena, pero estoy mala.*
  3. *Es caro, pero está barato.*

Preparation

- Ask students to get together with a classmate and share and discuss their Independent Starters. Then have pairs add context clues to the sentences to make the meaning clearer (e.g., *Jessica es una persona alegre y optimista, pero hoy está triste porque se murió su perrito. Ese perfume es caro, pero ahora está barato porque lo pusieron en oferta*). Ask students to share their sentences with the class. You may want to write some of their examples on the board. Then have students think of other examples to illustrate the different uses and meanings of *ser* and *estar* studied in this unit.

- Divide the class into five groups and assign each group one of these topics: *el pronombre se, pronombres de objeto directo e indirecto, verbos con preposición, artículos,* and *voz pasiva*. Have groups summarize, in their own words, their assigned topic and come up with four original examples to illustrate it. Then ask groups to present their grammar point to the class. Clarify any questions students may have.

120

Construcciones impersonales. El pronombre *se* (pág. 80)

EL PRONOMBRE SE IMPERSONAL
Se habla español en más de 20 países.

USO DE SE + VERBO EN TERCERA PERSONA
Se prohíbe comer en clase.
Se sabe que las verduras son saludables.
Se vende casa de campo.
Se necesitan cocineros con experiencia.

EL PRONOMBRE SE DE INVOLUNTARIEDAD
A mi padre se le perdieron las llaves.

Los verbos con preposición (pág. 92)

acostumbrarse a asistir a atreverse a ayudar a renunciar a	amenazar con casarse con contar con enojarse con soñar con
acordarse de alegrarse de darse cuenta de depender de despedirse de	confiar en consistir en fijarse en insistir en pensar en

La voz pasiva (pág. 104)

FORMACIÓN DE LA VOZ PASIVA

> sujeto paciente (receptor) + verbo en voz pasiva + complemento agente (con por)

El partido fue interrumpido por una tormenta.

USO DE LA VOZ PASIVA
- En español se usa poco la voz pasiva:
  - Con un objeto indirecto.
  - Con los tiempos progresivos.
  - Con verbos de percepción (ver, oír, sentir...) o emoción (querer, odiar...).
- En instrucciones no se suele usar la voz pasiva. Se prefiere la construcción se + verbo en 3.ª persona.

Los pronombres de objeto directo e indirecto (pág. 82)

PRONOMBRES DE OBJETO DIRECTO		PRONOMBRES DE OBJETO INDIRECTO	
me	nos	me	nos
te	os	te	os
lo, la	los, las	le (se)	les (se)

Ella va a dárselos./Ella se los va a dar.

Los artículos (pág. 94)

En español llevan artículo:
- Los nombres abstractos y los nombres usados con un sentido general.
- Las partes del cuerpo y las prendas de vestir.
- Los títulos (excepto don y doña).
- Los días, las horas y las fechas.
- Los nombres de las calles, los parques, etc.
- Los porcentajes y los números.

En español se omite el artículo:
- Para referirnos a seres u objetos no específicos.
- Con verbos como comprar, necesitar, dar, traer, hacer, etc., para hablar de nombres no contables en singular o de nombres contables en plural.
- Con el verbo ser, para hablar de oficios, cargos y ocupaciones.
- Con verbos como tener, llevar o ponerse, para referirnos al atuendo o a propiedades típicas de un objeto.

Ser y estar (pág. 106)

ADJETIVOS QUE CAMBIAN DE SIGNIFICADO

	SER	ESTAR
atento(a)	courteous	alert
callado(a)	reserved	quiet
listo(a)	smart	ready
malo(a)	bad	sick, ill
orgulloso(a)	arrogant	proud
rico(a)	rich	delicious
seguro(a)	safe	sure, certain
verde	green	unripe
vivo(a)	bright, sharp	alive

120 ciento veinte

Differentiated Instruction

DEVELOPING LEARNERS

- To strengthen students' understanding of *ser* and *estar*, ask them to review the uses, copy them in their notebooks, and beside each one write at least one original sentence. For example:

Ser
- *fecha y hora*: *Hoy es el 20 de marzo. Son las tres de la tarde.*
- *propósito o función*: *La canela es para el mate.*

Estar
- *estados*: *Estoy furiosa contigo.*
- *en expresiones idiomáticas*: *Estamos muertos de sueño.*

EXPANDING LEARNERS

- Refer students to the *verbos con preposición* and *verbos sin preposición* on page 92. Then ask them to work with a partner and create two or three short dialogues in which they use these verbs, along with others they may know. Invite pairs to act out their dialogues in front of the class. For example:
  A. *¿Te acordaste de traer las llaves?*
  B. *Por supuesto. Sabes que siempre puedes contar conmigo.*

DESAFÍO 1

4 **Fue involuntario.** Completa estas oraciones con los verbos del cuadro. Usa el pronombre *se* y el pronombre de objeto indirecto correspondiente.

> acabarse   caerse   olvidarse   perderse   romperse

1. Mi hermana tiene mala suerte. El verano pasado, ___1___ la cámara el segundo día del viaje y no pudo hacer más fotos.
2. Anoche no pude entrar en casa. ¡___2___ las llaves dentro!
3. Queríamos hacer un pastel de fresas para el cumpleaños de Laura, pero cuando lo estábamos preparando, ___3___ el azúcar… Así que tuvimos que comprar un pastel.
4. ¡Qué desastre! Al mesero ___4___ la bandeja al suelo y ___5___ todos los platos.

 DESAFÍO 2

5 **Sueños.** Completa estas oraciones. Usa las preposiciones adecuadas.

1. Desde pequeño(a), sueño…
2. No consigo acostumbrarme…
3. Mi familia y yo nos alegramos…
4. Siempre confío…
5. Lo siento mucho. No me acordé…
6. Antes no me atrevía…

 DESAFÍO 3

6 **¿Ser o estar?** Completa estas oraciones con los verbos *ser* o *estar*.

1. Yo siempre _____ atento en las clases para entender las explicaciones.
2. Mi hermano _____ muy orgulloso de sí mismo porque saca muy buenas notas.
3. He estudiado mucho, pero no _____ segura de la respuesta a este ejercicio.
4. Gonzalo me cae bien, aunque _____ muy callado y bastante tímido.

 CULTURA

7 **Comida, salud… y bodas.** Responde a estas preguntas.

1. ¿Qué son las tapas? ¿De dónde son típicas y por qué se llaman así?
2. ¿Quién es Manuel Patarroyo? ¿Cuál es su descubrimiento más importante?
3. ¿Qué tradiciones propias de la celebración de una boda en México conoces?

Activities

4. To extend this activity, have students work with a partner to choose one of the situations and write a paragraph to explain the scene. In their paragraphs, students should use *se* to express an involuntary or accidental action and verbs that require the use of a preposition. For example: *El mesero no se dio cuenta de que el comedor estaba lleno. Chocó contra un cliente y se le cayó la bandeja al suelo. El cliente lo ayudó a recoger los platos rotos.* Suggest to students that they illustrate their stories. Exhibit students' work in the classroom.

6. Have students write sentences like the ones in this activity for the rest of the adjectives (i.e., *listo, malo, rico, verde, vivo*). Then ask them to exchange their work with a classmate and complete each other's sentences.

Answer Key

4. 1. se le perdió   4. se le cayó
     2. Se me olvidaron   5. se le rompieron
     3. se nos acabó

5. Answers will vary. Sample answers:
     1. … con ser diseñadora.
     2. … a levantarme temprano.
     3. … de verte.
     4. … en ti.
     5. … de la cita.
     6. … a hablar en público.

6. 1. estoy   3. estoy
     2. está   4. es

7. Answers will vary. Sample answers:
     1. Son pequeñas porciones de comida. Son típicas de España.
     2. Es un científico colombiano que creó una vacuna contra la malaria.
     3. En las bodas mexicanas, el novio suele darle a la novia 13 monedas, conocidas como *arras*. También es común que los padrinos aten a los novios con un lazo.

Additional Resources

Fans Online activities
Practice Workbook

HERITAGE LANGUAGE LEARNERS

- Review the adjectives introduced in this unit that change meaning with *ser* and *estar*. Then ask students to write a list of other adjectives that change meaning with these verbs and explain the difference.

	con **ser**	*con* **estar**
aburrido	boring	to be bored
bueno	good	tasty
cansado	tiresome	tired
decidido	resolute	decided
consciente	aware	conscious
despierto	alert	awake
interesado	self-seeking	interested
loco	insane	nuts

MULTIPLE INTELLIGENCES:
Verbal-Linguistic Intelligence

- Ask students to write some advice on maintaining a healthful lifestyle. They may suggest a sound diet, exercise, maintaining their ideal weight, avoiding stress, getting proper health care, and keeping positive relationships with family and friends. Students should use *se* with a verb in the third person to express this advice. For example: *Se debe comer entre 4 y 5 porciones de verduras y frutas todos los días. Se prohíbe beber refrescos con azúcar.* Discuss students' suggestions and post them throughout the classroom.

121

PROYECTO

Sobre la salud

Presentation

- In this section, students will apply the vocabulary, grammar, and cultural information they have learned in this unit to create a comic strip to raise awareness about a health issue of their choice.

Activities	Standards	Resources
Paso 1	1.1, 3.1	
Paso 2	1.2, 3.1	
Paso 3	1.3, 3.1	
Paso 4	1.3, 3.1	
Paso 5	1.3, 3.1, 5.2	
Paso 6	1.3, 3.1, 5.2	

Teaching Suggestions

Warm-Up / Independent Starter

- Ask students to jot down some information (e.g., characters, plot) about a comic strip they know.

Preparation

- Have students share their Independent Starters. If the class is not familiar with some of the comic strips that students mention, have them describe what the comic is about. As a class, discuss some of the main features of comic strips as well as their aims (e.g., entertainment, propaganda, advertisement, education).

- Divide the class into small groups. Since images are an integral part of this project, try to place an artistically inclined student in each group. Suggest that groups divide the tasks (e.g., research, organization, writing the dialogues, drawing or taking pictures). However, all major decisions need to be discussed and made as a group.

Step-by-Step Instructions

Paso 1

- Suggest to groups that they create a short questionnaire to find out which health-related issues most concern the class. Then allow groups to administer their questionnaires and use the results to choose a topic for their comics. To avoid repetition of topics, have different groups focus their questionnaires on different health-related issues (e.g., physical health, mental health, lifestyle, social well-being).

Un cómic

sobre la salud

En pequeños grupos, van a elaborar un cómic para concienciar a sus compañeros(as) sobre algún tema relacionado con la salud.

PASO 1 Elige el tema

- Decidan sobre qué quieren hacer el cómic.

  Aquí tienen algunas ideas:
  - Concienciar sobre algún tema. Por ejemplo, la importancia de donar sangre.
  - Informar sobre la importancia de unos hábitos saludables. Por ejemplo, cuidar la alimentación, hacer deporte…
  - Dar consejos para evitar el estrés y la ansiedad.

  También pueden preguntar a sus compañeros(as) qué temas relacionados con la salud les preocupan o buscar en Internet qué problemas afectan a los(as) chicos(as) de su edad.

Mira, aquí en el folleto pone que la sangre no se puede fabricar y que se necesita para muchas operaciones por enfermedades y accidentes de tráfico.

PASO 2 Busca información

- Busquen información sobre el tema que eligieron y tomen notas. Apunten las dudas que tengan para intentar resolverlas con ayuda de un(a) médico(a) o experto(a).

PASO 3 Define los personajes

- Piensen en los personajes de su cómic.
  - ¿Cuántos personajes va a haber?
  - ¿Va a haber un protagonista?
  - ¿Los personajes van a ser conocidos: un superhéroe, un personaje de cómic, un actor o cantante famoso…? También pueden protagonizar el cómic ustedes mismos o sus compañeros(as).

- Si los personajes son inventados, completen una ficha para cada uno con estos datos y hagan un dibujo.

Mis personajes

Nombre: _____

Edad: _____

Características físicas: _____

Rasgos de personalidad: _____

Cómo va vestido(a): _____

Rubric for Evaluation

	Content	Organization	Presentation
1 point	Limited relevance. Information is incomplete or not based on research. Dialogues do not relate well to scenes.	Inefficient use of time. Scenes and sequence are disorganized or unclear. Connections are very general or hard to understand.	Unclear communication. Confusing images and captions. Delivery is not fluent. Many errors in vocabulary and grammar.
3 points	Mostly relevant. Information is correct but some of it lacks significance. Dialogues are related to the scenes.	Time is used well. Scenes are mostly organized but sequence lacks some clarity. Most connections are easy to understand.	Clear communication and fluent delivery. Images and captions mostly clear. Mostly correct vocabulary and grammar.

PASO 4 Escribe el guion

- Escriban el guion de su cómic. Especifiquen los siguientes aspectos para cada viñeta:

  – ¿Qué personajes intervienen?
  – ¿Dónde se desarrolla la escena?
  – ¿Qué hacen los personajes?
  – ¿Cuál es su estado de ánimo?

- Escriban los diálogos de las viñetas.

> **VIÑETA 1**
>
> Luis, Sonia y Roberto están en la puerta de la escuela. Están de pie, hablando. Al lado de la escuela hay un autobús para donar sangre.
>
> LUIS (contento): ¿Qué les parece que vayamos a donar?
> ROBERTO (poco animado): Mejor otro día, que esta noche hay fiesta...

PASO 5 Desarrolla las viñetas

- Decidan la forma y dimensiones de las viñetas y dibújenlas.

  Si los protagonistas son ustedes o sus compañeros(as), pueden hacer fotografías.

- Escriban los textos definitivos de las viñetas.

VIÑETA 2

PASO 6 Presenta tu cómic

- Presenten su cómic a sus compañeros(as). ¿Cuál les gusta más? ¿Por qué?

Unidad 2

Autoevaluación

¿Qué has aprendido en esta unidad?

Haz estas actividades para comprobar tu progreso.

Evalúa tus habilidades. Para cada punto, di Muy bien, Bien o Necesito practicar más.

a. ¿Puedes hablar sobre alimentos y restaurantes?

▶ Escribe una crítica sobre tu restaurante preferido o sobre el restaurante que menos te gusta.

b. ¿Puedes hablar sobre la salud?

▶ Escribe un resumen de lo que pasa en la enfermería de la escuela un día normal. Explica con qué tipo de dolores o enfermedades van ustedes allí generalmente y lo que la enfermera les suele decir que hagan.

c. ¿Puedes referirte a estados físicos y anímicos?

▶ Describe tu foto de familia favorita. Identifica a todas las personas, describe su postura en la foto y cuenta una breve anécdota sobre cada uno.

PROYECTO

Sobre la salud

Paso 2

- Make sure students understand the importance of using reputable sources. Students should keep a record of their sources. Remind them that if a piece of information is not common knowledge, they need to provide a source.

Paso 3

- Emphasize that comics are a visual medium. There is no space for a detailed character description, so characters should be shown.

Paso 4

- Remind students that in a comic strip they are breaking down the dialogue into sequences, or *viñetas*. The dialogue is usually preceded by a plot outline, like the one shown in the example. Emphasize that the dialogue should be "seen." Therefore, the characters' lines should be short.

Paso 5

- Suggest that students divide a blank page or large poster board into panels for their story. Then have them fill in the panels with their drawings or photos.

Paso 6

- You may want to allow students to promote their awareness campaigns in school.

Evaluation

- Distribute copies of the rubric to students. Discuss the evaluation criteria and explain how this project will be graded. Encourage students to refer to the rubric as they prepare their projects.

Content

- Explain that images should help the reader understand the message of the story, and convey emotion, mood, and action. The dialogues should be directly related to the scene and the characters easy to identify.

Organization

- Ask students to consider the sequence of their images carefully. Stress that the connections between the images and the dialogue should be easy to comprehend, and the progression of the action should be clearly understood.

Presentation

- You may wish to have groups role-play their comic strips.

	Content	Organization	Presentation
5 points	Relevant, interesting, significant, and well-researched information. Scenes and dialogues are well matched and enhance comprehension of the story.	Time is used wisely. Scenes are clearly organized in a logical sequence. Connections are clear and easy to understand.	Clear and fluent communication. Images and captions are easy to understand. Correct and complete vocabulary and grammar.

HACIA EL AP* EXAM

Interpretive Communication: Audio Texts

Presentation

- These pages present students with a sample activity from the "Interpretive Communication: Audio Texts" portion of the AP* Spanish Language and Culture Exam. Students will read an authentic text from the Spanish-speaking world, listen to an authentic audio selection, and answer multiple-choice questions based on the sources.

Activities	Standards	Resources
Interpretive Communication: Audio Texts	1.1, 1.2, 2.1, 2.2, 3.1, 3.2, 5.1, 5.2	Audio

Preparing for the Exam

About This Section

- The "Interpretive Communication: Audio Texts" section of the AP* Exam requires students to read and listen or simply listen to authentic sources from the Spanish-speaking world and answer comprehension questions based on their understanding. The section lasts approximately 55 minutes, and contains a total of 35 questions. These questions are divided among several activities, which may contain either print texts and audios, or simply audio selections. This section of the textbook, however, only contains one practice activity, so you may wish to prepare additional practice activities if you would like to simulate the conditions of an actual exam.

- The amount of time given for each source in the exam depends on the length and complexity of the text or audio, as well as the number of questions that follow. You may wish to set a strict time limit while administering the practice activity on these pages in order to simulate the testing conditions. Or, you may wish to allow students more time in order to put into practice the *estrategias* given. Students may need approximately four minutes to read the introduction and *Fuente número 1*. You may then give them approximately two minutes to read the introduction to the audio and preview the questions before playing the audio. Remind students that the audio will be played twice.

Hacia el AP* Exam

Interpretive Communication: Audio Texts

Presentación

La segunda prueba del examen AP* tiene dos partes: una que mide la comprensión de un texto oral y otra que combina la comprensión oral con la comprensión lectora. La prueba consta de varios textos y grabaciones de audio seguidos de preguntas de opción múltiple. Los textos y las grabaciones proceden de fuentes auténticas: periódicos, revistas, páginas web, cadenas de radio y otros medios de comunicación del mundo hispano.

En las preguntas que siguen a cada texto, tienes que escoger la opción que mejor contesta cada pregunta. Estas preguntas están basadas en los objetivos de aprendizaje establecidos por los organizadores del examen.

Estrategias

Antes de escuchar

- Lee el título de la grabación. Esto te permitirá tener una idea de cuál es el tema y predecir o anticipar el contenido de la grabación.

Primera escucha

- Identifica el tema central de la grabación y toma nota de las ideas principales.
- Intenta reconocer los cognados para facilitar la comprensión.

Segunda escucha

- Toma nota de los detalles específicos que apoyan la idea principal de la grabación.
- Haz un pequeño resumen de lo que has escuchado.

Lectura

- Aplica las estrategias de lectura que practicaste en la unidad anterior (ver página 66).

Preguntas

- Para responder las preguntas de opción múltiple, guíate por las palabras clave que señalaste en el texto y en tu resumen de la grabación.

Instrucciones para el examen

Directions: You will read a print text and then listen to an audio selection. You will first have a designated amount of time to read the print selection. You will then have a designated amount of time to read the introduction to the audio and preview the questions before the audio plays. The audio will be played twice. As you listen, you may take notes. For each question that follows, choose the answer that is best according to the audio and/or reading selection.

Instrucciones: Vas a leer un texto y luego vas a escuchar una grabación. Primero, vas a tener un tiempo determinado para leer el texto. Luego, vas a tener un tiempo determinado para leer la introducción de la grabación y prever las preguntas antes de que comience. Vas a escuchar la grabación dos veces. Mientras escuchas, puedes tomar apuntes. Para cada pregunta, elige la mejor respuesta según la grabación y/o el texto.

Language Expansion

VOCABULARY

- Students may have difficulty with the following words from the reading:

realzado	→	subrayado, alabado
lucha	→	batalla, combate
destacado	→	resaltado
reparten	→	distribuyen
aprovechar	→	sacar utilidad
aportados	→	contribuidos
gestionados	→	administrados

GRAMMAR STRUCTURES:
The *Vosotros* Form

- The *vosotros* form of address is used primarily in Spain, but is not common in Latin America. Therefore, students may not have sufficient exposure to use it, although they may understand it when they hear or see it used, as in the audio for this activity. To practice this verb form, have students listen to media from Spain and identify the verbs they hear that are used in the *vosotros* form. You may also have students rewrite texts that employ the *ustedes* form, this time using *vosotros*.

Fuente número 1: introducción

Este texto fue publicado originalmente en el diario El País (España) y se refiere a la celebración de los 25 años de la fundación del Banco de Alimentos de Barcelona.

Interpretive Communication: Audio Texts

EL PAÍS   25 de junio de 2012

El Banco de Alimentos cumple 25 años como aliado de la Administración

El Banco de Alimentos de Barcelona ha celebrado este lunes su 25 aniversario con un acto en el que representantes de las principales instituciones catalanas han realzado la labor social de esta ONG (Organización No Gubernamental) como gran aliada de la administración en la lucha contra la pobreza.

«Hay mucha gente que lo está pasando mal y es importante llegar a todos, pero la administración no lo puede hacer sola; se debe apoyar en el Banco de Alimentos para dar respuesta a la gente», ha destacado el alcalde de Barcelona, Xavier Trias. Esta ONG cuenta actualmente con 180 voluntarios y distribuirá este año más de 10 toneladas de comida de manera gratuita a 325 entidades benéficas que, a su vez, la reparten a las personas más necesitadas.

Nacido en 1987, el Banco de Alimentos es una fundación benéfica, privada e independiente que lucha para evitar que se destruyan alimentos consumibles que no se comercializan y se puedan aprovechar para los más desfavorecidos.

También organiza campañas de recogida de alimentos como la «Gran Recolecta» de las pasadas Navidades, en la que logró 1.095 toneladas de comida de donaciones particulares y de supermercados.

A la Fundación le ha llegado el 25 aniversario en el momento más crítico desde su creación: si en el año 2009 eran 70.000 personas las beneficiarias de la ayuda alimentaria, en 2011 fueron 114.000 y este año serán más de 120.000, solo en la provincia de Barcelona.

Actualmente hay 245 bancos de alimentos en 19 países europeos, de los que 53 están en España, uno en cada provincia.

En su primer año de funcionamiento, el Banco de Alimentos de Barcelona gestionó 227.000 kilos de alimentos aportados por 29 empresas donantes y, con 18 voluntarios, benefició a 1.500 personas. Veinticinco años después, el Banco reparte más de 10 toneladas de alimentos a más de 120.000 personas, con 320 empresas donantes y 180 voluntarios.

Entre 2010 y 2011, el total de kilos de alimentos gestionados ha pasado de 8.245 a 10.162, es decir, un 23% de incremento.

Fuente: http://www.elpais.com (selección)

Fuente número 2: introducción

Esta grabación trata de la cantidad de alimentos que se tiran a la basura. La entrevista fue transmitida el 24 de abril de 2011 en el programa *Punto de fuga* de la Cadena SER (España). La grabación dura aproximadamente seis minutos y en ella entrevistan a Agustín Alberti, representante de la Federación Española de Bancos de Alimentos.

ciento veinticinco 125

Strategies: Reading and Listening

- The audio sources for the exam come from sources in the Spanish-speaking world, and as such, represent authentic regional variations in pronunciation and vocabulary. In order to prepare students for these variations, you will probably want to expose them to authentic audios from around the Spanish-speaking world.

- The ability to synthesize information between two sources can be challenging in any language if students are not used to this type of task. As much as possible, incorporate a blend of sources and language skills—writing, reading, speaking, and listening—so that students have experience combining these skills in new and novel ways. For example, you may wish to have students speak to each other in class, then read a text, and then synthesize the information in a written paragraph. They might summarize their findings, compare and contrast the information, or apply what they learned from the conversation to the information presented in the reading.

Extension Activities

- After having students complete this activity, you may wish to take advantage of the activity by using the sources in a variety of different ways.

  - Have students research food banks in their community or state and prepare a two-minute presentation comparing their findings with the information presented in the sources.

  - Ask students to write a short persuasive essay about food banks, encouraging their community to support one at the local or state level, using information from these sources as support for their arguments.

  - Ask students to write additional questions based on the information in the two sources, and exchange these questions with a partner. Identifying the key information, as well as comparing and contrasting this information between two sources, is an excellent way to prepare for future comprehension activities.

More Practice

FINDING ADDITIONAL SOURCES

- Listening to Spanish from a multitude of places—with a wide variety of accents, vocabulary terms, and idiomatic expressions—may be extremely difficult for students to do in their everyday lives. Therefore, you may wish to search for as wide a variety as possible to give students additional practice. Most radio and television stations in Spanish-speaking countries have some of their programming available online. You may also wish to search for children's programming, sometimes available on sites like YouTube.com, as a stepping stone towards faster-paced presentations.

ADDITIONAL SOURCES

- You may find interesting audio selections and videos at these websites:
  - Bésame Radio (Costa Rica): www.besame.co.cr
  - W Radio (Mexico): www.wradio.com.mx
  - ADN Radio (Chile): www.adnradio.cl
  - Radio Continental (Argentina): www.continental.com.ar
  - Univisión (USA): www.univision.com
  - TVE (Spain): www.rtve.es
  - CNN en español: cnnespanol.cnn.com
- Be sure to review the selections to make sure the topic, length, and content are appropriate for your students.

Additional Resources

Español Santillana AP* Preparation Workbook

HACIA EL AP* EXAM

Interpretive Communication: Audio Texts

Presentation

- The fifteen multiple-choice questions on these pages comprise the reading comprehension activity that accompanies the text selection and audio recording on the previous page. Students will read the selection and listen to the audio, and then answer the comprehension questions based on the two sources.

Activities	Standards	Resources
Interpretive Communication: Audio Texts	1.1, 1.2, 2.1, 2.2, 3.1, 3.2, 5.1, 5.2	Audio

Preparing for the Exam

Critical Listening

- Listening critically is a skill that is often overlooked as students focus on merely comprehending the words they are listening to, rather than analyzing the underlying meaning, motives, and language tools that the speaker employs. You may wish to introduce students to the habit of listening critically by having them first practice with news reports in English. Have them listen once or twice to an audio, first writing a short summary of what they heard. Then, ask them critical thinking questions such as the ones listed below.

- The AP* Spanish Language and Culture Exam requires students to not only understand the listening selections, but also to listen critically. There are some types of questions and tasks that may be commonly asked.

  - Who is the intended audience?
  - What is the tone of the audio?
  - What is the audio's objective?
  - What literary device does the speaker use?
  - How does the speaker achieve his or her objective?
  - What does (a particular word or phrase) mean in this context?
  - What does (a particular word or phrase) refer to in this audio?
  - How could you best summarize the audio selection?

126

1 **¿Cuál es el objetivo del artículo?**

(A) Informar acerca de la campaña de recogida de alimentos llamada la «Gran recolecta».
(B) Analizar el momento crítico que atraviesan los bancos de alimentos en España.
(C) Informar sobre la celebración del 25 aniversario del Banco de Alimentos de Barcelona.
(D) Solicitar ayuda del Banco de Alimentos de Barcelona.

2 **¿Por qué, según Xavier Trias, la administración necesita el apoyo del Banco de Alimentos?**

(A) Porque en el Banco de Alimentos trabajan 180 voluntarios.
(B) Porque hay muchas personas que necesitan ayuda.
(C) Porque al alcalde no le gusta trabajar solo.
(D) Porque hay muchos alimentos para repartir.

3 **Según el artículo, ¿qué es el Banco de Alimentos?**

(A) Una fundación privada que recoge alimentos para los más necesitados.
(B) Una institución pública que recoge alimentos y los entrega a instituciones benéficas.
(C) Una fundación que lucha para que se destruyan alimentos consumibles que no se comercializan.
(D) Una ONG que exporta alimentos a países en vías de desarrollo.

4 **¿Qué sucedió en la «Gran recolecta» de las Navidades de 2011?**

(A) Que 70.000 personas se beneficiaron de la ayuda alimentaria.
(B) Que el Banco de Alimentos de Barcelona recogió 1.095 toneladas de comida de donaciones particulares.
(C) Que los supermercados y las grandes superficies no donaron alimentos.
(D) Que el Banco de Alimentos de Barcelona recogió más de mil toneladas de comida.

5 **¿Qué significa la frase «A la Fundación le ha llegado el 25 aniversario en el momento más crítico desde su creación»?**

(A) Que no hay suficientes alimentos para repartir.
(B) Que está aumentando el número de personas que necesitan ayuda.
(C) Que los alimentos están en mal estado.
(D) Que los voluntarios no quieren participar en la «Gran recolecta».

6 **Según el artículo, ¿qué factor contribuyó a que el Banco de Alimentos de Barcelona pudiera ayudar a 120.000 personas 25 años después de su fundación?**

(A) El aumento de bancos de alimentos en Europa.
(B) El aumento del número de personas necesitadas.
(C) El aprovechamiento de alimentos consumibles.
(D) La participación de un mayor número de empresas donantes.

7 **¿Qué afirma el artículo con relación a la cantidad de alimentos gestionados entre 2010 y 2011?**

(A) Que la cantidad de alimentos gestionados aumentó más de un 20%.
(B) Que el total de kilos de alimentos gestionados se ha mantenido igual desde la fundación del Banco de Alimentos.
(C) Que el incremento del 23% en la gestión de alimentos está relacionado con el 25 aniversario del Banco de Alimentos de Barcelona.
(D) Que la cantidad de alimentos gestionados ha pasado de 8.000 a 12.000 kilos.

More Information

FOOD BANKS IN SPAIN AND LATIN AMERICA

- The world's first food banks were established in the United States in the 1960s, and have since been set up all over the world. Currently, food banks often work within greater networks, such as Feeding America (U.S.), the Global FoodBanking Network (most of Latin America, Australia, India, etc.), and the European Federation of Food Banks (Spain and the rest of Europe). These networks provide training, support, and knowledge so that food banks can be more effective at combating hunger in their communities.

UNITED NATIONS WORLD FOOD PROGRAMME

- The UN World Food Programme (*Programa Mundial de Alimentos* in Spanish) is the world's largest humanitarian organization that addresses the problem of hunger. Funded entirely by donations, WFP aims to help more than 90 million people in more than 70 countries each year. Students can donate to the WFP and practice their Spanish at the same time through freerice.com, a website that quizzes you on Spanish (and a myriad of other subjects) and donates ten grains of rice for each correct answer.

8 ¿Por qué, según la grabación, se tira mucha comida en los aviones?

(A) Porque la comida de los aviones no es saludable.
(B) Porque no todas las personas compran comida cuando viajan.
(C) Porque no es bueno comer si estás viajando.
(D) Porque las compañías no conocen los bancos de alimentos.

9 ¿A quién se entrevista en la grabación?

(A) A un miembro de la Federación Española de Bancos de Alimentos.
(B) Al director del Banco de Alimentos de Madrid.
(C) Al alcalde de Barcelona.
(D) Al responsable de la creación de los Bancos de Alimentos en España.

10 ¿Por qué en España la ley no permite reutilizar la comida que sobra en restaurantes y supermercados?

(A) Porque a las empresas no les gusta donar la comida que sobra.
(B) Porque no es posible garantizar que los alimentos estén bien conservados.
(C) Porque muchos supermercados tiran la comida que no han vendido ese día.
(D) Porque los bancos de alimentos no son importantes en España.

11 ¿Cuál es el objetivo de la ley aprobada en el Parlamento italiano?

(A) Dar a conocer el trabajo de los bancos de alimentos en Italia.
(B) Crear un banco de alimentos en todas las ciudades del país.
(C) Reutilizar los alimentos que sobran.
(D) Prohibir a los supermercados la donación de alimentos.

12 ¿A qué se refiere Agustín Alberti cuando dice que hay empresas que tienen una responsabilidad social muy acusada?

(A) A que las empresas tienen poca responsabilidad social.
(B) A que las empresas no tienen ninguna responsabilidad social.
(C) A que las empresas tienen una alta responsabilidad social.
(D) A que las empresas acusan a otras empresas de falta de responsabilidad social.

13 ¿Qué factor influye en que las empresas no donen alimentos?

(A) Que hay empresas que devuelven a las compañías productoras los alimentos que no han vendido.
(B) Que las empresas no quieren cooperar con los bancos de alimentos y prefieren devolver la comida.
(C) Que hay empresas que tienen una alta conciencia solidaria.
(D) Que los bancos de alimentos tienen creados los mecanismos para distribuir alimentos.

14 ¿Qué iniciativa se está llevando a cabo en la Escuela Superior de Ingenieros Agrónomos?

(A) Un programa para no tirar comida en los aviones.
(B) Un nuevo sistema para almacenar comida en los bancos de alimentos.
(C) Una red social para estudiantes que trabajan en supermercados.
(D) Una red social para poner en contacto a las empresas con los bancos de alimentos.

15 ¿Qué tienen en común el artículo y la grabación?

(A) Que promocionan la campaña de la «Gran recolecta».
(B) Que destacan la importancia del trabajo realizado por los bancos de alimentos en España.
(C) Que celebran el 25 aniversario del Banco de Alimentos de Barcelona.
(D) Que hacen un análisis del crecimiento de la cantidad de alimentos gestionados.

ciento veintisiete **127**

Unit 2

HACIA EL AP* EXAM

Interpretive Communication: Audio Texts

Strategies: Answering Comprehension Questions

- Have students read the *Estrategias* box on page 124 again, this time focusing on the strategies that apply to *Preguntas*. What other strategies can they think of when dealing with a listening activity that has written questions? What strategies can they employ when taking notes that will facilitate answering the multiple-choice questions that follow?

- First listening: Taking notes while listening is a skill that requires practice to be developed, as it is not a common practice during everyday interactions. The first time students listen to the audio, have them listen primarily for meaning, noting—in shorthand, or even in quick sketches, but not word-for-word—the main ideas of the passage: who is talking, what they are talking about, main points in the story or argument. Dates and figures are easy to note down, but are only useful if they support one of these main ideas. Then, students should make an attempt to answer any of the questions that they previewed for which they already have the answer, but not spend time trying to decipher questions that require greater detail.

- Second listening: The second time, students should pay attention to the details, especially as they relate to the types of critical thinking questions previously mentioned. These might include the audio's intended audience, its purpose, and any words or phrases that stand out as important.

 AUDIO SCRIPT
See page 69N.

Answer Key

1. C	**4.** D	**7.** A	**10.** B	**13.** A
2. B	**5.** B	**8.** B	**11.** C	**14.** D
3. A	**6.** D	**9.** A	**12.** C	**15.** B

Additional Resources
Español Santillana AP* Preparation Workbook

Differentiated Instruction

DEVELOPING LEARNERS

- Differences in pronunciation and regional variants in vocabulary can impede understanding for some students. After completing this activity the first time, you may wish to provide students with the transcript of the audio passage so they can follow along visually while listening. They can therefore check their understanding of unfamiliar words and phrases, and more easily identify any sections that caused them difficulty. Have them generate a list of these problematic terms for further discussion and practice in class.

EXPANDING / HERITAGE LANGUAGE LEARNERS

- Have students write a list of three additional questions that they would like to ask Agustín Alberti about food banking in Spain. Ask them to work with a partner to conduct the "interview."

- Ask students to research food banking in their own country, and write a short essay about food banking in the U.S. and Spain. They might focus on a particular aspect, such as differences between the two, political considerations surrounding food banking, the history of food banks, etc.

Unit 3 Trabajamos

Objectives

- To talk about past actions.
- To describe school activities.
- To use past participles.
- To learn the uses of the present perfect and past perfect tenses.
- To connect future actions.
- To talk about banking, trade, and other economic activities.

- To add information about a noun using adjective clauses.
- To form and use the future perfect tense.
- To talk about job searches and applications.
- To express wishes.
- To state actions if certain conditions are met.

- To identify main ideas and significant details in a variety of texts.
- To write a wide variety of texts, including a résumé.
- To know and apply the different stages of the writing process: planning, writing, revising, and sharing.
- To explore Latin American economies.

Contents

Vocabulary

- Useful expressions used to talk about school and work, to say you do not remember something, to say someone works hard, and to cheer someone up.
- Review: Words for school, school subjects, the computer, employment, professions, job positions, and qualities.
- School. Math symbols and punctuation marks.
- Economic resources and activities. The bank.
- Work and professions.

Grammar

- The past participle.
- The present perfect tense and the past perfect tense.
- Relative pronouns.
- The future perfect tense.
- To express wishes.
- To express condition.

Culture

- The school calendar and curriculum in Hispanic countries.
- The cost of university education in Hispanic countries.
- *La Ciudad de las Artes y las Ciencias de Valencia.*
- The *salar de Uyuni* in Bolivia.
- *La Comunidad Andina de Naciones.*
- *Las monedas nacionales.*
- The Panama Canal as an engineering wonder in the world.
- *Conciliar la vida laboral y familiar.*
- Latin American economies.
- Hispanic companies in the world.

Evaluation Criteria

- Narrate and describe in the past using the different past tenses and differentiate the uses of each one of them.
- Talk about studies and school activities.
- Differentiate the uses of the past participle.
- Recognize and use the present perfect tense and the past perfect tense.
- Identify banking activities and transactions, and talk about trade and other economic resources and activities.

- Use adjective clauses to provide more information about a noun.
- Learn the formation and use of the future perfect tense.
- Identify different professions and employment possibilities, and talk about job searches and the application process.
- Express present and future wishes using the infinitive, the subjunctive mood, or the conditional tense.

- Express likely, unlikely, and impossible conditions.
- Express understanding of Latin American economies.
- Write a résumé.
- Read different types of texts and identify main ideas and significant details in them.
- Write guided texts giving information, describing, or narrating events.

Unit Plan

Las tareas/Antes de empezar

Estimated time: 2 sessions.

Text: *Estudiantes con futuro.*

Functions & forms:
- Useful expressions used to talk about school and work, to say you do not remember something, to say someone works hard, and to cheer someone up.
- Review of known vocabulary about school, school subjects, the computer, employment, professions, job positions, and qualities.

⚑DESAFÍO 1

Estimated time: 6 sessions.

Text: *Un intercambio cultural.*

Functions & forms:
- To talk about past actions.
- School. Math symbols and punctuation marks.
- The past participle.
- The present and past perfect tenses.

Culture:
- *El calendario escolar.*
- *El coste de la educación.*
- *La Ciudad de las Artes y las Ciencias de Valencia.*

Reading: *El plan de estudios.*

⚑DESAFÍO 2

Estimated time: 6 sessions.

Text: *El tesoro de Bolivia.*

Functions & forms:
- To connect future actions.
- Economic resources and activities. The bank.
- Relative pronouns.
- The future perfect tense.

Culture:
- *El salar de Uyuni (Bolivia).*
- *La Comunidad Andina de Naciones.*
- *Las monedas nacionales.*

Reading: *La globalización económica.*

⚑DESAFÍO 3

Estimated time: 6 sessions.

Text: *Una maravilla de la ingeniería.*

Functions & forms:
- To express wishes.
- Work and professions.
- To express wishes using the infinitive, the subjunctive mood, or the conditional tense.
- To express condition.

Culture:
- *Maravillas de la ingeniería.*
- *Solicitudes de empleo.*
- *Conciliar la vida laboral y familiar.*

Reading: *Un constructor de ecuaciones.*

Para terminar

Estimated time: 2 sessions.

Todo junto: Review of *Desafíos 1–3.*

Tu desafío:
- *Desafío A:* Find information and prepare a presentation about student exchange programs in a Spanish-speaking country.
- *Desafío B:* Find a piece of financial news in Spanish on the Internet and share the information with the class.
- *Desafío C:* Write an offer of employment for an ideal job.

MAPA CULTURAL

Estimated time: 1 session.

Mapa cultural: La economía de Latinoamérica.

ESCRITURA

Estimated time: 1 session.

Writing: *Tu currículum ideal.*

PROYECTO/EVALUACIÓN

Estimated time: 2 sessions.

Project: *Un premio a la empresa hispana del año.*

Self-evaluation: *Autoevaluación.*

HACIA EL *AP* EXAM*

Estimated time: 2 sessions.

Test: Interpersonal Writing: E-mail Reply.

Standards for Learning Spanish

COMMUNICATION

1.1 Interpersonal mode
- Exchange personal ideas, opinions, and experiences.
- Engage in oral conversations using personal knowledge and experience.
- Ask and answer questions on different topics.
- Compare information with a partner.
- Ask a partner questions and take notes from the answers given.
- Play a guessing game with a classmate.
- Write an advertising brochure.

1.2. Interpretive mode
- Demonstrate understanding of oral and written idiomatic expressions.
- Demonstrate understanding of questions relating to familiar and less familiar topics.
- Understand and obtain information from audio or video recordings.
- Understand written exchanges.
- Identify main ideas and significant details in a variety of texts.
- Extract information from an informative text.
- Draw conclusions and make judgments from oral and written texts.
- Interpret texts on topics of other cultures and relate them to personal knowledge and experience.
- Understand an employment advertisement.
- Understand new vocabulary presented in Spanish.
- Write sentences to explain images.

1.3. Presentational mode
- Produce and present an original creation orally.
- Dramatize a dialogue.
- Write an explanatory text about own experiences or as a result of a research activity.
- Write predictions.
- Write opinions on different topics.
- Write a formal, informative e-mail.
- Write a letter of recommendation.
- Write an employment advertisement.
- Write a résumé.
- Create a poster or a brochure.

CULTURE

2.1. Practices and perspectives
- Learn about the school calendar in Hispanic countries.
- Read about the cost of university education in Hispanic countries.
- Learn about economic activities and practices in Latin America.
- Read about the job application process in the United States and in Hispanic countries.

2.2. Products and perspectives
- Read about the *Ciudad de las Artes y las Ciencias* in Valencia, Spain.
- Learn about the *salar de Uyuni* in Bolivia and its natural resources.
- Learn about feats of engineering such as the Panama Canal.
- Learn about economic resources in Hispanic countries.

CONNECTIONS

3.1. Interdisciplinary connections
- Understand the similarities and differences between some aspects of grammar in English and in Spanish.
- Use the writing process to produce a résumé.
- Learn about energy resources.
- Learn about economic resources, activities, and institutions in Hispanic countries.

3.2. Viewpoints through language/culture
- Read dialogues, informative texts, and literary texts in Spanish that provide insight into Hispanic cultures.
- Learn about the importance of the economy in Hispanic societies and in the world.

COMPARISONS

4.1. Compare languages
- Compare the uses of the past participle in English and in Spanish.
- Compare the use of the present perfect and past perfect tenses in English and in Spanish.
- Compare the use of relative pronouns in English and in Spanish.
- Compare the use of the future perfect in English and in Spanish.
- Compare how to express wishes and condition in English and in Spanish.

4.2. Compare cultures
- Compare schools in the United States and in Hispanic countries.
- Compare the cost of university education in the United States and in Hispanic countries.
- Compare the job application process in the United States and in Hispanic countries.

COMMUNITIES

5.1. Spanish within and beyond the school setting
- Reflect on the benefits of cultural exchanges.
- Write a résumé.
- Research and obtain information on the Internet.

5.2. Spanish for lifelong learning
- Discuss skills, knowledge, and requirements needed for a future profession.
- Learn about the importance of economics for daily life.
- Learn the writing process.
- Use technology to learn.

Communicative Skills

Interpersonal Mode

		Activities
Speaking	• Exchange ideas, opinions, or experiences with classmates.	• 4, 9, 19, 28, 29, 30, 31, 49, *Lectura D1*, 52, 55, 62, *Lectura D3*, 77, 80, 82, *Proyecto*
	• Ask and answer questions or engage in conversation with a partner.	• 4, 6, 14, 24, 28, 39, 58, 68, 73
	• Compare and contrast information with a classmate.	• 10, 52, 82, *Proyecto*
	• Play a guessing game with a classmate.	• 45
Writing	• Take notes from a classmate's answers or summarize information in a list.	• 4, 39, 44, 62
	• Write an advertising brochure.	• 30
Listening	• Understand and obtain information from oral exchanges.	• 4, 5, 6, 9, 10, 14, 19, 24, 28, 29, 31, 39, 49, 52, 55, 58, 62, 73, 77, 80, 82, *Proyecto*
Reading	• Understand a résumé.	• *Escritura*

Interpretive Mode

		Activities
Listening	• Obtain information from conversations.	• 9, 19, 34, 68, 72
	• Understand descriptive or informative audios.	• 3, 38, 54, 58, 81
Reading	• Demonstrate comprehension of written exchanges or longer written dialogues.	• 1, 10, 26, 31, 33, 55, 57, 77, 80
	• Infer meanings based on a text.	• 2, 13, 27, 36, 60, 75
	• Reflect on cultural topics in relation to personal knowledge or experience.	• 11, 15, 20, 35, 40, 50, 59, 64, 69
	• Obtain information and draw conclusions from an informative text.	• 29, 48, 51, 52, 53, 83
	• Research using outside sources.	• 40, 59, 83, 84, 85, *Proyecto*
	• Understand an employment advertisement.	• 73, 79
Viewing	• Obtain information from an image.	• 6, 67

Presentational Mode

		Activities
Speaking	• Present information or an original creation to the class.	• 28, 30, 58, 59, 83, 84, 85, *Escritura*, *Proyecto*
	• Act out a dialogue.	• 54
Writing	• Write a descriptive or an explanatory text.	• 28, 29, 39, 53, 63
	• Write predictions or opinions on different topics.	• 48, 52, 55, 64, 77, 81
	• Write a formal informative e-mail or a letter of recommendation.	• 72, 78
	• Write a poem or a paragraph comparing and summarizing information.	• 76, 82
	• Write an employment advertisement or a résumé.	• 83, *Escritura*
Visually Representing	• Create a poster or a brochure.	• 59, *Proyecto*
	• Use photographs to illustrate information.	• *Proyecto*

Cross-Curricular Standards

Subject	Standard	Activities
Language Arts	• Compare elements of Spanish grammar with English equivalents. • Use the writing process to write a résumé.	• 16, 21, 41, 46, 65, 70 • *Escritura*
Social Studies	• Learn about economic resources, activities, and institutions in Latin America and in the world.	• 35, 40, 50, 51, 52, 53, 83, *Mapa cultural*
Science	• Learn about energy resources.	• 33, 34, 35, 48

Lesson Plans (50-Minute Classes)

Day	Objectives	Sessions	Activities	Time	Standards	Resources / Homework
1	To introduce secondary and post-secondary studies and employment, and the characters' challenges	**Trabajamos / Las tareas** (128–131) • Warm-Up: Topic orientation • Presentation: *Estudiantes con futuro*	1–2	15 m. 35 m.	1.1, 1.2, 2.1, 2.2	Practice Workbook
2	To learn useful expressions related to the unit topic and to review learned vocabulary	**Antes de empezar** (132–133) • Warm-Up: Independent Starter • *Expresiones útiles* • *Recuerda*	3–4 5–6	10 m. 15 m. 25 m.	1.1, 1.2, 2.1, 5.1	Audio Practice Workbook
3	To talk about past actions	**Desafío 1 – Un intercambio cultural** (134–135) • Warm-Up: Independent Starter • *Texto: Un intercambio cultural* • *Comparaciones: El calendario escolar*	7–10 11	5 m. 35 m. 10 m.	1.1, 1.2, 1.3, 2.1, 2.2, 3.1, 4.2	Audio
4	To communicate in the school setting	**Desafío 1 – Vocabulario** (136–137) • Warm-Up: Independent Starter • *Vocabulario: La escuela* • *Comparaciones: El coste de la educación*	12–14 15	5 m. 35 m. 10 m.	1.1, 1.2, 2.1, 3.1, 3.2, 4.2	Practice Workbook
5	To learn and use the past participle	**Desafío 1 – Gramática** (138–139) • Warm-Up: Independent Starter • *Gramática: El participio pasado* • *Cultura: La Ciudad de las Artes y las Ciencias de Valencia*	16–19 20	5 m. 35 m. 10 m.	1.1, 1.2, 1.3, 2.1, 2.2, 3.1, 3.2, 4.1, 5.1	Audio Practice Workbook
6	To learn and use the present perfect tense and the past perfect tense	**Desafío 1 – Gramática** (140–141) • Warm-Up: Independent Starter • *Gramática: El presente perfecto y el pluscuamperfecto*	21–25	5 m. 45 m.	1.1, 1.2, 1.3, 3.1, 4.1, 5.1	Audio Practice Workbook
7	To understand a written dialogue	**Desafío 1 – Lectura** (142–143) • Warm-Up: Independent Starter • *Lectura: El plan de estudios*	26–28	5 m. 45 m.	1.1, 1.2, 1.3, 2.1, 3.1, 5.1, 5.2	
8	To integrate vocabulary and grammar, and to assess student proficiency	**Desafío 1 – Comunicación / Evaluación** (144–145) • Warm-Up: Independent Starter • *Comunicación: Review* • *Final del desafío* • Quiz on *Desafío 1*	29–30 31	5 m. 25 m. 10 m. 10 m.	1.1, 1.2, 1.3, 2.1, 2.2, 3.1, 4.2, 5.1, 5.2	Practice Workbook
9	To connect future actions	**Desafío 2 – El tesoro de Bolivia** (146–147) • Warm-Up: Independent Starter • *Texto: El tesoro de Bolivia* • *Cultura: El salar de Uyuni (Bolivia)*	32–34 35	5 m. 35 m. 10 m.	1.1, 1.2, 1.3, 2.1, 2.2, 3.1, 3.2, 5.2	Audio

Day	Objectives	Sessions	Activities	Time	Standards	Resources / Homework
10	To talk about economic resources and activities	**Desafío 2 – Vocabulario** (148–149) • Warm-Up: Independent Starter • *Vocabulario: La economía* • *Cultura: La Comunidad Andina de Naciones*	36–39 40	5 m. 35 m. 10 m.	1.1, 1.2, 1.3, 2.1, 2.2, 3.1, 3.2, 5.1, 5.2	Audio Practice Workbook
11	To learn how to add information about a noun using adjective clauses	**Desafío 2 – Gramática** (150–151) • Warm-Up: Independent Starter • *Gramática: Los pronombres relativos*	41–45	5 m. 45 m.	1.1, 1.2, 1.3, 2.1, 2.2, 3.1, 4.1, 4.2, 5.2	Practice Workbook
12	To learn the future perfect tense	**Desafío 2 – Gramática** (152–153) • Warm-Up: Independent Starter • *Gramática: El futuro perfecto* • *Conexiones: Las monedas nacionales*	46–49 50	5 m. 35 m. 10 m.	1.1, 1.2, 1.3, 2.1, 2.2, 3.1, 3.2, 4.1, 5.1	Practice Workbook
13	To understand information about the global economy	**Desafío 2 – Lectura** (154–155) • Warm-Up: Independent Starter • *Lectura: La globalización económica*	51–52	5 m. 45 m.	1.1, 1.2, 1.3, 3.1, 3.2, 5.1	
14	To integrate vocabulary and grammar, and to assess student proficiency	**Desafío 2 – Comunicación / Evaluación** (156–157) • Warm-Up: Independent Starter • *Comunicación:* Review • *Final del desafío* • Quiz on *Desafío 2*	53–54 55	5 m. 25 m. 10 m. 10 m.	1.1, 1.2, 1.3, 2.1, 2.2, 3.1, 3.2, 4.2, 5.1, 5.2	Audio Practice Workbook
15	To express wishes about the future	**Desafío 3 – Una maravilla de la ingeniería** (158–159) • Warm-Up: Independent Starter • *Texto: Una maravilla de la ingeniería* • *Cultura: Maravillas de la ingeniería*	56–58 59	5 m. 35 m. 10 m.	1.1, 1.2, 1.3, 2.1, 2.2, 3.1, 3.2, 4.2, 5.1, 5.2	Audio
16	To talk about work and professions	**Desafío 3 – Vocabulario** (160–161) • Warm-Up: Independent Starter • *Vocabulario: Trabajo y profesiones* • *Comparaciones: Solicitudes de empleo*	60–63 64	5 m. 35 m. 10 m.	1.1, 1.2, 1.3, 2.1, 3.1, 3.2, 4.2, 5.1, 5.2	Practice Workbook
17	To express wishes	**Desafío 3 – Gramática** (162–163) • Warm-Up: Independent Starter • *Gramática: Expresar deseos* • *Comunidades: Conciliar la vida laboral y familiar*	65–68 69	5 m. 35 m. 10 m.	1.1, 1.2, 1.3, 2.1, 3.1, 3.2, 4.1, 5.1, 5.2	Audio Practice Workbook
18	To express condition	**Desafío 3 – Gramática** (164–165) • Warm-Up: Independent Starter • *Gramática: Expresar condición*	70–73	5 m. 45 m.	1.1, 1.2, 1.3, 2.1, 2.2, 3.1, 4.1, 5.1	Audio Practice Workbook

Day	Objectives	Sessions	Activities	Time	Standards	Resources / Homework
19	To understand a literary story	**Desafío 3 – Lectura** (166–167) • Warm-Up: Independent Starter • *Lectura: Un constructor de ecuaciones*	74–76	5 m. 45 m.	1.1, 1.2, 1.3, 2.2, 3.1	
20	To integrate vocabulary and grammar, and to assess student proficiency	**Desafío 3 – Comunicación / Evaluación** (168–169) • Warm-Up: Independent Starter • *Comunicación:* Review • *Final del desafío* • Quiz on *Desafío 3*	77–79 80	5 m. 25 m. 10 m. 10 m.	1.1, 1.2, 1.3, 2.1, 2.2, 5.1, 5.2	Practice Workbook
21	To integrate language in context	**Para terminar** (170–171) • Warm-Up: Independent Starter • *Todo junto* • *Tu desafío*	81–82 83	5 m. 25 m. 20 m.	1.1, 1.2, 1.3, 2.1, 2.2, 3.1, 3.2, 5.1, 5.2	Audio Practice Workbook *Tu desafío* work
22	To integrate language in context and to assess student proficiency	**Tu desafío / Evaluación** (171) • Warm-Up: Prepare *Tu desafío* presentations • *Tu desafío* presentations • Quiz on *Desafíos 1–3*		5 m. 25 m. 20 m.	1.2, 1.3, 2.1, 2.2, 3.1, 3.2, 5.1, 5.2	
23	To learn about Latin American economies	**Mapa cultural** (172–173) • Warm-Up: Independent Starter • *Mapa cultural: La economía de Latinoamérica*	84–85	5 m. 45 m.	1.2, 1.3, 2.1, 2.2, 3.1, 3.2, 5.1	Practice Workbook
24	To write a résumé	**Escritura** (174–175) • Warm-Up: Independent Starter • *Escritura: Tu currículum ideal*		5 m. 45 m.	1.1, 1.2, 1.3, 2.1, 5.1, 5.2	Project work
25	To learn about Latino-owned companies and to choose the best Hispanic company of the year	**Proyecto** (180–181) • Warm-Up: Prepare project presentations • Project presentations		10 m. 40 m.	1.1, 1.2, 1.3, 2.1, 2.2, 3.1, 5.2	**Repaso – Vocabulario** (176–177) **Repaso – Gramática** (178–179)
26	To assess student proficiency	**Assessment** • *Autoevaluación* (181) • Test		10 m. 40 m.	1.1, 1.2, 1.3, 2.1, 2.2, 5.1, 5.2	
27	To prepare for the AP* Exam	**Hacia el AP* Exam** (182–183) • Warm-Up: Test introduction • Test: Interpersonal Writing: E-mail Reply • Review and correction of the test		10 m. 15 m. 15 m.	1.2, 2.1, 2.2, 3.2	
28	To prepare for the AP* Exam	**Hacia el AP* Exam** (182–183) • Warm-Up: About the test • Review and correction of the test		10 m. 40 m.	1.2, 2.1, 2.2, 3.2	

Lesson Plans (90-Minute Classes)

Day	Objectives	Sessions	Activities	Time	Standards	Resources / Homework
1	To introduce secondary and post-secondary studies and employment, and the characters' challenges; to learn useful expressions related to the unit topic, and to review learned vocabulary	**Trabajamos / Las tareas / Antes de empezar** (128–133) • Warm-Up: Topic orientation • Presentation: *Estudiantes con futuro* • *Expresiones útiles* • *Recuerda*	1–2 3–4 5–6	15 m. 35 m. 15 m. 25 m.	1.1, 1.2, 2.1, 2.2, 5.1	Audio Practice Workbook
2	To talk about past actions and to communicate in the school setting	**Desafío 1 – Un intercambio cultural / Vocabulario** (134–137) • Warm-Up: Independent Starter • *Texto: Un intercambio cultural* • *Comparaciones: El calendario escolar* • *Vocabulario: La escuela* • *Comparaciones: El coste de la educación*	7–10 11 12–14 15	5 m. 30 m. 10 m. 35 m. 10 m.	1.1, 1.2, 1.3, 2.1, 2.2, 3.1, 3.2, 4.2	Audio Practice Workbook
3	To learn and use the past participle and to learn and use the present perfect tense and the past perfect tense	**Desafío 1 – Gramática** (138–141) • Warm-Up: Independent Starter • *Gramática: El participio pasado* • *Cultura: La Ciudad de las Artes y las Ciencias de Valencia.* • *Gramática: El presente perfecto y el pluscuamperfecto*	16–19 20 21–25	5 m. 35 m. 10 m. 40 m.	1.1, 1.2, 1.3, 2.1, 2.2, 3.1, 3.2, 4.1, 5.1	Audio Practice Workbook
4	To understand a written dialogue, to integrate vocabulary and grammar, and to assess student proficiency	**Desafío 1 – Lectura / Comunicación / Evaluación** (142–145) • Warm-Up: Independent Starter • *Lectura: El plan de estudios* • *Comunicación: Review* • *Final del desafío* • Quiz on *Desafío 1*	26–28 29–30 31	5 m. 40 m. 25 m. 10 m. 10 m.	1.1, 1.2, 1.3, 2.1, 2.2, 3.1, 4.2, 5.1, 5.2	Practice Workbook
5	To connect future actions and to talk about economic resources and activities	**Desafío 2 – El tesoro de Bolivia / Vocabulario** (146–149) • Warm-Up: Independent Starter • *Texto: El tesoro de Bolivia* • *Cultura: El salar de Uyuni (Bolivia)* • *Vocabulario: La economía* • *Cultura: La Comunidad Andina de Naciones*	32–34 35 36–39 40	5 m. 30 m. 10 m. 35 m. 10 m.	1.1, 1.2, 1.3, 2.1, 2.2, 3.1, 3.2, 5.1, 5.2	Audio Practice Workbook
6	To learn how to add information about a noun using adjective clauses and to learn the future perfect tense	**Desafío 2 – Gramática** (150–153) • Warm-Up: Independent Starter • *Gramática: Los pronombres relativos* • *Gramática: El futuro perfecto* • *Conexiones: Las monedas nacionales*	41–45 46–49 50	5 m. 35 m. 40 m. 10 m.	1.1, 1.2, 1.3, 2.1, 2.2, 3.1, 3.2, 4.1, 4.2, 5.1, 5.2	Practice Workbook

Day	Objectives	Sessions	Activities	Time	Standards	Resources / Homework
7	To understand information about the global economy, to integrate vocabulary and grammar, and to assess student proficiency	**Desafío 2 – Lectura / Comunicación / Evaluación** (154–157) • Warm-Up: Independent Starter • *Lectura: La globalización económica* • *Comunicación:* Review • *Final del desafío* • Quiz on *Desafío 2*	 51–52 53–54 55	5 m. 40 m. 25 m. 10 m. 10 m.	1.1, 1.2, 1.3, 2.1, 2.2, 3.1, 3.2, 4.2, 5.1, 5.2	Audio Practice Workbook
8	To express wishes about the future and to talk about work and professions	**Desafío 3 – Una maravilla de la ingeniería / Vocabulario** (158–161) • Warm-Up: Independent Starter • *Texto: Una maravilla de la ingeniería* • *Cultura: Maravillas de la ingeniería* • *Vocabulario: Trabajo y profesiones* • *Comparaciones: Solicitudes de empleo*	 56–58 59 60–63 64	 5 m. 30 m. 10 m. 35 m. 10 m.	1.1, 1.2, 1.3, 2.1, 2.2, 3.1, 3.2, 4.2, 5.1, 5.2	Audio Practice Workbook
9	To express wishes and to express condition	**Desafío 3 – Gramática** (162–165) • Warm-Up: Independent Starter • *Gramática: Expresar deseos* • *Comunidades: Conciliar la vida laboral y familiar* • *Gramática: Expresar condición*	 65–68 69 70–73	 5 m. 40 m. 10 m. 35 m.	1.1, 1.2, 1.3, 2.1, 2.2, 3.1, 3.2, 4.1, 5.1, 5.2	Audio Practice Workbook
10	To understand a literary story and to integrate vocabulary and grammar	**Desafío 3 – Lectura / Comunicación / Evaluación** (166–169) • Warm-Up: Independent Starter • *Lectura: Un constructor de ecuaciones* • *Comunicación:* Review • *Final del desafío* • Quiz on *Desafío 3*	 74–76 77–79 80	 5 m. 40 m. 25 m. 10 m. 10 m.	1.1, 1.2, 1.3, 2.1, 2.2, 3.1, 5.1, 5.2	Practice Workbook **Para terminar – Tu desafío** (171)
11	To integrate language in context and to assess student proficiency	**Para terminar / Evaluación** (170–171) • Warm-Up: Independent Starter • *Todo junto* • *Tu desafío:* work and presentations • Quiz on *Desafíos 1–3*	 81–82 83	 5 m. 25 m. 40 m. 20 m.	1.1, 1.2, 1.3, 2.1, 2.2, 3.1, 3.2, 5.1, 5.2	Audio Practice Workbook
12	To learn about Latin American economies and to write a résumé	**Mapa cultural / Escritura** (172–175) • Warm-Up: Independent Starter • *Mapa cultural: La economía de Latinoamérica* • *Escritura: Tu currículum ideal*	 84–85	 5 m. 40 m. 45 m.	1.1, 1.2, 1.3, 2.1, 2.2, 3.1, 3.2, 5.1, 5.2	Practice Workbook **Repaso – Vocabulario** (176–177) **Repaso – Gramática** (178–179) Project work

Day	Objectives	Sessions	Activities	Time	Standards	Resources / Homework
13	To learn about Latino-owned companies and to choose the best Hispanic company of the year, and to assess student proficiency	***Proyecto* / Assessment** (180–181) • Warm-Up: Prepare project presentations • Project presentations • *Autoevaluación* • Test		10 m. 45 m. 10 m. 25 m.	1.1, 1.2, 1.3, 2.1, 2.2, 3.1, 5.1, 5.2	
14	To prepare for the AP* Exam	***Hacia el* AP* Exam** (182–183) • Warm-Up: Test introduction • Test: Interpersonal Writing: E-mail Reply • Review and correction of the test		15 m. 15 m. 60 m.	1.2, 2.1, 2.2, 3.2	

3 Expresiones

1. Antes dedicaba mucho tiempo a mi trabajo, pero no tenía tiempo para mis *hobbies*, para estudiar o para ver a mi familia y a mis amigos. Ahora, en cambio, solo trabajo veinte horas a la semana y tengo mucho más tiempo para todo.
2. Cuando fui por primera vez a una entrevista de trabajo, lo pasé muy mal porque me hicieron una pregunta y se me olvidó lo que debía contestar. ¡No recordaba nada! Fue horrible.
3. Me gusta mi trabajo. Tengo mi propio negocio, pero no siempre es fácil. Hay que trabajar muy duro y tengo mucha responsabilidad, pero tiene sus compensaciones.
4. El sábado pasado participé en un maratón por mi ciudad, pero eran veintiséis millas y no fui capaz de correr ni una sola milla. Enseguida lo abandoné.

9 Buscando información

–¿Qué estás haciendo, Ethan?
–Estoy buscando en Internet más información sobre las escuelas en Chile. Quiero saber más cosas sobre el examen de ingreso.
–¿Y qué has encontrado?
–Pues mira, el examen tiene dos partes: una de Matemáticas y otra de Lengua.
–¿Matemáticas? ¡¡¡Uy!!! Voy a tener que empezar a estudiar ya. Es una de las asignaturas más difíciles para mí.
–A mí las Matemáticas no me preocupan, se me dan bien. Pero... ¿un examen de Lengua en español? Uf.
–Tranquilo, seguro que apruebas sin problemas.
–No puedo encontrar información sobre las pruebas de los exámenes. Me gustaría saber en qué consisten exactamente.
–Sí, sería bueno tener algún modelo para poder prepararnos bien.
–¿Crees que tendremos que escribir un ensayo en español?
–No sé. Lo mejor es que escriba de nuevo a la escuela y les pregunte.

19 Un museo interactivo

–¿Te has apuntado a la visita al museo, Sonia?
–¿A cuál? No me he enterado.
–A la que organiza la escuela. Es una visita al Museo de las Ciencias Príncipe Felipe. Está en la Ciudad de las Artes y las Ciencias de Valencia.
–¿Tú vas a ir?
–¡Sí! Es muy interesante porque no es un museo cualquiera; es un museo interactivo.
–¿Interactivo? Eso suena bien.
–Sí. Su lema es «Prohibido no tocar, no sentir, no pensar» porque los visitantes pueden hacer experimentos científicos.
–Uf, no sé... ¿Tú crees que eso es divertido?

–Claro. A mí me parece que está pensado para aprender. Con los experimentos puedes entender los fenómenos físicos, cómo funcionan los inventos... Ah, y también vamos a ir a uno de los talleres que el museo organiza para estudiantes de secundaria.
–¿Sabes de qué es el taller?
–Se titula *Magia química*. Creo que van a hacer demostraciones de cómo unas sustancias se transforman en otras mediante reacciones químicas. La profesora de Ciencias nos ha dicho que vamos a ver un reloj que se pone en marcha con jugo de naranja.
–¡Qué divertido! Vale, me has convencido, María. Me voy a apuntar.

23 ¿Ha hecho o había hecho?

1. Esta mañana he repasado mis apuntes de Matemáticas. ¡Voy a sacar una buena nota en el examen!
2. Cuando tenía quince años, viajé a México con mi familia durante las vacaciones de invierno. Fue un viaje inolvidable.
3. Después de trabajar varios días en el laboratorio, esta mañana he obtenido los datos para completar mi informe para la clase de Química.
4. Ayer terminó el plazo para solicitar la beca, pero yo ya había enviado mi solicitud.
5. Mis amigos me llamaron para ir al cine. Yo había estado estudiando toda la mañana para el examen, así que decidí ir al cine con ellos.

34 Bolivia tiene recursos

–Daniel, ¿has encontrado información para el debate?
–Sí, he visto algunos videos. ¿Y tú?
–Yo he leído varios artículos. Dicen que para el año 2020 el diez por ciento de los automóviles funcionarán con baterías eléctricas.
–¿Y estarán hechas de litio?
–Sí, parece que en el futuro habrá mucha demanda de este material.
–No lo dudo, pero ¿hay suficiente litio?
–Sí, lo que pasa es que no se está extrayendo todavía. Además del debate sobre quién debe tener los derechos de explotación del litio del salar de Uyuni, el problema es que es difícil llegar hasta allí.
–¿Y el litio solo se usa para las baterías de los autos eléctricos?
–No, el litio es un metal muy ligero que tiene muchas aplicaciones: se puede usar para fabricar celulares y otros productos electrónicos, y también se usa para hacer algunos medicamentos. Pero yo creo que el uso más interesante está en la industria automovilística.

–O sea que en el futuro, gracias al litio, no necesitaremos petróleo para los autos.

–Esa es la idea. Pero Bolivia tiene que decidir qué hacer con sus reservas de litio.

–Si lo extraen, sería muy bueno para su economía, ¿no?

–Sí, pero parece que el país no tiene los recursos suficientes para hacerlo. Y si extrae el litio una empresa de otro país, los bolivianos no se beneficiarían y además perderían una zona con un paisaje espectacular.

–¿Entonces...?

–Leí que el gobierno boliviano quiere ser líder en el desarrollo de los autos eléctricos. El presidente ha dicho que quiere que Bolivia construya la nueva generación de autos pero, desafortunadamente, ahora mismo no se puede.

–Pero eso no quiere decir que los recursos naturales de Bolivia queden en manos de otro país.

–Ya... Bueno, tenemos que buscar más argumentos para el debate. ¿Nos vemos mañana, después de clase?

–Claro. Hasta mañana.

38 El noticiero

1. El Ministerio de Defensa de Bolivia ha firmado un acuerdo de cooperación con el Ministerio de Defensa de la República Popular China. Este acuerdo, que tiene un valor de aproximadamente tres millones de dólares americanos, fortalecerá las relaciones entre las fuerzas armadas de ambos países.

2. Un informe publicado recientemente afirma que varias compañías petroleras y energéticas están entre las 10 empresas más grandes del mundo. Sus elevados ingresos hacen que controlen buena parte de la economía global.

3. Según datos del Instituto Boliviano de Comercio Exterior difundidos ayer, las exportaciones bolivianas ascendieron a 1.034 millones de dólares, mientras que las importaciones sumaron más de 718 millones, dejando un saldo comercial positivo. El incremento se debe en gran parte a la venta de gas natural a Brasil y Argentina.

4. La tasa de interés hipotecario bajó de nuevo esta semana. Se trata de la tasa más baja de este año. Algunos expertos señalan que esto apunta a que el mercado está cada vez más débil. Sin embargo, otros se muestran optimistas y dicen que este dato se traducirá en un aumento de las ventas de viviendas.

54 El futuro de mi compañía

1. Mi compañía no gana mucho dinero. Tenemos cinco oficinas y los gastos para mantenerlas todas son muy altos. Yo pienso que podríamos tener el mismo éxito con un número menor de oficinas.

2. Ahora mismo mi compañía genera mucho dinero. Vendemos nuestros productos en todo el país, pero creo que fuera hay un mercado que puede ser muy interesante.

3. Tengo ideas muy buenas, pero no cuento con el dinero para empezar un negocio. Sé bastante sobre comercio internacional, pero fundar una compañía internacional es muy caro.

4. Para tener una compañía exitosa, es necesario competir con el mercado global. Desafortunadamente, los costos de fabricar mis productos en mi país son enormes y por eso me es difícil venderlos a un precio competitivo.

5. Mi compañía genera muchos beneficios, así que estoy pensando en entrar en otros mercados. Sin embargo, no sé mucho sobre comercio internacional y tengo bastantes dudas.

6. Yo trabajo por cuenta propia. Tengo muy poco tiempo libre y no me ocupo de comprobar los movimientos de mi cuenta bancaria, ver los ingresos y gastos, etc. Siempre confío en que no haya errores.

58 ¡Ayúdame!

1. –Me gustaría saber si hay algún trabajo al que pueda presentarme como candidata.
   –¿Qué experiencia profesional tienes?
   –Tengo mi licenciatura en Español, pero todavía no tengo experiencia. Me encanta viajar y estudiar idiomas. Sin embargo, no me interesa hacerme profesora ni guía turística.

2. –Ana, debes empezar a pensar la profesión que te interesaría ejercer en el futuro.
   –Pero, ¿cómo puedo decidirlo?
   –Tienes que pensar en tus habilidades, tus conocimientos y tus destrezas.
   –No sé, no hago nada bien.
   –No pienses así, seguro que hay muchas cosas que haces muy bien. A ver, ¿cuál es tu clase favorita?
   –Bueno, si tuviera que elegir una, diría que me fascina la Anatomía. Es muy interesante saber cómo funciona el cuerpo humano.

3. –Dijiste que quieres estudiar Ingeniería, ¿verdad? ¿Por qué?
   –Pues porque pienso que un ingeniero se dedica a resolver problemas, y tú sabes que a mí eso me encanta.
   –Sí, es cierto. Eres capaz de analizar las causas y las consecuencias de cualquier situación. Si buscara consejo, te lo pediría a ti.
   –Gracias, Lucas, pero en este momento tengo un problema que no puedo solucionar. A ver si tú me puedes ayudar. Si en el futuro quiero ser ingeniera, ¿sería mejor matricularme en un programa para estudiar fenómenos físicos, químicos, biológicos, médicos...? Hay tantas posibilidades.

4. –Siempre me han interesado las Ciencias y tengo bastante habilidad para la Química. De hecho, estoy considerando estudiar Química en la universidad. Me gustaría dedicarme a investigar.

–Me parece una buena decisión, pero ten en cuenta que para ser investigador son imprescindibles la imaginación y la tenacidad. Y tendrás que trabajar duro.

68 Consejos paternos

–Javi, tenemos que pensar en tu futuro.

–¿En mi futuro? Creo que hay un partido de fútbol en mi futuro…

–No, en serio, hijo. Tienes que considerar qué profesión te gustaría tener: abogado, arquitecto, ingeniero…

–Pues todavía no lo sé, papá.

–Quizás podrías ser médico o fisioterapeuta. Las Ciencias se te dan muy bien.

–No sé… Es pronto para decidirlo. Y todas esas profesiones exigen muchos años de estudio, ¿no?

–Sí, por eso deberíamos empezar a considerar las posibilidades ahora.

–La verdad es que ahora prefiero que veas el partido de fútbol conmigo y dejemos lo de mi profesión para otro día.

–Es que estoy preocupado por ti; con el desempleo que hay…

–La verdad es que a mí lo que me gusta es el deporte, papá. Yo quiero ser futbolista.

–Pero también te interesan las Ciencias, ¿no? ¿No preferirías ser biólogo o químico?

–Por favor, vamos a ver el partido y ya hablaremos otro día. ¡Solo tengo quince años!

72 La entrevista

–Según su solicitud, usted quiere optar al puesto de traductora, pero no tiene experiencia previa. Hábleme un poco sobre su formación académica.

–Pasé cuatro años estudiando en París. Me licencié en Francés y tengo un título de profesora. Estoy segura de que haría muy bien el trabajo si usted me diera la oportunidad de trabajar como traductora para su empresa.

–Hablemos un poco de su experiencia en los Estados Unidos. Según su currículum, mientras estudiaba en la universidad, trabajaba en un museo, ¿no es así?

–Efectivamente. Me gustaba el puesto y las condiciones eran muy buenas. Trabajaba solo por las tardes y eso me permitía estudiar por las mañanas. A menos que ustedes me ofrezcan un puesto a tiempo parcial, preferiría trabajar a tiempo completo.

–Y en caso de que le diéramos el trabajo, ¿tendría usted disponibilidad para viajar los fines de semana?

–Sí, claro, no habría ningún problema.

–Bueno, volvamos a su currículum. Hábleme sobre su experiencia como profesora.

–Trabajé tres años como profesora de Francés en una escuela, pero era un trabajo muy duro y las condiciones económicas no eran buenas. Si trabajara en una empresa privada, creo que podría optar a un sueldo mejor.

–De acuerdo. Vamos a hacerle una prueba para el trabajo.

81 Una escuela diferente

Fuente: ADN Radio, Chile

–Estamos con Felipe Ríos, actor, director… Ahora está en un proyecto nuevo, que nos va a contar detalles. ¿Cómo estás, Felipe? Gracias por venir.

–Muy bien, ¿y tú? Gracias por la invitación. Muy contento de poder estar acá compartiendo este nuevo proyecto de la escuela de teatro musical de Projazz.

–Advierte que no se pudo tomar vacaciones, ¿eh? Ojo con eso.

–Pero nos queda energía todavía.

–¡Muy bien, así se dice! Bueno, cuéntanos. ¿Qué proponen ustedes con Teatro musical? Porque de esto se trata este proyecto.

–Claro, a ver. Esto es una escuela de teatro, de actuación. Está enfocada hacia el teatro musical porque tiene particularidades que… Tiene danza, tiene *jazz dance*, tiene *ballroom*, tiene *tap*, y tiene… Los cuatro años son clases de canto también, de voz hablada y voz cantada, además de la actuación. Entonces está enfocada a las tres áreas de interpretación: la música cantada, el cuerpo en danza y la actuación. Además de los ramos teóricos, por supuesto.

–Bueno, tú has estado involucrado justamente en proyectos que incorporan todas estas variantes. ¿Por qué surgió esta idea de una escuela que tuviera además este tipo de formación?

–Porque no existe acá. En Chile no existe ninguna escuela que dé herramientas tan amplias como las está dando Projazz en este minuto para armar este tipo de proyectos. A ver, todas las escuelas de teatro son… Hay muy buenas escuelas de teatro, pero están enfocadas solamente a la actuación. Tienen una pincelada superpequeña en el tercer semestre, cuarto semestre, de algún taller de baile o algún taller de voz cantada… Pero esto va a estar todos los semestres. Vas a tener danza, algún tipo de danza distinta, algún tipo de nivel de voz cantada y voz hablada, y actuación, por supuesto. Además de ramos teóricos que… ahora te voy a contar un poquito la malla.

–A ver, dale.

–Tenemos Teatro Musical 1, Voz para teatro musical, Actuación… Hay Ballet, Ballet clásico 1, *Jazz Dance*, Historia del teatro, Historia del teatro musical, Teoría musical, Solfeo, Lectura…

O sea, la gente además va a saber leer música. Está superenfocada en integrar todas las áreas y poder destacarse en cualquiera de las tres.

—Ah, bueno. Yo te iba a apuntar a eso en específico porque no es solamente para un actor que quiera desempeñarse en una obra cantando, sino que también esto puede ser atractivo para alguien que quiera dedicarse a la música y tener otras herramientas.

—Es que eso es lo bueno. Tienes las competencias en las tres áreas. Entonces, si quieres ser cantante, también puedes estudiar acá y vas a tener las competencias en actuación, que te van a servir para interpretar, por ejemplo. Si quieres ser bailarín, que cante y que baile, también lo podrías ser. Y si quieres integrar las tres áreas en una sola, que es el teatro musical, por ejemplo, en una obra de teatro musical, también

lo vas a poder hacer. Entonces te va a dar muchas más herramientas que solamente ser actor.

—Ahora, cuéntame un poquito. Estamos conversando con Felipe Ríos, actor, sobre este nuevo proyecto de Escuela de Teatro Musical. ¿Cuándo...? ¿Están abiertas hoy día las postulaciones? ¿Cómo están haciendo todo esto?

—Sí, están abiertas. Tenemos audiciones, que son la entrada a la admisión, y...

—O sea, que se necesita dar una prueba.

—Una prueba de admisión, que es la audición, que el día 27 hay una. O sea, pueden inscribirse hasta el 26 ahora de febrero. Y la próxima es el cinco de marzo. Los cupos se van a cerrar con cursos de veinte personas, no más.

—Felipe, un abrazo.

—Otro para ti. Gracias por la invitación. Felicidades.

—Chao, chao.

Unit 3
Trabajamos

The Unit

- The themes for Unit 3 are education and work. The participants will learn how to express recent and past actions, refer to future plans, make hypotheses, and express wishes. They will also discuss topics related to education, the economy, and work and professions.

- Andy and Diana, two veterans of *Fans del español*, will give the participants their tasks.

  - *Desafío 1.* Eva and Ethan have to find a student exchange program in Chile and prepare a proposal for the school's principal and their parents.

  - *Desafío 2.* Michelle and Daniel will participate in a debate about the salt flats of Uyuni, Bolivia.

  - *Desafío 3.* Asha and Lucas have to find out if there is a job position they can apply for at the Panama Canal.

Activities	Standards	Resources
Trabajamos	1.2, 2.1, 2.2	

Teaching Suggestions

Warm-Up / Independent Starter

- Have students write three sentences about things that they associate with each of these topics: school, the economy, and work.

Preparation

- Ask students to look at the photos and read the captions. Then have them predict what the topic for each challenge might be. For example, they may answer that the first image is about education in a Spanish-speaking country; the second is about natural resources or geographical features; and the last image may be about engineering projects or international trade. Then ask students to share their Independent Starters with the class.

- Have students read each *Desafío's* objective, as well as the vocabulary and grammar goals, then discuss how each image might relate to these objectives and goals.

128

Trabajamos
Los estudios y el trabajo

Paisaje en el salar de Uyuni (Bolivia).

DESAFÍO 1

▶ **Hablar de acciones pasadas**

Vocabulario
La escuela

Gramática
El participio pasado

El presente perfecto y el pluscuamperfecto

DESAFÍO 2

▶ **Relacionar acciones futuras**

Vocabulario
La economía

Gramática
Los pronombres relativos

El futuro perfecto

Profesor y estudiantes en una escuela (Chile).

128 ciento veintiocho

The Challenge

DESAFÍO 1
Profesor y estudiantes en una escuela
Secondary education in Chile lasts four years. There are three types of secondary schools: municipal (public, run by municipalities), private with a government subsidy (voucher), and private independent. After the first two years, students have to choose between a science-liberal arts diploma, which prepares them to enter a higher-learning institution (i.e., university or college) or a vocational-technical diploma, which prepares them for a trade. Students applying for university have to take an admissions exam, or *Prueba de Selección Universitaria* (*PSU*).

DESAFÍO 2
Paisaje en el salar de Uyuni
The *Salar de Uyuni* is located in southwestern Bolivia. At about 11,900 feet above sea level and extending for 4,000 square miles, the Uyuni salt flats make up the world's largest salt desert. However, during the wet season, this salt desert is transformed into a shallow salt lake. In addition to an abundance of salt, the *Salar de Uyuni* is rich in magnesium, potassium, and lithium. It is precisely the abundance of lithium beneath the crust of salt that has spurred an interest among mining companies in this remote corner of Bolivia.

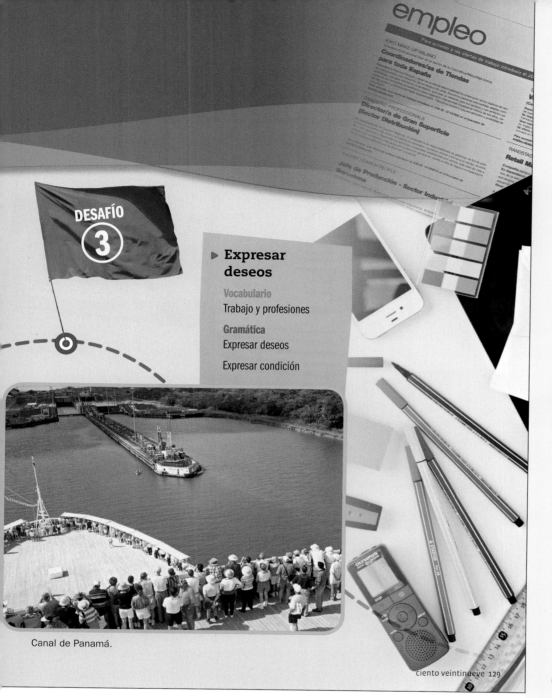

ciento veintinueve 129

3

▶ **Expresar deseos**

Vocabulario
Trabajo y profesiones

Gramática
Expresar deseos

Expresar condición

Canal de Panamá

The idea of connecting the Pacific and Atlantic Oceans across the Isthmus of Panama originated in the 16th century. However, it was not until 1881 when the French—who had built the Suez Canal in Egypt—started building a sea-level canal in Panama. But tropical diseases, bad planning, and economic difficulties derailed the effort. The United States took over the project in 1904 and decided to use a lock system to raise and lower ships instead of the sea-level canal planned by the French. The Americans successfully completed the Canal in 1914.

Trabajamos

Picture Discussion

▪ Ask students to look at the photos again and brainstorm what they know about the topics. Finally, have students review their predictions about each topic.

Profesor y estudiantes en una escuela (Chile)

▪ Ask students questions in order to help them describe the photo. For example: *¿Qué ven en esta foto? ¿Qué edades creen que tienen estos estudiantes? ¿En qué grado están? ¿Se parece esta escuela a la nuestra? ¿Hay algo que les llame la atención?* If there are students in your class who are familiar with school systems in other countries, invite them to share what they know with the class.

Paisaje en el salar de Uyuni (Bolivia)

▪ Ask students to locate the country of Bolivia on a map of South America. Then have them locate the region bordering Chile (i.e., Potosí and Oruro departments). Invite students to share what they know about this region of Bolivia. They may remember that this is an area of high plateaus—called *altiplano* in Spanish—which are part of the Andes mountain range. Students might also point out that this region is rich in minerals, especially silver, which was mined in Potosí.

Canal de Panamá

▪ Invite students to share what they know about the Panama Canal. You may want to ask them some of these questions: *¿En qué región y país se encuentra? (en Centroamérica, en Panamá) ¿Qué dos océanos une? (el Atlántico y el Pacífico) ¿Quiénes lo construyeron? (los estadounidenses) ¿Cómo funciona? (con un sistema de esclusas)*

Objectives

▪ By the end of Unit 3, students will be able to
- Discuss school and education.
- Talk about recent and past actions.
- Talk about the economy and banking.
- Provide essential and non-essential information.
- Refer to future actions.
- Talk about work and professions.
- Express wishes and condition.
- Familiarize themselves with some aspects of the education, economy, and employment practices of the Spanish-speaking world.

Unit 3
Las tareas

Presentation

- In this section, the three pairs receive a message from Andy and Diana, former participants in *Fans del español*, who describe the challenges that lie ahead. Students will preview useful expressions for talking about school and work. They will also preview expressions of encouragement.

Activities	Standards	Resources
Texto	1.2, 2.1, 2.2	
1.	1.1, 1.2, 2.2	
2.	1.1	

Teaching Suggestions

Warm-Up / Independent Starter

- Ask students to think about their future and jot down some of their academic and professional plans.

Preparation

- Acquaint or reacquaint students with Andy and Diana. Explain that Andy is from Atlanta, GA, and that he used to travel with his sister, Janet. Diana is from Lawrenceville, NJ, and she used to travel with her aunt, Rita.

- Invite volunteers to share their thoughts from the Independent Starter. Discuss with the class some of the steps that they would need to take in order to fulfill their goals.

- Discuss the word *trabajo* and its different meanings (i.e., job, labor, work, task, employment, effort). Ask students to find the word in the text and have them derive the meaning through the context.

- Have students scan the text on this page and the dialogue on the following page, and find two phrases used to talk about work or a job *(puesto de trabajo, trabajo a tiempo parcial)* and an expression of encouragement *(¡no se den por vencidos!)*.

Texto: Estudiantes con futuro

- Read the title aloud, and then have students observe the three images for a few moments. Ask students to describe the pictures. Are they able to identify some of the places?

130

Estudiantes con futuro

Los personajes reciben un mensaje que les envían Andy y Diana para explicarles sus nuevos desafíos. Esta vez están relacionados con los estudios y el trabajo. Lee el texto para saber en qué consisten.

DIANA: ¿Qué tal les va? Andy y yo ya tenemos listos sus nuevos desafíos. Van a tener que trabajar duro, pero estamos seguros de que les van a ser muy útiles para su futuro profesional. El primer desafío es para Ethan y Eva. Como sabemos que les encanta viajar y conocer lugares nuevos, van a buscar una escuela en Chile que tenga un programa de intercambio de estudiantes y establecer contacto con la escuela para obtener información. Tal vez puedan ir un tiempo a estudiar allí.

ANDY: Hola, amigos. Yo tengo preparado el desafío de Daniel y Michelle. Ustedes van a participar en un debate sobre el futuro del salar de Uyuni. Primero tendrán que averiguar por qué este tema es tan importante y buscar información sobre él. ¡Ah, y deberán prepararse muy bien para no quedarse en blanco en el debate!

DIANA: Por último, el desafío de Asha y Lucas tiene que ver con un lugar que seguro que conocen: el canal de Panamá. Les suena, ¿no? Bien, pues su tarea consiste en averiguar si hay algún puesto de trabajo al que puedan presentarse como candidatos. Y si no lo consiguen... ¡no se den por vencidos! Quizás lo logren más adelante.

130 ciento treinta

Differentiated Instruction

DEVELOPING LEARNERS

- Ask students the following questions:
  1. *Si Asha y Lucas no consiguen el trabajo, ¿qué les dice Diana? (Que no se den por vencidos.)*
  2. *¿Qué deben averiguar primero Daniel y Michelle? (Por qué el salar de Uyuni es un tema importante.)*
  3. *¿Por qué deben trabajar duro todas las parejas? (Los desafíos les van a ser muy útiles para su futuro profesional.)*
  4. *¿Por qué mandan a Eva y Ethan a buscar una escuela en Chile? (Saben que les encanta viajar y conocer lugares nuevos.)*

EXPANDING LEARNERS

- Have students consider the three *desafíos* that Andy and Diana set forth. Then, ask them to work with a partner and discuss the ideal characteristics, abilities, and interests that the participants should have in order to best execute these challenges. Ask students to write at least one paragraph outlining these qualities for each *desafío*. Invite pairs to read their paragraphs aloud.

¡Yo quiero ir a estudiar a Chile! ¿Crees que me aceptarán en alguna escuela?

¡Pues claro! ¡Si siempre sacas muy buenas notas!

El salar de Uyuni... ¿Te suena de algo?

¡Qué va! No tengo ni idea.

Este desafío es genial. ¿No te encantaría trabajar en el canal de Panamá?

Sí, pero me gustaría empezar por un trabajo a tiempo parcial.

1 ¿Comprendes?

▶ **Responde** a estas preguntas.

1. ¿Qué es un intercambio de estudiantes? ¿Quiénes van a participar en uno? ¿Dónde?
2. ¿Qué tienen que hacer Daniel y Michelle? ¿Qué saben sobre el salar de Uyuni?
3. ¿Qué sabes tú sobre el canal de Panamá? ¿Qué tienen que hacer Asha y Lucas?
4. ¿Qué desafío te parece más interesante? ¿Por qué?

2 Investiga

▶ **Busca** en el texto y en los bocadillos las expresiones para completar estas oraciones.

1. Si de pronto no recuerdas algo que sabías, dices que te has quedado en ___1___.
2. Un trabajo puede ser a tiempo completo o a tiempo ___2___.
3. Un sinónimo de *rendirse* es darse por ___3___.
4. Cuando alguien trabaja mucho, decimos que trabaja ___4___.
5. Si estudias mucho y haces bien los exámenes ___5___ buenas ___6___.

HERITAGE LANGUAGE LEARNERS

• Ask students to describe situations in which they would use each of the following expressions and write an example for each one: *quedarse en blanco, darse por vencido, sonarle a uno algo, empezar por, no tener ni idea, presentarse como.* Encourage students to add other expressions that have similar meanings and write a sentence for each one. Then have students share these expressions and their sentences with the rest of the class.

CRITICAL THINKING

• Remind students that Asha and Lucas's *desafío* has to do with working for the Panama Canal. Have students brainstorm related jobs for this location, and ask them to describe the position Asha and Lucas might have. Discuss what experience or special skills might be required of them and how they would go about securing the necessary documents for working outside of their country. Discuss the advantages or disadvantages of working abroad. Do students believe that such an experience would make them more marketable when they return home? Why?

■ Read the introduction to the text aloud, and then ask for three volunteers to read the messages from Diana and Andy aloud. Write down the following words on the board and ask students to associate a participant pair with each of these words according to their tasks: *programa de intercambio, debate, puesto de trabajo.* (Eva and Ethan, Michelle and Daniel, Asha and Lucas)

Activities

1. You may want to discuss question #4 as a class. How difficult do students think each *desafío* will be? Which pair will be most successful? Why?

2. Explore the vocabulary further by writing expressions or words on the board that might be unfamiliar to students or that they may not remember. For example: *ir un tiempo, tiene que ver con, ¿Te suena de algo?, ¡Pues claro!, ¡Qué va!* Do not translate them into English. Instead, explain their meaning with gestures or by using them in other contexts.

Answer Key

1. Answers will vary. Sample answers:
   1. Es cuando un estudiante vive y estudia en un país extranjero durante un periodo de tiempo limitado. Eva y Ethan van a participar en un intercambio de estudiantes en Chile.
   2. Tienen que participar en un debate sobre el futuro del salar de Uyuni. Ellos no saben nada de este salar.
   3. Answers will vary. Tienen que averiguar si hay algún puesto de trabajo en el canal de Panamá al que puedan presentarse como candidatos.
   4. Answers will vary.

2. 1. blanco   4. duro
   2. parcial   5. sacas
   3. vencido   6. notas

Additional Resources

Fans Online activities
Practice Workbook

131

Unit 3

Antes de empezar

Presentation

- In this section, students will learn a variety of useful expressions to talk about school and work. They will also learn expressions of encouragement.

- Students will also review vocabulary for talking about school, computers, jobs, and professions.

Activities	Standards	Resources
Expresiones útiles	1.2, 2.1	
3.	1.2, 2.1	Audio
4.	1.1, 2.1	
Recuerda	1.2	
5.	1.1	
6.	1.1, 5.1	

Teaching Suggestions

Warm-Up / Independent Starter

- Have students list words and phrases related to school and work in a two-column table.

Preparation

- Ask students to share their Independent Starter lists with the class. Then, give students a few moments to go over the *expresiones útiles* individually. Answer any questions they may have, and then use some of students' words and phrases from the Independent Starter to personalize and practice the *expresiones útiles*. For example, you may ask students: 1. *¿Si asistes a clase todos los días, sacas buenas notas?* 2. *¿Sueles quedarte en blanco cuando haces un examen?* 3. *¿Trabajar a tiempo parcial es lo mismo que trabajar media jornada?*

- Give students a few moments to read the *Recuerda* box silently. Then divide the class into seven groups—numbered from 1 through 7—and assign each group one of the following vocabulary categories: 1. *Asignaturas*; 2. *La escuela*; 3. *La computadora*; 4. *Profesiones* (half) and *Cargos* (half); 5. *Profesiones* (half) and *Cargos* (half); 6. *El trabajo*; 7. *Cualidades*. Have groups create a graphic organizer for each word in their vocabulary list. In each graphic organizer, students should include the word and part of speech, a short definition, a sample sentence and, if appropriate, a synonym or an antonym.

132

Antes de empezar

EXPRESIONES ÚTILES

Para hablar de los estudios:

Yo siempre **saco buenas notas**, pero mi hermano no.

Si **faltas a clase** no vas a salir bien en los exámenes.

Para decir que no recuerdas algo:

El día del examen me puse nervioso y me quedé **en blanco**: no me acordaba de nada.

Para referirse a las condiciones laborales:

Mis padres **trabajan a tiempo completo**, de 9 a. m. a 6 p. m.

Ahora **trabajo a tiempo parcial** porque tengo que estudiar.

Trabajo por cuenta propia: tengo una empresa de publicidad.

Para decir que alguien trabaja mucho:

Debes **trabajar duro** si quieres lograr tus objetivos.

Para animar:

No te des por vencida, Eva. Sigue intentándolo.

Sigue adelante, no te desanimes.

---

3 **Expresiones**

 ▶ **Escucha** a varias personas. ¿Qué oración corresponde a cada intervención?

a. Se quedó en blanco.

b. Trabaja a tiempo parcial.

c. Se da por vencida muy fácilmente.

d. Trabaja por cuenta propia.

4 **¿Qué opinas?**

▶ **Haz** estas preguntas a tu compañero(a) y toma nota de sus respuestas. Después, coméntenlas. ¿Están de acuerdo en todo?

1. ¿Qué hay que hacer para sacar siempre buenas notas?

2. Si un(a) estudiante saca malas notas en un examen, ¿es porque no ha estudiado o puede deberse a otras razones?

3. ¿Qué se puede hacer para no quedarse en blanco en un examen?

4. ¿Qué opinas de la gente que se da por vencida fácilmente? ¿Por qué?

5. ¿Qué se debe hacer si un(a) estudiante falta mucho a clase? ¿Por qué?

132 ciento treinta y dos

Differentiated Instruction

DEVELOPING LEARNERS

- Ask students to indicate which word does not belong and explain why.

Geografía	Química	Física (Geografía)
derechos	deberes	apuntes (apuntes)
emprendedor	impresora	teclado
(emprendedor)		
asignatura	pantalla	archivo
(asignatura)		
Matemáticas	jornada	contador (jornada)
eficiente	exigente	eficaz (exigente)
programador	impresora	arquitecta
(impresora)		
ambicioso	creativo	original
(ambicioso)		

EXPANDING LEARNERS

- Ask students the following:

1. *¿Qué consecuencias hay si faltas mucho a clase?*

2. *¿Qué te dicen en casa si sacas malas notas? ¿Y si sacas buenas notas?*

3. *¿Qué pasa si te quedas en blanco el día de un examen?*

4. *¿Siempre consigues el éxito si trabajas duro?*

5. *¿Cuándo es preferible trabajar a tiempo parcial?*

6. *¿Cómo animas a un(a) amigo(a) para que no se dé por vencido(a)?*

7. *¿Cómo te preparas para un examen final?*

RECUERDA

Asignaturas
la Biología
la Física
la Geografía
la Historia
la Literatura
las Matemáticas
la Química

La escuela
hacer un examen
levantar la mano
prestar atención
tomar apuntes

La computadora
la impresora
la pantalla
el ratón
el teclado
bajar/subir un archivo

Profesiones
el/la abogado(a)
el actor/la actriz
el/la administrativo(a)
el/la arquitecto(a)
el/la banquero(a)
el/la comerciante

el/la contador(a)
el/la empresario(a)
el/la ingeniero(a)
el/la periodista
el/la programador(a)
el/la traductor(a)

Cargos
el/la coordinador(a)
el/la director(a)

el/la empleado(a)
el/la presidente(a)

El trabajo
el contrato
los deberes
los derechos

la jornada completa
la media jornada
el sueldo

Cualidades
amable
ambicioso(a)
creativo(a)
eficiente

emprendedor(a)
exigente
organizado(a)
responsable

5 Definiciones

► **Escribe** las definiciones de tres palabras del cuadro Recuerda. Después, léeselas a tu compañero(a). Él/Ella tiene que adivinar de qué palabras se trata.

Modelo   A. *Es un acuerdo entre un empleador y un trabajador.*
  B. *El contrato.*

6 ¿Cuánto sabes?

► **Habla** con tu compañero(a). ¿A qué se dedican estas personas? ¿Qué hacen en su trabajo? ¿Qué tipo de condiciones crees que tienen: contrato, horario, sueldo...?

ciento treinta y tres **133**

HERITAGE LANGUAGE LEARNERS

• In addition to the *expresiones útiles* listed, ask students to come up with other ways to describe study habits, forgetting, work-related conditions, working hard, and to express encouragement. Ask students to make a five-column chart with the corresponding headers and relevant examples for each one. When students complete their charts, ask them to write a sample sentence for each new word or expression. Students will read the sentences to the rest of the class and explain the meaning of the new vocabulary.

SPECIAL-NEEDS LEARNERS

• Give students with auditory impairment a copy of the audio script for activity 3 before they listen to the recording. Then allow them to follow along with the script as they listen as many times as needed. Secure a quiet area in the classroom for these students, making sure they are seated away from windows, doors, or any other distractions. After students answer the questions, ask them to define or give examples of *quedarse en blanco, darse por vencido, trabajar a tiempo parcial,* and *trabajar por cuenta propia.*

Unit 3

Antes de empezar

■ Have groups 1, 2, and 3 get together and discuss their lists. Do the same with groups 4 and 6, and groups 5 and 7. Then have groups come up with sentences in which they combine several words from their lists. For example: *Es importante tomar apuntes en la clase de Historia.* Invite groups to share some of their sentences with the class.

Activities

4. Once pairs have finished this activity, ask them to get together with another pair. Then, have these small groups of four students discuss questions #1 and #3, and come up with a list of useful tips. Invite groups to share their advice with the class. Then discuss the most useful pieces of advice as a class.

6. To extend this activity, have students discuss the education and/or training required for each of the professions depicted. Then have students choose one of the three professions and role-play an interview in which one of the students will play the role of the professional and the other will be the interviewer. The interviewer will ask his or her interviewee about the educational requirements for the job, the job characteristics and duties, as well as salary, hours, etc. If time allows, ask for volunteer pairs to act out their interviews in front of the class.

 AUDIO SCRIPT
See page 127K.

Answer Key

3. a. 2 b. 1 c. 4 d. 3
4. Answers will vary.
5. Answers will vary.
6. Answers will vary.

Additional Resources

Fans Online activities
Practice Workbook

133

Unit 3
DESAFÍO 1

Hablar de acciones pasadas

Presentation

- In *Desafío 1*, Eva and Ethan have to find a student exchange program in Chile and prepare a proposal. Students will preview language used to talk about school, and verb structures used to talk about recently completed actions.

Activities	Standards	Resources
Texto	1.2, 2.1	
7.	1.2, 2.1	
8.	1.1, 1.2, 2.1	
9.	1.2, 2.1	Audio
10.	1.1, 1.3, 2.1, 4.2	
11. Comparaciones	1.1, 1.2, 2.1, 2.2, 3.1, 4.2	

Teaching Suggestions

Warm-Up / Independent Starter

- Ask students to write two or three sentences describing what they know about student exchange programs.

Preparation

- Invite students to share their Independent Starters. As a class, discuss some of the characteristics of these programs (e.g., study abroad, students stay with a host family). Then read the title and introduction aloud.

Texto: Un intercambio cultural

- Have students read the dialogue silently. Once they are finished, ask for two volunteers to play the roles of the characters and read the dialogue aloud.
- Invite students to share their impressions. What information do Eva and Ethan need to have before they apply for the program? How might they improve their chances of being accepted? Should they go for a full year instead of just one semester?

Activities

9. Have students correct the false statements. Then divide the class into small groups to discuss the question in the second part. Finally, have groups share their ideas with the class.

Un intercambio cultural

Ethan y Eva quieren participar en un programa de intercambio de estudiantes con una escuela de Santiago (Chile). Tienen que encontrar un programa y presentar su propuesta a la directora de su escuela... ¡y a sus padres! ¿La aceptarán?

ETHAN: ¡Qué interesante sería estudiar en un país hispano! ¿Te gustaría irte un semestre o todo el curso?

EVA: Yo creo que un semestre sería suficiente. Además, pasar todo el curso en Chile sería complicado porque tienen un calendario escolar muy distinto al nuestro. Me han dicho que el curso comienza a principios de marzo y tienen los exámenes parciales en julio y los finales en noviembre.

ETHAN: ¿Y cuándo tienen las vacaciones?

EVA: En julio tienen dos semanas de vacaciones de invierno. Y las vacaciones de verano son desde mediados de diciembre hasta principios de marzo.

ETHAN: Tienes razón, es mejor matricularse para un semestre. ¿Sabes si tienen información para estudiantes extranjeros?

EVA: Sí, he escrito a la escuela y les he pedido información sobre las becas que ofrecen. ¿Sabes? Cuando tomas el examen de ingreso, también te evalúan para concederte una beca.

ETHAN: ¿Un examen de ingreso? ¡Qué miedo! Voy a tener que repasar mis apuntes.

EVA: Yo ya he preparado el formulario de matriculación. Si apruebo todo, podré matricularme para el segundo semestre en el Colegio San Miguel, en Santiago.

ETHAN: ¿Y si repruebas algún examen?

EVA: ¡Espero que no! ¡Voy a seguir estudiando!

Panorámica de Santiago de Chile.

7 Detective de palabras

▶ **Completa** estas oraciones.

1. Eva cree que estudiar un _____ en Chile será suficiente.
2. En el calendario escolar chileno los exámenes _____ son en julio.
3. Ethan está de acuerdo en que es mejor _____ para un semestre.
4. A Ethan le asusta tener que tomar un examen de _____.
5. Para pasar el examen, Ethan va a tener que _____ sus apuntes.
6. Eva no cree que vaya a _____ ningún examen.

Differentiated Instruction

DEVELOPING LEARNERS

- To confirm students' comprehension of the dialogue, ask them to write a summary of it in the third-person narrative form. Suggest that they refer to their answers in activities 7 and 8 before they begin their summaries. Have them turn over their narratives to a student with superior language skills who will edit and query their work. After students discuss the suggested edits and queries, have them make the necessary corrections. Then, call on volunteers to read their work aloud.

EXPANDING LEARNERS

- Ask students to work with a partner and create a dialogue around their mutually agreed-upon ideal academic schedule. Students will need to address when the school year begins and ends, when daily classes start and end, and how long each class is. They will also need to include winter and summer vacations, holidays (including some to commemorate Hispanic figures or events), and policies regarding entrance exams and finals (or their elimination). Call on volunteers to act out their dialogues.

8 ¿Comprendes?

▶ **Responde** a estas preguntas.

1. ¿Por qué Eva prefiere ir solo un semestre a Chile?
2. ¿Cuándo terminan el curso en Chile?
3. ¿Cuándo son las vacaciones de verano en Chile?
4. ¿Para qué semestre y dónde quiere matricularse Eva?
5. ¿Quién crees que está más preparado para este desafío: Ethan o Eva? ¿Por qué?

9 Buscando información

 ▶ **Escucha** y decide si estas afirmaciones son ciertas o falsas.

1. Ethan está leyendo un folleto sobre las escuelas en Chile.
2. Ethan busca información sobre el calendario escolar.
3. A Eva le preocupa la prueba de Matemáticas del examen de ingreso.
4. Eva le recomienda a Ethan que comience a estudiar ya.
5. Ethan no ha encontrado suficiente información sobre los exámenes.
6. Eva le pide a Ethan que busque más información en Internet.

 ▶ **Habla** con tu compañero(a). ¿Qué pruebas incluirían ustedes en un examen de ingreso para una escuela?

10 Diferencias

▶ **Lee** de nuevo el diálogo de la página 134 y escribe una lista con las diferencias que encuentras entre la escuela de Chile y la tuya.

 ▶ **Habla** con tu compañero(a) y comparen sus listas. ¿Hay muchas diferencias? ¿Por qué creen que el calendario escolar es tan diferente?

 **COMPARACIONES**

El calendario escolar

El año escolar empieza y termina en cada país en distintas fechas, en función del clima y la situación geográfica. En España y en México, por ejemplo, el curso va de septiembre a junio. En la zona del ecuador, donde no existen grandes cambios estacionales, el año escolar comienza en enero y termina en noviembre. En cambio, en los países del hemisferio sur, suele comenzar en marzo, después de las vacaciones de verano, y terminar en diciembre.

 11 **Piensa.** ¿Cómo está organizado tu calendario escolar? ¿Por qué es así? ¿Cuáles son las ventajas y desventajas de esa organización?

ciento treinta y cinco **135**

HERITAGE LANGUAGE LEARNERS

- Ask students to describe the school year and daily schedule of classes in *una escuela* or *un colegio* from their heritage country. They should include what month the academic year traditionally begins and ends, and when seasonal vacations are taken and how long they last. Students should also address the daily school schedule, the average course load per student, and how students are evaluated for their progress. Encourage them to add other details, especially with regard to comparisons between their heritage country's schools and the one they are currently attending.

MULTIPLE INTELLIGENCES:
Verbal-Linguistic Intelligence

- Students will participate in a debate. The topic to be debated is whether or not to initiate an entrance exam for students wanting to enroll in a school that currently has no such requirement. Have students work in teams of four or five, who will debate another team. Assign some teams to argue in favor of initiating the requirement, and others to oppose the idea. Set time limits for arguments and rebuttals. Select some students to sit as judges and determine who has won each debate.

Hablar de acciones pasadas

10. To extend this activity, have small groups discuss what they like best about each school and come up with a few suggestions for changes in their school.

> **AUDIO SCRIPT**
> See page 127K.

COMPARACIONES

El calendario escolar

In the United States, most states require from 175 to 180 days of school per year. According to data published by UNESCO, there are variations in the average number of school days in the Spanish-speaking world: 200 in Bolivia, Mexico, and Peru; 190 in Chile and Ecuador; 180 in Argentina, Uruguay, and Guatemala; 175 in Spain. The number of years of compulsory education also varies: 13 in Argentina; 12 in Chile and Peru; 11 in Mexico and Spain; 10 in Colombia, Costa Rica, and Ecuador.

Answer Key

7.
1. semestre	4. ingreso
2. parciales	5. repasar
3. matricularse	6. reprobar

8.
1. Porque el calendario escolar es muy distinto.
2. Terminan en diciembre.
3. Son desde mediados de diciembre hasta principios de marzo.
4. Para el segundo semestre, en el Colegio San Miguel, en Santiago.
5. Answers will vary.

9. 1. F   2. F   3. C   4. F   5. C   6. F
▶ Answers will vary.

10. Answers will vary.
▶ Answers will vary.

11. Answers will vary.

Additional Resources

Fans Online activities

135

DESAFÍO 1

Vocabulario – La escuela

Presentation

- In this section, students will learn vocabulary related to school and education.

Activities	Standards	Resources
Vocabulario	1.2, 2.1, 3.1	
12.	1.1, 3.1	
13.	1.2	
14.	1.1	
15. Comparaciones	1.2, 2.1, 3.2, 4.2	

Teaching Suggestions

Warm-Up / Independent Starter

- Have students think about their school system and jot down some of its main characteristics (e.g., number of semesters, number of classes each semester, exams they take and frequency).

Preparation

- Call on eight volunteers to each read an entry from the chat. Then go over the highlighted words to emphasize pronunciation. You may want to ask students these questions to check their comprehension: *¿Cuándo comenzará Eva las clases en Chile? ¿Cuándo son los exámenes parciales? ¿Y los finales? ¿En qué consiste el examen de ingreso? ¿Qué debe hacer Eva si quiere optar a una beca?* Then read the words in the *Más vocabulario* section and have students repeat them after you.

- Have students work with a partner and, using their notes from the Independent Starter, write a brief description of their school system for an international exchange student who is new to the system. Invite volunteers to share their descriptions with the class.

Activities

13. To extend this activity, have students create four statements about their school, leaving out the vocabulary term. Then ask them to exchange their statements with a classmate and complete each other's activity. If time allows, invite volunteer students to share their sentences with the class.

Vocabulario

La escuela

Chat room

Colegio San Miguel
Me parece muy bien tu decisión de matricularte para el segundo semestre del curso académico. Comenzarás las clases después de los exámenes parciales.

Eva
¿Cuándo son esos exámenes?

Colegio San Miguel
En julio. Ya sabes que evaluamos la materia que los estudiantes han aprendido en un semestre, en este caso, entre marzo y julio. Y en diciembre tenemos los exámenes finales.

Eva
Gracias. Sé que tengo que hacer un examen de ingreso. ¿Puede decirme en qué consiste?

Colegio San Miguel
Es un examen para determinar el nivel en dos materias: Lengua y Matemáticas. La primera examina el nivel de español por medio de una lectura y la escritura de un párrafo de doce a quince oraciones sobre un tema específico. En la segunda hay que demostrar que se hacen sin problemas algunas operaciones básicas como las sumas, las restas, las multiplicaciones, las divisiones y las fracciones.

Eva
¿Y qué pasa si repruebo el examen?

Colegio San Miguel
Si normalmente sacas buenas notas, seguro que vas a aprobar. Pero debes esforzarte y hacerlo bien si quieres optar a una beca para ayudarte económicamente.

Eva
De acuerdo. Voy a ponerme a repasar mis apuntes de clase.

Participantes
- Colegio San Miguel

- Eva

Más vocabulario

Matemáticas

más	+	entre	÷
menos	−	igual a	=
por	×	por ciento	%

Lengua

mayúscula	A
minúscula	a
punto	.
coma	,
punto y coma	;
dos puntos	:

¡Atención!

descansar	to rest
restar	to subtract

12 **Operaciones matemáticas**

▶ **Escribe** una ecuación o expresión numeral para mostrar el significado de estos términos matemáticos.

1. resta   2. suma   3. porcentaje   4. división   5. fracción   6. multiplicación

 ▶ **Habla** con tu compañero(a). Túrnense para leer y completar estas operaciones.

1. $34 \times 2 =$ 2. $95 - 10 =$ 3. $120 \div 10 =$ 4. 10% de $100 =$

Differentiated Instruction

DEVELOPING LEARNERS

- Have students complete the following sentences with an appropriate word from the *Vocabulario* feature:
  1. *Al final de una oración declarativa se escribe...* (punto)
  2. *Si mencionas una serie de cosas en una oración, hay que escribir ... entre ellas.* (coma)
  3. *Tu nombre y apellido empiezan con una letra...* (mayúscula)
  4. *Los días de la semana y los meses del año se escriben con ... en español.* (minúscula)
  5. *Escribimos ... después del saludo de una carta formal.* (dos puntos)

EXPANDING LEARNERS

- Ask students to say aloud the following in Spanish:
  1. $2 \times 2 = 4$ *(dos por dos es igual a cuatro)*
  2. $35 \div 5 = 7$ *(treinta y cinco entre cinco/ dividido por cinco es igual a siete)*
  3. $21 + 2 = 23$ *(veintiuno más dos es igual a veintitrés)*
  4. 20% of 500 is 100 *(el veinte por ciento de quinientos es cien)*
  5. $87 - 8 = 79$ *(ochenta y siete menos ocho es igual a setenta y nueve)*
  6. Which is greater: ⅔ or ¾? *(¿Cuál es mayor: dos tercios o tres cuartos?)*

13 En la escuela

▶ **Completa** estas oraciones con palabras de la ficha de Vocabulario.

1. En esta escuela no hay exámenes _____, solo exámenes finales.
2. Para matricularte en esta escuela hay que hacer un examen de _____.
3. Ethan siempre tiene miedo de _____ los exámenes.
4. Si estudias y te _____, seguro que apruebas todas las asignaturas.
5. Además de estudiar todos los días, es conveniente _____ de vez en cuando.
6. Voy a solicitar una _____ para matricularme en la universidad.

14 Tu vida escolar

▶ **Habla** con tu compañero(a). Túrnense para hacerse estas preguntas.

1. ¿Cuándo te matriculaste en esta escuela?
2. ¿Cuál es tu asignatura favorita? ¿Y la que menos te gusta? ¿Por qué?
3. ¿Has recibido alguna vez una beca? ¿Esperas obtener alguna en el futuro? ¿Cuál?
4. ¿Reprobaste alguna materia en primaria? ¿Y en secundaria? ¿Por qué?
5. ¿Tienes algún sistema útil para repasar antes de los exámenes? ¿Cuál?
6. ¿Dónde te gustaría pasar un semestre como estudiante de intercambio? ¿Por qué?

COMPARACIONES

El coste de la educación

En los países hispanos hay universidades públicas y universidades privadas. En la mayoría de los países, la universidad pública es gratuita o semigratuita y el coste de la matrícula es bastante menor que en las universidades privadas. No obstante, el precio de la educación universitaria no alcanza el nivel de los Estados Unidos. Por ello, la mayor parte de los estudiantes no piden préstamos para pagar sus estudios.

Universidad de Santiago de Chile.

15 Explica.
¿Por qué crees que es tan caro el sistema educativo en los Estados Unidos? ¿Qué ventajas y desventajas tiene estudiar en una universidad pública? ¿Y en una privada?

---

14. Have students share their answers to question #5 in small groups and select the three most useful recommendations. Then have groups share their recommendations with the class.

15. Have student pairs research top-ranked U.S. universities—both private and public. To avoid repetition of information, you may want to assign a different institution to each pair (e.g., Harvard, Princeton, MIT, University of California, University of Virginia, University of Michigan). Students should prepare a report about their assigned university that includes costs, programs the university is known for, famous faculty members, and admission requirements.

COMPARACIONES

El coste de la educación

The United States has one of the best higher education systems in the world, but the cost of obtaining a college degree in America is also among the highest in the world. In order to pay for college, two-thirds of bachelor's degree recipients borrow money. Outstanding student loans total more than $1 trillion, and many graduates are struggling to pay their loans off. All the while, tuition has been rising at an annual rate of about 5%.

Answer Key

12. Answers will vary. Sample answers:

1. $30 - 9$	4. $100 \div 4$
2. $35 + 22$	5. ¾
3. 75%	6. 48×12

▶ 1. 68   2. 85   3. 12   4. 10

13.
1. parciales
2. ingreso
3. reprobar
4. esfuerzas
5. repasar
6. beca

14. Answers will vary.

15. Answers will vary.

Additional Resources

Fans Online activities
Practice Workbook

HERITAGE LANGUAGE LEARNERS

- Ask students to start their own *Cuaderno de puntuación*. Write the symbols for the following punctuation marks and ask students to identify them and to explain when they are used in Spanish: *el punto, la coma, el punto y coma, los dos puntos, los puntos suspensivos, el guion largo o raya, las comillas, los signos de interrogación y de admiración, el paréntesis, los corchetes*. Have students give examples for each one. Encourage them to share their explanations and examples with the rest of the class.

MULTIPLE INTELLIGENCES:
Verbal-Linguistic Intelligence

- Tell students that they are going to play a version of "Jeopardy" with the vocabulary. Explain that the categories will be *La escuela, Las Matemáticas,* and *La Lengua*. Have students play against one another in groups of four or five. Ask other students, who will not play, to write several answers, along with their corresponding questions, for each of these categories. For example: *No es un número entero. (¿Qué es una fracción?) Indica una pregunta. (¿Qué es un signo de interrogación?)*

DESAFÍO 1

Gramática – El participio pasado

Presentation

- In this section, students will review the formation of the past participle and how it may be used as an adjective, verb, or noun.

Activities	Standards	Resources
Gramática	1.2, 3.1	
16.	1.2, 3.1, 4.1	
17.	1.3, 3.1	
18.	1.3, 3.1	
19.	1.1, 1.2, 3.1, 5.1	Audio
20. Cultura	1.2, 1.3, 2.1, 2.2, 3.1, 3.2, 5.1	

Teaching Suggestions

Warm-Up / Independent Starter

- Have students read the grammar presentation silently, and then complete the following sentences with the past participle of the verb *emplear*:
  - *Carmen está … en una multinacional. (empleada)*
  - *Los … están descontentos. (empleados)*
  - *Ellos han … a dos ingenieros. (empleado)*

Preparation

- Review the Independent Starter as a class and call on volunteers to explain how the past participle is used in each case. (adjective, noun, verb) Then, discuss these sentences and the use of the past participle in each one: They have accused him. The accused denied the charges. The accused employee was fired. Next, have students translate the sentences into Spanish. (*Ellos lo han acusado. El acusado negó las acusaciones. El empleado acusado fue despedido.*)

Activities

17. Have students come up with sentences showing the use of *escrito* and *hecho* as adjectives and as nouns (e.g., *Las cartas están escritas y listas para enviar. Presenté un escrito de reclamación*).

19. You may want to have small groups prepare a short presentation about an interactive museum they have visited or would like to visit. They should include information about the museum's hours, exhibits, interactive activities, etc.

Gramática

El participio pasado

- El participio pasado (*past participle*) es una forma verbal que termina generalmente en -ado (hablado) o en -ido (comido), y se utiliza para formar los tiempos compuestos de los verbos: ha hablado, habíamos comido, habrán llamado.
- Algunos verbos como decir, escribir, hacer o ver tienen participios pasados irregulares: dicho, escrito, hecho, visto... Repasa los participios pasados irregulares en la página R12.

El participio pasado usado como adjetivo

- El participio pasado se puede usar como un adjetivo para describir un nombre. En este caso, el participio concuerda en género y número con el nombre al que se refiere.

  La puerta del salón está **abierta**.   Hay veinte estudiantes **inscritos**.

El participio pasado usado como verbo

- El participio pasado tiene dos usos como verbo:
  - Con el verbo auxiliar haber se utiliza para formar los **tiempos perfectos**: el presente perfecto, el pluscuamperfecto... En este caso, el participio siempre termina en -o.

    Habíamos **estudiado** antes de hacer el examen.   Tania ha **recibido** una beca.

  - Con el verbo auxiliar ser se utiliza para formar la **voz pasiva** de los verbos. En este caso, el participio concuerda en género y número con el sujeto.

    Las fechas de los exámenes **serán publicadas** en la página web.

El participio pasado usado como nombre

- El participio pasado de muchos verbos se usa también para formar nombres:

    Masculinos: el asado, el cocido, el empleado, el enamorado, el tejido...
    Femeninos: la llamada, la nevada, la propuesta, la salida, la subida...

16 **Compara.** ¿En inglés se usa también el participio pasado como adjetivo, como verbo y como nombre? ¿Hay diferencias entre estas formas?

17 **Preparativos**

▶ **Une** las columnas y escribe oraciones. Pon los verbos en la forma correcta del participio.

Ⓐ
1. Ethan y Eva han _____ (buscar)
2. Eva ha _____ (escribir)
3. Ethan y Eva están _____ (preocupar)
4. Eva nunca había _____ (hacer)
5. La propuesta será _____ (revisar)
6. Ethan y Eva aún no han _____ (resolver)

Ⓑ
a. por la directora de su escuela.
b. a una escuela para pedir información.
c. un examen para estudiar en otro país.
d. su desafío.
e. información sobre colegios en Chile.
f. por el examen de ingreso.

138 ciento treinta y ocho

Differentiated Instruction

DEVELOPING LEARNERS

- Have students complete the following sentences with the past participle of the verbs in parentheses:
  1. *¿Has (poner) la mesa? (puesto)*
  2. *Los astrónomos han (descubrir) una nueva estrella. (descubierto)*
  3. *He (cubrir) los muebles. (cubierto)*
  4. *Te he (ver) en el jardín. (visto)*
  5. *¿Cuántas cartas has (escribir)? (escrito)*
  6. *Siento que se haya (morir) tu mascota. (muerto)*
  7. *¿Quién ha (romper) el vaso? (roto)*
  8. *Han (volver) muy tarde. (vuelto)*

EXPANDING LEARNERS

- Ask students to translate the following sentences into Spanish:
  1. All the scholarships will be granted. (*Todas las becas serán concedidas.*)
  2. He has broken off relations with her. (*Ha roto relaciones con ella.*)
  3. I like fried eggs. (*Me gustan los huevos fritos.*)
  4. The books are not printed yet. (*Los libros no están impresos aún.*)
  5. I have solved the problem. (*He resuelto el problema.*)
  6. The schools are open. (*Las escuelas están abiertas.*)

AUDIO SCRIPT
See page 127K.

18 ¿Qué han hecho?

▶ **Piensa.** ¿Con qué verbos relacionas estos nombres? Escribe una oración con cada nombre.

Modelo   1. la empanada → *empanar*
Ayer preparé una empanada de espinacas deliciosa.

1. empanada   **2.** bajada   **3.** invitados   **4.** acampada   **5.** llegada   **6.** mirada

19 Un museo interactivo

 ▶ **Escucha** a dos estudiantes y responde a estas preguntas.

1. ¿Qué actividad ha organizado la escuela?

2. ¿Por qué dice María que «no es un museo cualquiera»?

3. ¿Cuál es el lema del museo?

4. ¿Cómo se titula el taller al que van a asistir?

 ▶ **Escucha** de nuevo y completa estas oraciones con los participios correctos.

1. María le pregunta a su amiga si se ha _____ a la visita al museo.

2. El lema del museo dice que está _____ no tocar, no sentir y no pensar.

3. María explica que el museo está _____ para aprender.

4. El museo ha _____ un taller para estudiantes de secundaria.

5. La profesora les ha _____ que verán un reloj que funciona con jugo de naranja.

6. María ha _____ a Sonia para que se apunte a la visita.

 ▶ **Habla** con tu compañero(a). ¿Alguna vez han visitado un museo interactivo? ¿Les gustaría ir a alguno? ¿Por qué?

 CULTURA

La Ciudad de las Artes y las Ciencias de Valencia

La Ciudad de las Artes y las Ciencias de Valencia (España), diseñada por los arquitectos españoles Santiago Calatrava y Félix Candela, es un conjunto de edificios destinados a la divulgación *(dissemination)* científica y cultural. El Museo de las Ciencias Príncipe Felipe y el Oceanogràfic —el mayor acuario de Europa— forman parte de este recinto, que se ha convertido en una de las principales atracciones turísticas de Valencia.

20 **Piensa y explica.** ¿Crees que es bueno que las ciudades apuesten por este tipo de proyectos? ¿Por qué?

ciento treinta y nueve **139**

Gramática – El participio pasado

AUDIO SCRIPT
See page 127K.

 CULTURA

La Ciudad de las Artes y las Ciencias de Valencia

The City of Arts and Sciences consists of several buildings that house a planetarium, an Imax cinema, an interactive museum of science, an aquarium, an opera house and performing arts center, and a multifunctional building for sports events, conventions, exhibitions, etc. Outdoor structures include a suspension bridge and a walkway, or promenade, surrounded by gardens and sculptures.

Answer Key

16. Sí, en inglés también se usa en esos tres casos, pero las formas no cambian: *the fruit has fallen from the tree; a fallen fruit; the fallen in a war.*

17. 1. (e) buscado   4. (c) hecho
2. (b) escrito   5. (a) revisada
3. (f) preocupados   6. (d) resuelto

18. 2. bajar   4. acampar   6. mirar
3. invitar   5. llegar

19. 1. Una visita al Museo de las Ciencias Príncipe Felipe.
2. Porque es un museo interactivo.
3. «Prohibido no tocar, no sentir, no pensar».
4. *Magia química.*

▶ 1. apuntado   4. organizado
2. prohibido   5. dicho
3. pensado   6. convencido

▶ Answers will vary.

20. Answers will vary.

Additional Resources

Fans Online activities
Practice Workbook

139

HERITAGE LANGUAGE LEARNERS

• Point out that some verbs have two past participle forms (e.g., *confesar: confesado, confeso*). In these cases, the regular participle is used with perfect verb tenses; the irregular participle is an adjective (e.g., *El asesino ha confesado. Él es el asesino confeso del crimen*). Ask students to write both past participle forms for the following verbs, explain the difference between the two, and write a sentence with each of them: *confundir, despertar, elegir, imprimir, suspender. (confundido/confuso; despertado/despierto; elegido/electo; imprimido/impreso; suspendido/suspenso)*

COOPERATIVE LEARNING

• Students will work in small groups and each one will research one of the buildings that make up *La Ciudad de las Artes y las Ciencias*. Then they will get back together with the group and create a plan for promoting tourism in *la Ciudad*. Students should be prepared to address the history of their building, events and exhibits held there, as well as hours of operation, fees, and any other pertinent or anecdotal information. Each group member will make a short oral presentation on his or her building and welcome questions from the class.

DESAFÍO 1

Gramática – El presente perfecto y el pluscuamperfecto

Presentation

- In this section, students will review and practice the present and past perfect tenses.

Activities	Standards	Resources
Gramática	1.2, 3.1	
21.	1.3, 3.1, 4.1	
22.	1.3, 3.1	
23.	1.2, 1.3, 3.1	Audio
24.	1.1, 5.1	
25.	1.3	

Teaching Suggestions

Warm-Up / Independent Starter

- Ask students to write five sentences about things they have done this week in school. For example: *He hecho un examen de Español.*

Preparation

- Have students read the grammar explanations silently. Then ask them to share their sentences from the Independent Starter with the class. You may wish to draw a timeline on the board and situate students' actions on the timeline.

- Ask students to rewrite their sentences using *ya* or *todavía* and the past perfect. Explain that they need to add new information so that the sentences make sense. For example: *Ya había repasado mis apuntes cuando hice el examen de Español.* Call on volunteers to share their examples with the class. Then, situate the actions on the timeline on the board.

Activities

23. Before playing the audio, have students analyze each statement and determine the tense that best completes it. Once students have finished the activity, ask them to use the recording and what they know about the participants to add one more sentence to each statement. For example: *Como no tenía los datos, Michelle no había podido completar el informe para su clase de Química. Pero esta mañana, ha obtenido los datos que necesitaba.*

Gramática

El presente perfecto y el pluscuamperfecto

El presente perfecto

- El presente perfecto *(present perfect)* se usa para hablar de acciones terminadas en un pasado inmediato o en un momento que todavía consideramos como presente.

Pasado ←———————→ Ahora

La tecnología **ha avanzado** mucho últimamente.

EXPRESIONES TEMPORALES DEL PRESENTE PERFECTO

> esta mañana/esta semana
> este siglo/año/mes
> hasta ahora
> hoy
> recientemente
> últimamente

- El presente perfecto se forma así:

presente del verbo haber + participio pasado

he llamado, has comido, ha venido

Repasa la conjugación del presente perfecto en la página R15.

El pluscuamperfecto

- El pluscuamperfecto *(past perfect)* se usa para hablar de acciones terminadas que se produjeron en un pasado no inmediato antes de otra acción también pasada.

Pasado ←———————→ Ahora

Juan se graduó porque **había aprobado** todas sus clases.

- El pluscuamperfecto se forma así:

imperfecto del verbo haber + participio pasado

había llamado, habías comido, había venido

Repasa la conjugación del pluscuamperfecto en la página R18.

Los adverbios *ya* y *todavía*

- El presente perfecto y el pluscuamperfecto se usan frecuentemente con los adverbios *ya* y *todavía*:
  - *Ya* equivale a *already*. Usamos *ya* + *presente perfecto* o *pluscuamperfecto* para expresar que la acción está realmente terminada.

    Cuando llegué, ella **ya había comido**. (= había terminado de comer)

  - *Todavía* equivale a *still*. Usamos *todavía* + *presente perfecto* o *pluscuamperfecto* para expresar que la acción no ha empezado o está en desarrollo. *Todavía* se usa frecuentemente en construcciones negativas.

    Ella **todavía no había comido**. (= no había empezado a comer o no había terminado)

 21 **Piensa.** Traduce al español estas oraciones.

  a. *Katie had already taken the math exam when I talked to her.*
  b. *Scientists have not yet discovered a cure for cancer.*

140 ciento cuarenta

Differentiated Instruction

DEVELOPING LEARNERS

- Ask students to use either *el presente perfecto* or *el pluscuamperfecto* of the verb in parentheses to complete the following sentences:
  1. *Hoy (nosotros – matricularse).* (nos hemos matriculado)
  2. *Carlos ya (repasar) los apuntes antes del examen.* (había repasado)
  3. *Cuando te llamé, tú todavía no (levantarse).* (te habías levantado)
  4. *Hasta ahora, Ana no (escribir) las cartas.* (ha escrito)
  5. *Mario consiguió la beca el año pasado porque (esforzarse).* (se había esforzado)

EXPANDING LEARNERS

- Tell students that the final exams have been stolen! Ask pairs to role-play an interview between a police officer and the suspect. The suspect will offer a variety of excuses and alibis. For example:
  A. *¿Dónde estaba usted el 5 de junio?*
  B. *Había ido a visitar a mi abuela.*
  A. *¿Y no entró en la escuela por la tarde?*
  B. *¡Imposible! No había vuelto de mi visita.*
- Give students time to practice, and then call on pairs to act out their dialogues.

22 La propuesta de Ethan y Eva

▶ **Completa** estas oraciones. Pon los verbos del cuadro en presente perfecto o en pluscuamperfecto.

> avanzar
> encontrar
> ir
> hacer
> escribir

1. Ethan está nervioso porque todavía no _____ su parte de la propuesta.
2. Ethan llamó a Eva para decirle que _____ un tercio de la propuesta.
3. Eva le preguntó si _____ la información que buscaba.
4. Ethan _____ bastante, pero no sabe cuándo va a terminar.
5. Ethan fue a hablar con la directora de la escuela, pero ella ya se _____.

23 ¿Ha hecho o había hecho?

▶ **Escucha** y completa estas oraciones. Usa el perfecto o el pluscuamperfecto.

1. Esta mañana Lucas... ⟶ *ha repasado sus apuntes de Matemáticas.*
2. Antes de los diecisiete años, Eva...
3. Esta mañana Michelle...
4. Antes de que terminara el plazo para solicitar la beca, Daniel...
5. Cuando lo llamaron sus amigos, Ethan...

24 ¿Alguna vez...?

▶ **Habla** con tu compañero(a). Túrnense para preguntar y responder.

Modelo A. ¿Alguna vez has recibido un premio?
B. *Sí, este semestre he recibido un premio por un proyecto de Ciencias.*

1. Recibir un premio.
2. Ir al extranjero como estudiante de intercambio.
3. Tomar clases de Anatomía.
4. Ser estudiante de honor.
5. Hacer un experimento científico.
6. Pensar en estudiar otra lengua.

25 Cuando cumplí quince años...

▶ **Escribe** si habías hecho o no estas actividades cuando cumpliste quince años. Usa los adverbios *ya* y *todavía*.

- Visitar un país hispano.
- Participar en una obra de teatro.
- Escribir un ensayo o un poema en español.
- Trabajar como voluntario(a).
- Ser miembro de un equipo en la escuela.
- Representar a tu escuela en un concurso de deletreo *(spelling)*.

Modelo
manejar un auto

⟶ *Cuando cumplí 15 años, todavía no había manejado un auto, pero ya había navegado en un velero.*

ciento cuarenta y uno **141**

Gramática – El presente perfecto y el pluscuamperfecto

25. After students have completed this activity, have them get together with a classmate and interview each other about what they had and had not done by the time they turned fifteen. Encourage partners to ask additional questions and to elaborate on the answers. They should try to keep the conversation going for a few minutes. For example:

A. *¿Habías visitado un país hispano cuando cumpliste quince años?*
B. *No, no había tenido la oportunidad.*
A. *¿Y has podido hacerlo?*
B. *No, no he podido, pero tengo un amigo hispano que me ha invitado a visitar su país.*
A. *¡Qué bien! ¿Y has hecho ya planes para ir?*

AUDIO SCRIPT
See page 127K.

Answer Key

21. a. Katie ya había hecho el examen de Matemáticas cuando hablé con ella.

b. Los científicos todavía no han descubierto una cura para el cáncer.

22. 1. ha hecho   4. ha avanzado
2. había escrito   5. había ido
3. había encontrado

23. 2. ... había viajado a México.
3. ... ha obtenido los datos que necesitaba.
4. ... había enviado la solicitud.
5. ... ya había estudiado para el examen.

24. Answers will vary.

25. Answers will vary.

Additional Resources

Fans Online activities
Practice Workbook

HERITAGE LANGUAGE LEARNERS

- Ask students to imagine that they are now ninety years old. Have them reflect on their long lives and then describe in several paragraphs what they *hicieron, hacían, han hecho,* and *habían hecho* in their studies, professions, and personal lives. Explain that they will need to use a combination of the preterite, imperfect, present perfect, and past perfect in their descriptions. Verify students' correct use of these tenses and have them make any necessary corrections. Then call on volunteers to read their work aloud.

MULTIPLE INTELLIGENCES:
Interpersonal Intelligence

- In pairs, have a student make a statement using the preterite or the past perfect. The partner will counter the statement with an exaggerated feat of his or her own using the past perfect. Then have partners switch roles. For example:
  A. *Hoy me desperté a las siete y media.*
  B. *¡Eso no es nada! Cuando yo me desperté, todavía no había salido el sol.*
- Call on volunteers to act out their dialogues.

LECTURA: TEXTO DIALOGADO

Presentation

- In this section, students will read a dialogue, review school vocabulary, and answer comprehension questions based on the reading.

Activities	Standards	Resources
Lectura: texto dialogado	1.1, 1.2, 2.1, 3.1	
26.	1.1, 1.2, 2.1	
27.	1.2, 3.1	
28.	1.1, 1.3, 3.1, 5.1, 5.2	

Teaching Suggestions

Warm-Up / Independent Starter

- Have students read the *Antes de leer* strategies silently. Then ask them to jot down some ideas to help them answer the questions.

Preparation

- Call on a volunteer to answer the first question in the *Antes de leer*. Then, as a class, discuss the answers to questions #2 and #3. Next, have students answer the following questions: *¿Qué asignaturas toman ustedes este semestre? ¿Cuáles de esas clases creen que serían más difíciles si tuvieran que tomarlas en español? ¿Por qué?*

- Read the dialogue aloud to students, modeling correct pronunciation and intonation. Then call on several pairs of students to alternate reading the dialogue aloud. Offer suggestions to improve their oral reading.

- Ask students to point out the uses of the present perfect in the dialogue. *(he elegido, he consultado)* Then have them note the vocabulary related to school (e.g., *cursar, asignaturas obligatorias u optativas, reprobar*). Encourage students to use context clues to try to figure out the meaning of new vocabulary.

- As a class, discuss the similarities and differences between the curriculum Eva has to follow in Chile and the curriculum students are following this semester. Would students find it easy to adapt to the school in Chile or is it too different from what they are doing? Which aspects would be the most difficult? Why?

Antes de leer: estrategias

1. Lee el título del texto. ¿Qué es un *plan de estudios*?
2. ¿Qué asignaturas crees que cursarán Ethan y Eva en Chile?
3. Busca en el texto nombres que se refieran a asignaturas. ¿Cuáles crees que pueden resultar más difíciles para un estudiante extranjero?

El plan de estudios

EVA: Ya tengo preparado mi plan de estudios en Chile. Tengo Lengua Castellana[1] y Comunicación, Matemáticas, Historia y Ciencias Sociales, y Educación Física. Esas asignaturas son obligatorias. Además he elegido tres asignaturas optativas: Biología y Química del área de Ciencias, y Artes Musicales del área de Educación Artística.

ETHAN: ¡Vas a estudiar siete asignaturas en español! ¡Qué valiente!

EVA: Sí, la verdad es que estoy un poco asustada. Espero acostumbrarme pronto al español y no reprobar ninguna asignatura.

ETHAN: ¡Tranquila! Eres muy buena estudiante.

EVA: Eso espero. He consultado también los programas de las asignaturas. En Matemáticas, por ejemplo, veremos raíces cuadradas[2], ecuaciones, triángulos rectángulos[3], algo de estadística…

ETHAN: ¡Ah! Entonces no vas a tener ningún problema.

EVA: Creo que en Matemáticas no. Pero tendré que estudiar mucho en Lengua Castellana. Eso seguro. Y tú, ¿ya sabes qué asignaturas vas a cursar?

ETHAN: Sí, son parecidas a las tuyas. Pero en vez de Artes Musicales, he elegido Artes Visuales. Me encanta el programa. Analizaremos todas las disciplinas contemporáneas, desde el cómic hasta el cine o el video.

EVA: ¡Qué interesante!

ETHAN: Sí, y lo que más me gusta es que desarrollaremos nuestro propio proyecto.

EVA: Lo harás fenomenal. Eres muy creativo.

ETHAN: ¡Muchas gracias, Eva!

---

1. *Spanish*   2. *square roots*   3. *right triangles*

Differentiated Instruction

DEVELOPING LEARNERS

- Ask students to correct the following false statements about Eva:
  1. *Va a tomar seis asignaturas. (siete)*
  2. *En Ciencias, piensa estudiar Física y Anatomía. (Biología y Química)*
  3. *Va a estudiar raíces cuadradas en la clase de Química. (de Matemáticas)*
  4. *Ethan no cree que Eva vaya a tener ningún problema con Historia. (Matemáticas)*
  5. *Cree que tendrá que dedicar horas de estudio a la Química. (Lengua Castellana)*
  6. *Piensa que Ethan es muy apasionado. (creativo)*

EXPANDING LEARNERS

- Ask students to compare and contrast Eva's proposed courses in Chile with those that they are studying. Ask them to write an essay of at least two paragraphs detailing the similarities and differences, as well as their opinion as to which program best prepares students for further studies or a profession. Explain to students that they must justify their opinions. Call on volunteers to read their essays aloud.

26 **¿Comprendes?**

▶ **Escribe.** ¿Qué asignaturas va a cursar Eva en Chile?

☐ Lengua Castellana y Comunicación
☐ Francés
☐ Matemáticas
☐ Historia y Ciencias Sociales
☐ Filosofía y Psicología
☐ Biología

☐ Física
☐ Química
☐ Artes Visuales
☐ Artes Musicales
☐ Educación Física
☐ Religión

▶ **Responde** a estas preguntas.

1. ¿Cómo se siente Eva respecto a su semestre en Chile? ¿Está tranquila?
2. ¿Confía Ethan en Eva? ¿Cree que le irá bien en Chile? ¿Por qué?
3. ¿En qué asignatura cree Eva que tendrá menos problemas? ¿Por qué?
4. ¿En qué asignatura cree Eva que tendrá que esforzarse más?
5. ¿Qué asignatura le hace más ilusión estudiar a Ethan? ¿Por qué?

27 **Palabras y expresiones**

▶ **Une** los contenidos con la asignatura correspondiente.

Ⓐ

1. La diversidad de civilizaciones
2. La música de concierto desde el siglo xx
3. Recursos verbales de la argumentación
4. Sistema nervioso: organización y función
5. Reacciones ácido-base
6. Deportes de colaboración y oposición
7. El diseño en la vida cotidiana
8. El movimiento circular uniforme

Ⓑ

a. Educación Física
b. Historia y Ciencias Sociales
c. Biología
d. Física
e. Química
f. Artes Visuales
g. Artes Musicales
h. Lengua Castellana y Comunicación

28 **Con tus propias palabras**

▶ **Piensa** en tu asignatura favorita y escribe lo que se estudia en el programa. ¿Puedes pensar en otros temas que se podrían añadir?

▶ **Habla** con tu compañero(a) y diseñen un proyecto que les gustaría desarrollar para esa asignatura. Después, preséntenlo.

Activities

27. After students have completed this activity, check the answers as a class. Then challenge students to show how much they know about each subject by providing at least one example for each case. For example: *En Historia y Ciencias Sociales estudiamos las civilizaciones precolombinas, por ejemplo, los aztecas, mayas, incas...* You may want to divide the class into small groups and turn this into a competition.

28. For the first part of this activity, encourage students to justify their choice of topics by indicating why the topics are important or intriguing. For the second part of this activity, the class may vote for the best project. Encourage students to consider proposing the project to their teacher.

Answer Key

26. Lengua Castellana y Comunicación, Matemáticas, Historia y Ciencias Sociales, Biología, Química, Educación Física, Artes Musicales.

▶ Answers will vary. Sample answers:
1. Está un poco asustada.
2. Sí. Le dice que es muy buena estudiante y que puede estar tranquila.
3. En Matemáticas porque le son familiares los temas que van a tratar.
4. En Lengua Castellana porque tendrá que estudiar mucho.
5. Artes Visuales porque le encanta el programa y analizarán todas las disciplinas contemporáneas.

27. 1. b   3. h   5. e   7. f
       2. g   4. c   6. a   8. d

28. Answers will vary.
▶ Answers will vary.

Additional Resources

Fans Online activities

HERITAGE LANGUAGE LEARNERS

• Ask students to compare and contrast Eva's proposed *plan de estudios* with one from their family's country of origin. If students have studied abroad, ask them to describe how the classes are organized, how exams are graded, the extent of family participation in their school, and how they and other students cope with studying a heavier course load than they usually carry here. If students have never studied abroad, discuss with them the possibility of inviting a speaker from their heritage country who is willing to talk about these similarities and differences.

CRITICAL THINKING

• Ask students to think about their class schedules and whether they would like to add some compulsory courses, eliminate others, or keep the status quo. Then take a class survey to record the results and identify these classes. Next, engage students in a classroom discussion in which they will explain why they have made these choices in responding to the survey. Remind students that they will need to justify their answers with logical and sound reasons.

DESAFÍO 1

Comunicación

Presentation

- In this section, students will integrate the vocabulary and grammar skills from *Desafío 1* in order to talk about a student exchange program, create a brochure for an exchange program in their school, and use the present and past perfect tenses in a dialogue.

Activities	Standards	Resources
29.	1.1, 1.2, 1.3, 2.1, 2.2, 5.1, 5.2	
30.	1.1, 1.2, 3.1	
31. Final del desafío	1.1, 1.2, 3.1	

Teaching Suggestions

Warm-Up / Independent Starter

- Ask students to think of three advantages and three disadvantages of studying abroad.

Preparation

- Have students share their Independent Starters in small groups. If there are differences in the groups regarding what some students consider advantages or disadvantages, have those students state their case and try to convince their peers. Then have groups decide on three advantages and three disadvantages that they all agree on and present those to the class. Do groups have similar lists or are there differences between the groups? Is there an advantage or disadvantage that only one group mentioned? If so, invite that group to explain their reasoning.

- Before students begin the activities, give them a few minutes to review the vocabulary and grammar topics for this *Desafío*. Be available to answer any questions students may have.

Activities

29. For the second part of this activity, ask pairs to also consider these questions: *¿Qué preguntas tienen ustedes sobre este programa? ¿Cómo se prepararían para participar en un programa de este tipo?* Then come together as a class and discuss some of students' answers to these and the rest of the questions in this activity.

Comunicación

29 Programas de intercambio

▶ **Lee** el texto y responde a estas preguntas.

Programas de intercambio en Educación Secundaria

Los programas de intercambio escolar en Chile son una gran experiencia porque proporcionan a los jóvenes la oportunidad de conocer una nueva cultura y adquirir destrezas en el idioma español, hablado por más de 400 millones de personas en el mundo, y, sobre todo, les permite crecer y desarrollar su personalidad.

La experiencia de intercambio significa que un joven vive con una familia chilena y asiste a un colegio de forma regular, participando en sus actividades y cumpliendo con las mismas obligaciones que el resto de sus compañeros.

Hay modalidades de intercambio que duran meses, semestres y un año. Los precios varían entre US$ 3.600 y US$ 8.000, lo que incluye pasajes y seguro médico. Los gastos académicos corren por parte del colegio que recibe al estudiante y su alojamiento es responsabilidad de la familia que lo acoge. A esto se deben sumar los gastos personales, que se estiman en US$ 250 al mes.

Para postular, el estudiante debe tener generalmente entre 15 y 18 años, y realizar una entrevista personal. Los postulantes deben tener conocimientos básicos de español.

Fuente: http://www.thisischile.cl (selección)

1. ¿Cuáles son las tres ventajas de este programa de intercambio escolar?
2. ¿Dónde se alojarán los estudiantes que participen en el programa?
3. ¿Quién paga los gastos de libros y otros materiales escolares?
4. ¿Qué requisitos debe cumplir un(a) estudiante que quiera participar en el programa?

 ▶ **Habla** con tu compañero(a). ¿Qué les parece este programa de intercambio? ¿Estarían dispuestos a participar en él? ¿Les parece caro? ¿Qué tipo de preguntas creen que les harían en la entrevista?

▶ **Escribe** un párrafo sobre las ventajas de participar en un intercambio de estudiantes.

Differentiated Instruction

DEVELOPING LEARNERS

- Ask students to match the words from both columns, and then write an original sentence with each of the words in the first column.

1. *proporcionar* (c)	a. *efectuar, hacer*
2. *asistir* (e)	b. *admitir a uno en su casa*
3. *modalidad* (f)	c. *dar*
4. *acoger* (b)	d. *solicitar*
5. *postular* (d)	e. *acudir*
6. *realizar* (a)	f. *categoría*

EXPANDING LEARNERS

- Ask students to work with a partner and prepare an interview between Eva and the principal of the school in Chile. First, students will need to brainstorm the kinds of questions a student who is going abroad to study might have. These questions may range from academics, living accommodations, and recreational activities to food, transportation, and weather. The "principal" might need to research answers to some of these questions before responding. Give students time to rehearse their interviews and call on pairs to present them to the class.

30 Un intercambio para tu escuela

▶ **Escribe** con dos compañeros(as) un folleto publicitario sobre un programa de intercambio entre tu escuela y otra de un país hispano.

 ▶ **Presenten** el programa y el folleto a la clase.

▶ **Elijan** entre todos(as) el mejor programa. Justifiquen sus respuestas.

Final del desafío

 31 ¿Lo conseguirán?

▶ **Completa** los bocadillos. Usa el presente perfecto o el pluscuamperfecto.

▶ **Habla** con tu compañero(a).

1. ¿Qué crees que contestó la directora a la pregunta de Eva?
2. ¿Crees que Ethan y Eva podrán participar en el programa de intercambio? ¿Por qué?

ciento cuarenta y cinco 145

---

30. As an alternative to creating a brochure, have small groups create a TV or Internet ad promoting their exchange program. All members will work collaboratively and contribute to writing a draft for the text of their ad. Other group members will look for images or take their own photos to include in the ad. Students may also consider creating a slogan and a mascot or symbol for their exchange program. If access to video recording equipment is available, you may want to allow students to record their ads. Then ask groups to present their commercials to the class. At the end of all the presentations, hold a vote to select the best ad.

Answer Key

29. Answers will vary. Sample answers:
1. Proporciona a los estudiantes la oportunidad de conocer otra cultura, adquirir destrezas en español y desarrollar su personalidad.
2. Vivirán con una familia chilena.
3. El colegio que recibe al estudiante.
4. Debe tener entre 15 y 18 años, poseer conocimientos básicos de español y realizar una entrevista.
▶ Answers will vary.
▶ Answers will vary.

30. Answers will vary.
▶ Answers will vary.
▶ Answers will vary.

31. 1. has hablado   5. ha encantado
2. había salido   6. han hecho
3. ha dicho   7. habíamos pensado
4. he enseñado
▶ Answers will vary.

Additional Resources

Fans Online activities
Practice Workbook

HERITAGE LANGUAGE LEARNERS

• Ask students to make an oral presentation or produce a video extolling the benefits of coming to their family's country of origin to study Spanish for a year. In addition to the academic program and participants' requirements, students might address the accommodations available, the historical and cultural sites, as well as other places of interest, the flora and fauna, day trips, recreational facilities, cultural events, and any other information that would entice students to enroll in an exchange program in their heritage country.

CRITICAL THINKING

• Ask students to think about how a host family might be enriched from housing a foreign student. Have students work in small groups and brainstorm the benefits of hosting such a student. Remind them to keep in mind any disadvantages or possible difficulties as well. Encourage students to suggest activities that the host family might like to engage in with a foreign student and why these would be culturally enriching. After groups have talked over the issue, lead the entire class in a discussion and encourage all students to share their opinions.

Presentation

- In *Desafío 2*, Michelle and Daniel have to participate in a debate about the salt flats of Uyuni, Bolivia. Students will preview language used in talking about the economy.

Activities	Standards	Resources
Texto	1.2, 2.1, 2.2, 3.1	
32.	1.1, 1.2, 2.1, 2.2	
33.	1.1, 1.2, 2.1, 2.2, 3.1	
34.	1.2, 1.3, 2.1, 2.2, 3.1	Audio
35. Cultura	1.2, 1.3, 2.1, 2.2, 3.1, 3.2, 5.2	

Teaching Suggestions

Warm-Up / Independent Starter

- Have students jot down what they know about Bolivia (e.g., location, capital city, indigenous cultures, geographical features).

Preparation

- Invite volunteers to share their Independent Starters. Then read the title of the dialogue and have students speculate on what the treasure might be. Encourage a discussion on what might constitute a treasure for a country's economy. Then, ask for a volunteer to read the introduction to the dialogue.

Texto: El tesoro de Bolivia

- Ask students to get together with a partner and read the dialogue. Have them write any words they can't identify or any constructions they don't understand. Review their lists as a class.
- With a show of hands, ask who agrees with Michelle and who feels more like Daniel does.

Activities

33. To expand this activity, ask small groups to come up with an argument in defense of Michelle's position as well as an argument that defends Daniel's position. Have groups share their arguments with the class. Hold a vote to see which side of the debate the class feels is more valid.

El tesoro de Bolivia

Michelle y Daniel tienen que participar en un debate sobre el futuro del salar de Uyuni (Bolivia). Pero primero deben averiguar cuál es el problema.

MICHELLE: ¿Tú sabes por qué tenemos que debatir sobre el salar de Uyuni?

DANIEL: Pues no. Sé que es el salar más grande del mundo y que se ve desde el espacio. Contiene once mil millones *(billion)* de toneladas de sal. Pero no sé por qué es tan importante.

MICHELLE: Por lo que he leído, lo importante no es la sal, sino el litio que contiene. Resulta que el salar de Uyuni es una de las mayores reservas de litio del mundo. ¿Y sabes qué cosas se fabrican con litio?

DANIEL: Las baterías de nuestros celulares. Y las de los autos eléctricos e híbridos. ¡Claro! Entonces el litio del salar de Uyuni es clave para la fabricación de los autos modernos.

MICHELLE: ¿Y por qué hay un debate? ¿Cuál es el problema?

DANIEL: Aquí dice que el problema es quién debe extraer el litio: los bolivianos o compañías de otros países.

MICHELLE: Yo pienso que si hay países que tienen más recursos que Bolivia para extraer el litio y procesarlo, deberían poder hacerlo. Es un producto muy necesario.

DANIEL: Yo no estoy muy de acuerdo con eso. Si Bolivia tiene las materias primas, son ellos quienes deben extraer el litio.

32 ### Detective de palabras

▶ **Completa** estas oraciones.

1. El salar de Uyuni es una de las mayores reservas de _____ del mundo.
2. Las baterías de los celulares se _____ con litio.
3. Es posible que participen en el proyecto _____ de otros países.
4. Hay países que tienen más _____ que Bolivia para extraer el litio.
5. El litio es un _____ muy necesario para el futuro.

Differentiated Instruction

DEVELOPING LEARNERS

- Have students complete the following sentences about *el salar de Uyuni*:

  1. *Es el ... más grande del mundo.* (c)
  2. *Se ve desde...* (d)
  3. *Se extiende por ... km.* (a)
  4. *También es un importante...* (e)
  5. *También contiene...* (f)
  6. *El ... se usa en las baterías.* (b)

  a. *doce mil*
  b. *litio*
  c. *salar*
  d. *el espacio*
  e. *destino turístico*
  f. *magnesio*

EXPANDING LEARNERS

- Have students imagine that they are tourists to the Uyuni salt flats. This is their first visit to the area and to Bolivia. Ask them to keep a journal for a few days during their stay and record their impressions of *el salar*. Encourage students to research Uyuni and find images that can serve as the foundation for their thoughts and feelings. They may even describe how it felt to spend their nights in a hotel made from salt blocks. Call on volunteers to read their journal entries aloud.

33 **¿Comprendes?**

▶ **Responde** a estas preguntas.

1. ¿Cuál es el tema del debate de Michelle y Daniel?
2. ¿Dónde está el salar de Uyuni?
3. ¿Por qué hay un debate sobre el salar de Uyuni?
4. ¿Cuál es la opinión de Michelle? ¿Y la de Daniel?

 34 **Bolivia tiene recursos**

 ▶ **Escucha** a Daniel y a Michelle, y elige la opción correcta.

1. Se predice que para el 2020 _____ de cada diez autos usará una batería de litio.
   a. uno   **b.** tres   **c.** seis
2. Una fuente potencial de litio está en _____ .
   a. el Círculo Polar Ártico   **b.** el océano   **c.** el altiplano boliviano
3. El litio es _____ que tiene diversos usos.
   a. una piedra natural   **b.** un metal   **c.** una madera

 ▶ **Escucha** de nuevo y decide si estas oraciones son ciertas o falsas. Después, corrige las oraciones falsas.

1. En el futuro, la mayoría de las baterías funcionarán con litio.
2. Los autos que funcionan con una batería de litio también necesitan petróleo.
3. Bolivia no quiere extraer y vender el litio porque ya tiene una economía fuerte.
4. El presidente de Bolivia no tiene planes para producir autos eléctricos.

 **CULTURA**

El salar de Uyuni (Bolivia)

El salar de Uyuni, con más de 12.000 kilómetros de extensión, es el salar más grande del mundo. Se formó por la evaporación de los mares que bañaban el continente hace miles de años. Contiene muchos recursos naturales, como sodio, potasio, magnesio y litio, el más importante desde el punto de vista económico, puesto que tiene un gran potencial para la fabricación de autos eléctricos. El espectacular paisaje que genera el reflejo del sol en el salar lo ha convertido en un importante destino turístico, especialmente para los amantes de la fotografía.

35 **Piensa.** ¿Qué ventajas y desventajas crees que tiene extraer el litio del salar para los habitantes de esa zona?

Relacionar acciones futuras

34. Before students listen to the audio recording, have them use what they know and what they have just read about the Uyuni salt flats to try to answer the questions. Then, as they listen to the audio, ask students to correct their answers.

 AUDIO SCRIPT
See page 127K.

 CULTURA

El salar de Uyuni (Bolivia)

Bolivia is believed to have some of the world's largest untapped deposits of lithium in the vast salt flats of Uyuni. However, the area is isolated and has very limited infrastructure, which increases the cost of extracting the lithium. Mining the lithium in Uyuni would require large investments. There is also opposition from the local population, who feel they will not benefit from the bounty.

Answer Key

32. 1. litio   4. recursos
      2. fabrican   5. producto
      3. compañías

33. 1. El futuro del salar de Uyuni.
      2. Está en Bolivia.
      3. Porque tiene grandes reservas de litio y no está claro quién debe extraerlo.
      4. Michelle cree que quienes tengan los medios deben extraer el litio. Daniel piensa que Bolivia debe hacerlo.

34. 1. a   2. c   3. b
      ▶ 1. C.
        2. F. No necesitarán petróleo.
        3. F. No tiene los recursos para hacerlo.
        4. F. Quiere ser líder en el desarrollo de los autos eléctricos.

35. Answers will vary.

Additional Resources

Fans Online activities

HERITAGE LANGUAGE LEARNERS

• Have students work in small groups to promote tourism to *el salar de Uyuni*. Students may choose any medium to advance tourism to this area: a brochure, poster, webpage, or TV or radio ads. Allow students to decide which medium they will use. Then they will distribute the tasks, from researching Uyuni and providing images, to contributing sections to a first draft and then finalizing their promotional material. Display their printed work in the classroom or have them make a video or audio presentation to the class.

MULTIPLE INTELLIGENCES:
Logical-Mathematical Intelligence

• Daniel says that Bolivia does not have the funds to mine its lithium reserves. Explain that having a budget and adhering to it is necessary for a government's or an individual's fiscal stability. Ask students to prepare a *presupuesto* for their own personal spending. They should indicate how much they earn from a job or allowance, and detail their spending habits over a week. Have them analyze their spending, and if they are not saving anything, ask them where they could make cuts.

Unit 3
DESAFÍO 2

Vocabulario – La economía

Presentation

- In this section, students will learn vocabulary related to the economy and bank transactions.

Activities	Standards	Resources
Vocabulario	1.2, 2.1, 2.2, 3.1, 3.2	
36.	1.2, 3.1	
37.	1.3	
38.	1.2, 1.3, 2.1, 2.2, 3.1	Audio
39.	1.1, 1.3, 3.1, 5.1, 5.2	
40. Cultura	1.2, 1.3, 2.2, 3.2	

Teaching Suggestions

Warm-Up / Independent Starter

- Have students jot down examples of *fabricar, importar,* and *exportar.*

Preparation

- Ask three volunteers to each read a paragraph of *La economía.* Then go over the highlighted words to emphasize pronunciation. To check students' comprehension of the text, you may ask them these questions: *¿Qué productos podría exportar Bolivia? ¿Qué necesita Bolivia para extraer el litio? ¿Por qué es importante el comercio internacional para Bolivia? ¿A quién debe beneficiar el negocio del litio según Daniel?*

- Call on volunteers to share their examples from the Independent Starter. Then have pairs come up with sentences explaining how those actions contribute to the world economy. Encourage students to use the target vocabulary.

Activities

37. Once students have finished this activity, have them get together with a partner and describe two bank transactions in detail. For example: *Para pedir un préstamo debes tener una cuenta bancaria. Tus ingresos tienen que ser mayores que tus gastos, y debes tener un saldo positivo en tu cuenta. Antes de firmar los documentos debes saber cuál es la tasa de interés.*

38. To extend this activity, play the recording a second time and ask students to write a brief news summary for two of the headlines.

148

Vocabulario

La economía

Gracias por invitarme a participar en este debate. Hoy hablamos del litio, un **recurso natural** presente en Bolivia, concretamente en el salar de Uyuni.

Algunos opinan que Bolivia debe extraer este mineral para **fabricar** y **exportar productos** como las baterías de los autos eléctricos. Esto le traería grandes beneficios, ya que son muchos los países que tienen que **importar** este mineral para fabricar mecanismos electrónicos. Pero hay expertos que señalan que Bolivia no cuenta con los recursos ni el **presupuesto** suficiente para extraer el litio. Por eso, opinan que se necesita el apoyo de **compañías** de otros países.

De hecho, muchas **multinacionales** han mostrado interés en participar en este proyecto.

El **comercio** internacional de **mercancías** es esencial para que Bolivia pueda competir en el mercado global, pero **llegar a un acuerdo** desfavorable no es la solución. En mi opinión, es esencial que el dinero que genere el **negocio** del litio beneficie a los bolivianos.

Más vocabulario

El banco

abrir una cuenta	to open an account	los gastos	expenses
ahorrar dinero	to save money	los ingresos	income
pedir una hipoteca	to apply for a mortgage	el saldo	bank balance
pedir un préstamo	to apply for a loan	la tasa de interés	interest rate

¡Atención!

ahorrar	to save	salvar	to rescue

36 **Términos económicos**

▶ **Une** las dos columnas.

(A)

1. recursos naturales
2. fabricar
3. exportar
4. multinacional
5. préstamo
6. cuenta

(B)

a. Crédito que se pide con garantía de devolución.
b. Depósito de dinero en un banco.
c. Compañía que tiene actividad en varios países.
d. Bienes que proporciona la Naturaleza.
e. Producir algo, generalmente por medios mecánicos.
f. Vender productos del propio país a otro.

148 ciento cuarenta y ocho

Differentiated Instruction

DEVELOPING LEARNERS

- Ask students to match words from both columns.

1. *no discutir* (d)   a. *recursos naturales*

2. *no son ahorros* (f)   b. *hipoteca*

3. *productos* (e)   c. *ahorrar*

4. *la ... de interés* (g) d. *llegar a un acuerdo*

5. *no gastar* (c)   e. *mercancías*
6. *el agua y el aire* (a) f. *los gastos*
7. *un tipo de préstamo* (b) g. *tasa*

EXPANDING LEARNERS

- Ask students to work with a partner and create a dialogue between a banker and a client. Encourage students to use other words that deal with finances, in addition to those on the page. For example:

  A. *Me gustaría abrir una cuenta.*
  B. *¿Una cuenta corriente o de ahorros?*
  A. *De ahorros. ¿Cuál es la tasa de interés?*
  B. *Con un depósito mínimo de $2.000, es del 2%.*

- Call on volunteers to act out their skits in front of the class.

37 En el banco

▶ **Completa** estas oraciones.

1. Si quieres ahorrar dinero, lo mejor es...
2. Para pedir una hipoteca, necesitas...
3. Si una empresa tiene demasiados gastos, debe...
4. Cuando una compañía no tiene ingresos, no puede...

38 El noticiero

▶ **Escucha** las noticias y toma nota de las palabras clave. Después, escribe un titular para cada noticia.

Modelo   1. *Bolivia y China firman un acuerdo militar.*

39 La economía de tu comunidad

▶ **Habla** con tu compañero(a) sobre la economía de tu comunidad. Utiliza estas preguntas como guía y toma notas.

1. ¿Cuáles son las compañías más grandes de tu comunidad?
2. ¿Qué se fabrica en tu comunidad?
3. ¿Qué recursos naturales tiene la zona donde vives?
4. ¿Cuáles son los productos que exporta tu comunidad?
5. ¿Qué productos importa tu comunidad?

▶ **Escribe** un breve informe sobre la economía de tu comunidad usando tus notas.

CULTURA

La Comunidad Andina de Naciones

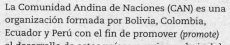

La Comunidad Andina de Naciones (CAN) es una organización formada por Bolivia, Colombia, Ecuador y Perú con el fin de promover (*promote*) el desarrollo de estos países y mejorar el nivel de vida de sus habitantes.

Entre sus objetivos está mejorar la posición de los estados miembros en el contexto económico internacional, favorecer su desarrollo económico y social, y fomentar la creación de empleo.

40 **Investiga.** ¿Qué crees que representa el emblema de la CAN? Visita la página web de la organización (www.comunidadandina.org) y averígualo.

ciento cuarenta y nueve 149

---

39. Give students the option of talking about their state. You may want to assign this activity as homework. Then ask students to report their findings to the class.

 AUDIO SCRIPT
See page 127L.

CULTURA

La Comunidad Andina de Naciones

The Andean Community of Nations was established on May 26, 1969. Its headquarters are located in Lima, Peru. The Andean Community's main goal is the economic integration of its members (Bolivia, Colombia, Ecuador, and Peru). These countries have adopted common regulations in several areas, including customs procedures, transport, and intellectual property. Social goals have gradually been added to the Community's agenda, an example of which is the signing of the Integrated Social Development Plan in 2004.

Answer Key

36. 1. d   2. e   3. f   4. c   5. a   6. b

37. Answers will vary. Sample answers:
  1. ... abrir una cuenta.
  2. ... pedir un préstamo al banco.
  3. ... ahorrar dinero.
  4. ... generar negocio.

38. Answers will vary. Sample answers:
  2. Diez empresas controlan la economía.
  3. Bolivia tiene un saldo comercial positivo.
  4. Baja la tasa de interés hipotecario.

39. Answers will vary.
  ▶ Answers will vary.

40. Answers will vary.

Additional Resources

Fans Online activities
Practice Workbook

HERITAGE LANGUAGE LEARNERS

• Ask students to research the *recursos naturales* that can be found in their heritage country. Have them list these natural resources, along with the quantities extracted, the products that can be made from them, and their impact on the country's economy. Encourage students to include information about conflicts with the processing of these resources and the possible negative impact on the environment. Should there be students from several Hispanic countries, ask them to compare and contrast their results.

COOPERATIVE LEARNING

• In small groups, have students research other multinational organizations in which Hispanic countries participate. You may want to suggest *MERCOSUR (Mercado Común del Sur), ODS (Organización para el Desarrollo Sostenible), OCDE (Organización para la Cooperación y el Desarrollo Económico),* and *UNASUR (Unión de Naciones Suramericanas).* Each student will research one aspect of the selected organization and coordinate this information with other group members. Groups will then make a brief presentation to the class.

DESAFÍO 2

Gramática – Los pronombres relativos

Presentation

- In this section, students will review and expand on the use of the relative pronouns *que, quien,* and *el que* in adjective clauses.

Activities	Standards	Resources
Gramática	1.2, 3.1	
41.	1.2, 3.1, 4.1	
42.	1.3, 2.1, 2.2	
43.	1.2, 3.1	
44.	1.3, 2.2	
45.	1.1, 2.1, 2.2, 4.2, 5.2	

Teaching Suggestions

Warm-Up / Independent Starter

- Write the following pairs of sentences on the board and ask students to join them using the pronoun *que*:
  1. a. *Las compañías fabrican baterías.*
     b. *Estas compañías importan litio. (Las compañías que fabrican baterías importan litio.)*
  2. a. *Los jóvenes pidieron un préstamo.*
     b. *Estos jóvenes no tenían ingresos. (Los jóvenes que pidieron un préstamo no tenían ingresos.)*

Preparation

- Ask volunteers to give the answers for the Independent Starter. Then have students note the word they used (i.e., *que*) to join the sentences. Next, have students read the first part of the grammar presentation silently. Then ask students to work with a partner to rewrite their sentences from the Independent Starter, placing a clause between commas. For example: *Las compañías que fabrican baterías importan litio. → Las compañías, que fabrican baterías, importan litio.* Discuss with students the differences between the sentences. In this case, for instance, the first sentence expresses that only the companies that manufacture batteries import lithium. In the second sentence, all the companies in question manufacture batteries, and therefore import lithium.

150

Gramática

Los pronombres relativos

Las cláusulas adjetivas

- En español, como en inglés, usamos con frecuencia cláusulas introducidas por el pronombre relativo que para dar información sobre un nombre. Estas cláusulas se llaman cláusulas adjetivas o de relativo.

  En mi ciudad hay una <u>fábrica</u> **que produce calzado deportivo.**
  noun — adjective clause

- Hay dos tipos de cláusulas adjetivas:
  - Cláusulas que dan una información esencial para identificar al nombre y, por tanto, no se pueden eliminar.

    El gobierno multó a las fábricas de papel **que contaminaban los ríos.**
    (Solo algunas fábricas contaminaban los ríos.)

  - Cláusulas que dan una explicación no esencial sobre el nombre y, por tanto, se pueden eliminar sin que el significado de la oración varíe. Estas cláusulas van entre comas.

    Las fábricas de papel, **que contaminaban los ríos,** tuvieron que pagar una multa.
    (Todas las fábricas contaminaban los ríos y todas fueron multadas.)

Los pronombres relativos

- Los pronombres relativos más frecuentes son que *(that)* y quien *(who)*.

  PRINCIPALES RELATIVOS

que	Se usa para personas y cosas.	Hay gobiernos **que** favorecen los tratados comerciales.
quien quienes	Se usan solo para personas.	Las empresarias de **quienes** te hablé tienen un supermercado.

- A diferencia del inglés, los pronombres relativos no se omiten en la lengua hablada.

  Este es el libro que compré.   *This is the book (that) I bought.*

Los relativos *el que, la que...*

- Usamos el que, la que, los que, las que en lugar del relativo que en estos casos:
  - Cuando la cláusula adjetiva comienza con una preposición (a, con, de, en...), en especial cuando el relativo se refiere a una persona.

    Tengo unos amigos mexicanos **con los que** siempre hablo en español.

  - Cuando la cláusula adjetiva va al principio de la oración.

    Los que quieran venir... Equivale a Los [chicos] que quieran venir...

  - Cuando el relativo se refiere a un nombre que está omitido.

    Ese niño es **el que** más sabe. Equivale a Ese niño es el [niño] que más sabe.

- En todos los casos, el artículo concuerda con el nombre en género y número.

  Describe el lugar **en el que** trabajas.   Describe los lugares **a los que** vas habitualmente.

41 **Compara.** Traduce estas oraciones al inglés. ¿Qué diferencias hay?
  a. La ropa que compré es importada.   b. Ella es la empresaria para quien trabajo.

Differentiated Instruction

DEVELOPING LEARNERS

- Ask students to complete these sentences by choosing the correct relative pronoun:
  1. *La directora de quien / que te hablé es mi vecina. (quien)*
  2. *El que / Quienes llegue tarde, no come. (El que)*
  3. *Las cuentas las que / que tenía ya están cerradas. (que)*
  4. *¿Conoces a que / los que exportan estos productos? (los que)*
  5. *Estas mercancías que / las que venden son de Bolivia. (que)*
  6. *Esta compañía es que / la que importa el litio. (la que)*

EXPANDING LEARNERS

- Ask students to write five or more sentences using a variety of relative pronouns, including *el/la que*. For example:
  1. *A veces importan productos que se fabrican en China.*
  2. *El banquero de quien te hablaron es el dueño de este banco.*
  3. *Los recursos naturales que se encuentran en esas selvas se están agotando.*
  4. *Los presupuestos de los que te hablé entran en vigor mañana.*
  5. *Llegaron a un acuerdo según el que no tendrán que pagar multas.*

42 Más información, por favor

▶ **Completa** estas oraciones.

Modelo   El litio es un recurso natural que... → *se encuentra en Bolivia.*

1. El salar de Uyuni es un lugar que...
2. Los autos eléctricos usan baterías que...
3. Bolivia es un país que...
4. Hay empresarios a quienes...

43 Más relativos

▶ **Elige** la opción correcta.

1. Esa es la empresa _____ trabaja mi madre.
   a. que   b. en la que   c. quien
2. Esos textiles, _____ se fabrican en Perú, se exportan a muchos países.
   a. quienes   b. que   c. en los que
3. Los empleados con _____ trabajo tienen mucho talento.
   a. quienes   b. lo que   c. el que
4. ¿Cuál es la multinacional _____ trabajas?
   a. para la que   b. para que   c. que

44 Hispanos famosos

▶ **Haz** con tu compañero(a) una lista de hispanos famosos: artistas, políticos, deportistas...

▶ **Escribe** oraciones sobre esas personas y su trabajo. Usa los pronombres relativos para dar más información sobre ellos(as).

Pablo
Picasso.

Modelo   *Pablo Picasso es un artista español.*
El Guernica, que es una de sus obras más famosas,
está en el Museo Reina Sofía, en Madrid.

45 ¡Adivina!

▶ **Habla** con tu compañero(a). Elige una de estas categorías y haz una descripción.
El / Ella tiene que adivinar a qué o a quién te refieres.

alimentos importados de América Latina
productos exportados por EEUU
recursos naturales
compañías internacionales
empresarios(as) famosos(as)

Modelo
A. *Es una fruta verde que se importa de México.*
B. *¿El melón?*
A. *No. Es un ingrediente que se usa...*

HERITAGE LANGUAGE LEARNERS

• Ask students to write two or three paragraphs describing the economy of their heritage country. They should address the nation's natural resources, the leading manufactured and agricultural products, major imports and exports, as well as the impact tourism has on the economy. Ask students to describe any major economic crises or changes in the standard of living, if pertinent. Encourage students to use relative pronouns in their writing. When they finish, call on volunteers to read their work aloud.

TOTAL PHYSICAL RESPONSE (TPR)

• Divide the class into six teams, corresponding to these relative pronouns: *que, quien/quienes, el que, la que, los que, las que*. Prepare sentences, leaving out the required relative pronouns, and read each sentence aloud. Teams will stand up according to the appropriate relative pronoun. If they are correct, they score one point. If they are wrong, one point is subtracted from their score. For example: *Voy a pedir un préstamo con ... pienso comprar un auto. (el que)*

Gramática – Los pronombres relativos

■ Go over the rest of the grammar explanations with students and clarify any points they did not understand. Explain that *que* is the default relative pronoun in Spanish.

Activities

43. Once students have finished this activity, have them get together with a partner and check their answers. Then call on volunteer pairs to explain their choice for each sentence. Next, to extend this activity, have pairs come up with sentences for the choices they didn't use. For example: 1. *Esta es la empresa que emplea a mi madre. Mi madre, quien trabaja en esa empresa, ha recibido el premio a la mejor empleada del año.*

44. To extend this activity, once student pairs have finished, ask them to get together with another student pair and present their lists of famous Hispanics to each other. Then have groups choose one of the personalities and research him or her in more detail. (You may wish to assign this part as homework.) Finally, have groups make a brief presentation to the class about their chosen person.

Answer Key

41. a. *The clothes I bought are imported.*
   b. *She is the businesswoman I work for.*
   En inglés se omitió el pronombre relativo en ambas oraciones.

42. Answers will vary. Sample answers:
   1. ... tiene mucho litio.
   2. ... se fabrican con litio.
   3. ... tiene muchos recursos naturales.
   4. ... les gustaría explotar el litio del salar de Uyuni.

43. 1. b   2. b   3. a   4. a

44. Answers will vary.
   ▶ Answers will vary.

45. Answers will vary.

Additional Resources

Fans Online activities
Practice Workbook

151

Unit 3
DESAFÍO 2

Gramática – El futuro perfecto

Presentation

■ In this section, students will learn and practice the future perfect tense to refer to actions that will be completed before a specific time in the future.

Activities	Standards	Resources
Gramática	1.2, 3.1	
46.	1.1, 3.1, 4.1	
47.	1.3, 3.1	
48.	1.2, 1.3, 2.1, 2.2, 3.2, 5.1	
49.	1.1, 5.1	
50. Conexiones	1.2, 1.3, 2.1, 2.2, 3.1, 3.2, 5.1	

Teaching Suggestions

Warm-Up / Independent Starter

■ Have students write a list of three things they plan to complete before they turn thirty (e.g., *Me graduaré de dentista*).

Preparation

■ Call on volunteers to read aloud the grammar presentation. Encourage students to ask questions about any explanations they do not understand and clarify this information for them.

■ Then have students change the verbs they used in their Independent Starter statements from the future to the future perfect (e.g., *me graduaré → me habré graduado*). Meanwhile, write this sentence starter on the board: *Antes de cumplir treinta años...* Then, have students rewrite their statements from the Independent Starter using this sentence starter and the future perfect tense (e.g., *Antes de cumplir treinta años, me habré graduado de dentista*).

Activities

47. Before completing this activity, ask students to conjugate the verbs in the box in the future perfect tense.

48. To extend this activity, have students use their predictions to compose a paragraph describing the future of natural gas vehicles in Peru. Invite students to share their paragraphs with the class.

152

Gramática

El futuro perfecto

• El futuro perfecto equivale a *will have + past participle*. Este tiempo se usa para hablar de una acción terminada antes de un momento futuro determinado.

Ahora ●————————————————————→ Futuro

firmar la hipoteca   martes a las 11:00 a. m.

El martes a las 11:00 a. m. ya **habremos firmado** la hipoteca.
(By 11:00 a. m. on Tuesday, we will have signed the mortgage.)

• También se usa para hablar de una acción terminada antes de otra acción futura.

Ahora ●————————————————————→ Futuro

cobrar el cheque   salir del banco

Cuando salgas del banco, ya **habrás cobrado** el cheque.
(By the time you leave the bank, you will have cashed the check.)

Formación del futuro perfecto

• El futuro perfecto se forma así:

> futuro del verbo haber + participio pasado

FUTURO PERFECTO. VERBOS REGULARES

	Comprar	Vender	Consumir
yo	habré **compr**ado	habré **vend**ido	habré **consum**ido
tú	habrás **compr**ado	habrás **vend**ido	habrás **consum**ido
usted, él, ella	habrá **compr**ado	habrá **vend**ido	habrá **consum**ido
nosotros(as)	habremos **compr**ado	habremos **vend**ido	habremos **consum**ido
vosotros(as)	habréis **compr**ado	habréis **vend**ido	habréis **consum**ido
ustedes, ellos(as)	habrán **compr**ado	habrán **vend**ido	habrán **consum**ido

46 **Compara.** ¿Cuándo se usa el futuro perfecto en inglés?

47 **Preparando el desafío**

▶ **Escribe.** Daniel y Michelle se preparan para el desafío. ¿Qué habrán hecho mañana?

ensayar tomar leer hacer

1. Mañana Daniel _____ apuntes sobre el futuro de la industria automovilística.

2. Mañana Michelle _____ artículos de finanzas sobre el litio.

3. Mañana Daniel _____ varias veces para preparar el debate.

4. Mañana Michelle _____ un esquema para preparar el debate.

Differentiated Instruction

DEVELOPING LEARNERS

• Have students work with a partner to write a dialogue in which they ask each other questions about their daily routines in the coming days, using the future perfect. Then have students role-play their dialogues. For example:

A. *¿Habrás desayunado antes de las 8?*
B. *Sí, para entonces habré desayunado. ¿Habrás enviado algún mensaje a esas horas?*
A. *No, pero habré repasado mis apuntes de Química porque tenemos examen. ¿Los habrás repasado tú?*
B. *No, pero Ana y yo habremos...*

EXPANDING LEARNERS

• Ask students to write at least one paragraph that describes what they will have done throughout the day and by the end of the day tomorrow. Remind them that they will need to use the future perfect as well as specific times. Encourage students to use the adverb *cuando* and the subjunctive. Then have them exchange papers with a partner and compare each other's activities for the day. Next, ask them to write a new paragraph that reflects what both of them will have done. Call on volunteers to read their work aloud.

48 Predicciones

▶ **Lee** el artículo y escribe tres predicciones sobre los autos de gas natural en Perú.

> **FINANZAS**
>
> ## Cada año más de 25.000 autos se convierten al gas natural
>
> **En los próximos cinco años, serán más de 230.000 autos los que ahorren en combustible.**
>
> Los vehículos que utilizan gas natural como combustible crecerán a un ritmo de 25.000 unidades anuales, con lo cual en los próximos cinco años el parque automotor, que actualmente tiene 130.000 vehículos, contará con más de 100.000 unidades adicionales, informó
>
> el gerente general de Cálidda Gas Natural del Perú, Adolfo Heeren. «Cada mes hay de 2.000 a 3.000 conversiones y esto ha hecho que el mercado de taxis en Lima se abastezca con gas natural», manifestó.
>
> Fuente: http://www.expreso.com.pe (selección)

49 El año 2050

▶ **Habla** con tu compañero(a). ¿Creen que en el año 2050 habrán pasado ya estos hechos? ¿Por qué?

> descubrir una cura para el cáncer
> extraer el litio del salar de Uyuni
> eliminar la dependencia del petróleo
> fabricar autos que vuelen
> descubrir nuevas fuentes de energía
> alcanzar la paz mundial

> ¿Crees que en el 2050 se habrá descubierto una cura para el cáncer?

> Sí, creo que se habrá descubierto una cura para el cáncer y también para otras enfermedades.

CONEXIONES: ECONOMÍA

Las monedas nacionales

Cada país tiene su propia moneda, pero en algunos casos los nombres coinciden. Por ejemplo, el peso es la moneda de México, Argentina, Chile y otros países.

La Organización Internacional de Normalización (ISO), que se encarga de establecer los estándares para el comercio internacional, estableció un código de tres letras para todas las monedas del mundo con el fin de evitar confusiones.

País	Moneda	Código
Argentina	peso argentino	ARS
Chile	peso chileno	CLP
Colombia	peso colombiano	COP
México	peso mexicano	MXN
República Dominicana	peso dominicano	DOP
Uruguay	peso uruguayo	UYU

50 Investiga. ¿Qué otros nombres de monedas coinciden en dos o más países?

ciento cincuenta y tres **153**

HERITAGE LANGUAGE LEARNERS

- Have students look up the exchange rate of the currency in their family's country of origin. Then, have them bring in ads—both from this country and the heritage nation—for some of the same common food or clothing items, as well as for some manufactured products, including the prices. Ask them to convert the foreign currency to the currency used here (and vice versa), and make a comparison between the price of goods sold abroad and those sold in this country.

CRITICAL THINKING

- Ask students to think about the advantages and/or disadvantages of introducing a common currency for all the Spanish-speaking countries in the Americas. Have them write an essay either endorsing this proposed common currency, or opposing it. Students may consider some of these advantages: it would eliminate currency exchange costs, make traveling easier, and it might give all member nations a sense of unity. They may also consider some disadvantages: the differences between the nations' economies and standards of living; the loss of identity by not having a national currency.

Gramática – El futuro perfecto

50. Ask students to work with a partner to research the history of a currency name that is shared by several countries (e.g., dollar, franc, pound, dinar). Have pairs report their findings to the class.

CONEXIONES: ECONOMÍA

Las monedas nacionales

The name *peso* was applied in 16th-century Spain to a large silver coin that had a value of eight *reales*. In other parts of Europe, the word *thaler*, or dollar, was used for a similar silver coin. The Spanish colonies of the Americas also used this silver coin, which was, in fact, made with Mexican or Bolivian silver. Following independence, the Spanish-speaking countries of the Americas began issuing their own currencies, but in many countries the name *peso* persisted.

Answer Key

46. En inglés, al igual que en español, el futuro perfecto se usa para hablar de una acción terminada antes de un momento futuro determinado o antes de otra acción futura.

47. 1. habrá tomado   3. habrá ensayado
2. habrá leído   4. habrá hecho

48. Answers will vary. Sample answers:
– En 5 años casi se habrá duplicado el número de vehículos que usan gas.
– Se habrá reducido la contaminación.
– Habrán desaparecido los taxis de gasolina.

49. Answers will vary.

50. Answers will vary. Sample answer:
El nombre *dólar* lo comparten las monedas de varios países, entre ellos EE. UU., Canadá, Australia y Nueva Zelanda.

Additional Resources

Fans Online activities
Practice Workbook

LECTURA: TEXTO INFORMATIVO

Presentation

- In this section, students will read an article describing the world economy and globalization. Students will review and practice vocabulary used to talk about the economy and finance, and they will express opinions regarding these topics.

Activities	Standards	Resources
Lectura: texto informativo	1.1, 1.2, 3.1, 3.2, 5.1	
51.	1.2, 1.3	
52.	1.2, 1.3, 3.1, 3.2, 5.1	

Teaching Suggestions

Warm-Up / Independent Starter

- Have students read the *Antes de leer* strategies silently. Ask them to jot down some notes and prepare to share their answers.

Preparation

- As a class, discuss the answers to the *Antes de leer* questions. To help students focus their answers, have them think of concrete examples of globalization (e.g., McDonald's in China, call centers in India, a smartphone sold in America but assembled in China with Korean components). Then, using their examples as a basis, have students think of positive and negative effects of globalization. Do most students see globalization as a positive or negative trend? This discussion will activate students' previous knowledge about the topic.

- Call on a volunteer to read the title, headings, and subheadings aloud. Based on the title and headings, have students infer the questions the article might answer (e.g., *¿Qué es la globalización? ¿Cuáles son sus características? ¿Cuáles son sus efectos?*).

- Have students read the article individually. As they read, ask them to create a list of 8–10 unfamiliar words. Then have students get together in groups of three and discuss their vocabulary lists. Allow students to use a dictionary to look up words that are unfamiliar to all the group members. Then have students read the article again in their groups.

154

Antes de leer: estrategias

1. Lee el título del texto. ¿Qué es la globalización? ¿Qué palabras asocias con ese término?
2. Piensa en un efecto positivo y en otro negativo de la globalización. Comparte tus ideas con tus compañeros(as).

La globalización económica

En la actualidad, las relaciones económicas entre los países son muy intensas: los capitales se invierten en casi cualquier lugar, se intercambian bienes[1] y servicios, e, incluso, han aumentado los movimientos laborales.

La *globalización* hace referencia a la escala mundial de todos estos fenómenos. Las relaciones económicas entre distintas partes del mundo han existido siempre, pero la diferencia es que ahora se producen con mucha más intensidad. La globalización se define como la interdependencia cada vez más estrecha e inmediata de las economías y políticas de todos los países.

Características de la economía global

El sistema económico mundial se basa en cuatro ejes[2]:

- **El crecimiento del comercio.** El volumen del comercio internacional de mercancías ha pasado de 300.000 millones de dólares en 1970 a más de 15,7 billones en 2008. En este sentido, la mejora y el abaratamiento de los transportes han sido decisivos. El tráfico marítimo es el principal medio de transporte en el comercio internacional.

- **La mundialización de la producción.** Gran parte de la producción y el comercio mundiales están controlados por las multinacionales, que son empresas registradas en un país, pero con filiales en otras partes del mundo.

  Las 1.000 empresas más grandes del mundo producen cuatro quintas partes de la producción industrial mundial y realizan más del 45 % de las exportaciones mundiales.

- **El *boom* de los flujos financieros.** Cada día se mueven en el mundo alrededor de un billón de dólares. La mayoría de las transacciones financieras no son pagos por una mercancía o servicio, sino que responden a operaciones especulativas en las que las grandes instituciones financieras buscan obtener beneficios.

- **La interrelación de todos los puntos del planeta.** Una decisión tomada en cualquier lugar por un gobierno, una gran empresa o una importante institución financiera provoca reacciones en el resto del mundo.

Differentiated Instruction

DEVELOPING LEARNERS

- To confirm students' comprehension of some new words that appear in the article, ask them to match the words in both columns.

  1. *actualidad* (e)   a. *causar*
  2. *escala* (i)   b. *admitir*
  3. *abaratamiento* (f)   c. *aumento*
  4. *decisivo* (h)   d. *ingresos*
  5. *filial* (g)   e. *presente*
  6. *provocar* (a)   f. *disminución de precio*
  7. *acoger* (b)   g. *sucursal*
  8. *rentas* (d)   h. *fundamental*
  9. *crecimiento* (c)   i. *proporción*

EXPANDING LEARNERS

- Ask students to write a three-paragraph essay that addresses one of the following topics:

  1. *¿Cuál es la relación entre la economía y la política de un país?*
  2. *Explica el impacto de la economía en tu comunidad y en tu vida.*
  3. *¿Cómo pueden ser más éticas las multinacionales?*
  4. *Si tuvieras los medios para hacerlo, ¿cuál sería tu solución para mejorar la vida de las personas que viven en países pobres?*

Efectos de la globalización

- Mayor oferta de productos baratos en los países ricos.
- Mayor especialización de los países en unas actividades económicas concretas y más productividad.
- Las multinacionales pueden fabricar con menores costes y ofrecer precios sin competencia.
- Aumento de las rentas[3] de la población de los países pobres que acogen empresas de los países desarrollados.
- Las crisis financieras pasan de unos países a otros.
- El crecimiento del comercio internacional ha beneficiado sobre todo a Europa occidental, América del Norte y Asia. En cambio, un gran número de países pobres, en particular los del África subsahariana, se ha quedado al margen[4] de esta globalización.
- Destrucción de los sistemas económicos tradicionales.
- Desempleo[5] entre los trabajadores en los sectores al margen del mercado.

Fuente: *Enciclopedia del estudiante. Geografía general.* Santillana.

1. productos   2. ideas fundamentales   3. *income*   4. excluido   5. *unemployment*

---

51 **¿Comprendes?**

▶ **Explica** estos epígrafes del texto con tus propias palabras.

1. El crecimiento del comercio.
2. La mundialización de la producción.
3. El *boom* de los flujos financieros.
4. La interrelación de todos los puntos del planeta.

52 **Con tus propias palabras**

▶ **Clasifica** en un gráfico como este los efectos de la globalización que menciona el texto. Después, añade un efecto más en cada columna.

EFECTOS POSITIVOS

EFECTOS NEGATIVOS

▶ **Escribe** un párrafo en el que expreses tu opinión. Después, compártelo con el resto de la clase. ¿Qué opinan tus compañeros(as)? ¿Están de acuerdo contigo?

Activities

51. Once students have completed this activity, have them write six true/false statements about the reading. Then, ask students to exchange their statements with a classmate and answer each other's activity.

52. You may want to assign the second part of this activity as homework so that students have more time to write a well-argued opinion piece. If time allows, hold a whole-class discussion about the pros and cons of globalization.

Answer Key

51. Answers will vary. Sample answers:
1. El volumen del comercio internacional y el tráfico marítimo han aumentado considerablemente debido al abaratamiento de los transportes.
2. La producción y el comercio están controlados en gran medida por 1.000 multinacionales.
3. Diariamente se mueve un billón de dólares en operaciones especulativas de las instituciones financieras.
4. Todo está relacionado, por lo que las decisiones que se tomen en un país afectan al resto del mundo.

52. Answers will vary. Sample answers:
Efectos positivos: más productos baratos, mayor especialización, más productividad, aumentan las rentas en los países pobres, mayor flujo de información y de ideas.
Efectos negativos: precios sin competencia, países que se quedan al margen, contagio de las crisis financieras, desempleo, beneficio de unos pocos, destrucción de los sistemas ecónomicos tradicionales, control de todo por pocas compañías.

▶ Answers will vary.

Additional Resources

Fans Online activities

HERITAGE LANGUAGE LEARNERS

- Ask students to research the multinational companies that have offices or factories in their family's country of origin. Then have them analyze the economic impact these companies have on the local or national economy in their heritage countries. Ask students to address both the positive and negative effects of these corporations. Engage students in a discussion on the pros and cons of keeping the status quo of these companies and how the local economy might be improved or worsened by their absence.

SPECIAL-NEEDS LEARNERS

- Help students who have language-processing difficulties improve their reading comprehension by pointing out the many cognates in the article. Allow students to look up new words or expressions in their dictionaries and ask them to identify the verb tenses. As students read the article aloud, have them paraphrase each sentence to verify their understanding of what is being described.

Unit 3
DESAFÍO 2
Comunicación

Presentation

- In this section, students will integrate the vocabulary and grammar skills from *Desafío 2* in order to read an article about sustainable banking and talk about improving a business. They will also hold a debate about mining Bolivia's lithium reserves.

Activities	Standards	Resources
53.	1.2, 1.3, 3.1, 4.2, 5.1, 5.2	
54.	1.1, 1.2, 3.1, 5.2	Audio
55. Final del desafío	1.1, 1.2, 1.3, 2.1, 2.2, 3.1, 3.2, 5.1	

Teaching Suggestions

Warm-Up / Independent Starter

- Have students list activities related to banking (e.g., *abrir una cuenta, pedir un préstamo*).

Preparation

- Spend some time reviewing the uses of relative pronouns and the future perfect tense. Then have students work in small groups to restate each grammar concept and provide examples of usage.
- To review some of the vocabulary for this *Desafío*, ask for volunteers to share their Independent Starters. Then, discuss with students what they know about the way banks operate. For example: *Los bancos reciben los depósitos de los clientes. Después prestan ese dinero, cobrando interés, a compañías o a otros clientes.*

Activities

53. After finishing the second part of this activity, have students work in small groups to share their writings. Have groups discuss the differences between a sustainable business (either a bank or a corporation) and an unsustainable one. To facilitate the discussion, students may first list the goals of each type of enterprise and how each of these business models goes about attaining its goals. Encourage a diversity of opinions.

Comunicación

53 **Banca sostenible**

▶ **Lee** el folleto de este banco y responde a las siguientes preguntas.

Triodos Bank, un banco donde cuenta algo más que el dinero

Triodos Bank es una entidad de crédito independiente que promueve desde 1980 una actividad bancaria transparente y sostenible. Somos pioneros en el desarrollo de un modelo de negocio financiero centrado en mejorar la calidad de vida de las personas y promover el respeto al medio ambiente, además de obtener rentabilidad económica.

Los ahorros de nuestros clientes nos permiten financiar iniciativas y organizaciones valiosas para la sociedad y para el futuro de las personas y el planeta. En la actualidad, contamos con 437.000 clientes en cinco países y hemos concedido más de 24.000 créditos a empresas y proyectos sostenibles. A través de nuestros Fondos de Inversión Socialmente Responsables y Fondos de Comercio Justo y Microcréditos, estamos presentes en más de 30 países de África, Europa del Este, América Latina y Asia.

NUESTRO TRABAJO

En Triodos Bank ponemos en contacto a ahorradores e inversores que quieren contribuir a mejorar la sociedad y el planeta con proyectos y empresas sostenibles cuya actividad se encamina hacia ese fin. Somos el único banco especializado en ofrecer financiación y oportunidades de inversión en actividades y empresas de carácter social, cultural y medioambiental en muchos países europeos. Las inversiones de Triodos Bank van dirigidas a sectores como las energías renovables, la agricultura ecológica, la bioconstrucción, el turismo sostenible, el comercio justo o las iniciativas culturales.

NUESTRA MISIÓN

- Contribuir a una sociedad que fomente la calidad de vida y la dignidad humana.
- Facilitar a personas, empresas y organizaciones un uso responsable del dinero.
- Proporcionar a nuestros clientes productos financieros sostenibles y un servicio de calidad.

Fuente: http://www.triodos.es (texto adaptado)

1. ¿Por qué Triodos Bank se define como un banco transparente y sostenible?
2. ¿En qué tipo de proyectos invierte dinero?
3. ¿Cómo financia los proyectos en los que invierte dinero?

▶ **Escribe.** ¿Conoces algún banco u otro tipo de compañía sostenible? Escribe un párrafo explicando a qué se dedica y cómo funciona.

Differentiated Instruction

DEVELOPING LEARNERS

- Ask students whether the following statements about Triodos Bank are true *(cierto)* or false *(falso)*. Have them correct the false statements.
  1. *Los ahorros de sus clientes se guardan y no se utilizan. (F; se usan para financiar iniciativas y organizaciones)*
  2. *Realiza inversiones en cuatro continentes. (C)*
  3. *Es solo uno de tres bancos que ofrecen financiación en asuntos sociales y medioambientales. (F; es el único)*
  4. *Invierte en iniciativas culturales. (C)*
  5. *Promueve el uso responsable del dinero. (C)*

EXPANDING LEARNERS

- Divide the class into three groups and ask students to go to the Triodos Bank website in Spain (triodos.es) and find the categories *Medio ambiente, Iniciativas sociales,* and *Cultura y ocio.* Assign each group one of these categories and have students work within the group to research their corresponding subcategories; for example, under *Cultura y ocio* students will find *Actividades culturales, Educación,* and *Ocio sostenible.* Ask students to read the information contained therein, including *los testimonios,* and make a brief report to the rest of the class.

54 El futuro de mi compañía

 ▶ **Escucha** y decide qué debe hacer cada empresario(a) para tener un negocio más exitoso.

1. Fabricar los productos en otro país e importarlos.
2. Pedir un préstamo al banco para financiar la compañía.
3. Verificar el saldo todos los días.
4. Firmar un contrato con otra compañía en el exterior.
5. Reducir los gastos cerrando algunas oficinas.
6. Exportar sus productos.

▶ **Habla** con tu compañero(a). Representen una conversación entre un(a) empresario(a) y un(a) experto(a) financiero(a) que le da sugerencias.

Final del desafío

DANIEL: ¿Estás lista para el debate?

MICHELLE: Sí. ¿Todavía tienes la misma opinión?

DANIEL: Pues, básicamente, sí. Pienso que son los bolivianos quienes tienen que beneficiarse de ese recurso natural que puede generar tantos beneficios a su país. Sin embargo, comprendo que al gobierno boliviano le hace falta una gran cantidad de dinero para realizar ese proyecto.

MICHELLE: ¿No leíste la información sobre el acuerdo que Bolivia firmó con China en 2011?

DANIEL: Sí, lo leí. Creo que hay empresas chinas que tienen mucho interés en Bolivia porque fabrican baterías y otros productos que requieren litio.

MICHELLE: Entonces, ¿estás a favor del acuerdo?

DANIEL: No del todo porque si Bolivia exporta el litio, todos los ingresos deberían ser para ellos, no para una compañía de otro país. ¿Tú qué opinas?

MICHELLE: Yo opino lo contrario. Pienso que...

55 Un debate muy controversial

▶ **Piensa.** ¿Qué opina Michelle? ¿Qué argumentos puede tener para apoyar su postura? Imagina qué le contestó a Daniel y escríbelo.

 ▶ **Habla** con tu compañero(a). ¿Cuál es su opinión sobre este tema? ¿Qué se debe hacer con las reservas de litio que hay en el salar de Uyuni? Hagan un debate exponiendo sus argumentos.

ciento cincuenta y siete 157

HERITAGE LANGUAGE LEARNERS

• Have students work with a partner and imagine that they are the founders of an ethical bank, one that promotes social and environmental responsibility in the financial sector. Students will need to find a suitable name for their bank, determine the founding city, and write a short descriptive paragraph, including all details that distinguish it from other financial institutions. Finally, they will create the bank's mission statement. Invite volunteer pairs to read their descriptions and mission statements aloud.

COOPERATIVE LEARNING

• Have students work in small groups and image that they are the board members of a new bank. Ask them to consider what their bank would offer customers and the community to distinguish it from other local financial institutions. Encourage all students in the group to contribute ideas to the discussion, and when a consensus is reached, have a member of the group write at least one paragraph describing the bank's distinguishing features. Invite groups to share their ideas with the rest of the class.

---

54. For the second part of this activity, ask students to imagine that they have a small business (e.g., a store, small construction or landscaping company, veterinary practice, coffee shop, design studio) that is not doing well. Give them a few minutes to jot down some of the things that are going wrong with their business before they get together with a classmate to exchange advice. If time permits, invite student pairs to present their conversations to the class. Encourage the class to comment on the advice given and to add their own advice or opinions.

 AUDIO SCRIPT
See page 127L.

Answer Key

53. Answers will vary. Sample answers:
1. Porque se basa en un modelo de negocio que busca mejorar la calidad de vida de las personas y promover el respeto al medio ambiente.
2. En actividades y empresas de carácter social, cultural y medioambiental, como por ejemplo, las energías renovables, la agricultura ecológica, la bioconstrucción, el turismo sostenible, el comercio justo o las iniciativas culturales.
3. Con los ahorros de sus clientes.
▶ Answers will vary.

54. 1. 4   2. 3   3. 6   4. 5   5. 1   6. 2
▶ Answers will vary.

55. Answers will vary. Sample answer:
Creo que Michelle piensa que el litio deben explotarlo los países y compañías que tengan los recursos para hacerlo porque es un producto muy necesario.
▶ Answers will vary.

Additional Resources

Fans Online activities
Practice Workbook

Unit 3
DESAFÍO 3

Expresar deseos

Presentation

- In *Desafío 3*, Asha and Lucas have to find out if there is a job position they can apply for at the Panama Canal. Students will preview language used for talking about jobs and professions and to express wishes and conditions.

Activities	Standards	Resources
Texto	1.2, 2.1, 2.2	
56.	1.2, 1.3, 2.1, 2.2	
57.	1.1, 1.2	
58.	1.1, 1.2, 1.3, 5.1, 5.2	Audio
59. Cultura	1.2, 1.3, 2.2, 3.1, 3.2, 4.2, 5.2	

Teaching Suggestions

Warm-Up / Independent Starter

- Ask students to list the steps to look for and apply for a job.

Preparation

- Have students share their Independent Starters. Then, brainstorm with students a list of jobs they could apply for. What kind of jobs are these? What qualifications are required?

Texto: Una maravilla de la ingeniería

- Read the introduction to the dialogue. Invite students to consider the types of jobs Asha and Lucas can do. Do students think those jobs will be available at the Panama Canal?

- Ask students to first read the dialogue silently. Then call on volunteers to role-play Lucas and Asha and read their parts convincingly in front of the class. Then have students work in pairs to write sentences summarizing the content.

Activities

57. To extend this activity, have students describe each job mentioned in the dialogue, give an example of the type of work, and identify the workplace. For example: *Los mecánicos trabajan con maquinaria pesada o vehículos. Reparan y les dan mantenimiento a estos equipos. Suelen trabajar en un taller.*

158

Una maravilla de la ingeniería

El canal de Panamá es una de las mayores obras de ingeniería del mundo. Hoy en día emplea alrededor de nueve mil personas. Asha y Lucas tienen que averiguar si hay algún trabajo al que puedan presentarse como candidatos. ¿Encontrarán alguno?

LUCAS: ¿Un puesto de trabajo en el canal de Panamá? Ojalá lo consigamos, suena muy exótico...

ASHA: Es posible. Si emplean a unas nueve mil personas, seguramente habrá algún puesto para nosotros.

LUCAS: ¿Sabes qué tipo de trabajos ofrecen?

ASHA: No sé, vamos a mirar en la página oficial. Es aquí, donde dice Empleos. Lucas, ¡mira la cantidad de ofertas que hay: ingenieros, mecánicos, químicos, trabajadores sociales... y hasta un fisioterapeuta!

LUCAS: ¿Un fisioterapeuta? ¿Los barcos necesitan fisioterapia?

ASHA: Muy gracioso... Supongo que con nueve mil empleados y sus familias, será necesario un fisioterapeuta. Aunque muchos de los puestos incluirán un seguro médico.

LUCAS: Ya, pero todavía no hemos visto ningún trabajo para nosotros. Si estuviéramos estudiando en la universidad, tendríamos más posibilidades.

ASHA: Quizá haya ofertas para estudiantes en prácticas. Pero si no lo conseguimos ahora, podemos intentarlo el año que viene. Yo quiero estudiar Ingeniería, ¿y tú?

LUCAS: A mí me gustaría ser intérprete.

56   Detective de palabras

▶ **Completa** estas oraciones.

1. Lucas y Asha esperan encontrar un ___1___ de trabajo en el canal de Panamá.
2. Hay muchas ___2___ porque el canal emplea a más de 9.000 personas.
3. A Lucas le sorprende que necesiten un ___3___ en el canal.
4. Asha cree que muchos de los puestos incluyen un ___4___ médico.
5. En el futuro, a Asha le interesa estudiar ___5___; a Lucas le gustaría hacerse ___6___.

Differentiated Instruction

DEVELOPING LEARNERS

- Point out the uses of the subjunctive mood in the dialogue (*consigamos, estuviéramos, haya*) and review its uses. Then, ask students to choose the correct mood for the following sentences and explain why:
  1. *No creo que consigas / consigues el puesto. (consigas)*
  2. *Es posible que hay / haya puestos. (haya)*
  3. *Buscan ingenieros que son / sean bilingües. (sean)*
  4. *Si Asha era / fuera universitaria, podría encontrar un puesto. (fuera)*
  5. *Seguro que mañana te van / vayan a entrevistar. (van)*

EXPANDING LEARNERS

- Ask students to imagine that they are looking for a job, either with the Panama Canal or locally. Have them write a list of their academics, after-school activities, special skills, interests, and work experience. Students should also include a brief paragraph describing the kind of job they are looking for and what makes them qualified for this work. Students should then send this information electronically to a partner, who will review it and use it in the next lesson.

57 ¿Comprendes?

▶ **Responde** a estas preguntas.

1. ¿En qué consiste el desafío de Asha y Lucas?
2. ¿Qué empleos menciona Asha?
3. ¿Qué tipo de ofertas espera encontrar Asha?
4. ¿Qué clases debería tomar Lucas para conseguir el trabajo que le gustaría?

58 ¡Ayúdame!

 ▶ **Escucha** los diálogos y decide qué oración completa mejor cada uno.

a. ¿Por qué no consideras estudiar para hacerte fisioterapeuta?

b. Estoy preparado para estudiar mucho. Sé que nada se consigue sin trabajo y esfuerzo.

c. Podrías solicitar un programa para estudiantes en prácticas. Así podrías trabajar con profesionales y eso te ayudaría a tomar una decisión.

d. ¿Por qué no te presentas como intérprete para una empresa internacional?

 ▶ **Habla** con tu compañero(a). Túrnense para preguntar y responder, y presenten la información a la clase.

1. ¿Dónde estará él/ella dentro de diez años?
2. ¿Qué oficio le gustaría ejercer? ¿Por qué?

 ## CULTURA

Maravillas de la ingeniería

El canal de Panamá es una de las grandes obras civiles del mundo. Une el océano Atlántico y el Pacífico a través del istmo de Panamá. Esta maravilla de la ingeniería es una ruta económica importantísima; cada año cruzan el canal más de 12.000 barcos.

El proyecto fue iniciado por Francia, pero finalmente lo realizaron los Estados Unidos. De 1904 a 1919 se emplearon casi 40.000 trabajadores para su construcción. Actualmente trabajan allí más de 9.000 personas.

59 **Investiga y explica.** ¿Conoces otras «maravillas de la ingeniería»? Busca información y haz un póster para presentarlas a la clase.

HERITAGE LANGUAGE LEARNERS

• Ask students to work in small groups and prepare an oral report on the Panama Canal. Each student will describe a different aspect of the Canal, including its early history and the first failed attempts at construction. Students may also include a description of the accidents and diseases the workers endured. Suggest that students address the physical characteristics of the Canal, its capacity, time taken for ships to pass through it, and the rates paid. Encourage them to address ownership of the Canal as well as the 21st century construction of new locks.

MULTIPLE INTELLIGENCES:
Intrapersonal Intelligence

• Ask students to imagine that they are among the workers who are helping to build the Panama Canal at the start of the 20th century. They will be separated from their families for many months or even years, and are in danger of succumbing to tropical diseases. Have students keep all of this in mind as they write their thoughts in a journal over the course of a few days. Call on volunteers to read some of their entries aloud.

---

58. For the second part of this activity, have students report their partner's answers to the class. Are most students staying in the area or are they planning to move? Which fields are students planning to work in? Is there a trend?

 AUDIO SCRIPT
See page 127L.

 ## CULTURA

Maravillas de la ingeniería

Feats of engineering are not exclusive to our modern world. In the pre-Hispanic Americas, the builders of the Sacsayhuaman complex, in Peru, fit together massive stones with such precision that a piece of paper cannot be inserted between them. In Teotihuacan, central Mexico, a civilization prior to the Aztecs built some of the largest pyramids in the Americas. At Chichen Itza, the Maya built surface water drainage systems that funneled the rainwater to a storage area.

Answer Key

56.
1. puesto
2. posibilidades
3. fisioterapeuta
4. seguro
5. ingeniería
6. intérprete

57. Answers will vary. Sample answers:
1. En averiguar si hay algún trabajo en el canal de Panamá al que puedan presentarse.
2. Ingenieros, mecánicos, químicos, trabajadores sociales y fisioterapeuta.
3. Ofertas para estudiantes en prácticas.
4. Clases de idiomas, Lingüística, Interpretación Simultánea...

58. a. 2   b. 4   c. 3   d. 1
▶ Answers will vary.

59. Answers will vary.

Additional Resources

Fans Online activities

DESAFÍO 3

Vocabulario – Trabajo y profesiones

Presentation

- In this section, students will learn and use target vocabulary to talk about various professions and jobs, and the job-seeking process.

Activities	Standards	Resources
Vocabulario	1.2, 5.1	
60.	1.2	
61.	1.2, 1.3, 5.1	
62.	1.1, 5.1	
63.	1.3, 5.1, 5.2	
64. Comparaciones	1.2, 1.3, 2.1, 3.1, 3.2, 4.2, 5.1	

Teaching Suggestions

Warm-Up / Independent Starter

- Have students answer the following questions in writing: *¿Qué trabajo te gustaría tener? ¿Qué conocimientos y habilidades se necesitan? ¿Cómo consigues ese tipo de trabajo?*

Preparation

- Have students share their Independent Starters. Ask students if any of them currently has a job and how they obtained the position. Then ask seven volunteers to each read a bullet point from the vocabulary presentation. After each bullet point is read, have students repeat the key words after you. Then, as a class, discuss some of the advice given in the text. Have students had experience looking for and applying for a job?
- Ask students to look at the *Más vocabulario* feature. Have them repeat the words after you to practice correct pronunciation. Encourage students to think of other professions they know and create their own lists of professions.

Activities

61. To expand this activity, have students use the information from their charts to create a curriculum vitae outline. Then ask them to exchange their outlines with a classmate and comment on each other's work.

160

Vocabulario

Trabajo y profesiones

Prepárate para conseguir un puesto de trabajo

Considera:

- Dónde puedes consultar ofertas de trabajo interesantes: en la sección de anuncios clasificados del periódico, en páginas web especializadas, en el tablón de anuncios de la escuela...
- Tus conocimientos, habilidades, intereses y experiencia previa.
- Las condiciones: el tipo de contrato y los seguros que incluye (seguro médico, dental o de vida), el horario (si es flexible, si ofrecen horas extraordinarias...), las vacaciones y días feriados, y el sueldo.

Prepárate para la entrevista:

- Fíjate bien en los requisitos y el perfil del puesto.
- Rellena la solicitud de empleo o redacta tu currículum vítae (CV) u hoja de vida. Incluye tus datos personales, formación académica, experiencia profesional, idiomas y otros datos de interés. Si puedes, añade referencias o pídele a alguien que te escriba una carta de recomendación.
- Busca información sobre la empresa y prepara algunas preguntas para el entrevistador.
- ¡No llegues tarde a la cita!

¡Atención!

| el currículum vítae | résumé |
| el resumen | summary |

Más vocabulario

El trabajo

el/la becario(a)	intern
(des)empleado(a)	(un)employed
el desempleo	unemployment
la plantilla	staff
contratar	to hire
despedir	to fire

Profesiones

el/la biólogo(a)	biologist
el/la fisioterapeuta	physical therapist
el/la geólogo(a)	geologist
el/la intérprete	interpreter
el/la químico(a)	chemist

60 **¿Qué quiere decir?**

▶ **Une** las dos columnas.

(A)

1. los requisitos
2. la entrevista
3. las referencias
4. las habilidades

(B)

a. Conversación entre la empresa y el candidato.
b. Informe sobre las cualidades de una persona.
c. Capacidades, aptitudes.
d. Condiciones necesarias para un puesto.

Differentiated Instruction

DEVELOPING LEARNERS

- Have students choose the best answer.
  1. *Los ... estudian minerales.* (b)
     a. *químicos*   b. *geólogos*
  2. *Si trabajas a tiempo completo, es probable que te ofrezcan...* (a)
     a. *seguro médico*   b. *desempleo*
  3. *Soy bilingüe y busco un puesto como...* (a)
     a. *intérprete*   b. *requisito*
  4. *Los ... no suelen cobrar sueldo.* (b)
     a. *biólogos*   b. *becarios*
  5. *Juan no trabaja porque lo han...* (a)
     a. *despedido*   b. *desempleado*

EXPANDING LEARNERS

- Have pairs create an interview between an employer and a job applicant. Have students bring the lists they wrote in the previous lesson to serve as a basis for the interview. Encourage students to use as much of the new vocabulary as they can. For example:
  A. *Usted tiene un currículum impresionante. ¿Por qué quiere trabajar con nosotros?*
  B. *Me han hablado muy bien de la empresa, y creo que con mi formación académica y habilidades podría contribuir a su éxito.*

61 La hoja de vida

▶ **Escribe** en una tabla como esta qué información hay que incluir en cada apartado del currículum. Después, anota tus datos.

Parte del CV	Tipo de información	Tus datos
Datos personales	Nombre y apellido(s), lugar de nacimiento, dirección, teléfono...	Osvaldo Sánchez
Formación académica		
Experiencia profesional		
Idiomas		
Otros datos		

62 Un nuevo profesor

▶ **Habla** con tu compañero(a). ¿Qué requisitos creen que debe cumplir un(a) profesor(a) de Ciencias? Hagan una lista.

Modelo   A. *Yo creo que el principal requisito es que sea licenciado en Química.*
                B. *Sí, y también es importante que tenga experiencia.*

63 El trabajo ideal

▶ **Escribe.** ¿Cuál es para ti el trabajo ideal? Incluye esta información:

- El puesto y sus funciones.
- La empresa o el lugar de trabajo.
- Los conocimientos y habilidades necesarios.
- Las condiciones: el horario, el sueldo...

 COMPARACIONES

Solicitudes de empleo

En muchos países hispanos es frecuente incluir una fotografía en el currículum. Sin embargo, en los Estados Unidos está prohibido, ya que se considera que puede ser un elemento discriminatorio. Lo mismo sucede con algunos datos personales, como el estado civil o la edad del candidato.

64   **Piensa.** ¿Qué información crees que puede aportar la fotografía en un currículum? ¿Qué ventajas y desventajas crees que tiene incluirla? Justifica tu opinión.

---

63. To extend this activity, have students write an ad for their ideal job, using the information from this activity. Then, set aside an area in the classroom (a bulletin board, a table, the blackboard) where students can "post" their job listings. Have the class read the different ads and "apply" for a job they like. If time allows, you may have pairs of students conduct job interviews.

 COMPARACIONES

Solicitudes de empleo

In several Spanish-speaking countries, job listings often specify a gender and/or age requirement. Therefore, a photo, date of birth, nationality, and marital status are usually required information in a résumé. During a job interview, candidates might be asked questions regarding marital and family status, country or region of origin, schools attended, common acquaintances, etc. However, an increasing number of countries are enacting laws that prohibit discrimination on the basis of age, sex, race, nationality, disability, or religion.

Answer Key

60. 1. d   2. a   3. b   4. c

61. Answers will vary. Sample answers:
Formación académica: estudios realizados.
Experiencia profesional: puestos de trabajo y labores realizadas en cada puesto.
Idiomas: lenguas que domina y el nivel.
Otros datos: programas informáticos que domina, pasatiempos, etc.

62. Answers will vary.

63. Answers will vary.

64. Answers will vary.

Additional Resources

Fans Online activities
Practice Workbook

HERITAGE LANGUAGE LEARNERS

- Ask students to explain the difference between the following: *tener conocimientos* and *poseer habilidades; ofertas de trabajo* and *puestos de trabajo; trabajar por cuenta propia* and *ser de la plantilla; solicitud de empleo* and *ofertas de trabajo; cartas de recomendación* and *referencias; currículum vítae* and *solicitud de empleo.* Students' explanations may be expressed orally or in writing. Encourage students to write a sentence with each of these terms or phrases and read them aloud.

MULTIPLE INTELLIGENCES:
Verbal-Linguistic Intelligence

- Ask students to write *una carta de recomendación* for a friend or family member who is seeking admission to a school, participation in an exchange program, or a job. Remind students to include information regarding the candidate's academic and work histories, any special skills or interests, extra-curricular activities, and insight into how this person interacts with others. Encourage students to state why this candidate would make worthy contributions to the organization in question.

DESAFÍO 3

Gramática – Expresar deseos

Presentation

- In this section, students will review verbs and structures used to express wishes or desires. They will also review when to use the subjunctive mood with these verbs or structures.

Activities	Standards	Resources
Gramática	1.2, 3.1	
65.	1.2, 3.1, 4.1	
66.	1.2, 3.1	
67.	1.3, 3.1	
68.	1.1, 1.2, 1.3, 5.1	Audio
69. Comunidades	1.2, 1.3, 2.1, 3.2, 5.1, 5.2	

Teaching Suggestions

Warm-Up / Independent Starter

- Have students write one wish for themselves, their parents, and their best friend.

Preparation

- Ask students to read the grammar explanations silently, take notes on any material they do not understand, and review the subjunctive verb forms (present and imperfect subjunctive) if they need to refresh their memory.

- Have students share their Independent Starters with the class and have the class correct each student's work to make sure that they made proper use of the contrast between infinitive and subjunctive. For further practice, ask students to rewrite their sentences using a different verb or structure. For example: *Ojalá consiga un buen trabajo este verano.* → *Me gustaría conseguir un buen trabajo este verano.*

Activities

65. To help students determine the different structures they use to express wishes in English, have them translate the examples provided in the grammar presentation into English. Encourage students to compare the verb forms they used in English with those used in Spanish.

162

Gramática

Expresar deseos

- Para expresar deseos, puedes usar esta expresión:

  | ojalá (que) + presente de subjuntivo |

  Ojalá consigamos un buen trabajo.

  Repasa la conjugación del presente de subjuntivo en las páginas R20 y R21.

- También puedes expresar un deseo con verbos como querer, esperar, preferir y desear seguidos de una cláusula con un verbo en infinitivo o en subjuntivo:
  - Usa el **infinitivo** cuando el verbo principal y la cláusula dependiente tienen el mismo sujeto.

    Espero recibir un sueldo justo por mi trabajo.

  - Usa el **subjuntivo** cuando el verbo principal y la cláusula dependiente tienen sujetos distintos.

    Mi abuelo **quiere** que **suba** su pensión de jubilación.

Expresar deseos hipotéticos o corteses

- Para expresar un deseo hipotético o un deseo formulado de una manera cortés, puedes usar el condicional seguido de una cláusula en infinitivo o en subjuntivo:
  - Usa el **infinitivo** cuando el condicional y la cláusula dependiente tienen el mismo sujeto.

    Me **gustaría jubilarme** a los 50 años.   **Desearíamos tener** más días feriados.

  - Usa el **imperfecto de subjuntivo** cuando el condicional y la cláusula dependiente tienen distintos sujetos.

    Me **apetecería** que **fuéramos** a Cancún.   Nos **gustaría** que todos **tuvieran** trabajo.

- También puedes usar la forma quisiera *(I wish)* para expresar deseos hipotéticos o corteses:

  | quisiera + infinitivo |

  Quisiera trabajar de arquitecta.

  | quisiera que + imperf. subjuntivo |

  Quisiera que me **llamaran** para una entrevista.

  Repasa la conjugación del imperfecto de subjuntivo en la página R22.

65 **Compara.** ¿De qué formas distintas expresas deseos en inglés?

66 **Los deseos de Asha y Lucas**

▶ **Completa** estas oraciones. Usa el infinitivo o el presente de subjuntivo.

1. Diana y Andy esperan que Asha y Lucas _____ el puesto.
   conseguir
2. Asha y Lucas desearían _____ como candidatos para un puesto.
   presentarse
3. Ellos quieren que el puesto _____ un seguro médico.
   incluir
4. Les gustaría que les _____ un puesto como estudiantes en prácticas.
   ofrecer

162 ciento sesenta y dos

Differentiated Instruction

DEVELOPING LEARNERS

- Have students complete the following sentences with the correct verb:
  1. *El becario quisiera que le pagaran / pagaron por su trabajo.* (pagaran)
  2. *Ojalá me ofrezcan / ofrecen un seguro médico.* (ofrezcan)
  3. *El director prefiere que no escribieras / escribas una carta de recomendación.* (escribas)
  4. *Espero que no tienes / tengas que trabajar este domingo.* (tengas)
  5. *Queremos despedir / que despidamos a los intérpretes.* (despedir)

EXPANDING LEARNERS

- Ask students to write ten things that they wish would happen using the verb *quisiera*. For example:
  1. *Quisiera que mis amigos me apoyaran.*
  2. *Quisiera que los gobiernos de esos dos países se pusieran de acuerdo.*
  3. *Quisiera que me tocara la lotería.*
  4. *Quisiera que el profesor me diera una buena nota en la clase.*
- Then ask students to explain why they would like to see these things happen.

67 **El que adelante no mira, atrás se queda**

▶ **Imagina.** ¿Cuáles pueden ser los deseos de estos(as) chicos(as) sobre su futuro profesional? Escribe oraciones siguiendo el modelo.

Modelo   1. *Elena quiere hacerse bióloga. Espera que sea posible estudiar las aves.*

ELENA

JUAN

ANA

DIEGO

68 **Consejos paternos**

▶ **Escucha** la conversación entre Javi y su padre. Después, completa cada oración con una respuesta lógica.

1. El papá quiere que Javi...
2. El papá espera que Javi...
3. Javi prefiere que su papá...
4. A Javi le gustaría...

▶ **Habla** con tu compañero(a). ¿Qué deseos tienen ustedes para su futuro? ¿Qué consejos les han dado sus familiares y sus profesores(as)?

Modelo   A. *A mí me gustaría ser actor.*
B. *A mí también, pero mis padres quieren que estudie Medicina.*

COMUNIDADES

CONCILIAR LA VIDA LABORAL Y FAMILIAR

Desde 1980, más de 70 millones de mujeres han ingresado al mercado laboral en Latinoamérica, según datos del Banco Mundial. Sin embargo, muchas mujeres intentan compatibilizar las obligaciones laborales y familiares, y se producen muchas situaciones de desigualdad. En España, por ejemplo, el 97,3% de las personas que trabajan a tiempo parcial para cuidar a sus hijos son mujeres. Afortunadamente, muchas empresas ofrecen medidas para conciliar la vida laboral y familiar, como la flexibilidad horaria o el teletrabajo.

69 **Piensa.** ¿Qué otras medidas de conciliación crees que podrían ofrecer las empresas? ¿Cómo crees que afectan al ambiente y a la productividad?

ciento sesenta y tres   163

Gramática – Expresar deseos

68. Hold a brief discussion with the class regarding stereotypical teenagers' wishes (e.g., a car, more free time to be with their friends) and what their parents usually want (e.g., better grades, more responsibility). Encourage students to explain how these wishes may clash and fuel conflict between teenagers and their parents.

 AUDIO SCRIPT
See page 127M.

COMUNIDADES

Conciliar la vida laboral y familiar

In the last two decades, the female economic participation rate in Latin America has grown from 42% to 52%. However, paternity leave is still uncommon in the region, and women are the main caretakers of children. But the issue of work-family balance is slowly gaining attention. Good and affordable childcare programs, such as *Chile crece contigo* and *Red Nacional de Cuido y Desarrollo Infantil* (Costa Rica), are becoming more common.

Answer Key

65. Se usan verbos como *wish, like* y *hope* con el infinitivo, el pasado o el condicional.

66. 1. consigan   3. incluya
       2. presentarse   4. ofrecieran

67. Answers will vary.

68. Answers will vary. Sample answers:
   1. ... piense en su futuro.
   2. ... estudie una carrera universitaria.
   3. ... vea el partido de fútbol con él.
   4. ... ser futbolista.
   ▶ Answers will vary.

69. Answers will vary.

Additional Resources

Fans Online activities
Practice Workbook

HERITAGE LANGUAGE LEARNERS

• Have students work with a partner. One will write a letter to an advice columnist, detailing his or her frustrated attempts at trying to find a job. The partner will answer with some sound suggestions. For example: *Recuerda que tu CV es la primera impresión que tienen de ti. Revísalo cuidadosamente antes de mandarlo. Verifica los datos y la ortografía. Indica lo que te gustaría lograr en el puesto que buscas e incluye lo que deseas aprender en el trabajo.* Call on pairs to read their letters and responses aloud.

CRITICAL THINKING

• After students read the *Comunidades* feature, engage them in a discussion of childcare options for working parents. How do they think that the statistics compare here to those cited from Spain? Encourage them to research this and also look into daycare centers in their community. Ask students to consider what other daycare alternatives are available locally to parents with young children. Finally, have students discuss what they consider to be the best options for combining a career and raising a family. You may also want students to debate this topic.

DESAFÍO 3

Gramática – Expresar condición

Presentation

- In this section, students will review how to express conditions. They will also learn some expressions to talk about conditions that have not yet been realized.

Activities	Standards	Resources
Gramática	1.2, 3.1	
70.	1.2, 3.1, 4.1	
71.	1.3, 3.1	
72.	1.2, 1.3	Audio
73.	1.1, 1.2, 1.3, 2.1, 2.2, 5.1	

Teaching Suggestions

Warm-Up / Independent Starter

- Write the following pair of sentences on the board and ask students to analyze the difference in meaning between them:
  - *Si consigo trabajo, compraré un auto.*
  - *Si consiguiera trabajo, compraría un auto.*

Preparation

- Have students read the grammar presentation with a partner and summarize the main points in their notebooks. Then ask volunteer pairs to explain each bullet point of the grammar presentation aloud to their classmates. Ask questions to guide the students' presentations. You may suggest to students that they look at the formulas for the formation of conditional sentences as if they were mathematical formulas, where variables are replaced.

- As a class, discuss the sentences from the Independent Starter. Call on volunteers to explain the difference between the first and the second sentence. (The first sentence refers to a real or likely condition. The second sentence refers to an unlikely or hypothetical condition.) If students are still having difficulties with this concept, ask them to translate these sentences into Spanish:
  - If I have the time, I'll help you. (*Si tengo tiempo, te ayudaré.*)
  - If I had the time, I'd help you. (*Si tuviera tiempo, te ayudaría.*)

164

Gramática

Expresar condición

Oraciones condicionales con si

- Para expresar lo que puede ocurrir si se cumple alguna condición, usamos generalmente la conjunción si *(if)*.

  <u>Si me llaman para una entrevista</u>, <u>iré</u>.
  condition   result

  <u>Envía tu CV</u> <u>si te interesa el puesto</u>.
  result   condition

- En español, como en inglés, hay varios tipos de condicionales:
  - Para hablar de **condiciones reales o probables**, utilizamos esta estructura:

si + presente indicativo +	presente indicativo futuro indicativo imperativo	Si trabajo horas extra, gano más dinero. Si necesito referencias, te las pediré. Si me llaman para un trabajo, avísame.

  - Para hablar de **condiciones hipotéticas, poco probables o contrarias a los hechos** referidas al presente o al futuro, usa esta estructura:

si + imperfecto subjuntivo + condicional	Si me ofrecieran el trabajo, lo aceptaría.

Otras expresiones de condición

- Tienen también valor condicional estas expresiones:

con tal de que *(provided that)* en caso de que *(in case)* + subjuntivo	Estoy dispuesto a viajar **con tal de que** me den el trabajo.

- Para expresar una condición que contradice *(contradicts)* lo que se dice en la cláusula principal, usa las siguientes estructuras:

a menos que *(unless)* a no ser que *(unless)* + subjuntivo salvo que *(unless)*	No te entrevistarán **a no ser que** tengas dos cartas de recomendación.

 70 **Compara.** Traduce al inglés las siguientes oraciones. ¿Qué tiempos verbales has usado en cada cláusula?

    a. No aceptaré el trabajo a no ser que paguen muy bien.

    b. Ten varias referencias listas en caso de que te las pidan.

71 **Condiciones**

▶ **Escribe** una respuesta para cada pregunta usando una condición.

Modelo   ¿Me ayudas a escribir mi currículum? ⟶ *Si tuviera tiempo, te ayudaría.*

1. ¿Me escribes una carta de recomendación?
2. ¿Sería posible trabajar desde casa?
3. ¿Cómo puedo decidir qué quiero estudiar?
4. ¿Hay algún puesto para estudiantes?

164   ciento sesenta y cuatro

Differentiated Instruction

DEVELOPING LEARNERS

- Ask students to choose the correct verb.
  1. *No te van a despedir a no ser que tienen / tengan que reducir la plantilla.* (tengan)
  2. *En caso de que te ofrecen / ofrezcan un seguro médico, ¡acéptalo!* (ofrezcan)
  3. *Si hay / hubiera muchas ofertas de trabajo, encontrarás un puesto rápidamente.* (hay)
  4. *Hay que trabajar los sábados a menos que son / sean días feriados.* (sean)
  5. *Si consigo / consiguiera una beca, me iría a la Universidad de Sevilla.* (consiguiera)
  6. *Aceptaré el trabajo con tal de que me dejan / dejen trabajar desde casa.* (dejen)

EXPANDING LEARNERS

- Ask pairs to look for job ads in Spanish-language newspapers. Have them select at least three that call for different skills and academic backgrounds, and respond to one of them with a cover letter and a CV from someone who may or may not be qualified for the position. Then, have the partners compose a letter in response to the applicant's CV. Remind students that all such letters will be formal and must use the *usted* form of the verbs. Call on volunteers to read their ads, letters, and responses aloud.

72 La entrevista

 ▶ **Escucha** una entrevista de trabajo y completa estas oraciones.

1. Marisol haría muy bien el trabajo si...
2. Ella preferiría trabajar a tiempo completo, a menos que...
3. Tendría disponibilidad para viajar los fines de semana en caso de que...
4. Podría optar a un sueldo mejor si...

▶ **Escribe.** Imagina que eres el / la jefe(a) de personal. Escríbele un correo a Marisol explicándole cuáles serían las condiciones de su empleo si decidiera aceptar el puesto.

73 ¡A trabajar!

▶ **Lee** estas ofertas para trabajar en el canal de Panamá y responde a estas preguntas.

1. ¿Qué puesto te interesaría más si te lo ofrecieran?
2. ¿Qué condiciones serían necesarias para que lo aceptaras?

ASISTENTE DE COMPUTACIÓN

REQUISITOS MÍNIMOS: Licenciatura en Sistemas Computacionales, Ciencias Computacionales, Informática u otras carreras equivalentes, o Diploma de Segundo Ciclo y un año de experiencia realizando las funciones de un(a) Asistente de Computación.

CÓMO INSCRIBIRSE: Ingrese al PORTAL DE EMPLEO, escoja el grupo de Informática, Electrónica y Telecomunicaciones, y seleccione Asistente de Computación.

ASISTENTE DE FISIOTERAPIA

REQUISITOS MÍNIMOS: Permiso para ejercer la profesión de Asistente de Fisioterapia emitido por el Consejo Técnico de Salud de Panamá.

CÓMO INSCRIBIRSE: Ingrese al PORTAL DE EMPLEO, escoja el grupo de Salud Ocupacional, Higiene Industrial y Bienestar, y seleccione Asistente de Fisioterapia.

TRADUCTOR(A) E INTÉRPRETE

REQUISITOS MÍNIMOS: Licenciatura en Inglés o la lengua extranjera requerida, o Diploma de Segundo Ciclo y un año de experiencia realizando las funciones de Traductor(a) o Intérprete.

CÓMO INSCRIBIRSE: Ingrese al PORTAL DE EMPLEO, escoja el grupo de Arte, Ciencias Sociales y Humanidades, y seleccione Traductor(a) e Intérprete.

Fuente: https://micanaldepanama.com

 ▶ **Habla** con tu compañero(a) sobre lo que has escrito en el apartado anterior y hazle más preguntas.

Modelo   A. *Me interesaría ser asistente de computación. Sin embargo, si tuviera que trabajar horas extraordinarias, no lo aceptaría.*
B. *¿Y qué harías si te ofrecieran un sueldo excelente?*

ciento sesenta y cinco **165**

Gramática – Expresar condición

Activities

71. Call on volunteers to share their answers with the class. Write some of the sentences on the board and analyze them with the class. Then, have students rewrite their answers using some of the expressions listed under *Otras expresiones de condición*. For example: *Te escribo la carta con tal de que tú me invites a comer.* Have students identify the condition that needs to be met in each sentence.

73. To expand this activity, have students choose one of the three jobs and role-play an interview. Suggest that they change partners for this. You may want to play the recording for activity 72 again so that students can use it as a model for their interviews.

 AUDIO SCRIPT
See page 127M.

Answer Key

70. a. *I will not accept the job unless it pays very well.*
b. *Have several references ready in case they ask for them.*
a. futuro y presente; b. imperativo y presente

71. Answers will vary. Sample answers:
1. Si te conociera mejor, te la escribiría.
2. Si fuera posible, no tendríamos oficinas.
3. Si hicieras prácticas en varias compañías, podrías decidir.
4. Si lo supiera, te lo diría.

72. 1. ... le dieran la oportunidad de trabajar.
2. ... le ofrecieran un puesto a tiempo parcial.
3. ... le dieran el trabajo.
4. ... trabajara en una empresa privada.
▶ Answers will vary.

73. Answers will vary.
▶ Answers will vary.

Additional Resources

Fans Online activities
Practice Workbook

Unit 3

LECTURA: TEXTO LITERARIO

Presentation

- In this section, students will read a short text about the creative process of a poet. As they read, they will review vocabulary related to mathematics. Students will also write a poem using words from the text.

Activities	Standards	Resources
Lectura: texto literario	1.1, 1.2, 2.2, 3.1	
74.	1.2, 1.3, 2.2, 3.1	
75.	1.2	
76.	1.3, 3.1	

Teaching Suggestions

Warm-Up / Independent Starter

- Ask students to list five things they associate with poetry, or the art of writing poems.

Preparation

- Call on individual students to share their ideas from the Independent Starter. Did any student think of mathematics as something related to poetry? Have students work with a partner to read the *Antes de leer* strategies and work on the two questions. Once pairs have finished working on the *Antes de leer* questions, discuss the answers as a class. Then read the title and ask: *¿Quiénes suelen "construir", o crear, ecuaciones en su trabajo? (los matemáticos, ingenieros, etc.)* Based on the questions in the *Antes de leer*, ask students to speculate on the profession of the "equation builder" in this reading.

- Ask for a volunteer to read the last sentence of the text aloud. Analyze with students the type of condition that is expressed by this sentence. Then, have students rewrite the sentence to express an unlikely or hypothetical condition. *(Si el deseo fuera una pregunta, la realidad sería un montón de respuestas.)*

- Read the text aloud to model pronunciation and have students follow along in their books. Then call on individual students to each read a paragraph aloud. Offer assistance with pronunciation. Finally, have students read the text again individually.

166

LECTURA: TEXTO LITERARIO

Antes de leer: estrategias

1. Escribe en español todas las palabras relacionadas con las matemáticas que recuerdes. Comparte tu lista con tus compañeros(as).

2. ¿Qué relación crees que puede haber entre la poesía y las matemáticas? Coméntalo con tus compañeros(as).

Un constructor de ecuaciones

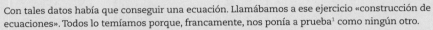

Yo tenía un profesor de matemáticas que nos obligaba a jugar con las ecuaciones. Nos ofrecía los resultados y a partir de estos nosotros teníamos que presentarle las ecuaciones de las cuales aquellos acababan derivándose.

> X igual a 7
> E igual a −3
> Z igual a 6,5

Con tales datos había que conseguir una ecuación. Llamábamos a ese ejercicio «construcción de ecuaciones». Todos lo temíamos porque, francamente, nos ponía a prueba[1] como ningún otro.

El profesor dejó claro que valoraría, más que cualquier otra cosa, la imaginación. Claro que nosotros no podíamos comprender cómo en una disciplina tan poco dada al malabarismo[2] como las matemáticas se nos iba a exigir que derrocháramos[3] imaginación. Y es que por entonces aún no sabíamos que imaginación y malabarismo se contradicen[4].

Cada vez que escribo un poema tengo la sensación de estar construyendo como entonces ecuaciones a partir de unos resultados que me ha ofrecido la realidad.

Los resultados que la realidad nos propone no pueden ser muy variables: amor, desasosiego[5], temor a la muerte, repugnancia por el paso del tiempo… Los de siempre. Meros números a partir de los cuales uno ha de presentar sus ecuaciones vertebradas[6] desde abajo, desde los resultados.

Creo que las matemáticas y la poesía tienen bastante que ver: pretenden expresar lo que existe mediante lo que no existe, o sea, mediante esos elementos que proceden de la imaginación.

Así pues mis poemas lo que persiguen es plantear una serie de ecuaciones cuyos resultados ya me había facilitado la realidad. Porque si el deseo es una pregunta cuya respuesta nadie conoce, la realidad es un montón de respuestas a las que el poeta debe plantearle sus preguntas.

JUAN BONILLA en Carlos Lomas, *La vida en las aulas* (selección)

1. *put us to the test*	3. usáramos en gran cantidad	5. intranquilidad
2. *expressiveness*	4. son contrarias, opuestas	6. organizadas, estructuradas

166   ciento sesenta y seis

Differentiated Instruction

DEVELOPING LEARNERS

- Ask students whether the following statements are true *(cierto)* or false *(falso)*. Have them correct the false ones.

  1. *El profesor les daba los resultados a los alumnos antes de darles las ecuaciones. (C)*
  2. *A los alumnos les parecía ese ejercicio muy fácil. (F; muy difícil)*
  3. *Según el autor, los resultados de la poesía vienen de la naturaleza. (F; de la realidad)*
  4. *El autor cree que la poesía y las matemáticas tienen bastante en común. (C)*
  5. *Según el autor, la realidad es una serie de preguntas. (F; de respuestas)*

EXPANDING LEARNERS

- Point out that Bonilla believes that both mathematics and poetry try to express what exists through what does not exist; that is, what comes from one's imagination. Ask students to consider this and to write at least one paragraph about an unlikely comparison between two school subjects, professions, countries, emotions, sports, the arts, or other topics of interest. Students must present their comparisons in an original manner and be prepared to justify the similarities.

74 ¿Comprendes?

 ▶ **Explica.**

1. ¿Qué oficio tiene el autor del texto?
2. ¿Qué quiere explicar con su texto?
3. ¿Qué relación establece entre las matemáticas y la poesía? ¿En qué parte del texto se establece esa relación?

▶ **Responde** a estas preguntas.

1. Para el autor del texto, ¿resultaba sencillo el ejercicio de construir ecuaciones?
2. ¿Qué era lo que el profesor apreciaba más de ese ejercicio?
3. ¿Qué relación existe entre la imaginación y el malabarismo, según el autor?
4. ¿Qué temas de su poesía se nombran en el texto?

75 Significa que...

▶ **Elige** la opción que equivale a la palabras destacadas.

1. Todos lo temíamos porque, francamente, **nos ponía a prueba** como ningún otro.
   a. nos divertía   b. nos exigía   c. nos hacía competir
2. El profesor **dejó claro** que valoraría, más que cualquier otra cosa, la imaginación.
   a. explicó   b. insinuó   c. pensó
3. Nosotros no podíamos comprender cómo en una disciplina **tan poco dada al** malabarismo como las matemáticas...
   a. tan alejada del   b. tan cercana al   c. tan poco regalada
4. Creo que las matemáticas y la poesía **tienen bastante que ver**.
   a. se distinguen   b. se parecen   c. son interesantes

76 Con tus propias palabras

▶ **Escribe** todas las palabras del texto de la página 166 relacionadas con las matemáticas y redacta un poema de cuatro versos (lines) usando algunas de esas palabras.

Ecuación

Cuánto le falta a 25 para ser 40
Inmersa estoy en sencilla situación
Una ecuación sin darme cuenta
Pronto le hallaré solución

Activities

74. You may want to ask students to work in pairs to answers the questions in this activity. One partner can, for instance, look for each answer in the text and read the corresponding section aloud. The other partner listens to what his or her partner is reading and then writes the answer to the question.

75. To extend this activity, have students write an original sentence with each of the four phrases listed in this activity. Then call on volunteers to share their sentences with the class.

76. Before students begin this activity, you may want to read some poems about poetry or math. The following are some examples: "Rima XXI" by Gustavo Adolfo Bécquer, "Teoría de conjuntos" by Mario Benedetti, "Oda a los números" by Pablo Neruda, "Números comparados" by Gloria Fuertes. Discuss with students unique rhyming or line patterns, and then have them try creating their own poems. You may want to have students work with a partner.

Answer Key

74. Answers will vary. Sample answers:
   1. Es poeta.
   2. La relación que hay entre las matemáticas y la poesía.
   3. Tanto las matemáticas como la poesía pretenden explicar lo que existe mediante lo que no existe. El autor explica esta relación en los últimos 4 párrafos.
   ▶ 1. No. Era un ejercicio que temía.
   2. La imaginación.
   3. Se contradicen.
   4. El amor, el desasosiego, el temor a la muerte, el paso del tiempo.

75. 1. b   2. a   3. a   4. b

76. Answers will vary.

Additional Resources

Fans Online activities

HERITAGE LANGUAGE LEARNERS

• Ask students to describe, in writing or orally, a past or current teacher who had some unique teaching methods and approaches to learning, and who inspired them to think analytically. Ask students to name the subject(s) taught, the grade level, and to describe how the teacher incorporated his or her methods in the classroom. Students should theorize as to what made these methods so unique. Encourage students to conjecture how these methods might be used for other classes and grade levels.

SPECIAL-NEEDS LEARNERS

• Have students who have language-processing difficulties work with a partner and take turns reading each sentence aloud. After they read, ask them questions to test their reading comprehension. For example (after the first sentence): *¿Qué los obligaba a hacer el profesor de Matemáticas? (Los obligaba a jugar con las ecuaciones.)* Should students answer incorrectly, ask them to read the sentence again. If they still have difficulties, simplify the sentence, or break it down into two or more sentences: *Yo tenía un profesor de Matemáticas. En su clase, teníamos que jugar con las ecuaciones.*

167

DESAFÍO 3

Comunicación

Presentation

- In this section, students will integrate the vocabulary and grammar skills from *Desafío 3* in order to talk about jobs and professions and to express wishes and conditions.

Activities	Standards	Resources
77.	1.1, 1.2, 1.3, 5.1	
78.	1.3, 2.2, 5.1	
79.	1.2, 1.3, 2.1, 2.2	
80. Final del desafío	1.1, 1.2, 1.3, 2.1, 2.2, 5.1, 5.2	

Teaching Suggestions

Warm-Up / Independent Starter

- Ask students to complete the following sentence starters with information about their academic and professional goals:
  - *Espero...*   – *Quisiera...*
  - *Me gustaría...*   – *Ojalá que...*

Preparation

- Call on students to share their Independent Starters. Then, review the structures they used to express wishes, as well as the use of the infinitive or subjunctive in each sentence. Next, have students rewrite their sentences to express the conditions that need or would need to be met for their wishes to come true. For example: *Espero que me acepten en una universidad reconocida.* → *Si saco buenas notas, me aceptarán en una universidad reconocida.*

Activities

77. Once students have finished this activity, write the following saying on the board and discuss it as a class: *Trabaja para vivir, no vivas para trabajar.* Do most students agree with this statement? Challenge students to think of obstacles they may encounter if they try to follow this advice. For instance, they may not be considered for a promotion if they do not put in as many hours as their coworkers.

Comunicación

77 El valor del trabajo

▶ **Lee** los testimonios de estos jóvenes. ¿Estás de acuerdo con ellos(as)? Escribe tu opinión y justifícala.

Dicen que los jóvenes de hoy en día no valoramos el esfuerzo, que hemos crecido con todo lo necesario y que por eso hemos perdido el espíritu de sacrificio. Pero yo no estoy de acuerdo. Estudio en la universidad por las mañanas y trabajo por las tardes para pagarme los estudios. ¿No es eso un ejemplo de esfuerzo?

Soy informático y me gusta mi trabajo, pero no quiero que sea el centro de mi vida. Me encanta viajar, así que le pedí a mi jefe tener unos días más de vacaciones al año (sin salario, claro). No suelo hacer horas extraordinarias, pero soy flexible: si un día hay que quedarse hasta más tarde, lo hago. Pero soy de los que piensan que hay que trabajar para vivir, no vivir para trabajar.

 ▶ **Habla** con tu compañero(a) sobre lo que has escrito. ¿Están ustedes de acuerdo? Compartan sus opiniones con la clase.

Modelo
A. *Yo no estoy de acuerdo con el chico. Si no estás dispuesto a sacrificarte, no conseguirás nunca un buen puesto.*
B. *Pues yo sí, porque...*

78 El empleado ideal

 ▶ **Escribe** una carta de recomendación para un(a) amigo(a) o para un personaje ficticio. Incluye algunos datos personales y toda la información de interés para que pueda conseguir el puesto de trabajo que imagines.

Modelo

Estimada Sra. Rivera:
Quisiera recomendarle a mi amiga Elisa Márquez para el puesto de química que ofrece su empresa. Aunque no tiene mucha experiencia, es una persona muy responsable y trabajadora. Si decide contratarla, le aseguro que...

Differentiated Instruction

DEVELOPING LEARNERS

- Ask students to complete the following sentences with the correct form of the verb in parentheses:
  1. *Si (esforzarte) más, te aumentarían el sueldo. (te esforzaras)*
  2. *Los becarios desean que el jefe les (escribir) una carta de recomendación. (escriba)*
  3. *Quisiera que los desempleados (encontrar) trabajo. (encontraran)*
  4. *Tendrás éxito con tal de que (llegar) a tiempo y (cumplir) con todo. (llegues; cumplas)*
  5. *Me gustaría que tú (enviar) la solicitud de trabajo. (enviaras)*

EXPANDING LEARNERS

- Ask students to work with a partner and exchange *las cartas de recomendación* they prepared for activity 78. Ask them to review their contents and write a positive response, setting up an interview. Then, have them create an interview for the position advertised. Next, have them reverse roles. Invite pairs to act out their interviews in front of the class.
- Have the class take a vote to decide who gets the job and be prepared to explain why.

79 Una oferta del canal de Panamá

▶ **Lee** este anuncio del canal de Panamá y responde a las preguntas.

> **Descripción del trabajo:** Trabajo a tiempo parcial para estudiante universitario. Desempeñará tareas relacionadas con su carrera universitaria bajo la coordinación directa de un trabajador del canal. Las funciones podrán ser de apoyo administrativo o técnico. Se le ofrecerá al estudiante un contacto con la realidad del ejercicio profesional para apoyar su crecimiento profesional y reafirmar su vocación. Trabajará en proyectos tales como el Proyecto de Construcción del Tercer Juego de Esclusas *(locks)* u otros proyectos en ejecución en el canal.
>
> **Requisitos mínimos:** Estar matriculado a tiempo completo en una universidad con un mínimo de 15 créditos semestrales o cuatrimestrales. Estar cursando los dos últimos años de su carrera universitaria. Tener un índice académico de 2,20 en una escala de 3,00 o equivalente.
>
> Fuente: https://apps.pancanal.com

1. ¿Sería posible que Asha y Lucas se presentaran como candidatos a este trabajo?
2. ¿Qué ventajas y desventajas crees que tiene este trabajo?
3. ¿Considerarías presentarte a este trabajo? Justifica tu respuesta.
4. Si tuvieras la oportunidad de negociar las condiciones de trabajo, ¿qué pedirías?

Final del desafío

ASHA: Si fuéramos estudiantes universitarios, sería posible trabajar en el canal de Panamá. Pero no cumplimos los requisitos mínimos.

LUCAS: Bueno, no hemos conseguido un puesto de trabajo en el canal de Panamá, pero hemos aprendido muchísimo. Además, si nos interesara podríamos intentarlo el año que viene. Venga, no estés tan desanimada.

80 ¿Desafío perdido?

▶ **Lee** el diálogo y responde a estas preguntas.

1. ¿Por qué no consiguen Asha y Lucas un puesto en el canal de Panamá?
2. ¿Qué podrían hacer Asha y Lucas para conseguirlo en el futuro?

 ▶ **Habla** con tus compañeros(as). ¿Qué piensas que significa esta afirmación del filósofo chino Confucio?

> *Elige un trabajo que te guste y no tendrás que trabajar ni un día de tu vida.*

HERITAGE LANGUAGE LEARNERS

- Direct students to the statement made by the young man in activity 77: [...] *le pedí a mi jefe tener unos días más de vacaciones al año (sin salario, claro)*. Even though he describes a vacation without pay, how likely are employers to grant this request? Ask students to discuss how this statement reflects the mindset of a country's culture regarding work and work-life balance. Have students compare how employers might react in their heritage country and how they would react here to such a request.

MULTIPLE INTELLIGENCES:
Verbal-Linguistic Intelligence

- Divide the class into two teams. One player from each team chooses a vocabulary word, or an expression or a verb that expresses *deseos* or *condiciones* (e.g., *becario, quisiera, en caso de que*) and writes it on the board for his or her team only. By turns, teammates will say a word that starts with each letter in the word on the board. For every correct word, the team scores one point. If a player fails to write a word, one point is subtracted from the score.

---

80. For the second part of this activity, divide the class into small groups and give each group a different quote to discuss: 1. *Si todo el año fuera fiesta, divertirse sería más aburrido que trabajar.* (William Shakespeare) 2. *Cuando alguien se queje de su trabajo, que lo pongan a no hacer nada.* (Blaise Pascal) 3. *El trabajo es todo lo que se está obligado a hacer; el juego es lo que se hace sin estar obligado a ello.* (Mark Twain) 4. *Yo creo bastante en la suerte. Y he constatado que, cuanto más duro trabajo, más suerte tengo.* (Thomas Jefferson) Then, have the groups come together in a whole-class discussion in which they share their assigned quotes and their opinions. You may want to post some of the quotes around the classroom.

Answer Key

77. Answers will vary.
   ▶ Answers will vary.
78. Answers will vary.
79. Answers will vary. Sample answers:
   1. No, porque aún no están en la universidad.
   2. Ventajas: trabajar en el área de estudio, adquirir experiencia, crecimiento profesional, trabajo en proyectos importantes.
      Desventajas: las tareas pueden ser un poco rutinarias, puede ser difícil estudiar a tiempo completo y trabajar a tiempo parcial.
   3. Answers will vary.
   4. Pediría trabajar en algo menos administrativo y que estuviera más relacionado con mi profesión.
80. Answers will vary. Sample answers:
   1. Porque no son estudiantes universitarios.
   2. Podrían volver a intentarlo cuando fueran estudiantes universitarios.
   ▶ Answers will vary.

Additional Resources

Fans Online activities
Practice Workbook

Unit 3
Para terminar

Presentation

- In this section, students will review the unit objectives and put them into practice. They will listen to a description of a school in Chile, and talk with a classmate about their future plans and goals. They will also select one of the following *desafíos* to develop: research a student exchange program in a Spanish-speaking country and present it to the class, look for a piece of news in Spanish that deals with the economy or finances and share it with the class, or think of an ideal job for a student their age and write a job offer.

Activities	Standards	Resources
81.	1.2, 1.3, 2.1, 2.2, 3.1, 3.2, 5.2	Audio
82.	1.1, 1.3, 5.2	
83. Tu desafío	1.2, 1.3, 2.1, 2.2, 3.1, 3.2, 5.1, 5.2	

Teaching Suggestions

Warm-Up / Independent Starter

- Have students write a paragraph describing an ideal curriculum for a semester abroad in a Spanish-speaking country. For example: *Me gustaría tomar una clase sobre el cine hispanoamericano. Quisiera que en la clase de Historia se estudiaran las civilizaciones precolombinas.*

Preparation

- Ask student pairs to read aloud their sentences from the Independent Starter. Then give pairs a few minutes to agree on a curriculum that both of them like and find interesting. Next, have pairs present their plans to the class. Hold a class vote to select the best curriculum.

- Ask students to change partners and have the new pairs consider the costs of a semester abroad and come up with a plan to pay for it. Students may, for instance, plan to apply for a summer job, open a savings account to deposit their earnings, ask for a loan, etc. As students work on this activity, allow them to go back and review the vocabulary and grammar sections in this unit. Then, ask pairs to present their plans to the class. As a class, discuss the feasibility of these plans.

170

Para terminar

Todo junto

ESCUCHAR Y ESCRIBIR

 81 **Una escuela diferente**

▶ **Escucha** el programa de radio que oyeron Ethan y Eva mientras buscaban escuelas en Chile y elige la opción correcta. Ten en cuenta que puede haber más de una.

1. Felipe Ríos es...
   a. cantante. b. profesor. c. actor.

2. En la escuela de teatro musical se puede estudiar...
   a. canto. b. jazz. c. escenografía.

3. Todos los semestres hay clases de...
   a. danza. b. piano. c. voz.

4. Para ser admitido en la escuela es imprescindible...
   a. una entrevista. b. una audición. c. una carta de presentación.

▶ **Escribe.** ¿Te gustaría matricularte en algún curso de esa escuela? ¿Por qué? Escribe un párrafo explicando tu respuesta.

HABLAR Y ESCRIBIR

 82 **Un futuro perfecto**

▶ **Habla** con tu compañero(a). Imaginen las cosas que ustedes habrán hecho en las siguientes fechas y compártanlas.

1. 2017 2. 2022 3. 2050 4. 2075

Modelo *En 2017 yo habré jugado el partido de baloncesto más importante de mi equipo. Habré terminado la escuela y habré conseguido una beca universitaria para estudiar en Argentina.*

▶ **Escribe** un párrafo comparando y contrastando todo lo que tú y tu compañero(a) habrán hecho en 2075 y compártelo con la clase.

170 ciento setenta

Differentiated Instruction

DEVELOPING LEARNERS

- Ask students to complete the following sentences:
  1. *Ojalá le paguen al...* (a)
     a. *becario* b. *saldo*
  2. *El año escolar se suele dividir en...* (b)
     a. *solicitudes* b. *semestres*
  3. *Si fueras bilingüe ... ser intérprete.* (b)
     a. *puedes* b. *podrías*
  4. *Me gustaría que ... más dinero.* (a)
     a. *ahorraras* b. *ahorres*
  5. *Cuando termines tus estudios universitarios, ya ... 22 años.* (a)
     a. *habrás cumplido* b. *cumplas*

EXPANDING LEARNERS

- Ask students which word does not belong, and then have them explain why.

1. *cuenta*	*saldo*	*punto (punto)*
2. *presupuesto*	*tasa*	*gastos (tasa)*
3. *reprobar*	*repasar*	*aprobar (repasar)*
4. *compañía*	*empresa*	*hipoteca (hipoteca)*
5. *recomendación*	*referencia*	*oferta (oferta)*
6. *conocimientos*	*habilidades*	*requisitos (requisitos)*
7. *mercancía*	*comercio*	*negocio (mercancía)*
8. *compatibilizar*	*conciliar*	*ejercer (ejercer)*

Tu desafío

83 Los desafíos

¿Recuerdas los desafíos que Andy y Diana les plantearon a los personajes? ¿Cuál te gusta más? Elige una de estas opciones y resuelve tu desafío.

DESAFÍO (A)

Busca información sobre programas de intercambio para estudiantes de secundaria en algún país hispanohablante. Elige el que más te guste y prepara una presentación para la clase. Incluye lo siguiente:

- A qué tipo de estudiantes está dirigido el programa.
- Qué requisitos son necesarios para participar en él.
- Qué información has obtenido a través de los testimonios de estudiantes que han participado en ese programa.

DESAFÍO (B)

Busca en Internet una noticia de finanzas de un periódico en español. Léela y comparte la información con la clase. Debes explicar:

- Cuál es la noticia y a qué país se refiere.
- Quiénes son los protagonistas de la noticia.
- Qué se puede aprender de esa noticia y cómo podría afectar a tu comunidad.

DESAFÍO (C)

Piensa en un trabajo ideal para estudiantes de tu edad y escribe una oferta de empleo. Incluye lo siguiente:

- Puesto de trabajo y funciones.
- Condiciones: tipo de contrato, horario...
- Requisitos necesarios.
- Información de contacto.

ciento setenta y uno **171**

HERITAGE LANGUAGE LEARNERS

- Ask students which *desafío* they would have liked to take part in, and why. Did the challenge focus on a country they know or would like to know? Was the challenge something that has always interested them or something they might be able to do soon? Then encourage students to create another challenge, based on those presented in this unit. For instance, they might choose a different country for a student exchange, present other economic issues, or choose a different site for possible employment.

MULTIPLE INTELLIGENCES:
Verbal-Linguistic Intelligence

- Ask students to work in groups of six or eight and identify a problematic economic or academic issue in their community that has divided, or has the potential to divide, the community into two camps. Students are going to debate this issue. Have them examine and define the opinions surrounding both sides of the topic. Next, have them divide their group in two, with each group taking one side of the debate. Finally, have them debate the matter in front of the other groups.

Activities

81. You may want to use this activity to practice listening comprehension techniques. With longer listening passages, it is easy to lose concentration. There may also be long sections where no information relevant to the exercise is given. Make students aware of this. Then have them read the four questions and list the information they would need in order to complete this activity (i.e., *profesión de Felipe, qué se estudia en la escuela, clases que se ofrecen todos los semestres, requisitos de admisión*). Then, play the recording and have students focus on getting the information they need to answer the four questions. Students should not get distracted by other information mentioned or by the small talk between the interviewer and interviewee.

82. Call on volunteers to share their paragraphs with the class. As a class, comment on any common trends among students' answers.

83. Display students' work in the classroom and have the class vote on the best entry in each category.

 AUDIO SCRIPT
See page 127M.

Answer Key

81. 1. c   2. a, b   3. a, c   4. b
   ▶ Answers will vary.

82. Answers will vary.
   ▶ Answers will vary.

83. Answers will vary.

Additional Resources

Fans Online activities
Practice Workbook

Unit 3

MAPA CULTURAL

La economía de Latinoamérica

Presentation

- This section presents information about the different economies of Latin America. The images serve as a reference point for additional cultural readings and activities that expand on the skills students learned in this unit.

Activities	Standards	Resources
Mapa cultural	1.2, 2.1, 2.2, 3.1, 3.2	
84.	1.2, 1.3, 2.1, 2.2, 3.1, 3.2, 5.1	
85.	1.2, 1.3, 2.1, 2.2, 3.1, 3.2, 5.1	

Cultural Topics

- **La industria en México.** Mexico has been labeled by some American journals as the "China next door," referring to the country's growing manufacturing power. Lately, manufacturing has been slowly moving away from China due to the increase of production costs there. This has helped Mexico, which already had a well-developed manufacturing industry. In fact, Mexico has become an important exporter of manufactured goods, rather than just exporting natural resources. Industries in Mexico include motor vehicles (cars, trucks, and parts), with manufacturing plants for all of the major brands; electronics, with Mexico being the second-largest supplier of electronics to the United States; chemicals and plastics; and aerospace manufacturing, with over 300 manufacturers.

- **Acuerdos comerciales.** The United States has bilateral trade agreements with several countries in Latin America. The largest of these agreements is the North American Free Trade Agreement (NAFTA), involving Canada, Mexico, and the U.S., and which went into effect in 1994. Other agreements have followed: U.S.-Chile Free Trade Agreement (2004), U.S.-Peru Trade Promotion Agreement or TPA (2009), U.S.-Panama TPA (2012), and the U.S.-Colombia TPA (2012).

Teaching Suggestions

Warm-Up / Independent Starter

- Ask students to list the countries where some of the products they buy or consume come from.

172

La economía de Latinoamérica

La agricultura, la ganadería y la minería han sido las principales actividades económicas de Latinoamérica y hoy continúan teniendo una gran importancia.

A lo largo de su historia, muchos países latinoamericanos se han especializado en algunos productos que han desempeñado un papel clave en su economía y han sido la base de sus exportaciones. Por eso, es frecuente encontrar en Latinoamérica amplias regiones dedicadas a un producto único o a una materia prima determinada: el banano, la soya, la carne, el petróleo…

Los países de clima tropical

Centroamérica, el Caribe y el norte de Suramérica (Ecuador, Colombia y Venezuela) son áreas de clima tropical y ecuatorial, donde la agricultura tiene un peso importante. En los países de esa zona se produce fundamentalmente café, bananos, caña de azúcar y otros productos tropicales, como la piña.

El café es fundamental para la economía de países como Colombia (tercer exportador mundial), Honduras, Guatemala y El Salvador.

Plantación de caña de azúcar.

Bananas y plátanos

El banano es una planta que puede producir dos tipos de frutos: uno pequeño, blando y dulce, que se suele consumir crudo, y otro más grande y menos dulce, que se consume cocinado. El primero se llama, según los países, banana, banano, plátano o guineo; y el segundo se llama plátano verde o plátano macho.

El cultivo de bananos está muy extendido por Centroamérica y el norte de Suramérica. Los principales países exportadores de bananas en el mundo son Ecuador, Costa Rica, Colombia y Guatemala.

En Latinoamérica el plátano cocinado es un ingrediente de muchos platos. Los tostones o chatinos (trozos de plátano verde aplastados y fritos) de Cuba, denominados patacones en Ecuador, acompañan muchas comidas tradicionales.

Las hojas de banano también se aprovechan. Se usan para envolver distintos platos, como los tamales.

Differentiated Instruction

DEVELOPING LEARNERS

- Ask students to complete the sentences with the name of the correct country or product.
  1. … es *el mayor productor de cobre.* (Chile)
  2. *Los países del sur de Suramérica exportan … y…* (soya y cereales)
  3. *México y Perú producen mucha…* (plata)
  4. *… es uno de los principales productores de estaño.* (Bolivia)
  5. *… es el tercer país exportador mundial de café.* (Colombia)
  6. *La carne de … es un producto importante de Argentina, Paraguay y Uruguay.* (vacuno)
  7. *Muchas piedras preciosas proceden de…* (Colombia)

EXPANDING LEARNERS

- Ask some students to look into the origin and history of one of the products mentioned in this section, and ask others to investigate legends related to these products. There are legends from around the world surrounding the origins of some of these food products. Encourage students to use the Internet or the school library for their research. Ask them to write at least three paragraphs to describe the history of a product and to write a short narrative to describe one of the legends. Call on volunteers to read their work aloud.

Los países de clima templado

Los países del sur de Suramérica (Paraguay, Argentina, Uruguay y Chile) son en su mayor parte países de clima templado, con una importante actividad agrícola. Los productos más importantes de esta zona son los cereales y la soya.

La ganadería tiene también mucho peso en la economía de Paraguay, Argentina y Uruguay. Los tres países están entre los principales exportadores mundiales de carne de vacuno, y la carne es una parte importante de la dieta de sus habitantes.

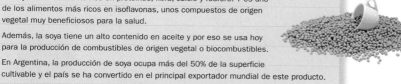

La soya

La soya es un alimento rico en proteínas, fibra, calcio y fósforo. Y es uno de los alimentos más ricos en isoflavonas, unos compuestos de origen vegetal muy beneficiosos para la salud.

Además, la soya tiene un alto contenido en aceite y por eso se usa hoy para la producción de combustibles de origen vegetal o biocombustibles.

En Argentina, la producción de soya ocupa más del 50% de la superficie cultivable y el país se ha convertido en el principal exportador mundial de este producto.

Explotación petrolífera.

Los países extractores

Latinoamérica es rica en recursos naturales. Y en muchos países, la extracción y exportación de esos recursos se ha convertido en una importante fuente de riqueza.

Chile es el principal productor de cobre del mundo. Ecuador, México, Venezuela y Argentina tienen importantes yacimientos de petróleo. Bolivia exporta gas natural y es uno de los grandes productores mundiales de estaño. México y Perú son los dos principales productores de plata del mundo. Colombia extrae piedras preciosas...

84 **Países productores**

▶ **Investiga.** ¿Has pensado alguna vez de dónde proceden los productos que consumes o utilizas diariamente? Haz un pequeño estudio y responde.

1. ¿Qué clases de frutas sueles encontrar en el supermercado? ¿De qué países proceden?
2. ¿En qué países se fabrica la ropa que usas? Mira las etiquetas de las prendas que utilizas para conocer esa información.

▶ **Intercambia** tu información con tus compañeros(as). ¿Qué países de Latinoamérica exportan alimentos y textiles a los Estados Unidos?

85 **Maquilas en la frontera**

▶ **Investiga** sobre las maquilas y presenta tus conclusiones. Da respuesta a estas cuestiones:

– ¿Qué son las maquilas? ¿En qué zonas se establecen?
– ¿Qué actividades se desarrollan en ellas? ¿Cómo funcionan?
– ¿Qué ventajas y qué inconvenientes económicos y sociales tienen?

HERITAGE LANGUAGE LEARNERS

• Ask students to research the major products and services from their family's country of origin and prepare a short oral report for the class. Have students indicate how these products impact the country's economy, how much is exported, and to where. You might also ask students to indicate the country's major imports and its principal trading partners. Encourage students to accompany their presentation with visuals and to welcome questions from the rest of the class.

MULTIPLE INTELLIGENCES:
Naturalistic Intelligence

• Have students work in groups and assign one of the geographical areas mentioned in the *Mapa cultural* to each one. Ask students to research the location, climate, landforms, and other natural phenomena in their assigned area. Based on this information, have students explain why this zone is ideal for the agricultural products and natural resources that flourish there. Have students prepare a short written or oral report and ask each group to present their findings to the class.

Unit 3

MAPA CULTURAL
La economía de Latinoamérica

Preparation

■ Invite students to share their Independent Starters. How many of the countries they mentioned are in Latin America? Some students might have mentioned Mexico, since Mexico is the third-largest supplier of goods to the United States. But many other Latin American countries also supply goods and natural resources to the American market. According to the Office of the United States Trade Representative, the following are the largest U.S. import categories from these Latin American countries: from Colombia → oil (crude), gold, coffee, cut flowers, bananas; from Chile → copper, edible fruits, wood, fish and seafood; from Guatemala → knit apparel, gold and silver, edible fruits, coffee; from the Dominican Republic → optical and medical instruments, precious stones, electrical machinery.

■ Have small groups read, analyze, and summarize the information provided in the *Mapa cultural*. To help students focus their summaries, you may want to suggest these or similar questions: What is this *Mapa cultural* about? What is the main idea? What important details illustrate and support the main idea? What would I tell my classmates about what I have just read?

Activities

84. You may want to divide the class into small groups and assign each group a different product to research. Other suggested products include electronic equipment, vehicles, fuel (e.g., oil), paper, footwear, coffee, and vegetables. Then, groups come together in a whole-class session and report their findings for their assigned product.

Answer Key

84. Answers will vary.
  ▶ Answers will vary.
85. Answers will vary.

Additional Resources

Fans Online activities
Practice Workbook

173

Unit 3
ESCRITURA
Tu currículum ideal

Presentation

- In this section, students will practice and extend their writing skills. They will apply the vocabulary and grammar they have learned in this unit to create an ideal curriculum vitae for a job they would like to have in the future.

Activities	Standards	Resources
Escritura	1.1, 1.2, 1.3, 2.1, 5.1, 5.2	

Teaching Suggestions

Warm-Up / Independent Starter

- Ask students to think about the process of applying for a job and to list the documents they would need to furnish and/or complete as part of the job application process.

Preparation

- Have students share their Independent Starters with the class. They might have mentioned *cartas de recomendación, referencias, formulario de solicitud,* and résumé. You may want to discuss each of these documents briefly. Students are probably familiar with résumés, but some of them may not know what a curriculum vitae (CV) is. The difference between these two documents can be partly explained by the meaning of each term. The word *résumé* is the past participle of the French verb *résumer*, which means "to summarize." The term *curriculum vitae* is Latin for "course of (one's) life." As the terms indicate, a CV is more comprehensive than a résumé. In America, a CV is usually requested for academic jobs, whereas a résumé is what most government institutions and private sector companies request. However, in most Spanish-speaking countries, a CV is generally expected. Explain that in some parts of Latin America, such as Colombia, Peru, Ecuador, and Venezuela, a CV is called *hoja de vida*.

- Ask for a volunteer to read *El currículum vítae* aloud. Explain that a CV is a biographical statement, listing and emphasizing the candidate's education, professional experience, achievements, and other information considered important for the position.

174

Tu currículum ideal

El currículum vítae

El currículum vítae u hoja de vida es un documento en el que se resumen los datos personales, la experiencia profesional y la formación académica de una persona.

El currículum es nuestra tarjeta de presentación a la hora de solicitar un trabajo. Por tanto, debe estar bien diseñado y perfectamente redactado, y debe presentar la información de una manera clara, concisa y ordenada en bloques: los datos personales, la formación, la experiencia profesional, los intereses...

En esta unidad vas a pensar en un trabajo que te gustaría tener en el futuro y vas a escribir el currículum perfecto para ese puesto.

Ten en cuenta que la limpieza, el orden y la claridad del escrito deben transmitir una imagen favorable de ti mismo(a).

Piensa

- ¿Qué profesión te gustaría tener? Te damos algunas ideas.

  - dependiente(a)
  - recepcionista
  - arquitecto(a)
  - ingeniero(a)
  - jardinero(a)
  - médico(a)
  - diseñador(a) de moda
  - monitor(a) de tiempo libre

- ¿Qué **formación académica** requiere esa profesión? Piensa en los estudios universitarios o en los cursos de formación relacionados con el trabajo que has elegido.

  Modelo

  Formación académica:
  Licenciado en Arquitectura

- ¿Qué **otros datos de interés** crees que podrías poner en tu currículum vítae? Selecciona aquella información que puede ser interesante para el puesto que has elegido. También puedes mencionar alguna característica personal favorable o hablar de aficiones relacionadas con el trabajo solicitado.

  Modelo

  Otros datos de interés:
  Informática: manejo a nivel usuario de programas de tratamiento de textos, bases de datos e Internet.
  Carné de conducir y vehículo propio.

Rubric for Evaluation

	Content	Organization	Conventions
1 point	Irrelevant or disjointed information. Missing key information. Limited or inaccurate word choices.	Layout could be improved. Style inconsistencies. Structure is not very effective. Unclear category selection.	Many errors in spelling, punctuation, grammar, and usage. Errors obscure meaning.
3 points	Mostly relevant and easy to understand information. Additional information may be needed. Some inaccurate word choices.	Attractive layout and mainly consistent style. Important information may not stand out. Appropriate choice of subject headers.	Some errors in spelling, punctuation, grammar, and usage. Errors don't interfere with meaning.

Expresiones útiles

Educación y formación:

Bachiller	*High School graduate*
Egresado(a) / Licenciado(a) en…	*Graduated in …*
Curso de…	*Course in …*

Capacidades y competencias personales:

Disponibilidad para…	*Availability to …*
Buenas dotes de…	*Good … skills*
Buen manejo de…	*Good command of …*

Escribe

■ Redacta el borrador de tu currículum. Utiliza las notas que escribiste antes y organiza la información en cuatro apartados:

– Datos personales.
– Formación académica.
– Experiencia profesional.
– Otros datos de interés.

■ No olvides que es fundamental cuidar el orden de la información y la claridad.

Revisa

■ Una vez finalizado tu borrador, revísalo.

– ¿La información es adecuada y está bien organizada?

– ¿El vocabulario es preciso y correcto?

– ¿La ortografía es correcta? ¿Tienes alguna duda ortográfica?

■ Pasa a limpio tu currículum e intercámbialo con tu compañero(a). Lee el suyo y analiza estas cuestiones:

– ¿Se diferencian claramente los distintos apartados? ¿La presentación es clara? ¿Facilita la lectura rápida de los datos?

– ¿La información es completa? ¿Es una información adecuada para el puesto que solicita?

– ¿Hay algún error gramatical o alguna falta de ortografía?

■ Devuelve el currículum a su autor(a) con tus sugerencias y revisa el tuyo teniendo en cuenta sus comentarios.

■ Pasa a limpio tu currículum con los errores corregidos.

Comparte

■ Presenta tu currículum a la clase. ¿Qué opinan tus compañeros(as)? ¿Eres un(a) buen(a) candidato(a) para ocupar el puesto que elegiste? ¿Reúnes los requisitos y las capacidades necesarias? ¿Por qué?

HOJA DE VIDA

Datos personales

Incluye:

– nombre y apellidos
– dirección completa
– teléfono y dirección de correo electrónico

Formación académica

Presenta la información ordenada cronológicamente. Indica la fecha y el lugar donde cursaste tus estudios.

Experiencia profesional

Incluye los trabajos realizados del más reciente al más antiguo. Especifica las fechas de inicio y fin, y el nombre de las empresas en las que desempeñaste cada puesto.

Otros datos de interés

Recoge toda la información interesante que pueda estar relacionada con el puesto.

---

5 points	Content	Organization	Conventions
	Relevant, complete, and easy to understand information. Precise and clear word choices.	Attractive layout and consistent style. Clear and purposeful structure. Excellent choice of subject headers.	Few, if any, errors in spelling, punctuation, grammar, and usage. Excellent command of the Spanish language.

ESCRITURA

Tu currículum ideal

Step-by-Step Instructions

Piensa

■ Explain that the following is information commonly included in a CV: educational background, career history, professional qualifications (e.g., certificates, accreditations), skills, awards, honors, publications, professional memberships, interests, and references. On average, a CV is two pages long. If time permits, allow students to look for CVs online to get ideas.

■ Clarify that students will be creating a CV for the type of job they would like to have in the future. Therefore, they will need to make up the information (e.g., educational background, professional experience, accreditations). Encourage students to decide on an ideal job and write a brief description of the position before they begin to plan their CVs.

Escribe

■ As students begin to write their CVs, remind them that they should target their skills, abilities, and strengths to match the position they are applying for. Students may want to do some research to better understand how they can tailor their CVs.

Revisa

■ Emphasize the importance of punctuation, spelling, good vocabulary choices, and correct grammar. In fact, according to some Human Resource Departments, poor spelling is one of the quickest ways of getting a rejection. Attention should also be placed on clarity. A prospective employer should be able to assess quickly if the applicant is a good match.

Comparte

■ Tell students to be prepared for constructive criticism from their classmates. Explain that they should try to view this activity as a useful rehearsal for real life (i.e., they can transfer some of the skills they learned and some of the feedback they received to a résumé or CV they create to apply for a real job).

Evaluation

■ Distribute copies of the rubric to students and discuss the evaluation criteria. Ask students to refer to the rubric as they prepare their writing and as they evaluate their classmates' CVs.

REPASO

Vocabulario

Presentation

- In this section, students will review all key vocabulary from the unit, organized by themes, to prepare for an assessment. Students will complete practice activities for each *Desafío*.

Activities	Standards	Resources
1.	1.2	
2.	1.2	
3.	1.2	

Teaching Suggestions

Warm-Up / Independent Starter

- Have students brainstorm as many key vocabulary words from the following categories as they can in three minutes: *La escuela*, *La economía*, and *Trabajo y profesiones*.

Preparation

- Ask student pairs to share their lists from the Independent Starter. Then, have pairs come up with three sentences for each vocabulary category. Encourage them to use as many target vocabulary words as possible in each sentence. For example: *Me esforcé mucho y aprobé el examen de ingreso, por lo que me concedieron una beca.* Call on volunteers to share some of their sentences with the class.

- Go over the *Repaso* presentation with the class, modeling pronunciation and intonation as necessary. Ask students to go through the vocabulary and make a list of cognates. How many did they find? Then have students look for false cognates. Did they find any? For instance, *suma* is not "sum" in this context, but "addition."

Activities

2. Once students have finished this activity, divide the class into small groups and ask each group to come up with their own list of eight golden rules of personal finance for students in their age group. Students may want to adapt some of the recommendations from this activity, search for tips on the Internet, or use their own experiences and those of people they know. Have groups create a poster with the selection they made, and ask each group to present their poster to the class.

REPASO Vocabulario

La escuela

la beca	scholarship	**Matemáticas**		**Lengua**	
el curso	course, year	la división	division	la oración	sentence
el examen…		la fracción	fraction	el párrafo	paragraph
de ingreso	entrance exam	la multiplicación	multiplication		
final	final exam	la resta	subtraction	mayúscula	uppercase
parcial	midterm exam	la suma	addition	minúscula	lowercase
el semestre	semester			punto	period
		más	plus	coma	comma
aprobar	to pass	menos	minus	punto y coma	semicolon
esforzarse	to make an effort	por	times	dos puntos	colon
matricularse	to register	entre	divided by		
repasar	to review	igual a	equals	**¡Atención!**	
reprobar	to fail	por ciento	percent	descansar	to rest
				restar	to subtract

La economía

el comercio	trade
la compañía	company
la mercancía	goods, merchandise
la multinacional	multinational company
el negocio	business
el presupuesto	budget
el producto	product
el recurso natural	natural resource
exportar	to export
fabricar	to make, to manufacture
importar	to import
llegar a un acuerdo	to come to an agreement
El banco	
abrir una cuenta	to open an account
ahorrar dinero	to save money
pedir una hipoteca	to apply for a mortgage
pedir un préstamo	to apply for a loan
los gastos	expenses
los ingresos	income
el saldo	bank balance
la tasa de interés	interest rate
¡Atención!	
ahorrar	to save
salvar	to rescue

Trabajo y profesiones

El trabajo	
el/la becario(a)	intern
(des)empleado(a)	(un)employed
el desempleo	unemployment
los días feriados	holiday
las horas extraordinarias	overtime
la plantilla	staff
el puesto de trabajo	position
los requisitos	requirements
el seguro de vida	life insurance
el seguro dental/médico	dental/health insurance
la carta de recomendación	letter of recommendation
los conocimientos	knowledge
la entrevista	interview
la formación académica	educational training
las habilidades	abilities
la oferta de trabajo	job offer
las referencias	references
la solicitud de empleo	job application
contratar	to hire
despedir	to fire
Profesiones	
el/la biólogo(a)	biologist
el/la fisioterapeuta	physical therapist
el/la geólogo(a)	geologist
el/la intérprete	interpreter
el/la químico(a)	chemist
¡Atención!	
el currículum vítae,	
la hoja de vida	résumé
el resumen	summary

Differentiated Instruction

DEVELOPING LEARNERS

- Ask students to complete the following sentences with the correct word(s):
  1. *Antes del examen final voy a … mis apuntes.* (repasar)
  2. *Si me dan una …, puedo estudiar en la universidad.* (beca)
  3. *En español las nacionalidades se escriben con…* (minúscula)
  4. *No discutas; intenta…* (llegar a un acuerdo)
  5. *El agua y los minerales son ejemplos de…* (recursos naturales)
  6. *Despidieron a Ana; ya no es parte de la … de la compañía.* (plantilla)

EXPANDING LEARNERS

- Ask students to explain the difference between the following pairs of words:
  1. *las habilidades / los requisitos*
  2. *el empleo / el desempleo*
  3. *importar / exportar*
  4. *el curso / el semestre*
  5. *la oración / el párrafo*
  6. *el biólogo / el químico*
  7. *aprobar / reprobar*
  8. *el recurso natural / el producto*
  9. *los ingresos / los gastos*
  10. *el puesto de trabajo / la solicitud de empleo*

DESAFÍO 1

1 **Estudios.** Elige la opción correcta.

1. Emily decidió _____ en un curso de Informática antes de ir a la universidad.
   a. examinarse   b. matricularse   c. esforzarse

2. He estudiado mucho, pero me preocupa no _____ el examen.
   a. reprobar   b. aprobar   c. repasar

3. 145 por 13… ¡Qué difícil! Las _____ no se me dan bien.
   a. divisiones   b. restas   c. multiplicaciones

4. Para poder matricularme en esa universidad, tengo que aprobar un _____.
   a. examen parcial   b. examen final   c. examen de ingreso

DESAFÍO 2

2 **Una buena economía.** Completa el texto con las palabras del cuadro.

ahorrar dinero	ingresos	gastos	pedir un préstamo
abrir una cuenta	gasto	presupuesto	tasa de interés

Consejos para una buena economía personal y familiar

La regla de oro para tener una buena economía es que el __1__ que realizas no supere tus __2__. Hacer un buen __3__ puede ayudarte a llegar sin problemas a fin de mes. Además, los expertos recuerdan la importancia de __4__; empieza por eliminar los __5__ innecesarios. Si piensas __6__, fíjate bien en las condiciones: no debes pagar una __7__ demasiado alta.

Es importante educar financieramente a los niños y a los jóvenes. __8__ bancaria a tus hijos puede ser una forma de enseñarlos a ahorrar.

DESAFÍO 3

3 **Busco trabajo.** Une las dos columnas y escribe oraciones completas.

Modelo 1. *Encontré una buena oferta de trabajo en un portal de empleo.*

A
1. oferta de trabajo
2. solicitud de empleo
3. formación académica
4. requisitos
5. habilidades
6. referencias

B
a. Licenciatura en Química
b. portal de empleo
c. carta de recomendación
d. currículum vítae
e. estudios de Música y un año de experiencia
f. resolver problemas y trabajar en equipo

3. To extend this activity, ask pairs of students to make a word web that associates at least four professions with the education and training that are needed to carry them out, the abilities, skills and knowledge required for a job in those fields, and the characteristics and benefits of a position in those areas. For example: *químico(a) → Licenciatura en Química; entender y transmitir información científica, usar metodología científica para resolver problemas, conocimientos avanzados de matemáticas; seguro médico y dental...* Then have students use the words in the web to describe each profession in detail.

Answer Key

1. 1. b   2. b   3. c   4. c

2. 1. gasto
   2. ingresos
   3. presupuesto
   4. ahorrar dinero
   5. gastos
   6. pedir un préstamo
   7. tasa de interés
   8. Abrir una cuenta

3. Answers will vary. Sample answers:
   2. (d) Con la solicitud de empleo se debe enviar un currículum vítae.
   3. (a) Mi formación académica consiste en una Licenciatura en Química.
   4. (e) Los requisitos mínimos son tener estudios de Música y un año de experiencia.
   5. (f) El puesto exige habilidades para resolver problemas y trabajar en equipo.
   6. (c) Necesito tres referencias o una carta de recomendación.

Additional Resources

Fans Online activities
Practice Workbook

HERITAGE LANGUAGE LEARNERS

- Ask students to compare and contrast labor practices here and in their heritage country. This might include how people search for a job, what they might include in their CV, and the interview process. Have students address some of the following: *¿Qué posibilidades hay de trabajar como becario? ¿En qué tipo de compañías suelen trabajar? ¿Dan las empresas mucho peso a las cartas de recomendación? ¿Cuáles suelen ser los beneficios más comunes? ¿Cómo son los horarios de trabajo? ¿Son iguales en el invierno y en verano? ¿Cuánto tiempo suelen dar de vacaciones?*

MULTIPLE INTELLIGENCES:
Mathematical-Logical Intelligence

- Have students imagine that they have finished their studies and are now working. Tell them what their monthly salary is, and have them come up with a workable *presupuesto*. Assign some students to continue living at home, others to share an apartment with a roommate, and others to live independently. They will need to list all their expenses, including any installment payments for items such as furniture or a car, plus student loans. Remind them to budget savings. Ask students to present their *presupuestos* in a graph or chart.

REPASO
Gramática

Presentation

- Students will review grammatical structures presented in the unit. Each grammar point is cross-referenced to the corresponding page on which it was introduced. The activities here provide systematic practice by *Desafío*.

Activities	Standards	Resources
4.	1.3, 3.1	
5.	1.3	
6.	1.2, 1.3	
7. Cultura	1.2, 1.3, 2.1, 2.2, 3.1	

Teaching Suggestions

Warm-Up / Independent Starter

- For each of the following sentences, have students come up with two separate sentences that convey a similar meaning. For example: *Ojalá que el examen final sea fácil. → Espero que el examen final sea fácil. Me gustaría que el examen final fuera fácil.*
  1. *Quisiera trabajar este verano.*
  2. *Deseamos que la economía mejore.*
  3. *A mis padres les gustaría que yo sacara mejores notas.*

Preparation

- Ask students to get together with a classmate and share and discuss their Independent Starters. How many variations of each sentence were they able to come up with? Ask pairs to share some of their sentences with the class. You may want to write some of their examples on the board to illustrate the different ways of expressing wishes studied in this unit. To check students' comprehension, have them come up with original sentences.
- Divide the class into five groups and assign each group one of these topics: *el participio pasado, el presente perfecto y el pluscuamperfecto, los pronombres relativos, el futuro perfecto,* and *expresar condición.* Ask groups to come up with four sentences to illustrate their grammar point. Have groups share their sentences with the class. If students need more reinforcement, write some of their examples on the board and explain the grammar point.

El participio pasado (pág. 138)

EL PARTICIPIO PASADO USADO COMO ADJETIVO
La puerta del salón está abierta.

EL PARTICIPIO PASADO USADO COMO VERBO
Habíamos estudiado antes de hacer el examen.
Las fechas de los exámenes serán publicadas en la página web.

EL PARTICIPIO PASADO USADO COMO NOMBRE
Los empleados trabajan de nueve a seis.

El presente perfecto y el pluscuamperfecto (pág. 140)

EL PRESENTE PERFECTO

presente del verbo haber + participio pasado

Hemos aprobado todos los exámenes.

EL PLUSCUAMPERFECTO

imperfecto del verbo haber + participio pasado

Cuando llegué a casa, tú ya te habías ido.

Los pronombres relativos (pág. 150)

LOS PRONOMBRES RELATIVOS

que: para personas y cosas.
Hay gobiernos que favorecen el comercio.

quien, quienes: para personas.
Ahí están las empresarias de quienes te hablé.

LOS RELATIVOS EL QUE, LA QUE...
Tengo unos amigos mexicanos con los que siempre hablo en español.

El futuro perfecto (pág. 152)

FUTURO PERFECTO. VERBOS REGULARES

COMPRAR	VENDER	CONSUMIR
habré comprado	habré vendido	habré consumido
habrás comprado	habrás vendido	habrás consumido
habrá comprado	habrá vendido	habrá consumido
habremos comprado	habremos vendido	habremos consumido
habréis comprado	habréis vendido	habréis consumido
habrán comprado	habrán vendido	habrán consumido

Expresar deseos (pág. 162)

ojalá (que) + presente de subjuntivo

Ojalá consigamos un buen trabajo.

desear esperar preferir querer	+ infinitivo/presente de subjuntivo

Espero recibir un sueldo justo.

EXPRESAR DESEOS HIPOTÉTICOS O CORTESES

condicional + infinitivo/imperfecto de subjuntivo

Desearíamos tener más días feriados.
Nos gustaría que todos tuvieran trabajo.

quisiera + infinitivo quisiera que + imperfecto de subjuntivo

Quisiera trabajar de arquitecta.
Quisiera que me dieran ese trabajo.

Expresar condición (pág. 164)

ORACIONES CONDICIONALES CON SI

Condicionales reales	Condicionales potenciales
si + presente indicativo + presente indicativo/futuro indicativo/imperativo	si + imperfecto subjuntivo + condicional
Si trabajo horas extra, gano más dinero.	Si tuviera trabajo, compraría un auto.

OTRAS EXPRESIONES DE CONDICIÓN

con tal de que en caso de que a no ser que a menos que salvo que	+ subjuntivo

Differentiated Instruction

DEVELOPING LEARNERS

- To give students more practice in expressing hopes and wishes, ask them to complete the following sentences:
  1. *Deseo que tú...*
  2. *Ojalá que la economía...*
  3. *Me gustaría que...*
  4. *Mis padres prefieren que yo...*
  5. *A los profesores les gustaría que...*
  6. *Mis amigos y yo esperamos que...*
  7. *¿Quieres que yo...?*
  8. *Quisiera que me...*
- Call on volunteers to read their completed sentences aloud.

EXPANDING LEARNERS

- Ask students to work with a partner and make predictions about this or another country's economic future. Explain that they will use the future perfect to complete this task. Suggest topics such as the changing job market and unemployment; tax hikes; cuts to social services; businesses that have gone bankrupt and new, emerging companies; changes in the country's imports and exports; new trade partners; and the role of sustainable and ethical companies. Have students prepare a list, chart, or graph with their forecasts. Display their work in the classroom.

DESAFÍO 1

4 **Tus experiencias.** ¿Qué cosas no habías hecho todavía en ese momento? ¿Qué cosas has hecho ya? Escribe cinco oraciones para cada grupo usando el pluscuamperfecto y el presente perfecto.

No lo había hecho todavía	Lo he hecho ya
Cuando tenía diez años, todavía no había viajado a ningún país hispano.	Ya he estado en México y en la República Dominicana.

 DESAFÍO 2

5 **En orden.** Ordena estos elementos y escribe las oraciones.

1. quiero comprar/me/El auto/muy caro./que/no es
2. gustaría/en/Esta es/la/la multinacional/que/me/trabajar.
3. trabajo/que/la/quinientos empleados./La compañía/para/tiene
4. su currículum/Quienes/la/podrán hacer/envíen/entrevista.

 DESAFÍO 3

6 **Deseos y condiciones.** Une las dos columnas para formar oraciones lógicas. Luego, elige cinco comienzos de la columna A y escribe tus propios finales.

Modelo 1. *Esperamos conseguir una beca para estudiar en los Estados Unidos.*

 A

1. Esperamos…
2. Si quisiera trabajar con ellos, …
3. Si terminara mis estudios este año, …
4. Mi padre quiere que…
5. A menos que tengas experiencia, …
6. Si trabajan horas extra, …

 B

a. trabajes en su empresa.
b. tener vacaciones en septiembre.
c. no conseguirás el trabajo.
d. les enviaría mi currículum.
e. encontraría trabajo enseguida.
f. ganarán más dinero.

 CULTURA

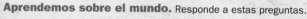

7 **Aprendemos sobre el mundo.** Responde a estas preguntas.

1. ¿Qué es la Ciudad de las Artes y de las Ciencias? ¿Dónde está?
2. ¿En qué países de Latinoamérica tienen el peso como moneda? Nombra tres.
3. ¿Qué dos océanos une el canal de Panamá?

ciento setenta y nueve **179**

Activities

4. After students have completed this activity, have them get together with a classmate and exchange the information. For example:
   A. *Cuando tenía diez años no había viajado a ningún país hispano, pero ya he visitado dos países hispanos. ¿Y tú?*
   B. *Yo sí había viajado a México a visitar a mis abuelos, y he vuelto varias veces.*

6. To extend this activity, have students choose one of their sentences and elaborate on it. For example: *Mi padre quiere que trabaje con él este verano en su oficina de contabilidad. Lo he pensado, pero prefiero trabajar en…*

Answer Key

4. Answers will vary.

5. 1. El auto que quiero comprar no es muy caro.
   2. Esta es la multinacional en la que me gustaría trabajar.
   3. La compañía para la que trabajo tiene quinientos empleados.
   4. Quienes envíen su currículum podrán hacer la entrevista.

6. 1. b   2. d   3. e   4. a   5. c   6. f
   Answers will vary. Sample answers:
   2. Si quisiera trabajar con ellos, solicitaría una entrevista.
   3. Si terminara mis estudios este año, buscaría trabajo en un país hispano.
   4. Mi padre quiere que estudie más.
   5. A menos que tengas experiencia, será difícil conseguir trabajo.
   6. Si trabajan horas extras, los ascienden.

7. Answers will vary. Sample answers:
   1. Es un conjunto de edificios destinados a la divulgación científica y cultural. Está en la ciudad de Valencia, España.
   2. En México, Colombia y Chile.
   3. El océano Pacífico y el Atlántico.

Additional Resources

Fans Online activities
Practice Workbook

HERITAGE LANGUAGE LEARNERS

- Customs and etiquette throughout the Spanish-speaking world can vary greatly. Explain to students that they are going to help their classmates have a successful stay abroad by writing a brochure that details the dos and don'ts of a "perfect" visitor's conduct, as well as insight into some lesser-known customs and practices. Students might work with a partner and brainstorm some advice, which can cover proper forms of address (*tú* vs. *usted*), table manners, accepting different meal times, and making proper introductions, complete with a handshake or kiss on the cheek.

CRITICAL THINKING

- Ask students to write an essay of at least two paragraphs that addresses one of the following questions:
  – *¿Cuáles son las ventajas de estudiar por lo menos un semestre en el extranjero?*
  – *¿Cuál será el mayor logro tuyo dentro de veinte años?*
  – *¿Cuáles serán los mayores logros en la economía de este país? ¿Y del mundo?*
  – *¿Habrá más cooperación entre países y gobiernos? Justifica tu respuesta.*
- Remind students to use the future perfect and the corresponding subjunctive when expressing wishes.

PROYECTO

La empresa hispana del año

Presentation

- In this section, students will apply the vocabulary, grammar, and cultural information they have learned in this unit to select a Hispanic-owned company that they would like to propose for a Best Hispanic Company award.

Activities	Standards	Resources
Paso 1	1.1, 1.2, 2.1, 2.2	
Paso 2	1.1, 1.2, 1.3, 2.1, 2.2, 3.1	
Paso 3	1.3, 2.1, 2.2	
Paso 4	1.1, 1.3, 2.1, 2.2	
Paso 5	1.1, 5.2	

Teaching Suggestions

Warm-Up / Independent Starter

- Ask students to list the top seven companies they patronize.

Preparation

- Have students share their Independent Starters with the class. What are some of the most popular companies students patronize? Ask students to share what they know about these companies (e.g., size, origin, CEO, sustainable practices, competitors). Then, as a class, discuss some of the characteristics that make these companies and the products or services they offer attractive.

- Call on a volunteer to read the introduction to the project aloud. Explain that the USHCC award recognizes Hispanic companies and entrepreneurs whose businesses have helped create employment and economic growth in innovative ways across the country. Then divide the class into small groups to work on the project.

Step-by-Step Instructions

Paso 1

- To help students narrow down the scope of their search, suggest that they classify the companies they listed in their Independent Starters by the type of product or service each company provides (e.g., *ropa y calzado, electrónica, ocio, salud, alimentación, comunicaciones*). Then, have groups select one of the categories and look for Hispanic-owned companies in that field.

PROYECTO

Un premio a

la empresa hispana del año

La *United States Hispanic Chamber of Commerce* (www.ushcc.com) premia todos los años a diez empresas, cinco propiedad de latinos y cinco propiedad de latinas, por su aportación a la comunidad empresarial hispana.

En este proyecto van a proponer ustedes a una empresa como candidata al premio a la mejor empresa hispana del año.

United States Hispanic Chamber of Commerce

USHCC

PASO 1 Selecciona una empresa

- Reúnete con tres o cuatro compañeros(as) y comenta. ¿Qué aspectos hacen que una empresa sea mejor que otras? ¿A qué tipo de empresa les gustaría premiar?
- Creen entre todos(as) una tabla que les permita evaluar las empresas.

BRIGHTSTAR

	Excelente	Normal	Mejorable
Productos y servicios que ofrece.			
Ganancias que obtiene.			
Innovación.			
Respeto al medio ambiente.			
Condiciones laborales.			
Beneficios sociales.			

GOYA

- Hagan un inventario de las empresas latinas que les interesen y reúnan información sobre ellas, especialmente sobre los aspectos de la tabla anterior. Pueden consultar la página de la USHCC (www.ushcc.org).
- Elijan entre todos(as) la empresa en la que quieran centrar el proyecto.

LibertyPower
Powerful Together

PASO 2 Busca información

- Haz una lista con la información que les interesa obtener sobre la empresa que han elegido y compártela con tus compañeros(as). Aquí tienes algunas ideas:
  - ¿Cuáles son sus productos estrella o qué servicios ofrece?
  - ¿En qué países y ciudades está representada?
  - ¿Quiénes son sus fundadores(as), propietarios(as), directivos(as)…?
  - ¿Cuántos(as) empleados(as) tiene?
  - ¿Cuántas mujeres hay en el equipo directivo?

ZARA

UNIVISION

Rubric for Evaluation

	Content	Organization	Presentation
1 point	Limited relevance. Information is incomplete or not based on research. Unconvincing defense of candidacy.	Inefficient use of time. Information is disorganized or unclear. Format is not appropriate or not used well.	Unclear communication. Delivery is not fluent. Many errors in vocabulary and grammar.
3 points	Mostly relevant and correct information, but some of it lacks significance. Mostly convincing defense of candidacy.	Time is used well. Information is mostly organized but lacks some clarity. Appropriate format.	Clear communication and fluent delivery. Mostly correct vocabulary and grammar.

- Investiguen para obtener información sobre la empresa elegida. Pueden visitar su página web.
- Busquen imágenes que sirvan para ilustrar su presentación.

PASO 3 Prepara tu presentación

- Elijan un formato adecuado para su presentación: un póster, una presentación de PowerPoint, un folleto… Tengan en cuenta que la presentación debe ser atractiva porque el objetivo es que sus compañeros(as) le den el premio a su empresa.
- Organicen toda la información recopilada de acuerdo con el formato que eligieron y escriban un borrador de su presentación. No olviden explicar por qué creen que su empresa se merece el premio.
- Revisen el borrador, corríjanlo y escriban los textos definitivos.

PASO 4 Presenta tu empresa

- Presenten su empresa a la clase y contesten a las preguntas que les hagan sus compañeros(as).

PASO 5 Concedan el premio

- Decidan entre todos(as) en qué consiste el premio y voten para elegir la mejor empresa hispana del año.

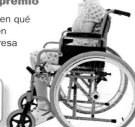

Y el premio a la mejor empresa hispana del año es para...

Unidad 3

Autoevaluación

¿Qué has aprendido en esta unidad?

Haz estas actividades para comprobar tu progreso.

Evalúa tus habilidades. Para cada punto, di Muy bien, Bien o Necesito practicar más.

a. ¿Puedes hablar de acciones pasadas?

▶ Describe lo que hiciste el viernes pasado cuando saliste de la escuela. ¿Qué habías hecho en cada clase?

b. ¿Puedes relacionar dos acciones futuras?

▶ Haz una lista de cosas que benefician a una persona o a una empresa desde el punto de vista económico.

▶ Di lo que habrás hecho para ahorrar dinero cuando llegues a la edad de jubilación.

c. ¿Puedes expresar deseos?

▶ Describe cómo quieres que sea tu futuro profesional. ¿Qué tipo de condiciones de trabajo esperas tener?

▶ Explica cómo será tu vida si encuentras un trabajo con esas condiciones. ¿Y qué pasaría si no consiguieras esas condiciones?

ciento ochenta y uno 181

PROYECTO

La empresa hispana del año

Paso 2

- Students should be able to find most of the information they need about their company on its webpage. However, encourage them to cross-reference some of the information using other sources. In this way, they will get a more balanced view of the company.

Paso 3

- Emphasize that they should not overwhelm their audience with facts and information about their company, but rather summarize what it does and highlight those aspects that make the company a good candidate for an award.

Paso 4

- Remind groups that their aim is to get their classmates to vote for their company, so their presentation should be upbeat and enticing.

Paso 5

- Hold a class discussion to decide on an award before groups begin their presentations. Encourage students to think of culturally significant symbols that may be used as part of the award.

Evaluation

- Distribute copies of the rubric to students. Discuss the evaluation criteria and explain how this project will be graded. Encourage students to refer to the rubric as they prepare their projects.

Content

- Ask groups to consider these questions: Is the information about our company relevant, interesting, accurate, and balanced? Does our presentation project an attractive image of the company? Do we have a solid and convincing argument for selecting our company for the award?

Organization

- Emphasize that the audience needs to know where the presentation is going. Ideas should flow in a logical way and the audience should be able to follow the presentation effortlessly. Stress the importance of creating an outline that organizes the talk.

Presentation

- Encourage students to speak clearly and to pause at the end of each point to give their audience time to process the information. Once they have finished, ask students to thank their audience and invite questions.

	Content	Organization	Presentation
5 points	Relevant, interesting, and well-researched information. Very convincing defense of candidacy.	Time is used wisely. Information is clearly organized, visually and logically. Excellent choice and use of format.	Clear and fluent communication. Very motivating, upbeat delivery. Correct and complete vocabulary and grammar.

HACIA EL AP* EXAM

Interpersonal Writing: E-mail Reply

Presentation

- These pages present students with a sample activity from the "Interpersonal Writing: E-mail Reply" portion of the AP* Spanish Language and Culture Exam. Students will read an e-mail and answer it in writing.

Activities	Standards	Resources
Interpersonal Writing: E-mail Reply	1.2, 2.1, 2.2, 3.2	

Preparing for the Exam

About This Section

- The "Interpersonal Writing: E-mail Reply" section of the AP* Exam requires students to read an e-mail about a real-life scenario and write an e-mail in which they reply and request additional information about the points contained in the original message. Students have 15 minutes to read and respond to the e-mail. This section accounts for 12.5% of the student's total score.

- While e-mails in general have a tendency to be less formal in structure than traditional letters, students will need to use the appropriate register in their response and include these elements: headers, a greeting, the body of the e-mail, and an appropriate closing. They will also need to use their response to show thorough comprehension of the original message as well as request further information. While students do not need to be superfluously wordy, they do need to take full advantage of the writing sample to show their mastery at interpersonal writing and communicative skills.

Strategies: Interpersonal Writing

- Students may associate writing e-mails with being informal and to-the-point, rarely dedicating the time necessary to include the appropriate parts of the correspondence (as outlined in the *Estrategias* box on page 182). Therefore, they may need as much practice with these communicative skills in English as in Spanish.

Hacia el AP* Exam

Interpersonal Writing: E-mail Reply

Presentación

Una de las pruebas del examen AP* está relacionada con la escritura interpersonal. Tendrás aproximadamente 15 minutos para leer un mensaje electrónico y escribir tu respuesta.

Estrategias

- Lee el mensaje atentamente y toma nota de la información que te piden.
- Para responder, utiliza el tratamiento adecuado (en los mensajes formales, la forma *usted*) y mantén un tono cortés.
- Organiza la información que quieres transmitir respetando las distintas partes que estructuran el mensaje electrónico:

  Encabezado. Incluye la dirección electrónica de la persona a la que va dirigido el mensaje y el tema o asunto del mensaje.

  Saludo. Emplea un saludo adecuado a la persona a la que te diriges.
  Querido(a) / Estimado(a):   Muy señor(a) mío(a):

  Cuerpo del mensaje. Responde a las preguntas o a los comentarios que te hacen. En el ejercicio que te proponemos, puedes comenzar con un párrafo agradeciendo la concesión de la beca. No olvides incluir los datos personales que consideres necesarios, tus preferencias para las actividades extracurriculares y sugerir en qué servicios de la universidad puedes colaborar.
  Le escribo este mensaje porque…
  Me alegra saber que…
  Aprovecho para…

  Despedida y firma. Para despedirte, utiliza el mismo tono que en el resto del escrito (generalmente un tono formal) y firma con tu nombre completo.
  Un cordial saludo.
  Atentamente.

Instrucciones para el examen

Directions: You will write a reply to an e-mail message. You have 15 minutes to read the message and write your reply.

Your reply should have a greeting and a closing and should respond to all questions and requests for information in the message. In your reply, you should also ask for more details about some aspects of the message. Also, you should use the appropriate register (formal or informal) given the context of the message.

Instrucciones: Vas a escribir una respuesta a un mensaje electrónico. Tendrás 15 minutos para leer el mensaje y escribir tu respuesta.

Tu respuesta debe incluir un saludo y una despedida, y debe responder a todas las preguntas y peticiones del mensaje original. En tu respuesta también debes pedir más detalles sobre algún aspecto del mensaje. Además, debes utilizar el registro apropiado (formal o informal) de acuerdo al contexto del mensaje.

Language Expansion

VOCABULARY

- Students may have difficulty with the following false cognates from the e-mail:

actual	→	del presente
concedida	→	otorgada, dada
realizar	→	hacer, efectuar

- Students may wish to use vocabulary and expressions like the following in their answers:

He recibido…	la documentación
En primer lugar...	el ocio
En contestación...	la colaboración
Me encantaría...	académico
No dude en...	aportar
A la espera de...	participar

GRAMMAR STRUCTURES:
Making Value Statements and Expressing Emotion

- The situation presented in the e-mail lends itself well to the use of value statements and expressions of emotion in the student's response. Students should be able to use expressions like *Es importante* (*que*) and *Prefiero* (*que*) in expressing their reaction to winning and responding to the inquiries about their preferences. They should therefore also employ the subjunctive, infinitive, and indicative appropriately. They may wish to use the *Resumen de gramática* at the back of the book to review these concepts.

Introducción

Este mensaje electrónico es del profesor Javier Gutiérrez, organizador del programa de becas «Me gusta el español». Has recibido este mensaje porque has sido ganador de una beca para estudiar español en Salamanca (España) durante el verano.

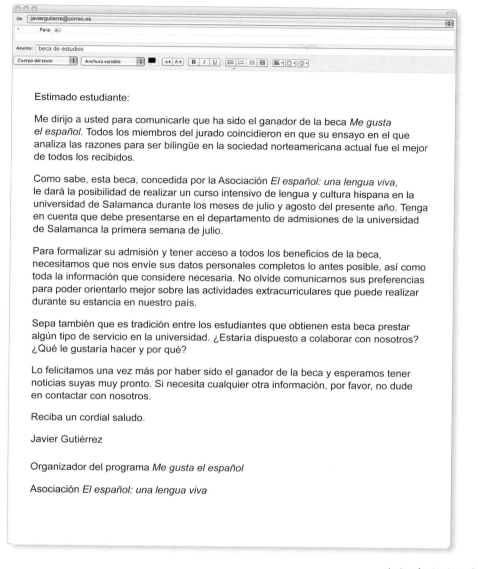

De: javiergutierre@correo.es

Para: ▲

Asunto: beca de estudios

Cuerpo del texto | Anchura variable | A+ A+ | **B** *I* U

Estimado estudiante:

Me dirijo a usted para comunicarle que ha sido el ganador de la beca *Me gusta el español*. Todos los miembros del jurado coincidieron en que su ensayo en el que analiza las razones para ser bilingüe en la sociedad norteamericana actual fue el mejor de todos los recibidos.

Como sabe, esta beca, concedida por la Asociación *El español: una lengua viva*, le dará la posibilidad de realizar un curso intensivo de lengua y cultura hispana en la universidad de Salamanca durante los meses de julio y agosto del presente año. Tenga en cuenta que debe presentarse en el departamento de admisiones de la universidad de Salamanca la primera semana de julio.

Para formalizar su admisión y tener acceso a todos los beneficios de la beca, necesitamos que nos envíe sus datos personales completos lo antes posible, así como toda la información que considere necesaria. No olvide comunicarnos sus preferencias para poder orientarlo mejor sobre las actividades extracurriculares que puede realizar durante su estancia en nuestro país.

Sepa también que es tradición entre los estudiantes que obtienen esta beca prestar algún tipo de servicio en la universidad. ¿Estaría dispuesto a colaborar con nosotros? ¿Qué le gustaría hacer y por qué?

Lo felicitamos una vez más por haber sido el ganador de la beca y esperamos tener noticias suyas muy pronto. Si necesita cualquier otra información, por favor, no dude en contactar con nosotros.

Reciba un cordial saludo.

Javier Gutiérrez

Organizador del programa *Me gusta el español*

Asociación *El español: una lengua viva*

ciento ochenta y tres 183

- You may wish to have students practice responding to letters and e-mails from their everyday lives using the appropriate language skills in English so that they can fully comprehend what is being asked of them, before having them practice in Spanish. The ability to use the formal register appropriately is difficult for many students to practice in real-world contexts, because they are often only in contact with other students their age. Have students practice writing to you, other teachers who may speak Spanish, and other Spanish-speaking adults in their community or country, all of whom should be addressed using formal language. They do not necessarily even have to send the e-mails; the emphasis should be on using the formal register (e.g., the *usted* form, formal expressions, fully appropriate verb forms) to express their thoughts.

Rubric for Evaluation

On the AP* Exam, each section is given a score between 0 (Unacceptable) and 5 (Strong). In order to earn a score of 5, the student's e-mail response should show:

– Content: All requested information is provided, and the student requests additional information. The student elaborates on the information provided frequently and with ease.
– Message: Student's response is fully understandable, with ease of expression and only occasional errors. The response is fully appropriate to the context given.
– Register: The register is appropriate for the situation and culture presented.
– Language: Vocabulary is varied and precise. Grammatical structures are used correctly. Few errors do not impede communication. Simple, compound, and complex sentences are used appropriately.

Additional Resources

Español Santillana AP* Preparation Workbook

183

More Practice

FINDING ADDITIONAL SOURCES

- Students may have difficulty coming across formally written e-mails in Spanish, directed toward them specifically, but they can practice responding to other sources. They can write e-mail responses to news articles from online sources or letters to the editor from Spanish-language newspapers and magazines. You may even find letters written in Spanish available from governmental organizations or NGOs. Students can respond from the point of view of the addressee, discussing the points outlined in the original text and asking for more information about any points that are unclear.

OTHER POSSIBLE TOPICS

- You may wish to have students write the initial e-mails about a variety of topics, then exchange their e-mails with a classmate to respond. Some possible topics include:
– An acceptance letter from a university.
– A letter of congratulations for a science project.
– An acceptance letter for a job application.
– A letter from a distant family member overseas.
– A letter from an elected official about an internship.
– A letter from an exchange student coming to the United States.

Unit 4 Nos divertimos

Objectives

- To express probability.
- To talk about leisure activities and entertainment.
- To express frequency.
- To learn the uses of the future and the conditional tenses to express conjecture or probability.
- To use the present perfect subjunctive in dependent clauses.

- To learn the use of indicative and subjunctive moods in the sequence of verbal tenses.
- To describe different means of traveling.
- To talk about different types of travel accommodations.
- To talk about the weather.
- To express cause.
- To express consequence.

- To identify main ideas and significant details in a variety of texts.
- To write a wide variety of texts, including a travel story.
- To know and apply the different stages of the writing process: planning, writing, revising, and sharing.
- To explore tourist attractions in Latin America.

Contents

Vocabulary

- Useful expressions to talk about free time, to tell how something went, and to talk about an entertainment performance.
- Review of known vocabulary about leisure time and entertainment events, trips, and cars.
- Leisure time and entertainment performances. Sports and free time. Board games.
- Trips. In the car. Trains and planes.
- Travel accommodations. Camping. Weather.

Grammar

- To express frequency.
- To express probability (I). Expressions with the indicative or the subjunctive, and *deber de* + infinitive.
- To express probability (II). The future and the conditional tenses.
- The present perfect subjunctive.
- To express cause.
- To express consequence.

Culture

- Cuban traditional *trova* music and the *nueva trova*, or New Cuban Song.
- Traditional games and toys among Spanish-speaking populations.
- Extreme sports in Nicaragua.
- The Ecuadorian Trans-Andean Railway and the Nariz del Diablo train.
- *El AVE (España).*
- *La Red Española de Albergues Juveniles.*
- *La Organización Mundial del Turismo.*
- Lake Titicaca.
- The Colombian writer Gabriel García Márquez.
- Tourist attractions in Latin America.

Evaluation Criteria

- Express probability or conjecture about present, past, and future actions.
- Talk about entertainment performances, sports, games, and leisure time.
- Express how often something is done.
- Talk about traveling by car, train, or plane.
- Learn the formation and use of the conditional perfect tense.
- Use the present perfect subjunctive.

- Use the indicative and subjunctive moods in the sequence of verb tenses.
- Describe and evaluate different types of travel accommodations.
- Talk about the weather.
- Give reasons for and express the cause of a situation.
- Express or emphasize the consequences of an event.

- Learn about tourist destinations and attractions in Latin American countries.
- Plan a trip.
- Write a travel story.
- Read different types of texts and identify main ideas and significant details in them.
- Write guided texts giving information, describing, or narrating.

Unit Plan

Las tareas/Antes de empezar

Estimated time: 2 sessions.

Text: ¡A divertirse!

Functions & forms:
- Useful expressions to talk about free time, to tell how something went, and to talk about an entertainment performance.
- Review of known vocabulary about leisure time and entertainment events, trips, and cars.

⚑ DESAFÍO 1

Estimated time: 6 sessions.

Text: Una trova auténtica.

Functions & forms:
- To express probability (I).
- Leisure time and entertainment performances. Sports and free time. Board games.
- To express frequency.
- To express probability (I). Expressions with the indicative or the subjunctive.

Culture:
- La trova y la nueva trova.
- Los juegos tradicionales.
- Deportes extremos (Nicaragua).

Reading: Una canción preciosa.

⚑ DESAFÍO 2

Estimated time: 6 sessions.

Text: Una maqueta misteriosa.

Functions & forms:
- To express probability (II).
- Trips. In the car. Trains and planes.
- To express probability (II). The future and the conditional tenses.
- The present perfect subjunctive.

Culture:
- El ferrocarril más difícil del mundo.
- El AVE (España).
- El condicional de rumor.

Reading: Como la vida misma.

⚑ DESAFÍO 3

Estimated time: 6 sessions.

Text: Un concurso para viajeros.

Functions & forms:
- To express cause and consequence.
- Travel accommodations. Camping. Weather.
- To express cause.
- To express consequence.

Culture:
- La Red Española de Albergues Juveniles (REAJ).
- La Organización Mundial del Turismo (OMT).
- El Titicaca: el lago místico de los incas.

Reading: Vivir para contarla.

Para terminar

Estimated time: 2 sessions.

Todo junto: Review of Desafíos 1–3.

Tu desafío:
- Desafío A: Find information and prepare a presentation about a Latin music genre.
- Desafío B: Find information and prepare a brochure about a famous amusement park in Latin America.
- Desafío C: Prepare a plan for travel and accommodations in a Spanish-speaking country and present it to the class.

MAPA CULTURAL

Estimated time: 1 session.

Mapa cultural: El turismo en Latinoamérica.

ESCRITURA

Estimated time: 1 session.

Writing: Un blog de viajes.

PROYECTO/EVALUACIÓN

Estimated time: 2 sessions.

Project: Un anuncio para promocionar un país.

Self-evaluation: Autoevaluación.

HACIA EL AP* EXAM

Estimated time: 2 sessions.

Test: Interpersonal Speaking: Conversation.

Standards for Learning Spanish

COMMUNICATION

1.1. Interpersonal mode
- Exchange personal ideas, opinions, and experiences.
- Engage in oral conversations using personal knowledge and experience.
- Ask and answer questions on different topics orally and in writing.
- Compare or share information with a partner.
- Invent or summarize a story.
- Write a joke with a partner.
- Write a tourism ad.

1.2. Interpretive mode
- Demonstrate understanding of oral and written idiomatic expressions.
- Demonstrate understanding of questions relating to familiar and less familiar topics.
- Understand and obtain information from audio or video recordings.
- Understand new vocabulary presented in Spanish.
- Understand written exchanges.
- Identify main ideas and significant details in a variety of texts.
- Extract information from an informative text.
- Draw conclusions and make judgments from oral and written texts.
- Interpret texts on topics of other cultures and relate them to personal knowledge and experience.
- Understand an e-mail or an online forum.
- Extract information from an image.

1.3. Presentational mode
- Produce and present an original creation orally.
- Dramatize a dialogue.
- Write a descriptive or an explanatory text about own experiences or the result of a research activity.
- Summarize information.
- Write song lyrics.
- Write a text to express probability or conjecture.
- Write opinions on different topics.
- Write sentences or a text to express cause.
- Write a travel story.
- Draw or use photographs to illustrate information.

CULTURE

2.1. Practices and perspectives
- Read about extreme sports people in Hispanic countries do in their leisure time.
- Learn about transportation practices and travel accommodations among Hispanic populations.
- Discuss the importance and effect of tourism on Hispanic countries.

2.2. Products and perspectives
- Learn about new and traditional Latin music.
- Read about traditional games and toys in Hispanic cultures.
- Learn about tourist sites and attractions in Hispanic countries.
- Research a renowned Colombian writer.

CONNECTIONS

3.1. Interdisciplinary connections
- Understand the similarities and differences between some aspects of grammar in English and in Spanish.
- Learn about traditional Cuban *trova* music and the *nueva trova*, and about other Latin music.
- Learn about the Colombian writer Gabriel García Márquez.
- Use the writing process to produce a travel story.
- Learn about tourism and tourist attractions in Hispanic countries.

3.2. Viewpoints through language / culture
- Read dialogues, informative texts, and literary texts in Spanish that provide insight into Hispanic culture.
- Learn about Latin music as a cultural manifestation and a form of societal expression.

COMPARISONS

4.1. Compare languages
- Compare the position of frequency-adverbs in English and in Spanish.
- Compare how to express probability and conjecture in English and in Spanish.
- Compare the sequence of verb tenses in English and in Spanish.
- Compare linguistic resources in journalistic language to refer to a rumor in English and in Spanish.
- Compare how to express cause in English and in Spanish.

4.2. Compare cultures
- Compare traditional games and toys in the United States and in Spanish-speaking countries.
- Compare feats of engineering in the United States and in Hispanic countries.
- Compare accommodations in youth hostels in the United States and in Spain.

COMMUNITIES

5.1. Spanish within and beyond the school setting
- Reflect on the relationship between music and social reality.
- Promote a positive attitude toward other cultures.
- Plan a trip.
- Research and obtain information on the Internet.

5.2. Spanish for lifelong learning
- Learn the writing process.
- Use technology to learn.
- Discuss ways in which Spanish can be used in future life experiences.

Communicative Skills

Interpersonal Mode

		Activities
Speaking	• Exchange ideas, opinions, or experiences with classmates.	• 22, 25, 26, 28, 30, 34, 45, 49, 51, 52, 54, 57, 69, 74, 76, *Proyecto*
	• Ask and answer questions or talk about cause or consequence with a partner.	• 12, 18, 68, 74, *Escritura*
	• Make conjectures or express probability with a partner.	• 22, 27, 38, 49, 78
	• Invent a story or compare information with a classmate.	• 33, 54
Writing	• Write questions and answers or a joke with a partner.	• 6, 12, 58, 69, *Escritura*
	• Write an ad to promote tourism.	• *Proyecto*
Listening	• Understand and obtain information from oral exchanges.	• 12, 18, 22, 25, 26, 27, 28, 30, 33, 34, 38, 45, 49, 51, 52, 54, 57, 69, 74, 76, *Proyecto*
Reading	• Understand a classmate's questions or a travel story.	• 6, 9, 58, *Escritura*

Interpretive Mode

		Activities
Listening	• Obtain information from conversations.	• 9, 17, 21, 34, 38, 57, 63, 75, 77
	• Understand descriptive or informative audios.	• 13
Reading	• Demonstrate comprehension of written exchanges and longer written dialogues.	• 1, 8, 23, 28, 52, 53
	• Infer meanings based on a text or demonstrate comprehension of an e-mail.	• 2, 22, 26, 32, 46, 47, 71
	• Reflect on cultural topics in relation to personal knowledge and experience.	• 10, 14, 19, 31, 35, 55, 64
	• Obtain information and draw conclusions from an informative text.	• 30, 46, 47, 50, 62
	• Research using outside sources.	• 59, 72, 79, *Proyecto*
	• Demonstrate comprehension of a literary story or literary quotations.	• 70, 71, 74
Viewing	• Obtain information from an image.	• 5, 33, 51, 68, *Proyecto*

Presentational Mode

		Activities
Speaking	• Present information or an original creation to the class.	• 18, 50, 72, 79, 80, *Proyecto*
	• Act out a dialogue or sing a song to the class.	• 25, 57
Writing	• Write sentences or a text summarizing information.	• 17, 26, 54, 63, 78, 79
	• Write a descriptive or an explanatory text.	• 24, 48, 58, 77, 79
	• Write song lyrics, a story, or a dialogue.	• 25, 33, 51
	• Write sentences or a text expressing probability, conjecture, or opinion.	• 27, 39, 44, 50
	• Write sentences or a text expressing cause or consequence.	• 67, 73, 74
	• Write a biography or a relevant anecdote of someone's life.	• 72
	• Write a travel story, a blog entry, or a script about travel experiences.	• 58, 76, *Escritura*
Visually Representing	• Draw a CD cover or illustrate a story.	• 9, 33
	• Use photographs to illustrate information.	• 72, *Proyecto*

Cross-Curricular Standards

Subject	Standard	**Activities**
Language Arts	• Compare elements of Spanish grammar with English equivalents.	• 5, 15, 20, 36, 40, 41, 60
	• Use the writing process to write a travel story.	• *Escritura*
	• Learn about the Colombian writer Gabriel García Márquez.	• *Lectura D3*, 72
Social Studies	• Learn about tourism and tourist attractions in Hispanic countries.	• 30, 31, 64, *Mapa cultural*, *Proyecto*
Music	• Learn about different Latin music.	• 9, 10, *Lectura D1*, 23, 26, 79

Unit 4 Nos divertimos

Lesson Plans (50-Minute Classes)

Day	Objectives	Sessions	Activities	Time	Standards	Resources / Homework
1	To introduce leisure time and trips, and the characters' challenges	**Nos divertimos / Las tareas** (184–187) • Warm-Up: Topic orientation • Presentation: ¡A divertirse!	1–2	15 m. 35 m.	1.2, 1.3, 2.1, 2.2, 5.1	Practice Workbook
2	To learn useful expressions related to the unit topic and to review learned vocabulary	**Antes de empezar** (188–189) • Warm-Up: Independent Starter • *Expresiones útiles* • *Recuerda*	3–4 5–6	10 m. 15 m. 25 m.	1.1, 1.2, 1.3, 2.1, 5.1	Practice Workbook
3	To express probability	**Desafío 1 – Una trova auténtica** (190–191) • Warm-Up: Independent Starter • *Texto: Una trova auténtica* • *Cultura: La trova y la nueva trova*	7–9 10	5 m. 35 m. 10 m.	1.1, 1.2, 1.3, 2.1, 2.2, 3.1, 3.2, 5.1, 5.2	Audio
4	To identify entertainment performances, sports, and other leisure activities	**Desafío 1 – Vocabulario** (192–193) • Warm-Up: Independent Starter • *Vocabulario: Ocio y espectáculos* • *Cultura: Los juegos tradicionales*	11–13 14	5 m. 35 m. 10 m.	1.1, 1.2, 1.3, 2.1, 2.2, 3.2, 4.2, 5.1, 5.2	Audio Practice Workbook
5	To express frequency	**Desafío 1 – Gramática** (194–195) • Warm-Up: Independent Starter • *Gramática: Expresar frecuencia* • *Cultura: Deportes extremos (Nicaragua)*	15–18 19	5 m. 35 m. 10 m.	1.1, 1.2, 1.3, 2.1, 2.2, 3.1, 3.2, 4.1, 5.1, 5.2	Audio Practice Workbook
6	To express probability	**Desafío 1 – Gramática** (196–197) • Warm-Up: Independent Starter • *Gramática: Expresar probabilidad (I)*	20–22	5 m. 45 m.	1.1, 1.2, 1.3, 2.1, 2.2, 3.1, 4.1	Audio Practice Workbook
7	To understand a written dialogue	**Desafío 1 – Lectura** (198–199) • Warm-Up: Independent Starter • *Lectura: Una canción preciosa*	23–25	5 m. 45 m.	1.1, 1.2, 1.3, 2.1, 2.2, 3.1, 3.2, 5.2	
8	To integrate vocabulary and grammar, and to assess student proficiency	**Desafío 1 – Comunicación / Evaluación** (200–201) • Warm-Up: Independent Starter • *Comunicación*: Review • *Final del desafío* • Quiz on *Desafío 1*	26–27 28	5 m. 25 m. 10 m. 10 m.	1.1, 1.2, 1.3, 2.1, 2.2, 3.1, 3.2, 5.1, 5.2	Practice Workbook
9	To express probability	**Desafío 2 – Una maqueta misteriosa** (202–203) • Warm-Up: Independent Starter • *Texto: Una maqueta misteriosa* • *Cultura: El ferrocarril más difícil del mundo*	29–30 31	5 m. 35 m. 10 m.	1.1, 1.2, 1.3, 2.1, 2.2, 3.1, 3.2, 4.2, 5.2	

Day	Objectives	Sessions	Activities	Time	Standards	Resources / Homework
10	To describe different modes of travel	**Desafío 2 – Vocabulario** (204–205) • Warm-Up: Independent Starter • *Vocabulario: Los viajes* • *Cultura: El AVE (España)*	32–34 35	5 m. 35 m. 10 m.	1.1, 1.2, 1.3, 2.1, 2.2, 4.2, 5.1, 5.2	Audio Practice Workbook
11	To express probability with the future and the conditional tenses	**Desafío 2 – Gramática** (206–207) • Warm-Up: Independent Starter • *Gramática: Expresar probabilidad (II). El futuro y el condicional* • *Conexiones: El condicional de rumor*	36–39 40	5 m. 35 m. 10 m.	1.1, 1.2, 1.3, 2.1, 3.1, 3.2, 4.1, 4.2	Audio Practice Workbook
12	To learn and use the present perfect subjunctive	**Desafío 2 – Gramática** (208–209) • Warm-Up: Independent Starter • *Gramática: El presente perfecto de subjuntivo*	41–45	5 m. 45 m.	1.1, 1.2, 1.3, 3.1, 4.1, 5.1	Audio Practice Workbook
13	To understand an informative article	**Desafío 2 – Lectura** (210–211) • Warm-Up: Independent Starter • *Lectura: Como la vida misma*	46–48	5 m. 45 m.	1.1, 1.2, 1.3, 2.1, 2.2, 3.1	
14	To integrate vocabulary and grammar, and to assess student proficiency	**Desafío 2 – Comunicación / Evaluación** (212–213) • Warm-Up: Independent Starter • *Comunicación: Review* • *Final del desafío* • Quiz on *Desafío 2*	49–50 51	5 m. 25 m. 10 m. 10 m.	1.1, 1.2, 1.3, 2.1, 2.2, 3.1, 3.2, 4.2, 5.1	Practice Workbook
15	To express cause and consequence	**Desafío 3 – Un concurso para viajeros** (214–215) • Warm-Up: Independent Starter • *Texto: Un concurso para viajeros* • *Comparaciones: La Red Española de Albergues Juveniles (REAJ)*	52–54 55	5 m. 35 m. 10 m.	1.1, 1.2, 1.3, 2.1, 2.2, 4.2, 5.2	
16	To talk about different types of accommodations and the weather	**Desafío 3 – Vocabulario** (216–217) • Warm-Up: Independent Starter • *Vocabulario: El alojamiento* • *Cultura: La Organización Mundial del Turismo (OMT)*	56–58 59	5 m. 35 m. 10 m.	1.1, 1.2, 1.3, 2.2, 5.1, 5.2	Audio Practice Workbook
17	To express cause	**Desafío 3 – Gramática** (218–219) • Warm-Up: Independent Starter • *Gramática: Expresar causa* • *Cultura: El Titicaca: el lago místico de los incas*	60–63 64	5 m. 35 m. 10 m.	1.1, 1.2, 1.3, 2.1, 2.2, 3.1, 3.2, 4.1	Audio Practice Workbook
18	To express consequence	**Desafío 3 – Gramática** (220–221) • Warm-Up: Independent Starter • *Gramática: Expresar consecuencia*	65–69	5 m. 45 m.	1.1, 1.2, 1.3, 2.1, 2.2, 3.1, 5.2	Practice Workbook

Day	Objectives	Sessions	Activities	Time	Standards	Resources / Homework
19	To understand a literary biography	**Desafío 3 – Lectura** (222–223) • Warm-Up: Independent Starter • *Lectura: Vivir para contarla*	70–72	5 m. 45 m.	1.1, 1.2, 1.3, 2.1, 2.2, 3.1, 3.2	
20	To integrate vocabulary and grammar, and to assess student proficiency	**Desafío 3 – Comunicación / Evaluación** (224–225) • Warm-Up: Independent Starter • *Comunicación:* Review • *Final del desafío* • Quiz on *Desafío 3*	73–75 76	5 m. 25 m. 10 m. 10 m.	1.1, 1.2, 1.3, 2.1, 2.2, 3.1, 5.1	Audio Practice Workbook
21	To integrate language in context	**Para terminar** (226–227) • Warm-Up: Independent Starter • *Todo junto* • *Tu desafío*	77–78 79	5 m. 25 m. 20 m.	1.1, 1.2, 1.3, 2.1, 2.2, 3.1, 3.2, 5.1, 5.2	Audio Practice Workbook *Tu desafío* work
22	To integrate language in context and to assess student proficiency	**Tu desafío / Evaluación** (227) • Warm-Up: Prepare *Tu desafío* presentations • *Tu desafío* presentations • Quiz on *Desafíos 1–3*		5 m. 25 m. 20 m.	1.2, 1.3, 2.1, 2.2, 3.1, 3.2, 5.1, 5.2	
23	To learn about tourism in Latin America	**Mapa cultural** (228–229) • Warm-Up: Independent Starter • *Mapa cultural: El turismo en Latinoamérica*	80	5 m. 45 m.	1.2, 1.3, 2.1, 2.2, 5.1, 5.2	Practice Workbook
24	To write a travel story	**Escritura** (230–231) • Warm-Up: Independent Starter • *Escritura: Un blog de viajes*		5 m. 45 m.	1.1, 1.2, 1.3, 3.1, 5.1	Project work
25	To create an ad to promote tourism in a Hispanic country	**Proyecto** (236–237) • Warm-Up: Prepare project presentations • Project presentations		10 m. 40 m.	1.1, 1.2, 1.3, 2.1, 2.2, 3.2, 5.1	**Repaso – Vocabulario** (232–233) **Repaso – Gramática** (234–235)
26	To assess student proficiency	**Assessment** • *Autoevaluación* (237) • Test		10 m. 40 m.	1.1, 1.2, 1.3, 2.1, 2.2, 5.1, 5.2	
27	To prepare for the AP* Exam	**Hacia el AP* Exam** (238–239) • Warm-Up: Test introduction • Test: Interpersonal Speaking: Conversation • Review and correction of the test		10 m. 20 m. 20 m.	1.1, 5.1	Audio
28	To prepare for the AP* Exam	**Hacia el AP* Exam** (238–239) • Warm-Up: About the test • Test: Interpersonal Speaking: Conversation • Review and correction of the test		10 m. 20 m. 20 m.	1.1, 5.1	Audio

Lesson Plans (90-Minute Classes)

Day	Objectives	Sessions	Activities	Time	Standards	Resources / Homework
1	To introduce leisure time and trips and the characters' challenges, to learn useful expressions related to the unit topic, and to review learned vocabulary	***Nos divertimos / Las tareas / Antes de empezar*** (184–189) • Warm-Up: Topic orientation • Presentation: *¡A divertirse!* • *Expresiones útiles* • *Recuerda*	 1–2 3–4 5–6	 15 m. 35 m. 15 m. 25 m.	1.1, 1.2, 1.3, 2.1, 2.2, 5.1	Practice Workbook
2	To express probability and to identify entertainment performances, sports, and other leisure activities	***Desafío 1 – Una trova auténtica / Vocabulario*** (190–193) • Warm-Up: Independent Starter • *Texto: Una trova auténtica* • *Cultura: La trova y la nueva trova* • *Vocabulario: Ocio y espectáculos* • *Cultura: Los juegos tradicionales*	 7–9 10 11–13 14	 5 m. 30 m. 10 m. 35 m. 10 m.	1.1, 1.2, 1.3, 2.1, 2.2, 3.1, 3.2, 4.2, 5.1, 5.2	Audio Practice Workbook
3	To express frequency and to express probability	***Desafío 1 – Gramática*** (194–197) • Warm-Up: Independent Starter • *Gramática: Expresar frecuencia* • *Cultura: Deportes extremos (Nicaragua)* • *Gramática: Expresar probabilidad (I)*	 15–18 19 20–22	 5 m. 35 m. 40 m. 10 m.	1.1, 1.2, 1.3, 2.1, 2.2, 3.1, 3.2, 4.1, 5.1, 5.2	Audio Practice Workbook
4	To understand a written dialogue, to integrate vocabulary and grammar, and to assess student proficiency	***Desafío 1 – Lectura / Comunicación / Evaluación*** (198–201) • Warm-Up: Independent Starter • *Lectura: Una canción preciosa* • *Comunicación:* Review • *Final del desafío* • Quiz on *Desafío 1*	 23–25 26–27 28	 5 m. 40 m. 25 m. 10 m. 10 m.	1.1, 1.2, 1.3, 2.1, 2.2, 3.1, 3.2, 5.1, 5.2	Practice Workbook
5	To express probability and to describe different modes of travel	***Desafío 2 – Una maqueta misteriosa / Vocabulario*** (202–205) • Warm-Up: Independent Starter • *Texto: Una maqueta misteriosa* • *Cultura: El ferrocarril más difícil del mundo* • *Vocabulario: Los viajes* • *Cultura: El AVE (España)*	 29–30 31 32–34 35	 5 m. 30 m. 10 m. 35 m. 10 m.	1.1, 1.2, 1.3, 2.1, 2.2, 3.1, 3.2, 4.2, 5.1, 5.2	Audio Practice Workbook
6	To express probability with the future and the conditional tenses and to learn and use the present perfect subjunctive	***Desafío 2 – Gramática*** (206–209) • Warm-Up: Independent Starter • *Gramática: Expresar probabilidad (II). El futuro y el condicional* • *Conexiones: El condicional de rumor* • *Gramática: El presente perfecto de subjuntivo*	 36–39 40 41–45	 5 m. 35 m. 10 m. 40 m.	1.1, 1.2, 1.3, 2.1, 3.1, 3.2, 4.1, 4.2, 5.1	Audio Practice Workbook

Day	Objectives	Sessions	Activities	Time	Standards	Resources / Homework
7	To understand an informative article, to integrate vocabulary and grammar, and to assess student proficiency	**Desafío 2 – Lectura / Comunicación / Evaluación** (210–213) • Warm-Up: Independent Starter • *Lectura: Como la vida misma* • *Comunicación:* Review • *Final del desafío* • Quiz on *Desafío 2*	46–48 49–50 51	5 m. 40 m. 25 m. 10 m. 10 m.	1.1, 1.2, 1.3, 2.1, 2.2, 3.1, 3.2, 4.2, 5.1	Practice Workbook
8	To express cause and consequence and to talk about different types of accommodations and the weather	**Desafío 3 – Un concurso para viajeros / Vocabulario** (214–217) • Warm-Up: Independent Starter • *Texto: Un concurso para viajeros* • *Comparaciones: La Red Española de Albergues Juveniles (REAJ)* • *Vocabulario: El alojamiento* • *Cultura: La Organización Mundial del Turismo (OMT)*	52–54 55 56–58 59	5 m. 30 m. 10 m. 35 m. 10 m.	1.1, 1.2, 1.3, 2.1, 2.2, 4.2, 5.1, 5.2	Audio Practice Workbook
9	To express cause and to express consequence	**Desafío 3 – Gramática** (218–221) • Warm-Up: Independent Starter • *Gramática: Expresar causa* • *Cultura: El Titicaca: el lago místico de los incas* • *Gramática: Expresar consecuencia*	60–63 64 65–69	5 m. 40 m. 10 m. 35 m.	1.1, 1.2, 1.3, 2.1, 2.2, 3.1, 3.2, 4.1, 5.2	Audio Practice Workbook
10	To understand a literary biography and to integrate vocabulary and grammar	**Desafío 3 – Lectura / Comunicación / Evaluación** (222–225) • Warm-Up: Independent Starter • *Lectura: Vivir para contarla* • *Comunicación:* Review • *Final del desafío* • Quiz on *Desafío 3*	70–72 73–75 76	5 m. 40 m. 25 m. 10 m. 10 m.	1.1, 1.2, 1.3, 2.1, 2.2, 3.1, 3.2, 5.1	Audio Practice Workbook **Para terminar – Tu desafío** (227)
11	To integrate language in context and to assess student proficiency	**Para terminar / Evaluación** (226–227) • Warm-Up: Independent Starter • *Todo junto* • *Tu desafío:* work and presentations • Quiz on *Desafíos 1–3*	77–78 79	5 m. 25 m. 40 m. 20 m.	1.1, 1.2, 1.3, 2.1, 2.2, 3.1, 3.2, 5.1, 5.2	Audio Practice Workbook
12	To learn about tourism in Latin America and to write a travel story	**Mapa cultural / Escritura** (228–231) • Warm-Up: Independent Starter • *Mapa cultural: El turismo en Latinoamérica* • *Escritura: Un blog de viajes*	80	5 m. 40 m. 45 m.	1.1, 1.2, 1.3, 2.1, 2.2, 3.1, 5.1, 5.2	Practice Workbook **Repaso –Vocabulario** (232–233) **Repaso – Gramática** (234–235) Project work

Day	Objectives	Sessions	Activities	Time	Standards	Resources / Homework
13	To create an ad to promote tourism in a Hispanic country, and to assess student proficiency	**Proyecto / Assessment** (236–237) • Warm-Up: Prepare project presentations • Project presentations • *Autoevaluación* • Test		10 m. 45 m. 10 m. 25 m.	1.1, 1.2, 1.3, 2.1, 2.2, 3.2, 5.1, 5.2	
14	To prepare for the AP* Exam	**Hacia el AP* Exam** (238–239) • Warm-Up: Test introduction • Test: Interpersonal Speaking: Conversation • Review and correction of the test		10 m. 40 m. 40 m.	1.1, 5.1	Audio
15	To practice oral skills in social interaction	**Final Activity** • Warm-Up: Presentation of the activity • Role-play activity		15 m. 75 m.	1.1, 1.2, 1.3, 2.1, 2.2, 5.1, 5.2	

Final Activity (Day 15)

Presentation

- Explain to students that they will be participating in a role-play situation related to one of the topics covered in this unit. You may wish to suggest the following situations:
  1. conducting a mock interview of a renowned Hispanic musician;
  2. planning a day of sports and leisure activities for a very diverse group of Hispanic tourists visiting your community;
  3. getting lost or missing a train or bus while traveling in a Spanish-speaking country;
  4. having a minor accident or road mishap while driving in a Spanish-speaking country;
  5. taking part in a local active-tourism activity while staying in a youth hostel in a Spanish-speaking country;
  6. experiencing adverse weather conditions while on a camping trip in a Spanish-speaking country.

Preparation

- Divide the class into small groups and assign a different situation to each group. Ask students to brainstorm the details of their assigned situation and the different characters who will take part in it. Then allow students time to write the script cooperatively. They should plan for a role-play of about five to six minutes.

Revision and Rehearsal

- Ask students to revise their scripts, paying attention to accurate use of vocabulary and grammar structures. At this point, students may also correct any inconsistencies in the storyline, add a punch line, or make other minor changes they deem appropriate. Then allow for rehearsal time. Explain to students that they will be able to improvise, or ad-lib. However, rehearsing their lines a few times will give them confidence and improve their fluency.

Dramatization and Evaluation

- Call on each group to role-play their assigned situation. Assess students on fluency, pronunciation, content, organization, and correct use of target vocabulary and grammar. You may want to prepare a short evaluation questionnaire that the class fills in at the end of each role-play. If time permits, discuss as a class the real-life situations upon which the role-plays were based.

Unit 4 Nos divertimos

9 La música cubana

—Este desafío me va a costar mucho.

—No te preocupes, Lucas. Tenemos que prepararnos bien, eso es todo.

—Investigué un poco sobre la música cubana para entender mejor las raíces de la trova.

—Qué bien. ¿Y qué has averiguado?

—Pues que la música cubana tiene sus orígenes culturales en Europa y en África. Como España dominó la isla mucho tiempo, hay influencias españolas en las melodías y en los instrumentos. Ya sabes que la trova se suele acompañar de guitarra española.

—Es cierto. ¿Y la influencia africana viene de los esclavos que llegaron a Cuba?

—Efectivamente. Ellos llevaron a la isla su cultura y su música. Por eso todavía hoy se habla de la música afrocubana. Ah, también leí que el *jazz* de los Estados Unidos influye en la música de Cuba.

—La verdad es que la música cubana es muy rica. ¿Y qué más estilos conoces, además de la trova?

—Pues la salsa, que es una variación del son y es el género más famoso. Y el bolero, que es otro género muy conocido.

—¿Y tú sabes diferenciarlos?

—La verdad es que no. Además es que muchos de estos géneros musicales tienen raíces comunes y se influyen entre sí. Bueno, ahora tengo que buscar la trova que vamos a interpretar. Quiero que sea muy conocida.

—Seguro que encuentras algo que nos guste.

13 ¿Cómo se van a entretener?

Muy buenos días, señoras y señores. La tripulación del barco Mar Fenomenal quiere ofrecerles una amplia oferta de actividades para que disfruten en nuestro próximo destino o, si lo prefieren, puedan entretenerse a bordo.

Si quieren conocer Cartagena y explorar los mejores rincones de esta bella ciudad, les recomendamos que vayan a la visita que organiza nuestro equipo de guías. La excursión dura todo el día.

Y si les interesa explorar y conocer la vida marina de esta zona privilegiada, apúntense a una clase para aprender a bucear. Podrán observar los peces tropicales y admirar unos fondos marinos espectaculares.

Para los que prefieran relajarse y tomar el sol, recuerden que la piscina estará abierta todo el día. Y si también quieren mantenerse en forma les recordamos que esta tarde hay una clase de ejercicios aeróbicos en el agua.

También hemos preparado un torneo de juegos de mesa para toda la familia, que se celebrará en el comedor a las cuatro de la tarde: habrá partidas de naipes, parchís, dominó, ajedrez...

Y, finalmente, esta noche después de la cena podrán asistir a un concierto de una fantástica banda de jazz. ¡Que disfruten del día!

17 La vida de una cantante

—Muy buenas tardes, radioyentes. Hoy tenemos con nosotros a la compositora y cantante Rita Castillo. Rita, es un placer hablar hoy con usted.

—El placer es mío.

—Imagino que está muy ocupada y por eso le agradecemos la oportunidad de hablar con usted antes del concierto de esta noche.

—Tiene razón. Mi trabajo nunca me da un descanso. Cada semana viajo a otra ciudad para dar un concierto y cuando no tengo un concierto, ensayo con los otros músicos.

—¿Y cuándo suele componer su música?

—¡Es una buena pregunta! No tengo tanto tiempo como quisiera... pero trato de tomarme un día de vez en cuando para sentarme en mi sala de música sin distracciones. Diría que compongo una canción al mes.

—¿Qué es lo más difícil de ser famosa?

—Creo que lo que más me ha costado ha sido estar lejos de mi familia. Trato de verlos cada semana, aunque a veces es difícil porque viajo mucho.

—A muchos nos encantaría ser cantantes famosos, pero la realidad es que, como dice usted, esta es una profesión que requiere estar mucho tiempo fuera de casa.

—Exacto. Yo suelo pedirle a mi asistente que me deje algo de tiempo libre para, simplemente, poder jugar con mis hijos. Tienen ocho y diez años, y quiero que su niñez sea lo más normal posible. Así que una vez a la semana, jugamos juntos todo el día.

—¿Viajan ellos con usted para pasar más tiempo juntos?

—Solo de vez en cuando porque prefiero que estén en casa y lleven una rutina. Pero hablamos todas las noches antes de que se duerman.

—Muchas gracias por hablarnos de su vida y que tenga un gran éxito en el concierto.

—Gracias por invitarme. ¡Y espero que se diviertan esta noche!

21 La nueva amiga de Lucas

—Hola, ¿qué tal? Tú acabas de matricularte en mi clase de Matemáticas, ¿no?

—Sí, mi familia se mudó aquí hace una semana. Soy Wendy, ¿y tú?

–Lucas. ¿Cómo te va por aquí?

–Pues la verdad es que no muy bien. Me ha sido un poco difícil acostumbrarme a la escuela y no conozco a mucha gente.

–¡Pues ahora me conoces a mí! Dime, ¿qué planes tienes para mañana?

–No lo sé. Es posible que ayude a mis padres con la nueva casa. Y también debería estudiar.

–Me parece muy bien, pero también hay que divertirse. A lo mejor puedes reunirte con mis amigos y conmigo para jugar al fútbol el próximo sábado. ¿Te apetece?

–Quizás vaya a jugar con ustedes, pero sé que mis padres quieren que arregle mi cuarto este fin de semana. Aún tengo que colocar un montón de ropa y libros.

–¿Y el fin de semana que viene?

–Es que mis abuelos nos vienen a visitar ese fin de semana. Quieren ver la nueva casa y es probable que pasemos toda la tarde jugando todos al parchís, a los naipes y esas cosas. Pero oye, seguro que mis padres me permiten invitarte. ¿Quieres venir?

–Vale, quizás no sea tanta tortura estar en casa con tu familia el sábado si estoy contigo. Nos divertiremos. ¡Chao, Wendy!

34 ¡Viajeros al tren!

–Es la primera vez que viajo en un tren nocturno.

–Yo he viajado otras veces, pero no en coche-cama. No sé si seré capaz de dormir con el movimiento. Estoy muy emocionado.

–Seguro que sí. Unos amigos viajaron así hace dos años y me dijeron que es muy cómodo y que apenas se nota el movimiento.

–Mira, es aquí.

–¡Es estupendo! Tiene bastante espacio. ¿Prefieres la cama de arriba o la de abajo?

–Elige tú, a mí me da igual.

–Dejemos las maletas y vayamos al vagón-restaurante, ¿quieres? Tengo hambre.

–¿Sabes si hay que tener asientos reservados?

–No sé, pero ahí está el revisor. Vamos a preguntarle.

–Buenas noches. Por favor, ¿podemos sentarnos en cualquier mesa?

–Buenas noches, señores. Sí, pueden sentarse en cualquier asiento libre.

–Muchas gracias.

–Creo que al fondo hay dos sitios libres. ¿Vamos?

38 ¿Dónde estará Ethan?

–¿Qué hora es, mamá?

–Habrán pasado unos veinte minutos desde la última vez que me lo preguntaste, así que serán las seis y media, más o menos. Tranquila, hija.

–Perdona, mamá. Es que estoy muy nerviosa con este desafío. ¿Crees que saldrá bien nuestra maqueta de la Nariz del Diablo?

–¡Claro que sí!

–¿Dónde estará Ethan?

–Se habrá demorado comprando los materiales para el proyecto. ¿A qué hora se fue?

–Serían las cinco y me dijo que estaría de regreso a las seis.

–Podrías llamarlo a su celular.

–Ya lo hice, pero no contestó; saltó el buzón de voz.

–Lo tendrá sin batería.

–No sería extraño. Le pasa con frecuencia.

–¿Sabes adónde fue a comprar los materiales?

–Habrá ido a ese almacén grande que hay en el centro.

–¡Uf! ¿En el centro? Oí por la radio que había un atasco enorme. Se habrá retrasado por eso.

–Tendría que haber ido con él porque...

–Hola, ya estoy aquí. ¿Por qué tienes esa cara, Eva?

42 ¡Al volante!

1. ¡Qué tarde es! ¡Y la reunión está a punto de empezar! No sé por qué habrá tanto tráfico. ¡Y además me estoy quedando sin gasolina! Tengo que encontrar una gasolinera cuanto antes.

2. –Ethan, me han puesto una multa. Llegaba tarde y manejaba un poco rápido. La policía fue muy amable, pero me multó y, encima, llegué aún más tarde.

   –Lo siento, Eva. Pero la próxima vez, tendrás que manejar más despacio.

3. –¿Qué te ha pasado? ¡Estás empapado!

   –No lo vas a creer. Venía de camino a la escuela y de repente se me ha pinchado una rueda. Y cuando salí del auto para poner la rueda de repuesto empezó a llover.

   –Ay, pobre...

4. –Vamos, Ethan. Nuestros amigos nos esperan.

   –Ya voy, ya voy. ¡Pero si todavía no te has puesto el cinturón de seguridad! Pues hasta que no te lo pongas, no arranco.

57 Compañeros de viaje

–¿Qué te parece si decidimos ya el destino y el alojamiento de nuestro viaje?

–Claro. ¿Tú ya has mirado algo?

–Sí, a mí me encantaría visitar la zona de las cataratas del Iguazú. He estado echando un vistazo en un sitio web que se llama viajeros.com y he pensado que, puesto que no tenemos mucho dinero, podríamos considerar alojarnos en un albergue juvenil. Además, si pasamos allí las vacaciones, podremos conocer a mochileros como nosotros de otras partes del mundo.

–¿Un albergue? Ay, Carla, es que no me gusta la idea de compartir habitación y baño con otras personas. Yo prefiero que nos alojemos en un hotel con todo incluido. Es mucho más cómodo.

–Ya, pero eso es carísimo. ¿Qué te parece si vamos de cámping?

–Pero si fuéramos de camping, tendríamos que pasar la noche al aire libre...

–¡Pues claro! Eso es lo bueno. Encontrar la paz y la armonía que hay en la naturaleza.

–¿Y qué pasaría si hubiera una ola de frío o si cayera un chaparrón?

–No te preocupes. Como me encanta la naturaleza, tengo todo el equipo necesario: dos sacos de dormir, una tienda, dos colchonetas y una nevera portátil. Además, antes de hacer nuestro viaje consultaremos el pronóstico de tiempo para ver si va a hacer bueno.

–No sé. Es que no soy un viajero muy aventurero, que digamos. ¿Qué tal si vamos a visitar una ciudad moderna? Podríamos ir a Buenos Aires. Considera las posibilidades... Ver un partido de fútbol del Boca o del River, visitar los museos, ir al barrio de La Boca... Si quieres encontrar la armonía con la naturaleza, podemos darnos un paseo por el zoológico. Anda, piénsalo.

63 Las razones perfectas

1. –Tengo tantas ganas de saber más sobre la historia de la civilización inca...

    –Claro, por eso vamos a pasar el verano recorriendo la ruta inca con nuestros amigos mochileros.

    –¡Qué emocionante!

2. –En la página web decían que una de las ventajas de este hotel son las hermosas vistas de las habitaciones.

    –Puede que sea una vista panorámica, pero hoy hay mucha neblina. No se ve nada.

3. –Vamos a elegir un alojamiento. Mira, hay hoteles con todo incluido: pensión completa, habitación con terraza y vistas al mar, baño privado, microondas, televisor de pantalla plana y piscina.

    –Pero, ¿cuánto nos va a costar tanto lujo?

    –¡Uy! Son quinientos dólares al día por una habitación doble.

4. –¡Qué día tan lluvioso! No podremos ir a la playa.

    –Es verdad. Además hay mucho viento y las olas son demasiado altas. Tendremos que pensar en hacer otras actividades. Ya sé. ¿Qué te parece si jugamos una partida de ajedrez en la sala de juegos del hotel?

75 Prepárate para ganar

–He pensado que podemos titular nuestro video *Michelle y Daniel: Los superviajeros extraordinarios.*

–Sí, tiene gracia. Pero si decimos que somos unos superviajeros, deberíamos tener claro qué características tiene que cumplir un viajero para ser un verdadero superviajero.

–Lo más importante es haber tenido una gran variedad de experiencias viajeras, como nosotros.

–Sí. Por nuestra afición a la naturaleza, mi familia y yo hemos ido muchas veces de cámping a parques nacionales de todo el mundo.

–Y puesto que no nos gusta la idea de dormir encima de una colchoneta, mi familia suele alojarse en hoteles con todo incluido. A mí también me encanta ver el mar y las montañas, y disfrutar de la naturaleza, pero yo prefiero disfrutar de esas vistas desde el balcón de un hotel.

–Entonces los superviajeros pueden tener distintas preferencias de alojamiento, ¿verdad?

–Eso es. También creo que es importante establecer cuáles son los beneficios de viajar. Yo creo que el principal es descubrir las tradiciones, la historia y las costumbres de las culturas que visitamos.

–Estoy de acuerdo. La curiosidad es una característica imprescindible en un "superviajero". Por ejemplo, mi familia y yo siempre intentamos conocer a la gente que vive en los lugares que visitamos y relacionarnos con ellos, en vez de estar todo el día metidos en los típicos hoteles para turistas.

–Claro, claro.

–Como nos encantan las aventuras, una vez fuimos de cámping a la orilla del lago Titicaca, en Bolivia. Pero nos alojamos un par de noches en casa de una familia de la zona. Fue una experiencia inolvidable.

–Debido a la variedad de experiencias que hemos vivido, estoy seguro de que vamos a ganar el concurso de "superviajeros". Por lo tanto... ¡vamos a decidir qué sitio queremos visitar y a elegir un albergue!

77 Un artista muy versátil

Fuente: Caracol Radio, Colombia

–Amigos de los Grandes Especiales de Caracol Radio, ¿qué tal? Aquí estamos con nuestra cita del fin de semana para compartir con ustedes todos los artistas que hacen noticia o que hicieron noticia y dejaron un legado musical, como el caso de hoy: Tito Rodríguez. Para eso hemos invitado a Ricardo Mendivil, que se ha vuelto parte ya de nuestra familia Caracol Radio. Ricardo, ¿qué tal? Buenas noches.

–Vicente, estoy muy contento. Primero, porque no lo veía desde hace muchos días y estábamos desconectados en estas tertulias musicales de los especiales de Caracol. Y segundo, la razón que me tiene aquí hoy es que Tito Rodríguez, que es mi artista favorito, está precisamente homenajeado porque el 4 de enero de 1923 nació, y el 28 de febrero, o sea muy cercano a esta fecha, falleció. Es un hombre que... Vamos a recorrer su historia, su vida musical, porque además es un personaje muy caribeño. Es el hijo de un dominicano, un padre dominicano, con una madre cubana, pero nacido en Puerto Rico. O sea, que es un hombre que recoge todo el sabor de las Antillas, y por eso es un hombre tan versátil en sus interpretaciones. Es un hombre que cantó bolero, que tocó mambos, que tocó chachachás, charangas... Incluso estuvo con Machito haciendo los inicios de la salsa.

–¿Y qué tal si comenzamos con una canción que lo identifique a él, a Tito Rodríguez?

–Vamos a empezar con un mambo que se llama *Mama Huela* y nos transportamos a los tiempos del Palladium en Nueva York.

Hacia el *AP* Exam.* Actividad 1

–Hola, ¿cómo estás? Habla Felipe. ¿Te gustaría ayudarme a organizar una exposición de arte local en la escuela?

–[...]

–La exposición es para celebrar la semana de la cultura. Me gustaría que fuera en la biblioteca de la escuela. Ah, y todas las obras deben ser de artistas locales. ¿Conoces a algún artista local? ¿Cómo podemos contactar con él?

–[...]

–¡Qué bien! Tenemos que comenzar a trabajar ya. Tengo otra idea: podríamos organizar un concurso de pintura entre los estudiantes. Por cierto, Cecilia, Alberto y yo vamos hoy por la tarde a ver un documental sobre los muralistas mexicanos. ¿Quieres venir con nosotros?

–[...]

–Es una pena que no vengas. El profesor de Arte nos dijo que es un documental excelente. Volviendo al tema, ¿qué crees que debemos hacer para promocionar nuestra exposición de arte local?

–¡Genial! Me parece una idea excelente. ¿Cuándo podemos reunirnos para comenzar a trabajar?

–[...]

–De acuerdo. ¡Gracias y hasta pronto!

Hacia el *AP* Exam.* Actividad 2

–[...]

–¡Hola, soy Alejandra! ¿Cómo estás?

–[...]

–Bien, pero un poco nerviosa. Resulta que he recibido una carta de una universidad de Chile aceptando mi solicitud. Pero también me han aceptado en una universidad mucho más cerca de mi casa, y no sé por cuál decidirme. ¿Tú qué opinas?

–[...]

–Ay, no sé... ¿Tú qué harías en mi lugar?

–[...]

–Muchas gracias. Voy a pensarlo y mañana te cuento qué he decidido. ¡Hasta mañana!

–[...]

Unit 4
Nos divertimos

The Unit
- The themes for Unit 4 are leisure time, entertainment, and travel. The participants will learn how to express frequency and probability as well as talk about the causes and consequences of events. They will also discuss topics related to musical traditions, modes of transportation, and lodging and travel options.
- Tess, a veteran of *Fans del español*, will give the participants their tasks.
  - *Desafío 1.* Asha and Lucas have to sing a traditional Cuban ballad at their school's music festival.
  - *Desafío 2.* Eva and Ethan have to make a scale model of a place in Ecuador called *Nariz del Diablo*.
  - *Desafío 3.* Michelle and Daniel have to participate in a travel competition sponsored by an association of youth hostels.

Activities	Standards	Resources
Nos divertimos	1.2, 2.1, 2.2	

Teaching Suggestions

Warm-Up / Independent Starter
- Have students associate each of the photos with one of the following topics: entertainment, travel, or lodging. Ask them to justify their associations in a three-sentence paragraph.

Preparation
- Ask volunteers to read their Independent Starters and initiate a class discussion on these topics. To expand the discussion, you may want to ask some of these questions: *¿Qué tipo de espectáculos musicales son comunes en nuestra comunidad? ¿Qué genero músical es más popular? ¿Saben algo sobre el origen de ese tipo de música? ¿Qué importancia tiene el ferrocarril en el transporte de pasajeros en este país? ¿Y en el transporte de mercancías? ¿Qué tipos de alojamientos conocen? ¿En qué se diferencian?*

184

UNIDAD 4
Nos divertimos
El ocio y los viajes

DESAFÍO 1

▶ **Expresar probabilidad (I)**

Vocabulario
Ocio y espectáculos.
Deportes y tiempo libre

Gramática
Expresar frecuencia
Expresar probabilidad (I)

DESAFÍO 2

Ferrocarril a Nariz del Diablo (Ecuador).

▶ **Expresar probabilidad (II)**

Vocabulario
Los viajes

Gramática
Expresar probabilidad (II).
El futuro y el condicional
El presente perfecto de subjuntivo

Casa de la Trova (Cuba).

184 ciento ochenta y cuatro

The Challenge

⚑ DESAFÍO 1

Casa de la Trova
During the first half of the 20th century, a group of Cuban musicians from Santiago de Cuba popularized *trova*, a form of ballad. Pepe Sánchez, Chicho Ibáñez, Manuel Corona, Sindo Garay, and María Teresa Vera are some of the names associated with the traditional Cuban *trova*. The *Casa de la Trova* was a small café that served as a meeting point for *trova* musicians during the 1950s. In the late 1980s, it was expanded and it now serves as a meeting place for music lovers who go there to enjoy the *trova* performances.

⚑ DESAFÍO 2

Ferrocarril a Nariz del Diablo
The town of Alausí, located in the Ecuadorian Andes, is the departure point for the *Nariz del Diablo* railway. On this section of the once-thriving railroad system that linked the coast with the highlands, trains are faced with a vertical wall of rock. At the time this rail line was developed, the engineers decided to build a railroad that went over, rather than around, the mountain. The train descends and ascends through a series of tight switchbacks carved into the rock; therefore, what the train lacks in speed, it makes up for in breathtaking views.

Nos divertimos

DESAFÍO

3

▶ **Expresar causa y consecuencia**

Vocabulario
El alojamiento.

El tiempo meteorológico

Gramática
Expresar causa

Expresar consecuencia

Letrero de un hostal (México).

ciento ochenta y cinco **185**

- Have students read each *Desafío's* objective, as well as the vocabulary and grammar goals, then discuss how each picture might relate to these objectives and goals.

Picture Discussion

- Ask students to look at the photos again and check their knowledge about the places and items pictured. Finally, ask students to review their predictions about each topic.

Casa de la Trova (Cuba)

- Invite students to share what they know about Caribbean music. Discuss with the class some features of Caribbean music (e.g., influenced by European, African, and indigenous rhythms and instruments, improvisation, rhythmic drive). If students do not know it, explain that a *trova* is a form of lyrical ballad that originated in Cuba more than a century ago.

Ferrocarril a Nariz del Diablo (Ecuador)

- Have students describe the train in this picture. Focus their attention on the word *Expreso* printed on the side of the train. Does this train look like a fast train? Elicit that this is a historic train and that it might have been considered *expreso* when it first started operating.

Letrero de un hostal (México)

- Based on the sign, invite students to comment on the type of lodging they think this hostel is. You may want to guide the discussion with these or similar questions: *¿Creen que es un alojamiento caro o barato? ¿Por qué? ¿Está en una gran ciudad o en una zona apartada? ¿Por qué creen eso?* If a student in your class has stayed in a hostel or knows what hostels are, invite him or her to share with the class.

Objectives

- By the end of Unit 4, students will be able to
  - Talk about entertainment and sports.
  - Express frequency.
  - Express conjecture or probability.
  - Talk about travel and modes of transportation.
  - Use the correct tense sequence to talk about events.
  - Talk about lodging and the weather.
  - Express cause and consequence.
  - Familiarize themselves with some aspects of the entertainment traditions, modes of transportation, and travel destinations of the Spanish-speaking world.

DESAFÍO 3

Letrero de un hostal

A youth hostel is a place that provides inexpensive accommodations. Hostels are usually aimed at young people and students, but they are open to people of all ages. In addition to affordable lodging, most hostels also offer breakfast or, in some cases, have a common kitchen where guests can prepare their meals. One of the disadvantages of hostels is the lack of privacy, since rooms and bathrooms are usually shared. However, hostels offer guests opportunities to socialize with fellow travelers in a more informal environment than hotels, and this is a big plus for many travelers.

Las tareas

Presentation

- In this section, the three pairs talk with Tess, who describes the challenges that lie ahead. Students will preview useful expressions for talking about leisure activities and entertainment. They will also preview expressions to say whether someone had a good time or not.

Activities	Standards	Resources
Texto	1.2, 2.1, 2.2	
1.	1.2, 1.3, 2.1, 2.2, 5.1	
2.	1.2, 1.3	

Teaching Suggestions

Warm-Up / Independent Starter

- Ask students to read the title of this section (*¡A divertirse!*) and think about the things they do for fun. Then have them list the top seven activities they do. To get students started, you may wish to share this list with them: *ir a un concierto, jugar al béisbol, tocar un instrumento musical, bailar, ir al cine, salir con los amigos.*

Preparation

- Invite students to share their lists from the Independent Starter with the class. You may want to keep a record of students' answers on the board, or ask the class to keep a record in their notebooks. Then, have the class categorize the activities into three types: *Actividades físicas* (e.g., *practicar algún deporte, montar en bicicleta, salir a pasear*); *Actividades artísticas* (e.g., *tocar un instrumento, realizar manualidades, ir a museos*); *Actividades sociales* (e.g., *salir con amigos, ir a fiestas, salir a comer*). Discuss with the class the results of their categorization. What would be a good description of your class: *activa, artística,* or *social*? Do students consider the results typical for young adults in their community? Invite them to explain any trends as well as any differences.

- Have students scan the text on this page and find expressions or phrases used to say that something is or will be fun, or to express enthusiasm. (*... lo van a pasar en grande. ¡Qué divertido! ¡Qué bien!*)

Las tareas

¡A divertirse!

Tess habla con los personajes para contarles cuáles son sus desafíos. ¿Quieres saber qué tendrán que hacer esta vez? Lee la conversación y averígualo. Una pista: están relacionados con la cultura y los viajes.

TESS: Hola, amigos. ¿Cómo están? A todos les gusta divertirse, ¿verdad? Pues esta vez lo van a pasar en grande, se lo aseguro. Tomen nota. Lucas, Asha, ¿saben qué es la trova?

LUCAS: Creo que es un tipo de música que se originó en Cuba.

TESS: Efectivamente. Pues su tarea consiste en cantar una trova delante de sus compañeros.

ASHA: ¡Qué divertido! Me gusta cantar.

LUCAS: Pues a mí me da mucha vergüenza...

TESS: ¡Ánimo, Lucas! Si ensayan, seguro que la actuación será un éxito.

EVA: ¿Y cuál es nuestra tarea, Tess?

TESS: Ustedes tienen que hacer una maqueta de la Nariz del Diablo.

ETHAN: ¿La Nariz del Diablo? ¿Eso qué es?

TESS: Es una de las mayores atracciones turísticas de Ecuador. Por allí pasa el ferrocarril más «difícil» del mundo...

EVA: Suena interesante. Tengo muchas ganas de empezar.

TESS: Michelle, Daniel, ¿se consideran unos superviajeros? Espero que sí, porque van a participar en un concurso para superviajeros organizado por una red de albergues juveniles. Y el premio merece la pena.

MICHELLE y DANIEL: ¡Qué bien! ¡Nos encanta viajar!

TESS: Me alegro. Bueno, espero que aprendan mucho y que se diviertan. ¡¡¡Buena suerte!!!

Differentiated Instruction

DEVELOPING LEARNERS

- Ask students to close their books as you have other students read the dialogue aloud. Then ask the developing students to explain in their own words what each of the pair's *desafíos* will be, as well as each pair's reaction to their challenge. If students have difficulty doing this, you may want to have the dialogue read again, or you may want to have developing students read it aloud, alternating roles. Ask students to predict which pair will complete their challenge with the most success, and to justify their answers.

EXPANDING LEARNERS

- Have students work with a partner and assign one of the dialogues on page 187 to them. Explain that they will need to role-play the current dialogue and then add several exchanges to it so that the final conversation will be about two to three minutes in length. Allow all pairs to first discuss, organize, and write their scripts, and then give them time to rehearse their lines. Call on volunteers to present their conversations in front of the class.

Yo no sé nada de la trova.

Yo tampoco sé mucho... Creo que se hizo muy popular en Cuba en los años 60 del siglo XX. Habrá que investigar.

A mí también. Tenemos que hacer un buen trabajo, Ethan.

Me encanta nuestra tarea. Además, me gustan mucho las manualidades.

¡Y yo! ¿Buscamos las reglas en Internet para planear una buena estrategia?

¡Yo quiero que ganemos el concurso!

1 ¿Comprendes?

▶ **Escribe.** ¿Qué tarea tiene que hacer cada pareja?

▶ **Responde** a estas preguntas.

1. ¿En qué país se originó la trova? ¿Cuándo logró más fama?
2. ¿Dónde está la Nariz del Diablo?
3. ¿Qué es un albergue juvenil? Si no lo sabes, averígualo.

▶ **Explica.** ¿Qué desafío te parece más difícil? ¿Por qué?

2 Investiga

▶ **Busca** tres palabras del texto que sean nuevas para ti y fíjate en el contexto. ¿Qué crees que significan? Escribe una oración con cada una.

ciento ochenta y siete **187**

HERITAGE LANGUAGE LEARNERS

• Asha and Lucas have been asked to sing a *trova*. Have students research some traditional songs or musical pieces from their family's heritage country. Then ask them to describe, sing, or bring in a recording of the musical numbers they selected. Encourage students to give a brief oral presentation about the music's origins, the population that is most closely associated with it, leading performers of the genre, and any other interesting facts or anecdotes they can share with the rest of the class.

CRITICAL THINKING

• Ask students what they think *la trova, la Nariz del Diablo,* and *los albergues* have in common, and why the *desafíos* associated with each of them have been included in a unit entitled *Nos divertimos*. Have students first work in small groups to discuss their ideas, and then enable a classroom discussion on these questions. Record the top reasons, and at the end of the unit ask students to evaluate their ideas with the reality of these events and places, as well as the *desafíos* connected to each one.

Texto: ¡A divertirse!

■ Call on a volunteer to read the introduction to the text aloud. Then point out the sentences in the text that have question marks or exclamation points. Model the pronunciation and intonation of these sentences and have students repeat after you. Assign the different roles of the dialogue to six students and remind them to emphasize the intonation and be careful with the pronunciation. Then have them read the dialogue aloud.

■ Work on comprehension through questions. For example: *¿Cuál de los participantes parece ser más tímido(a)? ¿Qué se debe hacer para que una actuación salga bien? ¿De qué tienen Eva y Ethan que hacer una maqueta? ¿Quiénes son los patrocinadores* (sponsors) *del concurso "superviajeros"?*

Activities

1. To expand this activity, have students work in small groups to pool what they know about Cuban music, the location and geographical features of Ecuador, and the various types of lodgings in which young people usually stay. Then, invite groups to share this information with the class.

Answer Key

1. Asha y Lucas: cantar una trova.
   Eva y Ethan: hacer una maqueta.
   Michelle y Daniel: participar en un concurso para superviajeros.
   ▶ Answers will vary. Sample answers:
   1. En Cuba. Se hizo muy popular en los años 60 del siglo xx.
   2. En Ecuador.
   3. Son lugares parecidos a un hotel, pero más baratos, donde se suelen alojar los estudiantes cuando viajan.
   ▶ Answers will vary.
2. Answers will vary.

Additional Resources

Fans Online activities
Practice Workbook

Unit 4

Antes de empezar

Presentation

- In this section, students will learn a variety of useful expressions to talk about leisure activities and entertainment. They will also learn expressions to say whether someone had a good time or not.

- Students will also review vocabulary for talking about leisure and entertainment activities, travel, and cars.

Activities	Standards	Resources
Expresiones útiles	1.2, 2.1	
3.	1.2, 2.1	
4.	1.2, 1.3, 2.1	
Recuerda	1.2	
5.	1.1, 1.3	
6.	1.1, 1.2, 1.3, 5.1	

Teaching Suggestions

Warm-Up / Independent Starter

- Have students think of the last three leisure activities in which they participated. Then ask them to write a sentence for each activity specifying what they did, when they did it, and with whom. For example: *El sábado fui al cine con mi amiga Laura.*

Preparation

- Go over the *expresiones útiles* as a class. Personalize the expressions by asking students these or similar questions: *¿Qué hacen el fin de semana para pasar el rato? ¿En qué actividades lo pasan en grande? ¿Qué los aburre como una ostra? ¿Han visto últimamente alguna película que haya sido un éxito?*

- Have students extend one of their sentences from the Independent Starter into a paragraph. Ask them to add information about the activity, explain why they participated in it, and say whether they had a good time or not and why. For example: *El sábado fui al cine con mi amiga Laura para entretenerme. Fuimos a la última sesión. La película había sido un éxito, y yo tenía muchas ganas de verla. Pero, me aburrí como una ostra porque...* Call on different volunteers to share their paragraphs with the class.

188

EXPRESIONES ÚTILES

Para hablar sobre el tiempo libre:
> Me gusta mirar fotografías para **pasar el rato**.
> Yo suelo **entretenerme** haciendo crucigramas.
> ¿Jugamos a algo para **matar el tiempo**?

Para decir cómo lo has pasado:
> Estuve en un parque de atracciones y **lo pasé en grande**.
> Ayer fui a una fiesta, pero **me aburrí como una ostra**.

Para hablar de un espectáculo:
> El sábado **fuimos a la última sesión** y el cine **estaba hasta la bandera**.
> La película *Lo imposible* **ha sido un éxito** inesperado.
> El Circo del Sol **prorroga su espectáculo** hasta el mes de marzo.

3 Diálogos

▶ **Completa** estos diálogos usando las expresiones útiles.

1. —Me encanta ir a la playa a tomar el sol.
   —Pues a mí no. En la playa me aburro como una ___1___.

2. —¿Qué tal la fiesta?
   —¡Genial! Lo pasamos en ___2___.

3. —Yo suelo hacer crucigramas o juego a los naipes para ___3___ el tiempo. ¿Y tú?
   —Yo prefiero pasar el ___4___ leyendo o escuchando música.

4. —El teatro estaba hasta la ___5___. Habían vendido todas las entradas.
   —O sea, que la función fue todo un ___6___.
   —Sí. Ojalá ___7___ la obra. Si puedo, volveré a verla. Pero tendré que ir a la última ___8___, porque salgo muy tarde del trabajo.

4 Dicho de otra forma

▶ **Transforma** estas oraciones con una expresión equivalente.

Modelo Mi hermana hace sudokus para **no aburrirse**.
→ *Mi hermana hace sudokus para pasar el rato.*

1. Cuando estuvimos en la discoteca, **nos divertimos mucho**.
2. La película no me gustó nada. **Me pareció muy aburrida**.
3. La sala de conferencias **estaba llena de gente**.
4. La obra de teatro **ha recibido muy buenas críticas**.
5. El espectáculo de danza **continuará** un mes más.

Differentiated Instruction

DEVELOPING LEARNERS

- To give students practice with some of the review vocabulary on page 189, ask them to interview a partner and ask: *¿Qué haces para pasar el rato o para matar el tiempo?* Encourage students to qualify their answers with an expression that indicates how often they do these activities (e.g., *cada mañana, todos los meses, de vez en cuando*). Then, ask partners to switch roles. Finally, ask students to get together with another pair and compare the results to see what they might have in common.

EXPANDING LEARNERS

- Give students more practice with the expressions in the *Expresiones útiles* section by having them explain, in writing, in which activities *lo pasan en grande* and which ones *los aburren como una ostra*. Explain that they should include at least three or four activities for each category. Then have students explain what makes each of these activities so enjoyable while others bore them. Call on students to read aloud some of the activities they listed along with the reasons they find them fun or boring.

RECUERDA

Ocio y espectáculos

el cine	el público
el concierto	la taquilla
la exposición	
el teatro	

la película cómica
la película de acción
la película de terror
la película policíaca
la película romántica

coleccionar monedas/sellos
jugar al ajedrez
montar a caballo
tocar la guitarra

Los viajes

la agencia de viajes
el andén
el boleto sencillo/de ida y vuelta
el equipaje
el mostrador del aeropuerto
los pasajeros
la tarjeta de embarque
el vuelo procedente de.../con destino a

El coche

arrancar	el cinturón de seguridad
estacionar	la ventanilla
manejar	el volante

---

5 **¿Cuánto sabes?**

 ▶ **Habla** con tu compañero(a). Describan dónde están las personas de las fotografías, qué están haciendo y qué va a pasar después.

① ②

▶ **Elige** una de las fotos y escribe un diálogo entre los personajes.

6 **Cuéntame más**

▶ **Responde** a estas preguntas.

1. ¿Alguna vez has ido al teatro? ¿Qué viste la última vez que fuiste?
2. ¿Cuál fue la última película que viste en el cine? ¿Qué tipo de película era?
3. ¿Adónde viajaste por última vez? ¿Cómo fuiste? ¿Con quién?

▶ **Lee** las respuestas de tu compañero(a) y escribe varias preguntas para saber más cosas sobre sus experiencias. Después, intercámbienselas y respondan por escrito.

ciento ochenta y nueve 189

HERITAGE LANGUAGE LEARNERS

• Ask students to think of other expressions that are used *para decir cómo se lo han pasado* and *para hablar de un espectáculo*. You might suggest the following: *lo hemos pasado bomba* (Spain), *estar padre/padrísimo* (Mexico); *el cine estaba de bote en bote/abarrotado/atestado*. Encourage students to use prior knowledge, research expressions in a dictionary, or ask family members for help. Then have students share these expressions with the rest of the class. Encourage all students to add these expressions to their notebooks.

TOTAL PHYSICAL RESPONSE (TPR)

• Divide the class into teams and explain that they are going to play a game of "Charades" with the activities listed on page 189 as well as any others they know (e.g., *nadar, bailar, patinar*). Write these activities on strips of paper and distribute one to each student. Set a time limit for each team member to pantomime the activity for his or her team. Award one point for each correct answer. If there is a tie, have the winning teams play against each other to see which one is the class champion.

■ Give students a few moments to read the *Recuerda* box silently. Then put them in pairs to take turns at guessing words by asking yes/no questions. To get pairs started, model how to guess the word *cine* by using the following questions: *¿Es una palabra relacionada con el ocio? ¿Es un lugar? ¿Se presentan películas? ¿Es el cine?*

■ Have pairs of students form small groups with another pair. Using some of the information generated by the guessing game, have pairs create word webs in which they categorize the words in the *Recuerda* box as well as other related words they know. For example: *Ocio y espectáculos: Lugares → auditorio, cine, estadio, teatro...*

Activities

3. Have students share their answers with a partner. For fluency practice, have partners read the mini-conversation aloud. Monitor for correct pronunciation, intonation, and stress.

5. If time allows, have students share the dialogue they created for the second part of this activity in small groups. Then have groups choose one of the dialogues to role-play. Allow for rehearsal time, and then invite groups to act out their dialogues for the class.

Answer Key

3.
1. ostra	5. bandera
2. grande	6. éxito
3. matar	7. prorroguen
4. rato	8. sesión

4.
1. ... lo pasamos en grande.
2. Me aburrí como una ostra.
3. ... estaba hasta la bandera.
4. ... ha sido un éxito.
5. ... se prorrogará un mes más.

5. Answers will vary.
▶ Answers will vary.

6. Answers will vary.
▶ Answers will vary.

Additional Resources

Fans Online activities
Practice Workbook

DESAFÍO 1

Expresar probabilidad (I)

Presentation

- In *Desafío 1*, Asha and Lucas have to sing a traditional Cuban ballad at their school's music festival. Students will preview language used to talk about entertainment and to express probability.

Activities	Standards	Resources
Texto	1.2, 2.1, 2.2	
7.	1.2, 1.3, 3.1	
8.	1.1, 1.2	
9.	1.1, 1.2, 1.3, 2.1, 2.2, 3.2	Audio
10. Cultura	1.1, 1.2, 2.1, 2.2, 3.2, 5.1, 5.2	

Teaching Suggestions

Warm-Up / Independent Starter

- Ask students to jot down what they know about the music from the Antilles.

Preparation

- Invite students to share their Independent Starters. As a class, discuss some of the musical genres from this region, such as son, merengue, salsa, and, most recently, reggaeton. Then ask for a volunteer to read the introduction to the dialogue.

Texto: Una trova auténtica

- Have students read the dialogue silently. Ask them to pay attention to how sure or unsure Asha and Lucas sound.

- Ask students whether or not they think Asha and Lucas are well suited for this *desafío*. Have them justify their answers using the dialogue.

Activities

8. In small groups, ask students to discuss ways in which Asha could help Lucas overcome his shyness and hesitation about singing in public. Encourage students to draw from their own experiences or from those of people they know.

9. Before playing the recording, have students use the dialogue and what they know about Cuban music to predict the answers.

190

Una trova auténtica

La escuela de Lucas y Asha celebra un festival internacional de música y ellos tienen que interpretar una trova. Tendrán que elegir un tema original de un compositor cubano, aprendérselo y actuar ante sus compañeros. ¿Lo harán bien?

LUCAS: ¿Realmente tenemos que cantar en el escenario delante de todos? ¿No te da vergüenza?

ASHA: Qué va, a mí me encanta actuar. De niña, mis amigas y yo solíamos entretenernos dando conciertos en casa para nuestros padres. Seguro que lo hacemos genial.

LUCAS: Pues a mí me da pánico cantar en público. ¿Y si yo me encargo del escenario? Tiene que parecer una auténtica casa de trova cubana.

ASHA: ¡Qué buena idea! Pero no estarás pensando en dejarme actuar sola, ¿no? ¿Por qué no cantamos juntos al menos el estribillo?

LUCAS: De acuerdo.

ASHA: Y a cambio tienes que ocuparte de elegir un tema sencillo de algún compositor famoso.

LUCAS: Trato hecho. Tú tocas la guitarra, ¿verdad?

ASHA: Sí... ¿Por qué?

LUCAS: Pues porque normalmente la trova se canta acompañada de guitarra.

ASHA: Ah, pues yo toco bastante bien.

LUCAS: Ya estoy más animado. Tal vez al final el público nos aplauda...

ASHA: ¡Pues claro, hombre! Oye, ¿y cómo son las trovas: tristes, alegres...?

LUCAS: Creo que muchas tratan temas sociales, pero es probable que también haya canciones de amor y otros sentimientos.

7 Detective de palabras

▶ **Completa** estas oraciones.

| hacer |
| encargarse |
| aplaudir |
| haber |

1. Seguro que Asha y Lucas lo _____ genial.
2. A lo mejor Lucas _____ del escenario.
3. Tal vez al final el público los _____.
4. Es probable que también _____ canciones de amor.

▶ **Compara** los verbos de esas oraciones. ¿En qué modos están conjugados? ¿Por qué?

190 ciento noventa

Differentiated Instruction

DEVELOPING LEARNERS

- Read the following false statements to students and ask them to make them true:
  1. *A Lucas le encanta actuar. (a Asha)*
  2. *Asha y sus amiguitas se entretenían bailando. (dando conciertos)*
  3. *Lucas se encargará de tocar la guitarra. (del escenario)*
  4. *Asha va a elegir el tema de la trova. (Lucas lo va a elegir.)*
  5. *La trova generalmente va acompañada de piano. (de guitarra)*
  6. *Lucas cree que muchas trovas tratan temas históricos. (temas sociales)*

EXPANDING LEARNERS

- Ask students to imagine that they are reporters from their school or local newspaper. Their assignment will be to conduct an interview with Asha and Lucas in order to gain insight into how the pair feels about their *desafío* and how well they will be able to execute it. Students will need to work in groups of three: two will be the participants and one will be the reporter. Give students time to organize their questions and answers and to rehearse their lines. Call on volunteers to conduct their interviews.

8 **¿Comprendes?**

▶ **Responde** a estas preguntas.

1. ¿Qué tienen que hacer Asha y Lucas?
2. ¿De qué se va a encargar Lucas? ¿Y Asha?
3. ¿Qué van a hacer los dos juntos?

▶ **Decide.** ¿Qué problema tiene Lucas con el desafío?

a. Que le da vergüenza cantar delante de sus compañeros(as).
b. Que no sabe tocar ningún instrumento.
c. Que piensa que al público no le va a gustar su actuación.

9 **La música cubana**

 ▶ **Escucha** y responde a estas preguntas.

1. ¿Qué tres influencias en la música cubana menciona Lucas?
2. ¿Qué géneros musicales cubanos conocen Asha y Lucas?

 ▶ **Escucha** de nuevo y escribe tres oraciones ciertas o falsas sobre la información que se da en esta conversación. Después, intercámbienlas y resuélvanlas.

Modelo *La flauta es un instrumento principal en la música cubana.*

 ▶ **Dibuja** con dos compañeros(as) una cubierta para un disco de música típica cubana. Después, expliquen a la clase qué elementos han incluido y por qué.

CULTURA

La trova y la nueva trova

La trova es un género musical originado en Francia en la Edad Media y está considerado como una de las raíces de la música cubana. En Cuba la popularizaron los trovadores en el siglo XIX, unos músicos que se ganaban la vida cantando y tocando la guitarra por los bares y las calles de Santiago de Cuba.

Actuación en una casa de trova (Cuba).

La trova se hizo famosa en todo el mundo en los años sesenta del siglo XX, después de la Revolución cubana, cuando nació la nueva trova, un estilo musical renovado en el que los compositores tratan temas sociales y políticos.

10 **Piensa y habla.** ¿Qué te parece que se traten temas sociales o políticos en la música? ¿Conoces algún grupo o algún compositor que lo haga? ¿Te gusta? ¿Por qué?

HERITAGE LANGUAGE LEARNERS

- Ask students to imagine that they are going to work with Lucas in order to carry out this *desafío.* You might suggest that first students work with a partner or in a small group in order to analyze why people are often confronted by stage fright and brainstorm ways of overcoming it. Then ask students to work independently and think of ways to encourage Lucas to overcome his fear of performing in public, and to incorporate these suggestions in a dialogue with Lucas or in a letter to him.

MULTIPLE INTELLIGENCES:
Interpersonal Intelligence

- Have student pairs identify a social or political topic that is of interest to them. After partners define the topic, ask them to think about how they would take their message to the public. Once they have agreed upon the medium (e.g., essay, letter to the editor, demonstration, interview, protest song), pairs will describe their topic to the rest of the class, and in the medium they have selected. Students should be prepared to defend the effectiveness of their chosen medium.

 Unit 4
DESAFÍO 1
Expresar probabilidad (I)

 AUDIO SCRIPT
See page 183K.

CULTURA

La trova y la nueva trova

Trova is a form of lyrical song. At the end of the 19th century and beginning of the 20th century, the first Cuban *trovadores* wandered through the streets of Santiago de Cuba singing love songs. In the late 1960s, a group of young Cuban musicians resurrected this genre. But, as a consequence of the political and social environment of that time, these new Cuban *trovadores* dealt with social and political themes, rather than love and romanticism.

Answer Key

7. 1. hacen/harán   3. aplauda
    2. se encarga   4. haya

▶ Algunos están en indicativo (hacen/harán, se encarga) y otros en subjuntivo (aplauda, haya), según el grado de probabilidad de que algo suceda.

8. 1. Van a interpretar una trova.
    2. Lucas se encarga del escenario y de elegir la canción. Asha va a tocar la guitarra y a cantar.
    3. Van a cantar el estribillo.
▶ a

9. 1. Española, africana y del *jazz.*
    2. La trova, la salsa, el son y el bolero.
▶ Answers will vary.
▶ Answers will vary.

10. Answers will vary.

Additional Resources

Fans Online activities

191

DESAFÍO 1

Vocabulario – Ocio y espectáculos

Presentation

- In this section, students will learn vocabulary related to leisure activities, sports, and entertainment.

Activities	Standards	Resources
Vocabulario	1.2	
11.	1.2	
12.	1.1, 5.1	
13.	1.1, 1.2	Audio
14. Cultura	1.2, 1.3, 2.1, 2.2, 3.2, 4.2, 5.2	

Teaching Suggestions

Warm-Up / Independent Starter

- Ask students to write their answers to the following question: *¿Qué actividades sueles realizar en tu tiempo libre?*

Preparation

- Call on two volunteers to read the dialogue between Asha and Lucas aloud. Then have students repeat the highlighted words after you. Check comprehension with these or similar questions: *¿Qué tipo de música le gusta a Asha? ¿Quién era Louis Armstrong? ¿Qué parte de las canciones cantaba la gente?*

- Review students' answers to the question in the Independent Starter as a class. Then have pairs go over the *Deportes y tiempo libre* section. Ask them to come up with two places they associate with each sport (e.g., *escalar → la montaña, las rocas*). Finally, have students go over the *Más vocabulario* individually and complete activity 11.

Activities

12. After finishing this activity, discuss with students some of the class's similarities and differences. Then, based on the results of this survey, ask students to come up with three words to describe the class. Invite students to share their words and justify their choices.

13. Remind students that the subjunctive mood is used in the dependent clause when making a recommendation—following verbs such as *recomendar, sugerir, aconsejar,* and *proponer*.

Vocabulario

Ocio y espectáculos

ASHA: Ayer fui a un concierto de música clásica. La orquesta tocó fenomenal. Y también actuaba un coro con unas voces increíbles. Fue todo un éxito.

LUCAS: ¡Qué casualidad! Yo también fui a un concierto, pero de una banda de jazz. Interpretaron algunas piezas musicales muy famosas del compositor Louis Armstrong.

ASHA: ¿La gente se sabía las canciones?

LUCAS: Toda la letra no, pero la gente sí cantaba los estribillos. ¡Incluso yo me animé!

Deportes y tiempo libre

escalar

practicar artes marciales

patinar sobre hielo

navegar

pescar

bucear

Más vocabulario

Juegos de mesa

la partida: conjunto de jugadas que se realizan hasta que alguien gana un juego.

hacer trampas: engañar, no seguir las reglas del juego.

tener mal perder: enfadarse cuando no se gana un juego.

la casilla	*square*	la ficha	*chip, token*
el dado	*die (dice)*	el tablero	*board*

¡Atención!

el éxito	*success*	la salida	*exit*

11 ¿Jugamos una partida?

▶ **Une** las dos columnas.

Ⓐ

1. jugar
2. avanzar
3. tirar
4. hacer
5. mover

Ⓑ

a. una ficha
b. una partida
c. trampas
d. una casilla
e. los dados

192 ciento noventa y dos

Differentiated Instruction

DEVELOPING LEARNERS

- Have students match words from both columns.

1. *navegar* (g)
2. *estribillo* (f)
3. *letra* (d)
4. *patinar sobre hielo* (b)
5. *escalar* (h)
6. *pescar* (e)
7. *ficha* (c)
8. *coro* (i)
9. *actuar* (a)

a. *interpretar*
b. *deporte de invierno*
c. *pieza de juego*
d. *palabras de una canción*
e. *cazar peces*
f. *se repite*
g. *ir en barco*
h. *subir*
i. *voces*

EXPANDING LEARNERS

- Ask students to choose the correct word to complete the following sentences:

1. *¿Conoces la … de esta canción?* (a)
   a. *letra*   b. *casilla*
2. *No me gusta jugar con Dan porque…* (b)
   a. *tiene partidas*   b. *tiene mal perder*
3. *Esa cantante siempre … bien.* (a)
   a. *actúa*   b. *hace trampas*
4. *El público cantó los…* (b)
   a. *dados*   b. *estribillos*
5. *Hay que adelantar las … por las…* (a)
   a. *fichas/casillas*   b. *casillas/fichas*

12 Las preferencias de la clase

▶ **Escribe** cinco preguntas para conocer las preferencias de ocio de tus compañeros(as). Puedes basarte en esta información.

Modelo *¿A ustedes cuál es el tipo de música que más les gusta?*

– Tipo de música preferido: *rock, pop, clásica, jazz...*

– Deportes que practican: jugar al baloncesto, practicar artes marciales...

– Juegos y pasatiempos: crucigramas, naipes, ajedrez...

– Actividades al aire libre: pescar, navegar, patinar sobre hielo...

– Otras actividades: conciertos, teatro, cine...

▶ **Haz** preguntas a tus compañeros(as) y responde a las suyas. ¿Con quién tienes más afinidades?

13 ¿Cómo se van a entretener?

▶ **Escucha** y escribe. ¿Qué actividades se ofrecen en el crucero?

▶ **Escucha** de nuevo y escribe una recomendación para estas personas.

Modelo La señora Rodrigo quiere entretenerse después de la cena.
→ *Le recomiendo que vaya al concierto de jazz de esta noche.*

1. Estela quiere explorar la ciudad, pero por la tarde quiere divertirse con sus amigas.
2. Lolita y Timo no quieren salir hoy del barco.
3. Miguel quiere ver los peces tropicales.
4. Mi hermana y yo queremos hacer alguna actividad física.

CULTURA
Los juegos tradicionales

En todos los países del mundo hay juegos y juguetes tradicionales, algunos de ellos autóctonos. La zaranda, por ejemplo, es originaria del suroeste de Venezuela y de los llanos de Colombia. Es un juguete que se fabrica a partir del fruto de la calabaza. El juego consiste en hacerla girar. Históricamente se jugaba en Semana Santa, aunque ahora se hace en cualquier época del año. Hoy en día se organizan festivales para contribuir a preservar los valores culturales indígenas, como el Festival del Trompo y la Zaranda.

14 Compara. ¿Qué juegos y juguetes tradicionales de tu cultura o de otras culturas conoces? ¿Todavía se mantienen? ¿Crees que se mantendrán? ¿Por qué?

ciento noventa y tres 193

Vocabulario – Ocio y espectáculos

AUDIO SCRIPT
See page 183K.

CULTURA
Los juegos tradicionales

In Mexico, people enjoy playing *Lotería*—a board game similar to bingo. However, instead of letters and numbers, it uses cards representing popular Mexican figures (e.g., *la calavera, el alacrán, el nopal*). The caller selects a card and creates a rhyme or a riddle alluding to the image on the card (e.g., the blanket for the poor → *el sol*). The players must guess the figure and, if they have it, mark it on their game board. As with bingo, the first player to complete a predetermined pattern shouts *¡Lotería!* and receives a prize.

Answer Key

11. 1. b   2. d   3. e   4. c   5. a

12. Answers will vary.
▶ Answers will vary.

13. Answers will vary. Sample answer:
Una excursión de un día por la ciudad, una clase de buceo, una clase de ejercicios aeróbicos, un torneo de juegos de mesa, un concierto de *jazz*.
▶ Answers will vary. Sample answers:
1. Le recomiendo que participe en el torneo de juegos de mesa.
2. Les propongo que vayan a la piscina.
3. Le aconsejo que asista a la clase de buceo.
4. Les sugiero que asistan a la clase de ejercicios aeróbicos.

14. Answers will vary.

Additional Resources

Fans Online activities
Practice Workbook

HERITAGE LANGUAGE LEARNERS

• Allow students to demonstrate their word power by seeing how many related words they can come up with for some of the new vocabulary. Have them write or say these word associations and encourage them to share this vocabulary with the rest of the class. Examples might include the following: *música clásica* → *ópera, concierto, sinfonía, director(a), cantante, soprano, tenor, barítono, músico(a); orquesta* → *instrumentos de cuerda, violín, violonchelo, bajo, instrumentos de viento, flauta, clarinete, trompeta*, etc.

COOPERATIVE LEARNING

• Ask students to work in small groups and assign one of the *Deportes y tiempo libre* activities, including jazz and *música clásica*, to each group. Tell students that they will need to prepare an ad to promote the activity assigned to them. Groups will discuss their assignment and each member of the group will have a specific task to complete; for example, compiling information on the activity, providing visuals, writing a first draft, proofing the final copy, or making an oral presentation to the class.

Unit 4
DESAFÍO 1

Gramática – Expresar frecuencia

Presentation

- In this section, students will review and expand on the use of adverbs and adverbial phrases to express how often something is done.

Activities	Standards	Resources
Gramática	1.2, 3.1	
15.	1.2, 3.1, 4.1	
16.	1.3	
17.	1.2, 1.3	Audio
18.	1.1, 1.3, 5.1	
19. Cultura	1.2, 1.3, 2.1, 2.2, 3.2, 5.2	

Teaching Suggestions

Warm-Up / Independent Starter

- Have students read the first bullet of the grammar presentation silently. Then have them assign an expression of frequency to each of the following activities based on how often they do them:
  - *jugar al ajedrez*   – *escalar*
  - *escuchar* jazz   – *pescar*
  - *ir a un concierto*   – *cantar*

Preparation

- Invite students to share their Independent Starters. Which activity is the most popular? Is there an activity that no one does? Next, ask students to read the second and third grammar bullets. Then, have them rewrite their sentences from the Independent Starter specifying how often they do those activities (e.g., *Canto una vez al mes*). Call on volunteers to share their sentences.

- Go over the rest of the grammar presentation as a class. Then have students answer these questions in writing: *¿Cada cuánto tiempo vas al cine? ¿Cuándo sales con tus amigos? ¿Qué sueles hacer los domingos?* Have students share their answers with a partner.

Activities

16. To extend this activity, have students share their sentences with a partner. Then ask pairs to write a paragraph comparing what both of them used to do as children for three or four more activities.

194

Gramática

Expresar frecuencia

Expresiones de frecuencia

- Recuerda: para expresar la frecuencia con la que hacemos algo, utilizamos adverbios y frases adverbiales como estas:

nunca   casi nunca   a veces   con frecuencia   muchas veces   casi siempre   siempre
        rara vez   a menudo

− ———————————————————————————→ +

- Para expresar de una forma más precisa la frecuencia con la que hacemos algo en un período de tiempo determinado, puedes utilizar estas estructuras:

| número + vez/veces + al/a la + tiempo |
Voy al cine **tres veces al mes.**
Voy al cine **una vez a la semana.**

| cada + número + tiempo |
Tengo clases de guitarra **cada dos días.**

| todos(as) + los(as) + tiempo |
Voy de compras **todos los fines de semana.**

- También puedes expresar frecuencia utilizando adverbios como diariamente *(daily)*, semanalmente *(weekly)*, mensualmente *(monthly)* o anualmente *(yearly)*.

  Charlo con mis amigos **diariamente,** pero salgo con ellos **semanalmente.**

Preguntar sobre la frecuencia de una acción

- Para preguntar por la frecuencia con la que alguien hace algo, usa ¿Con qué frecuencia...?, ¿Cuándo...? o ¿Cada cuánto tiempo...?

  ¿Con qué frecuencia vas al cine?   **¿Cada cuánto tiempo** ves a tus abuelos?

Soler + infinitivo

- Para hablar sobre acciones que desarrollamos habitualmente, usa esta estructura:

| soler *(to be in the habit of)* + infinitivo |
—¿Qué **sueles hacer** los fines de semana?
—**Suelo ir** al cine con mis amigos.

Atención: el verbo soler solo se conjuga en dos tiempos verbales: el presente (suelo, sueles...) y el imperfecto (solía, solías...).

15 **Compara.** Traduce estas oraciones al inglés. ¿Qué diferencias hay en el orden de las palabras entre el español y el inglés?

a. Doy **siempre** un paseo despúes de cenar.   **b.** No he navegado **nunca.**

16 **¿Con qué frecuencia?**

▶ **Escribe.** ¿Con qué frecuencia haces ahora y hacías de niño(a) las siguientes actividades?

Modelo   pescar ⟶ *Ahora pesco a veces, pero de niño no lo hacía nunca.*

1. jugar a juegos de mesa   2. enviar mensajes de texto   3. montar en bici

---

Differentiated Instruction

DEVELOPING LEARNERS

- Ask students to say how often they perform the following activities. Encourage them to use a variety of *expresiones de frecuencia* as well as the verb *soler.*

1. *navegar*
2. *pescar*
3. *escuchar* jazz
4. *escalar*
5. *bucear*
6. *cantar estribillos*
7. *practicar artes marciales*
8. *cantar en un coro*
9. *patinar sobre hielo*
10. *tocar un instrumento*

EXPANDING LEARNERS

- Ask students to imagine that they have a friend with some bad habits. Read the following statements to students and ask them to offer their friend better alternatives, and to justify their suggestions.

1. *Suelo hacer trampas cuando juego.*
2. *Casi nunca me lavo las manos.*
3. *Rara vez hago ejercicio.*
4. *Miento con frecuencia.*
5. *Nunca como verduras.*
6. *Casi siempre llego tarde a clase.*
7. *A menudo no termino las tareas.*

17 La vida de una cantante

▶ **Escucha** la entrevista y elige la opción correcta.

1. Rita presenta un concierto...
   a. semanalmente.   b. diariamente.   c. mensualmente.

2. Ella compone música...
   a. cada día.   b. todas las semanas.   c. una vez al mes.

3. Rita pasa tiempo con su familia...
   a. una vez al mes.   b. semanalmente.   c. cada día.

4. Ella tiene tiempo para jugar con sus hijos...
   a. diariamente.   b. semanalmente.   c. nunca.

5. Los niños de Rita viajan con ella...
   a. con frecuencia.   b. rara vez.   c. casi siempre.

▶ **Escribe** un resumen de la entrevista. Explica lo que hace y no hace Rita Castillo en su vida cotidiana.

18 Nuestros hábitos

▶ **Habla** con tu compañero(a) sobre sus hábitos. ¿Piensas que tiene un estilo de vida activo o sedentario? ¿Tiene unos hábitos y unos horarios regulares o varía mucho en su rutina? Hazle preguntas para averiguarlo.

> después de las clases
> después de cenar
> los viernes por la noche
> los fines de semana
> durante el verano

Modelo
A. *¿Qué sueles hacer por la mañana?*
B. *Suelo ducharme, desayunar y esperar el autobús para venir a la escuela.*

▶ **Compara** tus hábitos con los de tu compañero(a) y presenta tus conclusiones a la clase.

CULTURA

Deportes extremos (Nicaragua)

Escalar volcanes, recorrer la jungla, hacer *rafting* o *kitesurf*, bucear en las islas del Maíz para ver los restos de un galeón hundido o incluso bajar los 726 metros del volcán Cerro Negro en una tabla de *sandboard*; estos deportes, considerados de riesgo por su peligro y dificultad, son deportes extremos y una de las posibilidades de ocio que se pueden encontrar en Nicaragua, gracias a su riqueza geográfica.

Chico practicando *sandboard*.

19 Explica. ¿Te interesan los deportes extremos? ¿Por qué? ¿Cuáles te parecen más interesantes?

Gramática – Expresar frecuencia

18. Tell students to imagine that they are choosing a roommate, and ask them to interview several classmates. Encourage pairs to make compromises. For example:
A. *Veo que casi nunca ayudas en casa.*
B. *Bueno, una vez al mes paso la aspiradora.*
A. *¿Qué te parece si hacemos un horario?*
B. *Sí. ¡Buena idea!*

 AUDIO SCRIPT
See page 183K.

CULTURA

Deportes extremos (Nicaragua)

Some extreme sports have a long history in the Spanish-speaking world. *Andinismo*, or mountaineering in the Andes, caught the world's attention at the end of the 19th century when Edward Whymper climbed Chimborazo (Ecuador) and Edward Fitzgerald climbed Aconcagua (Argentina). Cliff diving at La Quebrada, in Acapulco (Mexico), has been popular since the 1930s. Divers leap from a 125-foot cliff into a narrow ocean cove below.

Answer Key

15. a. I *always* take a walk after dinner.
b. I have *never* gone sailing.
En estos dos casos la expresión de frecuencia va antes del verbo principal, pero en español puede ir detrás.

16. Answers will vary.

17. 1. a   2. c   3. b   4. b   5. b
▶ Answers will vary.

18. Answers will vary.
▶ Answers will vary.

19. Answers will vary.

Additional Resources

Fans Online activities
Practice Workbook

HERITAGE LANGUAGE LEARNERS

- Ask students to take a survey of their classmates' interest and/or participation in sports or hobbies. Have students make a graphic organizer with headings labeled *Nunca, Rara vez, A veces, A menudo,* and *Siempre*. Then, have students ask their classmates to list two sports or hobbies under each of these corresponding headings. When the results are complete, ask students to work with one another to compare and contrast the respondents' interests, and to draw conclusions as to the interest generated and the frequency of their participation.

TOTAL PHYSICAL RESPONSE (TPR)

- Divide the class into two teams and play a game of *¿Con qué frecuencia?* Have a student from one team call out *una expresión de frecuencia*. A student from the opposing team must use that expression along with an activity to make a logical and correct statement. If students are successful, they should stand up; if not, they stay seated. Have teams alternate roles. The first team with all members standing wins. Students may duplicate expressions, but not activities.

DESAFÍO 1

Gramática – Expresar probabilidad (I)

Presentation

- In this section, students will review and practice expressing probability by using certain structures and expressions.

Activities	Standards	Resources
Gramática	1.2, 3.1	
20.	1.2, 3.1, 4.1	
21.	1.2, 1.3	Audio
22.	1.1, 1.2, 2.1, 2.2	

Teaching Suggestions

Warm-Up / Independent Starter

- Ask students to write five sentences about what they are planning to do this weekend. Have them include things they are quite certain they will do as well as things they are not too sure they will be able to do. For example: *Seguro que voy a salir con mis amigos. Quizás vaya de compras. Es posible que lave la ropa.*

Preparation

- Have students read the first two bullets of the grammar presentation silently. Then ask them to review their Independent Starters and correct any mistakes they may have made. Next, invite students to share their sentences with the class. Write some of students' examples on the board and use them to clarify any questions the class might have regarding the use of the subjunctive or the indicative. Explain that for expressions that can be used with either the indicative or the subjunctive, the use of one mood or another can convey subtle differences in meaning, rather than one mood being the "correct" one.

- Ask students to read the last bullet of the grammar presentation in small groups. Explain that *deber de* + infinitive is used idiomatically to express conjecture. It is roughly equivalent to "must" in English, when "must" is not used to express obligation. For example: *Ella no me invitó a su fiesta. Debe de estar enfadada conmigo.* (She did not invite me to her party. She must be angry with me.)

Gramática

Expresar probabilidad (I)

Expresiones de probabilidad

- El español tiene diferentes expresiones para hablar sobre la posibilidad o la probabilidad de que una acción ocurra. Algunas de ellas implican un mayor o menor grado de certeza o de duda por parte del hablante.

  – La mayor parte de las expresiones de probabilidad llevan una cláusula dependiente con un verbo en subjuntivo.

  > Es probable que **llegue/llegara** tarde.
  > Puede que hoy **vayamos** a la playa.

  – Las expresiones *a lo mejor* y *seguro que* requieren un verbo en indicativo.

  > **A lo mejor** podéis/pudisteis/podréis/podríais hablar con él.
  > **Seguro que** el concierto es/era/fue/será/sería espectacular.

EXPRESIONES DE PROBABILIDAD	
Es posible/Es probable	
Es improbable	+ que + subjuntivo
Lo más probable es	
Puede (ser)	
A lo mejor	+ indicativo
Seguro + que	

- También podemos expresar probabilidad con un adverbio como *posiblemente* o *probablemente*. Aunque pueden ir con indicativo, los adverbios de probabilidad suelen ir con subjuntivo en estos casos:

  – Cuando se habla de una acción futura.

  > **Probablemente** vayamos mañana a pescar.

  – Cuando queremos expresar un mayor grado de duda.

  > **Tal vez** Javier esté ahora mismo en la biblioteca.

ADVERBIOS DE PROBABILIDAD	
Posiblemente	
Probablemente	+ indicativo
Seguramente	
Quizá(s)	+ subjuntivo
Tal vez	

- Para expresar probabilidad o conjetura usamos también la estructura *deber de* + *infinitivo*.

| deber de + infinitivo | La actriz **debe/debía de** estar muy feliz con su premio. |

20 **Piensa.** ¿Cómo se expresa la probabilidad en inglés? ¿Hay distintos grados?

21 La nueva amiga de Lucas

 ▶ **Escucha** y decide si estas oraciones son ciertas o falsas. Después, corrige las falsas.

1. Tal vez Wendy vaya a la playa mañana.
2. Es posible que Wendy juegue al fútbol con Lucas este fin de semana.
3. Probablemente Wendy limpie su habitación mañana.
4. Posiblemente los abuelos de Wendy vengan de visita la semana que viene.
5. Es improbable que Lucas vaya a casa de Wendy el fin de semana que viene.

Differentiated Instruction

DEVELOPING LEARNERS

- Ask students to choose the correct verb to complete each statement.

  1. *Es posible que conoces / conozcas la letra de esta trova.* (conozcas)
  2. *Seguro que lo pasas / pases bien en el concierto.* (pasas)
  3. *Debes estar / de estar orgulloso del trabajo que hiciste.* (de estar)
  4. *Tal vez Ana viene / venga, pero lo dudo.* (venga)
  5. *Puede ser que nos mudamos / mudemos a Barcelona.* (mudemos)
  6. *Ustedes deben leer / de leer las preguntas antes de contestar.* (leer)

EXPANDING LEARNERS

- Ask students to use some of the words that express probability mentioned on the page and write five statements of events that are most likely to happen in the next ten years, and five statements of events that are not likely to happen in the same period of time. Then, have students get together with a partner and compare their statements. Have pairs write at least one paragraph comparing and contrasting their predictions. Call on volunteers to read their paragraphs aloud.

22 Las dudas de Lucas

▶ **Lee** el mensaje que Lucas le envía a Asha y elige la opción correcta. Ten en cuenta que en algún caso puede haber dos respuestas posibles.

De: Lucas
Para: Asha
Asunto: El escenario

Hola, Asha. ¿Cómo estás? Te escribo para consultarte algunas dudas sobre nuestra actuación en la escuela. Como sabes, me comprometí a encontrar una trova original de un compositor cubano. Aún no me he decidido, pero tranquila, porque tengo varias opciones. Probablemente ___1___ un tema romántico porque creo que a nuestros compañeros les
<elijo/elija>
gustará mucho.

Lo que tengo menos claro es cómo decorar el escenario. Primero pensé llenarlo de fotos de intérpretes de trovas, pero puede que no ___2___ suficientes imágenes. Y, sobre todo,
<consigo/consiga>
seguro que no se ___3___ desde las últimas filas. Por eso pensé en poner algo más grande
<ven/vean>
y vistoso. ¿Qué te parece si les pedimos a tus compañeros que nos dibujen un mural con colores vivos? Tal vez ___4___ ayudarnos y quedaría muy bien.
<quieren/quieran>

Ah, también quería pedirte permiso para comprar la ropa que nos pondremos. ¡No vamos a salir con una camiseta y unos *jeans*, evidentemente!

Lo más probable es que ___5___ unas camisas
<compro/compre>
y unos pantalones blancos, y a lo mejor ___6___
<busco/busque>
algún complemento bonito. Yo puedo llevar un sombrero de yarey y tú unas flores en el pelo, por ejemplo.

¿Qué opinas? Espero tu respuesta. Un beso.

Lucas

 ▶ **Habla** con dos compañeros(as).

1. ¿Qué tipo de ropa creen que van a llevar finalmente Asha y Lucas en su actuación?
2. ¿Qué instrumentos utilizarán para acompañar mejor la trova?
3. ¿Cómo puede decorar Lucas el escenario?

Modelo
A. *Probablemente usen una guitarra porque es el instrumento típico de la trova.*
B. *Estoy de acuerdo.* Y *tal vez Lucas acompañe a Asha con unas maracas.*
   No es muy difícil.

ciento noventa y siete 197

Activities

21. Before playing the audio, have students draw a two-column chart with these headings: Wendy, Lucas. Then, ask them to add three rows to the chart and these headings: *Mañana, Este fin de semana, El fin de semana que viene*. As students listen to the recording, have them fill in the corresponding cells with the activities Wendy and Lucas are planning to do.

22. For the second part of this activity, encourage students to go online and research the typical dress and instruments of Cuban *trovadores*. This information will help them decide the answers to the questions. Call on volunteers to share their ideas with the class.

 AUDIO SCRIPT
See page 183K.

Answer Key

20. Se puede expresar con palabras como *could, may, maybe, might, must, possibly, probably, unlikely*. Estas palabras expresan distintos grados de probabilidad: *He must be late. He's probably/possibly late. He might/may be late. He could be late. It is unlikely that he is late.*

21. 1. F. Es posible que ayude a sus padres con la nueva casa.
2. C.
3. F. Posiblemente estudie.
4. F. Es seguro que los abuelos los visitarán.
5. F. Seguramente Lucas irá.

22. 1. elijo/elija   4. quieren/quieran
2. consiga   5. compre
3. ven   6. busco
▶ Answers will vary.

HERITAGE LANGUAGE LEARNERS

• Ask students to imagine that they are Asha and write a reply to Lucas's letter. They should answer all the comments, questions, and suggestions that Lucas is making. Encourage creativity; Asha might respond positively to her partner, or she might not agree with any of Lucas's suggestions and offer some new ideas in her reply. Suggest that students research some information on how *trovas* are presented to the public and on the musicians' typical attire in order to give Asha's comments more credibility.

SPECIAL-NEEDS LEARNERS

• Allow students with some minor hearing impairment to read the script of activity 21 as they listen to the recording. You may want to do this with all activities that have an audio portion. You may also want to ask heritage language learners to role-play the conversation as the special-needs learners listen. Encourage those students who are re-enacting the dialogue to make good use of body language in order to communicate more effectively.

Additional Resources

Fans Online activities
Practice Workbook

197

Unit 4

LECTURA: TEXTO DIALOGADO

Presentation

- In this section, students will read a dialogue about a *trova* song, answer comprehension questions, and create their own verses for a *trova*.

Activities	Standards	Resources
Lectura: texto dialogado	1.1, 1.2, 2.1, 2.2, 3.2	
23.	1.2, 2.1, 2.2	
24.	1.2, 1.3, 3.1	
25.	1.1, 1.3, 2.1, 2.2, 3.2, 5.2	

Teaching Suggestions

Warm-Up / Independent Starter

- Have students answer the first question in the *Antes de leer* section.

Preparation

- Call on several volunteers to share their Independent Starters. You may want to write some of the information they mention on the board (e.g., *país → Cuba*; *influencias → ritmos europeos y africanos*; *dos tipos de trova → trova tradicional y nueva trova*; *instrumento principal → la guitarra*). Have students copy this information and, as they read the dialogue and complete the activities on these pages, ask them to add information about the *trova* genre to their notes.

- As a class, answer questions #2 and #3 from the *Antes de leer*. Discuss with students some of the characteristics of love songs. Ask students for examples of love songs they know. What makes a love song live on through time? You may want to play the song *Veinte años* as interpreted by María Teresa Vega and Rafael Zequeira (you will find it online). The rhythm is slow and students should be able to understand the lyrics. Explain that María Teresa Vega was one of the most famous examples of the *vieja trova cubana* movement during the first half of the 20th century.

- Read the dialogue aloud to students, modeling correct pronunciation and intonation. Then call on several pairs of students to alternate reading aloud. Offer suggestions to improve their oral reading.

198

Antes de leer: estrategias

1. Lee el título del texto. ¿Qué sabes ya sobre la trova? Anótalo.
2. Busca la canción en el texto. ¿Qué tema trata?
3. Localiza el título de la canción y escríbelo.

Una canción preciosa

Lucas: Asha, he estado investigando sobre la trova cubana. Resulta que hay una trova tradicional, más antigua, y una nueva trova, la de los años sesenta y setenta del siglo XX.

Asha: ¡Ah! ¿Y cuál has elegido?

Lucas: He estado escuchando varias canciones y finalmente he encontrado una trova tradicional que me ha gustado mucho. Se titula *Veinte años* y la compuso María Teresa Vera en 1935.

Asha: ¡En 1935! ¡Qué antigua!

Lucas: Ya, pero desde entonces la han interpretado muchos artistas. ¿Quieres escucharla?

Asha: Claro.

Lucas: *Qué te importa que te ame,*
si tú no me quieres ya.
El amor que ya ha pasado
no se debe recordar.
Fui la ilusión de tu vida
un día lejano ya.
Hoy represento el pasado,
no me puedo conformar[1].

Asha: ¡Es preciosa! Me encantan la letra y la música.

Lucas: ¿Te atreverás a cantarla?

Asha: Tendré que ensayar mucho, pero lo conseguiré. Oye, ¡tú prometiste acompañarme en el estribillo! ¡Que no se te olvide!

Lucas: Sí, aunque me da mucha vergüenza cantar en público, ya lo sabes.

Asha: Tranquilo. Seguro que la canción les va a encantar a todos.

1. to resign myself

198 ciento noventa y ocho

Differentiated Instruction

DEVELOPING LEARNERS

- Ask students to correct the following false statements:
  1. *Lucas eligió una trova moderna.* (una tradicional)
  2. *Asha no quiere escucharla.* (sí quiere)
  3. *La trova elegida trata un tema social.* (un tema romántico)
  4. *A Asha no le gusta la trova.* (le encanta)
  5. *Asha no cree que haga falta ensayar.* (Cree que tendrá que ensayar mucho.)
  6. *Asha le pide a Lucas que la acompañe con el piano.* (en el estribillo)

EXPANDING LEARNERS

- Ask students to reread the lyrics to the *trova* on the page. Then, ask them to identify the line or lines that could be the refrain, or chorus, to *Veinte años*. Have students write at least one paragraph in which they first identify these lines and then explain why the words would be an appropriate chorus. Explain to students that they may also opt for writing new lines that would be a suitable chorus for this song, and justify their suggestions.

23 ¿Comprendes?

▶ **Responde** a estas preguntas.

1. ¿A qué tipo de trova corresponde la canción elegida por Lucas?
2. ¿Qué relación crees que hay entre el título de la canción y su letra?
3. ¿Qué le pasa al protagonista de la canción?
4. ¿Quién se muestra más seguro del éxito de la tarea, Asha o Lucas? ¿Por qué? ¿En qué palabras del texto se refleja esa actitud?

24 Palabras relacionadas

▶ **Completa** una tabla como esta a partir de los verbos que aparecen en el texto que has leído.

ACCIÓN (verbo)	CONCEPTO (nombre)	PERSONA (nombre)
cantar	canción	cantante
investigar		
		compositor
interpretar		

▶ **Escribe** un párrafo que contenga, al menos, cinco de las palabras anteriores.

Modelo

> A mí me encanta escuchar música, pero no suelo cantar porque no tengo buena voz. Mis cantantes y grupos preferidos son...

25 Con tus propias palabras

▶ **Completa** esta estrofa de la canción inventándote los versos que faltan.

▶ **Comparte** tu versión con tus compañeros(as). ¿Cuál les gusta más?

▶ **Busca** otra canción de la trova cubana tradicional o de la nueva trova. Escúchala y apréndete la letra. Si quieres, puedes cantársela a tus compañeros(as).

> ### VEINTE AÑOS
>
> Qué te importa que te ame,
> _____.
>
> El amor que ya ha pasado
> _____.
>
> Fui la ilusión de tu vida
> _____.
>
> Hoy represento el pasado,
> _____.

ciento noventa y nueve 199

Activities

23. Call on volunteers to share their answers with the class. Then, have students work with a partner to elaborate on question #3. Ask pairs to come up with a possible love story that gave rise to the song. You may wish to play the song again or have students look for the complete lyrics on the Internet. Have pairs write a two-paragraph "reconstruction" of what they think happened.

25. For the third part of this activity, you may want to suggest these songs and artists: *Cuando ya no me quieras* by Trío Matamoros, *Lágrimas negras* by Vieja Trova Santiaguera, and *El soldado* by María Teresa Vega.

Answer Key

23. Answers will vary. Sample answers:
1. A la trova tradicional.
2. Probablemente se trate de una pareja que lleva veinte años juntos, pero que ya ha perdido el amor.
3. Que aún está enamorado, pero su pareja ya no lo quiere.
4. Asha se muestra más segura pues cree que la canción le gustará al público. Así se lo dice a Lucas: «Seguro que la canción les va a encantar a todos».

24. Acción: componer.
Concepto: investigación, composición, interpretación.
Persona: investigador, intérprete.
▶ Answers will vary.

25. Answers will vary.
▶ Answers will vary.
▶ Answers will vary.

Additional Resources

Fans Online activities

HERITAGE LANGUAGE LEARNERS

• Explain to students that they are going to compose an original *trova*—one with a strong social message. Ask them to identify the song's theme and then give them time to write the lyrics. Students may read their lyrics to the class or, if they are musically inclined, they might sing the melody or accompany themselves, or have someone else in the class accompany them on a musical instrument. Encourage a classroom discussion on the effectiveness of the message through music.

CRITICAL THINKING

• In the dialogue, Lucas mentions that the *trova Veinte años* was composed in 1935. Point out that it is still sung and popular today. Ask students to think about the characteristics of songs that have been around for decades and why they continue to be popular. What elements contribute to their timelessness? Then, enable a classroom discussion on the long and popular life of certain songs. Encourage students to predict which songs that are popular today might still be enjoyed fifty years from now, and why.

199

DESAFÍO 1

Comunicación

Presentation

- In this section, students will integrate the vocabulary and grammar skills from *Desafío 1* in order to read and talk about an iconic place in the history of the *trova* music, make conjectures, and use different expressions to talk about the probability of an action taking place.

Activities	Standards	Resources
26.	1.1, 1.2, 1.3, 2.1, 2.2, 3.1, 3.2	
27.	1.1, 1.3	
28. Final del desafío	1.1, 1.2, 1.3, 5.1, 5.2	

Teaching Suggestions

Warm-Up / Independent Starter

- Ask students to read the headline and the lead sentence of the article in activity 26 and predict the content. Have students identify all of the cognates as well as other words they recognize. What type of place is being described?

Preparation

- Call on students to share their Independent Starters with the class. If possible, show the class some videos of *trova* musicians (you will find them online; search under *trova tradicional cubana*). Some songs students might enjoy include *La tarde* by Sindo Garay, *Mi última serenata* by Los Compadres, *Lágrimas negras* by Vieja Trova Santiaguera, and *Huellas del pasado* by Compay Segundo. Alternatively, you may want to play excerpts from the documentary *Buena Vista Social Club*. In this documentary, *trova* musicians—some in their eighties and nineties—are interviewed, and live performances in New York and Amsterdam are shown.
- If time permits, discuss with students their opinions about this music and how it might have influenced modern Latin music. For example:
  - *Seguro que la trova dio origen al bolero.*
  - *Es posible que la trova influenciara los ritmos caribeños modernos.*

Comunicación

26 **La Casa de la Trova**

▶ **Lee** el texto y escribe un breve resumen del origen de la Casa de la Trova Pepe Sánchez.

Casa de la Trova de Santiago de Cuba: santuario de la música cubana

Casa de la Trova Pepe Sánchez.

Hablar de la música cubana y Santiago de Cuba sin mencionar la Casa de la Trova Pepe Sánchez es imposible. Ese pequeño inmueble de la calle Heredia entre San Félix y San Pedro recoge entre sus paredes más historia de nuestra cultura que muchos otros espacios de mayor rango y renombre.

Su creador fue Virgilio Palais, allá por la década del 50 del siglo XX. Virgilio era torcedor de tabaco e intentaba mejorar su situación económica por distintas vías, pero eran años difíciles. Y para «matar el aburrimiento» se ponía a cantar *a capella*, cosa que al parecer no hacía mal con su voz de tenor. Amigos y trovadores se reunían en el lugar a acompañarlo. La presencia del trovador Ángel Almenares con su guitarra le dio sin duda un realce especial a esos encuentros.

Pronto el local, frecuentado por los choferes del Hotel Casa Granda que se encuentra al frente, comenzó a ser visitado por los amantes de la trova y la buena música, y se fue convirtiendo en un lugar habitual para el pueblo santiaguero.

Fuente: http://cubaensolfa.wordpress.com (selección)

▶ **Define** estos términos del texto con tus propias palabras.

1. inmueble   2. renombre   3. *a capella*   4. realce   5. frecuentado

 ▶ **Investiga.** ¿Continúa existiendo la Casa de la Trova Pepe Sánchez? ¿Qué actividades realiza? Comparte tus investigaciones con tu compañero(a).

Differentiated Instruction

DEVELOPING LEARNERS

- Have students complete a chart like the one below. These words should be filled in: *mencionar, creador, intentar, mejorar, aburrimiento, reunir,* and *frecuentado.*

Verbos	Nombres	Adjetivos
mencionar	(mención)	(mencionado)
(crear)	creador	(creado)
intentar	(intención)	(intentado)
mejorar	(mejora)	(mejorado)
(aburrir)	aburrimiento	(aburrido)
reunir	(reunión)	(reunido)
(frecuentar)	(frecuencia)	frecuentado

EXPANDING LEARNERS

- Ask students to imagine that they are the music critics for their local newspaper. They have just attended their first *trova* concert and need to write a review. Have students write several paragraphs for their article. Students will need to give some background information on the *trova*, a description of the pieces played, as well as some brief information on the performers. Students must also include their personal reaction to the performance. Call on volunteers to read their reviews aloud.

27 **Un momento de tensión**

▶ **Imagina** por qué Asha y Lucas salieron tarde al escenario. Escribe varias oraciones usando expresiones de probabilidad.

 ▶ **Habla** con dos compañeros(as) y compartan sus oraciones. ¿Qué explicación les parece más razonable?

Modelo

A. Es posible que Lucas se pusiera nervioso y no quisiera salir al escenario.

B. Pues yo pienso que quizás hubo un problema técnico, porque Lucas es muy responsable y nunca haría eso.

Final del desafío

ASHA: ¡Qué bien ha salido nuestra actuación!

LUCAS: ¡Sí, nos han aplaudido mucho!

ASHA: Oye, siento muchísimo que se me olvidara la guitarra en casa. ¿Crees que al público le molestó que saliéramos un poco tarde a actuar?

LUCAS: ¡Qué va! Seguro que ___1___ que yo estaba nervioso y no quería salir al escenario...

ASHA: Lo has hecho muy bien. Debes de ___2___ orgulloso, ¿no?

LUCAS: Sí, y tú también. ¿Sabes? Nunca pensé que ___3___ posible que yo cantara en público. ¡Todavía no me lo creo!

ASHA: Quizás este desafío te ___4___ a participar en más espectáculos.

LUCAS: No sé, no sé. Aunque tengo que reconocer que he aprendido mucho y que me ha dado más confianza en mí mismo. Muchas gracias por tu ayuda, Asha.

ASHA: No hay de qué. Ahora debemos ___5___ el éxito, ¿no te parece?

28 **Un gran éxito**

▶ **Completa** el diálogo con la forma correcta de estos verbos.

ser	celebrar	pensar	animar	estar

 ▶ **Habla** con tu compañero(a) sobre el final del desafío. ¿Debe estar orgulloso Lucas? ¿Alguna vez has vivido como Lucas una situación en la que no tenías confianza en ti mismo(a) pero al final todo salió bien?

doscientos uno 201

Activities

27. Once students have finished this activity, ask each small group to choose the most plausible explanation. Then have groups come up with the script for a dialogue defending their explanation. Finally, have groups role-play their conversations for the class. Once all of the groups have presented, hold a class vote to choose the most probable explanation.

28. To expand this activity, have pairs create a different *final del desafío*. Ask students to write a dialogue between Asha and Lucas that shows a different ending. Tell students that they can use the dialogue on page 201 as a guide for length. Allow pairs time to rehearse their lines and then have them present their *final del desafío* to the class. If time permits, discuss with the class the different endings presented by students. Encourage the class to talk about how probable they think some of these endings are. For example: *Es improbable que la actuación fuera un desastre porque Asha y Lucas se prepararon bien*.

Answer Key

26. Answers will vary.
▶ Answers will vary. Sample answers:
1. casa o apartamento
2. fama
3. sin acompañamiento musical
4. importancia, grandeza
5. visitado con frecuencia
▶ Answers will vary.

27. Answers will vary.
▶ Answers will vary.

28. 1. pensaron/pensaban   4. anime/anima
2. estar   5. celebrar
3. fuera
▶ Answers will vary.

Additional Resources

Fans Online activities
Practice Workbook

201

Unit 4

DESAFÍO 2

Expresar probabilidad (II)

Presentation

- In *Desafío 2*, Eva and Ethan have to make a scale model of a place called *Nariz del Diablo*. Students will preview language used to talk about train travel and to express conjecture or probability.

Activities	Standards	Resources
Texto	1.2, 2.2	
29.	1.2, 1.3, 3.1	
30.	1.1, 1.2, 2.2, 3.2, 5.2	
31. Cultura	1.2, 1.3, 2.1, 2.2, 3.2, 4.2	

Teaching Suggestions

Warm-Up / Independent Starter

- Have students list three places that have unusual or interesting names. If they cannot think of names in Spanish, they can list names in English or other languages. For example: Garganta del Diablo, Iguazú (Argentina); Salsipuedes, Argentina; Normal, IL; Boring, OR.

Preparation

- Invite volunteers to share their Independent Starters and discuss the place names as a class. Then read the title and introduction of the dialogue. What type of place do students think *Nariz del Diablo* is? Ask them to justify their answers.

Texto: Una maqueta misteriosa

- Pair students to read the dialogue. Have them write any words they cannot identify or any constructions they do not understand. Review their lists as a class.

- Have students compare the information they learned in the dialogue about *Nariz del Diablo* with their guesses from the Preparation activity.

Activities

29. Remind students that, in these cases, the use of the future and conditional tenses is idiomatic. If they are having difficulties with some of these sentences, have students locate the sentences in the dialogue and use context clues to determine the meaning.

Una maqueta misteriosa

Ethan y Eva tienen que hacer una maqueta de un lugar llamado Nariz del Diablo. ¿Por qué tendrá ese nombre? ¿Qué lugar será?

ETHAN: ¡Qué desafío tan misterioso!

EVA: Sí, pero eso de hacer una maqueta parece divertido.

ETHAN: ¿Por qué se llamará Nariz del Diablo?

EVA: No tengo ni idea. ¿Crees que Tess se habrá equivocado con el nombre?

ETHAN: No, no creo. Ella nos dio una pista: dijo que es una de las mayores atracciones turísticas de Ecuador y que allí está el ferrocarril más «difícil» del mundo. ¿Qué querría decir?

EVA: No sé. ¿Será que costó mucho construirlo?

ETHAN: Puede ser.

EVA: Vamos a buscar información en Internet y lo averiguamos. Y, de paso, podemos imprimir algunas fotos. Las vamos a necesitar.

ETHAN: Aquí está. Te lo leo: «En una parte de la montaña conocida como la Nariz del Diablo el tren tiene que avanzar en zigzag dentro de la roca». También dice que tardaron unos treinta años en realizar la obra y que murieron cientos de obreros... ¡Qué horrible! Ahora entiendo por qué Tess nos dijo que este era el ferrocarril más difícil del mundo.

EVA: Sí, tan difícil como nuestro desafío.

ETHAN: No te desanimes, Eva, ya verás como lo hacemos fenomenal. Vamos a buscar más fotos y a pensar qué materiales necesitaremos.

Ferrocaril a Nariz del Diablo (Ecuador).

29 Detective de palabras

▶ **Completa** estas oraciones con las formas verbales que se usan en el texto.

> llamarse
> equivocarse
> querer
> ser

1. ¿Por qué _____ Nariz del Diablo?
2. ¿Crees que Tess _____ con el nombre?
3. ¿Qué _____ decir?
4. ¿_____ que costó mucho construirlo?

▶ **Piensa.** ¿A qué tiempos verbales corresponden esas formas? ¿Qué expresan esas oraciones?

Differentiated Instruction

DEVELOPING LEARNERS

- Ask students to complete the following sentences with the correct word or phrase:

1. *A Eva le parece ... hacer una maqueta.* (b)
   a. *difícil*   b. *divertido*
2. *La Nariz del Diablo es un lugar en...* (a)
   a. *Ecuador*   b. *Perú*
3. *El ferrocarril es el más difícil del mundo por...* (a)
   a. *el terreno*   b. *el costo*
4. *La Nariz del Diablo se refiere...* (b)
   a. *al zigzag*   b. *a la montaña*
5. *Eva y Ethan tienen que buscar más...* (b)
   a. *ideas*   b. *fotos*

EXPANDING LEARNERS

- Ask students to work with a partner and together research some feats of ancient engineering: the Great Wall of China, the Great Pyramid of Giza, the Hanging Gardens of Babylon, the Pyramid of the Sun at Teotihuacan, Mexico, or any other one of their choosing. Confirm that each pair has selected a different topic. Then, ask them to present their engineering feat to the rest of the class, and have the class vote on the best presentation as well as the most challenging ancient construction.

30 De excursión

▶ **Lee** la información y responde a las preguntas.

NARIZ DEL DIABLO

Distancia: 12 km | Tiempo: 2h 30 min

Un recorrido donde el turista podrá deleitarse con los típicos paisajes andinos, la cultura, el folclore y la artesanía. Además disfrutará de una majestuosa obra de ingeniería única en el mundo por su peculiar forma en zigzag.

Excursión estándar (Alausí-Sibambe-Alausí)
De martes a domingo y feriados
Hora de salida: 8:00 a. m. / 11:00 a. m. / 3:00 p. m.

¡Escoge!

Excursión estándar | ida y vuelta $25
– Viaje en tren.

Excursión plus | ida y vuelta $35
– Viaje en tren (asientos laterales).
– El precio incluye $2 de consumo en el café del tren.
– Guía nativo.
– Entrada del Museo Cóndor Puñuna.

Viaje expreso | ida y vuelta $6.50
– Viaje en autoferro (asientos laterales).
– No incluye guía.

Viaje expreso (Alausí-Sibambe-Alausí)
De viernes a domingo y feriados
Hora de salida: 9:00 a. m.

1. ¿Cuál es la ruta de esta excursión? ¿Cuánto dura el viaje?
2. ¿Qué tiene de especial el recorrido?
3. ¿Qué crees que es un autoferro?

 ▶ **Habla** con tu compañero(a). Si pudieras hacer este viaje, ¿qué excursión elegirías? ¿Por qué?

 ## CULTURA
El ferrocarril más difícil del mundo

El Ferrocarril Transandino se empezó a construir en 1872 y pronto se le conoció como «el ferrocarril más difícil del mundo» por las características del trazado (*route*). Uno de los puntos más complicados fue la llamada Nariz del Diablo, una pared de roca casi vertical. En la actualidad funciona de nuevo gracias a un proyecto de restauración y es una atracción turística y una ruta importante para la economía de las comunidades cercanas.

 31 **Compara.** ¿Conoces alguna obra que fuera difícil de terminar en la historia de tu país? ¿Para qué se utilizaba? ¿Funciona en la actualidad?

DESAFÍO 2
Expresar probabilidad (II)

31. Divide the class into small groups and assign each group a different feat of engineering to research (e.g., Hoover Dam in Nevada, the First Transcontinental Railroad in the United States, the Golden Gate in San Francisco, the Brooklyn Bridge in New York City, the Big Dig in Boston, the Gateway Arch in Missouri). Then have groups share their information with the class.

CULTURA
El ferrocarril más difícil del mundo

The railroad connecting Guayaquil, Ecuador's largest port, and Quito, in the highlands, was of great economic significance during the first half of the 20th century. However, by the end of the 20th century, travel by road had replaced the train. Some sections of this historic railroad have been rehabilitated and are now in operation as charter or tourist trains. The ascent of a mountain known as *Nariz del Diablo* (Devil's Nose) is arguably the most spectacular section of this railroad.

Answer Key

29. 1. se llamará 3. querría
2. se habrá equivocado 4. Será
▶ Las formas verbales de las oraciones 1, 2 y 4 están en futuro; la 3 está en condicional. Expresan conjetura.

30. Answers will vary. Sample answers:
1. Es de Alausí a Sibambe, ida y vuelta. Dura dos horas y media.
2. Los paisajes andinos y la cultura de la región, así como la obra de ingeniería de las vías del ferrocarril en forma de zigzag.
3. Un tipo de vehículo parecido a un tren.
▶ Answers will vary.

31. Answers will vary.

Additional Resources

Fans Online activities

HERITAGE LANGUAGE LEARNERS

• Ask students to describe a scenic railroad or bus route in their family's country of origin. Have them include the cities this route links, the scenery one is likely to encounter along the way, the local towns' cultures, the products that are typically made and sold in these towns, and, if applicable, the languages spoken by the local people. Students might also mention the time it takes to reach certain points along the way, as well as the average ticket price, and the differences between the accommodations.

MULTIPLE INTELLIGENCES:
Verbal-Linguistic Intelligence

• Ask students to imagine that they are on the train that goes through *la Nariz del Diablo*. Have them research the sights and sounds they might encounter along this short route. Then, ask them to write a dialogue between them and several other passengers they meet on the train. These passengers' comments as well as their own should reflect impressions of the journey. Students may work in small groups to create a conversation and then present it to the rest of the class.

DESAFÍO 2

Vocabulario – Los viajes

Presentation

- In this section, students will learn vocabulary related to modes of transportation.

Activities	Standards	Resources
Vocabulario	1.2	
32.	1.2, 1.3	
33.	1.1, 1.3, 5.2	
34.	1.1, 1.2, 5.1	Audio
35. Cultura	1.2, 1.3, 2.1, 2.2, 4.2, 5.1	

Teaching Suggestions

Warm-Up / Independent Starter

- Have students list modes of transportation and uses for each one (e.g., *metro → en el centro de la ciudad; avión → largas distancias*).

Preparation

- Have volunteer pairs read the dialogue aloud. Then have students repeat the highlighted words after you and make sure they understand each word or phrase. Show pictures or give students examples. For instance, to explain *señales de tráfico*, show students different traffic signs. Go over the *Más vocabulario* section as a class. Then have students work in small groups to draw a car and a train on separate sheets of paper, and to label each drawing with the parts mentioned in the vocabulary presentation. Encourage them to add other words they know (e.g., *el volante, el acelerador, la ventanilla*). Have groups share their drawings and vocabulary with the class.

- Ask students to review their Independent Starter lists and add other means of transportation as needed (e.g., *tren de cercanías → del centro de la ciudad a los suburbios*). Then call on volunteers to share their lists with the class.

Activities

33. For the second part, have students draw a cartoon strip, consisting of several frames, to tell their story. Once they have written the story, students will present their cartoons to the class. Can the class reconstruct the story?

Vocabulario

Los viajes

EVA: ¡Hay miles de coches en esta autopista, llevamos más de diez minutos parados en este atasco!

ETHAN: No sé por qué hay tanto tráfico hoy. En esta ciudad la circulación no es mala y, en general, los conductores respetamos las normas de circulación y las señales de tráfico.

EVA: ¿Tú manejas con cuidado?

ETHAN: Pues claro. Siempre pongo el intermitente cuando voy a adelantar o a estacionar, cedo el paso a los peatones en los pasos de cebra...

EVA: Ay, Ethan, creo que es mejor y más rápido viajar en tren o en autobús...

ETHAN: Bueno, depende... ¿Te acuerdas de lo que nos pasó la última vez que fuimos en tren al aeropuerto? Llegamos tarde y tuvimos que poner una reclamación.

EVA: Fue porque el tren tuvo un problema técnico, como nos informó el revisor. Pero ¿te acuerdas del viaje que hicimos en el tren de alta velocidad en España? Fue extraordinario. Y todo lo que comimos en el vagón-restaurante estaba riquísimo.

ETHAN: Tienes razón. El AVE ofrece muchas comodidades y ventajas. ¡Y eso que viajamos en clase turista!

EVA: Ethan, ¿esa lucecita no quiere decir que tu coche está a punto de quedarse sin gasolina?

Más vocabulario

El coche

el maletero: lugar del coche en el que se guarda el equipaje.

la matrícula: placa oficial con letras y números que identifica el coche.

el pinchazo: perforación de la rueda que hace que pierda el aire.

la rueda de repuesto: rueda que se lleva en el maletero del coche para sustituir a otra.

El tren y el avión

el coche-cama	sleeper car
el tren de cercanías	commuter train
el tren de largo recorrido	long-distance train

¡Atención!

el/la conductor(a)	driver
el/la revisor(a)	(train) conductor

32 **Definiciones**

▶ **Lee** estas oraciones y escribe. ¿A qué palabras o expresiones de la ficha de Vocabulario se refieren?

1. Trenes que transportan pasajeros dentro de la ciudad o entre ciudades cercanas.
2. Vagón del tren dividido en compartimentos con camas.
3. Agente que se ocupa de comprobar que los viajeros llevan sus boletos.

▶ **Escribe** un ejemplo con otras tres palabras o expresiones del diálogo.

Differentiated Instruction

DEVELOPING LEARNERS

- Have students match words from both columns.

1. *intermitente* (j)	a. *placa*
2. *coche-cama* (h)	b. *perforación*
3. *gasolina* (g)	c. *empleado del tren*
4. *maletero* (i)	d. *pasar a otro coche*
5. *pinchazo* (b)	e. *persona a pie*
6. *matrícula* (a)	f. *reglas*
7. *normas* (f)	g. *hace funcionar el coche*
8. *revisor* (c)	h. *tren nocturno*
9. *adelantar* (d)	i. *para el equipaje*
10. *peatón* (e)	j. *indicador*

EXPANDING LEARNERS

- Ask students to complete the following sentences with the correct word(s):
  1. *En los atascos hay mucho... (tráfico)*
  2. *Hay que ... el paso a los... (ceder, peatones)*
  3. *Si tienes alguna queja, puedes poner una... (reclamación)*
  4. *La ... del coche es su identificación. (matrícula)*
  5. *Si tienes un ... hay que poner la... (pinchazo, rueda de repuesto)*
  6. *Los conductores tienen que seguir las ... de circulación. (normas)*
  7. *El coche se para si nos... (quedamos sin gasolina)*

33 Viajes accidentados

▶ **Describe** estas ilustraciones con detalle. ¿Qué les ha pasado a estas personas?

 ①    ②

 ▶ **Habla** con tu compañero(a). Elijan una de las viñetas, imaginen cómo continuó la historia y dibujen la viñeta final. Después, escriban la historia completa.

34 ¡Viajeros al tren!

 ▶ **Escucha** la conversación y elige la opción correcta.

1. Ethan y su papá viajan en un tren…
   a. expreso.   b. nocturno.   c. directo.

2. Ethan está emocionado porque es la primera vez que viaja en un tren…
   a. de alta velocidad.   b. con coche-cama.   c. de largo recorrido.

3. Ethan y su papá hablan con el inspector en…
   a. la estación.   b. el coche-cama.   c. el vagón-restaurante.

4. Ethan busca dos asientos…
   a. libres.   b. reservados.   c. ocupados.

 ▶ **Habla** con tu compañero(a) sobre un viaje que hayas hecho durante la noche. ¿Cómo y con quién fuiste? ¿Cuál era tu destino? ¿Cómo fue el viaje?

CULTURA
El AVE (España)

En el año 1992 se puso en servicio la primera línea de tren de alta velocidad española (AVE) entre Madrid y Sevilla. Esta línea une las dos ciudades en dos horas y media. En los años siguientes la red de alta velocidad se ha extendido desde Madrid a varias ciudades españolas, revolucionando el concepto de viaje. En la línea Madrid-Barcelona o Madrid-Valencia, los trenes llegan a 300 kilómetros por hora (186 mph). Además de la rapidez, los viajeros aprecian la comodidad y la garantía de puntualidad.

35 Piensa. ¿Cuáles serían las ventajas y dificultades de un tren como este en tu país?

doscientos cinco 205

Unit 4
DESAFÍO 2
Vocabulario – Los viajes

34. To extend the second part of this activity, have students take notes on their partner's trip and then report to the class. Hold a vote to select the most eventful trip.

35. Explain that higher gas prices and denser populations make rail travel attractive. However, building and operating a high-speed rail route can be extremely expensive. In a whole-class session, discuss the pros and cons of embarking on such an enterprise in this country.

 AUDIO SCRIPT
See page 183L.

CULTURA
El AVE (España)

In 1964, Japan opened the first high-speed rail route in the world. In Europe, in 1977, Italy was the first country to open a high-speed line between Rome and Florence. Spain opened its first high-speed rail in 1992, and has since expanded its network to include all major cities. Spain has also become an exporter of this technology and is currently building a high-speed rail in Saudi Arabia, connecting Medina and Mecca.

Answer Key

32. 1. tren de cercanías
      2. coche-cama
      3. revisor
      ▶ Answers will vary.

33. Answers will vary.
      ▶ Answers will vary.

34. 1. b   2. b   3. c   4. a
      ▶ Answers will vary.

35. Answers will vary.

Additional Resources

Fans Online activities
Practice Workbook

HERITAGE LANGUAGE LEARNERS

- Ask students to make a strong case for or against budgeting high-speed trains in their community or state. Students may select the medium through which they will appeal to the community and its leaders: a debate, a letter to the editor, a televised interview, etc. Students should provide several arguments in favor of or against providing funds to their project. Call on students to read or present their arguments to the rest of the class, and ask the class to determine who was the most convincing and why.

MULTIPLE INTELLIGENCES:
Logical-Mathematical Intelligence

- Ask students to calculate the time it takes the AVE to travel between Madrid and several other cities in Spain. Ask them to state the distances in both kilometers and miles, and to use a speed of 300 kph (186 mph). Then, have students identify major cities in North America, calculate distances between them, and determine the time needed to travel via the same high-speed trains. Call on volunteers to read some of their results.

205

DESAFÍO 2

Gramática – Expresar probabilidad (II). El futuro y el condicional

Presentation

■ In this section, students will review the use of the future tense to express conjecture in the present. They will also learn how to express conjecture in the past by using the conditional tenses.

Activities	Standards	Resources
Gramática	1.2, 3.1	
36.	1.2, 3.1, 4.1	
37.	1.2, 3.1	
38.	1.1, 1.2, 1.3	Audio
39.	1.3	
40. Conexiones	1.2, 1.3, 2.1, 3.1, 3.2, 4.1, 4.2	

Teaching Suggestions

Warm-Up / Independent Starter

■ Ask students to determine whether each of these conjectures refers to the present or past:
  – *No tendrá gasolina.* (presente)
  – *Habrá tenido un accidente.* (pasado)
  – *Se le olvidaría llamarte.* (pasado)

Preparation

■ Call on volunteers to share their Independent Starters. Invite students to try to explain how they knew. Clarify that this use of the future and conditional tenses does not have a direct translation into English. Then go over the grammar presentation as a class. You may wish to draw a timeline on the board and locate on it the different examples provided (e.g., *Estarán reservados →* presente; *Se habrá retrasado →* pasado reciente).

Activities

38. For the second part, encourage students to think of unusual reasons for Ethan's delay (e.g., *Se encontraría con su exnovia y la invitaría a comer*). Then ask pairs to decide on the funniest or most creative conjecture and write a paragraph describing what might have happened. Invite pairs to share their paragraphs with the class.

Gramática

Expresar probabilidad (II). El futuro y el condicional

Los tiempos del futuro

● Los tiempos del futuro se usan idiomáticamente para expresar conjetura o probabilidad:
  – El futuro (cantaré) puede expresar probabilidad en el presente. En este sentido equivale a *I suppose, I wonder, must* y *probably*.

  > —¿Por qué están libres esos asientos?
  > —No sé. **Estarán** reservados.

  – El futuro perfecto (habré cantado) puede expresar probabilidad en un pasado reciente.
  > Mario no ha llegado aún. Se **habrá retrasado** por el tráfico.

Los tiempos del condicional

● El condicional (cantaría) y el condicional perfecto (habría cantado) se pueden usar para expresar probabilidad en el pasado, seguidos generalmente de un verbo en pretérito o en imperfecto.

  > **Serían** las cuatro de la tarde cuando llegó Mario.
  > (= Probablemente eran las cuatro de la tarde…)
  > Eva **habría llegado** tarde al aeropuerto y por eso perdió el avión.
  > (= Probablemente Eva llegó tarde…)

● Observa en los ejemplos anteriores que el condicional (serían) presenta la acción sin terminar, mientras que el condicional perfecto (habría llegado) la presenta como una acción ya terminada.

● Como todos los tiempos compuestos, el condicional perfecto se construye con el verbo auxiliar haber.

VERBOS REGULARES. CONDICIONAL PERFECTO

	Viajar	Comer	Salir
yo	habría **viaj**ado	habría **com**ido	habría **sal**ido
tú	habrías **viaj**ado	habrías **com**ido	habrías **sal**ido
usted, él, ella	habría **viaj**ado	habría **com**ido	habría **sal**ido
nosotros(as)	habríamos **viaj**ado	habríamos **com**ido	habríamos **sal**ido
vosotros(as)	habríais **viaj**ado	habríais **com**ido	habríais **sal**ido
ustedes, ellos(as)	habrían **viaj**ado	habrían **com**ido	habrían **sal**ido

36 **Piensa.** ¿Qué expresiones y tiempos verbales usas en inglés para expresar probabilidad o conjetura sobre el pasado?

Differentiated Instruction

DEVELOPING LEARNERS

● Ask students to choose the correct answer.
  1. *¿Por qué no ha ido Ana a la fiesta? No la habrán / habrían invitado.* (habrán)
  2. *¿Por qué no contestaron estas preguntas? No sabrán / sabrían las respuestas.* (sabrían)
  3. *¿Por qué no llega Ethan? Estará / Estaría en un atasco.* (Estará)
  4. *¿Por qué no metió todo en el maletero? No habrá / habría espacio.* (habría)
  5. *¿Por qué se paró el coche? Se quedará / quedaría sin gasolina.* (quedaría)

EXPANDING LEARNERS

● Ask students to come up with a conjecture for each of the following sentences:
  1. *No aprobaste el examen.*
  2. *La policía le puso una multa a Carlos.*
  3. *María no metió nada más en el maletero.*
  4. *La circulación va muy bien ahora.*
  5. *Ellos no pudieron dormir en el tren.*
  6. *El coche no funciona.*
  7. *Ayer tuve que usar la rueda de repuesto.*
  8. *Ella toma el tren de cercanías.*

37 ¿Futuro o condicional?

▶ **Elige** la respuesta correcta.

1. ¿A qué hora llegaste a la estación? **Serán / Serían** las ocho.
2. ¿Por qué no ha subido Ethan al avión? **Habrá / Habría** olvidado el pasaporte.
3. ¿Por qué ha puesto Tess una reclamación? **Habrá / Habría** perdido una maleta.
4. ¿Por qué compra ahora Eva los boletos? **Serán / Serían** más baratos.

38 ¿Dónde estará Ethan?

▶ **Escucha** la conversación y decide si estas afirmaciones son ciertas o falsas. Después, corrige las oraciones falsas.

1. La mamá de Eva cree que Ethan se habrá demorado comprando los materiales.
2. Ethan se iría aproximadamente a las seis.
3. Si Ethan no contesta es porque habrá olvidado su celular en casa.
4. La mamá de Eva supone que Ethan se habrá retrasado por el tráfico.

▶ **Habla** con tu compañero(a). ¿Por qué crees que se retrasaría Ethan? ¿Qué le pasaría? Imaginen, al menos, tres posibles razones.

Modelo A. *Habría mucha gente en el almacén y por eso tuvo que esperar.*
B. *O se le habría olvidado lo que tenía que comprar cuando llegó al almacén.*

39 Probablemente...

▶ **Escribe** una conjetura para cada situación.

Modelo 1. *Habría habido un accidente.*

1. Ethan y Eva estuvieron en un atasco en la autopista durante dos horas.
2. Ethan estacionó su coche en un lugar prohibido.
3. Cuando Eva viaja, muchas veces tiene que pagar por exceso de equipaje.
4. El año pasado Ethan siempre iba a la escuela en el tren de cercanías de su ciudad.

CONEXIONES: LENGUA

La famosa actriz podría haberse casado en Hawaii

El condicional de rumor

Se conoce como condicional de rumor el uso del condicional (simple o compuesto) en el lenguaje periodístico para expresar que lo que se dice son suposiciones o rumores no confirmados. Equivale al uso de expresiones como *al parecer, se cree que, según se dice, según nos han informado*, etc.

40 Compara. ¿En inglés hay algún recurso lingüístico equivalente al condicional de rumor?

HERITAGE LANGUAGE LEARNERS

- Students are going to be journalists for a leading tabloid and practice using *el condicional de rumor.* Ask them to work with a partner and come up with at least eight tantalizing headlines about Hispanic celebrities or newsmakers. Students should also invent a name for their newspaper and arrange the headlines, complete with visuals, on the paper's front page. If time allows, ask students to read some of their work aloud and explain who the people featured are. Display students' papers in the classroom.

MULTIPLE INTELLIGENCES: Verbal-Linguistic Intelligence

- After the heritage language learners have presented their tabloid headlines, assign one to each student, or allow them to choose one, and ask students to counter the sensationalism of the headline with an article refuting the allegations. Then have students exchange their articles with a partner, who will proofread it and make any necessary corrections. Partners will return the articles to the authors, who will make a final copy and post it on the classroom bulletin board for all to read.

Gramática – Expresar probabilidad (II). El futuro y el condicional

39. To extend this activity, ask students to work with a partner and add one more conjecture to each situation (e.g., *Habría habido un accidente y no habrían retirado aún los vehículos accidentados*). Then have pairs share their answers with the class and discuss the most probable explanation for each case.

AUDIO SCRIPT
See page 183L.

CONEXIONES: LENGUA

El condicional de rumor

Although common in many Spanish-language newspapers, this use of the conditional is not a feature of Spanish; it is actually taken from French. Some style guides advise against its use, but the Royal Spanish Academy (RAE) does not condemn it. However, this structure should be avoided if a piece of news wants to be presented as factual.

Answer Key

36. Se usan expresiones como *could, may, might* o *probably* con tiempos del pasado.

37. 1. Serían 3. Habrá
2. Habrá 4. Serán

38. 1. C.
2. F. Serían las cinco cuando se fue.
3. F. Porque lo tendrá sin batería.
4. C.
▶ Answers will vary.

39. Answers will vary.

40. Answers will vary. Sample answer:
No hay un recurso específico. Se usan expresiones como *allegedly, it is rumored, it is said,* etc.

Additional Resources

Fans Online activities
Practice Workbook

DESAFÍO 2

Gramática – El presente perfecto de subjuntivo

Presentation

- In this section, students will review how and when to use the present perfect subjunctive. Students will also review the uses of the different tenses of the subjunctive mood.

Activities	Standards	Resources
Gramática	1.2, 3.1	
41.	1.2, 3.1, 4.1	
42.	1.2	Audio
43.	1.3	
44.	1.1, 1.3, 5.1	
45.	1.1, 1.3, 5.1	

Teaching Suggestions

Warm-Up / Independent Starter

- Write the following pairs of sentences on the board and ask students to explain the differences in meaning between each one:
  1. a. *Me sorprende que nunca viajes en tren.*
     b. *Me sorprende que nunca hayas viajado en tren.*
  2. a. *Es una pena que él no ponga el intermitente.*
     b. *Es una pena que él no haya puesto el intermitente cuando adelantó al otro coche.*

Preparation

- Ask students to read the first part of the grammar presentation silently. Next, have them situate the sentences from the Independent Starter on a timeline like the one on page 208. Then call on volunteers to explain the use of the present subjunctive and the present perfect subjunctive in the Independent Starter sentences. Elicit that the present perfect subjunctive refers to an action that is presented as completed before the action in the main clause.
- Go over the second part of the grammar presentation as a class. Even though the subjunctive mood is not used in English in these cases, both languages follow a similar sequence of tenses. To emphasize this point, you may want to complete activity 41 as a class.

Gramática

El presente perfecto de subjuntivo

El presente perfecto de subjuntivo

- Recuerda: usamos el presente perfecto de subjuntivo en el mismo tipo de cláusulas en las que usamos el presente de subjuntivo siempre que hablamos de una acción completada que es anterior a la acción de la cláusula principal.

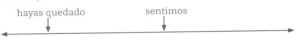

hayas quedado   sentimos

Sentimos que te **hayas quedado** sin gasolina en la autopista.

Repasa la formación del presente perfecto de subjuntivo en la página R21.

- Al igual que ocurre con el presente, el presente perfecto de subjuntivo puede referirse a acciones actuales o futuras.

VALOR TEMPORAL DEL PRESENTE Y EL PRESENTE PERFECTO DE SUBJUNTIVO

	INDICATIVO		SUBJUNTIVO
presente	Creo que Juan viene en tren.	presente	No creo que Juan venga en tren.
futuro	Creo que Juan vendrá en tren.		
presente perfecto	Creo que Eva ya ha comprado los boletos.	presente perfecto	No creo que Eva haya comprado todavía los boletos.
futuro perfecto	Creo que mañana Eva ya habrá comprado los boletos.		

Correlación de los tiempos verbales

- Recuerda: si la cláusula dependiente lleva un verbo en subjuntivo, el tiempo de ese verbo depende del verbo empleado en la cláusula principal.

CORRELACIÓN ENTRE EL INDICATIVO (TIEMPOS SIMPLES) Y EL SUBJUNTIVO

CLÁUSULA PRINCIPAL (modo indicativo)	CLÁUSULA DEPENDIENTE (modo subjuntivo)	
presente o futuro	presente (*acción sin completar*) presente perfecto (*acción completada*)	Me molesta que no respetes/hayas respetado las señales.
pretérito o imperfecto	imperfecto	Me molestó que no respetaras las señales.
condicional	imperfecto	Me molestaría que no respetaras las señales.

41 **Compara.** Traduce al inglés los ejemplos de la tabla. ¿Qué tiempos verbales has empleado?

Differentiated Instruction

DEVELOPING LEARNERS

- Ask students to complete the following sentences:
  1. *Pondré gasolina cuando el tanque esté / haya estado vacío.* (esté)
  2. *Es posible que se olviden / se hayan olvidado de mi cumpleaños porque no me llamaron.* (se hayan olvidado)
  3. *Me alegraría que hagamos / hiciéramos un viaje en tren.* (hiciéramos)
  4. *Ojalá que los conductores siempre respeten / hayan respetado a los peatones.* (respeten)
  5. *Temía que haya / hubiera atasco hoy.* (hubiera)

EXPANDING LEARNERS

- Have pairs ask each other the following questions. Students must use the subjunctive in their responses.
  1. ¿Qué temías cuando eras niño(a)?
  2. ¿Qué esperabas en tu pasado cumpleaños?
  3. ¿Qué te ha sorprendido de las últimas elecciones nacionales?
  4. ¿Qué no te gustó de la última película que viste?
  5. ¿Qué suelen lamentar los adolescentes?
  6. ¿Qué es lo que más te molesta de tu familia? ¿Y de tus profesores?
  7. ¿Por qué razones te enfadas?

42 ¡Al volante!

▶ **Escucha** y elige la opción correcta.

1. Eva echará gasolina cuando _____ del atasco.   **a.** haya salido   **b.** saldrá
2. Ethan siente que a Eva le _____ una multa.   **a.** pongan   **b.** hayan puesto
3. Eva lamenta que a Ethan se le _____ una rueda.   **a.** pinche   **b.** haya pinchado
4. Ethan arrancará cuando Eva se _____ el cinturón.   **a.** haya puesto   **b.** pondrá

43 Termínalas

▶ **Completa** las oraciones teniendo en cuenta la secuencia de tiempos verbales.

1. Ethan siempre teme que los conductores...
2. Eva esperaba que el atasco en la autopista...
3. A los asistentes de vuelo no les gusta que los viajeros...
4. Los viajeros lamentaron que el avión...
5. Los pasajeros quieren que los trenes de largo recorrido...
6. A los turistas les enojaría que el próximo verano...

44 Antes y ahora

▶ **Escribe** oraciones para expresar las opiniones de Ethan siguiendo el modelo. Usa algunos de los verbos del cuadro.

Modelo   1. *Antes a Ethan no le preocupaba que la gente no respetara las normas de circulación.*
           Sin embargo, ahora le molesta que los conductores no respeten a los peatones.

preocupar
molestar
sorprender
enojar
gustar
sentir
temer
querer
desear
esperar

45 En mis viajes

▶ **Habla** con tu compañero(a) sobre viajes. Usen estas preguntas.

A) En tu último viaje:
   1. ¿Qué esperabas que pasara?
   2. ¿Qué temías?
   3. ¿Qué suceso no te gustó?

B) En general, cuando viajas:
   1. ¿Qué esperas?
   2. ¿Qué te da miedo?
   3. ¿Qué te molesta?

HERITAGE LANGUAGE LEARNERS

• Ask student pairs to imagine that they are traveling by train. They will create a dialogue in which one plays the role of a difficult passenger, and the other is the peacemaker. Then have them present their dialogues. For example:

A. *Temo que este tren no llegue a tiempo.*
B. *Bueno, si no llegamos a tiempo, te sugiero que pongas una reclamación.*
A. *Me molestó que el revisor no me atendiera.*
B. *Siento que pienses así, pero él tiene mucho que hacer.*

CRITICAL THINKING

• Ask students to think about the advantages and disadvantages of traveling by car, train, or bus within this country, and to choose a route that could be covered by either of these three modes of transportation. Then, ask them to write an essay of at least three paragraphs detailing the pros and cons of each one. Students should conclude their essay by stating their preferred way to travel the route they have chosen, and why they believe it is the best way to cover this distance.

Gramática – El presente perfecto de subjuntivo

Activities

42. Before playing the recording, ask students to complete this activity with the verb tense they think makes more sense in each case. Then play the audio and have students check their answers.

43. First, have students identify the tense of the verb in the main clause. This will indicate to them which subjunctive tense should be used in the dependent clause.

45. To expand this activity, ask students to write two paragraphs comparing and contrasting their own and their partner's travel idiosyncrasies. Would they be compatible travel companions? Have students justify their answers.

AUDIO SCRIPT
See page 183L.

Answer Key

41. *It bothers me that you do not follow/have not followed the traffic signs.*
It bothered me that you did not follow the traffic signs.
It would bother me if you did not follow the traffic signs.
Se usa la misma secuencia de tiempos que en español, pero en el modo indicativo.

42. 1. a   2. b   3. b   4. a

43. Answers will vary. Sample answers:
   1. ... no respeten las normas.
   2. ... terminara cuanto antes.
   3. ... se levanten del asiento.
   4. ... se retrasara.
   5. ... sean cómodos.
   6. ... subieran de precio los pasajes.

44. Answers will vary.

45. Answers will vary.

Additional Resources

Fans Online activities
Practice Workbook

209

Unit 4

LECTURA: TEXTO INFORMATIVO

Presentation

- In this section, students will read a story about traffic in a big city. As they read, they will review vocabulary used to talk about cars and traffic. Students will also use context clues to determine the meaning of new words, and they will discuss the structure of narrative texts.

Activities	Standards	Resources
Lectura: texto informativo	1.1, 1.2, 2.2	
46.	1.1, 1.2, 1.3	
47.	1.2, 1.3, 2.1, 3.1	
48.	1.3	

Teaching Suggestions

Warm-Up / Independent Starter

- Have students complete the following sentence starters with their reactions about traffic congestion:
  - *Me molesta...*
  - *Me parece mal/bien que...*
  - *Me sorprende...*

Preparation

- Call on volunteers to share their Independent Starters. Do students have similar reactions? On the board, list some of the adjectives and verbs students used in their answers. Do most of these words convey positive or negative feelings? As a class, discuss some ways to alleviate traffic congestion (e.g., *ampliar la red de metro, fomentar el trabajo telemático, usar el transporte público*). Then have students work with a partner to answer the questions in the *Antes de leer* section.

- Divide the class into small groups of four students of varying abilities, and ask individual group members to each read a paragraph aloud. Encourage students to monitor their understanding during reading. First, they should concentrate on getting the gist, focusing on one paragraph at a time and identifying the most important information. Once they have finished reading, ask students to generate questions (e.g., who, what, when, where, why). As they answer each other's questions, they will review important ideas.

210

Antes de leer: estrategias

1. El texto que vas a leer está relacionado con el tráfico en una gran ciudad. ¿Reconoces las palabras destacadas? Si no, busca su significado.

2. ¿Cómo se siente la gente cuando está en un atasco? ¿Cómo reacciona?

Como la vida misma

Las nueve menos cuarto de la mañana. **Semáforo** en rojo, un rojo inconfundible. Las nueve menos trece, hoy no llego. **Atasco**. Doscientos mil coches apretujados[4] junto al tuyo. Escudriñas[2] al vecino. Está intolerablemente cerca.

Verde. Avanza, imbécil. ¿Qué hacen? No **arrancan**. No se mueven, los cretinos. Están de paseo, con la inmensa urgencia que tú tienes. Doscientos mil coches que han salido a pasear a la misma hora con el único fin de fastidiarte[3]. ¡Rojjjjjjjjjjo! ¡Rojo de nuevo!

No es posible. Las nueve menos diez. Hoy desde luego que no llegoooo. Alguien **pita** por detrás. Te sobresaltas, casi arrancas. De pronto adviertes que el semáforo sigue aún en rojo. ¿Qué quieres, que salga con el paso cerrado, imbécil? (en voz alta y quebrada[4] por la rabia). Pip, piiiiiiip. Te vuelves en el **asiento**. Gesticulas desaforadamente[5]. Los de atrás contestan con más gestos. Doscientos mil conductores solitarios encerrados en doscientos mil vehículos, todos ellos insultando gestualmente a los vecinos. En estas, la luz se pone verde y los de atrás del todo, a partir del coche doscientos mil uno, organizan un estrépito[6] verdaderamente portentoso. Ante tal algarabía reaccionas, recuperas el **volante**, al fin arrancas. Las nueve menos cinco.

La calle adquiere ahora una fluidez momentánea, puedes meter segunda, puedes meter tercera, te embriaga[7] el vértigo de la velocidad. Estás ya en la proximidad de tu destino, no hay posibilidades de **aparcar**.

De pronto descubres un par de metros libres, un milagroso pedacito de ciudad sin coche: pegas un **frenazo**, el corazón te late[8] apresuradamente.

Los conductores de detrás comienzan a **tocar la bocina**. Intentas **maniobrar**, pero los vehículos que te siguen te lo impiden. De pronto, uno de los coches de la fila se detiene, espera a que tú aparques. Intentas **retroceder** al hueco, pero la cosa está difícil. El vecino **da marcha atrás** para facilitarte las cosas, aunque apenas pueda moverse.

Tu agradecimiento es tal que te desborda[9], te llena de calor. Al fin aparcas y la fila continúa. Sales del coche, cierras la **portezuela**. Apresuras el paso para alcanzar al generoso conductor, detenido por el atasco a pocos metros. Llegas a su altura. Te inclinas sobre su **ventanilla**; muchas gracias, le dices en tono exaltado[10], aún tembloroso tras la batalla. El otro se sobresalta, te mira. Muchas gracias, insistes; soy el del coche azul, el que aparcaba. El otro palidece[11], al fin contesta con un hilo de voz: «Pero ¿qué quería usted, que me montara encima de los coches? No podía dar más marcha atrás». Tú por unos segundos no comprendes; al fin, enrojeces: «Pero si le estoy dando las gracias de verdad, oiga, le estoy dando las gracias». El hombre se pasa la mano por la cara, abrumado, y balbucea[12]: «Es que... este tráfico, estos nervios...». Reemprendes tu camino, sorprendido. Y mientras resoplas, te dices con filosófica tristeza, con genuino asombro: hay que ver lo agresiva que está la gente, no lo entiendo.

Rosa Montero. *El arrebato* (selección)

1. muy juntos	3. molestarte	5. con exceso	7. te apasiona	9. *overflows*	11. *turns pale*
2. Examinas	4. *broken*	6. mucho ruido	8. *beats*	10. exasperado	12. *stammers*

Differentiated Instruction

DEVELOPING LEARNERS

- To confirm developing learners' reading comprehension of *Como la vida misma*, pair them with more advanced students to read the story aloud. As they read, ask them to highlight any words they do not comprehend and have their partner provide synonyms or definitions for them. As they finish reading each paragraph, ask them to explain the content in their own words. Encourage the developing learners to write any new words, along with their meanings, in their notebooks and to write a sentence with each one.

EXPANDING LEARNERS

- Ask students to match words from both columns, and then have them write the word pairs in their notebooks.
  1. *atasco* (i)
  2. *arrancar* (g)
  3. *desaforado* (f)
  4. *portentoso* (h)
  5. *adquirir* (j)
  6. *vértigo* (c)
  7. *pedacito* (e)
  8. *retroceder* (a)
  9. *apresurar* (b)
  10. *reemprender* (d)

  a. *dar marcha atrás*
  b. *dar prisa*
  c. *mareo*
  d. *volver a empezar*
  e. *hueco*
  f. *desmedido*
  g. *empezar a andar*
  h. *asombroso*
  i. *embotellamiento*
  j. *conseguir*

46 ¿Comprendes?

▶ **Responde** a estas preguntas. ¿Qué palabras del texto justifican tus respuestas? Escríbelas.

1. ¿Quién es el protagonista del texto: un conductor o una conductora?
2. ¿Qué le sucede?
3. ¿Está tranquilo(a) el/la protagonista del texto?
4. ¿Crees que es una persona bien educada? ¿Se comporta adecuadamente?
5. ¿Por qué resulta irónico el final del texto?

▶ **Une** cada definición con la palabra correspondiente.

 A

1. Hacer gestos.
2. Preocupado, agobiado.
3. Darse prisa, acelerar.
4. Caos, alboroto.
5. Asustar o alterar a alguien de repente.

 B

a. sobresaltar
b. gesticular
c. apresurar el paso
d. algarabía
e. abrumado

47 Significa que...

▶ **Elige** la opción que mejor puede sustituir a las palabras destacadas.

1. Está **intolerablemente** cerca.
   a. muy   b. demasiado   c. un poco

2. Están de paseo, con la inmensa **urgencia** que tú tienes.
   a. inquietud   b. tranquilidad   c. prisa

3. De pronto **adviertes** que el semáforo sigue aún en rojo.
   a. te das cuenta de   b. avisas   c. alertas

4. Los coches organizan un estrépito verdaderamente **portentoso**.
   a. maravilloso   b. extraordinario   c. fenomenal

▶ **Lee** de nuevo el texto de Rosa Montero. ¿Puedes identificar en ese texto la estructura típica de los textos narrativos: Situación inicial–Acontecimiento inicial–Acciones–Situación final? Justifica tu respuesta con fragmentos extraídos del texto.

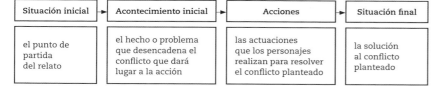

Situación inicial	Acontecimiento inicial	Acciones	Situación final
el punto de partida del relato	el hecho o problema que desencadena el conflicto que dará lugar a la acción	las actuaciones que los personajes realizan para resolver el conflicto planteado	la solución al conflicto planteado

48 Con tus propias palabras

▶ **Escribe** una descripción del protagonista del texto tal y como tú te lo imaginas. Piensa en detalles sobre su aspecto, su carácter, su trabajo, su familia, etc. ¿Conoces a alguien que se parezca a ese personaje?

doscientos once 211

Activities

46. You may want to have students work with a partner to complete the first part of this activity. Ask one partner to answer the questions while the other looks for quotes in the text that validate their answers.

47. For the second part of this activity, review with students the generic structure of narrative texts. First, the character(s) and place (setting) are introduced. Then a problem that needs to be resolved is presented. This conflict or problem gets worse and reaches a climax. At that point, a resolution begins to develop. The story ends with a resolution of the conflict. Have students complete this activity in small groups, and then invite them to share their answers with the class.

48. Invite students to share their descriptions of the main character with the class. How are their descriptions different and similar? What might account for the differences?

Answer Key

46. Answers will vary. Sample answers:

1. Un conductor. Se identifica así: «soy el del coche azul, el que aparcaba».
2. Está en un atasco y teme no llegar a tiempo. Así lo expresa: «Las nueve menos trece, hoy no llego. Atasco».
3. No, no está tranquilo: «Te vuelves en el asiento. Gesticulas desaforadamente».
4. A veces no, pues insulta a los demás: «¿Qué quieres, que salga con el paso cerrado, imbécil?».
5. Porque el conductor no ve su propia agresividad: «hay que ver lo agresiva que está la gente, no lo entiendo».

▶ 1. b   2. e   3. c   4. d   5. a

47. 1. b   2. c   3. a   4. b
▶ Answers will vary.

48. Answers will vary.

Additional Resources

Fans Online activities

HERITAGE LANGUAGE LEARNERS

• Have students imagine that they are one of the many stressed-out drivers who commute to work by car every day. Ask them to seek help in reducing their stress from an advice columnist by writing a letter that details their situation. After students write the letter, ask them to exchange it with a partner who will reply with some wise or humorous advice. Call on volunteers to read the letters and answers aloud. Ask the other students to vote on the best or most original advice.

MULTIPLE INTELLIGENCES:
Verbal-Linguistic Intelligence

• Using *Como la vida misma* as a model, ask students to write a narrative from the point of view of the other driver who is described. Encourage students to use the steps defined on the page when organizing their narrative (i.e., *situación inicial, acontecimiento inicial, acciones, situación final*), and to make a chart with these headings. When students finish writing, ask them to use phrases from their work to complete their graphic organizer. Call on volunteers to read their work aloud.

211

DESAFÍO 2

Comunicación

Presentation

- In this section, students will integrate the vocabulary and grammar skills from *Desafío 2* in order to read an article about travel in the future, write an opinion piece about high-speed rail networks, and create a dialogue using the future or the conditional to express probability and conjecture.

Activities	Standards	Resources
49.	1.1, 1.2, 1.3, 2.1, 3.2, 5.1	
50.	1.1, 1.3, 4.2, 5.1	
51. Final del desafío	1.1, 1.3, 2.2, 3.1	

Teaching Suggestions

Warm-Up / Independent Starter

- Have students write four sentences offering their predictions about travel in the future. For example: *Es probable que los aviones sean mucho más rápidos. Es posible que no existan las agencias de viaje y que todo se haga por Internet.*

Preparation

- Call on students to share their predictions from the Independent Starter. You may want to write some of their sentences on the board and analyze the sequence of tenses. For further practice with the sequence of tenses, have students rewrite their sentences to describe travel 50 years ago. For example: *Hace 50 años, era probable que los aviones fueran muy lentos. Es posible que las agencias de viajes hayan sido/fueran muy importantes porque no existía Internet.* Discuss with students how the tenses have changed to reflect that the sentences now refer to the past.

- For further practice using the future and conditional tenses, have pairs come up with two conjectures for each of the following statements:
  1. *El coche no arranca.*
  2. *Ella no cedió el paso.*
  3. *Ayer me pusieron una multa.*
  4. *El tren está retrasado.*

Comunicación

49 Viajar en el futuro

 ▶ **Lee** el texto y responde a las preguntas.

¿Cómo serán los viajes del futuro?

¿Cuáles serán los destinos de moda dentro de diez años? ¿Qué tipo de información turística requerirá la gente? ¿Qué pasará con los viajes de negocios? ¿Qué rol tendrán las agencias de viajes tradicionales? Estas son algunas de las previsiones para dentro de diez años.

Internet

En 2008, el 41% de los europeos reservó sus viajes de placer a través de Internet. Un informe de la consultora FastFuture sugiere que en pocos años se espera que esa cifra crezca y que estos viajeros reserven la mayor parte de sus viajes a través de Internet.

Agentes de viaje

Probablemente reinventarán su rol como asesores personalizados y como fuente fiable de información para competir y diferenciarse de la caótica avalancha de información que puede representar Internet. Los agentes deberán posicionarse a partir de su oferta de profesionalidad, confianza, consejos personalizados y la experiencia imprescindible para manejar itinerarios de viaje complejos.

Clases virtuales

Las clases de asientos tal como las conocemos hoy posiblemente se fragmentarán para dar lugar a clases virtuales o clases personalizadas. No solo habrá asientos diferenciados físicamente (como en el caso actual de las butacas de Economy o Business), sino que comenzarán a dividirse o categorizarse a partir de las necesidades y preferencias de los viajeros: comidas, acceso a servicios como wifi, juegos o entretenimiento, requerimiento de zonas de descanso o sin perturbaciones, etc.

Fuente: http://www.clarin.com (texto adaptado)

1. Según el artículo, ¿en qué cambiarán los viajes en los próximos años?
2. ¿Qué deberán hacer los agentes de viaje para poder competir con Internet?
3. ¿Cómo se diferenciarán en el futuro los asientos en un avión?

 ▶ **Habla** con tu compañero(a) acerca de las ideas del artículo. ¿Están de acuerdo? ¿Qué otras previsiones pueden hacer?

 ▶ **Habla** con dos compañeros(as) sobre sus predicciones para 2025. ¿Habrán cambiado mucho los viajes? ¿Existirán las agencias de viaje tradicionales? ¿Cómo habrán evolucionado los medios de transporte?

Differentiated Instruction

DEVELOPING LEARNERS

- Ask students to state whether the following topics were discussed in the article:
  1. *Describe los destinos de moda en el futuro.* (no)
  2. *Los agentes de viaje tendrán que asistir a clases especiales.* (no)
  3. *En el futuro los europeos usarán Internet para reservar la mayoría de sus viajes.* (sí)
  4. *Los agentes de viaje tendrán que adaptarse.* (sí)
  5. *Habrá una nueva categorización de las clases de asientos.* (sí)
  6. *Habla del futuro papel de los auxiliares de vuelo.* (no)

EXPANDING LEARNERS

- Ask students to think about the pros and cons of using a travel agent or the Internet when planning a trip and making reservations. Divide the class into several small groups and explain that they will debate each other on the topic of travel agent vs. Internet. Assign each group one side of the issue and allow time for students to consider their arguments. Set time limits for presentations and rebuttals, and when all groups have debated, take a class vote to select the most convincing argument on each side.

50 **El tren de alta velocidad**

▶ **Escribe.** Imagina que en tu región van a construir una red de trenes de alta velocidad para unir las ciudades principales. Escribe una columna de opinión para el periódico local en la que expliques:

– Por qué es necesaria o innecesaria esa red de trenes.
– Cuáles son las ventajas e inconvenientes del proyecto.
– Qué tendría que pasar para que el proyecto fuera un éxito.
– Qué te emociona y qué temes del proyecto.

▶ **Presenta** tu columna a un grupo de compañeros(as). ¿Están ustedes de acuerdo?

Final del desafío

LA NARIZ DEL DIABLO

51 **¿Prueba conseguida?**

▶ **Escribe** la conversación que tuvieron Ethan y Eva mientras terminaban su maqueta. Usa el futuro o el condicional de probabilidad y el presente perfecto del subjuntivo.

Modelo   Eva: ¿Cuánta gente participaría en la construcción de este ferrocarril?

▶ **Habla** con tu compañero(a). Compara la fotografía de la página 202 y la maqueta que han hecho Ethan y Eva. ¿Crees que han logrado el desafío? ¿Por qué?

doscientos trece 213

Activities

49. For the third part of this activity, ask students to use some of their predictions from the Independent Starter. Have groups discuss the viability of their classmates' predictions. For example:

A. *No creo que los aviones sean mucho más rápidos en el futuro.*
B. *¿Cómo puedes decir eso?*
A. *Es que en los últimos 20 años no han cambiado mucho.*
C. *Tienes razón. Es una pena que no haya aumentado la velocidad de los aviones. Por eso creo que en el futuro viajaremos más por tren.*

50. You may want to assign the first part of this activity as homework. Then, for the second part, you may wish to hold a class debate after the presentations.

51. Have students work with a partner to write the script for the dialogue. Then, allow them rehearsal time and invite volunteer pairs to role-play their dialogues for the class.

Answer Key

49. Answers will vary. Sample answers:
   1. Se reservarán los viajes en Internet, los servicios al viajero serán más personalizados y habrá clases virtuales.
   2. Deberán personalizar y diferenciar sus servicios, y ser fuentes fiables de información.
   3. Se diferenciarán según las necesidades y preferencias de los viajeros; por ejemplo: comidas, entretenimiento, acceso a wifi, etc.
   ▶ Answers will vary.
   ▶ Answers will vary.
50. Answers will vary.
   ▶ Answers will vary.
51. Answers will vary.
   ▶ Answers will vary.

Additional Resources

Fans Online activities
Practice Workbook

HERITAGE LANGUAGE LEARNERS

• Explain to students that they are going to play the role of dynamic travel agents specializing in trips to their family's country of origin. Ask them to gather relevant print materials from a travel agency, tourism bureau, or the Internet, or encourage them to create their own, based on family photos or images found online. Students should be prepared to describe unique excursions that visitors may make, recommend places to stay, and address different modes of transportation. Ask students to make an oral presentation before the class.

COOPERATIVE LEARNING

• Ask students to work in groups of three and imagine that they are going to take the trip of a lifetime! First, they will need to discuss where they are going, how they are getting there, if they will use a travel agent or buy tickets and make reservations online. They will also need to describe places they want to visit. Once their plans are final, each member of the group will describe one of these facets. All will work together in addressing what they hope to learn from this cultural experience.

Unit 4
DESAFÍO 3

Expresar causa y consecuencia

Presentation

- In *Desafío 3*, Michelle and Daniel have to participate in a travel competition sponsored by an association of youth hostels. Students will preview language used to talk about travel and lodging, as well as to express cause and consequence.

Activities	Standards	Resources
Texto	1.2, 2.1, 2.2	
52.	1.1, 1.2	
53.	1.2, 1.3, 2.1, 2.2	
54.	1.1, 1.2, 2.1, 2.2, 5.2	
55. Comparaciones	1.2, 1.3, 2.1, 2.2, 4.2, 5.2	

Teaching Suggestions

Warm-Up / Independent Starter

- Ask students to list the type of lodging facilities they have stayed in or know about (e.g., *hotel, balneario, motel, pensión, cámping*).

Preparation

- Have students share their Independent Starters. Discuss with the class the features of the different accommodations students mentioned. You may want to categorize these lodging facilities from cheapest to most expensive, from most uncomfortable to most comfortable, from most boring to most fun, etc. Do some of the facilities specialize in a certain type of clientele (e.g., families, business people)?

Texto: Un concurso para viajeros

- Read the title and introduction to the dialogue. Had students heard of *albergues juveniles* (youth hostels)? Invite them to describe this type of accommodation or explain what they think these *albergues* are.
- Call on volunteers to role-play Daniel and Michelle and read their parts convincingly in front of the class. Ask students whether they think Michelle and Daniel have a good chance of winning this competition.

214

Un concurso para viajeros

Una red de albergues juveniles en España y México está promocionando un concurso llamado ¿Eres un «superviajero»? El premio consiste en pasar tres noches en cualquier albergue de la red. ¿Conseguirán ganarlo Daniel y Michelle?

DANIEL: ¿En qué se diferencia un albergue juvenil de un hotel o de una pensión?

MICHELLE: En los albergues juveniles se suelen alojar estudiantes y gente joven. Las habitaciones tienen varias camas y puedes compartir habitación con otros viajeros; por eso son más baratos que los hoteles. Y algunos ofrecen actividades para jóvenes.

DANIEL: ¡Qué divertido! ¡Tenemos que ganar el concurso! Yo he viajado mucho, ¿y tú?

MICHELLE: Sí, yo también. Como a mi familia y a mí nos encanta la naturaleza, casi siempre vamos de cámping. ¡Hemos paseado nuestra tienda de campaña y nuestros sacos de dormir por todo el hemisferio! Y el año pasado recorrimos varios países europeos en tren.

DANIEL: ¡Qué suerte! Pues nosotros normalmente nos alojamos en hoteles ubicados en el centro de la ciudad porque nos resulta más cómodo. Pero un año, para variar, hicimos un viaje en caravana y disfruté un montón.

MICHELLE: Entre los dos hemos viajado tanto que podemos considerarnos unos «superviajeros». Y, puesto que tenemos un montón de experiencia, ¿qué te parece si hacemos un video para el concurso en el que mostremos los distintos tipos de viaje que hemos hecho?

52 ### Detective de palabras

▶ **Completa** estas oraciones.

1. Si ganan el concurso, Daniel y Michelle pasarán tres noches en un ___1___.
2. Como les encanta la naturaleza, Michelle y su familia van de ___2___: tienen una ___3___ y varios ___4___.
3. La familia de Daniel suele alojarse en ___5___ ubicados en el centro de la ciudad.
4. Una vez Daniel hizo un viaje en ___6___ con su familia.

 ▶ **Habla** con tus compañeros(as). ¿Qué opinas del plan de Daniel y Michelle para ganar el concurso? ¿Qué incluirías tú en el video? Justifica tu respuesta.

Differentiated Instruction

DEVELOPING LEARNERS

- Have students complete the following sentences:
  1. *Una compañía / red de albergues juveniles promociona el concurso.* (red)
  2. *Los viajeros comparten / no reservan habitación en los albergues.* (comparten)
  3. *A Michelle le encanta ir de cámping / en caravana.* (de cámping)
  4. *Michelle ha viajado por las Américas y Asia / Europa.* (Europa)
  5. *Daniel suele alojarse en hoteles / albergues juveniles.* (hoteles)
  6. *Para variar, un año Daniel viajó en tren / caravana.* (caravana)

EXPANDING LEARNERS

- Ask students to imagine that they are going on a family vacation with older siblings, parents, and grandparents. Everyone has different interests: the students and their siblings are into some extreme sports; the parents want to relax and take in some cultural events; and the grandparents are fans of nature and enjoy hiking. Explain to students that they must find a destination and accommodations that would suit everyone in the family. After students complete their research, ask them to make an oral presentation in front of the class.

53 **¿Comprendes?**

▶ **Responde** a estas preguntas.

1. ¿Por qué hay jóvenes que prefieren alojarse en albergues?
2. ¿Qué diferencias entre los albergues y los hoteles se mencionan en el diálogo?
3. ¿Qué servicios de los hoteles crees que no suelen ofrecer los albergues?
4. ¿Alguna vez te has alojado en un albergue? ¿Te gustaría hacerlo? ¿Por qué?

54 **El turismo activo**

▶ **Lee.** ¿Qué es un(a) *turista activo(a)*? Escribe una definición con tus propias palabras.

El turismo activo

En la actualidad, hay una demanda creciente de un turismo lleno de emociones fuertes que permita realizar hazañas deportivas, tener experiencias únicas o hacer algo que servirá para el crecimiento personal.

Utilizar las vacaciones para dar rienda suelta al afán de aventura y de superación personal, vivir intensas emociones o hacer cosas que nunca hacemos en un ambiente distinto del habitual son las motivaciones de aquellos que quieren romper con su rutina diaria. El turismo activo es una forma de vacaciones que favorece las actividades físicas o deportivas que se practican sirviéndose de los recursos que ofrece la naturaleza y que llevan implícito el factor riesgo, cierto grado de esfuerzo físico y, en algunos casos, cierta destreza para su práctica.

Fuente: http://www.uhu.es (texto adaptado)

▶ **Compara** tu definición con la de tu compañero(a). Según sus definiciones, ¿son ustedes turistas activos(as)? ¿Por qué?

COMPARACIONES

La Red Española de Albergues Juveniles (REAJ)

Los albergues juveniles en España reciben cada año a más de un millón de viajeros amantes del turismo activo, cultural y deportivo, que buscan conocer a otros jóvenes del mundo. La Red Española de Albergues Juveniles forma parte de Hostelling International, una red mundial que permite a los jóvenes elegir entre más de 4.000 albergues situados en países de todo el mundo.

Logo internacional de albergues juveniles.

55 **Investiga y explica.** ¿Hay una red de albergues juveniles en tu país? ¿En qué se parecen o se diferencian de los albergues que hay en España?

HERITAGE LANGUAGE LEARNERS

• Ask students to go online to find information about *albergues juveniles* in or near a city of interest in Spain or Mexico. Have them do an analysis of several *albergues* before creating an ideal one where they might like to stay. Students will then describe their youth hostel, detailing its location, accommodations, prices, activities offered, contact information, and any restrictions (e.g., limits on number of days one may stay). Ask students to arrange their material in a webpage format and display their work in the classroom.

SPECIAL-NEEDS LEARNERS

• For students with difficulties staying focused while reading longer passages, copy Daniel and Michelle's conversation onto index cards, one card for each exchange. Then ask students to work with a partner and read the parts together, in sequence. When they finish reading, mix up the index cards and ask them to put the conversation back together in the correct order and read it once again. Have the pairs continue to work together on the remaining activities on these pages.

DESAFÍO 3

Expresar causa y consecuencia

Activities

53. To extend this activity, have students discuss question #4. Encourage them to talk about the pros and cons of staying in a youth hostel.

54. Once students have completed this activity, ask pairs to come up with a list of seven activities that they think could be part of an active tourism vacation. Encourage students to consider ecological, adventure, educational, socially compatible, cultural, and low-impact activities. Have pairs share their lists with the class and hold a vote to choose the top ten activities.

COMPARACIONES

La Red Española de Albergues Juveniles

Hostelling International (HI) is a nonprofit organization that comprises more than 70 national youth hostel associations. The first youth hostel opened in Germany in 1912, and soon the movement spread to other parts of the world. It is now on six continents and it has more than four million members.

Answer Key

52. 1. albergue juvenil 4. sacos de dormir
2. cámping 5. hoteles
3. tienda de campaña 6. caravana
▶ Answers will vary.

53. Answers will vary. Sample answers:
1. Porque son baratos y suelen ofrecer actividades para jóvenes.
2. En los albergues se alojan jóvenes, y se comparte habitación con otros viajeros. También son más baratos.
3. Creo que no tienen baño privado en las habitaciones, ni restaurante.
4. Answers will vary.

54. Answers will vary.
▶ Answers will vary.

55. Answers will vary.

Additional Resources

Fans Online activities

DESAFÍO 3

Vocabulario – El alojamiento

Presentation

- In this section, students will learn and use target vocabulary to talk about lodging and the weather.

Activities	Standards	Resources
Vocabulario	1.2	
56.	1.3	
57.	1.1, 1.2, 1.3, 5.2	Audio
58.	1.1, 1.2, 1.3, 5.1	
59. Cultura	1.2, 1.3, 2.2, 5.2	

Teaching Suggestions

Warm-Up / Independent Starter

- Ask students to write a paragraph describing their ideal accommodations for a one-week vacation. Have them include the location, facilities, cost, etc.

Preparation

- Focus students' attention on the photo of the *albergue* on page 216. Then read the description aloud. Do students think that the price is reasonable for the location? (You can find the exchange rate online.) Next, call on four volunteer students to take the roles of Ignacio, Julio, Marcos, and Begoña and read their entries aloud. After each entry is read, have students repeat the key words after you. As a class, discuss some of the positive as well as the negative aspects of this hostel.

- Ask students to look at the *Más vocabulario* feature. Have them repeat the words after you to practice correct pronunciation. Finally, have students revise their Independent Starters, and call on volunteers to share their paragraphs with the class.

Activities

57. For the third part of this activity, play the recording again so that students get a feel for each character's personality and preferences. Then have pairs reach a consensus on a solution that they think would satisfy both characters. Next, allow partners time to write a script for the dialogue and rehearse their lines. Finally, have pairs role-play their dialogues for the class.

Vocabulario

El alojamiento

INICIO	HOTELES	DESTINOS	FOTOS	COMENTARIOS

ALBERGUE SAN PABLO

83 % ambiente   **92 %** limpieza   **86 %** ubicación

Ignacio Perfecto para hospedarse tanto en verano como en invierno. Se puede practicar montañismo, hacer rutas en bici, alquilar canoas, esquiar... En temporada alta conviene reservar con antelación, aunque tengas que pagar por adelantado.

Julio Una atmósfera agradable y un personal muy amigable. Incluso nos prestaron una nevera portátil para ir de excursión.

Marcos Excelentes zonas de uso común: biblioteca, sala de juegos y TV... Mi única queja es que debería haber wifi gratuito y disponible en todas las habitaciones.

Begoña No ofrece las grandes comodidades de un hotel (si quieres servicio de habitaciones o que el botones te suba el equipaje, este no es tu sitio), pero es un lugar perfecto para los mochileros que recorren el mundo con poco dinero y a quienes no les importa compartir habitación o baño con otros huéspedes.

ver más...

Descripción

Alojamiento limpio y cómodo, ubicado al pie de las montañas y con vistas panorámicas.

Tarifa: 30 €/persona y día en habitación doble.

Media pensión (desayuno y almuerzo o cena) o pensión completa.

Más vocabulario

El cámping

la tienda de campaña   la caravana

el saco de dormir   la colchoneta

Más vocabulario

El tiempo meteorológico

la brisa	breeze
el chubasco	downpour
la niebla	fog
la ola de frío	cold wave
caluroso(a)	hot
glacial	bitterly cold
caer un chaparrón	to pour down

56 **Hablando de alojamiento**

▶ **Escribe** oraciones completas con estas palabras y expresiones.

Modelo   1. *Nos hospedamos en ese hotel porque el personal era muy agradable.*

1. hospedarse
2. nevera portátil
3. huésped
4. tienda de campaña
5. media pensión
6. caravana

216 doscientos dieciséis

Differentiated Instruction

DEVELOPING LEARNERS

- Have students match words from both columns.

1. *glacial* (e)	a. *empleado de hotel*
2. *brisa* (d)	b. *invitado*
3. *ubicado* (g)	c. *nubes bajas*
4. *personal* (i)	d. *viento suave*
5. *gratuito* (f)	e. *muy frío*
6. *huésped* (b)	f. *sin cobrar*
7. *chubasco* (h)	g. *localizado*
8. *niebla* (c)	h. *chaparrón*
9. *botones* (a)	i. *trabajadores*

EXPANDING LEARNERS

- Ask students to complete the following sentences with the correct word:

1. *Voy a llevar paraguas por si cae un...* (chaparrón)
2. *Hay que pagar el hotel por...* (adelantado)
3. *El ... me sube las maletas.* (botones)
4. *Los ... prefieren hospedarse en los albergues.* (mochileros)
5. *Cuando voy de cámping monto la...* (tienda de campaña)
6. *A veces hay mucha ... cerca del mar y no vemos bien.* (niebla)
7. *En algunos albergues el desayuno es...* (gratuito)

57 **Compañeros de viaje**

 ▶ **Escucha** la conversación y decide si estas afirmaciones son ciertas o falsas. Después, corrige las falsas.

1. Diego y Carla quieren alojarse en un albergue juvenil.
2. Un hotel lujoso les costará menos que un albergue.
3. Diego está muy bien preparado para hacer cámping.
4. A Diego no le encanta la idea de compartir su desayuno con otros viajeros.
5. Carla está segura de que hará un tiempo agradable.

▶ **Habla** con tu compañero(a). ¿Preferirías viajar con Diego o con Carla? Explica por qué.

▶ **Representen** un diálogo en el que Diego y Carla solucionan su conflicto sobre adónde ir y dónde alojarse.

58 **Hablamos de viajes**

▶ **Escribe** un resumen sobre un viaje que has hecho. Usa estas preguntas como guía:

– ¿Dónde, cuándo y con quién fuiste?
– ¿Qué actividades realizaste? ¿Qué fue lo que más te gustó?
– ¿Qué tiempo hacía?
– ¿Dónde te alojaste? ¿Qué características tenía el alojamiento? ¿Echaste algo en falta?

▶ **Lee** el texto de tu compañero(a) y ponle un título. Después, escribe algunas preguntas para saber más cosas de su viaje y contesta a las suyas.

 **CULTURA**

La Organización Mundial del Turismo (OMT)

La OMT es el organismo de las Naciones Unidas encargado de la promoción de un turismo responsable, sostenible y accesible para todos. Tiene su sede en Madrid.

Como principal organización internacional en el ámbito turístico, la OMT aboga por un turismo que contribuya al crecimiento económico, a un desarrollo incluyente y a la sostenibilidad ambiental, y ofrece liderazgo y apoyo al sector para expandir por el mundo sus conocimientos y políticas turísticas.

Fuente: ©UNWTO, 9284403513

59 **Investiga.** Visita la página oficial de la OMT (www.unwto.org). Averigua qué actividades realiza esta organización. Comparte la información con tus compañeros(as).

doscientos diecisiete 217

Vocabulario – El alojamiento

58. You may want to ask students to prepare a visual presentation for their texts. Encourage them to bring pictures of their trip to class, a brochure from the hotel or place where they stayed (or they can search for its webpage), etc. Then have students present their trips in small groups.

 AUDIO SCRIPT
See page 183L.

 CULTURA

La Organización Mundial del Turismo (OMT)

Tourism is a significant source of income for millions of families and a central industry in many countries. In fact, tourism directly represents close to 3% of the global Gross Domestic Product (GDP) and employs over 100 million people worldwide. The World Tourism Organization is the leading organization in the field of tourism. It was created in 1970 and it currently has more than 155 member countries and over 400 affiliated members.

Answer Key

56. Answers will vary.

57. 1. F. Carla quiere alojarse en un albergue.
2. F. Les costará más.
3. F. Carla está bien preparada.
4. F. Compartir habitación y baño.
5. F. Va a consultar el pronóstico del tiempo.
▶ Answers will vary.
▶ Answers will vary.

58. Answers will vary.
▶ Answers will vary.

59. Answers will vary.

Additional Resources

Fans Online activities
Practice Workbook

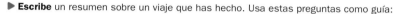

HERITAGE LANGUAGE LEARNERS

• Ask students to contact the tourism bureau that represents their family's country of origin. Explain to students that these government agencies are an excellent source for information on tourism. Encourage students to request brochures and recent data on accommodations, transportation, ecotourism, cultural events, and any other pertinent information. Ask students to share this information with the rest of the class. If students are not able to obtain printed materials from a tourism bureau, encourage them to go online, gather information, and report back to the class.

MULTIPLE INTELLIGENCES:
Interpersonal Intelligence

• Ask students to imagine that they are taking a trip with their best friend. One wants to stay at a youth hostel, the other prefers a hotel. Have students work with a partner and create a dialogue in which they express where they are going, how long they plan to stay, what they would like to visit, and where they plan to stay. Partners will need to work out a satisfactory solution as to their accommodations. Ask pairs to present their dialogues aloud.

DESAFÍO 3

Gramática – Expresar causa

Presentation

- In this section, students will review and expand on expressing the cause or reason for a situation.

Activities	Standards	Resources
Gramática	1.2, 3.1	
60.	1.2, 3.1, 4.1	
61.	1.2, 1.3	
62.	1.1, 1.2, 2.1, 2.2, 3.2	
63.	1.2, 1.3, 2.1, 2.2	Audio
64. Cultura	1.2, 1.3, 2.1, 2.2, 3.2	

Teaching Suggestions

Warm-Up / Independent Starter

- Have students answer these questions in writing: *¿Por qué hay más turistas en el verano? ¿Por qué se debe reservar hotel con antelación en temporada alta? ¿Por qué prefieren algunas personas los albergues?*

Preparation

- Have students read the grammar presentation with a partner and summarize the main points in their notebooks. Then ask volunteer pairs to explain each section of the presentation aloud to the class. Offer additional examples and ask questions to guide the students' presentations. Then ask pairs to rewrite their answers from the Independent Starter using some of the structures introduced in this grammar presentation (e.g., *Hay más turistas en verano debido a que mucha gente está de vacaciones*). Call on volunteers to share their answers. Does the class agree with their classmates' answers?

Activities

62. To expand this activity, have students write a question for each of the five statements. Then have them get together with a partner and check both their questions and answers.

63. After finishing this activity, play the recording a second time and have pairs continue one of the dialogues. Then invite volunteer pairs to act out their dialogues for the class.

Gramática

Expresar causa

Expresiones de causa

- Recuerda: para expresar la causa o la razón de una situación se usan estas estructuras:

| porque + indicativo | Nos quedamos en un albergue **porque** los hoteles **estaban** llenos. |

| por + infinitivo | **Por** no **reservar** un hotel, tuvimos que quedarnos en un albergue. |

Atención: porque + *indicativo* va siempre detrás de la cláusula principal; en cambio, por + *infinitivo* puede ir delante o detrás de la cláusula principal.

- También se usan estas otras estructuras en contextos formales y en el lenguaje escrito:

| ya que
puesto que + indicativo
dado que | **Puesto que** nos **gusta** nadar, fuimos a un hotel con piscina.
Pedro tuvo problemas, **ya que** no **había reservado** habitación. |

| debido a que + indicativo | No pasé frío **debido a que tenía** saco de dormir. |

| como + indicativo | **Como teníamos** una reserva, nos pudimos quedar en el parador. |

Como + *indicativo* va siempre delante de la cláusula principal. Las demás estructuras pueden ir delante o detrás.

Preguntar sobre la causa

- Recuerda: usa ¿Por qué...? + *indicativo* para preguntar por la causa o la razón de algo.

  ¿**Por qué** no **te quedaste** en la cabaña que habías reservado?

- En contextos más formales puedes usar estas estructuras:

| ¿Cuál es la razón/el motivo de...? + nombre | ¿A qué se debe(n)...? + nombre |

¿Cuál es el motivo de su cancelación?   ¿A qué se debe el retraso?

60 **Piensa.** Traduce estas oraciones de todas las maneras posibles.

a. *Since we love to cook, we rented an apartment and cooked our own food.*
b. *We didn't make a reservation because it was low season.*

61 **Preguntar sobre la causa**

▶ **Escribe** una pregunta para cada una de estas respuestas.

1. Porque los albergues eran más baratos que los hoteles.
2. Porque al viajar se aprende sobre las tradiciones y costumbres de otras culturas.
3. Porque Michelle y Daniel tienen mucha experiencia en viajes.
4. Por alojarse en un hotel de lujo.

218 doscientos dieciocho

Differentiated Instruction

DEVELOPING LEARNERS

- Have students use *una expresión de causa* to explain why they did each of the following. Sample answers are shown in parentheses.

  1. *Pedimos media pensión (porque no queríamos cenar en el hotel).*
  2. *(Por olvidar la tienda de campaña), tuvimos que dormir en el coche.*
  3. *(Debido a que cayó un chaparrón), nos mojamos.*
  4. *(Como no teníamos calefacción), pasamos mucho frío.*
  5. *(Puesto que nos encanta la naturaleza), buscamos un albergue en el campo.*

EXPANDING LEARNERS

- Have students work with a partner and create several short exchanges in order to practice *las expresiones de causa*. Taking turns, one student will make a statement using one of the expressions mentioned on the page (e.g., *Por no hacer la reserva con antelación...*). The partner will state the effect this has caused (e.g., *... tuvimos que cancelar nuestras vacaciones*). Then have students switch roles. Give pairs time to practice their exchanges and call on volunteers to act some of them out in front of the class.

62 **¿Por qué razón?**

▶ **Lee** la crítica de este hotel y completa las oraciones.

Hotel Puntarenas

Este encantador hotel está ubicado en Costa Rica, en la costa central del Pacífico, en uno de los últimos «zoológicos naturales» del mundo. Es una zona maravillosa, con playas paradisíacas de arena blanca y aguas de color turquesa. Y si lo que prefieres es el ecoturismo, puedes hacer rutas en el Parque Nacional Manuel Antonio, situado a pocos minutos del hotel.

El hotel cuenta con todos los servicios necesarios: las habitaciones tienen aire acondicionado, baño privado, televisor, acceso a Internet y caja de seguridad. Los huéspedes pueden también disfrutar de una gran piscina con *jacuzzi* y un patio con barbacoa.

Además de las habitaciones con terraza que dan al mar, recomiendo especialmente las que tienen vistas al parque nacional porque el paisaje es precioso y son muy tranquilas.

1. Como el hotel está bien situado…
2. Se recomienda visitar las playas de la zona, ya que…
3. En el hotel se puede comer al aire libre, puesto que…
4. Se le considera un buen hotel debido a que…
5. Se recomiendan las habitaciones con vistas al parque nacional por…

63 **Las razones perfectas**

 ▶ **Escucha** y escribe un resumen para cada mini-diálogo, utilizando las expresiones de causa de la ficha de Gramática.

Modelo   1. *Vamos a recorrer la ruta inca, ya que nos gusta mucho la Historia.*

 **CULTURA**

El Titicaca: el lago místico de los incas

El Titicaca, ubicado entre Perú y Bolivia, es el lago navegable más alto del mundo y el segundo más grande de Suramérica. El impacto del turismo en la zona es cada vez mayor, ya que en sus más de cuarenta islas se pueden hacer multitud de actividades: navegar, practicar senderismo, observar la fauna y la flora, conocer las costumbres locales, etc. En algunas islas los habitantes ofrecen alojamiento a los visitantes.

Hotel a orillas del lago Titicaca.

64 **Explica.** ¿Cuál puede ser el impacto de tantos turistas en esta zona? ¿Cuáles son las ventajas y desventajas de alojarte en casas privadas cuando viajas?

Gramática – Expresar causa

 AUDIO SCRIPT
See page 183M.

 CULTURA

El Titicaca: el lago místico de los incas

Lake Titicaca lies at about 12,500 feet above sea level and covers some 3,200 square miles. According to Incan mythology, the first Inca and his wife emerged from the waters of this lake to build the Incan Empire. However, archaeologists believe that the shores of Lake Titicaca have been inhabited by different civilizations since around 200 BCE, predating the Incas.

Answer Key

60. a. Como/Puesto que/Dado que/Ya que nos encanta cocinar, alquilamos un apartamento y preparamos la comida.

b. No reservamos debido a que/porque era temporada baja. Por ser/Como era temporada baja, no reservamos.

61. Answers will vary. Sample answers:
1. ¿Por qué se quedaron en albergues?
2. ¿Cuál es la razón de tus viajes?
3. ¿Por qué van a ganar el concurso Michelle y Daniel?
4. ¿Por qué gastaron tanto?

62. Answers will vary. Sample answers:
1. … ofrece muchas actividades al viajero.
2. … son paradisíacas.
3. … tiene un patio con barbacoa.
4. … cuenta con todos los servicios necesarios.
5. … el espectacular paisaje.

63. Answers will vary.

64. Answers will vary.

Additional Resources

Fans Online activities
Practice Workbook

219

HERITAGE LANGUAGE LEARNERS

• Ask students to research other hotels in Spanish-speaking countries that cater to ecotourism and to select one. Encourage students to look for those that may be located in their family's country of origin. Ask students to describe the area near the hotel, the typical flora and fauna one may observe, the measures taken to protect the environment and any species in danger of extinction, as well as excursions to observe nature. Encourage students to mention the hotel's accommodations, services, and any special activities.

MULTIPLE INTELLIGENCES:
Intrapersonal Intelligence

• Ask students to imagine that they are going to visit Lake Titicaca and the region around it. Have them keep a travel journal with their observations of the topography, indigenous people, local customs, and archaeological sites, as well as their impressions of their stay with a local family. Students need to do some research on the region so their observations are based on facts as well as their own feelings. Invite students to share their journals with the rest of the class.

DESAFÍO 3

Gramática – Expresar consecuencia

Presentation

- In this section, students will review and expand on how to express the consequences or conclusion of a previously stated event.

Activities	Standards	Resources
Gramática	1.2, 3.1	
65.	1.2, 3.1	
66.	1.2, 1.3, 3.1	
67.	1.2, 1.3	
68.	1.1	
69.	1.1, 1.3, 2.1, 2.2, 5.2	

Teaching Suggestions

Warm-Up / Independent Starter

- Write the following sentences on the board and ask students to identify both the cause and the consequence in each sentence:
  - *Había una ola de frío, así que no pudimos salir.*
  - *No habíamos reservado con antelación; por eso no pudimos quedarnos en el albergue.*
  - *Hacía mucho calor, por lo tanto, pusimos el aire acondicionado.*

Preparation

- As a class, discuss the Independent Starter. Call on three volunteers to identify the cause and the consequence in each sentence. Then have students identify the structures that express consequence. *(así que; por eso; por lo tanto)*
- Have students read the grammar presentation silently and ask them to prepare questions about what they do not understand. Then ask students to work in small groups to answer any questions their peers have.

Activities

68. To expand this activity, have pairs choose one of the situations and come up with a story. They should include some background information about the characters, explain what happened that provoked the depicted outcome, and conclude by saying how the situation was resolved. If time permits, have pairs illustrate their stories.

220

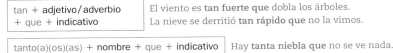

Expresar consecuencia

Expresiones de consecuencia

- Recuerda: para expresar las consecuencias o la conclusión de lo que se dice en la cláusula principal, usa estas estructuras:

así (es) que + indicativo	La Florida tiene un clima cálido, **así (es) que nieva** poco.
por eso + indicativo	Tuvimos una ola de frío; **por eso cerraron** las escuelas.

- Las siguientes estructuras se usan también comúnmente para expresar consecuencia:

en consecuencia por (lo) tanto + indicativo por consiguiente	Ha llovido y, **por consiguiente**, tenemos que cancelar la excursión.

Expresiones intensivas

- Para enfatizar la intensidad de un evento y sus consecuencias, usa estas estructuras:

tan + adjetivo/adverbio + que + indicativo	El viento es **tan fuerte que** dobla los árboles. La nieve se derritió **tan rápido que** no la vimos.

tanto(a)(os)(as) + nombre + que + indicativo	Hay **tanta niebla que** no se ve nada.

verbo + tanto + que + indicativo	Ayer **llovió tanto que** se inundaron las calles.

- Atención: en español nunca se omite la palabra *que* en las estructuras intensivas.

  Hacía tanto calor **que** *tuvimos que cancelar la caminata.*
  It was so hot (that) we had to cancel the hike.

65 **Piensa.** ¿Se puede alterar el orden de la cláusula que expresa consecuencia? ¿Por qué?

66 **Causas y consecuencias**

▶ **Decide** qué parte de estas oraciones expresa consecuencia. Después, transfórmalas escribiendo una consecuencia distinta.

Modelo   Los empleados estaban tan ocupados <u>que no tenían tiempo para ir de vacaciones</u>.
     ⟶ *Los empleados estaban tan ocupados que no nos atendieron tan bien como siempre.*

1. Nevaba tanto que no pudimos salir del hotel a esquiar.
2. Ana busca unas vacaciones de aventura; por eso viajará a las islas Galápagos.
3. Hace demasiado frío; por consiguiente, se ha cancelado la excursión.
4. Queremos ir de cámping, así es que necesitamos unos sacos de dormir.

220 doscientos veinte

Differentiated Instruction

DEVELOPING LEARNERS

- Ask students to complete these sentences by stating the consequences. Sample answers are shown in parentheses.
  1. *A Marcos le encanta la naturaleza, así que...* (*suele ir de cámping.*)
  2. *Era fiesta y fin de semana, por lo tanto...* (*no había habitaciones disponibles.*)
  3. *Hay niebla y, por consiguiente...* (*no vamos a navegar.*)
  4. *No tienen habitaciones privadas; en consecuencia...* (*tendremos que compartir.*)
  5. *Es un hotel pequeño, así que...* (*es mejor reservar con antelación.*)

EXPANDING LEARNERS

- Ask students to express the possible consequences in the following situations. Sample answers are shown in parentheses.
  1. *No piensas estudiar para el examen final...* (*así que es posible que no apruebes.*)
  2. *No sabes montar una tienda de campaña...* (*por lo tanto, tendrás que pedir ayuda.*)
  3. *Prefieres desayunar y almorzar en el hotel...* (*por eso pides media pensión.*)
  4. *Siempre cae un chaparrón por la tarde y...* (*por consiguiente, llevas el paraguas.*)

67 **Hay que saber más**

▶ **Completa** estas oraciones utilizando distintas expresiones de consecuencia.

Modelo   1. *Nos gustaría alojarnos en un castillo, así que vamos a preguntar en una buena agencia de viajes.*

1. Nos gustaría alojarnos en un castillo...
2. Los mochileros prefieren viajar económicamente...
3. Por la tarde cayó un chaparrón...
4. Mi madre no querrá compartir habitación...
5. Me encantaría viajar sola...
6. El hotel ofrece media pensión...

68 **Consecuencias**

▶ **Habla** con tu compañero(a) sobre las consecuencias de cada una de estas situaciones.

Modelo   1. *El autobús se rompió, por eso los chicos decidieron irse a pie.*

69 **Tan-tan**

▶ **Habla** con tu compañero(a) sobre el significado de estos chistes.

1. Era un hombre tan calvo, tan calvo, que se le veían las ideas.

2. Ella es tan dulce, tan dulce, que la echan en el café.

3. Era un hombre tan alto, tan alto, que se tropezó en un pueblo y se cayó en otro.

▶ **Escribe** con tu compañero(a) tres chistes más utilizando esta fórmula gramatical. Después, léanlos en alto para la clase.

doscientos veintiuno 221

Gramática – Expresar consecuencia

69. This is a good activity to use to play with the language and have fun. As pairs prepare their jokes, help them with pacing and stress. Remind students that fluency is key, since poor fluency hinders comprehension. Allow students time to rehearse. At the end, hold a class vote to choose the three funniest jokes.

Answer Key

65. No, porque esa cláusula expresa una consecuencia de la oración principal.

66. Answers will vary. Sample answers:
1. ... no pudimos salir del hotel a esquiar. Nevaba tanto que suspendieron las clases.
2. ... viajará a las islas Galápagos. Ana busca unas vacaciones de aventura; por eso se irá en un crucero por el río Amazonas.
3. ... se ha cancelado la excursión. Hace demasiado frío; por consiguiente, nos quedamos en casa.
4. ... necesitamos unos sacos de dormir. Queremos ir de cámping, así es que vamos a reservar lugar en el cámping.

67. Answers will vary. Sample answers:
2. ... por eso se quedan en albergues.
3. ... por lo tanto, no salimos del hotel.
4. ... por consiguiente, tenemos que reservar otra habitación para nosotros.
5. ... así es que me voy de vacaciones a Buenos Aires.
6. ... por eso desayunamos siempre en el hotel.

68. Answers will vary.

69. Answers will vary.
▶ Answers will vary.

Additional Resources

Fans Online activities
Practice Workbook

221

HERITAGE LANGUAGE LEARNERS

• After students complete activity 68, ask them to bring in two pairs of illustrations from magazines, newspapers, or from online. Each pair of images should be related, so that a brief story might be told using each set. Ask students to describe what is going on in the first illustration of one pair. Then, have them explain what the consequence is, according to the second illustration. Explain that they must use *una expresión de consecuencia* in their explanation. Have the class vote on the most original consequence.

COOPERATIVE LEARNING

• Have students work in small groups and explain to them that they will write a nonsense story that uses *expresiones intensivas* to exaggerate the personality traits and physical characteristics of the characters, as well as their abilities to carry out their actions. One member of the group will write the first line of the story and pass it on to the next, who will add to it. After each student has had two turns at writing, call time and have the groups read their work aloud.

LECTURA: TEXTO LITERARIO

Presentation

- In this section, students will read an excerpt from Gabriel García Márquez's autobiography, *Vivir para contarla*. As they read, they will review vocabulary related to travel by train.

Activities	Standards	Resources
Lectura: texto literario	1.1, 1.2, 2.1, 2.2, 3.1, 3.2	
70.	1.2, 1.3	
71.	1.3	
72.	1.2, 1.3, 2.1, 2.2	

Teaching Suggestions

Warm-Up / Independent Starter

- Ask students to observe the picture and write the answers to the questions in the *Antes de leer* section.

Preparation

- Call on individual students to share their Independent Starters. Ask students who have heard of Gabriel García Márquez or have read some of his writings to share what they know about this author with the class. Explain that *Vivir para contarla* is García Márquez's autobiography. It was published in 2002 and it focuses on his childhood and youth. You may wish to share with students this quote from *Vivir para contarla*: *La vida no es la que uno vivió, sino la que uno recuerda y cómo la recuerda para contarla.* If time allows, discuss with the class what García Márquez might have meant by this comment.

- Read the text aloud to model pronunciation and have students follow along in their books. Then call on individual students to each read a paragraph aloud. Offer assistance with pronunciation. Finally, have students read the text again individually.

Activities

70. To extend this activity, ask pairs to speculate on what might have caused the decline of the train. Invite students to share their theories with the class.

Antes de leer: estrategias

1. Lee el título. ¿A qué crees que se refiere el pronombre *la* en *Vivir para contarla*?
2. Haz una lista con todas las palabras que recuerdes relacionadas con los trenes. Después, compárala con la de tu compañero(a).

Vivir para contarla

Mi madre y yo llegamos a la estación pasadas las ocho, pero el tren estaba demorado[1]. Sin embargo, fuimos los únicos pasajeros. Ella se dio cuenta desde que entró en el vagón vacío, y exclamó con un humor festivo:

—¡Qué lujo! ¡Todo el tren para nosotros solos!

Siempre he pensado que fue un júbilo fingido[2] para disimular[3] su desencanto, pues los estragos[4] del tiempo se veían a simple vista en el estado de los vagones. Eran los antiguos de segunda clase, pero sin asientos de mimbre[5] ni cristales de subir y bajar en las ventanas, sino con bancas de madera curtidas por los fondillos[6] lisos y calientes de los pobres. En comparación con lo que fue en otro tiempo, no solo aquel vagón sino todo el tren era un fantasma de sí mismo. Antes tenía tres clases. La tercera, donde viajaban los más pobres, eran los mismos huacales[7] de tablas donde transportaban el banano o las reses de sacrificio, adaptados para pasajeros con bancas longitudinales de madera cruda. La segunda clase, con asientos de mimbre y marcos de bronce. La primera clase, donde viajaban las gentes del gobierno y altos empleados de la compañía bananera, con alfombras en el pasillo y poltronas[8] forradas de terciopelo rojo que podían cambiar de posición. Cuando viajaba el superintendente de la compañía, o su familia, o sus invitados de nota, enganchaban[9] en la cola del tren un vagón de lujo con ventanas de vidrios solares y cornisas doradas, y una terraza descubierta con mesitas para viajar tomando el té. No conocí ningún mortal que hubiera visto por dentro esa carroza[10] de fantasía. Mi abuelo había sido alcalde dos veces y además tenía una noción alegre del dinero, pero solo viajaba en segunda si iba con alguna mujer de la familia. Y cuando le preguntaban por qué viajaba en tercera, contestaba: «Porque no hay cuarta». Sin embargo, en otros tiempos, lo más recordable del tren había sido la puntualidad. Los relojes de los pueblos se ponían en la hora exacta por su silbato[11].

Aquel día, por un motivo o por otro, partió con una hora y media de retraso. Cuando se puso en marcha, muy despacio y con un chirrido[12] lúgubre[13] mi madre se persignó[14], pero enseguida volvió a la realidad.

GABRIEL GARCÍA MÁRQUEZ. *Vivir para contarla* (selección)

---

1. retrasado
2. no real
3. ocultar
4. daño, ruina
5. *wicker*
6. *bottoms*
7. *crates*
8. sillas amplias
9. *hooked up*
10. *carriage*
11. *whistle*
12. *squeak*
13. triste
14. *made the sign of the cross*

Differentiated Instruction

DEVELOPING LEARNERS

- Ask students to match words from both columns, and then have them write the word pairs in their notebooks.

  1. *demorar* (g)
  2. *fingido* (h)
  3. *disimular* (e)
  4. *desencanto* (b)
  5. *fantasma* (a)
  6. *poltrona* (i)
  7. *enganchar* (d)
  8. *noción* (j)
  9. *banca* (c)
  10. *partir* (f)

  a. *aparición*
  b. *decepción*
  c. *asiento de madera*
  d. *sujetar*
  e. *disfrazar*
  f. *salir*
  g. *tardar*
  h. *falso*
  i. *silla cómoda*
  j. *idea*

EXPANDING LEARNERS

- Ask students to imagine that a studio has decided to turn García Márquez's memoirs into a feature film and they will create the script. Have students rewrite the narrative as a dialogue, adding a conversation between mother and son, and possibly with the conductor or ticket agent. Encourage students to also indicate the main characters' destination and to explain, through their conversation, what they were doing in Aracataca. When students complete their scripts, have them assign the roles to other classmates who will act them out in front of the class.

70 ¿Comprendes?

▶ **Decide** si estas afirmaciones son ciertas o falsas. Después, corrige las falsas.

1. La madre se alegra mucho de que no haya más pasajeros en el tren.
2. Ahora en el tren hay tres clases de vagones.
3. Antes en los vagones de tercera clase viajaban juntos pasajeros y mercancías.
4. El director de la compañía bananera solía viajar en primera clase.
5. El abuelo del protagonista viajaba siempre en primera clase.
6. Antes el tren salía siempre con retraso.

▶ **Escribe** las diferencias entre el antiguo tren y el tren en el que se montan el protagonista y su madre.

El tren antiguo	El tren del relato
Los vagones de segunda tenían asientos de mimbre y cristales en las ventanas.	

71 Significa que...

▶ **Explica** el significado de estas oraciones con tus propias palabras.

1. Mi madre y yo llegamos a la estación pasadas las ocho, pero el tren estaba demorado.
2. Siempre he pensado que fue un júbilo fingido para disimular su desencanto.
3. Cuando viajaba el superintendente de la compañía, o su familia, o sus invitados de nota, enganchaban en la cola del tren un vagón de lujo.
4. No conocí ningún mortal que hubiera visto por dentro esa carroza de fantasía.
5. Cuando se puso en marcha, muy despacio y con un chirrido lúgubre, mi madre se persignó.

72 Con tus propias palabras

▶ **Investiga** sobre la vida del escritor, sobre su familia y sobre la región colombiana en la que vivió su niñez. Elige una anécdota de su vida que te haya gustado especialmente y escribe una página de su biografía.

"ME SIENTO LATINOAMERICANO DE CUALQUIER PAIS, PERO SIN RENUNCIAR NUNCA A LA NOSTALGIA DE MI TIERRA: ... , A LA CUAL REGRESE UN DIA Y DESCUBRI QUE ENTRE LA RE... Y LA NOSTALGIA ESTABA LA MATERIA PRIMA DE MI OBRA"

COLEGIO DEPARTAMENTAL DE BACHILLERATO AC...
Forjando el futuro de Maco...

▶ **Busca** fotografías para ilustrar tu texto y presenta tu trabajo a tus compañeros(as).

HERITAGE LANGUAGE LEARNERS

• Ask students to imagine that they are also passengers on the train that García Márquez and his mother are on. Ask them to write a short narrative from this new passenger's point of view and describe, among other things, the two passengers mentioned in the passage, the condition of the train, and the trip itself. Students might also explain why they were on the train and what they were doing in the town of Aracataca, along with any other interesting anecdote that will make the narrative more appealing.

CRITICAL THINKING

• Ask students to discuss the influence or role one's place of birth has—or may not have—on one's life story or on one's formation. Encourage them to consider the social factors (family, friends, language) as well as the physical ones (geography, weather, etc.). Then, ask students to write a short autobiography that includes a description of the impact—or lack thereof—that their place of birth has had on them. Post their autobiographies throughout the classroom and have students guess one another's identity.

LECTURA: TEXTO LITERARIO

72. You may want to assign this activity as homework and use the time in class for students to present their work. As a class, discuss some of the most interesting anecdotes or pieces of information.

Answer Key

70. Answers will vary. Sample answers:
1. F. Finge alegrarse, pero está decepcionada.
2. F. Solo hay una clase.
3. F. Era el mismo tipo de vagones, pero estaban adaptados para pasajeros.
4. C.
5. F. Viajaba en tercera o en segunda.
6. F. Antes el tren era puntual.
▶ El tren antiguo: Tenía tres clases. Viajaban muchos pasajeros de distintas clases sociales. La primera clase era muy lujosa. Era puntual.
El tren del relato: Los vagones de segunda tenían bancas de madera y no tenían cristales de subir y bajar en las ventanas. Solo tiene una clase. Ya no lo usa casi nadie; va vacío. No tiene lujos; está en mal estado. No es puntual.

71. Answers will vary. Sample answers:
1. Llegaron tarde, pero el tren no había llegado porque estaba retrasado.
2. Su alegría no fue real, pues estaba decepcionada, pero no quería que se notara.
3. Si iba el superintendente o sus allegados, le añadían al tren un vagón lujoso solo para ellos.
4. No conocía a nadie que hubiera estado en ese vagón de lujo.
5. El tren era lento y hacía ruido porque estaba viejo. La madre se asustó.

72. Answers will vary.
▶ Answers will vary.

Additional Resources

Fans Online activities

223

DESAFÍO 3

Comunicación

Presentation

- In this section, students will integrate the vocabulary and grammar skills from *Desafío 3* to express cause and consequence in various tasks. They will also write the script for a dialogue about travel.

Activities	Standards	Resources
73.	1.2, 1.3, 3.1	
74.	1.1, 1.3, 5.1	
75.	1.2	Audio
76. Final del desafío	1.1, 1.2, 1.3, 2.1, 2.2	

Teaching Suggestions

Warm-Up / Independent Starter

- Ask students to join the following sentences using appropriate structures to express consequence:
  1. *En los albergues se comparte habitación. Son más baratos.*
  2. *Daniel y Michelle han viajado mucho. Van a ganar el concurso.*
  3. *Está nublado y corre brisa. Va a llover.*
  4. *Vamos de cámping en temporada alta. Hay que reservar con antelación.*

Preparation

- Call on students to share their Independent Starters. Then, review the structures they used to express consequence. Next, give students a few moments to review the grammar presentation on page 218, and then have them rewrite their sentences from the Independent Starter using structures to express cause. For example: 1. *Como se comparte habitación, los albergues son más baratos.* 2. *Puesto que han viajado mucho, Daniel y Michelle van a ganar el concurso.* Invite students to share their sentences with the class. Provide additional examples, if necessary.

- For further vocabulary practice, assign small groups one of these accommodations: *un hotel de lujo, un balneario, una pensión, un albergue, un cámping.* Have groups describe their assigned lodging in detail to the rest of the class, and have the class guess the type of lodging.

Comunicación

73 **Consulta el clima**

▶ **Lee** este borrador de un texto sobre los viajes y escríbelo de nuevo usando expresiones de causa y consecuencia. No olvides ponerle un título.

> Es importante consultar las predicciones meteorológicas antes de planear un viaje a las montañas. A más altura, las temperaturas son generalmente más bajas. Hay que averiguar la altura del destino para anticipar las condiciones climáticas. Pero las predicciones nunca son del todo fiables. Es bueno llevar en tu maleta ropa de abrigo, algún impermeable y protección contra los rayos UV. Así, si falla la predicción, estarás preparado.
>
> El viento crea condiciones muy especiales en las montañas. La altura de las montañas altera las corrientes de aire. Las corrientes de aire crean microclimas. En las áreas montañosas la temperatura suele ser siempre más baja.
>
> También hay probabilidad de nieve y de frío. Las olas de frío y las nevadas son un factor que se debe tener en cuenta. Si hay mucha cantidad de nieve, los caminos se pueden congelar o bloquear y es posible que tengas que permanecer allí más tiempo del que esperabas.

74 **Los beneficios de viajar**

▶ **Habla** con tu compañero(a) sobre estas citas. Usa expresiones de causa y consecuencia.

Modelo
A. *Puesto que viajar es hoy mucho más fácil, es bueno hacerlo para aprender cómo vive otra gente.*
B. *Tienes razón. Por eso es importante explorar a fondo los lugares en vez de quedarse en los sitios turísticos o en los hoteles.*

Viajamos para cambiar no de lugar, sino de ideas.
Hipólito Taine, escritor francés

Viajar es imprescindible y la sed de viaje, un síntoma neto de inteligencia.
Enrique Jardiel Poncela, escritor español

▶ **Escribe** una entrada para un blog turístico titulado: *Sin viajar, el mundo es limitado y pequeño.* Habla sobre las causas y las consecuencias de viajar.

Differentiated Instruction

DEVELOPING LEARNERS

- Prepare index cards with *expresiones de causa, preguntas sobre la causa, expresiones de consecuencia,* and *expresiones intensivas.* Distribute several to students and have them ask questions or make statements using the expressions they were given. If students have *puesto que,* they might say: *Puesto que no queremos gastar mucho, vamos a hospedarnos en un albergue juvenil.* Should students have *debido a que,* their answer might be: *Debido a que queríamos hacer senderismo, buscamos un albergue ubicado en las montañas.* Encourage them to create sentences around the topics of lodging and climate.

EXPANDING LEARNERS

- Ask students to imagine that they have just returned from their first trip abroad. Ask them to name the country and cities visited, and to describe their first impressions of their experience. If students have traveled abroad, ask them to relate their impressions of their trip. Students should write at least two paragraphs describing their experience, and include what most surprised (or shocked) them, the most agreeable part of their trip (as well as the most disagreeable), and their own recommendations for future visits.

75 Prepárate para ganar

 ▶ **Escucha** y elige la opción correcta.

1. Según Daniel, un «superviajero» es una persona que:
   a. elige los mejores viajes.
   b. ha viajado mucho.
   c. suele ir de cámping.

2. Michelle opina que un «superviajero» se aloja:
   a. en los mejores hoteles.
   b. en lugares con buenas vistas.
   c. en cualquier lugar, según sus preferencias.

3. Una característica importante del «superviajero», según Michelle, es:
   a. la sociabilidad.
   b. la capacidad de improvisar.
   c. el gusto por el riesgo.

Final del desafío

MICHELLE: Por la variedad de experiencias que hemos vivido, nos va a salir un video fabuloso. ¡Si ganamos el concurso tendremos la oportunidad de pasar tres noches en cualquier albergue que escojamos! ¡Qué emocionante!

DANIEL: Sí, pero lo difícil será decidir adónde vamos.

MICHELLE: ¿Por qué no viajamos a un sitio que ni tú ni yo hayamos visitado antes?

DANIEL: Me parece bien. ¿Has oído la frase del filósofo francés Jean Jacques Rosseau que dice «Hay mucha diferencia entre viajar para ver países y para ver pueblos»? Tú y yo deberíamos inclinarnos por lo segundo, ¿no?

76 Los «superviajeros»

▶ **Escribe** el guion del video de Michelle y Daniel. Ten en cuenta que en él deben explicar por qué se consideran unos «superviajeros».

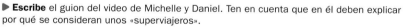 ▶ **Habla** con tus compañeros(as). ¿Qué significa la afirmación de Rousseau que cita Daniel? Justifica tu respuesta.

HERITAGE LANGUAGE LEARNERS

• Have students describe a place that they have never visited and would like to see. Ask them to justify why they want to travel to this spot and what they hope to learn from their trip. They should include details as to how they would travel there, what kind of accommodations they would look for, how long they plan to stay, and what kind of weather they might expect. Students also need to address the places and events of interest they would like to observe.

CRITICAL THINKING

• Ask students to think about how they would complete the statements in activity 75. Explain that they may opt to include answers that do not appear as options. Then, facilitate a classroom discussion on students' perceptions of a *superviajero* and have them be prepared to justify their opinions. Encourage students to talk about their own travel experience, or that of a family member. Ask if they consider themselves or any family member to be *superviajeros,* and why this term can be applied to them.

Activities

73. You may want to complete the first paragraph as a class. Explain to students that they should first identify the cause as well as the consequence in each pair of sentences. It might be possible to change the order of the sentences. For example: *A más altura, las temperaturas son generalmente más bajas; por eso, es importante consultar las predicciones…* There may also be several correct possibilities. For example: *Dado que a más altura las temperaturas son generalmente más bajas, es importante consultar…* Emphasize that the key to joining these sentences correctly is to know which is the cause and which is the consequence.

74. To extend this activity, have pairs search for additional quotes related to travel and choose one that they would like to talk about. Then ask students to share their quotes with the class.

76. Have students work in small groups to come up with the script for this video. If students have access to video recording equipment, encourage them to record their dialogues. Then have students watch the video and critique themselves.

AUDIO SCRIPT
See page 183M.

Answer Key

73. Answers will vary.

74. Answers will vary.
   ▶ Answers will vary.

75. 1. b   2. c   3. a

76. Answers will vary.
   ▶ Answers will vary.

Additional Resources
Fans Online activities
Practice Workbook

225

Presentation

- In this section, students will review the unit objectives and put them into practice. They will listen to a radio program about Caribbean music, and talk about what their classmates might have done by the end of the school year. They will also select one of the following *desafíos* to develop: prepare a presentation about a music genre from the Caribbean, look for information on a famous amusement park in Latin America and create a brochure, or present a plan for a trip to a Spanish-speaking country.

Activities	Standards	Resources
77.	1.2, 1.3, 2.1, 2.2, 3.2, 5.1	Audio
78.	1.1, 1.3, 5.1	
79. Tu desafío	1.2, 1.3, 2.1, 2.2, 3.1, 3.2, 5.1, 5.2	

Teaching Suggestions

Warm-Up / Independent Starter

- Have students write a sentence expressing a conjecture for each of the following situations:
  1. *Le pusieron una multa.*
  2. *Hay mucho tráfico en esta ciudad.*
  3. *Elena no me ha llamado desde que discutimos.*

Preparation

- Invite students to share their Independent Starters. Write some of the answers on the board and review the use of the future or the conditional to express conjecture. For additional practice, have students write three statements, similar to the ones in the Independent Starter, and exchange them with a partner. Pairs should write conjectures for each other's statements.

- To practice the weather vocabulary, discuss with the class the typical weather for each season in your community. Then compare and contrast the weather in your community with the weather in an opposite region of the country. For instance, if you are located in the Southeast, compare the weather there with the weather in the Northwest. Next, discuss the types of leisure activities and sports that can be practiced in both regions at different times of the year.

Todo junto

ESCUCHAR Y ESCRIBIR

77 **Un artista muy versátil**

 ▶ **Escucha** el programa de radio que Asha y Lucas oyeron cuando investigaban sobre la música del Caribe y decide si estas oraciones son ciertas o falsas.

1. El invitado del programa es Tito Rodríguez.
2. Tito Rodríguez nació en 1923.
3. La madre de Tito Rodríguez era dominicana.
4. Tito Rodríguez solo sabía cantar boleros.
5. La canción que ponen en el programa es un mambo.

Disco de Tito Rodríguez.

 ▶ **Escucha** el programa de nuevo y responde a las preguntas.

1. ¿Por qué Tito Rodríguez es un artista muy caribeño?
2. ¿Por qué Tito Rodríguez es un músico muy versátil?

▶ **Escribe** un párrafo dando respuesta a estas preguntas. Contesta usando tu propia experiencia.

1. ¿Qué tipo de música sueles escuchar?
2. ¿Cuál es tu artista favorito? ¿Por qué?
3. De todas sus canciones, ¿cuál prefieres? ¿Por qué?
4. ¿Hay alguna canción que te identifique a ti? ¿Cuál es? ¿Por qué?

HABLAR Y ESCRIBIR

78 **Para terminar el año**

 ▶ **Habla** con tu compañero(a). Piensen en la personalidad, los gustos y aficiones de sus compañeros(as) de clase e imaginen un viaje que uno(a) de ellos(as) habrá hecho cuando acabe el curso.

Modelo
A. *Es posible que a final de curso Shawn haya ido de viaje a Puerto Rico porque tiene familia allí y le encanta disfrutar del sol y la playa.*
B. *Sí, y es probable que Steve lo haya acompañado, porque es su mejor amigo.*

▶ **Escribe.** ¿Qué cosas habrás hecho cuando termine el curso? ¿A qué lugares habrás viajado?

Differentiated Instruction

DEVELOPING LEARNERS

- Have students complete the following sentences with the correct tense of the subjunctive mood:
  1. *Me enoja que tú...*
  2. *Llamaré al botones cuando...*
  3. *Me ha sorprendido que los peatones...*
  4. *Deseo que tú...*
  5. *¿Te sorprendió que yo no...?*
  6. *A la gente le suele molestar que...*
  7. *Me preocupaba que la ola de frío...*
  8. *Ellos querían que nosotros...*
  9. *Espero que el albergue...*
  10. *Temí que la caravana...*
  11. *Me gusta que la orquesta...*

EXPANDING LEARNERS

- Keeping in mind this unit's theme, ask students to think of other *desafíos* that would have been appropriate for each of the pairs. Have students work with a partner and discuss alternative challenges before deciding on the final three. After students describe the new *desafíos*, ask them to explain why they are appropriate, how they tie in to the unit's theme, and why they choose to assign a particular challenge to each of the pairs. You may have them do this orally in front of the class or in writing.

Tu desafío

79 **Los desafíos**

¿Recuerdas los desafíos que Tess les planteó a los personajes? ¿Cuál te gusta más? Elige una de estas opciones y resuelve tu desafío.

DESAFÍO Ⓐ

Elige entre el mambo, el bolero, la salsa, el chachachá o cualquier otra música del Caribe. Busca información para preparar una presentación. Incluye lo siguiente:

- Orígenes y descripción de esta música.
- Algunos cantantes o intérpretes famosos.
- Una canción representativa.

DESAFÍO Ⓑ

Busca información sobre algún parque de atracciones famoso de América Latina. Toma notas para preparar un folleto. Incluye lo siguiente:

- Ubicación y descripción del parque.
- Algunas de sus atracciones más famosas.
- Información sobre los días y las horas en las que se puede visitar.

DESAFÍO Ⓒ

Elige un país donde se hable español y prepara un plan de viaje y alojamiento para presentar a la clase. Incluye lo siguiente:

- Un itinerario con los lugares más interesantes.
- Información sobre los hoteles donde te vas a alojar.
- Las causas por las que elegiste estos lugares y hoteles.

doscientos veintisiete 227

HERITAGE LANGUAGE LEARNERS

- Ask students to imagine they are the owners of a new theme park that is opening in Latin America or Spain. Students must first determine where the park will be located and what the theme is going to be. Will it reflect something about the history or culture of the designated country? Or will it appeal to a worldview, and deal with, for example, enviromental concerns, sports, or films? Have students write at least three paragraphs to describe their new theme park and to explain their choices.

MULTIPLE INTELLIGENCES:
Musical-Rhythmic Intelligence

- Enable students who have sensitivity to rhythm and sound, and who are familiar with some of the dances mentioned on the page, to demonstrate the basic movements of mambo, bolero, salsa, cha-cha, or any other music from across the Spanish-speaking world. They will need to bring in recordings to accompany their demonstrations of each dance. Allow students time to practice and then hold a dance contest to see who are the champion pairs for two or three of these rhythms.

Unit 4
Para terminar

Activities

77. You may want to convert the third part of this activity into an intrapersonal intelligence exercise. Explain to students that by answering the questions in this section they will be relating what they have learned to their own lives. Ask them to try to determine what their answers might indicate about their personality, feelings, and beliefs. You may provide students with additional questions to help them with their introspections: *¿Con qué aspectos de la vida y obra de tu artista favorito te identificas más? ¿Qué emociones te produce la canción con la que te identificas? ¿Qué te impacta más de la canción: la letra, la música, la interpretación?* Encourage students to write their answers in the form of journal entries.

79. Display students' work in the classroom and have the class vote on the best entry in each category.

🎧 **AUDIO SCRIPT**
See page 183M.

Answer Key

77. 1. F   2. C   3. F   4. F   5. C
- ▶ Answers will vary. Sample answers:
    1. Porque su padre era dominicano, su madre cubana y él nació en Puerto Rico.
    2. Porque interpreta distintos géneros musicales en los que recoge todo el sabor de las Antillas: bolero, mambo, chachachá, charanga, etc.
- ▶ Answers will vary.

78. Answers will vary.
- ▶ Answers will vary.

79. Answers will vary.

Additional Resources

Fans Online activities
Practice Workbook

Unit 4

MAPA CULTURAL

El turismo en Latinoamérica

Presentation

- This section presents information about different tourist destinations in Latin America. The images serve as a reference point for additional cultural readings and activities that expand on the skills students learned in this unit.

Activities	Standards	Resources
Mapa cultural	1.2, 2.1, 2.2	
80.	1.3, 2.1, 2.2, 5.1, 5.2	

Cultural Topics

- **Turismo de aventura.** Adventure tourism is one of the fastest growing sectors of the tourism industry. Some activities usually included in this type of tourism are archaeological expeditions, backpacking, caving, climbing, hiking, and ziplining. Among Latin American countries, Chile, Costa Rica, Uruguay, Peru, and Argentina are important destinations for this type of tourism. Moreover, improving adventure tourism potential is a stated goal of the tourist industry of countries such as Mexico, Ecuador, Brazil, and Colombia.

- **Importancia del turismo en la economía.** According to the UN World Tourism Organization, total international visitor arrivals reached one billion in 2012. The contribution of tourism to a country's economy is measured as a percentage of the country's Gross Domestic Product (GDP). The following countries have the largest total (both direct and indirect) contribution of tourism to GDP in Latin America: Honduras (15.3%), Dominican Republic (15.2%), Panama (13.1%), Mexico (12.5%), Costa Rica (12.3%), Cuba (11%), Nicaragua (10.7%), and Argentina (10%). In comparison, total contribution of tourism to GDP in the United States is 8.6%.

Teaching Suggestions

Warm-Up / Independent Starter

- Ask students to rank the following types of vacations according to their preferences: adventure, beach, culinary, cultural and historical, ecological, rural, wildlife, winter (ski and other winter sports).

228

El turismo en Latinoamérica

Latinoamérica tiene numerosos atractivos turísticos, y el turismo representa una importante fuente de divisas para muchos países latinoamericanos. México, Argentina, República Dominicana y Puerto Rico son, junto con Brasil, los países de América Latina que reciben más turistas internacionales. El mayor número de visitantes de estos países procede de los Estados Unidos y de Canadá.

Riviera Maya

La Riviera Maya (México) está situada en la parte oriental de la península de Yucatán, cerca de la ciudad de Cancún. Alberga algunas de las playas más hermosas y extensas de México, y cuenta con el segundo arrecife de coral más largo del mundo. Entre sus atractivos destacan las localidades de Puerto Morelos y Playa del Carmen, las islas de Cozumel e Isla Mujeres, y las ciudades mayas de Tulum y Cobá.

Ruinas mayas de Tulum.

El turismo en México

México recibe cada año más de 23 millones de turistas internacionales y es, con diferencia, el país más visitado de Latinoamérica. Entre los destinos preferidos están la Ciudad de México, Baja California, Cancún y la Riviera Maya.

Kayak en el lago Patagonia (Bariloche).

Bariloche y la Patagonia argentina

La ciudad de San Carlos de Bariloche, situada al pie de los Andes en la Patagonia argentina, es un importante destino turístico internacional. Los argentinos consideran la ciudad como la capital nacional del turismo de aventura. Allí se puede practicar *trekking*, esquí, kayak, *canopy*, parapente, *mountain bike*, paseos en veleros y otras muchas actividades.

El turismo en la Argentina

Argentina recibe más de 5 millones de visitantes internacionales al año. Los destinos más visitados son Buenos Aires, Córdoba, las cataratas del Iguazú y la Patagonia.

228 doscientos veintiocho

Differentiated Instruction

DEVELOPING LEARNERS

- To help students organize the information presented here, ask them to make a three-column chart, with one column for each geographical area. Ask students to summarize, in a bulleted list, the information about each destination. The first entry should include the name of the country and where it is located; the second, the cities or other places of interest; the third, the number of tourists who visit each year; the fourth, special natural or cultural attractions; and the last entry might include any additional anecdotal information.

EXPANDING LEARNERS

- Ask students to compare and contrast the locations described in the *Mapa cultural* with places in the United States (or another country of their choice) that offer similar amenities: sandy beaches and waters for aquatic sports; national or state parks that offer a variety of both low- and high-impact activities; an old city steeped in history, etc. Ask students to research places in their country of choice that have these characteristics and evaluate them as ideal vacation spots alongside the three destinations of the *Mapa cultural*.

Santo Domingo

La capital de la República Dominicana es uno de los destinos más atractivos del Caribe. Fundada por Cristóbal Colón y su hermano Bartolomé en 1498, Santo Domingo es la ciudad más antigua de las Américas.

La zona colonial de Santo Domingo fue declarada Patrimonio de la Humanidad por la UNESCO en 1990. Entre sus tesoros destacan el alcázar de Colón, la catedral, la fortaleza Ozama, el Museo de las Casas Reales, el Jardín Botánico, el Malecón y el Palacio de Bellas Artes.

Catedral de Santo Domingo.

Alcázar de Colón.

El turismo en la República Dominicana

La República Dominicana recibe más de 4 millones de visitantes al año. Entre sus principales zonas turísticas están Punta Cana, Puerto Plata, Santo Domingo y La Romana.

80 De viaje por Hispanoamérica

▶ **Elige** uno de los tres destinos presentados y amplía la información que has leído:

– Lugares destacados.
– Actividades de interés.
– Información sobre el clima, el paisaje, etc.

▶ **Prepara** una presentación sobre el lugar que has elegido y busca imágenes que sirvan para ilustrarla.

  ▶ **Haz** tu presentación en clase y contesta a las preguntas de tus compañeros(as).

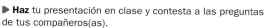

HERITAGE LANGUAGE LEARNERS

• Tell students that they will be promoting a very exclusive vacation spot. Everything must be near perfect and cost is no object! Students should address the transportation to and from home to the hotel that caters to every tourist's whim, on-site restaurants that go beyond five stars, a world-class spa, etc. Encourage students to accompany their brochures with images from print media or the Internet, and present them to the rest of the class, who will vote on the most appealing one.

CRITICAL THINKING

• Ask student pairs to create a list of rules for the ideal traveler. This list should include some practical tips (e.g., *infórmate sobre la ubicación y los servicios del alojamiento donde piensas hospedarte; haz las reservas en los hoteles o albergues con antelación; no te olvides de darle una propina al botones*). Students might also promote good manners (e.g., *aprende por lo menos unas expresiones de cortesía en el idioma del país que visitas*). After students complete their list of rules, enable a classroom discussion on what makes an ideal traveler.

Unit 4
MAPA CULTURAL
El turismo en Latinoamérica

Preparation

■ Invite students to share their Independent Starters. You may want to keep a tab of students' answers on the board. Which categories got the highest rakings among students? As a class, discuss the main features of students' top three choices. Then have students justify their choices.

■ Explain that tourists are increasingly seeking an engagement with nature and local culture during their vacations. There has also been an increase in the number of travelers looking for specialized trips that involve physical activity and adventure. In fact, a study from George Washington University found that the adventure market represents more than a quarter of the traveling population. Do the results of the Independent Starter survey support these trends among your students?

■ Before going over the *Mapa cultural* as a class, discuss with students some top Latin American travel destinations (e.g., Mexico, Costa Rica, Dominican Republic, Argentina, Peru). Which of these travel destinations appeal most to students? Why?

Activities

80. You may want to divide the class into small groups to work on this activity. To focus students' work, ask groups to first agree on a place. Then, as they search for additional information on the place, have students start a list of activities that are well suited to the weather, geography, and history of the place. Next, students may want to narrow down their choices of activities to what would appeal to students their age.

Answer Key

80. Answers will vary.
▶ Answers will vary.

Additional Resources

Fans Online activities
Practice Workbook

ESCRITURA

Un blog de viajes

Presentation

- In this section, students will practice and extend their writing skills. They will apply the vocabulary and grammar they have learned in this unit to create a post for a travel blog.

Activities	Standards	Resources
Escritura	1.1, 1.2, 1.3, 3.1, 5.1	

Teaching Suggestions

Warm-Up / Independent Starter

- Ask students to take a look back at the travel destinations described in this unit and choose one they would like to visit. Then, have students answer these questions about their destination in writing: *¿Por qué elegiste ese destino? ¿Con quién irías? ¿Cómo irías? ¿Dónde te alojarías? ¿Qué lugares visitarías?*

Preparation

- Invite students to share their Independent Starters with the class. What are some of the most common reasons students gave for choosing a particular destination? As a class, discuss some of the things that make for a memorable trip (e.g., accommodations, food, travel companions, places visited, people met during the trip). Discuss with students the role of a travel blog as a tool to share these memorable experiences with others.

- Ask for a volunteer to read *El texto narrativo* box aloud. Explain to students that narrative texts tell a story and, in this particular case, they will write a personal narrative about a trip they took. Have students read the introduction silently.

Step-by-Step Instructions

Piensa

- As students think about their different trips, encourage them to ask themselves which of those travel experiences would produce a strong narrative—one that holds the reader's attention. The event might be quite ordinary (e.g., a trip to Disney World), but it should have an angle that lends itself to the creation of an exciting narrative (e.g., being trapped in the Haunted Mansion due to a malfunction of the ride).

230

Un blog de viajes

El texto narrativo

Una narración es el relato de unos hechos reales o imaginarios que les suceden a unos personajes.

Una buena narración debe mantener el interés del lector. Por eso es preciso seleccionar los hechos que se narran, caracterizar adecuadamente a los personajes que intervienen, ambientar los hechos en el tiempo y el espacio de manera que resulten verosímiles, y presentarlos siguiendo un desarrollo temporal.

Las narraciones pueden hacerse en presente, cuando se narran hechos actuales, o en pasado. En las narraciones en pasado se combinan los verbos en pretérito, para contar los hechos, y los verbos en imperfecto, para describir a las personas y los ambientes.

Un blog o bitácora es un sitio web donde se recopilan cronológicamente textos de uno o varios autores sobre una temática en particular o sobre episodios personales del día a día.

Existen blogs de muchos tipos: de moda, de viajes, culturales, gastronómicos, etc. Todos ellos se caracterizan por dar una visión personal y subjetiva del tema que tratan y permitir que los lectores puedan incluir sus comentarios. Con frecuencia, están escritos en forma narrativa, aunque también hay blogs con un tono más descriptivo o argumentativo.

El blog debe actualizarse regularmente con nuevas entradas para lograr mantener el interés y la fidelidad de los lectores.

En esta unidad vas a escribir una entrada para un blog de viajes.

Piensa

- Piensa en los viajes que has realizado a lo largo de tu vida. ¿Cuál te gustaría compartir en un blog: el mejor, el peor, el más peligroso, el más divertido, el último que hiciste…?

- Haz memoria y escribe los detalles del viaje que vas a contar.
    - ¿Cuándo fue?
    - ¿Con quién viajaste?
    - ¿Desde dónde partiste? ¿Adónde fuiste?
    - ¿Qué medios de transporte utilizaste?
    - ¿Dónde te alojaste?
    - ¿Qué tiempo hacía?
    - ¿Qué lugares visitaste?
    - ¿Qué te llamó más la atención?
    - ¿Te pasó algo extraordinario?

- ¿Qué recomendaciones le harías a un viajero que quisiera realizar ese mismo viaje? Escríbelas.

Modelo

Viaja en tren. Así podrás disfrutar del paisaje durante el viaje.

- Busca alguna fotografía que pueda ilustrar el relato de tu viaje.

Rubric for Evaluation

	Content	Organization	Conventions
1 point	Posting provides minimal interest. Limited and unclear narrative. Limited, confusing, or vague word choices.	Very basic organization of information. Details are not in a logical order. Transitions are not present or not used well.	Many errors in spelling, punctuation, grammar, and usage. Errors obscure meaning.
3 points	Posting provides moderate interest. Clear narrative, but lacks details and supporting examples. Appropriate word choices.	Information is mostly organized. Details are not in the most effective order. Some effective transitions are present.	Some errors in spelling, punctuation, grammar, and usage. Errors don't interfere with meaning.

Expresiones útiles

En aquella ocasión...	*On that occasion ...*
No obstante / Sin embargo...	*Nevertheless ...*
De hecho...	*As a matter of fact ...*
En realidad...	*Actually ...*
No... sino...	*Not ... but ...*
No solo... sino que...	*Not only ... but ...*
Ni... ni...	*Neither ... nor ...*

Escribe

■ A partir de las ideas que anotaste, escribe el borrador de tu entrada de blog. Incluye los detalles del viaje y tus recomendaciones.

■ Elige un título que capte la atención del lector.

■ Encourage students to arrange the details of their trip in chronological order—a flow chart can help them with this task. Remind students that they will use the first-person point of view.

Escribe

■ Explain to students that they do not need a long introduction for this type of writing task. In fact, they can get right to the action. Emphasize the importance of including vivid descriptions. Encourage students to use their senses to describe how things looked, smelled, tasted, sounded, and felt to the touch. For example: *Al abrir la puerta de la habitación del hotel, me acarició la cara una brisa con olor a trópico: piñas, papayas, mangos...* Readers should be able to visualize and "feel" the writer's experiences.

■ Remind students to include concrete details in their narratives. These details, when narrated using concrete language, make the story and the images more real. Then, tell students to make sure their narratives have a beginning, middle, and end.

Revisa

■ Intercambia tu trabajo con tu compañero(a) y analiza estas cuestiones. Anota tus comentarios.

Contenido

¿Te ha gustado el relato del viaje? Después de leer el primer párrafo, ¿te apetecía seguir leyendo el texto? ¿Crees que falta algún detalle en concreto?

Redacción

¿El texto está escrito de manera clara, comprensible y atractiva? ¿Hay alguna parte que no entiendas?

Vocabulario, gramática y ortografía

¿Está bien escrito? ¿Tiene algún error gramatical o alguna falta de ortografía? ¿Se repiten mucho algunas palabras?

■ Devuelve el texto a su autor(a) con tus sugerencias y revisa el tuyo teniendo en cuenta sus comentarios.

■ Pasa a limpio tu texto e incluye la fotografía que seleccionaste para ilustrar tu relato.

Comparte

■ Lee tu artículo a la clase. Tus compañeros(as) pueden hacerte preguntas al final de tu relato.

■ Intenta publicar tu entrada en algún blog de viajes o creen su propio blog de viajes entre todos(as).

> ### Si diez años después (te vuelvo a encontrar, Punta del Este)
>
>
>
> Hace 10 años (en realidad 11, pero 10 suena mejor) pisé Punta del Este un verano. Me habían invitado a pasar una quincena ahí, con amigas, y dije que sí, pensando que eso equivaldría a «viajar». En ese viaje descubrí las medialunas calentitas (todavía me acuerdo de lo blanditas que eran), el puente de la Barra de Maldonado (ese que cuando lo atravesás* te da cosa en la panza) y las canciones de Joaquín Sabina.
>
> Fuente: http://viajandoporahi.com (selección)
>
> *atraviesas (en Argentina, Uruguay y Paraguay)

Revisa

■ Before students exchange their blog posts with a classmate, ask them to go back through their narratives and find places in the text where the details and descriptions could be improved to make them more real. Students may, for instance, use dialogue in one or two cases to show events happening rather than just telling how they happened.

Comparte

■ Suggest that students bring in additional photos of their trip to share with their classmates once they have presented their posts. Do the photos match the mental images triggered by the narrative?

Evaluation

■ Distribute copies of the rubric to students and discuss the evaluation criteria. Ask students to refer to the rubric as they prepare their writing and as they evaluate their classmates' blog posts.

	Content	Organization	Conventions
5 points	Posting piques interest. Clear narrative, rich in details and supporting examples. Word choices capture reader's attention and imagination.	Clearly organized information. Order of details is very effective. Effective use of transitions and logical sequencing.	Few, if any, errors in spelling, punctuation, grammar, and usage. Excellent command of the Spanish language.

REPASO

Vocabulario

Presentation

- In this section, students will review all key vocabulary from the unit, organized by themes, to prepare for an assessment. Students will complete practice activities for each *Desafío*.

Activities	Standards	Resources
1.	1.2, 1.3	
2.	1.2	
3.	1.2, 1.3	

Teaching Suggestions

Warm-Up / Independent Starter

- Ask students to review the vocabulary list. Then have them create a three-column chart with the following headings: *Ocio y espectáculos, Los viajes, El alojamiento* and *El tiempo meteorológico*. Have students think of associations among words within each category, and ask them to list these associations in the appropriate column. For example: *la orquesta → la pieza musical, interpretar; la rueda de repuesto → el pinchazo, el maletero.*

Preparation

- Have students share their associations from the Independent Starter with a partner. Then ask pairs to use their associations to write definitions in Spanish for the vocabulary. For example, *la orquesta: conjunto de músicos que interpretan una pieza musical; la rueda de repuesto: rueda que se lleva en el maletero para sustituir la rueda que tenga un pinchazo.*

- Have pairs present their definitions to the class without saying which word is being defined. The class will match the vocabulary word to the corresponding definition. Then go over the *Repaso* presentation with students.

Activities

1. Once students have finished this activity, have them write sentences using the vocabulary under *Ocio y espectáculos*. Challenge students to include as many target words as possible in each sentence (e.g., *El jugador movió su ficha las cinco casillas que indicaban los dados*). Invite students to share their sentences with the class.

232

Ocio y espectáculos

el/la compositor(a)	composer
el coro	chorus
el estribillo	refrain
la letra	lyrics
la música clásica	classical music
la orquesta	orchestra
la pieza musical	piece (of music)
actuar, interpretar	to perform

Deportes y tiempo libre

bucear	to scuba dive
escalar	to climb
patinar sobre hielo	to ice skate
pescar	to fish
practicar artes marciales	to practice martial arts
navegar	to sail

Juegos de mesa

la casilla	square
el dado	die (dice)
la ficha	chip, token
la partida	game, round
el tablero	board
hacer trampas	to cheat
tener mal perder	to be a sore loser

¡Atención!

el éxito	success
la salida	exit

Los viajes

las normas de circulación	traffic laws
el paso de cebra	crosswalk
el/la peatón(a)	pedestrian
la señal de tráfico	traffic sign/signal
el tráfico	traffic
adelantar	to pass
ceder el paso	to yield
poner el intermitente	to use a turn signal
quedarse sin gasolina	to run out of gasoline

El coche

el maletero	trunk
la matrícula	license plate
el pinchazo	flat tire
la rueda de repuesto	spare tire

El tren y el avión

el coche-cama	sleeper car
el tren de cercanías	commuter train
el tren de largo recorrido	long-distance train
el vagón-restaurante	dining car
poner una reclamación	to make a complaint

¡Atención!

el/la conductor(a)	driver
el/la revisor(a)	(train) conductor

El alojamiento

el botones	bellman, bellhop
las comodidades	comforts
el/la huésped	guest
el/la mochilero(a)	backpacker
la media pensión	half board
la pensión completa	full board
el personal	personnel, staff
el servicio de habitaciones	room service
las zonas de uso común	common areas
agradable	pleasant
disponible	available
gratuito(a)	free
ubicado(a)	located
hospedarse	to stay, to lodge
pagar por adelantado	to pay in advance
reservar con antelación	to reserve in advance

El cámping

la caravana	camper
la colchoneta	air mattress
la nevera portátil	cooler
el saco de dormir	sleeping bag
la tienda de campaña	tent

El tiempo meteorológico

la brisa	breeze
el chubasco	downpour
la niebla	fog
la ola de frío	cold wave
caluroso(a)	hot
glacial	bitterly cold
caer un chaparrón	to pour down

232 doscientos treinta y dos

Differentiated Instruction

DEVELOPING LEARNERS

- Ask students to identify the word that does not belong and explain why.

matrícula	maletero	tablero (tablero)
niebla	brisa	ficha (ficha)
actuar	bucear	escalar (actuar)
huésped	dado	casilla (huésped)
partida	dado	letra (letra)
chaparrón	colchoneta	chubasco (colchoneta)
pinchazo	revisor	rueda (revisor)
personal	mochilero	botones (mochilero)
adelantar	ubicar	ceder (ubicar)
caluroso	ola de frío	glacial (caluroso)
actuar	practicar	interpretar (practicar)

EXPANDING LEARNERS

- Ask students to identify the cognates as well as the false cognates in this *Repaso*. Have them create a two-column chart, with the first column dedicated to cognates, and the second to false cognates. For instance, *banda, compositor,* and *orquesta* are cognates; *letra, pensión,* and *revisor* are false cognates. Ask students to include the English-language equivalents for the false cognates. Have students also list synonyms for as many of the words as they can (e.g., *pieza – selección musical; hacer trampas – engañar; normas – reglas*).

DESAFÍO 1

1 **El intruso.** Decide qué palabra no corresponde a cada grupo. Justifica tu respuesta.

1
orquesta	estribillo
partida	compositora

2
coro	ficha
tablero	dado

3
casilla	pieza musical
estribillo	letra

DESAFÍO 2

2 **De viaje.** Elige la opción correcta.

1. El conductor no vio _____ y tuvo un accidente.
   a. las normas de circulación   b. la señal de tráfico   c. el pinchazo
2. Llevábamos tantas maletas que no nos cabían en el _____.
   a. coche-cama   b. equipaje   c. maletero
3. Si quieres adelantar a otro coche, tienes que _____.
   a. poner el intermitente   b. ceder el paso   c. echar gasolina
4. En un paso de cebra, los conductores deben _____.
   a. adelantar   b. ceder el paso   c. poner el intermitente

DESAFÍO 3

3 **Para todos los gustos.** Completa el foro con las palabras del cuadro. Después, escribe una experiencia personal de este tipo y compártela con tus compañeros(as).

agradable	botones	cámpings	comodidades	con antelación
caravana	disponible	ubicados	media pensión	tienda de campaña

Lisa **35 años** ⬚ Publicado: 07/04/2013 6:30 p. m.	¡Hola, amigos! Mi familia y yo siempre vamos de vacaciones a la playa. Nos gusta alojarnos en hoteles que estén ___1___ cerca del mar. No elegimos hoteles lujosos porque no necesitamos que el ___2___ nos suba el equipaje a la habitación, pero sí buscamos hoteles con las ___3___ básicas y preferimos régimen de ___4___ porque durante el día nunca estamos en el hotel. Siempre que es posible, elegimos hoteles pequeños; la atmósfera es más ___5___.
Juan **26 años** ⬚ Publicado: 07/04/2013 7:00 p. m.	Nosotros tenemos una ___6___; es una forma económica de viajar y nos permite estar en contacto con la naturaleza y conocer muchas ciudades. ¡Y es más cómoda que una ___7___! Para alojarnos buscamos ___8___ con buenas instalaciones y mucho espacio ___9___ para hacer deporte. Es muy importante hacer la reserva ___10___, especialmente si viajas en temporada alta.

---

2. To extend this activity, ask students to choose one of the four sentences and write a one- or two-paragraph narrative expanding on the incident or situation described by the sentence. For example: *El conductor iba hablando por teléfono. La conversación lo distrajo y no vio la señal de tráfico que indicaba que debía ceder el paso...* Call on volunteers to share their narratives with the class. You may want to have the class vote on the most interesting or creative story. Alternatively, have students read their narratives aloud to a partner.

3. Ask students to read each sentence through before attempting to complete it. Once they have finished this activity, have students work with a partner and write five comprehension questions (e.g., *¿Qué características tienen los hoteles donde se alojan Lisa y su familia? ¿Cómo viaja Juan?*). Then have pairs exchange their questions with another pair and answer each other's questions.

Answer Key

1. 1. partida: no se relaciona con la música
   2. coro: no se relaciona con los juegos de mesa
   3. casilla: no se relaciona con la música

2. 1. b   2. c   3. a   4. b

3.
1. ubicados	6. caravana
2. botones	7. tienda de campaña
3. comodidades	8. cámpings
4. media pensión	9. disponible
5. agradable	10. con antelación

Additional Resources

Fans Online activities
Practice Workbook

HERITAGE LANGUAGE LEARNERS

- Ask students to describe how their contemporaries in their family's country of origin typically spend their free time. Students should include activities during the week, on weekends, and during holidays and vacations, and draw comparisons to activities in this country. They might also include comparisons of how students and their families travel, the age at which students can officially drive (and their attitudes toward cars), as well as the popularity of camping and staying at *albergues*. Encourage them to share these comparisons with the rest of the class.

TOTAL PHYSICAL RESPONSE (TPR)

- Students will play a version of "Jeopardy." Define the categories and provide students with the answers. Then ask them to supply the corresponding questions by standing up and being the first to ask. For example:
  1. *Es un deporte de invierno.*
     (*¿Qué es patinar sobre hielo?*)
  2. *Detesto perder.*
     (*¿Qué es tener mal perder?*)
  3. *Sube las maletas a la habitación.*
     (*¿Qué es el botones?*)
  4. *Es la música de Mozart y Beethoven.*
     (*¿Qué es la música clásica?*)

REPASO

Gramática

Presentation

- Students will review grammatical structures presented in the unit. Each grammar point is cross-referenced to the corresponding page on which it was introduced. The activities here provide systematic practice by *Desafío*.

Activities	Standards	Resources
4.	1.1, 1.3	
5.	1.2, 1.3	
6.	1.2	
7. Cultura	1.2, 1.3, 2.1, 2.2	

Teaching Suggestions

Warm-Up / Independent Starter

- For each of the following sentences, have students come up with a conjecture, using the future or the conditional as appropriate:
  1. *Entre semana, Eduardo toma el tren de cercanías.*
  2. *La policía le puso una multa a mi hermano.*
  3. *Estamos esperando a Carlos, pero no llega.*
  4. *Diana tuvo un accidente de tráfico el año pasado cuando salía de la escuela.*

Preparation

- Ask students to get together with a classmate and share and discuss their Independent Starters. Possible answers: 1. *Vivirá en las afueras de la ciudad.* 2. *No respetaría las normas de circulación.* 3. *Habrá tenido un pinchazo.* 4. *Se habría distraído y no vio la señal de tráfico.* Then ask pairs to share some of their sentences with the class. You may want to write some of their examples on the board to illustrate the different ways of expressing conjectures studied in this unit.
- Go over the rest of the grammar topics from this *Repaso* with the class. If needed, provide additional examples and practice activities.

Activities

5. Remind students to first look at the tense of the verb in the main clause to determine which subjunctive tense should be used in the dependent clause.

Expresar frecuencia (pág. 194)

> número + vez / veces + al/a la + tiempo

Voy al cine tres veces al mes.

> cada + número + tiempo

Tengo clases de guitarra cada dos días.

> todos(as) + los(as) + tiempo

Voy de compras todos los fines de semana.

> soler *(to be in the habit of)* + infinitivo

¿Qué sueles hacer los fines de semana?

Expresar probabilidad (I) (pág. 196)

Es posible / Es probable + que Es improbable + que Lo más probable es + que Puede (ser) + que	+ subjuntivo
Posiblemente / Probablemente Seguramente Quizá(s) Tal vez	+ indicativo subjuntivo
A lo mejor Seguro + que	+ indicativo

> deber de + infinitivo

La actriz debe / debía de estar muy feliz con su premio.

Expresar probabilidad (II). El futuro y el condicional (pág. 206)

- El futuro y el futuro perfecto.
  Estos asientos estarán reservados.
  Mario no ha llegado. Se habrá retrasado por el tráfico.

- El condicional y el condicional perfecto.
  Serían las cuatro de la tarde cuando llegó Mario.
  Eva habría llegado tarde y por eso perdió el avión.

CONDICIONAL PERFECTO. VERBOS REGULARES

VIAJAR	COMER	SALIR
habría viajado	habría comido	habría salido
habrías viajado	habrías comido	habrías salido
habría viajado	habría comido	habría salido
habríamos viajado	habríamos comido	habríamos salido
habríais viajado	habríais comido	habríais salido
habrían viajado	habrían comido	habrían salido

El presente perfecto de subjuntivo (pág. 208)

Sentimos que te hayas quedado sin gasolina.

CORRELACIÓN DE LOS TIEMPOS VERBALES

Cláusula principal (indicativo)	Cláusula dependiente (subjuntivo)
presente o futuro	presente presente perfecto
pretérito o imperfecto	imperfecto
condicional	imperfecto

Expresar causa (pág. 218)

porque + indicativo	Fuimos a un albergue porque los hoteles estaban llenos.
por + infinitivo	Por no reservar en un hotel, tuvimos que ir a un albergue.
ya que puesto que + indicativo dado que	Pedro tuvo problemas, ya que no había reservado habitación.
debido a que + indicativo	No pasé frío debido a que tenía saco de dormir.
como + indicativo	Como teníamos una reserva, nos pudimos quedar en el parador.

Expresar consecuencia (pág. 220)

EXPRESIONES DE CONSECUENCIA

así (es) que por eso en consecuencia + indicativo por (lo) tanto por consiguiente

Nevó mucho; por eso cerraron la escuela.

EXPRESIONES INTENSIVAS

> tan + adjetivo / adverbio + que + indicativo

El viento es tan fuerte que dobla los árboles.

> tanto(a)(os)(as) + nombre + que + indicativo

Hay tanta niebla que no se ve la carretera.

> verbo + tanto + que + indicativo

Ayer llovió tanto que se inundaron las calles.

Differentiated Instruction

DEVELOPING LEARNERS

- Have students complete the following sentences:
  1. *Siento que tú (quedarse) sin gasolina.* (te hayas quedado)
  2. *Esperábamos que (haber) habitaciones disponibles en el albergue.* (hubiera)
  3. *Me gustaría que ustedes (navegar) conmigo.* (navegaran)
  4. *Me sorprende que hoy no (haber) atascos.* (haya)
  5. *Cuando nosotros (ir) de cámping llevaré la tienda de campaña.* (vayamos)
  6. *Me enoja que los conductores no (ceder) el paso a los peatones.* (cedan)

EXPANDING LEARNERS

- Ask students to write a narrative of at least two paragraphs to describe a recent stay (real or imaginary) at a hotel, *albergue*, or campsite. The description should include *expresiones de causa* and *de consecuencia* so that students might explain why something happened. Encourage students to work in, as naturally as possible, *expresiones intensivas* as well as *de probabilidad* (e.g., *Había una ola de frío tan intensa que es probable que no volvamos en esas fechas*). Invite volunteers to share their narratives with the class.

DESAFÍO 1

4 **Probabilidades.** Escribe explicaciones para estas situaciones. Usa estructuras de probabilidad: *posiblemente, puede que...*

1. El concierto de *jazz* de anoche no se pudo celebrar.
2. Mi vecino siempre toca la misma pieza musical al piano.
3. María siempre me gana cuando jugamos a los dados.
4. El hombre más rico del mundo se compró un barco y desapareció.

DESAFÍO 2

5 **Relación de tiempos.** Completa las oraciones teniendo en cuenta la secuencia de tiempos verbales.

1. Sentí mucho que Mario no ———— hacer el viaje en tren con nosotros.
   (poder)
2. Me preocuparía mucho que ustedes no ———— las normas de circulación.
   (respetar)
3. Temo que esta tarde ———— mucho tráfico y los chicos no ———— a tiempo al aeropuerto.
   (haber) (llegar)
4. Por favor, Manuela, envíanos un mensaje de texto cuando ya ———— en Nueva York.
   (aterrizar)
5. Me sorprendería que mis padres ———— en tren.
   (venir)

DESAFÍO 3

6 **Causas y consecuencias.** Une las dos columnas para formar oraciones lógicas y complétalas con las palabras del cuadro.

como	por	por eso	por consiguiente	ya que

(A)

1. ———— hace mucho calor...
2. Mi ciudad está muy al norte; ...
3. No pudimos alojarnos en el parador...
4. Se acerca una ola de frío polar y, ...
5. No hicimos la excursión a la montaña...

(B)

a. ———— comenzó a nevar.
b. ———— bajarán las temperaturas.
c. ———— no reservar con antelación.
d. elegiremos un hotel con piscina.
e. ———— hace tanto frío.

CULTURA

7 **Viajamos y nos divertimos.** Responde a estas preguntas.

1. ¿Qué es la trova? ¿Dónde y cuándo se hizo famosa?
2. ¿Qué es el AVE? ¿Qué ventajas ofrece?
3. ¿Dónde está el lago Titicaca? ¿Qué atractivos turísticos tiene?

doscientos treinta y cinco **235**

HERITAGE LANGUAGE LEARNERS

- Have students write at least two paragraphs about how they and their family spend their free time. Ask students to express how often they do these activities by using *expresiones de frecuencia*. Students should also mention what activities they and family members might do in the future by employing *expresiones de probabilidad*. For example: *Cada dos años solemos ir de cámping para practicar senderismo. Es posible que un día escale el Chimborazo con mi hermana.* Invite students to read their compositions aloud.

MULTIPLE INTELLIGENCES:
Verbal-Linguistic Intelligence

- Prepare index cards with some of the *expresiones de frecuencia, probabilidad, causa,* and *consecuencia*. Divide the class into teams and give one card (face down) to every student. Team members will take turns reading their cards aloud and then saying a sentence related to the unit content with that expression. For example: *como → Como nos hemos quedado sin gasolina, tendremos que pedir ayuda.* Award one point for every correct use; subtract one point for an incorrect answer.

Unit 4

REPASO

Gramática

6. To extend this activity, have students choose one of the sentences and, working together with a partner, come up with a short dialogue on the same topic. Call on volunteers to role-play their dialogues for the class.

Answer Key

4. Answers will vary. Sample answers:
  1. Puede ser que lloviera.
  2. Seguro que es su pieza favorita.
  3. Lo más probable es que tenga más suerte que tú.
  4. A lo mejor no había pagado los impuestos.

5. 1. pudiera   4. hayas aterrizado
  2. respetaran   5. vinieran
  3. haya; lleguen

6. 1. (d) Como hace mucho calor, elegiremos un hotel con piscina.
  2. (e) Mi ciudad está muy al norte; por eso hace tanto frío.
  3. (c) No pudimos alojarnos en el parador por no reservar con antelación.
  4. (b) Se acerca una ola de frío polar y, por consiguiente, bajarán las temperaturas.
  5. (a) No hicimos la excursión a la montaña ya que comenzó a nevar.

7. Answers will vary. Sample answers:
  1. Es un género musical de la Edad Media que se hizo popular en Santiago de Cuba a finales del s. XIX y principios del s. XX. En la década de los sesenta del s. XX, músicos cubanos popularizaron la nueva trova en todo el mundo.
  2. En un servicio de tren de alta velocidad en España. Es rápido, cómodo y puntual.
  3. Está entre Perú y Bolivia. En sus islas se puede navegar, practicar senderismo, visitar restos arqueológicos, observar la fauna y la flora, etc.

Additional Resources

Fans Online activities
Practice Workbook

235

Unit 4

PROYECTO

Promocionar un país

Presentation

- In this section, students will apply the vocabulary, grammar, and cultural information they have learned in this unit to prepare an advertisement to promote tourism to a Hispanic country.

Activities	Standards	Resources
Paso 1	1.1	
Paso 2	1.2, 2.1, 2.2, 3.2	
Paso 3	1.1, 2.1, 2.2	
Paso 4	1.1, 1.3, 2.1, 2.2	
Paso 5	1.3, 2.1, 2.2, 5.1	

Teaching Suggestions

Warm-Up / Independent Starter

- Have students list seven things they like doing when they travel (e.g., *ir a la playa, visitar museos*).

Preparation

- Ask students to share their Independent Starters. Based on students' answers, have the class come up with a list of different types of destinations (e.g., beach resort, large city, countryside, historical region, culinary hotspot) that would suit people in the class. Keep this list on the board.
- Have a volunteer read the introduction to the project aloud. Discuss ads that students have seen about different travel destinations. What are some of the features of those ads?

Step-by-Step Instructions

Paso 1

- Divide the class into small groups based on the activities they listed for the Independent Starter and the different types of destinations listed on the board. Grouping students with similar interests will serve to focus their ads so they generate a variety of ads with wide appeal.
- Encourage groups to choose a country that matches their type of destination, and then to concentrate on a region from the country. For example, if the group's type of destination is "large cities," they could choose Mexico as their country and Mexico City as their city.

Un anuncio para

promocionar un país

La mayoría de los países hacen anuncios para promocionar su imagen y sus atractivos turísticos. En estos anuncios se suelen mostrar imágenes de espacios urbanos, de paisajes naturales, de las costumbres y tradiciones de sus habitantes, de la gastronomía, etc.

En grupos van a hacer un anuncio para promocionar el país hispano que más les guste y animar a sus compañeros(as) a que visiten ese país. Pueden elegir el formato que deseen: un video, un póster, un *banner* de una página web, etc.

PASO 1 Elige un país

- Reúnete con tres o cuatro compañeros(as) para seleccionar el país que les interese y escribe las razones de la elección. Les damos algunas ideas.

Argentina

Perú

España

PASO 2 Reúne información sobre el país

- Busquen información en Internet, revistas de viajes o enciclopedias. Pueden fijarse en estos aspectos:
  - Las ciudades y los lugares más interesantes.
  - Los museos y los monumentos más importantes.
  - Los bailes típicos.
  - Los trajes tradicionales.
  - Los deportes que se pueden practicar.
  - La gastronomía.
  - Las fiestas y los eventos más destacados.
  - La artesanía.

236 doscientos treinta y seis

Rubric for Evaluation

	Content	Organization	Presentation
1 point	Information is incomplete or incorrect. The ad shows limited original ideas and is not persuasive.	Inefficient use of time. Information is disorganized or unclear. Simple or ineffective use of images.	Unclear communication. Delivery is not fluent. Many errors in vocabulary and grammar.
3 points	Information is correct but some of it lacks significance. The ad is creative and relatively persuasive.	Time is used well. Information is mostly organized but lacks some clarity. Images make a good point.	Clear communication and fluent delivery. Mostly correct vocabulary and grammar.

PASO 3 Determina la idea central del anuncio

- Analicen las siguientes cuestiones y decidan qué idea quieren transmitir:
  - ¿Qué imagen tienen los estadounidenses del país? ¿Es una imagen adecuada?
  - ¿Qué rasgos o qué características del país resultan más atractivos para los visitantes?
  - ¿En qué aspectos van a centrar ustedes la comunicación? ¿Qué imagen quieren transmitir del país?

- Busquen las imágenes que necesiten según el formato de su anuncio. Piensen que las imágenes tienen que hacer que su anuncio resulte atractivo.

PASO 4 Haz el anuncio

- Redacten los textos del anuncio y seleccionen las imágenes que van a utilizar para acompañarlos. Pueden buscar en Internet videos promocionales de varios países para tomar ideas.

- Si van a usar música de fondo, miren las imágenes que han seleccionado y piensen qué música es la que mejor las acompaña.

- Redacten un eslogan que refleje bien la idea central de su anuncio.

Lo que necesitas, seguro que lo encuentras en Perú.

- Revisen su anuncio y ensayen la presentación. Corrijan los aspectos que menos les gusten.

PASO 5 Presenta el anuncio

- Presenten su anuncio a la clase. ¿Cuál les ha gustado más? ¿Por qué?

Unidad 4

Autoevaluación

¿Qué has aprendido en esta unidad?

Haz estas actividades para comprobar tu progreso.

Evalúa tus habilidades. Para cada punto, di Muy bien, Bien o Necesito practicar más.

a. ¿Puedes hablar de hechos posibles o probables?

▶ Describe lo que crees que tu mejor amigo(a) está haciendo probablemente en este momento.

b. ¿Puedes expresar probabilidad sobre el pasado?

▶ Explica cómo crees que eran los viajes cuando tus abuelos(as) eran jóvenes. ¿Adónde irían, cómo viajarían y cómo serían las condiciones de aquellos viajes?

c. ¿Puedes expresar las causas y consecuencias de una acción?

▶ Describe unas vacaciones que no salieron bien. Explica qué ocurrió y da detalles sobre las causas y consecuencias de los hechos.

PROYECTO

Promocionar un país

Paso 2

- Suggest to students that they search for information on an official website. For example: Secretaría de Turismo de México, Servicio Nacional de Turismo de Chile, Instituto de Turismo de España, Compañía de Turismo de Puerto Rico. Even if students are concentrating on a specific region and a particular type of destination, they will still need to include some general information about the country.

Paso 3

- Images can make or break the effectiveness of an ad. Encourage students to consider the suitability of each image carefully.

Paso 4

- Stress the importance of visuals in advertising. The layout should be dramatic and engaging.

Paso 5

- Remind students that they are "selling" their destination to the class, so their presentations should be upbeat and enticing.

Evaluation

- Distribute copies of the rubric to students. Discuss the evaluation criteria and explain how this project will be graded. Encourage students to refer to the rubric as they prepare their projects.

Content

- Remind students that the main goal of their ads is to persuade. Potential visitors should be moved and ultimately persuaded to visit the place in the ad. Therefore, everything in the ad should be geared towards getting people excited about the destination.

Organization

- Due to the space and time limitations of an ad, format and organization are of utmost importance. Encourage students to make every word and image count.

Presentation

- Encourage students to show enthusiasm for their destination and to interact with their audience as they present their ads. If time permits, they may also answer questions the audience might have about the destination.

	Content	Organization	Presentation
5 points	Relevant, interesting, and well-researched information. The ad is creative, original, and persuasive.	Time is used wisely. Information is clearly organized, visually and logically. Very effective and convincing use of images.	Clear and fluent communication. Very motivating, upbeat delivery. Correct and complete vocabulary and grammar.

HACIA EL AP* EXAM

Interpersonal Speaking: Conversation

Presentation

- These pages present students with a sample activity from the "Interpersonal Speaking: Conversation" portion of the AP* Spanish Language and Culture Exam. Students will record a simulated conversation according to an outline.

Activities	Standards	Resources
Interpersonal Speaking: Conversation	1.1, 5.1	Audio

Preparing for the Exam

About This Section

- The "Interpersonal Speaking: Conversation" section of the AP* Exam requires students to participate in a simulated conversation based on an outline. Students will hear various exchanges and then have 20 seconds to record their response to each. This section accounts for 12.5% of the student's total score. On the exam, students will only take part in one conversation. We have provided two practice activities on these pages in order to give students more opportunities to practice their interpersonal speaking skills.

- You may wish to have students record their responses to each conversation, and then revise their answers immediately afterward, either independently or with a partner. They can evaluate their strengths and weaknesses, and devise a strategy for improving their spoken Spanish. At a later date, you may wish to have students complete the same activities, recording their responses again in order to compare their answers over time, see their progress, and reevaluate their plan for improvement.

Strategies: Interpersonal Speaking

- Students may have difficulty sustaining a conversation in Spanish, and/or elaborating on their ideas in a spontaneous way. Try to encourage conversation in Spanish, especially about themes that require expressing one's thoughts and ideas (as opposed to simply discussing everyday plans).

Hacia el AP* Exam

Interpersonal Speaking: Conversation

Presentación

Una de las pruebas del examen AP* consiste en participar en una conversación a partir de un esquema. El objetivo de la prueba es evaluar tu expresión oral. Durante la prueba tendrás que responder a cinco intervenciones de un interlocutor.

Estrategias

- Lee la introducción y el esquema de la conversación.
- Toma nota del vocabulario que conoces y que puede serte útil para el tema propuesto. Anota algunas expresiones de cortesía para saludar, despedirte, excusarte, etc. que sean adecuadas a la situación.
- Escucha atentamente la grabación y no te preocupes si no entiendes algún detalle.
- Fíjate bien en los verbos empleados en el esquema de la conversación para describir lo que tienes que comunicar. Trata de que tu respuesta esté de acuerdo con lo que te piden. Por ejemplo:

  Responde

  Da

  Acepta

  Explica

  Contesta

  Despídete

- Sigue el esquema de la conversación y responde con oraciones completas. Si no conoces una palabra específica en español, puedes utilizar otras palabras conocidas para explicar la misma idea. El uso de sinónimos o de circunloquios (circumlocution) te puede ayudar cuando no recuerdas una palabra precisa.
- Utiliza conectores para enlazar tus ideas: primero, después, debido a, por eso, en consecuencia...
- Sé creativo(a) y usa tu imaginación. Recuerda que tus respuestas no tienen que ser reales, pero sí deben seguir el esquema de la conversación.
- Habla con claridad y cuida tu pronunciación.

Instrucciones para el examen

Directions: You will participate in a conversation. You will have one minute to read a preview of the conversation. You will then take part in the conversation following the outline. Each time it is your turn to speak, you will have 20 seconds to record your response.

Instrucciones: Vas a participar en una conversación. Tendrás un minuto para leer el esquema de la conversación. Cada vez que tengas que intervenir, tendrás 20 segundos para grabar tu respuesta.

Language Expansion

VOCABULARY

- Students may wish to use vocabulary and expressions like the following in their conversation:

Actividad 1
por medio de
el/la escultor(a)
el/la diseñador(a)
el/la muralista
Siento mucho...
el compromiso
la cita
sugerir
recomendar

Actividad 2
felicitar
Creo que...
Yo que tú…
la ventaja
la desventaja
la decisión
depender de

GRAMMAR STRUCTURES:

Giving Advice and Making Recommendations

- The situation presented in the second practice activity asks students to give advice and make recommendations. They should therefore be able to use expressions and verb forms that are typically associated with this language function. Have students practice structures like Yo que tú + the conditional tense as well as Debes/Deberías and Recomiendo que + the subjunctive mood. See page 334 or the Resumen de gramática at the end of the book for a review of this topic.

Actividad 1

Imagina que tienes una conversación telefónica con Felipe, un compañero de tu clase de Arte. Él quiere hablar contigo porque está organizando una exposición de arte local en la escuela.

Las líneas en gris indican lo que escucharás en la grabación. Las líneas en blanco son las acciones que tú debes realizar.

Felipe: Te saluda y te hace una pregunta.
Tú: Responde al saludo y a su pregunta.
Felipe: Te explica en qué consiste el proyecto y te hace otra pregunta.
Tú: Responde afirmativamente y dale la información que pide.
Felipe: Te habla de un segundo proyecto y te hace una invitación.
Tú: No aceptes la invitación y explícale por qué.
Felipe: Reacciona a tu negativa y te pide una idea.
Tú: Respóndele aportando una idea.
Felipe: Te hace una pregunta.
Tú: Contesta la pregunta y despídete.
Felipe: Se despide.

Actividad 2

Imagina que recibes una llamada de teléfono de tu amiga Alejandra. Ella quiere hablar contigo para pedirte tu opinión.

Las líneas en gris indican lo que escucharás en la grabación. Las líneas en blanco son las acciones que tú debes realizar.

Tú: Contesta al teléfono.
Alejandra: Te saluda y se identifica.
Tú: Salúdala y pregúntale cómo está.
Alejandra: Te explica la situación y te pide tu opinión.
Tú: Dile lo que piensas y explícale por qué.
Alejandra: Te pide más argumentos para tomar una decisión.
Tú: Dale más argumentos.
Alejandra: Te da las gracias y se despide.
Tú: Despídete.

doscientos treinta y nueve **239**

Unit 4

HACIA EL AP* EXAM

Interpersonal Speaking: Conversation

- If possible, arrange for voice chats or video chats with a school in a Spanish-speaking country. Students can prepare topics ahead of time and practice speaking for 20 seconds about their thoughts on each topic. If you do not have access to a school in another country, even pairing students with other Spanish-speaking students in the school district can give them practice speaking in Spanish with unfamiliar people, accents, and ideas.

 AUDIO SCRIPT
See page 183N.

Rubric for Evaluation

On the AP* Exam, each section is given a score between 0 (Unacceptable) and 5 (Strong). In order to earn a score of 5, the student's verbal response should show:

- Content: Student participates with each exchange fully and appropriately, and elaborates on the information provided frequently and with ease.

- Message: Student's response is fully understandable, with ease of expression and only occasional errors. The response is fully appropriate to the context given.

- Register: The register is culturally and situationally appropriate.

- Language: Vocabulary is varied and precise. Grammatical structures are used correctly. Few errors do not impede communication, and self-correction improves comprehensibility. Simple, compound, and complex sentences are used appropriately.

- Speech: Pronunciation, rhythm, and pace are appropriate and contribute to comprehension.

Additional Resources

Español Santillana AP* Preparation Workbook

More Practice

CONVERSATION STARTERS

- You may wish to have students work in pairs to have extended conversations in Spanish about the following conversation starters:
  - *¿Por qué algunas personas no participan en programas de reciclaje? ¿Qué podríamos hacer para promover estos programas?*
  - *Si tu escuela tuviera un subsidio para construir o mejorar algo en la escuela, ¿qué recomendarías que se hiciera? ¿Por qué?*
  - *¿Cómo has cambiado desde que comenzaste el bachillerato (la preparatoria)? ¿Cómo crees que vas a cambiar después de graduarte?*

OTHER POSSIBLE TOPICS

- Topics of conversation that students can use to practice their interpersonal speaking skills should inspire elaboration on the topic and a respectful exchange of ideas. You will probably want to avoid extremely controversial topics, as well as topics that require excessive background knowledge or are uninteresting. Students may actually be the best source of ideas for further conversation starters. Have them brainstorm several prompts that they would genuinely like to discuss with their classmates. Collect them all and pull one out of a hat each day as a warm-up activity.

239

Unit 5 Participamos

Objectives

- To talk about historical events and figures.
- To express order or position in a series.
- To express certainty and doubt.
- To talk about politics and different government systems.
- To express the purpose of an action.
- To express an objection to or a difficulty with a fact or an event.
- To talk about social and environmental issues.
- To talk about contrary-to-fact or hypothetical conditions in the past.
- To express the time of an action or a sequence of events.
- To identify main ideas and significant details in a variety of texts.
- To write a wide variety of texts, including an essay exploring a topic.
- To know and apply the different stages of the writing process: planning, writing, revising, and sharing.
- To explore Hispanic immigration in the United States.

Contents

Vocabulary
- Useful expressions to introduce a topic, to introduce a positive or a negative fact, and to clarify or specify something said.
- Review of known vocabulary about history, society, and politics.
- History.
- Politics and government.
- Social and environmental issues.

Grammar
- Ordinal numbers.
- To express certainty and doubt.
- To express purpose.
- To express difficulty.
- To express condition.
- To express time.

Culture
- The Guayaquil Conference. Simón Bolívar and José de San Martín.
- The Chilean musical group Inti-Illimani and the *Canción Protesta* movement.
- Antonio Villaraigosa.
- María Eva Duarte de Perón.
- The Central American Indigenous Council and Latin American indigenous movements.
- *Voluntariado juvenil en Perú.*
- *La contaminación en la Ciudad de México.*
- Hispanic immigration in the United States.

Evaluation Criteria

- Describe an important event in the history of the Americas and talk about the historical figures who had a lead role in it.
- Learn the use of ordinal numbers.
- Express certainty and doubt using the indicative or the subjunctive.
- Describe different political and government systems in various Hispanic countries and in students' own country.
- Express the purpose of an action using constructions with infinitive or subjunctive.
- Provide information about events using expressions that imply objections or difficulties.
- Discuss crime and social problems.
- Talk about environmental problems and solutions.
- Express contrary-to-fact past conditions and their probable result in the past and present.
- Express time using the indicative or the subjunctive.
- Learn about Latin American immigrant populations in the United States.
- Write an essay exploring a topic.
- Read different types of texts and identify main ideas and significant details in them.
- Write guided texts giving information, describing, or narrating events.

Unit Plan

Las tareas/Antes de empezar

Estimated time: 2 sessions.

Text: *Nuestro pasado, nuestro presente.*

Functions & forms:
- Useful expressions to introduce a topic, to introduce a positive or a negative fact, and to clarify or specify something said.
- Review of known vocabulary about history, society, and politics.

DESAFÍO 1

Estimated time: 6 sessions.

Text: *El abrazo más famoso de la Historia.*

Functions & forms:
- To talk about historical events.
- History.
- Ordinal numbers.
- To express certainty and doubt.

Culture:
- *El «abrazo de Guayaquil».*
- *El significado de billón.*

Reading: *Bolívar y San Martín.*

DESAFÍO 2

Estimated time: 6 sessions.

Text: *Canciones con conciencia.*

Functions & forms:
- To express purpose and difficulty.
- Politics and government.
- To express purpose.
- To express difficulty.

Culture:
- *Inti-Illimani.*
- *Antonio Villaraigosa.*

Reading: *María Eva Duarte de Perón.*

DESAFÍO 3

Estimated time: 6 sessions.

Text: *Una obra de teatro con mensaje.*

Functions & forms:
- To talk about social problems.
- Social and environmental problems.
- To express condition.
- To express time.

Culture:
- *Movimientos indigenistas.*
- *Voluntariado juvenil en Perú.*
- *La contaminación en la Ciudad de México.*

Reading: *El exiliado.*

Para terminar

Estimated time: 2 sessions.

Todo junto: Review of *Desafíos 1–3*.

Tu desafío:
- *Desafío A:* Imagine a meeting and write a dialogue between two Hispanic leaders.
- *Desafío B:* Research and prepare a presentation about a Hispanic singer or musical group.
- *Desafío C:* Research the official webpage of the Central American Indigenous Council and prepare a presentation about it.

MAPA CULTURAL

Estimated time: 1 session.

Mapa cultural:
La inmigración hispana en los Estados Unidos.

ESCRITURA

Estimated time: 1 session.

Writing: *Un ensayo.*

PROYECTO/EVALUACIÓN

Estimated time: 2 sessions.

Project: *Un manifiesto para solucionar un problema de tu comunidad.*

HACIA EL *AP* EXAM*

Estimated time: 2 sessions.

Test: Presentational Writing: Persuasive Essay.

Standards for Learning Spanish

COMMUNICATION

1.1. Interpersonal mode
- Exchange personal ideas, opinions, and experiences.
- Engage in oral conversations using personal knowledge and experience.
- Ask and answer questions on different topics.
- Compare or share information with a partner.
- Invent a story.
- Write a dialogue or a response letter.
- Summarize ideas in a poster.
- Write a news article about current events.
- Write a manifesto.

1.2. Interpretive mode
- Demonstrate understanding of oral and written idiomatic expressions.
- Demonstrate understanding of questions relating to familiar and less familiar topics.
- Understand and obtain information from audio or video recordings.
- Understand new vocabulary presented in Spanish.
- Understand written exchanges.

- Identify main ideas and significant details in a variety of texts.
- Extract information from an informative text.
- Draw conclusions and make judgments from oral and written texts.
- Interpret texts on topics of other cultures and relate them to personal knowledge and experience.
- Extract information from an image.

1.3. Presentational mode
- Produce and present an original creation orally.
- Dramatize a dialogue.
- Write a descriptive or an explanatory text about experiences or the result of a research activity.
- Summarize information.
- Write personal reflections on different topics.
- Write a story.
- Write a dialogue in the context of politics.
- Write a political speech.
- Write an essay exploring a topic.
- Draw or use photographs to illustrate information.

CULTURE

2.1. Practices and perspectives
- Learn about an important historical meeting between two Latin American leaders.
- Read about politics and government systems in various Hispanic countries.
- Discuss the influence and role of protest music in Hispanic societies.
- Learn about indigenous movements in Latin America.

- Read about youth volunteer programs in Hispanic countries.
- Explore Latin American immigrant populations in the United States.

2.2. Products and perspectives
- Read about historical and political events and figures in Hispanic countries.
- Learn about musical groups and the *Canción Protesta* movement in Hispanic countries.

CONNECTIONS

3.1. Interdisciplinary connections
- Understand the similarities and differences between some aspects of grammar in English and in Spanish.
- Use the writing process to produce an essay.
- Learn about the history of Latin America.
- Identify historical and political figures in Hispanic countries.
- Learn about protest music in Latin America.

- Learn about Hispanic immigration in the United States.

3.2. Viewpoints through language / culture
- Read dialogues, informative texts, and literary texts in Spanish that provide insight into Hispanic cultures.
- Learn about Latin music as an expression of the society.
- Discuss current social issues.

COMPARISONS

4.1. Compare languages
- Compare the use of ordinals in English and in Spanish.
- Compare ways to express certainty and doubt in English and in Spanish.
- Compare expressing purpose in English and in Spanish.
- Compare ways to express difficulty in English and in Spanish.

4.2. Compare cultures
- Compare protest music and the need for indigenous movements in the United States and Latin America.
- Compare volunteer programs in the United States and in Hispanic countries.
- Compare pollution issues in the United States and in Hispanic countries.

COMMUNITIES

5.1. Spanish beyond the school setting
- Reflect on the relationship between music and social reality and on the role of politics.
- Promote a positive attitude toward other cultures.
- Learn about indigenous movements and volunteer programs.
- Discuss social and environmental issues.

5.2. Spanish for lifelong learners
- Learn the writing process.
- Write an essay.
- Use technology to learn.
- Discuss ways in which Spanish can be used in future life experiences.

Communicative Skills

Interpersonal Mode

		Activities
Speaking	• Compare or share information or invent a story with a classmate. • Discuss historical events or talk about political or social topics. • Exchange ideas, opinions, or experiences with classmates.	• 2, 5, 18, 36, 44, 51, 61, 67, 70 • 10, 14, 24, 26, 28, 38, 60 • 26, 28, 29, 38, 43, 48, 52, 53, 55, 59, 60, 75, 77, 79, 82, *Proyecto*
Writing	• Write a dialogue, a conversation, or summarize ideas in a poster. • Write a response letter or the end of a graphic novel. • Write a news story about current events or write a manifesto.	• 4, 30, 44 • 23, 31 • 60, *Proyecto*
Listening	• Understand and obtain information from oral exchanges.	• 2, 5, 10, 14, 18, 26, 28, 29, 36, 38, 43, 44, 48, 51, 52, 53, 55, 59, 60, 61, 67, 70, 73, 75, 77, 82, *Escritura*, *Proyecto*
Reading	• Understand a letter, an explanatory text, or an essay exploring a topic.	• 18, 23, *Escritura*

Interpretive Mode

		Activities
Listening	• Obtain information from conversations. • Understand descriptive or informative audios.	• 9, 22, 34, 57, 71 • 17, 28, 37, 60, 65, 80
Reading	• Demonstrate comprehension of written exchanges or longer written dialogues. • Infer meanings based on a text or obtain information from historical quotes. • Reflect on cultural topics in relation to personal knowledge and experience. • Obtain information and draw conclusions from an informative text. • Research using outside sources or understand a literary story.	• 1, 8, 24, 31, 33, 54, 55, 56, 79 • 3, 12, 13, 19, 25, 29, 48, 50, 74 • 35, 37, 39, 58, 62, 72 • 50, 52, 59, 76, 80 • 2, 11, 14, 51, 73, 80, 81, *Proyecto*
Viewing	• Obtain information from an image.	• 5, 10, 14, 17, 24, 53

Presentational Mode

		Activities
Speaking	• Present information, a speech, or an original creation to the class. • Act out a dialogue.	• 11, 27, 49, 53, 78, 81, *Escritura* • 4, 30
Writing	• Write a story, a text summarizing a song, or a personal reflection. • Write a descriptive or an explanatory text or an essay exploring a topic. • Write a formal letter or an e-mail giving opinions and suggestions. • Write a political speech or a fictitious dialogue in the context of politics. • Write a text about contrary-to-fact conditions and their consequences.	• 5, 44, 80 • 6, 18, 27, *Escritura* • 23, 54 • 49, 81 • 66, 67, 78
Visually Representing	• Draw a comic vignette or a poster. • Use photographs to illustrate information.	• 31, 53 • 18, 60, *Escritura*

Cross-Curricular Standards

Subject	Standard	Activities
Language Arts	• Compare elements of Spanish grammar with English equivalents. • Use the writing process to write an essay exploring a topic.	• 15, 20, 40, 45 • *Escritura*
Social Studies	• Learn about historical and political events and figures of Hispanic countries. • Learn about current social issues. • Learn about Hispanic immigration in the United States.	• *Texto D1*, 9, 13, 14, 17, *Lectura D1*, 28, 34, 39, *Lectura D2*, 51, 81 • 59, 60, 61, 62, 76, *Proyecto* • *Mapa cultural*
Music	• Learn about protest music in Latin American countries.	• *Texto D2*, 33, 35, 80, 81

Lesson Plans (50-Minute Classes)

Day	Objectives	Sessions	Activities	Time	Standards	Resources/ Homework
1	To introduce history and society, and the characters' challenges	**Participamos / Las tareas** (240–243) • Warm-Up: Topic orientation • Presentation: *Nuestro pasado, nuestro presente*	1–2	15 m. 35 m.	1.1, 1.2, 1.3, 2.1, 2.2, 5.2	Practice Workbook
2	To learn useful expressions related to the unit topic and to review learned vocabulary	**Antes de empezar** (244–245) • Warm-Up: Independent Starter • *Expresiones útiles* • *Recuerda*	3–4 5–6	10 m. 15 m. 25 m.	1.1, 1.2, 1.3, 2.1, 2.2, 3.1, 5.1	Practice Workbook
3	To talk about historical events	**Desafío 1 – El abrazo más famoso de la Historia** (246–247) • Warm-Up: Independent Starter • *Texto: El abrazo más famoso de la Historia* • *Conexiones: El «abrazo de Guayaquil»*	7–10 11	5 m. 35 m. 10 m.	1.1, 1.2, 1.3, 2.1, 2.2, 3.1, 4.2	Audio Practice Workbook
4	To talk about historical events and figures	**Desafío 1 – Vocabulario** (248–249) • Warm-Up: Independent Starter • *Vocabulario: Historia*	12–14	5 m. 45 m.	1.1, 1.2, 2.1, 2.2, 3.1, 3.2, 4.2	Practice Workbook
5	To indicate order or position in a series	**Desafío 1 – Gramática** (250–251) • Warm-Up: Independent Starter • *Gramática: Los numerales ordinales* • *Conexiones: El significado de billón*	15–18 19	5 m. 35 m. 10 m.	1.1, 1.2, 1.3, 2.1, 2.2, 3.1, 4.1, 5.1, 5.2	Audio Practice Workbook
6	To express certainty and doubt	**Desafío 1 – Gramática** (252–253) • Warm-Up: Independent Starter • *Gramática: Expresar certeza y duda*	20–23	5 m. 45 m.	1.1, 1.2, 1.3, 2.1, 2.2, 3.1, 4.1, 4.2	Audio Practice Workbook
7	To understand a written dialogue	**Desafío 1 – Lectura** (254–255) • Warm-Up: Independent Starter • *Lectura: Bolívar y San Martín*	24–26	5 m. 45 m.	1.1, 1.2, 2.1, 2.2, 3.1, 3.2	
8	To integrate vocabulary and grammar, and to assess student proficiency	**Desafío 1 –Comunicación / Evaluación** (256–257) • Warm-Up: Independent Starter • *Comunicación*: Review • *Final del desafío* • Quiz on *Desafío 1*	27–30 31	5 m. 25 m. 10 m. 10 m.	1.1, 1.2, 1.3, 2.2, 3.1, 3.2, 4.2, 5.1	Audio Practice Workbook
9	To express purpose and difficulty	**Desafío 2 – Canciones con conciencia** (258–259) • Warm-Up: Independent Starter • *Texto: Canciones con conciencia* • *Cultura: Inti-Illimani*	32–34 35	5 m. 35 m. 10 m.	1.1, 1.2, 1.3, 2.1, 2.2, 3.1, 4.2	Audio
10	To talk about politics and government	**Desafío 2 – Vocabulario** (260–261) • Warm-Up: Independent Starter • *Vocabulario: Política y gobierno* • *Cultura: Antonio Villaraigosa*	36–38 39	5 m. 35 m. 10 m.	1.1, 1.2, 1.3, 2.1, 2.2, 3.1, 4.2, 5.1	Audio Practice Workbook

Day	Objectives	Sessions	Activities	Time	Standards	Resources/ Homework
11	To express purpose	**Desafío 2 – Gramática** (262–263) • Warm-Up: Independent Starter • *Gramática: Expresar finalidad*	 40–44	5 m. 45 m.	1.1, 1.2, 1.3, 3.1, 4.1, 4.2, 5.1, 5.2	Practice Workbook
12	To express difficulty	**Desafío 2 – Gramática** (264–265) • Warm-Up: Independent Starter • *Gramática: Expresar dificultad*	 45–49	5 m. 45 m.	1.1, 1.2, 1.3, 2.2, 3.1, 4.1, 5.2	Audio Practice Workbook
13	To understand a biography	**Desafío 2 – Lectura** (266–267) • Warm-Up: Independent Starter • *Lectura: María Eva Duarte de Perón*	 50–51	5 m. 45 m.	1.1, 1.2, 1.3, 2.1, 2.2, 3.1, 3.2, 5.1	
14	To integrate vocabulary and grammar, and to assess student proficiency	**Desafío 2 – Comunicación / Evaluación** (268–269) • Warm-Up: Independent Starter • *Comunicación:* Review • *Final del desafío* • Quiz on *Desafío 2*	 52–53 54	5 m. 25 m. 10 m. 10 m.	1.1, 1.2, 1.3, 2.1, 2.2, 3.2, 5.1, 5.2	Practice Workbook
15	To talk about social problems	**Desafío 3 – Una obra de teatro con mensaje** (270–271) • Warm-Up: Independent Starter • *Texto: Una obra de teatro con mensaje* • *Comunidades: Movimientos indigenistas*	 55–57 58	5 m. 35 m. 10 m.	1.1, 1.2, 1.3, 2.1, 2.2, 3.2, 4.2	Audio
16	To talk about social and environmental problems	**Desafío 3 – Vocabulario** (272–273) • Warm-Up: Independent Starter • *Vocabulario: Problemas sociales y medioambientales* • *Comunidades: Voluntariado juvenil en Perú*	 59–61 62	5 m. 35 m. 10 m.	1.1, 1.2, 1.3, 2.1, 2.2, 3.1, 4.2, 5.1	Audio Practice Workbook
17	To express condition	**Desafío 3 – Gramática** (274–275) • Warm-Up: Independent Starter • *Gramática: Expresar condición*	 63–67	5 m. 45 m.	1.1, 1.2, 1.3, 3.1, 5.1	Audio Practice Workbook
18	To express time	**Desafío 3 – Gramática** (276–277) • Warm-Up: Independent Starter • *Gramática: Expresar tiempo* • *Comparaciones: La contaminación en la Ciudad de México*	 68–71 72	5 m. 35 m. 10 m.	1.2, 1.3, 2.1, 2.2, 3.1, 3.2, 4.2	Audio Practice Workbook
19	To understand a literary story	**Desafío 3 – Lectura** (278–279) • Warm-Up: Independent Starter • *Lectura: El exiliado*	 73–75	5 m. 45 m.	1.1, 1.2, 1.3, 2.2, 3.2	
20	To integrate vocabulary and grammar, and to assess student proficiency	**Desafío 3 – Comunicación / Evaluación** (280–281) • Warm-Up: Independent Starter • *Comunicación:* Review • *Final del desafío* • Quiz on *Desafío 3*	 76–78 79	5 m. 25 m. 10 m. 10 m.	1.1, 1.2, 1.3, 2.1, 2.2, 5.1	Practice Workbook

Day	Objectives	Sessions	Activities	Time	Standards	Resources/ Homework
21	To integrate language in context	**Para terminar** (282–283) • Warm-Up: Independent Starter • *Todo junto* • *Tu desafío*	80 81	5 m. 25 m. 20 m.	1.2, 1.3, 2.1, 2.2, 3.1, 3.2, 5.1, 5.2	Audio Practice Workbook *Tu desafío* work
22	To integrate language in context, and to assess student proficiency	**Tu desafío / Evaluación** (283) • Warm-Up: Prepare *Tu desafío* presentations • *Tu desafío* presentations • Quiz on *Desafíos 1–3*		5 m. 25 m. 20 m.	1.2, 1.3, 2.1, 2.2, 3.1, 3.2, 5.1, 5.2	
23	To learn about Hispanic immigration in the United States	**Mapa cultural** (284–285) • Warm-Up: Independent Starter • *Mapa cultural: La inmigración hispana en los Estados Unidos*	82	5 m. 45 m.	1.1, 1.2, 2.1, 2.2, 3.1, 3.2, 5.1, 5.2	Practice Workbook
24	To write an essay exploring a topic	**Escritura** (286–287) • Warm-Up: Independent Starter • *Escritura: Un ensayo*		5 m. 45 m.	1.1, 1.2, 1.3, 5.1, 5.2	Project work
25	To write a manifesto to demand solutions to community problems	**Proyecto** (292–293) • Warm-Up: Prepare project presentations • Project presentations		10 m. 40 m.	1.1, 1.2, 1.3, 2.1, 2.2, 3.1, 5.1, 5.2	**Repaso – Vocabulario** (288–289) **Repaso – Gramática** (290–291)
26	To assess student proficiency	**Assessment** • *Autoevaluación* (293) • Test		10 m. 40 m.	1.1, 1.2, 1.3, 2.1, 2.2, 5.1, 5.2	
27	To prepare for the AP* Exam	**Hacia el AP* Exam** (294–297) • Warm-Up: Test introduction • Test: Presentational Writing: Persuasive Essay		5 m. 45 m.	1.2, 1.3, 2.1, 2.2, 3.2, 5.1	Audio
28	To prepare for the AP* Exam	**Hacia el AP* Exam** (294–297) • Warm-Up: About the test • Review and correction of the test		5 m. 45 m.	1.2, 1.3, 2.1, 2.2, 3.2, 5.1	

Lesson Plans (90-Minute Classes)

Day	Objectives	Sessions	Activities	Time	Standards	Resources/ Homework
1	To introduce history and society and the characters' challenges, to learn useful expressions related to the unit topic, and to review learned vocabulary	**Participamos / Las tareas / Antes de empezar** (240–245) • Warm-Up: Topic orientation • Presentation: *Nuestro pasado, nuestro presente* • *Expresiones útiles* • *Recuerda*	1–2 3–4 5–6	15 m. 35 m. 15 m. 25 m.	1.1, 1.2, 1.3, 2.1, 2.2, 3.1, 5.1, 5.2	Practice Workbook
2	To talk about historical events and figures	**Desafío 1 – El abrazo más famoso de la Historia / Vocabulario** (246–249) • Warm-Up: Independent Starter • Texto: *El abrazo más famoso de la Historia* • Conexiones: *El «abrazo de Guayaquil»* • Vocabulario: *Historia*	 7–10 11 12–14	5 m. 30 m. 10 m. 45 m.	1.1, 1.2, 1.3, 2.1, 2.2, 3.1, 3.2, 4.2	Audio Practice Workbook
3	To indicate order or position in a series and to express certainty and doubt	**Desafío 1 – Gramática** (250–253) • Warm-Up: Independent Starter • Gramática: *Los numerales ordinales* • Conexiones: *El significado de* billón • Gramática: *Expresar certeza y duda*	 15–18 19 20–23	5 m. 35 m. 10 m. 40 m.	1.1, 1.2, 1.3, 2.1, 2.2, 3.1, 4.1, 4.2, 5.1, 5.2	Audio Practice Workbook
4	To understand a written dialogue, to integrate vocabulary and grammar, and to assess student proficiency	**Desafío 1 – Lectura / Comunicación / Evaluación** (254–257) • Warm-Up: Independent Starter • Lectura: *Bolívar y San Martín* • Comunicación: Review • Final del desafío • Quiz on *Desafío 1*	 24–26 27–30 31	5 m. 40 m. 25 m. 10 m. 10 m.	1.1, 1.2, 1.3, 2.1, 2.2, 3.1, 3.2, 4.2, 5.1	Audio Practice Workbook
5	To express purpose and difficulty and to talk about politics and government	**Desafío 2 – Canciones con conciencia / Vocabulario** (258–261) • Warm-Up: Independent Starter • Texto: *Canciones con conciencia* • Cultura: *Inti-Illimani* • Vocabulario: *Política y gobierno* • Cultura: *Antonio Villaraigosa*	 32–34 35 36–38 39	5 m. 30 m. 10 m. 35 m. 10 m.	1.1, 1.2, 1.3, 2.1, 2.2, 3.1, 4.2, 5.1	Audio Practice Workbook
6	To express purpose and to express difficulty	**Desafío 2 – Gramática** (262–265) • Warm-Up: Independent Starter • Gramática: *Expresar finalidad* • Gramática: *Expresar dificultad*	 40–44 45–49	5 m. 45 m. 40 m.	1.1, 1.2, 1.3, 2.2, 3.1, 4.1, 4.2, 5.1, 5.2	Audio Practice Workbook

Day	Objectives	Sessions	Activities	Time	Standards	Resources/ Homework
7	To understand a biography, to integrate vocabulary and grammar, and to assess student proficiency	**Desafío 2 – Lectura / Comunicación / Evaluación** (266–269) • Warm-Up: Independent Starter • *Lectura: María Eva Duarte de Perón* • *Comunicación:* Review • *Final del desafío* • Quiz on *Desafío 2*	50–51 52–53 54	5 m. 40 m. 25 m. 10 m. 10 m.	1.1, 1.2, 1.3, 2.1, 2.2, 3.1, 3.2, 5.1, 5.2	Practice Workbook
8	To talk about social and environmental problems	**Desafío 3 – Una obra de teatro con mensaje / Vocabulario** (270–273) • Warm-Up: Independent Starter • *Texto: Una obra de teatro con mensaje* • *Comunidades: Movimientos indigenistas* • *Vocabulario: Problemas sociales y medioambientales* • *Comunidades: Voluntariado juvenil en Perú*	55–57 58 59–61 62	5 m. 30 m. 10 m. 35 m. 10 m.	1.1, 1.2, 1.3, 2.1, 2.2, 3.1, 3.2, 4.2, 5.1	Audio Practice Workbook
9	To express condition and to express time	**Desafío 3 – Gramática** (274–277) • Warm-Up: Independent Starter • *Gramática: Expresar condición* • *Gramática: Expresar tiempo* • *Comparaciones: La contaminación en la Ciudad de México*	63–67 68–71 72	5 m. 40 m. 35 m. 10 m.	1.1, 1.2, 1.3, 2.1, 2.2, 3.1, 3.2, 4.2, 5.1	Audio Practice Workbook
10	To understand a literary story and to integrate vocabulary and grammar	**Desafío 3 – Lectura / Comunicación / Evaluación** (278–281) • Warm-Up: Independent Starter • *Lectura: El exiliado* • *Comunicación:* Review • *Final del desafío* • Quiz on *Desafío 3*	73–75 76–78 79	5 m. 40 m. 25 m. 10 m. 10 m.	1.1, 1.2, 1.3, 2.1, 2.2, 3.2, 5.1	Practice Workbook **Para terminar – Tu desafío** (283)
11	To integrate language in context, and to assess student proficiency	**Para terminar / Evalución** (282–283) • Warm-Up: Independent Starter • *Todo junto* • *Tu desafío:* work and presentations • Quiz on *Desafíos 1–3*	80 81	5 m. 25 m. 40 m. 20 m.	1.2, 1.3, 2.1, 2.2, 3.1, 3.2, 5.1, 5.2	Audio Practice Workbook
12	To learn about Hispanic immigration in the United States and to write an essay exploring a topic	**Mapa cultural / Escritura** (284–287) • Warm-Up: Independent Starter • *Mapa cultural: La inmigración hispana en los Estados Unidos* • *Escritura: Un ensayo*	82	5 m. 40 m. 45 m.	1.1, 1.2, 1.3, 2.1, 2.2, 3.1, 3.2, 5.1, 5.2	Practice Workbook **Repaso – Vocabulario** (288–289) **Repaso – Gramática** (290–291) Project work

Day	Objectives	Sessions	Activities	Time	Standards	Resources/ Homework
13	To write a manifesto to demand solutions to community problems, and to assess student proficiency	***Proyecto / Assessment*** (292–293) • Warm-Up: Prepare project presentations • Project presentations • *Autoevaluación* • Test		10 m. 45 m. 10 m. 25 m.	1.1, 1.2, 1.3, 2.1, 2.2, 3.1, 5.1, 5.2	
14	To prepare for the AP* Exam	***Hacia el* AP* Exam** (294–297) • Warm-Up: Test introduction • Test: Presentational Writing: Persuasive Essay • Review and correction of the test		10 m. 55 m. 25 m.	1.2, 1.3, 2.1, 2.2, 3.2, 5.1	Audio

9 El desafío

—Como no es posible inventar los hechos históricos, tendremos que investigar este famoso «abrazo» entre los líderes latinoamericanos Bolívar y San Martín.

—Sí, tenemos que averiguar más cosas de la historia del siglo XIX.

—Entonces, empecemos. En nuestro libro de Historia dice que Bolívar luchó por la independencia de Venezuela, y que participó también en la liberación e incorporación de los territorios al sur de Colombia.

—Yo he leído que no solo deseaba la independencia de estos territorios, sino que esperaba unir todas las regiones del continente para formar una gran República.

—Aquí hay más datos. ¿Sabías que San Martín vivió en España con su familia? Parece ser que estuvo en el ejército español y luchó contra las tropas de Napoleón.

—¡Qué curioso! Primero luchó para defender España y después, cuando volvió a Suramérica, luchó contra los españoles.

—Sí, es verdad. Mientras Bolívar liberaba el norte del continente, San Martín fue el libertador del sur. Claro, por eso se le llama «padre de la patria» en Argentina.

—Oye, hemos leído bastante sobre los libertadores, pero todavía no sabemos nada del famoso abrazo de Guayaquil...

—Bueno, sabemos que Bolívar y San Martín se encontraron en Guayaquil; que se sabe muy poco sobre la reunión porque no hubo testigos; y que después de ese encuentro Bolívar siguió luchando para lograr la independencia del continente.

—¿Y qué hizo San Martín?

—Dejó todos sus cargos y volvió a su casa, en Buenos Aires. Y pocos años después se trasladó a Europa, donde murió.

17 Escenas históricas

1. En 1486 Cristóbal Colón se reunió con los Reyes Católicos (Isabel de Castilla y Fernando de Aragón) para presentarles un proyecto para viajar a las Indias navegando hacia el oeste. Los reyes lo aceptaron y de esta manera Colón inició la aventura que llevaría a los españoles a las Américas.

2. Esta escena representa la llegada de Cristóbal Colón a la isla de Guanahani, que forma parte del archipiélago de las Bahamas. Este hecho tuvo lugar el doce de octubre de 1492, durante el primero de los cuatro viajes que realizó Colón a las Américas.

3. En esta escena vemos a Diego de Almagro y a Francisco Pizarro frente a Atahualpa. Los incas se enfrentaron a los españoles en 1532 y Atahualpa, hijo del difunto emperador inca Huayna Cápac, fue hecho prisionero por Francisco Pizarro.

4. Los venezolanos declararon su independencia el 5 de julio de 1811. Venezuela fue el tercer país de las Américas en independizarse, después de los Estados Unidos y Haití. En esta escena vemos el momento de la firma de la declaración de independencia.

22 ¿Cómo van con su trabajo?

—Ahora que sabemos más del encuentro entre San Martín y Bolívar, debemos explorar un poco más los elementos de las novelas gráficas. ¿Son como los cómics?

—Bueno, más o menos... Se puede decir que las novelas gráficas son un nuevo arte; no son un simple cómic para niños. Yo estoy convencido de que hoy en día este género tiene un prestigio comparable al de la literatura y otras formas de arte. ¿Empezamos?

—Claro.

—Es evidente que para hacer una novela gráfica lo primero es elegir un tema y un título, y eso ya lo tenemos, ¿verdad?

—Sí: «El famoso abrazo». Estoy segura de que el título está muy claro: se refiere al hecho histórico que presentamos y se expresa en una frase breve y sencilla.

—Pero es posible que nos haga falta identificar la época... Quizás sea mejor «El abrazo más famoso del siglo XIX».

—Genial. Sigamos. El segundo paso es crear una sinopsis para explicar quiénes son estos dos grandes líderes, en qué consistió este hecho histórico, qué consecuencias tuvo y por qué es tan importante. Daniel, ¿tú crees que es necesario incluir una biografía de cada uno de estos líderes? Yo no lo tengo muy claro.

—No es probable que a los lectores les interesen los detalles de su vida, ¿no crees?

—De acuerdo. Entonces, centrémonos en los hechos importantes, como la llegada de San Martín en barco.

—Bien. Y la segunda viñeta puede ser el recorrido de San Martín hasta el palacio donde lo esperaba Bolívar.

28 Cuatro héroes norteamericanos

1. Susan Brownell Anthony nació en 1820 en Massachusetts. Trabajó junto a Elizabeth Cady Stanton por los derechos de la mujer y, sobre todo, para garantizar su derecho al voto. Ambas visitaban las fábricas para investigar las condiciones laborales y los sueldos de las trabajadoras, que generalmente eran más bajos que los de los hombres. Susan defendió la coeducación y trabajó para que las universidades aceptaran a las mujeres como alumnas. También se interesó por la lucha para lograr la abolición de la esclavitud.

2. César Chávez nació en 1927 en Arizona, en una familia de inmigrantes de origen mexicano. En aquella época los trabajadores inmigrantes en Arizona y California sufrían

condiciones laborales muy malas. Chávez dedicó su vida a defender la justicia y la dignidad de su gente sin usar la violencia, mediante huelgas, manifestaciones, discursos, diálogo y negociación. En 1964 creó la National Farm Workers Association, el primer sindicato de trabajadores agrícolas.

3. Martin Luther King, Jr. nació el 15 de enero de 1929. Era uno de los principales líderes del movimiento para la defensa de los derechos fundamentales. Es famoso por sus métodos pacíficos y por sus discursos apasionados, que inspiraron a muchos a manifestarse en busca de la igualdad racial. Ganó el Premio Nobel de la Paz en 1964. Aunque había luchado de forma pacífica, King murió violentamente; fue asesinado en Memphis (Tennessee) en 1968.

4. El primero de diciembre se conmemora un hecho crucial que ocurrió en 1955, cuando el conductor de un autobús de Montgomery (Alabama) le dijo a Rosa Parks que le cediera su asiento a un pasajero blanco. Rosa se negó y fue encarcelada. Este hecho se convirtió en un símbolo de la desobediencia civil pacífica y ayudó a poner fin a la segregación racial en los Estados Unidos. En 1999, el Congreso le concedió a Parks la Medalla de Oro.

34 El gobierno militar de Chile

–Buenos días, clase. Hoy vamos a repasar un poco la historia de Chile. ¿Alguien recuerda quién era el presidente en 1973? Sí, Jamie...

–El presidente era Salvador Allende. Pero murió en septiembre de 1973 durante el golpe de Estado.

–Efectivamente. Y ¿quién fue el líder del golpe de Estado? A ver... Amanda.

–El general Augusto Pinochet. Después del golpe, Pinochet se convirtió en el jefe de Estado de Chile.

–Muy bien. Al principio de los años setenta, había bastante inestabilidad en Chile porque la economía no estaba muy fuerte. Como saben, Pinochet encabezó el golpe de Estado, instauró una dictadura y prohibió todos los partidos políticos. ¿Sí, Mateo?

–A mí no me parece justo que se prohíban los partidos políticos.

–Claro, tienes razón. Desgraciadamente, hubo muchas injusticias y violaciones de los derechos humanos durante la dictadura de Pinochet. Muchas personas murieron o desaparecieron por estar en contra del régimen. Dime, Nicole.

–¿Y cuándo terminó la dictadura?

–En 1980 se aprobó una nueva constitución, que entró en funcionamiento un año después. En ella se nombraba presidente a Pinochet durante ocho años. Y en 1988 se realizó un referéndum para prolongar el mandato presidencial por ocho años más. Pinochet perdió el referéndum y tuvo que convocar

elecciones. En 1990 dejó la presidencia, pero continuó siendo el jefe de las fuerzas armadas, así que no dejó definitivamente el poder hasta 1998.

–¿Y qué le pasó a Pinochet después?

–En 1998 fue detenido en Londres acusado de violación de los derechos humanos. En el año 2000 regresó a Chile, donde tuvo que enfrentarse a otros procesos judiciales. Murió a finales de 2006. Para mañana, quiero que lean este artículo sobre la situación sociopolítica en Chile después del régimen, ¿de acuerdo? Los veo mañana.

37 El sistema político argentino

En Argentina, como en otros muchos países, hay un sistema democrático basado en tres poderes: el ejecutivo, el legislativo y el judicial.

La rama ejecutiva corresponde al presidente, que es el jefe de Estado, y a la administración. Cada cuatro años se celebran elecciones. El vicepresidente, elegido con el presidente, también es el presidente del Senado.

La rama legislativa está representada en el Congreso Nacional. Consta de 72 senadores y 257 diputados. El número de diputados de una región se determina según la población y cada región elige a tres senadores: dos de la mayoría y uno de la minoría. Se eligen diputados cada cuatro años y senadores cada seis.

La rama judicial consiste en una Corte Suprema de nueve miembros designados por el presidente con la aprobación del Senado.

47 Conversaciones sobre política

1. –¿Al final tu candidato preferido ganó las elecciones?
   –Pues no. Tenía una campaña muy fuerte, pero los resultados muestran que la del otro candidato fue mejor.
   –Lo siento.
   –No pasa nada. Así son las elecciones.

2. –¿Crees que es buena idea limitar la duración de los cargos políticos?
   –Sí, porque así nadie puede tener el poder durante demasiado tiempo, aun cuando sean buenos líderes.
   –Claro, parece lógico.

3. –¿Crees que todavía hay demasiadas injusticias en nuestra sociedad?
   –Por supuesto. Por ejemplo, todavía hay mucha discriminación y violaciones de los derechos humanos. Hay muchas leyes para prevenir estos problemas, pero no siempre se cumplen y, lo que es peor, no siempre se castiga a quienes no las cumplen. Se pueden tener todas las leyes del mundo, pero si no se respetan, no valen nada.

4. –Acabo de oír que el presidente vetó un proyecto de ley para promover el comercio, pero no me lo creo.

–Yo lo oí también. Es un buen proyecto de ley, pero no hay recursos para financiarlo. Por eso creo que el presidente tuvo que vetarlo. En este momento, la opinión pública opina que no se debe gastar más dinero.

57 Una representante del CICA

–Muchas gracias por su ayuda, Luisa. Díganos, ¿desde cuándo es miembro del CICA?

–Desde el año en que nació la organización, o sea, desde 1995.

–¿Y cuál es el objetivo del CICA que más le gusta a usted, con el que se siente más comprometida?

–Uff, es difícil elegir uno. Todos están relacionados entre sí y todos buscan la defensa de los derechos de los indígenas y la recuperación de su cultura. Pero creo que la recuperación de las lenguas indígenas es la parte que más me fascina.

–¿Qué tipo de actividades organiza el CICA para lograr sus objetivos?

–Somos una organización muy activa. Organizamos cursos, talleres, conferencias...

–¿Y cómo funciona la organización?

–El CICA está formado por siete Consejos Nacionales correspondientes a los siete países que lo forman: Costa Rica, Belice, Panamá, Guatemala, El Salvador, Honduras y Nicaragua.

–Claro, los siete países de Centroamérica.

–Exactamente. Veo que les interesa mucho el tema. Pregúntenme todo lo que quieran.

60 Noticias nacionales

1. Hoy concluyó la construcción de los primeros aerogeneradores de la región que reemplazarán a la vieja planta nuclear que lleva treinta años contaminando nuestros acuíferos. Los vientos de los llanos generarán electricidad para todo el estado.

2. El análisis de los índices de criminalidad de los primeros seis meses del año muestra un aumento de la delincuencia en la región. Aunque los delitos con violencia han disminuido, han aumentado los robos en viviendas y los robos de vehículos. La policía está investigando para descubrir la raíz del problema.

3. Un total de doce personas han sido arrestadas acusadas de robar dinero de instituciones públicas para financiar proyectos privados. Entre los detenidos hay varios políticos locales, acusados de corrupción.

4. Aumentan preocupantemente los índices de pobreza debido a la situación general de crisis y el aumento del desempleo, según muestran los últimos estudios. Los trabajadores sociales alertan sobre todo de los índices de pobreza infantil y han presentado una serie de medidas de actuación.

65 Consecuencias

1. Perdí el autobús y tuve que esperar media hora hasta el siguiente. Por eso no llegué a tiempo para ver un programa muy interesante sobre el tráfico de armas en los países en desarrollo.

2. Me quedé dormido en el tren y cuando me desperté... ¡mi cartera había desaparecido! Hablé con el revisor y me dijo que tengo que ir a la policía a poner una denuncia.

3. Muchas personas no conocían los efectos negativos de los alimentos transgénicos en la salud y por eso los consumieron sin ninguna preocupación.

4. Hace unos años mi familia y yo íbamos a mudarnos a la Ciudad de México pero finalmente no lo hicimos por el alto nivel de contaminación. Mi mamá tiene asma y el médico no se lo recomendó.

5. A mis papás les preocupa mucho el futuro del medio ambiente y por eso desde hace dos años usamos energía solar para calentar la casa.

71 El desafío de Ethan y Eva

–¿Aló?

–Hola, Ethan, soy Eva. Te llamo solo para decirte que enseguida voy a tu casa para trabajar en el guion de la obra de teatro.

–¿Dónde estás?

–En la biblioteca. Saldré en cuanto termine de tomar algunas notas más sobre el indigenismo. Llegaré en cuanto pueda, pero no antes de las cinco.

–Estupendo. Yo me reuní con Luisa cuando terminé mis clases y me habló de diversas organizaciones indigenistas. No sabía que hubiera tantos grupos trabajando a favor de los derechos y la cultura de la población indígena.

–Sí, es sorprendente. ¿Y hablaron mucho?

–Sí, estuve con ella hasta que llegó Ricardo, un joven indígena de El Salvador que se ofreció a ayudarnos.

–¡Qué bien! ¿Y estaría dispuesto a actuar en la obra?

–Sí, pero antes de aceptar definitivamente quiere saber qué vamos a hacer.

–Bien. Entonces hoy trabajaremos hasta que tengamos un primer borrador para mostrárselo mañana.

–De acuerdo. Nos vemos en un rato.

–¡Hasta luego!

80 Una artista comprometida

Fuente: ADN Radio, Chile

—Esta tarde-noche, a las 20 horas, en la Plaza de Armas, hay un concierto tributo a Violeta Parra: 8 artistas invitados, 70 músicos de la orquesta sinfónica, van a formar parte de este homenaje, que es a las ocho y media. Es gratuito. Álvaro Henríquez, Claudia Acuña, Inti-Illimani Histórico, Ana Tijoux, Francisca Valenzuela, Camila Moreno, Javiera Parra y Los Imposibles... Además el invitado internacional, el músico argentino Pedro Aznar, que está con nosotros al teléfono y nos va a contar de este gran homenaje a la más grande de aquí. ¿Cómo estás, Pedro Aznar? Bienvenido.

—Muchas gracias, Diana. ¿Cómo estás?

—Muy bien. ¿Cómo se está preparando este gran concierto?

—Muy bien. Estuvimos haciendo dos ensayos que salieron realmente preciosos. El *show* va a ser un evento realmente conmovedor. La orquesta está sonando magníficamente bien y todos los artistas que estamos involucrados estamos muy emocionados de cantar estas canciones que son parte tan central del acervo cultural chileno, ¿verdad?

—¿Y cómo te enamoró, te conquistó con su música?

—En realidad, la música de Violeta la escuché desde chico pero empecé a transitarla con mayor hondura en estos últimos quince años, cuando empecé a grabar su música y a meterme realmente de lleno en su repertorio.

—¿Y cuál es el valor que le das a ella, a lo mejor en tu propia carrera musical, en tu propia formación como músico?

—Yo creo que ella es una gran referencia porque supo darle un valor universal a valores locales muy importantes, a la música de raíz y yo creo que ese es el gran legado de Violeta: haber puesto la música tradicional de Chile en un nuevo nivel de excelencia y ante los ojos de todo el mundo. Yo creo que eso es una gran enseñanza para todos los que componemos música.

—Estamos conversando con el músico argentino Pedro Aznar, que forma parte de los artistas que se van a presentar esta noche a las ocho y media en la Plaza de Armas de manera gratuita en un gran homenaje a Violeta Parra.

Hacia el *AP* Exam*

Fuente: BBC Mundo

—Este desierto podría cambiar el futuro de Bolivia. El salar de Uyuni contiene una de las mayores reservas mundiales de litio, el metal más ligero del planeta. Cerca del salar está en construcción la primera planta de litio del gobierno boliviano. Muchos apuestan a que este metal propulsará la próxima revolución industrial con la construcción en masa de autos eléctricos. Por eso, empresas de países como Japón, Corea del Sur y Francia quieren firmar contratos con el gobierno de Bolivia para su explotación. China, que tiene sus propias reservas de litio, le ha ofrecido cooperación en la extracción, desarrollo e infraestructura. Ha dicho, incluso, que fabricaría el primer satélite boliviano.

—Esta reserva es tan grande que es muy importante para Bolivia, no solo para este gobierno sino también para el futuro del país, implementar un proyecto que sea propiedad de Bolivia, que sea controlado por Bolivia y desarrollado por Bolivia. Pero algunos señalan que el país no cuenta con suficientes recursos para desarrollar la industria del litio.

—Si se hace una estrategia adecuada se puede tener toda la capacidad para llegar hasta cierto nivel de la cadena. Después seguramente ya se requieren inversiones para las cuales Bolivia no estaría en condiciones.

—Sin embargo el gobierno asegura que mantendrá el control del litio, del que tiene suficientes reservas para, según sus cálculos y a los niveles actuales de demanda, suministrarle este metal al mundo en los próximos cinco mil años.

Participamos

The Unit

- The themes for Unit 5 are history and society. The participants will learn to talk about historical facts and about political and social issues. They will also learn to express certainty, doubt, purpose, difficulties, conditions, and time.
- Tim and Andy, two veterans of *Fans del español*, have prepared some "historical challenges" for the participants.
  - *Desafío 1.* Michelle and Daniel have to create a graphic novel about an important historical event: the famous *abrazo de Guayaquil*.
  - *Desafío 2.* Asha and Lucas will have to write a "protest song," or a song associated with a social movement.
  - *Desafío 3.* Eva and Ethan must get in contact with an indigenous activist to learn about the indigenous movements and write the scene of a play.

Activities	Standards	Resources
Participamos	1.2, 2.1, 2.2	

Teaching Suggestions

Warm-Up / Independent Starter

- Have students look at the photos and come up with a one-paragraph description for one of the images. Ask them to describe the people in the photo, what they are wearing, what they look like, and what they are doing.

Preparation

- Ask students to read the captions and predict what the topic for each challenge might be. In order to recycle structures with *creer* to express opinion (e.g., *Creo que...*), have them guess what the *Monumento a los Libertadores* is about or what the indigenous people in Ecuador are doing.
- Have students read each *Desafío's* objective, as well as the vocabulary and grammar goals, then discuss how each picture might relate to these objectives and goals.

240

UNIDAD 5

Participamos
Historia y sociedad

Festival Internacional de la Canción de Viña del Mar (Chile).

DESAFÍO 1

▶ **Hablar de hechos históricos**

Vocabulario
Historia

Gramática
Los numerales ordinales

Expresar certeza y duda

DESAFÍO 2

▶ **Expresar finalidad y dificultad**

Vocabulario
Política y gobierno

Gramática
Expresar finalidad

Expresar dificultad

Monumento a los Libertadores. Guayaquil (Ecuador).

240 doscientos cuarenta

The Challenge

DESAFÍO 1

Monumento a los Libertadores. Guayaquil
Revolution was in the air during the early 19th century. The British colonies in America rose up in 1776, and in 1789, French citizens rebelled against the monarchy. In 1808, the people of Madrid revolted when Napoleon attempted to place his brother on the Spanish throne. This same spirit of independence spread to the Spanish colonies, and Bolívar and San Martín were two of the most influential figures leading the charge for a free, unified South America. While San Martín led the rebellion in the south, Bolívar took responsibility for the north.

DESAFÍO 2

Festival Internacional de la Canción de Viña del Mar
Protest songs became popular in Latin America in the 1960s and 1970s, with the so-called *nueva canción*, which was performed by well-known singers such as Violeta Parra, Víctor Jara, Mercedes Sosa, Silvio Rodríguez, Pablo Milanés, and Atahualpa Yupanqui, as well as by groups such as Inti-Illimani and Quilapayún. The songs criticized the status quo, and often expressed political ideas that were contrary to the governments in place. The *Festival Internacional de la Canción* has served as a venue for some of these artists.

Participamos

Picture Discussion

- Call on volunteers to read their descriptions from the Independent Starter, and share their predictions and any information they may have on these topics in a class discussion.

Monumento a los Libertadores. Guayaquil (Ecuador)

- Have students think about the word *Libertadores* and what it means. Remind them about the colonial history of the Americas. You may wish to tell the class briefly about generals Simón Bolívar and José de San Martín, who liberated South America from Spanish rule.

Festival Internacional de la Canción de Viña del Mar (Chile)

- Have students identify the musical instruments pictured. Some students may need help identifying some of the instruments, such as the *quena*, a traditional Andean flute. You may wish to show them images of some other instruments used by folkloric groups in South America, such as the *zampoña*, or panpipe, the *cajón*, a type of drum, or the *charango*, a small ten-stringed guitar.

Ritual indígena en Quito (Ecuador)

- Invite students to describe these people's clothes. Students may need help identifying some elements of Andean outerwear: poncho, *pollera* (a traditional embroidered skirt), *lliclla* or *manta* (a square woven cloth that covers the shoulders), *chumpi* or *chumbi* (a woven belt), *monteras* (hats), *ch'uspa* (a small woven bag). Then, ask students to describe what the people are doing as a way to recycle expressions such as *están de rodillas, tienen los ojos cerrados, otros están de pie*, etc. Ask them to guess what the ritual is about.

Objectives

- By the end of Unit 5, students will be able to
  - Talk about historical and political facts, and social issues.
  - Use ordinal numbers.
  - Express certainty and doubt.
  - Express purpose and difficulty.
  - Express condition.
  - Locate events in time and history.
  - Talk about important times and figures in the history of Latin America and Spain, and familiarize themselves with current politics and social issues of the Spanish-speaking world.

DESAFÍO 3

▶ **Hablar de problemas sociales**

Vocabulario
Problemas sociales y medioambientales

Gramática
Expresar condición.
El pluscuamperfecto de subjuntivo

Expresar tiempo

Ritual indígena en Quito (Ecuador).

doscientos cuarenta y uno 241

DESAFÍO 3

Ritual indígena en Quito

Ever since the arrival of the first Europeans, indigenous peoples of Latin America have fought to defend their identity and culture. However, in recent years, they have developed a movement to express their vision of how society should work. Among these ideas, the following may be highlighted: the Earth is the source of all life, and access to water is a fundamental human right; rejection of colonialism and defense of the self-government of indigenous communities; construction of multinational and multiethnic states; and promotion of self-determination.

Las tareas

Presentation

- In this section, Tim and Andy, two former participants, chat with the three pairs and describe the challenges that lie ahead. Students will preview ways to introduce a topic or a fact, and clarify something said.

Activities	Standards	Resources
Texto	1.2, 2.1, 2.2	
1.	1.2, 1.3, 2.2, 5.2	
2.	1.1, 1.2, 2.1, 2.2	

Teaching Suggestions

Warm-Up / Independent Starter

- To activate students' previous knowledge about the themes of this unit, have them create a three-column chart like the one below, in which they list examples from the Spanish-speaking world.

Personajes históricos	Cantantes	Tradiciones indígenas
Cristóbal Colón	María Teresa Vera	Día de Muertos

Preparation

- Invite volunteers to share their Independent Starters. Congratulate them on their knowledge of the people and cultures of the Spanish-speaking world, and discuss some of the historical figures, singers, and traditions they mentioned. If there are students who have first-hand knowledge of some of the traditions or artists mentioned, invite them to share their experiences and what they know with the class.

- Read the title of the dialogue aloud, and ask students to explain what they think it means. You may want to ask students what they think about learning history, and how knowing about our past may help us understand the present times. Ask them questions about the history of their own country, and about the type of government that their country has. You may ask these or similar questions to preview some of the vocabulary they will learn in this unit: *¿Es este país un reino o una república? ¿Qué partidos políticos son importantes en este país? ¿Cuándo tuvo lugar la lucha por la independencia?*

Nuestro pasado, nuestro presente

Tim y Andy les han preparado a los participantes unos «desafíos históricos». ¿Qué tendrán que hacer? Lee el chat para averiguarlo.

Mostrar mensajes de: Hoy | Esta semana | Últimos 30 días | Todos

Tim dice: 6:37
Hola a todos. ¿Cómo están? Andy y yo les hemos preparado unos desafíos bien interesantes. A todos les interesa la Historia, ¿no es cierto?

Michelle dice: 6:37
Sí. Por suerte, este año tengo clase de Historia de las Américas, así que estoy aprendiendo mucho.

Andy dice: 6:38
Pues me alegro, porque Daniel y tú van a crear una novela gráfica sobre un hecho histórico: el famoso «abrazo de Guayaquil».

Lucas dice: 6:51
¡Qué suerte! A mí me encantan los cómics y las novelas gráficas. ¿Nosotros también vamos a dibujar?

Tim dice: 6:53
No, pero también van a crear algo. Mejor dicho, van a escribir algo. Ustedes son muy creativos, ¿verdad? Pues tienen que escribir una canción protesta. Pueden inspirarse en el grupo chileno Inti-Illimani. Y cuando la hayan terminado podrán compartirla con nosotros.

Ethan dice: 7:01
¡Eso, eso! ¿Y cuál será nuestro desafío?

Tim dice: 7:02
Lo primero que tienen que hacer es ponerse en contacto con Luisa Itzel, una representante de un consejo indígena. Ella está de visita en California y los va a ayudar.

Eva dice: 7:03
¿Y qué vamos a hacer?

Tim dice: 7:04
Van a escribir una escena para una obra de teatro sobre los movimientos indigenistas en las Américas.

Ethan dice: 7:05
Perfecto. Yo me ocupo de escribirle hoy mismo. Por cierto, ¿tienes su dirección de correo electrónico, Tim?

Differentiated Instruction

DEVELOPING LEARNERS

- Ask students to correct the following false statements:
  1. *Daniel dice que tiene clase de Historia de las Américas. (Lo dice Michelle.)*
  2. *Michelle y Daniel van a crear una novela gráfica sobre Chile. (La novela será sobre el «abrazo de Guayaquil».)*
  3. *Lucas y Asha van a escribir una obra de teatro sobre los movimientos indígenas. (Van a escribir una canción protesta.)*
  4. *Asha pregunta si ella y Lucas van a dibujar algo. (Lo pregunta Lucas.)*
  5. *Luisa Itzel es una cantante famosa. (Es una representante de un consejo indígena.)*

EXPANDING LEARNERS

- Ask students to imagine that they are going to carry out similar *desafíos*. Ask them which famous event in Hispanic history they would depict. If they were writing *una canción protesta,* what would be its focus? And if they were writing the script for a play, what *movimiento indígena* would they highlight? Be sure to have students explain why they made these choices. You may wish to have them write their answers or be prepared to give a brief oral answer in front of the class.

¿Tú sabes qué es eso del «abrazo de Guayaquil»?

Sí. O, más bien, creo que sí. No estoy segura del todo.

Ya tengo los datos de contacto de la señora Itzel. Le voy a escribir un correo ahora mismo.

¡Perfecto!

Menos mal que a los dos nos interesa la música. ¿Tú sabes algo sobre la canción protesta?

No demasiado, pero suena interesante.

1 ¿Comprendes?

▶ **Responde** a estas preguntas.

1. ¿Quiénes se interesan por la Historia?
2. ¿Por qué le gusta a Lucas el desafío de Michelle y Daniel?
3. ¿Qué van a tener que hacer Lucas y Asha?
4. ¿De dónde es el grupo Inti-Illimani?
5. ¿Con quién tienen que comunicarse Ethan y Eva? ¿Para qué?

▶ **Escribe.** Si pudieras elegir, ¿qué desafío preferirías? ¿Por qué?

2 Investiga

▶ **Busca** información para responder a estas preguntas relacionadas con los desafíos.

1. ¿Cuándo sucedió el «abrazo de Guayaquil»? ¿Quiénes participaron en él?
2. ¿En qué año se formó el grupo Inti-Illimani? ¿Cuántos miembros tenía el grupo original?
3. ¿Qué activista indígena guatemalteca ganó el Premio Nobel de la Paz? ¿En qué año fue?

▶ **Compara** tus respuestas con las de tu compañero(a).

doscientos cuarenta y tres 243

Unit 5

Las tareas

Texto: Nuestro pasado, nuestro presente

■ Read the introduction to the text aloud, and discuss with the class the possible meaning of *desafío histórico*. Can students see that it is a play on words? Then, call on six volunteers to read the chat aloud. Write the following phrases on the board and ask students to associate a participant pair with each phrase according to their tasks: *novela gráfica*, *canción protesta*, *escena de teatro*. (Michelle and Daniel, Asha and Lucas, Eva and Ethan)

■ Then have students read the dialogues on page 243. As a class, discuss the participants' reactions and their level of preparation for each challenge. Which pair do students think is better prepared to perform well? Why?

Activities

1. To expand this activity, ask students questions about their favorite historical or political heroes. For example: *¿Quién es, en su opinión, uno de los personajes históricos más importantes? ¿Por qué? ¿Qué hizo?* You may want to ask students to write a brief description of their chosen figure.

Answer Key

1. Answers will vary. Sample answers:
   1. A todos les interesa.
   2. Porque le encantan los cómics y las novelas gráficas.
   3. Van a escribir una canción protesta.
   4. De Chile.
   5. Con Luisa Itzel, una representante de un consejo indígena, para que ella los ayude.
   ▶ Answers will vary.

2. Answers will vary. Sample answers:
   1. Ocurrió el 26 de julio de 1822 entre Simón Bolívar y José de San Martín.
   2. En 1967 y tenía cinco miembros.
   3. Rigoberta Menchú, en 1992.
   ▶ Answers will vary.

Additional Resources

Fans Online activities
Practice Workbook

HERITAGE LANGUAGE LEARNERS

• Encourage students to discuss how history can be viewed through other subjects, such as literature, music, art, architecture, and the sciences. Ask students to select one of these subjects that is of particular interest to them, do any necessary research, and then explain how they would integrate the subject's development alongside historical events. You may assign this as homework so students have time to develop their thoughts and then come to class ready to discuss their ideas. Encourage students to include images, where appropriate, alongside their descriptions and explanations.

CRITICAL THINKING

• Share with students your ideas on the impact that history has, not only on a nation's or a people's past, but how it can and does affect the present and the future. You might give students some examples. Then ask them to work in small groups to discuss their ideas on this topic. Explain that after they meet in their small groups, you will enable a classroom discussion on the role of history in the past, present, and future. Encourage all students to contribute their ideas, along with specific examples.

243

Unit 5
Antes de empezar

Presentation

- In this section, students will learn a variety of expressions used to introduce a topic, introduce a positive or a negative fact, and clarify something said.
- Students will also review vocabulary for talking about history, social issues, and politics.

Activities	Standards	Resources
Expresiones útiles	1.2, 2.1	
3.	1.3, 2.1	
4.	1.1, 1.3, 2.1	
Recuerda	1.2	
5.	1.1, 1.3	
6.	1.2, 1.3, 2.1, 2.2, 3.1, 5.1	

Teaching Suggestions

Warm-Up / Independent Starter

- Have students write a two-paragraph summary of a historic event that they are familiar with. You may want to get them started with these suggestions: *el atentado de las Torres Gemelas, la Guerra Civil estadounidense, la Batalla del Álamo, la llegada de los peregrinos a Massachusetts.*

Preparation

- Go over the *expresiones útiles* with the class. Explain that some of these expressions are used in conversation to refer to something already mentioned. For instance, *a propósito* introduces a topic related to another previously mentioned, and *mejor dicho* introduces a clarification of something previously stated.
- Call on students to share their Independent Starters. Then have them use their sentences and some of the *expresiones útiles* to add interest to their paragraphs. For example: *La llegada de los europeos a América promovió el intercambio cultural. Por desgracia, muchos indígenas murieron por las enfermedades que los europeos trajeron.*
- Give students a few moments to read the *Recuerda* box silently. Then divide the class into three groups and assign each group one of the vocabulary categories. Have students add other words they know to their assigned vocabulary list.

Antes de empezar

EXPRESIONES ÚTILES

Para introducir un tema:
Hay que escribir a Luisa. **Por cierto**, ¿tú tienes su dirección de correo electrónico?
Me voy a la biblioteca. **A propósito**, ¿consultaste el libro del que te hablé?

Para introducir un hecho positivo o negativo:
Por suerte, son muchos los países con un régimen democrático.
Menos mal que les gusta la Historia, porque su desafío se basa en un hecho histórico.
Por desgracia, todavía existen las desigualdades sociales.

Para aclarar o precisar lo que hemos dicho:
En la reunión habrá dos representantes y tres diputados. **O sea**, cinco legisladores.
Ustedes también van a crear algo. **Mejor dicho**, van a escribir algo.
Van a reformar la constitución. O, **más bien**, lo van a intentar.

3 **El examen de Historia**

▶ **Escribe** de nuevo el diálogo sustituyendo las palabras destacadas por estas expresiones.

por desgracia	menos mal	o sea	a propósito	por suerte

—Me gusta mucho la clase de Historia, pero **lamentablemente** tenemos muchos exámenes. **Por cierto**, ¿tienes los apuntes del martes pasado?

—Pues no, pero **afortunadamente** se los pedí a Luisa y me los va a pasar después.

—**Qué bien**, porque vamos a necesitarlos para preparar el próximo examen.

—¿Y cuándo es el próximo examen?

—A ver… El viernes. **Es decir**… ¡mañana!

4 **Tu propio diálogo**

▶ **Escribe** un diálogo con tu compañero(a) en el que incluyan al menos tres de las expresiones útiles. Memorícenlo y represéntenlo para la clase.

Modelo

A. *Las próximas vacaciones unos amigos y yo nos vamos a ir de viaje a Cancún. Por cierto, ¿tú no tenías una guía de viajes de México?*

B. *Sí. ¿Quieres que te la preste?*

A. *Sí, por favor.*

B. *Por suerte la tiene mi madre en su habitación porque ya sabes que soy bastante desordenada...*

244 doscientos cuarenta y cuatro

Differentiated Instruction

DEVELOPING LEARNERS

- Ask students to complete the following sentences with one of the expressions given:
  1. *Menos mal / Por desgracia, hay muchos conflictos en ese país.* (Por desgracia)
  2. *A propósito / Mejor dicho, ¿conoces a alguien de Ecuador?* (A propósito)
  3. *Marta ganó las elecciones. O sea / Más bien, es la nueva alcaldesa.* (O sea)
  4. *Por cierto / Por suerte, ¿sabes dónde está Guayaquil?* (Por cierto)
  5. *Menos mal / Más bien que ha terminado la guerra.* (Menos mal)

EXPANDING LEARNERS

- Have student pairs make a two-column chart, and label the columns *Palabras positivas* and *Palabras negativas*. Then, have students select ten of the words in the *Recuerda* feature and place them accordingly in their charts. Next, call on some pairs to explain why they have categorized their words this way. Take a quick survey of students' lists to see which words have more negative or positive connotations and discuss why students have classified them this way.

244

RECUERDA

Historia

la batalla	conquistar
la conquista	desaparecer
la guerra	descubrir
el imperio	excavar
la invasión	gobernar
el/la explorador(a)	invadir
el/la conquistador(a)	reconstruir

Sociedad

la convivencia	la diversidad
los deberes	la igualdad
los derechos	la integración

Política

comunista	la justicia
conservador(a)	la libertad
demócrata	la paz
liberal	el respeto
republicano(a)	la solidaridad
socialista	la tolerancia

el alcalde/la alcaldesa
el/la gobernador(a)
el rey/la reina
el/la senador(a)

---

5 **¿Cuánto sabes?**

▶ **Habla** con tu compañero(a). Elijan a uno de los siguientes personajes e inventen una historia en la que el personaje es protagonista. Usen palabras del cuadro Recuerda.

①  ②  ③

▶ **Escribe** la historia que tu compañero(a) y tú han inventado y compártela con la clase.

6 **Un poco de Historia**

▶ **Escribe** estos datos históricos.

1. El nombre de un explorador famoso.
2. El conquistador de México.
3. El defensor de los derechos humanos que fue asesinado en Memphis en los años 60.
4. El conflicto bélico en el que participaron los Estados Unidos en los años 60.
5. El presidente que abolió la esclavitud en los Estados Unidos.
6. La civilización que construyó la antigua ciudad de Machu Picchu.

▶ **Elige** uno de esos temas y escribe un texto breve con los datos que recuerdes.

Unit 5

Antes de empezar

- Next, ask groups to create a graphic organizer for each word in their list. In each graphic organizer, students should include the word and part of speech, a short definition, a sample sentence and, if appropriate, a synonym or an antonym.

- Encourage groups to come up with sentences in which they combine several words from their lists. For example: *Los conquistadores invadieron el imperio azteca, y después de ganar varias batallas, reconstruyeron la ciudad de Tenochtitlán.* Invite groups to share their graphic organizers and some of their sentences with the class.

Activities

4. To prepare for this activity, brainstorm with students situations where they would use the *expresiones útiles*. You may wish to start with these examples: *Por suerte, mañana es festivo. Por desgracia, tengo que trabajar en casa.*

6. To motivate students, you may wish to divide the class into teams and have them complete the questionnaire in a limited amount of time.

Answer Key

3. —... pero por desgracia... A propósito, ¿tienes los apuntes del martes pasado?
—... pero por suerte se los pedí...
—Menos mal, porque vamos a...
—O sea... ¡mañana!

4. Answers will vary.

5. Answers will vary.
▶ Answers will vary.

6. Answers will vary. Sample answers:
1. Henry Morton Stanley.
2. Hernán Cortés.
3. Martin Luther King, Jr.
4. La Guerra de Vietnam.
5. Abraham Lincoln.
6. La civilización inca.
▶ Answers will vary.

Additional Resources

Fans Online activities
Practice Workbook

HERITAGE LANGUAGE LEARNERS

- Ask students to consider the entries under *Sociedad* in the *Recuerda* feature. Ask them to list three that they consider to be the most important and then explain how these terms can be used to positively influence and improve society. Have students write their explanations in an essay of at least three paragraphs, justifying their choices and describing these terms' positive impact. Afterward, you may want to have students discuss their ideas and analyze the two leading characteristics on their lists.

CRITICAL THINKING

- Have small groups list the ten historical events that they believe have had the most impact on the world, either culturally, economically, or politically. Encourage students to support their choices with research on the influence of these events. Next, ask the groups to share their choice of events with one another and compare and contrast both the events and the influence put forth. You might have volunteers tabulate the results from all groups in order to see which events rank among the top ten.

Unit 5
DESAFÍO 1

Hablar de hechos históricos

Presentation

- In *Desafío 1*, Michelle and Daniel have to create a graphic novel about an important historical event that took place in Guayaquil, Ecuador. Students will preview language used to talk about history.

Activities	Standards	Resources
Texto	1.2, 2.1, 2.2, 3.1	
7.	1.2, 2.2, 3.1	
8.	1.2, 2.2, 3.1	
9.	1.2, 1.3, 2.2, 3.1	Audio
10.	1.1, 3.1, 4.2	
11. Conexiones	1.2, 1.3, 2.2, 3.1, 4.2	

Teaching Suggestions

Warm-Up / Independent Starter

- Ask students to brainstorm a list of historic events that have happened during their lifetimes.

Preparation

- Have students share their Independent Starters in small groups. Then, have groups write a "news flash" telling what happened during one of these events. They should include details pertaining to who, what, when, where, why, and how. As a class, discuss what students have learned from the events mentioned.

Texto: El abrazo más famoso de la Historia

- Read the title and point out the etching. Do they know of other famous historic "embraces"?
- Read the introduction, and then call on volunteer pairs to alternate reading the dialogue aloud. Have students note unknown words. Can they identify the meaning by studying the root of the word or the context clues?

Activities

9. Before working on this activity, ask students to find out ten "fun facts" about Bolívar, San Martín, and South American Independence, and share them with the class.

246

El abrazo más famoso de la Historia

Michelle y Daniel tienen que crear una novela gráfica sobre el encuentro entre dos importantes líderes latinoamericanos: el llamado «abrazo de Guayaquil». Lee el diálogo y averigua qué saben del tema.

Grabado que representa el encuentro entre Simón Bolívar y José de San Martín.

DANIEL: Me gusta mucho que tengamos que hacer una novela gráfica, pero ¿qué es eso del «abrazo de Guayaquil»? Es obvio que tiene que ver con Ecuador, pero no sé lo que es.

MICHELLE: ¿No recuerdas que nos lo explicaron en clase de Historia?

DANIEL: No, no me acuerdo.

MICHELLE: Sí, hombre. Es un hecho histórico famosísimo. También se llama «la entrevista de Guayaquil». Simón Bolívar y José de San Martín eran los generales de los dos ejércitos que lucharon para lograr la independencia de Suramérica de la monarquía española. Y después de muchas batallas los dos se encontraron en Guayaquil.

DANIEL: Ah, sí, ahora me acuerdo.

MICHELLE: Al final consiguieron liberar el continente, aunque no debió de ser fácil.

DANIEL: ¿Y qué pasó en aquella reunión? Porque ese es el punto central de nuestra novela.

MICHELLE: La verdad es que no se sabe exactamente porque fue una reunión secreta.

DANIEL: Entonces, ¿cómo vamos a hacer una novela gráfica sobre su encuentro? ¿Nos la podemos inventar?

MICHELLE: Dudo que podamos hacerlo. No sería muy riguroso, ¿no crees?

DANIEL: Pues está claro que tenemos un problema...

7 **Detective de palabras**

▶ **Completa** estas oraciones.

1. Daniel y Michelle van a investigar un hecho ___1___ que tiene que ver con la ___2___ de Suramérica de la monarquía española.
2. Bolívar y San Martín eran los ___3___ de dos ___4___.
3. Estos dos líderes lucharon en muchas ___5___.
4. Bolívar y San Martín consiguieron ___6___ el continente.

General José de San Martín.

Differentiated Instruction

DEVELOPING LEARNERS

- Ask students whether these statements are true (*cierto*) or false (*falso*), and to correct the false ones:
  1. *Daniel y Michelle estudian Historia.* (C)
  2. *Parece que Daniel tiene mala memoria.* (C)
  3. *El «abrazo de Guayaquil» también se llama el «encuentro de Guayaquil».* (F; «la entrevista de Guayaquil»)
  4. *Daniel y Michelle van a buscar un resumen de la conversación entre los dos generales.* (F; fue una reunión secreta y no se sabe qué hablaron)
  5. *Van a inventar lo que pasó en la reunión.* (F; no sería riguroso)

EXPANDING LEARNERS

- Ask students to match the related words.
  1. *encuentro* (e) a. *alcanzar*
  2. *tema* (g) b. *contienda*
  3. *averiguar* (h) c. *independizar*
  4. *famosísimo* (i) d. *audiencia*
  5. *lograr* (a) e. *reunión*
  6. *entrevista* (d) f. *combatir*
  7. *liberar* (c) g. *asunto*
  8. *riguroso* (j) h. *descubrir*
  9. *batalla* (b) i. *célebre*
  10. *luchar* (f) j. *preciso*

8 ¿Comprendes?

▶ **Responde** a estas preguntas.

1. ¿Qué sabe Michelle del «abrazo de Guayaquil»? ¿Y Daniel?
2. ¿Por qué piensa Daniel que tendrán un problema para realizar este desafío?
3. ¿Por qué Michelle no quiere inventarse lo que pasó en aquel encuentro?
4. ¿Qué dudas tienen Daniel y Michelle? ¿Cómo las solucionarías?

9 El desafío

▶ **Escucha** y decide si estas oraciones son ciertas o falsas. Después, corrige las falsas.

1. Bolívar quería unir todo el continente.
2. San Martín luchó por la monarquía española antes de rebelarse contra ella.
3. Bolívar liberó el sur del continente, mientras que San Martín luchó en el norte.
4. Después del encuentro con Bolívar, San Martín volvió a Argentina.

10 Te toca a ti

▶ **Habla** con tu compañero(a). Expliquen qué momento histórico ilustra cada imagen y qué están haciendo sus protagonistas.

1620 Plymouth (Massachusetts)

4 de julio de 1776

20 de julio de 1969

CONEXIONES: HISTORIA

El «abrazo de Guayaquil»

La entrevista o el abrazo de Guayaquil es el nombre con el que se conoce el encuentro entre los dos grandes libertadores de las Américas: Simón Bolívar y José de San Martín. Ambos se reunieron el 26 de julio de 1822 en Guayaquil (Ecuador) con el fin de aliarse para organizar los nuevos territorios liberados. Sin embargo, a partir de la entrevista San Martín puso su ejército a las órdenes de Bolívar y renunció a sus cargos.

11 **Investiga y explica.** ¿Conoces otras alianzas o reuniones históricas famosas? Busca información y preséntasela a la clase.

HERITAGE LANGUAGE LEARNERS

• Ask students to work with a partner and review what they know about the events depicted in the first two images of activity 10, or another historical event of their choosing. Encourage them to research additional information if necessary. Then, have them work together and create a brief dialogue to accompany one of these events. Give students time to practice their lines and then ask them to come in front of the class and state which event they have chosen, followed by their reenactment of the conversation.

SPECIAL-NEEDS LEARNERS

• Help students who have language-processing difficulties with their reading comprehension by pointing out cognates (e.g., *novela, obvio, histórico, generales*), allowing them to look up in a dictionary any unfamiliar words they cannot decode, and asking them to identify all the verb tenses that appear in the dialogue. As students read the conversation aloud, ask them to paraphrase each speaker's lines to verify that they understand what is being discussed.

DESAFÍO 1

Hablar de hechos históricos

10. Have students look at the photos and brainstorm a list of nouns and verbs that they might use. Then, ask students to conjugate the verbs in the preterite and the imperfect and to then narrate the events of the photos.

AUDIO SCRIPT
See page 239K.

CONEXIONES: HISTORIA

El «abrazo de Guayaquil»

The meeting between Bolívar and San Martín was not as successful as it looked. Both men had very different ideas on how to organize the governments of the liberated countries. At first, Bolívar's vision of a great republican union called *Gran Colombia* prevailed, but in the end, both *libertadores* witnessed in dismay the partition and infighting of the territories they had liberated.

Answer Key

7. 1. histórico
2. independencia
3. generales
4. ejércitos
5. batallas
6. liberar

8. 1. Michelle sabe que fue una reunión histórica entre Simón Bolívar y José de San Martín. Daniel no sabe casi nada.
2. Porque la reunión fue secreta y no se sabe qué pasó.
3. Porque eso no sería muy riguroso.
4. Answers will vary.

9. 1. C.
2. C.
3. F. Bolívar liberó el norte y San Martín el sur.
4. C.

10. Answers will vary.

11. Answers will vary.

Additional Resources

Fans Online activities

Unit 5

DESAFÍO 1

Vocabulario – Historia

Presentation

- In this section, students will learn key vocabulary to describe historical events.

Activities	Standards	Resources
Vocabulario	1.2, 2.2, 3.1, 4.2	
12.	1.2, 3.1	
13.	1.2, 2.1, 2.2, 3.1, 3.2	
14.	1.1, 2.2, 3.1, 3.2, 4.2	

Teaching Suggestions

Warm-Up / Independent Starter

- Ask students to create a two-column chart like the one below. Then have them list words they already know related to each topic.

La conquista	La independencia
invadir	la batalla

Preparation

- Have student pairs read the vocabulary presentation together. Then, using their charts from the Independent Starter, ask students to classify each of the new words in the appropriate column. Next, have pairs get together with another pair to review their charts. For each vocabulary word, see if students can come up with a list of related nouns, verbs, or adjectives (e.g., el navegante → navegar, navegable).

- To review the events listed in the text and the vocabulary associated with them, give each group of students a set of five index cards with the following dates written: 1492, 1810–1824, 1775, 1783, 1789. Ask groups to reenact what happened in each of those years or time periods. Then, distribute two to three blank index cards to each group. Ask them to brainstorm other historic events and to identify the years in which each event occurred. They should write each year on an index card and exchange them with other groups. Each group asks the other to identify the historic event that matches the year written on the card. You may want to convert this activity into a competition between groups.

248

Vocabulario

Historia

1492. La conquista de las Américas

En 1492, el navegante Cristóbal Colón llegó a las Antillas gracias al apoyo económico de los monarcas españoles, los Reyes Católicos. Él pretendía llegar a Asia navegando hacia el oeste y, sin saberlo, alcanzó un nuevo continente: el «Nuevo Mundo». En los siguientes años se realizaron otras expediciones y el dominio español fue extendiéndose por las Américas. Hernán Cortés conquistó el imperio azteca y Francisco Pizarro logró la conquista del imperio inca. Para gobernar y representar a la realeza en los nuevos territorios (o virreinatos), se creó la figura del virrey.

Cristóbal Colón.

Principios del siglo XIX. La independencia de las colonias

Siguiendo el ejemplo de los Estados Unidos, entre 1810 y 1824 las colonias españolas lucharon para lograr la independencia. Una de las causas que dio lugar a este proceso fue el descontento de los colonos que habían nacido en América (los llamados criollos) y los miembros de la clase media, debido a que el poder de los virreinatos seguía en manos de la nobleza de origen europeo.

El general Simón Bolívar, «el Libertador», y su ejército pelearon por la libertad en el norte de Suramérica. Además de liberar las colonias de la monarquía española, su sueño era unir los virreinatos en una sola república. Bolívar luchó también para abolir la esclavitud, declarando que, igual que las naciones, los hombres debían ser libres e independientes. En el sur, la campaña la inició José de San Martín, conocido en Argentina como el «padre de la patria». Estos procesos de independencia culminaron en diversas alianzas entre países y tratados de paz que dieron lugar a las nuevas repúblicas.

Simón Bolívar.

¡Atención!
| apoyar | to support |
| soportar | to put up with |

Más vocabulario

Historia

– En América del Norte, los colonos declararon la guerra a Inglaterra en 1775. En 1783 se firmó la paz y los ingleses reconocieron la independencia de las colonias.

– Una derrota se produce cuando alguien pierde en un enfrentamiento. Lo contrario es la victoria.

– En 1789 tuvo lugar la Revolución francesa.

12 El diccionario eres tú

▶ **Escribe.** ¿Qué palabra corresponde a cada definición?

1. Grupo de militares que lucha en una guerra.

2. Persona que gobernaba los territorios en nombre del rey.

3. Pacto o acuerdo que firman dos países después de una guerra.

4. Conseguir la libertad o la independencia.

5. Privación de libertad de un individuo por estar bajo el dominio de otro.

248 doscientos cuarenta y ocho

Differentiated Instruction

DEVELOPING LEARNERS

- Ask students to match the related words.

1. navegante (h)	a. eliminar
2. realeza (e)	b. aristocracia
3. ejército (f)	c. perder
4. derrota (c)	d. ganar
5. alianza (j)	e. monarquía
6. abolir (a)	f. tropa
7. nobleza (b)	g. rebelión
8. esclavitud (i)	h. marinero
9. victoria (d)	i. explotación
10. revolución (g)	j. acuerdo

EXPANDING LEARNERS

- Tell students that they are going to create their own section of a Spanish-language dictionary with the highlighted words from the article and the Más vocabulario feature. Ask students to work with a partner and define each of the terms in Spanish. You may get students started with these examples: Un navegante es alguien que hace viajes por el mar en barco. Unir es juntar cosas entre sí. Call on volunteers to read their definitions aloud, and have students write the most accurate ones in their notebooks.

13 **Bolívar: un héroe suramericano**

 ▶ **Lee** el texto y responde a las preguntas.

Tres héroes, por José Martí

Era su país, su país oprimido, que le pesaba en el corazón y no le dejaba vivir en paz. La América entera estaba como despertando. Un hombre solo no vale nunca más que un pueblo entero, pero hay hombres que no se cansan cuando su pueblo se cansa, y que se deciden a la guerra antes que los pueblos, porque no tienen que consultar a nadie más que a sí mismos. Ese fue el mérito de Bolívar, que no se cansó de pelear por la libertad de Venezuela, cuando parecía que Venezuela se cansaba.

«Un hombre solo no vale nunca más que un pueblo entero, pero hay hombres que no se cansan cuando su pueblo se cansa.»

Volvió un día a pelear, con trescientos héroes, con los trescientos libertadores. Liberó a Venezuela, a la Nueva Granada, al Ecuador, al Perú. Fundó una nación nueva, la nación de Bolivia. Ganó batallas sublimes con soldados descalzos, no defendió con tanto fuego el derecho de los hombres a gobernarse por sí mismos como el derecho de América a ser libre.

1. ¿Por qué se inquietaba Bolívar, según el texto?
2. ¿Qué significan las palabras del texto: «La América entera estaba como despertando»?
3. ¿A qué países liberó Bolívar?
4. ¿Qué cualidades crees que tenía Bolívar? ¿Qué palabras del texto te hacen pensar así?

14 **Otras figuras históricas**

▶ **Habla** con tu compañero(a). ¿Quiénes fueron estos personajes históricos? ¿Qué hicieron? Si no están seguros(as), investiguen para poder contestar.

Modelo *Hernán Cortés fundó Santa María de la Victoria, la primera población española en el virreinato de Nueva España.*

①  ②   ③  ④  ⑤

Hernán Cortés.   Atahualpa.   Moctezuma.   George Washington.   Abraham Lincoln.

doscientos cuarenta y nueve 249

Activities

12. To extend this activity, present students with other definitions, synonyms, or antonyms (e.g., *el antónimo de derrota*). Give students a time limit to come up with the answer (e.g., *la victoria*).

13. As students read, have them identify cognates and other words that they have already learned or that they can identify by isolating a prefix, a suffix, or the root of the word. For instance, they may not know *oprimido*; however, if they identify the infinitive, *oprimir*, they might be able to guess that it means "to be oppressed." As students answer the comprehension questions, insist that they refer to the text to explain how they know that their answers are correct.

14. To expand this activity, ask small groups to imagine that Cortés and Moctezuma are chatting with one another about the *conquista,* or that Washington, Atahualpa, and Lincoln are speaking about *liberación*. Have each group come up with the script for one of these conversations and role-play it for the class. Students in class "interview" these historic figures in an attempt to answer any questions that they may have.

Answer Key

12. 1. los soldados   4. liberar
    2. el virrey   5. la esclavitud
    3. el tratado

13. Answers will vary. Sample answers:
    1. Porque su país estaba oprimido.
    2. Significa que el continente se despertaba a la posibilidad de rebelarse y luchar por su independencia.
    3. A Venezuela, Nueva Granada (Colombia), Ecuador y Perú, y fundó Bolivia.
    4. Bolívar era incansable porque el texto dice: «hay hombres que no se cansan».

14. Answers will vary.

Additional Resources

Fans Online activities
Practice Workbook

HERITAGE LANGUAGE LEARNERS

• Ask students to imagine that they are the Public Relations person for one of the historical figures mentioned on these pages. Have students consider that person's greatest strengths and then plan his PR campaign accordingly in order to increase the client's credibility and popularity. Encourage students to enhance their knowledge with additional research on the person selected. Students may introduce their campaigns in an oral presentation to the class, a written communication for the media, or on a webpage. Take a class vote to see which campaign is the most effective.

MULTIPLE INTELLIGENCES:
Verbal-Linguistic Intelligence

• Ask students to make an argument against independence of the *virreinatos* from the Spanish crown. You may have students write an essay supporting their arguments or have them participate in a debate, with one side arguing for independence and the other for maintaining the status quo. Should you have students write essays, call on volunteers to read them aloud. If you hold a debate, establish time limits for arguments and take a class vote to see which debate team has been the most convincing.

DESAFÍO 1

Gramática – Los numerales ordinales

Presentation

- In this section, students will learn and practice how to use ordinal numbers.

Activities	Standards	Resources
Gramática	1.2, 3.1, 4.1	
15.	1.2, 3.1, 4.1	
16.	1.2, 3.1	
17.	1.2, 1.3, 2.2, 3.1	Audio
18.	1.1, 1.3, 5.1, 5.2	
19. Conexiones	1.2, 2.1, 3.1, 4.1	

Teaching Suggestions

Warm-Up / Independent Starter

- Write these two headings on the board: *Ordinales* and *Cardinales*. Underneath the appropriate heading, write: *primero, segundo, tercero* and *uno, dos, tres*. Ask students to write two examples for each word. Then have them brainstorm how these numbers are different in Spanish and in English.

Preparation

- Have two volunteers read the two sections of the grammar presentation aloud. Then review with students the examples they produced for their Independent Starters. For *primero* and *tercero*, make sure that students take off the -o before a masculine singular noun.

Activities

17. Before listening, ask students to *think, pair, and share* what they believe was happening in each of the pictures. After listening, extend this activity by asking students to write a brief paragraph of at least three sentences for each caption. Then, students can exchange paragraphs and decide what would be the best caption for the description of this historic event.

18. Call on pairs to present their interviews to the class. Encourage the class to ask follow-up questions that have not been answered in the interview.

Gramática

Los numerales ordinales

- Los numerales ordinales indican orden o posición.
- En español solo se usan los primeros ordinales. A partir del diez se suelen usar los números cardinales.

    La oficina no está en el **octavo piso**, está en el **piso trece**.

ORDINALES MÁS USADOS

1.º / 1.ª / 1.ᵉʳ	primero(a), primer	8.º / 8.ª	octavo(a)
2.º / 2.ª	segundo(a)	9.º / 9.ª	noveno(a)
3.º / 3.ª / 3.ᵉʳ	tercero(a), tercer	10.º / 10.ª	décimo(a)
4.º / 4.ª	cuarto(a)	11.º / 11.ª	undécimo(a) o décimo primer(o)(a)
5.º / 5.ª	quinto(a)	12.º / 12.ª	duodécimo(a) o décimo segundo(a)
6.º / 6.ª	sexto(a)	13.º / 13.ª	décimo tercer(o)(a)
7.º / 7.ª	séptimo(a)	14.º / 14.ª	décimo cuarto(a)

- Atención: primero y tercero pierden la -o final ante un nombre masculino singular.

    Francis Drake fue el **primer pirata** que atacó la ciudad de Santo Domingo.

Uso de los numerales ordinales

- Los ordinales concuerdan con el nombre en género y en número.

    Se cree que los **primeros habitantes** de las Américas venían de Asia.

- A diferencia del inglés, los ordinales no se usan para las fechas, aunque en algunos países hispanos se usa el ordinal para el día 1 de cada mes.

    Yo nací el **cinco de mayo**.   El **primero de mayo** se celebra el Día del Trabajo.

- La numeración romana que va detrás de la palabra siglo y del nombre de los reyes y de los papas se lee como numeral ordinal hasta el diez (X); a partir del once (XI), se lee como un número cardinal: siglo IV (cuarto), siglo XX (veinte); Isabel II (segunda), Juan XXIII (veintitrés). Atención: los nombres de los reyes y de los papas no llevan artículo.

15 **Compara.** ¿Es diferente el uso de los ordinales en inglés?

16 **Numerales**

▶ **Completa** estas oraciones con el ordinal o el cardinal correcto.

1. Se declaró la independencia el (4) _____ de julio de 1776.
2. Los dos generales se reunieron por (3) _____ vez antes de firmar el acuerdo.
3. El examen de Historia es en el aula (12) _____.
4. La nueva biblioteca de la escuela está en la (5) _____ planta.

Differentiated Instruction

DEVELOPING LEARNERS

- Ask students to write out the numbers in words.
  1. *Isabel (II) de Inglaterra ha reinado por muchos años.* (segunda)
  2. *Colón cruzó el Atlántico en el siglo (XV).* (quince)
  3. *El año 2013 fue el (500) aniversario de la llegada de Ponce de León a la Florida.* (quinientos)
  4. *Las gafas se inventaron en Italia en el siglo (XIII).* (trece)
  5. *¿Qué se inventó en el siglo (VI)?* (sexto)
  6. *¿Has leído la (2) parte del Quijote?* (segunda)

EXPANDING LEARNERS

- Explain to students that they are going to write about their favorite character of fiction, without revealing his or her name. The character could be someone from literature, film, theater, or even from a song. Then ask them to create this character's biography, again without mentioning his or her identity. Explain to students that they should make use of both ordinal and cardinal numbers in writing their biographies. Next, call on students to read their work aloud and ask the others to guess the character's name.

17 **Escenas históricas**

 ▶ **Escucha** y anota datos concretos sobre estas escenas: el hecho histórico, la fecha y qué ocurrió en cada caso. Después, escribe un pie de foto para cada ilustración.

①  ②  ③  ④

18 **La historia de tu vida**

▶ **Haz** una línea del tiempo con los cinco momentos más importantes de tu vida. Busca fotografías o haz dibujos para ilustrarlos y escribe textos breves para describirlos. Incluye oraciones con numerales ordinales o cardinales.

Modelo

2009   2010   2011   2012   2013

En el año 2009 hice mi primer viaje al extranjero. Era la primera vez que viajaba con mis compañeros de clase y fue muy emocionante. Pasamos dos semanas en México y...

▶ **Intercambia** lo que has escrito con tu compañero(a) y hazle preguntas para saber más cosas sobre su historia.

CONEXIONES: MATEMÁTICAS

El significado de *billón*

En español, un billón equivale a un millón de millones (1.000.000.000.000). Es decir, un billón en español equivale a lo que en inglés se denomina *trillion*, mientras que el inglés *billion* se traduce al español como *mil millones*. Sin embargo, en muchos medios de comunicación es frecuente encontrar errores de traducción en los que *billion* se traduce como *billón* y no como *mil millones* (1.000.000.000).

> Para el 2050, el número de personas que superen los 60 años será de casi dos billones

19 **Piensa.** Fíjate en este titular de prensa. ¿Crees que el titular es correcto o tiene algún error de traducción? ¿Cómo lo sabes?

doscientos cincuenta y uno 251

Gramática – Los numerales ordinales

19. For further practice of the terms *billón* and *mil millones,* ask students to research how various Spanish-speaking nations compare to one another in terms of population, Gross Domestic Product (GDP), national debt, etc.

 AUDIO SCRIPT
See page 239K.

 CONEXIONES: MATEMÁTIAS

El significado de *billón*

Another term for *mil millones* in Spanish is *millardo,* which is mainly used in Venezuela and in some financial publications. Both of these terms are equivalent to the term "billion" in English. Numbers and figures are also expressed differently. For instance, $3,000.50 would be expressed as $3.000,50 in most Spanish-speaking countries.

Answer Key

15. En inglés no hay concordancia, y los ordinales se usan en las fechas.

16. 1. cuatro   3. doce
       2. tercera   4. quinta

17. Answers will vary. Sample answers:
1. Colón se reunió con los Reyes Católicos en 1486, y ellos aceptaron su proyecto.
2. Colón llegó a la isla de Guanahani el 12 de octubre de 1492.
3. El emperador inca Atahualpa fue hecho prisionero por Francisco Pizarro en 1532.
4. Venezuela firmó la independencia el 5 de julio de 1811.

18. Answers will vary.
▶ Answers will vary.

19. Answers will vary.

Additional Resources

Fans Online activities
Practice Workbook

HERITAGE LANGUAGE LEARNERS

• Ask students to identify the ordinals beyond *décimo cuarto* (e.g., *décimo quinto, décimo sexto, décimo séptimo*), and then the ordinals from twentieth to one hundredth by tens (i.e., *vigésimo, trigésimo, cuadragésimo, quincuagésimo, sexagésimo, septuagésimo, octogésimo, nonagésimo, centésimo*). Have student pairs practice these numbers by imagining a skyscraper with more than 100 floors. Taking turns, one partner will write the number of the floor in numerals (92) and the other must identify it with an ordinal (*nonagésimo segundo*). Set a time limit to see how many floors are correctly identified.

MULTIPLE INTELLIGENCES:
Verbal-Linguistic Intelligence

• To play a game, prepare slips of paper with the ordinal numbers presented on page 250; be sure to show both the masculine and feminine forms. Prepare other slips of paper with dates, centuries, and names of monarchs. Place the slips of paper in a bag and have each student take one. If students pick an ordinal number, they have to make up a logical sentence with it. If they pick a date, century, or monarch's name, they must read it correctly. Award one point for each correct answer.

DESAFÍO 1

Gramática – Expresar certeza y duda

Presentation

- In this section, students will review the use of the indicative or the subjunctive when expressing certainty, doubt, or negation.

Activities	Standards	Resources
Gramática	1.2, 3.1	
20.	1.3, 3.1, 4.1	
21.	1.2, 1.3, 2.1, 2.2, 3.1	
22.	1.2, 1.3, 3.1	Audio
23.	1.1, 1.2, 1.3, 2.2, 3.1, 4.2	

Teaching Suggestions

Warm-Up / Independent Starter

- Ask students to complete the following sentences in writing:
  - *Dudo que...*
  - *Estoy seguro(a) de que...*
  - *Sabemos que...*
  - *Es improbable que...*

Preparation

- Write on the board (or project) a list of the infinitives used in the vocabulary presentation (i.e., *abolir, apoyar, declarar, firmar, liberar, luchar, pelear, soportar, unir*). Ask students to form the present and the imperfect subjunctive of these verbs. If students have trouble remembering, remind them that the present subjunctive is formed by using the *yo* form of the present indicative, while the imperfect subjunctive is formed by using the *ellos* form of the preterite.

- Remind students that the purpose of the indicative, as the name implies, is to "indicate" something. The purpose of the subjunctive is to express someone's "subjective" opinion, emotion, will, doubts, purpose, conditions, etc. regarding an action that may or may not take place. Call on volunteers to share their Independent Starters. Ask students to brainstorm their reasons for choosing either the indicative or the subjunctive for each of their sentences. Then, have students read the grammar presentation individually.

Gramática

Expresar certeza y duda

El indicativo con expresiones afirmativas de certeza

- Recuerda: en oraciones afirmativas, los verbos o expresiones que indican certeza requieren generalmente un verbo en indicativo en la cláusula dependiente.

  <u>Estamos convencidos</u> de que los dos países pronto **firmarán** la paz.

EXPRESIONES AFIRMATIVAS DE CERTEZA (INDICATIVO)

> Es verdad/Es cierto/Es evidente/Es obvio + que
> Estar convencido(a)/Estar seguro(a) + de que
> Está claro/Está demostrado + que
> Saber + que

El subjuntivo con expresiones afirmativas de duda

- Recuerda: en oraciones afirmativas, los verbos o expresiones que indican duda requieren un verbo en subjuntivo en la cláusula dependiente.

  <u>Es difícil creer</u> que en el siglo XXI aún **haya** guerras en el mundo.

EXPRESIONES AFIRMATIVAS DE DUDA (SUBJUNTIVO)

> Es dudoso/Es improbable + que
> Es posible/Es probable + que
> Es difícil creer/Parece mentira + que
> Dudar + (de) que

- El tiempo del verbo de la cláusula principal condiciona el tiempo del verbo de la cláusula dependiente.

CLÁUSULA PRINCIPAL (INDICATIVO)	CLÁUSULA DEPENDIENTE (SUBJUNTIVO)
presente	→ presente, presente perfecto, imperfecto, pluscuamperfecto
pasado o condicional	→ imperfecto
futuro	→ presente

  Es probable que **firmen/hayan firmado/firmaran/hubieran firmado** la paz.
  Era posible que **llegaran** a acuerdos.
  Será probable que **firmen** la paz.

El subjuntivo en oraciones negativas de certeza y duda

- Las siguientes expresiones negativas de certeza y duda requieren un verbo en subjuntivo:

EXPRESIONES NEGATIVAS DE CERTEZA Y DUDA (SUBJUNTIVO)

> No es verdad/No es cierto + que
> No es evidente/No es obvio + que
> No es posible/No es probable + que
> No está claro/No está demostrado + que
> No estar convencido(a)/No estar seguro(a) + de que

No está demostrado que los vikingos **fundaran** colonias en Norteamérica.

20 **Compara.** Traduce estas oraciones. ¿Qué tiempos y modos verbales has usado?
   a. *They were sure that they were going to win the war.*
   b. *They were not sure that they were going to win the war.*

Differentiated Instruction

DEVELOPING LEARNERS

- Ask students to complete the following sentences with the correct verb:
  1. *Es difícil creer que ellos no ... la paz.* (a)
     a. *firmaran*   b. *firmaron*
  2. *No es verdad que Colón ... el continente americano.* (b)
     a. *conquistó*   b. *conquistara*
  3. *Es dudoso que el país ... la monarquía.* (a)
     a. *aboliera*   b. *abolió*
  4. *Parece mentira que tú me ... esto.* (b)
     a. *dices*   b. *digas*
  5. *Es posible que esos colonos ... la guerra.* (a)
     a. *declaren*   b. *declaran*

EXPANDING LEARNERS

- Ask students to work with a partner and create several short dialogues between someone who continually makes affirmative statements and another who counters these with negative assertions. For example:
  A. *Estoy convencido de que se acabarán las guerras en el mundo.*
  B. *Dudo que eso suceda. No es probable que el ser humano sea capaz de eliminar la violencia.*

- Call on some pairs to present one or two exchanges before the rest of the class.

21 Oraciones completas

▶ **Completa** estas oraciones. Pon los verbos en el tiempo y modo correctos. Ten en cuenta que a veces puede haber más de una respuesta posible.

1. Sé que a San Martín lo _____ en Argentina el «padre de la patria».
   _{llamar}

2. Está claro que Bolívar y San Martín _____ dos grandes líderes.
   _{ser}

3. No está demostrado que Bolívar le _____ a San Martín que renunciara a sus cargos.
   _{pedir}

4. No está claro que los dos líderes _____ la misma opinión.
   _{tener}

5. Dudo que Bolívar y San Martín _____ de acuerdo en todo.
   _{estar}

22 ¿Cómo van con su trabajo?

▶ **Escucha** y une las dos columnas. Después, pon los verbos en el tiempo y modo correctos.

Ⓐ

1. Daniel está convencido de que la novela gráfica...

2. Es evidente que lo primero...

3. Michelle está segura de que el título...

4. Michelle duda que...

5. Para Daniel, no es probable que a los lectores...

6. Para Michelle, es obvio que...

Ⓑ

a. _____ muy claro.
   _{estar}

b. _____ un género de prestigio.
   _{ser}

c. _____ incluir una biografía.
   _{deber}

d. _____ elegir un tema y un título.
   _{ser}

e. _____ centrarse en los hechos importantes.
   _{deber}

f. les _____ los detalles biográficos.
   _{interesar}

23 La historia viva

▶ **Elige** dos personajes históricos de cualquier época e inventa una carta de uno al otro.

Modelo

> Carta de Simón Bolívar a George Washington.
>
> Estimado Sr. Washington:
>
> Es cierto que Ud. me ha inspirado a seguir luchando porque la independencia es más importante que nada. Es probable que Ud. ya sepa lo que pasa al sur de su país. Estaba claro que teníamos que hacer la revolución. No era posible que siguiéramos viviendo ni un día más bajo el dominio de la monarquía española....

▶ **Intercambia** tu carta con la de tu compañero(a) y respóndele con otra, poniéndote en el lugar del destinatario que él/ella ha imaginado.

Gramática – Expresar certeza y duda

■ Provide these sentences to students: *Es verdad que Colón fue un gran navegante. / Es posible que Colón fuera un gran navegante.* Ask students to articulate what each sentence communicates. Then, have them create their own contrasting sentences with some of the expressions on page 252.

Activities

21. After reviewing this activity, ask students to make all changes necessary in order to use the indicative instead of the subjunctive or the subjunctive instead of the indicative.

22. Before playing the recording, ask students to read the statements in column A and identify those that will require the use of the subjunctive with an "S" and those that will require the indicative with an "I". Then, suggest that they focus on the conjugation of each verb as they listen.

 AUDIO SCRIPT
See page 239.

Answer Key

20. a. Estaban seguros de que <u>iban</u> a ganar la guerra. (imperfecto de indicativo)
   b. No estaban seguros de que <u>fueran</u> a ganar la guerra. (imperfecto de subjuntivo)

21. 1. llaman/llamaban   4. tuvieran
   2. son/eran/fueron   5. estuvieran
   3. pidiera

22. 1. (b) es   4. (c) deban
   2. (d) es   5. (f) interesen
   3. (a) está   6. (e) deben

23. Answers will vary.
   ▶ Answers will vary.

Additional Resources

Fans Online activities
Practice Workbook

HERITAGE LANGUAGE LEARNERS

• Ask students to list three items, which might range from past or future events to their opinions about someone's character and trustworthiness, of which they have absolute certainty, and three that they believe are doubtful or uncertain. Then, have students write at least three paragraphs in which they detail these items and justify their feelings of certainty or doubt. Ask students to exchange their work with a partner, who will proofread it and make suggestions for improvement. After students review and consider the suggestions, call on them to read their compositions aloud.

MULTIPLE INTELLIGENCES: Visual-Spatial Intelligence

• Ask student pairs to think of a historic event they could describe and illustrate in *una novela gráfica*. Allow students time to research any additional information, such as direct quotes or confirmation of dates and names. Then have them illustrate one key scene and accompany it with speech bubbles and a brief introduction. Illustrations may be done by hand or can be cutouts from printed media. Ask pairs to display their work and read the dialogue.

Unit 5

LECTURA: TEXTO DIALOGADO

Presentation

- In this section, students will read and talk about the meeting that took place between Simón Bolívar and José de San Martín in Guayaquil, Ecuador, in 1822. Students will also answer comprehension questions based on the reading and use context clues to determine the meaning of new vocabulary.

Activities	Standards	Resources
Lectura: texto dialogado	1.2, 2.1, 2.2, 3.1	
24.	1.1, 1.2, 2.2, 3.1	
25.	1.2	
26.	1.1, 2.2, 3.1, 3.2	

Teaching Suggestions

Warm-Up / Independent Starter

- Have students answer the first two questions in the *Antes de leer* section.

Preparation

- Call on students to share their Independent Starters. Discuss the qualities of leadership that they have observed in these two historical figures, as well as other figures about whom they have spoken or written thus far in this unit. Then, direct students to discuss the following questions in small groups: ¿Qué nos enseña la Historia? ¿Creen que es importante estudiarla? ¿Cómo nos ayuda el conocimiento de la Historia a entender el presente?

- You may wish to assign question #3 of the *Antes de leer* section as homework. In this way, students can look up any of the names or places that they do not know before they come to class. Then, invite students to share the information learned.

- Make a copy of the dialogue and randomly label each of Michelle's and Daniel's lines as A, B, C, D, etc. Then, cut the characters' lines into strips and make enough copies so that each pair of students has a set of sentence strips. Ask students to work in pairs to logically order the conversation between Daniel and Michelle.

254

Antes de leer: estrategias

1. Lee el título del diálogo. Anota todo lo que ya sabes sobre estos dos personajes históricos.
2. Fíjate en la imagen de la actividad 24. ¿Qué momento histórico ilustra?
3. Busca los nombres propios que hay en el texto (personas, ciudades, etc.). ¿Los conoces todos?

Bolívar y San Martín

MICHELLE: Ya nos hemos documentado bastante. ¿Empezamos?

DANIEL: Sí. El encuentro duró dos días: del 26 al 27 de julio de 1822. He pensado que la novela puede comenzar con la llegada de San Martín a Guayaquil.

MICHELLE: Muy bien. Llegó en barco, ¿verdad?

DANIEL: Sí, había zarpado desde el puerto del Callao, en Perú, a bordo de la goleta *Macedonia*. Tenemos que buscar algún cuadro en el que aparezca un barco de aquella época para poder dibujarlo.

MICHELLE: Y la siguiente escena puede ser el camino de San Martín hasta el lugar del encuentro. Aquí dice que lo acompañó un batallón de infantería para hacerle los honores.

DANIEL: Pues tenemos que buscar información sobre los uniformes del ejército.

MICHELLE: Y la siguiente escena ya puede ser el encuentro. Al parecer, Bolívar esperaba a San Martín al final de la escalera de la casa en la que se iban a reunir.

DANIEL: En la reunión no hubo testigos así que he pensado que, para ilustrarla, podemos dibujar una puerta cerrada.

MICHELLE: Perfecto. Y como sabemos que el encuentro desilusionó mucho a San Martín, en la siguiente escena podemos dibujarlo saliendo apesadumbrado de la reunión.

DANIEL: ¿De qué hablarían? Supongo que sería una reunión cordial, dado que ellos eran aliados en la causa para lograr la independencia.

MICHELLE: Es posible, pero quizás tenían ideas muy diferentes sobre cómo lograr su meta.

DANIEL: Tal vez sí. Se sabe que esa misma tarde y al día siguiente volvieron a reunirse. Y la noche del 27, antes de la partida de San Martín, se celebró un banquete en su honor.

MICHELLE: Esa escena tenemos que dibujarla. ¡Voy a buscar imágenes para saber cómo eran los vestidos de las damas!

DANIEL: Y la última escena puede ser la despedida aquella noche. Bolívar acompañó a San Martín hasta el muelle.

MICHELLE: Nunca más volverían a verse. Debió de ser una despedida triste.

Differentiated Instruction

DEVELOPING LEARNERS

- Help students identify the cognates in the dialogue about Bolívar and San Martín. Cognates include *documentar, novela, a bordo, época, escena, acompañar, batallón, infantería, honores*. Encourage students to find more and to look up any new words that they cannot decode from the context. Have them add relevant new words in their notebooks for vocabulary enrichment and call on volunteers to say or write a sentence with some of them.

EXPANDING LEARNERS

- Ask students to work in small groups and research the events that led up to *el abrazo de Guayaquil*. Have them include in their research why the desire for independence from the Spanish crown was so widespread, what the rights and privileges of the various social classes were, as well as brief biographies of the two leading generals: San Martín and Bolívar. Each member of the group can focus on one aspect and then get back with the group and create a written report or make an oral presentation.

24 ¿Comprendes?

▶ **Responde** a estas preguntas.

1. ¿Cuál es la primera escena que van a dibujar Michelle y Daniel?
2. Según han leído Michelle y Daniel, ¿cómo fue recibido San Martín en Guayaquil?
3. ¿Por qué van a ilustrar la escena del encuentro dibujando una puerta cerrada?
4. ¿Qué escena le hace más ilusión dibujar a Michelle? ¿Por qué?

 ▶ **Fíjate** en esta imagen. ¿Qué momento del encuentro crees que representa? Habla con tus compañeros(as).

25 Palabras y expresiones

▶ **Busca** en el texto de la página 254 las palabras que corresponden a estas definiciones.

1. Buscar información sobre un tema.
2. Salir un barco.
3. Unidad del ejército que utiliza el mismo tipo de armas.
4. Quitar o perder la alegría.
5. Triste, apenado.
6. Comida a la que asisten muchas personas para celebrar algo.

Monumento a Simón Bolívar y José de San Martín. Guayaquil (Ecuador).

26 Con tus propias palabras

 ▶ **Habla** con tus compañeros(as). ¿Cuál es tu opinión sobre lo sucedido en la entrevista de Guayaquil y sobre el papel de las dos grandes figuras de la independencia de Hispanoamérica?

Modelo

A. *Es probable que los dos generales tuvieran algunas diferencias de opinión.*
B. *Puede ser, pero hay que tener en cuenta que...*

Unit 5
LECTURA: TEXTO DIALOGADO

- Remind students that using context clues is one way to identify the correct meaning of unknown words in a text. Have students scan the dialogue and list words or phrases they do not know. Next, have them use context clues to determine the meaning of each unknown word or phrase they listed. Once students have ordered the dialogue, ask volunteer pairs to read it to the class. Finally, have students open their books to page 254 to check their work.

Activities

24. Conduct a class discussion on students' opinions about Michelle and Daniel's progress thus far in creating the graphic novel for *el abrazo de Guayaquil*. What changes would the class make? What additions?

26. Conduct role-plays in which pairs of students interview Bolívar and San Martín, asking follow-up questions to find out further information. Encourage students to use expressions of certainty and doubt as they imagine what Bolívar and San Martín's responses might have been.

Answer Key

24. Answers will vary. Sample answers:
1. La escena de la llegada por barco de San Martín a Guayaquil.
2. Fue bien recibido y se celebró un banquete en su honor.
3. Porque en la reunión no hubo testigos y no se sabe qué pasó.
4. La escena del baile y el banquete porque quiere saber cómo eran los vestidos de las damas.
▶ Answers will vary.

25.
1. documentar
2. zarpar
3. batallón
4. desilusionar
5. apesadumbrado
6. banquete

26. Answers will vary.

Additional Resources

Fans Online activities

HERITAGE LANGUAGE LEARNERS

- Read the following quote attributed to San Martín and spoken about Bolívar: *Los resultados de nuestra entrevista no han sido los que me prometía para la pronta terminación de la guerra [...]. Desgraciadamente, ya estoy convencido íntimamente o que no ha creído sincero mi ofrecimiento de servir bajo sus órdenes, o que mi persona le es embarazosa [...].* Then ask students to comment on it, explaining how these words define each general's character. You may choose to have students write their comments or participate in a discussion on the topic.

CRITICAL THINKING

- Have students speculate about what was discussed at the meeting between San Martín and Bolívar. Have them consider any comments the two generals might have made to a trusted aide or written in a letter or diary. Explain that soon after their meeting, San Martín gave up his command and returned to Europe. Ask students why he might have done this. Could there have been a power struggle between these two generals? Could it be that San Martín no longer wanted to take part in wars or in leadership? Enable a classroom discussion on this topic.

DESAFÍO 1

Comunicación

Presentation

- In this section, students will integrate the vocabulary and grammar skills from *Desafío 1* in order to talk about historic events, as well as to use ordinal numbers and the subjunctive or the indicative after expressions of doubt or certainty.

Activities	Standards	Resources
27.	1.3, 5.1	
28.	1.1, 1.2, 2.2, 3.1, 4.2	Audio
29.	1.1, 1.2, 2.2, 3.1, 5.1	
30.	1.1, 1.3, 2.2, 3.1, 3.2	
31. Final del desafío	1.2, 1.3, 2.2, 3.1, 3.2	

Teaching Suggestions

Warm-Up / Independent Starter

- Write this proverb by Jacinto Benavente on the board: *Una cosa es continuar la historia y otra repetirla.* Ask students to use the vocabulary and grammar structures they learned in this *Desafío* to write a brief explanation for the proverb.

Preparation

- As a class, discuss students' answers to the Independent Starter. What do they think *continuar la historia* implies? And *repetirla*? Have students provide examples to justify their opinions. Then ask students: *¿Cómo creen que Bolívar y San Martín responderían a esas preguntas? ¿Y cómo creen que nuestro presidente respondería?* Remind students to use some of the expressions on page 252 in their responses.

Activities

27. You may want to compile the class's results in a chart on the board. As a class, discuss any trends and what they might indicate. Encourage a discussion with these or similar questions: *¿Cambian nuestros gustos o tenemos claro lo que queremos desde pequeños? ¿Influencia el entorno nuestros gustos?*

Comunicación

27 **En cada grado**

 ▶ **Escribe.** ¿Cuál era tu clase favorita en cada año escolar? ¿Por qué?

 ▶ **Contrasta** tus gustos con los de tu compañero(a).

Modelo

En primer grado, mi clase favorita era Matemáticas porque me resultaba fácil. Sin embargo, a partir de cuarto...

28 **Cuatro héroes norteamericanos**

▶ **Escucha** las biografías de estos personajes y toma notas sobre los hechos históricos en los que participaron y las características heroicas de cada uno.

Susan B. Anthony.

César Chávez.

Martin Luther King, Jr.

Rosa Parks.

 ▶ **Habla** con tu compañero(a). ¿A cuál de esos personajes admiras más? ¿Por qué? Comparen y contrasten los logros de esa persona con los de Bolívar.

29 **Citas**

 ▶ **Lee** estas citas y comenta con tu compañero(a) tu opinión sobre ellas. Usen expresiones de certeza y duda.

1. El sistema de gobierno más perfecto es aquel que produce mayor suma de felicidad posible, mayor suma de seguridad social y mayor suma de estabilidad política.

   Simón Bolívar

3. Sueño que mis cuatro hijos vivirán un día en un país en el cual no serán juzgados por el color de su piel, sino por los rasgos de su personalidad.

   Dr. Martin Luther King, Jr.

2. Ahora que, como resultado de la lucha por la igualdad de oportunidades y debido al uso de maquinaria, se ha operado una gran revolución en el mundo de la economía, de manera que donde pueda acudir un hombre a ganarse un dólar honradamente también puede ir una mujer, no hay forma de rebatir la conclusión de que esta tiene que estar investida de igual poder para poderse proteger. Y ese poder es el voto, el símbolo de la libertad y de la igualdad, sin el cual ningún ciudadano puede estar seguro de conservar lo que posee y, por lo tanto, mucho menos de adquirir lo que no tiene.

   Susan B. Anthony

Differentiated Instruction

DEVELOPING LEARNERS

- Ask students to read the comments made by the historical figures once again. Then, have them paraphrase these remarks using their own words and including expressions of certainty and doubt. For example: *Bolívar está convencido de que el gobierno más perfecto es el que ofrece seguridad social y estabilidad política. Susan B. Anthony dice que es evidente que el poder está en el voto.*

- You may want to pair developing students with heritage speakers to complete this activity.

EXPANDING LEARNERS

- After students read the comments made by the historical figures, ask them to think about a political or social issue in which they would like to play a major role. Have them write a few paragraphs, first defining the issue and then their role in it. Encourage students to follow this up with pertinent comments that could be considered inspirational to future generations, and would encourage others today to follow their leadership. Tell students to use expressions of certainty and doubt in their remarks. Then call on volunteers to read their comments aloud.

30 **Imagínate**

 ▶ **Habla** con tu compañero(a). Imaginen una conversación entre Bolívar y San Martín antes de comenzar a luchar por la independencia de Suramérica y escríbanla.

Modelo   A. *San Martín, amigo mío, dudo que vayamos a ganar muchas batallas durante los primeros años de esta guerra.*

   B. *Sin embargo, es cierto que vale la pena intentarlo. Confío en que con el tiempo lograremos la independencia. Y estoy convencido de que juntos...*

▶ **Memoricen** el diálogo y represéntenlo para la clase.

Final del desafío

EL ABRAZO MÁS FAMOSO DEL SIGLO XIX

Novela gráfica escrita por Daniel García y Michelle Liu

31 **La novela gráfica**

 ▶ **Lee** las primeras viñetas de la novela gráfica de Michelle y Daniel. ¿Cómo crees que puede continuar? Dibuja dos viñetas más con tu compañero(a) y escriban el texto que las acompaña.

HERITAGE LANGUAGE LEARNERS

- Share with students some pieces of advice that San Martín wrote for his daughter, Mercedes: *Amar la verdad y odiar la mentira. Estimular la caridad con los pobres. Respetar la propiedad ajena. Tratar con dulzura a los sirvientes, pobres y ancianos. Hablar poco y lo preciso. Amar la patria y la libertad. Amar el aseo y despreciar el lujo.* After sharing this with students, ask them which three pieces of advice they consider to be the most important and why, and what might be the consequences of not heeding this advice.

CRITICAL THINKING

- Students have read about heroism and some famous heroes. Now, have them consider the negative characteristics and personality traits of *los cobardes*. Ask students to write at least one paragraph in which they describe these characteristics and traits. Then, ask them to write one or more paragraphs in which they attribute remarks to a real or fictional coward who exhibits some, or all, of the aforementioned traits. Call on volunteers to read their character's remarks aloud. Alternatively, enable a classroom discussion on the roles that heroism and cowardliness play in society.

---

28. Before listening, have students pairs share what they know about these historical figures and the events in which they were involved. Encourage students to discuss what they believe these figures may have in common.

30. Before students conduct their conversations, ask them to brainstorm unit vocabulary and verbs that they may find useful in the creation of their dialogues. Emphasize that the dialogue should sound natural. After the groups present their dialogues, have students ask the "actors" follow-up questions to find out information that might not have been included in the original conversation.

AUDIO SCRIPT
See page 239K.

Answer Key

27. Answers will vary.

28. Answers will vary. Sample answers:
   1. Trabajó por los derechos de la mujer y para garantizar su derecho al voto. Visitaba las fábricas.
   2. Defendió los derechos de los trabajadores inmigrantes. Creó el primer sindicato de trabajadores agrícolas y defendió la lucha pacífica.
   3. Luchó por la igualdad racial. Usaba métodos pacíficos e inspiraba con sus discursos.
   4. Fue ejemplo de desobediencia civil pacífica al no cederle su asiento a un pasajero blanco.
   ▶ Answers will vary.

29. Answers will vary.

30. Answers will vary.
   ▶ Answers will vary.

31. Answers will vary.

Additional Resources

Fans Online activities
Practice Workbook

257

Unit 5

DESAFÍO 2

Expresar finalidad y dificultad

Presentation

- In *Desafío 2*, Asha and Lucas have to write a protest song about an issue in their community. Students will preview vocabulary related to politics and government, as well as expressions of purpose and difficulty.

Activities	Standards	Resources
Texto	1.2, 2.1, 2.2, 3.1	
32.	1.2, 1.3, 3.1	
33.	1.2, 2.1, 2.2, 3.1	
34.	1.1, 1.2, 1.3, 2.1, 2.2, 3.1	Audio
35. Cultura	1.1, 1.2, 2.1, 2.2, 4.2	

Teaching Suggestions

Warm-up / Independent Starter

- Ask students to think of artists or musicians whose work expresses a social or political message.

Preparation

- Call on students to talk about one of the artists or musicians from their Independent Starters. As a class, discuss how art and music can reflect society, and how often times artists are inspired by societal injustices or political issues. Have students read the title of the dialogue and ask them to interpret its meaning.

Texto: Canciones con conciencia

- Read the introduction aloud. Then, ask probing questions about Chile's history, such as *¿Saben algo sobre la década de los años sesenta o setenta en América Latina? ¿Qué tipo de gobierno tiene Chile ahora? ¿Y qué gobierno tenía antes?*
- Call on different volunteers to read the dialogue aloud. Ask students for some ideas about possible topics for Asha and Lucas's song.

Activities

32. To extend this activity, have students write two sentences about the dialogue, one using *de* + infinitive and one using *para que* + subjunctive.

258

Canciones con conciencia

Asha y Lucas tienen que escribir una canción protesta sobre alguna situación problemática de su comunidad. Deberán inspirarse en el estilo del grupo chileno Inti-Illimani. ¿Cómo será su música?

ASHA: Lucas, ¿tú sabes exactamente qué es una canción protesta?

LUCAS: Creo que es un tipo de música que se compone con el propósito de denunciar problemas sociales o políticos. Por eso tenemos que elegir un problema en nuestra comunidad.

ASHA: Sí, tiene sentido. Entonces, el grupo Inti-Illimani canta sobre los problemas en Chile, ¿no?

LUCAS: Supongo que sí. Piensa que en Chile hubo durante mucho tiempo un régimen militar liderado por el general Pinochet que, aunque tuvo partidarios, también provocó una gran oposición.

Actuación de Inti-Illimani.

ASHA: Creo que debemos empezar por escuchar alguna canción.

LUCAS: Buena idea. Mira, en su página web hay un video. Voy a ponerlo para que nos inspire.

ASHA: Me gusta su estilo. ¿Qué opinas?

LUCAS: Sí, a mí también. A ver qué más encontramos... Dice que este grupo pertenece al movimiento llamado Nueva Canción Chilena, que nació en la década de los sesenta del siglo XX.

ASHA: ¿Dice cuándo empezaron a tocar?

LUCAS: Sí, en 1967. Parece que estuvieron varios años en el exilio y que volvieron a Chile después de la dictadura.

ASHA: ¿Qué tal si leemos algunas de sus letras, a ver de qué temas hablan?

LUCAS: Bien pensado. Seguro que tratan sobre la libertad, la democracia, los derechos civiles...

32 **Detective de palabras**

▶ **Completa** estas oraciones con las formas verbales que se usan en el texto.

1. La canción protesta se compone con el propósito de _____ problemas sociales o políticos.

2. Voy a poner el video para que nos _____.

▶ **Compara** los verbos de las dos oraciones. ¿En qué forma están? ¿Por qué?

Differentiated Instruction

DEVELOPING LEARNERS

- Call on pairs to role-play the dialogue. As they complete each speaker's part, ask them to paraphrase the content in order to verify comprehension. For instance, after they read the first line they might say, *Asha le pregunta a Lucas si él sabe lo que es una canción protesta.* If students cannot answer correctly, ask them to read the line or lines again and try to paraphrase. If students continue to have difficulties, you might simply ask questions about the content (e.g., *¿Qué le pregunta Asha a Lucas?*).

EXPANDING LEARNERS

- Have small groups imagine that they are part of a TV broadcast that features an interview with Inti-Illimani. One student will be the host and the others will be part of the musical group. Students will need to research some background information on the group, their music, and the political atmosphere in Chile during the dictatorship. Give students time to do this, as well as to prepare their questions and answers, and to select a representational song. Then call on groups to present a segment of their interview before the class.

33 ¿Comprendes?

▶ **Responde** a estas preguntas.

1. ¿Qué es una canción protesta?
2. ¿Sobre qué tema tienen que escribir Asha y Lucas?
3. ¿Cómo van a inspirarse? ¿Cómo te inspirarías tú para resolver este desafío?
4. ¿Qué recuerda Lucas sobre la historia de Chile?
5. ¿Cuáles son los temas de las canciones de Inti-Illimani, según Lucas?
6. ¿Conoces algún movimiento en los Estados Unidos parecido a la canción protesta?

34 El gobierno militar de Chile

 ▶ **Escucha** y completa esta línea del tiempo.

1973   septiembre 1973   ☐ 5   ☐ 7   2006

| ___1___ era presidente de Chile. | Se produce un ___2___. ___3___ asume la presidencia y prohíbe todos los ___4___. | Se aprueba una nueva ___6___. | Pinochet deja la presidencia. | ☐ 8 |

 ▶ **Escucha** de nuevo y escribe tres oraciones ciertas y tres falsas sobre la información de la grabación.

> Modelo   *En 1974 Pinochet se convirtió en el jefe de Estado de Chile.*

▶ **Lee** tus oraciones a tu compañero(a). Él/Ella tiene que decidir si son ciertas o falsas.

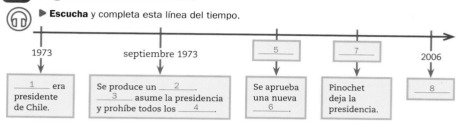

CULTURA

Inti-Illimani

La historia de la banda chilena Inti-Illimani comenzó en la Universidad Técnica del Estado en 1967, cuando un grupo de estudiantes universitarios se empezó a reunir para tocar música y así expresar sus ideas. El grupo estaba en Europa cuando Pinochet subió al poder y permaneció en el exilio hasta 1988.

Muchas de sus canciones hablan sobre la injusticia del régimen militar y las violaciones de los derechos humanos fundamentales.

35 Piensa y habla. ¿Conoces otros grupos musicales o artistas que denuncien problemas políticos o sociales? ¿Qué temas tratan en sus canciones?

doscientos cincuenta y nueve   259

HERITAGE LANGUAGE LEARNERS

- Asha and Lucas talk about the musical group Inti-Illimani in this lesson. Ask students what they know about other Hispanic musicians from the *canción protesta* movement. If students are not familiar with any of these musicians, ask them to research some and select one musician or group and describe their music, including the social messages of their songs. Encourage students to bring in some recordings of their music to share with the rest of the class. Heritage learners may want to provide a script or explanation of the songs' lyrics.

SPECIAL-NEEDS LEARNERS

- For students who are having difficulties staying focused while reading or listening to longer passages, copy the dialogue between Asha and Lucas onto copy paper and cut the conversation into six parts, one for each exchange between them. Then ask students to work with a partner and role-play their lines. After they read, mix up the exchanges and ask students to put the conversation back together by placing the exchanges in the correct order on a sheet of paper.

Unit 5

DESAFÍO 2
Expresar finalidad y dificultad

34. As an alternative to writing true/false statements, have small groups turn this into a game. Each group needs to write as many facts as they can about Chile's history within ten minutes. Then, groups compare their statements. They earn points for having a statement that other groups do not have.

 AUDIO SCRIPT
See page 239L.

CULTURA

Inti-Illimani

The name Inti-Illimani means "Sun of the Illimani," a mountain in Bolivia. After a long exile, the group returned to Chile and was surprised by the number of people who were waiting for them at the airport. Inti-Illimani is known internationally and has participated in concerts with Springsteen, Sting, Tracy Chapman, and Peter Gabriel, among others.

Answer Key

32. 1. denunciar (infinitivo, sigue a *de*)
     2. inspire (subjuntivo, después de *para que*)

33. 1. Un tipo de canción que denuncia problemas sociales o políticos.
     2. Sobre un problema en su comunidad.
     3. Van a ver un video de Inti-Illimani.
     4. Que hubo un régimen militar.
     5. Libertad, democracia, derechos civiles.
     6. Answer will vary.

34. 1. Salvador Allende   5. 1980
     2. golpe de Estado   6. constitución
     3. Augusto Pinochet   7. 1990
     4. partidos políticos   8. Muere.
     ▶ Answers will vary.
     ▶ Answers will vary.

35. Answers will vary.

Additional Resources

Fans Online activities

259

Unit 5
DESAFÍO 2

Vocabulario – Política y gobierno

Presentation

- In this section, students will learn vocabulary related to politics and government.

Activities	Standards	Resources
Vocabulario	1.2, 3.1	
36.	1.1, 1.3, 3.1	
37.	1.2, 1.3, 2.1, 2.2, 3.1, 4.2	Audio
38.	1.1, 3.1, 5.1	
39. Cultura	1.2, 1.3, 2.1, 2.2, 3.1, 5.1	

Teaching Suggestions

Warm-Up / Independent Starter

- Have students complete these sentences:
  – *El presidente de los Estados Unidos es…*
  – *El sistema político de este país es…*
  – *El alcalde o la alcaldesa de mi ciudad es…*

Preparation

- Review the Independent Starter with the class. To continue practicing previously learned vocabulary, ask students these or similar questions: *¿Qué partidos políticos hay en nuestro país? ¿Pueden nombrar un país donde exista una monarquía constitucional? ¿En qué países hay dictadura?*

- Have students read the vocabulary presentation silently. Once they have finished, read it aloud to them. Ask students to organize new vocabulary words into two categories: one list of words they associate with democracy and one list of words they associate with a military regime. After students have finished, ask them to share their responses. Next, have students write three statements, comparing democracies and military regimes.

Activities

36. To extend this activity, ask students to work in pairs and write additional definitions for five new vocabulary words. When they are finished, have them read the definitions aloud to the class without saying the word; their classmates need to identify the vocabulary word.

Vocabulario

Política y gobierno

La mayor parte de los países latinoamericanos viven hoy en democracia. Sin embargo, en el pasado muchos de ellos sufrieron golpes de Estado encabezados por una junta militar que dieron lugar a regímenes autoritarios en los que un dictador administraba todo el poder. Por lo general, en estos regímenes no se garantizaban los derechos civiles y se perseguía, detenía y encarcelaba a quienes no eran partidarios del régimen o eran sospechosos de tener una ideología distinta. Incluso algunos fueron ejecutados. Por eso muchas personas tuvieron que exiliarse o solicitar asilo político en otro país.

Debate en el Senado de Chile.

A diferencia de las dictaduras, en las que el poder se concentra en un solo individuo, los sistemas democráticos se basan en la división de poderes:

– El poder legislativo corresponde al Parlamento.
– El poder ejecutivo corresponde al Gobierno.
– El poder judicial corresponde a los Tribunales de Justicia.

Además, en los países democráticos se celebran periódicamente elecciones (primarias o generales) para que los ciudadanos elijan a sus representantes a nivel municipal, estatal o federal.
El derecho al voto de toda la población adulta se denomina sufragio universal. Durante la campaña electoral, los candidatos presentan su programa para lograr el apoyo de los votantes.

Más vocabulario

Acciones

abstenerse: renunciar a algo; por ejemplo, a votar en unas elecciones.

autorizar: permitir.

comprometerse: estar obligado a algo; por ejemplo, a cumplir un programa electoral.

oponerse: estar en contra.

¡Atención!
suceder — to happen
triunfar — to succeed

36 **Términos políticos**

▶ **Escribe** definiciones que ayuden a recordar el significado de estas palabras.

1. candidato(a)
2. elección primaria
3. votante
4. ideología
5. sufragio universal
6. gobierno municipal
7. democracia
8. asilo político

 ▶ **Habla** con dos compañeros(as). ¿Qué otros términos políticos conocen? Defínanlos y compártanlos con la clase.

Differentiated Instruction

DEVELOPING LEARNERS

- Ask students to match the related words.

1. *comprometerse* (g) a. *voto*
2. *encarcelar* (e) b. *permitir*
3. *sufragio* (a) c. *arrestar*
4. *autorizar* (b) d. *no estar de acuerdo*
5. *régimen* (f) e. *meter en la prisión*
6. *abstenerse* (h) f. *forma de gobierno*
7. *detener* (c) g. *obligarse*
8. *oponerse* (d) h. *privarse de algo*

EXPANDING LEARNERS

- Ask students to imagine that time has been turned back to when women did not have the right to vote. Have students work in small groups and prepare some slogans as well as a brochure that support this fundamental right in a Spanish-speaking country. Have groups read their slogans and display their brochures. Then, take a class vote to see which slogan is the most convincing and which brochure argues the issue most effectively. Remind students to keep in mind the political and social issues of the past.

37 El sistema político argentino

 ▶ **Escucha** y responde a estas preguntas.

1. ¿Cada cuántos años se elige al presidente de Argentina?
2. ¿Qué otro cargo tiene el vicepresidente de Argentina?
3. ¿Cuántos senadores hay en el Congreso Nacional? ¿Y diputados?
4. ¿Qué criterio determina el número de diputados de una región?
5. ¿Cuántos senadores elige cada región?
6. ¿Quién designa a los miembros de la Corte Suprema?

 ▶ **Escucha** de nuevo y toma notas. Compara el sistema político de Argentina con el sistema de tu país y completa un diagrama de Venn con tus conclusiones.

38 ¿Sabes?

 ▶ **Habla** con tu compañero(a) sobre la política del lugar donde viven. Usen estas preguntas como guía.

1. ¿Quiénes son los senadores? ¿De qué partido político son?
2. ¿Cuánto tiempo pueden mantener su cargo los senadores y los diputados? ¿Crees que ese tiempo es adecuado?
3. ¿Qué se está debatiendo ahora en el gobierno municipal? ¿Y en el gobierno federal?
4. ¿Qué proyecto de ley te gustaría que se presentara en el congreso? ¿Por qué?
5. Si te presentaras como candidato(a) a las elecciones municipales, ¿en qué temas basarías tu campaña electoral?

 CULTURA

Antonio Villaraigosa

Antonio Villaraigosa fue el primer alcalde hispano que tuvo Los Ángeles desde 1872. Ha sido calificado por la revista *Time* como uno de los veinticinco latinos más influyentes. Su interés por la política se remonta a sus años de estudiante en la UCLA. Fue elegido a la Asamblea Estatal de California en 1994 y, cuando terminó su cargo, empezó a trabajar en su comunidad. Fue elegido alcalde en 2005 y durante su mandato promovió la mejora del transporte en la ciudad, la seguridad y la producción de energía sostenible.

39 Piensa.
 ¿Conoces a otros políticos hispanos en el gobierno local o nacional? ¿En qué proyectos o reformas están involucrados?

Vocabulario – Política y gobierno

37. Before playing the recording, review the questions with students. After listening, review the answers before asking students to complete a Venn diagram. Finally, have students compare and contrast their diagrams with a partner's.

38. You may want to bring in a few recent newspapers or direct students to online newspapers, so that they can find stories about decisions being made in their local, state, and federal governments. Ask them to provide their opinions about the issues.

 AUDIO SCRIPT
See page 239L.

CULTURA

Antonio Villaraigosa

Born Antonio Villar in East Los Angeles, he was raised by a single mother. Villaraigosa dropped out of high school, but was persuaded to return and graduated from Theodore Roosevelt High School. He then attended UCLA, where he received a history degree. He was the mayor of Los Angeles for two consecutive terms (2005–2013).

Answer Key

36. Answers will vary.
  ▶ Answers will vary.
37. 1. Cada 4 años.　　4. La población.
  2. Presidente del Senado.　5. Tres.
  3. 72; 257.　　6. El presidente.
  ▶ Answers will vary.
38. Answers will vary.
39. Answers will vary.

Additional Resources

Fans Online activities
Practice Workbook

HERITAGE LANGUAGE LEARNERS

• Have Spanish speakers ask family members about, or research, the present form of government in their heritage country. Students should be prepared to explain when this form of government came into effect and what kinds of government preceded it. They should also elaborate on the various branches of government, including how they are elected or named; characteristics of the elections and when they are held; who has the right to vote; and any other anecdotal information. Students may write a report or give an oral presentation to the class.

CRITICAL THINKING

• Ask students to think about these two issues: how the world would be if women had not been given the right to vote, and compulsory voting. Then, have them choose one of these topics and write an essay of at least three well-developed paragraphs to support their ideas. Encourage students to research the history of women's right to vote in several countries. To help support their arguments, students should also look into which countries mandate compulsory voting and under which conditions. Call on volunteers to read their essays aloud.

DESAFÍO 2

Gramática – Expresar finalidad

Presentation

- In this section, students will review and expand on how to express the purpose of an action.

Activities	Standards	Resources
Gramática	1.2, 3.1	
40.	1.2, 3.1, 4.1	
41.	1.3, 3.1	
42.	1.2, 3.1	
43.	1.1, 1.2, 3.1	
44.	1.1, 1.2, 1.3, 4.2, 5.1, 5.2	

Teaching Suggestions

Warm-Up / Independent Starter

- Have students identify the conjugation of the underlined verbs in these sentences:
  1. *El pueblo votará para elegir al presidente.* (future, infinitive)
  2. *Los candidatos presentan sus propuestas con el propósito de que los votantes entiendan su ideología.* (present, present subjunctive)
  3. *El candidato dio un discurso para que los ciudadanos se enteraran de su programa electoral.* (preterite, imperfect subjunctive)

Preparation

- Review the Independent Starter with students. Compare the sequence of tenses, and then call on different students to read each bullet in the grammar presentation. Draw students' attention to the examples provided, and ask them to identify the verb forms of the main and subordinate clauses. Emphasize the meanings of the prepositions and conjunctions identified in the presentation.

- Revisit the sentences from the Independent Starter and give students a few moments to write a question for each of the sentences. Encourage them to use different expressions. For example: *¿Para qué votará el pueblo? ¿Con qué propósito presentan sus propuestas los candidatos? ¿Con qué fin dio un discurso el candidato?* Then, have students write two original statements and one question about politics and government.

262

Gramática

Expresar finalidad

- Para expresar el propósito de una acción, usa para (que) y a (que). Recuerda que a (que) se usa con verbos que indican movimiento, como ir, venir, subir, bajar, entrar o salir.

  Se presentó un proyecto de ley **para** mejorar la educación.
  Los ciudadanos **salieron a** protestar por el nuevo proyecto de ley.

- También puedes usar algunas expresiones más formales como a fin de (que) o con el propósito de (que), que equivalen a *so that, so as to* y *in order to*.

  Los ministros se reunieron **a fin de** elegir a un nuevo representante.

El infinitivo y el subjuntivo con expresiones de finalidad

- Cuando la cláusula principal y la dependiente tienen el mismo sujeto, usa estas estructuras:

para a a fin de con el propósito de	+ infinitivo

  El dictador prohibió las reuniones en lugares públicos **para evitar** las manifestaciones.

  Se realizó un referéndum **a fin de conocer** la opinión de los ciudadanos.

- Cuando la cláusula principal y la dependiente tienen distintos sujetos, usa estas otras estructuras:

para que a que a fin de que con el propósito de que	+ subjuntivo

  El presidente defendió su propuesta **para que** los diputados la **aprobaran**.

  El gobierno presentará los presupuestos **con el propósito de que** el Congreso los **autorice**.

Preguntar sobre la finalidad de una acción

- Para preguntar sobre el propósito o la finalidad de una acción, usa estas estructuras:

¿Para qué...? ¿A qué...? ¿Con qué fin...? ¿Con qué propósito...?	+ indicativo

  —¿**Con qué fin** salió el ejército a la calle?
  —El ejército salió a la calle **para controlar** la revolución.

40 **Compara.** Traduce al inglés los ejemplos de la ficha. ¿Qué expresiones de finalidad has usado en cada caso? ¿Por qué?

41 **Titulares**

▶ **Escribe** dos titulares ficticios de noticias de actualidad. Usa estas estructuras:

para + infinitivo para que + subjuntivo

Modelo   *El presidente convoca a los periodistas para presentar la nueva ley.*

Differentiated Instruction

DEVELOPING LEARNERS

- Ask students to complete the following sentences with the correct verb:
  1. *La junta militar suprimió la Constitución a fin de ... una dictadura.* (b)
     a. *imponga*   b. *imponer*
  2. *Se celebraron elecciones para que los ciudadanos ... alcalde.* (a)
     a. *eligieran*   b. *elijan*
  3. *Autorizaron la manifestación para ... los derechos civiles de los ciudadanos.* (b)
     a. *garantizara*   b. *garantizar*
  4. *El general prohibió las elecciones para ... su derrota.* (b)
     a. *evitara*   b. *evitar*

EXPANDING LEARNERS

- Ask students to answer the following questions about *la política* and *el gobierno* using an expression of purpose. Then call on volunteers to read some of their answers aloud.
  1. *¿Para qué se celebran elecciones?*
  2. *¿Por qué piden algunos inmigrantes el asilo político?*
  3. *¿Para qué sirve el poder judicial? ¿Y el poder legislativo?*
  4. *¿Para qué sirven las campañas electorales?*
  5. *¿Para qué se exilian algunas personas?*
  6. *¿Con qué fin controlan los dictadores el gobierno?*

42 La finalidad

▶ **Completa** estas oraciones con la forma correcta de los verbos del cuadro.

> oponerse   aprobar   elegir   trabajar   apoyar   expresar

1. Se convocaron elecciones primarias para _____ a los candidatos a las elecciones generales.
2. Casi todos los diputados votaron en contra a fin de _____ a la reforma de la Constitución.
3. Es necesario animar a los políticos a que _____ para mejorar las leyes.
4. La mayoría de los diputados va a votar a favor para que se _____ los presupuestos.
5. Muchos voluntarios participan en la campaña con el propósito de _____ al candidato.
6. Haremos un debate a fin de que todos _____ su opinión.

43 ¿Para qué?

 ▶ **Habla** con tu compañero(a). ¿Qué propósito crees que tienen estas normas y derechos?

Modelo   Hay elecciones primarias. → *Hay elecciones primarias para elegir a los representantes de los partidos políticos.*

1. Hay límites en la duración del cargo de presidente.
2. El presidente puede vetar un proyecto de ley.
3. La Constitución garantiza la libertad de expresión.
4. En democracia el poder se reparte en tres ramas: la legislativa, la judicial y la ejecutiva.

44 Mi punto de vista

▶ **Escribe** una reflexión sobre estas preguntas.

1. ¿Qué puedes hacer si no estás conforme con algún problema social?
2. ¿Cuál es el propósito de la canción protesta?
3. ¿Qué opinas sobre el hecho de que haya músicos que expresan sus ideas políticas a través de sus canciones?
4. ¿Con qué otros medios de expresión puedes comunicar tu punto de vista sociopolítico?

La cantante mexicana Lila Downs en un concierto.

▶ **Habla** con tu compañero(a). Comenten sus reflexiones del apartado anterior y hagan un póster con ideas para expresar opiniones políticas de una forma constructiva. Después, compártanlo con la clase.

Modelo

> Para expresar tu opinión sobre un tema determinado, puedes escribir una carta al director en algún diario.

doscientos sesenta y tres 263

HERITAGE LANGUAGE LEARNERS

• Ask students to research when citizens— both men and women—were first given the right to vote in their family's country of origin, and to describe the political, economic, and social issues that influenced giving citizens the right to vote. Encourage students to include the history of *el sufragio universal* and issues related to it in other Spanish-speaking countries. To avoid duplication of research, you might assign one or more countries for each student to research, in addition to his or her own. Have students share their findings with the class.

CRITICAL THINKING

• Remind students that while there are foreign-born citizens in the United States who hold elected offices, according to the U.S. Constitution these men and women can never be President. Enable a classroom debate with some teams arguing in favor of the status quo and others arguing in favor of changing the Constitution to enable these people to run for the presidency. Select some students to serve as judges in order to keep track of each team's time and ability to convince the audience. Alternatively, have students write an essay on this topic.

Unit 5

DESAFÍO 2

Gramática – Expresar finalidad

Activities

41. Call on students to share their headlines with the class. Then, to extend this activity, ask students to choose one of the headlines and write a one-paragraph summary of the news. They will make up the information, but it has to make sense. Invite volunteers to share their paragraphs with the class.

42. Before completing the sentences, have students identify whether the verb they need to complete each sentence will be in the subjunctive or infinitive, based on the preposition or conjunction that is used before the missing word.

43. Challenge more advanced learners to write two statements for each example: one with a preposition and the infinitive and a second with the conjunction and the subjunctive.

Answer Key

40. Answers will vary. Sample answers:
   – *The dictator forbade public gatherings to avoid demonstrations.*
   – *The president defended his proposal so that the representatives would approve it.*
   Cuando las cláusulas tienen el mismo sujeto, se usa el infinitivo. Cuando tienen sujetos distintos, se usa *that* en la expresión de finalidad, y esta va seguida de un sujeto y un verbo.

41. Answers will vary.

42. 1. elegir   4. aprueben
   2. oponerse   5. apoyar
   3. trabajen   6. expresen

43. Answers will vary.

44. Answers will vary.
   ▶ Answers will vary.

Additional Resources

Fans Online activities
Practice Workbook

263

DESAFÍO 2

Gramática – Expresar dificultad

Presentation

- In this section, students will review and expand on how to inform someone about events using expressions that imply objections, obstacles, or difficulties.

Activities	Standards	Resources
Gramática	1.2, 3.1	
45.	1.3, 3.1, 4.1	
46.	1.3, 3.1	
47.	1.2, 1.3	Audio
48.	1.1, 1.2, 1.3, 2.2, 3.1, 5.2	
49.	1.3, 3.1	

Teaching Suggestions

Warm-Up / Independent Starter

- Have students identify the conjugation of the following underlined verbs:
  1. a. *Prefiero la democracia, aunque no es perfecta.* (present indicative)
     b. *Prefiero la democracia, aunque no sea perfecta.* (present subjunctive)
  2. a. *A pesar de que era perseguido, seguía luchando.* (imperfect indicative)
     b. *A pesar de que fuera perseguido, seguía luchando.* (imperfect subjunctive)

Preparation

- Go over the grammar presentation with the class. Then, review the sentence pairs from the Independent Starter and discuss the difference in meaning between each pair of sentences. Next, ask students to work with a partner to translate some of the statements provided in the grammar presentation into English. Explain that, generally, *aunque* is translated as "even though" when followed by the indicative, and as "even if" when followed by the subjunctive.

Activities

45. Have students translate this sentence into Spanish: Even if the candidate wins the debates, he will lose the elections. (*Aunque el candidato gane los debates, perderá las elecciones.*)

Gramática

Expresar dificultad

- Para dar información sobre un evento que se cumple a pesar de que exista una objeción, un obstáculo o una dificultad, puedes usar las siguientes estructuras:
  - Aunque y a pesar de (que). Son las más habituales.
    Acabaremos con la crisis **aunque** *sea difícil.*
  - Aun cuando y pese a (que). Son más formales. Equivalen a *although*, *even though*, *even if* y *despite*.
    Aun cuando *esté ocupada, iré a votar.*
  - Aun + gerundio. Es también más formal. Expresa la idea de *although*, *even though* y *in spite of*, pero no tiene equivalencia exacta en inglés.
    Aun conociendo *a los candidatos, no sé a quién votar.*

  Observa en los ejemplos anteriores que la cláusula que expresa la dificultad puede ir antes o después de la cláusula principal.

EXPRESIONES DE DIFICULTAD
aunque
a pesar de (que)
aun cuando
pese a (que)
aun + gerundio

Intensificar la dificultad

- Si quieres intensificar la dificultad, puedes utilizar estas estructuras:

| por más + (nombre / adjetivo / adverbio) + que |
| por mucho(a)(os)(as) + (nombre) + que |
| por muy + adjetivo / adverbio + que |

  Por más *problemas* **que** *tenga, él es optimista.*
  Por mucho *esfuerzo* **que** *haga, no encuentra trabajo.*
  Por muy *difícil* **que** *sea, ganaremos las elecciones.*

El indicativo y el subjuntivo con expresiones de dificultad

- Las expresiones de dificultad llevan el verbo en **indicativo** cuando la cláusula tiene el sentido de *even though*. El indicativo expresa que el hablante siente la dificultad como un hecho real y relevante.
  Aunque **estaba** *ocupada, fue a votar. (Even though she was busy, she went to vote.)*
- Las expresiones de dificultad llevan el verbo en **subjuntivo** cuando la cláusula tiene el sentido de *even if*. El subjuntivo expresa que el hablante siente la dificultad:
  - Como un hecho hipotético en el futuro o en el pasado:
    Aunque **llueva** *(futuro), iré al cine.*   *Aunque* **lloviera** *(pasado), iba al cine.*
  - Como un hecho irreal en el pasado:
    Aunque **hubiera llovido** *(pasado), habría ido al cine.*
  - Como una objeción irrelevante:
    Aunque **esté lloviendo** *(presente o futuro), voy a ir al cine.*
- Por mucho y por muy llevan el verbo en subjuntivo.

45 **Piensa.** Traduce al español de todas las maneras posibles esta oración: *Even though the candidate won the debates, he lost the elections.*

Differentiated Instruction

DEVELOPING LEARNERS

- Ask students to complete the following sentences with the correct verb:
  1. *Aunque … la misma ideología que el candidato, no pienso votar por él.* (a)
     a. *comparto*   b. *comparte*
  2. *Por mucho que los políticos …, pocas veces cumplen con su palabra.* (a)
     a. *prometan*   b. *prometen*
  3. *Aunque el dictador … autorizado esas elecciones, no se habrían celebrado.* (a)
     a. *hubiera*   b. *haya*
  4. *Por muy difícil que … la lucha, vamos a lograr nuestros objetivos.* (b)
     a. *es*   b. *sea*

EXPANDING LEARNERS

- Ask students to identify a political issue in their community and to create a campaign to promote it. They may choose to write an ad for radio, TV, or the printed media, create a webpage, or design a poster. Encourage students to use sentences with expressions such as *aunque*, *a pesar de que*, *aun cuando*, and *por mucho* or *por muy* to show that in spite of the obstacles, their ideas for the campaign will overcome all difficulties. Invite students to present their campaigns and take a class vote to select the most effective one.

¿Qué expresión?

 46

▶ **Transforma** cada par de oraciones en una sola oración. Usa expresiones de dificultad.

Modelo Hay leyes para prevenir la violencia./Todavía hay crímenes.
  ⟶ *Aunque haya leyes para prevenir la violencia, todavía hay crímenes.*

1. El ministro ganó las elecciones primarias./No estaba seguro de conseguirlo.

2. El presidente vetó la ley./El público apoyaba la ley.

3. Él quería ser diputado./No ganó las elecciones.

4. Los candidatos gastan millones de dólares en sus campañas./Muchos no ganan.

Conversaciones sobre política

 47

▶ **Escucha** y completa las oraciones.

1. Su candidato preferido no ganó las elecciones por muy…

2. Cree que es buena idea limitar la duración de los cargos políticos a pesar de que…

3. Seguirá habiendo injusticias en la sociedad por más…

4. El presidente vetó el proyecto de ley pese a que…

Citas famosas

 48

▶ **Habla** con tu compañero(a). ¿Qué significan las palabras de estos célebres personajes?

① Por mucho que un hombre valga, nunca tendrá valor más alto que el de ser hombre.
Antonio Machado, escritor español

② Debemos amar a nuestro país aunque nos trate injustamente.
Voltaire, filósofo francés

③ La honradez es siempre digna de elogio, aun cuando no reporte utilidad, ni recompensa, ni provecho.
Cicerón, político, filósofo y escritor romano

▶ **Invéntate** una cita acerca de la política, la historia o la vida en general usando expresiones de dificultad. Compártela con la clase y comenten su significado.

Tu campaña para presidente

 49

▶ **Escribe** un discurso de campaña para presidente del país.
Explica lo que harás en tu campaña a pesar de estas dificultades.

1. El líder de la oposición es más conocido que tú.

2. No hay muchos fondos para tu campaña.

3. Tienes experiencia trabajando en varias ONG, pero no en política.

4. Hay conflictos con otros países.

▶ **Presenta** tu discurso a la clase.

doscientos sesenta y cinco 265

Gramática – Expresar dificultad

48. Ask students if they know any other famous quotes or proverbs and if they can explain what they mean. You may want to post some of these quotes and those that students create around the classroom.

49. As an alternative to this activity, have students write a campaign speech for a leadership position in their school, such as a class officer, captain of a sports team, the president of a club, or a position on student council. Have students create a campaign slogan and propaganda to accompany their speeches.

 AUDIO SCRIPT
See page 239L.

Answer Key

45. – Aunque/A pesar de que/Aun cuando/ Pese a que el candidato ganó los debates, perdió las elecciones.
– Aun ganando los debates, el candidato perdió las elecciones

46. Answers will vary. Sample answers:
1. Aunque no estaba seguro de conseguirlo, el ministro ganó las primarias.
2. A pesar de que el público apoyaba la ley, el presidente la vetó.
3. Aunque quisiera ser diputado, no ganó.
4. Pese a que gastan millones en sus campañas, muchos candidatos no ganan.

47. 1. … fuerte que fuera la campaña.
2. … sean buenos líderes.
3. … leyes que haya.
4. … es un buen proyecto.

48. Answers will vary.
▶ Answers will vary.

49. Answers will vary.
▶ Answers will vary.

Additional Resources

Fans Online activities
Practice Workbook

HERITAGE LANGUAGE LEARNERS

- Ask students to write at least three paragraphs about their thoughts on politics and government. Students may choose to focus on local, national, or international issues, governments, or politicians. Encourage students to integrate expressions of purpose and of difficulty throughout their compositions to express what should be done (e.g., *Debemos apoyar las democracias para evitar la dictadura*), as well as to express victory over obstacles (e.g., *Aunque sea difícil, eliminaremos el tráfico humano*). Call on volunteers to read their compositions aloud.

TOTAL PHYSICAL RESPONSE (TPR)

- Tell students that they are going to play a game. Prepare about thirty incomplete sentences and explain that they must complete them with either the gerund or the correct form of the subjunctive or indicative mood. Give each student three sheets of colored paper, and assign each sheet a particular verb form. As you read each sentence aloud, ask students to hold up the corresponding sheet for the required verb form. Then call on a student to say the sentence with the correct verb form in place.

LECTURA: TEXTO INFORMATIVO

Presentation

- In this section, students will read an article about Eva Duarte de Perón. They will learn information about her life and her political and social involvement in Argentina. Students will also learn transitional words to retell events, and will research the government of Juan Domingo Perón.

Activities	Standards	Resources
Lectura: texto informativo	1.2, 2.1, 2.2, 3.2	
50.	1.2, 2.1, 2.2	
51.	1.1, 1.2, 1.3, 2.1, 2.2, 3.1, 3.2, 5.1	

Teaching Suggestions

Warm-Up / Independent Starter

- Have students read the *Antes de leer* strategies silently. Then ask them to write the answers to the questions.

Preparation

- Call on volunteer students to share their answers for the *Antes de leer* section with the class. You may wish to write the responses on the board. Do not correct the answers at this point. Once students have read the article, have them correct their responses. Then, check the answers with the class.

- Have students skim the article, looking for the dates that are included and listing them in their notebooks. Ask them to identify what was happening around the world during this time period. If they cannot recall any historical events that took place during the first half of the 20th century, you may want to ask some probing questions, such as *¿Cuándo obtuvieron las mujeres el derecho al voto en los Estados Unidos? ¿Cuál era la situación económica mundial en los años treinta del siglo xx? ¿Qué dos guerras importantes se libraron en la primera mitad del siglo xx? ¿En qué años tuvo lugar la llamada «guerra fría» entre los Estados Unidos y la Unión Soviética?* You may also want to remind students about the gender inequalities during the first half of the 20th century.

LECTURA: TEXTO INFORMATIVO

Antes de leer: estrategias

1. Lee el título del texto y mira la fotografía. ¿Qué sabes de este personaje histórico? ¿En qué época nació? ¿Cuál era su nacionalidad? ¿Por qué fue conocida? ¿Sabes cómo la llamaban? Comparte la información con tus compañeros(as).

María Eva Duarte de Perón

Eva y Juan Domingo Perón saludan desde la Casa Rosada.

María Eva Duarte nació el 7 de mayo de 1919 en Los Toldos (provincia de Buenos Aires, en Argentina). Su niñez fue humilde. En 1935 viajó a Buenos Aires para convertirse en actriz de radioteatro y cine. En 1944 un acontecimiento fortuito[1] hizo que conociera al entonces coronel Perón. Un fuerte terremoto destruyó la ciudad de San Juan y Perón se puso a la cabeza de la ayuda enviada por el gobierno, mientras que Eva Duarte participó en uno de los festivales artísticos destinados a recaudar fondos. Un año más tarde eran marido y mujer.

Poco a poco la figura de Eva Duarte se transformó en un complemento del liderazgo de su esposo. En 1947 hizo un viaje a Europa y a partir de su regreso empezó a ser conocida como Evita. Ese mismo año encabezó la aprobación de la ley que otorgó el voto a las mujeres y comenzó la organización de la rama femenina del Partido Peronista.

Evita tenía a su cargo[2] la ayuda social directa a través de la Fundación de Ayuda Social María Eva Duarte de Perón —luego llamada, simplemente, Fundación Eva Perón— creada por ella en 1948. La Fundación se transformó en un vínculo[3] entre los sectores sociales más débiles y poco organizados. Evita solía atender cada uno de los reclamos[4] en forma personal, por lo cual eran habituales las largas colas ante el edificio de la Fundación.

Además de la ayuda social directa, la Fundación administró policlínicos, escuelas, hogares de tránsito y de ancianos, la Ciudad Infantil y la Ciudad Estudiantil, colonias de vacaciones y otros ámbitos de esparcimiento[5].

En 1951, cuando debía definirse el nombre del vicepresidente que acompañaría a Perón en las elecciones del 11 de noviembre, la Confederación General del Trabajo de la República Argentina (CGT) proclamó a Evita como candidata. Pero los altos jefes militares, que sentían un abierto recelo[6] hacia su figura, lograron vetar con éxito su candidatura. Evita debía comunicar la novedad ante una multitud que se había reunido frente al edificio de la CGT, en la intersección de las avenidas 9 de Julio y Belgrano, en Buenos Aires. Pero la presión popular fue tan grande que no se atrevió. Una semana más tarde, Eva comunicó su «renunciamiento»[7] por radio.

Differentiated Instruction

DEVELOPING LEARNERS

- The length of this text could be an impediment for some students. To help students better understand its contents, have them first identify the topic sentence of each paragraph. Then, have them skim the article, looking for unfamiliar words. If students are unable to decode these words using context clues, ask them to look these words up and write the meaning in their notebooks. Then, have students identify the supporting details in each paragraph. After students have read the text silently, call on individuals to read assigned paragraphs aloud.

EXPANDING LEARNERS

- Using the article about Eva Perón as a model, ask students to write a brief biography about another figure in Latin American politics. Give students time to research some individuals before choosing a subject from Latin America's early history or a contemporary figure. Encourage a cross-section of personalities to avoid duplication of biographies. In their composition, encourage students to use expressions of purpose and those of difficulty when describing their politician's background, role, and influence. Call on volunteers to read their compositions aloud.

Eva Perón murió el 26 de julio de 1952 a causa de un cáncer. Fue proclamada Jefa Espiritual de la Nación. Su cuerpo fue embalsamado[8] y mantenido en exposición en la CGT. Bajo una lluvia persistente, una multitud de millones de personas esperó horas y horas para saludarla por última vez. Mientras tanto, el gobierno empezó las obras del Monumento al Descamisado, que se había proyectado con base a una idea de Evita y que, según un nuevo plan, sería su tumba[9] definitiva. Cuando la Revolución Libertadora derrocó[10] a Perón el 23 de septiembre de 1955, el cadáver fue secuestrado y hecho desaparecer durante 16 años.

Fuente: http://www.kalipedia.com
(texto adaptado)

1. casual, accidental
2. se ocupaba, era responsable de
3. enlace, conexión
4. quejas
5. entretenimiento
6. desconfianza
7. abandono, dimisión
8. *embalmed*
9. *tomb*
10. obligó a dejar el poder

50 **¿Comprendes?**

 ▶ **Analiza** el texto que has leído. ¿Qué visión ofrece de la vida de Evita? ¿En qué partes del texto se aprecia esa visión? Escribe un párrafo justificando tu respuesta.

▶ **Une** las dos columnas y escribe oraciones lógicas.

Ⓐ

1. **A partir de** su regreso de Europa…
2. Evita atendía personalmente las peticiones en su Fundación, …
3. **Además de** la ayuda social directa, …
4. Eva Perón iba a ser proclamada candidata a la vicepresidencia, …
5. Eva Perón murió…
6. **Cuando** Perón fue derrocado, …

Ⓑ

a. **a causa de** un cáncer.
b. el cadáver de Eva Perón fue secuestrado.
c. **pero** los altos jefes militares lo impidieron.
d. empezó a ser conocida como Evita.
e. **por lo cual** eran habituales las largas colas en la puerta del edificio.
f. la Fundación administraba policlínicos, escuelas…

51 **Con tus propias palabras**

 ▶ **Busca** en Internet más información y videos sobre Eva Perón. ¿Cómo crees que era? ¿Qué rasgos de su personalidad destacarías? Coméntalo con tus compañeros(as).

 ▶ **Investiga** con tu compañero(a) sobre el gobierno de Juan Domingo Perón y recojan los acontecimientos más importantes en una línea del tiempo.

1946

Fue elegido presidente.

doscientos sesenta y siete **267**

▪ Divide the class into small groups of four students of varying abilities, and ask individual group members to each read one or two paragraphs aloud in their groups. Encourage students to monitor their understanding during the reading by paraphrasing the information. Then ask students to organize the data provided in the reading in a graphic organizer of their choosing.

Activities

50. Before completing this activity, have students use their graphic organizers from the Preparation activity to write a comprehension question about each paragraph. Then have students get together with a partner and quiz each other. Next, have students work individually to complete this activity.

51. As an alternative to the first part of this activity, you may provide students the choice of watching the movie *Evita* or researching the musical *Evita,* and writing a plot summary.

Answer Key

50. Answers will vary.
▶ 1. d   2. e   3. f   4. c   5. a   6. b
51. Answers will vary.
▶ Answers will vary. Sample answer:
1949: Se establece la Nueva Constitución.
1951: Perón gana su segundo mandato.
1952: Eva Perón muere.
Junio de 1955: intento de golpe de Estado por los sectores antiperonistas.
Septiembre de 1955: Perón deja el poder después de un golpe de Estado por parte de las Fuerzas Armadas.
1955–1973: Perón está en el exilio.
Octubre de 1973: Perón gana las elecciones y se convierte en presidente por tercera vez.
Julio de 1974: Perón muere.

Additional Resources
Fans Online activities

HERITAGE LANGUAGE LEARNERS

• Have pairs imagine that they are living in Buenos Aires when Evita was alive. One student will be a petitioner at *la Fundación Eva Perón;* the other will portray Evita. Have them imagine that the time has come for a meeting. The petitioner will define a social, academic, or professional need that can be met through *la Fundación.* Eva will ask some pertinent questions and make her decision known, followed by a brief exchange between the two. Give pairs time to practice and then call on volunteers to present their conversation to the class.

SPECIAL-NEEDS LEARNERS

• Help those students who have trouble focusing on the content of longer articles by having them read it aloud to a student with superior language skills. After students read each line, they should paraphrase the content to verify that they understand what is being described. At the conclusion of each paragraph, have the expanding or heritage learner ask one or more questions about its content, again to verify that the special-needs learner has understood. You may also call on this student to help the special-needs learner complete activity 50.

DESAFÍO 2

Comunicación

Presentation

- In this section, students will integrate the vocabulary and grammar skills from *Desafío 2* in order to read and discuss an article about graffiti as a form of expression, talk about political messages and create a poster to propose a bill to the local or federal government, and write an e-mail to Asha and Lucas about their *desafío*.

Activities	Standards	Resources
52.	1.1, 1.2, 2.1, 2.2, 3.2, 5.2	
53.	1.1, 1.3, 5.1	
54. Final del desafío	1.1, 1.2, 1.3, 5.1	

Teaching Suggestions

Warm-Up / Independent Starter

- Have students write a list of different political figures that they studied during this *Desafío* and ask them to write a description of two of them.

Preparation

- Go over the vocabulary and grammar topics from this *Desafío*. Clarify any questions students may have regarding when to use the infinitive, indicative, and subjunctive with the structures learned.
- Call on volunteers to share their Independent Starters. Ask students additional probing questions about the historical events of Chile and Argentina, and the different political leaders mentioned in this *Desafío*.
- Remind students of Lucas and Asha's challenge to write a song about a social problem in their community. As a class, discuss some of the issues Asha and Lucas might sing about, what the main purpose of their song should be, and the difficulties that may need to be overcome to address the issue. Then, discuss the effectiveness of protest songs as a way of making people aware of social and political issues. Encourage students to provide examples of these songs, some of the topics addressed, and artists who perform this genre.

DESAFÍO 2

Comunicación

52 Un *graffitero* chileno

 ▶ **Lee** el artículo y responde a las preguntas. Señala, en cada caso, qué palabras del texto justifican tus respuestas.

El *graffiti* ganó un reconocimiento social

El *graffiti* es más que una experiencia visual; es también una experiencia temporal y espacial. Su manifestación no encuentra límites y permite al creador interpretar libremente los contextos en los que acciona.

Para el *graffitero* chileno Ricardo Díaz Santander, esa libertad se manifiesta en la singularidad y la versatilidad que propone el *graffiti*: «Cada obra es distinta, siempre varía dependiendo de la situación personal que uno atraviesa y la del entorno que te rodea.» El joven de 25 años visualiza una reivindicación del *graffiti* como forma de expresión no muchos años atrás resistido y combatido por los oscuros gobiernos militares. «Hoy en día esta disciplina ganó un reconocimiento social muy grande. Cada vez son más frecuentes los espacios cedidos por las personas y las autoridades para que puedan ser intervenidos por artistas urbanos».

En una sociedad donde la información está supeditada a los discursos interesados de los medios, la intervención de los muros se vuelve tan necesaria como revolucionaria. Las consignas varían, pero todas denuncian algo. «Cuando estás pintando en la calle te encontrás[1] con muchas realidades que no se ven en la televisión, en Internet o en la radio. Tienes que estar ahí para ver la vida real tal cual es, y ahí es cuando te dices que puedes hacer cambios positivos para una sociedad mejor usando colores y formas en las paredes. Pensando positivamente siempre puedes llegar a conseguir cambios.»

[1] te encuentras (en Argentina, Uruguay y Paraguay)

Fuente: www.arteacieloabierto.com (selección)

1. ¿Para qué crean su arte los *graffiteros*, según el texto?
2. ¿A qué sale a la calle Ricardo Díaz Santander?
3. ¿Con qué fin ceden espacios públicos muchas personas y autoridades?
4. ¿Con qué propósito usa el *graffiti* Ricardo Díaz Santander?

 ▶ **Piensa.** ¿Qué opinas del *graffiti* como forma de expresión? ¿Crees que tiene valor artístico? Coméntalo con tus compañeros(as) de clase, argumentando tus opiniones.

 ▶ **Habla** con tus compañeros(as). Comparen y contrasten el *graffiti* y la canción protesta como formas artísticas en cuanto a sus contenidos y sus propósitos.

Differentiated Instruction

DEVELOPING LEARNERS

- Have students complete these sentences:
  1. *Los graffiteros pintan para que el pueblo (disfrutar) de su arte. (disfrute)*
  2. *Por mucho que ellos (denunciar) su arte, él seguirá pintando. (denuncien)*
  3. *Aunque el gobierno lo (prohibir), los ciudadanos van a protestar. (prohíbe/ prohíba)*
  4. *Los candidatos debaten para que los votantes los (conocer). (conozcan)*
  5. *Por muy liberales que ellos (ser), no van a autorizar la exposición. (sean)*
  6. *El dictador suprimió las elecciones a fin de (continuar) en el poder. (continuar)*

EXPANDING LEARNERS

- Ask student pairs to add several exchanges to the dialogue between Asha and Lucas in order to see how they complete their *desafío*. Students may describe the final outcome of the challenge, along with more details on the topics that Asha and Lucas focused on, and some lyrics to the song. Students may also give this an unhappy ending by concentrating on some obstacles along the way that are preventing Asha and Lucas from completing their *desafío*. Call on volunteer pairs to role-play their dialogues in front of the class.

53 Propaganda política

 ▶ **Lee** el cartel y habla con tu compañero(a). ¿Qué mensaje transmite? ¿Creen que lo hace de forma adecuada? ¿Les gusta? Argumenten sus opiniones.

 ▶ **Dibuja** con tu compañero(a) un cartel similar para promover un proyecto de ley de su gobierno municipal, estatal o federal. Después, preséntenlo a la clase.

Final del desafío

Asha: Creo que tenemos un montón de temas para escribir nuestra canción. Podemos cantar sobre la poca accesibilidad y adaptación de los lugares públicos para los discapacitados o hablar sobre la desigualdad de los sueldos entre hombres y mujeres.

Lucas: También podemos escribir sobre la falta de recursos para la gente que vive en la pobreza.

Asha: Sí, eso también es un gran problema de nuestra sociedad. Aunque hay algunos servicios para la gente sin hogar, podemos hacer mucho más por ellos.

Lucas: Quizá sea muy complicado, pero ¿qué te parece si escribimos una canción que trate varios temas?

Asha: Por muy complicado que sea, me gusta la idea. Vamos a intentarlo.

Lucas: Aunque sea una canción protesta, podemos darle un tono positivo. Me gustaría empezar transmitiendo un mensaje sobre los derechos civiles y la libertad.

Asha: Perfecto, aunque debemos ser algo críticos, ¿eh?

54 Un plan ambicioso

  ▶ **Escribe** un correo electrónico a Asha y a Lucas sobre el plan de su desafío. Hazles comentarios sobre su plan y ofréceles sugerencias.

Modelo

Hola, amigos:
Aunque tienen ideas muy buenas, para tener éxito en este desafío, les recomiendo que…

doscientos sesenta y nueve **269**

Activities

52. Explain that *graffiti* is the plural form of the Italian word *graffito*, which means "scratch" or "incised inscription." Modern graffiti exploded onto city walls and subway cars in New York in the 1970s. Opinions about graffiti are divided: some view it as a way of reclaiming public spaces and others regard it as vandalism. You may want to ask students if they know of any graffiti mural or graffiti work in their community and what the creator(s) might want to express with their public art.

53. To make this activity more authentic, you may want to send in some of the posters to your local municipal government. You may ask students to make them bilingual.

54. As an alternative to this activity, have students write their own songs!

Answer Key

52. Answers will vary. Sample answers:
   1. Los *graffiteros* crean su arte para que haya una experiencia visual, temporal y espacial en espacios públicos. Quieren interpretar libremente los contextos en los que actúan.
   2. Sale a la calle para expresarse y para ver la vida tal cual es.
   3. Ceden espacios públicos para que puedan ser intervenidos por artistas urbanos.
   4. Usa el *graffiti* a fin de lograr cambios positivos para la sociedad.
   ▶ Answers will vary.
   ▶ Answers will vary.
53. Answers will vary.
   ▶ Answers will vary.
54. Answers will vary.

Additional Resources

Fans Online activities
Practice Workbook

HERITAGE LANGUAGE LEARNERS

• Ask pairs to create an interview with a real *graffitero* such as Ricardo Díaz Santander, or a fictitious artist. Both partners will need to do some research in order to come up with meaningful questions and answers. Students may ask about the social content of the art, how the artist determined that this was his or her ideal medium, what projects are being worked on now, and what ideas he or she has for the future. Give students time to prepare their interviews and call on some pairs to present before the class.

COOPERATIVE LEARNING

• In small groups, have students come up with an idea for a graffiti mural. Students will first discuss if they want to promote or denounce something. Then, they will contribute ideas for a topic, discuss all of them, and select one. Students with artistic skills might make an outline of the work on poster boards or large sheets of paper; other group members may color the images. Students should also include a title for their work. Call on groups to display their work and make a brief explanation of their graffiti.

DESAFÍO 3

Hablar de problemas sociales

Presentation

- In *Desafío 3*, Ethan and Eva have to write a scene for a play dealing with the beginnings of the indigenous movement in Latin America. Students will preview language used to talk about social issues and contrary-to-fact conditions.

Activities	Standards	Resources
Texto	1.2, 2.1, 2.2	
55.	1.1, 1.2, 1.3, 2.1, 3.2	
56.	1.2, 1.3, 2.1, 2.2	
57.	1.2, 1.3, 2.1, 2.2	Audio
58. Comunidades	1.2, 1.3, 2.1, 2.2, 3.2, 4.2	

Teaching Suggestions

Warm-Up / Independent Starter

- Ask students to brainstorm and list the main features of plays.

Preparation

- Have students share their Independent Starters. If necessary, ask further questions to complete the list. Then, read the title of the dialogue and ask students to speculate on the meaning of *con mensaje*.

Texto: Una obra de teatro con mensaje

- Read the introduction to the dialogue and ask students to share with the class what they know about the indigenous movement in Latin America. Have students read the dialogue silently. Then, discuss the main ideas of the text with the class.

Activities

55. Discuss the answers with the class. What are the main causes of these problems? Can students think of possible solutions?

56. Have students work in small groups to discuss and list the advantages and disadvantages of globalization in their community, state, or country.

Una obra de teatro con mensaje

Ethan y Eva tienen que escribir una escena de una obra de teatro explicando el inicio del movimiento indigenista en las Américas. Los ayudará Luisa Itzel, una representante del CICA (Consejo Indígena de Centro América).

ETHAN: Buenas tardes, señora Itzel. Gracias por atendernos.

LUISA: Es un placer, chicos. Ha sido una suerte que contactaran conmigo justo cuando iba a viajar a su país. Si no hubiera estado aquí, no habría podido ayudarlos mucho.

EVA: Sí, hemos tenido mucha suerte. Díganos, ¿qué es el movimiento indigenista? ¿Tiene algo que ver con los derechos humanos?

LUISA: Sí. Desde la colonización ha habido muchas dificultades para la población indígena de Latinoamérica. Hemos sufrido el desempleo, la injusticia social, la discriminación e incluso la pobreza. Y hoy seguimos perdiendo nuestras lenguas, nuestras tierras y nuestras costumbres debido en gran parte a la globalización. El CICA busca lograr el reconocimiento y respeto a las formas de organización indígenas y la recuperación de nuestros valores culturales.

ETHAN: Pero yo siempre pensé que la globalización era una tendencia positiva.

LUISA: Es buena para algunas cosas. Por ejemplo, ahora las poblaciones indígenas pueden comunicarse entre sí más fácilmente. Pero cuéntenme ustedes, ¿cómo van a plantear la escena de la obra de teatro?

ETHAN: Pues no sabemos qué hacer. Si hubiéramos investigado un poco más antes de venir a verla, tendríamos alguna idea. Pero no nos ha dado tiempo.

LUISA: No se preocupen. ¿Qué les parece si la plantean a través de los ojos de un personaje? Por ejemplo, un niño o un joven indígena.

EVA: ¡Qué buena idea!

ETHAN: También podríamos hacerlo con un miembro del CICA. Así hablaría sobre los orígenes del movimiento indigenista, que es lo que nos interesa.

LUISA: Yo puedo contarles un montón de cosas. ¿Qué quieren saber?

55 **Detective de palabras**

▶ **Escribe.** ¿Qué cuatro problemas afectan a la población indígena, según el diálogo? Escribe una definición de cada problema.

 ▶ **Habla** con tu compañero(a). ¿Por qué creen que existen esos problemas?

Differentiated Instruction

DEVELOPING LEARNERS

- Ask students whether the following statements are true *(cierto)* or false *(falso)*, and to correct the false ones:
  1. *Asha y Lucas entrevistan a Luisa Itzel en Centroamérica. (F; en EE. UU.)*
  2. *El movimiento indigenista no tiene que ver con los derechos humanos. (F; tiene mucho que ver con ellos)*
  3. *Luisa dice que los indígenas han perdido lenguas, tierras y costumbres debido a la globalización. (C)*
  4. *La globalización ayuda a los pueblos indígenas a comunicarse entre sí más fácilmente. (C)*

EXPANDING LEARNERS

- After students have read the dialogue, ask them to write a narrative that describes what is happening in the conversation between Luisa, Eva, and Ethan. Explain to students that their narratives may be written from the more objective third-person point of view, or from the first-person point of view of one of the protagonists. The action may be in the present or in the past. Encourage students to do some research into the CICA (a good source of information is CICA's website) in order to add more meaningful information to their narratives. Call on volunteers to read their work aloud.

56 **¿Comprendes?**

▶ **Responde** a estas preguntas.

1. ¿Por qué dice Luisa que Ethan y Eva han tenido suerte?
2. ¿Qué consecuencias negativas de la globalización sufre la población indígena, según el texto?
3. ¿Qué es el CICA y qué función tiene?
4. ¿Qué opina Luisa sobre la globalización? ¿Qué parte del texto lo demuestra?
5. ¿Qué crees que quiere decir «valores culturales» en este contexto? Pon algunos ejemplos.

57 **Una representante del CICA**

▶ **Escucha** la conversación y elige la opción correcta.

1. Luisa pertenece al CICA desde _____.
   a. 2005　　　　　　b. 1985　　　　　　c. 1995
2. El objetivo que más le gusta a Luisa está relacionado con _____.
   a. la economía　　　b. los idiomas　　　c. la música
3. El CICA organiza _____.
   a. festivales　　　　b. talleres　　　　　c. viajes
4. _____ no pertenece al CICA.
   a. Chile　　　　　　b. Costa Rica　　　　c. Panamá

▶ **Escribe** dos preguntas más para Luisa Itzel sobre el CICA y sus objetivos.

 COMUNIDADES

Rigoberta Menchú.

MOVIMIENTOS INDIGENISTAS

Desde el comienzo de la colonización de las Américas, los pueblos indígenas han sufrido discriminación y opresión.

Esto ha dado lugar a la aparición de los movimientos indigenistas, que luchan para defender los derechos de los pueblos indígenas, otorgarles mayor participación política y terminar con la discriminación social y racial. También promueven los valores tradicionales de estas sociedades, caracterizadas por la solidaridad, la espiritualidad y el antimaterialismo.

Hoy en día muchos gobiernos latinoamericanos tienen en cuenta las reivindicaciones indigenistas en su labor de justicia política y social.

58 **Explica.** ¿Hay en los Estados Unidos algún movimiento indigenista semejante al de Latinoamérica? ¿Te parece necesario? Justifica tu respuesta.

---

57. After completing the activity, ask students to write the names of all the countries in Central America, and locate them on a map.

 AUDIO SCRIPT
See page 239M.

 COMUNIDADES

Movimientos indigenistas

The indigenous movement is an active political movement in Latin America with prominent activists and political leaders. Among them is Rigoberta Menchú from Guatemala, who was awarded the Nobel Peace Prize in 1992 for her defense of the rights of indigenous peoples. Evo Morales, the first member of an indigenous community to be elected president in Bolivia, is also associated with the indigenous movement.

Answer Key

55. El desempleo, la injusticia social, la discriminación y la pobreza.
　▶ Answers will vary.

56. Answers will vary. Sample answers:
1. Porque está de visita en Estados Unidos.
2. Han ido perdiendo sus lenguas, sus tierras y sus costumbres.
3. Es una organización que busca el reconocimiento y respeto a los diferentes grupos indígenas.
4. Cree que tiene consecuencias buenas, pero también negativas, y da ejemplos de ambos casos.
5. La lengua, el arte, las costumbres...

57. 1. c　2. b　3. b　4. a
　▶ Answers will vary.

58. Answers will vary.

Additional Resources

Fans Online activities

271

HERITAGE LANGUAGE LEARNERS

- Ask students to think about why indigenous peoples are often discriminated against and oppressed even though they are living on lands that have belonged to them for generations. Then, ask students to develop their thoughts in an essay of at least three paragraphs. Along with the answers to *¿por qué?*, have students explain how society should go about ending this discrimination. Call on volunteers to read their essays aloud and, if time permits, enable a classroom discussion on this topic.

CRITICAL THINKING

- Share CICA's mission statement with students: *El Consejo Indígena de Centro América es una organización que promueve y defiende los Derechos de los Pueblos Indígenas y genera políticas y estrategias de desarrollo para asegurar el buen vivir.* After reading this, ask students to define *el buen vivir*. Then, enable a classroom discussion on how their definition of a good life might differ from the perspective of an indigenous person of the Americas. Encourage all students to participate in the discussion.

DESAFÍO 3

Vocabulario – Problemas sociales y medioambientales

Presentation

- In this section, students will learn vocabulary related to social and environmental issues.

Activities	Standards	Resources
Vocabulario	1.2, 3.1	
59.	1.1, 1.3, 5.1	
60.	1.1, 1.2, 1.3, 4.2	Audio
61.	1.1, 1.3, 4.2, 5.1	
62. Comunidades	1.2, 1.3, 2.1, 2.2, 4.2, 5.1	

Teaching Suggestions

Warm-Up / Independent Starter

- Have students list some social and environmental problems in their community.

Preparation

- Call on volunteers to each read a paragraph from the vocabulary presentation aloud. Emphasize pronunciation of the highlighted words. To reinforce comprehension, you may ask: *¿Qué problemas nos suelen preocupar? ¿Qué problemas mundiales deberían ser una prioridad? ¿Qué se puede hacer para preservar el medio ambiente?* Then, have students share their Independent Starters. Do most students agree on the issues? Discuss possible solutions.

- Prepare flashcards with the new vocabulary, and give student pairs a set of flashcards. Next, have pairs write definitions for their assigned words without using the words being defined. Then, ask students to read their definitions to another pair to see if they can figure out the words.

Activities

61. For the second part of this activity, have a similar chart on the board and ask volunteers to complete it once they have finished their charts individually. When the chart is complete, start a whole-class discussion to talk about the results. As a class, have students decide on the best solutions for each problem.

Vocabulario

Problemas sociales y medioambientales

29 de abril de 2014

LOS PROBLEMAS MUNDIALES

por ANA SÁEZ

Es fácil pensar que los problemas que nos preocupan son los mismos que preocupan a todo el mundo. Hasta cierto punto, es verdad; todos nos alarmamos ante las guerras, el **hambre**, la **pobreza**, la **desigualdad**, la **discriminación**, el **analfabetismo**, los problemas medioambientales... Hoy en día, en parte debido a la globalización, muchos de estos problemas tienen una envergadura mundial. Sin embargo, no afectan por igual a todos los países.

Un estudio reciente demuestra que los ciudadanos de los países en desarrollo se preocupan menos por los temas económicos, como la **crisis** actual, que por problemas sociales, como la **corrupción** o la **delincuencia**.

En Colombia, por ejemplo, el desempleo es una de las mayores preocupaciones, muy por encima de los **conflictos armados** o el **terrorismo**.

No debemos perder de vista que algunos problemas mundiales dan lugar a otros muchos y afectan al desarrollo de los países, por lo que deberían ser una prioridad para las autoridades. Es el caso, por ejemplo, del **tráfico** y el **abuso de drogas**, que están relacionados con el **crimen organizado** y la **violencia**.

29 de abril de 2014

NUESTRO MUNDO

por GERARDO LEAL

Uno de los mayores problemas que tiene hoy la sociedad mundial es el impacto medioambiental creado por el alto nivel de **residuos tóxicos y radiactivos** producidos por la industrialización. Para preservar el medio ambiente deben potenciarse alternativas que favorezcan el **ahorro energético** y el **desarrollo sostenible**, como aprovechar el sol y el viento para producir **energía solar** y **eólica**, favorecer la **agricultura ecológica**, etc.

59 **Tus preocupaciones**

▶ **Piensa**. ¿Cuáles son los cinco problemas de la ficha de Vocabulario que más te preocupan? Haz una lista.

 ▶ **Habla** con dos compañeros(as). ¿Qué problemas les preocupan más a ellos(as)? Justifiquen sus respuestas.

Más vocabulario

Problemas sociales

las armas de fuego: pistolas, escopetas, fusiles, etc.
el delito: acción que va contra la ley.
el robo: quitarle la propiedad a alguien sin su permiso.

¡Atención!
perjudicar	to damage, to harm
el prejuicio	prejudice

272 doscientos setenta y dos

Differentiated Instruction

DEVELOPING LEARNERS

- Ask students to complete the sentences with the appropriate word: *armas de fuego, hambre, residuos, analfabetismo, organizado*.
  1. *Los ... tóxicos y radiactivos crean problemas medioambientales.* (residuos)
  2. *Las pistolas y las escopetas son...* (armas de fuego)
  3. *El tráfico de drogas y el crimen ... aumentan la violencia.* (organizado)
  4. *Una sociedad que tiene muchas personas que no saben ni leer ni escribir sufre de...* (analfabetismo)
  5. *Para reducir la pobreza hay que eliminar el...* (hambre)

EXPANDING LEARNERS

- Ask students to review the highlighted words on the page as well as those in the *Más vocabulario* feature. Then, have them make a two-column chart and classify these words under *Palabras positivas* and *Palabras negativas*. Ask students to explain in writing why they have classified the words this way. Review their work and call on students to read some of their explanations. Next, ask students to write a sentence for each of three positive words and three negative ones and share them with the rest of the class.

60 Noticias nacionales

 ▶ **Escucha** y escribe un titular para cada noticia.

 ▶ **Habla** con tu compañero(a). Escriban una noticia de actualidad de su país o estado. Incluyan un titular y una ilustración.

las drogas
pasan factura

Modelo

A. *Podemos escribir una noticia sobre el abuso de las drogas porque afecta a muchos jóvenes. Y el consumo empieza antes que hace unos años.*

B. *De acuerdo. El titular podría ser «Baja la edad de inicio en el consumo de drogas».*

61 Problemas y soluciones

▶ **Completa** una tabla como esta con algunos problemas sociales y medioambientales.

Problemas	Causa(s)	Consecuencia(s)
1. el analfabetismo		
2. el hambre		
3. la delincuencia		
4. ...		

 ▶ **Habla** con tu compañero(a). Compartan sus ideas y hagan una única tabla. Añadan otra columna con soluciones para cada problema a nivel local, nacional o internacional.

 **COMUNIDADES**

VOLUNTARIADO JUVENIL EN PERÚ

El Ministerio de Educación de Perú ha establecido un programa de voluntariado para los jóvenes peruanos con el objetivo de incrementar su participación en los tres ejes del programa: pobreza, asistencia en desastres y desarrollo. Este programa hace más eficiente el proceso: un joven o una organización que necesite voluntarios se inscriben en el sistema y este pone en contacto a los jóvenes con las organizaciones a la vez que hace un seguimiento y asesora a los voluntarios.

62 **Investiga.** ¿Hay algún programa así en tu país? ¿Cuáles son los beneficios de ese tipo de organización de voluntariado? ¿Hay alguna desventaja? Justifica tus respuestas.

doscientos setenta y tres **273**

Unit 5

DESAFÍO 3

Vocabulario – Problemas sociales y medioambientales

62. After completing this activity, ask students if they are or have been working as volunteers. Have those students share their experiences with the class. Do they recommend becoming volunteers? Why? For students who have not been volunteers, encourage them to think of volunteer activities in which they would like to participate.

 AUDIO SCRIPT
See page 239M.

 COMUNIDADES

Voluntariado juvenil en Perú

Similar to the diverse volunteer offerings in Perú, one of the major U.S. volunteer programs is the Peace Corps, which offers American college graduates the opportunity to participate in different technological, environmental, social, educational, and health programs—mainly in rural areas in developing countries. While the program is available in all continents, Latin America is one of the preferred areas for volunteering.

Answer Key

59. Answers will vary.
  ▶ Answers will vary.
60. Answers will vary. Sample answers:
  1. Nos llega la energía eólica
  2. Aumenta la delincuencia en la región
  3. Se acusa a políticos de corrupción
  4. Aumento alarmante de la pobreza
  ▶ Answers will vary.
61. Answers will vary.
  ▶ Answers will vary.
62. Answers will vary.

Additional Resources

Fans Online activities
Practice Workbook

273

HERITAGE LANGUAGE LEARNERS

- Ask students to describe the social and environmental problems that are foremost in their family's country of origin as well as those that are of most concern to them and to their families. Then, ask students to describe what is being done to eradicate the problem or improve the situation, and what organizations or associations are responsible for this. Encourage students to bring some relevant news articles that address the problems and their solutions, and share this information with the rest of the class.

CRITICAL THINKING

- Ask students one or all of the following questions in order to enable a classroom discussion on the corresponding topic:
  1. *¿Cómo contribuyen la pobreza y la ignorancia a la delincuencia?*
  2. *Para eliminar el papel del crimen organizado en el tráfico de drogas, ¿se debe legalizar su uso?*
  3. *¿Es más violento el mundo hoy que hace un siglo? ¿Por qué creen eso? Citen ejemplos.*
- Encourage all students to participate.

DESAFÍO 3

Gramática – Expresar condición

Presentation

- In this section, students will learn how to express unlikely, hypothetical, or contrary-to-fact conditions in the past.

Activities	Standards	Resources
Gramática	1.2, 3.1	
63.	1.2, 3.1	
64.	1.3	
65.	1.2	Audio
66.	1.3	
67.	1.1, 1.3, 5.1	

Teaching Suggestions

Warm-Up / Independent Starter

- Have students complete these sentences:
  - Si reciclamos...
  - Si los gobiernos luchan contra la corrupción...
  - Si ganara un millón de dólares...
  - Si ahorráramos energía...

Preparation

- Before students read the grammar presentation, have them review the grammar on page 164. Then, ask students to revise and correct (if necessary) their sentences from the Independent Starter.

- Ask students to read the *Gramática* feature on page 274 silently, and have them prepare questions about any points they do not understand. Clarify their questions in a class discussion. To emphasize the difference between the two types of sentences introduced in the presentation, complete activity 63 as a class.

- Have students transform their Independent Starter sentences into contrary-to-fact statements. For example: *Si hubiéramos reciclado, habría menos residuos. Si hubiera ganado un millón de dólares, habría destinado una parte a luchar contra el hambre.* Call on volunteers to read their sentences aloud and explain their meanings. You may want to have students translate some of their sentences into English so that they can see the parallelism in the sequence of tenses.

Gramática

Expresar condición

Oraciones condicionales irreales. El pluscuamperfecto de subjuntivo

- Para hablar de condiciones que no se cumplieron en el pasado (condicionales irreales), utilizamos el pluscuamperfecto *(past perfect)* de subjuntivo.

  Si hubiéramos ahorrado energía, ahora tendríamos más recursos.
  If we had saved energy, we would have more resources now.

- El pluscuamperfecto de subjuntivo se forma con el imperfecto de subjuntivo del verbo auxiliar haber.

PLUSCUAMPERFECTO DE SUBJUNTIVO. VERBOS REGULARES

	Ayudar	Comer	Vivir
yo	hubiera ayudado	hubiera comido	hubiera vivido
tú	hubieras ayudado	hubieras comido	hubieras vivido
usted, él, ella	hubiera ayudado	hubiera comido	hubiera vivido
nosotros(as)	hubiéramos ayudado	hubiéramos comido	hubiéramos vivido
vosotros(as)	hubierais ayudado	hubierais comido	hubierais vivido
ustedes, ellos(as)	hubieran ayudado	hubieran comido	hubieran vivido

Los tiempos verbales en las condicionales irreales

- Para expresar qué ocurriría en el presente si se hubiera cumplido una condición, usa esta estructura:

Si + pluscuamperfecto subjuntivo + condicional
si clause (condition)   main clause (result)

  Si hubiéramos acabado con la pobreza, ahora no existiría la injusticia social.

- Para expresar qué habría ocurrido en el pasado si se hubiera cumplido una condición, usa esta otra estructura:

Si + pluscuamperfecto subjuntivo + condicional perfecto
si clause (condition)   main clause (result)

  Si la policía no hubiera detenido a los terroristas, habrían cometido un atentado.

63 **Explica.** Lee estas oraciones. ¿Qué diferencia hay entre ellas?

  a. Si la economía hubiera crecido, no aumentaría el desempleo.
  b. Si la economía hubiera crecido, no habría aumentado el desempleo.

64 **Si hubiéramos...**

  ▶ **Completa** estas oraciones de forma lógica.

  1. Si hubiéramos usado más energía solar y eólica...
  2. Si hubiéramos potenciado el desarrollo sostenible...

274 doscientos setenta y cuatro

Differentiated Instruction

DEVELOPING LEARNERS

- Ask students to complete these sentences with the correct form of *el pluscuamperfecto* of the verb in parentheses:

  1. Si (nosotros – desarrollar) la energía eólica, habríamos ganado una fortuna. (hubiéramos desarrollado)
  2. Si los gobernantes no (ser) corruptos, ahora tendría más fe en los políticos. (hubieran sido)
  3. Si esas fábricas (emitir) residuos tóxicos, habrían dañado el medio ambiente. (hubieran emitido)
  4. Si ella no (cometer) el delito, ahora no estaría en la cárcel. (hubiera cometido)

EXPANDING LEARNERS

- Ask students the following questions. After they share their answers, encourage a whole-class discussion on these topics.

  1. Si hubieras sido el director de una escuela en la que fuera común el abuso de drogas, ¿qué habrías hecho para resolver el problema?
  2. Si hubieras sido presidente de EE. UU. a finales del siglo xx, ¿qué políticas de desarrollo sostenible habrías promovido?
  3. Si hubieras podido eliminar el crimen organizado, ¿cómo lo habrías hecho?

65 Consecuencias

▶ **Escucha** y elige la opción correcta.

1. **a.** Si Eva no hubiera perdido el autobús, habría visto el programa sobre las armas de fuego.
   b. Si Eva no hubiera perdido el autobús, vería el programa sobre las armas de fuego.

2. **a.** Si a Ethan no le hubieran robado la cartera, no habría denunciado el robo a la policía.
   b. Si a Ethan no le hubieran robado la cartera, no denunciaría el robo a la policía.

3. **a.** Si hubieran sabido los efectos, la gente no habría consumido alimentos transgénicos.
   b. Si hubieran sabido los efectos, la gente no consumiría alimentos transgénicos.

4. **a.** Si no hubiera habido tanta contaminación en México, Ethan se habría mudado allí.
   b. Si no hubiera habido tanta contaminación en México, Ethan se mudaría allí.

5. **a.** Si no les hubiera preocupado el futuro, no habrían usado energía solar en casa.
   b. Si no les hubiera preocupado el futuro, no usarían energía solar en casa.

66 ¿Qué habría pasado?

▶ **Escribe** oraciones condicionales irreales siguiendo el modelo.

Modelo El uso de fuentes de energía alternativas ayuda a preservar el medio ambiente.
 → *Si hubiéramos usado más fuentes de energía alternativas, ahora no habría tanta contaminación.*

1. Aumentaron los robos en tiendas.
2. Este año no se han creado suficientes puestos de trabajo para los jóvenes.
3. Hay nuevas enfermedades que se relacionan con el consumo de alimentos transgénicos.
4. Las guerras entre los carteles de la droga causaron cientos de muertes este año.
5. La utilización sostenible de los recursos naturales tiene muchas ventajas.
6. Los movimientos indigenistas incrementan su actividad en Latinoamérica.

67 Si yo hubiera...

▶ **Escribe** seis oraciones explicando condiciones que no se cumplieron en el pasado y que han afectado a tu vida presente.

Modelo *Si hubiera hecho más ejercicio, ahora estaría más atlética. Y si hubiera estudiado un poco más el año pasado, habría sacado mejores notas.*

▶ **Habla** con tu compañero(a) y comparen sus oraciones. ¿Son semejantes o muy diferentes?

doscientos setenta y cinco 275

HERITAGE LANGUAGE LEARNERS

• After students complete activity 66, ask them to look for articles in the Spanish-language press that deal with social or environmental issues. Students may find these papers online. They should select a few headlines that are similar in presentation to the sentences in activity 66. Ask students to write about what could have happened if people or circumstances had treated the situation differently. Call on volunteers to read one or two headlines and their corresponding sentences aloud.

MULTIPLE INTELLIGENCES:
Verbal-Linguistic Intelligence

• Ask students to work with their partners from activity 67. Have students write one or two paragraphs describing how their partners can improve their behavior. For example: *Si hubieras estudiado más, habrías sacado mejores notas. Pero, puedes modificar tus hábitos de estudio. A partir de hoy, debes dedicar dos horas diarias a las tareas.* Ask students to share these suggestions with their partners and address any disagreements they may have.

Unit 5

DESAFÍO 3

Gramática – Expresar condición

Activities

65. Before playing the recording, ask students to read the sentences and explain the differences in meaning between the pairs.

67. Before doing this activity, ask students to write two things they did not do this past year and the reasons for not doing them. Write on the board: *La profesora no viajó a Latinoamérica porque tuvo que trabajar. Si no hubiera tenido que trabajar, habría ido a Latinoamérica.* Discuss the example with the class, and then ask students to form sentences with their examples.

 AUDIO SCRIPT
See page 239M.

Answer Key

63. La primera oración expresa qué ocurriría ahora y la segunda expresa qué habría ocurrido en el pasado si se hubiera cumplido una condición.

64. Answers will vary. Sample answers:
1. ... habría menos contaminación.
2. ... nuestra economía sería más fuerte.

65. 1. a   2. b   3. a   4. a   5. b

66. Answers will vary. Sample answers:
1. Si la policía hubiera combatido la delincuencia, no habrían aumentado los robos.
2. Si se hubieran creado más puestos de trabajo, no tendríamos tantos jóvenes desempleados.
3. Si no hubiéramos consumido alimentos transgénicos, no tendríamos nuevas enfermedades.
4. Si se hubiera acabado con los carteles, no habría habido tantas muertes.

67. Answers will vary.
   ▶ Answers will vary.

Additional Resources

Fans Online activities
Practice Workbook

275

DESAFÍO 3

Gramática – Expresar tiempo

Presentation

- In this section, students will review and expand on how to express when actions take place in relation to one another in the present, past, and future.

Activities	Standards	Resources
Gramática	1.2, 3.1	
68.	1.2, 3.1	
69.	1.2	
70.	1.3, 3.1	
71.	1.2, 1.3	Audio
72. Comparaciones	1.2, 1.3, 2.1, 2.2, 3.2, 4.2	

Teaching Suggestions

Warm-Up / Independent Starter

- Write the following sentences on the board, and have students identify the conjugation of the underlined verbs:

  1. *Cuando hago la tarea, escucho música.* (present indicative, present indicative)

  2. *Cuando termine el curso, nos iremos de vacaciones.* (present subjunctive, future)

  3. *En cuanto comía, se acostaba.* (imperfect indicative, imperfect indicative)

Preparation

- Have students read the grammar presentation silently. Then go over the explanations, emphasizing that the use of subjunctive is linked to future actions while the indicative is linked to present or past actions. Draw students' attention to the fact that we use *antes/después de que* only when the main clause and the dependent clause have different subjects. If not, *antes/después de* + infinitive should be used.

- As a class, discuss the Independent Starter. Then have students change the sequence of tenses of the sentences (e.g., *Cuando haga la tarea, escucharé música*). Call on volunteers to read their new sentences, and then analyze with the class the changes in mood and/or tense for each sentence.

276

Gramática

Expresar tiempo

- Recuerda: para expresar el tiempo de una acción o una secuencia de eventos se utiliza generalmente cuando, antes de (que), después de (que) o mientras.

  Cuando reciclamos, preservamos el medio ambiente.

- Estas otras expresiones temporales son también frecuentes:
  - En cuanto (*as soon as*): Llámame **en cuanto** llegues.
  - Hasta que (*until*): No salgas **hasta que** te llame.
  - Siempre que (*whenever*): **Siempre que** viaja, me llama.
  - Al + *infinitivo*: Llámame por teléfono **al llegar**.

- La cláusula temporal puede ir delante o detrás de la cláusula principal.

EXPRESIONES DE TIEMPO

> cuando
> antes/después de (que)
> siempre que
> mientras
> al + infinitivo
> en cuanto
> hasta que

Indicativo y subjuntivo con expresiones de tiempo

- Las expresiones de tiempo, excepto antes de que, pueden introducir un verbo en indicativo o en subjuntivo. En general:
  - Usa el **indicativo** cuando la cláusula principal se refiere a eventos pasados, presentes o habituales.
  - Usa el **subjuntivo** cuando la cláusula principal se refiere a eventos futuros.

  Atención: estas expresiones de tiempo nunca van seguidas de un verbo en futuro.

INDICATIVO Y SUBJUNTIVO CON EXPRESIONES DE TIEMPO

	INDICATIVO (idea de pasado o de presente)	SUBJUNTIVO (idea de futuro)
cuando	Cuando **usamos** el transporte público, ahorramos energía.	Cuando **usemos** el transporte público, ahorraremos energía.
después de que	Después de que **cambiaste** las bombillas, bajó la factura eléctrica.	Después de que **cambies** las bombillas, bajará la factura eléctrica.
siempre que	Siempre que **uso** envases, los reciclo.	Siempre que **use** envases, los reciclaré.
en cuanto	Me apunté a la ONG en cuanto **pude**.	Apúntate a la ONG en cuanto **puedas**.
hasta que	Esa empresa no controló sus residuos tóxicos hasta que la **multaron**.	Esa empresa no controlará sus residuos tóxicos hasta que la **multen**.

- Recuerda: antes de que y después de que se usan cuando la cláusula principal y la dependiente tienen distintos sujetos. En cambio, cuando las dos cláusulas tienen el mismo sujeto, usamos antes de y después de + infinitivo.

  Lee la etiqueta **antes de que te vendan** un producto químico.
  Lee la etiqueta **antes de comprar** un producto químico.

 Explica. ¿Por qué crees que antes de que lleva siempre subjuntivo?

Differentiated Instruction

DEVELOPING LEARNERS

- Have students complete these sentences:

  1. *Después de que (ellos – multar) a esa fábrica, disminuirán las emisiones de residuos tóxicos.* (multen)

  2. *Cuando (nosotros – favorecer) el desarrollo sostenible, protegemos el medio ambiente.* (favorecemos)

  3. *Siempre que (haber) hambre, habrá pobreza.* (haya)

  4. *Habrá discriminación hasta que la sociedad (respetar) a todos los ciudadanos.* (respete)

  5. *Cuando (nosotros – resolver) los conflictos, el mundo será más seguro.* (resolvamos)

EXPANDING LEARNERS

- After students complete the activities on these pages, ask them to review the examples in the *Gramática* feature. Then, have students write their own sentences using different time expressions, but leaving a blank for the verb in the dependent clause. Explain that they should write some sentences that require the indicative and others that require the subjunctive. Encourage students to write about social and environmental problems. Next, ask them to exchange papers with a partner, who will complete each sentence. Have students check each other's work.

69 Por lógica

▶ **Une** las dos columnas y escribe oraciones lógicas.

(A)

1. El gobierno se preocupó por la violencia...
2. Ahorraremos energía...
3. Se redujo la contaminación...
4. El hambre y la pobreza no se acabarán...
5. La crisis acabará...

(B)

a. siempre que usemos el transporte público.
b. hasta que todos seamos más solidarios.
c. en cuanto baje el desempleo.
d. cuando aumentaron los robos.
e. después de que se limitó el tráfico.

70 ¿Indicativo o subjuntivo?

▶ **Completa** estas oraciones usando expresiones de tiempo.

1. Se seguirá destruyendo el medio ambiente...
2. El crimen y la violencia aumentan...
3. En las ciudades disminuirá el índice de delincuencia...
4. La injusticia social se evita...
5. Los pueblos indígenas exigirán la igualdad...

Danza indígena (San Salvador).

71 El desafío de Ethan y Eva

▶ **Escucha** y decide si estas oraciones son ciertas o falsas. Después, corrige las falsas.

1. Eva salió de la biblioteca después de tomar notas sobre el indigenismo.
2. Ethan se reunió con Luisa cuando terminaron sus clases.
3. Ethan estuvo con Luisa hasta que llegó Eva.
4. Ricardo no aceptará trabajar en la obra hasta que tenga más información.
5. Ethan y Eva van a trabajar hasta que tengan un primer borrador del guion.

COMPARACIONES

La contaminación en la Ciudad de México

La Ciudad de México es una de las mayores metrópolis del planeta. A causa del enorme tráfico y por estar situada en un valle rodeado de montañas, la contaminación ambiental alcanza niveles alarmantes. Para remediarlo, el gobierno ha puesto en marcha el plan *Hoy no circula*, que consiste en limitar la circulación de vehículos en determinados días y horas según su matrícula.

72 **Piensa.** ¿Qué medidas se han tomado en tu ciudad para reducir la contaminación?

doscientos setenta y siete **277**

Unit 5

DESAFÍO 3

Gramática – Expresar tiempo

Activities

70. While correcting the activity, ask students to identify the time clauses and to point out if they refer to a present, past, or future action.

72. After answering the question individually, divide the class into small groups and ask them to discuss whether the measures taken against pollution in your community are enough. If not, ask students to propose better solutions. If pollution is not an issue in your community, have students come up with other concerning issues.

 AUDIO SCRIPT
See page 239M.

 COMPARACIONES

La contaminación en la Ciudad de México

The program *Hoy no circula* began in 1989. In addition to limitations on days in which drivers can use their cars, there are other measures complementing the program to make it more effective. Among them, requiring emission tests every six months (exceptions are made for new, cleaner cars) and restricting foreign-plated and out-of-state vehicles.

Answer Key

68. Porque *antes de que* se refiere al futuro.
69. 1. d   2. a   3. e   4. b   5. c
70. Answers will vary.
71. 1. F. Saldrá cuando termine de tomar notas.
  2. C.
  3. F. Hasta que llegó Ricardo.
  4. C.
  5. C.
72. Answers will vary.

Additional Resources

Fans Online activities
Practice Workbook

HERITAGE LANGUAGE LEARNERS

• Ask students to cite examples of cities or areas in their family's country of origin where there are high indexes of air pollution. They may research this or talk to family members who have some familiarity with this issue. Ask students to address the solutions that are being discussed or implemented to cope with this problem. If there have been few positive results from these measures, ask students to propose some of their own and share these with the rest of the class.

MULTIPLE INTELLIGENCES:
Verbal-Linguistic Intelligence

• Have students work with a partner and devise a campaign that would reduce pollution in their community, or in another city that has contaminated air or water. Ask them to come up with a list of suggestions that residents should follow, such as *Hay que aumentar el uso del transporte público para reducir el uso de tantos coches.* Encourage students to use some of the expressions that indicate time to show the positive results of their campaign.

277

Unit 5

LECTURA: TEXTO LITERARIO

Presentation

- In this section, students will read a short story by Uruguayan author Cristina Peri Rossi. In addition to answering comprehension questions, students will discuss and analyze the text.

Activities	Standards	Resources
Lectura: texto literario	1.2, 2.2, 3.2	
73.	1.1, 1.2, 1.3, 2.2	
74.	1.1, 1.2	
75.	1.1	

Teaching Suggestions

Warm-Up / Independent Starter

- Ask students to read the title of the text and answer the first question in the *Antes de leer* section.

Preparation

- Call on individual students to share their definitions from the Independent Starter. Write on the board the most accurate definition. Then discuss with students some of the reasons that force people to seek asylum in a foreign country. You may want to explain that the law in the United States considers persecution due to race, religion, nationality, political opinion, or membership in a particular social group as grounds for seeking asylum. A person who seeks asylum must present credible evidence of his or her persecution.

- Have students answer questions #2 and #3 of the *Antes de leer* section individually. Then, conduct a whole-class discussion on these issues. To focus the discussion, you may ask these or similar questions: *¿Qué sentimientos creen que tiene un exiliado hacia su país? ¿Y hacia el país que lo recibe? ¿Creen que se espera que los exiliados se comporten mejor que los ciudadanos del país que lo recibe?* As a conclusion to this discussion, focus students' attention on the picture and ask them to explain how the picture relates to the idea and experience of exile.

278

Antes de leer: estrategias

1. Lee el título del texto. ¿Qué es un exiliado?
2. ¿Cómo crees que se siente un exiliado? Habla con tus compañeros(as) sobre sus sentimientos.
3. ¿Crees que es posible que un exiliado se sienta bien en la sociedad que lo recibe? Justifica tu respuesta.

El exiliado

Su acento lo delata[1]: arrastra un poco las eses y pronuncia de igual manera las b y las v. Entonces se produce cierto silencio a su alrededor.

A partir de ese instante (y también otros) él se siente en la necesidad de compensar a los demás. Oh, es cierto que él es un extranjero y debe hacerse perdonar. Agradece la buena voluntad ajena, esa que consiste en no preguntarle jamás de dónde viene, ni qué hacía antes, si ha solucionado o no los problemas de los papeles, cómo era el lugar donde vivía, si perdió algo en el camino, si se siente solo. Todos están dispuestos a disimular esa pequeña anomalía, a tomarlo en cuenta, pese a todo, a no hacerle preguntas y especialmente a no demostrar ninguna clase de curiosidad por su vida. Para corresponder a tanta amabilidad, él se obstina[2] en ignorar su pasado (hace como si no lo tuviera), reprime[3] cualquier malestar[4] y demuestra gran conocimiento de las plazas de la ciudad, los monumentos, el nombre y la ubicación de las calles, los servicios públicos y la escasa flora del lugar. Puede indicar con precisión la ruta de los autobuses y de los metros y la composición de la Alcaldía, pero, precisamente, el hecho de conocer todos estos datos crea cierta desconfianza a su alrededor y confirma que, en efecto, se trata de un extranjero que vive entre nosotros. Cuando alguien habla de un defecto nacional, él lo convierte de inmediato en una virtud. Por ejemplo, cuando su interlocutor[5], sin mirarlo especialmente fijo, menciona la mezquindad[6] de los habitantes de la ciudad, él afirma que se trata del sano sentido del ahorro que ha permitido prosperar a las familias; si se habla de la rudeza y falta de urbanidad[7] de los transeúntes[8], él asegura que es espontaneidad y falta de inhibiciones; si alguien comenta que en esa ciudad hay poca imaginación y sus habitantes son aburridos, él sugiere que, en realidad, se trata del sentido común de la raza, poco dada[9] —gracias a Dios— al delirio y a la aventura.

278 doscientos setenta y ocho

Differentiated Instruction

DEVELOPING LEARNERS

- Help students comprehend this short story by asking them to first scan it for unfamiliar words and to use the footnotes, cognates, and context clues to help decode the new vocabulary. Then ask students to imagine how they might act and react if they had to live in exile. Explain that showing empathy with the protagonist of the story may help them understand his reactions and attitudes. Now ask students to read the story silently before they take turns reading it aloud in a small group.

EXPANDING LEARNERS

- Ask students what they think about people's *buena voluntad* toward the protagonist when they do not ask him questions about his past. Do they agree with this assessment? Or do they think that asking such questions might lend itself to opening up a conversation that could lead to getting to know someone? Do they think that some foreigners overcompensate by knowing more about his or her new place than the local population? Ask students why they think foreigners might do this. Enable a classroom discussion to hear everyone's opinion.

Si el interlocutor persiste en enumerar los vicios y defectos del país, él da por[10] terminada la conversación con un enfático «¡Ustedes no saben lo que tienen!», y el ciudadano se interrumpe, mira alrededor, algo confuso, convencido de que el exiliado ama más el lugar que él. Pero de inmediato se recupera: no está dispuesto a que nadie hable de su patria superlativamente, si no nació allí. Es entonces cuando el Exiliado comprende que ha cometido una falta irreparable y que, por más esfuerzo que haga, siempre será un extranjero.

CRISTINA PERI ROSSI. *Cuentos.* (http://goo.gl/GD0y30) (selección)

1. lo descubre
2. insiste
3. contiene, domina
4. sensación incómoda

5. persona con la que se habla
6. mala intención, maldad
7. comportamiento adecuado a las normas

8. personas que pasan por un lugar
9. inclinada, orientada
10. considera

73 ¿Comprendes?

▶ **Responde** a estas preguntas y cita las palabras del texto en las que basas tus respuestas.

1. ¿Por qué se dan cuenta los demás de que el exiliado es un extranjero?
2. ¿Cómo se comportan los demás con él? ¿Y él con los demás?
3. ¿En qué consiste la «falta irreparable» que comete el exiliado?

▶ **Responde** a estas preguntas justificando tus respuestas. Después, coméntalas con tus compañeros(as) para averiguar si opinan lo mismo que tú.

1. ¿Crees que el exiliado es sincero cuando se refiere a la «buena voluntad» y la «amabilidad» de los demás? ¿Crees que realmente agradece su actitud?
2. ¿Qué crees que piensa realmente el exiliado de los habitantes de la ciudad?

74 Palabras y expresiones

▶ **Clasifica** las palabras del cuadro en una tabla como esta. Después, compara tu tabla con la de tus compañeros(as). ¿Coinciden en sus opiniones?

tener buena voluntad	ser desconfiado(a)	ser rudo(a)
no tener urbanidad	ser mezquino(a)	ser espontáneo(a)
no tener inhibiciones	tener poca imaginación	tener sentido común

Positivos	Negativos

75 Con tus propias palabras

¿Estás de acuerdo con estas palabras del texto? Coméntalo con tus compañeros(as) y justifica tu respuesta.

> Es cierto que él es un extranjero y **debe hacerse perdonar**.

doscientos setenta y nueve 279

■ Have students work with a partner and alternate reading several lines of the text aloud. After reading the entire text, have pairs write the main ideas of the text.

Activities

73. After completing this activity, ask students to take the role of somebody who lives in exile in a Spanish-speaking country and write a blog entry expressing his or her feelings and first impressions. Encourage them to use time expressions in their narration. If time allows, call on volunteers to share their blog entries with the class.

74. In order to ensure the comprehension of these phrases, have students reread the sentences in which they are used in the text. Then, you may ask students to write new sentences using these phrases in a different context.

Answer Key

73. Answers will vary. Sample answers:
1. Porque tiene un acento diferente: arrastra las eses y pronuncia de igual manera las b y las v.
2. Los demás se muestran indiferentes y no le preguntan nada sobre su vida anterior. Él ignora también su pasado y demuestra un gran conocimiento y admiración por la ciudad donde vive.
3. En intentar demostrar que ama a su nueva patria más que los propios ciudadanos.

▶ Answers will vary.

74. Answers will vary. Sample answers:
Positivos: tener buena voluntad, no tener inhibiciones, ser espontáneo(a), tener sentido común.
Negativos: no tener urbanidad, ser desconfiado(a), ser mezquino(a), tener poca imaginación, ser rudo(a).

75. Answers will vary.

Additional Resources

Fans Online activities

HERITAGE LANGUAGE LEARNERS

• Ask students to interview a family member or a family friend who has had the experience of being *un extranjero* in another land. Students might show the interviewee some passages from this short story and ask if any of the experiences or attitudes described reflect patterns from his or her life. Have students probe the differences between foreigners who surrender part of their identity when adapting to their new place and foreigners who refuse to adapt and what the consequences might be. Have students share their interviews with the class.

SPECIAL-NEEDS LEARNERS

• Allow students with information-processing difficulties to sit in a quiet area of the classroom so they can better process the directions to all the activities and the ideas presented in this literary text. Many students with information-processing difficulties can only concentrate for shorter periods of time. Allow these students additional time to complete reading the article and the activities on the page. Also allow them some breaks while they are working on their reading and the associated activities.

Unit 5
DESAFÍO 3
Comunicación

Presentation

- In this section, students will integrate the vocabulary and grammar skills from *Desafío 3* in order to read and talk about environmental and social issues. They will also make an oral presentation explaining what they do to be part of the solution.

Activities	Standards	Resources
76.	1.1, 1.2, 1.3, 2.1, 2.2, 5.1	
77.	1.1, 1.3, 5.1	
78.	1.3	
79. Final del desafío	1.1, 1.2, 2.1, 2.2	

Teaching Suggestions

Warm-Up / Independent Starter

- Have students list three to five issues that affect large cities, both in their country and in the world.

Preparation

- Ask students to share their Independent Starters. If students did not mention *sobrepoblación* (overpopulation), help them figure it out with questions such as, *¿Dónde viven más personas hoy en día: en el campo o en la ciudad? ¿Por qué? ¿Es esto un problema?*

- Have students work with a partner to think of how some of the problems that people have today in most large cities might have been prevented. Ask students to come up with at least three sentences. For example: *Si los gobiernos hubieran invertido en infraestructuras, no tendríamos tantos problemas de tráfico en las ciudades.*

Activities

76. After completing this activity, you may want to divide the class into small groups and have them discuss if the city where they live (or the nearest one) has some of the problems mentioned in the article. Then, have groups write a brief proposal to improve and/or avoid these problems in the future. Invite groups to present their proposals to the class.

280

Comunicación

 76 **Problemas en las ciudades**

 ▶ **Lee** el artículo y responde a las preguntas.

Editorial

El crecimiento de las ciudades

El aumento de habitantes en las ciudades latinoamericanas plantea una serie de problemas de organización social cuya previsión es indispensable. Un reciente informe de las Naciones Unidas muestra que las ciudades han experimentado un fuerte aumento en el número de pobladores. Actualmente, la mitad de la población vive en centros urbanos y el mayor grado de urbanismo se encuentra en Latinoamérica.

Las condiciones de la urbanización han contribuido a incrementar y consolidar grandes núcleos de pobreza, debido a que no se tomaron las previsiones para generar condiciones aceptables de vida. Además de las dificultades que sufren particularmente los habitantes pobres por las carencias de servicios indispensables y de viviendas adecuadas, los conglomerados se han convertido en lugares de asentamiento de redes de delito y en una fuente de problemas de seguridad que afectan en primer lugar a los pobladores locales. Los gobiernos deben tener en cuenta esta tendencia para, cuando menos, evitar el agravamiento de los problemas que genera.

Fuente: http://edant.clarin.com
(selección)

1. ¿Qué es lo que está causando problemas de organización social en las ciudades, según el texto?

2. ¿Cuáles son los problemas que se derivan del aumento de población en los centros urbanos?

3. ¿Qué significa la palabra *carencia*? ¿A qué tipo de servicios indispensables se refiere el texto?

4. ¿Cuál es el propósito de este artículo? ¿A quién está dirigido?

 ▶ **Habla** con dos compañeros(as). Preparen una lista de las medidas que podrían haber tomado los gobiernos para evitar los problemas de urbanización que describe el artículo.

Modelo   *Si se hubieran construido viviendas adecuadas en cuanto comenzó el crecimiento de las ciudades, los habitantes más pobres habrían…*

77 **Ciencia ficción**

▶ **Imagina.** ¿Qué problemas sociales y medioambientales habrá en el año 2100? ¿Cuáles se habrán solucionado? Escribe un párrafo siguiendo el modelo.

Modelo   *Estamos en el año 2100. Si no hubiéramos comenzado a reciclar hace muchos años, ahora no habría árboles. Además…*

 ▶ **Habla** con dos compañeros(as) y comparen sus predicciones. ¿Son optimistas o pesimistas?

280 doscientos ochenta

Differentiated Instruction

DEVELOPING LEARNERS

- Ask students to complete the following sentences with the correct form of the verb in parentheses:
  1. *Cuando (ver) al director, díselo. (veas)*
  2. *Antes de que (haber) más conflictos armados, debemos firmar una alianza. (haya)*
  3. *Hasta que ellos no (reducir) las emisiones tóxicas, habrá contaminación. (reduzcan)*
  4. *Cuando (llover), siempre bajan las temperaturas. (llueve)*
  5. *Después de que yo (regresar), te ayudaré con las tareas. (regrese)*

EXPANDING LEARNERS

- Ask students to work with a partner and make a list of what they consider the major crises of the world and of their community. Suggest that they include at least three items of concern in each category. Then, ask them to talk about how they would go about eliminating or ameliorating these problems and, based on this, write a few paragraphs describing their solutions to these challenges. Call on volunteers to share their ideas with the rest of the class.

78 **Tus decisiones**

 ▶ **Haz** una presentación oral. ¿Qué acciones realizas para lograr estos objetivos? Utiliza expresiones de tiempo.

Modelo   apoyar el comercio local
→ *Compro productos locales siempre que puedo para ayudar a los agricultores de mi comunidad.*

1. Evitar el consumo de alimentos transgénicos.
2. Cuidar el medio ambiente.
3. Rechazar la injusticia social.
4. Apoyar el comercio justo.

Final del desafío

Cuando tengas tiempo, podemos leer el guion en voz alta y ensayar la escena.

Perfecto. Me gusta mucho cómo han explicado el inicio del movimiento indigenista y el enfoque que le han dado a la escena: respeto a las culturas indígenas, igualdad de derechos...

Y díganme: ¿Qué soluciones se les ocurren para mejorar la situación de los pueblos indígenas?

79 **La escena**

▶ **Escribe.** ¿Qué problemas del cuadro crees que han tratado Ethan y Eva en el guion de la escena que han escrito? ¿Por qué?

| discriminación | robo | desigualdad | delincuencia | terrorismo |

▶ **Habla** con tu compañero(a). ¿Cómo responderían ustedes a la pregunta de Ricardo?

doscientos ochenta y uno 281

---

78. You may wish to turn this activity into a small group activity. Ask each group to prepare a visual presentation to share with the class. In addition to explaining what they do regarding the issues mentioned in the activity, encourage students to include a statement at the end of their presentation in which they call their classmates to action on these issues. Have the class vote for the best presentation.

79. In order to answer Ricardo's question, have student pairs create a colorful flyer with a proposal to improve the situation of the indigenous people. Encourage them to use images and to create a slogan for their campaign. You may want to post students' flyers around the classroom and invite the class to read them.

Answer Key

76. Answers will vary. Sample answers:
1. El aumento de la población en las ciudades latinoamericanas.
2. La pobreza, el delito y la inseguridad de los habitantes de las ciudades.
3. Es la falta de algo. En el texto se habla de servicios de salud, alimentación y vivienda como servicios indispensables.
4. Denunciar la falta de previsión ante el aumento de habitantes en las ciudades. Está dirigido a los gobiernos para que tomen las medidas necesarias.
▶ Answers will vary.

77. Answers will vary.
▶ Answers will vary.

78. Answers will vary.

79. Answers will vary.
▶ Answers will vary.

Additional Resources

Fans Online activities
Practice Workbook

HERITAGE LANGUAGE LEARNERS

• Ask students to compare and contrast urban neighborhoods in their family's country of origin with those in this country. Ask students to address the housing that is typically offered, the services and features that are commonly found in these neighborhoods, and how residents deal with environmental problems, crime and vandalism, water quality, population density, accessibility to public transportation, and green spaces. Ask students to make an oral presentation to the class. Encourage them to accompany their talk with images of neighborhoods from printed media or the Internet.

MULTIPLE INTELLIGENCES:
Visual-Spatial Intelligence

• Have students design a neighborhood that offers low-income residents features such as decent low-cost housing with city utilities, supermarkets, schools, libraries, access to public transportation, houses of worship, and green spaces with plenty of recreational areas for people of all ages. Ask students to work in small groups and come up with a description of the neighborhood and a design on poster board for it. Display students' work in the classroom.

Unit 5
Para terminar

Presentation

- In this section, students will review the unit objectives and put them into practice. They will learn about Violeta Parra, a famous Chilean songwriter and singer who revolutionized Chilean folk music. They will also select one of the following *desafíos* to develop: write an imaginary dialogue between two current Hispanic leaders, research a singer or musical group from the Spanish-speaking world who sings songs of social commentary, or research the *Consejo Indígena de Centro América (CICA)* and prepare a presentation about this organization.

Activities	Standards	Resources
80.	1.2, 1.3, 2.1, 2.2, 3.1, 3.2, 5.2	Audio
81. Tu desafío	1.2, 1.3, 2.1, 2.2, 3.1, 3.2, 5.1, 5.2	

Teaching Suggestions

Warm-Up / Independent Starter

- Ask students to think of a famous Hispanic political leader, social activist, or singer that they would like to learn more about. Have students jot down some of the things they would like to know about this person.

Preparation

- Have students go back and review the vocabulary and grammar sections in this unit. Then ask them to use their notes from the Independent Starter to write six questions about the person they chose. Encourage students to include questions about the person's life, his or her most important experiences, and the things this person is famous for. Have students include one or two questions that use expressions of certainty and/or doubt (e.g., *¿Es cierto que estudió en Colombia?*).

- Ask students to get together with a partner and read aloud their questions. Can the partners identify the person based on the questions? Once partners have identified the person, have them answers the questions they know and make guesses about the things they do not know (e.g., *Sé que estudió en Colombia. No estoy seguro de que su primer disco fuera un éxito*).

282

Para terminar

Todo junto

LEER, ESCUCHAR Y ESCRIBIR

80 **Una artista comprometida**

▶ **Lee** la información sobre la cantante Violeta Parra y completa las oraciones con la información que extraigas del texto.

Violeta Parra: una artista comprometida

Violeta Parra fue una cantante y compositora chilena que tuvo una gran influencia en la música, no solo chilena, sino de todo el mundo. Ella nació en una pequeña ciudad del sur de Chile en 1917 y murió en 1967. Durante toda su vida estuvo involucrada en movimientos progresistas y fue políticamente muy activa. Desde el punto de vista musical se la considera la inspiradora de la Nueva Canción Chilena, un estilo que incorporaba el folclore tradicional, la poesía y la protesta social. Una de las canciones más famosas de Violeta Parra fue *Gracias a la vida*, popularizada por la argentina Mercedes Sosa en toda Hispanoamérica, y por Joan Báez en los Estados Unidos.

1. Es cierto que… 2. Es probable que… 3. Es evidente que… 4. No hay duda de que…

▶ **Escucha** una noticia relacionada con el texto que has leído y elige la opción correcta.

1. El concierto es…
   a. por la mañana.   b. a mediodía.   c. por la noche.

2. En el concierto hay ocho artistas invitados y…
   a. 70 músicos.   b. 30 músicos.   c. 80 músicos.

3. El invitado internacional es…
   a. chileno.   b. argentino.   c. venezolano.

4. Pedro Aznar conoció la música de Violeta Parra…
   a. de niño.   b. a los 15 años.   c. cuando empezó a cantar.

5. Según Pedro Aznar, Violeta Parra dio gran popularidad a la música…
   a. sinfónica.   b. folclórica.   c. tradicional.

▶ **Investiga** sobre una de las canciones de Violeta Parra y escribe un párrafo. Explica:

1. ¿Cuál es el tema de la canción?
2. ¿A quién crees que está dirigida la canción? ¿Por qué?
3. ¿Te parece que tiene un contenido social? ¿Por qué?

282 doscientos ochenta y dos

Differentiated Instruction

DEVELOPING LEARNERS

- Explain to students that they are going to design a new logo for *el Consejo Indígena de Centro América*. Ask them to go to its webpage to see the current logo and to read about the organization in order to get ideas for images and possible words that may appear on the logo. When students complete their designs, call on volunteers to present the new logo and to give a brief explanation on the significance of the images, colors, words, and shapes they have chosen.

EXPANDING LEARNERS

- Ask students to work in small groups and explain that they are going to be protesting or supporting something today. First, they need to decide what kind of issue (e.g., political, social, environmental) they are going to protest or support. Next, ask them to select the medium through which they will channel their protests or support. They may choose a printed medium, a song or play, or a public demonstration. Give them time to prepare their "campaign" and ask them to share it with the rest of the class.

Tu desafío

81 **Los desafíos**

¿Recuerdas los desafíos que Tim y Andy prepararon para los personajes? ¿Cuál te gusta más? Elige una de estas opciones y resuelve tu desafío.

DESAFÍO Ⓐ

Imagínate un encuentro entre dos líderes hispanos(as) de la actualidad y escribe un diálogo entre ellos(as). Incluye lo siguiente:

- Las razones por las que es bueno reunirse.
- Un problema social o político que tienen que resolver.
- Los argumentos de cada uno.
- Ideas para resolver el problema.

DESAFÍO Ⓑ

Haz una investigación sobre un grupo o cantante hispano que cante canciones de contenido social. Prepara una presentación que incluya:

- Una breve biografía sobre el/la artista.
- Una explicación sobre los temas de sus canciones.
- Un fragmento de la letra de una de sus canciones que muestre ese contenido social.

El cantante Juanes en concierto.

DESAFÍO Ⓒ

Haz una investigación en la página oficial del Consejo Indígena de Centro América (www.cicaregional.org). Prepara un informe que incluya:

- Información histórica sobre el CICA y su finalidad.
- Una explicación sobre los proyectos que tienen.
- Uno de los temas en los que están trabajando que te gusta especialmente.

- Call on volunteer pairs to present their questions, answers, and guesses in front of the class. Does the class know some of the answers for the questions whose answers were guessed? If they know the answers, encourage students to share them (e.g., *Está demostrado que su primer disco no fue un éxito porque tardó varios años en volver a cantar*). Have students research (as homework or in class, if time allows) those questions whose answers no one knew. You may want to use some of the students' questions, answers, and guesses to assess their command of the vocabulary and grammar structures presented in this unit.

Activities

80. Call on a volunteer to read the text aloud. Ask students if they know the song *Gracias a la vida*. If you have access to Internet in the classroom, you may want to play the song and have students take notes as they listen. Before playing the recording for the second part of this activity, have students read the sentences and choices carefully. You may wish to talk about the differences between *música sinfónica*, *folclórica*, and *tradicional*.

81. Have students share their work in the classroom and have the class vote on the best entry in each category.

 AUDIO SCRIPT
See page 239M.

Answer Key

80. Answers will vary.
▶ 1. c   2. a   3. b   4. a   5. c
▶ Answers will vary.
81. Answers will vary.

Additional Resources

Fans Online activities
Practice Workbook

HERITAGE LANGUAGE LEARNERS

- Ask students to identify some social or political issues in their heritage country. Have them explain how these problems are progressing. Are they being solved amicably, or have they been resolved? Are they escalating? Is there reason to be concerned that a non-resolution will lead to a more serious, or even armed, conflict? Encourage students to compare these problems with those in this country. Students may express their ideas in writing or in a brief presentation to the class.

CRITICAL THINKING

- Ask students to predict what they think will be the major political, social, and environmental problems in the next century. Have students consider, for example, what we have learned from past armed conflicts, people's tendency to not always learn from their mistakes, what new political allies there will be, what indigenous groups will still survive and how they will be treated, the influence of the Spanish language, and the state of the environment. Enable a classroom discussion on this topic and encourage all to participate.

283

Unit 5
MAPA CULTURAL
La inmigración hispana en los Estados Unidos

Presentation

- This section presents information about Hispanic immigration to the United States. The images serve as a reference point for additional cultural readings and activities that expand on the skills students learned in this unit.

Activities	Standards	Resources
Mapa cultural	1.2, 2.1, 2.2, 3.1, 5.1	
82.	1.1, 2.1, 2.2, 3.2, 5.1, 5.2	

Cultural Topics

- **La comunidad puertorriqueña.** Puerto Ricans are American citizens, and as such are not immigrants. However, they generally self-identify as Hispanics of Puerto Rican origin. According to data from the 2010 Census, there are 4.6 million Puerto Ricans in the United States, comprising 9% of the Hispanic population in the country. Puerto Ricans are most likely to live in the Northeast, with 1.5 million residing in New York and New Jersey. Today, however, Florida has become the primary destination for many Puerto Ricans.

- **Población hispana de los Estados Unidos.** Hispanic immigrants are present in every state of the United States. However, as is the case with other immigrant groups, Hispanics are more numerous in certain urban areas and in certain states. According to data from the 2010 Census, Hispanics account for 29% of the total population in the West, 16% in the South, 13% in the Northeast, and 7% in the Midwest. Cities with the largest percentage (more than 80%) of Hispanics include Laredo (TX), Hialeah (FL), Brownsville (TX), McAllen (TX), and El Paso (TX). States with the largest Hispanic populations (of one million or more) are California, Texas, Florida, New York, Illinois, Arizona, New Jersey, and Colorado.

Teaching Suggestions

Warm-Up / Independent Starter

- Ask students to list the nationalities of the different Hispanic groups or communities who reside in their state.

284

La inmigración hispana en los Estados Unidos

Los Estados Unidos son el principal país de destino para los emigrantes de todo el mundo. Según datos de la Oficina del Censo, el año 2010 había en los Estados Unidos 40 millones de personas que habían nacido en otros países. El 53% de ellas procedían de Latinoamérica, especialmente de México, el Caribe (Cuba y República Dominicana) y Centroamérica (El Salvador, Guatemala y Honduras).

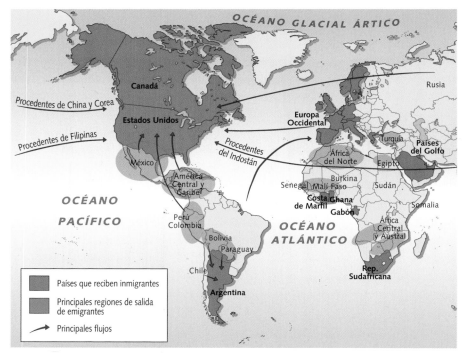

Principales flujos migratorios a finales del siglo XX y principios del XXI.

Differentiated Instruction

DEVELOPING LEARNERS

- Ask students to write some journal entries from the point of view of a student their age from Mexico, Cuba, the Dominican Republic, or any other Spanish-speaking country who has immigrated with his or her family to the United States. Have students record their first impressions of their new country, their difficulties expressing themselves in English, any discrimination they might have endured, their possible homesickness for their heritage country, any other problems they have encountered, and what they hope to accomplish in their newly adopted land.

EXPANDING LEARNERS

- Ask students to imagine what the United States would be like today if the Spaniards had made many more permanent settlements when they first came to America, and the British had not had a strong presence in the colonies. Have students predict how the Spanish influence would have shaped the culture, customs, religion, and language of the people, and how the architecture, music, and art would be affected. You may want to enable a classroom discussion, or ask students to put their thoughts in writing.

Los mexicanos

Según datos del censo, en 2010 había en los Estados Unidos cerca de 12 millones de inmigrantes mexicanos. Las comunidades mexicanas más numerosas están en California, Texas, Arizona, Illinois y Colorado, donde también se concentra la mayor parte de la población americana de origen mexicano.

> Se dice que Los Ángeles es la segunda ciudad del mundo con más personas de origen mexicano (inmigrantes y mexicanoamericanos), después de la Ciudad de México.

Los cubanos

Desde la segunda mitad del siglo XX muchos cubanos han abandonado su isla por motivos políticos y económicos, y se han instalado en los Estados Unidos, sobre todo en el Gran Miami. Allí se ha asentado una próspera comunidad que ha contribuido al crecimiento económico de la zona.

Los dominicanos

En los Estados Unidos viven cerca de un millón y medio de personas de origen dominicano. De ellas, cerca de 900.000 no tenían al nacer la nacionalidad americana.

Las comunidades de dominicanos más numerosas están actualmente en la ciudad de Nueva York y en los estados de New Jersey y la Florida.

> El Desfile Dominicano que se celebra durante el mes de agosto en la Sexta Avenida de Manhattan suele reunir a más de un millón de espectadores.

El Mes de la Herencia Hispana

Desde 1968 se celebra en muchas ciudades de los Estados Unidos el Mes de la Herencia Hispana. Entre el 15 de septiembre y el 15 de octubre se organizan desfiles, exposiciones y muchos otros actos culturales y festivos para reconocer la contribución de la comunidad hispana a la sociedad estadounidense.

82 **Hispanos famosos**

 ▶ **Habla** con tus compañeros(as). ¿Qué personaje de origen hispano admiras más? ¿Por qué?

doscientos ochenta y cinco **285**

MAPA CULTURAL

La inmigración hispana en los Estados Unidos

Preparation

- Invite students to share their Independent Starters. Is there a predominant nationality for Hispanics in your state? As a class, discuss what students know about the Hispanic immigrants in their state. You may want to consider some of these questions: How long ago did they come to this country? Why did they come? Is Spanish still their main language of communication?

- Explain that Hispanic immigrants are generally young and, on average, Hispanic families have more children than American families. However, these trends are slowly changing as the number of Hispanics arriving to the United States declines. Hispanics, as other immigrant groups before them, assimilate within two or three generations. For instance, more than half of third-generation Hispanics marry someone outside their ethnic group. Therefore, it seems that Hispanic immigrants are following similar assimilation trends to those followed by other immigrant groups who came to the United States in the past.

Activities

82. Encourage students to research Hispanics who have made important contributions in a variety of fields. You may want to give students the following list to get them started: Sonia Sotomayor (law), Jaime Escalante (education), Gustavo Dudamel (music), Soledad O'Brien (journalism), Sandra Cisneros (literature), France Anne Córdova (astrophysics), Eloy Rodríguez (biochemistry), Jovita Carranza (business), Roberto Clemente (sports), Isabel Toledo (design). The SACNAS Biography Project provides information on Hispanic scientists and engineers in America.

Answer Key

82. Answers will vary.

Additional Resources

Fans Online activities
Practice Workbook

HERITAGE LANGUAGE LEARNERS

- Ask students to define the issues that they believe most concern citizens of Hispanic descent living in the United States. Ask them to describe these issues in an essay of at least four paragraphs in which they also develop some solutions. Then ask students to compare their defined issues and proposed solutions to those that concern citizens in their family's country of origin. Have students note the ways in which these problems are similar and different, and ask them to comment on the effectiveness in solving these challenges in both countries.

COOPERATIVE LEARNING

- Ask students to work in small groups and assign one of these countries to each group: Spain, Mexico, Cuba, the Dominican Republic, Argentina, and Peru. Groups will decide which members are to research a particular aspect of their assigned country's contributions to the United States. Members will then report back to the group with the information and, together, will create a brochure describing how their assigned country enriches the American culture. Students may also elect to find or draw images to accompany their brochures.

ESCRITURA

Un ensayo

Presentation

- In this section, students will practice and extend their writing skills. They will apply the vocabulary and grammar they have learned in this unit to write an essay exploring a topic of their choosing about the history or social or political issues of the Spanish-speaking world.

Activities	Standards	Resources
Escritura	1.1, 1.2, 1.3, 5.1, 5.2	

Teaching Suggestions

Warm-Up / Independent Starter

- Have students list in their notebooks one area that interests them about each of the following topics: history (e.g., *la época precolombina en las Américas*), politics (e.g., *los golpes de Estado en Latinoamérica*), and social issues (e.g., *el desarrollo sostenible*).

Preparation

- Invite students to share their Independent Starters with the class. You may want to list the topics students mention on the board. If necessary, bring more possible areas of interest to light by asking additional questions. For example: *¿Existía la esclavitud en todas las colonias españolas de las Américas? ¿Quiénes dirigieron los movimientos independentistas en las colonias españolas? ¿Qué sistemas políticos existen actualmente en Latinoamérica? ¿Hay alguna dictadura? ¿Qué países de Latinoamérica tienen mayor igualdad social? ¿Y más desigualdad? ¿Existen todavía conflictos armados en alguna región de Latinoamérica? ¿Qué papel desempeñan los movimientos indigenistas en Latinoamérica?* Ask students to keep this list of topics or areas of interest in mind for the *Piensa* section.

- Ask for a volunteer to read the *Textos expositivos* box aloud. Explain that expository writing is the type of writing that most of us encounter in our daily lives. Students are probably familiar with these kinds of texts and they have probably written papers or essays for some of their classes. Invite them to share with the class some of the main features of expository writing. Elicit that these texts explain, inform, and describe.

ESCRITURA

Un ensayo

Textos expositivos

La palabra *exponer* remite, entre otras cosas, a la idea de explicar algo o hablar de algo para informar a los demás.

Los **textos expositivos** transmiten una información objetiva organizada según un determinado criterio.

En general, en los textos expositivos se utilizan los verbos en tercera persona, puesto que en ellos se habla de hechos y fenómenos objetivos, no de opiniones.

En esta unidad vas a escribir un ensayo sobre un tema histórico, social o político del mundo hispano que te interese.

Como sabes, un ensayo es un tipo de texto expositivo bastante extenso en el que se muestran los conocimientos que se poseen acerca de un tema concreto. Por tanto, un trabajo de este tipo debe estar bien documentado, redactado y presentado.

Piensa

- Elige el tema histórico, social o político sobre el que te gustaría escribir.

- Busca información sobre el tema que has elegido. Puedes utilizar enciclopedias, revistas especializadas, Internet... Anota las fuentes que utilices para incluirlas en la bibliografía de tu trabajo.

- Organiza tus ideas y elabora un guion para ordenar los contenidos que vas a tratar. Ese guion te servirá para la redacción posterior de tu ensayo. Sigue este esquema:

  – Una **introducción** para presentar el tema que vas a tratar y una explicación breve de la organización del ensayo.

  Modelo *En este trabajo propongo un análisis sobre las causas que motivaron los procesos de independencia en Latinoamérica a principios del s.XIX. En el primer capítulo analizo...*

  – Un **desarrollo** para explicar los hechos relacionados con el tema que elegiste: causas, consecuencias, etc.

  Modelo *Los procesos de independencia se debieron a...*

  – Una **conclusión** para resumir las ideas expuestas.

  Modelo *Entre 1810 y 1825, la mayor parte de los territorios del continente americano lograron la independencia.*

GUION PARA UN ENSAYO

El proceso de independencia de América Latina

1. Introducción
2. Desarrollo
   2. 1. Antecedentes
      - Causas internas
      - Causas externas
   2. 2. Desarrollo del proceso independentista
   2. 3. Grandes figuras de la independencia
      - Simón Bolívar
      - José de San Martín
   2. 4. Consecuencias de la independencia
3. Conclusión

Rubric for Evaluation

	Content	Organization	Conventions
1 point	Both the thesis and the essay's purpose are somewhat unclear. Inappropriate and/or unspecific word choices.	Focus on topic is not sustained. Details are not in a logical order. Few or no transitions between ideas.	Many errors in spelling, punctuation, grammar, and usage. Errors obscure meaning.
3 points	Thesis is clear and is supported with some evidence. Essay's purpose is mostly clear. Some inaccurate word choices.	Mostly clear focus. Details are not in the most effective order. Transitions are used, but some don't work well.	Some errors in spelling, punctuation, grammar, and usage. Errors don't interfere with meaning.

Escribe

■ Tomando como punto de partida el guion y las ideas que anotaste, escribe el borrador de tu ensayo.

Recuerda que en este tipo de textos es muy importante la claridad, el orden y la objetividad.

■ Selecciona imágenes que puedas incluir en tu ensayo.

■ Incorpora al principio del ensayo un índice con los títulos de los apartados y los subapartados en los que has organizado el texto.

■ Recopila la bibliografía que consultaste y ponla al final del ensayo.

Revisa

■ Una vez finalizado tu borrador, comprueba si incluiste toda la información que querías y si está bien organizada.

■ Intercambia tu ensayo con tu compañero(a). Lee el suyo y completa una tabla como esta con tus comentarios.

Criterio	Guía de preguntas	Comentarios
Contenido	– ¿El trabajo te parece interesante? – ¿Te aporta alguna información que desconocías? – ¿Crees que falta alguna información en concreto?	
Redacción	– ¿La redacción es clara y comprensible? – ¿Hay alguna parte del texto que no entiendas?	
Vocabulario	– ¿Se repiten mucho algunas palabras? – ¿El vocabulario es preciso y adecuado al registro?	
Gramática	– ¿El texto tiene algún error gramatical?	
Ortografía	–¿Tiene alguna falta de ortografía?	

■ Devuelve el ensayo a su autor(a) con tus sugerencias y revisa el tuyo teniendo en cuenta sus comentarios. Pásalo a limpio.

Comparte

■ Prepara una presentación de tu ensayo para tus compañeros(as). Ellos(as) deberán tomar notas para hacerte preguntas al final. ¡Suerte!

doscientos ochenta y siete **287**

Expresiones útiles

Causa:

A causa de…	*Because of …*
Debido a…	*Due to …*
Gracias a…	*Thanks to …*
Por culpa de…	*Because of …*

Consecuencia:

De manera que…	*So that …*
Por tanto…	*So …*
De ahí que…	*That's why …*
Entonces…	*So …*

Conclusión:

En resumen…	*In summary …*
Finalmente…	*Finally …*
En conclusión…	*In conclusion …*

	Content	Organization	Conventions
5 points	Clearly stated and fully supported thesis. Essay's purpose is clear. Accurate, rich, and purposeful word choices.	Distinct focus and clear structure that enhance the thesis. Effective use of transitions and logical sequencing.	Few, if any, errors in spelling, punctuation, grammar, and usage. Excellent command of the Spanish language.

Step-by-Step Instructions

Piensa

■ Have students use their Independent Starters and the discussion of the Preparation section to help them decide on a topic for their essays. Emphasize that they should narrow the focus by writing about just one area or aspect of their selected topic.

■ Explain to students that as they search for information, they will have to constantly weigh the sources and the value of the information they find. Emphasize the importance of an outline as an effective tool to organize their thoughts. The outline will help students keep a clear focus and direction throughout their essay.

Escribe

■ Students should begin with an introduction that contains a thesis statement that clearly states the focus of the essay, and a list of the major points the essay will address. Remind students that they should include facts, examples, and details in the body of their essay. Encourage students to think about their reasoning; it must be logical and clear. Transitions such as those in the *Expresiones útiles* box will help students link ideas, add coherence to their writing, and clarify their reasoning.

Revisa

■ As students revise their essays, ask them to pay attention to rhythm. In other words, their essays should read smoothly—the writing should flow.

■ Explain to students that clarity is one of the most important features of expository writing. Clarity requires strong organization; therefore, encourage students to provide directions to improve the organization of their classmates' essays.

Comparte

■ If time allows, you may want to hold a class debate on one of the topics at the end of all of the presentations. Alternatively, organize a question-and-answer session at the end of each presentation.

Evaluation

■ Distribute copies of the rubric to students and discuss the evaluation criteria. Ask students to refer to the rubric as they prepare their writing and as they evaluate their classmates' essays.

287

REPASO

Vocabulario

Presentation

- In this section, students will review all key vocabulary from the unit, organized by themes, to prepare for an assessment. Students will complete practice activities for each *Desafío*.

Activities	Standards	Resources
1.	1.3	
2.	1.2, 2.1, 2.2, 3.1	
3.	1.2, 1.3, 3.1	

Teaching Suggestions

Warm-Up / Independent Starter

- Ask students to imagine that they have to explain to a foreign exchange student an important historical event that took place in this country. Have students jot down some facts based on what they know about the event. They may use a timeline to help them situate the event in time.

Preparation

- Have students get together in small groups and share their notes from the Independent Starter. Tell students to withhold some information, such as the name of the event, main characters, or key years, and see if their classmates can guess the event and provide the missing information.

- If time allows, give students a few moments to go over the rest of the vocabulary categories (i.e., *Política y gobierno, Problemas sociales, El medio ambiente*). Answer any questions students may have regarding pronunciation, usage, or meaning. Then have them work on the activities.

Activities

1. Call on volunteer students to share some of their sentences with the class. If some of students' sentences refer to actual historical events, invite the class to expand on the information. Encourage students to share as much information about each historical event as they can. Alternatively, you may turn this into a competition in which small groups quiz each other on the historical events mentioned in the sentences students wrote for this activity.

REPASO Vocabulario

Historia

				Acciones	
la alianza	alliance	el tratado de paz	peace treaty	abolir	to abolish
la clase media	middle class	la victoria	victory	declarar la guerra	to declare war
la derrota	defeat	el virreinato	viceroyalty	firmar la paz	to sign a peace treaty
el ejército	army			liberar	to free
la esclavitud	slavery	el/la colono(a)	colonist	luchar, pelear	to fight
la independencia	independence	el/la criollo(a)	creole	unir	to unite
la nobleza	nobility	el/la general	general		
la realeza	royalty	el/la monarca	monarch	¡Atención!	
la revolución	revolution	el/la navegante	sailor	apoyar	to support
el territorio	territory	el virrey	viceroy	soportar	to put up with

Política y gobierno

el asilo político	political asylum
la campaña electoral	electoral campaign
la democracia	democracy
los derechos civiles	civil rights
las elecciones	elections
la ideología	ideology
la junta militar	junta
el poder ejecutivo	executive power
el poder judicial	judicial power
el poder legislativo	legislative power
el sufragio universal	universal suffrage
el/la candidato(a)	candidate
el/la votante	voter
estatal	state
federal	federal
municipal	city, local
partidario(a)	supporter

Acciones

abstenerse	to abstain
autorizar	to authorize
comprometerse	to commit
detener	to detain
ejecutar	to execute
encarcelar	to jail
exiliar(se)	to exile (oneself)
oponerse	to oppose
perseguir	to pursue, to persecute

¡Atención!

suceder	to happen
triunfar	to succeed

Problemas sociales

el abuso de drogas	drug abuse
el analfabetismo	illiteracy
el arma de fuego	firearm
el conflicto armado	armed conflict
la corrupción	corruption
el crimen organizado	organized crime
la crisis	crisis
la delincuencia	crime
el delito	crime
la desigualdad	inequality
la discriminación	discrimination
el hambre	hunger
la pobreza	poverty
el robo	robbery
el terrorismo	terrorism
el tráfico de drogas	drug trafficking
la violencia	violence

El medio ambiente

la agricultura ecológica	ecological agriculture
el ahorro energético	energy savings
el desarrollo sostenible	sustainable development
la energía eólica	wind energy
la energía solar	solar energy
los residuos radiactivos	radioactive waste
los residuos tóxicos	toxic waste

¡Atención!

perjudicar	to damage, to harm
el prejuicio	prejudice

Differentiated Instruction

DEVELOPING LEARNERS

- Have students match the related words.

  1. eólica (i)
  2. delincuencia (f)
  3. crisis (k)
  4. guerra (h)
  5. tóxico (j)
  6. derrota (a)
  7. ahorro (e)
  8. luchar (b)
  9. detener (d)
  10. unido (c)
  11. poder (g)

  a. perder
  b. pelear
  c. junto
  d. arrestar
  e. no gastar
  f. delito
  g. dominio
  h. conflicto
  i. de viento
  j. venenoso
  k. situación difícil

EXPANDING LEARNERS

- Ask students to imagine that they have just been elected mayor of their community with a rather free hand to get things done. Explain that plans will be approved by the city council and they have very few budgetary constraints. Ask students to identify the first problem they want to resolve and describe, orally or in writing, the plans they have for fixing it. These problems may be environmentally based, such as reducing air and water pollution, or they may be altruistic, such as ridding the community of discrimination and inequality.

DESAFÍO 1

1 **Alianzas de palabras.** Une las palabras de las columnas y escribe oraciones.

Ⓐ	Ⓑ	Ⓒ
1. firmar	la guerra	a los colonos
2. abolir	la colonia	con el virrey
3. declarar	la paz	en los estados del sur
4. unir	la esclavitud	en una sola provincia
5. liberar	los nuevos territorios	del poder de la monarquía

DESAFÍO 2

2 **Política en la Historia.** Completa el texto con las palabras del cuadro.

democracia   derechos civiles   elecciones   exiliarse

junta militar   oponerse   candidato   régimen

De la última dictadura a la democracia en Argentina

El 24 de marzo de 1976, una ___1___ dirigida por el general Jorge Videla se hizo con el poder en Argentina mediante un golpe de Estado. Desde entonces y hasta 1983, el país estuvo gobernado por una dictadura militar que suprimió los ___2___ y se caracterizó por la violación sistemática de los derechos humanos. Todos los sospechosos de ___3___ al ___4___ militar «desaparecieron», al tiempo que otras muchas personas tuvieron que ___5___.

El 30 de octubre de 1983 Argentina celebró ___6___ presidenciales. Las ganó el ___7___ de la Unión Cívica Radical (UCR), Raúl Alfonsín, y bajo su mandato la nación volvió a la ___8___.

Toma de posesión de Raúl Alfonsín.

 DESAFÍO 3

3 **Problemas.** Escribe. ¿A qué problemas sociales se refieren estos titulares?

① Una banda internacional obtiene en un golpe simultáneo 35 millones en cajeros de 27 países

② La mitad de la población del mundo no tiene acceso al consumo de agua

③ Unos 61 millones de niños en todo el mundo no van a la escuela

④ Doble ataque con coches bomba causa 9 muertos y 70 heridos

doscientos ochenta y nueve 289

HERITAGE LANGUAGE LEARNERS

• Ask students to research three or more dictators in Latin America and Spain during the 20th century. Some names you might suggest include: Alfredo Stroessner of Paraguay, Francisco Franco of Spain, the Somozas of Nicaragua, Rafael Trujillo of the Dominican Republic, Augusto Pinochet of Chile, and Fidel Castro of Cuba. Have students prepare a written or oral report on these men and describe the circumstances under which they seized power and held onto it. Students should also include how these dictatorships ended and what form of government these countries have now.

MULTIPLE INTELLIGENCES:
Verbal-Linguistic Intelligence

• Ask students to imagine that they are living under a dictatorship and are working relentlessly to rid the country of oppression and to initiate a democratic process of government. Students will need to deliver a powerful speech to their compatriots, urging them to join in the struggle to topple the current government. The speech students deliver must provoke and inspire without resorting to violence. After students deliver their speeches, ask the class to vote for the most effective one.

---

2. You may wish to have students research the period in Argentinean history known as *la Guerra Sucia*, and write a two- or three-paragraph summary stating the most relevant information. (This could be assigned as homework.) Then have students share their summaries with their classmates in small groups.

3. To extend this activity, have students get together with a partner to discuss the issues they listed for each of these headlines. Encourage them to give a short definition and provide examples for each one of the issues. For example: *Un delito es una violación de la ley. Puede castigarse con cárcel, dependiendo de la gravedad. Robar es un delito, así como la falsificación de documentos, la estafa, el homicidio...*

Answer Key

1. Answers will vary. Sample answers:
   1. Los rebeldes firmaron la paz con el virrey.
   2. En 1865 se abolió la esclavitud en los estados del sur.
   3. El rey declaró la guerra a los colonos.
   4. Los nuevos territorios se unieron en una sola provincia.
   5. Simón Bolívar liberó a las colonias del poder de la monarquía.

2. 1. junta militar   5. exiliarse
   2. derechos civiles   6. elecciones
   3. oponerse   7. candidato
   4. régimen   8. democracia

3. Answers will vary. Sample answers:
   1. el crimen organizado, la delincuencia, el delito, el robo
   2. la desigualdad, los problemas medioambientales, la pobreza
   3. el analfabetismo, la desigualdad, la pobreza
   4. el conflicto armado, el terrorismo, la violencia

Additional Resources

Fans Online activities
Practice Workbook

289

Unit 5
REPASO
Gramática

Presentation

- Students will review grammatical structures presented in the unit. Each grammar point is cross-referenced to the corresponding page on which it was introduced. The activities here provide systematic practice by *Desafío*.

Activities	Standards	Resources
4.	1.3, 3.1	
5.	1.3, 3.1	
6.	1.2, 1.3	
7. Cultura	1.2, 1.3, 2.1, 2.2	

Teaching Suggestions

Warm-Up / Independent Starter

- Have students complete these sentences:
  1. *Si Colón no hubiera llegado a las Américas...*
  2. *Si las colonias no hubieran ganado la guerra contra Inglaterra en 1776...*
  3. *Si los estados del sur hubieran ganado la guerra civil...*
  4. *Si el presidente no hubiera ganado las pasadas elecciones...*

Preparation

- Ask student pairs to discuss their sentences from the Independent Starter. Remind students that they can complete these sentences with the conditional to express a probable result in the present (e.g. *Si Colón no hubiera llegado a las Américas, no estaríamos hoy aquí*); or, they can use the perfect conditional to express a probable past result (e.g., *Si Colón no hubiera llegado a las Américas, no habría desaparecido el imperio azteca*).
- Go over the rest of the grammar topics from this *Repaso* with the class. If needed, provide additional examples and practice activities.

Activities

5. Explain to students that for sentences 3–5, either the subjunctive or the indicative is possible. Remind them that, generally, the subjunctive would be used in Spanish in sentences that use "even if" in English.

290

REPASO Gramática

Los numerales ordinales (pág. 250)

primero(a), primer	octavo(a)
segundo(a)	noveno(a)
tercero(a), tercer	décimo(a)
cuarto(a)	undécimo(a) / décimo primer(o)(a)
quinto(a)	duodécimo(a) / décimo segundo(a)
sexto(a)	décimo tercer(o)(a)
séptimo(a)	décimo cuarto(a)

Expresar certeza y duda (pág. 252)

EXPRESIONES AFIRMATIVAS DE CERTEZA (INDICATIVO)

Es verdad / Es cierto / Es evidente / Es obvio + que
Estar convencido(a) / Estar seguro(a) + de que
Está claro / Está demostrado + que
Saber + que

Sé que los dos países pronto firmarán la paz.

EXPRESIONES AFIRMATIVAS DE DUDA (SUBJUNTIVO)

Es dudoso / Es improbable + que
Es posible / Es probable + que
Es difícil creer / Parece mentira + que
Dudar + (de) que

Es difícil creer que aún haya guerras en el mundo.

EXPRESIONES NEGATIVAS DE CERTEZA Y DUDA (SUBJUNTIVO)

No es verdad / No es cierto + que
No es evidente / No es obvio + que
No es posible / No es probable + que
No está claro / No está demostrado + que
No estar convencido(a) / No estar seguro(a) + de que

No está demostrado que los vikingos fundaran colonias en Norteamérica.

Expresar condición (pág. 274)

PLUSCUAMPERFECTO DE SUBJUNTIVO. VERBOS REGULARES

AYUDAR	COMER	VIVIR
hubiera ayudado	hubiera comido	hubiera vivido
hubieras ayudado	hubieras comido	hubieras vivido
hubiera ayudado	hubiera comido	hubiera vivido
hubiéramos ayudado	hubiéramos comido	hubiéramos vivido
hubierais ayudado	hubierais comido	hubierais vivido
hubieran ayudado	hubieran comido	hubieran vivido

Expresar finalidad (pág. 262)

para a fin de	a con el propósito de	+ infinitivo
para que a fin de que	a que con el propósito de que	+ subjuntivo

Se hizo un referéndum a fin de elegir a un candidato.
Votamos para que gobiernen los mejores.

PREGUNTAR SOBRE LA FINALIDAD DE UNA ACCIÓN

¿Para qué...? ¿A qué...?	¿Con qué fin...? ¿Con qué propósito...?	+ indicativo

¿Con qué fin salió el ejército a la calle?

Expresar dificultad (pág. 264)

aunque a pesar de (que) aun cuando pese a (que) aun + gerundio	Aunque sea difícil, acabaremos con la crisis.

INTENSIFICAR LA DIFICULTAD

por más + (nombre/adj./adv.) + que
por mucho(a)(os)(as) + (nombre) + que
por muy + adjetivo/adverbio + que

Por más problemas que tenga, él es optimista.

Expresar tiempo (pág. 276)

cuando después de que siempre que	en cuanto hasta que	+	indicativo subjuntivo
antes de que + subjuntivo			
al + infinitivo			

LOS TIEMPOS EN LAS CONDICIONALES IRREALES

si + pluscuamperfecto subj. + condicional

Si hubiéramos acabado con la pobreza, ahora no existiría la injusticia social.

si + pluscuamperfecto subj. + condicional perfecto

Si la policía no hubiera detenido a los terroristas, habrían cometido un atentado.

Differentiated Instruction

DEVELOPING LEARNERS

- Have students complete these sentences:
  1. *Es dudoso que Ana (llegar) a tiempo. (llegue)*
  2. *No es verdad que (haber) ganado los liberales. (hayan)*
  3. *Antes de que (decir) algo, piénsalo bien. (digas)*
  4. *Si tú (estudiar) estudiado más Historia, ahora podrías contestarme. (hubieras estudiado)*
  5. *Por mucho que el candidato (pedir) perdón, el daño ya está hecho. (pida)*
  6. *Si ellos no (luchar) por su independencia, seguirían siendo colonos. (hubieran luchado)*

EXPANDING LEARNERS

- Ask students to complete the sentences with the correct form of these verbs: *ser, conocer, encarcelar, haber, robar, venir, llegar, tener.*
  1. *Por muchos votos que él ..., no va a ganar estas elecciones. (tenga)*
  2. *Es verdad que todavía ... discriminación y desigualdad. (hay)*
  3. *Si ... a ese delincuente, no ... el banco. (hubieran encarcelado, habría robado)*
  4. *Cuando tú ..., llámame. (llegues)*
  5. *No es verdad que esos residuos ... tóxicos. (sean)*
  6. *Si tú ... ayer, la... (hubieras venido, habrías conocido)*

DESAFÍO 1

4 **Certeza y dudas.** Completa estas oraciones para expresar certeza o duda.

1. Es cierto que...
2. Estoy convencido(a) de que...
3. Es poco probable que...

4. No es verdad que...
5. Parece mentira que...
6. No es posible que...

DESAFÍO 2

5 **A pesar de...** Completa estas oraciones con la forma correcta de los verbos del cuadro.

| estar | ser | comprometerse | prometer | ser |

1. Por muy popular que _____ el candidato, no conseguirá ganar las elecciones.
2. No dejaría de votar en unas elecciones aunque _____ muy decepcionada con los políticos.
3. Por más que el presidente _____ acabar con la crisis, no lo logró.
4. Aun cuando su ideología _____ diferente a la mía, nunca hemos discutido.
5. A pesar de que el candidato _____ a cumplir su programa electoral, no lo hizo.

DESAFÍO 3

6 **Una historia diferente.** Escribe un párrafo contando lo que podría haberle pasado a Marisol si hubiera actuado de otra forma o si no hubiera perdido el autobús.

¡Vaya día!

Marisol salió tarde de casa y perdió el autobús. ¡Qué mala suerte! Por fin había conseguido una prueba para una película y no podía llegar tarde. Intentó tomar un taxi, pero se celebraba un festival de cine en la ciudad y no encontró ni uno libre. De pronto empezó a llover y Marisol no llevaba paraguas, así que se mojó. ¡Qué desastre! Corrió para refugiarse en algún lugar y se le cayó el celular. Entró en un café y quiso llamar por teléfono para cambiar la prueba, pero ¡había perdido el celular! Para colmo, el director de la película entró en ese café, pero Marisol estaba tan preocupada que no lo vio y se fue. ¡Vaya día!

CULTURA

7 **Historia pasada y presente.** Responde a estas preguntas.

1. ¿Quiénes fueron los protagonistas del «abrazo de Guayaquil»?
2. ¿Quién es Antonio Villaraigosa?
3. ¿Cuándo y por qué surgieron los movimientos indigenistas en Latinoamérica?

doscientos noventa y uno **291**

---

6. Once students have finished this activity, have them get together with a classmate and compare and contrast their paragraphs. Do they have very different versions of events? Ask partners to write a new version together, using the most interesting, funny, or happiest parts from each of their stories. Call on student pairs to share their stories with the class. Then hold a class vote to choose the funniest or most interesting story.

Answer Key

4. Answers will vary. Sample answers:
   1. Es cierto que los colonos ganaron la guerra.
   2. Estoy convencida de que firmarán la paz.
   3. Es poco probable que los países se unan.
   4. No es verdad que el virrey fuera justo.
   5. Parece mentira que los derrotaran.
   6. No es posible que el general perdiera la guerra.

5. 1. sea
   2. estuviera
   3. prometió/prometiera
   4. es/sea
   5. se comprometió/se comprometiera

6. Answers will vary.

7. Answers will vary. Sample answers:
   1. Simón Bolívar y José de San Martín.
   2. El primer alcalde hispano que tuvo Los Ángeles desde 1872.
   3. Surgieron en las últimas décadas del siglo XX para defender los derechos de los pueblos indígenas y para luchar contra la discriminación social y racial que sufren.

Additional Resources

Fans Online activities
Practice Workbook

HERITAGE LANGUAGE LEARNERS

- Give students more practice with knowing when to use the subjunctive or the indicative by asking them to answer these questions orally:
  1. ¿Qué cosas no están demostradas?
  2. ¿De qué estás seguro(a)? ¿Y de qué no estás seguro(a)?
  3. ¿Con qué fin estudias español?
  4. ¿Qué no está demostrado de la conversación entre Bolívar y San Martín?
  5. ¿Qué es lo más difícil de creer sobre tu actor o cantante favorito(a)?

CRITICAL THINKING

- Explain to students that the following abstract words have been used in this unit: *democracia, libertad, paz, justicia, discriminación, terrorismo.* Ask students to choose one of these terms and write a brief essay, first defining what the word usually connotes to others and what it means personally to them. Then, ask students to describe the influence this word has had and continues to have on their lives, their community, country, and the world. Call on volunteers to read their essays aloud.

Unit 5
PROYECTO
Un problema de tu comunidad

Presentation

- In this section, students will apply the vocabulary, grammar, and cultural information they have learned in this unit to create a civic association and write a manifesto stating its goals.

Activities	Standards	Resources
Paso 1	1.1, 5.1, 5.2	
Paso 2	1.1, 1.3, 5.1, 5.2	
Paso 3	1.1, 1.2, 1.3, 3.1, 5.1, 5.2	
Paso 4	1.1, 1.3, 3.1, 5.1, 5.2	
Paso 5	1.1, 5.1, 5.2	
Paso 6	1.3, 3.1, 5.1, 5.2	

Teaching Suggestions

Warm-Up / Independent Starter

- Ask students to list three community issues they think need addressing (e.g., *la falta de áreas verdes, el vandalismo*).

Preparation

- Call on a volunteer to read the title and introduction to the project aloud. Then, have students share what they know about civic organizations. Encourage students to provide examples (e.g., Sierra Club, Rotary Club, American Cancer Society, Friends of the Earth, Salvation Army). Based on the examples they provided, have students mention some of the goals of these organizations and the kinds of issues they normally address.

- Ask students to write their lists from the Independent Starter on the board. Was the class aware of these issues or problem areas in their community? You may want to discuss some of the issues as a class. This will complete the first bullet point of *Paso 1*.

Step-by-Step Instructions

Paso 1

- Divide the class into small groups to work on the project. Encourage students to choose an issue that they care about or feel strongly about. Their manifesto will be more effective and they will have more to say if they identify with the issue.

292

Un manifiesto para solucionar

un problema de tu comunidad

En este proyecto van a crear una asociación ciudadana para luchar por un problema que les preocupa. Deberán escribir un manifiesto reivindicando soluciones para ese problema.

PASO 1 Elige el problema

- Entre todos(as), piensen qué problemas sociales, políticos o medioambientales afectan a su comunidad y anótenlos en la pizarra.

> Contaminación de un lago o de un río.
> Abandono y deterioro de un parque municipal.
> Mal uso y desperdicio del agua en riegos de jardines y parques.
> Ruido excesivo en algún barrio.
> Falta de servicios públicos.
> Falta de seguridad en algunas zonas.

- En pequeños grupos, elijan el problema que más les preocupa de los que han anotado en el paso anterior.

PASO 2 Define la asociación

- Decidan el nombre de su asociación. Aquí tienen algunos ejemplos para tomar ideas.

Jóvenes contra la intolerancia

Aire limpio para todos

El parque es nuestro

- Escriban un texto breve en el que expliquen quiénes son y cuáles son sus objetivos.

> **El parque es nuestro**
>
> **Quiénes somos**
>
> Somos un grupo de estudiantes de la escuela Kennedy preocupados por los problemas medioambientales de nuestra comunidad. Por ello, hemos creado una asociación con un objetivo claro: salvar el parque de los Castillos.
>
> No se trata de una asociación cerrada; está abierta para todos aquellos ciudadanos que quieran participar y contribuir a la mejora de...

292 doscientos noventa y dos

Rubric for Evaluation

	Content	Organization	Presentation
1 point	Goal is not clearly identified. The manifesto shows limited original ideas and is not persuasive.	Inefficient use of time. Information is disorganized. Includes a vague outline of an action plan.	Unclear communication. Delivery is not fluent. Many errors in vocabulary and grammar.
3 points	Goal is partially defined and its importance is somewhat highlighted. The manifesto is creative and persuasive.	Time is used well. Information is mostly organized. Includes details about an action plan.	Clear communication and fluent delivery. Mostly correct vocabulary and grammar.

PASO 3 Busca información

- Busquen información relacionada con el problema elegido. Pueden consultar en Internet, contactar con alguna asociación o preguntar a las personas afectadas por ese problema. Procuren responder a preguntas como estas:
  - ¿Cuáles son las causas que provocan ese problema? ¿Y las consecuencias?
  - ¿Se están tomando medidas para luchar contra ese problema? ¿Cuáles? ¿Creen que son suficientes?
- Organicen sus notas y escriban un breve texto en el que expongan cuál es el problema y cómo es la situación actual.

PASO 4 Propón las soluciones

- Analicen el problema y discutan las posibles soluciones. Hagan una lista con las medidas que crean necesarias para solucionar el problema.
- Organicen la lista y redacten cada uno de los puntos con claridad.

> **Qué queremos**
> - Que la administración se haga cargo de la limpieza y del cuidado de los jardines.
> - Que se pongan más papeleras en las zonas donde se puede hacer picnic.
> - Que se arreglen los columpios que están deteriorados.

PASO 5 Decide las acciones para dar a conocer la asociación

- Piensen en las acciones divulgativas y reivindicativas que van a llevar a cabo para que los ciudadanos conozcan su asociación y se involucren, y añádanlas al manifiesto. Por ejemplo:
  - Organizar una recogida de firmas.
  - Hacer una carrera por el parque.
  - Repartir pines con un eslogan.

PASO 6 Presenta el manifiesto

- Lean su manifiesto a sus compañeros(as) y coméntenles qué acciones van a realizar.

Unidad 5

Autoevaluación

¿Qué has aprendido en esta unidad?

Haz estas actividades para comprobar tu progreso.

> Evalúa tus habilidades. Para cada punto, di Muy bien, Bien o Necesito practicar más.

a. ¿Puedes hablar de hechos históricos?

▶ Describe algunos hechos históricos que ocurrieron en los últimos siglos: qué sucedió, dónde, cuándo, por qué, etc. Utiliza expresiones de certeza si estás totalmente seguro(a) y de duda si no sabes algún dato con exactitud.

b. ¿Puedes expresar finalidad y dificultad?

▶ Explica para qué sirven algunas instituciones gubernamentales, como el Departamento de Educación o el de Estado. ¿Con qué dificultades se encuentran y qué esperan lograr a pesar de esos obstáculos? Utiliza expresiones como *aunque*, *a pesar de que*, *por mucho que*, etc.

c. ¿Puedes hablar de problemas sociales?

▶ Elige un hecho histórico y explica cómo sería nuestra sociedad si ese hecho no hubiera ocurrido.

▶ Explica cuándo y cómo crees que se resolverán algunos problemas sociales o medioambientales. Usa expresiones de tiempo, como *hasta que*, *mientras*, etc.

PROYECTO

Un problema de tu comunidad

Paso 2

- Encourage students to choose a name for their civic organization that clearly reflects its goals. Then, students should clearly state the issue their organization intends to address, and make a solid case for its importance.

Paso 3

- Since this is an issue that affects the community, suggest to students that they interview their classmates to see how the problem is affecting them and to get their opinions. Relatives and neighbors may also be good sources of information.

Paso 4

- Encourage students to discuss specific strategies to achieve their goals, rather than propose general ideas. They may even wish to specify a timeline to give their planned measures a stronger focus and a sense of urgency.

Paso 5

- The students' aim is to get their audience involved and prompt them into action. Therefore, the proposed activities should promote community empowerment.

Paso 6

- Encourage students to show enthusiasm for their organization. They should strive to create a proactive awareness among their classmates.

Evaluation

- Distribute copies of the rubric to students. Discuss the evaluation criteria and explain how this project will be graded. Encourage students to refer to the rubric as they prepare their projects.

Content

- Presentations should include the goals of the civic organization, specific strategies to attain these goals, and planned outcomes.

Organization

- Encourage students to organize their information in a logical and interesting sequence. They should include a clear outline of their civic organization's plan of action.

Presentation

- Have the class vote on the best civic organization. You may wish to allow students to promote their organization in school.

	Content	Organization	Presentation
5 points	Goal is clearly defined and its importance is demonstrated. The manifesto is creative and persuasive.	Time is used wisely. Information is clearly organized. Includes a detailed outline of an action plan.	Clear and fluent communication. Very motivating, upbeat delivery. Correct and complete vocabulary and grammar.

293

HACIA EL AP* EXAM

Presentational Writing: Persuasive Essay

Presentation

- These pages present students with a sample activity from the "Presentational Writing: Persuasive Essay" portion of the AP* Spanish Language and Culture Exam. Students will read two authentic texts from the Spanish-speaking world, listen to an authentic audio selection, and write a persuasive essay based on the three sources and their own opinions.

Activities	Standards	Resources
Presentational Writing: Persuasive Essay	1.2, 1.3, 2.1, 2.2, 3.2, 5.1	Audio

Preparing for the Exam

About This Section

- The "Presentational Writing: Persuasive Essay" section of the AP* Exam requires students to read and listen to authentic sources from the Spanish-speaking world and write an essay supporting one point of view, based on their understanding of the sources and their own opinions. The section lasts approximately 55 minutes, and counts for 12.5% of the student's overall score on the test.

- Students will be given a certain amount of time to read the essay topic and the print sources. They will then listen to the audio source twice, during which they may take notes. Next, students will have 40 minutes to write their essays. You may wish to set a strict time limit while administering the practice activity on these pages in order to simulate the testing conditions. Or, you may wish to allow students more time in order to put into practice the *estrategias* given on page 294.

- In their essays, students should present the different points of view represented in the sources as well as their own. They should use the sources to thoroughly defend their essay, persuading the reader about their viewpoint. Remind them that they need to cite all three sources. Emphasize the importance of using mainly the sources—rather than personal opinions—to support the ideas expressed in the essay.

Hacia el AP* Exam

Presentational Writing: Persuasive Essay

Presentación

En el examen AP* vas a escribir un ensayo persuasivo en el que debes presentar y defender tu punto de vista. Tendrás aproximadamente 55 minutos para leer y escuchar las diferentes fuentes y escribir tu ensayo.

Estrategias

- Lee los textos y escucha la fuente auditiva. Toma nota de las ideas principales en las que se basa cada autor para apoyar su punto de vista.
- Decide la opinión que vas a defender en tu ensayo.
- Organiza la información de forma coherente y usa un lenguaje claro y persuasivo.
- Utiliza ejemplos y citas textuales de las diferentes fuentes para justificar y apoyar tu punto de vista.
- Para expresar tu opinión, puedes utilizar las siguientes expresiones:
    Considero que…
    Desde mi punto de vista…
    A mi modo de ver…
    En mi opinión…
    No me parece que…
- Revisa con cuidado tu trabajo. Es importante que no haya errores gramaticales u ortográficos.

Instrucciones para el examen

Directions: You are going to write a persuasive essay based on three sources, which present different viewpoints on the topic and include both print texts and an audio selection. First, you will have six minutes to read the essay topic and the print texts. You will then hear the audio twice. You may take notes while you listen. You will then have 40 minutes to write your essay. In your persuasive essay, you should present the various viewpoints on the topic as described in the sources, and also indicate and defend your own viewpoint. Use information from all sources to support your argument. As you refer to the sources, identify them appropriately.

Instrucciones: Vas a escribir un ensayo persuasivo basado en tres fuentes, que representan distintas perspectivas sobre el tema e incluyen textos impresos y una grabación. Primero, tendrás seis minutos para leer la introducción y las fuentes impresas. Después, escucharás la grabación dos veces. Puedes tomar apuntes mientras escuchas. Luego vas a tener 40 minutos para escribir tu ensayo. En tu ensayo persuasivo, debes presentar las distintas perspectivas sobre el tema que se incluyen en las fuentes, y también indicar y defender tu propio punto de vista. Usa información de las tres fuentes para apoyar tu postura. Al referirte a las fuentes, identifícalas apropiadamente.

Language Expansion

VOCABULARY

- Students may have difficulty with the following words from the readings:

portátil	→ *que se puede mover*
ligero	→ *no pesado*
planicie	→ *terreno plano o llano*
desechos	→ *residuos, basura*
adecuación	→ *acondicionamiento*
crianza	→ *alimentación y cuidado*
dichos	→ *previamente mencionados*
lixiviación	→ *filtrado por la tierra*
derramamiento	→ *verter o salirse un líquido*
descartada	→ *tirada, botada*
impulsar	→ *promover, estimular*

GRAMMAR STRUCTURES:

Expressing Opinions and Making Value Statements

- In order to write an essay that is persuasive, students will need to use appropriate expressions and grammatical structures. Some of these include expressing opinions and making value statements, which will require expressions such as *Considero que…* and *Es necesario que…* You may wish to review these structures with students before beginning the activity. Refer them to pages 320 and 322 and the *Resumen de gramática* at the end of the book for more review on this topic.

Tema del ensayo: ¿Se debe extraer litio del salar de Uyuni?

Fuente número 1

Introducción

Este fragmento trata sobre el impacto que puede tener en el medio ambiente la extracción de litio en el salar de Uyuni. Forma parte de un estudio realizado en mayo de 2010 por Rebecca Hollender y Jim Shultz para el Centro para la Democracia en Cochabamba (Bolivia).

Bolivia y su litio

¿Puede el «oro del siglo XXI» ayudar a una nación a salir de la pobreza?

I. El litio: el superhéroe de los metales

Cada vez que contestamos un teléfono celular o encendemos un iPod, vemos nuestros relojes o conectamos una computadora portátil, estamos contando con baterías que contienen litio. El litio también se utiliza en la producción de vidrio y cerámica, en medicación para el tratamiento del desorden bipolar, en el aire acondicionado, los lubricantes, las armas nucleares y otros productos. El más ligero de los metales de la tierra, el litio, es extraído de muchas fuentes, pero las más favorables económicamente son los salares subterráneos como los que se encuentran en abundancia en el vasto salar de Uyuni, en Bolivia.

II. La carrera por el litio boliviano

Incluso basándonos en las previsiones más conservadoras, las reservas de litio de Bolivia son las más grandes del mundo. El salar de Uyuni, una extensa planicie de 10.000 kilómetros cuadrados cubierta de minerales incrustados en sal, y localizada en el sudoeste del departamento de Potosí, es el punto cero para los sueños de litio bolivianos.

doscientos noventa y cinco **295**

More Practice

FINDING ADDITIONAL SOURCES

- Perhaps the easiest way to find additional sources for the essay section of the AP* Exam is to use current events as a topic. That way, you can find multiple sources about the same topic, often with several points of view involved. While news outlets like newspapers and television are a good source, you may also find interesting material at governmental and organization websites. These sources may also include visuals, such as charts, graphs, and tables, which either support or refute the points of view presented in other media.

ADDITIONAL SOURCES

- You may find interesting audio and video selections at the following governmental and organization websites:
  - Gobierno de EE. UU.: www.gobiernousa.gov
  - Cruz Roja Americana: www.redcross.org/cruz-roja
  - UNICEF: www.unicef.org/spanish
  - Naciones Unidas: www.un.org/es
  - Organización Mundial de la Salud: www.who.int/es
  - WWF Central America: www.wwfca.org
- Be sure to review the selections to make sure the topic, length, and content are appropriate for your students.

HACIA EL AP* EXAM

Presentational Writing: Persuasive Essay

Strategies: Reading and Listening

- Students may have prior knowledge about the topic, but they will need to cite specific information presented in these particular sources while writing their persuasive essays. This correlates directly with the concepts of "Writing from Sources" and "Text-Based Answers" that are presented in the Common Core State Standards for English Language Arts. Students should therefore practice reading and listening critically and taking accurate notes, rather than simply relying on previously learned information.

- Have students practice this skill by giving them an article to read in Spanish about a topic about which they are already familiar. Then ask them to answer questions that include information that is already known but not stated in the article. They should then go back and indicate where exactly in the article each answer is stated. They may find that they rely much more heavily on prior knowledge than they thought. Of course, prior knowledge is a good thing, and should be encouraged and emphasized frequently. However, it is important for students to be able to distinguish between what they read or hear in a source and what they already know (or think they know) about a topic.

Extension Activities

After having students complete this activity, you may wish to take advantage of the activity by using the sources in a variety of different ways.

- Have students write an e-mail (real or simulated) to an elected official about the topic of the Uyuni salt flats. They can persuade the official about their point of view, referring to the sources given here as well as others they may find.

- Students can hold a verbal debate about this topic as well. They should choose a side and do some additional research to support their argument. While it might be more effective to do this as a group activity, be sure each student participates in order for all students to practice speaking.

Additional Resources

Español Santillana AP* Preparation Workbook

HACIA EL AP* EXAM

Presentational Writing: Persuasive Essay

Presentation

- These pages present the continuation of the written and audio sources which serve as the basis for students' persuasive essays. When students finish reading and listening, they will prepare an essay based on the points of view described in the sources as well as their own.

Activities	Standards	Resources
Presentational Writing: Persuasive Essay	1.2, 1.3, 2.1, 2.2, 3.2, 5.1	Audio

Preparing for the Exam

Writing from Sources

- The Common Core State Standards require students to "write from sources," specifically to "draw evidence from informational texts to support analysis, reflection, and research." (CCSS.ELA-Literacy.WHST.6-8.9) The AP* Exam provides students with an exceptional activity that practices this skill. Students may have some prior knowledge about the topic of the essay or not, but the viewpoint they present in the persuasive essay needs to be supported by the information presented in the three authentic sources. This appeals to another shift demonstrated by the Common Core ELA standards: text-based answers.

- By incorporating these two facets, students show that they are not only capable of expressing themselves using the Spanish language, they are also able to use modern literacy skills in this foreign language, thus demonstrating even greater control of the language. They are able to communicate not only what is convenient to say, but what is clearly stated and why.

Strategies: Writing Persuasive Essays

- A five-paragraph essay is one of the most common organization patterns. Remind students of the outline: I. Introduction; II. Point #1 with supporting details; III. Point #2 with supporting details; IV. Point #3 with supporting details; V. Conclusion.

Impactos medioambientales

Perdida en la gran carrera del litio boliviano se encuentra una preocupación medioambiental muy seria y real. En nombre de proveer coches más limpios para los países ricos del norte, el hermoso y raro salar podría terminar en tierra de desechos. La adecuación de la estrategia ambiental de Bolivia para el desarrollo de litio en el sudoeste de Potosí es puesta en duda por algunas organizaciones medioambientales reconocidas en Bolivia.

Uno de los principales problemas que la producción de litio podría causar es una gran crisis de agua. La región ya sufre de una seria escasez del líquido que afecta a los productores de quinua, a la crianza de llamas, a la vital industria del turismo y a las fuentes de agua potable. Aunque los funcionarios bolivianos aseguran que las necesidades de agua para el proyecto de litio serán mínimas, sus estimaciones se basan en información muy limitada e incompleta.

La contaminación del aire, agua y suelos es también otra preocupación trascendental. Se necesitarán grandes cantidades de químicos tóxicos para procesar las estimadas 30.000 a 40.000 toneladas de litio anuales

que el proyecto pretende extraer. El escape de dichos químicos por medio de la lixiviación, derramamiento o emisiones atmosféricas pone en peligro a las comunidades y al ecosistema como un todo. Informes sobre el salar de Atacama en Chile describen un paisaje marcado por montañas de sal descartada y enormes canales llenos de agua azul contaminada con químicos.

La amenaza a las comunidades

¿Cómo se siente la gente y las comunidades que viven en el sudoeste de Potosí ante el hecho de que esta zona se convierta en la base de lo que pronto será uno de los proyectos industriales más grandes que el país jamás haya construido? De hecho, muchos grupos en la región han apoyado hace ya tiempo la explotación del litio, considerándola una oportunidad única para mejorar sus ingresos e impulsar su desarrollo. No obstante, existe también gran preocupación por lo que podría venir.

Fuente: www.democracyctr.org (texto adaptado)

More Information

THE UYUNI SALT FLATS

- The *salar de Uyuni* is the world's largest salt flat. Formed from a prehistoric lake, the salt flat now lies at an altitude of almost 12,000 feet above sea level and covers over 4,000 square miles—over 86 times larger than the Bonneville Salt Flats in Utah! While the salt flats have been attracting tourists for years, the increasing demand for lithium batteries has only recently brought this landscape to the forefront of international interest due to the vast reserves of lithium contained within.

EXTRACTION OF LITHIUM

- The United States currently imports around 80% of its lithium, mostly from sources in South America. But a discovery in early 2013 may be changing that. Researchers at the University of Wyoming Carbon Management Institute discovered a new lithium source near Rock Springs, Wyoming, that may be up to 150 times larger than the country's main source in Nevada—and which would be equivalent to about 720 years of current lithium production. This source has the potential to change the United States from a lithium importer to one of the world's lithium producers.

Fuente número 2

Introducción

Este gráfico sobre los usos del litio fue publicado en 2010 por www.rankia.com.

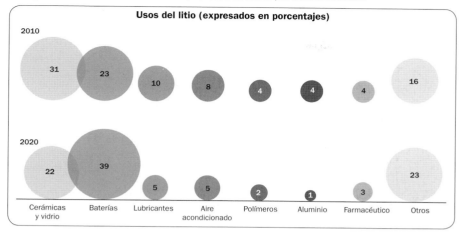

Usos del litio (expresados en porcentajes)

2010: Cerámicas y vidrio 31, Baterías 23, Lubricantes 10, Aire acondicionado 8, Polímeros 4, Aluminio 4, Farmacéutico 4, Otros 16

2020: Cerámicas y vidrio 22, Baterías 39, Lubricantes 5, Aire acondicionado 5, Polímeros 2, Aluminio 1, Farmacéutico 3, Otros 23

Fuente número 3

Introducción

 Esta grabación trata de la oportunidad que representa el mercado del litio para Bolivia. El reportaje original («El tesoro oculto de Bolivia») fue publicado por BBC Mundo el 15 de octubre de 2009 (www.bbc.co.uk).

El tesoro oculto de Bolivia

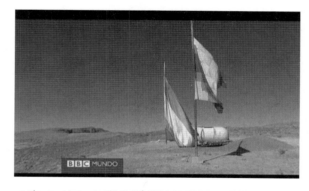

El salar de Uyuni, en el altiplano boliviano, contiene una de las principales reservas de litio a nivel mundial.

Presentational Writing: Persuasive Essay

- Since students will only have around 40 minutes to write, they should practice organizing their thoughts. They may also wish to begin taking notes within this outline, as they will find that they take far fewer unnecessary notes, and the ones they do take will contribute directly to assembling the final essay. Have students create a graphic organizer with transitional devices listed according to their role. For example: I. Introduction: *En principio...* II. Point #1: *En primer lugar... Para empezar...* III. Point #2: *En segundo lugar... Luego...* IV. Point #3: *Además de eso... Al mismo tiempo...* V. Conclusion: *En resumen... En conclusión...*

 AUDIO SCRIPT
See page 239N.

Rubric for Evaluation

On the AP* Exam, each section is given a score between 0 (Unacceptable) and 5 (Strong). In order to earn a score of 5, the student's essay should show:

– Comprehension: Demonstrates thorough comprehension of the print and audio sources.

– Content: Presents and defends viewpoint, with content from all three sources as support.

– Organization: Student's essay is organized, with transitions and other language devices facilitating and complementing the organization.

– Message: Student's response is fully understandable, with ease of expression and only occasional errors.

– Language: Vocabulary is varied and precise. Grammatical structures are used correctly. Few errors do not impede communication. Simple, compound, and complex sentences are used appropriately.

Differentiated Instruction

DEVELOPING LEARNERS

- Students may comprehend graphics, tables, and charts such as the one in this activity, but still have difficulties applying the information contained within in their essays. Have students practice summarizing visual elements in one or two sentences, or listing the most salient points in Spanish in their notes. That way, they will have the key information written explicitly when it comes time to include the information in their writing.

EXPANDING / HERITAGE LANGUAGE LEARNERS

- After completing this activity, have students exchange their essays with two other classmates. They should note the key points used by each classmate, and see if there are any points that are unsubstantiated by the sources. They can then work together to write a master essay which uses the strongest and most frequently cited points, and present their work to the class.

Additional Resources

Español Santillana AP* Preparation Workbook

297

Unit 6 Creamos

Objectives

- To talk about art and to describe an artwork.
- To talk about painting, architecture, and sculpture.
- To describe and compare people and things.
- To refer to a general concept or an abstract idea using the neuter article *lo*.
- To state opinions.
- To make value statements.

- To talk about literature.
- To express small size or affection using diminutives.
- To give advice and make recommendations.
- To identify main ideas and significant details in a variety of texts.
- To write a wide variety of texts, including a review of a novel.

- To know and apply the different stages of the writing process: planning, writing, revising, and sharing.
- To explore the flourishing of Latin American literature in the 1960s.

Contents

Vocabulary

- Useful expressions used to refer to very valuable artwork, to say that something happens in a moment, to say that something is looked at lightly, and to express that something is done in depth.
- Review of known vocabulary about art, architecture, shapes, colors, materials, and literature.
- Art and painting. Art styles.
- Architecture and sculpture. Materials.
- Literature. Literary genres.

Grammar

- Comparisons.
- The neuter article *lo*.
- To express opinion.
- To make value statements.
- Diminutives.
- To give advice and make recommendations.

Culture

- The Mexican Muralist movement and muralist painters Diego Rivera, David Alfaro Siqueiros, and José Clemente Orozco.
- The Colombian artist Fernando Botero.
- *El arte en la calle.*
- The Spanish architect Rafael Moneo.
- *La Ciudad Universitaria de Caracas.*
- The Spanish sculptor Eduardo Chillida.
- The Argentinean writer Jorge Luis Borges and his short story *El Sur*.
- *Premios literarios.*
- The Chilean writer Isabel Allende.
- Latin American literary boom in the 1960s.

Evaluation Criteria

- Talk about art, elements of art, and art styles.
- Describe and compare artwork.
- Talk about paintings, building types, and sculptures.
- Learn about works of art by Hispanic painters, architects, or sculptors.
- Compare and contrast people or things to express equality or inequality.
- Use the neuter article *lo* to refer to a general concept or an abstract idea.

- State personal opinions using different verbs and expressions.
- Make value statements using different expressions with the infinitive or the subjunctive.
- Talk about literature, literary genres, and literary works.
- Use diminutives to express small size or affection.
- Give advice and make recommendations using different expressions.

- Learn about Hispanic writers.
- Learn about the flourishing of Latin American literature in the 1960s.
- Write a review of a novel.
- Read different types of texts and identify main ideas and significant details in them.
- Write guided texts giving information, describing, or narrating events.

Unit Plan

Las tareas/Antes de empezar

Estimated time: 2 sessions.

Text: *Patrimonio cultural.*

Functions & forms:
- Useful expressions used to refer to very valuable artwork, to say that something happens in a moment, to say that something is looked at lightly, and to express that something is done in depth.
- Review of known vocabulary about art, architecture, shapes, colors, materials, and literature.

DESAFÍO 1

Estimated time: 6 sessions.

Text: *Paredes artísticas.*

Functions & forms:
- To describe and compare objects.
- Art and painting. Art styles.
- Comparisons.
- The neuter article *lo.*

Culture:
- *El muralismo mexicano.*
- *Fernando Botero.*
- *El arte en la calle.*

Reading: *Un gran mural.*

DESAFÍO 2

Estimated time: 6 sessions.

Text: *Una catedral vanguardista.*

Functions & forms:
- To give opinions and make value statements.
- Architecture and sculpture. Materials.
- To state opinions.
- To make value statements.

Culture:
- *Rafael Moneo.*
- *La Ciudad Universitaria de Caracas.*
- *Eduardo Chillida.*

Reading: *Rafael Moneo.*

DESAFÍO 3

Estimated time: 6 sessions.

Text: *Un cuento de Borges.*

Functions & forms:
- To give advice and make recommendations.
- Literature. Literary genres.
- Diminutives.
- Grammatical structures to give advice and make recommendations.

Culture:
- *Premios literarios.*
- *Isabel Allende.*
- *Gabriel García Márquez.*

Reading: *El Sur.*

Para terminar

Estimated time: 2 sessions.

Todo junto: Review of *Desafíos 1–3.*

Tu desafío:
- *Desafío A:* Research Velázquez's painting *Las Meninas* and prepare a presentation comparing it with Picasso's *Las Meninas.*
- *Desafío B:* Record a presentation about a building or a sculpture by a Hispanic artist.
- *Desafío C:* Research a Hispanic writer and prepare a presentation about him or her.

MAPA CULTURAL

Estimated time: 1 session.

Mapa cultural: *El «boom» de la literatura latinoamericana.*

ESCRITURA

Estimated time: 1 session.

Writing: *Una reseña.*

PROYECTO/EVALUACIÓN

Estimated time: 2 sessions.

Project: *Una exposición de las obras de arte favoritas.*

Self-evaluation: *Autoevaluación.*

HACIA EL *AP* EXAM*

Estimated time: 2 sessions.

Test: Presentational Speaking: Cultural Comparison.

Standards for Learning Spanish

COMMUNICATION

1.1. Interpersonal mode
- Exchange personal opinions and experiences.
- Engage in oral conversations using personal knowledge and experience.
- Describe and compare paintings, buildings, and sculptures.
- Compare and contrast information and drawings with a partner.
- Summarize the plot of a novel.
- Write a dialogue with a partner.
- Write a list of information about a topic.
- Write definitions.
- Write an e-mail to a partner.

1.2. Interpretive mode
- Demonstrate understanding of oral and written idiomatic expressions.
- Demonstrate understanding of questions relating to familiar and less familiar topics.
- Understand and obtain information from audio or video recordings.
- Understand new vocabulary presented in Spanish.
- Understand written exchanges.

- Identify main ideas and significant details in a variety of texts.
- Extract information from informative sentences or texts and from opinion texts.
- Draw conclusions and make judgments from oral and written texts.
- Interpret texts on other cultures and relate them to personal knowledge and experience.
- Extract information from an image.

1.3. Presentational mode
- Produce and present an original creation orally.
- Dramatize a dialogue.
- Describe and compare works of art.
- Write an explanatory text about own experiences or as result of a research activity.
- Summarize information or a literary story.
- Write value statements and opinions on different topics.
- Write a paragraph giving recommendations.
- Write a biography or a short story.
- Write a review of a novel.
- Draw or use photographs to illustrate information.

CULTURE

2.1. Practices and perspectives
- Reflect on the connection of Hispanic art to the history and socio-political reality of Latin America.
- Read about street art in Hispanic countries.
- Learn about literary prizes in the Hispanic world.
- Explore the Latin American literary boom in the 1960s.

2.2. Products and perspectives
- Learn about renowned Hispanic painters and paintings.
- Learn about Hispanic architecture and renowned Hispanic sculptors and their works.
- Learn about and research famous Latin American writers and literary works.

CONNECTIONS

3.1. Interdisciplinary connections
- Understand the similarities and differences between some aspects of grammar in English and in Spanish.
- Use the writing process to produce a review of a novel and to create a short story.
- Learn about renowned Hispanic artists and art masterpieces.
- Draw a sketch and make a poster.
- Learn about relevant Latin American writers and their works.

3.2. Viewpoints through language / culture
- Read dialogues, informative texts, and literary texts in Spanish that provide insight into Hispanic cultures.
- Learn about Latin American art as an expression of society and socio-political circumstances.
- Discuss the functionality of architecture in current society.
- Compare ancient and modern art.
- Reflect on the role of literature and art in one's life.

COMPARISONS

4.1. Compare languages
- Compare the use of comparative structures in English and in Spanish.
- Compare how to express abstract ideas in English and in Spanish.
- Compare asking for opinions in English and in Spanish.
- Compare how to make value statements in English and in Spanish.
- Compare diminutives in English and in Spanish.
- Compare making demands in English and in Spanish.

4.2. Compare cultures
- Compare street art in Hispanic countries and in one's own community.
- Compare paintings by different Hispanic artists.
- Compare ancient buildings and modern architecture.

COMMUNITIES

5.1. Spanish beyond the school setting
- Describe artwork.
- Reflect on the relationship between art and socio-political reality.
- Encourage the interest in art in one's own community.
- Promote a positive attitude toward other cultures.

5.2. Spanish for lifelong learning
- Encourage the love of art.
- Write a review of a novel.
- Use technology to learn.
- Discuss ways in which Spanish can be used in future life experiences.

Communicative Skills

Interpersonal Mode

		Activities
Speaking	• Exchange opinions, experiences, or information, summarize the plot of a novel, or give recommendations.	• 2, 19, 25, 28, 34, 38, 43, 48, 53, 60, 69, 73, 78, *Escritura*
	• Compare or share information, answers, or drawings with a classmate.	• 5, 51, 53, 65, 79
	• Describe and compare paintings, buildings, or sculptures.	• 6, 19, 34, 37, 38
Writing	• Make a list or a chart with information about a topic.	• 2, 28, 73, 75
	• Write a dialogue, definitions, or an e-mail to a classmate.	• 4, 12, 79
Listening	• Understand and obtain information from oral exchanges.	• 2, 5, 6, 19, 25, 28, 34, 37, 38, 43, 51, 53, 60, 65, 69, 73, 78,
Reading	• Understand an e-mail or a novel review.	• 79, *Escritura*

Interpretive Mode

		Activities
Listening	• Obtain information from conversations.	• 13, 18, 23, 34, 38, 52, 58, 68, 73, 78
	• Understand descriptive or informative audios, or take notes from an audio.	• 8, 30, 34
Reading	• Demonstrate comprehension of written exchanges and longer written dialogues.	• 1, 26, 31, 33, 43, 54, 77
	• Infer meanings based on a text.	• 3, 7, 11, 27, 36, 50, 59, 72
	• Reflect on cultural topics in relation to personal knowledge or experience.	• 2, 5, 10, 14, 20, 35, 39, 44, 55, 61
	• Research using outside sources.	• 10, 51, 57, 70, 80, *Proyecto*
	• Obtain information and draw conclusions from informative sentences or texts, or from opinion texts.	• 25, 29, 42, 47, 49, 52, 56, 74, R3
Viewing	• Obtain information from an image.	• 6, 9, 19, 44, 65

Presentational Mode

		Activities
Speaking	• Present information, a story, or an original creation to the class.	• 37, 51, 53, 76, 80, 81, *Escritura, Proyecto, Hacia el* AP* Exam
Writing	• Write descriptive and/or comparative sentences or texts.	• 19, 37, 38, 53, *Proyecto*
	• Write a text summarizing information or write a literary story.	• 30, 34, 52, 57, 70, 78, 81
	• Write texts making value statements or expressing opinions.	• 46, 47, 52, 80, 81, R5, *Proyecto*
	• Write questions for an interview, definitions, or an explanatory text.	• 51, 54, 59, 70
	• Write a paragraph giving arguments or making recommendations.	• 53, 69, 77, 80
	• Write a biography, a short story, or a review of a novel.	• 57, 76, *Escritura, Proyecto*
Visually Representing	• Draw a sketch.	• 31, 53
	• Use photographs to illustrate information.	• *Escritura, Proyecto*

Cross-Curricular Standards

Subject	Standard	Activities
Language Arts	• Compare elements of Spanish grammar with English equivalents.	• 16, 21, 40, 45, 62, 66
	• Use the writing process to write a short story or a review of a novel.	• 76, *Escritura*
Literature	• Read about and research relevant Hispanic writers and their works.	• *Texto D3*, 56, 57, 61, 70, *Lectura D3*, 71, 80, 81, *Mapa cultural*, R3
Art	• Learn about renowned Hispanic artists and works of art.	• *Texto D1*, 8, 10, *Vocabulario D1*, 13, 29, 30, *Texto D2*, 38, 42, 47, 48, *Lectura D2*, 51, 52, 80, *Proyecto*
	• Draw a sketch or make a poster.	• 31, 53, *Proyecto*

Unit 6 *Creamos*

Lesson Plans (50-Minute Classes)

Day	Objectives	Sessions	Activities	Time	Standards	Resources / Homework
1	To introduce art and literature and the characters' challenges	**Creamos / Las tareas** (298–301) • Warm-Up: Topic orientation • Presentation: *Patrimonio cultural*	1–2	15 m. 35 m.	1.1, 1.2, 1.3, 2.1, 2.2, 3.1, 5.2	Practice Workbook
2	To learn useful expressions related to the unit topic and to review learned vocabulary	**Antes de empezar** (302–303) • Warm-Up: Independent Starter • *Expresiones útiles* • *Recuerda*	3–4 5–6	10 m. 15 m. 25 m.	1.1, 1.2, 1.3, 2.1, 2.2, 3.1, 5.2	Practice Workbook
3	To describe and compare objects	**Desafío 1 – Paredes artísticas** (304–305) • Warm-Up: Independent Starter • *Texto: Paredes artísticas* • *Cultura: El muralismo mexicano*	7–9 10	5 m. 35 m. 10 m.	1.1, 1.2, 1.3, 2.1, 2.2, 3.1, 3.2, 5.2	Audio
4	To talk about art and painting	**Desafío 1 – Vocabulario** (306–307) • Warm-Up: Independent Starter • *Vocabulario: Arte y pintura* • *Cultura: Fernando Botero*	11–14 15	5 m. 35 m. 10 m.	1.1, 1.2, 1.3, 2.1, 2.2, 3.1, 5.2	Audio Practice Workbook
5	To make comparisons	**Desafío 1 – Gramática** (308–309) • Warm-Up: Independent Starter • *Gramática: Las comparaciones* • *Comunidades: El arte en la calle*	16–19 20	5 m. 35 m. 10 m.	1.1, 1.2, 1.3, 2.1, 2.2, 3.1, 4.1, 4.2, 5.1, 5.2	Audio Practice Workbook
6	To learn the uses of the neuter article *lo*	**Desafío 1 – Gramática** (310–311) • Warm-Up: Independent Starter • *Gramática: El artículo neutro 'lo'*	21–25	5 m. 45 m.	1.1, 1.2, 1.3, 2.2, 3.1, 3.2, 4.1, 5.1	Audio Practice Workbook
7	To understand a written dialogue	**Desafío 1 – Lectura** (312–313) • Warm-Up: Independent Starter • *Lectura: Un gran mural*	26–28	5 m. 45 m.	1.1, 1.2, 1.3, 2.1, 2.2, 3.1, 3.2, 5.1, 5.2	
8	To integrate vocabulary and grammar, and to assess student proficiency	**Desafío 1 – Comunicación / Evaluación** (314–315) • Warm-Up: Independent Starter • *Comunicación*: Review • *Final del desafío* • Quiz on *Desafío 1*	29–30 31	5 m. 25 m. 10 m. 10 m.	1.2, 1.3, 2.1, 2.2, 3.1, 3.2, 4.2, 5.1, 5.2	Audio Practice Workbook
9	To give opinions and make value statements	**Desafío 2 – Una catedral vanguardista** (316–317) • Warm-Up: Independent Starter • *Texto: Una catedral vanguardista* • *Cultura: Rafael Moneo*	32–34 35	5 m. 35 m. 10 m.	1.1, 1.2, 1.3, 2.2, 3.1, 4.2, 5.1, 5.2	Audio

Day	Objectives	Sessions	Activities	Time	Standards	Resources / Homework
10	To talk about architecture and sculpture	**Desafío 2 – Vocabulario** (318–319) • Warm-Up: Independent Starter • *Vocabulario: Arquitectura y escultura* • *Cultura: La Ciudad Universitaria de Caracas*	36–38 39	5 m. 35 m. 10 m.	1.1, 1.2, 1.3, 2.1, 2.2, 3.1, 4.2, 5.1, 5.2	Audio Practice Workbook
11	To state opinions	**Desafío 2 – Gramática** (320–321) • Warm-Up: Independent Starter • *Gramática: Expresar opinión* • *Cultura: Eduardo Chillida*	40–43 44	5 m. 35 m. 10 m.	1.1, 1.2, 1.3, 2.1, 2.2, 3.1, 4.1, 5.2	Practice Workbook
12	To make value statements	**Desafío 2 – Gramática** (322–323) • Warm-Up: Independent Starter • *Gramática: Hacer valoraciones*	 45–48	5 m. 45 m.	1.1, 1.2, 1.3, 2.2, 3.1, 4.1, 5.1	Practice Workbook
13	To understand a press interview	**Desafío 2 – Lectura** (324–325) • Warm-Up: Independent Starter • *Lectura: Rafael Moneo*	 49–51	5 m. 45 m.	1.1, 1.2, 1.3, 2.1, 2.2, 3.1, 3.2, 5.1	
14	To integrate vocabulary and grammar, and to assess student proficiency	**Desafío 2 – Comunicación / Evaluación** (326–327) • Warm-Up: Independent Starter • *Comunicación:* Review • *Final del desafío* • Quiz on *Desafío 2*	 52–53 54	5 m. 25 m. 10 m. 10 m.	1.1, 1.2, 1.3, 2.1, 2.2, 3.1, 3.2, 4.2, 5.1, 5.2	Audio Practice Workbook
15	To give advice and make recommendations	**Desafío 3 – Un cuento de Borges** (328–329) • Warm-Up: Independent Starter • *Texto: Un cuento de Borges* • *Conexiones: Premios literarios*	 55–56 57	5 m. 35 m. 10 m.	1.2, 1.3, 2.1, 2.2, 3.1, 3.2, 5.1	
16	To talk about literature	**Desafío 3 – Vocabulario** (330–331) • Warm-Up: Independent Starter • *Vocabulario: Literatura* • *Conexiones: Isabel Allende*	 58–60 61	5 m. 35 m. 10 m.	1.1, 1.2, 1.3, 2.2, 3.1, 5.1, 5.2	Practice Workbook
17	To learn and use diminutives	**Desafío 3 – Gramática** (332–333) • Warm-Up: Independent Starter • *Gramática: Los diminutivos*	 62–65	5 m. 45 m.	1.1, 1.2, 1.3, 3.1, 4.1	Practice Workbook
18	To give advice and make recommendations	**Desafío 3 – Gramática** (334–335) • Warm-Up: Independent Starter • *Gramática: Dar consejos y hacer recomendaciones* • *Conexiones: Gabriel García Márquez*	 66–69 70	5 m. 35 m. 10 m.	1.1, 1.2, 1.3, 2.1, 2.2, 3.1, 4.1	Audio Practice Workbook
19	To understand a literary story	**Desafío 3 – Lectura** (336–337) • Warm-Up: Independent Starter • *Lectura: El Sur*	 71–72	5 m. 45 m.	1.2, 1.3, 2.1, 2.2, 3.2	

Day	Objectives	Sessions	Activities	Time	Standards	Resources / Homework
20	To integrate vocabulary and grammar, and to assess student proficiency	***Desafío 3 – Comunicación / Evaluación*** (338–339) • Warm-Up: Independent Starter • *Comunicación: Review* • *Final del desafío* • Quiz on *Desafío 3*	73–76 77	5 m. 25 m. 10 m. 10 m.	1.1, 1.2, 1.3, 2.2, 3.1, 5.1, 5.2	Audio Practice Workbook
21	To integrate language in context	***Para terminar*** (340–341) • Warm-Up: Independent Starter • *Todo junto* • *Tu desafío*	78–79 80	5 m. 25 m. 20 m.	1.1, 1.2, 1.3, 2.1, 2.2, 3.1, 3.2, 5.1, 5.2	Audio Practice Workbook *Tu desafío* work
22	To integrate language in context and to assess student proficiency	***Tu desafío / Evaluación*** (341) • Warm-Up: Prepare *Tu desafío* presentations • *Tu desafío* presentations • Quiz on *Desafíos 1–3*		5 m. 25 m. 20 m.	1.1, 1.3, 2.1, 2.2, 3.2, 5.1, 5.2	
23	To learn about Latin American literature in the 20th century	***Mapa cultural*** (342–343) • Warm-Up: Independent Starter • *Mapa cultural: El «boom» de la literatura latinoamericana*	81	5 m. 45 m.	1.2, 1.3, 2.1, 2.2, 3.1, 3.2, 5.1, 5.2	Practice Workbook
24	To write a review of a novel	***Escritura*** (344–345) • Warm-Up: Independent Starter • *Escritura: Una reseña*		5 m. 45 m.	1.1, 1.2, 1.3, 3.1, 5.1	Project work
25	To organize an exhibition and describe works of art	***Proyecto*** (350–351) • Warm-Up: Prepare project presentations • Project presentations		10 m. 40 m.	1.2, 1.3, 2.1, 2.2, 3.1, 5.2	**Repaso – Vocabulario** (346–347) **Repaso – Gramática** (348–349)
26	To assess student proficiency	**Assessment** • *Autoevaluación* (351) • Test		10 m. 40 m.	1.1, 1.2, 1.3, 2.1, 2.2, 3.2, 5.1, 5.2	
27	To prepare for the AP* Exam	***Hacia el AP* Exam** (352–353) • Warm-Up: Test introduction • Test: Presentational Speaking: Cultural Comparison • Review and correction of the test		10 m. 20 m. 20 m.	1.3, 2.1, 2.2, 4.2, 5.1, 5.2	
28	To prepare for the AP* Exam	***Hacia el AP* Exam** (352–353) • Warm-Up: About the test • Test: Presentational Speaking: Cultural Comparison • Review and correction of the test		10 m. 20 m. 20 m.	1.3, 2.1, 2.2, 4.2, 5.1, 5.2	

Lesson Plans (90-Minute Classes)

Day	Objectives	Sessions	Activities	Time	Standards	Resources / Homework
1	To introduce art and literature and the characters' challenges, to learn useful expressions related to the unit topic, and to review learned vocabulary	**Creamos / Las tareas / Antes de empezar** (298–303) • Warm-Up: Topic orientation • Presentation: *Patrimonio cultural* • *Expresiones útiles* • *Recuerda*	 1–2 3–4 5–6	 15 m. 35 m. 15 m. 25 m.	1.1, 1.2, 1.3, 2.1, 2.2, 3.1, 5.2	Practice Workbook
2	To describe and compare objects and to talk about art and painting	**Desafío 1 – Paredes artísticas / Vocabulario** (304–307) • Warm-Up: Independent Starter • *Texto: Paredes artísticas* • *Cultura: El muralismo mexicano* • *Vocabulario: Arte y pintura* • *Cultura: Fernando Botero*	 7–9 10 11–14 15	 5 m. 30 m. 10 m. 35 m. 10 m.	1.1, 1.2, 1.3, 2.1, 2.2, 3.1, 3.2, 5.2	Audio Practice Workbook
3	To make comparisons and to learn the uses of the neuter article *lo*	**Desafío 1 – Gramática** (308–311) • Warm-Up: Independent Starter • *Gramática: Las comparaciones* • *Comunidades: El arte en la calle* • *Gramática: El artículo neutro 'lo'*	 16–19 20 21–25	 5 m. 35 m. 10 m. 40 m.	1.1, 1.2, 1.3, 2.1, 2.2, 3.1, 3.2, 4.1, 4.2, 5.1, 5.2	Audio Practice Workbook
4	To understand a written dialogue, to integrate vocabulary and grammar, and to assess student proficiency	**Desafío 1 – Lectura / Comunicación / Evaluación** (312–315) • Warm-Up: Independent Starter • *Lectura: Un gran mural* • *Comunicación*: Review • *Final del desafío* • Quiz on *Desafío 1*	 26–28 29–30 31	 5 m. 40 m. 25 m. 10 m. 10 m.	1.1, 1.2, 1.3, 2.1, 2.2, 3.1, 3.2, 4.2, 5.1, 5.2	Audio Practice Workbook
5	To give opinions and make value statements and to talk about architecture and sculpture	**Desafío 2 – Una catedral vanguardista / Vocabulario** (316–319) • Warm-Up: Independent Starter • *Texto: Una catedral vanguardista* • *Cultura: Rafael Moneo* • *Vocabulario: Arquitectura y escultura* • *Cultura: La Ciudad Universitaria de Caracas*	 32–34 35 36–38 39	 5 m. 30 m. 10 m. 35 m. 10 m.	1.1, 1.2, 1.3, 2.1, 2.2, 3.1, 4.2, 5.1, 5.2	Audio Practice Workbook
6	To state opinions and to make value statements	**Desafío 2 – Gramática** (320–323) • Warm-Up: Independent Starter • *Gramática: Expresar opinión* • *Cultura: Eduardo Chillida* • *Gramática: Hacer valoraciones*	 40–43 44 45–48	 5 m. 35 m. 10 m. 40 m.	1.1, 1.2, 1.3, 2.1, 2.2, 3.1, 4.1, 5.1, 5.2	Practice Workbook

Unit 6 Creamos

Day	Objectives	Sessions	Activities	Time	Standards	Resources / Homework
7	To understand a press interview, to integrate vocabulary and grammar, and to assess student proficiency	**Desafío 2 – Lectura / Comunicación / Evaluación** (324–327) • Warm-Up: Independent Starter • *Lectura: Rafael Moneo* • *Comunicación:* Review • *Final del desafío* • Quiz on *Desafío 2*	 49–51 52–53 54	 5 m. 40 m. 25 m. 10 m. 10 m.	1.1, 1.2, 1.3, 2.1, 2.2, 3.1, 3.2, 4.2, 5.1, 5.2	Audio Practice Workbook
8	To give advice and make recommendations and to talk about literature	**Desafío 3 – Un cuento de Borges / Vocabulario** (328–331) • Warm-Up: Independent Starter • *Texto: Un cuento de Borges* • *Conexiones: Premios literarios* • *Vocabulario: Literatura* • *Conexiones: Isabel Allende*	 55–56 57 58–60 61	 5 m. 30 m. 10 m. 35 m. 10 m.	1.1, 1.2, 1.3, 2.1, 2.2, 3.1, 3.2, 5.1, 5.2	Practice Workbook
9	To learn and use diminutives and to give advice and make recommendations	**Desafío 3 – Gramática** (332–335) • Warm-Up: Independent Starter • *Gramática: Los diminutivos* • *Gramática: Dar consejos y hacer recomendaciones* • *Conexiones: Gabriel García Márquez*	 62–65 66–69 70	 5 m. 40 m. 35 m. 10 m.	1.1, 1.2, 1.3, 2.1, 2.2, 3.1, 4.1	Audio Practice Workbook
10	To understand a literary story and to integrate vocabulary and grammar	**Desafío 3 – Lectura / Comunicación / Evaluación** (336–339) • Warm-Up: Independent Starter • *Lectura: El Sur* • *Comunicación:* Review • *Final del desafío* • Quiz on *Desafío 3*	 71–72 73–76 77	 5 m. 40 m. 25 m. 10 m. 10 m.	1.1, 1.2, 1.3, 2.1, 2.2, 3.1, 3.2, 5.1, 5.2	Audio Practice Workbook **Para terminar – Tu desafío** (341)
11	To integrate language in context and to assess student proficiency	**Para terminar / Evaluación** (340–341) • Warm-Up: Independent Starter • *Todo junto* • *Tu desafío:* work and presentations • Quiz on *Desafíos 1–3*	 78–79 80	 5 m. 25 m. 40 m. 20 m.	1.1, 1.2, 1.3, 2.1, 2.2, 3.1, 3.2, 5.1, 5.2	Audio Practice Workbook
12	To learn about Latin American literature in the 20th century and to write a review of a novel	**Mapa cultural / Escritura** (342–345) • Warm-Up: Independent Starter • *Mapa cultural: El «boom» de la literatura latinoamericana* • *Escritura: Una reseña*	 81	 5 m. 40 m. 45 m.	1.1, 1.2, 1.3, 2.1, 2.2, 3.1, 3.2, 5.1, 5.2	Practice Workbook **Repaso – Vocabulario** (346–347) **Repaso – Gramática** (348–349) Project work

Day	Objectives	Sessions	Activities	Time	Standards	Resources / Homework
13	To organize an art exhibition and describe works of art, and to assess student proficiency	***Proyecto / Assessment*** (350–351) • Warm-Up: Prepare project presentations • Project presentations • *Autoevaluación* • Test		10 m. 45 m. 10 m. 25 m.	1.1, 1.2, 1.3, 2.1, 2.2, 3.1, 3.2, 5.1, 5.2	
14	To prepare for the AP* Exam	***Hacia el* AP* Exam** (352–353) • Warm-Up: Test introduction • Test: Presentational Speaking: Cultural Comparison • Review and correction of the test		15 m. 40 m. 35 m.	1.3, 2.1, 2.2, 4.2, 5.1, 5.2	
15	To practice oral skills in social interaction	**Final Activity** • Warm-Up: Presentation of the activity • Role-play activity		15 m. 75 m.	1.1, 1.2, 1.3, 2.1, 2.2, 4.2, 5.1, 5.2	

Final Activity (Day 15)

Presentation

- Explain to students that they will be participating in a role-play situation related to one of the topics covered in this unit. You may wish to suggest the following situations:
  1. conducting a guided tour of a museum in which they compare and contrast two works of art by a Hispanic artist;
  2. planning a mural for the Spanish classroom and explaining the design choices;
  3. conducting a walking tour of the downtown area of a Spanish-speaking city and describing the main buildings;
  4. being part of a committee who has to decide on a new sculpture for their community;
  5. retelling a short story by a Hispanic writer;
  6. acting out a scene from a novel by a Hispanic writer (e.g., the windmills scene from *Don Quijote*).

Preparation

- Divide the class into small groups and assign a different situation to each group. Ask students to brainstorm the details of their assigned situation and the different characters who will take part in it. Then allow students time to write the script cooperatively. They should plan for a role-play of about five to six minutes.

Revision and Rehearsal

- Ask students to revise their scripts, paying attention to accurate use of vocabulary and grammar structures. At this point, students may also correct any inconsistencies in the storyline, add a punch line, or make other minor changes they deem appropriate. Then allow for rehearsal time. Explain to students that they will be able to improvise, or ad-lib. However, rehearsing their lines a few times will give them confidence and improve their fluency.

Dramatization and Evaluation

- Call on each group to role-play their assigned situation. Assess students on fluency, pronunciation, content, organization, and correct use of target vocabulary and grammar. You may want to prepare a short evaluation questionnaire that the class fills in at the end of each role-play. If time permits, discuss as a class the situations upon which the role-plays were based.

8 **El muralismo mexicano**

–Señores y señoras, por favor, pasen conmigo a la siguiente sala del museo. Aquí tenemos algunos murales de los pintores más conocidos del muralismo mexicano. Como saben, a principios del siglo xx México se recupera de una revolución. Muchos artistas empiezan a pintar murales como reacción a la realidad sociopolítica del momento, como este que vemos aquí.

–¿Quiénes eran los pintores más famosos de este movimiento?

–David Alfaro Siqueiros, José Clemente Orozco y el más conocido de todos: Diego Rivera. Ellos querían representar al pueblo mexicano y su historia.

–¿Y no hay más murales de otros artistas en el museo?

–Bueno, tenemos alguno más, pero los murales más conocidos no están aquí. La razón es que normalmente los artistas pintaban en las paredes de los edificios públicos parar poder comunicar sus mensajes al gran público. De hecho, en 1922, el presidente de México, Álvaro Obregón, promovió los murales en espacios públicos y en edificios del gobierno.

–¿Y de qué tratan esos murales?

–Muestran escenas de la conquista española, la Revolución mexicana, la industrialización, las tradiciones populares de México... También están retratadas algunas personas famosas de la cultura popular.

13 **Una obra maestra**

–Esta es una de las obras de Diego Rivera que más me gustan. Y debe de ser una de las mejores porque he leído que se vendió en una subasta en más de tres millones de dólares.

–¿En serio? ¡Es impresionante! ¿Y por qué te gusta tanto esta obra?

–Pues por la escena en sí. En esta obra Rivera no trata temas políticos ni de la historia de México, sino otro de los temas que trataban los muralistas: las tradiciones populares y el folclore, que a mí me parece muy interesante.

–Ah, ya entiendo. A ti te interesan las escenas de la vida cotidiana, ¿no?

–Exacto. En este cuadro se ve que los personajes van a bailar una danza tradicional. Fíjate en los detalles: van descalzos y llevan la ropa y los peinados típicos. También me gusta el estilo de la obra. Las formas son sencillas, pero lo que más destaca es el color. Los tonos son muy vivos y me encanta el contraste entre el primer plano, con colores más cálidos, y el verde del árbol del fondo.

–Sí, es verdad. Los colores son muy llamativos. Es un cuadro muy bonito, Eva.

18 **¿Más o menos?**

1. –Ethan, ¿sabes que el Museo del Prado de Madrid tiene más de veinte mil obras de arte?
   –No, no lo sabía. Pensaba que tenía menos. Pero... ¿estás segura de que se pueden ver tantas obras?
   –Es que no todas están expuestas porque no hay espacio suficiente para mostrarlas.

2. –Acabo de leer que Fernando Botero nació en 1932.
   –¡No lo sabía! Yo creía que había nacido en los años 50.
   –Pues no; en los años 50 ya había realizado su primera exposición.

3. –Ethan, ¿tienes la pintura para el mural?
   –Sí, pero no sabía cuánta cantidad necesitábamos y compré tres galones de cada color que me pediste.
   –¡Qué exagerado eres, no necesitamos tanta pintura! Bueno, al menos ya sabemos que no tendremos que comprar más...

4. –¿A qué lugar te gustaría viajar para poder ver alguna obra de arte?
   –Pues, si pudiera elegir, me gustaría ir a la Ciudad de México para ver los murales que hay en las paredes exteriores de los edificios. No tengo muchas ganas de visitar museos, pero me encantaría ver los grandes murales mexicanos.
   –¿Por qué no vamos? ¡Nos ayudaría mucho con el desafío!

23 **Una visita al Museo del Prado**

–Muy buenos días, señor Navarro. ¿Ha descansado bien?

–Sí, muchas gracias.

–¿En qué puedo ayudarlo?

–Querría visitar el Museo del Prado, pero no sé a qué hora hay menos gente.

–Es mejor ir después de comer. Por la mañana suele haber más gente.

–¿Cree que tendré que esperar mucho tiempo para entrar?

–Es un museo muy visitado. Lo más probable es que haya fila para entrar.

–Sí, lo suponía. Lo bueno es que el horario de visitas es muy amplio, así que tendré tiempo.

–Espero que lo disfrute. Hay cuadros muy interesantes de pintores italianos, flamencos, franceses, etc. Pero lo más importante es que vea las salas de los pintores españoles, son fantásticas.

–Muchas gracias por la información. ¿Sabe si hay visitas guiadas?

–Sí, las hay, pero tendría que haber hecho la reserva hace tiempo. Ahora creo que es tarde para conseguir una visita guiada.

–Bueno, no importa. Probablemente tengan audioguías. Hasta luego. Y gracias por su ayuda.

–De nada. Que pase un buen día.

30 Una exposición especial

Muy buenos días, señores y señoras, y bienvenidos a nuestra exposición. Vamos a comenzar con este fantástico mural de Diego Rivera, *Sueño de una tarde dominical en la Alameda Central*. Diego Rivera tenía casi sesenta años cuando el arquitecto de un hotel en construcción en la Ciudad de México le pidió que creara una obra para su edificio.

Rivera mezcla en esta obra sus recuerdos de la niñez y la historia de México, representada por algunos de sus protagonistas más emblemáticos. El artista incluyó unos ciento cincuenta retratos de familiares y personajes históricos. Ahora veremos algunos.

Para entender bien esta obra, divídanla en tres secciones. Comencemos por el lado izquierdo. En esta sección el artista hace un recorrido por la historia de México, representando la conquista, la época colonial, la Guerra de Independencia y algunos de los acontecimientos más importantes de principios del siglo XX. En esta parte tenemos retratados al conquistador Hernán Cortés y al presidente Juárez, entre otros muchos personajes.

El segundo segmento está compuesto por tres figuras fundamentales: la Catrina, que es esta calavera que representa la muerte. Como saben, la muerte tenía un sentido muy especial en la cultura mexicana. A su izquierda está el creador de este personaje: José Guadalupe Posada. Y a su derecha, un niño: es el autorretrato de Diego Rivera. Detrás podemos ver también a su tercera esposa: la pintora mexicana Frida Kahlo.

La tercera sección del mural representa al México de los años 40, identificado por construcciones como el Palacio de Bellas Artes y la plaza de toros. Aquí el artista trata los movimientos campesinos que culminaron en la revolución de 1910. El hombre montado a caballo es Emiliano Zapata, que está rodeado por otros revolucionarios y por una mujer armada, que representa a las mujeres que lucharon en la Revolución mexicana.

34 La catedral de Los Ángeles

–Fíjate en el exterior de esta catedral. Si no lo supiera, nunca habría adivinado que es una construcción religiosa. Se parece más a un museo.

–Sí, es cierto. Los expertos dicen que Moneo diseñó el edificio para ser un espacio público. Para él era importante que reflejara la diversidad de los ciudadanos de Los Ángeles.

–Me parece increíble que la arquitectura de un edificio pueda representar el concepto de la diversidad.

–Bueno es que la arquitectura es un arte. Es capaz de comunicar tanto como una pieza de música, una pintura o una escultura.

–Mira, ahí hay una placa con un poco de historia.

–¿Qué dice?

–Pues que en 1994 un terremoto causó tantos daños a la vieja catedral Santa Vibiana que era imposible construirla de nuevo. Por eso, decidieron construir una catedral nueva y convocaron un concurso internacional para elegir un arquitecto que la diseñara.

–Y ganó Rafael Moneo.

–Efectivamente. Al diseñar la catedral, tuvo que tener en cuenta que era necesario que la construcción resistiera los terremotos, que son bastante frecuentes en esta zona.

–He leído en una guía que la catedral tiene más de 4.000 metros cuadrados, o sea, más de 43.000 pies cuadrados. ¿Es posible que sea la tercera catedral más grande del mundo?

–Parece inmensa. Vamos a verla por dentro.

–Me encanta la luz. Está claro que Moneo ha empleado la luz natural para reflejar la espiritualidad del sitio. Y fíjate en las capillas. Ahora sí me parece una catedral…

38 Exploremos la escultura

–¿Cuáles son las esculturas más impresionantes que han visto en sus viajes por el mundo hispano? Empieza tú, Michelle.

–Yo lo tengo claro. Cuando viajamos a México, tuve ocasión de ver unas esculturas increíbles. Eran unas caras enormes de la época olmeca que fueron esculpidas en basalto, un tipo de piedra volcánica. Se cree que representan a los guerreros de aquella antigua civilización. Cada escultura pesa varias toneladas y algunas miden hasta cuatro metros de altura.

–Pues yo pude ver los moáis de la isla de Pascua.

–¡Qué suerte, Ethan! ¿Y qué te parecieron?

–Son impresionantes. Yo sabía que eran grandes, pero no tanto… También están hechos de piedra volcánica.

–¿Y tú, Eva? ¿Recuerdas alguna escultura que te haya llamado la atención?

–Sí, pero es totalmente distinta a las que han descrito ustedes, y mucho más moderna. ¿Conocen a Miró, el pintor español?

–Sí, he visto fotos de sus cuadros, pero no sabía que también era escultor.

–Pues sí. Cuando visité España con mi familia estuvimos unos días en Barcelona y visitamos el Parque Joan Miró. Allí hay una escultura enorme, mide más de 20 metros. Está hecha de cemento recubierto de cerámica de colores muy vivos y alegres. Se llama *Mujer y pájaro*. Si la miras con cuidado, puedes ver la forma de una mujer que lleva un sombrero. Y, sobre el sombrero, hay un pájaro, que es un motivo típico del artista. Luego les muestro unas fotos.

Unit 6 Creamos

52 **El encuentro entre dos artes**

–¿Qué te parece esta exposición, Flor?

–No sé, Diego. Es original, pero me parece un poco extraño que estos estudiantes se hayan inspirado en un diseñador de moda.

–Pues desde mi punto de vista los diseños son muy creativos.

–Eso sí. Y, ahora que lo pienso, Coco Chanel, la famosa diseñadora francesa, dijo que «la moda es arquitectura; solo es una cuestión de proporciones». O sea, que no es tan raro que dos artes se unan para crear algo tan innovador.

–Claro. Es bueno que los artistas se inspiren en cualquier elemento del mundo que los rodea. Como el mar Cantábrico inspiraba a Eduardo Chillida, el estudio de la técnica de Balenciaga ha inspirado a estos estudiantes.

–¿Crees que algún día serán famosos y se podrán comprar sus diseños en las tiendas?

–No creo que todos consigan hacerse famosos, pero seguro que tienen futuro en el mundo de la arquitectura y del diseño.

–¿Y qué te parece si nosotros diseñamos unos muebles inspirados en las pinturas cubistas de Picasso? A lo mejor también nos hacemos famosos.

–Muy graciosa…

58 **¿De qué hablan?**

1. –¿Ya has entendido el poema?
   –Sí, sí. Ahora que sé que la luna representa la muerte, el río la vida y el espejo el paso del tiempo, por fin lo he comprendido.

2. –¿Y ese libro?
   –Es de la biblioteca. Es de mi escritora favorita, he leído casi todas sus novelas. Son apasionantes.
   –Pues no la conozco. Me tienes que recomendar alguna de sus obras.

3. –¿Qué estás leyendo?
   –Una novela excelente, pero muy triste. Trata de un hombre que es acusado de asesinato, pero que en realidad es inocente. La novela cuenta cómo consigue demostrar su inocencia.

4. –¿Ya terminaste la novela?
   –Sí.
   –¿Y qué te ha parecido?
   –Es muy buena. El autor te sitúa tan bien en el lugar, da tantos detalles y lo describe con tanta precisión que parece que lo estás viendo.

5. –¡No te vas a creer quién era el asesino!
   –El hermano del protagonista. Leí la novela antes que tú, ¿no te acuerdas?

68 **Buenos consejos**

1. –¿Qué te pasa, Juan? Estás muy serio.
   –Es que mis padres están convencidos de que debo estudiar Economía, como ellos, para poder encargarme de su empresa en el futuro. Pero a mí eso no me gusta, yo prefiero estudiar Literatura. Mi sueño es ser escritor.
   –Yo que tú estudiaría Economía porque tienes el futuro asegurado.

2. –¡Estoy desesperada! ¡Se me ha estropeado la computadora y mañana tengo que entregar un trabajo en la escuela! Si no lo llevo, no aprobaré la asignatura.
   –Tranquila, Marisa. Te sugiero que hables con tu profesor. Seguro que si le explicas lo que ha pasado, te deja unos días más de plazo.

3. –¡He perdido mis apuntes! ¡No me lo puedo creer! Si ayer los tenía aquí, sobre mi mesa. Y el examen de Literatura es mañana. ¿Qué hago?
   –¡Ay, Carlos! Deberías llamar a un compañero de clase ahora mismo y preguntarle si pueden estudiar juntos.

4. –Hola, Mario. Soy Teresa. ¿Podemos hablar?
   –Claro. ¿Qué ocurre?
   –Es que me han llamado para hacer una entrevista de trabajo y estoy muy nerviosa. Sé que me van a hacer una prueba en francés y hace años que no lo hablo. Pero necesito ese trabajo, es una gran oportunidad.
   –¿Cuándo es la entrevista?
   –Dentro de dos semanas.
   –Tendrías que contratar a un profesor particular para que te diera clase todos los días. Es lo mejor.

73 **Un examen de Literatura**

–Repasemos, Lucas. ¿Qué recuerdas de *La casa de los espíritus*?

–A ver… *La casa de los espíritus*… Bueno, sé que la escribió la novelista chilena Isabel Allende. Y que narra la historia de Chile a través de varias generaciones de una familia. Pero no recuerdo cómo se llamaban los protagonistas…

–Yo sí. Eran Esteban y Alba.

–Ah, sí. Vale, ahora pregunto yo. ¿Recuerdas el cuento *Un día de estos*?

–¿El de Gabriel García Márquez?

–Sí. ¿Quién es el protagonista?

–¡Qué fácil! El protagonista del cuento es un dentista. Ahora me toca a mí. ¿Quién es el autor de *El laberinto de la soledad*?

–Este… ¡Paz! ¡El escritor mexicano Octavio Paz!

–¡Correcto! ¿Y te acuerdas del nombre del protagonista?

–¡Esa es una pregunta trampa! No hay protagonista porque es un ensayo. Pero, ¿recuerdas el tema?

—Sí, porque me impresionó mucho. Es un ensayo sobre la identidad mexicana.

—Bueno, creo que estamos listos para nuestro examen.

78 El arte al alcance de los niños

Fuente: Cadena SER, España

—*Hoy por hoy Madrid*. Con Marta González Novo.

—Lo cierto es que si a nosotros de pequeños nos hubiesen enseñado los cuadros de los pintores clásicos como se los enseñan a los niños ahora en el Museo del Centro de Arte Reina Sofía la verdad es que otro gallo nos habría cantado. De ello vamos a hablar con nuestro experto en arte, con Pablo Ortiz de Zárate. Pablo, hola.

—Hola, ¿qué tal? Muy buenas.

—¿Qué hacen en el Reina Sofía con los niños?

—Hay unas visitas guiadas especiales para Navidad, pero no las guía el clásico sabelotodo de museos.

—No es el empollón del museo.

—No. Son artistas de circo los que van a explicar no sé cómo varias obras. Pero tampoco han elegido las más famosas o fáciles de explicar, sino algunas de las más complicadas. Si yo tuviera que elegir la más difícil de explicar de todo el museo a un adulto, pues esas las han elegido. Se las van a contar a los niños unos actores de circo haciendo gestos... Todo un misterio.

—¿Y cuáles pueden ser, por ejemplo, las obras más difíciles de explicar?

—Pues, por ejemplo, hay una de Carl Andre, que es un artista de los años sesenta que lo que hizo fue una especie de tablero de ajedrez en el suelo. Tablero de ajedrez hecho de magnesio y de cobre. En teoría esta obra está hecha para pisarla. Hay que... el espectador debería poder pisarla. Hoy en día no se puede porque vale mucho mucho dinero; entonces, no dejan. Pero el objetivo era que la gente la pisara para protestar un poco. Es una especie de crítica contra el arte. Yo no sé si los actores de estas visitas guiadas para niños las van a llegar a pisar, pero me temo que algo intentarán.

—Vamos a preguntárselo a Berta Sureda, que es la directora de actividades públicas del Reina Sofía. Berta, hola.

—Hola, buenas tardes.

—¿Van a poder pisar este tablero de ajedrez?

—No.

—Ya me lo imaginaba, muy caro para...

—No van a poderlo pisar, pero sí van a poderlo entender, van a poder interactuar con él. Van a jugar alrededor del tablero como de muchas otras obras que, como decíais, verdaderamente son obras muy complicadas. No son las obras más fáciles. Es arte de los años 60 y 70. La cuestión es que estas obras tienen tanto en común con el circo... La práctica que desarrollaba el artista verdaderamente era, como también explicabais, era una práctica muy irónica, muy participativa, donde el público interviene... Entonces toda esta proximidad entre este arte que se hacía en los años 60 y 70, y las prácticas circenses nos ha hecho plantear este itinerario.

Creamos

The Unit

- The themes for Unit 6 are art and literature. The participants will learn about art, architecture, sculpture, and literature. They will also learn to compare works of art, express their opinions and value judgments, and make recommendations.

- Diana, a veteran of *Fans del español*, has prepared some tasks, and has created a website to inform the participants about them.

  – *Desafío 1.* Eva and Ethan will help some university students create a mural.

  – *Desafío 2.* In Los Angeles, Michelle and Daniel must prepare a digital tour of the cathedral.

  – *Desafío 3.* Asha and Lucas have to combine literature with the visual arts. They must choose and illustrate a short story by the famous Argentinean author Jorge Luis Borges, to include it in an anthology.

Activities	Standards	Resources
Creamos	1.2, 2.1, 2.2	

Teaching Suggestions

Warm-Up / Independent Starter

- Ask students to look at the photos on these pages and come up with a one-paragraph description for one of the images. This will reactivate the vocabulary they have previously learned about art, architecture, and literature.

Preparation

- Have students read the captions and ask them if they know the art or the artists featured. Encourage students to share with the class other painters or architects they know and other authors from the Spanish-speaking world they have read. Invite students to briefly describe some of the best-known works by these artists or writers.

- Have students read each *Desafío*'s objective, as well as the vocabulary and grammar goals, then discuss how each picture might relate to these objectives and goals.

298

Creamos

Arte y literatura

DESAFÍO 1

DESAFÍO 2

Rafael Moneo. Catedral de Los Ángeles (Estados Unidos).

▶ **Describir y comparar objetos**

Vocabulario
Arte y pintura

Gramática
Las comparaciones
El artículo neutro *lo*

▶ **Opinar y hacer valoraciones**

Vocabulario
Arquitectura y escultura

Gramática
Expresar opinión
Hacer valoraciones

Diego Rivera. *Sueño de una tarde de domingo en la Alameda Central* (1957).

298 doscientos noventa y ocho

The Challenge

DESAFÍO 1

Diego Rivera. *Sueño de una tarde de domingo en la Alameda Central*

The famous mural by Diego Rivera (Mexico, 1886–1957) features a summary of the history of Mexico, including the conquest by the Spaniards, the era of colonialism, and independence. The painting includes portraits of Moctezuma, Hernán Cortés, La Catrina (the skeleton lady in the middle), Frida Kahlo (Rivera's wife), and Diego Rivera as a boy. The mural is housed at the Museo Mural Diego Rivera, which is located in the Alameda district of Mexico City.

DESAFÍO 2

Rafael Moneo. Catedral de Los Ángeles

Some Spanish architects have acquired world fame in recent times. Among them, Rafael Moneo, best known for his National Museum of Roman Art in Mérida, Spain. After the original cathedral of Los Angeles was damaged by an earthquake in 1994, Moneo won an international contest to design the new church. He designed the church to represent the diversity of the citizens of Los Angeles. In the United States, Moneo has also designed the Davis Museum at Wellesley College and Columbia University's Northwest Corner building, among others.

Creamos

DESAFÍO

3

▶ **Dar consejos y hacer recomendaciones**

Vocabulario
Literatura

Gramática
Los diminutivos

Dar consejos y hacer recomendaciones

Exposición sobre el escritor argentino Jorge Luis Borges.

doscientos noventa y nueve **299**

Picture Discussion

- Have students look at the images again and describe them orally. Then, ask them to use their Independent Starters to initiate a discussion. What do they think of the painting? Do they like the building? Encourage students to express their opinions.

Diego Rivera. *Sueño de una tarde de domingo en la Alameda Central* **(1957)**

- You may wish to talk about the word *alameda*, which comes from *álamo* (poplar), a type of tree. Point out the fact that the *alameda* is often a promenade where people gather—especially on Sundays—to go for a stroll. Have them describe the people in the painting: *¿Quiénes son? ¿Qué representan?*

Rafael Moneo. Catedral de Los Ángeles (Estados Unidos)

- Review some vocabulary related to construction materials and shapes. You may need to preview words such as *ladrillo, piedra, cemento, metal, cuadrado, rectangular, redondo*. Ask students about the use of some buildings: *¿Para qué sirven las catedrales? ¿Y los ayuntamientos? ¿Qué es un castillo? ¿Y un palacio?*

Exposición sobre el escritor argentino Jorge Luis Borges

- Call students' attention to the library in the photo. Explain that libraries had a special meaning for Borges. Not only did he work as a librarian in Buenos Aires, but libraries often appear in his literature as a symbol of life and of the labyrinth-like nature of knowledge. Then have students discuss what they understand by an anthology: *¿Qué es una antología? ¿Pueden recomendar alguna antología a sus compañeros?*

Objectives

- By the end of Unit 6, students will be able to
  - Describe and compare works of art.
  - Express opinions and value judgments.
  - Talk about sculpture, architecture, and literature.
  - Make recommendations and give advice.
  - Talk about prominent figures in the arts, architecture, and literature of Latin America and Spain, and familiarize themselves with important works of art and literature of the Spanish-speaking world.

⚑ DESAFÍO 3

Exposición sobre el escritor argentino Jorge Luis Borges

Jorge Luis Borges is the author of numerous essays, poems, and short stories. He was a language perfectionist and a true intellectual. His writing is complex and reveals knowledge and erudition. He was one of the founders and promoters of the literary movement known as *ultraísmo* in the 1920s, which advocated for a language rich in metaphors. However, later in his life he refused any literary affiliation. His originality, brilliant thought, and precise prose made him the recipient of numerous literary awards.

299

Las tareas

Presentation

- Diana, a former participant, has prepared a website to explain the challenge to each pair. Students will preview ways to refer to a valuable piece of art, to express that something is done in depth or that it is looked at lightly, and to talk about something that occurs in an instant.

Activities	Standards	Resources
Texto	1.2, 2.1, 2.2, 3.1	
1.	1.2, 1.3, 2.1, 2.2, 3.1	
2.	1.1, 2.2, 3.1, 5.2	

Teaching Suggestions

Warm-Up / Independent Starter

- To activate students' previous knowledge about the themes of this unit, have them list the artists and writers they know from the Spanish-speaking world. You may want to help them remember with the following examples:

Artistas	Escritores
Frida Kahlo	Mario Vargas Llosa
Fernando Botero	Miguel de Cervantes

Preparation

- Invite volunteers to share their Independent Starters. Review the artists and writers of the Spanish-speaking world that they have jotted down, and discuss some of the works of art or pieces of writing that students know or have read.

- Read Pablo Picasso's quote aloud, which Diana includes in the introduction of her message. Picasso says that art is a lie that makes us understand reality. You may ask students to give their opinions about this citation and to guess what Picasso meant by it.

- On the board, write the following phrases from the reading on this page and the pairs' dialogue on page 301: *echen una ojeada, investigaremos a fondo, voy a echar un vistazo, vuelvo en un pispás*. Have students classify the phrases into these categories: *acción rápida, acción lenta*. How did they know? Encourage students to add other phrases to the list (e.g., *rápidamente, con cuidado*).

Las tareas

Patrimonio cultural

Diana ha preparado unos desafíos muy artísticos para los participantes y ha creado un sitio web para comunicárselos. ¿Quiénes van a hacer la obra maestra de este último desafío?

El último desafío

INFORMACIÓN	DESAFÍOS	PREGUNTAS

Hola, chicos:

Bienvenidos a su último desafío. ¿Sabían que el pintor español Pablo Picasso dijo: «El arte es una mentira que nos acerca a la verdad»? Pues bien, vamos a ver algunas de estas «mentiras» de la arquitectura, la escultura, la pintura y la literatura para saber lo que se puede aprender de ellas.

DESAFÍO 1

Ethan y Eva, preparen sus pinceles y paletas: van a ayudar a un grupo de estudiantes universitarios a pintar un mural al estilo de los grandes muralistas mexicanos. Ellos tienen todos los materiales necesarios, pero ustedes los van a ayudar a diseñar el mural. Para saber más sobre el muralismo como movimiento artístico, miren el enlace que les he enviado por correo electrónico.

DESAFÍO 2

Sé que Michelle y Daniel van a visitar a Ethan y a Eva en California, pero no se preocupen: allí encontrarán su desafío. Van a ir a la catedral de Los Ángeles para hacer un *tour* digital. Les he enviado información por correo electrónico. Echen una ojeada a las fotografías, verán que es una construcción muy interesante.

DESAFÍO 3

Lucas y Asha tienen un desafío doblemente artístico: van a mezclar la literatura con el arte visual. Tendrán que escoger un relato del escritor argentino Jorge Luis Borges e ilustrarlo para incluirlo en una antología. Les recomiendo que empiecen a trabajar enseguida porque hay mucho que leer. Pueden comenzar su investigación con los enlaces que les he enviado. Y recuerden: como dijo Borges, «El tiempo es el mejor antologista, o el único, tal vez».

Differentiated Instruction

DEVELOPING LEARNERS

- Ask students the following questions:
  1. *¿A quiénes ayudarán Ethan y Eva?* (A un grupo de estudiantes universitarios.)
  2. *¿Qué estilo van a seguir Ethan y Eva?* (El de los grandes muralistas mexicanos.)
  3. *¿Qué opina Diana sobre la catedral de Los Ángeles?* (Es una construcción muy interesante.)
  4. *¿A quiénes van a visitar Michelle y Daniel en California?* (A Ethan y a Eva.)
  5. *¿Quién es Jorge Luis Borges?* (Es un escritor argentino.)
  6. *¿Qué es una antología?* (Es una colección de textos literarios.)

EXPANDING LEARNERS

- After students have read the dialogue, ask them to comment on the quote attributed to Borges (i.e., *El tiempo es el mejor antologista, o el único, tal vez*). Remind students that *una antología es una colección de textos literarios*. Ask students why they think Borges equates *el tiempo* with *una antología*. Encourage students to discuss the similarities and differences between the two. You may also want to share another quote from Borges and have students comment: *El tiempo es la sustancia de la que estoy hecho*.

¿Muralistas mexicanos? Yo no conozco a ninguno. ¿Cómo vamos a lograr el desafío?

Investigaremos a fondo sobre ese estilo artístico.

Desde luego, esta catedral es una obra maestra de la arquitectura.

Supongo que hemos leído algo de Borges en la escuela, ¿no?

Sí, tengo muchas ganas de visitarla.

No lo sé. Voy a echar un vistazo al índice de nuestro libro de texto. Espérame aquí, vuelvo en un pispás.

 1 **¿Comprendes?**

▶ **Responde** a estas preguntas.

1. ¿En qué consiste el desafío de Ethan y Eva?
2. ¿Qué van a hacer Michelle y Daniel en Los Ángeles?
3. ¿Por qué el desafío de Lucas y Asha es doblemente artístico?
4. ¿Con qué categoría de arte se relaciona el desafío de cada pareja?
5. En tu opinión, ¿por qué dice Picasso que «el arte es una mentira que nos acerca a la verdad»? ¿Qué significan sus palabras?

  2 **Piensa**

▶ **Habla** con tu compañero(a). Hagan una lista de artistas y escritores(as) que conozcan. ¿Cuántos son de origen hispano? Comenten lo que saben sobre cada uno(a).

Modelo

A. Yo conozco a un arquitecto español muy famoso que se llama Gaudí. Sus obras más conocidas están en Barcelona y creo que son de finales del siglo XIX, pero no estoy muy segura.
B. Ah, sí, es el autor del templo de la Sagrada Familia.

trescientos uno 301

Texto: Patrimonio cultural

- Read the title aloud and ask students to explain the term *patrimonio cultural*. If students are having some difficulties with the word *patrimonio*, give them this synonym: *herencia*. Then invite students to provide examples of cultural heritage. Is there a consensus on the type of things that make up a cultural heritage?

- Read the introduction to the text aloud, and then ask for three volunteers to read the *desafíos* aloud. Write down two word categories on the board (*arte* and *literatura*), and ask students to associate words from the text with the corresponding category. For example: *arte* → *pinceles, paletas*; *literatura* → *relato, escritor*.

Activities

1. To expand this activity, ask students to describe the three challenges in detail. Brainstorm with them vocabulary used to talk about art, architecture, and literature, such as *pintura, escultura, diseño, edificio, poesía, novela,* etc.

2. Ask students to express themselves about artists that they admire, whether they are from the Spanish-speaking world or not. You may get them started with these or similar questions: *¿Por qué te gusta X? ¿En qué es diferente de Y? ¿En qué se parece?*

Answer Key

1. 1. Van a ayudar a un grupo de universitarios a pintar un mural.
   2. Van a preparar un *tour* digital de la catedral de Los Ángeles.
   3. Porque tienen que mezclar la literatura con el arte visual.
   4. Ethan y Eva: pintura; Michelle y Daniel: arquitectura; Asha y Lucas: literatura y artes visuales.
   5. Answers will vary.
2. Answers will vary.

Additional Resources

Fans Online activities
Practice Workbook

HERITAGE LANGUAGE LEARNERS

- Ask students to share with the class any information they may have (or can research) on leading muralists or other artists from their family's country of origin, as well as well-known architects or writers. Students may prepare a brief biography on one or two of these artists, and bring in images of their major works or read excerpts from some of their selected literary pieces. Encourage the rest of the class to ask questions about the lives and artistic contributions these individuals have made or continue to make.

MULTIPLE INTELLIGENCES:
Visual-Spatial Intelligence

- Ask students to imagine that they have been living abroad for several months and want to share their new surroundings with friends back home. First, they have to decide in which Spanish-speaking country they have been living. Then, they need to focus on a city and its landmarks. Next, they will prepare a "digital tour" of some key sites of their city with images taken from the web or from printed media. Students should be prepared to give background information on the selected images.

Unit 6
Antes de empezar

Presentation

- In this section, students will learn a variety of useful expressions to refer to a valuable piece of art, to talk about something that occurs in an instant, and to express that something is looked at lightly or that it is done in depth.

- Students will also review vocabulary for talking about art, architecture, shapes, colors, materials, and literature.

Activities	Standards	Resources
Expresiones útiles	1.2, 2.1	
3.	1.2, 1.3, 2.2, 3.1	
4.	1.2, 1.3, 2.1	
Recuerda	1.2	
5.	1.1, 1.3, 2.1, 2.2, 3.1	
6.	1.1, 3.1, 5.2	

Teaching Suggestions

Warm-Up / Independent Starter

- Have students write down information about a painting, sculpture, or building they have seen or heard about. You may want to turn this activity into a contest by awarding extra points to those students who are able to give more information in a timely manner about their chosen work of art (e.g., author or designer, location, when it was made, what materials were used to make it).

Preparation

- Go over the *expresiones útiles* with the class. Make students guess what *obra maestra* and *obra cumbre* mean. To help them, put these words in different contexts. Next, have students reflect about nouns related to *vistazo* (*vista*) and *ojeada* (*ojo*), and ask students to build sentences with these two expressions. Finally, compare and contrast the meanings of *por encima* and *a fondo*.

- Give students a few minutes to go over the vocabulary in the *Recuerda* box. Alternatively, project these words and have students explain their meanings to a partner using gestures, circumlocution, antonyms, or synonyms.

302

Antes de empezar

EXPRESIONES ÚTILES

Para referirse a una obra de gran valor artístico:

La *Gioconda* es la **obra maestra** de Leonardo da Vinci.
Cervantes escribió su **obra cumbre**, *El Quijote*, en 1605.

Para decir que algo sucede en un instante:

Espérame aquí, vuelvo **en un pispás**.
Escribí este poema **en un santiamén**. Debo revisarlo.
Préstame ese pincel, te lo devuelvo **en un periquete**.

Para decir que algo se lee o se mira sin profundizar:

No recuerdo bien ese libro, solo lo miré **por encima**.
¿Puedes **echar un vistazo** a mi boceto?
Quiero **echar una ojeada** a los planos del edificio.

Para expresar que algo se hace en profundidad:

Puedo escribir sobre esa época histórica porque la he estudiado **a fondo**.

3 Con otras palabras

▶ **Reescribe** este párrafo sustituyendo las expresiones destacadas por las expresiones útiles más apropiadas.

Los tres músicos es un cuadro que Picasso pintó en 1921. Si lo miras **superficialmente**, es difícil distinguir a los personajes, pero cuando lo estudias **con atención** puedes ver a los tres músicos con sus instrumentos y un perro a la izquierda. Es una **obra muy importante** del movimiento cubista.

Pablo Picasso. *Los tres músicos.*

4 ¿Qué dirías?

▶ **Elige** una de las siguientes situaciones y escribe un diálogo con tu compañero(a). Incluyan al menos cuatro de las expresiones útiles.

1. Estás escribiendo un ensayo y quieres que tu compañero(a) lo lea y te dé su opinión.

2. Tu compañero(a) y tú están haciendo un trabajo sobre un(a) pintor(a) importante y tienen que elegir su obra más representativa para estudiarla en profundidad.

 ▶ **Representa** el diálogo con tu compañero(a).

Differentiated Instruction

DEVELOPING LEARNERS

- Have students complete these sentences:
  1. *Las Meninas es la obra maestra / un vistazo de Velázquez.* (la obra maestra)
  2. *Hiciste un buen trabajo porque lo hiciste a fondo / por encima.* (a fondo)
  3. *No me interesa este artículo, pero le voy a echar una ojeada / un pispás.* (una ojeada)
  4. *No te preocupes, te devuelvo el libro en un santiamén / vistazo.* (santiamén)
  5. *Si no quieres estudiar algo seriamente, lo miras por encima / bien.* (por encima)

EXPANDING LEARNERS

- Have student pairs create short dialogues using the *expresiones útiles*. Before they start, ask partners to name some masterpieces of literature or art, tasks that can be done quickly, others that do not require much insight, and still others that involve deep analysis. For example: *Don Quijote es la obra maestra de Cervantes. Suelo desayunar en un santiamén. Leo las noticias por encima.* Have students base their dialogues on these statements.
  A. *¿Tardas mucho en desayunar?*
  B. *No. Suelo desayunar en un santiamén.*

RECUERDA

Arte

el color	el museo
el cómic	la obra de arte
el cuadro	
la escultura	el/la artista
la exposición	el/la pintor(a)
la fotografía	

Arquitectura

el/la arquitecto(a)	el exterior
la construcción	el interior
el edificio	el techo

Formas

cuadrado(a)	rectangular
ovalado(a)	redondo(a)

Colores

amarillo limón	gris claro
anaranjado brillante	rojizo
azul oscuro	verdoso

Materiales

el acero	el metal
el bronce	el papel
la cerámica	el plástico
la madera	el vidrio

Literatura

el cuento	el poema
la leyenda	
la novela	el/la escritor(a)
la obra de teatro	el/la protagonista

---

5 Un cuestionario de arte

▶ **Responde** a estas preguntas. Después, comprueba las respuestas con tus compañeros(as).

1. ¿Quién escribió El Quijote?
2. ¿Qué famoso muralista mexicano se casó con Frida Kahlo?
3. ¿Qué artista colombiano ha expuesto sus esculturas en las calles más famosas de todo el mundo?
4. ¿Quién es el autor de El Guernica?
5. ¿Qué puedes ver en el Museo del Prado de Madrid?

6 ¿Cuánto sabes?

▶ **Habla** con tu compañero(a). Describan estas obras y comenten lo que sepan de sus autores.

Salvador Dalí. *La persistencia de la memoria.*

Enrique Carbajal. *El caballito.*

Antonio Gaudí. *La Sagrada Familia.*

trescientos tres **303**

Antes de empezar

■ Then, divide the class into six groups and assign each group one of the categories in the *Recuerda* box. Give each group several index cards and have students write a sentence for each word in which they leave a blank space to be filled in with one of the words. Then, have groups get together with another group and exchange the cards. Have groups complete each other's sentences. Finally, ask groups to write several examples for each word on the back of the corresponding card.

Activities

3. To extend this activity, give students other contexts with words or expressions to be substituted. For example: *Una de las obras más importantes de Shakespeare es Romeo y Julieta. Terminé el examen rápidamente. Hay que leer el artículo cuidadosamente.*

5. To extend this activity, have student pairs add other information they know about each of these artists or writers. Then, come together as a class and have pairs share their answers.

6. You may wish to bring additional photos of well-known works, and have students describe them using the words in the *Recuerda* box.

Answer Key

3. – superficialmente: por encima
   – con atención: a fondo
   – obra muy importante: obra maestra / obra cumbre
4. Answers will vary.
   ▶ Answers will vary.
5. Answers will vary. Sample answers:
   1. Miguel de Cervantes.
   2. Diego Rivera.
   3. Fernando Botero.
   4. Pablo Picasso.
   5. Obras de pintores como Diego Velázquez, Francisco de Goya y El Greco, entre otros.
6. Answers will vary.

Additional Resources

Fans Online activities
Practice Workbook

HERITAGE LANGUAGE LEARNERS

• Have students add to the list of colors in the *Recuerda* box by having them create a bilingual list of shades of color to share with the rest of the class. Get them started by suggesting "-ish" shades, such as *azulado* (bluish), *amarillento* (yellowish), *grisáceo* (grayish), and *negruzco* (blackish). Then, have students use the verb *tirar* to indicate that a color has a certain hue: *un amarillo fuerte tirando a naranja* (a bright orangish yellow). You may establish a time limit and see how many different shades of color students can come up with.

MULTIPLE INTELLIGENCES: Visual-Spatial Intelligence

• Ask students to look for images of some of Botero's paintings of musicians. Have them select one of these paintings, and then write a few paragraphs comparing it to Picasso's *Los tres músicos.* Students should address the style of each painting, the colors, the shapes of the figures, and the kinds of instruments depicted. Students should also give their opinion on which painting they prefer and why. Call on students to make a brief oral presentation to the class, using their written work as notes.

DESAFÍO 1

Describir y comparar objetos

Presentation

- In *Desafío 1*, Ethan and Eva will have to help a group of students design a mural for their community. Students will preview language used to talk about art and paintings.

Activities	Standards	Resources
Texto	1.2, 2.1, 2.2, 3.1	
7.	1.2, 3.1	
8.	1.2, 1.3, 2.1, 2.2, 3.1	Audio
9.	1.1, 1.3, 2.2, 3.1, 3.2	
10. Cultura	1.2, 2.1, 2.2, 3.1, 3.2, 5.2	

Teaching Suggestions

Warm-Up / Independent Starter

- Have students jot down what they know about murals and muralists. You may want to mention Diego Rivera to get students started.

Preparation

- Ask students to share their Independent Starters. Call on volunteers to describe the styles of these artists and the time period during which they lived. Discuss with students some features of murals (e.g., large size, painted directly on walls, usually located in public places).

- Focus students' attention on the mural that appears with the dialogue and invite them to interpret the scene. What seems to be the topic of this mural?

Texto: Paredes artísticas

- Read the introduction to the dialogue. Ask students what the connection is between the title of the dialogue and Ethan and Eva's *desafío*.

- Call on several pairs of volunteers to alternate reading the dialogue aloud. Ask students to identify the artists who are mentioned in the dialogue and the goals of the muralists.

Activities

8. Before listening to the recording, have students read the statements and make predictions about which ones are true and which are false.

Paredes artísticas

Un grupo de estudiantes va a diseñar un mural al estilo de los muralistas mexicanos. Ethan y Eva tienen que ayudarlos a diseñarlo. ¿Cómo lo harán?

ETHAN: Hola, chicos. ¿Conocen a algún muralista mexicano?

TOMÁS: Sí, yo he oído hablar de Diego Rivera. Era pintor, pero también creó murales muy famosos.

EVA: En efecto. Diego Rivera es uno de los muralistas mexicanos más conocidos, pero no es el único...

MARGARITA: Es verdad. David Alfaro Siqueiros y José Clemente Orozco también son representantes importantísimos de este movimiento artístico. Saben que los murales son obras de grandes dimensiones, ¿no?

EVA: Sí, lo sabemos.

TOMÁS: Por eso necesitamos una pared enorme para pintar. Y, por supuesto, pinceles y pintura de varios colores.

ETHAN: También debemos conseguir una hoja de papel muy grande para dibujar el boceto antes de comenzar a pintar sobre la pared.

EVA: Aún no hemos hablado del tema del mural. No olvidemos que el propósito de los muralistas mexicanos era educar a la población sobre la historia del país y sobre temas sociales y políticos, utilizando las paredes de edificios públicos como si fueran lienzos. ¿Qué tema político o social les gustaría comunicar con su mural?

TOMÁS: Pues... tenemos que pensarlo. ¿Nos ayudarán a decidirlo?

ETHAN: Claro.

José Clemente Orozco.
Lucha por la independencia de México.

---

7 **Detective de palabras**

▶ **Busca** en el diálogo las palabras que corresponden a estas definiciones.

1. Pintura hecha sobre una pared.
2. Objeto que se utiliza para pintar.
3. Dibujo que se hace antes de comenzar una obra.
4. Tela sobre la que se pinta.

Differentiated Instruction

DEVELOPING LEARNERS

- Ask students the following questions:
  1. *¿Qué pintaba Diego Rivera? (Pintaba murales y cuadros.)*
  2. *¿Quiénes son los otros muralistas que menciona Margarita? (Siqueiros y Orozco.)*
  3. *¿De qué tamaño suelen ser los murales? (Suelen ser grandes.)*
  4. *¿Qué necesita Tomás para pintar el mural? (Necesita una pared, pinceles y pintura.)*
  5. *¿Qué van a hacer antes de pintar? (Van a dibujar un boceto.)*
  6. *¿Cuál era el propósito de los muralistas mexicanos? (Educar a la población sobre la historia del país y sobre temas sociales.)*

EXPANDING LEARNERS

- Ask students to keep in mind current socio-political problems and how they are affecting their country or community. Have small groups discuss what they would like to depict in a mural in order to educate the public on these matters, or to offer their support of these issues. They should be prepared to explain their choices. After groups have brainstormed some ideas, ask them to share their best suggestions for a mural with the class. Hold a class vote to see which topic becomes the theme for the mural.

Describir y comparar objetos

 8 **El muralismo mexicano**

 ▶ **Escucha** a la guía de un museo y decide si estas afirmaciones son ciertas o falsas. Después, corrige las falsas.

1. El muralismo mexicano es un movimiento artístico de principios del siglo XIX.
2. José Clemente Orozco es el muralista mexicano más conocido.
3. Los murales representan a la clase alta y a la aristocracia.
4. Se pueden encontrar murales en los espacios públicos.
5. El presidente mexicano Álvaro Obregón apoyaba el muralismo.
6. Los murales representan escenas históricas de Europa.

9 **Un mural de Rivera**

▶ **Habla** con tu compañero(a) sobre lo que observan en esta pintura mural.

▶ **Escribe** un párrafo sobre esta obra. Descríbela y explica qué mensaje crees que quería comunicar su autor.

Diego Rivera. *Historia de México: de la conquista al futuro* (1929-1935).

 CULTURA

El muralismo mexicano

Uno de los movimientos artísticos más representativos de México es el muralismo, que nació a principios del siglo XX, después de la Revolución mexicana. Los artistas, apoyados por el gobierno, trataban temas sociopolíticos en sus obras con el fin de educar a la población y mostrarle el valor de su cultura y de sus orígenes. Por eso muchos murales están en las fachadas de edificios públicos del país, a la vista de todo el mundo, como muestra la fotografía.

Fachada de la Universidad Nacional Autónoma de México.

10 **Investiga.** Investiga sobre la historia de México a principios del siglo XX. ¿Por qué crees que el gobierno apoyaba a los muralistas?

trescientos cinco **305**

9. Ask student pairs to discuss the colors, style, theme, scene, and possible message of the mural. Before students write their paragraphs, ask them to share in small groups what they discussed with their partner.

 AUDIO SCRIPT
See page 297K.

 CULTURA

El muralismo mexicano

Mexican *muralismo* is an artistic movement that was supported by the Mexican government after the Mexican Revolution, lasting from the 1920s to about the 1970s. Since many people were illiterate during this time period, a majority of the murals were painted in public spaces, in order to educate people visually. In this way, the message reached a large audience. Most scenes in these murals relate back to Mexican history and culture, including all the flora and fauna that is typically present in the background.

Answer Key

7. 1. mural   3. boceto
     2. pincel   4. lienzo

8. 1. F. De principios del siglo XX.
     2. F. Diego Rivera.
     3. F. Representan al pueblo mexicano y su historia.
     4. C.
     5. C.
     6. F. Representan escenas de la historia de México.

9. Answers will vary.
     ▶ Answers will vary.

10. Answers will vary.

Additional Resources

Fans Online activities

HERITAGE LANGUAGE LEARNERS

- Ask students to research the scenes in Rivera's mural *Historia de México*. You might assign one or more students to research one of the three walls that depict the story. Explain to them that the wall on the right shows the pre-Columbian world ruled by the god Quetzalcoatl. Harmony between industry and nature are depicted on the left wall, and the effects of the Spanish conquest on Mexico are shown on the center wall. Ask students to provide details and have them share their information with the rest of the class.

CRITICAL THINKING

- Ask students to research what was happening in Mexico at the start of the 20th century. (the Mexican Revolution and the post-revolutionary labor movements and land redistribution) Then, have them think about what might have been the consequences if government policies and muralists' depictions did not coincide. Ask students to explain how murals might educate or enlighten, or how they might even increase misunderstanding and misinterpretation. Encourage a whole-class discussion.

Unit 6
DESAFÍO 1

Vocabulario – Arte y pintura

Presentation

- In this section, students will learn vocabulary used to talk about paintings and artistic styles.

Activities	Standards	Resources
Vocabulario	1.2, 2.1, 2.2, 3.1	
11.	1.2	
12.	1.1, 1.3, 3.1	
13.	1.2, 1.3, 2.2, 3.1	Audio
14.	1.1, 3.1	
15. Cultura	1.2, 2.2, 3.1, 5.2	

Teaching Suggestions

Warm-Up / Independent Starter

- Ask students to create a two-column chart and label the columns with these headings: *Colores vivos, Colores apagados*. Have students list colors they associate with each category.

Preparation

- Go over the vocabulary presentation with students. Ask them to identify the colors they observe in the two paintings and state which colors are *vivos* and which are *apagados*. Have students refer back to their lists from the Independent Starter. As a class, discuss how the color affects the message of the painting.

- Have students work with a partner to prepare comprehension questions using the text. Then have them quiz another student pair.

Activities

11. To extend this activity, have students write their own lists of four words to share with the class, and call on volunteers to identify the word that does not belong.

12. As an alternative to this activity, ask students to write definitions for six vocabulary words that appear in the text or in the *Más vocabulario* feature, and then have their partner identify the correct word. Or, if you have access to small whiteboards, say a definition to students and have them write the correct word on their boards. You may wish to turn this into a competition.

306

Vocabulario

Arte y pintura

El pintor mexicano José Clemente Orozco realizó este mural en 1967. Es una obra de gran tamaño; mide 5,90 × 4,50 metros. La escena muestra la alegría del pueblo ante la llegada del presidente Juárez, a quien vemos en el centro. Frente a él, en primer plano, un grupo de niñas le ofrecen flores. Al fondo vemos a las tropas de Porfirio Díaz.

El estilo de Orozco se caracteriza por el uso de líneas simples y pinceladas precisas, pero sobre todo destaca el contraste de colores vivos y apagados.

José Clemente Orozco. Entrada triunfal de Benito Juárez al Palacio Nacional acompañado de su gabinete (1967).

Los muralistas Diego Rivera y Orozco influyeron en gran medida en Fernando Botero, que también trata temas sociales y políticos en sus obras.

Botero se caracteriza por un innovador tratamiento de la figura humana, que presenta un volumen exagerado. En este cuadro juega con la proporción y con la perspectiva. Sus pinceladas muestran muchos detalles en las formas.

Fernando Botero. Los músicos (1980). Óleo sobre lienzo.

Más vocabulario

Pintura

la acuarela: pintura sobre papel o cartón con colores diluidos en agua.

el boceto: dibujo que se realiza antes de la obra.

el paisaje: pintura que representa el terreno.

el pincel: instrumento alargado con pelos en uno de sus extremos que se usa para pintar.

el retrato: pintura de una persona.

Estilos artísticos

arte figurativo: estilo artístico que representa la realidad de forma concreta y reconocible, al contrario que el arte abstracto.

cubismo: estilo artístico basado en el uso de formas geométricas.

surrealismo: estilo artístico que representa lo imaginario y lo irracional.

¡Atención!

darse cuenta *to realize*   **realizar** *to achieve*

11 **El intruso**

▶ **Busca** el intruso en cada serie y justifica tu respuesta.

1. volumen - perspectiva - proporción - lienzo
2. retrato - pincel - mural - paisaje
3. vivo - oscuro - apagado - preciso

306 trescientos seis

Differentiated Instruction

DEVELOPING LEARNERS

- Ask students to match the words.

1. *influir* (g)	a. *proyecto*
2. *exagerado* (j)	b. *exacto*
3. *fondo* (f)	c. *tipo de pintura*
4. *boceto* (a)	d. *resaltar*
5. *óleo* (c)	e. *comprender*
6. *paisaje* (h)	f. *zona alejada*
7. *destacar* (d)	g. *ejercer un efecto*
8. *darse cuenta* (e)	h. *representación del terreno*
9. *preciso* (b)	i. *brillante*
10. *vivo* (i)	j. *excesivo*

EXPANDING LEARNERS

- Ask students to indicate which word does not belong and explain why.

1. *óleo* · *pincel* · *acuarela* (pincel)
2. *vivo* · *preciso* · *apagado* (preciso)
3. *figuras* · *formas* · *escenas* (escenas)
4. *retrato* · *boceto* · *paisaje* (boceto)
5. *mural* · *tamaño* · *volumen* (mural)
6. *figura* · *fondo* · *primer plano* (figura)
7. *paisaje* · *proporción* · *perspectiva* (paisaje)
8. *lienzo* · *escena* · *cartón* (escena)
9. *realizar* · *destacar* · *conseguir* (destacar)
10. *realista* · *abstracto* · *figurativo* (abstracto)

12 Arte incompleto

▶ **Completa** estas afirmaciones con tus propias explicaciones.

1. Un autorretrato es…
2. Los murales son obras que…
3. En las obras con colores vivos…
4. Los artistas innovadores…
5. El primer plano es…
6. La perspectiva es…

13 Una obra maestra

 ▶ **Escucha** y decide. ¿Cuál de estas obras de Diego Rivera describe Eva? Anota las palabras y oraciones que justifican tu respuesta.

Civilización tarasca.

La vendedora de alcatraces.

Baile en Tehuantepec.

14 Tu estilo preferido

 ▶ **Habla** con tu compañero(a). ¿Cuál es el tipo de pintura que más te gusta? ¿Por qué?

 **CULTURA**

Fernando Botero

Nacido en Medellín (Colombia) en 1932, Fernando Botero es uno de los artistas contemporáneos más notables. En algunas de sus obras retrata la vida cotidiana, con escenas familiares y de ocio; en otras, plasma acontecimientos históricos, sociales o políticos. Su estilo, que algunos llaman «Boterismo», se caracteriza por el uso exagerado del volumen y la desproporción, que utiliza de forma irónica o crítica.

Fernando Botero. Familia.

15 Explica. ¿Qué opinas del estilo de Botero? ¿Te gusta? ¿Te parece innovador? Argumenta tus opiniones.

trescientos siete 307

---

13. After listening to the audio, ask students to write a description of the two paintings that are not described in the conversation.

 AUDIO SCRIPT
See page 297K.

 CULTURA

Fernando Botero

Fernando Botero's paintings and sculptures are easy to identify due to his use of volume and exaggeration. In addition to paintings that depict family life and political topics, Botero has also done interpretations of other famous paintings, such as Velázquez's *Infanta Margarita* and da Vinci's *Mona Lisa*. He is an icon of popular culture in Colombia, and has his own museum in Bogotá.

Answer Key

11. 1. lienzo: es un material, no una descripción
2. pincel: es un instrumento, no un tipo de pintura
3. preciso: no describe el color

12. Answers will vary. Sample answers:
1. … el retrato que hace el pintor de sí mismo.
2. … tratan temas sociales y políticos.
3. … hay mucha luz.
4. … tienen su propio estilo.
5. … el área más cercana de la escena.
6. … el punto de vista.

13. *Baile en Tehuantepec.* «Van a bailar una danza tradicional». «Van descalzos y llevan la ropa y los peinados típicos». «Los tonos son muy vivos». «[…] el verde del árbol del fondo».

14. Answers will vary.

15. Answers will vary.

Additional Resources

Fans Online activities
Practice Workbook

HERITAGE LANGUAGE LEARNERS

• After students have looked at the images of *Civilización tarasca*, *La vendedora de alcatraces*, and *Baile en Tehuantepec*, ask them what other popular images they would depict from their family's country of origin. If students' heritage country is Mexico, ask them if the three paintings by Rivera shown on this page represent something familiar to them and, if so, to provide more information on their significance. Ask students whose families come from other Hispanic cultures to describe or find two images that would represent familiar cultural perspectives to them and explain why.

CRITICAL THINKING

• Ask students to work in small groups and to choose ten events from our country's history as well as some current events and others that they predict may happen in the next thirty years. Explain that these events will become the focus of a mural. Have students list the events and their corresponding dates, and organize them in a three-paneled mural to represent our country's past, present, and future. If possible, students may accompany the events with images, but the primary focus should be on why they have made these choices.

DESAFÍO 1

Gramática – Las comparaciones

Presentation

- In this section, students will review and expand on making comparisons of equality and inequality.

Activities	Standards	Resources
Gramática	1.2, 3.1	
16.	1.2, 3.1, 4.1	
17.	1.3, 3.1	
18.	1.2, 1.3, 2.2, 3.1	Audio
19.	1.1, 1.3, 2.2, 3.1, 5.1, 5.2	
20. Comunidades	1.2, 2.1, 2.2, 3.1, 4.2, 5.1, 5.2	

Teaching Suggestions

Warm-Up / Independent Starter

- Ask students to write down some key words to describe a mural by José Clemente Orozco and a painting by Fernando Botero.

Preparation

- Call on two volunteers to read the first part of the grammar presentation (*Las comparaciones*) aloud. Call students' attention to the formulas presented, and have them take their notes from the Independent Starter and write statements comparing a mural by Orozco to a painting by Botero. Ask students to write two statements of equality and three statements of inequality. Then have students share their examples with the class. You may want to write some of their sentences on the board to illustrate the different structures students used to compare and contrast. Be sure to include sentences that make use of irregular comparative forms.

- Have students read the second part of the grammar presentation silently. Answer any questions they may have, and then ask them to translate the examples provided in this section. (It is a more complex piece of art than you think. He/She sold fewer paintings than he/she was hoping for. I paint less than I should.) As a class, compare the English sentences with the Spanish equivalents and then do activity 16.

Gramática

Las comparaciones

Las comparaciones

- Recuerda: podemos comparar la cantidad, las características o las cualidades de dos o más seres, entidades u objetos utilizando estas estructuras: igual que y tan/tanto como para expresar igualdad, y más que o menos que para expresar desigualdad.

COMPARACIONES DE IGUALDAD

verbo + igual que
igual de + adjetivo/adverbio + que
verbo + tanto como
tanto(a)(os)(as) + nombre + como
tan + adjetivo/adverbio + como

Ese artista pinta **igual que** Salvador Dalí.
Ese músico es **igual de** bueno **que** el otro.
Los pintores trabajan **tanto como** los escultores.
Los retratos tienen **tantos** colores **como** los paisajes.
Rembrandt es **tan** famoso **como** Rubens.

COMPARACIONES DE DESIGUALDAD

más/menos + adjetivo/adverbio/nombre + que
verbo + más/menos que

La acuarela se seca **más** rápido **que** el óleo.
Yo dibujo **menos que** tú.

- Los adjetivos bueno(a), malo(a), grande y pequeño(a), y los adverbios bien y mal tienen formas comparativas específicas: mejor, peor, mayor y menor.

  Diego Rivera era **mayor** que su esposa Frida Kahlo.

  Sin embargo, cuando hablamos de tamaño, es frecuente usar más grande y más pequeño(a). Y también usamos más pequeño(a) cuando hablamos de la edad.

  Los murales son **más grandes** que los iconos.   ¿Tu hermano es **más pequeño** que tú?

FORMAS COMPARATIVAS

bueno(a)/bien	→	mejor
malo(a)/mal	→	peor
grande	→	mayor
pequeño(a)	→	menor

Las comparaciones con *de* + artículo

- En las comparaciones de desigualdad usamos a veces de + *artículo* + que en lugar de que en el segundo término de la comparación. Esta estructura se usa frecuentemente con verbos como decir, creer, pensar, parecer, necesitar o esperar cuando comparamos algo con una referencia: lo que dijiste, lo que pensaba, lo que parecía, etc.

COMPARACIONES CON DE + ARTÍCULO

más/menos + adjetivo + de lo que
más/menos + nombre + del (de la, de los, de las) que
verbo + más/menos de lo que

Es una obra **más** compleja **de lo que** crees.
Vendió **menos cuadros de los que** esperaba.
Pinto **menos de lo que** debería.

 16 **Piensa.** ¿Cómo dirías en inglés Este pintor es más creativo que ese? ¿Y El pintor creó un cuadro más bonito de lo que esperaba?

Differentiated Instruction

DEVELOPING LEARNERS

- Have students complete these sentences:
  1. *Esos murales son más importantes del que / de los que / de lo que piensas.* (de lo que)
  2. *Me gustaría pintar mejor que / mejor de / mejor a Picasso.* (mejor que)
  3. *Necesito más pinturas de las que / del que / de lo que me diste.* (de las que)
  4. *Uso menos colores de los que / de lo que / del que tengo.* (de los que)
  5. *La pintura es tanto / tan importante como / que la escultura.* (tan, como)
  6. *Dalí era más tímido de que / las que / lo que piensas.* (lo que)

EXPANDING LEARNERS

- Ask students to find images of two pieces of art. Then have them work with a partner and describe these images to one another. Next, have students make comparisons between two of the images, or between all four. Explain that students should use expressions of both equality and inequality, as well as comparisons with *de* plus the article. Ask students to make up brief dialogues using these comparisons. Allow them time to rehearse, and then call on volunteer pairs to present their dialogues.

17 **Comparaciones**

▶ **Elige** la opción correcta y escribe oraciones completas.

1. Las pinceladas de Van Gogh son menos precisas (**que/de lo que/como**) las de Botero.
2. Este cuadro es mucho más grande (**que/de lo que/de los que**) pensaba.
3. Pienso que Picasso era igual de talentoso (**que/de lo que/como**) Velázquez.

 18 **¿Más o menos?**

 ▶ **Escucha** los diálogos y completa estas afirmaciones.

1. En el Museo del Prado hay más obras _____ pensaba Ethan.
2. Botero es mayor _____ creía Eva.
3. Eva y Ethan tienen más pintura _____ necesitan.
4. Eva tiene tantas ganas de viajar a la Ciudad de México _____ Ethan.

19 **Compara las obras**

▶ **Escribe** con tu compañero(a) ocho oraciones comparando estos cuadros.

Francisco de Goya. *La duquesa de Abrantes* (1816).

Pablo Picasso. *Retrato de Marie-Thérèse* (1937).

 COMUNIDADES

EL ARTE EN LA CALLE

La gran riqueza artística y cultural del mundo hispano se puede apreciar en sus calles, donde hay verdaderas obras de arte. Por ejemplo, el mural que retrata la historia azteca en la pared exterior de la biblioteca de la Universidad Nacional Autónoma de México, el mosaico de Joan Miró en Las Ramblas de Barcelona o el Parque de las Esculturas de Medellín, con obras de Fernando Botero.

Mosaico de Joan Miró (Barcelona).

20 **Compara.** ¿Hay arte en los espacios públicos de tu comunidad? ¿Qué ventajas y desventajas tiene exponer el arte en la calle en vez de hacerlo en museos?

HERITAGE LANGUAGE LEARNERS

• Explain to students that many years ago, portraits served the same purpose as our photographs today. They are records of people, places, pets, things, and events that have had an impact on our lives. Ask students what or whom they would paint if they were artists. Have them name a family member, a friend, or someone in the news, as well as an event or place that has had an influence on them. Students should be prepared to explain why this person, place, thing, or event is worthy of their artistic talent.

COOPERATIVE LEARNING

• Ask students to imagine that they work for their local government and want to promote art in public places throughout their community. Working in small groups, have students come up with the best plan for exhibiting this kind of art. Group members will need to figure out the kind of art they want to promote. They will also need to establish whether there will be permanent exhibits, or seasonal ones. They may consider a theme for the art, and any lectures to accompany the exhibits. Call on groups to explain their plans to the class.

Unit 6

DESAFÍO 1

Gramática – Las comparaciones

Activities

18. Before playing the recording, have students read each statement and determine the type of comparison that is being made. Then ask them to complete the statements and check their answers after listening to the dialogue.

19. Ask students to compare and contrast the colors, perspective, shapes, volume, background, foreground, and style.

 AUDIO SCRIPT
See page 297K.

 COMUNIDADES

El arte en la calle

Many people believe that it is important to add beauty to cities and to create a connection between the people, their culture, and their environment. And in many cities of the Spanish-speaking world, one does not need to go to a museum to see art. Just by walking through a plaza, park, or street, public art can be admired. For instance, in the city of Caracas, Venezuela, there are more than 400 works of art in public spaces.

Answer Key

16. *This painter is more creative than that one. The painter created a nicer painting than he was hoping for.*

17. 1. que
2. de lo que
3. que

18. 1. de las que   3. de la que
2. de lo que   4. como

19. Answers will vary.

20. Answers will vary.

Additional Resources

Fans Online activities
Practice Workbook

309

DESAFÍO 1

Gramática – El artículo neutro *lo*

Presentation

- In this section, students will learn and practice the use of the neuter article *lo* to refer to a general concept or an abstract idea. Students will also learn that this article has no plural and does not refer to a gendered word.

Activities	Standards	Resources
Gramática	1.2, 3.1	
21.	1.2, 1.3, 3.1, 4.1	
22.	1.3, 3.1	
23.	1.2, 1.3	Audio
24.	1.2, 1.3, 3.1	
25.	1.1, 1.2, 2.2, 3.1, 3.2, 5.1	

Teaching Suggestions

Warm-Up / Independent Starter

- Ask students to complete the following sentences:
  1. *Lo importante en la vida es…*
  2. *Lo más difícil de la escuela es…*
  3. *Lo primero que haré cuando me gradúe es…*

Preparation

- Have students read the introduction to the grammar presentation silently. Then read the first part (*Usos del artículo neutro* lo) aloud to students. Next, ask students to revise their sentences from the Independent Starter and determine the structure that was used in each case. Call on volunteers to share their sentences.

- Ask students to translate their sentences from the Independent Starter. (1. The important thing about life is… 2. The most difficult part/thing about school is… 3. The first thing I'll do when I graduate is…) Note to students that they may be tempted to translate these statements as *La cosa importante/difícil es…* since the article *lo* does not have an exact equivalent in English. However, they should use the article *lo* in these cases.

- Have students work with a partner to read the last section of the grammar presentation (*El artículo* lo *enfático*). Then have pairs work on activity 21.

Gramática

El artículo neutro *lo*

- Usamos con frecuencia el artículo neutro lo delante de un adjetivo o de una cláusula. Este artículo no se usa nunca con nombres y no tiene un equivalente exacto en inglés.

  lo importante *(the important thing/part)*   lo que me dijiste *(what you told me)*

  Atención: no debes confundir el artículo neutro lo, que es invariable, con el pronombre de objeto directo lo, que varía en género y número.

  <u>Lo</u> bueno es que <u>lo/la</u> vi cuando entraba al museo y <u>lo/la</u> pude saludar.
  article   pronoun   pronoun

Usos del artículo neutro lo

- El artículo neutro lo se usa principalmente en estos casos:

  – Delante de un adjetivo masculino singular:

  | lo + adjetivo |

  Todos admiramos lo bello. (= las cosas bellas).
  We all admire what is beautiful.

  | lo más/menos + adjetivo + de/que |

  La técnica es lo más difícil de la pintura.
  Technique is the most difficult thing about painting.

  | lo + adjetivo + ser + que |

  Lo bueno es que hemos visto muchos cuadros.
  The good thing is that we have seen many paintings.

  – En construcciones posesivas:

  | lo + pronombre posesivo |

  Lo mío es tuyo.
  What is mine is yours.

  | lo de + pronombre personal/nombre |

  Lo de ella es tuyo.   Lo de María es tuyo.
  What is hers is yours.   *What is María's is yours.*

  – Delante de un numeral ordinal para expresar orden o secuencia:

  | lo + ordinal |

  Lo primero es observar los colores.
  The first thing is to look at the colors.

  – Delante del pronombre relativo que para introducir una cláusula:

  | lo que + cláusula |

  Tengo lo que necesito.
  I have what I need.

El artículo lo enfático

- El artículo lo se usa también delante de un adjetivo o un adverbio en construcciones enfáticas. En este caso, el adjetivo puede variar en género y en número:

  | lo + adjetivo + que |

  Sé lo difíciles que son algunos cuadros.
  I know how difficult it is to understand some paintings.

  | lo + adverbio + que |

  ¿Sabes lo bien que pinta este artista?
  Do you know how well this artist paints?

21 **Piensa.** Traduce estas oraciones al español. ¿Qué estructuras con lo usaste?

a. *We always do what is right.*   b. *I understand how important art is.*

Differentiated Instruction

DEVELOPING LEARNERS

- Ask students to form sentences.
  1. *pintar? / lo / ¿Sabes / que / difícil / es* (¿Sabes lo difícil que es pintar?)
  2. *colores. / debes / elegir / Lo / que / es / primero / hacer / los* (Lo primero que debes hacer es elegir los colores.)
  3. *interesante / de / las / más / ese / la / proporción / figuras. / cuadro / Lo / es / de* (Lo más interesante de ese cuadro es la proporción de las figuras.)
  4. *ver / rápido / que / Hay / pintas. / que / lo* (Hay que ver lo rápido que pintas.)
  5. *nuestro / tuyo. / Lo / es* (Lo nuestro es tuyo.)

EXPANDING LEARNERS

- Ask students to work with a partner and complete these phrases:
  1. *Lo más fácil de la clase de Español es … y lo más difícil es…*
  2. *Lo que más distingue a un buen artista de uno mediocre es…*
  3. *Lo importante en la obra de un artista es…*
  4. *Lo primero que debes hacer al llegar a la escuela es…*
  5. *En el arte, lo bueno es que…*
- Call on student pairs to read their statements aloud.

22 **De nuevo**

▶ **Ordena** estos elementos y escribe las oraciones.

Modelo   no comenzaron/malo/que/el mural./es/Lo
→ *Lo malo es que no comenzaron el mural.*

1. un/primero/Lo/boceto./hacer/es
2. los temas/importante/Lo/es que/analices/mural./del
3. en espacios públicos./interesante/Lo/tantos murales/es/haya/que

23 **Una visita al Museo del Prado**

▶ **Escucha** la conversación y completa estas oraciones.

1. _____ es que visite el museo por la tarde.
2. _____ es que haya fila para entrar.
3. _____ es que el horario de visitas es muy amplio.
4. _____ es que hay cuadros de muchos pintores.
5. _____ es que vea las salas de los pintores españoles.
6. _____ es que tengan audioguías.

Fachada del Museo del Prado (Madrid).

24 **Preparándose para pintar**

▶ **Lee** las respuestas de Eva. ¿Qué palabras imaginas que pudo decirle Ethan? Escríbelas.

Modelo   ETHAN: *Pasé mucho tiempo buscando un libro sobre Siqueiros, pero por fin lo encontré.*
EVA: *Lo importante es que lo encontraste.*

1. **Lo** difícil será hacer una pintura de un tamaño tan grande.
2. **Lo** que más tiempo nos llevará será elegir el tema del mural.
3. **Lo** más interesante de este desafío será trabajar en equipo.
4. Sí, ya **lo** tenemos todo: el papel, los lápices, la pintura...
5. **Lo** primero que hay que hacer es dibujar un boceto.

▶ **Analiza** cada respuesta de Eva y decide. ¿*Lo* es artículo neutro o pronombre de objeto directo?

25 **Palabras de Orozco**

▶ **Lee** estas palabras del muralista mexicano José Clemente Orozco. ¿Estás de acuerdo con ellas? Habla con tus compañeros(as) y justifica tu respuesta.

> No importan las equivocaciones. Lo que vale es el valor de pensar en voz alta, es decir las cosas tal como se sienten en el momento en que se dicen. Ser lo suficientemente temerario para proclamar lo que uno cree que es la verdad sin importarle las consecuencias.

trescientos once 311

Gramática – El artículo neutro *lo*

Activities

24. To extend this activity, have students add a few more statements and answers. Then ask them to practice these mini-conversations with a partner. For example:

A. *No soy un artista muy bueno. Es más, pinto muy mal.*

B. *No te preocupes. Lo importante es que haces el esfuerzo.*

25. Before students discuss this quote from Orozco, ask them to rewrite some of the sentences using different structures with *lo*. For example: *Lo importante no son las equivocaciones. Lo primero es decir las cosas...*

 AUDIO SCRIPT
See page 297K.

Answer Key

21. a. Siempre hacemos lo correcto.
(lo + adjetivo)
b. Entiendo lo importante que es el arte.
(lo + adjetivo + que)

22. 1. Lo primero es hacer un boceto.
2. Lo importante es que analices los temas del mural.
3. Lo interesante es que haya tantos murales en espacios públicos.

23. 1. Lo mejor   4. Lo interesante
2. Lo más probable 5. Lo más importante
3. Lo bueno   6. Lo más probable

24. Answers will vary.

▶ 1. neutro   4. objeto directo
2. neutro   5. neutro
3. neutro

25. Answers will vary.

Additional Resources

Fans Online activities
Practice Workbook

HERITAGE LANGUAGE LEARNERS

• Ask students to write an essay of at least three paragraphs that begins with the following words: *Lo más importante en la vida es...* Explain to students that they need to compare and contrast what is important in this culture with what is valued in the culture of their heritage country. Students might also consider the cultural shock that may occur when one goes on to live in another culture. Call on students to read their essays aloud, and enable a classroom discussion on these similarities and differences.

CRITICAL THINKING

• Ask students to explain in writing what they consider to be the most important virtue and why, and to give examples of how it impacts their lives. Then, have them name what they consider to be the most overrated virtue, why they think it lacks importance, and state why others might not agree with their assessment. Call on volunteers to read their work aloud and, after a classroom discussion on virtues, see which ones receive top rating and which ones are considered to be valued too highly, and without merit.

311

Unit 6

LECTURA: TEXTO DIALOGADO

Presentation

- In this section, students will read a dialogue, and research and discuss Hispanics that have made positive contributions to the United States. Students will also answer comprehension questions and complete vocabulary activities based on the reading.

Activities	Standards	Resources
Lectura: texto dialogado	1.2, 2.1, 2.2, 3.1	
26.	1.2, 1.3, 2.2, 3.1	
27.	1.2, 1.3, 2.1, 2.2	
28.	1.1, 1.3, 2.2, 3.1, 3.2, 5.1, 5.2	

Teaching Suggestions

Warm-Up / Independent Starter

- Have students list three themes that Mexican murals typically depict.

Preparation

- Call on students to share their Independent Starters. You may want to start a list on the board with their answers. Then focus students' attention on the first question of the *Antes de leer* section and have them predict the theme that Eva and Ethan will choose for their mural. Ask students if they recognize the people pictured on page 313 and have them share what they know about these Hispanic personalities. Then have students answer the second and third questions from the *Antes de leer* in pairs. Check their answers as a class.

- Remind students that identifying cognates can be a useful reading strategy. Ask them to focus on the italicized text and identify ten cognates that could help them to understand this part of the reading.

- Ask students to read the dialogue silently, noting any words they do not understand. Next, read the dialogue aloud, modeling correct pronunciation and intonation. Then have students work in groups of three to read the dialogue aloud and clarify their vocabulary questions.

312

Antes de leer: estrategias

1. Lee el título del diálogo y fíjate en las imágenes de la página 313. ¿Cuál crees que será el tema del mural que van a pintar los personajes?
2. Fíjate en el párrafo que va en cursiva. ¿Qué tipo de texto es: narrativo, descriptivo, expositivo, argumentativo…?
3. Echa un vistazo rápido al diálogo. ¿Qué palabras se repiten más?

Un gran mural

EVA: He pensado que, ya que estudiamos español, podemos dedicar el mural a mostrar la herencia hispana en los Estados Unidos. ¿Qué les parece, amigos?

TOMÁS: ¡Qué buena idea!

MARGARITA: Así el mural estará listo para celebrar el próximo Mes de la Herencia Hispana.

EVA: Si les parece bien, podemos inspirarnos en estas palabras que encontré en la página web del gobierno:

Hoy más que nunca los estadounidenses de origen hispano desempeñan un papel integral en el desarrollo y crecimiento del país. Cada vez más hispanos alcanzan posiciones de liderazgo en el Gobierno, el sistema judicial, la aeronáutica, los negocios, las fuerzas armadas, los deportes, las ciencias de la salud y del medio ambiente, las artes y muchas otras ocupaciones clave en el crecimiento económico y desarrollo social del país. La influencia de la cultura hispana se refleja en múltiples aspectos de la vida cotidiana de los estadounidenses, contribuyendo a su progreso y diversificación.

ETHAN: ¡Sí! Podemos pintar retratos de personajes hispanos muy conocidos: políticos, artistas, periodistas…

EVA: Y mezclarlos con retratos de personas de origen hispano que conozcamos: amigos, familiares, profesores…

ETHAN: Lo más importante es que el mural refleje las aportaciones de la comunidad hispana a la sociedad.

EVA: Estoy de acuerdo, pero no olviden que debemos imitar el estilo y los colores que utilizaban Diego Rivera o José Clemente Orozco.

ETHAN: Muy bien. Ahora entre todos debemos decidir a qué personas vamos a retratar.

EVA: ¡Eso será lo más complicado!

312 trescientos doce

Differentiated Instruction

DEVELOPING LEARNERS

- Have students compete against each other in making a word family chart based on words from the dialogue. Then have students write sentences with some of the words.

Verbo	Nombre
pensar	pensamiento
dedicar	dedicación
mostrar	muestra
heredar	herencia
celebrar	celebración

EXPANDING LEARNERS

- Have small groups brainstorm other ideas for Eva and Ethan's mural. Students may consider the history of another Hispanic country or of their own community. They may portray social, environmental, or political issues and propose solutions to them. Students may also depict positive messages for young people, from encouraging them to continue their education, to volunteering their time in the community. Ask the groups to summarize their ideas in writing or in an oral presentation.

26 ¿Comprendes?

▶ **Responde** a estas preguntas.

1. ¿Qué tema han elegido Ethan y Eva para su mural?
2. ¿Por qué le parece a Eva un tema apropiado?
3. ¿Qué áreas de trabajo se mencionan en la cita que lee Eva? Pon ejemplos de profesiones que relacionas con cada una de esas áreas.
4. ¿Qué es lo más importante para Ethan?
5. ¿Qué es lo más difícil para Eva?
6. ¿En qué pintores se van a inspirar?

César Chávez.

27 Palabras y expresiones

▶ **Escribe** de nuevo este texto sustituyendo las palabras destacadas por otras que signifiquen lo mismo. Piensa en vocabulario que conoces o usa un diccionario.

Modelo
Hoy más que nunca los estadounidenses de origen hispano realizan un papel...

Sonia Sotomayor.

> *Hoy más que nunca los estadounidenses de origen hispano **desempeñan** un papel integral en el desarrollo y crecimiento del país. Cada vez más hispanos **alcanzan** posiciones de liderazgo en el Gobierno, el sistema judicial, la aeronáutica, los negocios, las fuerzas armadas, los deportes, las ciencias de la salud y del medio ambiente, las artes y muchas otras **ocupaciones** clave en el crecimiento económico y desarrollo social del país. La influencia de la cultura hispana **se refleja** en múltiples aspectos de la vida cotidiana de los estadounidenses, **contribuyendo** a su progreso y diversificación.*
>
> Fuente: http://www.usa.gov

John Danny Olivas.

28 Con tus propias palabras

▶ **Piensa** en tres personajes hispanos que incluirías en el mural. Justifica tu elección.

▶ **Habla** con tus compañeros(as). Entre todos(as), hagan una lista con los diez personajes hispanos que incluirían en el mural.

Modelo   *A mí me gustaría incluir a Sonia Sotomayor porque fue la primera jueza hispana en la Corte Suprema.*

trescientos trece 313

HERITAGE LANGUAGE LEARNERS

• In the dialogue, Eva says they should imitate the style and colors of Rivera and Orozco. Have student pairs research other—past and present—muralists. You may want to suggest the following: Oswaldo Guayasamín, Judy Baca, Cecilia Álvarez, Maceo Montoya, Alfredo Guido. Then ask student pairs to choose the muralist whose style and colors they like best. Next, have pairs use this information to write a brief essay encouraging Eva and Ethan to imitate this artist's style in their mural. Finally, call on pairs to present their chosen muralist to the class.

MULTIPLE INTELLIGENCES:
Visual-Spatial Intelligence

• Explain that a mural can be painted on any surface, including a ceiling, and that the most famous of such ceiling murals is the one Michelangelo painted in the Sistine Chapel. Have students research this work of art, as well as some of the earliest murals, including those painted on cave walls or in Egyptian tombs thousands of years ago. Assign different types of murals to small groups so there is no duplication of research. Call on groups to present their findings to the class, including images.

Activities

26. For question #3, ask students what other areas they could include that are not already mentioned in the dialogue. Then have them brainstorm famous Hispanics for the areas that are mentioned in the dialogue.

27. Remind students that they must maintain the appropriate part of speech and suggest that they use a dictionary or a thesaurus. You can extend this activity by asking students to substitute three additional words that do not already appear in bold.

28. To expand this activity, ask students to work with a partner and select one person they would like to research more about for homework. Then have students share their information with the class.

Answer Key

26. Answers will vary. Sample answers:
1. La herencia hispana en EE. UU.
2. Porque estudian español.
3. Las áreas de Gobierno, el sistema judicial, la aeronáutica, los negocios, las fuerzas armadas, los deportes, las ciencias de la salud y del medio ambiente y las artes. Ejemplos de profesiones: senador(a), juez(a), astronauta, empresario(a), teniente, beisbolista, médico(a), ingeniero(a) ambiental, escultor(a).
4. Que el mural refleje lo que la comunidad hispana aporta a la sociedad.
5. Decidir a qué personas van a retratar.
6. En Diego Rivera y José Clemente Orozco.

27. Answers will vary. Sample answers:
– alcanzan: logran, consiguen
– ocupaciones: profesiones, trabajos
– se refleja: se manifiesta, se revela
– contribuyendo: ayudando, aportando

28. Answers will vary.
▶ Answers will vary.

Additional Resources

Fans Online activities

313

DESAFÍO 1

Comunicación

Presentation

- In this section, students will integrate the vocabulary and grammar skills from *Desafío 1* in order to talk about art. Students will read about an art exhibit and make comparisons.

Activities	Standards	Resources
29.	1.2, 1.3, 2.1, 2.2, 3.1, 3.2	
30.	1.2, 1.3, 2.2, 3.1, 3.2	Audio
31. Final del desafío	1.2, 1.3, 2.1, 2.2, 3.1, 4.2, 5.1, 5.2	

Teaching Suggestions

Warm-Up / Independent Starter

- Have students write five comparison statements about pieces of artwork or artists they have studied during this *Desafío*.

Preparation

- Ask students to share their Independent Starters with a partner. Have students check their partner's work, verifying the comparison structures against the formulas on page 308. Once students have reviewed their own work again, have them share their responses with the class.

- Discuss with students what they have learned about Mexican murals and their relationship to Mexican history and culture. Then have them complete the following statements:
  – *Lo que me gusta de los murales es…*
  – *Los murales mexicanos son más … de lo que pensaba.*
  – *Lo más interesante de los murales es…*
  Call on volunteers to share their answers.

Activities

29. Before completing the article, have students identify the part of speech for each of the words. Review the completed article as a class before students answer the comprehension questions. Ask students to recall the events related to Chile that they studied in Unit 5.

Comunicación

29 **Muralismo mexicano en Chile**

▶ **Completa** este artículo con las palabras del cuadro. Ten en cuenta que no todas son válidas.

sala	expuestas	inaugurada	pintura	exposición
obras	muralistas	museo	descolgadas	retratos

EL UNIVERSAL   Domingo, 18 de noviembre de 2012

Obras de Rivera, Orozco y Siqueiros, a Chile

El ___1___ Nacional de Bellas Artes de Chile montará el próximo año una muestra de los ___2___ mexicanos Diego Rivera (1886-1957), David Alfaro Siqueiros (1896-1974) y José Clemente Orozco (1883-1949), informó hoy la edición digital del diario *La Tercera*.

El periódico chileno señaló que la ___3___, que debía haber sido ___4___ en septiembre de 1973, se montará en la ___5___ Matta del museo y estará abierta entre septiembre y diciembre de 2013.

El 13 de septiembre de 1973 debía abrirse en el Museo de Bellas Artes una muestra de 167 ___6___ de Rivera, Orozco y Siqueiros, pero el golpe militar del 11 de septiembre de ese año contra el presidente chileno Salvador Allende cambió los planes. Las obras fueron ___7___ tras el golpe y llevadas de regreso a un avión mexicano, el mismo que había sido ofrecido por el gobierno de México para sacar de Chile, rumbo al exilio, al poeta Pablo Neruda.

Esta vez solo serán ___8___ 80 obras de Rivera, Orozco y Siqueiros que pertenecen al Museo Carrillo Gil de la Ciudad de México, las que se unirán a cartas, catálogos y grabaciones de audio hechas por Fernando Gamboa, curador de la fallida muestra de 1973.

Fuente: http://www.eluniversal.com.mx (selección)

▶ **Responde** a estas preguntas.
1. ¿Por qué es especial esta muestra de murales mexicanos en Santiago? ¿Qué palabras del texto te lo indican?
2. ¿Por qué no se celebró la exposición en 1973?
3. ¿Qué hicieron con las obras?
4. ¿Cuántas obras habrá en la exposición de 2013?
5. ¿Qué otros recursos habrá en la exposición, además de los murales?

▶ **Escribe** oraciones comparando la exposición planeada en 1973 y la muestra de 2013.

Modelo   *Las obras de la muestra son tan famosas como las de la exposición original.*

Differentiated Instruction

DEVELOPING LEARNERS

- After students listen to the description of Rivera's work in activity 30, ask them to work with a partner and create a dialogue commenting on this mural. Explain that they should use the neuter article *lo* whenever possible. For example:
  A. *Lo que más me llama la atención es la figura en el centro.*
  B. *Sí, a mí me parece lo más original de la obra.*
  A. *Lo interesante es cómo Rivera se representa a sí mismo.*
- Call on pairs to act out their dialogues.

EXPANDING LEARNERS

- Ask students to work with a partner and find two magazine or newspaper articles that describe an artistic event (e.g., an art exhibit). Next, students will read both articles and then compare and contrast the two events. Finally, ask students to create short dialogues with these comparisons and present them to the class. For example:
  A. *Los cuadros de esta pintora son tan buenos como los de los muralistas mexicanos.*
  B. *Sí, pero son mucho más pequeños porque no son murales.*

Diego Rivera. *Sueño de una tarde de domingo en la Alameda Central* (1947).

 30 **Una exposición especial**

 ▶ **Escucha** la explicación del mural de Diego Rivera y toma notas de la información más importante. Después, escribe un resumen.

Final del desafío

ETHAN: ¿Estamos listos para empezar?

TOMÁS: Sí, tengo el boceto para ayudarnos. ¿Saben? Elegir el tema fue al final menos difícil __1__ había pensado.

EVA: Sí, lo difícil viene ahora. Me gustaría pintar tan bien __2__ los muralistas mexicanos, pero son mejores artistas __3__ nosotros.

MARGARITA: Lo importante es lo que vamos a comunicar. Ya dijimos que lo que el mural expresa es más importante __4__ la calidad de las pinceladas. Como los muralistas, vamos a representar el pasado, el presente y nuestras esperanzas para el futuro de la comunidad.

EVA: Ya, pero creo que pintar una obra de este tamaño será más complicado __5__ ustedes piensan.

ETHAN: El boceto tiene tres partes, así que podemos dividirlo. Ustedes pueden hacer dos, y Eva y yo una. Como tenemos menos experiencia…

MARGARITA: Lo cierto es que ustedes han hecho tanto trabajo __6__ nosotros, así que me parece bien.

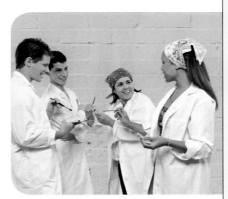

31 **¡Listos para pintar!**

▶ **Completa** el diálogo con las palabras para comparar que faltan.

▶ **Dibuja** el boceto de un mural que represente a tu comunidad. Como los personajes, divídelo en tres secciones: el pasado, el presente y el futuro.

trescientos quince 315

HERITAGE LANGUAGE LEARNERS

• Have students research the life and work of one of the Mexican muralists mentioned in the article, or one of their own choosing. Ask students to explain the historical, social, political, or cultural significance of this artist's work. Then have students select one mural and describe the artist's style, the figures depicted in the foreground and background, how the work expresses the artist's values, and how it might be used to educate or unite people. Students may present a written report or make an oral and visual presentation to the class.

SPECIAL-NEEDS LEARNERS

• Assist students with language-processing difficulties in completing activity 30. These students may find it difficult to listen, process, and encode the information presented in the audio. Provide a written script for these students so they can gather the information, view the mural in their textbooks, and take notes. You might do this for all other activities of this type, with or without images. Students may find it less stressful to write one or two sentences about each aspect of the mural before attempting to write a summary.

---

30. Before playing the recording, have students observe the mural. Tell them to divide it into three sections (i.e., left, center, and right) and analyze each section independently. Remind students to pay attention to all the details, including what they see in the background.

31. Have students point out clues in the sentences that can help them determine the appropriate comparison word. Before students create their sketches, have them discuss in small groups historical events of your community and any well-known individuals that have made positive contributions to your community.

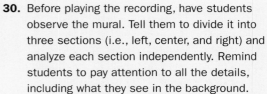 **AUDIO SCRIPT**
See page 297L.

Answer Key

29. 1. Museo 5. sala
2. muralistas 6. obras
3. exposición 7. descolgadas
4. inaugurada 8. expuestas

▶ Answers will vary. Sample answers:
1. Porque la exposición original no pudo presentarse en 1973 en Chile debido al golpe militar que tuvo lugar dos días antes.
2. Por el golpe de Estado.
3. Las descolgaron y devolvieron a México.
4. Ochenta.
5. Habrá cartas, catálogos y grabaciones de audio hechas por el curador de la exposición original.

▶ Answers will vary.

30. Answers will vary.

31. 1. de lo que 4. que
2. como 5. de lo que
3. que 6. como

▶ Answers will vary.

Additional Resources

Fans Online activities
Practice Workbook

315

Unit 6
DESAFÍO 2
Opinar y hacer valoraciones

Presentation

- In this section, Michelle and Daniel have to prepare a digital tour of the Los Angeles Cathedral and show it to their school. Students will preview language used to talk about architecture and to express opinions.

Activities	Standards	Resources
Texto	1.2, 2.2, 3.1	
32.	1.2, 1.3, 2.2, 3.1	
33.	1.2, 1.3, 2.2	
34.	1.1, 1.2, 1.3, 2.2, 3.1, 4.2	Audio
35. Cultura	1.2, 1.3, 2.2, 3.1, 5.1, 5.2	

Teaching Suggestions

Warm-Up / Independent Starter

- Write this definition of *vanguardia* on the board: *parte de una fuerza armada que va delante del cuerpo principal.* Ask students to consider this definition as they brainstorm an answer to this question: *¿Cómo es posible que una catedral sea una obra vanguardista?*

Preparation

- Ask students to discuss their Independent Starters in small groups. Then share photos of the cathedral with the class. Have students express their ideas as to how this cathedral might be considered *vanguardista*.

Texto: Una catedral vanguardista

- Read the introduction, and then call on four volunteers to alternate reading the dialogue. Ask students to explain how this cathedral is different from others they may have seen.

Activities

34. Before listening, conduct a "Think, pair, share" with this question: *¿Cómo es la arquitectura capaz de comunicar?* To get students thinking, show them images of world landmarks (e.g., the Statue of Liberty, pyramids, the Coliseum in Rome, the Great Wall of China). Have pairs report their thoughts to the class.

316

Una catedral vanguardista

Michelle y Daniel visitan a Ethan y a Eva para ver la catedral de Los Ángeles. Para lograr el desafío, tendrán que preparar un *tour* digital sobre la catedral y presentarlo en su escuela.

MICHELLE: ¿Qué les parece la catedral?

DANIEL: Lo primero que me llama la atención es que no se parece a ninguna de las que he visto. Pienso que esta catedral es diferente, aunque muy bonita en su estilo. Ahora no recuerdo quién la diseñó.

EVA: Rafael Moneo, un arquitecto español. Me parece que tiene otras construcciones en los Estados Unidos. Yo lo considero muy creativo: el color del exterior reproduce el color de las antiguas misiones de California.

DANIEL: Sí, pero no creo que la forma de la catedral sea similar a la de las misiones.

MICHELLE: Tenemos que hacer fotos y grabar imágenes para hacer un *tour* muy atractivo. Podemos comenzar por el exterior: la fachada, los materiales...

DANIEL: Yo no creo que debamos empezar con la catedral. Es mejor que primero hablemos un poco del arquitecto, su vida y su trabajo. Pero a mí no me gusta hablar frente a la cámara. ¿Michelle...?

MICHELLE: Vale, lo haré yo. ¡Un día me convertiré en una estrella de cine de Los Ángeles!

---

32 **Detective de palabras**

▶ **Completa** estas oraciones extraídas del diálogo anterior.

1. Pienso que esta catedral _____ diferente.
2. Me parece que Moneo _____ otras construcciones en los Estados Unidos.
3. No creo que la forma de la catedral _____ similar a la de las misiones.
4. No creo que _____ empezar con la catedral.

▶ **Decide.** ¿Qué oraciones llevan el verbo en indicativo? ¿Y en subjuntivo? Explica por qué crees que es así.

316 trescientos dieciséis

Differentiated Instruction

DEVELOPING LEARNERS

- Have students choose the correct answer.
  1. *El color de la catedral de Los Ángeles representa el color...* (b)
     a. *favorito de Moneo*　　b. *de las misiones*
  2. *¿En qué parte está la fachada?* (b)
     a. *en el interior*　　b. *en el exterior*
  3. *¿Quién quiere empezar el tour por el exterior?* (b)
     a. *Daniel*　　b. *Michelle*
  4. *¿Qué premio recibió Moneo?* (a)
     a. *el Pritzker*　　b. *el Nobel*
  5. *¿Cuál es la otra pasión del arquitecto?* (a)
     a. *la enseñanza*　　b. *la pintura*

EXPANDING LEARNERS

- After students have completed activity 32, ask them to write at least five sentences based on information from the dialogue and to use verbs that indicate either a positive or negative opinion, such as *imaginar, juzgar, opinar, suponer, (no) considerar, (no) creer, (no) parecer, (no) pensar.* For example:
  1. *Supongo que la catedral de Los Ángeles es la más innovadora de California.* 2. *No creo que sea buena idea comenzar el video sin música.* 3. *Pienso que a Michelle le encanta estar delante de la cámara.*

33 **¿Comprendes?**

▶ **Responde** a estas preguntas.

1. ¿En qué consiste el desafío de Michelle y Daniel?
2. ¿Cómo es la catedral de Los Ángeles? ¿Qué palabras del diálogo justifican tu respuesta?
3. ¿Con qué contenido van a empezar el *tour* digital?
4. ¿Qué no le gusta hacer a Daniel? Compara su actitud con la de Michelle.
5. ¿Por qué crees que Moneo se inspiró en las antiguas misiones al diseñar esta catedral?

34 **La catedral de Los Ángeles**

 ▶ **Escucha** la conversación entre Michelle y Daniel mientras visitan la catedral. Después, escribe un resumen usando estas palabras.

| exterior | terremoto | luz | diseñar | reflejar | diversidad | construir |

 ▶ **Habla** con tu compañero(a). Comparen la antigua catedral de Los Ángeles y la nueva diseñada por Moneo. ¿Cuál les gusta más? ¿Por qué? Compartan sus opiniones con la clase.

 **CULTURA**

Rafael Moneo

Museo del Prado (Madrid).

Rafael Moneo nació en España en 1937. Siempre ha combinado sus dos pasiones: la arquitectura y la enseñanza. Desde 1985 hasta 1990, fue decano de la facultad de Arquitectura de Harvard. La mayor parte de sus obras se encuentran en España, Suecia y los Estados Unidos. En 1996 recibió el Premio Pritzker, considerado el Premio Nobel de la arquitectura porque se entrega a arquitectos que hayan realizado construcciones funcionales de buena calidad, con un alto nivel de creatividad y que contribuyan al enriquecimiento de la humanidad.

35 **Piensa y explica.** Para ti, ¿cómo puede enriquecer un edificio a la humanidad?

trescientos diecisiete **317**

HERITAGE LANGUAGE LEARNERS

• Explain to students that Spanish missions played an important role in the history of the United States, especially in the southwest. Ask students to research this role, and include some of the history of the missions, the characteristics of their structures, their purpose, and the impact the missions had on the indigenous populations. Invite students to make a presentation before the class based on their research. Encourage students to accompany their presentations with images of some of the better-known missions, especially those along *el Camino Real*.

CRITICAL THINKING

• If students were doing a digital tour of an interesting structure or building in their community, ask them which one they would select and why. After discussing this in small groups, have groups make a final selection, and justify their choices. Students should also explain how they would start their tour: with a brief history of the community, a short biographical sketch of the architect, or some other strategy to get viewers' attention. After all groups make their presentations, have the class select the definitive landmark for their tour.

Unit 6

DESAFÍO 2

Opinar y hacer valoraciones

35. To extend this activity, have students write two or three questions for Rafael Moneo about architecture and its role in society. Ask volunteers to pretend to be Moneo and sit on the "hot seat" and rapidly answer questions posed by the class.

 AUDIO SCRIPT
See page 297L.

CULTURA

Rafael Moneo

Rafael Moneo believes that architecture is an art that is capable of communicating as much as a song, a painting, or a sculpture. Before designing a building, he considers its location carefully, which is the reason his buildings are extremely site-specific—as if woven into the landscape. This approach produces buildings that are understated, yet functional.

Answer Key

32. 1. es   3. sea
2. tiene   4. debamos

▶ 1.–2. indicativo: opinión afirmativa
3.–4. subjuntivo: opinión en negativo

33. Answers will vary. Sample answers:
1. En preparar un *tour* digital de la catedral de Los Ángeles.
2. Es original. Daniel dice: «no se parece a ninguna de las que he visto».
3. Comenzarán hablando del arquitecto.
4. No le gusta hablar frente a la cámara, pero a Michelle sí le gusta.
5. Answers will vary.

34. Answers will vary.
▶ Answers will vary.

35. Answers will vary.

Additional Resources

Fans Online activities

317

Unit 6

DESAFÍO 2

Vocabulario – Arquitectura y escultura

Presentation

- In this section, students will learn vocabulary to talk about architecture and sculpture.

Activities	Standards	Resources
Vocabulario	1.2, 2.1, 2.2, 3.1	
36.	1.3, 3.1	
37.	1.1, 1.3, 2.1, 2.2, 3.1, 4.2, 5.1, 5.2	
38.	1.1, 1.2, 2.1, 2.2, 3.1, 5.1	Audio
39. Cultura	1.2, 1.3, 2.1, 2.2, 3.1, 5.1	

Teaching Suggestions

Warm-Up / Independent Starter

- Ask students to create a two-column chart with these headings: *Nombres, Adjetivos.* Then have them read the first paragraph of the vocabulary presentation silently and classify the highlighted words in their charts.

Preparation

- Read the vocabulary presentation and the *Más vocabulario* feature aloud to demonstrate correct pronunciation, and have students repeat the highlighted words after you. Then ask them to complete their charts. Next, have students fill in the *Adjetivos* column with adjectives that would form logical pairs with the nouns in the *Nombres* column (e.g., *catedral – vanguardista*). Invite students to share their charts with a partner and come up with six to seven sentences in which they use some of their noun-adjective pairs.

- For further practice with this vocabulary, ask students to research one of the works mentioned in the presentation for homework. They should prepare to present their work to the class.

Activities

36. Have students write definitions for some of the words they listed. Then ask them to have their peers guess the vocabulary defined. You may wish to turn this into a competition.

318

Vocabulario

Arquitectura y escultura

La arquitectura es el arte de diseñar edificios y construcciones de todo tipo: edificios religiosos como catedrales, mezquitas, templos o sinagogas, con impresionantes arcos y columnas o altísimas torres, y también lujosos palacios y viviendas.

A lo largo de la historia las distintas civilizaciones nos han ido dejando verdaderas obras de arte, no solo pertenecientes al período clásico de los griegos y los romanos (como el famoso acueducto de Segovia, del siglo I), sino también a la arquitectura moderna y contemporánea. De hecho, muchos rascacielos (como el famosísimo Empire State) y puentes (como el Golden Gate) se consideran maravillas arquitectónicas.

Actualmente no solo se emplean materiales tradicionales como la piedra, el granito, el cemento o el concreto, sino otros más modernos como el cristal o el aluminio y otros metales.

Hotel Santos Porta Fira (Barcelona).

Conjunto escultórico de la Sagrada Familia (Barcelona).

En muchas ocasiones, la escultura está íntimamente unida a la arquitectura, como es el caso de la fachada de la Sagrada Familia de Gaudí. Las figuras fueron esculpidas por varios artistas dirigidos por el propio Gaudí.

Más vocabulario

Materiales

el hierro	iron
el ladrillo	brick
el mármol	marble

¡Atención!

actualmente	currently
de hecho	actually

36 **Categorías**

▶ **Escribe** una lista de términos para cada categoría. Incluye palabras de la ficha de Vocabulario y otras que conozcas.

1. Materiales. → *acero, bronce, hierro...*
2. Tipos de edificios y construcciones. → *iglesia...*
3. Partes de edificios. → *fachada...*
4. Acciones asociadas con arquitectos y escultores. → *diseñar...*

318 trescientos dieciocho

Differentiated Instruction

DEVELOPING LEARNERS

- Ask students to match the words.

1. *acueducto* (g)	a. *en realidad*
2. *rascacielos* (f)	b. *material de construcción*
3. *puente* (h)	c. *residencia de un monarca*
4. *actual* (i)	d. *piedra*
5. *ladrillo* (b)	e. *residencia*
6. *fachada* (j)	f. *edificio muy alto*
7. *de hecho* (a)	g. *lleva el agua*
8. *mármol* (d)	h. *va sobre un río*
9. *vivienda* (e)	i. *presente*
10. *palacio* (c)	j. *parte exterior de un edificio*

EXPANDING LEARNERS

- Ask students to imagine that their city council is considering demolishing an emblematic building in their community in order to put up a shopping mall. Some students will be in favor of this plan, while others oppose it. All students will write a letter to convince their community government to either go ahead with their plans and tear down the building or to preserve it. Students will need to state the advantages of their argument and the disadvantages of the opposition. Call on students to read their letters aloud.

37 ¿Cómo es?

▶ **Escribe** una descripción de cada uno de estos edificios. ¿Cuál te gusta más? ¿Por qué?

1

Torre de las Comunicaciones.
Montevideo (Uruguay).

2

Misión de Santa Bárbara.
California (Estados Unidos).

3

Casa Rosada.
Buenos Aires (Argentina).

▶ **Habla** con tu compañero(a). Comparen estos edificios con los de su comunidad. Después, presenten sus conclusiones a la clase.

38 Exploremos la escultura

▶ **Escucha** y responde a estas preguntas.

1. ¿Qué representaban las esculturas que vio Michelle en México? ¿De qué material son?
2. ¿Qué famosas esculturas describe Ethan? ¿De qué material están hechas?
3. ¿Cómo se llama la escultura que describe Eva? ¿De qué material es?
4. ¿Qué tienen en común las tres esculturas que describen los personajes?

▶ **Habla** con tu compañero(a) sobre la escultura más impresionante que conoces. Después, escribe un párrafo comparándola con la que ha descrito tu compañero(a).

CULTURA

La Ciudad Universitaria de Caracas

Conocida como la «Ciudad museo», la Ciudad Universitaria de Caracas, del famoso arquitecto venezolano Carlos Raúl Villanueva, se considera una obra maestra de la arquitectura moderna y fue declarada Patrimonio de la Humanidad por la UNESCO en el año 2000. En este espacio el arquitecto logró combinar de forma magistral las edificaciones y la naturaleza, es decir, el arte como parte del espacio. Además del conjunto de edificios, la Ciudad Universitaria de Caracas cuenta con más de cien obras de artistas de todo el mundo, como Alexander Calder y Jean Arp.

39 Piensa. ¿Te gusta la arquitectura moderna o prefieres los edificios antiguos? ¿Por qué?

trescientos diecinueve 319

HERITAGE LANGUAGE LEARNERS

- Ask students to research some architectural landmarks in their heritage country. Explain that they may consider not only public buildings, but also bridges, parks, private residences, and structures such as stadiums, towers, *glorietas* (roundabouts), and fountains. Have students bring in images of these landmarks and be prepared to give some background information on the piece, including its history, architect, materials used, date of construction, and any other anecdotal information. Ask students to share this information with the rest of the class.

CRITICAL THINKING

- Ask students to imagine that their community wants to commission a sculpture, but has not decided who or what it should represent and where the art will be exhibited. Have students write a proposal to the local government, proposing a sculpture, where it should be located and why, the material(s) that would be used to make it, the style of the piece, the approximate dimensions of the finished art, and any other information that might help sway the community in their favor. Students might also assign their art a name.

---

38. After listening, project or show photos of the sculptures described in the conversation and ask students to match each image with the description heard. Have students chat with a partner to describe which of the sculptures they like best.

AUDIO SCRIPT
See page 297L.

CULTURA

La Ciudad Universitaria de Caracas

Carlos Raúl Villanueva began work on this new campus in 1945. Villanueva's vision was to integrate the new architectural forms and contemporary art of the 20th century with university buildings. One of the most notable buildings is the Aula Magna, which contains a sculpture by Alexander Calder—a prominent American sculptor.

Answer Key

36. Answers will vary. Sample answers:
   1. piedra, cemento, concreto, cristal, granito
   2. catedral, mezquita, templo, sinagoga, rascacielos, palacio, acueducto, puente
   3. arco, columna, torre, ventana
   4. esculpir, representar, construir, crear

37. Answers will vary.
   ▶ Answers will vary.

38. 1. Guerreros olmecas. Son de basalto.
   2. Los moáis de la isla de Pascua. Son de piedra volcánica.
   3. Se llama *Mujer y pájaro*. Es de cemento.
   4. Son muy grandes y representan figuras humanas.
   ▶ Answers will vary.

39. Answers will vary.

Additional Resources

Fans Online activities
Practice Workbook

319

DESAFÍO 2

Gramática – Expresar opinión

Presentation

- In this section, students will review and expand on how to express opinions.

Activities	Standards	Resources
Gramática	1.2, 3.1	
40.	1.2, 3.1, 4.1	
41.	1.3, 3.1	
42.	1.2, 1.3, 2.1, 2.2, 3.1	
43.	1.1, 1.2, 2.1, 2.2, 3.1	
44. Cultura	1.2, 1.3, 2.2, 3.1, 5.2	

Teaching Suggestions

Warm-Up / Independent Starter

- Ask students to note any patterns that they observe in the use of the indicative and the subjunctive in these sentences:
  1. *Creo que la catedral es innovadora.*
  2. *Daniel no piensa que la catedral se parezca a las misiones.*
  3. *Los expertos consideran que las obras de Moneo enriquecen a la humanidad.*
  4. *A mí no me parece que la arquitectura comunique tanto como la literatura.*

Preparation

- Ask students to share their Independent Starters. Then, have them go over the grammar presentation with a partner. Next, ask pairs to change the sentences from the Independent Starter to express the opposite view (e.g., *No creo que la catedral sea innovadora*). Finally, ask students to form questions (e.g., *¿Qué te parece la catedral?*). Invite them to share their work.

- For further practice, show students pictures of famous buildings and sculptures and ask them for their opinions. For example: *¿Qué piensan de la Torre Eiffel?* They must use different expressions of opinion in their answers.

Activities

42. Before reading, ask students to look at the sculpture and read the title. Then have them write two or three sentences stating their opinions of this sculpture and its name.

Gramática

Expresar opinión

- Para expresar una opinión personal, puedes usar los siguientes verbos y expresiones:

VERBOS DE OPINIÓN

considerar	opinar
creer	parecer
imaginar	pensar
juzgar	suponer

Creo que este cuadro es de estilo cubista.
Me pareció que la fachada era lo más valioso de la catedral.
Considero que esta es la iglesia más bonita.

EXPRESIONES DE OPINIÓN

En mi opinión	Desde mi punto de vista
Para mí	A mi juicio

A mi juicio, el ladrillo es mejor material que el cemento.

El indicativo y el subjuntivo con los verbos de opinión

- El verbo de la cláusula dependiente de un verbo de opinión puede ir:
  - En **indicativo**, si la cláusula principal es afirmativa.

    Me parece que la catedral **es** del siglo XVII.

  - En **subjuntivo**, si la cláusula principal es negativa y el verbo de opinión está en primera persona (singular o plural).

    Yo no creo que esa escultura **sea** románica.

CONSTRUCCIONES AFIRMATIVAS (INDICATIVO)

considerar que	opinar que
creer que	parecer que
imaginar que	pensar que
juzgar que	suponer que

CONSTRUCCIONES NEGATIVAS (SUBJUNTIVO)

no considerar que	no parecer que
no creer que	no pensar que

Pedirle a alguien su opinión

- Para pedir a alguien su opinión sobre algo, usa las siguientes construcciones:

PREGUNTAR SOBRE OPINIONES

¿Qué crees que...?
¿Qué piensas/opinas de (que)...?
¿Qué te parece...?

—¿**Qué te parece** la arquitectura moderna?
—¡Me encanta!

—¿**Qué opinas de** aplicar estuco a las fachadas?
—En mi opinión, es algo demasiado costoso.

40 **Compara.** ¿Qué estructuras se emplean en inglés para pedirle a alguien su opinión?

41 **Opiniones opuestas**

▶ **Transforma** estas opiniones afirmativas en negativas.

1. Pienso que ese puente se construyó en el siglo XIII.
2. Considero que el acueducto de Segovia es el mejor ejemplo de la arquitectura romana.
3. Creo que la escultora ha creado una obra muy innovadora.

Differentiated Instruction

DEVELOPING LEARNERS

- Ask students to change these affirmative statements to negative ones:
  1. *Creo que la torre es de piedra. (No creo que sea...)*
  2. *Considero que Moneo tiene mucha creatividad. (No considero que tenga...)*
  3. *Pienso que esa escultura representa muy bien la ciudad. (No pienso que represente...)*
  4. *Me parece que la fachada es de otro escultor. (No me parece que sea...)*
  5. *Creíamos que el palacio era del siglo XVII. (No creíamos que fuera...)*
  6. *Pienso que el color le da mucha vida al edificio. (No pienso que le dé...)*

EXPANDING LEARNERS

- Ask students to choose seven of the verbs or expressions presented on this page and write a sentence with each of them that reflects their thoughts or opinions related to architecture. For example: *A mi juicio la comunidad debe construir más viviendas para las personas de pocos recursos. Pienso que los arquitectos deben respetar la naturaleza del lugar donde se construyen sus edificios. Considero que la mayoría de los rascacielos son feos y no creo que nuestra comunidad deba construir más.* Then have students work in groups of four to compare and contrast their opinions.

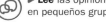

42 Peine del viento

▶ **Lee** la descripción de esta famosa obra escultórica. Después, completa las oraciones como si tú fueras el escultor, Eduardo Chillida.

El *Peine del viento* XV es, probablemente, la obra más conocida del escultor español Eduardo Chillida. Es un conjunto de esculturas situado en un extremo de la bahía de La Concha, en San Sebastián (España). Lo forman tres esculturas de acero, de 10 toneladas de peso cada una, incrustadas en unas rocas azotadas por las olas que dan al mar Cantábrico.

1. Considero que esta obra...
2. Supongo que la construcción...
3. No creo que el mar...
4. Me parece que el lugar donde está esta obra...
5. No pienso que los materiales...
6. Opino que el gran valor de esta obra...

43 Opiniones diversas

▶ **Lee** las opiniones de estos estudiantes sobre arquitectura y escultura, y coméntenlas en pequeños grupos. ¿Están de acuerdo con ellas? ¿Por qué?

1. «Desde mi punto de vista, el arte moderno no tiene ningún valor.» Natalia, 16 años.

2. «A mí no me parece que la arquitectura sea un arte, como lo son la pintura o la escultura.» Jaime, 17 años.

3. «Opino que las esculturas de Chillida son hermosísimas. Me encantaría que mi ciudad tuviera una.» Alicia, 16 años.

CULTURA

Eduardo Chillida

Eduardo Chillida nació en 1924 en San Sebastián (España). Abandonó los estudios de Arquitectura para dedicarse al dibujo y a la escultura, sus grandes pasiones. Empezó esculpiendo en hierro y madera, pero pronto empezó a experimentar con materiales como el acero. La naturaleza era para él fuente de inspiración; de ahí que muchas de sus grandes obras estén situadas en espacios naturales abiertos.

Eduardo Chillida. *Elogio del horizonte.* Gijón (España).

44 **Piensa y explica.** Fíjate en las dos fotografías de esta página. ¿Por qué piensas que Chillida les puso esos títulos a sus obras? ¿Qué nombres les habrías dado tú?

Gramática – Expresar opinión

43. In order to provide and evaluate their own authentic opinions, have students complete this activity while viewing images of other works by Chillida (they will find them online). Students should speak in complete sentences and include expressions of opinion in their answers.

CULTURA

Eduardo Chillida

Eduardo Chillida claimed that space itself was his main building material. Perhaps for this reason, most of his sculptures are open-air pieces. Chillida worked in cement, stone, steel, and iron, which he forged himself. There are several sculptures by Chillida in public places in the United States. Among them, *Around the Void V* in the courtyard of the World Bank headquarters in Washington, D.C. and *De música*, outside the Morton H. Meyerson Symphony Center in Dallas, TX.

Answer Key

40. Estructuras como: *What do you think of...? How do you feel about...? What's your opinion of...? What are your views on...?*

41. 1. No pienso que ese puente se construyera en el siglo XIII.
2. No considero que el acueducto de Segovia sea...
3. No creo que la escultora haya creado...

42. Answers will vary. Sample answers:
1. ... se adapta al entorno.
2. ... es fuerte y duradera.
3. ... dañe las esculturas.
4. ... muestra la fuerza del mar.
5. ... se oxiden.
6. ... es su simbolismo.

43. Answers will vary.

44. Answers will vary.

Additional Resources

Fans Online activities
Practice Workbook

HERITAGE LANGUAGE LEARNERS

- Have students work with a partner and ask pairs to select a piece of art, building, piece of sculpture, or a well-known artist, architect, or sculptor. Explain to students that they will create a conversation based on their opinions of that art, architecture, or its creator, but one of them will always make affirmative statements, and the other, negative ones. If needed, allow students some time to research the art or artist/architect in order to make logical and insightful comments.

MULTIPLE INTELLIGENCES:
Naturalistic Intelligence

- Ask students to imagine that they are sculptors and have been thinking about creating a spectacular sculpture that they want to integrate with nature in their community or region. Have students write several paragraphs that will define and describe their ideas surrounding the piece they wish to create. Then, ask them to mention several places where their art could be ideally integrated with nature and how it could be exhibited. Call on volunteers to share their ideas with the class.

DESAFÍO 2

Gramática – Hacer valoraciones

Presentation

■ In this section, students will review the use of the infinitive and the subjunctive in clauses introduced by expressions that make a value judgment.

Activities	Standards	Resources
Gramática	1.2, 3.1	
45.	1.2, 3.1, 4.1	
46.	1.3, 3.1, 5.1	
47.	1.2, 1.3, 2.2, 3.1	
48.	1.1, 2.2, 3.1	

Teaching Suggestions

Warm-Up / Independent Starter

■ Ask students to rewrite the following sentences to express what the person(s) in parentheses should do:

1. *Es importante estudiar la arquitectura moderna. (tú) (Es importante que estudies...)*

2. *Es aconsejable emplear una gran variedad de materiales. (los escultores) (Es aconsejable que los escultores empleen...)*

3. *Es fantástico tener obras de arte en las calles de las ciudades. (nosotros) (Es fantástico que tengamos...)*

Preparation

■ Give students time to go over the grammar presentation individually. Then, ask them to revise and if necessary, correct their sentences from the Independent Starter. They should note that when expressing a judgment about the action of another, the subjunctive must be used in the dependent clause. Call on volunteers to share their Independent Starters.

■ For further practice, distribute individual whiteboards and markers (or index cards) to students. Read a few incomplete sentences aloud and ask students to complete each one with the infinitive or the subjunctive of the verb provided. After each sentence, ask students to hold up the whiteboards (or index cards) with their answers written. For example: *(tener) Es importante que las ciudades ... una arquitectura variada. (tengan)*

Gramática

Hacer valoraciones

Expresiones para hacer valoraciones

● Recuerda: para hacer valoraciones puedes utilizar las siguientes construcciones:

EXPRESIONES PARA HACER VALORACIONES

Es aconsejable/conveniente… Es importante… Es necesario/preciso… Es bueno/malo… Es mejor/peor… Es sorprendente/fantástico/peligroso… Es un error/un problema/una tontería…	+ infinitivo + que + subjuntivo

> **Es importante** aprender a reconocer los distintos estilos artísticos.
> **Es una pena** que no se conserven las antiguas murallas.

● Para hacer una valoración personal puedes usar también la expresión me parece seguida de una palabra que exprese valoración: un adverbio (bien, mal), un adjetivo (extraño, imprescindible, perfecto) o un nombre (una pena, una maravilla, un error).

> **Me parece bien** que haya visitas guiadas gratuitas a los museos.

El infinitivo y el subjuntivo con expresiones de valoración

● Usa el **infinitivo** en afirmaciones o negaciones generales en las que no hay un sujeto.

> **Sería necesario restaurar** el edificio.

● Usa el **subjuntivo** cuando la cláusula dependiente se refiere a un sujeto en particular.

> **Fue una lástima** que no **consiguiéramos** entradas para la exposición.

45 **Compara.** ¿Cómo expresas las valoraciones impersonales en inglés? ¿Y las personales?

46 **¿Qué piensas tú?**

▶ **Escribe** estas oraciones con la forma verbal correcta.

1. Es preciso que la arquitecta _____ la luz y el espacio.
   (considerar)
2. Sería aconsejable que la construcción _____ el estilo del entorno.
   (reflejar)
3. Es una tontería _____ que la arquitectura no es un arte.
   (pensar)
4. Me pareció fatal que no _____ esta obra en la exposición.
   (incluir)
5. Sería una lástima no _____ visitar el museo.
   (poder)

▶ **Escribe** seis oraciones valorando el edificio de tu escuela u otro edificio de tu comunidad. Usa distintas estructuras de la ficha de Gramática.

Differentiated Instruction

DEVELOPING LEARNERS

● Write or say ten sentences using *las expresiones de valoración* on the page and an infinitive (e.g., *Es aconsejable estudiar los distintos estilos arquitectónicos*). Then ask students to rewrite each sentence, using the subjunctive (e.g., *Es aconsejable que estudiemos los distintos estilos arquitectónicos*). Remind students that they must use the subjunctive when there is a change of subject and when the value statement is followed by the relative pronoun *que*. Then, ask students to read their sentences aloud.

EXPANDING LEARNERS

● Explain to students that they will work with a partner and create a dialogue based on a familiar structure or piece of art in their community. They will take turns using some of the value statements on the page to talk about the structure or artwork. For example:
  A. *Es un error que tiren la antigua biblioteca.*
  B. *Sí, tiene bastante valor histórico, pero es importante que la comunidad tenga una biblioteca más grande.*

● Call on pairs to act out their dialogues.

47 ¿Qué opinas de la catedral?

▶ **Lee** las características de la catedral de Los Ángeles y escribe una valoración sobre la información que se da en cada punto.

Modelo

Moneo incorporó muchísima luz natural en el diseño de la catedral de los Ángeles.
→ *Es bueno que Moneo incorporara mucha luz porque así se ahorra electricidad.*

1. Está situada en el centro de la ciudad. El proyecto incluye una gran plaza, jardines, una cafetería y una tienda de regalos.
2. La catedral tiene capacidad para más de 3.000 personas. Cuenta con un estacionamiento subterráneo con 600 plazas.
3. El proyecto incluye varias salas de reuniones con conexión a Internet.
4. El edificio fue proyectado para resistir terremotos de hasta 8,4 grados en la escala de Richter.
5. Aunque es de estilo moderno, posee elementos tradicionales, como la torre con el campanario o la planta de la catedral, en forma de cruz.

48 La arquitectura urbana

▶ **Habla** con tu compañero(a) sobre estos otros edificios de Moneo. Usen expresiones para hacer valoraciones.

Modelo *En mi opinión, es una lástima que el Palacio de Congresos sea tan grande porque no se ve la montaña que hay detrás.*

1

Edificio Bankinter en Madrid (España).

2

Palacio de Congresos y Auditorio de Kursaal en San Sebastián (España).

3

Ayuntamiento de Logroño (España).

trescientos veintitrés 323

HERITAGE LANGUAGE LEARNERS

- Heritage learners often do not know why they must use the subjunctive. Ask students to write or say at least seven original sentences: some that state a fact and others that make a value statement. Then ask students to explain why they used the indicative, infinitive, or subjunctive. For example: *Creo que el arte es muy necesario en una ciudad.* (indicativo: una opinión afirmativa) *Es mejor usar el ladrillo como material de construcción.* (infinitivo: una valoración sin cambio de sujeto) *Es mejor que usemos...* (subjuntivo: una valoración con cambio de sujeto)

MULTIPLE INTELLIGENCES: Verbal-Linguistic Intelligence

- Tell students that we probably all know someone who is very opinionated and will not agree with our ideas. Ask students to share an opinion with their partner by making a value statement using one of the expressions on the page. Partners will respond with a contrary opinion. For example:
  A. *Es un error que construyan esas viviendas al lado de la playa.*
  B. *¡Qué va! Es aconsejable construirlas muy cerca, porque a la gente le encanta estar al lado del mar.*

Gramática – Hacer valoraciones

Activities

46. Ask students to explain each of their verb selections. After completing this activity, have students do all changes necessary in order to use a different verbal mood for each sentence. For example: 1. *Es preciso considerar la luz y el espacio.* 3. *Es una tontería que pensemos que la arquitectura no es un arte.* Check students' answers as a class.

47. Before beginning this activity, show images of the exterior and interior of the cathedral.

48. Ask students to enter an imaginary essay contest, *Un edificio que enriquece nuestra ciudad,* held in Madrid or another city. Each participant explains his or her opinion as to how the building chosen enriches the city where it is located. Students should compare and contrast it to other buildings seen in this *Desafío.*

Answer Key

45. Se usan expresiones como: *It is important..., It is better..., It would be a mistake...* o *I think/believe that...*

46. 1. considere   4. incluyeran
    2..reflejara   5. poder
    3. pensar
    ▶ Answers will vary.

47. Answers will vary. Sample answers:
1. Me parece perfecto que tenga una gran plaza y que esté en el centro de la ciudad.
2. Es importante que toda la gente que quiera ir tenga lugar para estacionar.
3. Es un error que tenga conexión a Internet porque eso puede distraer a la gente.
4. Es necesario que resista terremotos porque hay varias fallas en California.
5. Me parece bien que se mezclen los estilos.

48. Answers will vary.

Additional Resources

Fans Online activities
Practice Workbook

323

Presentation

- In this section, students will read an interview with Rafael Moneo, a Spanish architect, and answer comprehension questions based on the reading. Students will also learn more about the philosophy and works of this Spanish architect and compose questions that they would like to ask him.

Activities	Standards	Resources
Lectura: texto informativo	1.2, 2.1, 2.2, 3.1, 3.2	
49.	1.2, 1.3, 2.1, 2.2	
50.	1.2	
51.	1.1, 1.2, 1.3, 2.1, 2.2, 3.1, 5.1	

Teaching Suggestions

Warm-Up / Independent Starter

- Have students list three to five facts they have learned about the life and works of Rafael Moneo.

Preparation

- Call on students to share their Independent Starters. Award one point for each item mentioned that no other student has written. You may wish to reward the winning student with a "no homework" pass redeemable at his or her convenience. Use the information students provided to discuss the second question of the *Antes de leer* section as a class. Then give students a few moments to work on question #1 individually.

- Before reading, show students images of Moneo's works, and read this quote from the interview: *Lo hermoso de la arquitectura es cuando no tiene tanta necesidad de hacerse presente.* Using some of the images of Moneo's works as a reference, discuss this quote as a class. You may want to prompt students with these or similar questions: *¿Les parecen llamativos* (flashy) *los edificios de Moneo? ¿Cómo son las líneas de estos edificios: rectas o curvas? ¿Cómo creen que es el interior? ¿Consideran que estos edificios se adaptan al entorno* (surroundings)?

324

Antes de leer: estrategias

1. Observa el título, el texto y su disposición. ¿Qué tipo de texto es?
2. ¿Qué sabes del protagonista del texto? ¿Y de su estilo artístico?

Rafael Moneo.

Rafael Moneo

«Confundir arquitectura con obra de arte da lugar a muchos excesos»

«Max Aub dijo que uno es de donde ha hecho el bachillerato». Rafael Moneo (Tudela, 1937) recuerda esta frase para hablar de su infancia y su pueblo, de las calles, plazas y viviendas navarras, de la importancia que tiene la geografía para un arquitecto: «Nacer en un pueblo, crecer en un lugar con contornos bien definidos, geográficos y sociales, sin duda ayuda a entender lo importantes que son los límites, las condiciones de partida, tanto para la vida como para un proyecto. Conocer las ciudades es siempre necesario para iniciar una obra de arquitectura».

Museo de Arte Moderno. Estocolmo (Suecia).

PREGUNTA. Ha dicho en alguna ocasión que «lo hermoso de la arquitectura es cuando no tiene tanta necesidad de hacerse presente». ¿Qué valor tiene para usted lo que pasa desapercibido, la sencillez[1]?

RESPUESTA. La arquitectura anónima convive con la obra singular. En ambas puede encontrarse todo aquello que se pide a una obra de arquitectura. Una gran obra de arquitectura acaba estando tan incorporada al medio que no reclama atención. Se la entiende como parte de él.

P. Los espacios interiores que diseña son bastante particulares y complejos. ¿Diría que ese es su mayor rasgo distintivo?

R. Lo que se llamó en el siglo XX «arquitectura moderna» pretendía[2] no hacer distinción entre interior y exterior. La obra de arquitectura disfrutaba de[3] una autonomía tal que llevaba a ignorar el medio en el que se incluía. Siempre he creído que esto no era así.

Que la obra de arquitectura debía contar con el medio –ciudad o paisaje– y que su inclusión en él propiciaba[4] la distinción entre interior y exterior de la que antes hablaba. Un proyecto puede así resolverse desde la condición urbana y ser en su interior otra cosa. La luz, naturalmente, desempeña[5] un papel mediador entre interior y exterior.

P. ¿Qué se espera de la arquitectura hoy en día?

R. Algunos reclamarían[6] la novedad y con ella la condición espectacular que seduce. Otros, la contribución de la arquitectura a una construcción racional en el planeta, lo que implicaría, a mi modo de ver, establecer la continuidad con lo construido. Particularmente, me considero más próximo a estos que a los primeros.

P. ¿Cómo está viviendo la arquitectura este momento de globalización? ¿Aporta mayor internacionalización para la arquitectura española?

R. La globalización ha llegado en un momento en que la arquitectura española gozaba[7] de una cierta visibilidad.

Differentiated Instruction

DEVELOPING LEARNERS

- Ask students whether the following statements are true *(cierto)* or false *(falso)*. Have them correct the false ones.
  1. *Moneo cree que una obra de arquitectura no debe llamar la atención. (C)*
  2. *Moneo no hace distinción entre el interior y el exterior. (F; el interior es distinto al exterior)*
  3. *Según Moneo, la luz juega un papel importante entre interior y exterior. (C)*
  4. *Moneo dice que la arquitectura ha sido un conocimiento exclusivo de cada civilización. (F; ha sido un conocimiento compartido)*

EXPANDING LEARNERS

- Ask students to think about the following statement that Moneo makes in the interview: *La obra de arquitectura debía contar con el medio —ciudad o paisaje— en el que se incluye.* Promote a classroom discussion on the importance of harmony, or lack thereof, between a work of architecture and its surroundings. Ask students to review the architectural pieces described and shown in this unit and any others they may know. Encourage all students to share their opinions and participate in the discussion.

No es raro encontrar arquitectos españoles trabajando en una escuela, dando conferencias, formando parte de jurados, construyendo, etc., fuera de España.

P. Para alguien tan apegado a su tierra natal, ¿qué sentido tiene la idea de «no lugar»?

R. Hace siglos, miles de años, que la arquitectura no ha estado estrictamente localizada. Basta pensar en la arquitectura romana, en el Gótico, en la difusión de la arquitectura en el Renacimiento, para entender que la arquitectura ha sido un conocimiento compartido, extenso. En un momento como el actual, naturalmente, la discusión de los problemas que tiene la arquitectura es global. Todos participamos en él. Pero ello no es óbice[8] para que ese modo común de entender las cosas encuentre acomodo,

se ajuste a un lugar. Hasta el extremo de que quepa[9] decir que el lugar es el origen de la arquitectura. Los «no lugares» actuales, solo hasta cierto punto, lo son.

P. Ha confesado que no solo tiene pasión por la arquitectura, sino también por la pintura. ¿Sigue encontrando tiempo para pintar? ¿Qué es lo último que ha dibujado?

R. Dibujo todos los días, todavía me gusta ayudarme del dibujo para entrever[10] lo que una arquitectura puede ser. Y ello me lleva a dibujar continuamente. Desgraciadamente pinto poco. Pero la pintura sigue atrayéndome, así como muchas otras cosas: la lectura, viajar por España, beber un buen vino.

Fuente: http://www.elcultural.es
(selección)

---

1. discreción
2. quería, deseaba
3. tenía
4. favorecía
5. realiza, cumple
6. pedirían, exigirían
7. tenía
8. impedimento
9. sea posible
10. imaginar

---

49 **¿Comprendes?**

▶ **Responde** a estas preguntas. Señala, en cada caso, qué palabras del texto justifican tus respuestas.

1. ¿Qué relación debe haber entre las obras de arte y el lugar donde se ubican, según Moneo?
2. ¿Qué diferencia las construcciones de Moneo de las obras de la llamada «arquitectura moderna»?
3. ¿Cómo ha afectado la globalización a la arquitectura española?
4. ¿Por qué dibuja Moneo cada día? ¿Qué relación encuentra entre el dibujo y la arquitectura?

50 **Palabras y expresiones**

▶ **Explica** con tus palabras el significado de estas expresiones que aparecen en el texto.

1. pasar desapercibido
2. reclamar atención
3. estar próximo
4. estar apegado

51 **Con tus propias palabras**

▶ **Escribe** tres preguntas que harías a Moneo si pudieras entrevistarlo. Compártelas con dos compañeros(as) y elijan las cinco preguntas más relevantes.

▶ **Investiga** sobre otras construcciones de Moneo. Elige una que te llame la atención, busca información e imágenes, y preséntala en clase.

■ Have students form groups of three to read the selection. Each student will have a different responsibility as they read: a "vocabulary expert," who lists unknown words and uses a dictionary or the context clues to write definitions; a "summarizer," who writes a summary for each of Moneo's answers (in ten words or less); a "questioner," who records two to three questions that the group has after reading each of Moneo's answers.

Activities

49. After completing this activity, have students form new groups of three and ask each group to imagine that they are on the 1996 selection committee for the Pritzker Prize. They will role-play a discussion of why they believe that Moneo should win this most prestigious prize. Ask students to justify their answers by referring to the interview they have just read and to specific buildings designed by Moneo.

Answer Key

49. Answers will vary. Sample answers:
1. La obra debe incorporarse al medio: «[…] la obra de arquitectura debía contar con el medio».
2. La distinción entre el interior y el exterior: «Un proyecto puede […] ser en su interior otra cosa».
3. De forma positiva. Moneo dice: «No es raro encontrar arquitectos españoles […] fuera de España».
4. Dibujar lo ayuda a imaginar la obra: «me gusta ayudarme del dibujo para entrever lo que una arquitectura puede ser».

50. Answers will vary. Sample answers:
1. No se nota.
2. Llamar la atención; se nota mucho.
3. Estar cerca.
4. Sentir cariño por algo o alguien.

51. Answers will vary.
▶ Answers will vary.

Additional Resources

Fans Online activities

HERITAGE LANGUAGE LEARNERS

• After students have completed activity 51, explain that they will play the role of Rafael Moneo and answer some of the questions that students have posed. Heritage learners will research the life and works of Moneo to be better equipped to answer these questions. Allow students time to rehearse their questions and answers and then call on groups to present their interview as if they were participating in a roundtable discussion made for television, complete with host and guests.

SPECIAL-NEEDS LEARNERS

• The article presents challenges because of its length, complexity, and new vocabulary. Help those students who have difficulty focusing on articles of this nature by pairing them with a student who has superior language skills, or by working directly with them. Ask the special-needs learner to read the article aloud and to paraphrase each sentence or paragraph, as needed. His or her partner will offer help by asking questions to test comprehension and to help decode new vocabulary. You may also ask students to rewrite the interview as a third-person narrative to verify their comprehension.

Unit 6
DESAFÍO 2
Comunicación

Presentation

- In this section, students will integrate the vocabulary and grammar skills from *Desafío 2* in order to express their opinions about topics related to architecture and sculpture.

Activities	Standards	Resources
52.	1.2, 1.3, 2.1, 2.2, 3.1, 3.2, 5.2	Audio
53.	1.1, 1.3, 2.1, 4.2, 5.1, 5.2	
54. Final del desafío	1.1, 1.2, 1.3, 2.1, 2.2, 3.1	

Teaching Suggestions

Warm-Up / Independent Starter

- Project or show an image of one of Chillida's sculptures and ask students to write a two-paragraph description of it. They should mention the material(s), shape, style, size, surroundings, as well as their personal opinion of this piece.

Preparation

- Call on volunteers to share their Independent Starters. Record some of their sentences on chart paper. What aspects of Chillida's work caught students' attention? What do they think of the choice of materials? What do they like most about Chillida's work? And least? Then, ask students to use some of the sentences you recorded as well as the class discussion to write value statements. For example: *Es una lástima que Chillida no use madera en sus esculturas.* Call on volunteers to share some of their statements.

Activities

52. Before reading the article, show students images of several of Balenciaga's iconic dresses (you will find them on the webpage of the Museo Cristóbal Balenciaga). Then ask students to draw a piece of furniture that might be inspired by one of these designs. Next, have them get together with a partner and comment on each other's designs.

Comunicación

 52 El encuentro entre dos artes

 ▶ **Lee** este artículo sobre una exposición de arte y responde a estas preguntas.

1. ¿En qué consiste el proyecto de los estudiantes de Arquitectura? ¿Qué opinas sobre él?
2. ¿Qué significa que el proyecto «se ha basado en el estudio de una serie de vestidos del diseñador desde un punto de vista constructivo y conceptual»?
3. ¿Qué significa en este contexto «mantener una relación muy estrecha»?

EL PAÍS   12 de abril de 2013

Lámparas inspiradas en Balenciaga

Los estudiantes del Grado en Fundamentos de Arquitectura han sido los creadores de este proyecto

La sala Axular de Bizkaia Aretoa ha inaugurado este viernes la exposición *Balenciaga Argitzen*, en la que se podrá ver el proyecto compuesto por ocho lámparas creadas por diez estudiantes de la Escuela Técnica Superior de Arquitectura de la Universidad del País Vasco. Las lámparas se han creado inspirándose en diferentes vestidos de Cristóbal Balenciaga. Además de las lámparas realizadas por los alumnos, los visitantes de la exposición podrán conocer cuál ha sido el proceso que se ha seguido mediante paneles explicativos y varios videos. La elaboración de estas lámparas se ha basado en el estudio de una serie de vestidos del diseñador desde un punto de vista constructivo y conceptual.

Como ha explicado Amaia Casado, profesora y responsable del proyecto, «a lo largo del curso hemos mantenido una relación muy estrecha con el Museo Balenciaga y hemos tenido la oportunidad de conocer muy de cerca los diseños del modisto».

La exposición permanecerá en la sala Axular hasta el próximo 26 de abril y la entrada será gratuita. Es una iniciativa que se repetirá en cursos venideros, aunque para el próximo curso se ha previsto diseñar y crear sillas inspiradas en los trabajos del modisto.

Fuente: http://ccaa.elpais.com (texto adaptado)

 ▶ **Escucha** las opiniones de dos asistentes a la exposición de lámparas y completa estas oraciones.

1. A Flor le parece raro...
2. Diego opina que...
3. A Flor no le sorprende...
4. Diego cree que es bueno...

 ▶ **Escribe** un ensayo presentando el proyecto de estos estudiantes de Arquitectura y tu opinión sobre él.

326 trescientos veintiséis

Differentiated Instruction

DEVELOPING LEARNERS

- Ask students to complete these sentences:
  1. ¿No te parece extraño que diseñan / diseñen esas lámparas? (diseñen)
  2. No creo que es / sea lógico hacerlo. (sea)
  3. Pienso que este proyecto va / vaya a tener éxito. (va)
  4. Es bueno que no cobran / cobren la entrada. (cobren)
  5. Es lógico que la exposición tiene / tenga lugar en el País Vasco. (tenga)
  6. Considero aconsejable que vamos / vayamos al museo. (vayamos)

EXPANDING LEARNERS

- Ask students to choose a work of architecture mentioned in this unit, or to explore and research other buildings or structures on their own, and write a well-developed paragraph describing the work they have chosen. Students will describe what is important, good or bad, necessary, surprising, or original about the structure. They will use some of the value statements from this unit, as well as verbs or phrases that express their opinions. Call on volunteers to read their work aloud.

53 Te toca a ti

▶ **Dibuja** un boceto de una escultura o un edificio para tu ciudad. Después, escribe una descripción detallada (tamaño, forma, materiales, ubicación...) y justifica por qué consideras que es apropiado para tu ciudad.

 ▶ **Habla** con tu compañero(a). Explícale tu proyecto y comparen sus diseños. Después, háganse recomendaciones para mejorar sus respectivos proyectos.

▶ **Presenta** tu diseño a la clase y explica tu proyecto detalladamente. ¿Quién tiene la escultura más creativa? ¿Y el edificio más innovador?

Parque de las Esculturas en Santiago (Chile).

Final del desafío

MICHELLE: Aprendimos mucho sobre este edificio, ¿no?

DANIEL: Sí. Y sabemos muchas más cosas sobre arquitectura.

MICHELLE: Yo creo que es conveniente que en el *tour* digital incluyamos algunos datos sobre el tamaño de la catedral. Me parece fundamental. ¿A ti qué es lo que más te ha sorprendido?

DANIEL: Para mí es impresionante que el arquitecto haya conseguido reflejar la historia de la región y las misiones en un edificio tan moderno.

MICHELLE: Sí, debemos mencionar eso. Y también que para Moneo era importante que las obras fueran comprendidas por los ciudadanos.

DANIEL: ¿No te parece increíble que la arquitectura sea capaz de comunicar tanto?

 54 El *tour* digital

▶ **Lee** el diálogo y responde a estas preguntas.

1. ¿Cuál es para Michelle el rasgo más importante de la catedral de Moneo?
2. ¿Qué le ha llamado más la atención a Daniel?
3. ¿Qué has aprendido tú sobre Moneo y sus construcciones? ¿Qué opinas de su estilo?
4. ¿Cómo crees que va a responder Michelle a la última pregunta de Daniel?

 ▶ **Escribe** con tu compañero(a) el esquema del *tour* digital de la catedral de Los Ángeles. Incluyan las ideas más importantes en cada parte: introducción, desarrollo y conclusión.

trescientos veintisiete **327**

 Unit 6

DESAFÍO 2
Comunicación

53. Before drawing, have students list sculptures and/or buildings that exist in their town. Lead a whole-class discussion with these or similar questions: *¿Qué conmemoran o celebran estas obras? ¿De qué manera es el tamaño, la forma, los materiales y la ubicación de estas obras un reflejo de la ciudad?* Once students have presented, hold a class vote to select *la escultura más creativa* and *el edificio más innovador.*

🎧 **AUDIO SCRIPT**
See page 297M.

Answer Key

52. Answers will vary. Sample answers:
1. En crear lámparas inspiradas en vestidos de Balenciaga. Answers will vary.
2. Se ha analizado cómo se hicieron los vestidos, así como la idea o concepto que transmiten.
3. Han estado en comunicación frecuente.
▶ Answers will vary. Sample answers:
1. ... que se hayan inspirado en un diseñador de moda.
2. ... los diseños son muy creativos.
3. ... que la moda y la arquitectura se unan para crear algo tan innovador.
4. ... que los artistas se inspiren en cualquier elemento que los rodea.
▶ Answers will vary.

53. Answers will vary.
▶ Answers will vary.
▶ Answers will vary.

54. 1. El tamaño de la catedral.
2. Que Moneo haya conseguido reflejar la historia de la región en el edificio.
3. Answers will vary.
4. Answers will vary.
▶ Answers will vary.

Additional Resources

Fans Online activities
Practice Workbook

HERITAGE LANGUAGE LEARNERS

• Have students refer to Daniel's last question in the *Final del desafío* and answer it in their own words. Students should give examples of how the architect achieves this communication or, if they so choose, they may explain why architecture does not communicate that much to us. Ask students to cite examples of buildings and other structures in their explanation. Encourage students to use examples from their heritage country. Call on volunteers to read their work or make a brief oral and visual presentation to the class.

MULTIPLE INTELLIGENCES:
Visual-Spatial Intelligence

• Explain to students that it is now their turn to design something original. Distribute some fashion magazines to small groups or have them search for designers and their fashions online. After groups make their selections, have them discuss what piece of furniture or accessory for the home they will design, based on the clothing item they selected. Finally, ask students to work together and create their design. Take a class vote to select the most original one.

 327

Unit 6

DESAFÍO 3

Dar consejos y hacer recomendaciones

Presentation

- In *Desafío 3*, Asha and Lucas have to illustrate a short story by Borges, the famous Argentinean writer. Students will preview language used to talk about literature and to give advice.

Activities	Standards	Resources
Texto	1.2, 2.1, 2.2	
55.	1.2, 1.3, 2.2	
56.	1.2, 1.3, 2.1, 2.2, 3.2	
57. Conexiones	1.2, 1.3, 2.1, 2.2, 3.1, 5.1	

Teaching Suggestions

Warm-Up / Independent Starter

- Have students make a list of short stories they have read and liked.

Preparation

- Call on students to share their lists with the class. Are there short stories that are common to most students? What is the plot and who are the characters of those stories? Which authors seem to be most popular? Why? Then have students discuss the main characteristics of short stories by contrasting them with novels they know.

Texto: Un cuento de Borges

- Ask students to read the dialogue silently. Once they are finished, ask for three volunteers to play the role of the characters and read the dialogue aloud.
- Have students find words in the dialogue related to literary analysis. Point out that *relato / cuento* and *escritor / autor* have the same meaning in this context.

Activities

- **56.** After completing this activity, ask students to work in small groups to research Borges's biography in more detail. Have students write new facts that they discovered, and ask them to share this information with the class.

328

Un cuento de Borges

Asha y Lucas tienen que ilustrar un cuento del escritor argentino Jorge Luis Borges para incluirlo en una antología que prepara la universidad de su ciudad. ¡Pero no han leído nada de este autor! ¿Lograrán su desafío?

ASHA: ¡Lucas, no sabemos nada de Borges! Yo solo sé que fue un autor argentino de mucho prestigio y que es muy famoso por sus cuentos. Pero he quedado con nuestra profesora de Literatura para que nos ayude.

* * *

ASHA: Señora Amato, ¿podría ayudarnos a elegir un relato de Borges? Es que tenemos que leer uno e ilustrarlo.

SRA. AMATO: Claro, pero les aconsejo que lean varios cuentos antes de elegir uno. ¿Sabían que en su prosa trata el mundo de los sueños y que emplea muchos símbolos, como los laberintos y los espejos?

LUCAS: Parece un poco surrealista.

SRA. AMATO: Bueno, sí, pero en realidad no fue un escritor surrealista. Tomen este libro que explica muy bien su estilo literario y, si tienen alguna duda, vengan a verme.

* * *

LUCAS: Te propongo que empecemos a leer para conocer el ambiente y los personajes de los cuentos de este escritor.

ASHA: De acuerdo, vamos a la biblioteca. Por cierto, ¿sabes que Borges también fue bibliotecario?

LUCAS: No. ¡Qué curioso!

55 **Detective de palabras**

▶ **Completa** estas oraciones.

1. Borges fue un _____ argentino muy importante.
2. Asha y Lucas tienen que ilustrar un _____ de Borges.
3. En la _____ de Borges se repiten símbolos como los laberintos o los espejos.

▶ **Escribe.** ¿Qué más palabras relacionadas con la Literatura conoces?

Modelo *poeta, verso…*

328 trescientos veintiocho

Differentiated Instruction

DEVELOPING LEARNERS

- Ask students to correct the following false statements:
  1. *La profesora les aconseja que lean varias poesías de Borges.* (varios cuentos)
  2. *Los sueños son los símbolos más abundantes en la literatura de Borges.* (los laberintos y los espejos)
  3. *La Sra. Amato dice que Borges fue un escritor surrealista.* (no fue surrealista)
  4. *Lucas quiere empezar a leer sobre los símbolos que emplea Borges.* (sobre el ambiente y los personajes)
  5. *Asha dice que Borges fue secretario.* (bibliotecario)

EXPANDING LEARNERS

- After students read the dialogue and the biography of Borges, ask them to work with a partner and rewrite their version of a conversation between Asha and Lucas as they start to gather and organize information for their *desafío*. This time students should exclude the presence of Sra. Amato, and have Asha and Lucas be responsible for finding pertinent information on the life and works of Borges. Encourage students to be creative and even add humor to their dialogues as they go about finding information.

56 Datos biográficos

▶ **Lee** el texto y responde a las preguntas.

Jorge Luis Borges. Biografía

(Buenos Aires, 1899 - Ginebra, 1986)

Poeta, ensayista y escritor argentino. Estudia en Suiza e Inglaterra. Vive en España desde 1919 hasta su regreso a Argentina en 1921. Colabora en revistas literarias francesas y españolas, donde publica ensayos y manifiestos. En 1923 publica su primer libro de poemas, *Fervor de Buenos Aires*, y en 1935 *Historia universal de la infamia*, compuesto por una serie de relatos breves.

Durante los años treinta su fama crece en Argentina y publica diversas obras en colaboración con Bioy Casares, de entre las que cabe subrayar *Antología de la literatura fantástica*. Durante estos años su actividad literaria se amplía con la crítica literaria y la traducción de autores como Virginia Woolf, Henri Michaux o William Faulkner.

Es bibliotecario en Buenos Aires de 1937 a 1945, conferenciante y profesor de Literatura inglesa en la Universidad de Buenos Aires, presidente de la Sociedad Argentina de Escritores, miembro de la Academia Argentina de las Letras y director de la Biblioteca Nacional de Argentina desde 1955 hasta 1974. Desde 1964 publica indistintamente (*equally*) en verso y en prosa.

Borges utiliza un singular estilo literario, basado en la interpretación de conceptos como los de tiempo, espacio, destino o realidad. La importancia de su obra se ve reconocida con el Premio Miguel de Cervantes en 1979.

Fuente: © Departamento de Bibliotecas y Documentación. Instituto Cervantes (selección)

1. Según el texto, ¿en qué países vivió Borges?
2. ¿A qué género literario corresponde *Fervor de Buenos Aires*?
3. Además de escribir, ¿qué otros trabajos realizó Borges?
4. ¿Cómo describirías la vida de Borges? ¿Qué partes del texto te hacen pensar así?

CONEXIONES: LITERATURA

Premios literarios

Dentro del mundo hispánico hay premios literarios que reconocen a escritores que escriben en español. Entre los más importantes están el premio Cervantes, que se concede a un autor por toda su obra, y los premios Alfaguara y Nadal, que se conceden a una novela no publicada. Además, varios escritores hispanos como Gabriel García Márquez, Octavio Paz o Mario Vargas Llosa han recibido el premio literario más importante del mundo: el Premio Nobel de Literatura.

José Manuel Caballero Bonald. Premio Cervantes (2013).

57 Investiga.
Averigua quiénes han sido los últimos ganadores de los cuatro premios citados. Elige a uno de los escritores y escribe una breve reseña biográfica.

Dar consejos y hacer recomendaciones

57. In order to make this activity more productive, divide the class into small groups and assign each group one of the literary awards mentioned in the text (you may also want to add the Planeta-Casa de América Award). Ask groups to write a short biography of the last writer who won each award, and share it with the class. Encourage students to use visuals in their presentations.

CONEXIONES: LITERATURA

Premios literarios

Literary prizes are common in many countries. In the United States, the most important are the Pulitzer and the National Book Award. In Great Britain, the Man Booker Prize recognizes an outstanding novel from the British Commonwealth and Ireland each year. In Latin America, the Planeta-Casa de América Award is one of the most important. While most of the prizes are a way to recognize the prestige of a writer, they also result in hefty royalties and visibility for an author and his or her work.

Answer Key

55. 1. autor   2. cuento   3. prosa
▶ Answers will vary.

56. Answers will vary. Sample answers:
1. Vivió en Suiza, Inglaterra, España y Argentina.
2. A la poesía.
3. Fue crítico literario, traductor, bibliotecario, conferenciante y profesor de Literatura inglesa.
4. Borges estuvo siempre vinculado a la literatura, tanto como autor como en sus diversas profesiones.

57. Answers will vary.

Additional Resources

Fans Online activities

HERITAGE LANGUAGE LEARNERS

- Ask students to name one writer from their heritage country. Have them explain whether this author writes fiction or non-fiction, if he or she writes one type of genre exclusively (e.g., only short stories), and to describe the main topics in this author's work. Students should also be prepared to give some basic biographical information, as well as which other writers have influenced him or her. You may ask students to write a report or give an oral presentation to the class. Also encourage students to bring in an excerpt from this writer.

CRITICAL THINKING

- Explain to students that some readers describe novels as "light" reading and consider that non-fiction works such as biographies, history, or books that deal with the sciences, psychology, medicine, economics, or the social sciences provide more critical thinking skills. However, reading fiction enriches one's imagination and, by serving as example, helps to improve the reader's writing skills. Ask students to consider both fiction and non-fiction books they have read and to explain which ones they are more attracted to, or if they are equally interested in both, and why.

DESAFÍO 3

Vocabulario – Literatura

Presentation

- In this section, students will learn words to discuss literary works.

Activities	Standards	Resources
Vocabulario	1.2, 2.2, 3.1	
58.	1.2, 3.1	Audio
59.	1.3, 3.1	
60.	1.1, 1.3, 3.1, 5.2	
61. Conexiones	1.2, 1.3, 2.2, 3.1, 5.1	

Teaching Suggestions

Warm-Up / Independent Starter

- Ask students to list words they already know related to literature. You may suggest that they start the list with words from the dialogue on page 328.

Preparation

- Ask for two volunteers to play the roles of Lucas and Asha in the vocabulary presentation, and read their parts aloud. Emphasize pronunciation as needed. Then focus students' attention on the *Más vocabulario* section. Call on a volunteer to read the word definitions under *Literatura* aloud, emphasizing pronunciation. Have students repeat after you the words listed under *Géneros literarios*. Then ask students to write a short definition in Spanish for each of the *géneros literarios*. Have different volunteers share their definitions.

- Invite students to share their lists from the Independent Starter. Did students list any words not included on pages 328 or 330? Invite the class to write these words in their notebooks and use them, when appropriate, in this *Desafío*.

Activities

58. Before playing the recording, have students write a short definition for each word. Then call on volunteers to share their definitions with the class.

59. To extend this activity, have students provide an example for each word. Encourage them to use well-known examples from English or Spanish literary works.

330

Vocabulario

Literatura

Lucas: Ayer me reuní con mi club de lectura. ¿A que no sabes qué leímos?

Asha: No me digas que leyeron algo de Borges...

Lucas: ¡Sí! Qué casualidad, ¿eh? Es un autor fascinante, te va a encantar. Al principio parece difícil porque usa un lenguaje figurado, metáforas y símbolos.

Asha: ¡Lucas, eres todo un experto!

Lucas: No, qué va. Pero ya verás como los cuentos son interesantísimos. Leímos uno que se titula *El Sur*.

Asha: ¿Y cuál es el argumento?

Lucas: El protagonista es un bibliotecario de Buenos Aires. Un día, al volver a casa, se da un fuerte golpe en la cabeza. Como está muy grave, lo ingresan en un sanatorio para operarlo. El desarrollo del cuento parece un poco confuso porque, de pronto, el narrador describe el viaje del protagonista a la casa que tiene al sur del país. Pero, en realidad, no sabemos si está viajando de verdad o está soñando mientras se recupera en el hospital.

Asha: ¿Y cuál es el desenlace?

Lucas: No pienso contártelo. Tendrás que leer el relato tú misma para saber cómo acaba.

Más vocabulario

Literatura

el ambiente: circunstancias que rodean la acción, como el lugar, la época, etc.

la poesía: poema; composición literaria de varios versos generalmente agrupados en estrofas.

la prosa: forma habitual de la escritura que no se ajusta a las normas del verso.

Géneros literarios

el ensayo	*essay*
la fábula	*fable*
la novela negra	novela policíaca
la novela rosa	novela romántica

¡Atención!

el carácter	*personality*
el personaje	*character*

58 ¿De qué hablan?

 ▶ **Escucha** y relaciona cada diálogo con la palabra adecuada.

a. ambiente   b. desenlace   c. autor   d. argumento   e. símbolos

330 trescientos treinta

Differentiated Instruction

DEVELOPING LEARNERS

- Ask students to match the words.

1. *argumento* (h)		a. *conjunto de versos*
2. *protagonista* (i)		b. *historia*
3. *estrofa* (a)		c. *especie de comparación*
4. *narrador* (f)		d. *lugar*
5. *desenlace* (g)		e. *acción*
6. *relato* (b)		f. *el que cuenta*
7. *prosa* (j)		g. *conclusión*
8. *desarrollo* (e)		h. *asunto*
9. *ambiente* (d)		i. *personaje principal*
10. *metáfora* (c)		j. *no es poesía*

EXPANDING LEARNERS

- Ask students to answer these questions:

1. ¿Cuál es la diferencia entre metáfora y símil?
2. ¿Quién es el/la protagonista de tu novela favorita? ¿Cómo es?
3. Explica el papel que juega el narrador de un relato.
4. Describe tu poema favorito en menos de tres oraciones.
5. ¿Prefieres leer prosa o poesía? ¿Por qué?
6. ¿Crees que las fábulas son solo para niños? ¿Por qué?
7. Antes de leer una novela o un cuento, ¿te gusta saber cuál es el argumento? ¿Por qué?

59 Definiciones

▶ **Escribe** una definición para cada uno de estos términos usando tus propias palabras.

1. el/la protagonista
2. el desarrollo
3. el desenlace
4. el argumento
5. la metáfora
6. el lenguaje figurado

60 Tus gustos literarios

▶ **Completa** una ficha como esta sobre tu novela favorita.

Mi novela favorita

Título: _____

Autor(a): _____

Género: _____

Nombre del/de la protagonista: _____

Otros personajes importantes: _____

Tema de la novela: _____

Argumento: _____

 ▶ **Habla** con tu compañero(a). Hazle un resumen del argumento de tu novela favorita sin decirle el título. Él/Ella tiene que adivinarlo.

> A mí me encanta la novela negra. Mi obra favorita trata de una mujer que...

CONEXIONES: LITERATURA

Isabel Allende

La escritora chilena Isabel Allende es una de las autoras más leídas en lengua española. En 1973, tras el golpe de Estado militar en su país, se exilió a Venezuela y después fijó su residencia en California.

La obra de Allende destaca por su lirismo y descripción precisa de los sentimientos. Su obra más conocida es *La casa de los espíritus*. Ha sido traducida a más de 25 idiomas y llevada al cine.

 61 Piensa. ¿Qué efecto tiene la descripción detallada de sentimientos en una obra literaria? ¿Qué obras conoces con esta característica?

HERITAGE LANGUAGE LEARNERS

• Encourage students to share their opinions by asking them to give detailed answers to these questions: *¿Qué te atrae más en una obra de ficción: el argumento o el desarrollo de los protagonistas? ¿Cómo suelen ser los protagonistas de las historias que te gusta leer? Nombra un protagonista que te hubiera gustado conocer y explica por qué. ¿Quién es el escritor más representativo de tu cultura? ¿Por qué?* Encourage students to share their opinions with the rest of the class, and encourage the class to ask heritage learners more questions.

CRITICAL THINKING

• Ask students to consider the parallels between writing and painting, and to think about which form best expresses ideas and feelings. Enable a classroom discussion on the differences between the ways painters or other visual artists express these ideas and feelings (e.g., with lines, colors, shapes, materials), and how writers may do this with only words, and which form is more effective. Have students share their ideas on the effectiveness of messages in print or in images or ask them to write a brief essay on this topic.

---

61. In order to help students complete this activity, read this quote from *La casa de los espíritus*: *Tuve la visión de la rabia creciendo dentro de mí como un tumor maligno, ensuciando las mejores horas de mi existencia, incapacitándome para la ternura o la clemencia. Pero, [...] el sentimiento más fuerte que recuerdo haber tenido esa noche, fue el deseo frustrado.*

 AUDIO SCRIPT
See page 297M.

CONEXIONES: LITERATURA

Isabel Allende

Allende is part of a rich tradition of Latin American women writers that includes Elena Poniatowska and Ángeles Mastretta in Mexico, Luisa Valenzuela in Argentina, Cristina Peri Rossi in Uruguay, and Gabriela Mistral in Chile, to name a few. While most female writers in Latin America have embraced a progressive political position and have defended feminist positions, their work is also recognized for its insight and lyricism.

Answer Key

58. a. 4   b. 5   c. 2   d. 3   e. 1

59. Answers will vary. Sample answers:
1. personaje principal
2. secuencia de acciones
3. cómo termina la obra
4. la historia, lo que sucede
5. figura retórica que usa una palabra o frase por otra
6. lenguaje que no usa el significado literal

60. Answers will vary.
▶ Answers will vary.

61. Answers will vary.

Additional Resources

Fans Online activities
Practice Workbook

DESAFÍO 3

Gramática – Los diminutivos

Presentation

■ In this section, students will learn how to form and use diminutive forms.

Activities	Standards	Resources
Gramática	1.2, 3.1	
62.	1.2, 3.1, 4.1	
63.	1.3	
64.	1.1, 1.2, 1.3, 3.1	
65.	1.1, 1.3, 3.1	

Teaching Suggestions

Warm-Up / Independent Starter

■ Write the following sentences on the board and ask students to decide whether the underlined word refers to size or expresses affection:

1. *Visitamos un pueblito de cien habitantes.* (size)
2. *Mi gatito ya tiene dieciséis años.* (affection)
3. *Mis abuelitos viven con nosotros.* (affection)
4. *La sillita del bebé está en el coche.* (size)

Preparation

■ Call on volunteers to share their Independent Starters. Did all students agree on the shade of meaning conveyed by the diminutive in each sentence? How did they know? Then have students read the grammar presentation silently. Encourage them to ask questions about any explanations they did not understand. Next, read the examples of the grammar presentation aloud, emphasizing contrast between regular and irregular forms and spelling changes.

■ You may want to clarify that in addition to expressing small size and affection, diminutives can also be used to add other shades of meaning. For example: to strike a friendly tone → *Te ayudo en un ratito*; to talk to children → *Dame la manita*; to intensify → *Está cerquita*; to express irony → *¡Qué calladita estás hoy!*; to soften the meaning → *Está gordito*; to say something is unimportant → *Compré unas cosillas en la tienda*. Remind students that for nouns and adjectives, diminutive suffixes show gender and number information. For example: nariz (fem.) → *naricita*; pequeñas (fem., pl.) → *pequeñitas*.

Gramática

Los diminutivos

● Los diminutivos son sufijos que se añaden al final de los nombres y de algunos adjetivos y adverbios para expresar tamaño pequeño u otros valores (afecto, ironía...).

perro ⟶ perrito   gordo ⟶ gordito   pronto ⟶ prontito

● En español hay varios sufijos diminutivos. El más común es -ito/-ita. **SUFIJOS DIMINUTIVOS**

Ayer leí un *poemita* de cuatro versos.
Los **abuelitos** nos visitan todos los veranos.

-ito/-ita	-ico/ica
-illo/-illa	-ín/-ina

● Los diminutivos pueden variar de un país a otro, pero en general se forman así:

DIMINUTIVOS REGULARES

Palabras de varias sílabas terminadas en vocal no acentuada.	Suprimen la vocal y añaden -ito/-ita.	gato ⟶ gatito elefante ⟶ elefantito
Palabras de varias sílabas terminadas en consonante distinta de-n o -r.	Añaden -ito/-ita.	animal ⟶ animalito nariz ⟶ naricita

DIMINUTIVOS IRREGULARES

Palabras de una sílaba.	Añaden -ecito/-ecita.	flor ⟶ florecita pez ⟶ pececito Pero pie ⟶ piececito
Palabras de dos sílabas terminadas en vocal acentuada.	Añaden -cito/-cita.	café ⟶ cafecito Pero papá ⟶ papaíto o papito y mamá ⟶ mamaíta o mamita
Palabras de dos sílabas terminadas en -e, -n o -r.	Añaden -cito/-cita.	coche ⟶ cochecito canción ⟶ cancioncita mujer ⟶ mujercita

● Atención: al formar el diminutivo se pueden producir algunos cambios ortográficos:

z > c: taza ⟶ tacita   c > qu: flaco ⟶ flaquito   g > gu: amigo ⟶ amiguito

62 **Compara.** ¿Cómo se expresa en inglés el diminutivo?

63 **¡A practicar!**

▶ **Escribe** el diminutivo de estas palabras con el sufijo -ito / -ita. Recuerda hacer los cambios ortográficos necesarios.

1. libro ⟶ *librito*
2. amigo
3. novela
4. nariz
5. tren
6. banco
7. calor
8. grande

Differentiated Instruction

DEVELOPING LEARNERS

● Ask students to say or write a diminutive ending in -ito(a) for the following words. Then, have them write sentences with five of the diminutives.

1. *cosa (cosita)*
2. *árbol (arbolito)*
3. *lápiz (lapicito)*
4. *choza (chocita)*
5. *cerca (cerquita)*
6. *dolor (dolorcito)*
7. *pobre (pobrecito)*
8. *sol (solecito)*
9. *loco (loquito)*
10. *lago (laguito)*

EXPANDING LEARNERS

● Explain to students that –uelo(a) can denote diminutive and pejorative at the same time (*tonto → tontuelo*), and may be used to form new words (*paño → pañuelo*). Provide student pairs with these words: *polluelo, ladronzuelo, cazuela, jovenzuelo, arroyuelo, riachuelo, callejuela*. Next, have pairs determine the base word. (*pollo, ladrón, cazo, joven, arroyo, río, calle*) Then, ask them to determine if the word denotes diminutive (*polluelo, arroyuelo*), both diminutive and pejorative (*ladronzuelo, jovenzuelo, callejuela*), or if it is a new word (*cazuela, riachuelo*). Finally, have students write sentences.

Gramática – Los diminutivos

64 **¿Qué expresan?**

▶ **Decide.** ¿Qué matices añaden los sufijos diminutivos en estas oraciones? ¿Se refieren al tamaño o la duración de algo, o aportan algún otro valor? Justifica tus respuestas.

1. Vamos a hacer un viajecito de tres días por la costa.
2. Tengo que leerme esta novelita de 500 páginas. ¡No terminaré nunca!
3. La profesora nos ha pedido que escribamos un poemita de ocho versos.
4. Mercedes, ¿quieres que te lea un cuentito antes de irte a dormir?
5. Me encanta el cochecito de Marga. Es perfecto para circular por la ciudad.
6. Me he comprado un vestidito precioso para la fiesta.
7. Mónica debería perder peso, está un poco gordita.
8. Dale un besito a papá.

▶ **Escribe** tres ejemplos más usando diminutivos. Léeselos a tu compañero(a) para que decida qué matices aportan en cada oración.

65 **Con detalle**

▶ **Escribe** un pie de foto para cada imagen usando diminutivos.

Modelo   1. *A Asha le encanta salir a pasear con su perrito.*

①    ②    ③

④    ⑤

 ▶ **Habla** con tu compañero(a). Comparen lo que han escrito y decidan si los diminutivos que han elegido describen bien las imágenes.

trescientos treinta y tres **333**

Activities

63. After finishing this activity, ask students to write five new words and their diminutive forms in their notebooks. You may want to check their work for accuracy. Then have student pairs test each other using the words they listed in their notebooks.

64. Clarify that a diminutive can express several things. For instance, the word *cuentito* in #4 could express both small size and affection. To expand this activity, have student pairs choose one of the sentences to create a conversation. Challenge students to keep the conversation going for as long as they can. Emphasize that they should not use English at any point.
For example:

A. *Vamos a hacer un viajecito de tres días por la costa.*

B. *¡Qué bien! ¿Y qué van a ver?*

A. *Pues tenemos pensado ir a unos pueblitos de pescadores muy pintorescos.*

Answer Key

62. Se usan adjetivos como *little, tiny, small*. También hay algunos nombres en diminutivo (e.g., *auntie, kitty, doggy, dearie, blanky, birdie*) y algunos apodos (e.g., Johnny, Susie, Jimmy).

63.
1. librito	5. trenecito
2. amiguito	6. banquito
3. novelita	7. calorcito
4. naricita	8. grandecito

64.
1. duración	5. tamaño
2. ironía	6. afecto
3. tamaño	7. afecto
4. tamaño/afecto	8. afecto

▶ Answers will vary.

65. Answers will vary

▶ Answers will vary

Additional Resources

Fans Online activities
Practice Workbook

HERITAGE LANGUAGE LEARNERS

• Explain that the suffixes *–ón, –azo, –ote,* and *–udo* indicate large size or excess, but can also add a pejorative tone. For example: *cuchara → cucharón, soltero → solterón, bueno → buenazo, coche → cochazo, libro → librote, palabra → palabrota, barba → barbudo, nariz → narigudo.* Ask students to come up with a list of ten words with these suffixes. Then have them explain whether the suffix indicates just large size or adds a pejorative tone. Next, have students write a sentence with each of their words. Finally, invite students to share some of their sentences with the class.

MULTIPLE INTELLIGENCES:
Verbal-Linguistic Intelligence

• Explain that the diminutive suffix *-ete/-eta* is often used to denote affection and add humor. For example: *amigo → amiguete, gordo → regordete.* This suffix can also add a new meaning to a word. For example: *avión → avioneta, camión → camioneta, historia → historieta, camisa → camiseta, libro → libreta.* Ask students to work with a partner and find more examples of words with this suffix. Then have them write a sentence with each word they find. See how many sentences student pairs can write correctly.

333

Unit 6

DESAFÍO 3

Gramática – Dar consejos y hacer recomendaciones

Presentation

- In this section, students will review how to give advice and make recommendations.

Activities	Standards	Resources
Gramática	1.2, 3.1	
66.	1.2, 3.1, 4.1	
67.	1.2, 1.3, 3.1	
68.	1.2, 1.3, 3.1	Audio
69.	1.1, 1.2, 3.1	
70. Conexiones	1.2, 1.3, 2.1, 2.2, 3.1	

Teaching Suggestions

Warm-Up / Independent Starter

- Ask students to write four recommendations to Asha and Lucas for a successful completion of their *desafío*.

Preparation

- Have students go over the grammar presentation individually and if necessary, correct their sentences from the Independent Starter. Then call on volunteers to share some of their sentences with the class. Use their sentences to clarify any questions they may have. Next, ask them to rewrite their sentences using a different structure from page 334. For example: *Asha y Lucas tienen que leer varios cuentos de Borges.* → *Les aconsejo que lean varios cuentos de Borges.*

Activities

69. To extend this activity, have students think of their favorite author. Then ask them to write three recommendations for this author. Call on volunteers to read their recommendations aloud without mentioning the name of the author. Can the class guess the author's identity?

70. Have some volunteers read their texts aloud. Review with the class the main characteristics of *realismo mágico*. Then, have student pairs write a brief description of an imaginary town using the techniques of *realismo mágico*. If time allows, invite pairs to share their writing.

334

Gramática

Dar consejos y hacer recomendaciones

- Para dar consejos y hacer recomendaciones, puedes usar las siguientes estructuras:

CONSEJOS Y RECOMENDACIONES NEUTROS

aconsejar animar a proponer recomendar sugerir	+ infinitivo + que + subjuntivo

El profesor nos **aconsejó escribir** una fábula.
El profesor nos **aconsejó** que **escribiéramos** una fábula.

CONSEJOS Y RECOMENDACIONES CON MATIZ DE OBLIGACIÓN

deber (presente o condicional) haber que (presente o condicional) + infinitivo tener que (presente o condicional)

Debes/Deberías ir al teatro.
Hay/Habría que leer más.
Tienes/Tendrías que promocionar más tu obra.

- Para dar un consejo o hacer una recomendación poniéndote en el lugar de otra persona, puedes usar estas estructuras:

Yo en tu lugar Yo que tú	+ condicional

Yo en tu lugar centraría mi ensayo en los protagonistas del cuento.

El imperativo para dar consejos y hacer recomendaciones

- Según el contexto y el tono, el imperativo se puede usar como una sugerencia, un consejo o una recomendación, y no como una orden.

    No leas tan rápido. No te va a entender nadie.

    Repasa la formación del imperativo afirmativo y negativo en las páginas R22 y R23.

66 **Compara.** ¿Cómo comunicas distintos grados de imposición *(demand)* o énfasis cuando das consejos y haces recomendaciones en inglés?

67 **Recomendaciones**

▶ **Transforma** las siguientes órdenes en recomendaciones usando las estructuras de la ficha de Gramática.

1. Toma, lee *Cien años de soledad*. Te va a encantar.
2. David, estudia más para sacar buenas notas.
3. Póngase las gafas de sol en cuanto salga a la calle.
4. Busca información sobre Borges en Internet.
5. Visita el puente del Alamillo cuando estés en Sevilla.
6. Comunícate con el escritor para hacerle la entrevista.

334 trescientos treinta y cuatro

Differentiated Instruction

DEVELOPING LEARNERS

- Have students write the correct form of the verb in parentheses.
  1. *Te aconsejo que (leer) los cuentos de Borges.* (leas)
  2. *El profesor nos animó a que (ir) a la biblioteca.* (fuéramos)
  3. *Yo que tú no (comer) tanta pizza.* (comería)
  4. *Propongo que usted (recibir) este premio literario.* (reciba)
  5. *Yo en tu lugar no (decir) esto.* (diría)
  6. *Ellos sugieren que nosotros (llegar) a tiempo.* (lleguemos)
  7. *Te recomiendo que (comprar) esa novela.* (compres)

EXPANDING LEARNERS

- Ask students to imagine that they have a friend who is constantly telling them what they should do. Have students write a letter from this friend, using as many of the expressions on page 334 as they can. Then ask students to exchange letters with a partner, who will counter these recommendations with comments or other suggestions. Encourage creativity and humor. For example:
  A. *Yo en tu lugar no leería este libro.*
  B. *Pero como no estás en mi lugar, no deberías aconsejarme.*

Gramática – Dar consejos y hacer recomendaciones

68 Buenos consejos

 ▶ **Escucha** a cuatro personas y escribe qué problema tiene cada una.

▶ **Escucha** de nuevo. ¿Qué recomendación le hacen a cada persona? Completa estas oraciones.

1. El amigo de Juan le recomienda...
2. A Marisa su amiga le sugiere...
3. La madre de Carlos le propone...
4. Mario le aconseja a Teresa...

▶ **Escribe.** ¿Qué le aconsejarías tú a cada una de esas personas para solucionar sus problemas?

Modelo *Juan debería hablar seriamente con sus padres y explicarles cómo se siente.*

69 Soy escritor y...

 ▶ **Habla** con tu compañero(a). Hagan recomendaciones para escritores(as) en estas situaciones.

Modelo «Quiero vender muchos libros.»
    A. *Si un escritor quiere vender muchos libros, yo le aconsejo escribir libros cómicos.*
    B. *No estoy de acuerdo. Yo le recomendaría escribir libros de misterio porque...*

1. «Quiero ganar un premio literario.»
2. «Me gustaría formar un club de escritores.»
3. «Tengo un bloqueo mental desde hace semanas que me impide escribir.»
4. «No soy capaz de decidir el desenlace de mi novela.»

CONEXIONES: LITERATURA

Gabriel García Márquez

El escritor y premio nobel colombiano Gabriel García Márquez es uno de los padres del llamado «boom» de la narrativa hispanoamericana que se produjo en los años 60 del pasado siglo y uno de los mejores exponentes del realismo mágico, que mezcla lo fantástico con la realidad cotidiana. Su obra *Cien años de soledad* (1967) es para muchos la novela más importante de las letras hispánicas en el siglo XX. En ella cuenta la historia de un pueblo imaginario llamado Macondo a lo largo de varias generaciones de la familia Buendía.

70 Investiga. Busca información sobre el realismo mágico y escribe un párrafo explicando las características de esta corriente literaria.

 AUDIO SCRIPT
See page 297M.

 CONEXIONES: LITERATURA

Gabriel García Márquez

García Márquez's work has been recognized for its powerful imagination and lexical richness. In addition to *Cien años de soledad*, novels such as *El amor en los tiempos del cólera*, *El otoño del patriarca*, *Crónica de una muerte anunciada*, and *El coronel no tiene quién le escriba* have become canonical works in world literature. He is also a well-recognized author of short stories.

Answer Key

66. Se usan estructuras como: *I advise you to... I recommend/suggest/propose that you... I encourage you to... You must... You have to... You should... Perhaps you should...*

67. Answers will vary.

68. 1. Sus padres quieren que estudie Economía, pero él prefiere estudiar Literatura.
2. Necesita entregar un trabajo y se le ha estropeado la computadora.
3. Ha perdido sus apuntes para el examen.
4. Necesita practicar francés para una entrevista de trabajo.

▶ 1. ... que estudie Economía porque tiene el futuro asegurado.
2. ... que hable con el profesor.
3. ... que estudie con un compañero.
4. ... que contrate a un profesor particular de francés.

▶ Answers will vary.

69. Answers will vary.

70. Answers will vary.

Additional Resources

Fans Online activities
Practice Workbook

HERITAGE LANGUAGE LEARNERS

• Ask students to write a letter to an advice columnist to help them resolve some problems they are having with a friend, a family member, or one of their teachers. (For privacy reasons, suggest that students make up their problems.) Have students exchange their letters with a partner who will play the role of the advice columnist and make some recommendations. Encourage students to use some of the verbs and expressions on the page, as well as any others they know. Call on volunteers to read their letters aloud.

TOTAL PHYSICAL RESPONSE (TPR)

• Divide the class into teams to play "Charades" against each other. Prepare slips of paper with the titles of well-known books that also lend themselves to being pantomimed (e.g., *Cien años de soledad, La casa de los espíritus, Como agua para chocolate, Lo que el viento se llevó, El viejo y el mar, El señor de los anillos*), and place them in a bag. Then ask each member of the teams to select one. Establish a time limit for guessing the title and have the winning teams play against each other to see which one will be the class champion.

335

Unit 6

LECTURA: TEXTO LITERARIO

Presentation

- In this section, students will read a short story by Argentinean author Jorge Luis Borges.

Activities	Standards	Resources
Lectura: texto literario	1.2, 2.1, 2.2, 3.2	
71.	1.2, 1.3, 2.1, 2.2, 3.2	
72.	1.2	

Teaching Suggestions

Warm-Up / Independent Starter

- Ask students to look at the picture and answer the first question in the *Antes de leer* section.

Preparation

- Call on volunteers to share their responses from the Independent Starter. On the board, write the list of topics mentioned by students. Then have student pairs work on question #2. As most of the geographical names in the text are located in Buenos Aires, bring a map to class (or search for one online), and ask students to locate streets mentioned in the text. Next, have students read the text silently and ask them to mark down words or sentences they have difficulties understanding. Then call on individual students to each read a paragraph aloud.

- Borges's writing can be difficult and even confusing for a first-time reader. Therefore, consider working with the class to discuss and clarify some passages. You may want to give students additional background information to help them understand the story. Explain that Dahlmann had undergone surgery in a Buenos Aires hospital as a consequence of a head injury. At the hospital, he came close to dying due to an infection. Read the following excerpt, which explains that Dahlmann has been discharged from the hospital: *Otro día, el cirujano le dijo que estaba reponiéndose y que, muy pronto, podría ir a convalecer a la estancia. Increíblemente, el día prometido llegó.* Then, Dahlmann takes a taxi across the city to the train station.

336

LECTURA: TEXTO LITERARIO

Antes de leer: estrategias

1. Lee el título del texto y mira la fotografía. ¿De qué tema crees que trata este cuento de Borges?
2. Localiza los nombres geográficos del texto. ¿A qué país corresponden?

El Sur

EL hombre que desembarcó en Buenos Aires en 1871 se llamaba Johannes Dahlmann y era pastor de la Iglesia evangélica; en 1939, uno de sus nietos, Juan Dahlmann, era secretario de una biblioteca municipal en la calle Córdoba y se sentía hondamente argentino. Su abuelo materno había sido aquel Francisco Flores, del 2 de infantería de línea, que murió en la frontera de Buenos Aires, lanceado[1] por indios de Catriel. A costa de[2] algunas privaciones, Dahlmann había logrado salvar el casco[3] de una estancia en el Sur, que fue de los Flores: una de las costumbres de su memoria era la imagen de los eucaliptos balsámicos y de la larga casa rosada que alguna vez fue carmesí. Las tareas y acaso la indolencia lo retenían en la ciudad. Verano tras verano se contentaba con la idea abstracta de posesión y con la certidumbre[4] de que su casa estaba esperándolo, en un sitio preciso de la llanura[5]. En los últimos días de febrero de 1939, algo le aconteció.

Nadie ignora que el Sur empieza del otro lado de Rivadavia. Dahlmann solía repetir que ello no es una convención y que quien atraviesa esa calle entra en un mundo más antiguo y más firme. Desde el coche buscaba entre la nueva edificación, la ventana de rejas[6], el llamador[7], el arco de la puerta, el zaguán[8], el íntimo patio.

En el *hall* de la estación advirtió que faltaban treinta minutos. Recordó bruscamente que en un café de la calle Brasil (a pocos metros de la casa de Yrigoyen) había un enorme gato que se dejaba acariciar por la gente, como una divinidad desdeñosa[9]. Entró. Ahí estaba el gato, dormido. Pidió una taza de café, la endulzó lentamente, la probó y pensó, mientras alisaba[10] el negro pelaje[11], que aquel contacto era ilusorio y que estaban como separados por un cristal, porque el hombre vive en el tiempo, en la sucesión, y el mágico animal, en la actualidad, en la eternidad del instante.

A lo largo del penúltimo andén el tren esperaba. Dahlmann recorrió los vagones y dio con uno casi vacío. Acomodó en la red la valija[12]; cuando los coches arrancaron, la abrió y sacó, tras alguna vacilación, el primer tomo[13] de *Las Mil y Una Noches.*

A los lados del tren, la ciudad se desgarraba[14] en suburbios; esta visión y luego la de jardines y quintas demoraron el principio de la lectura. La verdad es que Dahlmann leyó poco; la felicidad lo distraía de Shahrazad y de sus milagros superfluos; Dahlmann cerraba el libro y se dejaba simplemente vivir.

El almuerzo (con el caldo servido en boles de metal reluciente, como en los ya remotos veraneos de la niñez) fue otro goce[15] tranquilo y agradecido.

Differentiated Instruction

DEVELOPING LEARNERS

- After reading, ask students to match the words.

  1. *Juan Dahlmann* (d)   a. *soldado*
  2. *un color* (i)   b. *hacienda*
  3. *un ser divino* (e)   c. *el vagón*
  4. *lo que lee* (g)   d. *secretario*
  5. *casi vacío* (c)   e. *el gato*
  6. *estancia* (b)   f. *el caldo*
  7. *un recuerdo de su niñez* (f)   g. *Las mil y una noches*
  8. *un abuelo* (a)   h. *durmió*
  9. *lo que hizo en el tren* (h)   i. *carmesí*

EXPANDING LEARNERS

- Have students answer the following questions:

  1. ¿Por qué quiere ir Dahlmann al Sur? (*Para visitar una estancia suya.*)
  2. ¿Por qué lee Las mil y una noches? (*Quizás quiere distraerse o le gusta la fantasía o le sirve de contraste a la vida aburrida que tiene.*)
  3. ¿Qué relación ves entre Shahrazad y Borges? (*Los dos cuentan historias.*)
  4. ¿Cómo puede ser la soledad perfecta y hostil a la vez? (*Es perfecta para la contemplación y hostil porque nadie te ayuda.*)

Alguna vez durmió y en sus sueños estaba el ímpetu[16] del tren. Ya el blanco sol intolerable de las doce del día era el sol amarillo que precede al anochecer y no tardaría en ser rojo. Afuera la móvil sombra del vagón se alargaba hacia el horizonte. No turbaban[17] la tierra elemental ni poblaciones ni otros signos humanos. Todo era vasto, pero al mismo tiempo era íntimo y, de alguna manera, secreto. En el campo desaforado[18], a veces no había otra cosa que un toro. La soledad era perfecta y tal vez hostil, y Dahlmann pudo sospechar que viajaba al pasado y no solo al Sur.

JORGE LUIS BORGES. «El Sur», *Artificios* (selección)

---

1. *speared*	6. barras de hierro	11. pelo de un animal	16. intensidad, fuerza
2. *at the expense of*	7. *doorknocker*	12. equipaje	17. cambiaban su estado natural
3. casa principal	8. *hall*	13. *volume*	18. muy extenso
4. seguridad	9. *scornful*	14. *tore up*	
5. *plain*	10. *smoothed*	15. placer	

71 ¿Comprendes?

▶ **Decide.** ¿Por qué este cuento se titula *El Sur*?

a. Porque transcurre en Buenos Aires.
b. Porque el protagonista viaja al sur del país.
c. Porque el autor nació en Buenos Aires.
d. Porque el protagonista quiere comprar una casa en el sur del país.

▶ **Responde** a estas preguntas.

1. ¿Cómo dirías que es el carácter del protagonista? ¿Por qué?
2. ¿En qué parte del texto se muestra el juego entre la posibilidad de que el protagonista esté viajando o todo sea un sueño?
3. ¿Qué crees que significa la frase «A los lados del tren, la ciudad se desgarraba en suburbios» en este contexto?
4. ¿Cómo imaginas el final del cuento: triste, feliz, misterioso...? ¿Por qué?

72 Palabras y expresiones

▶ **Une** las dos columnas. ¿A qué significado corresponden estas palabras del texto?

Ⓐ		Ⓑ	
1. reluciente		a. roja	
2. carmesí		b. tocar suavemente	
3. acontecer		c. darse cuenta	
4. advertir		d. brillante	
5. bruscamente		e. encontrar	
6. acariciar		f. de pronto, de repente	
7. demorar		g. suceder, ocurrir	
8. dar con algo		h. retrasar	

■ Remind students that Borges plays with the concepts of time and space. Things might not be what they seem. Ask students to read the last sentence of the third paragraph and note how the scene with the cat is described: *y pensó [...] que aquel contacto era ilusorio y que estaban como separados por un cristal.* Then, read aloud the last sentence: *[...] y Dahlmann pudo sospechar que viajaba al pasado y no solo al Sur.* Discuss with the class whether Dahlmann's trip to *el Sur* was real. Ask students to quote from the text to support their opinions.

Activities

71. After completing the activity, have students work in small groups to discuss where they think the protagonist would have traveled if the story had taken place in the United States. Ask them to justify their answers. Then have groups share their conclusions with the class. What type of places did students mention?

72. In order to facilitate their word associations, have student pairs reread the text and search for the words in the left column. Once they have completed the activity, have pairs create an original sentence for each word.

Answer Key

71. b

▶ Answers will vary. Sample answers:
1. Indolente, solitario, tranquilo, metódico.
2. Donde dice: «Alguna vez durmió y en sus sueños estaba el ímpetu del tren».
3. El tren va saliendo ya de la ciudad; está en las afueras.
4. Answers will vary.

72. 1. d   3. g   5. f   7. h
2. a   4. c   6. b   8. e

Additional Resources

Fans Online activities

HERITAGE LANGUAGE LEARNERS

• Explain to students that the story they have just read in their textbooks is an excerpt and several scenes have been omitted. Ask them to read the complete short story and to write a synopsis of the plot. Then have students comment on the topics in this narrative, the parallels between the protagonist and the writer, the symbolism Borges uses, and what students perceive to be the real ending of the story. Ask students to share their insights with the rest of the class.

MULTIPLE INTELLIGENCES:
Verbal-Linguistic Intelligence

• Ask students to write their own ending to the story as it appears on these pages. They may have the protagonist arrive at his destination, or they may keep him traveling on the train, looking for his final stop and making observations along the way. Students may make inferences regarding the meaning of the phrase *"que viajaba al pasado y no solo al Sur."* Encourage students to add other elements, characters, and scenes to the story and elaborate on Dahlmann's life before he stepped onto the train.

Unit 6
DESAFÍO 3
Comunicación

Presentation

- In this section, students will integrate the vocabulary and grammar skills from *Desafío 3* in order to make recommendations, and to analyze and talk about a literary text.

Activities	Standards	Resources
73.	1.1, 1.2, 1.3, 2.2, 3.1	Audio
74.	1.1, 1.2, 1.3, 5.1, 5.2	
75.	1.1, 1.3, 5.1, 5.2	
76.	1.3, 5.2	
77. Final del desafío	1.2, 1.3, 2.2	

Teaching Suggestions

Warm-Up / Independent Starter

- Have students think about the last three books they read. Ask them to complete the following information for their favorite one: author, title, plot, setting, main characters, and ending.

Preparation

- Call on students to share their Independent Starters with the class. After each presentation, ask students to explain why they recommend the book to their classmates.

- Write this poem by Manuel Machado on the board and have students analyze the use of the diminutive forms: *Hermanita y compañera, / la de los ojitos negros / y la carita morena. / Tú eras buena y eras mala / todito te lo pasaba. / No te quiero decir nada, / no quiero que se te ponga / la carita colorada.* Discuss how the use of diminutives contributes to the poem's expressiveness.

Activities

73. Before listening, ask students to look at the chart and fill in information they may know. For the second part, have students add three rows to the chart, but with missing information. Finally, ask each pair to exchange their chart with another pair and complete it.

Comunicación

 73 **Un examen de Literatura**

▶ **Escucha** a Asha y a Lucas mientras repasan para su examen y completa una tabla como esta.

Autor	Título	Género	Protagonista(s)	Tema
	La casa de los espíritus	novela		
Gabriel García Márquez	Un día de estos			venganza contra la corrupción política
	El laberinto de la soledad			

 ▶ **Habla** con tu compañero(a). Agreguen tres filas más a la tabla con otros autores y otras obras en español que conozcan.

 74 **Problemas que te afectan**

▶ **Lee** estos titulares y, con tu compañero(a), escribe recomendaciones que podrían ayudar a mejorar o solucionar esos problemas.

Modelo   1. *El gobierno debería hacer una campaña publicitaria para fomentar la lectura.*

① **Los jóvenes ven la televisión más de 6 horas al día y leen un promedio de 1 hora a la semana**

② **Aumenta el número de estudiantes que no termina la enseñanza secundaria**

③ **Próximo cierre de la biblioteca local por falta de fondos**

④ **Un informe revela que los jóvenes deben mejorar sus habilidades de lectura y escritura**

 75 **Diez razones**

▶ **Escribe.** Con dos compañeros(as), haz una lista de diez razones por las que los jóvenes deben leer.

Modelo   *Yo creo que leer es bueno para desarrollar la imaginación.*

 ▶ **Presenten** su lista a la clase y, entre todos(as), hagan un póster con las diez razones que más les gusten para ponerlo en el salón de clases.

Differentiated Instruction

DEVELOPING LEARNERS

- If students are still having problems using the subjunctive or the infinitive after verbs that express advice or recommendations, ask them to write the verbs from page 334 in their notebooks and guide them as they write two sentences for each verb. Explain that one sentence should use the infinitive and the other, the subjunctive. For example: *Mi abuelo me aconsejó leer otros cuentos de Borges. Mi abuelo me aconsejó que leyera otros cuentos de Borges.*

EXPANDING LEARNERS

- Ask students to work with a partner and create short dialogues in which one gives some advice or makes a recommendation to the other regarding their reading habits or favorite authors. The other student will react to this negatively and counter it with some other advice or an entirely different recommendation. For example:
  A. *Si te gusta la poesía, te recomiendo que leas algo de Neruda. Es genial.*
  B. *La poesía es muy aburrida; prefiero las novelas. Deberías leer más novelas.*

76 Érase una vez...

▶ **Elige** uno de los siguientes cuentos infantiles y escribe una nueva versión cambiando algún aspecto: el protagonista, el conflicto o el desenlace.

- Cenicienta
- La bella durmiente
- Caperucita roja
- Ricitos de oro
- Los tres cerditos
- El hombre de jengibre

▶ **Presenta** tu versión del cuento a la clase. Analiza cómo ha afectado el cambio al argumento del cuento.

Final del desafío

ASHA: Me encanta nuestro dibujo del protagonista de *El Sur*, Lucas.

LUCAS: Sí, yo también estoy contento con el resultado. Pero deberíamos acercarnos más al texto.

ASHA: ¿Qué quieres decir?

LUCAS: Pues que podemos incluir detalles sobre el ambiente. Por ejemplo, como sabemos que el personaje viaja al sur del país, podíamos dibujar el paisaje de esa zona como fondo de esta ilustración.

ASHA: Me parece genial. Vamos a buscar algunas fotos en Internet.

77 Un cuento ilustrado

▶ **Lee** el diálogo y responde a estas preguntas.

1. ¿Cómo cree Lucas que pueden mejorar los dibujos que han hecho para ilustrar el cuento de Borges?
2. ¿Qué cosas crees que hay que tener en cuenta para ilustrar un relato?

▶ **Escribe.** ¿Qué recomendaciones les harías a Asha y a Lucas? ¿Cómo pueden mejorar sus ilustraciones?

Modelo *Les sugiero que les den un aire misterioso, porque creo que encaja con el cuento que han elegido.*

75. You may turn this activity into a contest. Ask small groups to prepare a colorful poster with ten reasons for reading more. Then have each group present their poster. Display students' posters around the classroom and have the class vote for the best one. If possible, display the winning poster in school.

76. Once students present their "new" stories, have the class decide on the version they prefer for each tale. Ask students to justify their choices.

🎧 **AUDIO SCRIPT**
See page 297M.

Answer Key

73. Autor: Isabel Allende; Octavio Paz.
Género: cuento; ensayo.
Protagonista(s): Esteban y Alba; un dentista; no hay protagonistas.
Tema: historia de Chile a través de varias generaciones de una familia; la identidad mexicana.
▶ Answers will vary.

74. Answers will vary.

75. Answers will vary.
▶ Answers will vary.

76. Answers will vary.
▶ Answers will vary.

77. Answers will vary. Sample answer:
1. Cree que pueden acercarse más al texto, incluyendo algunos detalles sobre el ambiente del cuento; por ejemplo, el paisaje de la zona.
2. Answers will vary.
▶ Answers will vary.

Additional Resources

Fans Online activities
Practice Workbook

HERITAGE LANGUAGE LEARNERS

- Ask students to bring in some children's classics from their heritage country and, if they are not too long, read them to the class. They should be prepared to explain some of the more difficult vocabulary, provide some cultural or historical background, and point out the typical wording at the start and conclusion of such stories. For example: *Érase una vez* (once upon a time), *colorín colorado, este cuento se ha acabado* (to indicate the end of a story), and *fueron felices y comieron perdices* (to show that they lived happily ever after).

CRITICAL THINKING

- Ask students to write a persuasive essay of at least three paragraphs that is a defense for either electronic books or for traditional printed books. Students need to justify their preference, showing the advantages of one format over the other, as well as outlining the disadvantages of the other format. Explain to students that they may start their essay with a statement in defense of their choice, and then list and detail at least three reasons that justify their assertion. Call on volunteers to read their essays aloud.

Unit 6
Para terminar

Presentation

- In this section, students will review the unit objectives and put them into practice. They will learn how art is presented to children in a Spanish museum and will write an e-mail to a classmate. Students will also select one of the following *desafíos* to develop: research the most famous painting by Velázquez, *Las Meninas*, and compare it to a version by Picasso; select a famous sculpture or building by a Hispanic designer and record a presentation for the class; prepare a presentation about a famous writer from the Spanish-speaking world.

Activities	Standards	Resources
78.	1.1, 1.2, 1.3, 2.1, 2.2, 3.1, 3.2, 5.2	Audio
79.	1.1, 1.3, 3.1, 5.1	
80. Tu desafío	1.3, 2.1, 2.2, 3.1, 3.2, 5.2	

Teaching Suggestions

Warm-Up / Independent Starter

- Have students go back and review the vocabulary and grammar sections in this unit.

Preparation

- Ask students to work on the following individually: 1. write a paragraph comparing two paintings or two buildings; 2. write four sentences expressing their opinions about a book they have read recently; 3. make recommendations to a Spanish-speaking tourist about places to visit and things to see in their town.

- Once students have finished, have them get together with a partner and check each other's work. Tell students that they may use their textbooks as reference. Answer any questions students may have about their partner's work.

- Have students switch partners and give each new pair a photo (or show them an online image) of a famous painting, sculpture, or building. Have pairs describe their assigned piece in terms of colors, shapes, materials used, style, etc. Then, have them share their photos and opinions with the class.

340

Para terminar

Todo junto

ESCUCHAR, ESCRIBIR Y HABLAR

 78 El arte al alcance de los niños

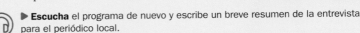

▶ **Escucha** un programa cultural y decide si estas afirmaciones son ciertas o falsas. Después, corrige las falsas.

1. El Museo Reina Sofía ofrece visitas guiadas para los niños en Navidad.
2. Unos artistas de circo explican las obras a los niños cantando.
3. Los niños pueden pisar (*step on*) una de las obras.
4. Los niños van a poder interactuar con varias obras.
5. Las obras elegidas son fáciles de entender para todo el mundo.

 ▶ **Escucha** el programa de nuevo y escribe un breve resumen de la entrevista para el periódico local.

 ▶ **Habla** con tu compañero(a) sobre tu experiencia con el arte. Túrnense para hacerse estas preguntas.

1. ¿Qué museos y monumentos visitaste durante tu infancia? ¿Con quién fuiste?
2. ¿Qué prefieres: la pintura, la escultura o la arquitectura? ¿Por qué?
3. ¿Qué pintor(a) o escultor(a) te gusta más? ¿Por qué?
4. ¿Tienes alguna reproducción de un(a) artista famoso(a) en tu cuarto? ¿Cómo es?
5. ¿Piensas que el arte es importante? ¿Por qué?

ESCRIBIR, LEER Y HABLAR

79 La arquitectura y yo

▶ **Escribe** un correo electrónico a tu compañero(a) recomendándole que visite un edificio famoso que te gusta. Explícale:

- Qué es lo que más te gusta de ese edificio.
- Por qué crees que le va a gustar a él/ella.
- Qué te parece más interesante de su construcción y su diseño.
- Qué le recomiendas que haga cuando lo visite.

 ▶ **Lee** el correo de tu compañero(a) y comparen los edificios que han elegido teniendo en cuenta estos aspectos: antigüedad, diseño y materiales.

Differentiated Instruction

DEVELOPING LEARNERS

- Ask students to match the author or artist to his or her work.

1. *Orozco* (f)	a. *Los músicos*
2. *G. Márquez* (b)	b. *Cien años de soledad*
3. *E. Chillida* (g)	c. *la Sagrada Familia*
4. *Gaudí* (c)	d. *Guernica*
5. *Borges* (h)	e. *La casa de los espíritus*
6. *I. Allende* (e)	f. *Lucha por la independencia*
7. *D. Rivera* (i)	g. *El peine del viento*
8. *Picasso* (d)	h. *El Sur*
9. *Botero* (a)	i. *Historia de México*

EXPANDING LEARNERS

- Ask students to think about their favorite novel or short story; it could be one originally written in Spanish or in any other language. Have students consider a scene that they especially liked and contemplate how they might change it. Then, have them take into account their ideas and start rewriting the scene. When they finish, call on students to first identify the work and its author and then give a brief summary of the original scene. Then ask students to read their version aloud.

Tu desafío

80 Los desafíos

¿Recuerdas los desafíos que Diana les planteó a los personajes? ¿Cuál te gusta más? Elige una de estas opciones y resuelve tu desafío.

DESAFÍO Ⓐ

Busca información sobre *Las Meninas*, el famoso cuadro de Diego Velázquez. Luego, compáralo con *Las Meninas* de Picasso y haz una presentación. Incluye estos datos:

- Breve biografía de los pintores.
- Época(s) en que fueron pintados los cuadros.
- Estilo de los cuadros.
- Tu opinión sobre los dos cuadros.

Pablo Picasso.
Las Meninas (1957).

DESAFÍO Ⓑ

Elige un edificio o una escultura de un(a) artista hispano(a) y graba una presentación para la clase. Incluye:

- Algunos datos biográficos.
- Estilo y materiales empleados en la obra.
- Tu opinión sobre la obra.

Rogelio Salmona. *Torres del Parque.*
Bogotá (Colombia).

DESAFÍO Ⓒ

Busca información sobre un(a) escritor(a) hispano(a), como Gabriel García Márquez, Octavio Paz, Mario Vargas Llosa, Camilo José Cela o Gabriela Mistral. Prepara una presentación que incluya:

- Una breve biografía.
- El argumento de una de sus obras más importantes.
- Género y estilo de esa obra.
- Una recomendación para que tus compañeros(as) de clase lean esa obra.

Gabriela Mistral.

trescientos cuarenta y uno **341**

HERITAGE LANGUAGE LEARNERS

- Ask students to describe a museum from their heritage country. It may be an art museum, a natural history or science museum, or one dedicated to children's interests. Ask students to describe the permanent collections featured or one particular exhibit that was especially successful. Ask students how visitors to the museum can interact with the exhibits. If there is no interaction, ask students to describe how they would remedy this and what they would like to see exhibited in the future.

MULTIPLE INTELLIGENCES:
Visual-Spatial Intelligence

- Explain to students that they are going to create a *boceto* for a mural, and they will be the subjects depicted in the art. Students will represent scenes from their own past, present, and what they perceive as their future. They may choose to draw their images or represent them with photos or even images taken from the Internet. Ask students to explain the significance of the images and where they would like to exhibit their work. Display students' sketches throughout the classroom.

Activities

78. Before playing the recording, have students read the statements and make sure they understand the vocabulary. You may wish to clarify that the Museo Reina Sofía is in Madrid, Spain, and that it is named after the current queen of Spain. You may also inform students that this museum hosts one of Picasso's most famous paintings, *Guernica*. Next, have students guess which of the statements may be true and which may be false, and explain why. For the third part of this activity, ask students to compare and contrast their opinions with those of their partner, and then share them with the class.

79. To expand this activity, you may want to ask student pairs to prepare a brief presentation for the class that includes photos, the description and comparison of the two buildings chosen, and two sentences recommending a visit to the buildings.

80. Display students' work in the classroom and have the class vote on the best entry in each category.

AUDIO SCRIPT
See page 297N.

Answer Key

78. 1. C.
2. F. Las explican haciendo gestos.
3. F. No pueden pisarla.
4. C.
5. F. No son las obras más fáciles.
▶ Answers will vary.
▶ Answers will vary.
79. Answers will vary.
▶ Answers will vary.
80. Answers will vary.

Additional Resources

Fans Online activities
Practice Workbook

MAPA CULTURAL

El «boom» de la literatura latinoamericana

Presentation

- This section presents information about the flourishing of Latin American literature in the 1960s. The images serve as a reference point for additional cultural readings and activities that expand on the skills students learned in this unit.

Activities	Standards	Resources
Mapa cultural	1.2, 2.1, 2.2, 3.1, 3.2	
81.	1.2, 1.3, 2.1, 2.2, 3.1, 5.1, 5.2	

Cultural Topics

- **El trasfondo del «boom».** The literary period known as the "Boom" emerged in Latin America in the midst of political turmoil, rapidly changing economics, and artistic movements that broke with tradition. On the political front, the Cuban Revolution (1959), the military regimes that ruled in several Latin American countries, and the Cold War were defining events. In terms of the economy, an increasingly urban population gave rise to a larger middle class. And, artistically, the Modernist literature of the early 20th century opened the door to new literary techniques.

- **El «post-boom».** By the mid-1970s, a new group of writers had begun to deviate from the Boom. This new literary movement, called "Post-Boom," comprised a heterogeneous group who exhibited a great variety of styles, making the Post-Boom more difficult to define than the Boom. However, one of its few characterizing features was the emergence of a group of women writers, including Elena Poniatowska (Mexico) – *La noche de Tlatelolco* (1971), Luisa Valenzuela (Argentina) – *Como en la guerra* (1977), Isabel Allende (Chile) – *La casa de los espíritus* (1982), and Cristina Peri Rossi (Uruguay) – *La nave de los locos* (1984), among others.

Teaching Suggestions

Warm-Up / Independent Starter

- Ask students to list all of the Latin American writers they know and some details about each one.

342

El «boom» de la literatura latinoamericana

A comienzos de los años sesenta del siglo XX publicaron sus primeras obras con un gran éxito un conjunto de jóvenes escritores latinoamericanos que escribían en español y planteaban una ruptura con las formas tradicionales del relato. Entre esos jóvenes estaban autores tan importantes como Gabriel García Márquez (Colombia), Mario Vargas Llosa (Perú), Carlos Fuentes (México), Julio Cortázar (Argentina), José Lezama Lima (Cuba) o José Donoso (Chile). Este es el fenómeno al que se conoce como el «boom» de la novela latinoamericana.

Gabriel García Márquez

El colombiano Gabriel García Márquez (1928) es uno de los grandes narradores hispanoamericanos. *La hojarasca*, *El coronel no tiene quien le escriba*, *Crónica de una muerte anunciada* y *El amor en los tiempos del cólera* son algunas de sus novelas. Pero su obra fundamental es *Cien años de soledad*.

En 1982 Gabriel García Márquez recibió el Premio Nobel de Literatura.

Cien años de soledad (1967) fue la obra que consagró a Gabriel García Márquez como uno de los mejores escritores del siglo XX. Se considera la novela emblemática del realismo mágico, basado en la mezcla de realismo, leyenda y sueño. Cuenta la historia de un pueblo, Macondo, desde su fundación hasta su desaparición a través de la historia de la familia Buendía.
«Muchos años después, frente al pelotón de fusilamiento, el coronel Aureliano Buendía había de recordar aquella tarde remota en que su padre lo llevó a conocer el hielo.»

¿Sabías que...?

Cien años de soledad ha sido traducida a 35 idiomas y se han vendido más de 20 millones de ejemplares desde su publicación.

Realismo mágico

En el realismo mágico lo real, lo cotidiano, lo mítico y lo imaginario se encuentran enlazados de forma estrecha y verosímil, intentando reflejar la identidad de América.

342 trescientos cuarenta y dos

Differentiated Instruction

DEVELOPING LEARNERS

- Ask students whether the following statements are true (*cierto*) or false (*falso*). Have them correct the false ones.
  1. *El «boom» tiene lugar a finales del siglo XX.* (F; *en los 60*)
  2. *En el realismo mágico se mezcla lo real con lo imaginario.* (C)
  3. *En* Cien años de soledad *se hace una crítica a la sociedad peruana.* (F; *en* La ciudad y los perros)
  4. *Carlos Fuentes fue un escritor colombiano.* (F; *mexicano*)
  5. *Tanto García Márquez como Vargas Llosa recibieron el Nobel de Literatura.* (C)

EXPANDING LEARNERS

- Explain to students that they are going to compete with the prestigious Guatemalan short story writer Augusto Monterroso. Monterroso is credited with writing one of the world's shortest stories: *Cuando desperté, el dinosaurio todavía estaba allí.* Using Monterroso's work as a model, ask students to work with a partner and see if together they can create a "story" with fewer than twenty words. After student pairs read their stories aloud, take a class vote to see which one will win a special literary prize for brevity and creativity.

Mario Vargas Llosa

El escritor peruano Mario Vargas Llosa (1936) encabezó el «boom» con su primera obra, *La ciudad y los perros*, en la que se hace una crítica a la sociedad peruana. Otras novelas interesantes son *La casa verde*, *Pantaleón y las visitadoras*, la autobiográfica *La tía Julia y el escribidor* y *La guerra del fin del mundo*. Entre sus últimas publicaciones destacan *La Fiesta del Chivo*, *El paraíso en la otra esquina*, *El sueño del celta* y *El héroe discreto*.

Mario Vargas Llosa ganó el Premio Nobel de Literatura en 2010.

> Mario Vargas Llosa, como otros escritores del «boom», se interesó por las dictaduras americanas en obras como **Conversación en La Catedral** (1970) o **La Fiesta del Chivo** (2006).
>
> *«Urania. No le habían hecho un favor sus padres; su nombre daba la idea de un planeta, de un mineral, de todo, salvo de la mujer espigada y de rasgos finos, tez bruñida y grandes ojos oscuros, algo tristes, que le devolvía el espejo. ¡Urania! Vaya ocurrencia. Felizmente ya nadie la llamaba así, sino Uri, Miss Cabral, Mrs. Cabral o Doctor Cabral.»*

Carlos Fuentes

La obra del mexicano Carlos Fuentes (1928-2012) se caracteriza por el análisis de la problemática social y política de su país. *La muerte de Artemio Cruz* supuso su consagración. Otros títulos destacables son *La región más transparente*, *Cambio de piel*, *La cabeza de la hidra* y *Una familia lejana*.

> ***La muerte de Artemio Cruz*** (1962) supuso la consagración de Carlos Fuentes. A través de los recuerdos de un dirigente político corrupto que agoniza, se reconstruye la historia mexicana desde la Revolución. La novela se estructura mediante tres narradores distintos y presenta abundantes saltos espacio-temporales.
>
> *«Yo siento esa mano que me acaricia y quisiera desprenderme de su tacto, pero carezco de fuerzas. Qué inútil caricia. Catalina. Qué inútil. ¿Qué vas a decirme? ¿Crees que has encontrado al fin las palabras que nunca te atreviste a pronunciar? ¿Hoy? Qué inútil. Que no se mueva tu lengua. No le permitas el ocio de una explicación. Sé fiel a lo que siempre aparentaste; sé fiel hasta el fin. Mira: aprende de tu hija. Teresa. Nuestra hija. Qué difícil. Qué inútil pronombre. Nuestra. Ella no finge. Ella no tiene nada que decir.»*

81. Cuéntame un cuento

▶ **Lee** un cuento de uno de estos autores y preséntalo en clase. Incluye estos aspectos:

- – Resumen del cuento.
- – Comentarios sobre el estilo del autor.
- – Tu opinión personal sobre el relato.

> Gabriel García Márquez
>
> Julio Cortázar
>
> Augusto Monterroso

HERITAGE LANGUAGE LEARNERS

- Explain that when Vargas Llosa accepted the Nobel in 2010, he stated in his acceptance speech: *Aprendí a leer a los cinco años [...]. Es la cosa más importante que me ha pasado en la vida. [...] La lectura convertía el sueño en vida y la vida en sueño y ponía al alcance del pedacito de hombre que era yo el universo de la literatura.* Ask students to imagine that they have become great authors and have been awarded a top honor. Have them deliver a speech extolling the virtues of reading and literature.

TOTAL PHYSICAL RESPONSE (TPR)

- Students will play a version of "Jeopardy" to see how many literary works and authors they can identify. You will give them the title of a work and they will identify the author, or you will name an author and give a brief description of one of his or her works so that students will guess the title. The first to stand up and ask the question correctly scores a point. For example: La muerte de Artemio Cruz. *¿Quién es Carlos Fuentes?* Obra que consagró a García Márquez. *¿Qué es Cien años de soledad?*

MAPA CULTURAL

El «boom» de la literatura latinoamericana

Preparation

- Call on students to share their Independent Starters. As a class, discuss some of these authors' works, their styles, and some biographical information. Encourage students to critique some of the works they have read from these authors.

- Explain that, in addition to the three authors highlighted in the *Mapa cultural*, other important authors and works of the Boom period include Juan Rulfo (Mexico) with *Pedro Páramo* (1953), Alejo Carpentier (Cuba) with *Los pasos perdidos* (1953), Julio Cortázar (Argentina) with *Rayuela* (1963), and Manuel Puig (Argentina) with *Boquitas pintadas* (1969). You may wish to read some excerpts from works by Boom authors to give students a taste of this literature.

Activities

81. Remind students of some of the features of short stories, such as limited length and number of characters, clearly defined conflict, focused nature, and precise narration. However, explain that modern short stories tend to be more flexible and some of these elements may not be present. It is also important to keep in mind that some authors play with time and space. You may want to suggest some of the following stories: García Márquez → "Un día de estos," "Ladrón de sábado," "Algo muy grave va a suceder en este pueblo," "La muerte en Samarra;" Cortázar → "Continuidad de los parques," "Los amigos," "Historia verídica," "Instrucciones para dar cuerda al reloj;" Monterroso → "El eclipse," "La honda de David," "La mosca que soñaba que era águila," "La rana que quería ser una rana auténtica."

Answer Key

81. Answers will vary.

Additional Resources

Fans Online activities
Practice Workbook

ESCRITURA

Una reseña

Presentation

- In this section, students will practice and extend their writing skills. They will apply the vocabulary and grammar they have learned in this unit to write a book review about a novel they have read.

Activities	Standards	Resources
Escritura	1.1, 1.2, 1.3, 3.1, 5.1	

Teaching Suggestions

Warm-Up / Independent Starter

- Have students list four features they look for and like in a novel. Explain that these features may include the genre (e.g., *aventura, ciencia ficción, romance, misterio*), the type of ending (e.g., *feliz, abierto, trágico, sorprendente*), and the type of main character (e.g., *héroe, antihéroe, cómico*).

Preparation

- Invite students to share their Independent Starters with the class. Then, discuss some of the basic elements of fiction with students: plot (*el argumento*), setting (*el marco o escenario*), characters (*los personajes*), conflict (*el conflicto*), point of view (*el punto de vista narrativo*), theme (*el tema*). You may want to use a novel most of the class knows well to illustrate these elements.

- Ask for a volunteer to read the *Texto expositivo-argumentativo* box aloud. You may want to bring to class some examples of this type of writing (e.g., letters to the editor, movie or book reviews). Before you or volunteer students read each text aloud, note the purpose of the text and its target audience. As a class, talk about the features of each text and discuss the specific language and techniques employed by the writer.

Step-by-Step Instructions

Piensa

- Explain to students that the structure of their book review should flow; it should be clear and easy to read. The format suggested here is the most common, and their readers are probably familiar with it, so encourage students to follow this format closely. Remind them that their text should have a clear-cut introduction, body, and conclusion.

Una reseña

Texto expositivo-argumentativo

Los textos expositivo-argumentativos tienen como objetivo convencer de algo a alguien mediante una serie de argumentos. En ellos se expone una información, pero también se adopta una posición personal respecto al tema. Son textos que abundan en la comunicación escrita; los artículos de opinión, las críticas de espectáculos, las cartas de los lectores, etc. pertenecen al género expositivo-argumentativo.

Los textos de este tipo aúnan la objetividad de la exposición y la subjetividad de la argumentación. A menudo su carácter expositivo no es más que otro recurso de la argumentación.

Una reseña es un tipo de texto que tiene por objeto dar a conocer una obra literaria o una película informando sobre su contenido y añadiendo una valoración crítica de la misma. Su finalidad es que alguien que no conoce la obra pueda hacerse una idea lo suficientemente clara y completa sobre ella.

Internet ofrece actualmente muchos blogs literarios en los que los lectores comparten con otras personas sus lecturas y reseñan sus obras favoritas.

En esta unidad vas a escribir una reseña sobre una novela que hayas leído.

Piensa

- Elige la novela sobre la que vas a escribir la reseña: tu preferida, la última que leíste…
- Anota tus ideas para desarrollar las diferentes partes de la reseña, siguiendo este esquema:

Presentación	Busca los datos bibliográficos para presentar la novela: autor, título, género literario, editorial, año y lugar de publicación, y número de páginas.
Resumen del contenido	Toma notas para hacer un resumen del libro. Fíjate en estos aspectos: – ¿Cuándo y dónde ocurre la historia? – ¿Cuáles son los personajes principales? – ¿Qué problemas tienen esos personajes? ¿Cómo se resuelven?
Comentario crítico	Para elaborar tu opinión personal sobre el texto, puedes responder a estas preguntas: – ¿Crees que el título de la novela anima a la lectura? – ¿Qué opinas del estilo y el lenguaje empleados? – ¿Los personajes están bien descritos? – ¿Cómo es el final: lógico, sorprendente, decepcionante…?
Conclusión	Recoge las ideas fundamentales de tu reseña. Debe quedar claro que la valoración de la novela corresponde a tu opinión personal y que el lector deberá formar la suya propia.

Rubric for Evaluation

	Content	Organization	Conventions
1 point	Missing key details about the book. Vague recommendation statement. Limited vocabulary.	Unclear formatting. Details are not in a logical order. Few or no transitions present. Ineffective conclusion.	Many errors in spelling, punctuation, grammar, and usage. Errors obscure meaning.
3 points	Missing one or two details about the book. Provides a clear recommendation, but it lacks support. Some inaccurate word choices.	Format is close to the suggested model. Some effective transitions are present. Conclusion restates thesis, but is not very effective.	Some errors in spelling, punctuation, grammar, and usage. Errors don't interfere with meaning.

Escribe

■ Redacta una primera versión de la reseña. Utiliza las notas que escribiste y sigue estas recomendaciones:

– El resumen de la novela debe ser breve, pero tiene que contener los elementos esenciales para que el lector se haga una idea clara del argumento. Obviamente, no puedes desvelar el final.

– El comentario crítico debe recoger tu opinión sobre la historia y los personajes, y también puedes valorar el estilo literario, comparar la obra con otras que hayas leído, etc.

Revisa

■ Intercambia tu reseña con tu compañero(a) y revisa la suya. Fíjate en estos aspectos:

– ¿Te has hecho una idea clara de la novela?

– ¿Queda clara la opinión de tu compañero(a) sobre la novela?

– ¿El texto está redactado de manera clara y comprensible?

– ¿Se repiten mucho algunas palabras?

– ¿Tiene algún error gramatical, por ejemplo, en el uso del indicativo y del subjuntivo? ¿Tiene alguna falta de ortografía?

■ Devuelve la reseña a su autor(a) con tus sugerencias y revisa la tuya teniendo en cuenta sus comentarios. Modifica lo que creas necesario y pásala a limpio. Si quieres, puedes incluir la imagen de la cubierta del libro.

Comparte

■ Lee tu reseña a la clase. ¿Alguno de tus compañeros(as) ha leído esa novela? ¿Comparte tu opinión sobre ella?

■ Después de escuchar todas las reseñas, comenta con tus compañeros(as) qué novela(s) te gustaría leer y por qué. Pueden publicarlas en un blog.

Vocabulario útil

la alusión	*allusion*
la imagen	*image*
la ironía	*irony*
el paralelismo	*parallelism*
la parodia	*parody*
el punto de vista	*point of view*
el ritmo	*rhythm*
ágil	*agile*
entretenido(a)	*enjoyable*
lento(a)	*slow*
magnífico(a)	*magnificent*
monótono(a)	*boring*
recomendable	*advisable*
sorprendente	*amazing*

Libro de mal amor
Fernando Iwasaki
Novela
Editorial Alfaguara
Madrid, 2007
N.º de páginas: 180

Libro de mal amor es la historia de los fracasos amorosos de un joven que, para alcanzar a la mujer de sus sueños, se hace deportista, patinador, político, vegetariano, judío y experto en *ballet*. El joven es un antihéroe que se vuelve camaleónico en su intento desesperado de conquistar a las mujeres.

Es un libro muy entretenido que, con mucho humor, narra diez fracasos amorosos a cual más divertido. Con un estilo sencillo y muchos juegos de palabras, este libro es muy accesible para los adolescentes a los que va dirigido. En mi opinión es una lectura muy recomendable.

	Content	Organization	Conventions
5 points	Includes all necessary information about the book. Provides a well-supported recommendation. Accurate, rich, and purposeful word choices.	Follows the suggested format. Effective use of transitions and logical sequencing. Conclusion binds review together.	Few, if any, errors in spelling, punctuation, grammar, and usage. Excellent command of the Spanish language.

ESCRITURA
Una reseña

Escribe

■ Emphasize to students the importance of using precise vocabulary. Correct usage of appropriate words will make their review sound professional and knowledgeable, as well as clear and to the point. Encourage students to use both the *Vocabulario útil* on this page and the *Repaso de vocabulario* on page 346 as reference.

■ Remind students that they should include a critical evaluation of the book. This critique usually contains reactions to the novel, describes how it could be improved, comments on the overall successes and failures of the book, and analyzes how well the book has achieved its goal. Encourage students to cite specific examples or sections from the novel to support their arguments.

Revisa

■ Ask students to read through their own text before they exchange it with a classmate. Have students try to look at their text from the point of view of someone who has not read the book and who is trying to decide whether to read it or not. Tell students to make sure their book review addresses important points in the novel, includes some of the key events and provides examples, and offers a critique of the book.

Comparte

■ If time allows, have a whole-class discussion about the types of novels students have chosen. Is there a trend among students? What motivates them to want to read a particular book?

Evaluation

■ Distribute copies of the rubric to students and discuss the evaluation criteria. Ask students to refer to the rubric as they prepare their writing and as they evaluate their classmates' book reviews.

REPASO

Vocabulario

Presentation

■ In this section, students will review all key vocabulary from the unit, organized by themes, to prepare for an assessment. Students will complete practice activities for each *Desafío*.

Activities	Standards	Resources
1.	1.2, 3.1	
2.	1.2, 1.3, 3.1	
3.	1.2, 3.1	

Teaching Suggestions

Warm-Up / Independent Starter

■ Ask students to leaf through this unit and choose a work of art, architecture, or literature that catches their attention in a special way. Then, ask them to jot down words and expressions that they can use to describe the work.

Preparation

■ Have students get together with a classmate and describe the work they chose for their Independent Starters. Tell students to withhold the name of the work, its author, location, etc. They should just concentrate on describing the work itself. For example: *El fondo es negro, y en el primer plano tenemos un retrato bastante preciso. Parece ser un óleo...* Students can leaf through the unit as they listen to their partner's description. Then, once they think they have located the work being described, they should show it to their partner to see if they guessed correctly. If time allows, ask students to switch partners and repeat the activity.

■ Go over the *Repaso* presentation with the class, modeling pronunciation, stress, and intonation. Then have students work on the activities.

Activities

2. To extend this activity, have student pairs write a paragraph describing a work of architecture they both like. Explain that they need to describe the main features of the work, mention some of the building materials that were used, and give some information about the architect. If time allows, invite students to share their paragraphs with the class.

REPASO Vocabulario

Arte y pintura

la acuarela	watercolor
el boceto	sketch
el fondo	background
la forma	shape
el lienzo	canvas
el mural	mural
el óleo	oil
el paisaje	landscape
la perspectiva	perspective
el pincel	brush
la pincelada	brushstroke
el primer plano	foreground
la proporción	proportion
el retrato	portrait
el tamaño	size
el volumen	volume
apagado(a)	subdued
exagerado(a)	exaggerated
innovador(a)	innovative
preciso(a)	precise
vivo(a)	vivid
destacar	to stand out
influir	to influence

Estilos artísticos

el arte abstracto	abstract art
el arte figurativo	representational art
el cubismo	cubism
el surrealismo	surrealism

¡Atención!

darse cuenta	to realize
realizar	to achieve

Arquitectura y escultura

el acueducto	aqueduct
el arco	arch
la catedral	cathedral
la columna	column
la construcción	construction
la fachada	facade
la mezquita	mosque
el palacio	palace
el puente	bridge
el rascacielos	skyscraper
la sinagoga	synagogue
el templo	temple
la torre	tower
la vivienda	home
lujoso(a)	luxurious
esculpir	to sculpt

Materiales

el aluminio	aluminum
el cemento	cement
el cristal	glass
el concreto	concrete
el granito	granite
el hierro	iron
el ladrillo	brick
el mármol	marble
la piedra	stone

¡Atención!

actualmente	currently
de hecho	actually

Literatura

el ambiente	atmosphere	la prosa	prose
el argumento	plot	el relato	story, tale
el desarrollo	development	el símbolo	symbol
el desenlace	dénoument, ending	el verso	verse, line
la estrofa	verse, stanza		
la lectura	reading	el/la autor(a)	author
el lenguaje figurado	figurative language	el/la narrador(a)	narrator
la metáfora	metaphor		
la poesía	poetry		

Géneros literarios

el ensayo	essay
la fábula	fable
la novela negra	crime novel
la novela rosa	romance novel

¡Atención!

el carácter	personality
el personaje	character

Differentiated Instruction

DEVELOPING LEARNERS

• Ask students to indicate which word does not belong.

1. *retratos* *símbolos* *metáforas (retratos)*
2. *arcos* *ladrillos* *columnas (ladrillos)*
3. *paisaje* *óleo* *acuarela (paisaje)*
4. *versos* *estrofas* *pinceladas (pinceladas)*
5. *granito* *hierro* *boceto (boceto)*
6. *pincel* *cristal* *lienzo (cristal)*
7. *palacio* *fachada* *vivienda (fachada)*
8. *narrador* *proporción* *perspectiva (narrador)*
9. *fondo* *desarrollo* *desenlace (fondo)*
10. *puente* *torre* *acueducto (torre)*

EXPANDING LEARNERS

• Have students answer the following questions:

1. ¿Cómo definirías el arte surrealista? ¿Y el cubismo?
2. ¿Qué has aprendido sobre la arquitectura en esta unidad?
3. ¿Qué valor tienen los murales hoy en día?
4. Si pudieras elegir a cualquier pintor para que pintara tu retrato, ¿a quién elegirías? ¿Por qué?
5. ¿Con qué escritor —del presente o pasado— te gustaría conversar? ¿Por qué?
6. ¿Con qué personaje de ficción te identificas? Explica tu respuesta.

DESAFÍO 1

1 **Mucho arte.** Decide. ¿A qué palabras relacionadas con el arte corresponden estas definiciones?

1. Tela preparada para pintar sobre ella.
2. Esquema o dibujo que se realiza antes de la obra.
3. Trazo dado con el pincel sobre una superficie.
4. Pintura de una persona.
5. Pintura que se obtiene disolviendo colores en aceite.

DESAFÍO 2

2 **Grupos.** Clasifica las palabras del cuadro en una tabla como esta. Luego, escribe cinco oraciones con ellas.

| mezquita | columna | concreto | arco | fachada |
| ladrillo | piedra | puente | rascacielos | torre |

Edificios o tipos de construcción	Partes de una construcción	Materiales de construcción

DESAFÍO 3

3 **Obras maestras.** Completa estas notas sobre obras maestras de la literatura hispanoamericana con las palabras del cuadro. Ten en cuenta que no todas son válidas.

| estrofa | desenlace | autor | novela |
| lectura | ambiente | narradora | autora |

Rayuela (1963)

Inspirado en el juego infantil que consiste en saltar sobre una figura dibujada en el suelo, el argentino Julio Cortázar escribió una ___1___ que propone una ___2___ diferente a la tradicional; en lugar de leer los capítulos en orden, se puede seguir el orden que da el ___3___.

La casa de los espíritus (1982)

Se trata, sin duda, del libro más famoso de Isabel Allende. En él, la ___4___ principal nos cuenta la historia de una gran familia, los Trueba, a través de la lectura de los cuadernos de su abuela Clara, la verdadera protagonista de la novela, las cartas de su madre, los testimonios de su abuelo y sus propios recuerdos. La ___5___ decidió cómo escribir el ___6___ del relato después de un sueño donde se vio a sí misma sentada con un libro frente a su abuelo.

HERITAGE LANGUAGE LEARNERS

- Words that are easily confused by both native and non-native speakers include *carácter, realizar,* and *actualmente.* Encourage students to start a list of such words and expressions and their English-language equivalents, and to add to it from time to time. To get students started, suggest these word pairs: *asistir* (to attend)/ *atender* (to take care of); *idioma* (language)/ *modismo* (idiom); *sensible* (sensitive)/ *sensato* (sensible); *disgusto* (displeasure)/ *asco* (disgust); *pretender* (to try)/ *fingir* (to pretend). Ask students to share these words with the rest of the class.

MULTIPLE INTELLIGENCES:
Verbal-Linguistic Intelligence

- Ask students to think about what a conversation might be like between an author and one of his or her characters. Have students work with a partner to create such a dialogue. One student will be the author, and the other, one of his or her characters. You may want to assign this as homework to allow students more time. When their conversations are complete, call on pairs to act them out in front of the class.

---

3. Call on two volunteers to each read one of the notes aloud, and have the class check their answers. Then, provide the class with the following quotes from the two works of literature mentioned in this activity, and have students identify the book and its author: 1. *En casi todas las familias hay algún tonto o un loco, hijita. [...] A veces no se ven, porque los esconden, como si fuera una vergüenza. Los encierran en los cuartos más apartados, para que no los vean las visitas. Pero en realidad no hay de que avergonzarse, ellos también son obra de Dios.* (*La casa de los espíritus,* Isabel Allende); 2. *Lo que mucha gente llama amar consiste en elegir a una mujer y casarse con ella. La eligen, te lo juro, los he visto. Como si se pudiese elegir en el amor, como si no fuera un rayo que te parte los huesos y te deja estaqueado en la mitad del patio.* (*Rayuela,* Julio Cortázar) Were students able to identify the works of literature and the authors? What features provided students with clues?

Answer Key

1.
1. el lienzo
2. el boceto
3. la pincelada
4. el retrato
5. el óleo

2. Edificios o tipos de construcción: mezquita, puente, rascacielos, torre.
Partes de una construcción: columna, arco, fachada.
Materiales de construcción: ladrillo, piedra, concreto.

3.
1. novela
2. lectura
3. autor
4. narradora
5. autora
6. desenlace

Additional Resources

Fans Online activities
Practice Workbook

347

REPASO

Gramática

Presentation

- Students will review grammatical structures presented in the unit. Each grammar point is cross-referenced to the corresponding page on which it was introduced. The activities here provide systematic practice by *Desafío*.

Activities	Standards	Resources
4.	1.2, 1.3, 2.2, 3.1	
5.	1.3, 2.2, 3.1	
6.	1.2, 1.3	
7. Cultura	1.3, 2.1, 2.2, 3.1	

Teaching Suggestions

Warm-Up / Independent Starter

- Have students use these statements to write sentences about the Los Angeles Cathedral:
  1. *Lo bueno/malo es que...*
  2. *... es lo más/menos interesante de la catedral.*
  3. *Lo primero que se observa es...*

Preparation

- Call on several volunteers to share their Independent Starters. Write some of their sentences on the board and review the uses of the neuter article *lo*. Then, divide the class into five groups and assign each group one of the remaining grammar topics on this page. Have groups summarize their assigned topic and come up with four original examples to illustrate it. Then ask groups to present their grammar point to the class. You may want to verbally quiz the class after each presentation to ensure comprehension of these grammar points.

Activities

4. To expand this activity, have student pairs research two of their favorite artists. They should get information about the style, materials they used, colors, etc. for the two artists. If possible, ask students to look for pictures on the Internet. Once students have gathered the information, have them write a two-paragraph text comparing and contrasting the two artists. Call on pairs to show the pictures and read their paragraphs.

Las comparaciones (pág. 308)

COMPARACIONES DE IGUALDAD

verbo + igual que
igual de + adjetivo / adverbio + que
verbo + tanto como
tanto(a)(os)(as) + nombre + como
tan + adjetivo / adverbio + como

COMPARACIONES DE DESIGUALDAD

más / menos + adjetivo / adverbio / nombre + que
verbo + más / menos que

COMPARACIONES CON DE + ARTÍCULO

más / menos + adjetivo + de lo que
más / menos + nombre + del (de la, de los, de las) que
verbo + más / menos de lo que

El artículo neutro *lo* (pág. 310)

USOS DEL ARTÍCULO NEUTRO *LO*

- Delante de un adjetivo masculino singular.

lo + adjetivo
lo más / menos + adjetivo + de / que
lo + adjetivo + ser + que

- En construcciones posesivas.

lo + pronombre posesivo
lo de + pronombre personal / nombre

- Delante de un numeral ordinal.

lo + ordinal

- Delante del pronombre relativo *que*.

lo que + cláusula

EL ARTÍCULO *LO* ENFÁTICO

lo + adjetivo / adverbio + que

Expresar opinión (pág. 320)

INDICATIVO Y SUBJUNTIVO CON VERBOS DE OPINIÓN

Construcciones afirmativas con indicativo	considerar que creer que imaginar que juzgar que	opinar que parecer que pensar que suponer que
Construcciones negativas con subjuntivo	no considerar que no creer que	no parecer que no pensar que

Hacer valoraciones (pág. 322)

EXPRESIONES PARA HACER VALORACIONES

Es aconsejable / conveniente… Es importante… Es necesario / preciso… Es bueno / malo…	+ infinitivo
Es mejor / peor… Es sorprendente / fantástico… Es un error / un problema…	+ que + subjuntivo

Los diminutivos (pág. 332)

DIMINUTIVOS REGULARES

Palabras de varias sílabas terminadas en vocal no acentuada.	Suprimen la vocal final y añaden -ito(a): gatito
Palabras de varias sílabas terminadas en consonante distinta de -n, -r.	Añaden -ito(a): animalito

DIMINUTIVOS IRREGULARES

Palabras de una sílaba.	Añaden -ecito(a): florecita
Palabras de dos sílabas terminadas en vocal acentuada.	Añaden -cito(a): cafecito
Palabras de dos sílabas terminadas en -e, -n, -r.	Añaden -cito(a): cochecito

Dar consejos y hacer recomendaciones (pág. 334)

CONSEJOS Y RECOMENDACIONES NEUTROS

aconsejar animar a proponer	+ infinitivo
recomendar sugerir	+ que + subjuntivo

CONSEJOS Y RECOMENDACIONES CON MATIZ DE OBLIGACIÓN

deber (presente o condicional) haber que (presente o condicional) tener que (presente o condicional)	+ infinitivo
Yo en tu lugar Yo que tú	+ condicional

Differentiated Instruction

DEVELOPING LEARNERS

- Ask students to complete these sentences with the correct form of the verb in parentheses:
  1. *No creo que a ella le (gustar) el estilo de Picasso. (guste)*
  2. *Es importante que (prepararte) a fondo para el examen. (te prepares)*
  3. *Es mejor que (nosotros – hacer) un boceto antes de pintar el mural. (hagamos)*
  4. *Yo en tu lugar le (hacer) caso. (haría)*
  5. *Es importante (reconocer) los diferentes estilos de arquitectura. (reconocer)*
  6. *No considero que (ser) práctico aprender todos estos datos. (sea)*

EXPANDING LEARNERS

- Ask students to work with a partner and explain that they are going to compare two pieces of art. Partners will decide if they are going to compare a painting, a sculpture, or an architectural piece. After they select two different images, they will need to work alone and make a brief description of their art. Then, they will get together with their partner and, based on their notes and observations of both pieces, make their comparisons. Call on volunteers to share their comparisons with the rest of the class.

DESAFÍO 1

4 **Comparaciones artísticas.** Completa estas oraciones.

1. Los cuadros de Picasso son tan...
2. Van Gogh es mucho más...
3. Este pintor es igual de...
4. Voy a menos exposiciones de arte de lo...
5. Para mí, este retrato es mejor...
6. Los pintores trabajan tanto...

DESAFÍO 2

5 **En mi opinión...** Escribe tu opinión sobre cada uno de estos temas o artistas. Usa distintas estructuras y expresiones.

la pintura abstracta	Eduardo Chillida	los museos	Fernando Botero
la arquitectura	la escultura al aire libre	los *graffiti*	Rafael Moneo

5. Have students exchange their opinions with a classmate. For those areas in which they have different opinions, have students try to influence their partner's opinion. For example:

A. *No considero que la pintura abstracta sea atractiva. Es más, creo que está sobrevalorada.*

B. *Es una pena que pienses así. Te propongo que estudies la pintura de Dalí...*

Answer Key

4. Answers will vary. Sample answers:
1. ... caros como los de Monet.
2. ... conocido que Botero.
3. ... innovador que Picasso.
4. ... que me gustaría.
5. ... de lo que dicen los críticos de arte.
6. ... como los escultores.

5. Answers will vary. Sample answers:
– Me parece que la pintura abstracta es muy compleja.
– No creo que la sociedad valore la arquitectura como se debe.
– Considero que la obra de Eduardo Chillida es muy original.
– No pienso que los *graffiti* sean arte.

DESAFÍO 3

6 **Buenas recomendaciones.** Completa estas oraciones con la forma correcta de los verbos del cuadro.

hacer
ir
leer
perderse
ver

1. La profesora nos recomendó que _____ el libro antes de ver la película.
2. Yo en tu lugar no _____ la exposición de Dalí del Museo Reina Sofía.
3. Tendrías que _____ estas esculturas de Antonio López. ¡Te encantarían!
4. Mis amigos me animaron a que _____ con ellos al museo.
5. Ana, te propongo que _____ los dos juntos el trabajo sobre la novela hispanoamericana.

6. 1. leyéramos   4. fuera
2. me perdería   5. hagamos
3. ver

 CULTURA

7 **Arte y cultura.** Responde a estas preguntas.

1. ¿Cómo es el estilo de Fernando Botero?
2. ¿Qué se conoce con el nombre de «Ciudad museo»? ¿Quién la diseñó?
3. Nombra algún escritor hispano que haya recibido el Premio Nobel de Literatura.

7. Answers will vary. Sample answers:
1. El estilo de Botero, llamado *boterismo*, se caracteriza por el volumen exagerado de sus figuras.
2. La Ciudad Universitaria de Caracas, en Venezuela. Fue diseñada por el arquitecto venezolano Carlos Raúl Villanueva.
3. Entre los escritores hispanos que han recibido el Premio Nobel de Literatura se encuentran Gabriel García Márquez, Octavio Paz y Mario Vargas Llosa.

trescientos cuarenta y nueve **349**

Additional Resources

Fans Online activities
Practice Workbook

HERITAGE LANGUAGE LEARNERS

• Share with students these two quotes from Jorge Luis Borges that extol the virtues of reading: 1. *Uno llega a ser grande por lo que lee y no por lo que escribe.* 2. *Que otros se jacten de las páginas que han escrito; a mí me enorgullecen las que he leído.*

• Ask students to comment on these statements and then have them work with a partner and create another quote worthy of Borges that praises reading and encourages others to read more.

COOPERATIVE LEARNING

• Ask students to work in small groups and select what they consider to be their community's ugliest building or landmark and propose ways to "fix it," either through remodeling or demolishing it and building something attractive in its place. Encourage students to bring in or draw "before" and "after" images of the structure in question. Then have the group share in making an oral presentation of their project. Encourage the use of verbs and phrases that express comparisons, opinions, value judgments, and recommendations.

Unit 6
PROYECTO
Las obras de arte favoritas

Presentation

- In this section, students will apply the vocabulary, grammar, and cultural information they have learned in this unit to organize an art exhibit.

Activities	Standards	Resources
Paso 1	2.2, 3.1	
Paso 2	1.3, 2.2, 3.1	
Paso 3	1.2, 1.3, 2.1, 2.2, 3.1	
Paso 4	1.3, 2.2, 3.1, 5.2	
Paso 5	1.3, 2.2, 3.1	
Paso 6	1.3, 2.2, 3.1	

Teaching Suggestions

Warm-Up / Independent Starter

- Have students think of their favorite artistic style (e.g., *abstracto, minimalista, arte pop, barroco*). Then have them list an artist associated with this style and three features that characterize the style.

Preparation

- Have students share their Independent Starters. As a class, discuss some of the most representative artists and works of art from the styles students mentioned. The following are some examples students might know: American Regionalism → *American Gothic* by Grant Wood; Realism → *Nighthawks* by Edward Hopper; Post-Impressionism → *Sunflowers* by Vincent van Gogh; Surrealism → *La persistencia de la memoria* by Salvador Dalí; street art → the embedded sculptures of Mark Jenkins.

- Call on a volunteer to read the title and introduction. Then have students observe the pictures on the page and discuss some of the main features and artistic styles of these works.

Step-by-Step Instructions

Paso 1

- In order to narrow down their search, suggest to students that they use their Independent Starters. Students may want to visit the websites for these museums: Museo del Prado (Madrid), Museo Nacional de Arte (Mexico City), Museo Nacional de Colombia, Museo Nacional de Bellas Artes (Buenos Aires), and the Smithsonian Latino Center.

350

PROYECTO

Una exposición de
las obras de arte favoritas

En este proyecto van a organizar una exposición con las obras de arte favoritas de la clase.

PASO 1 Elige tu obra de arte favorita

- Piensa en la obra de arte de un pintor, escultor o arquitecto hispano que te guste mucho. Aquí tienes algunas sugerencias.

Salvador Dalí. *Enigma sin fin.*

Fernando Botero. *El gato.*

Remedios Varo. *Ciencia inútil o el Alquimista.*

Ricardo Legorreta. Catedral Nueva de Managua.

Rodrigo Arenas. *Monumento a la raza.*

Antonio Gaudí. *La Pedrera.*

PASO 2 Busca información

- ¿Qué sabes sobre la obra que has elegido? Busca información y completa una ficha como esta.

Mi obra favorita
Autor(a): Pablo Ruiz Picasso
Título de la obra: Guernica
Fecha: 1937
Técnica: Óleo sobre lienzo
Medidas: 349,3 x 776,6 cm
Ubicación: Museo Reina Sofía (Madrid)

350 trescientos cincuenta

Rubric for Evaluation

	Content	Organization	Presentation
1 point	Limited relevance. Information is incomplete or not focused. Limited descriptions.	Inefficient use of time. Information is disorganized. Minimal formatting; images are confusing.	Unclear communication. Delivery is not fluent. Many errors in vocabulary and grammar.
3 points	Relevant and focused information, but some of it lacks significance. Appropriate descriptions.	Time is used well. Information is mostly organized. Attractive formatting and good use of images.	Clear communication and fluent delivery. Mostly correct vocabulary and grammar.

PASO 3 Amplía la información

- Busca información sobre el/la autor(a) de la obra y escribe una breve biografía. Busca también una foto suya y varias imágenes de la obra que has elegido.
- Investiga más sobre la obra elegida:
  - ¿Qué representa? ¿A qué estilo artístico pertenece?
  - Si es una pintura, ¿cómo se ha usado el color? ¿Y la luz?
  - Si es una escultura o una construcción, ¿qué materiales se han empleado?
  - ¿Qué relación tiene con su contexto geográfico, artístico, económico, político, social o religioso?

PASO 4 Describe la obra

- Escribe una descripción detallada de la obra y explica lo que representa. Añade una breve valoración personal.

PASO 5 Organiza la información

- Reúne toda la información y prepara un póster.

Pablo Ruiz Picasso. *Guernica* (1937). Óleo sobre lienzo (349,3 x 776,6 cm.). Museo Reina Sofía (Madrid).

La obra: El cuadro representa la crueldad de la guerra. A la izquierda hay un toro, símbolo de la brutalidad. Debajo, una mujer llora con su hijo muerto en brazos. En el suelo hay un hombre muerto con una espada rota y una flor en la mano como un símbolo de esperanza.

El autor: Pablo Ruiz Picasso. Málaga (España) 1881 – Mougins (Francia) 1973. Pintor, dibujante y escultor. Inició su aprendizaje en el mundo de la pintura a través de su padre, profesor de Bellas Artes. Es uno de los grandes maestros del siglo XX y uno de los creadores del movimiento cubista.

PASO 6 Monta la exposición

- Reúnan todos los pósteres elaborados por la clase y monten la exposición. Expliquen las obras a los visitantes y contesten sus preguntas.

Unidad 6

Autoevaluación

¿Qué has aprendido en esta unidad?

Haz estas actividades para comprobar tu progreso.

Evalúa tus habilidades. Para cada punto, di Muy bien, Bien o Necesito practicar más.

a. ¿Puedes describir y comparar obras de arte?

▶ Describe tu cuadro favorito y compáralo con otro que conoces.

b. ¿Puedes opinar y hacer valoraciones sobre esculturas y construcciones?

▶ Escribe tu opinión sobre el edificio de tu escuela. ¿Qué te parece más interesante o sorprendente desde el punto de vista arquitectónico?

c. ¿Puedes dar consejos y recomendaciones sobre obras literarias?

▶ ¿Cuáles son tus tres libros favoritos? Explica por qué te gustan y haz un resumen del argumento de uno de ellos.

▶ Recomiéndale un libro a un(a) amigo(a) para que lo empiece a leer este fin de semana. Explica por qué crees que le gustaría.

	Content	Organization	Presentation
5 points	Relevant, focused, and interesting information. Vivid sensory details and striking descriptions.	Time is used wisely. Information is clearly organized. Very attractive formatting and excellent choice of images.	Clear and fluent communication. Very motivating, upbeat delivery. Correct and complete vocabulary and grammar.

PROYECTO

Las obras de arte favoritas

Paso 2

- Using 4" x 6" index cards, have students create an "ID Card" for their chosen work of art. They may wish to put a border around it. Explain that this will be their label for the poster, just like the labels used in museums to identify the different works of art.

Paso 3

- Ask students to try to get as much information as they can about their work of art. Then, they should carefully decide what is relevant and interesting enough to be included in the poster.

Paso 4

- Emphasize the importance of including detailed and vivid descriptions. Students may also want to briefly speculate about the meaning of the work in their personal critique.

Paso 5

- Encourage students to try to achieve a good mix of text and images, as well as attractive formatting.

Paso 6

- Suggest to students that they prepare index cards with additional information about their chosen artist and work of art to be prepared for questions from the public.

Evaluation

- Distribute copies of the rubric to students. Discuss the evaluation criteria and explain how this project will be graded. Encourage students to refer to the rubric as they prepare their projects.

Content

- Encourage students to include original comments and analyses in their descriptions. Remind them that they should use precise art terminology.

Organization

- Remind students to keep in mind the importance of headings and captions when organizing the different sections and images of their posters.

Presentation

- Encourage students to ask good questions and to be thoughtful listeners. Stress that the conversations should stick to art topics.

HACIA EL AP* EXAM

Presentational Speaking: Cultural Comparison

Presentation

- These pages present students with a sample activity from the "Presentational Speaking: Cultural Comparison" portion of the AP* Spanish Language and Culture Exam. Students will prepare and deliver a two-minute oral presentation about a cultural topic.

Activities	Standards	Resources
Presentational Speaking: Cultural Comparison	1.3, 2.1, 2.2, 4.2, 5.1, 5.2	

Preparing for the Exam

About This Section

- The "Presentational Speaking: Cultural Comparison" section of the AP* Exam requires students to consider a prompt about a topic of cultural interest. They will then prepare an oral presentation in which they compare their own culture(s) and the culture(s) of the Spanish-speaking world with which they are familiar in terms of the aspect described in the prompt. This section lasts approximately six minutes and counts for 12.5% of the student's overall score on the test.

- Students will have four minutes to prepare the presentation and two minutes to speak. Because the purpose of this activity is to evaluate students' spoken expression in Spanish and their cultural and cross-cultural understanding, it is important that they take full advantage of the two-minute time allowance, in order to give as complete a speaking sample as possible to the test scorers.

- You may wish to set a strict time limit while administering the practice activities on these pages in order to simulate the testing conditions. Or, you may wish to allow students more time in order to put into practice the *Estrategias* given. You may also want to have students record their presentation so that they can evaluate their strengths and weaknesses, and devise a strategy for improving their spoken Spanish.

Hacia el AP* Exam

Presentational Speaking: Cultural Comparison

Presentación

Para terminar el examen AP* vas a hacer una presentación de dos minutos sobre un tema cultural. En tu presentación, debes comparar aspectos culturales de tu comunidad con lugares del mundo hispano que conozcas. El objetivo de esta presentación es evaluar los conocimientos que has adquirido sobre la cultura del mundo hispano y tus habilidades para exponer un tema en español.

Estrategias

- Lee la pregunta que te plantean para la presentación y decide qué elementos vas a comparar. Puedes organizar tu presentación mediante un gráfico o una serie de preguntas. Por ejemplo:
  - ¿Qué fiestas representan la herencia cultural de tu comunidad?
  - ¿Qué fiestas representan la herencia cultural de la comunidad hispana que has elegido?
  - ¿En qué se parecen estas fiestas? ¿En qué aspectos se diferencian?
  - ¿Por qué son importantes estas fiestas?
- Cita ejemplos de materiales culturales que has leído, visto y escuchado. También puedes apoyarte en tus experiencias personales.
- Intenta que tu presentación sea original y trata de despertar el interés de la audiencia.
- Emplea un registro adecuado a la situación: usa la forma *usted(es)*, un vocabulario preciso y estructuras complejas y bien construidas.
- Aplica las estrategias de expresión oral que practicaste en la unidad 4 (ver página 238).

Instrucciones para el examen

Directions: You will make an oral presentation on a particular topic of cultural interest. You will have four minutes to read the presentation topic and prepare your presentation. You will then have two minutes to record your presentation.

In your presentation, you should compare your community with an area of the Spanish-speaking world with which you are familiar. You should show your understanding of cultural elements of the Spanish-speaking world. You should organize your presentation clearly and logically.

Instrucciones: Vas a hacer una presentación oral sobre un tema cultural. Tendrás cuatro minutos para leer la introducción y preparar tu presentación. Luego tendrás dos minutos para grabar tu presentación.

En tu presentación, debes comparar tu comunidad con un área del mundo hispanohablante que conozcas. Debes demostrar tu comprensión de elementos culturales del mundo hispanohablante. Organiza tu presentación de una forma clara y lógica.

Language Expansion

VOCABULARY

- Students may find it easier to begin speaking about each of these three topics if they have a list of useful vocabulary about each. Have them brainstorm vocabulary about the topics of festivals and holidays, new technology, and art. Remind them that their lists should include not only nouns, but also verbs, adjectives, adverbs, and other expressions. They should use the dictionary to include terms with which they are not already familiar. Have them share their lists in small groups and add more terms, or create a master list for the class.

GRAMMAR STRUCTURES: Comparing and Contrasting

- In their presentations, students will need to compare and contrast their home culture with the culture(s) of the Spanish-speaking world. They will therefore need to use grammatical structures for comparing and contrasting, as well as related transitional words and phrases. Have students review the grammar presentation on page 308 before beginning this activity. They can also refer to the *Resumen de gramática* at the end of the book. Have them brainstorm transitional words that would be useful in making these comparisons.

Actividad 1

Imagina que tienes que hacer una presentación oral en tu clase de Español sobre este tema:

> **Tema de la presentación:**
>
> ¿Qué fiestas representan la herencia cultural de tu comunidad?
>
> Compara las fiestas que representan la herencia cultural de tu comunidad con las de una comunidad del mundo hispano que conozcas. Puedes referirte, en tu presentación, a lo que has experimentado, aprendido y observado.

Actividad 2

Imagina que tienes que hacer una presentación oral en tu clase de Español sobre este tema:

> **Tema de la presentación:**
>
> ¿Cómo afecta el uso de las nuevas tecnologías a la vida de las personas en tu comunidad?
>
> Compara tus observaciones acerca de las comunidades en las que has vivido con tus observaciones de alguna región del mundo hispano que te sea familiar. En tu presentación puedes referirte a lo que has estudiado, vivido, observado, etc.

Actividad 3

Imagina que tienes que hacer una presentación oral en tu clase de Español sobre este tema:

> **Tema de la presentación:**
>
> ¿Qué papel desempeña el arte en tu comunidad?
>
> Compara la presencia que tiene y la importancia que se le da al arte (arquitectura, pintura, teatro, etc.) en tu comunidad y en alguna región del mundo hispano que conozcas. Puedes basarte en lo que has visto y leído o en tus propias experiencias.

trescientos cincuenta y tres 353

More Practice

OTHER POSSIBLE TOPICS

• The six course themes for the AP* Spanish Language and Culture Exam provide excellent ideas for other topics with which students can practice their Cultural Comparison presentations. These themes are: Global Challenges, Science and Technology, Contemporary Life, Personal and Public Identities, Families and Communities, and Beauty and Aesthetics. The *Curriculum Framework,* published by the College Board, provides additional information about these themes. You can find this publication online at http://apcentral.collegeboard.com.

ADDITIONAL SOURCES

• You may find additional sources of cultural information at the following websites:
  – UNESCO: www.unesco.org/new/es
  – Centro Regional para la Salvaguardia del Patrimonio Cultural Inmaterial de América Latina: www.crespial.org
  – Instituto Distrital de Patrimonio Cultural de Colombia: www.patrimoniocultural.gov.co
  – Instituto Nacional de Patrimonio Cultural del Ecuador: inpc.gob.ec
  – Instituto del Patrimonio Cultural de España: ipce.mcu.es

Strategies: Presentational Speaking

■ The questions contained in the *Estrategias* box are examples that refer to the topic of *Actividad 1*. Have students read the estrategias silently. Then, with a partner, have them come up with a list of guiding questions for the other two activities. They can compile their list with that of other groups before beginning the practice activities.

■ The task of comparing elements between two or more cultures can get very complex. Help students design a graphic organizer with which they can organize their thoughts. For example, you may want to have students vary a Venn diagram in such a way that it can be used to discuss a series of points. Have students present their graphic organizers and choose the one that works best for them.

Rubric for Evaluation

On the AP* Exam, each section is given a score between 0 (Unacceptable) and 5 (Strong). In order to earn a score of 5, the student's oral presentation should show:

– Content: Student presents and elaborates on his or her cultural comparison, including supporting details.

– Organization: Student's presentation is organized, with transitions and other language devices facilitating and complementing the organization.

– Message: Student's response is fully understandable, with ease of expression. Few errors do not impede communication, and self-correction improves comprehensibility.

– Language: Vocabulary is varied and precise. Grammatical structures are used correctly. Simple, compound, and complex sentences are used appropriately.

– Speech: Pronunciation, rhythm, and pace are appropriate and contribute to comprehension.

Additional Resources

Español Santillana AP* Preparation Workbook

RESUMEN DE GRAMÁTICA

Nouns

Nouns are words for people, animals, places, and things. Spanish nouns have gender (masculine or feminine) and number (singular or plural).

Gender of nouns. Most nouns that end in -o are masculine, and most nouns that end in -a are feminine. Nouns that end in -e or in a consonant can be either masculine or feminine.

Masculine form	Feminine form	Examples
Ends in -o.	Changes -o to -a.	el niño → la niña
Ends in a consonant.	Adds -a.	el profesor → la profesora

Exceptions:

- Masculine nouns that end in -a: día, mapa, planeta.
- Feminine nouns that end in -o: foto, moto.
- Masculine nouns of Greek origin that end in -ma: clima, drama.
- Masculine and feminine nouns with the same ending:

-ista: artista, periodista	-e: agente, cantante	-o: modelo, piloto

Number of nouns. Nouns can be singular (one person or thing) or plural (more than one person or thing).

Singular form	Plural form	Examples
Ends in a vowel.	Adds -s.	el edificio → los edificios
Ends in a consonant.	Adds -es.	el ascensor → los ascensores

Articles

Articles agree in gender and number with the noun they accompany.

Definite articles are used with people, objects, or entities that are unique, that are specified, that are known, or that have been previously identified.

Indefinite articles are used with people, objects, or entities that are unknown, that are unspecified, or that have not been previously identified.

DEFINITE ARTICLES

	Masculine	Feminine
Singular	el	la
Plural	los	las

INDEFINITE ARTICLES

	Masculine	Feminine
Singular	un	una
Plural	unos	unas

Remember: a + el → al; de + el → del.

Presence and absence of the article

Unlike in English, in Spanish, articles are used in these situations:

- With abstract nouns and with nouns used in a general sense: El amor es el sentimiento más fuerte.
- With body parts and clothing: Lleva un suéter en la mano.
- With titles (except don and doña): El doctor García es mexicano.
- With days, dates, and times: Los viernes salgo pronto del trabajo. But Hoy es lunes, 12 de octubre.
- With the names of streets, parks, etc.: Vivo en la calle Mayor.
- With percentages and numbers: El 80 por ciento aprobó el examen.

In Spanish, it is common to use the noun without an article in these cases:

- To refer to unspecified people or objects: Compra helado.
- With the verb ser, to talk about professions, jobs, and occupations: Mi padre es médico.
- With verbs like tener, llevar, or ponerse, to refer to attire or to typical properties of an object: ¿Tienes coche? Lleva falda. Tiene ascensor.
- With verbs like comprar, necesitar, querer, dar, traer, hacer, etc., to talk about singular uncountable nouns or plural countable nouns: Quiero sopa. Necesito camisas.

The neuter article *lo*

The neuter article *lo* is never used with nouns, and does not have an exact equivalent in English. It is used primarily in these cases:

- Before a singular masculine adjective.

| lo + adjective
lo más / menos + adjective + de / que
lo + adjective + ser + que | Todos admiramos lo bello. |

- In possessive constructions.

| lo + possessive pronoun
lo de + personal pronoun / noun | Lo mío es tuyo. |

- Before an ordinal number to express sequence.

| lo + ordinal | Lo primero es observar los colores. |

- Before the relative pronoun que to introduce a clause.

| lo que + clause | Tengo lo que necesito. |

- In emphatic constructions.

| lo + adjective / adverb + que | Sé lo difícil que es pintar. |

Adjectives

Adjectives describe nouns. In Spanish they usually follow the noun: el músico **calvo**, la cantante **morena**.

Spanish adjectives can be masculine or feminine, singular or plural.
They must agree with the noun in both gender and number.

End in -o: 4 forms	el chico simpático los chicos simpáticos la chica simpática las chicas simpáticas
End in -e: 2 forms	el niño inteligente los niños inteligentes la niña inteligente las niñas inteligentes
End in a consonant: usually, 2 forms	el señor débil los señores débiles la señora débil las señoras débiles

Adjectives that express nationality also have variation of gender and number.

End in -o or in a consonant: 4 forms	el niño español la niña española	los niños españoles las niñas españolas
End in -e: 2 forms	el señor canadiense la señora canadiense	los señores canadienses las señoras canadienses

Position of descriptive adjectives

- In Spanish, adjectives that express types of people or things, as well as their individual qualities or properties, go after the nouns they modify: Cartagena de Indias es una ciudad turística.

- Conversely, adjectives that express typical qualities of the noun precede it: A lo lejos se veían las altas montañas.

- Many adjectives can be placed before or after the noun for style reasons, but some have differences in meaning depending on their position.

ADJECTIVES WITH MEANING CHANGES

Adjective	Before the noun	After the noun
antiguo(a)	former, ex-	ancient, antique
viejo(a)	long-standing	old, elderly
nuevo(a)	different, other	brand new
gran, grande	great, famous	big, large
pobre	unfortunate	penniless
único(a)	only	unique

APOCOPATED ADJECTIVES

bueno → buen
malo → mal   + masculine singular noun
grande → gran

Demonstrative adjectives and pronouns

To indicate where something or someone is located in relation
to the person speaking, use demonstratives. Demonstrative adjectives
and pronouns show gender and number.

Demonstrative pronouns can be used to indicate or to avoid repetition.
They mean *this one/that one* or *these/those*.

Distance from speaker	Singular			Plural	
	Masculine	Feminine	Neuter	Masculine	Feminine
Near	este	esta	esto	estos	estas
At a distance	ese	esa	eso	esos	esas
Far away	aquel	aquella	aquello	aquellos	aquellas

Neuter forms esto, eso, and aquello are always pronouns. They are used
to refer to situations or facts, and to present or to refer to unknown
objects.

Possessive adjectives and pronouns

Possessive adjectives and pronouns express ownership. Possessive
adjectives agree with the noun they accompany. They agree with the thing
(or person) possessed, not with the owner. They can be placed before
or after the noun they accompany.

	Before the noun (*mi tío*)				After the noun (*un tío mío*) or pronouns			
	Singular		Plural		Singular		Plural	
	Masculine	Feminine	Masculine	Feminine	Masculine	Feminine	Masculine	Feminine
my	mi		mis		mío	mía	míos	mías
your (inf.)	tu		tus		tuyo	tuya	tuyos	tuyas
his, her, your	su		sus		suyo	suya	suyos	suyas
our	nuestro	nuestra	nuestros	nuestras	nuestro	nuestra	nuestros	nuestras
your (inf.)	vuestro	vuestra	vuestros	vuestras	vuestro	vuestra	vuestros	vuestras
their, your	su		sus		suyo	suya	suyos	suyas

Numbers

Cardinal numbers

Cardinal numbers express quantity in a precise way: uno, cien, mil.

Ordinal numbers

Ordinal numbers indicate order or position. In Spanish, only the first ordinal numbers are used. After ten, we generally use cardinal numbers. Unlike in English, ordinal numbers are not used for dates, and the names of kings and popes do not require an article.

1.º / 1.ª / 1.ᵉʳ	primero(a), primer*	6.º / 6.ª	sexto(a)
2.º / 2.ª	segundo(a)	7.º / 7.ª	séptimo(a)
3.º / 3.ª / 3.ᵉʳ	tercero(a), tercer*	8.º / 8.ª	octavo(a)
4.º / 4.ª	cuarto(a)	9.º / 9.ª	noveno(a)
5.º / 5.ª	quinto(a)	10.º / 10.ª	décimo(a)

* Use primer and tercer + *masculine singular noun*.

Other numbers

Some numbers express a part of something: medio, la mitad (de), un tercio (de), un cuarto (de), la tercera parte (de), la cuarta parte (de).

Other numbers are used to multiply: el doble, el triple, el cuádruple, dos veces más, tres veces más, etc.

Indefinites

Indefinites indicate existence or quantity in an imprecise way, or absence.

ningún*, ninguno(a)	*no, (not) any, none*	alguien	*someone*
algún*, alguno(a)(os)(as)	*a few, any, one, some*	algo	*something*
poco(a)(os)(as)	*some, few*	nadie	*nobody*
mucho(a)(os)(as)	*many, a lot of*	nada	*nothing*
demasiado(a)(os)(as)	*too much, too many*	cualquier(a)	*any, whichever*
todo(a)(os)(as)	*all, every, throughout*	otro(a)(os)(as)	*another*
varios(as)	*several*	bastante(s)	*enough*
		suficiente(s)	*enough*

* Use ningún and algún + *masculine singular noun*.

Alguien and nadie refer to people. Algo and nada refer to things.

Comparatives

verb + igual que	... as much as ...
igual de + adjective / adverb + que	as ... as
verb + tanto como	... as much as ...
tanto(a)(os)(as) + noun + como	as much / many ... as
tan + adjective / adverb + como	as ... as

COMPARISONS OF INEQUALITY

más / menos + adjective / adverb / noun + que	more / less ... than
verb + más / menos que	... more / less than
más / menos + adjective + de lo que	more / less ... than
más / menos + noun + del (de la, de los, de las) que	more / less ... than
verb + más / menos de lo que	... more / less than

COMPARATIVE FORMS

bueno(a) / bien	→	mejor
malo(a) / mal	→	peor
grande	→	mayor
pequeño(a)	→	menor

Nevertheless, when we talk about size, we use más grande and más pequeño(a). We can also use más pequeño(a) when referring to age.

Superlatives

The superlative is used to express an extreme degree of an adjective.
Use muy + *adjective* to express the same idea.

Adjectives ending in a consonant.	Add -ísimo, -ísima, -ísimos, -ísimas. popular + ísimo → popularísimo
Adjectives ending in a vowel.	Drop the vowel and add the superlative ending. triste + ísimo → tristísimo

The relative superlative is used to describe a noun in comparison to a larger group: Este es el lugar más bonito del mundo.

el / la / los / las + noun + más / menos + adjective + de... / que...

Pronouns

Subject pronouns

Subject pronouns identify the person who is performing an action.

Singular		Plural	
yo	I	nosotros nosotras	we
tú	you (informal)	vosotros vosotras	you (informal)
usted él ella	you (formal) he she	ustedes ellos ellas	you they they

Direct object and indirect object pronouns

To avoid repeating words that have already been mentioned, you can replace the direct object or the indirect object with a pronoun. The object pronoun is necessary:

- With pronominal verbs: Marta nunca se queja.
- When the indirect object is a + *pronoun* (a mí, a ti, a usted…) or a + *noun:* Le envié un mensaje a Pedro.
- When the object noun goes in front of the verb: Estas fresas las compré ayer.

DIRECT OBJECT PRONOUNS

Singular		Plural	
me	*me*	nos	*us*
te	*you* (informal)	os	*you* (informal)
lo la	*you* (formal), *him, it* *you* (formal), *her, it*	los las	*you, them* *you, them*

INDIRECT OBJECT PRONOUNS

Singular		Plural	
me	*to / for me*	nos	*to / for us*
te	*to / for you* (informal)	os	*to / for you* (informal)
le	*to / for you* (formal), *him, her*	les	*to / for you,* *them*

Direct and indirect object pronouns are placed before the conjugated verb, or attached to the infinitive, the present participle, or the affirmative command.

Direct and indirect object pronouns may be used in the same sentence. In this case, the indirect object pronoun goes before the direct object pronoun. Le and les become se when placed in front of a direct object pronoun.

The pronoun *se*

When speaking about an action without saying exactly who performs it, we use this construction:

se + verb in 3rd person	Se habla español en más de 20 países.

In constructions with se + *verb in the 3rd person*, the verb can be in singular or plural.

se + verb in 3rd person singular with a singular noun, an infinitive, or a clause starting with que	Se prohíbe comer en clase.
se + verb in 3rd person plural with a plural noun	Se necesitan cocineros.

With verbs like caer, olvidar, perder, and romper, to present the action as an accident or something involuntary, we use this construction:

se + indirect object pronoun (me, te, le, nos, os, les) + verb in 3rd person	A mi padre se le perdieron las llaves.

Adverbs

Adverbs and phrases of frequency

These adverbs and adverbial phrases express how often something is done:

nunca	*never*	muchas veces	*many times, often*	diariamente	*daily*
casi nunca	*almost never*	casi siempre	*usually, normally*	semanalmente	*weekly*
rara vez	*seldom, rarely*	siempre	*always*	mensualmente	*monthly*
a veces	*sometimes*	todos los días	*every day*	anualmente	*yearly*

To express the frequency with which we do something during a period of time in a precise way, we can use these structures:

number + vez / veces + al / a la + time	Voy al cine tres veces al mes.
cada + number + time	Tengo clases de guitarra cada dos días.
todos(as) + los(as) + time	Voy de compras todos los fines de semana.

To talk about actions that we do habitually, we can use the structure soler (in the present or imperfect tense) + *infinitive*: Los fines de semana suelo salir con mis amigos.

Adverbs of quantity

Some verbs and adjectives can be modified by a word that expresses quantity.

nada	poco	bastante	mucho	demasiado
not at all	*little, not much*	*quite, enough*	*a lot, much*	*too, too much*

Adverbs and phrases about the future

When you express intention or future plans, you can use these adverbs or expressions:

ahora	*now*	mañana	*tomorrow*
luego, después	*later*	pasado mañana	*the day after tomorrow*
en un rato	*in a while*	mañana por la mañana	*tomorrow morning*
en media hora	*in half an hour*	mañana por la tarde	*tomorrow afternoon / evening*
en dos horas	*in two hours*	mañana por la noche	*tomorrow night*
hoy	*today*	el lunes que viene / el próximo lunes	*next Monday*
esta mañana	*this morning*	el mes que viene / el próximo mes	*next month*
esta tarde	*this afternoon*	el año que viene / el próximo año	*next year*
esta noche	*tonight*		

Adverbs and phrases about the past

These adverbs and time expressions refer to the past tense:

antes	*before*	la semana pasada	*last week*
anoche	*last night*	el mes pasado	*last month*
ayer	*yesterday*	el año pasado	*last year*
anteayer	*the day before yesterday*		

These time expressions often accompany the present perfect tense:

esta mañana / esta semana	*this morning / this week*	hoy	*today*
este siglo / este año / este mes	*this century / this year / this month*	recientemente	*recently*
hasta ahora	*until now*	últimamente	*lately*

The present perfect and the past perfect are frequently used with the adverbs ya and todavía.

- Ya (*already*) is used to express that the action is actually finished: Cuando llegué, ella ya había comido.

- Todavía (*still*) is used to express that the action has not started or is still in progress. Todavía is frequently used in negative constructions: Él todavía no había comido.

Use hace to express the amount of time elapsed since an action was completed.

hace + time expression + que + verb in the preterite tense	Hace una hora que espero.
verb in the preterite tense + desde hace + time expression	Espero desde hace una hora.

Use hacía to describe an action or event that began in the past and continued for some time.

hacía + time expression + que + verb in the imperfect tense	Hacía una hora que esperaba.
verb in the imperfect tense + desde hacía + time expression	Esperaba desde hacía una hora.

Adverbs and phrases of location

Many words and phrases are used to show location.

aquí, acá	*here*	encima de	*on, on top of*
ahí	*there*	debajo de	*under*
allí, allá	*over there*	delante de	*in front of*
		detrás de	*behind*
al lado de	*next to*		
a la derecha de	*to the right of*	cerca de	*near, close to*
a la izquierda de	*to the left of*	lejos de	*far from*

Adverbs ending in -*mente*

Many adverbs are formed from adjectives by adding the suffix -mente to the feminine singular form.

Adjectives ending in -o.	Change -o to -a and add -mente.	lento → lentamente
Adjectives ending in -e or in a consonant.	Add -mente.	frecuente → frecuentemente habitual → habitualmente

Diminutives

Diminutives are suffixes that are added to the end of nouns and some adjectives and adverbs to express small size or other values (affection, irony, etc.). In Spanish, there are several diminutive suffixes: -ito / -ita (the most common), -ico / -ica, -illo / -illa, and -ín / -ina.

REGULAR DIMINUTIVES

Words of two or more syllables that end with an unaccented vowel.	Eliminate the final vowel and add -ito(a): gatito
Words of two or more syllables that end with a consonant other than -n or -r.	Add -ito(a): animalito

IRREGULAR DIMINUTIVES

Monosyllabic words.	Add -ecito(a): florecita Exception: pie → piececito
Words of two or more syllables that end with an accented vowel.	Add -cito(a): cafecito Exception: papá → papaíto, papito; mamá → mamaíta, mamita
Words of two or more syllables that end with -e, -n, or -r.	Add -cito(a): cochecito

Prepositions

Prepositions of place

en	*at, in, on, inside* (to express location)	de	*from* (to express origin)
a	*to* (after the verb *ir* indicating destination)	desde... hasta de... a	*from … to* (to express direction or destination)

The personal *a*

The preposition a works like a marker before certain direct objects:

direct objects referring to a definite or specific person or people, or a definite pet
direct object pronouns referring to people, such as alguien, nadie, alguno, ninguno, or todos

Prepositions *por* and *para*

Por and *para* can usually be translated as *for* in English.

Uses of *por*		Uses of *para*
«in exchange for»	approximate time	deadline
ratio, proportion, «per»	approximate place	purpose
mode of communication	time periods during the day	opinion
mode of transportation	cause or reason	movement toward a place
«on behalf of»	movement within an area	recipient of an action
object of an errand	agent of an action	comparison, «considering»

Verbs with prepositions

Many verbs require a complement that is introduced by a preposition.

Verbs with *a*	Verbs with *con*	Verbs with *de*	Verbs with *en*
acostumbrarse a to get used to	amenazar con to threaten to	acordarse de to remember	confiar en to trust
asistir a to attend	casarse con to marry	alegrarse de to be pleased to	consistir en to consist of
atreverse a to dare	contar con to count on	darse cuenta de to realize	fijarse en to notice
ayudar a to help	enojarse con to get mad at	depender de to depend on	insistir en to insist on
renunciar a to give up	soñar con to dream of	despedirse de to say good-bye to	pensar en to think about

Some verbs that require a preposition in English are used without a preposition in Spanish when they refer to a thing: agradecer (*to be grateful for*), buscar (*to look for*), escuchar (*to listen to*), esperar (*to wait for*), mirar (*to look at*), pedir (*to ask for*): Busco un libro. Busco a Juan.

Interrogatives

Interrogatives are words that are used to ask questions. Normally, interrogatives go at the beginning of a sentence.

¿Qué? What?	¿Cuál(es)? Which?	¿Cuánto(a)? How much?	¿Por qué? Why?	¿Cómo? How?	¿Adónde? Where to?
¿Quién(es)? Who?	¿Cuándo? When?	¿Cuántos(as)? How many?	¿Para qué? What for?	¿Dónde? Where?	¿De dónde? Where from?

Relative pronouns

Relative pronouns introduce clauses that give information about a noun.
Unlike in English, relative pronouns are not omitted in spoken Spanish.

que *that*	Used for people and things.
quien, quienes *who*	Used only for people.
el que, la que, los que, las que *which, the one(s) that*	Used when the adjective clause starts with a preposition, especially when the relative pronoun refers to a person; when the adjective clause is at the beginning of the sentence; or when the relative pronoun refers to a noun that has been omitted.

Use the indicative to describe someone or something that exists
or is known: Conozco a un chico que habla seis idiomas.

Use the subjuntive to describe someone or something that doesn't exist,
is unknown, or whose existence is in question: No hay ningún celular que
funcione con energía solar. Necesito una casa que tenga jardín. ¿Hay algo
que no entiendas?

Verbs

Verbs are words that express actions and events, and place them in time
(past, present, and future). Spanish verbs fall into three conjugations:
-ar (*hablar, estudiar...*), -er (*aprender, comer...*), and -ir (*vivir, subir...*).

The infinitive

1st conjugation: -ar	comprar, hablar, estudiar...
2nd conjugation: -er	comer, tener, vender...
3rd conjugation: -ir	abrir, pedir, escribir...

The present participle

The present participle (gerundio) is formed by adding the following endings
to the verb stem:

-ando for -ar verbs	lavar → lavando
-iendo for -er, -ir verbs	hacer → haciendo escribir → escribiendo

Irregular present participle forms

e > i		o > u
decir → diciendo	servir → sirviendo	dormir → durmiendo
medir → midiendo	vestir → vistiendo	morir → muriendo
pedir → pidiendo		poder → pudiendo

The past participle

The past participle (participio) of a verb can be used as an adjective to describe a noun. In addition, the past participle is used with the verb estar to express the state or condition of a subject as a result of a previous action:

Luis hizo las tareas. Las tareas están hechas.

The past participle has two uses in verb formations:

- With the auxiliary verb haber to form the perfect tenses: the present perfect, the past perfect, etc. In this case, the participle always ends in -o.
- With the auxiliary verb ser to form the passive voice. In this case, the participle agrees in gender and number with the subject.

Regular past participle forms

-ar verbs	Add the ending -ado to the verb stem.	pintar → pintado
-er and -ir verbs	Add the ending -ido to the verb stem.	vestir → vestido

Irregular past participle forms

abrir → abierto	escribir → escrito	resolver → resuelto
cubrir → cubierto	hacer → hecho	romper → roto
decir → dicho	morir → muerto	ver → visto
descubrir → descubierto	poner → puesto	volver → vuelto

The present tense

We use verbs in the present tense in these situations:

- To talk about actions and situations that are occurring while you are speaking.
- To describe repeating routines or actions.
- To describe constant situations or make statements of a general nature.
- To present past occurrences as though they were current.
- To talk about schedules and planned or foreseen future events.

Regular verbs (-ar, -er, -ir)

		Comprar (to buy)	Vender (to sell)	Abrir (to open)
Singular	yo	compro	vendo	abro
	tú	compras	vendes	abres
	usted él, ella	compra	vende	abre
Plural	nosotros(as)	compramos	vendemos	abrimos
	vosotros(as)	compráis	vendéis	abrís
	ustedes ellos(as)	compran	venden	abren

Stem-changing verbs

		Cerrar (e > ie) *(to close)*	Poder (o > ue) *(can, to be able)*	Pedir (e > i) *(to ask)*	Adquirir (e > ie) *(to acquire)*	Jugar (u > ue) *(to play)*
Singular	yo	cierro	puedo	pido	adquiero	juego
	tú	cierras	puedes	pides	adquieres	juegas
	usted él, ella	cierra	puede	pide	adquiere	juega
Plural	nosotros(as)	cerramos	podemos	pedimos	adquirimos	jugamos
	vosotros(as)	cerráis	podéis	pedís	adquirís	jugáis
	ustedes ellos(as)	cierran	pueden	piden	adquieren	juegan

Verbs with irregular yo forms

		Dar *(to give)*	Conocer[1] *(to know)*	Hacer *(to do)*	Poner *(to put)*	Saber *(to know)*	Traer[2] *(to bring)*	Ver *(to see)*	Salir *(to leave)*
Singular	yo	doy	conozco	hago	pongo	sé	traigo	veo	salgo
	tú	das	conoces	haces	pones	sabes	traes	ves	sales
	usted él, ella	da	conoce	hace	pone	sabe	trae	ve	sale
Plural	nosotros(as)	damos	conocemos	hacemos	ponemos	sabemos	traemos	vemos	salimos
	vosotros(as)	dais	conocéis	hacéis	ponéis	sabéis	traéis	veis	salís
	ustedes ellos(as)	dan	conocen	hacen	ponen	saben	traen	ven	salen

[1] In general, verbs ending in -ecer and -ucir add a z in the yo form like conocer (parecer: yo parezco; traducir: yo traduzco).

[2] The verb caer is conjugated like traer (yo caigo).

Verbs *ser* and *estar*

Ser *(to be)*			
Singular		**Plural**	
yo	soy	nosotros(as)	somos
tú	eres	vosotros(as)	sois
usted él, ella	es	ustedes ellos(as)	son

Estar *(to be)*			
Singular		**Plural**	
yo	estoy	nosotros(as)	estamos
tú	estás	vosotros(as)	estáis
usted él, ella	está	ustedes ellos(as)	están

- Use ser to identify people, places, and things, and to describe physical characteristics and personality traits: La señora Flores **es** mi profesora. Ella **es** muy inteligente.

  Additionally, the verb ser is used in Spanish to express dates and times, possession, location of events, price, material, mathematical equations, and purpose or function (used with para).

- Use estar to express feelings and conditions or when talking about the result of a process: Ellos **están** tristes porque **están** enfermos. Luis **está** muy guapo con esa camisa.

  In addition, the verb estar is used in Spanish to express state, with bien and mal, in progressive tenses, and in idiomatic expressions with de.

Many adjectives change meaning when they are used with ser or with estar.

	Ser	Estar		Ser	Estar		Ser	Estar
atento(a)	courteous	alert	malo(a)	bad	sick, ill	seguro(a)	safe	sure, certain
callado(a)	reserved	quiet	orgulloso(a)	arrogant	proud	verde	green	unripe
listo(a)	smart	ready	rico(a)	rich	delicious	vivo(a)	bright, sharp	alive

The verb ir

- To say where someone is going, use ir a + *place*.
- To express intention or future plans, use ir a + *infinitive*.

Ir *(to go)*			
Singular		Plural	
yo	voy	nosotros(as)	vamos
tú	vas	vosotros(as)	vais
usted él, ella	va	ustedes ellos(as)	van

The verb haber

- To say that someone or something exists or to ask about the existence of something, use the form hay (*there is, there are*).
- To make recommendations and to express obligation and necessity, use these structures:

hay que + infinitive	tener que + infinitive	deber + infinitive

Verbs like *gustar* (a mí me...)

Many verbs that express likes, interests, feelings, and emotions follow the same pattern as the verb gustar: they are generally conjugated in the third person (singular or plural), with an indirect object pronoun: me, te, le, nos, os, les.

Gustar *(to like)*		
	Singular	Plural
(A mí)	me **gusta**	me **gustan**
(A ti)	te **gusta**	te **gustan**
(A usted) (A él/a ella)	le **gusta**	le **gustan**
(A nosotros/as)	nos **gusta**	nos **gustan**
(A vosotros/as)	os **gusta**	os **gustan**
(A ustedes) (A ellos/a ellas)	les **gusta**	les **gustan**

Verbs like *gustar*		
aburrir	divertir	fascinar
alegrar	doler	importar
apetecer	emocionar	interesar
asustar	encantar	molestar
caer bien / mal	enfadar	parecer
dar miedo	enojar	preocupar
dar pena	extrañar	sorprender
deprimir		

Pronominal verbs

Pronominal verbs (arrepentirse, atreverse, enterarse, quejarse, etc.) are conjugated with a reflexive pronoun: me, te, se, nos, os, se. The pronoun agrees with the subject: ¿Tú te atreves?

Peinarse (to comb one's hair)			
Singular		**Plural**	
yo	me **pein**o	nosotros(as)	nos **pein**amos
tú	te **pein**as	vosotros(as)	os **pein**áis
usted él, ella	se **pein**a	ustedes ellos(as)	se **pein**an

Verbs with changes in meaning							
acabar *to finish*	acabarse *to end, to run out*	ir *to go*	irse *to leave, to go away*	quedar *to arrange to meet*	quedarse *to stay*
acordar *to agree*	acordarse *to remember*	levantar *to lift*	levantarse *to get up*	romper *to break something*	romperse *to get broken*
aprender *to learn*	aprenderse *to memorize*	parecer *to seem*	parecerse *to look like*	salir *to leave, to go out*	salirse *to go beyond the limits*
dormir *to sleep*	dormirse *to fall asleep*	poner *to put*	ponerse *to put on*	volver *to come back*	volverse *to turn*
estudiar *to study*	estudiarse *to learn*				

Reflexive verbs

Reflexive verbs (acostarse, lavarse, levantarse, maquillarse, vestirse, etc.) are pronominal verbs that express an action that is reflected back onto the subject.

Reciprocal verbs

Reciprocal verbs (abrazarse, ayudarse, besarse, conocerse, escribirse, hablarse, llamarse, mirarse, pelearse, perdonarse, quererse, saludarse, verse, etc.) are pronominal verbs that express reciprocal actions. They are conjugated like reflexive verbs, but always in the plural: ¡Abrácense y perdónense!

The present perfect

The present perfect (presente perfecto) is equivalent to *have + past participle*. Use the present perfect tense:

- To describe actions that already happened at the time we consider to be the present: He vivido en esta casa toda mi vida.
- To describe actions that have recently ended: He llegado hace un minuto.

Hablar (to speak)			
Singular		**Plural**	
yo	he **hablado**	nosotros(as)	hemos **hablado**
tú	has **hablado**	vosotros(as)	habéis **hablado**
usted él, ella	ha **hablado**	ustedes ellos(as)	han **hablado**

The preterite tense

Use the preterite tense to talk about past actions presented as completed, without mentioning the duration.

		Comprar (to buy)	Comer (to eat)	Escribir (to write)
Singular	yo	compré	comí	escribí
	tú	compraste	comiste	escribiste
	usted él, ella	compró	comió	escribió
Plural	nosotros(as)	compramos	comimos	escribimos
	vosotros(as)	comprasteis	comisteis	escribisteis
	ustedes ellos(as)	compraron	comieron	escribieron

Verbs ending in -car, -gar, and -zar require a spelling change in the yo form of the preterite tense: buscar → yo busqué; llegar → yo llegué; empezar → yo empecé.

Irregular verbs: *ser, ir, decir, tener, estar, hacer,* and *traer*

		Ser (to be), ir (to go)	Decir (to say)	Tener (to have)	Estar (to be)	Hacer (to make, to do)	Traer (to bring)
Singular	yo	fui	dije	tuve	estuve	hice	traje
	tú	fuiste	dijiste	tuviste	estuviste	hiciste	trajiste
	usted él, ella	fue	dijo	tuvo	estuvo	hizo	trajo
Plural	nosotros(as)	fuimos	dijimos	tuvimos	estuvimos	hicimos	trajimos
	vosotros(as)	fuisteis	dijisteis	tuvisteis	estuvisteis	hicisteis	trajisteis
	ustedes ellos(as)	fueron	dijeron	tuvieron	estuvieron	hicieron	trajeron

Irregular verbs: *pedir* and *dormir*

In Spanish, -ir verbs that are e > i stem-changing in the present tense (pedir > pido) have the same change in the third person of the preterite tense.

The verbs dormir and morir are also irregular in the third person (o > u).

		Pedir (to ask)	Dormir (to sleep)
Singular	yo	pedí	dormí
	tú	pediste	dormiste
	usted él, ella	pidió	durmió
Plural	nosotros(as)	pedimos	dormimos
	vosotros(as)	pedisteis	dormisteis
	ustedes ellos(as)	pidieron	durmieron

Irregular verbs: *dar, poder, poner, querer, saber,* and *venir*

		Dar (to give)	Poder (to be able)	Poner (to put)	Querer (to want)	Saber (to know)	Venir (to come)
Singular	yo	di	pude	puse	quise	supe	vine
	tú	diste	pudiste	pusiste	quisiste	supiste	viniste
	usted él, ella	dio	pudo	puso	quiso	supo	vino
Plural	nosotros(as)	dimos	pudimos	pusimos	quisimos	supimos	vinimos
	vosotros(as)	disteis	pudisteis	pusisteis	quisisteis	supisteis	vinisteis
	ustedes ellos(as)	dieron	pudieron	pusieron	quisieron	supieron	vinieron

The imperfect tense

Use the imperfect tense:
- To talk about habitual actions or actions that happened repeatedly in the past.
- To talk about past actions as actions that lasted an undetermined amount of time, without mentioning their end.
- To describe characters and setting, and to explain the circumstances surrounding an event.
- To make a polite request.

		Viajar (to travel)	Volver (to return)	Salir (to leave)
Singular	yo	viajaba	volvía	salía
	tú	viajabas	volvías	salías
	usted él, ella	viajaba	volvía	salía
Plural	nosotros(as)	viajábamos	volvíamos	salíamos
	vosotros(as)	viajabais	volvíais	salíais
	ustedes ellos(as)	viajaban	volvían	salían

Irregular verbs

		Ser (to be)	Ir (to go)	Ver (to see)
Singular	yo	era	iba	veía
	tú	eras	ibas	veías
	usted él, ella	era	iba	veía
Plural	nosotros(as)	éramos	íbamos	veíamos
	vosotros(as)	erais	ibais	veíais
	ustedes ellos(as)	eran	iban	veían

The past perfect

Use the past perfect (pluscuamperfecto) to describe an action that was completed before another action in the past: Cuando él llegó, María ya se había ido.

Hablar *(to speak)*			
Singular		**Plural**	
yo	había **habl**ado	nosotros(as)	habíamos **habl**ado
tú	habías **habl**ado	vosotros(as)	habíais **habl**ado
usted él, ella	había **habl**ado	ustedes ellos(as)	habían **habl**ado

The future

Use the future tense to talk about things that will happen in the future.

The future tense is also sometimes used idiomatically in Spanish to express conjecture or probability in the present.

		Entrar *(to come in)*	Comer *(to eat)*	Seguir *(to follow)*
Singular	yo	entrar**é**	comer**é**	seguir**é**
	tú	entrar**ás**	comer**ás**	seguir**ás**
	usted él, ella	entrar**á**	comer**á**	seguir**á**
Plural	nosotros(as)	entrar**emos**	comer**emos**	seguir**emos**
	vosotros(as)	entrar**éis**	comer**éis**	seguir**éis**
	ustedes ellos(as)	entrar**án**	comer**án**	seguir**án**

Irregular verbs

poder → podr-	**tener** → tendr-	**decir** → dir-	**saber** → sabr-
poner → pondr-	**venir** → vendr-	**hacer** → har-	**haber** → habr-
salir → saldr-	**valer** → valdr-	**querer** → querr-	**caber** → cabr-

The future perfect

The future perfect (equivalent to *will have + past participle)* is used:

* To talk about an action that will be finished before a particular moment in the future: El martes ya habremos firmado la hipoteca.

- To talk about an action that will be finished before another future action: Cuando salgas del banco, ya habrás cobrado el cheque.

- To express probability in the recent past: Mario no ha llegado aún. Se habrá retrasado por el tráfico.

Comprar (to buy)			
Singular		Plural	
yo	habré **compr**ado	nosotros(as)	habremos **compr**ado
tú	habrás **compr**ado	vosotros(as)	habréis **compr**ado
usted él, ella	habrá **compr**ado	ustedes ellos(as)	habrán **compr**ado

The conditional

The conditional is used:

- To express wishes for the present or the future: Me gustaría ir a la fiesta.

- To give advice by putting yourself in the place of the other person: Yo no iría.

- To make polite requests: ¿Podrías prestarme un lápiz?

- To express probability in the past: Serían las cuatro de la tarde cuando llegó Mario.

- In conditional sentences, to express what would occur in the present if a condition had been met: Si hubiéramos acabado con la pobreza, ahora no existiría la injusticia social.

		Entrar (to come in)	Comer (to eat)	Seguir (to follow)
Singular	yo	entraría	comería	seguiría
	tú	entrarías	comerías	seguirías
	usted él, ella	entraría	comería	seguiría
Plural	nosotros(as)	entraríamos	comeríamos	seguiríamos
	vosotros(as)	entraríais	comeríais	seguiríais
	ustedes ellos(as)	entrarían	comerían	seguirían

Irregular verbs

poder → podr-	**tener** → tendr-	**decir** → dir-	**saber** → sabr-
poner → pondr-	**venir** → vendr-	**hacer** → har-	**haber** → habr-
salir → saldr-	**valer** → valdr-	**querer** → querr-	**caber** → cabr-

The conditional perfect

The conditional perfect is used:

- To express probability in the past: Eva habría llegado tarde al aeropuerto y por eso perdió el avión.
- In conditional sentences, to express what would have occurred in the past if a condition had been met: Si la policía no hubiera detenido a los terroristas, habrían cometido un atentado.

Viajar (to travel)			
Singular		**Plural**	
yo	habría **viaj**ado	nosotros(as)	habríamos **viaj**ado
tú	habrías **viaj**ado	vosotros(as)	habríais **viaj**ado
usted él, ella	habría **viaj**ado	ustedes ellos(as)	habrían **viaj**ado

The present subjunctive

Use the subjunctive to express wishes, feelings, emotions, or opinions, to express doubt or uncertainty, and to express value judgments.

		Cantar (to sing)	**Comer** (to eat)	**Vivir** (to live)
Singular	yo	cant**e**	com**a**	viv**a**
	tú	cant**es**	com**as**	viv**as**
	usted él, ella	cant**e**	com**a**	viv**a**
Plural	nosotros(as)	cant**emos**	com**amos**	viv**amos**
	vosotros(as)	cant**éis**	com**áis**	viv**áis**
	ustedes ellos(as)	cant**en**	com**an**	viv**an**

Verbs ending in -car, -gar, -zar, -ger, -gir, and -guir have spelling changes.

-car → -que: sacar → saque, saques…	-ger, -gir → -ja: dirigir → dirija, dirijas…
-gar → -gue: llegar → llegue, llegues…	-guir → -ga: seguir → siga, sigas…
-zar → -ce: abrazar → abrace, abraces…	

Irregular verbs

Irregular verbs in the yo form of the present indicative are also irregular in the present subjunctive.

yo hago → haga, hagas, haga…	yo tengo → tenga, tengas, tenga…
yo conozco → conozca, conozcas, conozca…	yo traigo → traiga, traigas, traiga…

Stem-changing verbs

		Pensar *(to think)*	Jugar *(to play)*	Volver *(to return)*	Pedir *(to ask)*	Dormir *(to sleep)*
Singular	yo	piense	juegue	vuelva	pida	duerma
	tú	pienses	juegues	vuelvas	pidas	duermas
	usted él, ella	piense	juegue	vuelva	pida	duerma
Plural	nosotros(as)	pensemos	juguemos	volvamos	pidamos	durmamos
	vosotros(as)	penséis	juguéis	volváis	pidáis	durmáis
	ustedes ellos(as)	piensen	jueguen	vuelvan	pidan	duerman

Irregular verbs: *dar, estar, saber, ser,* and *ir*

		Dar *(to give)*	Estar *(to be)*	Saber *(to know)*	Ser *(to be)*	Ir *(to go)*
Singular	yo	dé	esté	sepa	sea	vaya
	tú	des	estés	sepas	seas	vayas
	usted él, ella	dé	esté	sepa	sea	vaya
Plural	nosotros(as)	demos	estemos	sepamos	seamos	vayamos
	vosotros(as)	deis	estéis	sepáis	seáis	vayáis
	ustedes ellos(as)	den	estén	sepan	sean	vayan

The present perfect subjunctive

Use this tense in the same types of sentences in which you would use
the present subjunctive, when the action in the dependent clause
is presented as completed: Me alegro de que te hayas casado.

Cantar *(to sing)*			
Singular		Plural	
yo	haya **cant**ado	nosotros(as)	hayamos **cant**ado
tú	hayas **cant**ado	vosotros(as)	hayáis **cant**ado
usted él, ella	haya **cant**ado	ustedes ellos(as)	hayan **cant**ado

The imperfect subjunctive

Use this tense in the same situations in which you would use the present subjunctive when the verb in the main clause is in the past.

		Cantar (to sing)	Comer (to eat)	Vivir (to live)
Singular	yo	cantara	comiera	viviera
Singular	tú	cantaras	comieras	vivieras
Singular	usted él, ella	cantara	comiera	viviera
Plural	nosotros(as)	cantáramos	comiéramos	viviéramos
Plural	vosotros(as)	cantarais	comierais	vivierais
Plural	ustedes ellos(as)	cantaran	comieran	vivieran

If a verb is irregular in the preterite, it is also irregular in the imperfect subjunctive: No sabía que fueras abogado.

The past perfect subjunctive

The past perfect subjunctive is used to talk about conditions that were not completed in the past (hypothetical or contrary-to-fact conditions): Si hubiéramos ahorrado energía, ahora tendríamos más recursos.

Ayudar (to help)			
Singular		Plural	
yo	hubiera **ayud**ado	nosotros(as)	hubiéramos **ayud**ado
tú	hubieras **ayud**ado	vosotros(as)	hubierais **ayud**ado
usted él, ella	hubiera **ayud**ado	ustedes ellos(as)	hubieran **ayud**ado

Affirmative commands

We use affirmative commands to give orders or ask someone to do something. We use the nosotros(as) command to express what we have to do or to suggest something.

	Caminar (to walk)	Comer (to eat)	Escribir (to write)	
Singular	camina	come	escribe	tú
Singular	camine	coma	escriba	usted
Plural	caminemos	comamos	escribamos	nosotros(as)
Plural	caminad	comed	escribid	vosotros(as)
Plural	caminen	coman	escriban	ustedes

Irregular verbs: *tener*, *hacer*, *poner*, *venir*, and *salir*

	Tener (to have)	Hacer (to do, to make)	Poner (to put)	Venir (to come)	Salir (to leave)	
Singular	ten	haz	pon	ven	sal	tú
	tenga	haga	ponga	venga	salga	usted
Plural	tengamos	hagamos	pongamos	vengamos	salgamos	nosotros(as)
	tened	haced	poned	venid	salid	vosotros(as)
	tengan	hagan	pongan	vengan	salgan	ustedes

Irregular verbs: *ser*, *decir*, *ir*, and *dar*

	Ser (to be)	Decir (to say)	Ir (to go)	Dar (to give)	
Singular	sé	di	ve	da	tú
	sea	diga	vaya	dé	usted
Plural	seamos	digamos	vayamos	demos	nosotros(as)
	sed	decid	id	dad	vosotros(as)
	sean	digan	vayan	den	ustedes

Negative commands

Use negative commands when telling someone what not to do.

	Caminar (to walk)	Comer (to eat)	Escribir (to write)	
Singular	no camines	no comas	no escribas	tú
	no camine	no coma	no escriba	usted
Plural	no caminemos	no comamos	no escribamos	nosotros(as)
	no caminéis	no comáis	no escribáis	vosotros(as)
	no caminen	no coman	no escriban	ustedes

Irregular verbs: *dar*, *estar*, *ir*, and *ser*

	Dar (to give)	Estar (to be)	Ir (to go)	Ser (to be)	
Singular	no des	no estés	no vayas	no seas	tú
	no dé	no esté	no vaya	no sea	usted
Plural	no demos	no estemos	no vayamos	no seamos	nosotros(as)
	no déis	no estéis	no vayáis	no seáis	vosotros(as)
	no den	no estén	no vayan	no sean	ustedes

The passive voice

Use the passive voice to emphasize the receiver or product of an action rather than the performer:

> **Subject** (receiver) + **verb** (ser + past participle) + **agent** (with por)
>
> Esta pirámide fue construida por los mayas.

In Spanish, the passive voice with ser is less common than in English and is rarely used:

- With an indirect object.
- With progressive tenses.
- With verbs of perception (ver, oír, sentir...) or emotion (querer, odiar...).
- In instructions. In this case, use the construction se + verb in the 3rd person.

Progressive tenses

Progressive tenses are used to speak about past, present, or future actions that are in progress. Progressive tenses are formed with the verb estar and the present participle (gerundio) of a verb: Ahora María está leyendo y antes estaba haciendo la comida.

Lavar (to wash)			
Singular		Plural	
yo	estoy lavando	nosotros(as)	estamos lavando
tú	estás lavando	vosotros(as)	estáis lavando
usted él, ella	está lavando	ustedes ellos(as)	están lavando

In Spanish, the progressive tenses are not normally used with the verbs ir, venir, conocer, saber, or creer. And remember that to express future plans, we use the future tense or the expression ir a + infinitive, not the progressive tenses.

Sentence structures

Expressing probability

To express probability, we use various expressions that are generally accompanied by a clause in the indicative or in the subjunctive.

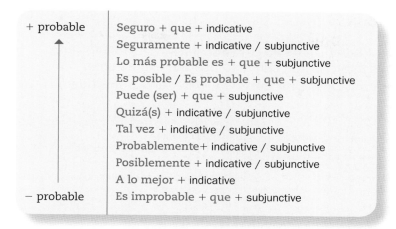

+ probable	Seguro + que + indicative
↑	Seguramente + indicative / subjunctive
	Lo más probable es + que + subjunctive
	Es posible / Es probable + que + subjunctive
	Puede (ser) + que + subjunctive
	Quizá(s) + indicative / subjunctive
	Tal vez + indicative / subjunctive
	Probablemente+ indicative / subjunctive
	Posiblemente + indicative / subjunctive
	A lo mejor + indicative
− probable	Es improbable + que + subjunctive

In addition, to express probability or conjecture, we can also use the structure deber de + *infinitive*, and the future and conditional tenses.

Expressing certainty and doubt

Verbs and expressions that indicate certainty generally require that the dependent clause be in the indicative when the sentence is affirmative.

Es verdad		Estar convencido(a)	+ de que + indicative
Es cierto		Estar seguro(a)	
Es evidente	+ que + indicative	Está claro	+ que + indicative
Es obvio		Está demostrado	
		Saber	

Verbs and expressions that indicate doubt require that the dependent clause be in the subjunctive when the sentence is affirmative.

Es dudoso		Es difícil creer	+ que + subjunctive
Es improbable		Parece mentira	
Es posible	+ que + subjunctive		
Es probable		Dudar	+ (de) que + subjunctive

The following negative expressions of certainty and doubt require a verb in the subjunctive.

No es verdad		No está claro	+ que + subjunctive
No es cierto		No está demostrado	
No es evidente			
No es obvio	+ que + subjunctive		
No es posible		No estar convencido(a)	+ de que + subjunctive
No es probable		No estar seguro(a)	

Expressing opinion

Use verbs like creer, opinar, parecer, pensar, suponer, considerar, imaginar, juzgar, or parecer. You can also use the expressions En mi opinión, Para mí, Desde mi punto de vista, and A mi juicio.

verb + que + indicative	When the verb in the main clause states an opinion in the affirmative: Creo que esta foto es bonita.
no + verb + que + subjunctive	When the verb in the main clause states an opinion in the negative: No creo que esta foto sea bonita.

Expressing value statements

To make value statements, you can use the following constructions:

Es aconsejable / conveniente... Es importante... Es necesario / preciso...	+ infinitive	In general affirmative or negative sentences when there is no subject stated: Es necesario restaurar el edificio.
Es bueno / malo... Es mejor / peor... Es sorprendente / fantástico / peligroso... Es un error / un problema / una tontería... Me parece + adverb / adjective / noun	+ que + subjunctive	When the dependent clause refers to a particular subject: Es una lástima que no podamos ir a la exposición.

Expressing wishes, likes, and preferences

Use verbs like gustar, apetecer, desear, preferir, etc.

verb + infinitive	When there is no subject change: Me gustaría ir a Cancún.
verb + que + subjunctive	When there are two subjects: Me gustaría que fuéramos a Cancún.

You can also use the formula ojalá (que) + *present subjunctive*.

Expressing feelings

Use verbs like alegrar, asustar, divertir, molestar, etc.

verb + infinitive	When the main clause and the dependent clause refer to the same person: Nos encanta jugar.
verb + que + subjunctive	When the main clause and the dependent clause refer to different people: Me molesta que hagas ruido.

Giving advice and making recommendations

To give advice and make recommendations, use these structures:

aconsejar animar a proponer recomendar sugerir	+ infinitive + que + subjunctive	Neutral advice and recommendations: El profesor nos aconsejó escribir una fábula.
deber (present or conditional) haber que (present or conditional) tener que (present or conditional)	+ infinitive	Advice and recommendations with an obligatory tone: Deberías ir al teatro.
Yo en tu lugar Yo que tú	+ conditional	Putting yourself in the other person's place: Yo en tu lugar centraría mi ensayo en los protagonistas del cuento.
command		No leas tan rápido. No te va a entender nadie.

Expressing location

Use donde, adonde, de / desde donde, or por donde.

donde adonde de / desde donde por donde	+ indicative	When the main clause refers to a known, definite, or real place: Fuimos de excursión por donde pasa el río.
	+ subjunctive	When the main clause refers to an unknown, indefinite, or hypothetical place: Prefiero comer en restaurantes donde no haya mucha gente.

Expressing time

Use the following structures:

cuando después de que siempre que en cuanto hasta que	+ indicative + subjunctive	Use the indicative when the main clause refers to past, present, or habitual events: Cuando usamos el transporte público, ahorramos energía. Use the subjunctive when the main clause refers to future events: Cuando usemos el transporte público, ahorraremos energía.
antes de que	+ subjunctive	Lee la etiqueta antes de que te vendan un producto químico.
al antes de después de	+ infinitive	Llámame por teléfono al llegar.

Expressing difficulty

We use the following structures:

aunque a pesar de (que) aun cuando pese a (que) por más / menos + (noun / adjective / adverb) + que	+ indicative + subjunctive	Use the indicative when the clause conveys *even though*: Aunque estaba ocupada, fue a votar. Use the subjunctive when the clause conveys *even if*: Aunque esté ocupada, irá a votar.
por mucho(a)(os)(as) + (noun) + que por muy + adjective / adverb + que	+ subjunctive	Por muchos problemas que tenga, él es optimista.
aun	+ present participle	Aun conociendo a los candidatos, no sé a quién votar.

Expressing condition

Use conditional sentences with **si** *(if)* clauses to express what could happen if some condition is met.

si + present indicative, present indicative / future indicative / command	To refer to real or likely conditions in either the present or the future: Si termino pronto las tareas, veré el partido en la televisión.
si + imperfect subjunctive, conditional	To express unlikely, hypothetical, or contrary-to-fact conditions in either the present or the future: Si terminara pronto las tareas, vería el partido en la televisión.
si + past perfect subjunctive, conditional	To express what would happen in the present if a condition had been met: Si hubiéramos acabado con la pobreza, ahora no existiría la injusticia social.
si + past perfect subjunctive, conditional perfect	To express what would have occurred in the past if a condition had been met: Si la policía no hubiera detenido a los terroristas, habrían cometido un atentado.

These expressions are also used to express condition:

con tal de que en caso de que a menos que a no ser que salvo que	+ subjunctive	Estoy dispuesto a viajar con tal de que me den el trabajo. No te entrevistarán a no ser que tengas dos cartas de recomendación.

Expressing purpose

Use the following structures:

para a a fin de con el propósito de	+ infinitive	When there is no subject change: Salí a tomar el sol.
	+ que + subjunctive	When there are two subjects: Traigo fotos para que las veas.

Expressing cause

We use the following structures:

porque ya que puesto que dado que debido a que como	+ indicative	No saldré porque tengo que estudiar. Puesto que nos gusta nadar, fuimos a un hotel con piscina. No pasé frío debido a que tenía saco de dormir. Como teníamos una reserva, nos pudimos quedar en el parador.
por	+ infinitive	Saldré por acompañarte.

Expressing consequence

We use the following structures:

así (es) que por eso en consecuencia por lo tanto por consiguiente tan + adjective / adverb + que tanto(a)(os)(as) + noun + que verb + tanto + que	+ indicative	Llovió mucho, así que se inundó la calle. Hubo un terremoto; por eso se derrumbaron varios edificios. Ha llovido y, por consiguiente, tenemos que cancelar la excursión. El viento es tan fuerte que dobla los árboles. Hay tanta niebla que no se ve nada. Ayer llovió tanto que se inundaron las calles.

Reported speech

To speak in reported speech (estilo indirecto), use a verb like decir, contar, or responder followed by que.

reporting verb + que + indicative	To relay information: El profesor dice que el examen es el viernes.
reporting verb + que + subjunctive	To relay a request or a command: El profesor dice que estudiemos para el examen.

With the verb preguntar, in indirect yes/no questions, use si instead of que:
El profesor me pregunta si estudiamos mucho.

In reported speech, it may be necessary to change the verb tense to match the moment of speaking: El profesor me dijo que había pocos errores en mis tareas.

GLOSARIO ESPAÑOL-INGLÉS

A

a *to* 1
a bordo de *on (board)* 254
a caballo *on horseback* 101
a cambio *in return* 190
a causa de *because of* 5
a comienzos de *at the beginning of* 342
a continuación *then, next* 47
a diario *daily* 50
a dieta *on a diet* 106
a diferencia de *unlike* 36
a favor (de) *in favor (of)* 157
a fin de (que) *so that, in order to* 262
a finales de *at the end of* 284
a fondo *in depth* 302
A la espera de sus noticias, le(s) saluda... *I look forward to hearing from you ...* 59
a lo largo de *throughout* 172
a lo lejos *in the distance* 24
a lo mejor *maybe* 196
a mano *by hand* 38 *handy* 117
a mediodía *at noon* 282
a menos que *unless* 164
a menudo *often* 194
a mi juicio *in my opinion* 320
a no ser que *unless* 164
a partir de *from* 166
a pesar de (que) *despite, although* 264
a pie *on foot* 221
a principios de *at the beginning of* 134
A propósito, *By the way,* 244
a punto de *about to, on the verge of* 204
a que *to* 262
¿A qué...? *What ... for?* 262
¿A qué se debe(n)...? *What's the reason for ...?* 218
a simple vista *at first sight* 222
a tiempo *on time* 10
a tiempo completo *full-time* 131
a tiempo parcial *part-time* 131
a través de *through* 29
a veces *sometimes* 194
abajo *below* 166
abandonado(a) *abandoned* 51
abandonar *to leave* 50
el **abaratamiento** *fall in price* 154
abastecerse con (irreg.) *to use* 153
abierto(a) *open* 138
el/la **abogado(a)** *attorney* 47
abogar por *to advocate* 217
abolir *to abolish* 248
abrazarse *to hug* 36
el **abrazo** *hug* 17
abreviar *to abbreviate* 69
la **abreviatura** *abbreviation* 66
abrir (irreg.) *to open* 28
abrir una cuenta *to open an account* 148
abrumado(a) *overwhelmed* 210
abrumador(a) *overwhelming* 110
abstenerse (irreg.) *to abstain* 260

abstracto(a) *abstract* 94
el/la **abuelo(a)** *grandfather/ grandmother* 162
los **abuelos** *grandparents* 6
la **abundancia** *abundance* 295
abundante *abundant* 117
abundar *to be abundant* 344
aburrido(a) *bored* 75 *boring* 188
el **aburrimiento** *boredom* 200
aburrir *to bore* 22
aburrirse *to get bored* 188
aburrirse como una ostra *to be bored stiff* 188
el **abuso de drogas** *drug abuse* 272
acabar *to finish, to end* 34 *to end up* 49
acabar con *to put an end to* 264
acabar de... *to have just ...* 11
acabarse *to end, to run out* 34
la **academia** *academy* 329
académico(a) *academic* 136
la **acampada** *camping* 139
acariciar *to caress* 336
acaso *perhaps* 336
acceder a *to have access to* 45
la **accesibilidad** *accessibility* 269
accesible *affordable* 217 *accessible* 345
el **acceso** *access* 7
accidentado(a) *eventful* 112
accidental *accidental* 80
el **accidente** *accident* 4
la **acción** *action* 2 *act* 272
Acción de Gracias *Thanksgiving* 74
accionar *to act* 268
el **aceite** *oil* 75
la **aceituna** *olive* 79
acelerar *to hurry* 211
el **acento** *accent* 278
acentuado(a) *stressed* 332
aceptable *acceptable* 280
aceptado(a) *accepted* 110
aceptar *to accept* 88
acerca de *about* 68
acercar *to bring closer* 1
acercarse *to come closer* 46 *to approach* 67
el **acero** *steel* 303
ácido(a) *acid* 106
aclarar *to clarify* 244
la **aclimatación** *acclimatization* 117
acoger *to welcome (into a home)* 59 *to receive* 155
la **acogida** *welcome, reception* 58
el **acogimiento** *welcome, reception* 59
acomodar *to place* 336
acomodarse *to make oneself comfortable* 38
el **acomodo** *place* 325
acompañado(a) *accompanied* 23
acompañar *to go with* 79 *to accompany* 100
aconsejable *advisable* 117
aconsejar *to advise* 91
acontecer (irreg.) *to happen* 336
el **acontecimiento** *event* 211
acordar (irreg. **ue**) *to agree* 34

acordarse (irreg. **ue**) *to remember* 34
acordarse de (irreg. **ue**) *to remember* 92
acostado(a) *lying down* 102
acostarse (irreg. **ue**) *to lie down* 36
acostumbrarse a *to get used to* 92
la **actitud** *attitude* 22
la **actividad** *activity* 3
el/la **activista** *activist* 243
activo(a) *active* 104
el **acto** *event* 125
el **actor** *actor* 25
la **actriz** *actress* 24
la **actuación** *performance* 186
actual *present, current* 1 *modern* 23
la **actualidad** *current situation* 1
actualizarse *to be updated* 230
actualmente *currently* 318
actuar *to perform* 192 *to act* 275
la **acuarela** *watercolor* 306
el **acuario** *aquarium* 139
acudir *to go* 256
el **acueducto** *aqueduct* 318
el **acuerdo** *agreement* 133
la **acumulación** *accumulation* 90
acusado(a) *marked, distinct* 127
acusar *to accuse* 127
la **adaptación** *adjustment, adaptation* 69
adaptado(a) *adapted* 5
adaptar(se) *to adjust, to adapt* 67
la **adecuación** *suitability* 296
adecuadamente *appropriately* 96
adecuado(a) *appropriate* 22
adelantar *to pass* 204
adelante *ahead* 130
Adelante. *Go on. (to encourage action)* 1
adelgazar *to lose weight* 92
además *also* 27
además de *as well as* 18
adicional *additional* 153
el **adiós** *goodbye* 109
adivinar *to guess* 61
el **adjetivo** *adjective* 24
adjetivo(a) *adjectival* 150
la **administración** *government* 125
administrar *to hold* 260 *to manage* 266
administrativo(a) *administrative* 169
el/la **administrativo(a)** *office worker* 133
admirar *to admire* 310
la **admisión** *admission* 183
admitido(a) *admitted* 170
admitir *to allow* 21 *to admit* 44
la **adolescencia** *adolescence* 103
el/la **adolescente** *adolescent* 96
adónde *where* 189
adoptar *to take* 97
adornar *to decorate* 19
el **adorno** *ornament* 101
adquirir (irreg. **ie**) *to acquire* 2
adulto(a) *adult* 103
el/la **adulto(a)** *adult* 69
adverbial *adverbial* 194

el **adverbio** *adverb* 48
advertir (irreg. **ie, i**) *to notice* 210
la **aeronáutica** *aeronautics* 312
el **aeropuerto** *airport* 189
el **afán de** *urge for* 215
afectar *to affect* 57
el **afecto** *affection* 21
la **afición** *hobby* 58
el/la **aficionado(a)** *fan* 49
aficionado(a) a *fond of* 85
la **afiliación** *affiliation* 106
la **afinidad** *affinity* 193
la **afirmación** *statement* 2 *affirmative statement* 322
afirmar *to say, to state* 69
afirmativamente *affirmatively* 239
afirmativo(a) *affirmative* 1
afligir *to afflict* 96
afortunadamente *fortunately* 38
afuera *outside* 337
agachado(a) *crouching* 102
la **agencia de viajes** *travel agency* 189
el **agente** *agent* 96
ágil *quick* 31 *agile* 345
agobiado(a) *overwhelmed* 211
agonizar *to be dying* 343
agradable *pleasant* 216
agradecer (irreg.) *to be grateful for, to thank* 92
agradecido(a) *grateful* 336
el **agradecimiento** *gratitude* 58
el **agravamiento** *worsening* 280
agregar *to add* 338
agresivo(a) *aggressive* 22
agrícola *agricultural* 173
el/la **agricultor(a)** *farmer* 281
la **agricultura ecológica** *ecological agriculture* 272
agrupado(a) *grouped* 330
el **agua** *water* 33
el **aguacate** *avocado* 78
agudo(a) *high-pitched* 53
ah *oh* 18
ahí *there* 25 *then* 268
ahora *now* 2
ahora mismo *right now* 63
el/la **ahorrador(a)** *saver* 156
ahorrar *to save* 148
el **ahorro** *saving* 156
el **ahorro energético** *energy savings* 272
el **aire** *air* 7
el **aire acondicionado** *air conditioning* 219
aislado(a) *isolated* 7
el **ajedrez** *chess* 189
ajeno(a) *of others* 278
ajustarse a *to fit in with* 325
al aire libre *in the open air* 22 *open-air* 193
al alcance *within reach* 91
al contado *cash (adjective)* 117
al contrario que *unlike* 306
al extranjero *abroad* 141
al fin *finally* 109
al final *at the end* 91 *in the end* 201
al frente *opposite* 200

al horno *baked* 78
al lado (de) *next (to)* 123
al menos *at least* 5
al pie de *at the foot of* 216
al principio *in the beginning* 87 *at first* 93
al revés *inside out* 36
la **alameda** *tree-lined avenue* 298
alargado(a) *long* 306
alargarse *to grow longer* 337
alarmante *alarming* 277
alarmarse *to be alarmed* 272
el **alba** *dawn* 33
la **alberca** *swimming pool* 56
albergar *to hold* 228
el **albergue (juvenil)** *(youth) hostel* 186
el **alboroto** *din* 211
el **alcalde** *mayor (man)* 104
la **alcaldesa** *mayor (woman)* 245
la **alcaldía** *city council* 278
alcanzar *to reach* 137 *to catch* 210 *to achieve* 345
el **alcatraz** *big yellow-flowered Mexican plant* 307
el **alcázar** *fortress* 229
el **alcohol** *alcohol* 96
alegrar *to make happy* 22
alegrarse *to be happy* 102
alegrarse de *to be glad to (followed by infinitive)* 16 *to be pleased to (followed by infinitive)* 92
alegre *happy* 111 *happy-go-lucky* 222
la **alegría** *happiness* 33
alejado(a) de *different from* 167
el **alejamiento** *growing apart* 67
la **alergia** *allergy* 58
alertar *to warn* 45
la **alfombra** *carpet* 222
la **algarabía** *din* 210
algo *something* 5 *anything* 26
alguien *someone* 16
algún, alguno(a) *any (in questions)* 19 *some* 48
alguna vez *ever (in questions)* 15
el/la **aliado(a)** *ally* 125
la **alianza** *alliance* 248
aliarse *to form an alliance* 247
la **alimentación** *food* 57 *diet* 122
alimentario(a) *food (adjective)* 125
alimenticio(a) *food (adjective)* 11
los **alimentos** *food* 72
los **alimentos transgénicos** *GM foods* 275
las **alitas de pollo** *chicken wings* 78
allá por... *some time around ...* 200
allí *there* 7
el **almacén** *store, shop* 207
almacenar *to store* 127
la **almendra** *almond* 112
el **almuerzo** *lunch* 86
el **alojamiento** *accommodation* 144
alojarse *to stay (at a hotel, etc.)* 7
alquilar *to rent* 10 *to hire* 216
el/la **alquimista** *alchemist* 350
alrededor (de) *around* 108
el **altavoz** *loudspeaker* 44

alterar *to upset* 211 *to alter* 220
la **alternativa** *alternative* 272
alternativo(a) *alternative* 275
el **altiplano** *high plateau* 147
alto(a) *high* 11 *tall* 221
la **altura** *position* 210 *height* 224
el **aluminio** *aluminum* 318
el/la **alumno(a)** *student* 63
la **alusión** *allusion* 345
la **amabilidad** *kindness* 278
amable *kind, nice* 17
amanecer *to dawn* 26
el/la **amante** *lover* 147
amar *to love* 198
amargo(a) *bitter* 76
amarillo(a) *yellow* 54
amarillo limón *lemon yellow* 303
ambicioso(a) *ambitious* 133
ambiental *environmental* 217
ambientar *to set* 230
el **ambiente** *atmosphere* 330
la **ambigüedad** *ambiguity* 116
el **ámbito** *sector (of economy)* 217
ambos(as) *both* 247
la **amenaza** *threat* 69
amenazar con *to threaten to (followed by infinitive)* 92
americano(a) *American* 285
amigable *friendly* 216
el/la **amigo(a)** *friend* 3
la **amistad** *friendship* 17
amistoso(a) *friendly* 17
el **amor** *love* 17
amoroso(a) *love (adjective)* 39
ampliar *to enlarge* 98 *to expand* 351
ampliarse *to expand* 329
amplio(a) *roomy* 7 *wide* 56 *extended* 91 *broad* 172
el **analfabetismo** *illiteracy* 272
el **análisis** *analysis* 127
el **análisis de sangre** *blood test* 75
analizar *to analyze* 68
anaranjado(a) *orange* 303
la **anatomía** *anatomy* 141
ancestral *age-old* 31
el/la **anciano(a)** *old person* 50
Anda, *Go on, (to encourage)* 100
el **andén** *platform* 189
andino(a) *Andean* 149
la **anécdota** *anecdote* 5
animado(a) *cheerful* 123
el **animal** *animal* 15
animar *to cheer up* 11 *to encourage* 132 *to drive, to motivate* 344
animarse *to cheer up* 192
anímico(a) *emotional (state, etc.)* 102
¡Ánimo! *Come on!* 186
el **aniversario** *birthday* 54 *anniversary* 125
anoche *last night* 86
el **anochecer** *dusk* 337
la **anomalía** *anomaly* 278
anónimo(a) *anonymous* 324
anormal *abnormal* 90
anotar *to note down* 27
la **ansiedad** *anxiety, nervous tension* 122

aumentar de peso   *to gain weight* 75

el **aumento**   *increase* 126

aún   *still* 14 *yet* 38

aun cuando   *even though* 264

aunar   *to combine* 344

aunque   *although* 264

la **ausencia**   *absence* 94

auténtico(a)   *genuine* 66 *real* 77

el **auto**   *car* 15

autobiográfico(a)   *autobiographical* 343

el **autobús**   *bus* 56

autóctono(a)   *indigenous* 193

la **autoevaluación**   *self-assessment* 65

el **autoferro**   *type of train* 203

automotor   *motor vehicle (adjective)* 153

automovilístico(a)   *car, automobile (adjective)* 152

la **autonomía**   *independence* 324

la **autopista**   *freeway* 204

el/la **autor(a)**   *author* 11 *creator* 26

la **autoridad**   *authority* 268

autoritario(a)   *authoritarian* 260

autorizar   *to authorize* 260

el **autorretrato**   *self-portrait* 307

auxiliar   *auxiliary* 138

la **avalancha**   *avalanche* 212

el **avance**   *advance* 98

avanzado(a)   *advanced* 114

avanzar   *to advance* 140 *to make progress* 141 *to move forward* 192 *to move on* 210

el **ave**   *bird* 163

la **avenida**   *avenue* 31

la **aventura**   *adventure* 108

avergonzado(a)   *embarrassed* 102

avergonzar (irreg. **ue**)   *to embarrass* 102

averiguar   *to find out* 14

el **avión**   *airplane* 63

avisar (a alguien)   *to let someone know* 164

ayer   *yesterday* 4

la **ayuda**   *help* 47 *aid* 98

ayudar   *to help* 1 *to assist* 90

ayudar a   *to help* 92

ayudarse   *to help each other* 36

el **ayuntamiento**   *city hall* 323

azotar   *to lash* 321

azteca   *Aztec* 248

el **azúcar**   *sugar* 77

azul   *blue* 35

el **bacalao**   *cod* 78

el/la **bachiller**   *high school graduate* 175

el **bachillerato**   *high school* 324

la **bahía**   *bay* 321

bailar   *to dance* 3

el **baile**   *dance* 11

la **bajada**   *descent* 139

bajar   *to download* 133 *to come down* 195 *to lower* 222 *to fall, to drop* 235

---

bajar de peso   *to lose weight* 11

bajo   *under 50 in* 267

bajo(a)   *low* 224

la **balanza**   *scale* 32

el **baloncesto**   *basketball* 170

balsámico(a)   *balsamic* 336

la **banana**   *banana* 172

bananero(a)   *banana (adjective)* 222

el **banano**   *banana tree* 172 *banana* 222

la **banca**   *banking* 156 *bench* 222

bancario(a)   *banking (adjective)* 156

el **banco**   *bank* 29 *bench* 50

la **banda**   *band* 192 *gang* 289

la **bandeja**   *tray* 121

la **bandera**   *flag* 61

el/la **banquero(a)**   *banker* 133

el **banquete**   *banquet* 254

el **bañador**   *swimming trunks* 56

bañarse   *to take a bath* 36

el **baño**   *bath* 7

el **bar**   *bar* 191

barato(a)   *cheap* 114

la **barba**   *beard* 17

la **barbacoa**   *barbecue* 219

el **barco**   *ship* 158 *boat* 193

la **barra**   *bar* 337

el **barrio**   *neighborhood* 58

el **barro**   *clay* 18

basado(a) en   *based on* 42

basarse (en)   *to be based on* 154 *to base one's argument on* 193

la **base**   *base* 143 *basis* 172

la **base de datos**   *database* 174

las **bases**   *rules* 67

básicamente   *basically* 157

básico(a)   *basic* 66

bastante   *quite* 48

bastante(s)   *enough, quite a few* 48

bastar   *to be enough* 325

la **batalla**   *battle* 210

el **batallón**   *battalion* 254

la **batería**   *battery* 53

el **bautizo**   *christening* 100

beber   *to drink* 76

la **bebida**   *drink* 10

la **beca**   *scholarship* 136

el/la **becario(a)**   *intern* 160

las **bellas artes**   *fine arts* 229

bello(a)   *beautiful* 39

beneficiar   *to benefit* 125

beneficiario(a)   *beneficiary* 125

beneficiarse   *to benefit* 126

el **beneficio**   *profit* 52 *benefit* 55

beneficioso(a)   *beneficial* 80

benéfico(a)   *charitable* 125

benigno(a)   *benign* 96

la **berenjena**   *eggplant* 78

besarse   *to kiss* 36

el **beso**   *kiss* 17

Besos.   *Love, (in letters)* 20

el **bestiario**   *bestiary* 50

la **bibliografía**   *bibliography* 286

bibliográfico(a)   *bibliographical* 344

la **biblioteca**   *library* 46

---

el/la **bibliotecario(a)**   *librarian* 328

la **bici**   *bicycle* 194

bien   *good* 7 *fine* 16 *well* 322

Bien pensado.   *Good thinking.* 258

los **bienes**   *goods* 148

el **bienestar**   *welfare* 114

la **bienvenida**   *welcome* 84

bienvenido(a)   *welcome* 300

el **bigote**   *mustache* 17

bilingüe   *bilingual* 183

el **billón**   *trillion* 154

el **biocombustible**   *biofuel* 173

la **bioconstrucción**   *green building* 156

la **biografía**   *biography* 223

biográfico(a)   *biographical* 253

la **Biología**   *biology* 133

el/la **biólogo(a)**   *biologist* 160

biomédico(a)   *biomedical* 89

bipolar   *bipolar* 295

la **bitácora**   *blog* 230

blanco(a)   *white* 20

blando(a)   *soft* 96

el **bloque**   *block* 174

bloquear   *to block* 224

el **bloqueo mental**   *mental block* 335

bobo(a)   *silly* 100

el **bocadillo**   *speech bubble* 33

el **boceto**   *sketch* 306

la **bocina**   *horn* 210

la **boda**   *wedding* 71

el **bol**   *bowl* 336

el **bolero**   *bolero* 226

el **boleto**   *ticket* 189

boliviano(a)   *Bolivian* 146

el **bolsillo**   *pocket* 108

el **bolso**   *purse* 21

la **bomba**   *bomb* 289

la **bombilla**   *light bulb* 76

bondadoso(a)   *kind* 20

bonito(a)   *pretty, nice* 19

el **bono**   *voucher* 67

el **borrador**   *draft* 95

el **botiquín**   *first-aid kit* 116

el **botón**   *button* 44

el **botones**   *bellman, bellhop* 216

el **brazo**   *arm* 5

breve   *short, brief* 25

brillante   *bright* 303

la **brisa**   *breeze* 216

la **broma**   *joke* 20

el **bronce**   *bronze* 222

bruñido(a)   *bright* 343

bruscamente   *suddenly* 336

brusco(a)   *sudden* 110

la **brutalidad**   *brutality* 351

bucear   *to scuba dive* 192

buen, bueno(a)   *good* 24

Buenas tardes   *Good afternoon* 30

Bueno,   *Well,* 20

el **bus**   *bus* 56

buscar   *to look for* 4 *to look up* 26 *to search for* 89

la **búsqueda**   *search* 68

la **butaca**   *seat* 212

el **buzón**   *mailbox* 32

C

el **caballo** *horse* 101
la **cabaña** *hut, cabin* 218
caber *to fit* 8
la **cabeza** *head* 75
cada *each* 9 *every* 194
cada vez más *more and more* 39
el **cadáver** *body, corpse* 267
la **cadena** *network* 44
caer (irreg.) *to fall* 19
caer bien/mal *to like/to dislike* 20
caer un chaparrón *to pour down* 216
caerse (irreg.) *to drop* 80 *to fall* 119
el **café** *coffee* 172 *café* 203
la **cafetera** *coffee maker* 7
la **cafetería** *cafeteria* 323
la **caja** *box* 19
la **caja de seguridad** *safe-deposit box* 219
el **cajero** *ATM* 289
la **calabacita** *squash* 78
la **calabaza** *pumpkin* 76
el **calcio** *calcium* 173
calcular *to calculate* 96
el **caldo** *broth* 336
el **calendario** *calendar* 134
la **calidad** *quality* 81
cálido(a) *warm* 220
caliente *hot* 76 *warm* 222
calificar *to describe* 261
calificativo(a) *qualifying* 24
callado(a) *quiet* 106 *reserved* 106
callar *to be quiet* 100
la **calle** *street* 6
calmar *to soothe* 92
el **calor** *heat* 8 *warmth* 210
caluroso(a) *hot* 216
calvo(a) *bald* 17
el **calzado** *footwear* 57
la **cama** *bed* 204
camaleónico(a) *chameleon-like* 345
la **cámara** *camera* 54
cambiar *to change* 11
el **cambio** *change* 2 *exchange* 116
caminar *to walk* 7
la **caminata** *hike* 220
el **camino** *path* 31 *way* 50
el **camión** *bus* 56
la **camisa** *shirt* 36
la **camiseta** *T-shirt* 56
el **campanario** *belfry* 323
la **campaña** *campaign* 99
la **campaña electoral** *electoral campaign* 260
el/la **campesino(a)** *peasant* 40
el **cámping** *camping* 5 *campground* 216
el **campo** *field* 40 *country* 80
la **cana** *gray hair* 20
el **canal** *channel* 44 *canal* 129
canario(a) *Canary (adjective)* 42
la **cancelación** *cancellation* 218
cancelar *to cancel* 220
el **cáncer** *cancer* 8

cancerígeno(a) *carcinogenic* 96
canceroso(a) *cancerous* 96
la **canción** *song* 14
el/la **candidato(a)** *candidate* 260
la **candidatura** *candidacy* 43
la **canela** *cinnamon* 78
el **cangrejo** *crab* 78
la **canoa** *canoe* 216
cansado(a) *tired* 34
cansarse *to get tired* 249
el/la **cantante** *singer* 54
cantar *to sing* 18
la **cantidad** *quantity, amount* 31 *number* 79
el **canto** *singing* 170
la **caña** *straw* 84
la **caña de azúcar** *sugar cane* 172
el **caos** *chaos* 211
caótico(a) *chaotic* 212
la **capacidad** *ability* 43 *skill* 103 *capacity* 323
capaz de *able to* 6
el **capital** *capital* 154
la **capital** *capital* 2
el **capítulo** *chapter* 50
captar *to detect, to grasp* 66 *to grab* 231
la **cara** *face* 20
el **carácter** *nature* 156 *personality* 330
la **característica** *feature* 20
característico(a) *characteristic* 23
caracterizado(a) *characterized* 50
caracterizar *to portray* 230
caracterizarse por *to be characterized by* 230
el **caramelo** *sweet* 117
la **caravana** *camper* 216
el **carbón** *coal* 37
cardinal *cardinal* 250
el/la **cardiólogo(a)** *cardiologist* 90
carecer de (irreg.) *to lack* 343
la **carencia** *lack* 280
el **cargo** *post, position* 94
caribeño(a) *Caribbean* 226
la **caricia** *caress* 343
cariñoso(a) *affectionate* 17
carmesí *crimson* 336
la **carne** *meat* 75
la **carne de res** *beef* 75
el **carné de conducir** *driver's license* 174
caro(a) *expensive* 32
la **carrera** *race* 14 *university course* 165
la **carretera** *road* 234
la **carta** *letter* 32
la **carta de recomendación** *letter of recommendation* 160
el **cartel** *poster* 14 *sign* 38 *cartel* 275
la **cartera** *pocketbook* 275
el/la **cartero(a)** *mail carrier* 32
el **cartón** *cardboard* 19
la **casa** *home* 3 *house* 6
casarse con *to marry* 92
casi *almost* 20
casi nunca *hardly ever* 194
casi siempre *almost always* 194
la **casilla** *square* 192

el **caso** *case* 2
castaño(a) *chestnut, brown* 17
el **castellano** *Spanish (language)* 67
el **castillo** *castle* 221
la **casualidad** *coincidence* 192
el **catalán** *Catalan (language)* 67
catalán(a) *Catalan* 125
el **catálogo** *catalogue* 314
las **cataratas** *falls* 228
el **catarro** *cold* 75
la **catedral** *cathedral* 318
la **categoría** *category* 151
categorizarse *to be categorized* 212
católico(a) *Catholic* 26
el **caucho** *rubber* 56
la **causa** *cause* 96 *reason* 227
causar *to cause* 39
cazar *to hunt* 109
la **cazuela** *pot* 109
el/la **cebador(a)** *person who prepares a maté drink* 77
cebar *to prepare (maté)* 77
ceder *to hand over* 268
ceder el paso *to yield (when driving)* 204
la **celebración** *celebration* 5
celebrar *to celebrate* 14 *to hold* 31
celebrarse *to take place, to be held* 14
célebre *famous* 265
celoso(a) *jealous* 17
celta *Celt* 343
la **célula** *cell* 90
el **celular** *cell phone* 44
el **cemento** *cement* 318
la **cena** *dinner* 47
cenar *to have dinner* 8
el **censo** *census* 284
el **centavo** *cent* 106
centenario(a) *century-old* 31
centrado(a) en *centered on* 156
central *central* 19
centrar *to center* 89
centrarse en *to concentrate on, to focus on* 253
el **centro** *center* 57
el **centro comercial** *shopping mall* 37
el **centro de salud** *clinic* 114
el **centro urbano** *town center* 7
la **cerámica** *ceramics* 295
cerca *near* 58 *close* 210
cerca de *around* 38 *near* 58
cercano(a) *close* 167 *nearby* 203
el/la **cerdito(a)** *piglet* 339
el/la **cerdo(a)** *pork* 75
el **cereal** *cereal* 173
el **cerebro** *brain* 114
la **ceremonia** *ceremony* 85
la **cereza** *cherry* 78
cerrado(a) *closed* 210
cerrar (irreg. **ie**) *to close* 157
la **certeza** *certainty* 196
el **certificado(a)** *certified* 30
el **ceviche** *Peruvian dish consisting of raw fish marinated in lemon juice* 72
el **chachachá** *cha-cha* 227
el **champú** *shampoo* 36

la **charla** *talk* 72
charlar *to chat* 84
el **charro** *Mexican cowboy in traditional dress* 101
el/la **chasqui** *Inca messenger or courier* 12
los **chatinos** *fried plantain* 172
el **cheque** *check* 152
la **chica** *girl* 59
el **chicle** *chewing gum* 117
el **chico** *boy* 20
chicos *guys (when greeting)* 72
chileno(a) *Chilean* 134
chino(a) *Chinese* 157
el **chiste** *joke* 221
el **chivo** *goat* 343
el **chocolate** *chocolate* 85
el/la **chofer** *chauffeur* 200
el **chubasco** *downpour* 216
las **chuletas de cordero** *lamb chops* 78
la **cicatriz** *scar* 17
el **ciclo** *season* 47 *series* 88 *cycle* 102 *course* 165
ciego(a) *blind* 20
cielito *darling (term of endearment)* 23
la **ciencia** *science* 350
las **ciencias de la salud** *medical sciences* 312
científico(a) *scientific* 114
el/la **científico(a)** *scientist* 70
cientos *hundreds* 38
el **cierre** *closure* 338
cierto(a) *true* 2 *certain* 46
la **cifra** *figure* 212
el **cine** *cinema* 44
el **cinturón (de seguridad)** *safety belt* 189
el **circo** *circus* 188
la **circulación** *traffic* 204
circular *circular* 143 *to drive* 277
circulatorio(a) *circulatory* 90
el **Círculo Polar Ártico** *the Arctic Circle* 147
las **circunstancias** *circumstances* 6
la **ciruela** *plum* 78
la **cirugía** *surgery* 5
la **cita** *appointment* 92 *date* 93 *quote* 224
citado(a) *mentioned* 329
citar *to mention* 117 *to quote* 225
la **ciudad** *city, town* 24 *complex* 139
el/la **ciudadano(a)** *citizen* 114
cívico(a) *civic* 289
civil *civil* 159
la **civilización** *civilization* 4
claramente *clearly* 175
la **claridad** *clarity* 174
clarificar *to make clearer* 67
claro (que)... *of course ...* 8
claro(a) *clear* 96 *light* 303
la **clase** *class* 2
la **clase media** *middle class* 248
clásico(a) *classical* 38
clasificado(a) *classified* 160
clasificar *to classify* 7
la **cláusula** *clause* 80
la **clave** *key* 66

el/la **cliente(a)** *client* 38 *customer* 44
el **clima** *climate* 9
climático(a) *climatic* 224
la **clínica** *clinic* 117
el **club náutico** *yacht club* 106
cobarde *cowardly* 20
la **cobertura sanitaria** *health coverage* 114
la **cobertura wifi** *Wi-Fi connection* 7
cobrar *to cash (a check)* 152
el **cobre** *copper* 173
cocer (irreg. **ue**) *to boil* 108
el **coche** *car* 189
el **coche-cama** *sleeper car* 204
el **cocido** *stew* 138
la **cocina** *cuisine* 112 *cooking* 116
cocinado(a) *cooked* 172
cocinar *to cook* 73
el/la **cocinero(a)** *cook* 80
el **código** *code* 67
el **código postal** *ZIP code* 32
el **cognado** *cognate* 124
coherente *coherent* 294
la **coincidencia** *coincidence* 53
coincidir *to coincide* 26
coincidir en/en que *to agree on/ that ...* 183
la **cola** *rear* 222 *line* 266
la **colaboración** *collaboration* 143
el/la **colaborador(a)** *contributor* 69
colaborar *to collaborate* 68
colaborar en *to write for* 44 *to help with* 59 *to help in* 182
colaborativo(a) *collaborative* 67
la **colchoneta** *air mattress* 216
coleccionar *to collect* 189
el **colectivo** *bus* 56
colectivo(a) *collective* 86
el **colegio** *school* 67
el **cólera** *cholera* 342
el **colesterol** *cholesterol* 90
colgar (irreg. **ue**) *to hang* 19 *to put* 38 *to upload* 52
colocar *to put, to place* 5
colombiano(a) *Colombian* 54
la **colonia** *cologne* 91 *colony* 248
la **colonia de vacaciones** *summer camp* 266
colonial *colonial* 7
la **colonización** *colonization* 270
el/la **colono(a)** *colonist* 248
el **color** *color* 219
la **columna** *column* 318
el **columpio** *swing* 293
la **coma** *comma* 136
combatir *to combat* 268
combinar *to combine* 124
el **combustible** *fuel* 153
comentar *to discuss* 44 *to say, to remark* 108
el **comentario** *comment* 28
comenzar (irreg. **ie**) *to begin* 20
comer *to eat* 10
comer como una fiera/como una lima *to eat like a horse* 74
comercial *commercial* 91 *trade (adjective)* 150
comercializarse *to be sold* 125
el/la **comerciante** *vendor* 133

el **comercio** *trade* 148
el **comercio justo** *fair trade* 156
cometer *to commit* 274 *to make* 279
el **cómic** *comic (strip)* 122
cómico(a) *comic* 189
la **comida** *food* 5 *meal* 28 *dish* 79 *lunch* 86
el **comienzo** *beginning* 179
como *as* 2 *like* 7 *since, as* 218 *such as* 318
como consecuencia de *as a result of* 96
como dos gotas de agua *identical* 20
como una bestia *hard* 40
¿Cómo...? *How ... like?* 3 *How ... ?* 16
¿Cómo estás? *How are you?* 16
¿Cómo te va? *How are you doing?* 16
las **comodidades** *comforts* 216
cómodo(a) *comfortable* 102 *convenient* 214
el **compadre** *friend* 56
el/la **compañero(a) (de clase)** *classmate* 3
la **compañía** *company* 148
la **comparación** *comparison* 308
comparar *to compare* 17
comparativo(a) *comparative* 308
compartido(a) *shared* 325
el **compartimento** *compartment* 204
compartir *to share* 25
compatibilizar *to make compatible* 163
compensar *to compensate* 278
la **competencia** *competition* 31 *competence* 175
el/la **competidor(a)** *competitor* 31
competir (irreg. **i, i**) *to compete* 83
la **complejidad** *complexity* 43
complejo(a) *complex* 212
el **complemento** *complement* 92 *accessory* 197
el **complemento agente** *agent* 104
completamente *completely* 43
completar *to complete* 5
completo(a) *complete* 4
complicado(a) *complicated* 87
el **componente** *component* 96
el/la **componente** *member* 49
componer (irreg.) *to make up* 58 *to compose* 195
el **comportamiento** *behavior* 102
comportarse *to behave* 211
la **composición** *composition* 278
la **composición literaria** *literary work* 330
el/la **compositor(a)** *composer* 192
la **compra** *shopping* 3
comprar *to buy* 10
comprender *to understand* 44
comprensible *understandable* 117
la **comprensión** *understanding* 57 *comprehension* 66
comprensivo(a) *understanding* 17
comprobar (irreg. **ue**) *to check* 49
comprometerse *to commit* 260

el **despertador** *alarm clock* 6

despertar (irreg. **ie**) *to wake up* 26 *to awaken* 352

despertarse (irreg. **ie**) *to wake up* 34

el **desprecio** *contempt* 21

desprenderse de *to be drawn from* 109

la **desproporción** *disproportion* 307

después *then* 2 *later* 23 *after* 24

después de (que) *after* 276

destacable *notable* 343

destacado(a) *highlighted* 24 *prominent* 236

destacar *to highlight, to emphasize* 43 *to stand out* 306

destapar *to open* 83

destinado(a) *intended, aimed* 139

el/la **destinatario(a)** *addressee* 32

el **destino** *destination* 114 *destiny, fate* 329

la **destreza** *skill* 144

la **destrucción** *destruction* 155

destruir (irreg.) *to destroy* 96

desvelar *to reveal* 345

la **desventaja** *disadvantage* 105

detalladamente *in detail* 107

detallado(a) *detailed* 327

el **detalle** *detail* 38

la **detección** *detection* 96

detectar *to detect* 98

el/la **detective** *detective* 18

detener (irreg.) *to detain* 260

detenerse (irreg.) *to stop* 210

deteriorado(a) *damaged* 293

el **deterioro** *deterioration* 292

determinado(a) *definite* 94 *certain* 96 *specific* 124

determinar *to determine* 136 *to help determine* 261

detrás *back* 210

detrás de *behind* 11 *after* 22

la **devolución** *repayment* 148

devolver (irreg.) *to give back* 59 *to return* 127

el **día** *day* 2

el **día feriado** *holiday* 160

el **día festivo** *holiday* 24

la **diabetes** *diabetes* 90

el **diablo** *devil* 184

diagnosticar *to diagnose* 97

el **diagnóstico** *diagnosis* 75

el **diagrama** *diagram* 261

el **dialecto** *dialect* 67

dialogado(a) *dialogue (adjective)* 26

el **diálogo** *dialogue* 16

diariamente *daily* 194

el **diario** *newspaper* 45 *diary* 119

diario(a) *daily* 7

el/la **dibujante** *draftsman/ draftswoman* 351

dibujar *to draw* 41

el **dibujo** *drawing* 41

el **diccionario** *dictionary* 66

dicho(a) *said, aforementioned* 296

el/la **dictador(a)** *dictator* 260

la **dictadura** *dictatorship* 258

didáctico(a) *didactic* 116

diestro(a) *right-handed* 20

la **dieta** *diet* 11

la **diferencia** *difference* 19

diferenciado(a) *differentiated* 212

diferenciarse (de) *to stand out (from)* 175 *to be different (from)* 214

diferente *different* 69

diferentes *different* 17 *various* 22

difícil *difficult* 39

la **dificultad** *difficulty* 90 *disadvantage* 205 *problem* 264

dificultar *to hinder* 67

el/la **difunto(a)** *deceased* 113

la **difusión** *spreading* 325

digital *digital* 44

la **dignidad** *dignity* 156

diluido(a) *diluted* 306

la **dimensión** *dimension* 123

el **diminutivo** *diminutive* 332

la **dimisión** *resignation* 267

dinámico(a) *dynamic* 46

el **dinero** *money* 10

Dios *God* 40

el **diploma** *diploma* 165

el/la **diputado(a)** *representative* 244

la **dirección** *address* 32

directamente *directly* 37

directivo(a) *manager* 180

el/la **directivo(a)** *managerial* 180

directo(a) *direct* 36

el/la **director(a)** *director* 67 *principal* 134 *editor* 263

el/la **dirigente** *leader* 343

dirigir *to address* 40 *to direct* 89

dirigirse a *to head for* 47 *to address* 58

discapacitado(a) *disabled* 269

la **disciplina** *discipline* 142

el **disco** *record* 191

la **discoteca** *nightclub, disco* 188

la **discreción** *discretion* 325

discreto(a) *discreet* 343

la **discriminación** *discrimination* 272

discriminatorio(a) *discriminatory* 161

el **discurso** *speech* 265 *discourse* 268

la **discusión** *discussion* 325

discutir *to argue, to discuss* 44

el/la **diseñador(a) (de moda)** *(fashion) designer* 174

diseñar *to design* 10

el **diseño** *design* 65

disfrutar (de) *to enjoy* 45

disimular *to hide* 278

disminuir (irreg.) *to decrease* 11

disolver (irreg.) *to dissolve* 347

la **dispersión** *spreading* 97

disponer de (irreg.) *to have* 114

la **disponibilidad** *availability* 165

disponible *available* 216

la **disposición** *layout* 324

dispuesto(a) a *prepared to, willing to* 144

la **distancia** *distance* 31

distante *faraway* 31

la **distinción** *distinction* 324

distinguir *to distinguish* 57 *to make out* 302

distintivo(a) *distinctive* 324

distinto(a) *different* 134

distintos(as) *different* 24 *various* 31

distraer (irreg.) *to distract* 336

la **distribución** *distribution* 56

distribuir (irreg.) *to distribute* 125

el **distrito** *district* 31

la **diversidad** *diversity* 101

la **diversificación** *diversification* 312

diverso(a) *varied* 57

diversos(as) *various* 41

divertido(a) *fun, enjoyable* 17 *funny, amusing* 61

divertir (irreg. **ie, i**) *to entertain, to amuse* 22

divertirse (irreg. **ie, i**) *to enjoy oneself* 3

dividido(a) *divided* 204

dividir(se) *to divide* 204

la **divinidad** *divinity* 336

las **divisas** *foreign currency* 228

la **división** *division* 136

divorciado(a) *divorced* 59

divulgativo(a) *informative* 293

doblar *to bend* 220

doble *double* 216

el **doble** *double* 48

doblemente *doubly* 300

el/la **doctor(a)** *doctor* 59

el **documental** *documentary* 44

documentar *to document* 286

documentarse *to do research* 254

el **documento** *document* 174

el **dólar** *dollar* 106

la **dolencia** *ailment* 91

doler (irreg. **ue**) *to hurt* 22

el **dolor** *pain* 119

doméstico(a) *domestic* 59

dominar *to control* 279

dominicano(a) *Dominican* 153

el **dominio** *mastery* 38 *control, rule* 248

don *Mr.* 94

la **donación** *donation* 115

el/la **donante** *donor* 115

donar *to donate* 88 *to give* 122

donde *where* 6

dónde *where* 19

doña *Mrs.* 94

dorado(a) *golden* 222

dormido(a) *asleep* 336

dormir (irreg. **u, ue**) *to sleep* 34

dormirse (irreg. **u, ue**) *to fall asleep* 34

los **dos puntos** *colon* 136

las **dotes** *skills* 175

la **droga** *drug* 272

ducharse *to take a shower* 36

la **duda** *doubt, question* 58

dudar *to hesitate* 183 *to doubt* 246

dudoso(a) *doubtful* 252

dulce *sweet* 37

el **dulce** *sweet* 19

el **dulce de leche** *milk caramel* 77

duodécimo(a) *twelfth* 250

la **duquesa** *duchess* 309

la **duración** *duration* 263

durante *during* 23 *for* 40

durar to last 5
el **durazno** peach 78
durmiente sleeping 339
duro(a) hard 103

echar to mail 37 to add 76 to put 108
echar de menos to miss 14 to notice it's missing 117
echar en falta to notice it's missing 217
echar la culpa to blame 17
echar un vistazo a to have a quick look at 301
echar una ojeada a to take a quick look at 300
el **eco** echo 33
la **economía** economy 1 finances 177
económicamente economically 136 cheaply 221
económico(a) economic 9 cheap 79
el **ecosistema** ecosystem 296
el **ecoturismo** ecotourism 219
la **ecuación** equation 136
ecuatorial equatorial 172
la **edad** age 58
la **edición** edition 314
la **edificación** building 319
el **edificio** building 24
el **editorial** editorial 44
la **editorial** publisher 344
la **educación** education 9
educado(a) polite 58
educar to educate 177
educativo(a) educational 137
efectivamente exactly 186
efectivo(a) effective 89
el **efecto** effect 38
eficaz effective 38
eficiente efficient 133
egoísta selfish 17
el/la **egresado(a)** graduate 175
¿eh? OK? 41 isn't it? 330
el **eje** central idea 273
la **ejecución** execution, implementation 169
ejecutar to execute 260
ejecutivo(a) executive 67
el **ejemplar** copy 342
el **ejemplo** example 39
ejercer to practice 159
el **ejercicio** exercise 11
el **ejército** army 248
la **elaboración** preparation 67 manufacture 326
elaborar to prepare 77 to make 122 to develop 344
la **elección** choice 41 election 260
las **elecciones** elections 53
la **electricidad** electricity 323
eléctrico(a) electric 146
electrónico(a) e-mail (adjective) 33 electronic 148
el **elefante** elephant 332
elegante elegant 7
elegido(a) chosen 50

elegir (irreg. **i, i**) to choose 4 to elect 260
elemental pristine 337
el **elemento** element 49
eliminar to remove, to eliminate 69
el **elogio** praise 321
embarazada pregnant 102
el **emblema** emblem 61
emblemático(a) emblematic 342
las **emergencias** emergency (room) 116
el/la **emigrante** emigrant 284
la **emisión** emission 296
emitir to show, to broadcast 102 to issue 165
la **emoción** emotion 22 excitement 38
emocionado(a) excited 20
emocionante exciting 225
emocionar to thrill, to excite 22
la **empanada** pastry 139
empanar to bread 139
empaquetar to pack 50
empezar (irreg. **ie**) to begin 1
empleado(a) employed 68
el/la **empleado(a)** clerk 32 employee 138
emplear to use 21 to employ 158 to spend 208
el **empleo** job 114 employment 149
emprendedor(a) entrepeneurial 133
la **empresa** company 45
empresarial business (adjective) 180
el/la **empresario(a)** businessman/ businesswoman 133
en in 1 on 2 at 3 about 10
en cambio on the other hand 24
en caso de (que)... in case ... 164
en comparación con compared to 222
en común in common 76
en conclusión in conclusion 287
en concreto specific 231
en consecuencia consequently 220
en contra against 260
en cuanto as soon as 276
en cuanto a as regards 268
en cuestión in question 110
en curso in progress 46
en efecto indeed 109
en el extranjero abroad 58
en equipo as a team 177
en especial especially 150
en función de depending on 135
en general in general 94
en gran medida to a large extent 306
en grupo in a group 3
en la actualidad currently, nowadays 50
en lugar de instead of 57
en mal estado spoiled (food) 126
en mi opinión in my opinion 320
en nombre de on behalf of 248
en peligro at risk 45
en pleno(a) in the middle of 7
en prácticas intern 158

en realidad actually 231
en resumen in summary 287
en un periquete in a jiffy 302
en un pispás in a jiffy 302
en un principio at first 38
en un santiamén in a jiffy 302
el/la **enamorado(a)** lover 138
enamorado(a) (de) in love (with) 17
enamorarse (de) to fall in love 17
el **encabezado** heading 182
encabezar to lead 260
encajar to fit 27
encaminarse hacia to be aimed at 156
encantado(a) de que delighted that 14
encantador(a) charming, lovely 219
encantar to love, to really like 22
encarcelar to jail 260
encargado(a) de in charge of 217
encargar to commission 39
encargarse de to undertake, to take care of 18 to be in charge of 153
encender (irreg. **ie**) to turn on 295
encerrado(a) locked up 210
la **enciclopedia** encyclopedia 97
encima de on top of 108
encontrar (irreg. **ue**) to find 4
encontrarse (irreg. **ue**) to feel 48 to be 200 to meet 246
el **encuentro** meeting 200
la **encuesta** survey 3
encuestar to survey 86
endulzar to sweeten 336
energético(a) energy (adjective) 272
la **energía** energy 38
enfadado(a) angry (at each other) 37
enfadar to anger 22
enfadarse to get angry 46
el **enfado** anger 110
el **énfasis** emphasis 334
enfático(a) emphatic 310
enfatizar to emphasize 220
la **enfermedad** illness 90
la **enfermería** nurse's office 123
el/la **enfermero(a)** nurse 95
enfermo(a) ill 16
el/la **enfermo(a)** patient 88
el **enfoque** approach 281
el **enfrentamiento** confrontation 248
engañar to deceive 192
el **enigma** enigma 15
el **enlace** link 64
enlazar to link 238
enojado(a) angry 75
enojar to anger 22
enojarse con to get mad at 92
enorme huge 19
enriquecer (irreg.) to enrich 109
el **enriquecimiento** enrichment 317
enrojecer (irreg.) to blush 210
la **ensalada** salad 78
ensayar to rehearse 29
el/la **ensayista** essayist 329

el **ensayo** *essay* 330

enseguida *at once* 93 *very soon* 179

la **enseñanza** *lesson* 109 *teaching* 317 *education* 338

enseñar *to teach* 43 *to show* 145

entender (irreg. **ie**) *to understand* 66

entenderse (irreg. **ie**) *to understand each other* 36

enterarse (de) *to find out (about)* 34

entero(a) *whole* 249

la **entidad** *entity* 94 *organization* 125 *institution* 156

entonar *to sing* 54

entonces *then* 8

el **entorno** *environment* 268

la **entrada** *entry* 7 *ticket* 188 *admission* 326

entrar *to enter, to come in* 38

entre *between* 2 *among* 3 *divided by* 136

entregar *to deliver* 32 *to hand over* 84 *to award* 317

entrenar *to train* 75

entretenerse (irreg.) *to pass the time* 188

entretenido(a) *enjoyable, entertaining* 345

el **entretenimiento** *entertainment* 52

la **entrevista** *interview* 160

la **entrevista de trabajo** *job interview* 4

el/la **entrevistado(a)** *interviewee* 69

el/la **entrevistador(a)** *interviewer* 160

entrevistar *to interview* 45

enumerar *to list* 279

envejecer (irreg.) *to get old* 102

la **envergadura** *scale, extent* 272

enviar *to send* 32

envidiar *to envy* 39

envidioso(a) *envious* 20

el **envío** *shipment* 32

envolver (irreg.) *to wrap* 51

eólico(a) *wind (adjective)* 272

el **epígrafe** *heading* 155

el **episodio** *event* 230

la **época** *era* 77 *season* 193 *time* 253

equipado(a) *fitted* 7

el **equipaje** *baggage* 189

el **equipo** *team* 23

la **equivalencia** *equivalence* 264

equivalente *equivalent* 51

equivaler (irreg.) *to be equivalent* 140

la **equivocación** *mistake* 311

equivocarse *to make a mistake* 17

la **era** *age, era* 38

Érase una vez... *Once upon a time ...* 339

erróneo(a) *mistaken* 116

el **error** *mistake, error* 47

erudito(a) *erudite* 39

la **escala** *scale* 154

escalar *to climb* 192

la **escalera** *stairs* 254

los **escalofríos** *chills* 75

el **escape** *leak* 296

la **escasez** *shortage* 296

escaso(a) *scarce* 278

la **escena** *scene* 107

el **escenario** *stage* 190

la **escenografía** *set design* 170

la **esclavitud** *slavery* 248

escoger *to choose* 66

escolar *school (adjective)* 134

el/la **escolar** *schoolboy/schoolgirl* 13

esconder *to hide* 19

la **escopeta** *shotgun* 272

el/la **escribidor(a)** *writer* 343

escribir (irreg.) *to write* 3

escribirse (irreg.) *to write to each other* 36

el **escrito** *text* 174

escrito(a) *written* 30

el/la **escritor(a)** *writer* 33

la **escritura** *writing* 30

escuchar (a) *to listen (to)* 2

el **escudo** *shield* 61

la **escuela** *school* 11

esculpir *to sculpt* 318

el/la **escultor(a)** *sculptor* 308

escultórico(a) *sculptural* 318

la **escultura** *sculpture* 300

esencial *essential* 148

esforzarse (irreg. **ue**) *to make an effort* 136

el **esfuerzo** *effort* 159

el **esguince** *sprain* 90

el **eslogan** *slogan* 14

espacial *spatial* 268

el **espacio** *space* 50 *program* 52 *place* 200 *room* 233 *area* 236

espacio-temporal *space-time (adjective)* 343

la **espada** *sword* 351

la **espalda** *back* 31

el **español** *Spanish (language)* 1

español(a) *Spanish* 47

especial *special* 37

la **especialidad** *specialty* 115

el/la **especialista** *specialist* 90

la **especialización** *specialization* 155

especializado(a) *specialized* 115

especialmente *especially* 58

la **especie** *kind, sort* 30

especificar *to specify* 94

específico(a) *specific* 66

espectacular *spectacular* 93

el **espectáculo** *show* 188 *entertainment* 192

el/la **espectador(a)** *spectator* 285

especulativo(a) *speculative* 154

el **espejo** *mirror* 328

la **espera** *wait* 114

la **esperanza** *hope* 315

la **esperanza de vida** *life expectancy* 115

esperanzado(a) *hopeful* 102

esperar *to await* 1 *to hope* 24 *to expect* 38 *to wait for* 92

espigado(a) *slender* 343

las **espinacas** *spinach* 75

el **espíritu** *spirit* 168

espiritual *spiritual* 267

la **espiritualidad** *spirituality* 271

la **espontaneidad** *spontaneity* 278

espontáneo(a) *spontaneous* 96

la **esposa** *wife* 33

el **esposo** *husband* 11

el **esquema** *outline* 152 *diagram* 347

el **esquí** *skiing* 228

esquiar *to ski* 216

la **esquina** *corner* 343

la **estabilidad** *stability* 256

estable *stable* 2

establecer (irreg.) *to set* 66 *to establish* 130 *to formulate* 167 *to implement* 273

establecerse (irreg.) *to set up business* 173

el **establecimiento** *establishment* 91

la **estación** *station* 205

estacional *seasonal* 135

el **estacionamiento** *parking lot* 323

estacionar *to park* 204

la **estadística** *statistics* 142

el **estado** *state* 9

el **estado civil** *marital status* 161

el **estado de ánimo** *state of mind* 75

estadounidense *American, US* 52

el/la **estadounidense** *American* 237

la **estampilla** *stamp* 32

la **estancia** *stay* 58 *ranch* 336

estándar *standard* 203

el **estándar** *standard* 153

el **estaño** *tin* 173

estar (irreg.) *to be* 1

estar claro (que) *to be clear (that)* 252

estar conforme (con) *to be happy (with)* 263

estar convencido(a) (de que) *to be convinced (that)* 252

estar de acuerdo *to agree* 96

estar de buen/mal humor *to be in a good/bad mood* 102

estar demostrado (que) *to be a fact (that)* 252

estar mal visto *to be frowned upon* 84

estar para chuparse los dedos *to be absolutely delicious* 74

estar peleados(as) *to have fallen out* 39

estar presente *to be present* 116

estar seguro(a) (de que) *to be sure (that)* 252

estatal *state (adjective)* 260

la **estética** *aesthetic* 43

estilístico(a) *stylistic* 24

el **estilo** *style* 39

el **estilo de vida** *lifestyle* 195

la **estimación** *estimate* 296

estimado(a) *estimated* 229

Estimado(a)... *Dear ...* 59

estimarse *to be estimated* 144

el **estómago** *stomach* 95

estornudar *to sneeze* 75

la **estrategia** *strategy* 26

estrecho(a) *close* 154

la **estrella** *star* 19

el **estrés** *stress* 122

estresado(a) *stressed* 2

el **estribillo** *refrain* 192

estrictamente _strictly_ 325
estricto(a) _strict_ 20
la estrofa _verse, stanza_ 330
la estructura _structure_ 8
estructurado(a) _structured_ 166
estructurar _to structure_ 182
el estuco _stucco_ 320
el/la estudiante _student_ 48
estudiantil _student (adjective)_ 266
estudiar _to study_ 2
estudiarse _to learn_ 34
el estudio _study_ 45
los estudios _studies_ 47
estupendo _great (adverb)_ 29
estupendo(a) _great (adjective)_ 7
la etapa _stage_ 103
la eternidad _eternity_ 336
la etiqueta _label_ 173
la etnicidad _ethnicity_ 271
el eucalipto _eucalyptus_ 336
europeo(a) _European_ 19
el euskera _Basque (language)_ 67
evaluar _to evaluate, to assess_ 65
evangélico(a) _evangelical_ 336
la evaporación _evaporation_ 147
el evento _event_ 2
evidente _obvious, evident_ 252
evidentemente _obviously, evidently_ 197
evitar _to avoid_ 82 _to prevent_ 125
evocar _to recall_ 31
evolucionar _to develop_ 39
exactamente _exactly_ 80
la exactitud _precision_ 293
exacto(a) _precise, right_ 222
exagerado(a) _exaggerated_ 306
el examen _exam_ 2
el examen de ingreso _entrance exam_ 136
el examen final _final exam_ 136
el examen físico _physical examination_ 75
el examen parcial _midterm exam_ 136
examinar _to examine_ 95
examinarse _to take an exam_ 177
excavar _to excavate_ 245
excelente _excellent_ 11
excepcional _exceptional_ 43
excepto _except_ 82
excesivo(a) _excessive_ 45
el exceso _excess_ 207
excitante _exciting_ 50
exclamar _to exclaim_ 222
excluido(a) _excluded_ 155
exclusivo(a) _exclusive_ 7
la excursión _excursion, trip_ 65
excusarse _to excuse yourself_ 238
exigente _demanding_ 133
exigir _to demand_ 117
el/la exiliado(a) _exile_ 278
exiliar(se) _to exile (oneself)_ 260
el exilio _exile_ 258
existir _to exist_ 21
el éxito _success_ 192
exitoso(a) _successful_ 112
exótico(a) _exotic_ 158
expandir _to expand_ 217

la expedición _expedition_ 248
la experiencia _experience_ 23
la experiencia profesional _work experience_ 160
experimentar _to experience_ 80 _to undergo_ 280 _to experiment_ 321
el experimento _experiment_ 141
experto(a) _expert_ 87
el/la experto(a) _expert_ 122
la explicación _explanation_ 101
explicar _to explain_ 5
explicativo(a) _explanatory_ 326
el/la explorador(a) _explorer_ 245
explorar _to explore_ 193
la explotación _mining_ 296
la explotación petrolífera _oilfield_ 173
el exponente _exponent_ 335
exponer (irreg.) _to set out_ 157 _to explain_ 286 _to exhibit_ 303 _to present_ 352
la exportación _export_ 154
el/la exportador(a) _exporter_ 172
exportar _to export_ 148
la exposición _exhibition_ 80 _display_ 267 _presentation_ 344
expositivo(a) _explanatory_ 286
expresar _to express_ 10
la expresión _expression_ 16
la expresión idiomática _idiom_ 106
la expresión oral _oral skills_ 238
expreso(a) _express_ 203
extenderse (irreg. ie) _to spread_ 205
extendido(a) _widespread_ 101
la extensión _area_ 147
extenso(a) _large_ 228 _long_ 286 _extensive_ 325
exterior _outside_ 309
el exterior _foreign country_ 157 _outside_ 303
externo(a) _external_ 286
la extracción _mining_ 173
extractor(a) _extracting_ 173
extraer (irreg.) _to mine_ 146 _to extract_ 173
extranjero(a) _foreign_ 44
el/la extranjero(a) _foreigner_ 278
extrañar _to surprise_ 22
extraño(a) _strange_ 322
extraordinario(a) _extraordinary_ 204
la extremidad _limb_ 5
el extremo _end_ 306 _extreme_ 325
extremo(a) _extreme_ 195

F

la fábrica _factory_ 150
la fábrica de papel _paper mill_ 150
la fabricación _manufacture_ 146
fabricar _to make, to manufacture_ 148
la fábula _fable_ 330
fabuloso(a) _fabulous_ 99
la fachada _facade_ 318
fácil _easy_ 14
facilitar _to make possible_ 67 _to make easy_ 124 _to provide_ 166

fácilmente _easily_ 103
el factor _factor_ 115
la factura _bill_ 276
la facultad _faculty_ 317
la falda _skirt_ 94
fallar _to be wrong_ 224
fallido(a) _unsuccessful_ 314
falso(a) _false_ 2
la falta _lack_ 127
la falta de ortografía _spelling mistake_ 175
faltar _to be missing_ 28 _to lack_ 49 _to need_ 83
faltar a clase _to be absent (from class)_ 132
la fama _reputation_ 38 _fame_ 329
la familia _family_ 3
familiar _family (adjective)_ 11 _familiar_ 352
el/la familiar _relative_ 27
famoso(a) _famous_ 28
la fantasía _fantasy_ 50
el fantasma _ghost_ 222
fantástico(a) _fantastic_ 53
farmacéutico(a) _pharmaceutical_ 88
la farmacia _drugstore_ 91
la farmacia de guardia _pharmacy on duty_ 91
el fármaco _medicine, drug_ 97
fascinante _fascinating_ 14
fascinar _to fascinate_ 22
fatal _terrible, awful_ 322
la fauna _fauna_ 219
el favor _favor_ 343
favorable _favorable_ 174
favorecer (irreg.) _to help_ 105 _to favor_ 150
favorito(a) _favorite_ 65
la fe _faith_ 38
la fecha _date_ 94
la federación _federation_ 125
federal _federal_ 260
la felicidad _happiness_ 39
felicitar _to wish well (on birthday)_ 14 _to congratulate_ 58
feliz _happy_ 106
felizmente _luckily_ 343
femenino(a) _feminine_ 138
fenomenal _great, terrific_ 142
el fenómeno _phenomenon_ 57
la feria _fair_ 72
el feriado _holiday_ 203
el ferrocarril _railroad_ 184
el fervor _fervor_ 329
festejar _to celebrate_ 54
el festival _festival_ 190
festivo(a) _cheerful_ 222 _festive_ 285
fiable _reliable_ 45
la fibra _fiber_ 173
la ficción _fiction_ 65
la ficha _box_ 35 _index card_ 122 _chip, token_ 192
ficticio(a) _fictional_ 168 _fictitious_ 262
la fidelidad _faithfulness_ 17 _loyalty_ 230
la fiebre _fever_ 75
fiel _faithful_ 17

G

gordito(a) overweight 332
gordo(a) fat 40
la **gota** drop 33
la **grabación** recording 42
el **grabado** engraving 12
grabar to record 238
gracias thank you 11
gracias a thanks to 287
gracias a Dios thank God 278
gracioso(a) funny 5
el **grado** degree 196 grade 256 (university) degree 326
la **graduación** graduation 19
gradualmente gradually 117
graduarse to graduate 93
el **gráfico** chart 66 diagram 155
la **gramática** grammar 2
gramatical grammatical 57
gran, grande big, great 24
la **gran superficie** department store 126
el **granito** granite 318
el **granizo** hail 40
la **granja** farm 108
el/la **granjero(a)** farmer 108
la **grasa** fat 11
gratis free 39
la **gratuidad** condition of being free 115
gratuito(a) free 216
grave low 53 serious 90
griego(a) Greek 318
la **gripe** flu 75
gris gray 54
gritar to shout 47
el **grupo** group 3 cluster 12 set 69
la **guagua** bus 56
guapo handsome 37
guaraní Guarani 77
guardar to keep 109 to put away 204
guatemalteco(a) Guatemalan 243
gubernamental government (adjective) 293
la **guerra** war 108
el/la **guerrero(a)** warrior 103
la **guía** guide, guidance 28 guide (book) 81
el/la **guía** guide 203
guiado(a) guided 322
guiar to guide 1
guiarse por to be guided by 66
el **guineo** banana 172
el **guion** outline 123 script 225
el **guisante** pea 75
la **guitarra** guitar 2
gustar to like 22
el **gusto** taste (of person) 72 taste (of food) 108 like 225
los **gustos** likes 22

H

haber (irreg.) to have (auxiliary) 140
haber que to have to 334
había there was 6 there were 7
la **habilidad** ability, skill 65

la **habitación** room 7 bedroom 196
el/la **habitante** inhabitant 42
el **hábito** habit 11
habitual usual, common 6 regular 200
habitualmente usually, regularly 47
el/la **hablante** speaker 57
hablar de to talk 1 to speak 2
hablarse to talk to each other 36
habrá there will be 80
hace poco not long ago 72
hacer (irreg.) to do, to make 2
hacer frente a to face up to 110
hacer ilusión to thrill 143
hacer memoria to try to remember 230
hacer trampas to cheat 192
hacerse (irreg.) to become 158
hacerse cargo (de) to take care (of) 293
hacerse daño to hurt 119
hacérsele la boca agua a alguien to make someone's mouth water 74
hacia toward 54
la **hacienda** country estate 7
el **hambre** hunger 272
harto(a) (de) fed up (with) 102
hasta until 2 to 31 up to 67 even 158
hasta la bandera packed 188
Hasta la vista. See you later. 16
Hasta luego. See you later. 16
Hasta pronto. See you soon. 16
hasta que until 276
hay there are 6 there is 20
la **hazaña** feat 215
el **hecho** event 1 fact 39
hecho(a) de made of 19
el **helado** ice cream 22
el **hemisferio** hemisphere 135
heredar to inherit 96
hereditario(a) hereditary 96
la **herencia** inheritance 41
el/la **herido(a)** wounded 289
la **hermana** sister 2
el **hermano** brother 17
hermoso(a) beautiful 100
el **héroe** hero 249
heroico(a) heroic 256
la **herramienta** tool 67
hervir (irreg. **ie, i**) to boil 108
híbrido(a) hybrid 146
la **hidra** hydra 343
el **hielo** ice 83
el **hierro** iron 318
el **hígado** liver 115
la **higiene** hygiene 36
la **hija** daughter 90
el **hijo** son 11
los **hijos** children (offspring) 9
hinchado(a) swollen 75
la **hipoteca** mortgage 148
hipotético(a) hypothetical 162
hispánico(a) Hispanic 329
hispano(a) Hispanic 1
hispanoamericano(a) Spanish-American 47

hispanohablante Spanish-speaking 116
el/la **hispanohablante** Spanish speaker 56
la **historia** history 1 story 25
históricamente historically 31
histórico(a) historic 242
el **hogar** home 266
la **hoja** sheet (of paper) 8 leaf 33
la **hoja de vida** résumé 160
la **hojarasca** dead leaves 342
hola hello 11
el **hombre** man 24
el **homenaje** tribute 41
hondamente deeply 336
hondureño(a) Honduran 271
el **hongo** mushroom 78
el **honor** honor 141
honradamente honestly 256
la **hora** hour 5 time 36
el **horario** timetable, schedule 2 opening hours 91 working hours 133
las **horas extraordinarias** overtime 160
el **horizonte** horizon 321
horrible horrible 119
la **hortaliza** vegetable 11
hospedarse to stay, to lodge 216
el **hospital** hospital 59
el **hostal** guesthouse 185
hostil hostile 337
el **hotel** hotel 7
hoy today 20
hoy en día nowadays 30
hubo there were 31 there was 201
el **hueco** space 210
el/la **huésped** guest 216
el **huevo** egg 78
los **huevos revueltos** scrambled eggs 78
la **humanidad** world 43 mankind 317
las **humanidades** humanities 229
humano(a) human 43
humilde modest, humble 20
el **humor** humor 50 mood 110
hundir to sink 195

I

el **icono** icon 65
ida y vuelta round-trip 189
la **idea** idea 5
ideal ideal 7
idéntico(a) identical 20
la **identidad** identity 23
identificar to identify 98
identificarse con to identify with 110
la **ideología** ideology 260
el **idioma** language 2
idiomáticamente idiomatically 206
idiomático(a) idiomatic 106
la **iglesia** church 100
ignorar to ignore 67 not to know 336
igual like it 25 the same 80
igual a equals 136

limpiar *to clean 84*

la **limpieza** *neatness 174 cleanliness 216 cleaning 293*

limpio(a) *clean 87*

lindo(a) *pretty 23 nice 73*

la **línea** *railroad track 205 line 306*

la **línea del tiempo** *timeline 251*

el **linfoma** *lymphoma 96*

el/la **lingüista** *linguist 67*

lingüístico(a) *linguistic 207*

el **líquido** *liquid 117*

el **lirismo** *lyricism 331*

liso(a) *smooth 222*

la **lista** *list 10*

listo(a) *ready 106 smart 106*

literal *literal 100*

literario(a) *literary 50*

la **literatura** *literature 1*

el **litio** *lithium 146*

la **lixiviación** *lixiviation, leaching 296*

la **llamada** *call 138*

llamado(a) *called 86 so-called 114*

llamar *to call 45*

llamar la atención (a/de alguien) *to catch (someone's) attention 86*

llamarse *to be called 17 to call each other 36*

los **llanos** *plains 193*

la **llanta** *tire 56*

la **llave** *friend 56 key 80*

la **llegada** *arrival 103*

llegar *to arrive 2 to come 109 to make it 210*

llegar a *to reach 125*

llegar a fin de mes *to make ends meet 177*

llegar a hacer algo *to get to do something 115*

llegar a un acuerdo *to come to an agreement 148*

llenar (de) *to fill (with) 84 to cover (with) 197*

llenarse *to fill up 33*

lleno(a) *full 28 full (up) 74*

llevar *to take (things) 19 to carry 30 to have been 38 to wear 94 to have 94 to take (time) 311*

llevar (a alguien) a *to lead (someone) to 89*

llevar a cabo *to carry out 127*

llevar al cine (una novela) *to adapt for film 331*

llevarse *to take 50*

llevarse (bien/mal) *to get along (well/badly) 17*

llorar *to cry 39*

llover (irreg. **ue**) *to rain 6*

la **lluvia** *rain 267*

lluvioso(a) *rainy 22*

Lo malo es que... *The problem is that ... 311*

lo que más *most 21*

lo que menos *least 21*

local *local 213*

el **local** *establishment, premises 200*

la **localidad** *town 228*

localizado(a) *localized 96*

localizar *to find 26 to locate 106*

---

loco(a) (por) *crazy (about) 44*

lógico(a) *logical 163*

lograr *to manage 5 to win 29 to achieve 114 to obtain 125*

el **logro** *achievement 256*

el **lomo** *loin 78*

la **loncha** *slice 79*

longitudinal *lengthwise (adjective) 222*

el **lote** *batch, lot 67*

el **lubricante** *lubricant 295*

la **lucha** *fight 96*

luchar *to struggle 110 to fight 248*

luego *then 41 later 266*

el **lugar** *place 1*

el **lugar de nacimiento** *birthplace 161*

el **lugar de trabajo** *workplace 161*

el **lujo** *luxury 218*

lujoso(a) *luxurious 318*

luminoso(a) *bright 19*

la **luna** *moon 94*

el **lunar** *mole (on skin) 17*

la **luz** *light 40*

la **maceta** *flowerpot 11*

la **madera** *wood 147*

la **madre** *mother 59*

la **madrina** *maid of honor 100*

la **madurez** *adulthood 103*

el/la **maestro(a)** *master 351*

mágico(a) *magic 38 magical 336*

magistral *masterly 319*

el **magnesio** *magnesium 147*

magnífico(a) *magnificent 345*

el **maíz** *corn 195*

majestuoso(a) *majestic 203*

mal *badly, terribly 18 bad (adjective) 24 ill 75*

el **mal de altura** *altitude sickness 117*

la **mala pata** *bad luck 107*

la **malaria** *malaria 88*

la **maldad** *evil 279*

el **malecón** *waterfront 229*

maleducado(a) *bad-mannered, rude 20*

el **malentendido** *misunderstanding 56*

la **maleta** *suitcase 63*

el **maletero** *trunk (of car) 204*

maligno(a) *malignant 96*

la **malla** *swimming trunks 56*

malo(a) *bad 106 sick, ill 106*

la **mamá** *mom 86*

el **mambo** *mambo 226*

mandar *to send 32*

el **mandato** *term (of office) 261*

manejar *to handle 110 to drive 141*

el **manejo** *command 175*

la **manera** *way 39*

la **manifestación** *demonstration 262 display 268*

manifestar (irreg. **ie**) *to express 153*

---

manifestarse (irreg. **ie**) *to become apparent 268*

el **manifiesto** *manifesto 292*

maniobrar *to maneuver 210*

la **mano** *hand 1*

el/la **mano(a)** *friend 56*

la **mansión** *mansion 107*

mantener (irreg.) *to keep 182 to keep up 230 to have 326*

mantenerse (irreg.) *to remain 126*

el **manual** *manual 67*

las **manualidades** *crafts 187*

mañana *tomorrow 8*

la **mañana** *morning 6*

el **mapa** *map 56*

la **maqueta** *model 43*

la **maquila** *assembly plant 173*

maquillarse *to make oneself up 36*

la **maquinaria** *machinery 256*

el/la **mar** *sea 147*

la **maraca** *maraca 197*

la **maravilla** *wonder 158*

maravilloso(a) *wonderful 109*

el **marcador** *marker 98*

marcar *to mark 103*

marcharse *to leave 119*

el **marco** *frame 222*

mareado(a) *dizzy 75*

marearse *to get dizzy 90*

el **mariachi** *mariachi 23*

el **marido** *husband 47*

la **mariposa** *butterfly 54*

el **marisco** *seafood 78*

marítimo(a) *sea (adjective) 154*

el **mármol** *marble 318*

más *more 3 most 26 (the) most 27 again 29 any more 72 plus 136*

más adelante *later 130*

más bien *rather 244*

más de/que *more than 308*

masculino(a) *masculine 24*

masivo(a) *mass (adjective) 67*

matar el aburrimiento *to relieve the boredom 200*

matar el tiempo *to kill time 188*

el **mate** *maté 76 maté gourd 76*

matear *to drink maté 77*

las **matemáticas** *mathematics 22*

matemático(a) *mathematical 106*

la **materia** *subject 136*

la **materia prima** *raw material 146*

el **material** *material 106*

materno(a) *mother (adjective) 56 on his mother's side 336*

matero(a) *maté drinker 84*

el **matiz** *meaning 333*

la **matrícula** *enrollment 137 license plate 204*

la **matriculación** *register 134*

matriculado(a) *registered 169*

matricularse *to register 136*

el **matrimonio** *marriage 93*

maya *Mayan 228*

mayor *older 17 bigger 33 highest 52 greater 98 biggest 139 more 155 higher 196 greatest 272*

la **mayor parte (de)** *majority (of), most (of) 48*

la **mayoría** *majority 48*

la **mayúscula** *uppercase* 136

Me alegro de verte. *I'm glad to see you.* 16

Me dirijo a usted(es)... *I am addressing you ...* 59

Me pongo en contacto con usted(es)... *I have contacted you ...* 59

mecánico(a) *mechanical* 148

el/la **mecánico(a)** *mechanic* 158

el **mecanismo** *mechanism* 127

la **media jornada** *part-time* 133

la **media pensión** *half board* 216

mediador(a) *mediating* 324

mediados de *middle of (a month, week, etc.)* 134

la **medialuna** *croissant* 231

mediante *by means of* 97

la **medicación** *medication* 295

el **medicamento** *medicine (drug)* 91

la **medicina** *medicine (science)* 88

médico(a) *medical* 5

el/la **médico(a)** *doctor* 8

la **medida** *measure* 97

las **medidas** *size* 350

el **medio** *means* 97

el **medio ambiente** *environment* 272

el **medio de expresión** *medium* 263

el **medio de transporte** *means of transport* 154

el **medio de vida** *living (earning money)* 39

medio(a) *ordinary, average* 39 *half* 48

medioambiental *environmental* 156

los **medios de comunicación** *media* 44

medir (irreg. **i, i**) *to measure* 306

mejor *better* 8 *best* 11

Mejor dicho, *Rather,* 242

la **mejora** *improvement* 154

mejorar *to improve* 98

el **melanoma** *melanoma* 96

la **melodía** *melody* 27

el **melón** *melon* 75

la **memoria** *memory* 336

mencionar *to mention* 6

menor *lower, smaller* 114

menor de *under (an age)* 68

menos *less* 29 *least* 123 *minus* 136

menos de/que *less than* 308

menos mal (que) *thank God* 243

el **mensaje** *message* 11

el/la **mensajero(a)** *messenger* 30

mensualmente *monthly* 194

mental *mental* 86

mentir (irreg. **ie, i**) *to lie* 4

la **mentira** *lie* 300

el **menú** *menu* 7

el **mercado** *market* 148

el **mercado laboral** *labor market* 163

la **mercancía** *goods, merchandise* 148

merecer la pena *to be worthwhile, to be worth it* 186

merecerse (irreg.) *to deserve* 181

el **mérito** *merit* 249

mero(a) *mere* 166

el **mes** *month* 8

la **mesa** *table* 86

el/la **mesero(a)** *waiter/waitress* 82

el **mesón** *inn, tavern* 79

la **meta** *goal* 254

la **metáfora** *metaphor* 330

el **metal** *metal* 147

metálico(a) *metallic* 76

la **metamorfosis** *metamorphosis* 50

la **metástasis** *metastasis* 96

meteorológico(a) *weather (adjective)* 216

meter *to put in* 40 *to go into (a gear)* 210

meterse *to set* 26 *to get involved* 39

el **metro** *meter* 195 *subway* 278

la **metrópolis** *metropolis* 277

mexicano(a) *Mexican* 3

el/la **mexicanoamericano(a)** *Mexican American* 285

la **mezcla** *mixture* 342

mezclar *to mix* 112

mezquino(a) *mean* 279

la **mezquita** *mosque* 318

el **microclima** *microclimate* 224

el **microcrédito** *microcredit* 156

el **miedo** *fear* 22

la **miel** *honey* 78

el **miembro** *member* 58

mientras *while* 276

mientras que *whereas* 206

mientras tanto *meanwhile* 267

migratorio(a) *migratory* 284

mil *thousand* 48

el **milagro** *miracle* 38

milagroso(a) *miraculous* 109

miles de *thousands of* 147

militar *military* 149

el/la **militar** *soldier* 248

el **millón** *million* 48

el **mineral** *mineral* 11

la **minería** *mining* 172

el **mini-diálogo** *mini-dialogue* 219

el **mínimo** *minimum* 169

mínimo(a) *minimum* 165

el **ministerio** *department, ministry* 273

el/la **ministro(a)** *minister* 262

la **minúscula** *lowercase* 136

el **minuto** *minute* 17

la **mirada** *look, gaze* 139

mirar *to look (at)* 92 *to check* 158

mirar fijo a *to stare at* 278

mirarse *to look at each other* 36

la **misión** *mission* 31

mismo(a) *same* 25

el **misterio** *mystery* 335

misterioso(a) *mysterious* 14

místico(a) *mystic* 219

la **mitad** *half* 48

mítico(a) *mythical* 342

el/la **mochilero(a)** *backpacker* 216

la **modalidad** *type* 144

el **modelo** *model (example)* 3 *model (design)* 25

moderno(a) *modern* 8

el/la **modisto(a)** *fashion designer* 326

el **modo** *way* 39 *mood (in gramar)* 190

mojarse *to get wet* 291

molestar *to bother* 22 *to upset* 22 *to annoy* 23

las **molestias** *ache* 90

molido(a) *ground* 78

momentáneo(a) *momentary* 210

el **momento** *time* 19 *moment* 64

el/la **monarca** *monarch* 248

la **monarquía** *monarchy* 246

la **moneda** *coin* 100 *currency* 153

el/la **monitor(a)** *monitor* 174

monótono(a) *monotonous* 345

la **montaña** *mountain* 24 *mountains* 63

el **montañismo** *mountaineering* 216

montañoso(a) *mountainous* 224

montar *to ride* 189 *to get onto* 223 *to organize* 314

montarse *to get onto* 210

el **montón** *heap* 29

el **monumento** *monument* 61

la **mora** *blackberry* 78

moreno(a) *dark-haired* 20

morir (irreg.) *to die* 102

el/la **mortal** *mortal* 222

el **mosaico** *mosaic* 309

el **mostrador** *counter* 189

mostrar (irreg. **ue**) *to show* 21

mostrarse (irreg. **ue**) *to be* 199

la **motivación** *motive* 215

motivar *to cause* 286

el **motivo** *reason* 218

mover (irreg. **ue**) *to move* 192

moverse (irreg. **ue**) *to move* 33

el **móvil** *cell phone* 67

el **movimiento** *motion* 143 *movement* 262

Mucha suerte. *Good luck.* 14

el/la **muchacho(a)** *boy/girl* 50

mucho *a lot, much* 15 *much (in negatives)* 17

mucho(a) *a lot of* 7

muchos(as) *many, a lot of* 1

mudarse *to move* 107

mudo(a) *mute* 20

el **mueble** *piece of furniture* 24

el **muelle** *dock* 254

la **muerte** *death* 33

muerto(a) *dead* 289

muerto(a) de hambre *very hungry* 102

muerto(a) de sed *very thirsty* 102

muerto(a) de sueño *very sleepy* 102

la **muestra** *evidence* 43 *proof* 67 *sign* 84 *exhibition* 314

la **mujer** *woman* 38 *wife* 39

la **multa** *fine* 150

multar *to fine* 150

la **multinacional** *multinational company* 148

múltiple *multiple* 66

múltiples *many, numerous* 312

la **multiplicación** *multiplication* 136

multiplicar *to multiply* 48

la **multitud** *crowd* 266

multitud de *many* 219

mundial *world (adjective)* 88
la **mundialización** *globalization* 154
el **mundo** *world* 1
municipal *city, local* 260
el/la **muñeco(a)** *doll* 18
el **mural** *mural* 197
el **muralismo** *mural painting* 300
el/la **muralista** *muralist* 300
la **muralla** *wall* 322
el **muro** *wall* 268
el **museo** *museum* 116 *art gallery* 151
la **música** *music* 3
musical *musical (adjective)* 23
el/la **músico(a)** *musician* 191
muy *very* 4

nacer *(irreg.)* *to be born* 67
nacido(a) *born* 125
el **nacimiento** *birth* 161
la **nación** *nation* 149
nacional *national* 3 *domestic* 273
la **nacionalidad** *nationality* 106
nacionalizarse *to become naturalized* 50
nada *nothing* 8 *at all* 22 *anything* 26
nadar *to swim* 59
nadie *nobody* 6 *anybody* 249
el **naipe** *card* 188
la **naranja** *orange* 77
la **nariz** *nose* 332
la **narración** *story* 6
el/la **narrador(a)** *narrator* 330
narrar *to tell, to recount* 230
la **narrativa** *narrative, fiction* 335
narrativo(a) *narrative* 211
natal *native* 325
la **natilla** *custard* 112
nativo(a) *native* 203
natural *natural* 9
la **naturaleza** *nature* 7
la **naturalidad** *naturalness* XXII
naturalmente *of course* 324
las **náuseas** *nausea* 90
navarro(a) *Navarrese* 324
navegable *navigable* 219
el/la **navegante** *sailor* 248
navegar *to sail* 192
la(s) **Navidad(es)** *Christmas* 19
navideño(a) *Christmas (adjective)* 32
necesario(a) *necessary* 58
la **necesidad** *necessity* 38 *need* 43
necesitado(a) *needy* 125
necesitar *to need* 7
la **negación** *negative* 322
negarse *(irreg. ie)* *to refuse* 92
la **negativa** *refusal* 239
negativo(a) *negative* 7
negociar *to negotiate* 169
el **negocio** *business* 148
los **negocios** *business* 38
negro(a) *black* 54
los **nervios** *nerves* 119
nervioso(a) *nervous* 75

neto(a) *clear* 224
el **neumático** *tire* 56
neutro(a) *neuter* 310 *neutral* 334
la **nevada** *snowfall* 138
nevar *(irreg.ie)* *to snow* 111
la **nevera portátil** *cooler* 216
ni *not even, not a single* 17 *nor/or* 32
ni idea *no idea* 15
ni siquiera *not even* 33
ni... ni... *neither ... nor ...* 225
la **niebla** *fog* 216
los **nietos** *grandchildren* 105
la **nieve** *snow* 220
ningún(o)(a) *(not) any, no (adjective)* 48 *any other (pronoun)* 83
la **niñez** *childhood* 6
el/la **niño(a)** *child* 6
el **nivel** *level* 11
el **nivel de vida** *standard of living* 9
no *not* 2 *no* 15
no obstante *however, nevertheless* 91
no... sino... *not ... but ...* 231
no solo... sino que... *not only ... but ...* 231
la **nobleza** *nobility* 248
la **noche** *night* 37 *evening* 195
la **noción** *notion* 222
nocturno(a) *night (adjective)* 205
nombrar *to mention* 94 *to refer to* 104 *to name* 179
el **nombre** *name* 4 *noun* 24
el **nombre propio** *proper noun* 254
la **norma** *rule* 263
normal *normal* 50
la **normalización** *standardization* 153
normalmente *normally* 41
las **normas de circulación** *traffic laws* 204
las **normas de comportamiento** *standards of behavior* 116
el **norte** *North* 57
norteamericano(a) *North American* 86
la **nota** *mark* 11
notable *remarkable* 307
notablemente *considerably* 33
la **noticia** *news (item)* 44
el **noticiero** *news (program)* 44
la **novedad** *news* 266 *novelty* 324
novedoso(a) *new* 5
la **novela** *novel* 33
la **novela gráfica** *graphic novel* 242
la **novela negra** *crime novel* 330
la **novela rosa** *romance novel* 330
noveno(a) *ninth* 250
el **noviazgo** *engagement* 33
el/la **novio(a)** *boyfriend/girlfriend* 4 *bride/groom* 100
nuclear *nuclear* 295
el **núcleo** *area* 280
el **nudo** *knot* 30
nuevo(a) *new* 1
la **nuez** *nut* 78
la **numeración** *numerals* 250
el **numeral** *numeral* 250
el **número** *number* 33

numeroso(a) *numerous* 43
nunca *(not) ever* 33 *never* 194
la **nutrición** *nutrition* 5

o *or* 2
o sea, *that is,* 244
la **objeción** *objection* 264
la **objetividad** *objectivity* 287
el **objetivo** *aim, objective* 9
el **objeto** *object* 4
el **objeto directo/indirecto** *direct/indirect object* 82
la **obligación** *obligation* 144
obligado(a) a algo *required to do something* 260
obligar *to force* 166
obligatorio(a) *compulsory* 82
la **obra** *work* 50
la **obra cumbre** *outstanding work* 302
la **obra de arte** *work of art* 303
la **obra de teatro** *play* 303
la **obra maestra** *masterpiece* 302
el/la **obrero(a)** *worker* 202
observar *to notice* 22 *to watch* 50 *to look at* 310
obsesionado(a) *obsessed* 86
obstaculizar *to hinder* 69
el **obstáculo** *obstacle* 264
la **obstrucción** *obstruction* 90
obtener *(irreg.)* *to obtain* 38 *to make* 154
obviamente *obviously* 345
obvio(a) *obvious* 246
la **ocasión** *chance* 24 *occasion* 112
occidental *Western* 23
el **océano** *ocean* 147
el **ocio** *leisure* 192
octavo(a) *eighth* 250
el/la **oculista** *ophthalmologist* 75
ocultar *to hide* 222
oculto(a) *hidden* 297
la **ocupación** *occupation (job)* 94
ocupacional *occupational* 165
ocupado(a) *busy* 2 *taken* 205
ocupar *to take up* 173 *to hold* 175
ocuparse de hacer algo *to be in charge of doing something* 190
la **ocurrencia** *idea* 343
ocurrir *to happen* 2
ocurrírsele algo a alguien *to think of something* 73
odiar *to hate* 104
odiarse *to hate each other* 36
el **oeste** *West* 248
la **oferta** *supply* 155 *offer* 158
la **oferta de trabajo** *job offer* 160
oficial *official* 116
oficiar *to officiate at* 104
la **oficina** *office* 145
la **oficina de correos** *post office* 32
el **oficio** *job, profession* 38
ofrecer *(irreg.)* *to present* 59 *to offer* 91 *to have* 204
¡oh! *Oh!* 278
el **oído** *ear* 94

la **peca** *freckle* 17
el **pecho** *chest* 90
la **pechuga** *breast* 78
peculiar *peculiar* 203
el **pedazo** *piece* 210
el/la **pediatra** *pediatrician* 75
el **pedido** *order* 39
pedir (irreg. **i, i**) *to ask* 10 *to order* 72 *to ask for* 92 *to apply for* 148
pegado(a) a *glued to* 44
el **pegamento** *glue* 29
pegar un frenazo *to brake hard* 210
peinarse *to comb one's hair* 37
el **peine** *comb* 321
pelear *to fight* 248
pelearse *to argue* 36
la **película** *movie* 22
el **peligro** *danger* 69
peligroso(a) *dangerous* 96
el **pelo** *hair* 20
el **pelotón de fusilamiento** *firing squad* 342
la **pena** *sadness* 56 *embarrassment* 56 *pity, shame* 322
la **península** *peninsula* 228
pensado(a) *planned* 84
pensar (irreg. **ie**) *to think* 2
pensar en (irreg. **ie**) *to think about* 92
la **pensión** *pension* 162 *rooming house* 214
la **pensión completa** *full board* 216
penúltimo(a) *second-to-last* 336
peor *worst* 230 *worse* 308
el **pepino** *cucumber* 78
pequeño(a) *small* 5 *little* 17 *short, brief* 124
la **pera** *pear* 112
la **percepción** *perception* 104
percibir *to perceive* 110
perder (irreg. **ie**) *to lose* 5 *to miss* 24
perder de vista *to lose sight of* 272
perder el conocimiento *to lose consciousness* 90
perder la cuenta *to lose count* 39
perderse (irreg. **ie**) *to get lost* 80 *to miss* 349
la **pérdida** *loss* 52
perdido(a) *lost* 169
el **perdón** *forgiveness* 17
perdonar *to forgive* 39
perdonarse *to forgive each other* 36
la **pereza** *laziness* 49
perezoso(a) *lazy* 17
perfecto *fine, great* 242
perfecto(a) *perfect* 86
el **perfil** *profile* 160
la **perforación** *perforation* 204
periódicamente *periodically* 260
el **periódico** *newspaper* 45
el/la **periodista** *journalist* 38
periodístico(a) *journalistic* 95
el **período** *period* 31
perjudicar *to damage, to harm* 272
permanecer (irreg.) *to stay* 224

el **permiso** *permission* 37 *license, permit* 165
permitir *to allow* 33
pero *but* 1
peronista *Peronist* 266
el **perro** *dog* 302
perseguido(a) *persecuted* 260
perseguir (irreg. **i, i**) *to pursue, to be after* 166 *to pursue, to persecute* 260
persistente *persistent* 267
persistir *to persist* 279
la **persona** *person* 8
el **personaje** *character* 6 *celebrity* 41
personal *personal* 17
el **personal** *personnel, staff* 165
la **personalidad** *personality* 20
personalizado(a) *personal* 212
personalizar *to personalize* 45
personalmente *personally* 89
la **perspectiva** *perspective* 306
persuadir *to persuade* 344
persuasivo(a) *persuasive* 294
pertenecer a (irreg.) *to belong to* 258
perteneciente a *from* 318
la **perturbación** *disturbance* 212
peruano(a) *Peruvian* 54
pesado(a) *heavy* 32
pesar *to weigh* 61 *to grieve* 249
el **pescado** *fish* 78
pescar *to fish* 192
pese a *despite* 264
pesimista *pessimistic* 9
el **peso** *weight* 11 *peso* 39 *weight (importance)* 172
la **petición** *request* 39
el **petróleo** *oil* 147
petrolífero(a) *oil (adjective)* 173
el **pez** *fish* 193
el **pez espada** *swordfish* 78
el **piano** *piano* 170
picante *hot (spicy)* 92
picar *to itch* 75
el **picnic** *picnic* 293
el **pie** *foot* 119
el **pie de foto** *caption* 32
la **piedra** *stone* 318
la **piel** *skin* 96
la **pieza musical** *piece (of music)* 192
la **píldora** *pill* 75
la **pileta** *swimming pool* 56
el **pimiento** *pepper (vegetable)* 78
el **pincel** *brush* 306
la **pincelada** *brushstroke* 306
pinchar *to give an injection* 123
pincharse *to get a puncture* 209
el **pinchazo** *flat tire* 204
pintar *to paint* 268
el/la **pintor(a)** *painter* 300
la **pintura** *painting* 300 *paint* 304
la **piña** *pineapple* 79
el/la **pionero(a)** *pioneer* 156
el **pionono** *long rolled-up cake filled with sweet or savory ingredients* 112
el/la **pirata** *pirate* 250
pisar *to set foot in* 231 *to step on* 340

la **piscina** *swimming pool* 56
el **piso** *floor* 250
la **pista** *clue* 30
la **pistola** *pistol* 272
pitar *to honk* 210
la **pizarra** *chalkboard* 292
la **placa** *plate* 204
el **placer** *pleasure* 212
el **plan** *plan* 9 *program* 277
el **plan de estudios** *syllabus* 142
la **plana** *page* 44
planear *to plan* 2
el **planeta** *planet* 102
la **planicie** *plain* 295
planificado(a) *planned* 2
planificar *to plan* 10
el **plano** *plan* 302
la **planta** *floor* 6 *plant* 77 *plan* 323
la **plantación** *plantation* 172
plantear *to propose* 55 *to set out (a problem)* 166 *to raise (questions)* 166 *to pose* 280
plantearse *to consider, to think* 67
la **plantilla** *staff* 160
plasmar *to portray* 307
el **plástico** *plastic* 303
plástico(a) *plastic* 5
la **plata** *silver* 4
la **plataforma** *platform* 67
el **plátano** *banana* 172
el **plato** *dish* 3 *helping* 74 *course, meal* 78
la **playa** *beach* 7
la **playera** *T-shirt* 56
la **plaza** *square* 50 *parking space* 323
el **plazo** *deadline* 141
el **plural** *plural* 22
la **población** *population* 52 *town* 249
el/la **poblador(a)** *inhabitant* 280
pobre *poor, penniless* 24 *unfortunate* 24 *poor (showing sympathy)* 111
los **pobres** *poor* 222
la **pobreza** *poverty* 272
poco *little (adverb)* 48
poco a poco *little by little* 266
poco(a) *little* 48
pocos(as) *few* 48
poder (irreg. **ue, u**) *can* 4 *to be able* 8
el **poder** *power* 248
el **poema** *poem* 33
la **poesía** *poetry* 330
el/la **poeta** *poet* 166
poético(a) *poetic* 39
la **poetisa** *poetess* 38
polar *polar* 147 *icy* 235
la **polera** *T-shirt* 56
el/la **policía** *policeman/policewoman* 47
la **policía** *police* 47
policíaco(a) *detective (adjective)* 189
policial *police (adjective)* 47
policlínico(a) *polyclinic* 266
el **polímero** *polymer* 297
la **política** *politics* 45 *policy* 217
políticamente *politically* 282
político(a) *political* 191

el/la **profesor(a)** *teacher* 8 *professor* 329

la **profundidad** *depth* 302

profundizar *to go into depth* 302

el **programa** *program* 44

la **programación** *programming* 44

el/la **programador(a)** *programmer* 133

progresista *progressive* 282

progresivo(a) *progressive* 46

el **progreso** *progress* 46

prohibido(a) *forbidden* 161 *prohibited* 207

prohibir *to forbid* 80 *to prohibit* 127 *to ban* 259

la **proliferación** *proliferation* 96

el **promedio** *average* 115

prometer *to promise* 198

la **promoción** *promotion* 217

promocional *promotional* 237

promocionar *to promote* 14

promover (irreg. **ue**) *to promote* 68

el **pronombre** *pronoun* 22

pronominal *pronominal* 34

pronto *soon* 14 *quickly* 40

la **pronunciación** *pronunciation* 56

pronunciar *to pronounce* 278

la **propaganda** *propaganda* 269

la **propensión** *tendency* 96

la **propiedad** *property* 24 *ownership* 180

el/la **propietario(a)** *owner* 180

la **propina** *tip* 79

propio(a) *typical* 24 *own* 27

proponer (irreg.) *to suggest, to propose* 14

la **proporción** *proportion* 306

proporcionar *to provide* 52

el **propósito** *purpose* 58 *intention* 258

la **propuesta** *suggestion, proposal* 41

prorrogar *to extend* 188

la **prosa** *prose* 330

prosperar *to prosper* 278

la **prosperidad** *prosperity* 111

próspero(a) *prosperous* 285

el/la **protagonista** *main character* 49 *subject* 171

protagonizar *to be the main character in* 122

la **protección** *welfare* 114 *protection* 224

proteger *to protect* 256

protegerse *to protect oneself* 96

la **proteína** *protein* 173

la **protesta** *protest* 242

protestar *to protest* 262

proveer (irreg.) *to provide* 296

la **provincia** *province* 125

provocar *to cause* 29 *to give rise to* 154

la **proximidad** *vicinity* 210

próximo(a) *next* 8 *close* 105

la **proyección** *screening* 23

proyectar *to screen* 47 *to design* 267 *to plan* 323

el **proyecto** *project* 64 *plan* 283

el **proyecto de ley** *bill* 261

la **prueba** *test* 66 *audition* 291

la **psicología** *psychology* 143

el/la **psicólogo(a)** *psychologist* 75

el/la **psiquiatra** *psychiatrist* 92

la **publicación** *publication* 66

publicado(a) *posted* 11 *published* 54

publicar *to publish* 33 *to post* 102

la **publicidad** *advertising* 47

publicitario(a) *publicity (adjective)* 145

el **público** *public* 4 *audience* 49

público(a) *public* 61

el **pueblo** *people* 18 *town, village* 40

el **puente** *bridge* 318

la **puerta** *door* 38 *gate* 119

el **puerto** *port* 254

pues *then* 1 *well* 14

el **puesto de trabajo** *position, job* 160

puesto que *because* 147 *since* 218

el **pulmón** *lung* 115

el **pulso** *pulse* 91

el **punto** *point (in time)* 19 *point (in games, etc.)* 49 *period (in writing)* 136 *place* 154

el **punto de partida** *starting point* 211

el **punto de vista** *point of view* 147

el **punto y coma** *semicolon* 136

la **puntuación** *punctuation* 117

la **puntualidad** *punctuality* 205

Q

que *that* 1

qué *what* 3

¿Qué crees que...? *What do you think ...?* 320

Que descanses. *Sleep well.* 16

Que pasen un buen fin de semana. *Have a good weekend.* 16

¿Qué piensas/opinas de (que)...? *What do you think of ...?* 320

Que se diviertan. *Enjoy yourselves.* 14

¿Qué tal? *How are you doing?* 16

¿Qué tal...? *How about ...?* 76

Que te mejores. *Get well soon.* 16

¿Qué te parece...? *What do you think of ...?* 320

Que te vaya bien. *Take care.* 16

Que tengas buen viaje. *Have a good journey.* 16

Que tengas un buen día. *Have a good day.* 16

quechua *Quechua* 77

quedar *to arrange to meet* 34 *to be left* 49 *to suit, to fit* 94 *to look* 197

quedarse *to stay* 34 *to keep* 47 *to be left* 108

quedarse (alguien) en blanco *to go blank (someone's mind)* 130

quedarse sin gasolina *to run out of gasoline* 204

la **queja** *complaint* 7

quejarse *to complain* 34

la **quemadura** *burn* 90

quemar *to burn* 19

querer (irreg.) *to want* 8 *to like* 59 *to love* 104

quererse (irreg.) *to love each other* 36

querido(a) *dear* 37

el **queso** *cheese* 75

quien *who* 18 *whom* 85

quién *who* 9 *whom* 19

quieto(a) *still* 17

la **Química** *chemistry* 133

químico(a) *chemical* 96

el/la **químico(a)** *chemist* 160

la **quimioterapia** *chemotherapy* 97

la **quinceañera** *celebration of a girl's fifteenth birthday in parts of Latin America* 105

la **quincena** *two weeks* 231

la **quinta** *country house* 336

quinto(a) *fifth* 48

la **quinua** *quinoa* 296

quirúrgico(a) *surgical* 114

quitar *to remove* 87 *to take away* 255

quitarse *to take off* 94

quizá(s) *maybe* 15

R

la **rabia** *rage* 210

racial *racial* 271

racional *rational* 324

racionalizado(a) *rationalized* 49

la **radiación** *radiation* 96

radiactivo(a) *radioactive* 272

radical *radical* 289

la **radio** *radio* 52

la **radiografía** *X-ray* 75

el **radioteatro** *radio drama* 266

la **radioterapia** *radiation therapy* 97

la **raíz** *root* 8

la **rama** *branch* 33

el **ramo** *bouquet* 100

el **rango** *standing, prestige* 200

la **rapidez** *speed* 205

rápido *quickly, fast* 107

rápido(a) *quick, fast* 41

rara vez *seldom* 194

raro(a) *strange* 30 *unusual* 39 *rare* 296

el **rascacielos** *skyscraper* 318

el **rasgo** *trait* 20 *feature* 237

el **rato** *while* 47

el **ratón** *mouse* 104

el **rayo** *ray* 96

la **raza** *race* 278

la **razón** *reason* 24

razonable *reasonable* 20

la **reacción** *reaction* 143

reaccionar *to react* 40

reactivo(a) *reactive* 98

reafirmar *to strengthen* 169

real *royal* 31 *real* 65

el **realce** *enhancement* 200

la **realeza** *royalty* 248

la **realidad** *reality* 67

el **realismo** *realism* 335

realizar to carry out 3 to perform 5 to do 66 to make 109 to achieve 306

realmente really 39

rebatir to refute 256

rebelarse to rebel 247

recaudar to collect 266

la **recepción** reception 7

el/la **recepcionista** receptionist 174

el/la **receptor(a)** recipient 104

la **receta** prescription 75 recipe 79

rechazar to reject 69

el **rechazo** rejection 67

Reciban un cordial saludo. Please accept my cordial greetings. 59

recibir to receive 32 to be awarded 89

reciclar to recycle 102

el/la **recién nacido(a)** newborn baby 115

reciente latest 45 recent 96

recientemente recently 140

el **recinto** area 139

el **recipiente** container 76

recíproco(a) reciprocal 36

la **reclamación** complaint 204

recoger to gather 64 to collect 126 to contain 200 to show 345

la **recogida** collection 125

la **recolecta** collection 125

recomendable advisable 7

la **recomendación**. recommendation 11

recomendar (irreg. **ie**) to recommend 11

reconciliarse to make up 17

reconocer (irreg.) to recognize 23 to admit 86 to acknowledge 285

reconocible recognizable 306

reconocido(a) renowned 23

el **reconocimiento** recognition 38

reconstruir (irreg.) to reconstruct 245

recopilar to collect 181 to compile 230

recordable memorable 222

recordar (irreg. **ue**) to remember 1 to remind 177

recorrer to travel through 31

el **recorrido** route 203

rectangular rectangular 303

el **recuerdo** souvenir 61 memory 343

la **recuperación** recovery 270

recuperar(se) to recover 38

el **recurso** means, resort 68 resource 146

el **recurso natural** natural resource 148

la **red** network 37 Internet 45 net 336

la **redacción** wording 117 writing 286

redactar to write 38

redondo(a) round 303

reducir (irreg.) to reduce 11

reemprender to resume 210

reescribir (irreg.) to rewrite 51

la **referencia** reference 160

el **referéndum** referendum 262

referido(a) a relating to 164

referirse a (irreg. **ie, i**) to refer to 34 to mean 69

reflejar to reflect 36 to show 59

el **reflejo** reflection 52

la **reflexión** thought 263

reflexivo(a) reflexive 36

la **reforma** reform 261

reformar to reform 244

el **refresco** soft drink 83

el **refrigerador** refrigerator 63

refugiarse to take refuge 291

regalar to give as a present 29

el **regalo** present 10

el **régimen** regime 244

la **región** region 9

registrado(a) registered 154

registrar to register 31 to record 52

registrarse to register 68

el **registro** register 58

la **regla** rule 81

el **reglamento** rules 116

regresar to come back 108

el **regreso** return 266

la **regulación** regulation 67

regular regular 2 average 7

regularmente regularly 230

la **reina** queen 245

reinventar to reinvent 212

reír (irreg. **i**) to laugh 20

la **reivindicación** claim 268

reivindicar to claim 292

reivindicativo(a) of protest 293

la **relación** relationship 14 relation 40

relacionado(a) related 9

relacionar to link 9

relajado(a) relaxed 75

relajarse to relax 75

relativo(a) relative 150

relativo(a) a relating to 116

el **relato** story, tale 25

relevante important 72

la **religión** religion 106

religioso(a) religious 101

rellenar to fill in 160

relleno(a) filled 78

el **reloj** clock 139 watch 295

reluciente gleaming 336

remediar to solve 277

la **remera** T-shirt 56

el/la **remitente** sender 32

remitir to refer 286

remontarse a to date back to 261

remoto(a) remote 44 distant 336

el **Renacimiento** Renaissance 325

rendirse (irreg. **i**) to give up 131

el **renombre** fame 200

renovable renewable 156

renovado(a) renewed 191

la **rentabilidad** profitability 156

renunciar a to give up 92

renunciar a hacer algo to refuse to do something 260

repartir to deliver 33 to distribute 125

repasar to revise 2 to review 136

el **repaso** revision 60

la **repetición** repetition 82

repetidamente repeatedly 6

repetir (irreg. **i, i**) to repeat 2

repetitivo(a) repetitive 7

el **reportaje** feature 38 report 52

reposar to brew (tea) 87

el/la **representante** representative 125

representar to represent 55 to perform 57 to mean 69

representativo(a) representative 227

reprobar (irreg. **ue**) to fail 136

la **reproducción** reproduction 340

reproducir (irreg.) to reproduce 43

la **república** republic 248

republicano(a) republican 245

la **repugnancia** disgust 166

requerido(a) required 165

el **requerimiento** request 212

requerir (irreg. **ie, i**) to require 4 to demand 212

el **requisito** requirement 7

resaltar to highlight 43

la **reseña** profile 329 review 344

reseñar to review 344

la **reserva** reserve 146 reservation 218

reservado(a) shy 17 reserved 205

reservar to book 86

las **reses** cattle 222

la **residencia** residence 54

los **residuos tóxicos** toxic waste 272

resistir to withstand 323

resolver (irreg.) to solve 55

resolverse (irreg.) to be solved 293

resoplar to snort 210

respectivo(a) respective 327

respecto a compared to 45 regarding 143

respetar to respect 17

el **respeto** respect 57

respirar to breathe 75

responder to answer 3

la **responsabilidad** responsibility 127

responsable responsible 133

el/la **responsable** person in charge 127

la **respuesta** answer 31

la **resta** subtraction 136

restablecer (irreg.) to resume 86

restar to subtract 136

restar importancia a to play down the importance of 21

la **restauración** restoration 203

el **restaurante** restaurant 72

restaurar to restore 322

el **resto** rest 41

los **restos** leftovers 87 wreckage 195

el **resultado** result 3

resultar to be 38 to turn out (to be) 117

el **resumen** summary 45

resumir to summarize 38

retener (irreg.) to hold back 336

retrasar to delay 337

retrasarse to be late, to be delayed 207

el **retraso** delay 218

retratar to portray 307

el **retrato** *portrait* 306
retroceder *to go back* 210
la **reunión** *meeting* 35
reunir *to meet* 175 *to gather* 236 *to bring together* 285
reunirse *to meet* 3
reutilizar *to reuse* 127
revelar *to show* 338
revisar *to check* 59
la **revisión médica** *medical checkup* 75
el/la **revisor(a)** *(train) conductor* 204
la **revista** *magazine* 48
revivir *to revive* 31
la **revolución** *revolution* 26
revolucionar *to revolutionize* 205
revolucionario(a) *revolutionary* 268
el **rey** *king* 23
los **Reyes Magos** *the Three Wise Men* 37
rico(a) *rich* 39 *delicious* 74
ridículo(a) *ridiculous* 86
el **riego** *watering* 292
el **riesgo** *risk* 86
riguroso(a) *rigorous* 246
el **rincón** *corner* 31
el **riñón** *kidney* 115
el **río** *river* 150
la **riqueza** *wealth* 173 *richness* 195
el **ritmo** *rhythm* 153
el **rito** *rite* 14
el **ritual** *ritual* 77
rizado(a) *curly* 17
robar *to steal* 5 *to rob* 29
el **robo** *robbery* 272
la **roca** *rock* 202
la **rodaja** *slice* 77
rodeado(a) *surrounded* 54
rodear *to surround* 6
la **rodilla** *knee* 102
rojizo(a) *reddish* 303
rojo(a) *red* 63
el **rol** *role* 212
el **rollo** *roll* 112
el **romance** *romance* 38
románico(a) *Romanesque* 320
romano(a) *Roman* 250
romántico(a) *romantic* 22
romper (irreg.) *to break up* 4 *to break* 19
romperse (irreg.) *to get broken* 34 *to break* 80
la **ronda** *round* 84
la **ropa** *clothes* 25
la **ropa de abrigo** *warm clothing* 224
la **rosa** *rose* 33
rosado(a) *pink* 266
roto(a) *broken* 75
la **rudeza** *rudeness* 278
rudo(a) *rough* 40
la **rueda** *round* 84
la **rueda de repuesto** *spare tire* 204
el **ruido** *noise* 22
la **ruina** *ruin* 222
el **rumbo** *course* 314
el **rumor** *rumor* 207
la **ruptura** *break* 342
rural *rural* 31

la **ruta** *route* 159
la **rutina** *routine* 2

S

saber (irreg.) *to know* 1 *to be able to, can* 40
el **sabor** *taste* 76 *flavor* 112
sacar *to get* 11 *to take* 100 *to take out* 108
sacar buenas notas *to get good marks* 132
el **sacerdote** *priest* 105
el **saco de dormir** *sleeping bag* 216
sacrificarse *to make sacrifices* 168
el **sacrificio** *sacrifice* 168
sagrado(a) *holy* 301
la **sal** *salt* 35
la **sala** *room* 188
la **sala de urgencias** *emergency room* 90
el **salar** *salt flat* 128
el **salario** *salary* 168
el **saldo** *bank balance* 148
la **salida** *exit* 192
salir (irreg.) *to go out* 3 *to leave* 34 *to turn out* 38 *to come out* 54
salirse (irreg.) *to go beyond the limits* 34
el **salmón** *salmon* 75
el **salón** *hall* 10 *living room* 138
el **salón de clases** *classroom* 338
la **salsa** *sauce* 92 *salsa* 227
saltar *to hop* 347
el **salto** *leap* 343
la **salud** *health* 11
saludable *healthy* 11
saludar *to say hello* 63 *to greet* 266
saludarse *to greet each other* 34
el **saludo** *greeting* 16
salvar *to rescue* 148 *to save* 292
salvo que *unless* 164
San *Saint* 114
el **sanatorio** *hospital* 330
la **sandía** *watermelon* 75
sangrar *to bleed* 90
la **sangre** *blood* 75
sanguíneo(a) *blood (adjective)* 98
sanitario(a) *health (adjective)* 98
sano(a) *healthy* 278
santiaguero(a) *from Santiago de Cuba* 200
el **santo** *saint's day* 26
el/la **santo(a)** *saint* 26
el **santuario** *sanctuary* 200
el **sarcoma** *sarcoma* 96
satisfacer (irreg.) *to satisfy* 109
satisfecho(a) *satisfied* 145
saturado(a) *saturated* 11
Se me da bien... *I'm good at ...* 18
Se me da mal... *I'm bad at ...* 41
Se ruega silencio. *Silence, please.* 104
secarse *to dry* 308
la **sección** *section* 44
seco(a) *dry* 87
el/la **secretario(a)** *secretary* 145
el **secreto** *secret* 38

secreto(a) *secret* 246
el **sector** *sector* 83
la **secuencia** *sequence* 209
secuestrado(a) *kidnapped* 267
la **secundaria** *secondary education* 137
secundario(a) *secondary* 96
la **sed** *thirst* 224
la **seda** *silk* 106
la **sede** *headquarters* 217
sedentario(a) *sedentary* 96
seducir (irreg.) *to attract* 324
seguido(a) *followed* 66
el/la **seguidor(a)** *follower* 47
el **seguimiento** *monitoring* 98 *follow-up* 273
seguir (irreg. i, i) *to follow* 4 *to keep* 14 *to continue* 84
seguir adelante *to go ahead* 132
según *according to* 3 *depending on* 21
el **segundo** *second* 67
segundo(a) *second* 250
seguramente *probably* 14
la **seguridad** *security* 116 *safety* 189 *certainty* 337
la **seguridad social** *social security* 114
seguro *definitely* 32
el **seguro** *insurance* 114
el **seguro de vida** *life insurance* 160
el **seguro dental/médico** *dental/health insurance* 160
seguro(a) *confident* 17 *safe* 106 *sure, certain* 106
la **selección** *selection* 111
seleccionar *to select* 58
el **sello** *stamp* 189
la **selva** *jungle* 4
el **semáforo** *traffic light* 210
la **semana** *week* 6
semanal *weekly (adjective)* 86
semanalmente *weekly (adverb)* 194
sembrar (irreg. ie) *to sow* 11
semejante *similar* 271
la **semejanza** *similarity* 19
semestral *one-semester* 169
el **semestre** *semester* 136
semigratuito(a) *almost free* 137
el **senado** *senate* 260
el/la **senador(a)** *senator* 245
sencillo(a) *simple* 76
el **senderismo** *hiking* 219
el **sendero** *path* 7
la **sensación** *feeling* 166 *sensation* 279
sensato(a) *sensible* 20
sensible *sensitive* 20
sentado(a) *seated* 102
sentarse (irreg. ie) *to sit* 106
el **sentido** *sense* 39 *meaning* 94
el **sentido común** *common sense* 278
el **sentido del humor** *sense of humor* 20
el **sentimiento** *feeling* 22
sentir (irreg. ie, i) *to feel* 23 *to be sorry* 92
sentirse (irreg. ie, i) *to feel* 61

el **tacto** *touch* 343
tal *such (pronoun)* 67 *such (adjective)* 210
tal (y) como *just as* 39
tal vez *perhaps* 196
el **talento** *talent* 38
talentoso(a) *talented* 309
el **taller** *workshop* 47
el **tamal** *corn meal and meat empanada wrapped in corn or banana leaves* 172
el **tamaño** *size* 306
también *also* 7
tampoco *neither* 94
tan *so* 8
tanto *so much* 214
tanto como *as much as* 308
tanto(a) que *so much that* 220
la **tapa** *tapa* 79
tapar *to cover* 79
la **taquilla** *box office* 189
tardar (en) *to delay* 32
tarde *late* 6
la **tarde** *afternoon* 2 *evening* 5
la **tarea** *task* 10 *homework* 37
las **tareas domésticas** *housework* 59
la **tarifa** *price* 216
la **tarjeta de embarque** *boarding pass* 189
la **tarjeta de felicitación** *greeting card* 32
la **tarjeta de presentación** *card* 174
la **tarjeta navideña** *Christmas card* 32
la **tarjeta postal** *postcard* 32
el **tarro** *jar* 108
la **tasa de interés** *interest rate* 148
la **taza** *cup* 332
el **té** *tea* 76
Te felicito. *Congratulations.* 11
el **teatro** *theater* 23
el **techo** *ceiling* 303
el **teclado** *keyboard* 133
la **técnica** *technique* 5
técnico(a) *technical* 43
la **tecnología** *technology* 44
tecnológico(a) *technological* 98
el **tejido** *tissue* 115
la **tela** *fabric* 304
la **tele** *TV* 3
las **telecomunicaciones** *telecommunications* 165
telefónico(a) *telephone (adjective)* 239
el **teléfono** *telephone* 8
la **telenovela** *soap opera* 4
el **teletrabajo** *telecommuting* 163
la **televisión** *television* 44
el **televisor** *television set* 219
el **tema** *subject* 14 *song* 190
la **temática** *subject* 230
tembloroso(a) *trembling* 210
temer *to fear, to be afraid of* 166
temerario(a) *reckless* 311
temerse que *to be afraid that* 83
el **temor** *fear* 166
la **temperatura** *temperature* 224
templado(a) *warm* 173
el **templo** *temple* 318

la **temporada** *time* 110 *season* 216
temporal *time (adjective)* 140
temprano *early* 35
temprano(a) *early* 97
la **tendencia** *trend* 270
tener *(irreg.)* *to have* 2
tener claro(a) *to be sure about* 197
tener en cuenta *to bear in mind, to take into account* 27
tener ganas de *to look forward to* 186
tener lugar *to take place* 5
tener mal perder *to be a sore loser* 192
tener que *to have to* 334
tener razón *to be right* 17
tener sentido *to make sense* 30
el **tenor** *tenor* 200
la **tensión** *tension* 201
tercer(o)(a) *third* 250
el **tercio** *third* 48
el **terciopelo** *velvet* 222
terco(a) *stubborn* 20
la **terminación** *ending* 4
terminado(a) *finished* 140
el **terminal** *terminal* 67
terminar *to end* 4 *to finish* 95
terminar con *to put an end to* 271
terminarse *to finish* 49
el **término** *term* 67
la **ternera** *veal* 78
la **terraza** *balcony* 219 *terrace* 222
el **terremoto** *earthquake* 266
el **terreno** *ground* 98 *land* 306
el **territorio** *territory* 43
el **terrorismo** *terrorism* 272
el/la **terrorista** *terrorist* 274
el **tesoro** *treasure* 146
el/la **testigo** *witness* 254
el **testimonio** *testimony* 97
el **textil** *textile* 31
el **texto** *text* 5
textual *textual* 294
la **tez** *skin* 343
el **tiempo** *time* 3 *tense* 22 *weather* 216
la **tienda** *store* 25
la **tienda de campaña** *tent* 216
la **tierra** *land* 41 *Earth* 295
tímido(a) *shy* 17
el/la **tío(a)** *uncle/aunt* 105
típico(a) *typical* 3 *traditional* 14
el **tipo** *type, kind* 7
la **tira** *strip* 98
tirar *to throw* 111 *to throw away* 127
la **tiroides** *thyroid gland* 96
titulado(a) *named* 224
el **titular** *headline* 44
el **título** *title* 26
el **tobillo** *ankle* 90
tocar *to play* 23 *to touch* 139
todavía *still* 140
todo *everything* 2
todo(a) *all* 22
todos(as) *every* 6 *everyone* 11
la **tolerancia** *tolerance* 245
la **toma de posesión** *inauguration* 289

tomar *to take* 6 *to drink* 76 *to eat* 79 *to sit (an exam)* 134
tomar el pelo *to trick, to tease* 20
tomar el sol *to sunbathe* 188
tomar en cuenta *to bear in mind, to take into account* 278
tomar nota de *to note down* 26
la **tonelada** *metric ton* 80
el **tono** *tone* 58
la **tontería** *stupid thing (to say)* 322
el/la **torcedor(a)** *tobacco factory worker* 200
la **tormenta** *storm* 22
el **toro** *bull* 337
la **toronja** *grapefruit* 78
la **torre** *tower* 318
la **torta** *cake* 112
la **tos** *cough* 90
toser *to cough* 75
los **tostones** *fried plantain* 172
el **total** *total* 125
totalmente *totally* 39
tóxico(a) *toxic* 272
trabajador(a) *hard-working* 17
el/la **trabajador(a)** *worker* 95
trabajar *to work* 11
trabajar por cuenta propia *to be self-employed* 132
el **trabajo** *work* 6 *job* 33 *essay* 64
la **tradición** *tradition* 18
tradicional *traditional* 14
tradicionalmente *traditionally* 76
la **traducción** *translation* 251
traducir *(irreg.)* *to translate* 22
el/la **traductor(a)** *translator* 133
traer *(irreg.)* *to bring* 2 *to give as a present* 37 *to carry* 108
el **tráfico** *traffic* 204
el **tráfico de drogas** *drug trafficking* 272
el **traje** *suit* 54 *costume* 236
el **traje de baño** *swimming trunks* 56
la **tranquilidad** *calm* 38
tranquilo(a) *calm* 75 *quiet, peaceful* 219
Tranquilo(a). *Don't worry.* 90
la **transacción** *transaction* 154
transandino(a) *trans-Andean* 203
transcurrir *to take place* 337
la **transformación** *transformation* 51
transformar *to transform* 67 *to change* 188 *to turn (into)* 265
transformarse en *to turn into* 266
la **transición** *transition* 110
transmitir *to pass on* 30 *to broadcast* 125
transparente *open* 156 *transparent* 343
transportar *to transport* 204
el **transporte** *transportation* 116
el **tranvía** *streetcar* 50
tras *after* 108
trascendental *extremely important* 296
trasgresor(a) *transgressive* 67
el **trasplante** *transplant* 5
el **trastorno** *disorder* 98
el **tratado** *treaty* 150
el **tratado de paz** *peace treaty* 248

el **tratamiento** *form of address* 57 *treatment* 97

el **tratamiento de textos** *text processing* 174

tratar (de) *to be about* 23

tratarse de *to be* 133

Trato hecho. *It's a deal.* 190

travieso(a) *mischievous* 17

el **trazo** *stroke* 347

el **tren** *train* 92

el **tren de cercanías** *commuter train* 204

el **tren de largo recorrido** *long-distance train* 204

el **tribunal** *court* 260

el **trigo** *wheat* 80

el **triple** *triple* 48

triste *sad* 22

la **tristeza** *sadness* 56

triunfal *triumphal* 306

triunfar *to succeed* 260

la **trompeta** *trumpet* 23

el **trompo** *spinning top* 193

las **tropas** *troops* 306

tropezar (irreg. **ie**) *to stumble* 221

tropical *tropical* 172

la **trova** *ballad* 184

el/la **trovador(a)** *troubadour* 191

el **trozo** *piece* 74

la **trusa** *swimming trunks* 56

la **tumba** *grave* 4

el **tumor** *tumor* 96

el **turismo** *tourism* 114

el/la **turista** *tourist* 203

turístico(a) *tourist (adjective)* 24

turnarse *to take turns* 35

el **turno** *turn* 33

turquesa *turquoise* 219

u *or* 66

la **ubicación** *location* 216

ubicado(a) *located* 216

ubicarse *to be located* 325

últimamente *lately* 140

último(a) *last* 23 *latest* 25 *recent* 33

Un beso. *Love, (in letters)* 83

un montón (de) *a lot (of)* 29

Un saludo. *Regards.* 59

undécimo(a) *eleventh* 250

único(a) *only, unique* 24

la **unidad** *unit* 1

unido(a) *joined* 82

uniforme *uniform* 143

el **uniforme** *uniform* 254

la **uniformidad** *uniformity* 67

la **unión** *union* 289

unir *to join* 4 *to connect* 31 *to unite* 248

universal *universal* 2

la **universalización** *universality* 114

la **universidad** *university* 47

universitario(a) *university (adjective)* 137

unos(as) *some* 18

el **urbanismo** *city planning* 280

la **urbanización** *urbanization* 280

urbano(a) *urban* 7

la **urgencia** *emergency* 90 *urgency* 210

urgente *urgent* 32

uruguayo(a) *Uruguayan* 153

usado(a) *used* 94

usar *to use* 2

el **uso** *use* 33

el/la **usuario(a)** *user* 45

el **utensilio** *tool, utensil* 85

el **útero** *uterus* 89

útil *useful* 16

la **utilidad** *usefulness* 116

la **utilización** *use* 69

utilizado(a) *used* 66

utilizar *to use* 8

la **uva** *grape* 75

¡Uy! *Gosh!* 42

las **vacaciones** *vacation* 5

la **vacilación** *hesitation* 336

vacío(a) *empty* 222

la **vacuna** *vaccine* 90

la **vacunación** *vaccination* 116

vacunarse *to get vaccinated* 99

el **vacuno** *cattle* 173

el **vagón** *train car* 204

el **vagón-restaurante** *dining car* 204

vale *OK* 123

valer (irreg.) *to be worth* 8 *to count* 311

valer la pena *to be worthwhile, to be worth it* 257

válido(a) *valid* 110

valiente *brave* 20

valioso(a) *valuable* 43

el **valle** *valley* 277

el **valor** *value* 2 *courage* 311

la **valoración** *value statement* 322

valorar *to value* 166

vanguardista *avant-garde* 316

vanidoso(a) *vain* 20

variable *variable* 166

la **variación** *variation* 48

la **variante** *variation* 77

variar *to vary* 7 *to change* 310

la **variedad** *variety* 11

varios(as) *several* 4

la **vasija de barro** *earthenware vessel* 29

el **vaso** *glass* 34

vasto(a) *vast* 295

el/la **vecino(a)** *neighbor* 35 *person next to you* 210

vegetal *plant (adjective)* 173

vegetariano(a) *vegetarian* 79

el **vehículo** *vehicle* 153

la **vela** *candle* 28

el **velero** *sailboat* 141

la **velocidad** *speed* 204

vencer *to beat (in competition)* 83

el/la **vendedor(a)** *salesperson* 22 *seller* 307

vender *to sell* 8

venezolano(a) *Venezuelan* 282

¡venga! *come on!* 30

la **venganza** *revenge* 338

venidero(a) *future* 326

venir (irreg.) *to come* 4

la **ventaja** *advantage* 98

la **ventana** *window* 47

la **ventanilla** *window (of car)* 189

ver (irreg.) *to see* 2 *to watch* 3

el **veraneo** *summer vacation* 336

el **verano** *summer* 2

verbal *verbal* 34

el **verbo** *verb* 2

la **verdad** *truth* 109

¿verdad? *aren't you?/don't you?/ etc.* 14

verdaderamente *truly* 210

verdadero(a) *true* 47

verde *green* 106 *unripe* 106

verdoso(a) *greenish* 303

la **verdura** *vegetable* 10

la **vergüenza** *embarrassment* 56

verificar *to check* 157

verosímil *believable* 230

versátil *versatile* 226

la **versatilidad** *versatility* 268

verse (irreg.) *to see each other* 36

la **versión** *version* 26

la **versión original** *original version* 44

el **verso** *verse, line* 330

vertical *vertical* 203

el **vértigo** *dizziness* 210

el **vestido** *dress* 35 *clothes* 36

vestido(a) *dressed* 54

vestirse (irreg. **i, i**) *to get dressed* 36

vetar *to veto* 263

la **Veterinaria** *veterinary science* 59

la **vez** *time* 11

la **vía** *way* 200

viajar *to travel* 24

el **viaje** *journey, trip* 5 *travel* 8

el/la **viajero(a)** *traveler* 7

la **vicepresidencia** *vice presidency* 267

el/la **vicepresidente(a)** *vice president* 261

el **vicio** *vice* 279

la **victoria** *victory* 248

la **vida** *life* 33

el **video** *video* 29

el **videojuego** *videogame* 3

el **vidrio** *glass* 222

viejo(a) *old* 18

el **viento** *wind* 23

el/la **vikingo(a)** *Viking* 252

el **vinagre** *vinegar* 75

el **vino** *wine* 79

la **viñeta** *comic frame* 123

la **violación** *violation* 259

la **violencia** *violence* 272

la **virgen** *virgin* 101

el **virreinato** *viceroyalty* 248

el **virrey** *viceroy* 248

virtual *virtual* 37

la **virtud** *virtue* 278

el **virus** *virus* 96

la **visibilidad** *visibility* 324

la **visión** *view* 9

la **visita** *visitor* 84 *visit* 139

GLOSARIO INGLÉS-ESPAÑOL

A

a lot mucho 15
a lot (of) un montón (de) 29
a lot of muchos(as) 1 mucho(a) 7
abandoned abandonado(a) 51
to **abbreviate** abreviar 69
abbreviation la abreviatura 66
ability la capacidad 43 la habilidad 65
able to capaz de 6
abnormal anormal 90
to **abolish** abolir 248 suprimir 289
about sobre 4 de 6 en 10 acerca de 68
about to a punto de 204
above por encima de 272
above all sobre todo 14
abroad en el extranjero 58 al extranjero 141
absence la ausencia 94
to **abstain** abstenerse (irreg.) 260
abstract abstracto(a) 94
abundance la abundancia 295
abundant abundante 117
academic académico(a) 136
academy la academia 329
accent el acento 278
to **accept** asumir 39 aceptar 88
acceptable aceptable 280
accepted aceptado(a) 110
access el acceso 7
to **access** ingresar 165
accessibility la accesibilidad 269
accessible accesible 345
accessory el complemento 197
accident el accidente 4
accidental accidental 80
acclimatization la aclimatación 117
accommodation el alojamiento 144
accompanied acompañado(a) 23
to **accompany** acompañar 100
to **accomplish** conseguir (irreg. i, i) 53
according to según 3 de acuerdo con 66
account la cuenta 7
accountant el/la contador(a) 133
accumulation la acumulación 90
accuracy la precisión 98
to **accuse** acusar 127
ache las molestias 90
to **achieve** lograr 114 realizar 306 alcanzar 345
achievement el logro 256
acid ácido(a) 106
to **acknowledge** reconocer (irreg.) 285
to **acquire** adquirir (irreg. ie) 2
act la ley 127 la acción 272
to **act** actuar 275 accionar 268
action la acción 2
active activo(a) 104
activist el/la activista 243
activity la actividad 3
actor el actor 25

actress la actriz 24
actually en realidad 231 de hecho 318
ad el anuncio 99
to **adapt** adaptar(se) 67
to **adapt for film** llevar al cine (una novela) 331
adaptation la adaptación 69
adapted adaptado(a) 5
to **add** añadir 17 echar 76 sumar 144 agregar 338
addition la suma 136
additional adicional 153
address la dirección 32
to **address** dirigir 40 dirigirse a 58
addressee el/la destinatario(a) 32
adjectival adjetivo(a) 150
adjective el adjetivo 24
to **adjust** adaptar(se) 67
adjustment la adaptación 69
administrative administrativo(a) 169
to **admire** admirar 310
admission la admisión 183 la entrada 326
to **admit** admitir 44 reconocer (irreg.) 86
admitted admitido(a) 170
adolescence la adolescencia 103
adolescent el/la adolescente 96
adult el/la adulto(a) 69 adulto(a) 103
adulthood la madurez 103
advance el avance 98
to **advance** avanzar 140
advanced avanzado(a) 114
advantage la ventaja 98
adventure la aventura 108
adverb el adverbio 48
adverbial adverbial 194
advertising la publicidad 47
(piece of) advice el consejo 334
advisable recomendable 7 aconsejable 117 conveniente 137
to **advise** aconsejar 91 asesorar 273
adviser el/la asesor(a) 212
to **advocate** abogar por 217
aeronautics la aeronáutica 312
aesthetic la estética 43
to **affect** afectar 57
affection el afecto 21
affectionate cariñoso(a) 17
affiliation la afiliación 106
affinity la afinidad 193
affirmative afirmativo(a) 1
affirmative statement la afirmación 322
affirmatively afirmativamente 239
to **afflict** afligir 96
affordable accesible 217
aforementioned dicho(a) 296
after detrás de 22 después 24 tras 108 después de (que) 276
afternoon la tarde 2
again más 29
against contra 29 en contra 260
age la era 38 la edad 58
agent el agente 96 el complemento agente 104

age-old ancestral 31
aggressive agresivo(a) 22
agile ágil 345
to **agree** acordar (irreg. ue) 34 concordar 80 (irreg. ue) estar de acuerdo 96
to **agree on/that ...** coincidir en/en que 183
agreement el acuerdo 133
agricultural agrícola 173
ahead adelante 130
aid la ayuda 98
ailment la dolencia 91
aim el objetivo 9 el fin 210
to **aim for** optar a 136
aimed destinado(a) 139
air el aire 7
air conditioning el aire acondicionado 219
air mail el correo aéreo 32
air mattress la colchoneta 216
airplane el avión 63
airport el aeropuerto 189
aisle el pasillo 222
alarm clock el despertador 6
alarming alarmante 277
alchemist el/la alquimista 350
alcohol el alcohol 96
alert atento(a) 106
alive vivo(a) 43
all todo(a) 22
allergy la alergia 58
alliance la alianza 248
to **allow** admitir 21 permitir 33
allusion la alusión 345
ally el/la aliado(a) 125
almond la almendra 112
almost casi 20
almost always casi siempre 194
almost free semigratuito(a) 137
alone solo(a) 50
already ya 140
also también 7 además 27
to **alter** alterar 220
alternative la alternativa 272 alternativo(a) 275
although aunque, a pesar de (que) 264
altitude sickness el mal de altura 117
aluminum el aluminio 318
always siempre 6
amazed asombrado(a) 123
amazement el asombro 210
amazing portentoso(a) 210 sorprendente 322
ambiguity la ambigüedad 116
ambitious ambicioso(a) 133
American, US estadounidense 52 el/la estadounidense 237 americano(a) 285
among entre 3
amount la cantidad 31
to **amuse** divertir (irreg. ie, i) 22
amusement park el parque de atracciones 188
amusing divertido(a) 61
analysis el análisis 127
to **analyze** analizar 68

anatomy   la anatomía 141
ancient   antiguo(a) 24
and   y 1
anecdote   la anécdota 5
anger   el enfado 110
to anger   enfadar, enojar 22
angry   enojado(a) 75
angry (at each other)   enfadado(a) 37
animal   el animal 15
ankle   el tobillo 90
anniversary   el aniversario 125
to announce   anunciar 67 comunicar 266
to annoy   molestar 23
annual   anual 153
anomaly   la anomalía 278
anonymous   anónimo(a) 324
another   otro(a) 8
answer   la respuesta 31
to answer   responder 3 contestar 65
anthologist   el/la antologista 300
anthology   la antología 300
antibiotic   el antibiótico 75
to anticipate   anticipar, prever 124
antihero   el antihéroe 345
anti-materialism   el antimaterialismo 271
antique   antiguo(a) 24
antiquity   la antigüedad 340
anxiety   la ansiedad 122
anxious   ansioso(a) 42
any   cualquier(a) 22
(not) any   ningún(o)(a) 48
any (in questions)   algún, alguno(a) 19
any more   ya 25 más 72
any other (pronoun)   ningún(o)(a) 83
anybody   nadie 249
anything   algo, nada 26
apart from   aparte de 91
apart from that   por lo demás 7
to appeal   atraer (irreg.) 325
to appear   aparecer (irreg.) 41 surgir 291
appearance   el aspecto 54 la apariencia 106 la aparición 271
to applaud   aplaudir 190
appliance   el aparato 116
applicant   el/la postulante 144
application   la aplicación 98
to apply   aplicar 85 postular 144
to apply for   solicitar 137 pedir (irreg. i, i) 148 presentarse 169
to appoint   designar 261
appointment   la cita 92
to appreciate   apreciar 17
approach   el enfoque 281
to approach   acercarse 67
appropriate   adecuado(a) 22 apropiado(a) 95
appropriate for   dado(a) a 166
appropriately   adecuadamente 96 apropiadamente 294
approval   la aprobación 266
to approve   aprobar (irreg. ue) 290
approximately   aproximadamente 31

aquarium   el acuario 139
aqueduct   el acueducto 318
arable   cultivable 173
arch   el arco 318
archeological   arqueológico(a) 4
archeologist   el/la arqueólogo(a) 4
architect   el/la arquitecto(a) 9
architectural   arquitectónico(a) 318
architecture   la arquitectura 174
ardor   el fuego 249
area   la zona 7 el área 9 el recinto 139 la extensión 147 la superficie 173 el espacio 236 el núcleo 280
aren't you?/don't you?/ etc.   ¿verdad?   14
Argentinean   argentino(a) 23
to argue   pelearse 36 discutir 44 argumentar 68
argument   el argumento 157
argumentative   argumentativo(a) 230
to arise   surgir 58
aristocracy   la aristocracia 305
arm   el brazo 5
armchair   el sillón 38
armed conflict   el conflicto armado 272
armed forces   las fuerzas armadas 312
army   el ejército 248
around   cerca de 38 alrededor (de) 108
to arrange to meet   quedar 34
arrival   la llegada 103
to arrive   llegar 2
arrogant   orgulloso(a) 106
art   el arte 29
art gallery   el museo 151
artery   la arteria 90
article   el artículo 36 el/la artista 151 el/la creador 268
artistic   artístico(a) 29
as   como 218 igual de 308
as a matter of fact   de hecho 231
as a result of   como consecuencia de 96
as a team   en equipo 177
as far as I'm concerned   para mí 320
as much as   tanto como 308
as regards   en cuanto a 268
as soon as   en cuanto 276
as well as   además de 18
to ask   pedir (irreg. i, i) 10 preguntar 29
to ask for   pedir (irreg. i, i) 92
asleep   dormido(a) 336
aspect   el aspecto 7
to assassinate   asesinar 245
assembly   la asamblea 261
assembly plant   la maquila 173
to assess   evaluar 95
to assist   ayudar 90
assistance   la asistencia 273
assistant   el/la asistente 165
to associate with   asociar a/con 112
associated   asociado(a) 26
association   la asociación 67
assumption   la suposición 207

to assure   asegurar 14
asthma   el asma 90
at   en 3 ante 306
at all   nada 22
at first   en un principio 38 al principio 93
at first sight   a simple vista 222
at least   al menos 5 cuando menos 280
at noon   a mediodía 282
at once   enseguida 93
at risk   en peligro 45
at the beginning of   a principios de 134 a comienzos de 342
at the end   al final 91
at the end of   a finales de 284
at the foot of   al pie de 216
at the same time   paralelamente 67
athletic   atlético(a) 74
ATM   el cajero 289
atmosphere   la atmósfera 216 el ambiente 330
atmospheric   atmosférico(a) 296
to attach postage to   franquear 61
attack   el ataque 289
to attack   atacar 104
to attend   asistir a 92
attention   la atención 92
attentively   atentamente 47
attentiveness   las atenciones 109
attitude   la actitud 22
attorney   el/la abogado(a) 47
to attract   seducir (irreg.) 324
attraction   la atracción 139
attractive   atractivo(a) 61
audience   el público 49 la audiencia 52
audio   el audio 124
audio guide   la audioguía 311
audiovisual   audiovisual 69
audition   la audición 170 la prueba 291
auditorium   el auditorio 323
auditory   auditivo(a) 294
aunt   la tía 105
author   el/la autor(a) 11
authoritarian   autoritario(a) 260
authority   la autoridad 268
to authorize   autorizar 260
autobiographical   autobiográfico(a) 343
automobile (adjective)   automovilístico(a) 152
autumn   el otoño 47
auxiliary   auxiliar 138
availability   la disponibilidad 165
available   disponible 216
avalanche   la avalancha 212
avant-garde   vanguardista 316
avenue   la avenida 31
average   regular 7 medio(a) 39 el promedio 115
avocado   el aguacate 78
to avoid   evitar 82
to await   esperar 1
to awaken   despertar (irreg. ie) 352
to award   conceder 134 entregar 317
awarding   la concesión 182

aware *concienciado(a)* 102
awareness *la conciencia* 127
awful *fatal* 322
Aztec *azteca* 248

back *la espalda* 31 *atrás, detrás* 87
background *los antecedentes* 286 *el fondo* 306
background (adjective) *de fondo* 237
backpacker *el/la mochilero(a)* 216
bad *malo(a)* 106
bad (adjective) *mal* 24
bad luck *la mala pata* 107
badly *mal* 18
bad-mannered *maleducado(a)* 20
baggage *el equipaje* 189
baked *al horno* 78
balcony *la terraza* 219
bald *calvo(a)* 17
ballad *la trova* 184
balsamic *balsámico(a)* 336
to **ban** *prohibir* 259
banana *la banana, el guineo, el plátano* 172 *el banano* 222
banana (adjective) *bananero(a)* 222
banana tree *el banano* 172
band *la banda* 192
bang *el golpe* 330
bank *el banco* 29
bank balance *el saldo* 148
banker *el/la banquero(a)* 133
banking *la banca* 156
banking (adjective) *bancario(a)* 156
banquet *el banquete* 254
bar *el bar* 191 *la barra* 337
barbecue *la barbacoa* 219
barefoot *descalzo(a)* 249
barely able to speak *con un hilo de voz* 210
base *la base* 143
to **base** *apoyar* 157
to **base one's argument on** *basarse (en)* 193 *apoyarse en* 352
based on *basado(a) en* 42
basic *básico(a)* 66
basic principles *los fundamentos* 326
basically *básicamente* 157
basin *la cuenca* 77
basis *la base* 172
basketball *el baloncesto* 170
Basque (language) *el euskera* 67
batch *el lote* 67
bath *el baño* 7
battalion *el batallón* 254
battery *la batería* 53
battle *la batalla* 210
bay *la bahía* 321
to **be** *estar (irreg.)* 1 *ser (irreg.)* 2 *resultar* 38 *tratarse de* 133 *mostrarse (irreg. ue)* 199 *encontrarse (irreg. ue)* 200

to **be a fact (that)** *estar demostrado (que)* 252
to **be a good idea** *convenir (irreg.)* 216
to **be a sore loser** *tener mal perder* 192
to **be able** *poder (irreg. ue, u)* 8
to **be able to** *saber (irreg.)* 40
to **be about** *tratar (de)* 23
to **be absent (from class)** *faltar a clase* 132
to **be absolutely delicious** *estar para chuparse los dedos* 74
to **be abundant** *abundar* 344
to **be afraid of** *temer* 166
to **be afraid that** *temerse que* 83
to **be after** *perseguir (irreg. i, i)* 166
to **be aimed at** *encaminarse hacia* 156
to **be alarmed** *alarmarse* 272
to **be awarded** *recibir* 89
to **be based on** *basarse (en)* 154
to **be bored stiff** *aburrirse como una ostra* 188
to **be born** *nacer (irreg.)* 67
to **be called** *llamarse* 17 *denominarse* 97
to **be carried out** *desarrollarse* 173
to **be categorized** *categorizarse* 212
to **be characterized by** *caracterizarse por* 230
to **be clear (that)** *estar claro (que)* 252
to **be concentrated** *concentrarse* 260
to **be confident that** *confiar en que* 257
to **be convinced (that)** *estar convencido(a) (de que)* 252
to **be delayed** *demorarse, retrasarse* 207
to **be derived from** *derivarse de* 166
to **be different (from)** *diferenciarse (de)* 214
to **be difficult** *costar (irreg. ue)* 39
to **be discouraged** *desanimarse* 53
to **be drawn from** *desprenderse de* 109
to **be due to** *deberse a* 132
to **be dying** *agonizar* 343
to **be enough** *bastar* 325
to **be equivalent** *equivaler (irreg.)* 140
to **be estimated** *estimarse* 144
to **be flooded** *inundarse* 220
to **be frowned upon** *estar mal visto* 84
to **be glad to (followed by infinitive)** *alegrarse de* 16
to **be grateful for** *agradecer (irreg.)* 92
to **be guided by** *guiarse por* 66
to **be happy** *alegrarse* 102
to **be happy (with)** *estar conforme (con)* 263
to **be hard work** *costar (irreg. ue)* 202
to **be held** *celebrarse* 14
to **be higher than** *superar* 177
to **be in a good/bad mood** *estar de buen/mal humor* 102

to **be in charge of** *encargarse de* 153
to **be in charge of doing something** *ocuparse de hacer algo* 190
to **be in the habit of** *soler (irreg. ue)* 194
to **be inspired by** *inspirarse en* 242
to **be interested in** *interesarse por* 243
to **be introduced** *introducirse (irreg.)* 67
to **be known** *conocerse (irreg.)* 91
to **be late** *retrasarse* 207
to **be left** *quedar* 49 *quedarse* 108 *sobrar* 127
to **be located** *ubicarse* 325
to **be missing** *faltar* 28
to **be more than** *superar* 251
to **be noticed** *apreciarse* 309
to **be on ... (expenses)** *correr por parte de...* 144
to **be pleased to (followed by infinitive)** *alegrarse de* 92
to **be present** *estar presente* 116
to **be quiet** *callar* 100
to **be right** *tener razón* 17
to **be satisfied with** *contentarse con* 336
to **be self-employed** *trabajar por cuenta propia* 132
to **be sold** *comercializarse* 125
to **be solved** *resolverse (irreg.)* 293
to **be sorry** *sentir (irreg. ie, i)* 92
to **be startled** *sobresaltarse* 210
to **be supported by** *sustentarse en* 43
to **be sure (that)** *estar seguro(a) (de que)* 252
to **be sure about** *tener claro(a)* 197
to **be the main character in** *protagonizar* 122
to **be the responsibility of** *corresponder a* 260
to **be updated** *actualizarse* 230
to **be useful** *servir (irreg. i, i)* 42
to **be worth** *valer (irreg.)* 8
to **be worth it** *merecer la pena* 186 *valer la pena* 257
to **be worthwhile** *merecer la pena* 186 *valer la pena* 257
to **be wrong** *fallar* 224
beach *la playa* 7
bean *el frijol* 75
to **bear in mind** *tener en cuenta* 27 *tomar en cuenta* 278
beard *la barba* 17
to **beat** *superar* 45 *vencer* 83 *ganar* 235
beautiful *precioso(a)* 21 *bello(a)* 39 *hermoso(a)* 100
because *porque* 2 *puesto que* 147 *debido a que* 218
because of *a causa de* 5 *por culpa de* 287
to **become** *convertirse en (irreg. ie, i)* 38 *ponerse (irreg.)* 102 *hacerse (irreg.)* 158 *volverse (irreg.)* 268
to **become apparent** *manifestarse (irreg. ie)* 268

to **become independent** independizarse 105

to **become naturalized** nacionalizarse 50

bed la cama 204

bedroom el cuarto 92 la habitación 196

beef la carne de res 75

before antes 24 ante 75 antes de (que) 276

to **begin** empezar (irreg. ie) 1 comenzar (irreg. ie) 20 iniciar 159

beginning el principio 40 el inicio 175 el comienzo 179

to **behave** comportarse 211

to **behave well** portarse bien 37

behavior el comportamiento 102

behind detrás de 11 atrás 163

being el ser 94

belfry el campanario 323

believable verosímil 230

to **believe** considerar 67

bellhop el botones 216

bellman el botones 216

to **belong to** pertenecer a (irreg.) 258

below abajo 166 debajo 175

bench el banco 50 la banca 222

to **bend** doblar 220

beneficial beneficioso(a) 80

beneficiary beneficiario(a) 125

benefit el beneficio 55

to **benefit** beneficiar 125 beneficiarse 126

benign benigno(a) 96

best mejor 11

best man el padrino 100

better mejor 8

between entre 2

bibliographical bibliográfico(a) 344

bibliography la bibliografía 286

bicycle la bici 194

big gran, grande 24

bigger mayor 33

biggest mayor 139

bilingual bilingüe 183

bill el proyecto de ley 261 la factura 276

biofuel el biocombustible 173

biographical biográfico(a) 253

biography la biografía 223

biologist el/la biólogo(a) 160

biology la Biología 133

biomedical biomédico(a) 89

bipolar bipolar 295

bird el ave 163

birth el nacimiento 161

birthday el cumpleaños 14 el aniversario 54

birthplace el lugar de nacimiento 161

bitter amargo(a) 76

bitterly cold glacial 216

black negro(a) 54

blackberry la mora 78

to **blame** echar la culpa 17

to **bleed** sangrar 90

blind ciego(a) 20

block el bloque 174

to **block** bloquear 224

blog la bitácora 230

blood la sangre 75

blood (adjective) sanguíneo(a) 98

blood pressure la presión arterial 90

blood test el análisis de sangre 75

to **blow** soplar 28

blue azul 35

to **blush** enrojecer (irreg.) 210

board el tablero 192 la tabla 195 el panel 326

board game el juego de mesa 192

boarding pass la tarjeta de embarque 189

boat el barco 193

body el cuerpo 36 el cadáver 267

to **boil** cocer (irreg. ue), hervir (irreg. ie, i) 108

bolero el bolero 226

Bolivian boliviano(a) 146

bomb la bomba 289

bone (adjective) óseo(a) 96

book el libro 24

to **book** reservar 86

border la frontera 173

to **bore** aburrir 22

bored aburrido(a) 75

boredom el aburrimiento 200

boring aburrido(a) 188

born nacido(a) 125

boss el/la jefe(a) 40

both ambos(as) 247

to **bother** molestar 22

bouquet el ramo 100

bow el lazo 100

bowl el bol 336

box el cuadro 5 la caja 19 la ficha 35

box office la taquilla 189

boy el chico 20 el muchacho 50

boyfriend el novio 4

brain el cerebro 114

to **brake hard** pegar un frenazo 210

branch la rama 33

brave valiente 20

to **bread** empanar 139

break la ruptura 342

to **break** romper (irreg.) 19 romperse (irreg.) 80

to **break up** romper (irreg.) 4 fragmentarse 212

breakfast el desayuno 216

breast la pechuga 78

to **breathe** respirar 75

breeding la crianza 296

breeze la brisa 216

to **brew (tea)** reposar 87

brick el ladrillo 318

bride el novio 100

bridge el puente 318

brief breve 25 pequeño(a) 124

bright luminoso(a) 19 brillante 303 bruñido(a) 343

to **bring** traer (irreg.) 2

to **bring closer** acercar 1

to **bring together** reunir 285

to **bring under control** controlar 262

broad amplio(a) 172

to **broadcast** emitir 102 transmitir 125

brochure el folleto 113

broken roto(a) 75

bronze el bronce 222

broth el caldo 336

brother el hermano 17

brown castaño(a) 17

brush el pincel 306

brushstroke la pincelada 306

brutality la brutalidad 351

budget el presupuesto 148

to **build** construir (irreg.) 202

building el edificio 24 la construcción 318 la edificación 319

built construido(a) 324

bull el toro 337

bulletin board el tablón de anuncios 160

bump el golpe 330

burn la quemadura 90

to **burn** quemar 19

bus el autobús, el bus, el camión, el colectivo, la guagua 56

business los negocios 38 el negocio 148

business (adjective) empresarial 180

businessman/businesswoman el/la empresario(a) 133

busy ocupado(a) 2

but pero 1 sino 67

butterfly la mariposa 54

button el botón 44

to **buy** comprar 10

by por 3

by hand a mano 38

by means of mediante 97 por medio de 136

By the way, Por cierto, 28 A propósito, 244

by then para entonces 8

by yourself solo(a) 125

C

cabin la cabaña 218

cabinet el gabinete 306

café el café 203

cafeteria la cafetería 323

cake el pastel 28 la torta 112

calcium el calcio 173

to **calculate** calcular 96

calendar el calendario 134

call la llamada 138

to **call** convocar 43 llamar 45

to **call each other** llamarse

called denominado(a) 36 llamado(a) 86

calm la tranquilidad 38 tranquilo(a) 75

camera la cámara 54

campaign la campaña 99

camper la caravana 216

campground el cámping 216

camping el cámping 5 la acampada 139

to **consult** *consultar* 116
consultancy firm *la consultora* 212
to **consume** *consumir* 117
consumed *consumido(a)* 77
consumption *el consumo* 11
contact *el contacto* 130
to **contact** *contactar (con)* 183
contagious *contagioso(a)* 90
to **contain** *contener (irreg.)* 19 *recoger* 200
container *el recipiente* 76
contemporary *contemporáneo(a)* 142
contempt *el desprecio* 21
content *el contenido* 11
contents *el contenido* 19
contest *el concurso* 67
contestant *el/la concursante* 76
context *el contexto* 149
continent *el continente* 147
to **continue** *continuar* 16 *seguir (irreg. i, i)* 84
continuity *la continuidad* 324
contract *el contrato* 133
contrast *el contraste* 306
to **contrast** *contrastar* 170
to **contribute** *contribuir (irreg.)* 99 *aportar* 125
contribution *la cuota* 114 *la aportación* 180 *la contribución* 285
contributor *el/la colaborador(a)* 69
control *el control* 110 *el dominio* 248
to **control** *controlar* 154 *dominar* 279
convenient *cómodo(a)* 214
convention *la convención* 336
conversation *la conversación* 2
conversion *la conversión* 153
to **convey** *comunicar* 263
to **convince** *convencer (irreg.)* 229
convinced *convencido(a)* 38
convincing *convincente* 55
cook *el/la cocinero(a)* 80
to **cook** *cocinar* 73
cooked *cocinado(a)* 172
cooking *la cocina* 116
cooler *la nevera portátil* 216
to **cooperate** *cooperar* 69
to **coordinate** *coordinar* 115
coordination *la coordinación* 169
coordinator *el/la coordinador(a)* 133
copper *el cobre* 173
copy *el ejemplar* 342
coral *el coral* 228
corn *el maíz* 195
corner *el rincón* 31 *la esquina* 343
cornice *la cornisa* 222
corporate *corporativo(a)* 67
corpse *el cadáver* 267
correct *correcto(a)* 5
to **correct** *corregir (irreg. i, i)* 2
correctness *la corrección* 58
correlation *la correlación* 208
to **correspond to** *corresponderse con* 27 *corresponder a* 30
corresponding *correspondiente* 9
corrupt *corrupto(a)* 343

corruption *la corrupción* 272
cosmetic *cosmético(a)* 114
cosmetics *la cosmética* 91
cost *el coste* 137
to **cost** *costar (irreg. ue)* 217
costume *el traje* 236
cough *la tos* 90
to **cough** *toser* 75
cough syrup *el jarabe* 92
council *el consejo* 165
to **count** *contar (irreg. ue)* 30 *valer (irreg.)* 311
to **count on** *contar con (irreg. ue)* 92
countable *contable* 94
counter *el mostrador* 189
country *el país* 3 *el campo* 80
country estate *la hacienda* 7
country house *la quinta* 336
coup (d'état) *el golpe de Estado* 260
couple *la pareja* 39 *el par* 210
courage *el valor* 311
course *el plato* 78 *el curso* 136 *el ciclo* 165 *el rumbo* 314
court *el tribunal* 260
courteous *atento(a)* 106
courtyard *el patio* 219
cousin *primo(a)* 73
cover *la cubierta* 191
to **cover** *cubrir (irreg.)* 31 *tapar* 79
to **cover (with)** *llenar (de)* 197
cowardly *cobarde* 20
crab *el cangrejo* 78
crafts *las manualidades* 187 *la artesanía* 203
craziness *el delirio* 278
crazy (about) *loco(a) (por)* 44
cream *la crema* 91
to **create** *crear* 25
created *creado(a)* 98
creation *la creación* 69
creative *creativo(a)* 39 *creador(a)* 43
creativity *la creatividad* 317
creator *el/la autor(a)* 26 *el/la creador(a)* 98
credit *el crédito* 156
creole *criollo(a)* 248
cretin *el/la cretino(a)* 210
crime *el crimen* 265 *la delincuencia, el delito* 272
crime novel *la novela negra* 330
crimson *carmesí* 336
crisis *la crisis* 272
criterion *el criterio* 117
critical *crítico(a)* 125
criticism *la crítica* 329
croissant *la medialuna* 231
crop *el cultivo* 172
croquette *la croqueta* 79
cross *la cruz* 323
to **cross** *cruzar* 159 *atravesar (irreg. ie)* 231
crosswalk *el paso de cebra* 204
crossword *el crucigrama* 188
crouching *agachado(a)* 102
crowd *la multitud* 266
to **crown it all** *para colmo* 291
cruelty *la crueldad* 351

cruise *el crucero* 193
to **cry** *llorar* 39
Cuban *cubano(a)* 38
Cubism *el cubismo* 306
Cubist *cubista* 302
cucumber *el pepino* 78
cuisine *la cocina* 112
cultural *cultural* 23
culture *la cultura* 14
cup *la taza* 332
curator *el/la curador(a)* 314
to **cure** *curar* 8
curiosity *la curiosidad* 108
curly *rizado(a)* 17
currency *la moneda* 153
current *actual* 1
current situation *la actualidad* 1
currently *en la actualidad* 50 *actualmente* 318
custard *la natilla* 112
custom *la costumbre* 1
customer *el/la cliente(a)* 44
cut *el corte* 90
to **cut** *cortar* 53
to **cut oneself** *cortarse* 90
cycle *el ciclo* 102

dad *el papá* 21
daily *diario(a)* 7 *a diario* 50 *cotidiano(a)* 58 *diariamente* 194
damage *el daño* 222
to **damage** *perjudicar* 272
damaged *deteriorado(a)* 293
dance *el baile* 11 *la danza* 170
to **dance** *bailar* 3
danger *el peligro* 69
dangerous *peligroso(a)* 96
to **dare** *atreverse a* 92
dark *oscuro(a)* 268
dark-haired *moreno(a)* 20
darling (term of endearment) *cielito* 23
data *los datos* 98
database *la base de datos* 174
date *la cita* 93 *la fecha* 94
to **date back to** *remontarse a* 261
to **date from** *situarse en* 79
daughter *la hija* 90
dawn *el alba* 33
to **dawn** *amanecer* 26
day *el día* 2 *la jornada* 54
dead *muerto(a)* 289
deadline *el plazo* 141
deaf *sordo(a)* 20
to **deal with** *atender (irreg. ie)* 39
dean *el/la decano(a)* 317
dear *querido(a)* 37
Dear ... *Estimado(a)...* 59
death *la muerte* 33
debate *el debate* 130
to **debate** *debatir* 52
debut *la presentación en sociedad* 105
decade *la década* 200
deceased *el/la difunto(a)* 113
to **deceive** *engañar* 192

to **decide** *decidir* 2
to **decide to** *decidirse a* 38
decision *la decisión* 11
decisive *decisivo(a)* 154
to **declare** *declarar* 248
décor *la decoración* 7
to **decorate** *adornar* 19 *decorar* 197
decoration *la decoración* 10
to **decrease** *disminuir (irreg.)* 11
  descender (irreg. ie) 33
deeply *hondamente* 336
defeat *la derrota* 248
to **defend** *defender (irreg. ie)* 249
defender *el/la defensor(a)* 38
to **define** *definir* 65
definite *determinado(a)* 94
  definido(a) 95
definitely *seguro* 32
definition *la definición* 44
definitive *definitivo(a)* 59
degree *la licenciatura* 165 *el grado* 196
(university) degree *el grado* 326
delay *el retraso* 218
to **delay** *tardar (en)* 32 *demorar* 336
  retrasar 337
to **delete** *suprimir* 67
delicious *delicioso(a)* 28 *rico(a)* 74
delighted that *encantado(a) de que* 14
to **deliver** *entregar* 32 *repartir* 33
demand *la demanda* 215
to **demand** *exigir* 117 *requerir (irreg. ie, i)* 212
demanding *exigente* 133
democracy *la democracia* 260
democrat *el/la demócrata* 245
democratic *democrático(a)* 244
demonstration *la demostración* 67
  la manifestación 262
dénouement (literary) *el desenlace* 330
to **denounce** *denunciar* 258
dense *denso(a)* 109
dental *dental* 160
dental/health insurance *el seguro dental/médico* 160
dentist *el/la dentista* 75
departing for *con destino a* 189
department *el departamento* 183
  el ministerio 273
department store *la gran superficie* 126
departure *la partida* 254
to **depend on** *depender de* 92
dependence *la dependencia* 153
dependent on *supeditado(a) a* 268
depending on *según* 21 *en función de* 135
deposit *el depósito* 148
to **depress** *deprimir* 22
depressed *desanimado(a)* 102
depth *la profundidad* 302
dermatologist *el/la dermatólogo(a)* 90
descent *la bajada* 139
to **describe** *describir (irreg.)* 1
  calificar 261
description *la descripción* 58

descriptive *descriptivo(a)* 230
to **deserve** *merecerse (irreg.)* 181
design *el diseño* 65
to **design** *diseñar* 10 *proyectar* 267
(fashion) designer *el/la diseñador(a) (de moda)* 174
desired *deseado(a)* 39
desperate *desesperado(a)* 38
despite *pese a, a pesar de (que)* 264
dessert *el postre* 78
destination *el destino* 114
destiny *el destino* 329
to **destroy** *destruir (irreg.)* 96
destruction *la destrucción* 155
detail *el detalle* 38
detailed *detallado(a)* 327
to **detain** *detener (irreg.)* 260
to **detect** *captar* 66 *detectar* 98
detection *la detección* 96
detective *el/la detective* 18
detective (adjective) *policíaco(a)* 189
deterioration *el deterioro* 292
to **determine** *determinar* 136
to **develop** *evolucionar* 39 *desarrollar* 43
developed *desarrollado(a)* 155
development *el desarrollo* 98
devil *el diablo* 184
to **devote** *dedicar* 11
diabetes *la diabetes* 90
to **diagnose** *diagnosticar* 97
diagnosis *el diagnóstico* 75
diagram *el gráfico* 155 *el diagrama* 261 *el esquema* 347
dialect *el dialecto* 67
dialogue *el diálogo* 16
dialogue (adjective) *dialogado(a)* 26
diary *el diario* 119
dictator *el/la dictador(a)* 260
dictatorship *la dictadura* 258
dictionary *el diccionario* 66
didactic *didáctico(a)* 116
die *el dado* 192
to **die** *morir (irreg.)* 102
diet *la dieta* 11 *la alimentación* 122
difference *la diferencia* 19
different *diferentes* 17 *distintos(as)* 24 *diferente* 69 *distinto(a)* 134
different from *alejado(a) de* 167
differentiated *diferenciado(a)* 212
difficult *difícil* 39
difficulty *la dificultad* 90
digital *digital* 44
dignity *la dignidad* 156
diluted *diluido(a)* 306
dimension *la dimensión* 123
diminutive *el diminutivo* 332
din *la algarabía* 210 *el alboroto* 211
dining car *el vagón-restaurante* 204
dinner *la cena* 47
diploma *el diploma* 165
direct *directo(a)* 36
to **direct** *dirigir* 89

direct/indirect object *el objeto directo/indirecto* 82
directly *directamente* 37
director *el/la director(a)* 67
disabled *discapacitado(a)* 269
disadvantage *el inconveniente* 97 *la desventaja* 105 *la dificultad* 205
disadvantaged *desfavorecido(a)* 125
to **disappear** *desaparecer (irreg.)* 33
disappearance *la desaparición* 342
disappointed *decepcionado(a)* 291
disappointing *decepcionante* 344
disappointment *el desengaño* 49 *el desencanto* 222
disaster *el desastre* 121
discarded *descartado(a)* 296
discipline *la disciplina* 142
disco *la discoteca* 188
discourse *el discurso* 268
to **discover** *descubrir (irreg.)* 1
discovery *el descubrimiento* 4
discreet *discreto(a)* 343
discretion *la discreción* 325
discrimination *la discriminación* 272
discriminatory *discriminatorio(a)* 161
to **discuss** *discutir, comentar* 44
discussion *la discusión* 325
to **disembark** *desembarcar* 336
disgust *la repugnancia* 166
dish *el plato* 3 *la comida* 79
disheartened *apesadumbrado(a)* 254
to **disillusion** *desilusionar* 254
disorder *el trastorno* 98 *el desorden* 295
display *la exposición* 267 *la manifestación* 268
disproportion *la desproporción* 307
to **dissolve** *disolver (irreg.)* 347
distance *la distancia* 31
distant *lejano(a)* 33 *remoto(a)* 336
distinct *acusado(a)* 127
distinction *la distinción* 324
distinctive *distintivo(a)* 324
to **distinguish** *distinguir* 57
to **distract** *distraer (irreg.)* 336
to **distribute** *distribuir (irreg.), repartir* 125
distribution *la distribución* 56
district *el distrito* 31
distrust *la desconfianza* 267
distrustful *desconfiado(a)* 279
disturbance *la perturbación* 212
diversification *la diversificación* 312
diversity *la diversidad* 101
to **divide** *dividir(se)* 204
divided *dividido(a)* 204
divided by *entre* 136
divinity *la divinidad* 336
division *la división* 136
divorced *divorciado(a)* 59
dizziness *el vértigo* 210
dizzy *mareado(a)* 75
to **do** *hacer (irreg.)* 2 *realizar* 66

to **do for a living** *dedicarse a* 113
to **do research** *documentarse* 254
to **do something again** *volver a hacer algo* 40
dock *el muelle* 254
doctor *el/la médico(a)* 8 *el/la doctor(a)* 59
doctor's office *la consulta (médica)* 75
document *el documento* 174
to **document** *documentar* 286
documentary *el documental* 44
dog *el perro* 302
doll *el/la muñeco(a)* 18
dollar *el dólar* 106
domestic *doméstico(a)* 59 *nacional* 273
Dominican *dominicano(a)* 153
Don't worry. *Tranquilo(a).* 90
to **donate** *donar* 88
donation *la donación* 115
donor *el/la donante* 115
door *la puerta* 38
double *el doble* 48 *doble* 216
doubly *doblemente* 300
doubt *la duda* 58
to **doubt** *dudar* 246 *poner en duda* 296
doubtful *dudoso(a)* 252
download *la descarga* 67
to **download** *descargar* 111 *bajar* 133
downpour *el chubasco* 216
draft *el borrador* 95 *la corriente de aire* 224
draftsman/draftswoman *el/la dibujante* 351
to **draw** *dibujar* 41
to **draw out (a sound)** *arrastrar* 278
drawback *el inconveniente* 97
drawing *el dibujo* 41
dream *el sueño* 33 *la ilusión* 198
to **dream of** *soñar con (irreg. ue)* 92
dress *el vestido* 35
dressed *vestido(a)* 54
dried fruits and nuts *los frutos secos* 75
to **drink** *beber, tomar* 76
to **drink maté** *matear* 77
drinking *potable* 296
to **drive** *manejar* 141 *conducir (irreg.)* 174 *circular* 277 *animar* 344
driver *el/la conductor(a)* 204
driver's license *el carné de conducir* 174
drop *la gota* 33
to **drop** *caerse (irreg.)* 80 *bajar* 235
drug *el fármaco* 97 *la droga* 272
drug abuse *el abuso de drogas* 272
drug trafficking *el tráfico de drogas* 272
drugstore *la farmacia* 91
dry *seco(a)* 87
to **dry** *secarse* 308
duchess *la duquesa* 309
due *debido(a)* 117
due to *debido a* 238
duration *la duración* 263
during *durante* 23

dusk *el anochecer* 337
duties *los deberes* 245
duty *la función* 161
dynamic *dinámico(a)* 46

each *cada* 9
ear *el oído* 94
early *temprano* 35 *temprano(a)* 97
to **earn** *ganar* 179 *ganarse* 256
to **earn a living** *ganarse la vida* 191
Earth *la tierra* 295
earthenware vessel *la vasija de barro* 29
earthquake *el terremoto* 266
easily *fácilmente* 103 *con facilidad* 110
East *el oriente* 37
Eastern *oriental* 228
easy *fácil* 14
to **eat** *comer* 10 *tomar* 79
to **eat like a horse** *comer como una fiera/como una lima* 74
to **eat one's fill** *ponerse las botas* 74
echo *el eco* 33
ecological agriculture *la agricultura ecológica* 272
economic *económico(a)* 9
economically *económicamente* 136
economy *la economía* 1
ecosystem *el ecosistema* 296
ecotourism *el ecoturismo* 219
edition *la edición* 314
editor *el/la director(a)* 263
editorial *el editorial* 44
to **educate** *educar* 177
education *la educación* 9 *la enseñanza* 338
educational *educativo(a)* 137
educational training *la formación académica* 160
effect *el efecto* 38
effective *eficaz* 38 *efectivo(a)* 89
efficient *eficiente* 133
effort *el esfuerzo* 159
egg *el huevo* 78
eggplant *la berenjena* 78
eighth *octavo(a)* 250
to **elect** *elegir (irreg. i, i)* 260
election *la elección* 260
elections *las elecciones* 53
electoral campaign *la campaña electoral* 260
electric *eléctrico(a)* 146
electricity *la electricidad* 323
electronic *electrónico(a)* 148
elegant *elegante* 7
element *el elemento* 49
elephant *el elefante* 332
elevator *el ascensor* 94
eleventh *undécimo(a)* 250
to **eliminate** *eliminar* 69
e-mail *el correo (electrónico)* 28
e-mail (adjective) *electrónico(a)* 33
to **embark upon** *apostar por (irreg. ue)* 139

to **embarrass** *dar vergüenza* 29 *avergonzar (irreg. ue)* 102
embarrassed *avergonzado(a)* 102
embarrassment *la pena, la vergüenza* 56
embedded *incrustado(a)* 295
emblem *el emblema* 61
emblematic *emblemático(a)* 342
emergency *la urgencia* 90
emergency room *la sala de urgencias* 90 *las emergencias* 116
emigrant *el/la emigrante* 284
emission *la emisión* 296
emotion *la emoción* 22
emotional (state, etc.) *anímico(a)* 102
emphasis *el énfasis* 334
to **emphasize** *destacar* 43 *enfatizar* 220
emphatic *enfático(a)* 310
empire *el imperio* 4
to **employ** *emplear* 158
employed *empleado(a)* 68
employee *el/la empleado(a)* 138
employment *el empleo* 149
empty *libre* 210 *vacío(a)* 222
to **encourage** *animar* 132 *fomentar* 149
encyclopedia *la enciclopedia* 97
end *el final* 6 *el fin* 156 *la finalidad* 262 *el extremo* 306
to **end** *terminar* 4 *acabar(se)* 34 *culminar* 248
to **end up** *acabar* 49
ending *la terminación* 4 *el desenlace* 330
endless *sin fin* 350
energy *la energía* 38
energy (adjective) *energético(a)* 272
energy savings *el ahorro energético* 272
energy source *la fuente de energía* 45
engagement *el noviazgo* 33 *el compromiso* 100
engineer *el/la ingeniero(a)* 133
engineering *la ingeniería* 158
English *inglés(a)* 329
English (language) *el inglés* 21
engraving *el grabado* 12
enhancement *el realce* 200
enigma *el enigma* 15
to **enjoy** *disfrutar (de)* 45 *deleitarse con* 203
to **enjoy oneself** *divertirse (irreg. ie, i)* 3
Enjoy yourselves. *Que se diviertan.* 14
enjoyable *divertido(a)* 17 *entretenido(a)* 345
to **enlarge** *ampliar* 98
enough *bastante(s)* 48 *suficiente* 49 *suficientemente* 311
to **enrich** *enriquecer (irreg.)* 109
enrichment *el enriquecimiento* 317
enrollment *la matrícula* 137

to **enter** *entrar* 38 *presentar* 113
ingresar 163 *inscribirse (en)*
(irreg.) 165
to **entertain** *divertir (irreg. ie, i)* 22
entertaining *entretenido(a)* 345
entertainment *el entretenimiento*
52 *el espectáculo* 192
entity *la entidad* 94
entrance *el ingreso* 136
entrance exam *el examen de*
ingreso 136
entrepreneurial *emprendedor(a)*
133
entry *la entrada* 7
envelope *el sobre* 32
envious *envidioso(a)* 20
environment *el entorno* 268 *el*
medio ambiente 272
environmental *medioambiental*
156 *ambiental* 217
to **envy** *envidiar* 39
equality *la igualdad* 245
equals *igual a* 136
equation *la ecuación* 136
equatorial *ecuatorial* 172
equivalence *la equivalencia* 264
equivalent *equivalente* 51
era *la era* 38 *la época* 77
error *el error* 47
erudite *erudito(a)* 39
to **escape** *fugarse* 34
especially *especialmente* 58 *en*
especial 150
essay *el trabajo* 64 *el ensayo* 330
essayist *el/la ensayista* 329
essential *fundamental* 50 *esencial*
148
to **establish** *establecer (irreg.)* 130
establishment *el establecimiento*
91 *el local* 200
estimate *la estimación* 296
estimated *estimado(a)* 229
eternity *la eternidad* 336
ethnicity *la etnicidad* 271
eucalyptus *el eucalipto* 336
European *europeo(a)* 19
to **evaluate** *evaluar* 65
evangelical *evangélico(a)* 336
evaporation *la evaporación* 147
even *incluso* 21 *hasta* 158
even though *aun cuando* 264
evening *la tarde* 5 *la noche* 195
event *el hecho* 1 *el evento* 2
el acto 125 *el acontecimiento* 211
el episodio 230
eventful *accidentado(a)* 112
ever (in questions) *alguna vez* 15
every *todos(as)* 6 *cada* 194
everyday *cotidiano(a)* 51
everyone *todos(as)* 11
everything *todo* 2
evidence *la muestra* 43
evident *palpable* 67 *evidente* 252
evidently *evidentemente* 197
evil *la maldad* 279
exactly *exactamente* 80
efectivamente 186
exaggerated *exagerado(a)* 306
exam *el examen* 2

to **examine** *examinar* 95
example *el ejemplo* 39
to **excavate** *excavar* 245
excellent *excelente* 11
excelling *la superación* 215
except *excepto* 82
exceptional *excepcional* 43
excerpt *el fragmento* 33
excess *el exceso* 207
excessive *excesivo(a)* 45
exchange *el cambio* 116 *el*
intercambio 130
to **exchange** *intercambiar* 9
to **excite** *emocionar* 22
excited *emocionado(a)* 20
excitement *la emoción* 38
exciting *excitante* 50 *emocionante*
225
to **exclaim** *exclamar* 222
excluded *excluido(a)* 155
exclusive *exclusivo(a)* 7
excursion *la excursión* 65
to **excuse yourself** *excusarse* 238
to **execute** *ejecutar* 260
execution *la ejecución* 169
executive *ejecutivo(a)* 67
exercise *el ejercicio* 11
to **exhibit** *exponer (irreg.)* 303
exhibition *la exposición* 80 *la*
muestra 314
exile *el exilio* 258 *el/la exiliado(a)*
278
to **exile (oneself)** *exiliar(se)* 260
to **exist** *existir* 21
exit *la salida* 192
exotic *exótico(a)* 158
to **expand** *expandir* 217 *ampliarse*
329 *ampliar* 351
to **expect** *esperar* 38
expedition *la expedición* 248
expenses *los gastos* 144
expensive *caro(a)* 32 *costoso(a)*
320
experience *la experiencia* 23
to **experience** *experimentar* 80
experiment *el experimento* 141
to **experiment** *experimentar* 321
expert *experto(a)* 87 *el/la*
experto(a) 122
to **explain** *explicar* 5 *indicar* 278
exponer (irreg.) 286
explanation *la explicación* 101
explanatory *expositivo(a)* 286
explicativo(a) 326
to **explore** *explorar* 193
explorer *el/la explorador(a)* 245
exponent *el exponente* 335
export *la exportación* 154
to **export** *exportar* 148
exporter *el/la exportador(a)* 172
express *expreso(a)* 203
to **express** *expresar* 10 *manifestar*
(irreg. ie) 153
expression *la expresión* 16
to **extend** *prorrogar* 188
extended *amplio(a)* 91
extensive *extenso(a)* 325
extent *la envergadura* 272
external *externo(a)* 286

to **extract** *extraer (irreg.)* 173
extracting *extractor(a)* 173
extraordinary *extraordinario(a)*
204
extreme *extremo(a)* 195 *el*
extremo 325
extremely *sumamente* 110
extremely important *trascendental*
296
eye *el ojo* 19

fable *la fábula* 330
fabric *la tela* 304
fabulous *fabuloso(a)* 99
facade *la fachada* 318
face *la cara* 20 *la pared* 203
to **face up to** *hacer frente a* 110
facilities *las instalaciones* 233
fact *el hecho* 39
factor *el factor* 115
factory *la fábrica* 150
faculty *la facultad* 317
to **fail** *reprobar (irreg. ue)* 136
failure *el fracaso* 345
fair *la feria* 72
fair trade *el comercio justo* 156
faith *la fe* 38
faithful *fiel* 17
faithfulness *la fidelidad* 17
fall *el otoño* 47
to **fall** *caer (irreg.)* 19 *caerse (irreg.)*
119 *bajar* 235
to **fall asleep** *dormirse (irreg. u, ue)*
34
to **fall in love** *enamorarse (de)* 17
fall in price *el abaratamiento* 154
falls *las cataratas* 228
false *falso(a)* 2
fame *el renombre* 200 *la fama* 329
familiar *familiar* 352
familiarity *la confianza* 57
family *la familia* 3
family (adjective) *familiar* 11
famous *famoso(a)* 28 *célebre* 265
fan *el/la aficionado(a)* 49
fantastic *fantástico(a)* 53
fantasy *la fantasía* 50
far (from) *lejos (de)* 7
faraway *distante* 31 *la despedida*
254
farm *la granja* 108
farmer *el/la granjero(a)* 108 *el/la*
agricultor(a) 281
to **fascinate** *fascinar* 22 *apasionar*
210
fascinating *apasionante,*
fascinante 14
fashion designer *el/la modisto(a)*
326
fashionable *de moda* 212
fast *rápido(a)* 41 *rápido* 107
apresuradamente 210
fat *la grasa* 11 *gordo(a)* 40
fate *el destino* 329
father *el padre* 24
fault *el defecto* 278

full (up) *lleno(a)* 74
full board *la pensión completa* 216
full-time *a tiempo completo* 131 *la jornada completa* 133
fun *divertido(a)* 17
function *la función* 106
functional *funcional* 317
fund *el fondo* 156
fundamental *fundamental* 50
funeral *el funeral* 43
funny *gracioso(a)* 5 *divertido(a)* 61
furious *furioso(a)* 102
future *futuro(a)* 2 *el futuro* 8 *venidero(a)* 326

to **gain** *ganar* 98
to **gain weight** *aumentar de peso* 75
Galician (language) *el gallego* 67
galleon *el galeón* 195
gallery *la galería* 64
game *el juego* 59 *el partido* 120 *la partida* 192
game show *el concurso* 44
gang *la banda* 289
garage *el garaje* 47
garden *el jardín* 7
gardener *el/la jardinero(a)* 174
garment *la prenda (de vestir)* 94
gas *el gas* 153
gasoline *la gasolina* 204
gastronomic *gastronómico(a)* 79
gastronomy *la gastronomía* 72
gate *la puerta* 119
to **gather** *recoger* 64 *reunir* 236
gaze *la mirada* 139
gender *el género* 48
general *general* 66 *el/la general* 246
generally *generalmente* 22
to **generate** *generar* 147
generation *la generación* 43
generous *generoso(a)* 17
genetic *genético(a)* 96
genius *el genio* 43
genre *el género* 330
gently *suavemente* 337
genuine *auténtico(a)* 66 *genuino(a)* 210
geographic *geográfico(a)* 56
geography *la Geografía* 133 *la geografía* 324
geologist *el/la geólogo(a)* 160
geometric *geométrico(a)* 306
germinative *germinativo(a)* 96
to **gesticulate** *gesticular* 210
gesture *el gesto* 210
to **get** *sacar* 11 *conseguir (irreg. i, i)* 83
to **get a puncture** *pincharse* 209
to **get along (well/badly)** *llevarse (bien/mal)* 17
to **get angry** *enfadarse* 46
to **get bored** *aburrirse* 188
to **get broken** *romperse (irreg.)* 34
to **get dizzy** *marearse* 90
to **get dressed** *vestirse (irreg. i, i)* 36

to **get fit** *ponerse en forma* 11
to **get good marks** *sacar buenas notas* 132
to **get in touch** *ponerse en contacto* 242
to **get involved** *meterse* 39 *involucrarse* 293
to **get lost** *perderse (irreg. ie)* 80
to **get mad at** *enojarse con* 92
to **get off** *descender (irreg. ie)* 50
to **get old** *envejecer (irreg.)* 102
to **get onto** *montarse* 210 *montar* 223
to **get ready** *prepararse* 103
to **get tired** *cansarse* 249
to **get to do something** *llegar a hacer algo* 115
to **get up** *levantarse* 34
to **get used to** *acostumbrarse a* 92
to **get vaccinated** *vacunarse* 99
Get well soon. *Que te mejores.* 16
to **get wet** *mojarse* 291
ghost *el fantasma* 222
giant *el gigante* 83
ginger *el jengibre* 339
girl *la muchacha* 50 *la chica* 59
girlfriend *la novia* 4
to **give** *dar (irreg.)* 1 *donar* 122 *conceder* 134 *aportar* 239
to **give (a name)** *poner (irreg.)* 26
to **give a prize to** *premiar* 180
to **give an injection** *pinchar* 123
to **give as a present** *regalar* 29 *traer (irreg.)* 37
to **give back** *devolver (irreg.)* 59
to **give free rein to** *dar rienda suelta a* 215
to **give guidance to** *orientar* 183
to **give recognition to** *consagrar* 342
to **give rise to** *provocar* 154
to **give up** *renunciar a* 92 *darse por vencido(a)* 130 *rendirse (irreg. i)* 131
given that *dado que* 218
glass *el vaso* 34 *la copa* 54 *el vidrio* 222 *el cristal* 318
gleaming *reluciente* 336
global *global* 148
globalization *la globalización, la mundialización* 154
glucose *la glucosa* 98
glue *el pegamento* 29
glued to *pegado(a) a* 44
GM foods *los alimentos transgénicos* 275
to **go** *ir (irreg.)* 3 *acudir* 256
to **go ahead** *seguir adelante* 132
to **go away** *irse (irreg.)* 34
to **go away on a trip** *ir de viaje* 8
to **go back** *retroceder* 210
to **go beyond the limits** *salirse (irreg.)* 34
to **go blank (someone's mind)** *quedarse (alguien) en blanco* 130
to **go into (a gear)** *meter* 210
to **go into depth** *profundizar* 302
Go on, (to encourage) *Anda,* 100

Go on. (to encourage action) *Adelante.* 1
to **go out** *salir (irreg.)* 3
to **go shopping** *ir de compras* 34
to **go through** *atravesar (irreg. ie)* 110
to **go to** *pasar* 186
to **go unnoticed** *desapercibido(a)* 324
to **go up** *subir* 262
to **go with** *acompañar* 79
goal *la meta* 254
goat *el chivo* 343
God *Dios* 40
gold *el oro* 4
golden *dorado(a)* 222
good *bien* 7 *buen, bueno(a)* 24
Good afternoon. *Buenas tardes.* 30
Good luck. *Mucha suerte.* 14
good manners *de buena educación* 84
Good thinking. *Bien pensado.* 258
goodbye *el adiós* 109
goods *los bienes, la mercancía* 148
to **govern** *gobernar* 245
government *el gobierno* 43 *la administración* 125
government (adjective) *gubernamental* 293
government employee *el/la funcionario(a)* 296
governor *el/la gobernador(a)* 245
to **grab** *captar* 231
grade *el grado* 256
gradually *gradualmente* 117
graduate *el/la egresado(a)* 175
to **graduate** *graduarse* 93
graduate (in) *el/la licenciado(a) (en)* 114
graduated (in) *licenciado(a) (en)* 175
graduation *la graduación* 19
grammar *la gramática* 2
grammatical *gramatical* 57
grandchildren *los nietos* 105
grandfather/grandmother *el/la abuelo(a)* 162
grandparents *los abuelos* 6
granite *el granito* 318
to **grant** *otorgar* 266
grape *la uva* 75
grapefruit *la toronja* 78
grapevine *la parra* 282
graphic novel *la novela gráfica* 242
to **grasp** *captar* 66
grateful *agradecido(a)* 336
gratitude *el agradecimiento* 58
grave *la tumba* 4
gray *gris* 54
gray hair *la cana* 20
great *gran, grande* 24 *genial* 131 *fenomenal* 142 *perfecto* 242
great (adjective) *estupendo(a)* 7
great (adverb) *estupendo* 29
greater *mayor* 98
greatest *mayor* 272
Greek *griego(a)* 318
green *verde* 106

green building la bioconstrucción 156
greenish verdoso(a) 303
to **greet** saludar 266
to **greet each other** saludarse 34
greeting el saludo 16
greeting card la tarjeta de felicitación 32
to **grieve** pesar 249
groom la novia 100
ground molido(a) 78 el terreno 98 el suelo 347
group el grupo 3 el conjunto 139
grouped agrupado(a) 330
to **grow** crecer (irreg.) 102
to **grow longer** alargarse 337
growing creciente 98
growing apart el alejamiento 67
growth el crecimiento 52 el desarrollo 90
Guarani guaraní 77
guarantee la garantía 148
to **guarantee** garantizar 127
Guatemalan guatemalteco(a) 243
to **guess** adivinar 61
guest el/la invitado(a) 10 el/la huésped 216
guesthouse el hostal 185
guidance la guía 28
guide la guía 28 el/la guía 203
to **guide** guiar 1
guide (book) la guía 81
guided guiado(a) 322
guitar la guitarra 2
guys (when greeting) chicos 72
gym el gimnasio 10

habit el hábito 11 la costumbre 336
hail el granizo 40
hair el pelo 20
half la mitad, medio(a) 48 el medio 285
half board la media pensión 216
hall el salón 10
ham el jamón 78
hand la mano 1
to **hand over** entregar 84 ceder 268
to **handle** manejar 110
handsome apuesto 17 guapo 37
handwriting la letra 38
handy a mano 117
to **hang** colgar (irreg. ue) 19
to **happen** ocurrir 2 pasar 4 suceder 260 acontecer (irreg.) 336
happiness la alegría 33 la felicidad 39
happy contento(a) 102 feliz 106 alegre 111
happy-go-lucky alegre 222
hard como una bestia 40 duro(a) 103
hardly apenas 210
hardly ever casi nunca 194
hardship las privaciones 336
hard-working trabajador(a) 17

to **harm** perjudicar 272
harvest la cosecha 40
hat el sombrero 197
to **hate** odiar 104
to **hate each other** odiarse 36
to **have** tener (irreg.) 2 poseer (irreg.) 38 presentar 43 sufrir 90 llevar 94 disponer de (irreg.) 114 consumir 117 contar con (irreg. ue) 153 ofrecer (irreg.) 204 mantener (irreg.) 326
to **have (auxiliary)** haber (irreg.) 140
to **have a feast** darse un atracón, darse una comilona 74
Have a good day. Que tengas un buen día. 16
Have a good journey. Que tengas buen viaje. 16
Have a good weekend. Que pasen un buen fin de semana. 16
to **have a great time** pasarlo en grande 188
to **have a hard time** pasarlo mal 125
to **have a quick look at** echar un vistazo a 301
to **have access to** acceder a 45
to **have been** llevar 38
to **have breakfast** desayunar 3
to **have dinner** cenar 8
to **have fallen out** estar peleados(as) 39
to **have just ...** acabar de... 11
to **have to** deber 11 haber que, tener que 334
head el/la jefe(a) 5 la cabeza 75
to **head for** dirigirse a 47
head of state el/la jefe(a) de Estado 259
heading el epígrafe 155 el encabezado 182
headline el titular 44
headquarters la sede 217
health la salud 11
health (adjective) sanitario(a) 98
health care la asistencia sanitaria 115
health care (adjective) asistencial 115
health coverage la cobertura sanitaria 114
healthy saludable 11 sano(a) 278
heap el montón 29
to **hear** oír (irreg.) 23
heart el corazón 33
heart attack el infarto 90
heat el calor 8
heavenly paradisíaco(a) 219
heavy pesado(a) 32 fuerte 330
height la altura 224
heist el golpe 289
hello hola 11
help la ayuda 47
to **help** ayudar 1 contribuir (irreg.) 67 ayudar a 92 favorecer (irreg.) 105
to **help determine** determinar 261
to **help each other** ayudarse 36
to **help in** colaborar en 182
to **help with** colaborar en 59

helping el plato 74
hemisphere el hemisferio 135
here aquí 14
hereditary hereditario(a) 96
heritage el patrimonio 43
hero el héroe 249
heroic heroico(a) 256
to **hesitate** dudar 183
hesitation la vacilación 336
hidden oculto(a) 297
to **hide** esconder 19 ocultar 222 disimular 278
high alto(a) 11
high plateau el altiplano 147
high school el bachillerato 324
high school graduate el/la bachiller 175
higher superior 127 mayor 196
highest mayor 52
to **highlight** destacar, resaltar 43
highlighted destacado(a) 24
high-pitched agudo(a) 53
hike la caminata 220
hiking el senderismo 219
to **hinder** dificultar 67 obstaculizar 69
to **hint** insinuar 167
to **hire** contratar 160 alquilar 216
Hispanic hispano(a) 1 hispánico(a) 329
historic histórico(a) 242
historically históricamente 31
history la historia 1
hobby la afición 58
to **hold** celebrar 31 desempeñar, ocupar 175 albergar 228 administrar 260
to **hold back** retener (irreg.) 336
holiday el día festivo 24 el día feriado 160 el feriado 203
holy sagrado(a) 301
home la casa 3 el inicio 216 el hogar 266 la vivienda 318
homeland la patria 248
homeless sin hogar 269
homework la tarea 37 los deberes 133
Honduran hondureño(a) 271
honestly honradamente 256
honey la miel 78
to **honk** pitar 210
honor el honor 141
to **hop** saltar 347
hope la esperanza 315
to **hope** esperar 24
hopeful esperanzado(a) 102
horizon el horizonte 321
horn el cuerno 29 la bocina 210
horrible horrible 119
horse el caballo 101
hospital el hospital 59 el sanatorio 330
to **hospitalize** ingresar 90
hostile hostil 337
hot caliente 76 caluroso(a) 216
hot (spicy) picante 92
hour la hora 5
house la casa 6

to **inform** *informar 5 comunicar 183*
informal *informal 10*
information *la información 29 los datos 58*
informational *informativo(a) 38*
informative *divulgativo(a) 293*
informed *informado(a) 44*
infusion *la infusión 76*
ingredient *el ingrediente 77*
inhabitant *el/la habitante 42 el/la poblador(a) 280*
to **inherit** *heredar 96*
inheritance *la herencia 41*
inhibition *la inhibición 278*
initial *inicial 211*
initiative *la iniciativa 67*
injury *la lesión 96*
injustice *la injusticia 259*
inn *el mesón 79*
inner *interior 324*
innovation *la innovación 180*
innovative *innovador(a) 306*
inside *dentro de 29 dentro 76 el interior 303 interior 324*
inside out *al revés 36*
to **insinuate** *insinuar 167*
to **insist on** *insistir en 92*
inspector *el/la inspector(a) 205*
inspiration *la inspiración 39*
to **inspire** *inspirar 253*
inspired *inspirado(a) 326*
inspirer *el/la inspirador(a) 282*
instant *el instante 109*
instantaneous *instantáneo(a) 67*
instead of *en lugar de 57*
institute *el instituto 3*
institution *la institución 125 la entidad 156*
institutional *institucional 67*
instructions *las instrucciones 1*
instrument *el instrumento 23*
to **insult** *insultar 210*
insurance *el seguro 114*
integral *integral 312*
integration *la integración 245*
intelligence *la inteligencia 224*
intelligent *inteligente 61*
to **intend** *pretender 67*
intended *destinado(a) 139*
intense *intenso(a) 215*
to **intensify** *intensificar 264*
intensity *la intensidad 154*
intensive *intensivo(a) 183*
intention *el propósito 258 la intención 279*
to **interact** *interactuar 340*
interactive *interactivo(a) 139*
interdependence *la interdependencia 154*
interest *el interés 22*
to **interest** *interesar 22*
interest rate *la tasa de interés 148*
interested *interesado(a) 69*
interesting *interesante 15*
interior *el interior 303*
intern *(el/la estudiante) en prácticas 158 el/la becario(a) 160*
internal *interno(a) 286*
international *internacional 44*

internationalization *la internacionalización 324*
Internet *el/la Internet 7 la red 45*
interpersonal *interpersonal 67*
to **interpret** *interpretar 268*
interpretation *la interpretación 50*
interpreter *el/la intérprete 160*
interrelation *la interrelación 154*
intersection *la intersección 266*
intervention *la intervención 268*
interview *la entrevista 160*
to **interview** *entrevistar 45*
interviewee *el/la entrevistado(a) 69*
interviewer *el/la entrevistador(a) 160*
intimate *íntimo(a) 336*
intimately *íntimamente 318*
intolerably *intolerablemente 210*
intolerance *la intolerancia 292*
to **introduce** *introducir (irreg.) 92*
to **introduce oneself** *presentarse 58*
introduction *la introducción 66 la presentación 170*
intruder *el/la intruso(a) 78*
to **invade** *invadir 96*
invariable *invariable 310*
invasion *la invasión 245*
to **invent** *inventar 113*
to **invest** *invertir (irreg. ie, i) 154*
invested with *investido(a) de 256*
investment *la inversión 156*
investor *el/la inversor(a) 156*
invitation *la invitación 10*
to **invite** *invitar 18*
to **involve** *consistir en 19 implicar 196*
involved *involucrado(a) 261*
iron *el hierro 318*
ironic *irónico(a) 211*
irony *la ironía 345*
irrational *irracional 306*
irregular *irregular 2*
irreparable *irreparable 279*
island *la isla 13*
isn't it? *¿eh? 330*
isoflavone *la isoflavona 173*
isolated *aislado(a) 7*
to **issue** *emitir 165*
isthmus *el istmo 159*
It depends. *Depende. 204*
It's a deal. *Trato hecho. 190*
It's hard to believe ... *Parece mentira... 252*
Italian *italiano(a) 127*
italics *la cursiva 312*
itch *picar 75*
itinerary *el itinerario 212*

to **jail** *encarcelar 260*
jar *el tarro 108*
jealous *celoso(a) 17*
Jewish *judío(a) 345*
job *el trabajo 33 el oficio 38 el empleo 114 el puesto de trabajo 160*

job application *la solicitud de empleo 160*
job interview *la entrevista de trabajo 4*
job offer *la oferta de trabajo 160*
to **join** *unir 4 apuntarse a 139*
joined *unido(a) 82*
joke *la broma 20 el chiste 221*
journalist *el/la periodista 38*
journalistic *periodístico(a) 95*
journey *el viaje 5*
joy *el júbilo 222*
jubilation *el júbilo 222*
judge *el/la juez(a) 313*
to **judge** *juzgar 320*
juzged *juzgado(a) 256*
judicial *judicial 260*
juice *el jugo 77*
jungle *la selva 4 la jungla 195*
junta *la junta militar 260*
jury *el jurado 183*
just *justo 270*
just as *tal (y) como 39*
justice *la justicia 245*
to **justify** *justificar 39*

to **keep** *seguir (irreg. i, i) 14 quedarse 47 guardar 109 mantener (irreg.) 182 conservar 256*
to **keep up** *mantener (irreg.) 230*
key *la clave 66 la llave 80*
keyboard *el teclado 133*
kidnapped *secuestrado(a) 267*
kidney *el riñón 115*
to **kill time** *matar el tiempo 188*
kilo *el kilo 50*
kilometer *el kilómetro 31*
kind *el tipo 7 amable 17 bondadoso(a) 20 la especie 30 cordial 59*
kindness *la delicadeza 39 la amabilidad 278*
king *el rey 23*
kinship *el parentesco 106*
kiss *el beso 17*
to **kiss** *besarse 36*
kiwi *el kiwi 106*
knee *la rodilla 102*
kneeling *de rodillas 102*
knife *el cuchillo 90*
knot *el nudo 30*
to **know** *saber (irreg.) 1 conocer (irreg.) 2*
knowledge *los conocimientos 160 el conocimiento 278*
known *el/la conocido(a) 94*

label *la etiqueta 173*
labor *laboral 47*
labor market *el mercado laboral 163*
laboratory *el laboratorio 70*

ownership *la propiedad* 180
oyster *la ostra* 188

to **pack** *empaquetar* 50
package *el paquete* 32
packed *hasta la bandera* 188
pact *el pacto* 248
page *la página* 2 *la plana* 44
pain *el dolor* 119
paint *la pintura* 304
to **paint** *pintar* 268
painter *el/la pintor(a)* 300
painting *el cuadro* 254 *la pintura* 300
pair *la pareja* 15 *el par* 265
palace *el palacio* 318
palette *la paleta* 300
panic *el pánico* 190
panoramic *panorámico(a)* 216
panoramic view *la panorámica* 134
pants *los pantalones* 197
paper *el papel* 8
paper mill *la fábrica de papel* 150
papers (identification) *los papeles* 278
parade *el desfile* 5
paradise *el paraíso* 343
paradox *la paradoja* 50
paragliding *el parapente* 228
paragraph *el párrafo* 19
parallelism *el paralelismo* 345
parasite *el parásito* 98
parents *los padres* 6
to **park** *estacionar* 204 *aparcar* 210
park *el parque* 59
parking lot *el estacionamiento* 323
parking space *la plaza* 323
parliament *el parlamento* 127
parody *la parodia* 345
part *la parte* 48
participant *el/la participante* 31
participation *la participación* 126
particular *particular* 37
particularly *particularmente* 280
partner *la pareja* 3
part-time *a tiempo parcial* 131 *la media jornada* 133
party *la fiesta* 10 *el partido* 261
to **pass** *pasar* 18 *superar* 103 *adelantar* 136 *aprobar (irreg. ue)* 204
to **pass on** *transmitir* 30
to **pass the time** *entretenerse (irreg.)*, *pasar el rato* 188
passage *el fragmento* 26 *el pasaje* 66 *el paso* 166
passenger *el/la pasajero(a)* 189
passing *el paso* 103
passion *la pasión* 33
passionate *apasionado(a)* 20
passive *paciente, pasivo(a)* 104
passport *el pasaporte* 207
past *el pasado, pasado(a)* 1
pastime *el pasatiempo* 193
pastry *la empanada* 139

patent *la patente* 88
paternal *paterno(a)* 163
path *el sendero* 7 *el camino* 31
patience *la paciencia* 10
patient *el/la paciente* 75 *el/la enfermo(a)* 88
to **pause** *interrumpirse* 279
to **pay** *pagar* 39
to **pay attention** *prestar atención* 86
to **pay attention (to)** *fijarse en* 17
to **pay attention to** *cuidar* 58
payment *el pago* 117
pea *el guisante* 75
peace *la paz* 248
peace treaty *el tratado de paz* 248
peaceful *tranquilo(a)* 219
peach *el durazno* 78
pear *la pera* 112
peasant *el/la campesino(a)* 40
peculiar *singular* 38 *peculiar* 203
pedestrian *el/la peatón(a)* 204
pediatrician *el/la pediatra* 75
peel *la corteza* 77
to **pen an account** *abrir una cuenta* 148
pencil *el lápiz* 311
peninsula *la península* 228
penniless *pobre* 24
pension *la pensión* 162
people *el pueblo* 18 *la gente* 23
pepper (vegetable) *el pimiento* 78
per *por* 11
to **perceive** *percibir* 110
percent *por ciento* 136
percentage *el porcentaje* 94
perception *la percepción* 104
perfect *perfecto(a)* 86
perforation *la perforación* 204
to **perform** *realizar* 5 *representar* 57 *actuar, interpretar* 192
performance *la actuación* 186 *la función* 188
performer *el/la intérprete* 197
perhaps *tal vez* 196 *acaso* 336
period *el período* 31
period (in writing) *el punto* 136
periodically *periódicamente* 260
permission *el permiso* 37
permit *el permiso* 165
Peronist *peronista* 266
to **persecute** *perseguir (irreg. i, i)* 260
persecuted *perseguido(a)* 260
to **persist** *persistir* 279
persistent *persistente* 267
person *la persona* 8
person attending *el/la asistente* 326
person in charge *el/la responsable* 127
person next to you *el/la vecino(a)* 210
personal *personal* 17 *el personal* 165 *personalizado(a)* 212
personal details *los datos personales* 160
personality *la personalidad* 20 *la forma de ser* 58 *el carácter* 330
to **personalize** *personalizar* 45

personally *personalmente* 89
perspective *la perspectiva* 306
to **persuade** *persuadir* 344
persuasive *persuasivo(a)* 294
Peruvian *peruano(a)* 54
peso *el peso* 39
pessimistic *pesimista* 9
pharmaceutical *farmacéutico(a)* 88
pharmacy on duty *la farmacia de guardia* 91
phenomenon *el fenómeno* 57
philosopher *el/la filósofo(a)* 169
philosophical *filosófico(a)* 210
philosophy *la filosofía* 143
phosphorus *el fósforo* 173
photograph *la fotografía* 5
photographic *fotográfico(a)* 72
photography *la fotografía* 33
phrase *la frase* 194
to **phrase** *formular* 116
physical *físico(a)* 20
physical examination *el examen físico* 75
physical therapist *el/la fisioterapeuta* 160
physical therapy *la fisioterapia* 158
physically *físicamente* 21
physics *la Física* 133
piano *el piano* 170
picnic *el picnic* 293
pie *la empanada* 139
piece *el trozo* 74 *el pedazo* 210
piece (of music) *la pieza musical* 192
piece of furniture *el mueble* 24
piglet *el/la cerdito(a)* 339
pill *la píldora* 75
pineapple *la piña* 79
pink *rosado(a)* 266
pioneer *el/la pionero(a)* 156
pirate *el/la pirata* 250
pistol *la pistola* 272
pitcher *la jarra* 79
pity *la lástima, la pena* 322
place *el lugar* 1 *el sitio* 44 *el punto* 154 *el espacio* 200 *el acomodo* 325
to **place** *colocar* 5 *acomodar* 336
plain *la planicie* 295
plains *los llanos* 193
plan *el plan* 9 *el proyecto* 283 *el plano* 302 *la planta* 323
to **plan** *planear* 2 *planificar* 10 *proyectar* 323
planet *el planeta* 102
planned *planificado(a)* 2 *previsto(a)* 49 *pensado(a)* 84
plant *la planta* 77
plant (adjective) *vegetal* 173
plantation *la plantación* 172
plastic *plástico(a)* 5 *el plástico* 303
plate *la placa* 204
platform *la plataforma* 67 *el andén* 189
play *el juego* 50 *la obra de teatro* 303

to **play** *jugar (a) (irreg. ue)* 2 *tocar* 23 *desempeñar* 172 *practicar* 193
to **play (jokes)** *gastar* 21
to **play down the importance of** *restar importancia a* 21
play on words *el juego de palabras* 345
player *el/la jugador(a)* 29
playing *el juego* 50
pleasant *agradable* 216
please *por favor* 11
Please accept my cordial greetings. *Reciban un cordial saludo.* 59
pleasure *el placer* 212
plot *el argumento* 330
plum *la ciruela* 78
plural *el plural* 22
plus *más* 136
pocket *el bolsillo* 108
pocketbook *la cartera* 275
poem *el poema* 33
poet *el/la poeta* 166
poetess *la poetisa* 38
poetic *poético(a)* 39
poetry *la poesía* 330
point (in games, etc.) *el punto* 49
point (in time) *el punto* 19
point of view *el punto de vista* 147
to **point out** *señalar* 148
pointing at *orientado(a) hacia* 84
polar *polar* 147
police *la policía* 47
police (adjective) *policial* 47
policeman/policewoman *el/la policía* 47
policy *la política* 217
polite *educado(a)* 58 *cortés* 162
political *político(a)* 191
political asylum *el asilo político* 260
politically *políticamente* 282
politician *el/la político(a)* 151
politics *la política* 45
to **pollute** *contaminar* 150
pollution *la contaminación* 275
polyclinic *policlínico(a)* 266
polymer *el polímero* 297
poor *pobre* 24 *los pobres* 222
poor (showing sympathy) *pobre* 111
poor suburbs *los suburbios* 336
popular *popular* 3
popularity *la popularidad* 282
to **popularize** *popularizar* 83
popularized *popularizado(a)* 282
population *la población* 52
pork *el/la cerdo(a)* 75
port *el puerto* 254
portal *el portal* 116
portion *la porción* 79
portrait *el retrato* 306
to **portray** *caracterizar* 230 *plasmar, retratar* 307
to **pose** *plantear* 280
position *la posición* 24 *el cargo* 94 *la postura* 103 *el puesto de trabajo* 160 *la altura* 210
to **position oneself** *posicionarse* 212
positive *positivo(a)* 7

positively *positivamente* 268
possession *la posesión* 106
possessive *posesivo(a)* 36
possibility *la posibilidad* 67
possible *posible* 37
possibly *posiblemente* 196
post *el cargo* 94
to **post** *publicar* 102
post office *la oficina de correos* 32
postage *el franqueo* 32
postcard *la tarjeta postal* 32
posted *publicado(a)* 11
poster *el cartel* 14 *el póster* 65
pot *la olla* 19 *la cazuela* 109
potassium *el potasio* 147
potato *la papa* 78
potential *el potencial* 98 *potencial* 147
to **pour down** *caer un chaparrón* 216
poverty *la pobreza* 272
power *el poder* 248 *la fuerza* 337
powerful *fuerte* 266
practical *práctico(a)* 39
practice *la práctica* 4
to **practice** *practicar* 10 *ejercer* 159
praise *el elogio* 321
prawn *el langostino* 78
to **precede** *preceder* 337
precipice *el precipicio* 42
precise *exacto(a)* 222 *preciso(a)* 306
precisely *precisamente* 278
precision *la exactitud* 293
pre-Columbian *precolombino(a)* 77
predisposition *la predisposición* 96
to **prefer** *preferir (irreg. ie, i)* 45
preferable *preferible* 69
preference *la preferencia* 45
pregnant *embarazada* 102
prejudice *el prejuicio* 272
preliminary *preliminar* XXII
premises *el local* 200
preparation *la elaboración* 67 *la preparación* 118
preparations *los preparativos* 18
to **prepare** *preparar* 11 *elaborar* 77
prepared to *dispuesto(a) a* 144
preposition *la preposición* 92
pre-read *la prelectura* 66
to **prescribe** *prescribir (irreg.)* 97
prescription *la receta* 75
prescriptive *prescriptivo(a)* 116
presence *la presencia* 200
present *actual* 1 *el presente* 2 *el regalo* 10 *presente* 46
to **present** *presentar* 2 *ofrecer (irreg.)* 59 *exponer (irreg.)* 352
presentation *la presentación* 55 *la exposición* 344
to **preserve** *preservar* 193
preserved *conservado(a)* 127
presidency *la presidencia* 259
president *el/la presidente(a)* 45
presidential *presidencial* 53
press *la prensa* 44
prestige *el prestigio* 114 *el rango* 200
to **pretend** *fingir* 343
pretty *bonito(a)* 19 *lindo(a)* 23

to **prevent** *prevenir (irreg.)* 96 *impedir (irreg. i, i)* 97 *evitar* 125
prevention *la prevención* 96
previous *anterior* 4 *previo(a)* 160
price *el precio* 45 *la tarifa* 216
priest *el sacerdote* 105
primary *primario(a)* 115
primary education *la primaria* 137
prince *el príncipe* 114
principal *el/la director(a)* 134
to **print** *imprimir (irreg.)* 202
printed *impreso(a)* 45
printer *la impresora* 133
priority *la prioridad* 272
pristine *elemental* 337
private *privado(a)* 114 *particular* 125
prize *el premio* 54
probably *seguramente* 14 *probablemente* 39
problem *el problema* 1 *la dificultad* 264
problematic *problemático(a)* 258
problems *la problemática* 343
process *el proceso* 67
to **process** *procesar* 146
to **proclaim** *proclamar* 266
to **produce** *producir (irreg.)* 147
producer *el/la productor(a)* 173
producing *productor(a)* 127
product *el producto* 148
production *la producción* 154
productivity *la productividad* 155
profession *la profesión* 9 *el oficio* 38
professional *profesional* 81 *el/la profesional* 86
professionalism *la profesionalidad* 212
professor *el/la profesor(a)* 329
profile *el perfil* 160 *la reseña* 329
profit *el beneficio* 52
profitability *la rentabilidad* 156
profits *las ganancias* 180
program *el programa* 44 *el espacio* 52 *el plan* 277
programmer *el/la programador(a)* 133
programming *la programación* 44
progress *el progreso* 46
progressive *progresivo(a)* 46 *progresista* 282
to **prohibit** *prohibir* 127
prohibited *prohibido(a)* 207
pro-independence *independentista* 286
project *el proyecto* 64
proliferation *la proliferación* 96
prominent *destacado(a)* 236
to **promise** *comprometerse a* 197 *prometer* 198
to **promote** *promocionar* 14 *promover (irreg. ue)* 68 *fomentar* 149 *potenciar* 272
promotion *la promoción* 217
promotional *promocional* 237
pronominal *pronominal* 34
pronoun *el pronombre* 22
to **pronounce** *pronunciar* 278
pronunciation *la pronunciación* 56

proof *la muestra* 67
propaganda *la propaganda* 269
proper *debido(a)* 117
proper noun *el nombre propio* 254
property *la propiedad* 24 *el inmueble* 200
proportion *la proporción* 306
proposal *la propuesta* 41
to **propose** *proponer (irreg.)* 14 *plantear* 55 *presentar* 261
prose *la prosa* 330
to **prosper** *prosperar* 278
prosperity *la prosperidad* 111
prosperous *próspero(a)* 285
to **protect** *proteger* 256
to **protect oneself** *protegerse* 96
protection *protección* 224
protein *la proteína* 173
protest *la protesta* 242
to **protest** *protestar* 262
proud *orgulloso(a)* 106
to **provide** *proporcionar* 52 *aportar* 55 *facilitar* 166 *prestar* 183 *proveer (irreg.)* 296
to **provide (medical) attention** *prestar atención* 115
provided (that) *con tal de (que)* 164
province *la provincia* 125
psychiatrist *el/la psiquiatra* 92
psychologist *el/la psicólogo(a)* 75
psychology *la psicología* 143
public *el público* 4 *público(a)* 61
publication *la publicación* 66 *la aparición* 342
publicity (adjective) *publicitario(a)* 145
to **publish** *publicar* 33
published *publicado(a)* 54
publisher *la editorial* 344
pulse *el pulso* 91
pumpkin *la calabaza* 76
punctuality *la puntualidad* 205
punctuation *la puntuación* 117
punctuation mark *el signo de puntuación* 117
purpose *el propósito* 58 *la finalidad* 262
purse *el bolso* 21
to **pursue** *perseguir (irreg. i, i)* 166
to **put** *poner (irreg.)* 2 *colocar* 5 *colgar (irreg. ue)* 38 *echar* 108
to **put an end to** *acabar con* 264 *terminar con* 271
to **put away** *guardar* 204
to **put in** *meter* 40
to **put in contact with** *poner en contacto con* 127
to **put on** *poner (irreg.)* 3 *ponerse (irreg.)* 34
to **put up with** *soportar* 248 *sufrir* 270

qualifying *calificativo(a)* 24
quality *la cualidad* 24 *la calidad* 81

quantifier *el cuantificador* 48
quantity *la cantidad* 31
quarter *el cuarto* 48
quarter (of) *la cuarta parte (de)* 48
Quechua *quechua* 77
queen *la reina* 245
question *la pregunta* 3 *la duda* 58 *la cuestión* 173
to **question** *poner en duda* 296
questionnaire *el cuestionario* 303
quick *ágil* 31 *rápido(a)* 41
to **quicken one's pace** *apresurar el paso* 210
quickly *pronto* 40 *rápido* 107
quiet *callado(a)* 106 *tranquilo(a)* 219
quinoa *la quinua* 296
quite *bastante* 48
quite a few *bastante(s)* 48
quote *la cita* 224
to **quote** *citar* 225

R

race *la carrera* 14 *la raza* 278
racial *racial* 271
radiation *la radiación* 96
radiation therapy *la radioterapia* 97
radical *radical* 289
radio *la radio* 52
radio drama *el radioteatro* 266
radioactive *radiactivo(a)* 272
rage *la rabia* 210
railroad *el ferrocarril* 184
railroad track *la línea* 205
rain *la lluvia* 267
to **rain** *llover (irreg. ue)* 6 *entrenar* 75
raincoat *el impermeable* 224
rainy *lluvioso(a)* 22
to **raise** *levantar* 35
to **raise (questions)** *plantear* 166
raisin *la pasa* 78
ranch *la estancia* 336
rare *raro(a)* 296
raspberry *la frambuesa* 78
rather *más bien* 244
Rather, *Mejor dicho,* 242
rational *racional* 324
rationalized *racionalizado(a)* 49
raw *crudo(a)* 172
raw material *la materia prima* 146
ray *el rayo* 96
to **reach** *llegar a* 125 *alcanzar* 137
to **reach (years of age)** *cumplir* 125
to **react** *reaccionar* 40
reaction *la reacción* 143
reactive *reactivo(a)* 98
read *leído(a)* 331
to **read** *leer (irreg.)* 3
reader *el/la lector(a)* 45
reading *la lectura* 26
reading (adjective) *lector(a)* 124
ready *preparado(a)* 1 *listo(a)* 106
real *real* 65 *auténtico(a)* 77
realism *el realismo* 335
reality *la realidad* 67
to **realize** *darse cuenta de* 92

really *realmente* 39
to **really like** *encantar* 22
rear *la cola* 222
reason *la razón* 24 *el motivo* 218 *la causa* 227
reasonable *razonable* 20
reasoning *la argumentación* 143
to **rebel** *rebelarse* 247
to **recall** *evocar* 31
to **receive** *recibir* 32 *acoger* 155
recent *último(a)* 33 *reciente* 96
recently *recientemente* 140
reception *la recepción* 7 *la acogida* 58 *el acogimiento* 59
receptionist *el/la recepcionista* 174
recipe *la receta* 79
recipient *el/la receptor(a)* 104
reciprocal *recíproco(a)* 12
reckless *temerario(a)* 311
recognition *el reconocimiento* 38 *la consagración* 343
recognizable *reconocible* 306
to **recognize** *reconocer (irreg.)* 23
to **recommend** *recomendar (irreg. ie)* 11
recommendation *la recomendación* 11
reconcile *conciliar* 163
reconciliation *la conciliación* 163
to **reconstruct** *reconstruir (irreg.)* 245
record *el disco* 191
to **record** *registrar* 52 *grabar* 238
recording *la grabación* 42
to **recount** *narrar* 230
to **recover** *recuperar(se)* 38
recovery *la recuperación* 270
rectangular *rectangular* 303
to **recycle** *reciclar* 102
red *rojo(a)* 63
reddish *rojizo(a)* 303
to **reduce** *reducir (irreg.)* 11
reef *el arrecife* 228
to **refer** *remitir* 286
to **refer to** *referirse a (irreg. ie, i)* 34 *nombrar* 104
reference *la referencia* 160
referendum *el referéndum* 262
to **reflect** *reflejar* 36
reflection *el reflejo* 52
reflexive *reflexivo(a)* 36
reform *la reforma* 261
to **reform** *reformar* 244
refrain *el estribillo* 192
refrigerator *el refrigerador* 63
refusal *la negativa* 239
to **refuse** *negarse (irreg. ie)* 92
to **refuse to do something** *renunciar a hacer algo* 260
to **refute** *rebatir* 256
Regards. *Un saludo.* 59
regarding *respecto a* 143
regime *el régimen* 244
region *la región* 9
register *el registro* 58 *la matriculación* 134
to **register** *registrar* 31 *registrarse* 68 *matricularse* 136

Saint *San* 114
saint *el/la santo(a)* 26
saint's day *el santo* 26
salad *la ensalada* 78
salary *el sueldo* 133 *el salario* 168
salesclerk *el/la dependiente* 174
salesperson *el/la vendedor(a)* 22
salmon *el salmón* 75
salsa *la salsa* 227
salt *la sal* 35
salt flat *el salar* 128
same *mismo(a)* 25
sanctuary *el santuario* 200
sand *la arena* 219
sarcoma *el sarcoma* 96
satisfied *satisfecho(a)* 145
to **satisfy** *satisfacer (irreg.)* 109
saturated *saturado(a)* 11
sauce *la salsa* 92
to **save** *ahorrar* 148 *salvar* 292
saver *el/la ahorrador(a)* 156
saving *el ahorro* 156
to **say** *decir (irreg.)* 4 *contar (irreg. ue)* 39 *afirmar* 69 *comentar* 108
to **say goodbye to** *despedirse de (irreg. i, i)* 92
to **say hello** *saludar* 63
scale *la balanza* 32 *la escala* 154 *la envergadura* 272
scar *la cicatriz* 17
scarce *escaso(a)* 278
scene *la escena* 107
schedule *el horario* 2
scholarship *la beca* 136
school *la escuela* 11 *el colegio* 67
school (adjective) *escolar* 134
schoolboy/schoolgirl *el/la escolar* 13
schooner *la goleta* 254
science *la ciencia* 350
scientific *científico(a)* 114
scientist *el/la científico(a)* 70
scornful *desdeñoso(a)* 336
scrambled eggs *los huevos revueltos* 78
screen *la pantalla* 8
to **screen** *proyectar* 47
screening *la proyección* 23
script *el guion* 225
to **scuba dive** *bucear* 192
to **sculpt** *esculpir* 318
sculptor *el/la escultor(a)* 308
sculptural *escultórico(a)* 318
sculpture *la escultura* 300
sea *el/la mar* 147
sea (adjective) *marítimo(a)* 154
seafood *el marisco* 78
search *la búsqueda* 68
to **search for** *buscar* 89 *consultar* 160
season *el ciclo* 47 *la época* 193 *la temporada* 216
seasonal *estacional* 135
seat *el asiento* 203 *la butaca* 212
seated *sentado(a)* 102
second *el segundo* 67 *segundo(a)* 250
second-to-last *penúltimo(a)* 336
secondary *secundario(a)* 96

secondary education *la secundaria* 137
secret *el secreto* 38 *secreto(a)* 246
secretary *el/la secretario(a)* 145
section *el apartado* 25 *la sección* 44
sector *el sector* 83
sector (of economy) *el ámbito* 217
security *la seguridad* 116
sedentary *sedentario(a)* 96
to **see** *ver (irreg.)* 2
to **see each other** *verse (irreg.)* 36
See you later. *Hasta la vista. Hasta luego.* 16
See you soon. *Hasta pronto.* 16
to **seem** *parecer (irreg.)* 34 *aparentar* 343
seldom *rara vez* 194
to **select** *seleccionar* 58
selection *la selección* 111
self-assessment *la autoevaluación* 65
self-interested *interesado(a)* 268
selfish *egoísta* 17
self-portrait *el autorretrato* 307
to **sell** *vender* 8
seller *el/la vendedor(a)* 307
semester *el semestre* 136
semicolon *el punto y coma* 136
senate *el senado* 260
senator *el/la senador(a)* 245
to **send** *enviar, mandar* 32
sender *el/la remitente* 32
sensation *la sensación* 279
sense *el sentido* 39
sense of humor *el sentido del humor* 20
sensible *sensato(a)* 20
sensitive *sensible* 20
sentence *la frase* 14 *la oración* 136
to **separate** *separar* 42
separated *separado(a)* 336
sequence *la secuencia* 209
serenade *la serenata* 28
series *la serie* 44 *el ciclo* 88
serious *serio(a)* 17 *grave* 90
seriously *seriamente* 335
to **serve** *servir (irreg. i, i)* 79 *atender (irreg. ie)* 220
service *el servicio* 5
session *la sesión* 188
set *el juego* 67 *el grupo* 69
to **set** *meterse* 26 *establecer (irreg.)* 66 *ambientar* 230
set design *la escenografía* 170
to **set foot in** *pisar* 231
to **set off** *ponerse en marcha* 222
to **set out** *exponer (irreg.)* 157
to **set out (a problem)** *plantear* 166
to **set sail** *zarpar* 254
to **set up** *instalar* 37
to **set up business** *establecerse (irreg.)* 173
to **settle** *asentarse (irreg. ie), instalarse* 285
settlement *el asentamiento* 280
seventh *séptimo(a)* 250
several *varios(as)* 4

shadow *la sombra* 337
shame *la lástima, la pena* 322
shampoo *el champú* 36
shape *la forma* 18
to **share** *compartir* 25
shared *compartido(a)* 325
sharp *fuerte* 280 *definido(a)* 324
sheet (of paper) *la hoja* 8
shield *el escudo* 61
ship *el barco* 158
shipment *el envío* 32
shirt *la camisa* 36
shoe *el zapato* 36
shop *el almacén* 207
shopping *la compra* 3
shopping mall *el centro comercial* 37
shores *las orillas* 219
short *corto(a)* 24 *breve* 25 *pequeño(a)* 124
short story *el cuento* 40
shortage *la escasez* 296
shortened *apocopado(a)* 24
shotgun *la escopeta* 272
should *deber* 11
to **shout** *gritar* 47
show *el espectáculo, la función* 188
to **show** *mostrar (irreg. ue)* 21 *reflejar* 59 *demostrar (irreg. ue)* 67 *emitir* 102 *enseñar* 145 *revelar* 338 *recoger* 345
shrewd *astuto(a)* 20
to **shy** *reservado(a), tímido(a)* 17
sick *malo(a)* 106
side *el lado* 44
sightseeing *de paseo* 210
sign *el cartel* 38 *la muestra* 84 *el letrero* 185 *el signo* 337
to **sign** *firmar* 32
to **sign a peace treaty** *firmar la paz* 248
to **sign up for** *apuntarse a* 139
signature *la firma* 32
to **signify** *suponer (irreg.)* 67
silence *el silencio* 104
Silence, please. *Se ruega silencio.* 104
silk *la seda* 106
silly *bobo(a)* 100
silver *la plata* 4
similar *similar* 7 *semejante* 271
similar to *parecido(a) a* 142
similarity *la semejanza* 19
simple *sencillo(a)* 76 *simple* 98
simply *simplemente* 266
simultaneous *simultáneo(a)* 289
since *desde* 26 *como, puesto que, dado que, ya que* 218
sincere *sincero(a)* 17
to **sing** *cantar* 18 *entonar* 54
singer *el/la cantante* 54
singing *el canto* 170
singing its praises *superlativamente* 279
single *solo(a)* 27
single (adjective) *individual* 58
singular *singular* 22 *el singular* 36
to **sink** *hundir* 195
to **sip** *sorber* 85

Sir/Madam *señor(a)* 182
sister *la hermana* 2
to **sit** *sentarse (irreg. ie)* 106
to **sit (an exam)** *tomar* 134
situation *la situación* 2 *la posición* 149
sixth *sexto(a)* 250
size *el tamaño* 306 *las medidas* 350
skater *el/la patinador(a)* 345
sketch *el boceto* 306
to **ski** *esquiar* 216
skiing *el esquí* 228
skill *la habilidad* 65 *la capacidad* 103
skills *las aptitudes* 160 *las dotes* 175
skimming (read) *por encima* 302
skin *la piel* 96 *la tez* 343
skinny *flaco(a)* 332
skirt *la falda* 94
skyscraper *el rascacielos* 318
slavery *la esclavitud* 248
to **sleep** *dormir (irreg. u, ue)* 34
Sleep well. *Que descanses.* 16
sleeper car *el coche-cama* 204
sleeping *durmiente* 339
sleeping bag *el saco de dormir* 216
slender *espigado(a)* 343
slice *la rodaja* 77 *la loncha* 79
slim *fino(a)* 8
slogan *el eslogan* 14 *el lema* 139 *la consigna* 268
slow *lento(a)* 7
slowly *despacio* 222 *lentamente* 336
small *pequeño(a)* 5
smaller *menor* 114
smart *listo(a)* 106
to **smell** *oler (irreg.)* 74
smooth *curtido(a), liso(a)* 222
snack *el aperitivo* 79
to **sneeze** *estornudar* 75
to **snort** *resoplar* 210
snow *la nieve* 220
to **snow** *nevar (irreg. ie)* 111
snowfall *la nevada* 138
so *así* 7 *tan* 8 *así (es) que* 220
so as to *con el propósito de (que)* 262
so much *tanto* 214
so much that *tanto(a) que* 220
so that *para que* 19 *a fin de (que)* 262
so that ... *de manera que...* 287
soap opera *la telenovela* 4
so-called *llamado(a)* 114
soccer *el fútbol* 6
sociability *la sociabilidad* 225
social *social* 1
social security *la seguridad social* 114
socialist *socialista* 245
socially *socialmente* 156
society *la sociedad* 38
sociopolitical *sociopolítico(a)* 263
sodium *el sodio* 147
soft *blando(a)* 96
soft drink *el refresco* 83

soil *el suelo* 296
solar *solar* 272
soldier *el/la militar* 248 *el/la soldado* 249
solidarity *la solidaridad* 245
solitude *la soledad* 54
solution *la solución* 82
to **solve** *solucionar* 40 *resolver (irreg.)* 55 *remediar* 277
some *unos(as)* 18 *algún, alguno(a)* 48
some time around ... *allá por...* 200
someone *alguien* 16
something *algo* 5
sometimes *a veces* 194
son *el hijo* 11
song *la canción* 14 *el tema* 190
soon *pronto* 14
to **soothe** *calmar* 92
sophisticated *sofisticado(a)* 79
sort *la especie* 30
sound *el sonido* 44
to **sound** *sonar (irreg. ue)* 55
soup *la sopa* 35
source *la fuente* 3
South *el sur* 19
South African *sudafricano(a)* 284
South American *suramericano(a)* 249
southwest *el suroeste* 193 *el sudoeste* 295
souvenir *el recuerdo* 61
sovereign *el/la soberano(a)* 31
to **sow** *sembrar (irreg. ie)* 11
soy bean *la soya* 172
space *el espacio* 50 *el hueco* 210
space-time (adjective) *espacio-temporal* 343
Spanish *español(a)* 47
Spanish (language) *el español* 1 *el castellano* 67
Spanish (subject) *la Lengua* 67
Spanish speaker *el/la hispanohablante* 56
Spanish-American *hispanoamericano(a)* 47
Spanish-speaking *hispanohablante* 116
spare tire *la rueda de repuesto* 204
spatial *espacial* 268
to **speak** *hablar de* 2 *intervenir (irreg.)* 238
speaker *el/la hablante* 57
special *especial* 37
specialist *el/la especialista* 90
specialization *la especialización* 155
specialized *especializado(a)* 115
specialty *la especialidad* 115
specific *específico(a)* 66 *determinado(a)* 124 *en concreto* 231
specifically *concretamente* 148
to **specify** *especificar* 94 *precisar* 244
spectacular *espectacular* 93
spectator *el/la espectador(a)* 285

speculative *especulativo(a)* 154
speech *el discurso* 265
speech bubble *el bocadillo* 33
speed *la velocidad* 204 *la rapidez* 205
spelling *la ortografía* 117
spelling (adjective) *ortográfico(a)* 4
spelling mistake *la falta de ortografía* 175
to **spend** *pasar* 58 *pasarse* 92 *emplear* 208 *gastar* 265
spilling *el derramamiento* 296
to **spin** *girar* 193
spinach *las espinacas* 75
spinning top *el trompo* 193
spirit *el espíritu* 168
spiritual *espiritual* 267
spirituality *la espiritualidad* 271
spoiled (food) *en mal estado* 126
spontaneity *la espontaneidad* 278
spontaneous *espontáneo(a)* 96
sport *el deporte* 192
sports (adjective) *deportivo(a)* 47
sportsman/sportswoman *el/la deportista* 151
sprain *el esguince* 90
to **spread** *extenderse (irreg. ie)* 205
spreading *la dispersión* 97 *la difusión* 325
spring (of drinking water) *la fuente* 296
square *la plaza* 50 *la casilla* 192 *cuadrado(a)* 303
squash *la calabacita* 78
squashed *aplastado(a)* 172
stability *la estabilidad* 256
stable *estable* 2
staff *el personal* 165 *la plantilla* 160
stage *la etapa* 103 *el escenario* 190
stairs *la escalera* 254
stamp *la estampilla* 32 *el sello* 189
stance *la posición* 344
to **stand out** *sobresalir (irreg.)* 50 *destacar* 306
to **stand out (from)** *diferenciarse (de)* 175
to **stand up** *levantarse* 108
standard *el estándar* 153 *estándar* 203
standard of living *el nivel de vida* 9
standardization *la normalización* 153
standards of behavior *las normas de comportamiento* 116
standing *de pie* 102 *el rango* 200
stanza *la estrofa* 330
star *la estrella* 19
to **stare at** *mirar fijo a* 278
start *el inicio* 175
to **start** *poner en marcha* 86 *arrancar* 189
to **start doing something** *ponerse a hacer algo* 136
starting point *el punto de partida* 211
state *el estado* 9

to **take part** *participar 5 intervenir (irreg.)* 123
to **take place** *tener lugar 5 celebrarse 14 producirse (irreg.) 52 desarrollarse 123 transcurrir 337*
to **take refuge** *refugiarse 291*
to **take turns** *turnarse 35*
to **take up** *ocupar 173*
to **take up residence** *fijar residencia* 331
taken *ocupado(a)* 205
tale *el relato* 25
talent *el talento* 38
talented *talentoso(a)* 309
talk *la charla* 72
to **talk** *hablar de 1 conversar* 69
to **talk to each other** *hablarse* 36
tall *alto(a)* 221
tapa *la tapa* 79
task *la tarea* 10
taste *el sabor* 76
taste (of food) *el gusto* 108
taste (of person) *el gusto* 72
tasteless *soso(a)* 35
tavern *el mesón* 79
tea *el té* 76
to **teach** *enseñar* 43
teacher *el/la profesor(a)* 8
teaching *la enseñanza* 317
team *el equipo* 23
to **tease** *tomar el pelo* 20
technical *técnico(a)* 43
technique *la técnica* 5
technological *tecnológico(a)* 98
technology *la tecnología* 44
telecommunications *las telecomunicaciones* 165
telecommuting *el teletrabajo* 163
telephone *el teléfono* 8
telephone (adjective) *telefónico(a)* 239
television *la televisión* 44
television set *el televisor* 219
to **tell** *contar (irreg. ue) 1 decir (irreg.) 14 narrar 230 indicar 278*
temperature *la temperatura* 224
temple *el templo* 318
tendency *la propensión* 96
tenor *el tenor* 200
tense *el tiempo* 22
tension *la tensión* 201
tent *la tienda de campaña* 216
tenth *décimo(a)* 250
term *el término* 67
term (of office) *el mandato* 261
terminal *el terminal* 67
terrace *la terraza* 222
terrible *fatal* 322
terribly *mal* 18
terrific *fenomenal* 142
to **terrify** *dar pánico* 190
territory *el territorio* 43
terrorism *el terrorismo* 272
terrorist *el/la terrorista* 274
terrorist attack *el atentado* 274
test *la prueba* 66
testimony *el testimonio* 97
text *el texto 5 el escrito* 174

text processing *el tratamiento de textos* 174
textbook *el libro de texto* 65
textile *el textil* 31
textual *textual* 294
to **thank** *agradecer (irreg.)* 92
thank God *menos mal (que) 243 gracias a Dios* 278
thank you *gracias* 11
thanks to *gracias a* 287
Thanksgiving *Acción de Gracias* 74
that *que* 1
that can be eaten *consumible* 125
that is, *o sea,* 244
that's why *de ahí 79 por eso 220 de ahí que* 287
the other (before noun) *los/las demás* 218
The problem is that … *Lo malo es que…* 311
the same *igual* 80
the Three Wise Men *los Reyes Magos* 37
theater *el teatro* 23
then *pues 1 después 2 entonces 8 luego 41 a continuación 47 ahí* 268
there *allí 7 ahí* 25
there are *hay* 6
there is *hay* 20
there was *había 6 hubo* 201
there were *había 7 hubo* 31
there will be *habrá* 80
therefore *por (lo) tanto* 220
thick *denso(a)* 109
thin *fino(a) 8 delgado(a)* 106
thing *la cosa* 1
to **think** *pensar (irreg. ie) 2 creer (irreg.) 7 parecer (irreg.) 22 opinar 59 plantearse 67 juzgar que* 320
to **think about** *pensar en (irreg. ie)* 92
to **think of something** *ocurrírsele algo a alguien* 73
third *el tercio 48 tercer(o)(a)* 250
thirst *la sed* 224
this way *así* 11
thousand *mil* 48
thousands of *miles de* 147
threat *la amenaza* 69
to **threaten to (followed by infinitive)** *amenazar con* 92
to **thrill** *emocionar 22 hacer ilusión* 143
throat *la garganta* 94
through *por 1 a través de* 29
throughout *a lo largo de* 172
to **throw** *tirar* 111
to **throw away** *tirar* 127
to **throw up** *vomitar* 90
thyroid gland *la tiroides* 96
ticket *el pasaje 144 la entrada 188 el boleto* 189
tidy *ordenado(a)* 106
to **tie** *atar* 100
time *el tiempo 3 la vez 11 el momento 19 la hora 36 la corbata 54 la temporada 110 la época* 253

time (adjective) *temporal* 140
timeline *la línea del tiempo* 251
times *por* 176
timetable *el horario* 2
tin *el estaño* 173
tip *la propina* 79
tire *la goma, la llanta, el neumático* 56
tired *cansado(a)* 34
tissue *el tejido* 115
title *el título* 26
to *a 1 para 2 hasta 31 a que* 262
to a large extent *en gran medida* 306
to and fro *de un lado a otro* 44
to be honest, *la verdad,* 15
tobacco *el tabaco* 96
today *hoy* 20
together *juntos(as)* 3
together with *junto con* 228
token *la ficha* 192
tolerance *la tolerancia* 245
tomorrow *mañana* 8
tone *el tono* 58
tongue *la lengua* 343
too (before adjective) *demasiado* 48
too many *demasiado(a)* 149
too much *demasiado(a) 48 demasiado* 61
tool *la herramienta 67 el utensilio* 85
total *frontal 67 el total* 125
totally *totalmente* 39
touch *el tacto* 343
to **touch** *tocar* 139
tourism *el turismo* 114
tourist *el/la turista* 203
tourist (adjective) *turístico(a)* 24
toward *hacia* 54
tower *la torre* 318
town *la ciudad 24 el pueblo 40 la localidad 228 la población* 249
town center *el centro urbano* 7
toxic *tóxico(a)* 272
toxic waste *los residuos tóxicos* 272
toy *el juguete* 193
trade *el comercio* 148
trade (adjective) *comercial* 150
tradition *la tradición* 18
traditional *típico(a), tradicional* 14
traditionally *tradicionalmente* 76
traffic *la circulación, el tráfico* 204
traffic jam *el atasco* 204
traffic laws *las normas de circulación* 204
traffic light *el semáforo* 210
traffic sign *la señal de tráfico* 204
train *el tren* 92
train car *el vagón* 204
training *la formación* 174
trait *el rasgo* 20
transaction *la operación, la transacción* 154
to **transform** *transformar* 67
transformation *la transformación* 51
transgressive *trasgresor(a)* 67

transition *el paso* 103 *la transición* 110
to **translate** *traducir (irreg.)* 22
translation *la traducción* 251
translator *el/la traductor(a)* 133
transparent *transparente* 343
transplant *el trasplante* 5
to **transport** *transportar* 204
transportation *el transporte* 116
trash can *la papelera* 293
travel *el viaje* 8
to **travel** *viajar* 24
travel agency *la agencia de viajes* 189
to **travel through** *recorrer* 31
traveler *el/la viajero(a)* 7
tray *la bandeja* 121
treasure *el tesoro* 146
treatment *el tratamiento* 97
treaty *el tratado* 150
tree *el árbol* 220
tree-lined avenue *la alameda* 298
trembling *tembloroso(a)* 210
trend *la tendencia* 270 *la corriente* 335
tribute *el homenaje* 41
trick *el artificio* 337
to **trick** *tomar el pelo* 20
to **trigger** *desencadenar* 211
trillion *el billón* 154
trip *el viaje* 5 *la excursión* 65
triple *el triple* 48
triumphal *triunfal* 306
troops *las tropas* 306
tropical *tropical* 172
troubadour *el/la trovador(a)* 191
true *cierto(a)* 2 *verdadero(a)* 47
truly *verdaderamente* 210
trumpet *la trompeta* 23
trunk (of car) *el maletero* 204
trust *la confianza* 17
to **trust** *confiar en* 92
truth *la verdad* 109
try *el intento* 345
to **try** *intentar* 29 *probar (irreg. ue)* 72
to **try on** *probarse (irreg. ue)* 94
to **try to remember** *hacer memoria* 230
T-shirt *la camiseta, la playera, la polera, la remera* 56
tumor *el tumor* 96
tuna *el atún* 75
turkey *el pavo* 78
turn *el turno* 33
to **turn** *ponerse (irreg.)* 11 *volverse (irreg.)* 34
to **turn (into)** *transformar* 265
to **turn into** *convertirse en (irreg. ie, i)* 38 *convertir en (irreg. ie, i)* 51 *transformarse en* 266
to **turn on** *poner (irreg.)* 42 *conectar, encender (irreg. ie)* 295
to **turn out** *salir (irreg.)* 38
to **turn out (to be)** *resultar* 117
turn signal *el intermitente* 204
to **turn up** *subir* 42 *presentarse* 183
turquoise *turquesa* 219
twelfth *duodécimo(a)* 250

type *el tipo* 7 *la modalidad* 144
typical *típico(a)* 3 *propio(a)* 24

umbrella *el paraguas* 291
unbearable *intolerable* 337
uncertain *incierto(a)* 19
uncle *el tío* 105
uncomfortable *incómodo(a)* 102
uncovered *descubierto(a)* 222
under *bajo* 50
under (an age) *menor de* 68
to **undergo** *sufrir* 51 *someterse a* 114 *experimentar* 280
underground *subterráneo(a)* 295
to **underline** *subrayar* 329
to **understand** *comprender* 44 *entender (irreg. ie)* 66
to **understand each other** *entenderse (irreg. ie)* 36
understandable *comprensible* 117
understanding *comprensivo(a)* 17 *la comprensión* 57
to **undertake** *encargarse de* 18
undifferentiated *indiferenciado(a)* 96
unease *la intranquilidad* 166
unemployed *desempleado(a)* 160
unemployment *el desempleo* 160
unexpected *inesperado(a)* 188
unfavorable *desfavorable* 148
unfortunate *pobre* 24
unfortunately *por desgracia* 244 *desgraciadamente* 325
unhappiness *el descontento* 248
unhappy *descontento(a)* 102
uniform *uniforme* 143 *el uniforme* 254
uniformity *la uniformidad* 67
unimportant *irrelevante* 264
unintentional *involuntario(a)* 80
unintentionality *la involuntariedad* 80
union *la unión* 289
unique *único(a)* 24 *singular* 324
uniqueness *la singularidad* 268
unit *la unidad* 1
to **unite** *unir* 248
universal *universal* 2
universal suffrage *el sufragio universal* 260
universality *la universalización* 114
university *la universidad* 47
university (adjective) *universitario(a)* 137
university course *la carrera* 165
unless *a menos que, a no ser que, salvo que* 164
unlike *a diferencia de* 36 *al contrario que* 306
unlikely *improbable* 196
unmistakable *inconfundible* 210
unnecessary *innecesario(a)* 177
unripe *verde* 106
unsuccessful *fallido(a)* 314
untidy *desordenado(a)* 244

until *hasta* 2 *hasta que* 276
unusual *inusual, raro(a)* 39
to **unwind** *desconectar* 7
up to *hasta* 67
upholstered *forrado(a)* 222
to **upload** *colgar (irreg. ue)* 52 *subir* 98
upper *superior* 5
uppercase *la mayúscula* 136
to **upset** *molestar* 22 *alterar* 211
urban *urbano(a)* 7
urbanization *la urbanización* 280
urge for *el afán de* 215
urgency *la urgencia* 210
urgent *urgente* 32
Uruguayan *uruguayo(a)* 153
use *el uso* 33 *la utilización* 69 *el aprovechamiento* 126
to **use** *usar* 2 *utilizar* 8 *emplear* 21 *aprovechar* 114 *abastecerse con (irreg.)* 153 *poner* 204
used *utilizado(a)* 66 *usado(a)* 94
useful *útil* 16
usefulness *la utilidad* 116
useless *inútil* 343
user *el/la usuario(a)* 45
using gestures *gestualmente* 210
usual *habitual* 6
usually *habitualmente* 47
utensil *el utensilio* 85
uterus *el útero* 89

vacation *las vacaciones* 5
vaccination *la vacunación* 116
vaccine *la vacuna* 90
vague *impreciso(a)* 48
vain *vanidoso(a)* 20
valid *válido(a)* 110
valley *el valle* 277
valuable *valioso(a)* 43
value *el valor* 2
to **value** *apreciar* 17 *valorar* 166
value statement *la valoración* 322
variable *variable* 166
variation *la variación* 48 *la variante* 77
varied *diverso(a)* 57
variety *la variedad* 11
various *diferentes* 22 *distintos(as)* 31 *diversos(as)* 41
to **vary** *variar* 7
vast *vasto(a)* 295
veal *la ternera* 78
vegetable *la verdura* 10 *la hortaliza* 11
vegetarian *vegetariano(a)* 79
vehicle *el vehículo* 153
vehicle fleet *el parque automotor* 153
velvet *el terciopelo* 222
vendor *el/la comerciante* 133
Venezuelan *venezolano(a)* 282
verb *el verbo* 2
verbal *verbal* 34
versatile *versátil* 226
versatility *la versatilidad* 268

worried *preocupado(a)* 40
worry *la preocupación* 42 *la inquietud* 211
to worry *preocuparse* 18 *preocupar* 22 *inquietarse* 249
worse *peor* 308
worsening *el agravamiento* 280
worst *peor* 230
wounded *el/la herido(a)* 289
to wrap *envolver (irreg.)* 51
wreckage *los restos* 195
wrinkle *la arruga* 20
to write *escribir (irreg.)* 3 *redactar* 38
to write for *colaborar en* 44
to write to each other *escribirse (irreg.)* 36

writer *el/la escritor(a)* 33 *el/la escribidor(a)* 343
writing *la escritura* 30 *la redacción* 286
written *escrito(a)* 30

X-ray *la radiografía* 75

yacht club *el club náutico* 106
yard *el jardín* 7

year *el año* 1
yearly *anualmente* 194
yellow *amarillo(a)* 54
yes *sí* 15
yesterday *ayer* 4
yet *aún* 38
to yield (when driving) *ceder el paso* 204
young *joven* 61 *juvenil* 273
young person *el/la joven* 3
youth *la juventud* 3

ZIP code *el código postal* 32
zoo *el zoológico* 219

ÍNDICE GRAMATICAL

CRÉDITOS FOTOGRÁFICOS (TEACHER'S EDITION)

Cubierta: Helen Chelton López de Haro/Jorge Cueto; Jan Sochor/A. G. E. FOTOSTOCK; Alamy Images/ACI AGENCIA DE FOTOGRAFÍA; Thinkstock/GETTY IMAGES SALES SPAIN **Contracubierta:** C. Díez Polanco; Jaume Gual/A. G. E. FOTOSTOCK; GARCÍA-PELAYO/JUANCHO; Ulf Andersen/GETTY IMAGES SALES SPAIN **T1** Helen Chelton López de Haro/Jorge Cueto **T4** Helen Chelton López de Haro/Jorge Cueto **T5** Museo Mural Diego Rivera, Mexico City, Mexico/The Bridgeman Art Library/INDEX **T7** Javier Larrea/A. G. E. FOTOSTOCK **T8** I. Preysler/Atrezzo: Helen Chelton; SEIS x SEIS **T9** C. Díez Polanco; FUNDACIÓN SANTILLANA **T10** I. Preysler/Atrezzo: Helen Chelton **T13** I. Preysler/Atrezzo: Helen Chelton **T15** Helen Chelton López de Haro/Jorge Cueto; ARCHIVO SANTILLANA **T18** I. Preysler/Atrezzo: Helen Chelton **T20** Amos Morgan/A. G. E. FOTOSTOCK **T28** I. Preysler/Atrezzo: Helen Chelton

CRÉDITOS FOTOGRÁFICOS (STUDENT BOOK)

Cubierta: Helen Chelton López de Haro/Jorge Cueto; Jan Sochor/A. G. E. FOTOSTOCK; Alamy Images/ACI AGENCIA DE FOTOGRAFÍA; Thinkstock/GETTY IMAGES SALES SPAIN **Contracubierta:** C. Díez Polanco; Jaume Gual/A. G. E. FOTOSTOCK; GARCÍA-PELAYO/JUANCHO; Ulf Andersen/GETTY IMAGES SALES SPAIN **I** Helen Chelton López de Haro/Jorge Cueto **IV** Michael Langford, Travel Ink/GETTY IMAGES SALES SPAIN; I. PREYSLER **V** GETTY IMAGES SALES SPAIN; I. PREYSLER **VI** A. Guerra; A. Martínez; Olivier Goujon/A. G. E. FOTOSTOCK **X** Tono Balaguer/A. G. E. FOTOSTOCK **XI** Prats i Camps/I. Rovira; Helen Chelton López de Haro/Jorge Cueto; Hughes Herve/hemis.fr/GETTY IMAGES SALES SPAIN **XII** Steve St. John/GETTY IMAGES SALES SPAIN **XIII** Helen Chelton López de Haro/Jorge Cueto; Thinkstock/GETTY IMAGES SALES SPAIN **XIV** Kristian Sekulic/GETTY IMAGES SALES SPAIN **XV** Barry Winiker/A. G. E. FOTOSTOCK; Martin Bernetti/GETTY IMAGES SALES SPAIN **XVI** Alamy Images/ACI AGENCIA DE FOTOGRAFÍA **XVII** ARCO/Loos K., Robert Francis/A. G. E. FOTOSTOCK **XVIII** Photo Researchers/A. G. E. FOTOSTOCK **XIX** José de la Cuesta/CORDON PRESS; LatinContent/Rafael Sánchez Fabres/GETTY IMAGES SALES SPAIN **XX** Richard Nebesky/GETTY IMAGES SALES SPAIN **XXI** Javier Larrea/A. G. E. FOTOSTOCK; Leo La Valle/EFE; **000** Helen Chelton López de Haro/Jorge Cueto **001** I. PREYSLER **002** Thinkstock/GETTY IMAGES SALES SPAIN; I. PREYSLER **003** Prats i Camps **004** REUTERS/CORDON PRESS; I. PREYSLER **005** Pietro Scozzari, Ulrich Niehoff/A. G. E. FOTOSTOCK **006** I. PREYSLER **007** Thinkstock/GETTY IMAGES SALES SPAIN; I. PREYSLER; ISTOCKPHOTO **008** Samsung; I. PREYSLER **009** David Buffington, David Young-Wolff, Thinkstock/GETTY IMAGES SALES SPAIN; AbleStock.com/HIGHRES PRESS STOCK **010** I. PREYSLER **012** DEA/G. DAGLI ORTI, Wendy Connett/A. G. E. FOTOSTOCK **013** Helen Chelton López de Haro/Jorge Cueto; C. Fernández/EFE **014** Helen Chelton López de Haro/Jorge Cueto; I. PREYSLER; ISTOCKPHOTO **015** Helen Chelton López de Haro/Jorge Cueto; Thinkstock/GETTY IMAGES SALES SPAIN; Getty Images Sales Spain/ISTOCKPHOTO **016** Helen Chelton López de Haro/Jorge Cueto; J. Jaime; Prats i Camps; PhotoAlto/AlixMinde/GETTY IMAGES SALES SPAIN **017** C. Contreras; Prats i Camps; Chris Ted, Just One Film/GETTY IMAGES SALES SPAIN **018** Helen Chelton López de Haro/Jorge Cueto; Thinkstock/GETTY IMAGES SALES SPAIN **019** Prats i Camps; Dianna Sarto/John Lun/A. G. E. FOTOSTOCK **020** Prats i Camps; UpperCut Images/GETTY IMAGES SALES SPAIN **021** Helen Chelton López de Haro/Jorge Cueto; Thinkstock/GETTY IMAGES SALES SPAIN **023** Alamy Images/ACI AGENCIA DE FOTOGRAFÍA; Paul Bradbury/GETTY IMAGES SALES SPAIN **024** Thinkstock/GETTY IMAGES SALES SPAIN **026** Helen Chelton López de Haro/Jorge Cueto **027** Helen Chelton López de Haro/Jorge Cueto; Cristian Lazzari, Thinkstock/GETTY IMAGES SALES SPAIN **029** Helen Chelton López de Haro/Jorge Cueto **030** A. Toril; Photos.com Plus/Getty Images Sales Spain; Helen Chelton López de Haro/Jorge Cueto; SERIDEC PHOTOIMAGENES CD; Photos.com Plus/GETTY IMAGES SALES SPAIN; A. G. E. FOTOSTOCK/the Granger Collection **031** Prats i Camps; AFP/AizarRaldes/GETTY IMAGES SALES SPAIN **032** Helen Chelton López de Haro/Jorge Cueto; Prats i Camps **033** Helen Chelton López de Haro/Jorge Cueto; S. Padura; CONTIFOTO **036** Prats i Camps **037** Prats i Camps **038** HankaSteidle/A. G. E. FOTOSTOCK **040** Helen Chelton López de Haro/Jorge Cueto; I. Preysler; J. Jaime; Robert Llewellyn, Thinkstock/GETTY IMAGES SALES SPAIN; I. PREYSLER **041** Helen Chelton López de Haro/Jorge Cueto; Prats i Camps **042** Helen Chelton López de Haro/Jorge Cueto **043** FURITA/M.ª ÁNGELES SÁNCHEZ; E. Ferro **044** Photos.com Plus, Thinkstock/GETTY IMAGES SALES SPAIN **045** Prats i Camps **047** Prats i Camps **049** CORDON PRESS **050** Helen Chelton López de Haro/Jorge Cueto; S. Enríquez **052** Jeff Greenberg/A. G. E. FOTOSTOCK **053** Helen Chelton López de Haro/Jorge Cueto; E. Ferro **054** Mario Guzmán/EFE **055** Prats i Camps/I. Rovira; Helen Chelton López de Haro/Jorge Cueto; Corbis/A. G. E. FOTOSTOCK; I. PREYSLER **056** J. M.ª Escudero; Thinkstock/GETTY IMAGES SALES SPAIN; ISTOCKPHOTO **057** Helen Chelton López de Haro/Jorge Cueto; S. Padura; Joaquín Salvador Lavado (Quino)/todoMafalda/Editorial Lumen **058** A. G. E. FOTOSTOCK **061** Photos.com Plus, Thinkstock/GETTY IMAGES SALES SPAIN **063** Thinkstock/GETTY IMAGES SALES SPAIN; ISTOCKPHOTO **064** COMSTOCK; Photos.com Plus/GETTY IMAGES SALES SPAIN; ISTOCKPHOTO **065** Photos.com Plus, Thinkstock/GETTY IMAGES SALES SPAIN; ISTOCKPHOTO **067** Getty Images Sales Spain/ISTOCKPHOTO **070** Helen Chelton López de Haro/Jorge Cueto; Thinkstock/GETTY IMAGES SALES SPAIN **071** M L Sinibaldi/A. G. E. FOTOSTOCK; David Malan/GETTY IMAGES SALES SPAIN **072** Helen Chelton López de Haro/Jorge Cueto; I. PREYSLER **073** Helen Chelton López de Haro/Jorge Cueto; Oscar Garces/A. G. E. FOTOSTOCK; Thinkstock/GETTY IMAGES SALES SPAIN **074** Helen Chelton López de Haro/Jorge Cueto; Prats i Camps **075** AbleStock.com/HIGHRES PRESS STOCK **076** Helen Chelton López de Haro/Jorge Cueto; Getty Images Sales Spain/ISTOCKPHOTO **077** Helen Chelton López de Haro/Jorge Cueto; J. Jaime; Kerstin Reiger/A. G. E. FOTOSTOCK; Photos.com Plus, Thinkstock/GETTY IMAGES SALES SPAIN; I. PREYSLER **078** Helen Chelton López de Haro/Jorge Cueto **079** FOODFOLIO/A. G. E. FOTOSTOCK **083** Helen Chelton López de Haro/Jorge Cueto; Mauritius/Photononstop/P. Revilla **084** Helen Chelton López de Haro/Jorge Cueto **085** Prats i Camps; Sol de Zuasnabar Brebbia/GETTY IMAGES SALES SPAIN **086** Kristian Sekulic/GETTY IMAGES SALES SPAIN **087** Helen Chelton López de Haro/Jorge Cueto **088** Helen Chelton López de Haro/Jorge Cueto; J. F. Moreno/EFE; Getty Images Sales Spain/ISTOCKPHOTO **089** Leonardo Muñoz/EFE; Photo division/GETTY IMAGES SALES SPAIN **091** S. Padura; Thinkstock/GETTY IMAGES SALES SPAIN **093** Prats i Camps; S. Padura; Roy Morsch/A. G. E. FOTOSTOCK; Thinkstock/GETTY IMAGES SALES SPAIN; PHOTODISC/SERIDEC PHOTOIMAGENES CD **095** Helen Chelton López de Haro/Jorge Cueto **097** SPL/A. G. E. FOTOSTOCK **098** S. Padura **099** Helen Chelton López de Haro/Jorge Cueto; ISTOCKPHOTO **100** Helen Chelton López de Haro/Jorge Cueto/E. Talavera **101** Helen Chelton López de Haro/Jorge Cueto; Jeremy Woodhouse/GETTY IMAGES SALES SPAIN **102** Prats i Camps; Photos.com Plus, Thinkstock/GETTY IMAGES SALES SPAIN; ISTOCKPHOTO **103** Prats i Camps; S. Padura; Cezary Wojtkowski/A. G. E. FOTOSTOCK; Thinkstock/GETTY IMAGES SALES SPAIN **105** John Lund/Tiffany Schoepp, Thinkstock/GETTY IMAGES SALES SPAIN **108** Pixtal/A. G. E. FOTOSTOCK; ISTOCKPHOTO **110** ISTOCKPHOTO **111** Helen Chelton López de Haro/Jorge Cueto; Dennis MacDonald/A. G. E. FOTOSTOCK **113** David R. Frazier/A. G. E. FOTOSTOCK; Elvira Urquijo/EFE; I. PREYSLER **114** Nick Halverson/nickhalverson@gmail.com;

HOLMES/GARCÍA-PELAYO/JUANCHO **315** Helen Chelton López de Haro/Jorge Cueto; Museo Mural Diego Rivera, Mexico City, Mexico/The Bridgeman Art Library/INDEX; Getty Images Sales Spain/ISTOCKPHOTO **316** Helen Chelton López de Haro/Jorge Cueto; Lonely Planet/GETTY IMAGES SALES SPAIN **317** F. Ontañón; Art on File, Robert Harding World Imagery/Richard Cummins/CORBIS/CORDON PRESS **318** C. Pérez; ARCO/La TerraMagica/A. G. E. FOTOSTOCK **319** Demetrio Carrasco, JTB Photo, Miguel Ángel Muñoz, Waldhaeusl.com/A. G. E. FOTOSTOCK **321** JaumeGual, Javier Larrea/A. G. E. FOTOSTOCK **323** Helen Chelton López de Haro; S. Padura; Bruce Bi/A. G. E. FOTOSTOCK **324** Fernando Camino/Cover, Universal Images Group/Arcaid/GETTY IMAGES SALES SPAIN **326** ARGAZKI PRESS **327** Helen Chelton López de Haro/Jorge Cueto; Eco Images/UIG, Kul Bhatia/A. G. E. FOTOSTOCK **328** Helen Chelton López de Haro/Jorge Cueto; MATTON-BILD **329** Chema Moya/EFE **330** Helen Chelton López de Haro/Jorge Cueto **331** Sigefredo/Archdc/KORPA/ZUMAPRESS.com/EFE; Thinkstock/GETTY IMAGES SALES SPAIN **333** Helen Chelton López de Haro/Jorge Cueto **334** Helen Chelton López de Haro/Jorge Cueto **335** Ballesteros/EFE; AbleStock.com/HIGHRES PRESS STOCK **339** Helen Chelton López de Haro/Jorge Cueto; Thinkstock/GETTY IMAGES SALES SPAIN **340** Tomas Abad/A. G. E. FOTOSTOCK **341** Carl & Ann Purcell, The Granger collection/A. G. E. FOTOSTOCK; MUSEU PICASSO, BARCELONA/GARCÍA-PELAYO/JUANCHO **342** Helen Chelton López de Haro/Jorge Cueto; EFE; S. Padura **343** Prats i Camps; S. Enríquez; **345** Helen Chelton López de Haro/Jorge Cueto; GARCÍA-PELAYO/JUANCHO **347** alan64/A. G. E. FOTOSTOCK **349** SYGMA/CONTIFOTO; The Bridgeman Art Library/MUSEUM ICONOGRAFÍA **350** TEATRO MUSEO DALÍ, FIGUERAS/ORONOZ; R. Manent; Jane Sweeney, Oscar Garces/A. G. E. FOTOSTOCK; MUSEO NACIONAL CENTRO DE ARTE REINA SOFÍA/GARCÍA-PELAYO/JUANCHO **351** A. Quier/SIPA-PRESS/EFE; MUSEO NACIONAL CENTRO DE ARTE REINA SOFÍA/GARCÍA-PELAYO/JUANCHO; Thinkstock/GETTY IMAGES SALES SPAIN; ARCHIVO SANTILLANA

Agradecimientos: Cruz Roja Española